Masonic Rivalries and Literary Politics

from Jonathan Swift to Henry Fielding

Marsha Keith Schuchard

Front cover: *Royal Arch Tracing Board,* John Harris, published 8 April 1844.
Back cover: *Ancient of* Days (1794) Watercolor etching by William Blake.

ISBN: 1717258646
ISBN-13: 978-1717258649

DEDICATION

To Patrick Geay and Gauthier Pierozak, with admiration and gratitude.

TABLE OF CONTENTS

ACKNOWLEDGMENTS

The independent publication of this book is a new adventure for me, and I am most grateful to Gauthier Pierozak for encouraging me to undertake it and for offering to edit and prepare the text. For many years, potential readers of my lengthy scholarly works have complained about the high price, which has prevented them and even their libraries from acquiring them. I thus determined to explore the newly emerging methods of independent publishing, which make possible much less expensive production. Nevertheless, I am grateful to my earlier academic publishers, and I wish them continuing success in the challenging future of traditional book publication.

In this volume, I have tried to address the problem of overly-generalized or narrowly-focused studies of Freemasonry by providing a detailed, chronological, and international analysis of Masonic-related British literary works and their political context from the 1680s to the 1750s. In the process, I have been assisted by many scholars, who generously contributed their expertise, even when they did not agree with all of my interpretations.

I am most grateful to the French historians who have encouraged my research, including Edward Corp, Antoine Faivre, Patrick Geay, André Kervella, Gauthier Pierozac, and Louis Trebuchet. I have benefitted from the important studies and constructive criticism of the English scholars Ric Berman, Jane Clark, Robert Collis, Aubrey Newman, Andrew Pink, Ricky Pound, and the indomitable Eveline Cruickshanks. Among my American colleagues, thanks go to Allison Coudert, John Patrick Deveney, Shawn Eyer, Matt Goldish, Kathryn King, Brent Morris, and the extraordinarily generous Alexander Pettit, who donated to me his valuable "Orator" Henley transcripts. The Irish archivist Tom Gilgariff provided copies of the unpublished Charles Wogan/ Jonathan Swift documents in the Galway Diocesan Archives, which the Irish historian Eamonn O'Ciardha had urged me to explore. Once again, I drew upon material provided by the Swedish scholars Susanna Åkerman, Robert Carlson, Kjell Lekeby, Harriet Sandvall, and the late Olle Hjern. From Australia, Bob James has raised provocative questions. From Poland, Peter Pininski provided rare information on the later Stuarts. From Hungary, the groundbreaking historian Róbert Péter has greatly enlarged the scope of scholarship on eighteenth-century British Freemasonry.

And finally, I must pay tribute to the Japanese scholar, Hashinuma Katsumi, who in an important article, "Jonathan Swift and Freemasonry" (1997), observed that his subject "has been a kind of blind spot in the history of Swift studies." He lamented that the arguments by Irish Masonic historians for Swift's affiliation have "never elicited serious attention from Swift scholars"; thus, "it might be worthwhile reopening the subject, giving it, I hope, a fresh importance." Yes, indeed, it is worthwhile.

All historians of the eighteenth century can now benefit from the *Eighteenth-Century Collections Online* (ECCO), which has made accessible many rare publications. But, of course, comprehensive research is still dependent upon the expert assistance of traditional library staffs. I have received invaluable assistance from them at the Houghton Library at Harvard, British Library, Bodleian Library, Christ Church Library at Oxford, British National Archives at Kew, Royal Society of Sciences, Royal Archives at Windsor, Wellcome Institute of the History of Medicine, University of Nottingham, Library of United Grand Lodge of England, Library of Grand Lodge of Scotland, Library of Grand Lodge of Ireland, Royal Order of Scotland Archives, Galway Diocesan Archives, Riksarkivet and Svensk Frimurarorden Arkiv at Stockholm, and Stiftsbibliotek at Linköping, Sweden. As always, special praise goes to Marie Hansen of the Interlibrary Loan Office at Emory University for finding the "unfindable."

I am grateful also for the patience and good humor of my husband, Ronald Schuchard, and our three daughters, five grand-children, and one great-grand-child.

INTRODUCTION

In 1972 the English historian J.M. Roberts published an important book, *The Mythology of the Secret Societies*, in which he lamented the lack of serious academic study of Freemasonry and its related fraternities: "Because the historian passed by, the charlatan, the axe-grinder and the paranoiac long had the field to themselves," which led to the publication of "a mountain of rubbish."[1] Roberts explained that he would not examine the secret societies themselves but rather the "mythology" that had developed around them in the 18th and 19th centuries, which he did with rather broad strokes but little detailed investigation. To his credit, unlike most historians of 18th-century British Freemasonry, he placed "English" developments alongside European movements, and he drew on the recent, substantive work of French historians. Three years later, when I prepared my Ph.D. dissertation, "Freemasonry, Secret Societies, and the Continuity of the Occult Traditions in British Literature," I found his repeated usage of the word "nonsense" for the significant influence of the Cabalistic and Hermetic traditions on various Masonic systems to be not only misinformed but misleading.[2] Moreover, he gave short shrift to the role of Scottish Freemasonry within the international Jacobite movement, referring to it as the "legendary Scottish origin," and concluding that "the only definite thing that can be said about Scottish masonry is that it did not come from Scotland."[3] Even more surprising, he did not discuss Ireland as part of 18th-century "British" Masonry, making only a brief reference to the United Irishmen in the late 1790s.[4]

Because my interest in the literary history of British Freemasonry began with the modern Irish writers William Butler Yeats and James Joyce, who took me back to Jonathan Swift, I realized that I would have to take a less Anglo-centric approach if I wanted to explore the esoteric references and political contexts of writers – throughout the British Isles – who were

---

[1] J.M. Roberts, *The Mythology of the Secret Societies* (1972; London, 1974), 25.
[2] *Ibid.*, 11, 15, 127. Marsha Keith Schuchard, "Freemasonry, Secret Societies, and the Continuity of the Occult Traditions in British Literature" (University of Texas at Austin: Ph.D. Dissertation, 1975). I use the spelling "Cabala," rather than the more modern "Kabbalah," because the former was the most common spelling in the 17th and 18th centuries. I also capitalize Freemason and Mason for a similar reason.
[3] J. Roberts, *Mythology*, 53, 110.
[4] *Ibid.*, 220-21.

influenced (positively or negatively) by Masonic developments.[5] For example, Swift anonymously published *A Letter from the Grand Mistress of the Female Freemasons to Mr. Harding the Printer* (Dublin, 1724), in which he countered in burlesque style the recently published, official *Constitutions of the Freemasons* (London, 1723), written by the Reverend James Anderson, an anti-Jacobite, Scottish Presbyterian. Having learned about Scots-Irish Masonry in Trinity College, Dublin, in 1688, and in a lodge in Omagh, Ulster, in 1695, Swift gave a rollicking counter-account of the Cabalistic-Hermetic-Rosicrucian themes of traditional Stuart Freemasonry:

> The Branch of the Lodge of Solomon's Temple, afterwards called the Lodge of St. John of Jerusalem is as I can easily prove, the Antientist and Purest now on Earth. The famous old Scottish Lodge of Kilwinnin of which all the Kings of Scotland have been from Time to Time Grand masters without Interruption down from the days of Fergus, who Reign'd there more than 2000 Years ago, long before the Knights of St. John of Jerusalem or the Knights of Maltha, to which two Lodges I must nevertheless allow the Honour of having adorn'd the Antient Jewish and Pagan Masonry with many Religious and Christian Rules.
>
> Fergus being eldest Son to the chief King of Ireland, was carefully instructed in all the Arts and Sciences, especially in the natural Magick, and the Caballistical Philosophy (afterwards called the Rosecrution)… Fergus before his Descent upon the Picts in Scotland rais'd that famous Structure, call'd to this Day Carrick-Fergus after his Name, the most mysterious Piece of Architecture now on earth, …as any Skillful Free-Mason may easily perceive by examining it according to the Rules of the Art…[6]

With many plays upon Hebrew letters, Swift referred to "the Enigmaticall Terms of Free-Masonry, or more properly speaking of the Cabala, as Masonry was call'd in those Days."[7]

From his access to seventeenth-century Scots-Irish traditions, Swift was probably familiar with an important poem, *The Muses Threnodie* (Edinburgh, 1638), in which Henry Adamson revealed the esoteric and royalist themes already present in Stuart Freemasonry. Calling upon King Charles I to repair at Perth a great stone bridge "so stately with eleven arches," which had collapsed in 1621, Adamson reassured his friends and local stonemasons: "Therefore I courage take, and hope to see/ A bridge yet built, although I aged be":

> For we be brethren of the *Rosie Crosse*;
> We have the *Mason word*, and second sight,
> Things for to come we can foretell aright,
> And shall we show what misterie we mean
> In fair acrosticks *Carolus Rex* is seen.[8]

---

[5] In the five-volume *British Freemasonry: 1717-1813* (London, 2016), Róbert Péter presents documentation to deconstruct "the Anglo-centric historiography of Freemasonry in the British Isles"; he also notes the need to "improve the current state of research into the literary aspects of Freemasonry in the British Isles (see Vol. I, xxviii, xxx).

[6] [Anon.], *Letter from the Grand Mistress of the Female Free-Masons to Mr. Harding the Printer* (Dublin, 1724); reprinted in Appendix to Jonathan Swift, *The Prose Writings of Jonathan Swift*, ed. Herbert Davis (Oxford, 1962), V, 328. The evidence for Swift's authorship will be discussed in Chapters Two and Nine.

[7] *Ibid.*, V, 330.

[8] Henry Adamson, *The Muses Threnodie* (Edinburgh, 1638), 31-32.

These early works by Adamson and Swift seemed aligned with Yeats's claim that an Irish-descended William Blake learned Cabala from a Jewish Rosicrucian in London and with Joyce's portrayal of Leopold Bloom as a Jewish Mason in Catholic Dublin.[9] But they did not align with the majority of histories of 18th-century British Freemasonry, which portrayed a rationalistic, deistic, Newtonian fraternity. In her provocative book, *The Radical Enlightenment: Pantheists, Freemasons, and Republicans* (1988), Margaret Jacob affirmed that "In Hanoverian England, Whiggery provided the beliefs and values, while Freemasonry provided one temple wherein some of its most devoted followers worshipped the God of Newtonian science."[10] Certainly, that was true for an important type of Masonry in England, but there were other competing types in greater Britain, with deeper roots in seventeenth-century Scotland and Ireland and with significant interests in Renaissance esoteric sciences.

In the same year when Jacob defined her Masonic temple of Newtonian science, David Stevenson published two ground-breaking books – *The Origins of Freemasonry: Scotland's Century, 1590-1710* (1988), and *The First Freemasons: Scotland's Early Lodges and Their Members* (1988), which challenged the long-held presumption that "modern" Freemasonry originated in England. Drawing on Scottish documents dating back to the 1590s and surviving lodge records from the 17th century, Stevenson presented a compelling and credible narrative of organized Masonry, which preserved Hermetic and Rosicrucian mysticism alongside the technical training involved in operative, architectural, "craft" Masonry. Differing from those historians who portray Freemasonry as a generically Enlightenment institution, Stevenson argued that the fraternity contained elements "that appear highly incongruous in the Age of Enlightenment":

> In essence freemasonry is a late Renaissance phenomenon. Its astonishing expansion in the eighteenth century saw it adapt itself to some extent to a new age, but in many ways it remained a movement which fits better into the world of the late sixteenth and early seventeenth centuries than into the world of the Enlightenment.[11]

The Scottish system was supported by the Stuart kings, with James VI and I bringing it south to England in the early 1600s. Like Swift two and a half centuries earlier, Stevenson criticized James Anderson's first "official" history of the fraternity, noting that the anti-Stuart Presbyterian recognized that,

> The Scots in general were very unpopular in England and for much of the eighteenth century. To admit that much of freemasonry, which the *Constitutions* sought to popularize in England, was derived from her despised northern neighbours would have discredited it. Moreover, Anderson was creating

---

[9] Edwin Ellis and W.B. Yeats, eds., *The Works of William Blake* (London, 1893), I, 24-25; he was wrong about his *belief* in Blake's Irish descent. For Bloom and Masonry, see James Joyce, *Ulysses* (1914; New York, 1961), 514. For the complex Yeatsian-Rosicrucian-Masonic traditions, see Marsha Keith Schuchard, "Yeats and the 'Unknown Superiors': Swedenborg, Falk, and Cagliostro," in Marie Roberts, ed., *Secret Texts: The Literature of Secret Societies* (New York, 1995), 114-68.

[10] Margaret Jacob, *The Radical Enlightenment: Pantheists, Freemasons, and Republicans* (London, 1981), 121.

[11] David Stevenson, "The Scottish Origins of Freemasonry," in Jennifer Carter and Joan Pittock, eds., *Aberdeen in the Enlightenment* (Aberdeen, 1987), 39.

a mythology for the English, and it was therefore appropriate and proper to fill past centuries with eminent English freemasons and thus create a far more acceptable and respectable past than a Scottish dominated masonic one could ever have been.[12]

Stevenson briefly referred to the immigration to Ireland in 1617 of William St. Clair of Rosslyn, traditional head of Scottish Masonry, but he did not discuss the infusion of Scottish traditions into northern Irish Masonry that Swift would later describe.[13] After Stevenson's revisionist publications, the description by Professor Roberts of 18th-century Freemasonry as "so peculiarly English," when it crossed the Channel, is no longer historically credible.[14] Moreover, the dominant system in Europe and Scandinavia became *Écossaisme*, which fused together Scottish, Irish, and French themes of Cabalistic mysticism and chivalric ideals.[15]

During the two decades after I completed my dissertation, when I worked as a medical writer and international lecturer on drug education, I visited diplomatic, literary, and Masonic archives in many countries where I continued my independent research into Masonic literary and political history. I was especially interested in the role of Freemasonry in transmitting Cabalistic, Hermetic, and Rosicrucian traditions into 17th- and 18th- century British literature. The result was a lengthy book, *Restoring the Temple of Vision: Cabalistic Freemasonry and Stuart Culture* (Leiden: Brill, 2002), in which I provided the real-world, historical grounding for the flights of visionary Temple building that were later expressed in the rituals of "high-degree," *Écossais* Masonry. Tracing the concepts of Solomonic architecture, Hermetic masques, and Rosicrucian science from their Jewish origins through their Stuart development until 1695, I explained the persistent and potent attraction of early Scottish-Stuart Masonry; its ramifications in England, Wales, and Ireland; and its links to relevant developments in Europe.

During that research, I learned about the little-known support of Protestant Sweden for the Stuart dynasty, from the 17th into the 18th centuries, and about Sweden's often close relationship with royalist and Jacobite Scotland. Once again, Swift and his Scottish and Irish associates were central to that relationship. In 1719, when Swift dedicated his proposed history of England to Count Carl Gyllenborg, the Swedish ambassador arrested in London for his organization of the Swedish-Jacobite plot in 1717, he revealed that he had considered moving to Stockholm to serve Gyllenborg and King Carl XII, if the Whig government's persecution of him intensified.[16] Gyllenborg, a talented writer, contributed influential pamphlets in English to the Tory-Whig literary wars that emerged in newly Hanoverian Britain. His pamphlets were often translated and reprinted on the Continent, where they effected significant political decisions. And, as the Franco-Swedish historian Claude Nordmann has shown, the continuing Swedish-Jacobite plots, led by the

---

[12] David Stevenson, *The First Freemasons: Scotland's Early Lodges and Their Members*, 2nd ed. (1988; Edinburgh, 2001), 149.

[13] David Stevenson, *The Origins of Freemasonry: Scotland's Century, 1590-1710* (1988; Cambridge, 1993), 56-57.

[14] J. Roberts, *Mythology*, 45.

[15] Pierre Chevallier, *Les Ducs sous l'Acacia, ou les Premiers Pas de la Franc-Maçonnerie Française, 1725-1743* (Paris, 1964); and *Le Première Profanation du Temple Maçonnique* (Paris, 1968). Also, René Le Forestier, *La Franc-Maçonnerie Templière et Occultiste au XVIIIe et XIXe Siècles*, ed. Antoine Faivre (Paris, 1970).

[16] J. Swift, *Prose*, V, 11-12. For his possible move to Sweden in 1714 and 1718, see Jonathan Swift, *The Correspondence of Jonathan Swift*, ed. David Wooley (Frankfurt am Main, 2001), I, 646 and n. 3; II, 289 and n. 9-11.

Gyllenborg family (often with Scottish and Irish involvement), were undertaken by an international Masonic network.[17]

Having already written about the influence of radical, occultist Swedish Freemasons on William Blake in the 1780s and 90s, in *Why Mrs. Blake Cried: William Blake and the Sexual Basis of Spiritual Vision* (London: Random House, 2006), I undertook a biography of Emanuel Swedenborg, the celebrated mystical scientist, which revealed his involvement in Swedish political-Masonic efforts to support the Stuart cause (efforts which lasted from the 1650s into the 1780s).[18] In *Emanuel Swedenborg, Secret Agent on Earth and in Heaven: Jacobites, Jews, and Freemasons in Early Modern Sweden* (Leiden: Brill, 2012), I demonstrated how Sweden's support for the Jacobites had a significant influence on British and European politics and religious history. After that publication, I decided to re-focus on British literature and pick up where I had left off in *Restoring the Temple of Vision*, which terminated in 1695, and to prepare a study of the factions and rivalries within British Freemasonry that influenced and were reflected in literature from the 1680s to 1750s. I define "British" as inclusive of England, Scotland, Ireland, and Wales, as well as Anglophone writers in the Jacobite diaspora in Europe and Scandinavia. Fortunately, the energetic revisionism that has emerged in international Jacobite and Masonic studies over the past two decades means that many previously suppressed or inaccessible documents have become available.[19] It is now possible to more precisely locate Masonic literary references (Whig and Tory, Hanoverian and Jacobite, rationalist and mystical) within their local and international historical context, often on a daily, not just yearly, basis.

Until quite recently, the "conventional academic wisdom" held that Freemasonry began in 1717 in London, when four lodges formed the Grand Lodge of London and Westminster, dedicated to the Hanoverian succession and Whig politics.[20] Frank McLynn, the pre-eminent biographer of Prince Charles Edward Stuart, was initially skeptical about the role of Masonry in the Jacobite movement when he wrote *Charles Edward Stuart: A Tragedy in Many Acts* (1988). From his scrupulous research in the unpublished Stuart Papers and international diplomatic archives, he came to realize that the conventional wisdom was wrong: "The primary impetus for the rise of freemasonry in the first quarter of the eighteenth century came from the Jacobites. The great names of early freemasonry were all partisans of the House of Stuart."[21] Moreover, "The first lodges in England, France, Spain, and Italy were extended Jacobite Clubs." But, he added, by the 1730s, the Jacobite lodges were infiltrated by British intelligence: "Freemasonry ceased to be a Jacobite secret society and seemed likely to become a Hanoverian fifth column." In 1988 McLynn acknowledged that the eighteen year-old Charles Edward "showed great interest in this secret organization," but he did not advance "beyond simple curiosity," and the many

---

[17] Claude Nordmann, *Le Crise du Nord au Début de XVIIIe Siècle* (Paris, 1962), 10, 153 n. 148; and *Grandeur et Liberté de la Suède* (Paris, 1971), 199, 424.

[18] Republished in paperback as *Why Mrs. Blake Cried: William Blake and the Erotic Imagination* (London, 2007); and *William Blake's Sexual Path to Spiritual Vision* (Rochester, 2008).

[19] R. Péter's edition, *British Freemasonry* (2016), provides a wealth of previously inaccessible and rare documents from 1721 to 1813. Though the editors do not deal extensively with Jacobite Freemasonry, they recognize its existence and political role (see V, 141-47, 287-92, 402-04).

[20] *Ibid.*, V, lxxv-lxxvi; Cécile Révauger's comments on the relative significance of the English Grand Lodge in 1717.

[21] Frank McLynn, *Charles Edward Stuart: A Tragedy in Many Acts* (1988; Oxford, 1991), 532.

lodges allegedly founded by the prince "turn out to be so many myths."[22] However, by 2004, after researching more thoroughly in diplomatic archives, McLynn changed his mind and portrayed the Stuart prince and "his fellow freemasons," noting that the adult Charles Edward was "deeply versed in the thinking of the philosophes"; was "the personal friend" of Voltaire, Montesquieu, Helvetius, and other liberal Masons; and became "a leading light in eighteenth-century freemasonry."[23]

The growing sense that the Masonic fraternity was a very broad church, with many factions and rivalries, influenced Margaret Jacob's next book on the subject, *Living the Enlightenment: Freemasonry and Politics in Eighteenth-Century Europe* (1991). After reading David Stevenson's argument for Scottish origins and French historians on Jacobite (*Écossais*) lodges, Jacob expressed her puzzlement at the preoccupation of so many Continental Masonic rites with so-called "Scottish" Masonry, which did not fit comfortably into her earlier Whig-Hanoverian "temple of Newtonian science." She observed that,

> Generally historians have not known quite what to do with the stalwart but exiled Jacobites except to see them as romantic patrons of an essentially lost, and backward-looking cause. When their cause merges with a commitment to freemasonry, defined as progressive and modern in its aspirations and outlook, the historian is confounded by an ostensible paradox.[24]

While major historians like McLynn and Jacob revised their arguments, in the light of increasing international evidence, "official" English Masonic historians continued to claim that the fraternity was apolitical. Róbert Péter observes that "in accordance with the self-definition of Freemasonry as a non-political movement," Masonic historians often belittled or denied the links between "some masonic lodges and political movements" while claiming that "lodges were (and are) politically and religiously neutral spaces."[25] Or, as Professor Roberts stated in 1972, English Freemasonry in the eighteenth century continued "its respectable, blameless, and increasingly insular course."[26] He argued further that "overt political activity by masons remains exceptional and easily explicable on non-masonic grounds."[27] That "self definition" of non-political British Masonry was still maintained in 2000 by John Hamill, official spokesman for the United Grand Lodge of England, who dismissed a Jacobite-Masonic role as a "romantic invention," "nonsense," and "just so much blowing in the wind."[28]

But the winds of change are blowing even through the English Grand Lodge, for one member – the historian Ric Berman – is currently challenging that apolitical version with his important books, *The Foundations of Modern Freemasonry* (2011), and *Schism: The Battle that Forged Freemasonry* (2013), which make clear that Hanoverian Masonry was often employed in "overt political activity," while it strove to counter the political intrigues and

---

[22] *Ibid.*, 533.

[23] Frank McLynn, *1759: The Year that Britain Became Master of the World* (2004; New York, 2007), 79, 223.

[24] Margaret Jacob, *Living the Enlightenment: Freemasonry and Politics in Eighteenth-Century Europe* (New York, 1991), 206.

[25] R. Péter, British Freemasonry, I, xv.

[26] J. Roberts, *Mythology*, 44.

[27] *Ibid.*, 69.

[28] John Hamill, "The Jacobite Conspiracy," *Ars Quatuor Coronatorum*, 113 (2000), 97-113. [Henceforth cited as *AQC*].

plots of Jacobite, Tory, and opposition Whig Masonry – at home and abroad. In *Espionage, Diplomacy and the Lodge* (2017), Berman argues that "the lodge was used overtly as a vehicle to promote a political and diplomatic agenda, and covertly to gather intelligence."[29] Moreover, "in direct contrast to what is often posited, from the mid-1720s through to the 1740s it was not freemasonry that influenced the government but rather the opposite." For many writers with Masonic affiliations or interests (both loyalist and disaffected), this manipulation influenced either their pro-government publications or their anti-government protests, in what became a Masonic-literary chess game of spy and counter-spy.[30]

The British literary world was not immune to these governmental factions and disputes, both petty and serious, but the resultant writings were frequently cloaked in high-minded rhetoric, obfuscating allegory, strict anonymity, or bizarre pseudonymity, for the consequences of explicit communication were often hazardous. The Masonic and political rivalries were expressed by writers from the Tory-Jacobite side (such as Jonathan Swift, Alexander Pope, John Arbuthnot, Richard Savage, Duke of Wharton, Earls of Orrery, Viscount Bolingbroke, Charles Wogan, William Meston, Allan Ramsay, Aaron Hill, John Byrom, Samuel Johnson, William King, Thomas Carte, Paul Whitehead, Moses Mendes, Eliza Haywood, and Chevalier Ramsay), and conversely from the Whig-Hanoverian side (such as Richard Steele, Daniel Defoe, John Toland, Earl of Shaftesbury, James Anderson, J.T. Desaguliers, Charles Johnson, Colley Cibber, "Orator" Henley, William Hogarth, James Thomson, Edward Young, Horace Walpole, Lord Hervey, James Arbuckle, and Henry Fielding). Serious students and practitioners of architecture, who had access to operative and speculative developments in Masonry, wrote about them from a Tory-Jacobite perspective (Christopher Wren, Earl of Mar, James Gibbs, Earl of Burlington) or a Whig-Hanoverian position (John Vanbrugh, William Benson, Colen Campbell, Batty Langley). Caught between and intrigued by the competing traditions were philosophers such as John Locke and David Hume, who tried to apply rational evaluation and criticism to the more archaic and esoteric themes of Rosicrucianism and Freemasonry.

In the current century, as Scottish, Irish, French, Swedish, German, Spanish, Italian, Hungarian, and Russian scholars move beyond the "peculiarly English" origins and Hanoverian-Whig development of Freemasonry, it is important to place England, Scotland, Ireland, and Wales within a more inclusive British literary history, and to place that history within an international context. I will thus define literature as another broad church – one that includes poems, novels, dramas, ballads, pamphlets, newspapers, diaries, letters, diplomatic and espionage reports. I will also define Masonic affiliation broadly, for surviving lodge lists are notoriously incomplete and do not include private and "irregular" Masons. Moreover, the stress on secrecy meant that members rarely recorded their own initiations.[31] I will consider a writer or activist as possibly or definitely "Masonic" if there

---

[29] Ric Berman, *Espionage, Diplomacy and the Lodge* (Goring Heath, 2017), 17.

[30] In *British Freemasonry*, I, xix, R. Péter notes that "an increasing number of scholars are interested in the different forms of communication and networks of the members of eighteenth-century secret societies and spying circles," as they investigate "encrypted, anonymous and pseudonymous writings," which convey subversive politics and heterodox spirituality.

[31] The Irish Masonic historian W.J. Chetwode Crawley reported that "It was a point of honour with the Irish Freemasons…to prevent any written information or authorization, concerned with the Craft, from

is any evidence of his affiliation, and if the personal and historical context lends credibility to the affiliation. I also recognize that initiates may have only occasionally (or never) attended officially *organized* lodge meetings, while still considering themselves as "brothers," for there is evidence of surreptitious, private, occasional, outdoor, battle-field, "hedge or bush" induction ceremonies. In the process, I will examine the political and Masonic rivalries that produced charges and counter-charges, Hanoverian accusations and Jacobite defenses, Whig propaganda and Tory polemics – all of which found expression in the multi-faceted literature of "Greater Britain" in the first half of the eighteenth century.

---

passing out of fraternal keeping. The Irish Freemason held it to be his plain duty to destroy any document, public or private, historical or evidential, sooner than let it pass to the hands of outsiders. Warrants, Certificates, Lodge Registers and Minute Books shared the common fate"; see his "Notes on Early Irish Freemasonry, No. VII, *AQC*, 16, part 1 (1903), 69.

CHAPTER ONE

JAMES VII AND II AND THE JACOBITE-MASONIC DIASPORA
(1685-1691)

And after many days Charles did reign in ye land and lo his blood was spilled upon ye earth even by ye traitor Cromwell. Behold now ye return of pleasant [illegible] for doth not ye Son of ye Blessed Martyr rule over ye whole land...

Long may he reign in ye land and govern ye Craft. Is it not written ye shall not hurt ye Lords anointed.

Thomas Treloar, "Ye History of Masonry" (MS. 1665).

The Mason Word... its like a Rabbinical tradition in a way of comment on Jachin and Boaz the two pillars erected in Solomon's Temple; with an addition of some secret signe delivered from hand to hand, by which they know, and become familiar with one another.

Robert Kirk, *The Secret Commonwealth* (1691).

In January 1685 James Stuart, Duke of York, was on the point of leaving London and returning to Edinburgh to head another Scottish Parliament, but he soon learned that he needed support from the northern kingdom for his disputed claim to the English throne.[1] The death of his brother, King Charles II, on 6 February, intensified anti-Catholic and Whig agitation to deprive James, a Catholic convert, of the hereditary succession. In March he appealed to his Scottish friends to travel to London, which provoked them to publish a bizarre manifesto of Masonic support for his rightful claim. Hugh Ouston argues that the versified broadside, entitled *Caledonia's Farewell to the most Honourable James, Duke of Perth, etc. Lord High Chancellor, and William, Duke of Queensbury, etc. Lord High Treasurer of Scotland, When Called up by the King*, was published by the Edinburgh

---

[1] This introductory chapter recapitulates some material given in the concluding chapter of M. Schuchard, *Restoring the Temple of Vision*.

Freemasons.[2] According to Drummond family tradition, James Drummond, 1st Duke of Perth, and his brother, John, 4th Earl of Melfort, were Freemasons.[3] William Douglas, 1st Duke of Queensbury, was currently working closely with royalist architects and operative Masons on the re-building of Drumlanrig Castle, which became one of Scotland's greatest examples of castellar, Baroque palace design. Thus, there was a tightly-knit Masonic context for the unusual manifesto.[4]

The tract targeted James's opponents in England, and its author utilized mystical Masonic mathematics to prove the antiquity and legitimacy of his claim to the throne:

> Go on, My Lords, and prosper; Go, repair
> To Court; and Kiss the Hands of the TRUE HEIR
> Of Fivescore Kings and Ten, Four Diadems,
> And Kingdoms Three: an Heir, whose Royal Stems
> From British, Saxon, Danish, Norman Blood;
> With Scots and Irish, makes His Title good
> 'Gainst all Seclusion. And whose Entry's blest
> With an auspicious Peace, and he possest
> O' th' Thrones of His Ancestors, without stirr
> From any discontented snarling Curr,
> An Heir refus'd (but by no Builders) strange
> Is now Chief Corner-Stone! O happy change,
> And ne'r a Sword Unsheath'd! Lo, Slighted He,
> Seems strangely by the Fates, ordain'd to be
> The Basis of Our Rest: Let those go pry,
> Who hidden Virtus say, in Numbers ly,
> Who speaks the * HUNDREDTH and ELEVENTH, since He
> Stands such from FERGUS, in the Royal Tree.
> Consult but Euclid, take the Architect
> Alongst; try, what One Figure doth direct
> those Arts of Kind; see, what Support the All
> Of the Cementing Trade...[5]

The asterisk pointed to a lengthy footnote which demonstrated James's legitimacy by mathematical and architectural proofs:

> * The number of an hundredth and eleven, when Ciphered, is but the first Figure in Arithmetick, by position thus thrice repeated (111) and which, by advancing the middlemost, after this manner disposed ∴. Makes, when handsomly in right angles conjoyned, a straight aequilateral Triangle △ and such is reckoned to be the first Figure in Geometrie (parallel Lines without some closing Ligament, never being lookt upon as any denominated Figure) and

---

[2] Hugh Ouston, "York in Edinburgh: James VII and the Patronage of Learning in Scotland, 1679-1688," in John Dwyer, Roger Mason, and Alexander Murdoch, eds., *New Perspectives on the Politics and Culture of Early Modern Scotland* (Edinburgh, 1983), 153-54. Rare copy of broadside in National Library of Scotland.
[3] J. Yarker, "Drummond – Earls of Perth," *AQC*, 14 (1901),138. Also, Edward Corp, "Melfort: a Jacobite Connoisseur," *History Today* (October 1995), 46.
[4] Miles Glendenning, Ranald Macinnes, and Aonghus Mackechnie, eds., *A History of Scottish Architecture* (Edinburgh, 1996), 85. For more details on the Masonic context, see M. Schuchard, *Restoring the Temple*, 740-42.
[5] *Caledonia's Farewell* (Edinburgh, 1685).

> this Triangle is said to be in Architecture, of all aedificial Superstructures, the first truest and firmest Basis whence the Grecians denominated a King...

Later Jacobite Masons utilized the emblem of three dots forming a triangle (∴) as a sign of their membership in the fraternity.

The Scottish poet produced further convoluted calculations, coupled with historic and dynastic claims, which would throw all exclusionist arguments "out of doors":

> if you can but in this cryptick way of compting, allow the three ticks to pass for Crowns, see then but, reflect and consider, by what strange and mysterious Algebra, this our Hundredth and eleventh KING, may be said, and is found to *Basis Tou Laou* [in Greek letters: "Base of the People"].

At the conclusion of the footnote, an emblem of an equilateral triangle with number 111 inside rested on the base of SCOTLAND, while ENGLAND and IRELAND lay on the upper angles. Perth and Queensbury were urged to inform the English that this "Riddle, open'd with a thinking Skill,/ Might well have made the COMMONS cast their Bill." The Scottish Freemasons evidently hoped to influence their brethren in the south. The main text continued with a peroration that "CALEDONIA loves the STUARTS well" and prophesied the intensification of ties of loyalty between the Scottish mother and royal father of Great Britain.

James, as Duke of York, had earned the respect of royalists and Freemasons in Scotland, when he resided in Edinburgh in 1679-82 and took a keen interest in architectural projects. While he encouraged the architectural work of William Bruce, Robert Mylne, and James Smith (all allegedly Masonic initiates), he "led an artistic renaissance with the rebuilding of much of Holyrood Palace."[6] Remembering the epithet applied to his grandfather, James VI and I, as not only Scotland's but Great Britain's Solomon, York determined to revive the Stuart image of Solomonic architecture and learning. He had been sent to Scotland by Charles II to keep him out of the way of an English Commons inflamed by the phony "Popish Plot" and Whig attempts to exclude him from the succession. The anti-Catholic hostility he experienced from radical Dissenters and Whigs reinforced his belief in "liberty of conscience," and while in Scotland he encouraged a policy of religious toleration, which included law-abiding Catholics, Presbyterians, Quakers, and Jews. As he associated with architects and operative Masons, the Scottish lodges increased their openness to multi-class, multi-religious members. For example, surviving lodge records from Aberdeen, written circa 1679-80, indicate the presence of Quakers, as well as "landowners, merchants, and craftsmen," among the operative Masons.[7] In the portraits of two members of the Aberdeen lodge there appear in the background the pillars of Jachin and Boaz, suggesting their Masonic initiation into Solomon's Temple.[8]

Given his Masonically-related activities and friendships in Edinburgh, new questions need to be raised about the long-held assumption among Masonic historians that James VII and II was the first Stuart king in four reigns who did not become a Freemason.

---

[6] For their Masonic affiliation see M. Schuchard, *Restoring the Temple*, Index; for York's architectural accomplishments, see E. Cruickshanks, *The Glorious Revolution* (London, 2000), 47.

[7] D. Stevenson, *First Freemasons*, 136-39, 142.

[8] D. Stevenson, *Origins of Freemasonry*, 147.

According to the first official Masonic historian, the Reverend James Anderson (an anti-Jacobite, Presbyterian Whig), James VII and II's grandfather, father, and brother were all "Mason Kings, "but he was not "a Brother Mason."[9] Anderson further claimed that "the Art was much neglected, and People of all Sorts were otherwise engag'd in this Reign." Later in the eighteenth century, the Scottish Mason and Newtonian mathematician John Robison lamented the "heap of rubbish with which Anderson disgraced his *Constitutions of Free Masonry,*" which had unfortunately become "the basis of Masonic history." Robison then made an ambiguous statement about James II's Masonic affiliation:

> We also know that Charles II. was made a Mason, and frequented the Lodges... His brother and successor James II. was of a more serious and manly cast of mind, and had little pleasure in the frivolous ceremonies of Masonry. He did not frequent the Lodges.[10]

Rather than repeating Anderson's claim that James was *not* a "Brother Mason," Robison implied that he did not attend often or enjoy lodge meetings. Moreover, Robison added that the lodges had become the rendezvous of "accepted" Masons who had no association with actual building projects – which suggests that James did not "frequent" English lodges. In Scotland and Ireland, the lodges continued to be closely associated with "craft" stonemasonry and practical architecture.

Thus, it is certainly possible that James, as Duke of York, had carried on the Stuart tradition of Masonic affiliation. After all, he had long experience with military Masonry, especially during the Interregnum in the 1650s, when he frequently worked with Scottish and Irish engineers serving with him in the French army.[11] The military positions of engineers, fortification experts, and quartermasters were part of Scottish and Irish "operative" Masonry. His Scottish royalist colleagues, Sir Robert Moray, and Alexander Bruce, 2nd Earl of Kincardine, were involved in not only military but mystical Masonry.[12] When James arrived in Edinburgh, Kincardine was instrumental in bringing factions together to welcome him as the first Stuart prince since 1603 to establish a royal court in Scotland. During the 1670s, James as Duke of York collaborated with the 1st Duke of Perth in the colonization of New Jersey, and the historian R.W.D. Magregor argues that both men were Freemasons.[13] David Stevenson acknowledges that various Aberdeen Masons immigrated to New Jersey, but notes that MacGregor does not provide documentation for this claim.[14] However, Stevenson was evidently unaware of the Masonic publication of *Caledonia's Farewell.* Thus, it is plausible (though not provable) that James was initiated in a military field lodge on the Continent or while working with architects and Masons in Scotland, but not in England, which led James Anderson to eliminate him from his Anglicized, anti-Jacobite version of Masonic history. If true, this would explain the oral

---

[9] James Anderson, *The Constitutions of the Freemasons (1723) and (1738)*, facs. rpt (Abingdon, 1976), 105-06.

[10] John Robison, *Proofs of a Conspiracy Against all the Religions and Governments of Europe*, 3rd rev. ed. (1797; Philadelphia, 1798), 27.

[11] F.M.G. Higham, *King James the Second* (London, 1934), 44.

[12] David Stevenson, "Masonry, Symbolism and Ethics in the Life of Sir Robert Moray, FRS," *Proceedings of Society of Antiquaries of Scotland*, 114 (1984), 405-31.

[13] R.W.D. Macgregor, "Contributions to the Early History of Freemasonry in New Jersey," *The Master Mason, 1 (1925-27), 98-100.*

[14] D. Stevenson, *First Freemasons*, 138-43, 79 n.59.

tradition voiced by Jonathan Swift and later members of Franco-Scottish (*Écossais*) rites that "all the Kings of *Scotland* have been from time to time Grand Masters without Interruption."[15]

The Scottish Masons were not the only supporters who valued the Stuarts' Solomonic traditions, for the Jewish community in London was determined that James II would continue his brother's tolerant policies. Moreover, the Jews remembered that Charles II had welcomed the Jewish architect, Jacob Jehudah Leon, when the Dutch rabbi visited London in 1675 to exhibit his famous models of the Tabernacle and Temple. In preparation for his journey, Leon prepared a booklet in English, entitled *A Relation of the Most Memorable Things in the Tabernacle of Moses and the Temple of Salomon*, which was printed in Amsterdam in early 1675. The title-page included the coat of arms of the Stuart kings, thus signifying royal approval and patronage. The preface was dedicated to Charles II and included suggestively Masonic terms:

> the love of the Divine Worship, that imparalleld Pietie of your Majestie, ...call for the Protection, not of the most magnificent structure of this World, but of a building, though made with hands, yet that hath God Himself for the Architect thereof; Vouchsafe, therefore, most Potent Prince... to cast a Benign eye upon what is here represented to your Sacred Majestice, it being the Exact form of the Tabernacle, so as it was in the Wilderness, with the struction of Salomon's Temple, the Holy Vessels, Garments and Utensils... The which was graciously owned [acknowledged] with devoted affection 30 years ago and upwards by the Serene Queen, your Majesties Mother..[16]

Unfortunately, no records survive of Leon's experiences in England, but in 1788 the Jewish author David Franco Mendes published an account, in Hebrew, of his visit:

> In the year 1675 he [Leon] made his way with the model of the Temple... He was received at the King's palace with honour and showed him the Model of the Temple and the utensils and the King was very glad to see them and hear about their quality and use. He also gave him a letter sealed and signed that permission is given to him alone and no one else to show the work in all the Kingdom.[17]

Mendes did not mention a Masonic connection, which had earlier been published by Laurence Dermott, an Irish Mason from a mixed Protestant-Catholic family, who examined Leon's papers in 1759-60, when Leon's grandson exhibited the model in London. In *Ahiman Rezon* (1764), Dermott described Rabbi Jacob Jehudah Leon as a Masonic "brother."[18] Though some English Masonic historians question the veracity of Dermott,

---

[15] Jonathan Swift, *Prose Works of Jonathan Swift*, ed. Herbert Davis (Oxford, 1962), v, 329.

[16] Arthure Shane, "Jacob Jehudah Leon of Amsterdam (1602-1675) and His Models of the Temple of Solomon and the Tabernacle," *AQC*. 96 (1983), 146-69.

[17] David Franco Mendes, *Ha-measef* [Hebrew] (Berlin-Koenigsberg, 1788), IV, 297-301; translated in A. Shane, "Jacob Jehudah Leon," 161.

[18] *Ibid.*, 146. Sean Murphy argues that Dermott had Jacobite connections in "Irish Jacobitism and Freemasonry," *Eighteenth-Century Ireland*, 9 (1994), 82. However, Ric Berman argues that while other members of the Dermott family were Catholics, he was almost certainly a Protestant and not a Jacobte; see his *Schism*, 22-23, 27-28.

most Jewish scholars see no reason to dispute the tradition of Leon's Masonic influence in London. Richard Popkin asserts that he addressed Charles II "as if he and the monarch were part of co-equal worlds" and that their meeting was significant for the development of Freemasonry.[19] Lucien Wolf argues that the Masonic coat of arms "is entirely composed of Jewish symbols" and belongs to the highest and most mystical domain of Hebrew symbolism.[20] He also reports a version of Leon's design on a seventeenth-century Masonic panel.

During Leon's visit, Robert Hooke and Christopher Wren were immersed in major building projects, and they perceived Leon's work as relevant to their own. In 1675 Wren wrote but did not publish a tract entitled "Of Architecture; and Observations on Antique Temples," which linked Jewish Temple traditions with Stuart political concerns:

> Architecture has its political use, publick buildings being the ornament of a country... The obstinate valour of the Jews, occasioned by the love of their Temple, was a cement that held together that people, for many ages, through infinite changes... Architecture aims at eternity.[21]

He concluded that the craft of architecture was rooted in nature and primeval Hebrew traditions. Vaughn Hart stresses that Wren drew upon the Solomonic traditions of operative Masonry for his Hiramic-Tyrean notions.[22] Though Rabbi Leon returned to Holland and soon died, his son Solomon Jehudah Leon continued to display the Temple model and explanatory treatises; a document in Wells Cathdral refers to this exhibit in 1680. Leon's coat of arms was subsequently adopted by Irish Masons, evidently in the seventeenth century, and Dermott's account of "brother" Leon served his effort to revive "Antient" traditions of Scots-Irish Freemasonry.

Ten years after Rabbi Leon's visit, the Jews perhaps sensed a common cause with the Scottish and royalist Masons. In 1685, during the first two months of James II's reign, Jewish representatives presented to him a loyal address on parchment and visited his palace five times.[23] Their actions would long be remembered and resented by anti-Jacobites, who preserved an odd tradition about the Jews' claim of heavenly support for James's succession. Writing in 1748, in the wake of the recently crushed Jacobite rebellion, the Whig propagandist and novelist Henry Fielding attacked the insidious combination of Jacobites, Jews, and Freemasons. In passing, he referred to the Jews' loyalty to James II, as expressed on the day of his brother's death:

> the *Jacobite* rabbins tell us, that on *Friday, Feb.* 6, 1684/5, one of the Angels, I forget which, came to *Whitehall* at Noon-day, without being perceived by anyone, and brought with him a Commission from Heaven, which he

---

[19] Richard Popkin,, "Some Aspects of Jewish-Christian Theological Interchange in Holland and England, 1640-1700," in J. Van den Berg and E.G.E. Van der Wall, eds., *Jewish-Christian Relations in the Seventeenth Century* (Dordrecht, 1988), 24.

[20] Lucien Wolf, "Anglo-Jewish Coats of Arms," *Transactions of the Jewish Historical Society of England (1894-95)*, 153-57, 156-57. Henceforth cited as *TJHSE*.

[21] Christopher Wren, *Parentalia* (London, 1750), 351.

[22] Vaughan Hart, *St. Paul's Cathedral, Christopher Wren* (London, 1995), 9, 24n.25.

[23] David Katz, *The Jews in the History of England* (Oxford, 1994), 146-52.

delivered to the then Duke of York, by which the said duke was indefeasibly created King of *England*, *Scotland*, and *Ireland*...

And as there is so great an Analogy between the *Jews* and *Jacobites*, so hath there been the same likeness between their Kings.[24]

In May 1685 the Jews were forced to petition for protection, when a group of City merchants argued that Charles II's endenizations of Jews were no longer valid and that they should now pay customs duty. The Jews were supported by Sir Peter Killigrew, who ordered the arrest of the complaining customs officials. His kinsman, Sir Thomas Killigrew, had earlier signed Charles II's statements of toleration for the Jews and Rabbi Leon's patent to exhibit the Temple model. Over the next months, further attacks on the community were mounted, so the Jewish leaders were enormously relieved in November when James II followed his brother's example and issued an order to stop all proceedings against the Hebrew community: "His Majesty's Intention being that they should not be troubled upon this account, but quietly enjoy the free exercise of their Religion, whilst they behave themselves dutifully and obediently to his Government."[25] R.D. Barnett stresses the historical importance of James's order: "Here was a clear statement of toleration, well in line with, or even ahead of, the most advanced notions in Europe." David Katz agrees that James "gave the Jews of England what amounted to a Declaration of Indulgence," but he also notes that it was inextricably linked with the disputed issue of the king's prerogative.[26] Thus, the Jews realized that their rights were closely connected with Catholic rights, which partially explains the later loyalty of the Jacobite Jews to the Stuart cause. Moreover, the most famous Jacobite Jew, Francis Francia, would reportedly use his Masonic connections for that cause.[27]

Despite the opposition of parliamentary Whigs to royal and ecclesiastical building projects, James II always supported Christopher Wren, who, according to Anderson, was elected Grand Master of the Free Masons in July 1685.[28] As anti-Catholic political turmoil threatened his architectural agenda, Wren selected certain craftsmen to form a loyal corps around him.[29] Perhaps sensing the growing significance of Freemasonry in the royalist cause, the antiquarian John Aubrey recorded in his manuscript "Natural History of Wiltshire" (1686) information about Masonry that he had earlier received from Wren and William Dugdale. The brackets enclose Aubrey's corrections:

about Henry the third's time, the Pope gave a Bull or diploma [patent] to a company of Italian architects [Freemasons] to travell up and downe all over Europe to build Churches. From those are derived the *Fraternity of Free-Masons* [Accepted Masons]. They are known to one another by certayn Signes and Marks [scratched out] and Watch-Words; it continues to this day. They have Severall Lodges in severall Counties for their reception; and when any

---

[24] Henry Fielding, *The Jacobite's Journal and Related Writings*, ed. W.B. Coley (Middletown, 1975), 282, 285.

[25] R.D. Barnett, "Mr. Pepys' Contacts with the Spanish and Portuguese Jews in London," *TJHSE*, 29 (1986), 31.

[26] David Katz, "The Jews of England and 1688," in Olle Grell, Jonathan Israel, and Nicholas Tyacke, eds., *From Persecution to Toleration: The Glorious Revolution and Religion in England* (Cambridge, 1994), 223-24.

[27] See ahead, Chapter Six.

[28] J. Anderson, *Constitutions (1738)*, 106.

[29] Bryan Little, *Sir Christopher Wren: A Historical Biography* (London, 1979), 137.

of them fall into decay, the brotherhood is to relieve him, etc. The manner of their Adoption is very formall, and with an Oath of Secrecy.[30]

Like his Masonic friends Elias Ashmole and the late Robert Moray, who attempted similar research into the fraternity's history, Aubrey merged occult with Masonic studies. While writing the "Natural History," he also made notes on the Cabalistic significance of the Jewish pentalpha (used by Moray as a Mason's Mark), on Rosicrucian recipes for "Invisibility," and on the fertility and sexual rituals supposedly carried out by the Knights Templar and visitors to the Temple Church in London.[31]

Aubrey and Ashmole may have urged their friend Dr. Robert Plot to investigate further the role of Masonry in England. Plot's interest in architecture and operative Masonry had first been expressed in his book, *The Natural History of Oxfordshire* (1677), dedicated to Charles II, in which he described the architectural designs of the Gothic buildings of the university and methods of cutting and setting freestone.[32] Citing many Hebraic and Hermetic writings, he perceived architecture as part of a Christian-Cabalistic tradition of natural history.[33] For his *Natural History of Staffordshire* (1686), he revived the Solomonic tributes to the Stuart kings, praising James II as "Israel's King," for "'tis by you/ That we enjoy a happy Canaan too." What Plot found in England was a tradition that differed significantly from the ancient, nationalistic, and occasionally politicized Freemasonry of Scotland. He noted that the fraternity had spread all over England, but it was particularly strong in the moorlands in the south. This regional concentration of operative Masons was associated with the location of stone quarries which, as Howard Colvin notes, served as "nurseries of masons" during this period.[34]

Plot recognized the value of the secret signs used by Accepted Masons for regulating and improving the skills, integrity, and prestige of the craft, but he suspected that some of the Masons' secrets ("to which they are sworn after their fashion") were much worse than hand signs or giving of gloves. He warned that it is "still to be feared these Chapters of Freemasons do as much mischeif as before, which if one may examine the penalty, was anciently so great, that perhaps it might be useful to examin them now."[35] His concern was based mainly on the combinations of craftsmen who could raise prices – the point of the fourteenth- and sixteenth-century penalties against them. However, some readers of his book thought he hinted at potential conspiracies against the state. The moorland sites suggested the Scottish practice of meetings in isolated places, which evoked memories of the field conventicles of radical Covenanters, who included Masons among their leaders in 1638.[36]

As a Catholic loyal to James II, his patron and friend, Plot possibly influenced the king to firm up Masonic support in England, for a royalist Masonic initiative was

---

[30] The work remained in MS. unti 1847; see Robert Freke Gould, *History and Antiquities of Freemasonry*, 3rd rev. ed. (1882-87; New York, 1951), II, 128-31.

[31] John Aubrey, *Remains of Genitilisme and Judaisme* (London, 1688), 48, 51, 97. The MS. was completed by February 1687.

[32] Robert Plot, *The Natural History of Oxfordshire* (Oxford, 1677), 75-109, 268.

[33] *Ibid.*, 229-32, 282, 343.

[34] Howard Colvin, *A Biographical Dictionary of British Architects*, 3rd ed. (New Haven, 1955), 22.

[35] Robert Plot, *The Natural History of Staffordshire* (Oxford, 1686), 316-18.

[36] D. Stevenson, *Origins*, 199, and *First Freemasons*, 15; also, M. Schuchard, *Restoring the Temple*, 439-40

subsequently undertaken. In 1686 a London Freemason made an elaborate, five-foot long transcript on parchment of the traditional constitutions of the Company of Accepted Masons.[37] Featuring the coats of arms of the royal family, the City of London, and the Masons' Company, it charged the initiated brother to keep truly all the "Counsells that ought to be kept by way of Masonrye," to be "true to God and holy Church," to be a "true liege man to the King of England without Treason or any Falsehood," and to "warne the King or his Counsell" if he hears any treason. The stress on loyalty and worry about sedition were probably provoked by James's toleration policies, which roused intensifying anti-Catholic opposition. As Whig opposition blocked his agenda, his supporters sought alternative methods for funding his policies. At Oxford, Plot tried to convince James that he could finance his government by "an inexhaustible supply of gold from alchemical transmutations which would make parliaments permanently unnecessary."[38] Plot counted on help from Ashmole, for the Hermetic gold factory would be located in the Ashmolean Museum, where it would be protected by Oxford's royalist officials.

Encouraged by the support his moderate policies received earlier in Scotland, James issued a Declaration of Indulgence for the northern kingdom in February 1687. His action provoked a wave of anti-Catholic propaganda, which claimed that the toleration policy was a Jesuitical plot.[39] Even more alarming to the opposition was the Indulgence issued in England in April, when the king suspended the penal laws against Catholics and Dissenters. As F.M. Higham observes,

> Political equality between men of all religions was to be accompanied by freedom of worship. Unfortunately, James, though he accomplished much, had only been able to do so by stretching his prerogative to the utmost. The legality of his piecemeal preferments was at best questionable. He set his heart on the Parliamentary repeal of the Test and the Penal Laws which should give substance to what he had achieved in skeleton form.[40]

The belief in "political equality between men of all religions" (within the lodges) would become the public creed of eighteenth-century Freemasonry. Thus, it is relevant that the lodge of Aberdeen recorded an egalitarian statement about this time (circa 1687). In its surviving Mark Book, a list of names and Mason's Marks for its eclectic membership – ranging from noblemen to artisans – emphasized the equality maintained within the lodge: "we entreat all our good successors in the mason craft to follow our Rule as your patterns and not to strive for place, for here you may see above [on the list] wherein and amongst the rest of our names, persons of a mean degree are inserted by great persons of quality."[41]

Meanwhile in England, despite anti-Catholic agitation, the king's policy was popular among artisans and merchants. On 12 June officials from Coventry presented a large parchment address, signed by over a thousand citizens, in appreciation of James's

[37] Edward Conder, *Records of the Hole Craft and Fellowship of Masons* , eds. Louis Williams and Robin Carr (1894; facs. rpt. Bloomington, 1988), 207, 215.
[38] Michael Hunter, *Science and the Shape of Orthodoxy* (Woodbridge, 1995), 129.
[39] John Evelyn, *The Diary of John Evelyn*, ed. E.S. De Beer (Oxford, 1955), IV, 535-36.
[40] F. Higham, *James II*, 257.
[41] R. Gould, *History*, II, 55 (spelling modernized). For the dating, see D. Stevenson, *First Freemasons*, 126-30.

"granting a liberty of conscience."[42] The presenters claimed that "this was not the application of one party only, but the unanimous address of Church of England men, Presbyterians, Independents, and Anabaptists." By removing "all dissensions and animosities," the policy of toleration would enable them to improve trade and develop future industry. A delighted James promised to establish toleration "by law, that it should never be altered by his successors."

In May 1688, when James issued a second Declaration of Indulgence, the anti-Catholic campaign accelerated in England and Scotland. Against this background, the publication by the English royalist Randle Holme of *An Academie of Armoury* (1688), with its praise of Freemasonry, suggests an infusion of Scottish-style Masonry into the lodge at Chester, located on the northwest border between England and Wales. A strategically important garrison town from which troops passed from England to Ireland, Chester was home to many royalists and Catholics.[43] Thus, there was possibly an infusion of military Masonry from Scots-Irish visitors. Holmes wrote that "I cannot but Honour the Fellowship of the Masons, because of its Antiquity; and the more, as a Member of that Society, called Free-Masons."[44] Among Holmes's papers was a membership list and a copy of the Old Charges, which revealed a similarity to Scottish lodges in which "the first members who were not operative masons were drawn from the other building crafts."[45]

Meanwhile in Scotland, despite troubling divisions within some lodges, James launched an ambitious charter to the Edinburgh Town Council for the building of new streets and bridges. He continued his support of virtuoso scientific culture by founding a new university in Edinburgh, in order to make the city a fitting capital for the royalist aristocracy. Hugh Ouston observes, "Although these intentions were not fulfilled, the initiative which they represented was to contribute through individuals and institutions to the society of eighteenth-century Edinburgh in which the Enlightenment took root."[46] Unfortunately, the heavy-handed actions of several Catholics whom James appointed to official positions disrupted these promising projects, just when the Whigs became most threatened by an unexpected royal birth.

On 10 June 1688 James's queen, Mary of Modena, delivered a baby boy, James, Prince of Wales – an event that shocked the anti-Catholic opposition into a radical new course. Bishop Gilbert Burnet, once a royalist friend of Sir Robert Moray but now a supporter of the exclusionist Whigs, spread false stories that there was no Stuart birth but that an infant was brought from outside in a warming pan. Radical Protestants then published broadsheets accusing Edward Petre, James's Jesuit confidant, of practicing black magic and fathering the infant on a nun.[47] Of such fables are revolutions made! At The Hague, Burnet convinced James's daughters, the Protestant princesses Mary and Anne, that the birth was fraudulent. The controversy about the legitimacy of the king's own succession was thus heightened, and various Whigs and Anglican bishops secretly communicated to

---

[42] J. Evelyn, *Diary*, IV, 553-54.

[43] Eveline Cruickshanks, ed., *By Force or Default? The Revolution of 1688-89* (Edinburgh, 1989), 35-37, and *Glorious Revolution*, 29.

[44] Douglas Knoop, G.P. Jones, and Douglas Hamer, *Early Masonic Pamphlets* (London, 1978), 34f. Henceforth cited as *EMP*.

[45] D. Stevenson, *Origins*, 224-25.

[46] H. Ouston, "York in Edinburgh," 153.

[47] David Mitchell, *The Jesuits: A History* (London, 1980), 165.

Prince William of Orange, Mary's husband and James's nephew, their desire for him to replace James on the throne. These turbulent events provide the context for a comical account of Freemasonry presented at Trinity College, Dublin, soon after Prince James's birth. That Jonathan Swift contributed to the satire lends it a special significance in Masonic literary history.

*
* *

As a witty and irreverent student at Trinity, Swift contributed to a satirical *Tripos* composed by his friends for the Commencement ceremonies on 11 July 1688.[48] The *Tripos* was named for the three-legged stool upon which the university jester sat in medieval times, and it furnished comic relief during the scholastic disquisitions delivered by candidates for degrees. At Trinity the satire was written by a group or club of students, in "a hideous mixture of dog Latin and bog English."[49] The occasion drew a large audience of university officials, military officers, and fashionable ladies and gentlemen. In 1688 the authors especially aimed their satire at the virtuosos of the Dublin Philosophical Society, whose supposedly useless and manic experiments were mocked via references to Samuel Butler's *Hudibras*, the Duke of Buckingham's *The Rehearsal*, and Thomas Shadwell's *The Virtuoso*.[50] More explicitly than their English models, Swift and his fellow comics linked the New Science to Freemasonry, which was portrayed as a contributor to the eager innovations and frenetic activities characteristic of scientific-virtuoso culture.

The students drew upon their observations of the Masonic lodge at Trinity College, which had been established some years earlier during a period of active college building.[51] Designed by the craftsman-architect Thomas Lucas, the main front and central portion of Trinity reflected recent trends in Parisian architecture.[52] According to the student authors,

> It was lately ordered, that, for the honour and dignity of the University, there should be introduced a society of Freemasons, consisting of gentlemen, mechanics, porters, parsons, ragmen, hucksters, coblers, poets, justices, drawers, beggars, aldermen, paviours, sculls, freshmen, bachelors, scavingers, masters, sow-gelders, doctors, ditchers, pimps, lords, butchers, tailors, who shall bind themselves by an oath, never to discover their mighty no-secret; and to relieve whatsoever strolling distressed brethren they meet with, after the example of the fraternity of Freemasons in and about Trinity College...[53]

[48] The case for Swift's contribution is presented persuasively by George Mayhew, "Swift and the Tripos Tradition," *Philological Quarterly*, 45 (1966), 85-101; and Katsumi Hashinuma, "Jonathan Swift and Freemasonry," *Hitotsubashi Journal of Arts and Sciences*, 38 (1997), 13-22.

[49] R.E. Parkinson, "The Lodge in Trinity College, Dublin, 1688," *AQC*, 54 (1941), 96-107.

[50] The *Tripos* manuscript was discovered in the archives of Trinity College, Dublin, by John Barrett, and published by him in *An Essay on the Earlier Part of the Life of Swift* (London, 1808). It was included in Sir Walter Scott's edition, *The Works of Jonathan Swift* (Edinburgh, 1824), VI, 240-59.

[51] John Heron Lepper and Philip Crossle, *History of the Grand Lodge of Free and Accepted Masons of Ireland* (Dublin, 1925), I, 36-37.

[52] Rolf Loeber, "Early Classicism in Ireland before the Georgian Era," *Architectural History*, 22 (1979), 58.

[53] J. Swift, *Works*, ed. Scott, VI, 242-43.

While some benefactors gave a pair of old shoes, a bundle of godly ballads, or a slice of Cheshire cheese, Sir Warren gave five shillings "for being freemasonized the new way." Irish Masonic historians consider this a reference to speculative rituals that went beyond the basic requirements of Masonic initiation. Hinting at a Caledonian Masonic influence on the "new" Masonry, the *Tripos* described a Scots-Irish gentleman – "Sir Fitzsimmons, who always dropt after, (as our town of Berwick-upon Tweed) into a thistle, which still retains its primitive roughness" – and quoted the Scottish Presbyterian historian George Buchanan.[54] James II's recent revival of the Order of the Thistle, which included Scottish Freemasons among its knights, may be relevant.[55] There were striking similarities between the oaths and rituals of the Thistle and Freemasonry.[56]

Swift and his club exploited the sinister rumors about Masonry in their portrayal of "the admirable Ridley" as an initiated brother. Notorious as a spy and informer who made his living "by betraying Catholic priests to their doom under the inhuman penal laws," Ridley was embalmed and stuffed after his death.[57] His body was hung in the Trinity College library, where the medical students examined it and noticed that "the Freemasons' mark" was branded on his buttocks. In "An Elegy Upon Ridley," the *Tripos* authors lamented:

> Unhappy brother, what can be
> In wretchedness compared to thee,
> Though grief and shame of our society!
> Had we in due time understood
> That thou were of the brotherhood,
> By fraud or force thou had'st got loose
> From shameful tree and dismal noose:
> And now perhaps with life been blest,
> A comely brother as the best,
> Not thus exposed to monumental jest;
> When lady longs for college beer,
> Or little dame or country squire
> Walk out an afternoon, to look
> On thee, and devil-raising book;
> Who kindly rather chose to die,
> Than blemish our fraternity;
> The first of us e'er hang'd for modesty.[58]

The sly hints at magical practices among the Freemasons were followed by the narrator's hint at sexual horseplay, when he concluded good-naturedly that "the Freemasons will banish me their lodge, and bar me the happiness of kissing long Lawrence."

The references to Masonry appeared within a context of political satire upon the polarized politics of Trinity and Dublin in 1688. Despite composing the vast majority of

---

[54] *Ibid.*, VI, 247-48.
[55] Matthew Glozier, "The Earl of Melfort, the Catholic Party, and the Foundation of the Order of the Thistle," *Scottish Historical Review*, 79 (2000), 233-38.
[56] N.H. Nicholas, *The Statutes of the Order of the Thistle* (London, 1828), [ii].
[57] J.E.S. Tuckett, "The French-Irish Family of Walsh," *AQC*, 38 (1925), 190.
[58] J. Swift, *Works*, ed. Scott, VI, 244-45.

the Irish population, Catholics were not allowed to attend Trinity, which was controlled by the Anglican church. Some Protestants protested the attempt of the royal government to force the university to accept "the infamous Bernard Doyle" as a Fellow, merely "on the merit of conforming to the religion of James II."[59] When Doyle refused to take the Anglican religious oath, his critics charged him with debauchery, drunkenness, and theft. The university then resisted the king's order, and Doyle spread slanders about the Trinity authorities. In the *Tripos*, the students made obscene allusions to Doyle's mistress Nelly, who was said to like a man "on the prick of preferment" and who has "mandrakes from the King." Doyle's tattered and filthy breeches were given Masonic associations: "By their shreds of all nations, you would have thought they belonged to one of the Freemasons who built Babel."

The satirists also hinted at larger targets. While under attack, Doyle petitioned Richard Talbot, 1st Earl of Tyrconnell, for support. Though James had maintained Protestants in the role of Lord Lieutenant for two years, in 1687 he appointed Tyrconnell, an Irish Catholic, to the post, and the latter's opening up of positions for native Catholics intensified the fears of the more militant Anglicans and Presbyterians.[60] From London, James repeatedly sent orders that his Irish Protestant subjects should be treated fairly and that no one should be deprived of office because of religion. However, bitter grudges on all sides frustrated this attempt at enlightened royal policy – a policy opposed by Swift as undermining the Anglican hegemony. The Trinity students were also aware of Tyrconnell's great interest in Palladian architecture, which he expressed in ambitious building projects.[61] Edward Corp suggests that the 3rd Earl of Tyrconnell's membership in the Jacobite lodge in Paris in 1725-26 was based on family tradition.[62] Thus, the *Tripos* authors may have indirectly targeted Tyrconnell among their eclectic Masonic crew.

Further jibes were directed at Sir Michael Creagh, the mayor of Dublin and an outspoken supporter of King James. Opponents complained that he was "foisted upon Dublin by Tyrconnell."[63] Creagh boasted to a rival alderman about the birth of the Prince of Wales: "We have a brave young prince, and the world's our own." In order to silence rumors about the warming-pan substitution, Creagh had ordered a day of general celebration for the royal birth, which included the distribution of wine to the citizens of Dublin.[64] In the *Tripos*, the alderman accepts the drink but raises questions about Creagh's own legitimacy. The narrator recognized that he was treading on dangerous ground, and he followed this scene with a defensive explanation that he brought all these characters out "for nothing at all, as Bayes did his beasts" (in Buckingham's satiric *Rehearsal*). Just what Swift's attitude was to Freemasonry is difficult to determine, given the comic license and public performance of the skit. At the end, the narrator announced regretfully that "If I take myself to the library, Ridley's ghost will haunt me, for scandalizing him with the name of free-mason," and the brothers "will banish me their lodge."

---

[59] *Ibid.*, VI, 248-52.
[60] E. Cruickshanks, *Glorious Revolution*, 54-55.
[61] R. Loeber, "Early Classicism," 56-57.
[62] Edward Corp, ed., *Lord Burlington – The Man and His Politics* (Lewiston, 1998), 11, 20. The 3rd Earl was Richard Talbot, great-great nephew of the 1st Earl; he became a prominent military officer in France.
[63] Hugh Ormsby-Lennon, *Hey Presto! Swift and the Quacks* (Newark, 2011), 291.
[64] G. Mayhew, "Swift and the Tripos," 95.

Despite his plea of comic tradition, the narrator – John Jones, a close friend of Swift – was punished by Trinity authorities "for false and scandalous reflections in his *Tripos*." John Barrett, who first discovered the manuscript of the *Tripos* in Trinity archives, argued that Swift was the major contributor, if not the sole author, of the satire.[65] He concluded that Swift was also punished and forced to leave the university in January 1689. However, Hugh Ormsby-Lennon disputes this, noting that though the officials disapproved, their punishments were not severe nor long-lasting.[66] Nevertheless, the experience was instructive for Swift, who tried to cover up the affair. While still at Trinity, he began writing *A Tale of a Tub*, which further satirized religious sectarians and Rosicrucian virtuosos, but he refined and developed the techniques of the *Tripos* in order to more carefully conceal his encoded political allusions.

*

* *

In the seven months between the rollicking *Tripos* and Swift's exit from Trinity, the fate of James II's government underwent dramatic changes. Reinforcing the radical Presbyterians in Scotland, a secret coalition of Whigs and Anglicans urged William of Orange to come to London and take over the government. Hoping to gain England's assistance in his war against Louis XIV, William issued a manifesto which catalogued James's alleged misdeeds and questioned the legitimacy of the Prince of Wales. James was shocked and incredulous at the disloyalty of his daughter and son-in-law, and he was ill-prepared to deal with William's invasion of England in November 1688. Despite William's public claims that he had no designs on the throne and was only interested in protecting Protestantism, he had long planned the invasion – with a powerful army in which his Catholic mercenaries outnumbered James's Catholic troops.[67]

In Scotland rebellious Whigs, inflamed by anti-Catholic propaganda, went on iconoclastic rampages, in which they especially targeted monuments of "Papist" architecture. In November the "rabble" attacked Roslin Castle and Chapel, where they defaced many of the Gothic sculptures so admired by Freemasons.[68] The St. Clair family, keepers of Roslin castle, embodied Stuart Masonic traditions from the sixteenth into the eighteenth centuries. In 1697, when the English Jacobite, George Hickes, was hiding in Scotland from the Whig government, he studied the history and practices of operative Masons:

> I went to Halbertshire. This is a strong, high tower house built by the Laird of Roslin in King James the 5th time. The Lairds of Roslin have been great architects and patrons of building for many generations. They are obliged to receive the mason's word, which is a secret signall masons have thro' out the world to know one another by. They alledge 'tis as old as Babel when they could not understand one another and they conversed by signs. Others

---

[65] J. Barrett, *Essay*, 13, 20-21.
[66] H. Ormsby-Lennon, *Hey Presto!, 278-99.*
[67] E. Cruickshanks, *Glorious Revolution*, 23-25; Jonathan Israel, *The Anglo-Dutch Moment: Essays on the Glorious Revolution and Its World Impact* (Cambridge, 1991), 1-13.
[68] Richard Hay, *A Genealogie of the Saintclaires of Rosslyn* (Edinburgh, 1835), 107.

would have it no older than Solomon. However it is, he that hath it will bring his mason to him without calling to him or your perceiving the sign.[69]

From his earlier experience in Scotland, when he served as chaplain to the Duke if Lauderdale in 1678, Hickes came to be considered an expert on Highland lore about second sight, which was traditionally associated with Freemasonry. In 1700 he answered inquiries about the phenomenon from Samuel Pepys, and recounted his questioning of a second-sighted teenage girl: "I asked...to know whether the second sight was by outward representation; which I call apparition, or by inward representation on the theater of the imagination caused by some spirit, or...whether these *second-sight folks* were seers or visionists."[70] From his continuing inquiries, Hickes learned that some "visionists" claimed that they could teach an initiate how to achieve the visionary state, which perhaps explains the linkage with Masonic rituals and training.

In November 1688, not content with rabbling Roslin Castle and Chapel, radical Presbyterians overpowered the royalist guard at Holyrood Palace, where they desecrated the tombs of the Scottish kings and sacked the chapel. They were especially determined to destroy "all the curious workmanship" of fine wood and stone sculpture that James had commissioned for the chapel to honor the Order of the Thistle, and "several parcels of these Pieces of work" were burned at the Cross of Edinburgh.[71]

Despite the political divisions within some lodges, the Masonic veterans of Charles II's restoration campaign remained loyal and urged the king to mount an armed resistance against the Dutch "usurper."[72] But James, who seems to have suffered a minor stroke, became confused and fearing for his life, tried to escape from London.[73] He was captured and placed under Dutch guard, but in December managed to flee to France and the protection of Louis XIV. His flight, inaccurately called his abdication by his enemies, launched the international Jacobite movement. According to eighteenth-century Scottish-French-Swedish-German traditions, his flight also planted the seeds for the later growth of *Écossais* Freemasonry, which developed Cabalistic, Rosicrucian, and chivalric high degrees, as well as international networks of support for the Jacobite cause.

Though there is no surviving contemporary documentation, references to a lodge formed by Jacobite partisans at St. Germain in 1688-89 appeared frequently in eighteenth-century writings.[74] Gustave Bord argues further that the Jacobites in France revived the political-military Masonic strategy utilized earlier by the exiled Charles II – i.e., they introduced Masonic organization and formed a political party within each regiment.[75] The Scots-Irish regiments then became "les agents exécutifs" and their lodges "le pouvoir

---

[69] *Historical Manuscripts Commission 29: 13th Report. Portland M.SS.*, appendix ii (1893-94), II, 56. Henceforth cited as *HMC*.

[70] Michael Hunter, *The Occult Laboratory: Magic, Science and Second Sight* (Woodbridge, 2001), 177.

[71] Alexander Nisbet, *A System of Heraldry, Speculative and Practical* (Edinburgh, 1722), II, 123.

[72] For details of the Scottish resistance and Masonic context, see M. Schuchard, *Restoring the Temple*, 762-70, 775-81.

[73] His sudden nosebleed and subsequent languor suggested not only stress but a minor stroke.

[74] Pierre Chevallier, *Histoire de la Franc-Maçonnerie* (Paris, 1974), I, 4-5; Phillipe Morbach, "Les régiments écossais et irlandais à St. Germain-en-Laye: mythe ou réalité maçonnique?," in Edward Corp, ed., *L'Autre Exil: Les Jacobites en France au Début de XVIII-Siècle* (Montpellier, 1993), 143-55.

[75] Gustave Bord, *La Franc-Maçonnerie en France de Origines à 1815* (1908; facs. rpt. Paris, 1985), I, 51.

directeur" of the Stuart cause. In 1772 the French lodge *Parfaite Égalité* in the Regiment of Walsh succeeded in securing recognition of its claim to date its constitution from 1688:

> This regiment was formerly called the Royal Irish, and went into exile in France following the Jacobite defeat of 1691. It was renamed the Regiment of Walsh after 1770, in reference to its commander Antoine Joseph Phillipe Walsh...member of a family prominent for its support of Jacobitism.[76]

One of James's most ardent supporters was the Irish officer James Walsh, who reportedly established a lodge within his regiment on 25 March 1688.[77] A new regiment was raised by Theobald Dillon, 7th Viscount Dillon, who agreed to send it to France in exchange for Louis XIV's troops bound for Ireland. Led by the viscount's son, Arthur Dillon, the troops arrived in France in May 1690, and Dillon allegedly established a regimental lodge at St. Germain.[78] Like the Fitzjameses, the Walsh and Dillon families would play active roles in the lodges of the Stuart diaspora.

In Scotland, while strong resistance was led by the architect Sir William Bruce (the Grand Master, according to James Anderson), and John Graham of Claverhouse (Viscount Dundee), the anti-Jacobites pressured enough nobles in the Scottish Convention to accept William and Mary on 11 April 1689. Despite the heroism of the charismatic Dundee, who led a furious Highland charge at the precipitous pass of Killiecrankie, the Williamite forces were victorious and Dundee was killed, "only to live on in Jacobite song and poetry as 'Bonnie Dundee.'" According to later (and controversial) traditions, he wore a Templar cross, emblematic of his role in chivalric Masonry.[79] John Graham was an expert in military mathematics, and his surviving brother David served as quartermaster in John's regiment, which makes plausible their association with military Masonry. Moreover, the city of Dundee was an ancient stronghold of royalist Masonry. David Stevenson points out that during Viscount Dundee's residence, there were two levels of Masonry – the public Society of Masons and the secret lodge of Dundee, which were different aspects of the same organization.[80]

Adding some degree of plausibility to the Templar claims was John Graham's acknowledged fascination with chivalric orders, which he perhaps infused into the rituals of the secret lodge in Dundee. Moreover, in a 1745 lodge history, the Dundee Masons claimed to have been founded by medieval veterans of the crusades.[81] After David Graham escaped to France, the exiled James II honored the family's chivalric ideals by making him a Knight of the Thistle.[82] James obviously believed that the continuance or revival of chivalric orders was important for building morale and fraternity among his embattled supporters. Like Elias Ashmole, the royalist Freemason, James probably saw the Templars and Knights of Malta as brothers, and he now took a renewed interest in the latter

---

[76] S. Murphy, "Irish Jacobitism," 77.

[77] J. Tuckett, "French-Irish Family," 189-96.

[78] P. Chevallier, *Histoire*, I, 5; P. Morbach, "Les régiments," 143-44; Albert Lantoine, *Histoire de la Franc-Maçonnerie Française* (Genève, 1982), 105, 127, 132.

[79] For the Dundee-Templar controversies, see Michael Baigent and Richard Leigh, *The Temple and the Lodge* 1989; London, 1993) 228-34, 376-77; M. Schuchard, *Restoring the Temple*, 767-70.

[80] D. Stevenson, *Origins*, 195.

[81] R. Gould, *History*, II, 61.

[82] R. Corp, *Burlington*, 23.

order.[83] While he was in Dublin and attempting to link his Irish campaign with Dundee's in Scotland, he wrote the Grand Master of Malta and obtained permission to revive in Britain the Grand Priory of the Knights of Malta.[84] His efforts were supported by Tyrconnell, who since 1687 had worked on plans to restore to the Knights Hospitallers their ancient Priory at Kilmainham, which currently housed a royal military hospital.[85] James had sent his natural son, Henry Fitzjames, to Malta in 1687, where he visited the Grand Master, who conferred upon him the diamond cross of the order. James now named him Grand Prior of Britain and gave him command of an Irish regiment. Fitzjames was befriended by the Scottish Earl of Melfort, a Freemason and Thistle knight, and the two men possibly collaborated in an infusion of chivalric ideals into the Jacobite field lodges.[86] As we shall see, Jonathan Swift would later refer to Masonic "lodges" of "the Knights of St. John of Jersualem" and "the Knights of Maltha," and Fitzjames continued to serve as Grand Prior until 1701.[87] His exiled family would subsequently play a leading role in *Écossais* Freemasonry in France.[88]

As William's seasoned troops defeated the Jacobites in Scotland and James's army at the Battle of the Boyne in Ireland, Gaelic bards and Latin poets extolled the heroism of the defeated Jacobites. Dr. Archibald Pitcairne, a royalist physician, published an eloquent Latin epitaph upon Dundee, as the last protector of the authentic "Temple" of Stuart governance. It was then "English'd" by John Dryden under the title, "Upon the Death of the Earl of Dundee":

> O last and best of *Scots*! who dids't maintain
> Thy Country's freedom from a Foreign Reign;
> New People fill the Land now thou art gone,
> New Gods the Temples, and new Kings the Throne.
> *Scotland* and thou did each in other live,
> Thou wouldst not her, nor could she survive;
> Farewell! who living didst support the State,
> And couldst not fall but with thy Country's Fate.[89]

*
* *

While the structure of the Stuarts' Solomonic kingship crumbled before the Dutch conqueror, the Jewish community in London was placed in a precarious position. Would new Gods fill their Temples, their synagogues protected by the later Stuart kings? Thus,

---

[83] Elias Ashmole, *The Institution, Laws, and Ceremonies of the Most Noble Order of the Garter* (1672; facs. rpt. London, 1971), 47; M. Schuchard, *Restoring the Temple*, 767.

[84] H.J.A. Sire, *The Knights of Malta* (New Haven, 1994), 125-26, 187-88.

[85] E.J. King and the Earl of Scarborough, *The Grand Priory of the Hospital of St. John of Jerusalem in England* (London, 1924), 65.

[86] On Fitzjames and Melfort, see *The Journal of John Stevens*, ed. Robert H. Murray (Oxford, 1912), 72-73.

[87] J. Swift, *Works*, V, 328-29.

[88] E. Corp, *Burlington*, 10-11, 20-21.

[89] John Dryden, *The Works of John Dryden*, eds. E.N. Hooker and H.T. Swedenberg (Berkeley, 1956), III, 222.

they waited anxiously to see if William III would extend traditional Dutch toleration to his new kingdom.

It was well known that William had long relied on Jewish military suppliers in Holland, who contributed to his successful invasion of England. However, to the dismay of the London Jews, William implemented policies that greatly worsened their condition. His Toleration Act of 1689 exempted "Their Majesties' Protestant subjects, dissenting from the Church of England, from the penalties of certain laws," but the Jews were not exempted.[90] Even worse, the seventeenth clause of the Act expressly excluded from its benefits "any person that shall deny in his preaching or writing the doctrine of the blessed Trinity." Thus, the royal protection of liberty of conscience – including the Jews – enacted by James II was now abandoned in the newly-titled "Glorious Revolution."

As William prepared to invade Ireland, his English Protestant partisans determined to impose an exorbitant tax on the Jewish community in London in order to finance the campaign. The Jews struggled to defend themselves, even vowing in November that they would "remove their effects into Holland" rather than pay the "imposition which Parliament has designed to lay upon them." Their resistance to William's war tax was remembered in anti-Jacobite propaganda in 1748, when Henry Fielding cited the tradition of the "Jacobite Rabbins" who claimed that the same angel who announced James II's legitimate succession made "a second Appearance" in December 1688 and "convey'd away the King, together with his divine Commission, to another Country," where the Stuarts' divine rights were preserved for his heirs.[91]

This "rabbinical" controversy provides a provocative context for a Masonic discussion, which took place in London on 6 October 1689, between a Scottish Presbyterian minister, Robert Kirk, and a Williamite Anglican bishop, Dr. Edward Stillingfleet. As a student of Gaelic and Scottish folklore, Kirk had gathered much rare and secret information about Scottish traditions. At the London dinner, Stillingfleet quizzed him about "the 2nd Sight, only heard of in the highlands of Scotland."[92] When Stillingfleet expressed skepticism about the reality or permissibility of second sight, Kirk affirmed its reality but suggested that it might be "an extended form of natural eyesight," like that of cats or lynxes at night or telescope-aided human sight. Despite Kirk's semi-scientific argument, Stillingfleet maintained that the devil was involved. Kirk then gave a partial explanation of the Mason Word, which moved the bishop to declare it "a Rabbinical mystery."

Perhaps provoked by this discussion, Kirk visited the Bevis Marks Synagogue on 25 January 1690 in order to observe the ceremonies. He probably learned that the officiating rabbi, Solomon Allyon, came from Safed, "the centre of cabbalistic studies in Palestine and arguably in the entire Jewish world."[93] Also present in London at the time was Solomon Jehudah Leon Templo, son of the Masonic Rabbi Leon. Unfortunately, we do not know if Kirk met Templo, but his subsequent writing makes the possibility relevant. After returning to Scotland, Kirk published in 1691 the result of his Jewish-Masonic investigation:

---

[90] D. Katz, *Jews in History*, 161-65.
[91] H. Fielding, *Jacobite's Journal*, 282-83.
[92] See account in D. Stevenson, *Origins*, 132-33.
[93] D . Katz, *Jews in History*, 161-62.

> The Mason-Word, which tho some make a Misterie of it, I will not conceal a little of what I know; its like a Rabbinical tradition in a way of comment on Jachin and Boaz the two pillars erected in Solomon's Temple; with an addition of some secret signe delivered from hand to hand, by which they know, and become familiar with another. This Second Sight so largely treated of before.[94]

Kirk had written extensively on second sight in the pages leading up to his explication of the Mason Word, and he evidently connected it to Masonry.

David Stevenson observes that the Scottish antiquarian hinted at Jewish mystical associations for the Mason Word:

> Kirk does not actually identify them [Jachin and Boaz] as words that were part of the Word, but the masonic catechisms reveal that Boaz was the word given to the entered apprentice, Jachin that given to the fellow craft. When Kirk explained this to Stillingfleet the latter called it a "Rabbinical mystery"; as the words of the Mason Word were connected with Solomon's Temple it was natural to connect their use with Jewish tradition, and Stillingfleet probably had in mind the Cabbala...[95]

These words should be remembered when we read Swift's reference to "the *Cabala*, as *Masonry* was call'd in those Days."[96]

Though the influence of Rabbi Leon on Restoration Freemasonry disappeared from contemporary records in England, it may have been carried to Ireland by royalist Masons who appreciated his loyalty to the Stuart cause. Leon Huehner notes that in the 1660s, when Irish genealogists published the characteristics of different nationalities, they "strangely enough" represented the Jews "as being pre-eminent as builders."[97] Given this popular Irish belief that "For building the noble Jews are found," an interest in Leon's architectural and heraldic designs would be natural for royalist Masons in Ireland. There is a hazy tradition that "ancient" Irish Masons secretly used Leon's Masonic coat of arms in the 1680s.[98]

Meanwhile in England, a new wave of propaganda emerged, aimed at converting the Jews. Bishop Stillingfleet and other Williamite churchmen talked excitedly of Protestant victories against the Papacy, which they linked with an outburst of millenarian prophecies about the imminent conversion of the Jews.[99] After William defeated the Jacobite armies at the Battle of the Boyne (July 1690), he returned to London determined to make the English Jews contribute financially to his military campaign, which now included war against France. Pressured by English merchants, the king in October levied customs duties on all English exports effected by foreign merchants, including Jews previously

---

[94] Robert Kirk, *The Secret Commonwealth and a Short Treatise of Charms and Spirits*, ed. Stewart Sanderson (1691; London, 1976), 88-89.

[95] D. Stevenson, *Origins*, 133-34.

[96] J. Swift, *Works*, V, 328-29.

[97] Leon Huehner, "The Jews of Ireland: an Historical Sketch," *TJHSE*, 5 (1902-05), 232. The characterization was documented in *MacFirbis's Book of Genealogies*, finished in 1666.

[98] A. Shane, "Jacob Jehudah Leon," 164-65.

[99] D. Katz, *Jews in History*, 161-62.

naturalized under the Stuarts. By December the negative effect on trade led Parliament to abolish the increased alien duties.

Though David Katz initially defines William's actions as "a deliberate policy of near persecution," he later concludes that the king had no ideological reason for his attacks on the London Jews, whom he merely regarded "as a dormant financial asset which might be tapped in this, the Crown's hour of need."[100] Norman Roth goes further, however, and views the Williamites' attempt to prohibit the Jews from trading in gold and silver as dangerously discriminatory:

> unlike the legal issues involving oaths, where the distinction was made be-
> tween those who would swear an oath as Christians on the Christian Bible
> and those who would not, this is the first case of clear discrimination against
> the Jews simply for being Jews in a situation that applied without distinction
> to all subjects of the realm. In vain did the Jews point out in their petition ,
> which...was not even allowed a hearing (contrary to the procedure under
> Stuart kings when all Jewish petitions were at least considered), their contri-
> butions to trade and the economy...[101]

By judicious bribery, the London Jews were able to alleviate some of these attacks, but it is small wonder that many of them remained privately sympathetic to the Jacobite cause. Moreover, as discontent with the Williamite settlement simmered in Scotland, anti-Jacobite propaganda increasingly characterized the Scots as Jews. In 1691, when a reader inquired of the popular *Athenian Mercury*, "Why do Scotch-men hate swines flesh?" the London editor replied that it was a borrowing from the Jews.[102] In September, when the Williamite Dean of Guild in Edinburgh tried to deny trading privileges to David Brown, "a profess'd Jew," the old treasurer Hugh Blair successfully argued for Brown's legal rights and for the historical importance of the Jews to Scottish Protestantism. Arthur Levy notes that this decision "may be regarded as the Charter of Liberty for the Jews of Seventeenth Century Edinburgh."[103]

*
* *

In 1690 a Presbyterian minister, William Geddes, printed in Edinburgh "An *Encomiastick Epigram* Upon the *Antient* and *Honourable Trade* of MASONS," a poem which summed up the Hebrew and royalist traditions of Scottish Freemasonry. David Stevenson observes that it "adds to the evidence of the interest taken by non-Masons in Scotland in the myths and organization of the mason craft that were giving birth to freemasonry." In the text,

---

[100] Ibid., 173; D. Katz, "Jews...and 1688," 242.

[101] Norman Roth, "Social and Intellectual Currents in England in the Century Preceding the Jew Bill of 1753" (Ph.D. Dissertation: Cornell University, 1978), 189-90.

[102] Arthur Williamson, "'A Pil for Pork-Eaters': Ethnic Identity, Apocalypic Premises, and the Strange Creation of the Judeo-Scots," in R.B. Waddington and Arthur Williamson, eds., *The Expulsion of the Jews: 1492 and After* (New York, 1994), 249, 257n.34.

[103] Arthur Levy, "The Origins of Scottish Jewry," *TJHSE*, 20 (1959-61), 136.

The legend of the two antediluvian pillars in which human knowledge was preserved is repeated, the importance of symbolism to masons stressed, reference made to the secrets relating to identification that masons had, and it is emphasized how it is masons who provide the settings for the grandeur and pomp of great courts. A rather more unusual touch is the claim that God himself was a stonemason, for with mallet and chisel He engraved the Ten Commandments on stone for Moses.[104]

The broadside was headed by a woodcut of the Scottish royal coat of arms, commonly used to head official acts and proclamations. Because the poem so clearly expresses the essence of Stuart Masonry, which influenced the fraternity's eighteenth-century development, it is worth quoting at length:

Among Mechanicks, MASONS I extoll
And with best I doubte not to Enroll.
Before the *Flood* Antiquity they Claime,
The MASON then must have an antient Name.
When Godly *Enoch* by his *Divine Art*,
He did foretell how that the World should smart
By Fire and Water, he two Pillars made,
The one with *Brick*, and one with *Stone* was laid:
He wrote thereon all *Sciences* and *Arts*,
Some knowledge to Diffuse in all Men's hearts.
If water came, the *Stone* might it endure;
The *Brick* the Fire; so all continue sure.
The Moral-Law, in writ none could it have,
Till GOD himself in *Stone* he must it Grave.
For *Hewing Stone*, none can put to shame,
The *Corner Stone*, to JESUS is a Name:
For this I think the MASON must be Blest,
From antient times he hath a *Divine Crest*.
A *Character* whereby they know each other,
And yet so *Secret*, none knows but a Brother.
All Temples, Turrets, Pallaces of Kings,
All Castles, Steeples, and such other things:
Do owe all what they have to Masons cure.
All Courts great Grandeur, and Magnifick State,
What Pomp they have, from MASONS they do get:
The strictest Laws they have for *Common-well*,
The *greatest Charity* when BRETHREN fail.
Symbols Divine, Pomp, Dwelling, Law, and *Love*;
Few are the *Men who do such Tradesmen* prove.[105]

The fate of Stuart Freemasonry during the early Williamite regime is difficult to piece together, because of destruction of documents and increasing secrecy maintained by Jacobite resisters and exiles. In 1738 James Anderson noted that "many of the Fraternity's records" from Charles II's reign were lost during James II's reign and "at the

---

[104] D. Stevenson, *First Freemasons*, 206.
[105] *Ibid.*, 207-08. The poem was discovered in 1999, and a single copy is in the Scottish National Library.

Revolution." William III was preoccupied with European war plans and paid little attention to architecture in his new kingdom. After a hiatus in 1689, Christopher Wren managed to resume his rebuilding projects. However, as John Summerson observes, during the next decade, "this vacant interval," few churches were built in England.[106] French and Continental historians argue that Wren maintained his private Jacobite sympathies, while he worked discretely and cautiously under the new regime.[107] Paul Jeffrey suggests that the lack of written documents about Wren's work during these years was deliberate:

> his tracks are usually well-hidden. His early brushes with authority had taught him to be wary of committing himself to paper and of exposing his ideas to public criticism and debate... he may just have carried on, unwilling to record decisions on paper, but secure in the knowledge that he had the support of the Commissioners [of Building], even though their attention was largely diverted elsewhere..[108]

Wren soon realized that William III deliberately avoided the monumental stone construction beloved by his Stuart predecessors. However, when Queen Mary, James's daughter, requested a rebuilding of Hampton Court Palace, Wren began a set of ambitious designs. Then, in summer 1689 William appointed a triumvirate of his supporters – William Talman, George London, and William Bentinck, Earl of Portland (his Dutch favorite) to oversee the building work. Their collaboration "was close and often inimical to Wren's own plans."[109] Talman especially tried to undermine Wren, even accusing him of causing the deaths of workmen in a collapsed building at Hampton Court. "A man of colic and irritability," Talman developed "a peculiarly intimate relationship with the king."[110] Covetous of Wren's position, he hoped to replace him. In later years, Talman become the confidential friend of John Theophilus Desaguliers, who with James Anderson, would help to develop the anti-Jacobite Grand Lodge of England.

In December 1689, when William and Mary moved into Kensington Palace, extensive renovations were required, but Wren was not allowed to carry out the expensive stonework that he favored. John Harris explains that Williamite "court architecture was brick ornamented with stone," because "stone architecture required the expensive talents of sculptors to make it effective."[111] He then laments that "the best of baroque architecture is built of stone, not brick." The neglect of the highest quality skills of operative Masons, which frustrated Wren, sheds some light on a note made by John Aubrey on 18 May 1691, which has long provoked controversy among Masonic historians:

> MDM, this day...is a great convention at St. Paul's church of the Fraternity of the Accepted ["Free" being struck out] Masons where Sr. Christopher Wren is to be adopted a Brother; and Sr. Henry Goodric...of ye Tower, &

---

[106] John Summerson, *Architecture in Britain, 1530-1830* (London, 1935), 184.

[107] G. Bord, *Franc-Maçonnerie*, 55-57; M. Jacob, *Living the Enlightenment*, 92.

[108] Paul Jeffrey, *The City Churches of Christopher Wren* (London, 1996), 28-29.

[109] John Harris, "The Architecture of the Williamite Court," in R.P. Maccubin and M. Hamilton-Phillips, eds., *The Age of William III and Mary II: Power, Politics, and Patronage, 1688-1702* (Williamsburg, 1989), 227.

[110] H. Colvin, *Biographical Dictionary*, 949; John Harris, *William Talman: Maverick Architect* (London, 1982), 20-32.

[111] J. Harris, "Architecture," 231.

divers ["sev'l" being struck out] others, there have been Kings, that have been of this Sodalitie.[112]

Aubrey added this "Memorandum" to his MS. "Natural History of Wiltshire," which was then being transcribed for the archives of the Royal Society. B.G. Cramer, clerk to the society, copied the note with one possibly significant change – i.e., writing "Adopted" instead of Aubrey's "Accepted" Masons. John Evelyn also recorded the ceremony of 18 May, noting that "Sr Christopher Wren (Architect of St Paules) was at a Convention...of Free-masons, adopted a brother of that Society, shore have Kings ben of this sodality."[113]

By participating in this unusual public ceremony, did the privately Jacobite Wren hope to allay suspicion that he maintained an inner circle of Accepted Masons, who worked with him on earlier Stuart projects. Perhaps Wren hoped to give Acception a more public and thus acceptable status. Aubrey first wrote "Free" and then inserted "Accepted" in his more public transcript. Wren's companion in adoption, Sir Henry Goodricke, had secured the city of York for William at the Revolution and was subsequently rewarded with the position of Lieutenant-General of the Ordinance and Privy Councillor. Thus, he would certainly lend respectability to Wren and his craftsmen.

Goodricke was also interested in architecture and operative Masonry, for he had supervised the demolishing and rebuilding of the ancient stone edifice at Ribston ("Tympill Ribstayne"), originally constructed by the Knights Templar and later sold to Goodricke's ancestors by the Knights Hospitallers.[114] Goodricke had been a royalist before William's actual arrival in England, and he was then friendly with various architecturally-interested Jacobites. In 1691, after his shift of loyalty, he enjoyed enormous powers of patronage and rewarded court supporters with jobs, money, favors.[115] The Freemasons who performed the public ceremony probably hoped to gain aristocratic and popular support for Wren's ambitious agenda and for their craft. Disappointingly, over the next years, the use of stone for building material would be largely superseded by brick: "This resulted in a decline in the Mason trade" in England, while "stone remained the main building material in Scotland."[116]

In his pro-Williamite history of Freemasonry, James Anderson initially ignored this decline and tried, unconvincingly, to provide the Dutch king with an English Masonic role. Writing in 1722-23, at a time of Jacobite-Hanoverian struggles for control of Masonry, Anderson asserted:

> after the Revolution, Anno 1688, King William, though a war-like Prince, having a good Taste of Architecture, carried on the aforesaid two famous Hospitals of Greenwich and Chelsea, built the fine part of his royal Palace of Hampton Court, and founded and finish'd his incomparable Palace at Loo in Holland, & the bright Example of that glorious Prince, (who by most is

---

[112] Quoted in Michael Baigent and Bernard Williamson, "Sir Christopher Wren and Freemasonry: New Evidence," *AQC*, 109 (1996), 88-89.

[113] British Library: Evelyn MS. 173.f.9 [Henceforth cited as BL].

[114] Charles A. Goodricke, *Ribston...Seat of the Goodricke Family* (London, 1902), 69-79.

[115] E. Cruickshanks, *Glorious Revolution*, 62. For the Whig-Masonic diplomatic activities of his descendant, Sir John Goodricke, in Sweden in the 1760-70s, see M. Schuchard, *Emanuel Swedenborg*, chapters 17 to 21.

[116] George Draffen, "Freemasonry in Scotland in 1717," *AQC*, 83 (1979), 366.

reckon'd a Free-Mason) did influence the Nobility, the Gentry, the Wealthy
and the Learned of Great-Britain, to affect much of the Augustan Style.[117]

In terms of architectural history, this purported influence of William is erroneous.
Moreover, according to Aubrey and Evelyn, the Masonic affiliation of kings was in the
past. In his 1738 edition, Anderson admitted the decline in the craft during the Williamite
years ("Particular lodges were not so frequent and mostly occasional in the South").[118]
But with Wren then dead and unable to contradict him, Anderson now claimed that King
William was "privately made a Free Mason, approved of their Choice of G. Master Wren,
and encourag'd him." No other source speaks of this or grants William architectural importance in England. Of course, it is possible that he was initiated into a military field
lodge, for he worked closely with his personal regiment of Dutch and Huguenot engineers. As the Williamite revolution gained the title of the "Glorious Revolution," the
Jacobites at home and abroad developed secret networks of communication as they
struggled against the victorious Whigs, and some found that Freemasonry provided a
valuable vehicle for their cause, which soon began to emerge in literary expression.

---

[117] J. Anderson, *Constitutions (1723)*, 42-43.
[118] J. Anderson, *Constitutions (1738)*, 106-07.

CHAPTER TWO

FREEMASONS, ROSICRUCIANS, AND RADICAL CLUBS
(1691-1698)

> Divertissements: these are to give notice, that the Modern Green-Ribbond Caball, together with the Ancient Brotherhood of the Rosy Cross; the Hermetick Adepti; and the Company of Accepted Masons, intend all to dine together... Having already given order for great store of Black-swan Pies, Poach'd Phoenix Eggs, Haunches of Unicorns, etc.
>
> *Poor Robin's Intelligencer* (10 October 1676).

> Having thought it needful to warn you of the Mischiefs and Evils practiced In the sight of God by those called Freed Masons, I say take care lest their secret Swearings take hold of you...For this devilish Sect of Men are Meeters in Secret which swear against all without their Following. They are the Anti Christ which was to come leading Men from Fear of God.
>
> M. Winter, *To All godly People, in the Citie of London* (1698).

While James II and his supporters continued to plot his restoration to the British throne, Jacobite Freemasonry went largely underground in the British Isles. However, according to eighteenth-century traditions, the exiles took their Masonic organization to France, from where their dispersed brothers established clandestine networks of fraternally-bonded initiates. In 1737 the French Mason Bertin de Rocheret wrote that Freemasonry was brought to France in 1689 by supporters of James II.[1] In 1797 the Scottish Mason John Robison wrote that the "most zealous supporters" of James II "took Free Masonry with them to the continent, where it was immediately received by the French ," and "All the Brethren on the Continent agree in saying, that Freemasonry was imported from Great Britain about the beginning of this century [ca.

---

[1] Quoted in André Kervella, *Aux Origines de la Franc-maçonnerie Française (1689-1750)* (Rouvray,1996), 31 n. 19.

1700] and this in the form of a mystical society."[2] The mysticism consisted of the traditional Cabalistic and Hermetic symbolism of the Scottish lodges, but Robison also described a special chivalric degree created by the Jacobites at St. Germain, with an emblem alluding "to the dethronement, the captivity, the escape and asylum of James II. and his hopes of re-establishment by the help of the loyal Brethren." Robison was not sure whether this degree of *Chevalier Maçon Écossais* was added "immediately after King James's abdication, or about the time of the attempt to set his son on the British throne."

These claims of chivalric developments within Jacobite Masonry continue to provoke arguments among historians, because of the dearth of contemporary documents until the 1730s. However, an oblique reinforcement comes from Jonathan Swift, who drew upon his experiences in Dublin in 1688 and Ulster in 1695-96 to later describe the chivalric (as well as Cabalistic, Lullist, and Rosicrucian) interests of Scots-Irish Freemasonry. In *A Letter from the Grand Mistress of the Female Freemasons* (Dublin, 1724), Swift's comical summary of "Celtic" traditions in "a Lodge of Free-Masons at O---h in U----r" (Omagh in Ulster) throws a retrospective light on developments in the fraternity in the 1690s.[3]

In 1689 Swift fled the political turmoil in Dublin and moved to England, where he became amanuensis to the retired diplomat Sir William Temple at Moor Park. Temple shared Swift's skeptical interest in Rosicrucianism, which he had encountered in its radical form in Ireland during the 1650s.[4] He also dealt with operative Masons there, who drew on Scots-Irish traditions. After the Restoration, Temple was employed on delicate secret missions for Charles II and Lord Arlington, both allegedly Masons, and he was kept abreast of Scottish affairs while serving at The Hague. In 1668 Arlington sent Temple a paper written by the prominent Mason Sir Robert Moray and praised the Scot's expertise in chemistry (which included Moray's alchemical experiments).[5] Two years later Temple met Moray, who sought his assistance for the export to Holland of building stone quarried by his Scottish Masonic brother, Alexander Bruce, Second Earl of Kincardine. The enterprise also involved Sir William Bruce, the architect, who had utilized his Masonic connections to help General Monk organize the restoration of Charles II, and Sir William Davidson, who had handled the exiled king's overture to the Jews.[6] Thus, when

---

[2] J. Robison, *Proofs*, 27-28, 541. Though historians rightfully scoff at Robison's sweeping charges of radical Masonic conspiracy in the 1790s, they have not examined his accounts of his personal experiences in *Écossais* lodges on the Continent in the 1770s, when he collected documents on the esoteric and chivalric higher degrees. The latter material is important for its rare "British" insight into the Scottish-Jacobite traditions preserved in various European Masonic rites.

[3] J. Swift, *Works*, V, 324. The dismissal by some modern critics of Swift as the author is puzzling, given the publishing history of the pamphlet. After anonymous publication by Harding and his widow in 1724 and 1730, it was advertised and reprinted in 1731 by George Faulkner, Swifts' good friend and publisher, with himself as dedicatee rather than the late Harding. Swift was identified as the author by Faulkner's London agents, who reprinted it in *Miscellanies by Dr. Swift* (London, 1746),XI, 173-86. Faulkner himself included it in his "great edition" of Swift's complete works in 1762. It was also featured in the collections issued at London (1755), Hamburg (1760), and London (1774). Paul Monod notes that "Swift is now acknowledged to have been the author"; see his *Solomon's Secret Arts* (New Haven, 2013), 381 n. 16.

[4] William Temple, *Miscellaneous Essays*, ed. Samuel Holt (Ann Arbor, 1963), 200-01; "Sir William Temple," *ODNB*.

[5] Arlington, Henry Bennett, Earl of, *The Right Honourable Earl of Arlington's Letters to Sir William Temple*, ed. Thomas Babington (London, 1701), 450.

[6] See M. Schuchard, *Restoring the Temple*, 529-51, 575-87.

Temple discussed with Swift the secret diplomacy of Charles II, he may have revealed the role of Freemasonry in Stuart politics.

Swift was disappointed that Temple could not secure him a clerical position in England, and he grudgingly agreed to take over the Anglican ministry at Kilroot in northern Ireland, where he immediately faced political and Masonic problems. During this period, economic conditions in Scotland deteriorated so badly that thousands of Scottish Presbyterians migrated to Ulster, where they were soon at loggerheads with the Episcopal establishment, which felt increasingly betrayed by William's concessions to the non-conformists. Into this volatile situation, riven by bitter theological and political disputes, the newly-ordained Anglican priest was sent in January 1695. In the parish of Kilroot, Scots-Irish Presbyterians were a majority, while the struggling Episcopal churches suffered from negligent and corrupt ministers.[7] Swift expected to take over the ministry of Robert Mylne, who had been charged with non-residence, intemperance, and incontinence. But Mylne had supporters who petitioned the bishop to sustain his position. Though little is known about Swift's year in Ulster, he gained more knowledge about Rosicrucianism and Freemasonry during his residence – knowledge which he incorporated into *A Tale of a Tub* (1704) and *A Letter from the Grand Mistress of the Female Free-Masons* (1724), both published anonymously.

The influence of Scottish Freemasonry had long been felt in Ulster, where William St. Clair of Roslin, hereditary patron of the Scottish Masons, had emigrated in 1617 and died in 1650.[8] The remaining St. Clairs in Scotland were still considered the heads of Scottish Masonry, and there were many ties between Masons in Scotland and northern Ireland. Swift's predecessor in Ulster, Robert Mylne, was kinned to the famous Scottish family of Master Masons, who claimed to have initiated James VI and I and then served his Stuart successors.[9] Robert emigrated to Ireland in 1657, where he initially served as a Presbyterian minister.[10] Between 1657 and 1660, the Mylnes in Scotland participated in important Masonic activity, including assistance to General Monk's restoration scheme.[11] In 1660 the Anglican priest Jeremy Taylor hurried from Ireland to London to support Monk in his final campaign.[12] On Taylor's return to Dublin, he was instrumental in converting Robert Mylne to Anglicanism, and he ordained the new priest in 1662. While serving in Kilroot, Mylne maintained contact with Scots who were privy to their native Masonic traditions. When Mylne's supporters contested Swift's appointment, the new priest had to work to develop good relationships with his parishioners. From Swift's later allusion to a lodge of Freemasons at Omagh, it seems likely that he gained access to "Celtic" Masonic traditions or even participated in a lodge during his residence.

In *A Letter from the Grand Mistress*, Swift revealed an "ancient" Scots-Irish Masonic tradition that included Cabalistic, Rosicrucian, and chivalric themes, which he had learned about in 1695-96 and which foreshadowed the emergence of *Écossais* higher degrees in

[7] Irvin Ehrenpreis, *Swift: The Man, His Works, and the Age* (London, 1962), I, 159-62.
[8] Lepper and Crossle, *Freemasonry*, I, 37-38, 115.
[9] Robert S. Mylne, *The Master Masons to the Crown of Scotland and their Works* (Edinburgh, 1893), 128-29.
[10] Louis Landa, *Swift and the Church of Ireland* (Oxford, 1954), 12-21.
[11] For details, see M. Schuchard, *Restoring the Temple*, 573-90.
[12] C.J. Stranks, *The Life and Writings of Jeremy Taylor* (London, 1952), 201, 233, 245.

the 1740s. Though his letter was quoted in the Introduction, it is worth repeating its salient points:

> The Branch of the Lodge of Solomon's Temple, afterwards call'd the Lodge of St. John of Jerusalem...is...the Antientest and Purest now on Earth. The famous old Scottish lodge of Kilwinnin of which all the Kings of Scotland have been from Time to Time Grand Masters without Interruption, down from the days of Fergus, who Reign'd there more than 2000 Years ago, long before the Knights of St. John of Jerusalem or the Knights of Maltha, to which two Lodges I must nevertheless allow the Honour of having adorn'd the Antient Jewish and Pagan Masonry with many Religious and Christian Rules. Fergus being the eldest Son to the chief King of Ireland, was carefully instructed in all the Arts and Sciences, especially in the natural Magick, and the Caballistical Philosophy (afterwards called the Rosecrution)...[13]

Swift added that the printer Mr. Harding, if duly encouraged by subscribers, will publish also "a Key to Raymundus Lullius, without whose help...it's impossible to came at the Quintessence of Freemasonry."[14]

Swift's burlesque of the operative Masons' craft histories written in various Old Charges drew on specific Scots-Irish traditions in Omagh and Carrickfergus. Moreover, during his frequent visits to Carrickfergus, he would have seen in St. Nicholas' Church the engraved tablet in praise of the restoration of the edifice: "This worke was begune 1614...and wrought by Thomas Paps free-mason...*Vivat Rex Jacobus.*" Philip Crossle argues that Swift had this tablet in mind when writing his *Letter from the Grand Mistress*.[15] Also displayed in the church was a Mason's chair, which featured elaborate Masonic carvings (including an Irish harp with square and compasses), the mysterious initials A.J.R.K.C.B., and date 1685.[16] The chair was an Irish version of a Scottish chair from Berwick-on-Tweed, a Masonic location Swift and his friends mentioned earlier in the Trinity *Tripos.*

Disgusted by the sectarian hostilities he encountered in his parish, Swift worked on the draft of *A Tale of a Tub*, which he had started writing at Trinity College, when he also contributed to the Masonic satire of the *Tripos*.[17] The earliest part of *A Tale* was the allegory of a dying father who bequeaths to each of his sons a new coat, with instructions to care for it and to "live together in one House like Brethren and Friends, for then you will be sure to thrive, and not otherwise."[18] The allegory drew on earlier versions of the story of three rings, which represented the Jewish, Christian, and Moslem religions. Swift made the three brothers and their coats represent the current factions of the Christian church – i.e., the Papist (Peter), Episcopalian (Martyn), and Presbyterian-Dissenter (Jack).

---

[13] J. Swift, *Works*, V, 328-29.

[14] For the influence of Lull on early Scottish Freemasonry, see M.K. Schuchard, *Masonic Esotericism and Politics: The "Ancient" Stuart Roots of Bonnie Prince Charlie's Role as Hidden Grand Master. La Règle d'Abraham, Hors-série no. III, June 2017* (Columbia, 2017).

[15] Philip Crossle, "Freemasonry in Ireland, circa 1725-31," *The Lodge of Research, No. CC. Ireland. Transactions for the Year 1924* (Dublin, 1931), 94; also, Terence de Vere White, "The Freemasons," in T. Desmond Williams, ed., *Secret Societies in Ireland* (New York, 1973), 48.

[16] Lepper and Crossle, *History*, I, 33, 38.

[17] For the important connection of *Tripos* and *Tub*, see H. Ormsby-Lennon, *Hey Presto!*, 278-309.

[18] Jonathan Swift, *A Tale of a Tub*, eds. A.C. Guthkelch and D. Nichol Smith, 2nd ed. (Oxford, 1958), 74.

Having experienced the Jacobite-Williamite struggles in Dublin while still at Trinity, he was further provoked in Ulster to satirize the bitter sectarian hostilities that undermined church and state in the British Isles. When he targeted the enthusiastic, zealous, bigoted, and "Illuminated" Jack, he connected radical Presbyterian-Dissenter beliefs with the original Continental Rosicrucian movement.[19] The sub-title, "Written for the Universal Improvement of Mankind," was taken from Triano Boccalini's *Ragguagli di Parnaso*, which was printed together with the *Allgemeine und General Reformation der gantzen weiten Welt. Beneben der Fama Fraternitatis, dess Löblichen Ordens des Rosenkreutzer* (1614).[20]

From Swift's later statements (in *Letter from the Grand Mistress*) about the importance of Cabala to Rosicrucianism and Freemasonry, it is significant that he already held that opinion when writing *A Tale of a Tub*. He wrote mockingly about Cabalistic letter-number manipulations which were used as an aid to prayerful meditation"

> And First, I have couched a very profound Mystery in the Number of O's multiplied by Seven and divided by Nine. Also, if a devout Brother of the *Rosy Cross* will pray fervently for sixty three Mornings, with a lively Faith, and then transpose certain Letters and Syllable according to the Prescription… they will certainly reveal into a full Receit of the *Opus* Magnum.[21]

Even more absurd to Swift were the claims that this Cabalistic technique would produce the ultimate Rosicrucian "illumination":

> Lastly, Whoever will be at the Pains to calculate the whole Number of each Letter in this Treatise, and sum up the Difference exactly between the several Numbers, assigning the true natural Cause for every such Difference; the Discoveries in the Product, will plentifully reward his Labour. But then he must beware of *Bythus* and *Sigé*, and be sure not to forget the Qualities of *Acamoth*… wherein *Eugenius Philalethes* that committed an unpardonable Mistake.[22]

Swift would later assume the pseudonym "Phil-Alethes" when writing another satire on irrationality and corruption.[23]

As we shall see from John Toland's experiences in Ulster, Swift could well have met Rosicrucians or Freemasons who were interested in the occult sciences and radical reform. The earliest parts of *A Tale* that seem most likely to have been written in Kilroot describe scathingly the Scots who made grandiose claims for their ancient lineage (drawing upon the founding myth of the marriage of the Egyptian Scota to the Greek Gathelus).[24] These radical Scots preached seditiously against the Episcopal church and English regime, while they claimed Cabalistic and Rosicrucian illumination.[25] He even got in jabs against the

---

[19] Philip Pinkus, "A Tale of a Tub and the Rosy Cross," *Journal of English and Germanic Philology*, 59 (1960), 669-79.

[16⁹] J. Swift, *Tale of a Tub*, 353.

[21] *Ibid.*, 187.

[22] *Ibid.*, 187.

[23] See ahead, Chapter Eleven.

[24] See William Matthews, "The Egyptians in Scotland: The Political History of a Myth," *Viator*, 1970), 291-92.

[25] J. Swift, *Tale of a Tub*, 58, 99, 138-39, 153-54.

Order of the Thistle and the Judaized Scots'aversion to pork (hinting at anti-Stuart propaganda that claimed the Scots were descended from the Jews).[26] The current heirs of the radical Presbyterianism of John Knox ("Knocking Jack of the North") could only organize their "Epidemick Sect of Aeolists" because the Anglican church (Martyn) "at this time happened to be extremely flegmatick and sedate." Certainly, this was the case in Kilroot, where the Episcopal ministers were so negligent or absent that their parishioners had to attend Presbyterian services if they wanted any Protestant church experience at all.

Swift read widely in Hermetic and Rosicrucian literature, including Paracelsus, Boehme, Sendivogius, Heydon, the *Comte de Gabalis*, and Thomas Vaughan (Eugenius Philalethes), as well as the parodists of that literature, Buckingham, Shadwell, and Butler.[27] When he left Kilroot in 1696 and returned to Sir William Temple's employment at Moor Park, the two men must have discussed their mutual experience with Scots-Irish "illuminists." In 1690 Temple had written sardonically of abandoned libertines, extravagant debauchees, and dabblers in chemistry, characters he observed during his service in Ireland. Even worse, while there he had known in the family of some friends "a keeper deep in the Rosicrucian principles."[28]

Though Swift drew upon occultist literary publications, his precise description of the seditious Presbyterian Jack suggests his observation of actual Scottish Rosicrucians and/or Freemasons in Ulster. With traditional Stuart-Jacobite Freemasonry driven underground, various quasi-Masonic societies were organized, which preserved in some cases older Rosicrucian themes and in others encouraged newer deistic trends. The restless explorers of this shadowy Masonic world sometimes crossed political lines to pursue their researches and experiments. And Swift seemed to point to the flamboyant Ulsterman, John Toland, who embodied these shifting boundaries, as he moved from Catholicism to Episcopalianism to Presbyterianism to Pantheism. Swift would later view Toland's works as dangerous expressions of the occultist-radicalism of the "Knocking Jacks of the North." In her important but controversial book, *The Radical Enlightenment: Pantheists, Freemasons, and Republicans* (1981), Margaret Jacob argued that Toland was involved in 1710 in a "private Masonic lodge" at The Hague, known as "the Knights of Jubilation," but she did not examine his earlier experiences in Ireland and Scotland that stimulated his interest in secret societies.[29]

Baptized as Johannes Eugenius (Sean Owen) in 1670 in northern Ireland and raised as a Gaelic-speaking Catholic, Toland converted to Anglicanism in 1686, became a protégé of the bishop of Derry, and entered Glasgow University in 1687.[30] According to Dr. Edmund Gibson, who knew Toland in 1694, he soon became a controversial figure:

> wanting a Competent he apply'd himself to the Archbishop of Glasgow, under pretence of being a great admirer of Church Government and Episcopacy. But not meeting with the encouragement he expected (for his Grace had been armed with a Character of him, tho something he did get) he struck in very zealously with the Presbyterians, went to their meetings, and was very

---

[26] *Ibid.*, 48, 50; plus, A. Williamson, "Pil for Pork-Eaters", 237-58.
[27] J. Swift, *Tale of a Tub*, 353-60, the "Notes on Dark Authors."
[28] W. Temple, "Of Poetry,"in *Miscellaneous Essays*, 200-01.
[29] M. Jacob, *Radical Enlightenment*, xv, 233.
[30] J.G. Simms, "John Toland (1670-1722), a Donegal Heretic," *Irish Historical Studies*, 16 (1969), 304-20.

liberal in his abuses not only of the Arch Bp, but of the whole Order. He got a rabble together, and at the Head of them in the Market place burn't the Pope; upon which occasion he made a formal Speech against the then Magistrates o' the Town for being Episcopal... He fail'd not to cast in his mite when the Episcopal Clergy were *rabbled*... He pretended to work wonders by some secret arts, and so seduced a number of young students.[31]

Toland remained in Glasgow until late 1689, where he "may have dabbled in some occult arts (and later would be referred to as a Rosicrucian)."[32] Toland scholars have been puzzled by these occultist activities, for they were unaware of the long Rosicrucian-Masonic tradition in Scotland (and among the Scottish enclaves in Ulster). Many of the radical Presbyterians who opposed James II remembered the militant Protestant crusade of the early Continental Rosicrucians. Among those who favored a return to Covenanting ideals was Andrew Fletcher of Saltoun, who accompanied William's invasion force to England and then returned to Scotland in spring 1689. Fletcher and other anti-monarchists organized "the Club," an eclectic nationalist group that struggled for constitutional reform.[33] According to his 1798 biographer, the radical Freemason Robert Watson, Fletcher drew upon the quasi-Masonic organizing tactics of late seventeenth-century Covenanters in Glasgow:

> the people took an oath, called the solemn league and covenant, not unlike the oath of the united irishmen [in 1798], by which they bound themselves to support one another, and persevere until they obtained a redress of grievances.*
>
> ....
> * [Footnote]. It is worth remarking, that the Scots, in the neighborhood of Glasgow, were the first people who took a secret oath to counteract the encroachments of despotism...[34]

A.T.Q. Stewart argues that there was a strong Masonic component in the United Irishmen.[35] As we shall see, Fletcher was interested in architecture and operative Masonry, as well as occult phenomenon and clairvoyance. If Toland met Fletcher or his Glasgow network, it would explain his own fusion of Covenanting, Rosicrucian, and Masonic ideas.

Toland received a certificate from the Glasgow magistrates that he had behaved himself as "ane trew protestant and loyal subject."[36] He then transferred to Edinburgh University in late 1689, during the period of Fletcher's radical campaign. Dr. Gibson, in a follow-up letter, reported on Toland's occult activities in Edinburgh:

> he mov'd to Edinburrow, and set up there for a Rosacrucian: gave them the nice name of Sages, and printed a Book in French and English, with this

---

[31] Bodleian: Rawlinson MSS.D.923, f.317 (Dr. Edmund Gibson to Rev. Dr. Charlett); quoted in F.H. Heinemann, "John Toland and the Age of Enlightenment," *Review of English Studies*, 20 (1944), 127-28.

[32] Stephen Daniel, *John Toland: His Methods, Manners, and Mind* (Montreal, 1984), 6.

[33] James Halliday, "The Club and the Revolution in Scotland," *Scottish Historical Review*, 45 (1966), 143-59.

[34] Robert Watson, *The Political Works of Fletcher of Salton* (London, 1798), 39.

[35] A.T.Q. Stewart, *A Deeper Silence: The Hidden Roots of the United Irishmen* (London, 1993), 156-57, 163-78, 184-85.

[36] J. Simms, "Toland," 305.

Title, *The Sage of the Time.* He had contriv'd that there should be some appearance of a flame in a closet near a Street, and no harm done. When all
was safe and the House not burnt down or injur'd, as the Neighbours expected, his reputation grew upon it quickly, but whether under the name
ofConjuror, or what other title, I know not. An acquaintance of his tells me,
he has heard him express a very favourable opinion of Popery.[37]

Toland's movement between different political and religious camps was not unusual
during this period, when many Scots became so disillusioned with William III's policies
that radical Whigs began to collaborate with Jacobites. Robert Sullivan notes that Toland's "introduction to the world of secret societies, which fascinated him throughout
his life," probably took place in Scotland.[38] His later comments (in 1721) on Scottish
operative Masonry reveal his access to the local craft fraternity.[39] We will return to Toland's esoteric and exoteric activities when he becomes a target of Swift's wrath from
1696 onward.

*

* *

In England William III's preoccupation with European war plans meant that he paid
little attention to architecture. When James Anderson noted the decline in Freemasonry
under the Williamite regime, he made an exception for lodges formed "in or near the
Places where great Works were carried on":

Thus Sir Robert Claytor [Clayton] got an Occasional Lodge of his Brother
Masters to meet at St. Thomas's Hospital Southwark, A.D. 1693, and to advise the Governours about the best Design of rebuilding that Hospital as it
now stands most beautiful; near which a stated Lodge continued long afterwards.[40]

Clayton, a wealthy City financier, was the son of a carpenter, who spurred his lifelong
interest in practical building projects and architectural design. On 12-15 October 1677
Clayton invited John Evelyn to visit him in order to examine his expensive new house.[41]
Evelyn then tried to persuade Clayton to rebuild the dilapidated church on his property.
Perhaps influenced by Evelyn, on 20 October Clayton used his political influence as a
London alderman to recommend to the Lord Mayor and Court of Aldermen that the
"present charter" of the Company of Masons be extended seven miles around the city as
"an advantage" to it.[42] Throughout 1679 Clayton consulted with the Robert Hooke on

---

[37] Bodleian: Ballard MS. v.27 (Dr. Gibson to Dr. Charlett); in F.H. Heinemann, "John Toland, France,
Holland, and Dr. Williams," *Review of English Studies*, 25 (1949), 347. Gibson also heard that he was born in
France of Franco-Irish parents.

[38] Robert Sullivan, *John Toland and the Deist Controversy: A Study in Adaptations* (Cambridge, 1982), 3.

[39] See ahead, Chapter Seven.

[40] J. Anderson, *Constitutions* (1738), 106-07.

[41] J. Evelyn, *Diary*, III, 9-10.

[42] M. Jacob, *Living the Enlightenment*, 70, 241n.80.

various architectural projects.[43] In 1695, two years after the Masonic meeting at St. Thomas's, he helped Evelyn and Wren survey the construction of Greenwich Hospital.[44]

That Clayton was an activist Whig, who campaigned against James II's accession, has led some scholars to assume that the "Occasional Lodge of his Brother *Masters*" had radical associations.[45] That assumption seems untenable, for Clayton maintained Masonic friendships with many royalists who shared an interest in architecture. For example, he collaborated with Hooke, who worked closely with Wren, throughout the Exclusion Crisis, when he and they were on opposite political sides. However, Clayton may have utilized what he learned about Masonic organization to further his political agenda. He had earlier participated in the Green Ribbon Club, which was lumped together with Freemasons and Rosicrucians in a satirical article in *Poor Robin's Intelligencer* (10 October 1676):

> Divertissements: these are to give notice, that the Modern Green-Ribbond Caball, together with the Ancient Brotherhood of the Rosy Cross; the Hermetick Adepti; and the Company of Accepted Masons, intend all to dine together on the 31 of November...having already given order for great store of Black-swan Pies, Poach'd Phoenix Eggs, Haunches of Unicorns, etc. To be provided for that occasion; All idle people who can spare so much time from the Cone-house, may prepare to be Spectators of the Solemnity. But are advised to provide themselves Spectacles of Malleable Glass; for otherwise 'tis thought the said Societies will (as hitherto) make their Appearance Invisible.[46]

Though Clayton remained a lifelong supporter of free-thinkers, he soon became disillusioned with the Williamite regime. Within a year of the "Glorious Revolution," he was criticized for not representing strongly the court's interest in the City.[47] A religious moderate, he was further criticized by Daniel Defoe for failing to lead the Non-conformist cause. Thus, his Masonic affiliation seems motivated by his architectural interests rather than radical political beliefs. He was a principled Whig, who maintained non-partisan architectural friendships, while sympathizing with the young deists and pantheists who dared to think unconventionally. Thus, when Toland returned from Holland to London in 1693-94, Clayton befriended him, and both men attended the radical Calves' Head Club, which celebrated the beheading of Charles I. Toland would subsequently be accused of participating in a "secret Club, who set themselves with a great deal of Industry to destroy all Reveal'd Religion."[48] This must have been too radical for Clayton, who eventually joined the Anglican church.

Christopher Wren continued his cautious career, but Robert Hooke's architectural activities evidently ended in 1693, when he made his last surveying visits to City

---

[43] Robert Hooke, *The Diary of Robert Hooke*, eds. H.W. Robinson and W. Adams (London, 1935), 399, 415, 425, 430.

[44] J. Evelyn, *Diary*, III, 317.

[45] M. Goldie, "Roots," 205; M. Jacob, *Radical*, 88-89. For criticism of Jacob's argument, see S. Daniel, *Toland*, 218-19; D. Stevenson, *Origins*, 226-27.

[46] *EMP*, 30-31.

[47] Perry Gauci, "Sir Robert Clayton," in Eveline Cruickshanks, Stuart Handley, and D.W. Hayton, *The House of Commons, 1690-1715* (Cambridge, 2002), III, 606-1715.

[48] R. Sullivan, *Toland*, 14-16.

churches.[49] At the same time, Hooke was dismayed at the decline of the Royal Society, which was accelerated by William's lack of interest in science and failure to support virtuoso enterprises.[50] Under a series of non-scientist presidents, the control of the society passed to the secretaries, who were responsible for publishing the *Transactions*. As in the early days of the society, there were still some activist Masonic members. Sir Hans Sloane, who became secretary in 1693, was a Mason, though the date of his initiation is unknown. Born to a Scottish landholder in Ulster, Sloane was a moderate Whig who maintained friendships with many Jacobites. He was also an inveterate collector, who amassed bizarre specimens and rare manuscripts, which included many Cabalistic, Rosicrucian, and Masonic works.[51]

Working and quarreling with Sloane was Dr. John Woodward, who evidently became a Mason in the 1690s.[52] Woodward's Masonic affiliation was linked with his investigations of stone quarries, where he collected fossil shells, and of Roman antiquities, which were discovered during the rebuilding of St. Paul's and other churches.[53] In 1691 he planned to tour Europe, in order to prepare a book on architecture, antiquities, museums, and libraries. In 1693 he was nominated to the Royal Society by his friend Hooke, who shared his multifarious "Masonic" interests, which included Athanasius Kircher's writings on the hieroglyphs. As Hooke noted, fossil shells were "Records of Antiquity," just like the ancient monuments and hieroglyphics.[54] Woodward studied reports from travellers to Egypt, and he began a lifelong effort to prove that the Egyptians borrowed not only their magical religion but their architectural prowess from the Jews. In his eclectic scientific career, Woodward represented a continuing virtuoso-Masonic tradition rooted in Moray's early tenure in the Royal Society. He would later become the target of Swift's satire.

For Jacobite Masons, their situation became increasingly vulnerable, which necessitated even more scrupulous secrecy. Eveline Cruickshanks observes that the persistent tradition of a Masonic lodge at St. Germain perhaps explains the Jacobite capacity to maintain clandestine communication, despite the proliferation of Williamite spies: "If there was indeed a masonic lodge at the exiled Stuart court, its existence was the best-kept secret of all. It could have provided an additional means of contacting secret supporters in both England and Scotland."[55]

As Jacobite Masons went underground and acted in the shadows, there was growing interest among virtuosos in the esoteric as well as architectural traditions of the craftsmen. While Swift endured his residency in Ulster, John Aubrey enthusiastically corresponded with Scottish and English students of the occultist and architectural sciences. Though no record has been found documenting Masonic membership for Aubrey, he had long been in contact with operative Masons; was close to Moray, Ashmole, and Evelyn; and was familiar with Wren's role in the fraternity. In the 1690's Aubrey drafted "an

[49] Paul Jeffery, *The City Churches of Christopher Wren* (London, 1996), 36; H. Colvin, *Biographical Dictionary*, 507.

[50] M. Hunter, *Science and Shape*, 154.

[51] Arthur Mac Gregor, ed., *Sir Hans Sloane* (London, 1994), 263-77; E. St. John Brooks, *Sir Hans Sloane* (London, 1954).

[52] Michael Spurr, "William Stukeley: Antiquarian and Freemason," *AQC*, 100 (1987), 118.

[53] Joseph Levine, *Dr. Woodward's Shield* (Berkeley, 1977), 23-30, 151.

[54] *Ibid.*, 32, 75-77.

[55] E. Cruickshanks, "Introduction," *Stuart Court*, xxiii.

unfinished Piece, Entitled *Architectonica Sacra*, which treats of the Manner of our Church-Building in England for Several Ages."[56] He also planned to publish *Monumenta Britannica*, which included "Chronologia Architectonica," a pioneering study of English architecture from the Dark Ages to his own time, and he devised a broadsheet expounding *Elements of Architecture*, which he hop'd that young men might "relish & like, and so fall to the study."[57] At the same time, he planned to write a "Treatise of Hermetique Philosophie" and allowed Evelyn to make notes from the manuscript.

In January 1694 Aubrey's Scottish correspondent Dr. James Garden sent from Aberdeen an account of the Highlanders' gift of second sight, which he connected with rumors of Rosicrucian activities in England: "as strange things are reported with you of 2d sighted men in Scotland so with us here of ye Rosicruzians in England."[58] Garden then told the story of David Williamson, a Scottish schoolmaster, who was invited to London by an English friend, who took him to a stately house in the country where a company of Rosicrucians asked him to join the society. When Williamson refused, his host boxed his ears and the scene disappeared. Garden advised Aubrey to question Williamson's son James, who now served as an Anglican minister near Canterbury and who could give him more details. In May Garden wrote Aubrey: "Its likely your book of hermetick philosophie (which I conceive will be very diverting to the reader) may contain some account of the Rosicrucians; if not, pray, let me know if there be any persons in England that goe under that name & what may be beleeved concerning them."[59]

Curiously, at Oxford Aubrey had recently met Toland, whose Rosicrucian activities in Scotland were described by their mutual acquaintance, the Oxford fellow Edmund Gibson, in June 1694.[60] Toland agreed with Aubrey's and Garden's theories on the Druidic origins of Stonehenge, and he may have recounted his own Rosicrucian experiences to Aubrey. In March 1695 Garden reminded Aubrey of his request for an account of the Rosicrucians, while in April John Archer complained after seeing the list of contents of Aubrey's proposed *Miscellanies*, "You see what a Volume of Rosicrusian philosophy we may expect."[61] In May Aubrey solicited information about the origins and nature of the Rosicrucians from his friend William Holder, Dean of Windsor, who evidently shared his interest in occult phenomenon.[62]

Another friend of Aubrey, the physician and philosopher John Locke, was also curious about the Rosicrucians and second sight, and Aubrey allowed him to copy Garden's letter on both phenomena. With Wren and Boyle, Locke had earlier studied under the Rosicrucian chemist Peter Sthael, but Locke's "turbulent spirit, clamorous, and never contented" caused complaint.[63] Nevertheless, Locke did collaborate with Sthael in preparing chemical medicines, which he preserved in a cabinet.[64] In 1679, while traveling in

---

[56] John Aubrey, *Miscellanies*, 2nd rev. ed. (London, 1721), ix.

[57] Michael Hunter, *John Aubrey and the Realm of Learning* (London, 1975), 162, 218.

[58] John Locke's transcription of Garden's letter; in Bodleian: MS. Locke, C.31, f.122. See also M. Hunter, *Occult Laboratory*, 42-43,, 151

[59] M. Hunter, *Aubrey*, 140; also 103-04, 141-47.

[60] *Ibid.*, 205; F. Heinemann, "John Toland," 126.

[61] M. Hunter, *Aubrey*, 140.

[62] *Ibid.*, 123.

[63] Anthony à Wood, *Athenae Oxonienses*, 3rd rev. ed., ed. Philip Bliss (London, 1813), I, lii-liii.

[64] Maurice Cranston, *John Locke: A Biography* (1957; London, 1966), 76.

France, Locke recorded an account of Rosicrucian deception given to him by his friend Nicolas Toinard:

> About the year 1618 or 20...they produced their paper which was the draught of a program to be posted up in Paris to tell the people that there were certain persons of a brotherhood come to town to cure all diseases... That which put them first upon doeing this was to play a trick to Lullyists who were then in vogue at Paris & cried up as men that had more then ordinary skill in the secrets of nature...[65]

Though Locke recorded the trickery involved in this Rosicrucian affair, he also took notes on the dissection of Cardinal Richelieu, which revealed that the Frenchman's incredible powers of sight and hearing were made possible by an extraordinary double number of optic and auditory nerves.[66] In 1690, when Locke published *An Essay Concerning Human Understanding*, he argued against the "romance way of physick," but he continued to privately investigate reports of extraordinary powers of vision.

Perhaps Locke read Reverend Kirk's treatise of 1691, which explained the Scottish capacity for second sight as a natural extension of the optical capacity. As Locke transcribed Garden's letter, he read that second sight relates only to things which will shortly come to pass (within six years), and that the adepts see everything visibly before their eyes.[67] The seers do not know where the gift comes from, but some have offered to teach it upon certain conditions. This offer perhaps explains the Scottish Freemasons' claim to possess (or acquire through instruction) the gift of second sight. From his Cabalistic studies, Locke may have recognized the similarities between Scottish clairvoyance and Cabalistic vision. In 1679 he not only discussed with Toinard the Rosicrucians but also the Zoharists, while both men tried to get copies of the *Kabbala Denudata* (1677-84), the Latin translation of thirteenth-century Jewish mystical texts.[68] By 1688 Locke was in touch with the editors Frances Mercurius Van Helmont and Knorr von Rosenroth, and the latter sent him a Cabalistic commentary on the *Abrégé* of Locke's forthcoming *Essay Concerning Human Understanding*. In his fascinating critique of Locke's theories, Rosenroth argued:

> That the understanding is a *tabula rasa* was not the teaching of the ancient Hebrews or of those philosophers who built on their foundations, namely Pythagoras and Plato. For they determined that the source of knowledge was reminiscence... God, being infinitely luminous...at the same moment produced all souls, which in the single body of the Messiah constituted a single luminous mass with one understanding and one will, by means of which faculties they were fashioned by the Messiah in the contemplation and love of God in order to obtain union with God.... By this argument the understanding could be called a *tabula rasa*, since it contained nothing that was not printed on it by divine light.

---

[65] Patrick Romanell, "Locke's Medico-Philosophical Papers," *Journal of the History of Ideas*, 25 (1964), 110.

[66] *Ibid.*, 112.

[67] Bodleian: Locke MS. c. 31, 111-18.

[68] John Locke, *The Correspondence of John Locke*, ed. E.S. de Beer(Oxford, 1976), II, 30, 46.

> The source of ideas here is said to be twofold: sensation and reflection. Rightly indeed if (1) the sixth sense is acknowledged or (counting the internal ones) the eighth or ninth, that is, internal vision. It may, on the one hand, be passive, i.e. perception of things communicated internally either divinely (through a dream, vision, trance, etc.) or by other spirits...or by another soul, whether through an embryo (Ibbur in Hebrew) concealed within us, or a Maggid, i.e., a voice expounding something to us, to which also infused feelings are relevant...[69]

Rosenroth's commentary must have fueled Locke's curiosity about Cabalistic notions of cognition and vision, and in October 1693 he was joined by Van Helmont, who stayed with him at Lady Masham's until February 1694.[70] At this time, Van Helmont was considered a Judaizing Rosicrucian by his critics.

During Van Helmont's Continental travels, he had also become friendly with Gottfried Wilhelm Leibniz and other mathematicians who utilized Cabala as they developed the *arte combinatoria*. Moreover, Van Helmont and Leibniz dreamed of establishing Rosicrucian-style societies of polymathia and pansophia.[71] Locke shared with Van Helmont a desire to inaugurate a tolerant, ecumenical society of "Pacifick Christians," and he sketched out possible rules for such a brotherhood.[72] Since the publication of Adrien Baillet's *Vie de Monsieur Descartes* in 1691, questions about the early Rosicrucian fraternity and its alleged contemporary disciples circulated in the scholarly and scientific world. Locke, an early reader of Descartes, was always interested in information about him.[73] Adrien Auzout, who knew Descartes in Paris, and Leibniz, who possessed original communications, assisted Baillet, which rendered the latter's Rosicrucian account uncomfortably plausible. That Auzout and Leibniz were foreign Fellows of the Royal Society also placed Rosicrucianism in a virtuoso context. Baillet demonstrated the conformity of Descartes's ideas with those of Francis Bacon, godfather of British natural science.

On the first plate of *Vie de Descartes*, "Earthly Truth" holds a wand with the All-Seeing Eye, a symbol that soon gained Masonic as well as Rosicrucian connotation. According to Baillet, Descartes wanted to meet and converse with the brothers of the Rose Cross, for it was claimed that their society had only a view to research the truth of natural things and the true science.[74] Baillet then gave a history of the original Rosicrucians and recounted Descartes's attempt to contact them in Germany, which led to charges when he returned to Paris that he was an initiate of the fraternity. Given the current debate about the reality or validity of Rosicrucian science, Locke's investigations of supra-natural perceptual phenomena were *à la mode*.

By 1694 Locke was also friendly with Fletcher of Saltoun, who shared his radical political ideas and interest in second sight. While Locke advised Fletcher about his family's

---

[69] *Ibid.*, III, 400-03.

[70] *Ibid.*, IV, 730; V, 7. For Locke's friendship with Van Helmont, see Allison Coudert, *The Impact of the Kabbalah in the Seventeenth Century: The Life and Thought of Francis Mercurius Van Helmont* (Leiden, 1999).

[71] Allison Coudert, *Leibniz and the Kabbalah* (Dordrecht, 1995); also, M. K. Schuchard, "Leibniz, Benzelius, and Swedenborg: The Cabalistic Roots of Swedish Illuminism," in Richard Popkin and Gordon Weiner, eds., *Leibniz, Mysticism, and Religion* (Dordrecht, 1998).

[72] J. Locke, *Correspondence*, V, 3-4; Bodleian: MS. Locke, c.17.f.80; see A. Coudert, *Van Helmont*.

[73] H.R. Fox Bourne, *The Life of John Locke* (New York, 1876), I, 63-71.

[74] Adrien Baillet, *La vie de Monsieur Descartes* (Paris, 1691), I, 87.

medical problems, the Scot informed Locke about his researches in Egyptian history and religion. Evidently unaware of the Scottish origin myth of the Greek Gathelus and his Egyptian wife Scota, Locke was surprised that Fletcher could find the "footsteps" of Egyptian mysteries and priestcraft while ensconced in his northern study.[75] Fletcher would later recommend to Locke a Scottish friend, Martin Martin, who planned to publish *A Description of the Western Islands of Scotland*, which included "A Particular Account of the Second Sight, or Faculty of foreseeing things to come, by way of vision, common among them." Fletcher assured Locke that he would be "mightyly pleased with his account concerning that which is called the Second, but more properly the first or prophetick sight; as well as smell and hearing."[76]

In 1694-95 Locke was in contact with Sir Edward Harley, who had been a Masonic friend of the late Moray, and with Harley's son Robert, who would become a Mason and maintain secretive bonds with certain Scottish Masons.[77] He was friendly with other Freemasons, such as Sloane and Woodward, and he met Toland, who showed Locke his manuscript of *Christianity Not Mysterious* before its publication in late 1695.[78] As Toland compared the early Jewish and Greek mystery religions to Christianity, he utilized terms that would later surface in the higher degrees of Masonry: "All the Excluded were ...stil'd the PROFANE, as those not in Orders with us the LAITY. But the cunning PRIESTS...thought fit to *initiate* or instruct certain Persons in the meaning of their Rites."[79] The initiates were sworn to secrecy, passed through degrees, and were assured that ultimately they would dwell with the gods: "The Heathens had five degrees necessary to Perfection. First, common Purgation; Secondly, more private Purgation; Thirdly, a liberty of standing among the initiated; Fourthly, Initiation; and, Lastly, the right of seeing everything, or being Epopts."[80] Arguing that early Christians copied these Jewish and Pythagorean rites, Toland quoted the church fathers on the Christian "mystery": "Clemens Alexandrinus tell us that...the Christian Discipline was called Illumination, because it brought hidden things to light, the Master (CHRIST) alone removing the Cover of the Ark, that is, the Mosaick Vail.[81]

Locke's network of reformist political and scientific thinkers included the Molyneux brothers in Dublin, whose family had a long history of Masonic interests. Their father Samuel served as Irish Clerk of the Works and master gunner, and he subsequently gained fame as "an experimentalist in the science of gunnery."[82] His sons William and Thomas were enthusiastic virtuosos who maintained interests in mathematics, mechanics, medicine, and architecture. William Molyneux translated Descartes's *Meditations* in 1680, helped found the Dublin Philosophical Society in 1683, and was elected FRS in 1685.

---

[75] J. Locke, *Correspondence*, V, 81, 275; VIII, 436. For the Gathelus and Scota tradition, see W. Matthews, "The Egyptians in Scotland," 289-306.

[76] J. Locke, *Correspondence*, VII, 471.

[77] *Ibid.*, V, 59, 148. For the Masonic relationship between Edward Harley and Robert Moray, see M. Schuchard, *Restoring the Temple*, 640-43,660-61. For evidence that Edward's son Robert was considered "an honest mason," see Paula Backsheider, *Daniel Defoe* (Baltimore, 1989), 214.

[78] J. Locke, *Correspondence*, V, 114, 127, 737, 506; VI, 35, 320; S. Daniel, *Toland*, 8.

[79] John Toland, *Christianity Not Mysterious*, 2nd ed. (London, 1702), 68.

[80] *Ibid.*, 161.

[81] *Ibid.*, 114.

[82] R. Loeber, "Early Classicism," 51-52; "Thomas and William Molyneux," *DNB*.

For three years, he served as chief engineer and surveyor-general of the king's buildings and works, in which capacity he rebuilt Dublin Castle. Through his brother Thomas, who met Locke in Holland when both were studying medicine, he became an enthusiastic disciple of Lockean philosophy.

The Molyneux family amassed a rare and extensive collection of architectural pattern books, from Palladio to Evelyn, including materials on domestic building and military fortification. In February 1711, while Thomas designed a large townhouse in Dublin, he recorded or copied a Masonic catechism, with a memorandum about signs and words. Douglas Knoop suggests that it was "a mason's *aide de mémoire*" and represents "a link between the operative masonry of the seventeenth century and the speculative masonry of the eighteenth century."[83] Thomas was probably a member of the Trinity College lodge, well-known since 1688, and his manuscript was deposited in the college library. This "Trinity College, Dublin MS." drew on Scottish traditions, and it closely resembled the "Edinburgh Register House MS." of 1696, which was titled "Some Questions Anent the Mason Word." We will return to the Scottish document when we deal with secret Jacobite-Masonic activities in 1696. Knoop suggests further that Molyneux's document had a non-operative origin:

> Whereas operative masonry, so far as the Mason Word was concerned, apparently recognized only two classes of masons, viz., either entered apprentices and fellowcrafts, or fellow-crafts and masters, this MS. distinguishes three classes, viz., entered apprentices, fellow craftsmen, and masters, each with its own secrets. It is the earliest-known MS. to make such a distinction.[84]

This context of a Lockean circle or network with known Masonic interests raises new questions about a letter of 1696, attributed (controversially) to Locke, in which he asserted his desire to become a Freemason. The letter was first published as *Ein Brief Von dem Berüchtigt herrn Johann Locke, betressend die Frey-Maureren* (Frankfurt, 1748); it was then reprinted in the *Gentleman's Magazine* (September 1753). In summer 1754 it was published in *A Masons' Creed, to Which will be Subjoin'd, a Curious Letter from Brother Locke, Author of the Essay on Human Understanding.*[85] Locke's early biographer H.R. Fox Bourne accepts the letter as Locke's but guesses that it is satirical, while adding that "Locke's learned historical and philosophical notes sufficiently attest his curiosity."[86] Locke's later editor E.S. de Beer notes that "it is more likely to be spurious" and does not reprint it in Locke's *Correspondence*.[87] However, neither of these scholars examined the context of Locke's Masonic friends and his interest in Scottish second-sight, which lend new plausibility to his authorship of the letter, though not to the authenticity of the old manuscript itself.[88] The

---

[83] Douglas Knoop, "The Mason Word," *AQC*, 51 (1938), 210.

[84] *Ibid.*, 210.

[85] R. Péter, *British Freemasonry*, I, xlv, n.90. *The Masons' Creed* was advertised in the *Public Advertiser* (26 June and 8 July 1754), and in *The Monthly Review* (July 1754).

[86] Fox Bourne, *Locke*, II, 307-08.

[87] J. Locke, *Correspondence*, V, 631. See also J.R. Clarke, "John Locke and Freemasonry," *AQC*, 78 (1965), 168-71.

[88] In "The Philologist and the Forger," *The Bodleian Quarterly*, 26 (1920), 27, the supposed 15th century Leland MS. is deemed a forgery, for no such MS. has "ever come to light and Mr. Madan, in his Summary Catalogue, refers to it as mythical." Another librarian points out that the word "kymistrye" (chemistry) is

Masonic historian Ric Berman keeps the question open, noting that the letter, "if genuine," provides "an example of early scholarly interest in Freemasonry."[89] In the following discussion, I will accept Locke as the *possible* author.

Dated 6 May 1696 and written to "the Rt Hon*** Earl of ****," Locke recounted his study of a sixteenth-century Masonic manuscript:

> My Lord,
>
> I have at length by the help of Mr. C----ns procured a Copy of that MS. in the Bodleian Library, which you were so curious to see... Most of the Notes annex'd to it, are what I made Yesterday for the Reading of my Lady MAS-HAM, who is become so fond of masonry, as to say, that she now more than ever wishes herself a Man, that she might be capable of Admission into the Fraternity... the Original is said to have been in the Hand-writing of K.H.VI [King Henry VI] Where that Prince had it is at present an Uncertainty: But it seems to me to be an Examination (taken perhaps before the king) of some one of the Brotherhood of MASONS: among whom he entered himself, as 'tis said, when he came out of his Minority, and thenceforth put a Stop to a Persecution that had been raised against them...[90]

After making comments on the manuscript, Locke concluded:

> I know not what effect the sight of this old paper may have upon your LORDSHIP; but for my own part I cannot deny, that it has so much raised my curiosity; as to induce me to enter myself into the fraternity; which I am determined to do (if I may be admitted) the next time I go to LONDON, (and that will be shortly).[91]

Fox Bourne identifies the recipient as Thomas Herbert, 8th Earl of Pembroke, who had befriended Locke in 1676, when both were on the Continent. Playing "the ambiguous role of a moderate Tory," Pembroke was subsequently employed by the Stuart and Williamite regimes.[92] He was a generous patron of Locke, who dedicated his *Essay Concerning Human Understanding* (1690) to him. A mathematician and virtuoso, he was elected an FRS in 1685 and served as the society's president in 1689-90. According to Fox Bourne, "it would seem that the Earl of Pembroke was anxious for information on freemasonry, and especially anxious to know the contents of an old document" in the Bodleian.[93] His curiosity may have been piqued by a family history of Masonic affiliation, for James Anderson listed William Herbert, 3rd Earl of Pembroke, as Grand Master in 1618.[94] Moreover, the 8th earl's son, Henry Herbert, 9th Earl of Pembrok, was "later a prominent

---

not found in English until around 1600; see N.W.J. Haydon, "Lelande-Locke MS.," *AQC*, 50 (1940), 128. However, they do not go further to deem Locke's letter itself a forgery.

[89] R. Berman, *Foundations*, 14.

[90] "Ancient MS. on Free Masonry," *Gentleman's Magazine*, 23 (September 1753), 417.

[91] *Ibid.*, 420.

[92] "Thomas Herbert, 8th Earl of Pembroke," *ODNB*.

[93] Fox Bourne, *Locke*, II, 307-08.

[94] J. Anderson, *Constitutions (1738)*, 99.

Freemason."[95] Fox Bourne then speculates that Locke's assistant was Anthony Collins but admits that he cannot trace the connection.[96] Margaret Jacob mistakenly states that the *recipient* was the freethinker Anthony Collins and assumes that the "Mr C-----s" mentioned was the same man.[97] However, Anthony Collins did not correspond with or meet the philosopher until 1703; from that date, over the next eighteen months, he visited Locke five times at Oates and acted as his agent in the city, buying books, contacting friends, and reporting news.[98] Thus, Locke could not have referred to Anthony Collins in the Masonic letter.

However, in 1696, when the letter was written, Locke may have been assisted by William Collins, a prominent operative Mason, who was then working as the partner of Edward Strong, an Oxfordshire Mason and Master of the Masons' Company in London.[99] Through Strong, who worked closely with Wren and other architecturally-minded Fellows of the Royal Society (such as Evelyn and Hooke), Collins may well have met Locke and assisted him in finding the old Masonic manuscript. At that time, many manuscripts in the Bodleian were still uncatalogued, and a request from a prominent aristocrat like Pembroke to borrow one would probably be fulfilled. More importantly, Collins certainly could have sponsored Locke for "acception" or "adoption" in the London Masons' Company, for non-stonemasons and gentlemen were permitted to join if they paid a higher fee.[100] Berman suggests that the "fraternity" mentioned in the letter was "the 'Acception,' an inner circle among the London Company of Masons."[101]

Claude Jones observes that while "there is no incontrovertible proof" that Locke's letter and the manuscript were genuine, the antiquarian pieces in the *Gentleman's Magazine* were "published in good faith."[102] Moreover, "the editors were conscious of their Masonic readers," for they carried reports of current Masonic activities in the same issue. In the November 1753 issue, a Masonic reader in Norwich wrote about the great interest in Locke's letter among local brethren. It subsequently appeared in Jonathan Scott's *Pocket Companion and History of Free-Masons* (1759); in William Preston's *Illustrations of Masonry* (1772); in William Hutchinson's *The Spirit of Masonry in Moral and Elucidatory Lectures* (1775); in Laurence Dermott *Ahiman Rezon* (1778), the official handbook of the Grand Lodge of the "Antients." In 1804 Alexander Lawrie, a rationalist Scottish Mason, reinforced the argument: "The style of the letter...and the acuteness of the annotations, resemble so much that philosopher's manner of writing, and the letter is so descriptive of Mr. Locke's real situation at the time when it was written, that it is almost impossible to deny their authenticity."[103] Thus, for five decades after its publication, the letter was

---

[95] R. Berman, *Foundations*, 243 n.42. Róbert Péter notes that the term Grand Master probably pre-dates the Grand Lodge phase and was used to address the Master of a lodge, before it became reserved for the Master of the Grand Lodge; see *British Freemasonry*, IV, 397 n.7.

[96] Fox Bourne, *Locke*, I, 518.

[97] M. Jacob, *Living the Enlightenment*, 63.

[98] James O'Higgins, *Anthony Collins: The Man and His Works* (The Hague, 1970), 3-4.

[99] E. Conder, *Hole Craft*, 239-40; H. Colvin, *Biographical Dictionary*, 936.

[100] Henrik Bogdan and Jan Snoek, eds., *Handbook of Freemasonry* (Leiden, 2014), 75.

[101] R. Berman, *Foundations*, 14.

[102] Claude Jones, "Locke and Masonry," *Neuphilologische Mitteilungen*, 67 (1966), 72-78.

[103] M. Jacob, *Living the Enlightenment*, 239n.50; Alexander Lawrie, *The History of Masonry* (Edinburgh, 1804), 97.

accepted as genuine. Margaret Jacob notes that "throughout the eighteenth century, English Masons claimed Locke as one of their own, and the 18th-century portrait gallery of the Grand Lodge includes him"; nevertheless, she characterizes the 1696 letter as "of very dubious origin."[104] Given the continuing controversy about Locke's alleged Masonic affiliation, it is worth examining his real situation at the time and what he may have found attractive and provocative in the Masonic manuscript (whether genuine, spurious, or a credulously mis-dated copy).

To the question, "What mote ytt be," Locke annotated "that is, what may this mystery of MASONRY be?"

> The answer imports, that it consists in natural, mathematical, and mechanical knowledge, some part of which (as appears by what follows) the masons pretend to have taught the rest of mankind, and some part they still conceal.[105]

The question, "Howe comede ytt yn Engelonde?" was answered by "Peter Gower a Grecian," who "journeyedde ffor kunnynge yn Egypte,...where fromme, yn Processe of Tyme, the Arte passed yn Engelonde." Locke enjoyed teasing out this one:

> I was puzzled at first to guess who Peter Gower should be, the name being perfectly English...but as soon as I thought of Pythagoras, I could scarce forebear smiling, to find that Philosopher had undergone a Metempsychosis he never dreamt of. We need only consider the French pronunciation of his Name Pythagore, that is, Petagore, to conceive how easily such a mistake might be made by an unlearned clerk. That Pythagoras travelled for knowledge into Egypt is known to all the learned, and that he was initiated into several different orders of Priests, who in those days kept all their learning secret from the vulgar, is as well known. Pythagoras also made every Geometrical theorem a secret, and admitted only such to the knowledge of them, as had undergone a five years silence...[106]

Locke was intrigued by the answer to "Do the Maconnes descover here Artes unto Others?" He noted:

> This Paragraph hath something remarkable in it. It contains a justification of the secrecy so much boasted of by Masons, and so much blamed by others; asserting that they have in all ages discover'd things as might be useful, and that they conceal such only as would be hurtful either to the world or themselves. What these secrets are, we see afterwards.[107]

The Masons claimed to teach "the Artes Agricultura, Architectura, Astronomia, Geometria, Numeres, Musica, Poesie, Kymistrye, Governmente, and Relygyonne." Morevoer, they themselves "haveth allein the Arte of fyndynge neue Artes, which Arte the ffyrste

---

[104] M. Jacob, *Radical*, 88. She later asserts that the letter was "a forgery," but that was "not known in the eighteenth century"; see *Living*, 63.

[105] *Gentleman's Magazine* (1753), 418.

[106] *Ibid.*, 77.

[107] *Ibid.*, 78.

Maconnes receaved from Godde; by the whyche they fyndethe whatte Artes" they please. Locke commented:

> The art of inventing arts, must certainly be a most useful art. My Lord Bacon's Novum Organum, is an attempt towards somewhat of the same kind. But I must doubt, that if ever the Masons had it, they have now lost it; since so few new arts have been lately invented, and so many are wanted. The Idea I have of such an art is, that it must be something proper to be apply'd in all the sciences generally, as Algebra is in numbers, by the help of which new rules of arithmetic are and may be found.[108]

Locke's guess came strikingly close to the Lullist *Ars Magna*, which Swift would later claim provided the key to Freemasonry.[109] Did Thomas Molyneux also learn this in the Trinity College lodge?

"Whatt do the the Maconnes concele, and hyde?" The answer further piqued Locke's curiosity:

> They concelethe the Arte of ffyndynge neue Artes, and thattys for here owne Proffytte, and Preise; they concelethe the Arte of kepynge Secretes, that soe the World mayethe nothinge concele from them. Thay concelethe the arte of Wunderwerckynge, and of fore sayinge thynges to comme, thatt so thay same artes may not be usedde of the wyckedde to evylle Ende; they also concelethe the Arte of chaunges, the Wey of Wynnynge the Facultye of Abrac, the Skylle of becommynge gude and parfyghte wythouten the Holpynges of Fere, and Hope; and the Universelle Longage of Maconnes.[110]

Locke suggested that the "Arte of chaunges" referred to "the transmutation of metals," but he was "utterly in the dark" about the "Facultye of Abrac." A reader of Locke's comment wrote to the *Gentleman's Magazine* (November 1753) "that by the *Facultye of Abrac* is meant the chimerical virtues ascribed to the magical term ABRACADABRA," where it appears in the seventh row of the usual triangular writing.

Locke indeed travelled to London in late May, but it is unknown if he pursued his Masonic inquiries. Thus, the question of his alleged Masonic affiliation remains open. Soon after he supposedly wrote the letter to Pembroke, his association with Toland placed him in a vulnerable position, especially concerning any charges of affiliation with a secret society. Though Toland anonymously published *Christianity Not Mysterious* in December 1695, by summer 1696 his vanity provoked him into "allowing his name to be attached to what was proving to be a *succès de scandale*."[111] Already attacked as a participant in "a Club of Prophane Wits," he was now suspected of organizing a Socinian sect. Boldly placing his name on the title-page of a second edition, Toland learned that his book was presented by the Grand Jury of Middlesex, and he prepared to flee England for Ireland. At the same time, Locke learned about the arrest of a student in Edinburgh for espousing essentially Tolandian beliefs. He followed the Scottish trial with great interest and

---

[108] *Ibid.*, 79.
[109] J. Swift, *Prose*, V, 328.
[110] *Gentleman's Magazine* (1753), 80.
[111] R. Sullivan, *Toland*, 7.

perhaps fear, for the accusations against Thomas Aikenhead "the Atheist" threatened to tar Locke as well as Toland.

Aikenhead was the son of an apothecary ("chirurgeon"), who had earlier been accused of "selling poisonous and amorous drugs and philters to provoke lust," resulting in the near death of one woman.[112] That the son may have learned something of chemistry and even alchemy from his father's craft became relevant to the later charges against Thomas. As a student at the University of Edinburgh in 1693-96, Thomas fearlessly and recklessly explored the writings of "free thinkers" such as Vanini, Hobbes, Blount, Spinoza, Locke and, almost certainly, Toland (his *Christianity Not Mysterious*). Like Toland, he was accused of trying to recruit young men to his radical beliefs and of setting up as a magician.[113] Michael Graham suggests that Toland's earlier Rosicrucian activity influenced Aikenhead, but he also notes that Freemasonry was more prevalent than Rosicrucianism in Scotland.[114] However, it is certainly possible that both Toland and Aikenhead had some kind of contact with Masons interested in Rosicrucianism, for such combined interests were traditional in Scotland throughout the seventeenth-century.[115]

The four student accusers of Aikenhead charged that he was familiar with theories (and possibly techniques) of natural magic. He allegedly called the New Testament "the History of the Impostor Christ," who had learned magic in Egypt:

> returning from Egypt into Judea, he picked up a few blockish ignorant fisher-fellows, whom he knew by his [magical] skill and phisiognomie, had strong imaginations, and that by the help of exalted imagination he play'd his pranks as you blasphemously terme the working of his miracles. Lyke as you affirmed Moses, if ever you say ther was such a man, to have also learned magick in Egypt, but that he was both the better artist and better politician than Jesus...[116]

Aikenhead also asserted that "baptisme was a magicall ceremony," that "the Revelations was ane alchimy book for finding out the philosopher's stone," and that "he could make himself immortal." Merging his deist-pantheist notions with magical theories of the imagination, he declared:

> that God-man was as great a contradictione as *quadratum_rotundum*,... that God, the world, and nature, were all one thing, and that the world was from eternitie; ...that man's imaginatione duely exalted by airt and industry might create a world, and produce any thing produceable...[117]

From his prison cell, Aikenhead defended himself by claiming that many students shared his skeptical opinions, but when he faced the guilty verdict from the privy council,

---

[112] T.B. Howell, *A Complete Collection of State Trials* (London, 1809-28), XIII, 918.

[113] Michael Hunter, "'Aikenhead the Atheist': The Context and Consequences of Articulate Irreligion in the Late Seventeenth Century," in Michael Hunter and David Wooton, eds., *Atheism from the Reformation to the Enlightenment* (Oxford, 1992), 221-54.

[114] Michael Graham, *The Blasphemies of Thomas Aikenhead: Boundaries of Belief on the Eve of the Enlightenment* (Edinburgh, 2008), 27.

[115] See Schuchard, *Restoring the Temple*, chapter 7.

[116] T. Howell, *State Trials*, XIII, 919.

[117] *Ibid.*, XIII, 926.

he recanted and offered himself as a martyr to the battle against deism: "it is my earnest desire [to the Lord] that my blood may give a stop to that rageing spirit of atheism which hath taken such footing in Britain, both in practice and profession. And of his infinite mercy recover those who are deluded with these pernicious principles."[118] Despite his petitions for mercy and the support of moderate clergymen, the Presbyterian General Assembly wanted him dead. Thus, the Privy Council sustained the order for his execution by hanging on 18 January 1697.

Despite the harangues of Covenanting preachers against him, Aikenhead did have enough supporters to make the authorities fear disturbances, and they ordered two troops of armed guards to escort him to the gallows. One significant sympathizer was Robert Mylne, the prominent architect and Master Mason, who wrote that the young student had "acknowledged God, father, son, and Holy Ghost and sang a psalm. But some Presbyterian ministers followed him to death."[119] Michael Graham suggests that Aikenhead knew Mylne earlier, for he acquired a flat in a new stone townhouse constructed by Mylne, and they were close neighbors.[120] If so, Aikenhead may have learned that Robert Mylne's Masonic forebears were praised in *The Muses Threnodie* (1638), the Scottish poem that linked Masonry, Rosicrucianism, and second sight.[121] In February 1697, a Scottish opponent of Aikenhead's execution, James Johnston, sent to his friend Locke ("to satisfie your curiositie") a packet of materials on Aikenhead's case, including a manuscript copy of the prisoner's personally drafted *Cygnea Cantio* ("Swan Song").[122]

Michael Graham observes that in his troubled testimony, Aikenhead proclaimed the need for free inquiry "in the style of a Galileo or many of the *philosophes* who people the intellectual histories of the Enlightenment."[123] He described "a deistic God, entirely bound by logic, and only minimally related to the God of the Christian and Hebrew scriptures," and he rejected the charge that he practiced magic and conversed with devils. Locke was intrigued and disturbed by Aikenhead's "Swan Song," and he asked for a transcript of the trial, which his Scottish friend promised to send on 20 March. Johnston lamented the death of the twenty year-old student, believing that he should have been reprieved on grounds of "youth, levity, docility, and no designe upon others." The last qualification, which was not believed by his judges, was especially relevant to Locke's relationship with Toland, who would soon be compared to Aikenhead by his critics.[124]

While Locke collected materials on the executed Aikenhead (and the related burning of seven Scottish witches), his protégé Toland returned to Ireland in early 1697.[125] He was initially welcomed by William Molyneux, who wrote Locke that he admired Toland as a "candid Free-Thinker, and a good scholar," but especially for his "Acquaintance and

---

[118] *Ibid.*, XIII, 930.

[119] Mylne's annotations to Mungo Craig's attack on Aikenhead in his *Satyr Against Atheistical Deism* (1696); notes in copies of the work in the National Library of Scotland and British Library. See M. Graham, *Blasphemies*, 11, 122, 125n.39.

[120] Michael Graham (private communication, March 2012).

[121] For the Master Mason John Mylne (d. 1621) and the poem, see M. Schuchard, *Restoring the Temple*, 320-22.

[122] J. Locke, *Correspondence*, VI, 17-19, 56-57. The Aikenhead documents now comprise MS. Locke, b.4.fos.86-106 (Bodleian Library).

[123] M. Graham, *Blasphemies*, 118-20.

[124] R. Sullivan, *Toland*, 10-11, 44.

[125] M. Hunter, "Aikenhead," 236-37.

Friendship to you." However, by May, both Molyneux and Locke were apprehensive about the intense hostility aroused by Toland in Ireland. That month Peter Browne, an Anglican clergyman in Trinity College, published *A Letter in Answer to a Book, Entitl'd Christianity Not Mysterious; as Also to All Those Who Set Up for Reason and Evidence in Opposition to Revelation and Mysteries* (Dublin, 1697). Browne claimed to have traced Toland's background "from the time he first gave out he wou'd be *Head* of a Sect before he was thirty years of age," until he became an author, and from thence to "his coming into this Kingdom to spread his Heresies and put his designs in execution."[126] Through his knowledge of magic and his skeptical attitude, Toland implies that we cannot distinguish the delusions of the devil, feats of goblins and witches, and those "conjurers which he speaks of," from those supernatural phenomena produced by "the finger of God."[127] Further suggesting that Toland exploited the occult sciences for seditious purposes, Browne scorned his quotation from Clemens Alexandrinus that the Christian discipline consisted of "Illumination," charging that "we may call this New Old Sect of his, the Gnosticks of our Age." Browne was a fellow student and friend of Swift at Trinity, though Swift sometimes made fun of his character, noting that Browne "is a capricious gentleman," who must be flattered "monstrously upon his learning"; you must tell him that that "you have read his book against Toland a hundred times."[128]

Locke wrote William Molyneux about his regret that Toland had not visited him to receive advice about his behavior before he left for Dublin. William replied that Toland was bandying Locke's name around while he irritated all parties. The Molyneuxs and their political allies – who now resented William III's repressive policies towards Ireland – also suspected Toland of acting as a secret agent for the new Lord Chancellor, the strong Whig John Methuen, who arrived from London in June.[129] After the Irish Commons ordered that *Christianity Not Mysterious* be burned by the common hangman, Toland returned to England in September, where he found that Locke wanted nothing more to do with him.

When Locke complained (in his alleged letter to Pembroke) that the Masonic art of finding new arts, which he speculated was a mathematical technique, was evidently now lost, he pointed to a problem caused by the anti-Catholic biases that excluded many areas of inquiry from English students. Under the Stuart king James VI, training in the Art and Science of Memory – a visualization and mnemonic technique based on architectural imaging – had been required of Scottish operative Masons.[130] Among radical English Protestants, the Art of Memory – developed by Lull and Bruno as a key to all arts and sciences – was condemned as a Catholic image-making superstition.[131] Nevertheless, on the Continent innovative thinkers like Leibniz were willing to utilize the techniques of the Lullist *Ars Magna* in mathematical, philosophical, and theological speculations.

In order to appease English iconoclastic opposition but still utilize the mnemonic technique, a Huguenot refugee in London, Marius d'Assigny, published a Protestant,

---

[126] See Peter Browne, *A Letter in Answer to... Christianity Not Mysterious* (Dublin, 1697), 148, 199.

[127] *Ibid.*, 185, 204, 214, 228.

[128] I. Ehrenpreis, *Swift*, I, 75.

[129] R. Sullivan, *Toland*, 8-10.

[130] D. Stevenson, *Origin*, 45, 49-50, 87-96.

[131] Francis Yates, *The Art of Memory* (London, 1966), 278; and "The Art of Ramon Lull," *Journal of the Warburg and Courtauld Institute*, 17 (1954), 115-68.

word-oriented *Art of Memory* (1697), dedicated to young students at Cambridge and Oxford and designed to improve their speaking and preaching skills. D'Assigny admitted that the Art of Memory could be used in studying all manner of sciences, but he scorned that application as awkwardly Catholic:

> The Fancies of some Ingenious Men, and a Method which they lay down, and which may sometimes be useful I confess for the assistance of an Artificial Memory…
>
> It Consists in Places and Images, etc. Now some prescribe the Imagination of a fair and regular Building, divided into many Rooms and Galleries…which the Party must fancy to stand before him as so many Repositories where he is to place the Things or Ideas which he desires to remember… But this method of remembering things is cumbersome and fantastical, and perhaps may not be suitable to every Temper and Person.[132]

Throughout his treatise, d'Assigny hid his sources (Lull, Bruno, etc.) and hedged his instructions, in order to avoid charges that his publication was crypto-Papist. He cited Calvin and Luther as experts in the Art and urged Protestant students to learn it in order to convert audiences through "pulpit efficacy."

D'Assigny's version of the Art of Memory was the opposite of that traditionally taught by Scottish Freemasons. Thus, it is curious that the "Edinburgh Register House MS." of 1696, drafted while d'Assigny worked on his treatise, was prepared for a symbolic "lodge of the mind, a temple of memory."[133] In the manuscript, according to David Stevenson, "Certainly we have a building visualised in the mind in which features and objects are associated with concepts to be remembered"; more striking is "the general avoidance of overtly religious references":

> To have peopled the lodge of the mind with human images might seem to smack of idolatry, both to the Calvinist masons themselves and to the censorious ministers of the Church of Scotland. However crude and limited the lodge and its symbolism as described in the early catechisms may seem when compared to the classical art of memory, it may nonetheless have its origins in the concept of a temple of memory illustrating eternal truths and moral principles through images appropriate to the mason craft.[134]

As we shall see, d'Assigny's iconoclastic Protestant version of the Art found readers among Dissenters, and it was no coincidence that the prolific writer Daniel Defoe – who probably became a Freemason in Scotland in 1706 – acquired a copy of the work.[135] Fifield d'Assigny, a descendant, would later become a prominent Whig Freemason in Ireland.[136]

After Aikenhead was executed in the last *auto da fé* in the British isles, an unrepentant Toland found a kindred spirit in Giordano Bruno, who was burned for heresy in 1600. In 1698 Toland acquired Queen Elizabeth's copy of Bruno's *Spaccio della bestia trionfante*

---

[132] Marius d'Assigny, *The Art of Memory* (London, 1697), 81-84.
[133] D. Stevenson, *Origins*, 140.
[134] *Ibid.*, 142-43.
[135] The Bodleian copy of D'Assigny's *Art of Memory* is from Defoe's library.
[136] See ahead, Chapter Nineteen.

("The Expulsion of the Triumphant Beast"), which he enthusiastically circulated among his friends.[137] Bruno disguised his universalist pantheism in allegorical form, while he urged his readers to be guided by the "intellectual sun" and to recognize "an element of truth in all religions." He then satirized the contradictions and sectarian divisions within Christianity and revealed his admiration for the Hermetic mystery religion of Egypt. In the process, Bruno denigrated the Jews as mere inheritors of the superior traditions of the Egyptians. While in Paris, Bruno attended and admired the preaching of Jewish rabbis, whom he considered superior to their Christian contemporaries, but he scorned the ancient Jews as ancestors of the Christianity he was determined to transcend. However, Bruno did respect Cabala and recognized its importance to his hero Lull. As Arthur Imerti notes, "Since Bruno was attracted not only by the Pythagorean belief in metempsychosis but also, to a lesser extent, by its employment of numbers as symbols, we can readily understand the philosopher's interest in the numerical symbolism of the Cabala."[138]

In the *Spaccio*, Bruno argued that the "Cabala of the Jews (whatever wisdom may be found in its genus) has proceeded from the Egyptians, among whom Moses was instructed"; furthermore, let no one infer that "the sufficiency of the Chaldaean magic has come out of, and is derived from, the Jewish Cabala; because the Jews have been proved to be the excrement of Egypt, and there is no one who could have imagined that Egyptians have taken some worthy or unworthy principle from them."[139] For Toland, this was heady stuff, because the establishment theologians of his day credited the Jews with priority over the Egyptians. As Toland immersed himself in Bruno's writings, he learned more about the master's admiration for Pythagorean initiation and Lullist mnemonics. When Bruno boasted of being able to teach the Art of Memory in one hour, Toland may have seen possiblities for similar instruction among his secret sectarians. If he was aware of the Scottish Masons' instruction in the Art of Memory, he would have found Bruno's linkage of the mnemonic arts with invention and geometry relevant to a contemporary secret fraternity.[140]

In 1698 Toland reinforced his image as a seditious heretic when he published his *Life of Milton*. Claiming that Charles I did not write *Eikon Basilike*, a widely revered royalist apologia, Toland suggested that the books of the New Testament were perhaps equally pseudonymous. Critics promptly compared his ideas to those of the recently executed Aikenhead, and Toland found himself shunned by many of his previous friends. As earlier, he found refuge among the radical Presbyterians in the Scottish enclaves of London, and he solicited the protection of Sir Robert Clayton, a Freemason and fellow Whig. Within this context, in which Toland was charged with Rosicrucianism and other secret society affiliations, an anti-Masonic leaflet issued in 1698 seemed to target him and his fellow free-thinkers. Entitled *To All Godly People, in the Citie of London*, the anonymous author charged the Freemasons with heretical activities:

---

[137] James Jacob says Toland purchased a copy of the *Spaccio* in 1690; see his "Newtonian Theology and the Defense of the Glorious Revolution," in *Age of William and Mary*, 163; however, the acquisition is dated 1698 by R. Sullivan, *Toland*, 198, and S. Daniel, *Toland*, 200.

[138] Giordano Bruno, *The Expulsion of the Triumphant Beast*, trans. and ed. Arthur Imerti (New Brunswick, 1964), 306n.27.

[139] *Ibid.*, 240, 251.

[140] *Ibid.*, 6, 12, 17.

Having thought it needful to warn you of the Mischiefs and Evils practised in the sight of God by those called Freed Masons, I say take care lest their Ceremonies and secret Swearings take hold of you; and be wary that none cause you to err from Godliness. For this devilish Sect of Men are Meeters in Secret which swear against all without their Following. They are the Anti Christ which was to come leading Men from Fear of God. For how should Men meet in secret Places and with secret Signs taking care that none observe them to do the Work of God; are not these the Ways of Evil-doers? Knowing how that God observeth privily them that sit in Darkness they shall be smitten and the Secrets of their Hearts layed bare. Mingle not among this corrupt People lest you be found so at the World's Conflagration.[141]

These shadowy stirrings of eclectic activities within Freemasonry suggest the emergence of political and religious polarizations within the formerly operative fraternity in England. As radical Whigs became increasingly disenchanted with the limitations of William III's reforms, they were sometimes willing to cooperate with opposition Tories and even Jacobites. As knowledge about Freemasonry leaked out in antiquarian and journalistic sources, the oaths, rituals, and symbols that protected the brothers' secrets evidently proved attractive to a variety of men disaffected from the current government. Moreover, as the Jacobites became more aggressive in their efforts to overturn the Williamite regime, the government's surveillance over its critics made secrecy increasingly important for the motley crew of opposition.

---

[141] Anon., *To All Godly People, in the Citie of London* (London, 1698); also, *EMP*, 35.

CHAPTER THREE

JACOBITES, WILLIAMITES, AND DISPUTED ARCHITECTURAL TRADITIONS (1695-1703)

The Divine Architect has been pleased to honour this Excellent Art…
The Holy Ghost stiles the Mechanick Knowledge of Bezaleel and Aholiab,
Etc. the Spirt of God, Wisdom…. Our Blessed Redeemer was Pleased
to exercise this Art of Architecture, and to be a Mechanick, viz. a Carpenter
…which is no small honour to the Mechanick and Architect.

Richard Neve, *The City and Country Purchaser* (1703).

The God of Wealth was therefore made
Sole Patron of the Building Trade.

Jonathan Swift, "Van Brug's House" (1703).

By 1695 various former Williamites who were now crypto-Jacobites, began to maneuver themselves into positions of power. In 1738 James Anderson made the following claim in his revised, official Masonic history:

> This year [1695] our most noble Brother Charles Lennox Duke of Richmond and Lennox (Father of the present Duke) Master of a Lodge at Chichester, coming to the annual Assembly and Feast at London, was chosen Grand Master and approv'd by the King. Sir Christopher Wren was D.G. Master, who acted as before at the Head of the Craft, and was again chosen Grand Master, A.D.1698. Edward Strong, sen., Edward Strong, jun. Grand Wardens.[1]

---

[1] J. Anderson, *Constitutions (1738)*, 107.

Lennox was the natural son of Charles II and Louise de Keroualle, Duchess of Portsmouth, and he reportedly inherited a Franco-Scottish Masonic tradition through his own and his mother's connections.[2] Though Charles had been fond of Lennox, James II hated the Duchess of Portsmouth and stripped her child of certain offices. However, after Lennox was raised as a Catholic in France, he regained James's favor and volunteered to accompany him to Ireland. He was turned down because of his youth and instead received training in a French regiment. When Louis XIV disappointed him by not promoting him higher, Lennox secretly departed for England in February 1692. It was reported that he had stolen his mother's jewels, and she thought he was out of his senses. In London Lennox "found it convenient to change both his politics and religion"; he was received into the Church of England and made his peace with William III, who accepted him as 1st Duke of Richmond.[3]

Though Anderson claimed that William approved Richmond's assumption of the Grand Mastership, the duke soon came under suspicion for secret Jacobite intrigues. In 1696, while French troops waited at Dunkirk and Calais for orders to invade England, he initiated a man in the southern city of Chichester, a strategic port.[4] During this year, concerns that he was a secret Jacobite were at their height. According to French tradition, in the early 1700s Richmond maintained a lodge in his territory of Aubigny in France.[5] From a rare surviving document in Dunblane, Scotland, it is clear that Jacobite Masons were currently involved in new intrigues against William – intrigues that crossed the channel to the Stuart court at St. Germain. In January 1695, the minute book records the founding of the lodge at Dunblane.[6] According to David Stevenson,

> the first moves to found the lodge were being made by then, perhaps with those who were to form the lodge being initiated in advance to the secrets of the Mason Word by members...who had already been initiated elsewhere... Of thirteen members only four were operative masons, and seven were gentlemen non- operatives... it is immediately evident that the lodge had a strongly Jacobite political bias.[7]

Though Stevenson notes that "there is no sign that the lodge as such was connected with Jacobite political activities," the broader international context of Jacobite and Masonic activities suggests the contrary.

In February James Fitzjames, 1st Duke of Berwick – the natural son of James II and Arabella Churchill – made a secret journey from St. Germain to London to solicit support for a planned French invasion and Jacobite rising. Berwick's brother Henry currently served as titular Grand Prior of the British Knights of Malta which, as Swift suggested, possibly had Masonic associations in Scotland and Ireland.[8] While remaining incognito in London, Berwick attended a masked ball at Draper's Hall, where he whispered Jacobite

[2] Jean-André Faucher, *Dictionnaire Historique des Francs-Maçons* (Paris, 1988), 53.
[3] "Charles Lennox, First Duke of Richmond," *ODNB*.
[4] D. Stevenson, *Origins*, 225.
[5] P. Chevallier, *Histoire*, I, 10-11.
[6] A.F. Hatton,"The Early Minute Book of the Lodge of Dunblane,"*AQC*,67(1955), 84-119.
[7] D. Stevenson, *First Freemasons*, 107-08.
[8] M. Schuchard, *Restoring the Temple*, 744, 768-69.

tidings to potential supporters among the disguised guests.[9] Returning to St. Germain, Berwick reported to James that many persons of highest rank had engaged themselves to support the restoration but that they were unable to "take off the mask" and act until a body of troops had landed from France.[10] James did not reveal this cautious condition to Louis XIV; instead, his agents from St. Germain increased their efforts to suborn military and naval officers in England for a Jacobite rising.

Berwick did not reveal to James that he had learned of a plan to assassinate William III – a plan strikingly similar to the Rye House Plot to kill Charles II in 1683. An Irish Catholic participant in the new plot, Thomas Prendergast, betrayed the plan to the Earl of Portland and was richly rewarded by the government.[11] If the assassination plot included a Masonic element, then Portland was in a good position to discover suspicious signs, for William had earlier assigned him to work closely with (and possibly spy on) Wren and his Masons. Interestingly, Swift would later castigate Thomas Prendergast as "him who sham'd our Isle, traitor...Assassin, Informer vile."[12] He would heap additional scorn on his son Thomas, when the younger Prendergast served as a Whig Grand Warden in Irish Freemasonry. In the wake of the exposed plot, scores of high-ranking conspirators were arrested, and the government mounted intense surveillance over suspects, which drove Jacobite sympathizers even deeper underground. In such circumstances, the Masonic technique of maintaining loyalty, non-written communication, and secrecy would have been invaluable.

Thus, the increased emphasis on secrecy in the Edinburgh Register House MS. (1696) was probably a response to the dangerous political situation. One section was titled, "Some Questions that Masons use to put to those who have the word before they will acknowledge them," while another read, "The form of giving the mason word."[13] The questions, answers, and threatened penalties went far beyond the requirements of merely operative Masons. "Are you a Mason?" and "How shall I know it?" were answered, "You shall know it in time and place convenient" (with annotation, "Remark the fors[ai]d answer is only to be made when there is company present who are not masons. But if there be no such company by, you should answer by signes, tokens and other points of my entrie"). Did Berwick utilize these identification techniques while he whispered to guests at the masked ball? Edward Corp notes that the first documented lodge in Paris in 1725-26 included young Jacobites whose parents were probably members of the lodge at St. Germain – including a son of Berwick.[14] Moreover, Berwick's descendants would play active roles in *Écossais* Masonry throughout the eighteenth century.

In the Edinburgh MS., the catechist asks "What is the first point?" and the initiate responds, "Tell me the first point ile tell you the second. The first is to heill [hide, keep secret] and conceall; second, under no less pain, which is then cutting of your throat" (annotated "For you must make that sign when you say that"). "Where shall I find the

---

[9] Paul Monod, "Pierre's White Hat: Theatre, Jacobitism, and Popular Protest in London, 1689-1760," in E. Cruickshanks, *By Force or Default*, 167.

[10] Eveline Cruickshanks, "Attempts to Restore the Stuarts, 1689-96," in E. Corp and E. Cruickshanks, *Stuart Court in Exile*, 8-9.

[11] "Sir Thomas Prendergast, *ODNB*.

[12] J. Swift, *Complete Poems*, 550.

[13] D. Knoop, "Mason Word," 195-98.

[14] E. Corp, *L'Autre Exil*, 17.

key of your lodge" evoked an odd reply, "under the lap of my liver where all my secrets of my heart lie," while "Which is the key of your lodge" evoked "a weel hung tongue." The oath was administered to the candidate only "after a great many ceremonies to frighten" him, which included "1,000 ridiculous postures and grimaces" before being given the sign, postures, and words of entry. Douglas Knoop points out that the fellowcraft or master mason had secrets distinct from those of an entered apprentice and that the "five points of fellowship" ("foot to foot, Knee to Knee, Heart to Heart, Hand to Hand, and ear to ear") were given only in the higher degree. The apprentice made a vow of loyalty to the master and undertook a stringent oath of secrecy, in which he swore not to reveal by word or writing any part of what he should see or hear, nor to draw it with the point of a sword, or any other instrument upon snow or sand.[15]

The stress on secrecy was reinforced by the stress on the Solomonic origins of Freemasonry, which in Scotland would recall the widely-known Solomonic identification of the Stuart kings:

> Q. 8: What is the name of your lodge? *Ans.* Kilwinning.
> Q. 9: How stands your lodge? *Ans.* East and West as the Temple of Jerusalem.
> Q.10: Where was the first lodge? *Ans.* In the porch of Solomon's Temple.
> ....
> Q.1: [Annotation]. Then make the sign of fellowship and shake hand and you will be acknowledged a true mason. The words are in the 1 of the Kings ch 7, v 21, and in 2 Chr: ch 3 verse last [i.e., "And he set up the pillars in the porch of the temple; and he set up the right pillar, and called the name therof Jachin: and he set up the left pillar, and called the name thereof Boaz," etc.]

According to R.B. Scott, the full Hebrew interpretation of Jachin was "he (Yahweh) will establish the throne of David, and his kingdom to his seed for ever," and the coronations of later kings of the Davidic dynasty took place by this pillar.[16] He suggests that Boaz signified "In the strength of Yahweh shall the king rejoice."

By the late seventeenth century, many Scottish lodges possessed manuscript copies of the Old Charges and catechisms, which were guarded with intensifying secrecy. This suggests an increase in speculative Masonry – and recruitment of gentleman Masons – at a time when operative masonry was suffering from lack of royal support. Moreover, the risky use of written *aides de mémoire* was perhaps necessitated by the lack of time or desire of speculative (and political Masons) to learn the difficult Art of Memory, traditionally associated with architectural and mathematical visualization techniques and taught orally.

The failure of the Franco-Jacobite campaign diminished the prospect of full military support from France. By September 1697, Louis recognized that his country was exhausted by war, and he signed the peace treaty of Ryswick with William, recognizing the Dutch "usurper" as English king *de facto*. However, he refused to expel the Stuarts from St. Germain, and he continued to treat James as king *de jure*. Louis's contradictory position accelerated the deteriorating morale of Jacobites in England, for the cause now seemed

---

[15] *Ibid.*, 197.
[16] R.B.Y Scott, "The Pillars of Jachin and Boaz," *Journal of Biblical Literature*, 58 (1939), 143-39; in Stevenson, *Origins*, 146.

doomed. John Evelyn, who had been shocked by the violent plans of 1696, shifted from pity for "King James' condition" to sad acceptance of the status quo.[17] In a reflective mood, Evelyn prepared *An Account of Architects and Architecture* (1697), an enlarged edition of *Parallel of Architecture Ancient and Modern* (1664), his translation of Roland Fréart's French treatise. In his dedication to Wren, "Master Surveyor of Works," Evelyn recalled the sorrowful time when St. Paul's Cathedral was "full of horses and drunken soldiers" and the happier time when "you and I were named by the late King Charles to survey the dilapidations." He noted that some of the workmen at St. Paul's thanked him for his earlier book on architecture, which had helped them, and he then revealed a new respect for operative masons (whose secrecy had earlier frustrated him when he tried to investigate their craft):

> [From Vitruvius] you may see how necessary it is that an accomplished Master-builder should be furnished beyond the vulgar... An Architect is not to be taken for the common illiterate Mechanick (which may bring it into contempt), but the person who superintends, and presides over him with so many advantages. Yet neither is this to the dishonour of those excellent men who make use of their hands and tools in the grosser materials, since God himself, and Nature, the universal builders, are by translation truly styl'd architects, both as to what they have excogitated so wisely, and wrought so artificially.[18]

Evelyn's spirits were temporarily lifted on 5 December 1697, when the first service was held in St. Paul's since the great fire. However, on 5 January 1698, he recorded disconsolately, "Whitehall burnt, nothing but walls and ruins left." William III confessed that the loss of the Stuart palace did not affect him personally, "since I cannot live there," but when someone unearthed Inigo Jones's beautiful plans for a new Whitehall, he was strongly tempted to re-build, "for the mere fun of the thing."[19] Wren responded with alacrity to a comment that "his majestie designes to make it a noble palace" a stone baroque architecture at last – and he produced magnificent designs for the project.[20] According to Anderson, Wren was re-elected Grand Master in 1698.[21] But neither William nor Parliament were willing to finance Wren, and his attempted revival of the royalist architecture of Inigo Jones and the Stuart kings remained in "the realm of make-believe."

While Wren dreamed of a Stuart revival, Jonathan Swift – returned from Ulster and living with Temple at Moor Park – expressed his own ambivalence towards the Williamite regime in a poem entitled "On the Burning of Whitehall in 1698." Swift planned to date the poem 30 January, an Anglican holy day commemorating the martyrdom of Charles I, a monarch he increasingly admired while scorning the other Stuart kings who once inhabited Whitehall. "Northern James dishonoured every room/ With filth and palliardism [lechery] brought from home," while his grandson "sauntering Charles" polluted the hall with "Bawds, pimps and pandars."[22] James II brought in "assistant herds of

---

[17] J. Evelyn, *Diary*, III, 322, 332.

[18] John Evelyn, *Miscellaneous Writings*, ed. William Upcott (London, 1825), 357.

[19] Nesca Robb, *William of Orange* (1962; London, 1966), 422.

[20] J. Harris, "Architecture of Williamite Court," 231.

[21] J. Anderson, *Constitutions (1738)*, 107.

[22] J. Swift, *Complete Poems*, 80.

preaching cowls," until he was driven out; but, "He gone, the rank infection still remains." Then, in a surprising turn, Swift asserted that not even William III, "great Nassau," can cleanse the palace, which is corrupted by Dutch-inspired financial speculators and political operators:

> Most greedy financiers, and lavish too,
> Swarm in, in spite of all that prince could do,
> Projectors, peculates the palace hold,
> Patriots exchanging liberty for gold,
> Monsters unknown in this blessed land of old.
> Heaven takes the cure in hand, celestial ire
> Applies the oft-tried remedy of fire;
> ....
> Down come the lofty roofs, the cedar burns,
> The blended metal to a torrent turns.
>
> ....
> But mark how providence with watchful care,
> Did Inigo's famed theatre spare,
> That theatre produced an action truly great,
> On which eternal acclamations wait,
> Of kings deposed most faithful annals tell,
> And slaughtered monarchs would a volume swell.
> Our happy chronicle can show alone
> On this day tyrants executed – one.

Jones's theater somehow survived the fire, which gave Swift's tribute to Charles I a certain political ambivalence and nostalgia.[23] Coupled with his near-scatological satire, this complicated world-view would characterize Swift's future writings.

*
* *

In 1697 the Treaty of Ryswick not only brought a much-needed peace but also a confusing realignment in international diplomacy. Despite their disappointment at Louis XIV's withdrawal of military support, the Jacobites determined to take advantage of the shifting alliances. In the process, they accelerated the international spread of Stuart-style Freemasonry that had begun earlier in France and in the English occupation of Tangier.[24] J.H. Lepper asserts that the seventeenth-century army was "a great disseminator of the true light," for "our militant forefathers found that the secrets of a mason were very useful pieces to carry with them on a campaign."[25] J.F. Smith argues further that ambulatory military lodges were directly responsible for the world-wide spread of Masonry in the seventeenth and eighteenth centuries.[26]

---

[23] On the poem's anti-Williamite implications, see Ian Higgins, *Swift's Politics: A Study in Disaffection* (Cambridge, 1994), 49-50, 68.

[24] For Tangier, see M. Schuchard, *Restoring the Temple*, 639-46.

[25] J.H. Lepper, *The Differences between English and Irish Masonic Rituals Treated Historically* (Dublin, 1920), 17.

[26] James Fairburn Smith, *The Rise of the Ecossais Degrees*. Proceedings of the Lodge of Research of the Grand Chapter of Royal Arch Masons of the State of Ohio, vol. X (Dayton, 1965), 10.

The Jacobites were especially interested in Carl XII, the fifteen year-old king of Sweden, whose father, Carl XI, had granted in the 1650s privileges to a clandestine Scottish lodge in Gothenburg, which supported the Stuart restoration.[27] Carl XII's beloved mentor was Carl Magnus Stuart, a brilliant military office of Scottish descent.[28] Serving as quartermaster general, Stuart instructed the boy in geometry, fortifications, gunnery, and the history of war. Like Moray, Hamilton, and Tessin earlier, Stuart was probably familiar with the military Masonic tradition in Scottish regiments, and he may have informed his young protégé about Scottish Masonic lore.

Even more promising was the twenty-five year-old Czar of Russia, Peter I, who also employed expatriate Scots in important positions. Peter inherited a strong sympathy for the Stuart cause from his father, who was so shocked by the execution of Charles I that he expelled all English merchants from Moscow and then tried to help Charles II during his exile.[29] Like Carl XII, Peter had been tutored by a pro-Stuart Scottish refugee from an earlier conflict, Paul Menzies.[30] A more important Scot was General Patrick Gordon of Auchleuchries, who served in the Swedish army under Carl XI, before moving on to Poland and Russia. After James II's defeat, Gordon pressed the Stuart case with the Czar and ensured that he remain pro-Jacobite and anti-William III, whom he called a "Pretender." According to Robert Collis, Gordon maintained important links with Scottish Freemasons while he served the Czar.[31] Over the next decades, an important network of Jacobites operated in Russia and influenced foreign policy decisions. They would also utilize Freemasonry to recruit sympathetic Russians – including, allegedly, the Czar.

In 1697 Peter determined to visit the West in order to study new developments in ship-building, mechanics, and technology. His great admirer Leibniz reported that Peter's "maxim" was to learn all the details of an art or craft.[32] He passed through all the military degrees among his own troops, in order to develop a more effective service. In Holland he performed manual labor in the construction of a ship, in order to learn the structure of vessels from "la qualité de garçon jusqu'a celle d'Architecte." Peter was accompanied by General Francis Lefort, who joined a Masonic lodge in Holland – probably an operative, "craft" lodge like the one Sir Robert Moray joined forty years earlier.[33] It is unknown whether Peter also attended a Dutch lodge, but he was disappointed at his inability to gain instruction in the higher principles of design and construction, despite his acquisition of manual and technical skills. He thus accepted William III's invitation to visit London, where he stayed (in loose incognito) from January to April 1698.

While the Russian party resided in (and vandalized) John Evelyn's house, the Czar met Gilbert Burnet, who praised him in Solomonic terms.[34] Burnet may also have

[27] M. Schuchard, *Restoring the Temple*, 542.

[28] Raghnild Hatton, *Charles XII of Sweden* (Cambridge, 1968), 49-50.

[29] Rebecca Wills, *The Jacobites and Russia, 1715-1750* (West Linton, 2002), 38-39.

[30] Steve Murdoch, "Soldiers, Sailors, Jacobite Spy: Russo-Jacobite Relations 1688-1750," *Slavonica*, 3 (1996-97), 7-8.

[31] Robert Collis, "Patrick Gordon and his Links to Stuart and Jacobite Freemasonry," *Faravid*, 28 (2004), 73-90.

[32] Gottfried Wilhelm Leibniz, *Sämtliche Schriften und Briefe* (Berlin, 1923-93), S.1, B.13, pp.758-59.

[33] Tatiana Bakounine, *Le Répertoire Biographique des Francs-Maçons Russes* (Bruxelles, 1940), 290.; G Dielemans, "Een maconnicke (liefde) Brief uit Maastricht A.D. 1658," *Acta Macionica*, 10 (2000), 181-82; M. Schuchard, *Restoring the Temple*, 545.

[34] T.E.S. Clarke and H.C. Foxcroft, *A Life of Gilbert Burnet* (Cambridge, 1907), 348.

informed Peter about the Masonic influence on the early Royal Society, for they discussed mathematics and mechanics – subjects Burnet had learned from his earlier Masonic friends Moray and Kincardine. Peter's main concern was naval architecture, which was included in the operative training and ritual instruction of Stuart-style Masonry.[35] Thus, the Russian tradition that Peter was initiated into Freemasonry by Christopher Wren, who maintained loyalty to Stuart traditions, is quite plausible.[36] When the Czar returned to Russia, Patrick Gordon reportedly founded a lodge, in which he served as Senior Warden with Peter as Junior Warden.[37] General Lefort served as "maître en chaire" in a lodge founded by Peter.[38] The Czar also acted as Warden in a select secret club known as the "Neptune Society," which some historians believe was a quasi-Masonic group. The Neptunians met in the School of Mathematics and Navigation in Moscow and included as members two Scottish mathematicians, Henry Farquarson and General James Bruce.[39] Further evidence suggesting the Czar's Masonic affiliation would appear in the 1714 correspondence between the Earl of Mar and his cousin Dr. Thomas Erskine, the Czar's physician.[40]

Peter may also have learned of the Cabalistic and Rosicrucian interests of many Scottish Freemasons, for General Bruce – who reportedly became a Grand Master in the Moscow lodge – earned a reputation for sorcery because of his interest in chemistry and astronomy (i.e., alchemy and astrology).[41] Certainly, the non-sectarian aims of contemporary Rosicrucians would have appealed to Peter, for he was determined to break the power of the Russian Orthodox Church by implementing religious toleration.[42] When Leibniz asserted that F.M. Van Helmont would make an admirable advisor to the Czar, if only Van Helmont were not eighty years old, he was probably aware of Peter's interest in neo-Rosicrucian orders like the "Philadelphian Society."[43] While in London, Peter collaborated with Dr. Francis Lee, an erudite Cabalist and leader of the Philadelphian Society, who had earlier recruited Van Helmont to his group. Lee featured in his treatises the Rosicrucian-Masonic emblem of the "All-Generating Eye" or "Divine Magical Eye," and the Philadelphians attracted some members of Jacobite Masonic lodges.

---

[35] J. Anderson, *Cosntitutions (1738)*, 107. Also, see references to naval architecture in Christopher Wren, "Discourse on Naval Architecture," *Wren Society*, 19 (1942), 140, and in C.N. Batham, "Chevalier Ramsay: A New Appreciation," *AQC*, 81 (1968), 302.

[36] T. Bakounine, *Répertoire*, 84, 184.

[37] A.G. Cross, "British Freemasons in Russia during the Reign of Catherine the Great," *Oxford Slavonic Papers* (1971), 43.

[38] T. Bakounine, *Répertoire*, 290; Ernest Zitser, "The Petrine Round Table: Chivalry, Travesty, and Fraternalism at the Court of Peter the Great," in Andreas Önnerfors and Robert Collis, eds., *Freemasonry and Fraternalism in Eighteenth-Century Russia*, Volume II (Sheffield, 2009), 7-32.

[39] S. Murdoch, "Soldiers," 8.

[40] For the description of Peter as a "brother mechanic" with the "Masson Word," see Robert Paul, ed., *Letters and Documents Relating to Robert Erskine, Physician to Peter the Great, Czar of Russia, 1677-1720*. Miscellany of the Scottish Historical Society, II (1904), 408. Also, Robert Collis, "Hewing the Rough Stone: Masonic Influence in Peter the Great's Russia," in A. Önnerfors and R. Collis, *Freemasonry and Fraternalism*, 33-61.

[41] A. Cross, "British Freemasons," 42.

[42] Ian Grey, "Peter the Great in England," *History Today*, 6 (1956), 225.

[43] G. Leibniz, *Sämlichte Schriften*, S.1., B. 13, pp. 758-59.

In the *Theosophical Transactions* (1697), Lee announced that the reason for "the Foundation and Promotion of Our Society" is to achieve universal peace and fraternity.[44] He hoped to combine the secretive organization of the Rosicrucian commune maintained earlier by John Pordage on Ashmole's estate with the "process of initiation into the heavenly mysteries" or "alchemical apprenticeship of the adept" described by Jane Lead.[45] At the Czar's request, Lee presented a pansophic plan for national regeneration in Russia, which would be brought about by the establishment of seven colleges.[46] Merging the goal of Bacon's *New Atlantis* with the current French and English scientific societies, the colleges would bring together Christians, Jews, and Moslems for religious reform and scientific progress. The ecumenical colleges would combine the visionary training of the ancient Hebrew schools of prophecy, and they would sponsor collective ceremonies of meditation in which the whole Russian populace would pray for peace, brotherhood and the restoration of Israel. This was perhaps an attempt at Cabalistic *Tikkun* or cosmic reintegration through collective meditative magic. Lee became such an expert Cabalist that he was called "Rabbi Lee," and he made clear in the *Theosophical Transactions* that the visionary techniques of the *Sepher Yetzirah* contained the key to the Cabalistic art. Though Peter had to cut short his Masonic and Philadelphian explorations when he received news of the revolt of his royal guards, his visit to London may have revived the hopes of various Masons and Rosicrucians about the possibility of pansophic Solomonic reform.

An opposer of such "spiritualist" programs, John Toland, published *An Inquiry Concerning Virtue* (1699), whose anonymous author was Anthony Ashley-Cooper, 3rd Earl of Shaftesbury. Though Shaftesbury was angered by this unauthorized publication, he also began a secretive collaboration with Toland to promote Whig policies and free-thinking philosophy. At the same time, Toland worked discretely for Sir Robert Harley, now leader of the Country Party which opposed William III's attempt to maintain a standing army. As noted earlier, Harley had been interested in the trial of Thomas Aikenhead and collected documents related to the affair.[47] He was not put off by Toland's radicalism and opportunism, which proved politically useful.[48] Pleased by Toland's tract, *The Militia Reformed* (1698), Harley privately encouraged him to publish *The Oceana of James Harrington and his Other Works* (1700), in which the radical republican argued against the antiquity and legitimacy of the Scottish royal line and posited instead a classical Commonwealth. Toland eulogized the Whig Freemason Sir Robert Clayton as "the father of the city," who showed great courage "in bringing in the bill for excluding a Popish successor from the crown."[49] Clayton's heir had died in 1698, and Toland hoped to "insinuate himself as a successor in the aging man's affections and fortune."[50] It was perhaps at this time that Harley acquired a Masonic manuscript (Harleian MS. 2054), entitled "The free Masons

---

[44] *Theosophical Transactions by the Philadelphian Society* (1697), III, 195.

[45] Hillel Schwartz, *The French Prophets* (Berkeley, 1980), 47.

[46] Lee's proposals were published posthumously in Francis Lee *Apoleipomena* (London, 1752), I, 1-12.

[47] M. Graham, *Blasphemies*, 140, 153n.50.

[48] R. Sullivan, *Toland*, 9.

[49] James Harrington, *The Oceana and Other Works*, ed. John Toland. Rpt. of London edition of 1771. (Germany, 1963), iv.

[50] R. Sullivan, *Toland*, 12-13.

orders and Constitutions," an English copy of the old charges in the handwriting of the antiquarian Randle Holme (who died in March 1700).[51]

Meanwhile in Scotland, increasing disenchantment with the Williamite government raised Whig concerns about increasing numbers of Jacobite sympathizers in the northern kingdom – including the former republican Fletcher of Saltoun, who was currently researching the tyranny of Egyptian religion and priestcraft (an interest he shared with John Locke). In January 1700 Fletcher appealed to Locke to help James Garden, who was ejected from his professorship in Aberdeen because of his refusal to sign the Williamite oaths. Brother of George Garden, whose writing on second sight so intrigued Locke, James was praised by Fletcher for his "steady adherance to that freedom of mind, and a scorning to be limited and confined to any compacted... Confessions of Faith. A crime that recommends!"[52] Like the Philadelphians, the Gardens were intrigued by the theosophical teachings of Antoinette Bourignon and the Christian Cabalism of various Continental Boehmenists.[53] Did Fletcher view their religion of spiritual "illumination" as an antidote to Egyptian-style priestcraft? That the Gardens were open Jacobites reveals how far the old Scottish republican was shifting in his political loyalties.

For Toland, Shaftesbury, and their free-thinking circle, these Cabalistic developments must have seemed ominous. Under the influence of Bruno, who denigrated the Jews in the name of a higher Egyptian religion, Toland moved away from his earlier Presbyterian sympathies. He may also have moved away from Scottish-style Freemasonry, which continued to cherish its Jewish and Cabalistic heritage and which was becoming better known in London. Among the Masonic papers collected by Hans Sloane was a manuscript entitled "A Narrative of the Freemasons Word and Signes," which is dated "circa 1700."[54] Now called "Sloane MS. 3329," the document shows some signs of English influence in the wording, but "most if not all of its contents are Scottish in origin."[55] The manuscript repeats much of the material in a 1659 report made by Thomas Martin, who was evidently a Cromwellian spy and hostile to Masonry.[56] It adds a peculiar third word – Mahabyn – to the traditional Jachin and Boaz, and notes that Mahabyn is always divided in two. David Stevenson suggests that the explanation for this ritual change "lies in the obscure process by which the two grades of the seventeenth-century Scottish lodges were converted into a three-grade system":

> This is first visible in the Sloane Manuscript itself. In describing the quorum for lodge meetings it specifies two entered apprentices, two fellow crafts, and two masters; and it describes separate grips for handshakes for fellow crafts and masters... It is therefore possible that the Sloane catechism reflects the extension of developments in the Edinburgh Lodge to ritual matters. The masters now have a separate grip from the fellow crafts; and after briefly referring to the secret words "J and B" the catechism announces "Another they have called the masters word and is Mahabyn." It would thus appear

[51] G.W. Speth, ed., *Masonic Reprints of the Lodge Quatuor Coronati, #2076*, vol. III (1891), 1, lvi.

[52] J. Locke, *Correspodence*, VII, 469-70.

[53] "George and James Garden," *ODNB*.

[54] D. Knoop, "Mason Word," 205-06.

[55] D. Stevenson, "Origins," 137.

[56] For the contents and context, see M. Schuchard, *Restoring the Temple*, 576-79.

that this is a special word for a new type of master, concealed from the fellow crafts/masters."[57]

Like its 1659 predecessor, the Sloane MS. also stressed the international spread of Masonry, referring to brothers in France, Spain, and Turkey.

The political worries of anti-Jacobite Whigs became more acute after the death of Princess Anne's only child, the Duke of Gloucester, which raised new questions about the succession. In June 1701 Parliament's Act of Settlement placed the succession in the House of Hanover, currently headed by the Dowager Electress Sophia, grand-daughter of James I and daughter of Elizabeth Stuart, the "Winter Queen of Bohemia." The Act was widely resented in Scotland, which determined to choose its own monarch. Then, in September 1701, James II died at St. Germain, and a guilt-stricken Louis XIV recognized his thirteen year-old son James "III" as the legitimate British king. Within this politically fraught atmosphere, Toland was invited to join the Williamite delegation to Hanover to discuss the succession with the Electress Sophia. He took along his copy of Bruno's *Spaccio*, and he sought out Leibniz and other Protestant pansophists who had earlier demonstrated interests in Rosicrucian-style societies, who corresponded with Philadelphians, and who now supported the Hanoverian succession.

Toland wrote to Shaftesbury about his Brunonian campaign, but his reckless indiscretion worried the earl. Toland also referred to a pamphlet he and Shaftesbury planned to write but, as Robert Voitle observes, "secrecy is so much a part of the relationship between the two men that we will never know how closely they worked [together]."[58] Robert Sullivan notes that Toland's contact with Rosicrucians at the Hanoverian court reinforced his "ever elusive implication in the secret societies, perhaps in an international network."[59] These secretive and risky developments provide a revealing context for Shaftesbury's drafting of an amusing satire on enthusiastic occultists, whose fraternity boasts of international political influence. On l9 January 1702 the earl began a ten thousand word manuscript entitled "The Adept Ladys or the Angelick Sect," written as "a Letter to a Brother." Shaftesbury hinted at his acquaintance with members of Rosicrucian and/or Philadelphian societies and then mocked their psycho-erotic enthusiasm and endless gullibility. It seems likely that Toland was "a Brother" and that Shaftesbury hoped to warn him about renewed associations with occultist societies.

Writing from Chelsea, Shaftesbury recounted his recent experience of the evils of superstition and enthusiasm "in the persons of some of our acquaintance."[60] Two old friends, Chrysogenes and his accomplished spouse Chrysogenia, arrived at his door, accompanied by "a Woman in Quakers Dress." Chrysogenes revealed that God had a great work in hand and reminded him of earlier secret prophecies concerning kings and parliaments. The Quaker woman then "appear'd in great agitation...in a Double Labour, both of Body, and Mind," until she drew out a bundle of writings on "the Subjects." It seems certain that Shaftesbury satirized Jane Lead, the elderly embodiment of "Virgin Wisdom," who was the idol of the Philadelphian society. A disciple of the late Dr.

---

[57] D. Stevenson, "Origins," 151-52.

[58] Robert Voitle, *The Third Earl of Shaftesbury, 1671-1713* (Baton Rouge, 1984), 204-05.

[59] R. Sullivan, *Toland*, 19.

[60] Anthony Ashley Cooper, Third Earl of Shaftesbury, *Standard Edition*, ed. Gerd Hemmerich and Wolfram Benda (Stuttgart, 1981), B.I, t.1, p.378.

Pordage, she had published his *Theologia Mystica* and her own vivid, eloquent, and often lurid accounts of prophetic visions and angelic visitations. Lead and her co-sectarians were frequently called Quakers by their critics, and they published instructions for meditation and silent waiting for spiritual illumination that seemed exaggerations of Quaker practice. Since 1693, when a group of German admirers visited Lead and called themselves "the true Rosicrucians," the Philadelphians were considered a Rosicrucian extension of Quakerism.

The "Adept Lady" then revealed to Shaftesbury her discovery that human excrement can be transmuted into gold. In a comical scene, she tried to get the fastidious earl to touch, smell, and taste this miraculous substance. When he pretended to smell it, the visitors assumed that he was "allready initiated in their reverend Misteryes."[61] The belief that excrement could be transmuted was held by many alchemists, and it was based on Cabalistic-Hermetic beliefs that divinity was implicit in materiality. Curiously, the belief would endure in Sweden throughout the eighteenth century, where it was promoted by Masonic alchemists at Gustaf III's court.[62] Thus, when the adepts praised Carl XII, "the Young Hero of Sweden" for his "Love to Religion," they hinted at actual contacts between Philadelphians and Swedish visitors.[63] Shaftesbury became more alarmed when they boasted of sending Carl XII prophesies and admonitions about his role as king, and then revealed their supernatural means of communicating with other sovereign princes by means of "Sublime Aeriall Messengers."

A.O. Aldridge argues that Shaftesbury's next target was F.M. Van Helmont, who died in 1698 but whose reputation was on the rise.[64] Both Leibniz and Hans Sloane were determined to procure Van Helmont's manuscript memoirs and other papers.[65] Shaftesbury had met Van Helmont, whom he later described as "a notable enthusiast," one of those "whom in this age we usually call philosophers, a successor of Paracelsus, a master in the occult science." He had also read Van Helmont's treatise, *The Natural Hebrew Alphabet*, which he subsequently mocked in *Characteristics of Men, Manners, Opinions, Times* (1711). That Van Helmont was not only a Quaker but a Philadelphian, and that he was called a Rosicrucian in the London press, makes the identification convincing. Moreover, Toland may have sent information from Hanover about the adept, for both Leibniz and the Electress were great admirers of Van Helmont's mystical and scientific expertise. Was Shaftesbury worried that Toland was being seduced back into his earlier Rosicrucian fantasies? Or, did he believe that Toland's increasingly radical pantheism was a form of Rosicrucian natural magic?

Shaftesbury's most comical satire targeted the psychoerotic fantasies of Mrs. Lead, whose works expressed a breathlessly naive "Divine Lust." She described love-melting powers and divine ejaculations that awakened her in the night, when she received angelic

---

[61] *Ibid.*, 390.

[62] Carl-Michael Edenborg, *Gull och Mull* (Magister-uppsats i idéhistoria vid Stockholms Universitet (September 1995). Includes Count Gustaf Bonde's drawing of an alchemist sitting on his chamber pot and excreting the transmutable gold.

[63] The Swedish scholar Eric Benzelius, future brother-in-law of Swedenborg, visited the Philadelphians while in London in 1699, and he may have informed Carl XII about the Czar's interest in the society; see my article, "Leibniz, Benzelius, and Swedenborg," 84-106.

[64] A. Owen Aldridge, "Shaftesbury's Rosicrucian Ladies," *Anglia*, 103 (1985), 303-04.

[65] On Leibniz and Van Helmont, see Allison Coudert, *Leibniz and the Kabbalah* (Dordrecht, 1995).

visitors (often handsome males).[66] Thus, Shaftesbury parodied her account of "her first Salutation by the Angell of God" when she was "in a Middle State, neither as waking, nor as Dreaming," which the Quakeress cautiously described as a female angel. But she later revealed that "she had constant Night-Convers with 12 Male Angells in personable Human-Bodyes...the last of these (whome she call'd her Night Friend) seen also by Chrysogenes and His Family, both Young and Old."[67] When the Quakeress tried to cure Shaftesbury's lung ailment, she utilized such erotic terms that he blushed: "Sometimes she described the Conjunction, mutuall Love, and Kind Embraces of these sweet Subjects, that you would have thought they had been Male and Female, whom She conveniently & kindly, brought together for Procreation."[68] At this time, the Philadelphians were suffering much negative publicity because of the orgiastic ceremonies held by some of their more radical German devotées.

In a post-script, Shaftesbury added a "gallant" tale about the sect's attempt to trick him into marriage with the Quakeress's virginal daughter, who turned out to be a whore. In an accompanying poem, "The Golden Dream," he described the sect as a "Pilgrim Band/ of wand'ring Saints that sought the Promised Land," but when the "sprightly youth of heav'nly Meen" impregnated the female leader, "by Luck her Thought was hitt./ She wak'd and found herself Be---- [Beshit]."[69] In another attached poem, "The Golden Lovers," Shaftesbury featured "a Dialogue between Mick of the North, & Nan of the Town." When "jolly Lad Mick went to chear up his Nancy," he found her surrounded by boiling crucibles and excremental fumes in an alchemical lab.[70] Each stanza ends, "But who can Endure a Chimicall Spouse?" Aldrich argues that the poem draws on Johann Valentin Andreae's *Chemical Wedding* and that Mick is Shaftesbury and Nan is a female Rosicrucian, while Voitle argues that Mick is Thomas Micklethwayte and Nan is Nancy Ewer, sister of Shaftesbury's future wife.[71] It seems more likely that Mick of the North referred to Toland, who came from northern Ireland and practiced Rosicrucianism in Scotland. When the Quakeress described "her meeting Persons (those of her own Society) constantly, without appointment, by only walking abroad in the fields, or other Places," Shaftesbury seemed to hint at the secret recognition signs used by Freemasons and possibly their Rosicrucian affiliates.[72]

After Toland returned from his German mission, he continued his clandestine collaboration with Shaftesbury, who paid him a pension. However, like Locke, Shaftesbury would later try to conceal his collaboration with Toland, and both men destroyed their correspondence with the increasingly notorious pantheist. In the meantime, Toland continued to write Hanoverian propaganda and to secretly work for Robert Harley. If he was a Freemason with Rosicrucian ties on the Continent, he could supply Harley with important intelligence. Moreover, given an increase in Jacobite intrigue between Scotland and the exiles in Europe, access to Masonic lodges would be critical. As we shall see,

---

[66] See passages in Lead's *A Fountain of Gardens*; N. Thune, *Behmenists*, 175.

[67] Shaftesbury, *Standard Edition*, I, 1, 406.

[68] *Ibid.*, 396.

[69] *Ibid.* 436.

[70] *Ibid.*, 440.

[71] A. Aldridge, "Shaftesbury's Rosicrucian Ladies," 304; R. Voitle, *Shaftesbury*, 196.

[72] *Ibid.*, 412.

Toland would later reveal his inside knowledge of General Monk's restorationist strategy, which he accused his former employer Harley of attempting to replicate in 1713.

*
* *

Shortly before the death of James VII and II in September 1701, the increasingly impoverished Colin Lindsay, 3rd Earl of Balcarres, member of an old Masonic family, received permission from William III to return to Scotland. While in exile, he had written *Memoirs Touching the Revolution in Scotland* (1691), at the request of James, and he gained the admiration of Dutch and French free-thinkers for his promotion of religious toleration.[73] The Duke of Queensberry argued that the highly-respected earl would provide "an instance of the folly of Jacobitism, and, when he comes, the party may see in him the fate of their extravagances."[74] However, when Balcarres arrived, he found that sympathy for the Stuart cause was growing, as patriotic motives led many Whigs to join with Jacobites in a struggle for Scotland's interests. Once again, as during Charles II's restoration campaign, architects and Masons played an important role in the secretive negotiations.

One of Balcarres's contacts was John Erskine, Sixth Earl of Mar, whose dying father had earlier disappointed Dundee by acquiescing to the Williamite revolution in 1689. Young John was educated in Edinburgh and Leiden, before indulging his artistic and architectural interests on the Grand Tour. On his accession to the title, the heavily indebted Mar prudently adopted a policy of political conformity which enabled him to take a seat in the Scottish Parliament in 1698. At his family estate of Alloa, near Stirling Castle, he energetically designed new buildings and gardens that would provide "an enduring symbol of Scotland's independence."[75] Mar was inspired by Fletcher, who shared his political and architectural ideals and who may have taught him draughtsmanship. As Margaret Stewart observes:

> Alloa was not so much a case of Scots "pride and poverty" as wealth and virtue. It exemplified the civic virtue propounded in the writings of Andrew Fletcher of Saltoun. From the turn of the century Saltoun, in order to avert the necessity of incorporating union with England, had been urging the landowners of Scotland to undertake economic improvements. The wealth produced by these schemes was to be directed into radical social reform and great public buildings. Only financial security and the maintenance of our ancient liberties, Saltoun argued, could protect Scotland from the financial "corruption" and colonial ambitions of England.[76]

Like Balcarres who was friendly with the Continental free-thinkers Bayle and Leclerc, Fletcher came to merge Whiggish liberalism with Jacobite sympathy. Moreover, Fletcher advocated Italian-style villa planning and "magnificency" of Masonic construction, which

---

[73] Anne Barbeau Gardiner, "For the Sake of Liberty of Conscience: Pierre Bayle's Passionate Defense of James II," *1650-1850*, 8 (2003), 235-55.
[74] Lindsay, *Lives of Lindsays*, 191.
[75] Margaret Stewart, "Lord Mar's Gardens at Alloa, c. 1700-1732," in Frew and Jones, *Aspects*, 33-40.
[76] *Ibid.*, 36.

would express the values of antiquity and the enterprise of free citizens.[77] As noted earlier, Fletcher's eighteenth-century biographer suggested that he was a Freemason. From later evidence, it is clear that Mar was also a Mason.[78]

After the death of James II, Mar and a group of Jacobite noblemen sponsored a Continental study tour by Alexander Edward, who was ejected from his Episcopal ministry in 1689 and then studied architecture under Sir William Bruce, the former Scottish Grand Master (according to Anderson). Edward's public commission in France was to "view, observe and take draughts of the most curious and remarkable Houses, Edifices,...land improvements, coal works, mines, water works, and other curiosities of art and nature" – a Masonic commission which expressed the interests of Moray, Kincardine, and Bruce four decades earlier. That he definitely undertook restorationist and possibly Masonic intrigues also repeated the earlier pattern. Despite the dearth of information on Freemasonry during this period, André Kervella suggests that the exiled Jacobite Masons in Brest, France, had already recruited certain French officers in Brest.[79] At this time, the Jacobites in northern French ports were well-served by the Scottish exile Robert Arbuthnot, who had fought with "Bonnie Dundee" at Killiecrankie in 1689 and then fled to Rouen after the Williamite victory. Robert developed a profitable banking business and subsequently supplied ships and arms for emerging Jacobite plots. He evidently assisted Edward in France, and he would later become the admired friend of Swift, Alexander Pope, and their literary circle in London.

Robert Arbuthnot's younger brother John did not take part in the Scottish military actions and instead studied medicine, while maintaining his Jacobite sympathies. After the death of their father, a Non-juring Episcopal minister in 1691, John Arbuthnot moved to London, where he taught mathematics and published a small, anonymous book, *Of the Laws of Chance* (1692). He was also interested in architecture and, as a friend of Mar and Fletcher, he evidently become a Freemason during his visits to Scotland. He acquired important architectural treatises by Scamozzi, Vitruvius, and Palladio, and a manuscript "history of masonry."[80] These readings influenced his *Essay on the Usefulness of Mathematical Learning* (1701), which also drew on his familiarity with operative Masonry.[81] He maintained his Masonic association in England, where in 1704 he served as the Junior Grand Warden in a London lodge.[82] In his *Essay*, Dr. Arbuthnot argued for the importance of mathematical learning to the practice of designing and construction:

> As for civil architecture...there is hardly any part of mathematics but is some way subservient to it. Geometry and arithmetic for the due measure of the several parts of a building, the plans, models, computation of materials, time and charges; for ordering right its arches and vaults, that they may be both firm and beautiful; mechanics for its strength and firmness, transporting and

---

[77] M. Glendenning, et al., *History*, 104.

[78] R. Paul, "Letters," 408.

[79] André Kervella, *La Maçonnerie Écossaise dan le France de la Ancien Régime, les Années Obscures (1720-1755)* (Paris, 1996), 167, 316.

[80] *A Catalogue of the Capital and Well Known Library of Books, of the late celebrated Dr. Arbuthnot* (London, 1779), 296, 389, 390, 393, 395.

[81] George Aitken, *The Life and Works of John Arbuthnot* (1892; New York, 1968), 66-69, 77, 85.

[82] M. Spurr, "William Stukeley," 118.

raising materials; and optics for the symmetry and beauty. And I would not have any assume the character of architect without a competent skill in all of these. You see that Vitruvius requires these and many more for making a complete architect.[83]

Arbuthnot's fortunes dramatically improved after the death of William III on 12 April 1702, for he soon gained favor with the new queen. The accession of Queen Anne, who was devoted to the Anglican Church, inspired new hopes among the Scottish Jacobites, many of whom suffered repression by the ruling Presbyterian faction. Balcarres traveled to London, where he called upon the new queen and urged her to ameliorate the condition of Episcopalians in Scotland.[84] Rumors circulated that Anne privately favored her half-brother James for the succession, rather than the House of Hanover. As Edward, Mar, Fletcher, and Bruce carried out their ambitious nationalist projects of industrial and architectural development, there was a resurgence of Stuart-style enthusiasm for virtuoso culture in Scotland.

Among their like-minded friends was the Jacobite Martin Martin, whose scientific interests included second sight. Encouraged by Fletcher, Martin researched the natural and cultural history of the western islands of Scotland and, after sending preliminary reports to the Royal Society in London, published his findings in 1703. In a chapter titled "A Particular Account of the *Second Sight*, or Faculty of foreseeing things to come, by way of Vision," Martin gave a naturalistic description of second sight, noting that "at the sight of a vision, the eye-lids of the person are erected, and the eyes continue staring until the object vanishes."[85] When one man sees a vision, "the inner part of his eye-lids turns so far upwards" that afterwards "he must draw them down with his fingers, and sometimes employs others to draw them down." Though Martin could not learn how the gift is transmitted, he noted that the novices become skillful seers through some kind of discipline or training. As we shall see, Toland would later mount an attack on Martin, criticizing his descriptions of not only second sight but of operative Masonry in Scotland.[86]

One skeptic who became convinced of the reality of second sight was George Mackenzie, 1st Viscount Tarbat, currently serving as Queen Anne's secretary of state in Scotland.[87] Tarbat had encountered the phenomena in Scotland in the 1650s, and he described his findings to Robert Boyle, the eminent chemist and FRS.[88] Another skeptic who changed his mind was General Monk, who became a Freemason during his military occupation of Edinburgh, and who subsequently told John Evelyn that reports about second sight were true in Scotland, "tho at first he much doubted of it."[89] Evelyn's note follows "a long and revealing account" of the Scottish Mason Word, which he had heard from his Masonic friend, Sir Robert Moray. Thus, in 1703 the old Masonic tradition that

---

[83] G. Aitken, *Arbuthnot,*

[84] Lindsay, *Lives of Lindsays*, 191.

[85] Martin Martin, *A Description of the Western Islands of Scotland* (London, 1703), 321.

[86] See ahead, Chapter 7.

[87] M. Martin, *Description*, 340-41.

[88] Michael Hunter, *The Occult Laboratory: Magic, Science, and Second Sight* (Woodbridge, 2001), 2.

[89] *Ibid.*, 4.

initiates attain prophetic vision perhaps took on new political significance, as Scots of all parties wondered about Anne's rumored Jacobite sympathies.[90]

Another believer in this capacity for enhanced vision was the Jacobite George Garden, whom Fletcher had recommended to Locke. Soon after Anne's accession, Garden appealed to her in *The Case of the Episcopal Clergy...as to Granting Them Toleration and Indulgence* (1703). Making positive references to James II's edicts of toleration, Garden argued for a new era "when the Mass and the Meeting House are then set up peaceably beside one another."[91] He then used suggestive "Masonic" imagery, portraying Jesus as a "Master Builder" and a national religion as "one City compactly built together" and "not like that of a Heap of Stones thrown together by force, but as Lively Stones built up into a Spiritual House by the Cement of Love and Charity.[92] In September 1703 Garden added harsh words about the destructive impact of William's reign on Scottish development: "his late Majesty King William, the greatest Friend to Presbyterie that ever sat upon a Throne, and yet in whose Reign, some complained that the Rights, Liberties, and Priviledges of the People of Scotland, as an Independent State, a Free People, and partakers of the same Human Nature with others, were most trampled upon.[93] However, he stressed that Queen Anne sympathized with "the hard plight" of Episcopalians in Scotland and that she subsequently instructed the Privy Council to implement toleration for them.

Meanwhile, in England, Swift shared many of the concerns and hopes of his fellow Episcopalians in Scotland. In 1703 he revived his earlier architectural theme of disaffection from Williamite culture (expressed in 1698 in "The Burning of Whitehall") in order to lampoon the Flemish-descended soldier turned playwright turned architect, John Vanbrugh. Swift had recently been involved in practical architectural projects in Ireland, where he supervised the building of a parish church and "sturdy parsonage" at Laracor.[94] He praised William King, the Anglican archbishop of Ireland, for his program of church building and palace restoration. Having resumed his friendship with John Jones (co-author of the Masonic satire of the 1688 *Tripos*), Swift also utilized Masonic imagery in his political writing (he portrayed the faction-ridden House of Commons as "an over-extended pair of compasses").[95] Thus, when he drafted "Van Brug's House. An. 1703. Built from the Burnt Ruins of Whitehall," he revealed his approval of Vitruvian-Stuart architectural theory and his scorn for modern-Whig architectural practice.

Already annoyed by Vanbrugh's play *The Provok'd Wife* (1697), which satirized the Anglican clergy, Swift was further irritated by the upstart architect's presumption in building a private residence on the site of Whitehall Palace, where Vanbrugh even used stones from the former royal dwelling. When the Treasury ministers granted Vanbrugh the right to build in 1701, they confirmed Wren's fears that a new Whitehall Palace was now out of the question.[96] Even worse, Vanbrugh designed an essentially anti-Vitruvian building, with disproportionate and dissonant features that led critics to call it the "Goose-pie House." As John Fischer observes, the house and its placement provided "a densely

---

[90] See R. Wodrow, *Early Letters*, 248-51.
[91] George Garden, *The Case of the Episcopal Clergy*, 2nd rev. ed. (Edinburgh, 1703), part I, 20.
[92] *Ibid.*, 5.
[93] *Ibid.*, part II, 55 (published 1704).
[94] I. Ehrenpreis, *Swift*, II, 94-101.
[95] *Ibid.*, II, 15, 52.
[96] Kerry Downes, *Vanbrugh* (London, l077), 12.

significant topography" to Swift, for Wren's ambitious plan to utilize Inigo Jones's designs came to nothing: "the great seat of the Tudors and Stuarts was allowed to perish in an England that had learned to crown its kings by convocation... Swift apparently felt deeply that both the site and style of house formed an irreverent comment on the past and a bleak prophecy for the future".[97]

Swift drafted his poem around three motifs – the myth of Amphion whose musical harmonies magically drew stones into a massive protective wall; the insect-like deterioration of modern literature into webs spun out of the self or snail-houses carried on one's back; and the comparison of "piddling restorations such as Vanbrugh's building with the great notion of restoration expressed in the phoenix myth."[98]

> In times of old, when Time was young,
> And Poets their own Verses sung,
> A Song could draw a Stone or Beam,
> That now would overload a Team,
> Lead them a Dance of many a Mile,
> Then rear 'em to a goodly Pile,
> Each Number had it's diff'rent Power;
> Heroick strains could build a Tower...
>
> ....
>
> Now Poets find this Art is lost,
> Both to their own and Landlord's cost...
>
> ....
>
> The God of Wealth was therefore made
> Sole Patron of the building Trade...
>
> ....
>
> Sing Muse the House of Poet Van
> In higher Strain than we began.
> Van, (for 'tis fit the Reader know it)
> Is both a Herald and a Poet;
> No wonder then, if nicely skill'd
> In each Capacity to build:
> As Herald, he can in a Day
> Repair a House gone to decay...
>
> ....
>
> A Type of Modern Witt and Style,
> The Rubbish of an antient Pile.[99]

Fischer comments, "To an eye accustomed to seeking in architecture the symbolic representation of a binding universal harmony," the Goose-pie House must have seemed an "antitype of art."[100]

For Swift, the only positive outcome of Vanbrugh's rise was the fall of William Talman, who was displaced by Vanbrugh from his position as the late William III's Comptroller of the King's Works in May 1702. After he attempted to undermine Christopher

---

[97] John Irwin Fischer, *Swift's Poetry* (Gainesville, 1978), 75.
[98] *Ibid.*, 75.
[99] Jonathan Swift, *The Complete Poems of Jonathan Swift*, ed. Pat Rogers (New Haven, 1983), 581-83.
[100] J. Fischer, *Swift's Poetry*, 80.

Wren, Talman became the major designer of country houses for the Whig aristocracy, and he had no interest in the kind of ecclesiastical and royal architecture admired by Swift. Even worse, he was "an arrogant and argumentative man with an inflated idea of his own worth," whose frequent overcharging of patrons led to "vexations" with his clients.[101] That he later became the close friend of J.T. Desaguliers, an organizer of the modern, Whig-Hanoverian version of Freemasonry, would also be "vexatious" to Swift.

Swift's poetic lamentation over the Whig debasement of royalist architecture was echoed by the practical criticism of an actual English builder, who seemed to draw on Irish and Scottish Masonic traditions. "Philomath" (Richard Neve) dedicated his treatise, *The City and Countrey Purchaser and Builders' Dictionary or the Compleat Builder's Guide* (London, 1703), to John and Robert Baker of Sussex and, more significantly, to Robert Knight, Treasurer of the Honourable Irish Society in London, which oversaw the "plantation" of Ulster. In 1698 Sir Robert Clayton, a Whig Freemason, served as President of the society and presented the city of Derry's petition to William III for compensation for the damage to buildings caused by his battle with the Jacobite forces.[102] The Irish Society was still involved in architectural reconstruction, and Richard Neve was evidently familiar with the same Scots-Irish Masonic traditions that Swift would later reveal in his *Letter from the Grand Mistress of the Female Freemasons.*

Neve stressed that he interviewed "many handicraftsmen, whose Imployments solely depended on building," as well as "some observing Gentlemen and others who were sometimes Masters of such Buildings"; moreover, most of his material "was never made publick before." Like Swift and Wren's Master Masons, Neve lamented the decline in English Masonic skills, and he published the book to improve the education, morale, and status of architectural craftsmen. Expressing the Hebraic and Solomonic traditions of Stuart Freemasonry, Neve used a long Proem to praise the spiritual and royalist significance of architecture. "*The Divine Architect* of the World hath been pleased to honour this Excellent *Art*," despite the current condemnation and slighting by some, "because it depends upon *Mechanicks* or *Handicraftsmen* Practice":

> But the *Holy Ghost* stiles the *Mechanick* Knowledge of *Bezaleel*, and *Aholiab*, etc. the Spirit of God, Wisdom, etc.... Our Blessed Redeemer...was pleased to exercise this Art of Architecture, and to be a *Mechanick*, viz. a *Carpenter*... which is no small Honour to the Mechanick and Architect."

Neve titled one section "Free-Masons Work" but noted that it involved so many skills that he would define the "Particulars" in their proper places in the Alphabet. Under "House," he described,

> Some ingenious Workmen that understand the Speculative Part of Architecture or Building: But of these knowing sort of Artificers there are few because but few workmen look any further than the Mechanical, Practick or Working part of Architecture; not regarding the Mathematical or Speculative part of Building, thinking it to be of little or no use... such men affirm that

---

[101] "William Talman," *ODNB.*
[102] P. Gauci, "Clayton," III, 609.

the Theory or Speculative part of Architecture was of no use, because, they say, it is false.[103]

He stressed that "it is very well known that many Gentlemen of good Rank and Quality in this Nation, are often conversant with Handicraft employments." However, the situation is much better in France, where high-ranking nobles participate in building and craft projects, and the king has established an academy of architecture.

Given the "auld alliance" between France and Scotland, and their history of shared architectural traditions, Neve hinted at Stuart traditions that had weakened in England. Scottish and Irish Freemasonry had long encouraged the collaboration between educated, "speculative" gentlemen and operative craftsmen, with the latter often elevated to high social status by their mastery of mathematical and designing skills. Christopher Wren had maintained these traditions, but he had been undermined by the Williamite government. Despite the Whig ascendancy in the government, Jacobites and Tories hoped that Queen Anne would revive the architectural themes and policies of her Stuart forebears.

Among those Stuart (and possibly Masonic) themes was a desire to revive chivalric traditions. In 1701 Anne's half-brother Henry Fitzjames married and thus had to resign as titular Prior of the British Knights of Malta.[104] Though the British order then went into abeyance, it is possible that its traditions and rituals were absorbed into the Knight of Malta degree of Jacobite Freemasonry.[105] In his *Letter from the Grand Mistress*, Swift praised the Knights of St. John of Jerusalem and the Knights of Malta as "two Lodges" which "adorn'd the Antient Jewish and Pagan Masonry with many Religious and Christian Rules."[106] With the resurgence of Jacobite hopes, various Scottish courtiers persuaded Anne in December 1703 to bring back the Order of the Thistle, which had been suppressed at the Revolution. However, the queen revised the order's vow, so that the knights must swear to defend "the true reformed Protestant religion."[107] With the Catholic exiles Melfort and Perth, knights in James II's revived Thistle, now playing important roles at the Stuart court in France, the queen's limitation of membership to Protestants seemed a necessary precaution.

Part of the motivation for the queen's revival of the Thistle was the urgent need to secure the loyalty of important Scottish nobles in the wake of the northern parliament's defiant passage of the Act of Security in August 1703, which affirmed Scotland's right to choose its own sovereign, "being always of the royal line of Scotland, and of the true Protestant religion," if there was no heir of Anne's body.[108] Thus, in January 1704 Anne appointed seven Scottish nobles as Knights of the Thistle. All of these men would come under intense pressure from the court to support the unification of Scotland and England. Ironically, the Act of Security – a high watermark of Scottish nationalism – provoked so much fear in England that it led to a unionist campaign that eventually cost Scotland the very independence it was designed to protect.[109]

---

[103] Philomath [Richard Neve], *The City and Countrey Purchaser and Builder's Dictionary: or the Complete Builders' Guide* (London, 1703), 181. See also W.J. Williams, "The Use of the Word 'Freemason" before 1717," *AQC, 48* (1939), 187.

[104] H. Sire, *Knights*, 188.

[105] For the 18th-century links between the knights and the fraternity, see Desmond Caywood, "Freemasonry and the Knights of Malta," *AQC*, 83 (1979), 71-73.

[106] J. Swift, *Works*, V, 329.

[107] N. Nicolas, *Statutes*, [x]

[108] William Ferguson, *Scotland's Relations with England: A Survey to 1707* (Edinburgh, 1977), 210.

[109] P.H. Scott, *Andrew Fletcher and the Treaty of Union* (Edinburgh, 1994), 87-88.

CHAPTER FOUR

JUDAIZED SCOTS, JACOBITE JEWS,
AND THE PROBLEM OF "FALSE BROTHERS"
(1702-1712)

The First Christian Prince that expelled the Jews out of his territories was that heroic King, our Edward the first, who was such a scourge also to the Scots, and it is thought diverse families of those banished Jews fled to Scotland, where they have propagated since in great number, witness the aversion that nation hath above all others to hogs-flesh.

> James Howell, *History of the Latter Times of the Jews* (London, 1699).

I am perfectly Unsuspected as Corresponding with anybody in England. I Converse with Presbyterian, Episcopall-Dissenter, Papist, and Non Juror... I have faithfull Emissaries in Every Company... And am Entirely confided in.

> Daniel Defoe to Robert Harley (Edinburgh, 1706).

We are buzzed with prophecies, dreams and visions in a trance, all of the King's return.

> Bishop William Nicholson to Thomas Innes (Edinburgh, 1706).

The Scottish resistance to England's choice of a Hanoverian successor provoked a flood of anti-Scottish pamphlets that revived the old charge that the Scots were essentially Jews. These charges came in the wake of a Whig-sponsored bill that was bitterly resented in London's Jewish community. William III owed a great deal of money to his Dutch-Jewish war suppliers, whom he tried to pacify by dining with and then knighting Solomon de Medina in 1700.[1] Ambiguously tolerated and financially exploited, the Jews acted cautiously under the Williamite regime. Rabbi Solomon Allyon resigned his post in 1701, "in less than friendly circumstances with a whiff of Sabbatian heresy about him," and he was replaced by Rabbi David Nieto, who promptly published a pamphlet which consisted of a prayer by the congregation "offered up to God to help

---

[1] D. Katz, *Jews in History*, 188.

King William III with his government of the country."[2] However, Nieto's panegyric did not prevent a Whig attack on the religious rights of the community.

In 1702 a Jewish girl who converted to Protestantism became a minor *cause célèbre*, when a Whig committee – led by Toland's Masonic friend Sir Robert Clayton – passed "a bill compelling Jews to support their children converted to any version of Protestantism."[3] Jewish leaders argued against this thinly-disguised conversionist campaign and spent large sums in trying to defeat the bill, but Clayton's committee voted against them in May. Among the protesters was Moses Francia, whose kinsman Francis Francia emerged as a Jacobite partisan. A native of Bordeaux, Francis Francia was the son of a wine merchant who became wealthy through Franco-British trade. Though "An Act to Oblige the Jews to Maintain and Provide for their Protestant Children" was initiated under William, it became law under Anne in June 1702. The queen evidently knew nothing about it, and the Jews did not blame her for it.

At the same time that Moses Francia lobbied against the bill, Francis Francia appeared as a witness in the prosecution of a man who expressed doubts about the legitimacy of Queen Anne. On 11 May an anonymous tipster reported to the government about "some scandalous words against the Queen" – i.e., "If the Queen were King James' daughter, I am sorry she is crowned."[4] On 15 May Francia testified that he and others heard the following exchange in a tavern: "Mr. Pott said, "We have now a lawful and rightful Queen of our own country, King James' daughter, and I like her the better and thank God for her." Mr. Wostenholme then said he did not know whether she was King James' daughter or not, but, if she was, he liked her the worse."[5] The incident may seem minor, but Francia's defense of Anne's Stuart legitimacy foreshadowed his role as a committed Jacobite over the next four decades. He would become a major player in a succession of international Franco-Swedish-Jacobite plots, and he would organize "a noble club" or "society" of Jews which was evidently a Masonic lodge dedicated to a Stuart restoration.[6] As a Jewish "brother," he could draw upon the earlier Stuart-Jewish-Masonic tradition, expressed in the Treloar manuscript of 1665, which was copied by John Raymond in 1705. The document featured quotations in Hebrew, Solomon's Seal (the hexalpha within a circle), an elaboration of Hiramic-Jewish lore, and a merger of Stuart royalism with fervent Solomonic mysticism.[7]

As Jacobite sentiment intensified in Scotland, the English ministers increased their pressure for "an incorporating union," which would essentially make Scotland a province of England. Some pro-unionist propagandists blatantly insulted the Scots, as an inferior race who were historically subject to British domination. Martin Martin had already complained that English propagandists refused to see the Scots "as partakers of the same Human Nature as others."[8] Many Jacobites remembered the charge by James Howell, an English royalist-turned-Cromwellian, that the Scots were descended from the Jews: "The

---

[2] *Ibid.*, 196.

[3] *Ibid.*, 192-96.

[4] *Calendar of State Papers, Domestic Series, of the Reign of Anne, 1702-03*, ed. R.P. Mahaffy (London, 1916), I, 59.

[5] *Ibid.*, I, 66.

[6] Marcus Lipton, "Francis Francia--the Jacobite Jew," *TJHSE*, 11 (1928), 190-205; John Shaftesley, "Jews in Regular English Freemasonry," *TJHSE*, 25 (1977), 159.

[7] Wallace McLeod, "Additions to the List of Old Charges," *AQC*, 96 (1983), 98-99.

[8] M. Martin, *Case*, part II, 55.

first Christian Prince that expelled the Jews out of his territories was that heroick King, our Edward the first, who was such a scourge also to the Scots, and it is thought diverse families of these banished Jews fled to Scotland, where they have propagated since in great number, witness the aversion that nation hath above all others to hogs-flesh"[9] Howell's work, first published in 1652, was reprinted many times, with the most recent in 1699, so the charge was familiar to many anti-English Scots.

One Jacobite who accepted proudly the tradition of Judaized Scots was the Episcopalian poet William Forbes of Disblair, who published *A Pil for Pork-Eaters: or, a Scots Lancet for an English Swelling* (1705), in which the poet turned Howell's charge against him. On the title-page was a quote from the royalist poet Abraham Cowley – "Curs'd be the Man...who thinks it brave/ and great, his Country to enslave."[10] Equating the "Mungrel, Hackney State-scriblers in Ordinary to Old England" with non-Jewish "Pork-Eaters," Forbes made a bawdy and passionate call to arms for "all true honest hearted Scotsmen":

> Heav'ns! Are we such a Servile Nation grown,
> Beneath our Ancestors so vastly thrown,
> That every English scribling Tool-o'late,
> (Base Miscreants, and Vermin of the State,
> Hir'd by the Mob, and licens'd now to prate)
> Dares thus arraign our Justice and our Laws...
> ....
> Had we pack't Juries, such damn'd Hellish Things,
> By which you decently have Murder'd Kings;
> ....
> Here were no Juries of old Bradshaw's Spawn,
> Who for Revenge, their Necks and Souls would pawn;
> ....
> May England for its Luxury be damn'd,
> Base Epicures with Pork and Pudding cramm'd;
> ....
> And London, thou curs'd Sodom o' the Isle,
> Who drains our Wealth, and laughs at us the while...[11]

Forbes defended the Duke of Hamilton and Fletcher of Saltoun, both reportedly Masons, as patriots who would never sell out their country for English gold, unlike the "brib'd fawning Parasites" who receive court pensions. His Jacobite-Jewish sentiments were made more threatening by tributes to ancient Scottish heroes whose armies defeated the English. In the face of English bullying, Scotland's only hope was a military pill to purge the pork-eaters:

> To Prophesie, tho' I have no Pretence,
> Yet I'll adventure to Divine for once;
> When Swans grow Black, and Ravens shall grow White
> Proud England then with Scotland shall unite;

---

[9] James Howell, *The Wonderfull, and Most Deplorable History of the Latter Times of the Jews* (1652; London, 1653), Epistle Dedicatory. For the context, see Schuchard, *Restoring the Temple*, 528-29.

[10] For Cowley's Masonic associations, see M. Schuchard, *Restoring the Temple, 604-07.*

[11] William Forbes, *A Pil for Pork-Eaters* (Edinburgh,1705), 3-4.

Unless we purg' em with some Warlike Pills,
And tame their Insolence against their Wills.[12]

Praising the "auld alliance" with France, Forbes hinted at the clandestine but continuing contact between Scottish Jacobites and their supporters across the water. Thus, it is curious that a Masonic song appeared in the confiscated papers of Joseph Huchet, a vendor of prohibited books, in Paris in June 1705. Titled "Les Freimaçons, Vau de Ville sur un air anglois," it was obviously a translation of verses in English, which as a "vau de ville" (voice of the city) was a "Chanson de circonstance," which circulated in the town and whose "air" was easy to sing.[13] Boasting that no one has penetrated their sacred sign or mark, the author noted that from all eternity, "our masons have been visible everywhere and unknown everywhere." Then, affirming pride in their architectural work, he proclaimed that "by our masons the world was vaulted." Moreover, never has a "Belle Libre maçon" refused what is proposed; "autant de toisé," all work is easy to our masons. At that time, the Masons calculated in *toises*, the old French lineal measurement of approximately two metres. The song seemed to draw on Scottish and Irish traditions, in which the operative masons collaborated and sang with gentleman "brothers." Admitting that the evidence is not definitive, Alain Mothu concludes that the document appears to provide a serious indication of a Continental Masonry earlier than 1725, probably of Jacobite inspiration.

While the Jacobite poet Forbes proudly affirmed Scotland's ancient Jewish heritage, the Whigs exploited that identification to attack the Scots. John Toland joined the anti-Jacobite Whigs who believed the tradition that after England expelled the Jews in 1290, many of them escaped to Scotland and that the Scots' abhorrence of pork and black pudding came from their Jewish heritage. Thus, he also entered the fray.[14] In *Letters to Serena* (1704), he drew on his philosophical conversations with Queen Sophie-Charlotte of Prussia to issue propaganda for the Hanoverian succession. In order to undermine the Jewish-Jacobite claim, Toland rejected the pretense maintained by "Jews and a world of Christians" that "the Egyptians had all their learning from Abraham."[15] While giving Brunonian praise to the Egyptians, he revealed his increasing knowledge about ancient Jewish and gentile mystery religions, as well as his grudging respect for Spinoza (who had been excommunicated by the Amsterdam rabbis).

In *Letters to Serena*, Toland also began to hint at his emerging belief in the practices of secret societies, with their esoteric secrets for the initiated and exoteric statements for the public. Though he mocked the inside-language or cant of various professions, he also suggested his familiarity with operative Masonry: "In most Professions (especially in those they repute Mechanick) the Members are sworn not to discover the Mystery of their Trade, which very Notion of Mystery makes others imagine that there's something extraordinary in very trivial matters thus artfully disguised; and your Mysterys of State (tho not to be pry'd into by Vulgar Eyes, but to be admir'd with Veneration) are

---

12 *Ibid.*, 8.
13 Alain Mothu and Charles Porset, "A Propos du Secret des Francs-Maçons: une Référence Jacobite (1705)?," in Charles Porset, ed., *Studia Latomorum & Historica: Mélange offerts à Daniel Ligou* (Paris, 1998), 326-33.
14 See his remarks in *Reasons for Naturalizing the Jews in Great Britain and Ireland* (London, 1714), Dedication, 37.
15 John Toland, *Letters to Serena* (London, 1704), 39-41, 131.

sometimes as airy and imaginary, as slight and ridiculous as any others."[16] As we shall see, in 1721 Toland will refer more explicitly to his familiarity with Scottish operative Masonry.

Toland's oddest contribution to the Judaized Scots controversy was his anonymous translation from the French of La Créquinière's *Agreement of the Customs of the East-Indians with Those of the Jews* (London, 1705). Toland evidently hoped that La Créquinière's rejection of the originality of Hebrew religious practices would undermine the Scots' claim to be a uniquely Covenanted nation. By showing the priority of Indian to Jewish customs and by equating Oriental fakirs to Jewish Cabalists, he struck a bizarre blow at the Jacobites. La Créquinière argued that since circumcision was not unique to the Jews it could not be a unique sign of Covenant between Israel and God. By studying Oriental customs, one could decipher many difficult texts of scripture, for the Jews drew on earlier practices among Indians and Egyptians. In passages relevant to current architectural and Masonic controversies, he compared the high status given to monumental stone architecture by Orientals and Jews:

> The Pagod[a]s and other publick Edifices of the Gentiles, are commonly built of great Black stones of an extraordinary length: the Pillars...are almost all of one piece, and support the Rafters...of Stone... They join them all together, and put a little Lime between them... in these great Buildings there is not one bit of Wood.
>
> The difficulty they meet with, to find out these Stones, to transport them, and put them in their places, makes them to be of great Price... the Walls of Jerusalem were built, *Lapides pretiosi muri sui Jerusalem.*
>
> Solomon made use of them also, to lay the Foundations of his House, and of that which he built for the Daughter of Pharaoh, according to that Passage: *And the Foundation was of costly stones, even great stones, stones of ten Cubits, and stones of eight Cubits*, I King.10. Which contributed very much to the duration of these famous Buildings, which held out against the Injury of times, and the Revolution of Ages. The Mode at present, is very much, whether any thing we do will be grateful to our Posterity, we consult only our own Ease, and take care to please our selves.[17]

Perhaps Toland expected Robert Harley, who secretly employed him, to be interested in these passages, given Harley's Masonic associations. Ironically, La Créquinière's criticism of ephemeral and self-serving architecture would later be echoed by Swift in his continuing attacks on the Whig builder Vanbrugh.

Toland was especially attracted to the techniques of concealment and revelation practised by Phoe, an Indian philosopher in Ceylon, who published his doctrine of metempsychosis in the time of Solomon. Phoe had "two sorts of doctrines, one Internal, or Secret, and another External, or Publick":

> His Internal Doctrine which he Communicated only to his most beloved Disciples (whom he knew to be entirely addicted to him, and of whose

---

[16] *Ibid.*, 11.
[17] La Créquinière, *The Agreement of the Customs of the East-Indians with Those of the Jews* [trans. John Toland] (London, 1705), 63.

fidelity he was certain) asserted...the Annihilation of the Soul after Death... after it was separated from the Body, it was scattered in the *Air*, and resolved into an ethereal Matter; which is in effect...*Atheism*, such as some pretend, is still followed by the generality of the Learned *Chinese*.[18]

The common people were taught the external doctrine of transmigration of souls, in order to control them morally.

Even the Cabala, the sacred oral tradition of the Jews, was merely derivative of earlier Indian beliefs:

'Tis pretended, that the *Cabala* has taken a great part of its Follies from the Philosophy of Phoe...And in this confus'd Heap of *Rabbinism* and *Magick*, something is discover'd that comes near to the Doctrine of the Learned Chinese, concerning the Heaven and Etherial Matter... the *Cabalists* had no less strange Ideas about the Matter of which the Heaven was fram'd; they believe this Matter to be animated, and pretend that the Queen of Heaven, *Regina Coeli*, mentioned in *Jerem.* c.44, is the Soul of this Material Heaven which appears to our Eyes...[19]

Toland would later be suspected of organizing a Masonic lodge based on Phoe's philosophy of esoteric and exoteric beliefs. Instead of concealing supernatural mysteries, however, he and his *frères* would conceal natural philosophy (i.e, deism, pantheism, even atheism).[20]

Toland's oblique attack upon the Judaized Scots may have hit its target, for an anti-unionist Presbyterian issued a Judaized defense of his nation's resistance to English pressure. William Wright, in *The Comical History of the Marriage-Union Betwixt Fergusia and Heptarchus* (Edinburgh and London, 1706), lamented that "Salomoni Pacifico" (the Scottish James VI) made "Fergusia" (Scotland) a widow when he moved south to London (and became the English James I). Scots do not object to the succession of the "Grand-child of Salomoni Pacifico" (Queen Anne) but she must sometimes dwell in her northern palace, or they will choose their own tenant. Then, appealing to Scotland's unique role as a covenanted nation, Fergusia upholds (despite Toland) the unique Jewishness of circumcision:

I am obliged to be circumcised by this marriage, and you are uncircumcised still... I must not marry till you be circumcised too... I'm a Sovereign Independent Lady, and I have the Honour to be so, for one Third of the World's Age... I'd rather have a Highland-Plaid with Liberty, than the greatest Dainties, with a Hook, at the Heart of it.[21]

This anti-unionist tract revealed that non-Jacobite nationalists were currently the strange bedfellows of their Jacobite countrymen. Rumors of an imminent Stuart invasion inspired the more mystical Jacobites, leading the Catholic bishop William Nicholson to

---

[18] *Ibid.*, 57.

[19] *Ibid.*, 102-03.

[20] See M. Jacob, *Radical Enlightenment*, 151-59.

[21] [William Wright], *The Comical History of the Marriage-Union Betwixt Fergusia and Heptarchus* (Edinburgh and London, 1706), 21-25.

report, "We are buzzed with prophecies, dreams and visions in a trance, all of the King's return."[22]

Robert Harley eventually recognized that the reckless, cynical Toland was not suited to deal with the complexities of Scottish affairs. Though he continued to secretly employ Toland for intelligence and propaganda work, he needed more discrete agents to work in Scotland, where bipartisan antagonism to the proposed union was growing daily. Led by Hamilton and Fletcher, the opposition roused popular opinion against the Scottish courtiers in London. In order to secure the support of the Earl of Mar and Hugh Campbell, 3rd Earl of Loudoun, Queen Anne made them knights of the Thistle on 10 August 1706 – a move which Mar praised as demonstrating that the unionists "are much in favour" at court.[23] It is unknown if Loudoun was a Mason, but his son, John Campbell, 4th Earl of Loudoun, would serve as the Hanoverian Grand Master of the English Grand Lodge in 1736.

Despite their opposite political stances, Mar was determined to maintain his Masonic friendship with Fletcher. On 18 August he wrote his brother James Erskine: "I hope Salton and I shall still be in speaking terms tho' not of the same opinion in this measure of the Union. I have not forgot his case of instruments... if the Union should fail I see not what possiblie we can do to save our country from ruin."[24] The case contained mathematical-surveying instruments for Fletcher's architectural projects. John Erskine reported to Mar on 20 August that Fletcher angrily condemned the "damn'd villainous Union," until Erskine switched to the more congenial subject of the "building of houses."[25]

Mar possibly reminded Harley of the capacity of Scottish Masonic networks to influence political affairs. Moreover, Harley could have learned from his father, Edward Harley, about the Masonic network utilized by Moray, Bruce, and Monk in 1659-60.[26] In August 1706, when Harley selected Daniel Defoe to serve as his secret agent in Scotland, he chose someone familiar with Freemasonry. Since 1694, when Defoe owned a prosperous tile and brick factory, he worked closely with builders, and he dealt with Evelyn during the construction of the Greenwich sailor's home. In his *Essay on Projects* (1697), Defoe hinted at the traditional craft lore of the building guilds, when he presented the origins of "the projecting humour" in the construction of Noah's Ark and the Tower of Babel.[27] Echoing the earlier proposals of the royalist architect Balthazar Gerbier, Defoe proposed a royal military academy that would instruct English gentry in mathematics, dialing, fortification, delineation, surveying, and architecture (all traditionally the provenance of Stuart operative Masonry), and he lamented the lack of training of English youth in these fields.[28] In *The Consolidator* (1705), Defoe pointed to Czar Peter as the embodiment of his ideal "projector," who was willing to learn the operative craft of military

---

[22] William Nicholson to Thomas Innes (Edinburgh, 17 August 1706); quoted in Daniel Szechi, *1715: The Great Jacobite Rebellion* (New Haven, 2006), 63. Spelling modernized.

[23] *HMC. Report on the Manuscripts of the Earl of Mar and Kellie, Preserved at Alloa House* (London, 1904), 272.

[24] *Ibid.*, 272.

[25] *Ibid.*, 263.

[26] On this network, see M. Schuchard, *Restoring the Temple*, 521-94.

[27] Henry Morley, *The Earlier Life and the Chief Earlier Works of Daniel Defoe* (London, 1889), 38-39.

[28] *Ibid.*, 143.

masons, ship-builders, and city designers, and he may have heard rumors that Peter had been initiated into craft Masonry.[29]

By the time *The Consolidator* came out, Defoe had been secretly working for Harley for two years. The tract included unusual praise of the Scots, as people justifiably opposed to a union until trade relations could be worked out. Thus, Defoe would be seen by the Scots as friendly to their national interests. Harley, who used the Masonic technique of "giving three knocks" at the door before secretly meeting his private agents, evidently hoped that Defoe could ingratiate himself with the Freemasons in Scotland. According to Paula Backsheider, Harley and Defoe utilized Masonic techniques and language in their secret political communications.[30] The two had already worked out an intelligence plan, which Defoe called "a Method how the Scotts may be brought to reason."[31] Arguing that "the Most Usefull Thing at home is Secrecy" and "Dissimulation," Defoe brazenly justified his false conduct in religious terms: "This is the Dissimulation I Recommend, which is Not Unlike what the Apostle Sayes of himself; becoming all Things to all Men, that he might Gain Some. This Hypocrise is a Vertue." The secretaries of state should form an inner cabinet for the queen, maintain a "Secret Management" of their agents, and keep them ignorant of the identities of their superiors and fellow agents. Later in the eighteenth-century, this notion of "unknown superiors" and hierarchical networks of secret agents would be viewed as an insidious Masonic development.

In April 1706 Defoe worked closely with the Scottish commissioners (appointed by the queen) who came to London to negotiate the treaty of union, and in May he published *An Essay on Removing National Prejudices Against a Union with Scotland*. Perhaps intentionally, the *Essay* was published in Edinburgh "as propaganda *against* the Union."[32] When Defoe arrived in Edinburgh in late September 1706, he immediately sought out members of clubs and societies, including the Freemasons. He recorded his admiration for the great stone constructions in the city, and he would long admire the work of Sir William Bruce and other Scottish architects.[33] While he sent Harley intelligence reports and produced anonymous pro-Union tracts, he pretended to sympathize with the opposition and even claimed that he would move permanently to Scotland. One of Defoe's recruits was evidently the Duke of Hamilton, who accepted bribes from the English ministry while he pretended to lead the anti-Union forces. Hamilton's shift in loyalties has long puzzled historians who voice suspicions of some secret deal with Harley.[34] Perhaps a clue lies in Hamilton's correspondence with Harley, in which he warmly addressed the English unionist as "an honest Mason," suggesting that they shared Masonic bonds.[35] Defoe probably shared them also; at this time, "the mutual confidence and close working relationship between Defoe and Harley was at its zenith."

A barrage of unionist propaganda – and secret bribes – soon took its toll on the opposition. In November 1706 Defoe boasted of passing as an oracle among the anti-

[29] *Ibid.*, 265-66.

[30] Paula Backsheider, *Daniel Defoe: His Life* (Baltimore, 1989), 156, 182, 214; plus personal communication (April 1997).

[31] Daniel Defoe, *The Letters of Daniel Defoe*, ed. George Healey (Oxford, 1955), 38-43.

[32] *Ibid.*, 208.

[33] *Ibid.*, 209.

[34] P. Scott, *Andrew Fletcher*, 118-20, 142-44.

[35] P. Backsheider, *Defoe*, 214, 222, 247.

unionist Presbyterians, "owing to that Secret Management for which I suppose my Mission hither is designed."[36] Describing his pretended friends as "a hardened, refractory, and Terrible people," he warned Harley of "an Association forming in the North and West," composed of fifty thousand Scots who have taken "an Oath that they will stand by One Another in defense of the present Establishment in Church and state." Defoe further charged that the opposition uses the "Cant of the Old Times," calling themselves "the Lords Covenanted people," while they are really "known Jacobites and Episcopall men." As noted earlier, there was a Masonic element in the earlier Covenanting movement, as well as in subsequent royalist, nationalist efforts. On 26 November Defoe boasted to Harley:

> I am Perfectly Unsuspected as Corresponding with anybody in England. I Converse with Presbyterian, Episcopall-Dissenter, Papist and Non Juror, and I hope with Equall Circumspection... I have faithfull Emissaries in Every Company And I talk to Everybody in Their Own Way. To the Merchants I am about to settle Here in Trade, Building ships, etc.... I am privy to their folly, I wish I could not call it Knavery, and am Entirely Confided in.[37]

In December Defoe reported the Jewish pretensions of the nationalists, who "have gone in parliament just as Nehemiah did at the Wall of Jerusalem with the sword in one hand and the mattock in the other."[38] This Biblical image would later emerge in Jacobite Masonic rituals. In January 1707 he reported, "I have Incognito gotten into the company" of Fletcher and the Duke of Atholl, who planned to petition the commission and encourage rebellion, but were "like the Pharissees in the Gospell, that bound heavy Burthens on Other Mens shoulders but would not Touch them." He had acquired a volume of Fletcher's anti-union speeches to the Scottish parliament (1703), and he recognized the popular influence of the fiery, anti-unionist republican.[39] By March he boasted of having spies and pensioners in every place – "I confess tis the Easyest thing in the World to hire people here to betray their friends."[40] Despite the passionate opposition of the vast majority of Scots, Harley's secret "management" won the day, and the bribed commissioners signed away Scotland's independence on 25 March. In an especially cynical letter to Harley on 3 April, Defoe wrote: "The Great Men are posting to London for places and Honours. Every Man full of his Own Merit, and afraid of Every One Near him. I Never saw so much Trick, sham, pride, Jealousy, and Cutting of Friends Throats as there is Among the Noblemen."[41] As the Scottish poet Robert Burns, an admirer of the Jacobites and a republican Freemason, would later write, Scottish independence was "Bought and sold for English gold" by "a parcel of rogues in a nation."[42]

---

[36] D. Defoe, *Letters*, 140.

[37] *Ibid.*, 67-68.

[38] *Ibid.*, 186.

[39] *Librorum ex Bibliothecis Philippi Farewell, D.D. et Danielis De Foe, Gen. Catalogus* (London, 1731), #1022.

[40] D.Defoe, *Letters*, 211-13.

[41] *Ibid.*, 213.

[42] Robert Burns, *The Best Laid Schemes: Selected Poetry and Prose of Robert Burns*, ed. Robert Crawford and Christopher MacLachlan (Princeton, 2009), 145.

Fletcher was so disgusted at the Union that he proclaimed that the nation was now "only fit for the slaves that sold it."[43] While he made plans to leave Saltoun, he kept in touch with Scottish Freemasons in England. On 21 April the Scottish mathematician David Gregory wrote Fletcher from London, with greetings from Dr. John Arbuthnot: "We miss no opportunity of all grateful remembring you and hope to see you here for all that has happened and if you are resolved not to come to London, I hope to see you at Salton."[44] Since 1705 Arbuthnot had been a Fellow of the Royal Society, where he shared his Vitruvian interests with his fellow Mason and friend Christopher Wren, to whom he transmitted various architectural inquiries from Fletcher.[45] Fletcher had met Wren earlier in London, and he had expressed his interest in the design of the Covent Garden Church. Wren now replied (via Gregory) to Fletcher's technical questions about the construction of some stone outbuildings at Saltoun. Despite Fletcher's vow to leave his enslaved country, he stayed on and was suspected of collaboration with the Jacobites.

In July Defoe, who kept his eye on Fletcher and his anti-unionist supporters, warned Harley about new intrigues by Atholl, St. Clair, and several other of the Popish and Jacobite gentlemen: "The Jacobites Report their K Ja. VIII will be on show quickly, some report he is Arriv'd Incog., but all Agree there is some Mischief in hand."[46] Defoe gained intelligence about Jacobite overtures to the young Swedish king Carl XII, who was making a sensational military campaign across Europe. He thus published attacks on Carl in his *Review*, written in Edinburgh and published in London in August and September 1707. The Swedish ambassador in London, Christoffer Leijoncrona, complained bitterly to Queen Anne and Harley, and rumors reached Edinburgh that Defoe would be bound and handed over to "the insulted Sweedes." Leijoncrona's embassy secretary, Count Carl Gyllenborg, would become so infuriated by Defoe's continuing attacks on Carl XII that he would later help organize the Swedish-Jacobite plot (which included a significant Masonic component).[47] On 20 December Defoe wrote to a friend that he "is yet alive in Spite of Scotch Mobs, Swedish Monarchs, or Bullying Jacobites and is going to London to shew his Face to the worst of his Enemies and bid them defiance."

On 5 January 1708 Defoe was in London incognito, and he asked Harley to give him orders about future clandestine activities. However, he was shocked to learn that Harley was on the verge of resignation, for the minister's rivals exploited the discovery that William Gregg, who worked as a translator in his office, served as a spy for France. Queen Anne was apparently not informed that Gregg had been planted by the Jacobites at St. Germain, and she allowed Dr. Arbuthnot, his friend, to attend Gregg as he awaited execution.[48] At this time, Arbuthnot's brother Robert utilized his position in French banking to serve the court at St. Germain. After Harley's resignation on 11 February, Defoe had the grim satisfaction of watching his predictions of Jacobite resistance come true. In March the nineteen year-old James VIII and III was carried to the coast of Scotland by a French ship, which was then driven away by bad weather and Admiral Byng's superior

[43] P.Scott, *Andrew Fletcher*, 210.

[44] *Ibid.*, 210-11.

[45] G. Aitken, *John Arbuthnot*, 66-69, 77, 85.

[46] D.Defoe, *Letters*, 230, 248.

[47] For various historians' arguments suggesting a Masonic component, see M. Schuchard, *Emanuel Swedenborg*, 107-15, 119-29.

[48] E. Cruickshanks and E. Corp, *Stuart Court*, xxi; G. Aitken, *Arbuthnot*, 33-34.

English fleet.[49] Lord Godolphin, ministerial victor over Harley, now sent Defoe back to Scotland, where a mass arrest of Scottish nobles was implemented. Among the prisoners was Fletcher, who was sent to Stirling Castle. From London, Mar instructed his brother to look after their old friend and architectural collaborator.

Within months of the Union, many Scots who had supported it changed their minds, as the reality of Scotland's losses became apparent. One pamphleteer noted that the "voluntary" marriage of Israel and Egypt, consummated in 1707 B.C., was at first happy but soon deteriorated because the Egyptians treated the Jews "as a Parcel of beggarly strangers."[50] Then "God himself chaulked out the methods" followed by Moses and Aaron to leave Egypt. "In the sight of God, the Israelites were absolv'd from all allegiance to the King of Egypt"; moreover, "it was lawful for them to use even violent methods towards withdrawing themselves from their oppressors." Outrage over England's repressive policies also spread to Ireland, where an English official reported, "You would hardly believe there should be such a creature as an Irish Protestant Jacobite, and yet 'tis most certain there are a great many such monsters."[51] By the time of the attempted Jacobite invasion, the Duke of Hamilton was suspected of complicity, arrested, and transported to London, while the former unionist Mar became steadily disillusioned. As Presbyterians, Episcopalians, Papists, and even Republicans became odd bedfellows in the Scottish-Irish resistance movement, the usage of Masonic-style communication and organization became more widespread.

However, as far as the main English public was concerned, Freemasonry was still an operative organization. In a revised edition of *A New View of London* (1708), Edward Hatton described the seventeenth-century craftsman's fraternity which met at Masons Hall in Basinghall Street:

> This company was Incorporated about the year 1410, having been called the Free Masons, a Fraternity of great account who have been honoured by several Kings and very many of the Nobility and Gentry being of their Society. They are governed by a Master, 2 Wardens, 25 Assistants and there are 65 on the Livery.[52]

Given the abandonment of Stuart building projects, the operative fraternity in England was in a severe decline. Anderson recalled that after the Union of 1707, "in the South the Lodges were more and more disused."[53]

That some Whigs suspected the Scots of using Masonry for political ends is suggested by the effort made in 1708 to transcribe Thomas Martin's manuscript "Narrative of the Free Masons Word and Signs" (1659) and enter it into the register book of the Royal Society.[54] Sir Isaac Newton, a staunch Whig, was now president of the society, but it was probably the Ulster-born Hans Sloane who provided the original manuscript from his collection.[55] Martin had apparently acted as a Cromwellian spy, who reported to the

---

[49] Bruce Lenman, *The Jacobite Risings in Britain, 1689-1746* (London, 1980), 88-89.
[50] Anon., *An Historical Account of the Union, Betwixt the Egyptians and Israelites* (Edinburgh, ca. 1709-10), 4-8.
[51] I. Ehrenpreis, *Swift*, II, 170.
[52] Anon., *A New View of London* (London, 1708), II, 168.
[53] J. Anderson, *Constitutions (1738)*, 108.
[54] Royal Society, London: MS. Register Book(C), IX,ff.240-52.
[55] See British Library: Sloane MS. 3323,f.209.

Commonwealth government on the beliefs and activities of the Masons.[56] The relevance of his hostile account in the aftermath of the 1708 Jacobite invasion lies in its detailed descriptions of secret identification signs and codes, means of secretly exchanging money, recognition technique of three knocks on a door, ritual toasts passed over water glasses, and bonded loyalty between Masonic brothers toward the king. A Scottish influence on the manuscript is suggested by the emphasis on the Jews and Egyptians and a chivalric reference to the lodge at "the Holy Chappel of St. John" (maintained by the Knights of St. John of the Hospital). As we shall see, Jonathan Swift would later draw on this tradition when he referred to lodges of the "Knights of St. John of Jerusalem."[57]

That Harley continued to use Masonic techniques, while he struggled to rebuild his political base, is suggested by the activities of two of his agents, John Toland and Richard Steele, in 1708-10. Sent to Holland by Harley in 1708, Toland was unaware that his patron was shifting from his previous Whig loyalties to new collaboration with the Tories. While Toland sent intelligence reports and acquired rare books and manuscripts for Harley, he and his friends organized a secret society at The Hague, called "The Knights of Jubilation." Margaret Jacob argues (controversially) that the Knights "adopted most of the aspects of the new speculative Masonry."[58] The brothers were drawn from a network of free-thinking publishers and booksellers, who gathered for ritualized initiations under their Grand Master, who led them in jovial discussions of heterodox topics (accompanied by bawdy jests and heavy drinking). Toland had already hinted at his fascination with secret societies and ancient mysteries, but in *Adeisdaemon* ("The Unsuperstitious Man"), published at The Hague in 1709, he explicitly advised secrecy as "a means to an end, as a way of arriving at the true esoteric philosophy, the knowledge that God and Nature are one."[59] Toland's strategy of esoteric secrecy and exoteric political manipulation evidently appealed to Defoe, who acquired a rare copy of *Adeisdaemon* (1709); he would continue to collect Toland's works over the next decade.[60]

At this time, Toland was immersed in Bruno's writings, which inspired him to make another attack on ancient Hebrew traditions. He appended to *Adeisdaemon* a section on *Origines Judaicae*, in which he denied that the Old Testament was the word of God or the production of his spirit.[61] Moses did not write the Torah, which was thus an uncertain, fallible authority. According to Robert Sullivan, Toland believed that

> Moses was an Egyptian priest and provincial governor who led a confused and rebellious mob. Like any pagan legislator, he invoked the supernatural in order to legitimate his state, which was now a theocracy... Moses sought to insinuate an esoteric teaching differing from that which he promulgated to his followers. He thus set a pattern for the imposture that marked the subsequent history of Judaism. The oracles conveyed by the patriarchs and

---

[56] For more on the context and his role as a spy, see M. Schuchard, *Restoring the Temple*, 576-78.
[57] J.Swift, *Works*, V, 329.
[58] M. Jacob, *Living the Enlightenment*, 75; and *Radical Enlightenment*, 153-76.
[59] *Ibid.*, 169-70.
[60] *Librorum...De Foe*, part 1, #1456, 1077; part II, 257.
[61] S. Daniel, *Toland*, 202.

prophets were raptures and dreams, comparable to the hallucinations of other men.[62]

This was heady but hazardous stuff for Toland and his friends, who found refuge, sociability, and fraternity in their secret society.

The Knights of Jubilation specialized in radical and libertine publications, indulged in feasting and drinking, and lambasted the evils of womanhood. In the surviving minute of a meeting, one member was chastised for breaking his oath "to abstain from all love, whether clandestine or matrimonial, since love is the complete opposite of all joy, and marriage the grave of all laughter and fun."[63] The free-thinkers' rejection of heterosexuality gave rise to rumors about homosexuality in their circles (with Shaftesbury a particular target). Toland's group – and possible affiliates in London – evidently provoked Richard Steele to lampoon them in his new journal *The Tatler*, where he compared a similar group of effeminate libertines to the Freemasons. Steele, an Irish-born Protestant, may have learned about military Masonry when he served in the Duke of Ormonde's regiment and in the Cold Stream Guards (formed by Monk in 1659). A student of Rosicrucianism and alchemy in 1703-05, Steele was probably aware of Toland's earlier "adeptship."[64] Harley, despite his fall, managed to get Steele appointed Gazetteer for the Whig ministry, where Steele could provide inside information for his ever-dissembling patron. When Steele started publishing *The Tatler* in May 1709, he received much foreign news from The Hague, which was probably supplied by Toland. Though Steele was a staunch Whig, he was not a free-thinker, and he occasionally poked fun at Toland in *The Tatler*.

Within this context, Steele's allusions to Freemasons on 9 June 1709 seemed to be targeted at the Knights of Jubilation or an affiliated society led by Shaftesbury. A correspondent appeals to Bickerstaff (Steele's persona) to put a stop to "an insinuating, increasing set of people," who assume the name of "pretty fellows" and "even get new names":

> Some of them I have heard calling to one another...by the names of Betty, Nelly, and so forth. You see them accost each other with effeminate airs: they have their signs and tokens like freemasons: they rail at women-kind; receive visits on their beds in gowns, and do a thousand other unintelligible prettinesses that I cannot tell what to make of.[65]

On 29 December Steele lampooned an effeminate dandy, who included a volume of Toland's *Christianity Not Mysterious* among his pomades and perfumes, and on 2 May 1710 he mocked "the Order of Insipids," who have "some secret intimation of each other like the freemasons."[66]

While Harley's Whig agents imitated or mocked Freemasonry, his new secret allies among the High Tories organized a "semi-Masonic" society, "The Loyal Brotherhood," which recruited crypto-Jacobites. As Linda Colley notes, "The Brothers borrowed some

[62] R. Sullivan, *Toland*, 202.
[63] M. Jacob, *Radical*, 268.
[64] George Aitken, *The Life of Richard Steele* (1889; rpt. New York, 1968), I, 141-45.
[65] *The Tatler*, ed. George Aitken (New York, 1899), I, 216.
[66] *Ibid.*, I, 417; III, 274-75.

of the more decorative elements of freemasonry" and "underwent an initiation ceremony," while they regularly met in taverns that "had masonic associations."[67] In the surviving minutes, from 7 July 1709 to 5 June 1713, it is clear that the brothers went through an "adoption" process and vowed to avoid all religious controversy.[68] The first president was Henry Somerset, 2nd Duke of Beaufort ("a thorough-going Tory"), whose grandson Henry, 5th Duke of Beaufort, would later serve as the crypto-Jacobite Grand Master of the English Grand Lodge in 1766-72.[69] The Loyal Brotherhood subsequently initiated the Duke of Hamilton (Harley's Masonic ally) in June 1711 and Charles Middleton, Second Earl of Middleton (leader of the "Compounders" or moderate Jacobites) in May 1712.[70] Swift was friendly with Hamilton, and he later recorded that he had known Middleton, whom he and Temple admired.[71] Other members, such as the Earl of Scarsdale and Lord North and Grey would later be implicated in Jacobite plotting in 1715 and 1722.

When Henry St. John and Swift organized the "Society of Brothers" in summer 1711, they were influenced by the Loyal Brotherhood, and both fraternities supported the Tory-Jacobite cause. In January 1712 Swift recorded that the Duke of Beaufort wanted to join the society and, after some resistance from the duke's kinsman, James Butler, 2nd Duke of Ormonde, he became a member in February.[72] Ormonde evidently worried that Beaufort was too overtly Jacobite, and Swift initially shared his reluctance, but after Beaufort joined, the two became friendly. Despite the fraternal theme, the society soon reflected the political rivalries between St. John and Harley. While St. John determined to consolidate his hold on the leadership of the Tory party, he excluded his rival Harley from the "Brothers," but friends of Harley such as Dr. Arbuthnot and Ormonde (both Jacobite Masons) sometimes served as president of the society."[73] An important member was George Granville (later Baron Lansdowne), an aspiring poet and friend of Pope, who was "ever conscious of his family's loyalty to the Stuarts."[74] Like his friend Swift, he tried to reconcile Harley and Bolingbroke, which led the latter to threaten him with expulsion from the "Brothers" for "doing Harley's bidding." As we shall see, Granville's paternal kinship with General Monk and his access to private family papers about Monk's role in the Restoration will provide a clue to the oral tradition that Monk utilized Masonic networks to organize Charles II's return. Though it is unknown if Granville was a Mason, he would later work closely with Lord Mar, Colonel Arthur Dillon, Chevalier Ramsay, and the Jacobite Masons in Paris.

Another Masonic-like fraternity – the mock "Corporation of the Ancient Borough of Walton-le-Dale" – met at the Unicorn Inn, on the outskirts of Preston in northeast

---

[67] Linda Colley, "The Loyal Brotherhood and the Cocoa Tree: the London Organization of the Tory Party," *The Historical Journal*, 20 (1977), 80-83.

[68] BL. Add. MSS. 49,360, ff.1-95: "Minute Book of the Board of Brothers."

[69] For the 5th Earl of Beaufort's secret Jacobite-Masonic intrigues, see M. Schuchard, *Emanuel Swedenborg*, 677-78, 690-96, 737.

[70] See entries in *ODNB*.

[71] Jonathan Swift, *Journal to Stella*, ed. Abigail Williams (Cambridge, 2013), 251, 368, 379-81, 456; Ian Higgins, *Swift's Politics: A Study in Disaffection* (Cambridge, 1994), 75.

[72] J. Swift, *Journal to Stella*, 371, 392, 415, 517.

[73] I. Ehrenpreis, *Swift*, II, 502-04; G. Aitken, *Arbuthnot*, 46.

[74] "George Granville," *ODNB*.

England.[75] Formed in 1700 as a cover for its Jacobite and Catholic members, "its raison d'être was to flout authority, giving mock offices to the families whose hereditary county posts had been removed after James II's flight."[76] While appointing comical officers, such as "slut kisser" and "custard-eater," the corporation also named more serious officers, maintained strict rules, and developed elaborate rituals and symbolic paraphernalia.[77] Francis Skeet argues that it was "in reality a secret society which under the cloak of jollity and conviviality concealed a deep political purpose." W.E. Moss notes that the initiates "met in secret, practised secret ceremonies, had passwords, and a mace and other insignia," and he concludes that "the *mise en scene* is Masonic."[78] Initially headed by great Northumbrian magnates, such as the Catholic Thomas Howard, 8th Duke of Norfolk, the corporation seemed to draw on older Stuart Masonic traditions, and it is significant that James Anderson, the later official Whig historian of Masonry, claimed that Freemasonry was inherited in the Howard family, with Thomas Howard, 2nd Earl of Arundel, serving as Grand Master, and Inigo Jones appointed as his deputy in 1633. And indeed the 8th Duke of Norfolk would become the crypto-Jacobite Grand Master of the London Grand Lodge in 1729.[79]

The mock corporation became more politically significant when James Radcliffe, 3rd Earl of Derwentwater, was elected Mayor of the Corporation in 1710. A grandson of Charles II and Moll Davis, Radcliffe had been raised as a Catholic at St. Germain, where he became the intimate friend of the young James III. Through the influence of his relative, the "plain-speaking" Dr. John Radcliffe (physician to Queen Anne and an Anglican Jacobite), and the doctor's friend Ormonde, he was allowed to return to his estates in 1709. Swift, who was friendly Dr. Radcliffe, was probably aware of Derwentwater's return to England. On his extensive northern properties, the earl undertook ambitious stone building projects, especially at his family home of Dilston, which kept him in touch with operative Masons, many of whom would follow him into battle in the 1715 Jacobite rebellion. W.E. Moss argues that Derwentwater and his younger brother Charles were Freemasons before 1715.[80] James Radcliffe reportedly maintained ancient Stuart themes within the fraternity, and Charles would later undertake a *revival* of those Jewish mystical and Christian chivalric traditions in the *Écossais* lodges in France.[81] Leo Gooch stresses the importance of Freemasonry in northern Catholic life, noting that "Certainly, Jacobite lodges flourished in Newcastle and in the Tyne valley where the Radcliffes lived."[82] It was at Newcastle that Freemasons from Edinburgh admitted Sir Robert Moray and earlier royalist Masons into a mobile military lodge in 1641.[83]

During this same period in Ireland, a leak of the Masons' secret language and rituals occurred in an amusing context. In 1710 Arthur St. Leger, 1st Viscount Doneraile, held a

---

[75] L. Gooch, *Desperate Faction*, 38-40; Frederick Pick, "Preston – the Guild and the Craft," *AQC*, 59 (1948), 105.

[76] F. Alison Wright, "The Layburnes and their World circa 162-1720: The English Catholic Community and the House of Stuart" (Ph.D. Thesis: St. Andrews University, 2002), 265.

[77] P. Monod, *Jacobitism*, 298-99.

[78] Francis Skeet, *The Life of the Right Honourable James Radcliffe, Third Earl of Derwentwater* (London, 1929), 42-43.

[79] See ahead, Chapter 12.

[80] W. Moss, "Freemasonry," 105.

[81] P. Chevallier, *Histoire*, I, 22.

[82] L. Gooch, *Desperate Faction*, 38-40.

[83] M. Mylne, *Master Masons*, 167-69; M. Schuchard, *Restoring the Temple*, 450.

lodge in his residence of Doneraile Court in County Cork.[84] His young daughter Elizabeth accidently witnessed the ceremonies and was subsequently initiated in order to ensure her secrecy. She remained a lifelong patron of the order, subscribed to Masonic publications, and wore a Masonic jewel and apron for her portrait. Doneraile received his title from Queen Anne while at court in London in 1703, and he evidently knew Swift, who would later draw on Elizabeth's initiation in his *Letter from the Grand Mistress of the Female Freemasons.* According to David Dickson, early Freemasonry in Cork – in which the St. Legers were involved – was Tory and "tolerant of passive Jacobitism."[85]

Not long after Elizabeth's initiation, Thomas Molyneux copied a Masonic manuscript in Dublin in February 1711 that drew on Scottish practices, included a third Master's degree, and probably "had a non-operative origin."[86] Swift knew the Molyneux brothers and was possibly aware of their family's Masonic interests. These developments within Irish Freemasonry provide a suggestive background for the publication of Swift's attack on Vanbrugh's architecture in 1710. He revised his 1705 manuscript to include references to Vanbrugh's even greater violations of Vitruvian principles – i.e., the massive palace of Blenheim built to honor the Duke of Marlborough, whose victories over France made him a Whig hero. He now worked for Harley and published propaganda against Marlborough in *The Examiner.* For Swift the overweening arrogance and secular greed of Marlborough and his wife was expressed in Blenheim's grandiose design. In "The History of Vanbrugh's House," he charged that the amateurish Vanbrugh pilfered the design for the "Goose-pie House" from a child's house of cards:

> Van's genius, without thought or lecture,
> Is hugely turned to architecture:
> He saw the edifice, and smiled,
> Vowed it was pretty for a child:
> It was so perfect in its kind,
> He kept the model in his mind.[87]

Even worse, he copied some other boys' mud house:

> With true delight oberved'em all
> Raking up mud to build a wall;
> The plan he much admired, and took
> The model in his table-book;
> Thought himself now exactly skilled,
> And so resolved a house to build;

Now the Whigs at court have enabled Vanbrugh to create the ultimate monstrosity for the ultimate duke of corruption:

> From such deep rudiments as these
> Van is become by due degrees

---

[84] Edward Conder, "The Hon. Miss St. Leger and Freemasonry," *AQC*, 8 (1895), 16-19; Lepper and Crossle, *History*, I, 38-39.
[85] David Dickson, *Old World Colony: Cork and South Munster, 1630-1830* (Cork, 2005), 275.
[86] D. Knoop, "Mason Word," 210.
[87] J. Swift, Complete Poems, 91-92.

> For building famed, and justly reckoned
> At court, Vitruvius the second.
> No wonder, since wise authors show,
> That best foundations must be low.
> And now the Duke has wisely taken him
> To be his architect at Blenheim.
>
> But raillery for once apart,
> If this rule holds in every art,
> Or if his Grace were no more skilled
> The art of battering walls than building;
> We might expect to see next year
> A mousetrap-man chief engineer.

Certainly, the individualistic-secular Whig architecture was far removed from the royalist-religious Jacobite architecture advocated by Dr. Arbuthnot, who was closely involved with Swift at this time. Moreover, Swift and his Tory Masonic friends were probably aware that Whig interference with Wren's work in 1709 so disgusted the famed architect that he stopped attending the Commission on Building, where Vanbrugh dominated the meetings.[88] At the same time, Wren encouraged the young Scottish architect James Gibbs, who was recommended by his enthusiastic patron Lord Mar.[89] Gibbs had earlier been forced to leave Scotland because of his Catholicism, and he subsequently studied in Italy. Wren "was much Gibbs' friend and was pleased with his drawings." He also appreciated the Stuart loyalties of the young Scot, who opposed the architectural "Whiggery" of Vanbrugh. According to Anderson, "Brother Gib, the Architect" was a Freemason.[90]

During this period, Mar – whom Swift currently knew and admired – pushed his architectural conceptions "beyond the merely practical to the visionary."[91] At Alloa he proposed a vast, Versailles-inspired layout of formal tree-lined avenues, with vistas to Stirling Castle and other historic landmarks. Reflecting his desire to unify Scottish Presbyterians and Episcopalians (a unionist and Masonic dream), he built a chapel for an Anglican service, "betwixt the bare unbecoming nakedness of the Presbiterian service in Scotland, and the gadie, affected and ostensive way of the Church of Rome."[92] Like Swift, he despised the English Whig architectural styles that had no national or symbolic meaning. He considered decorative embellishments on modern palaces as "trifling gimcrack insignificant ornaments worthy of nobody but Vanbruge" – certainly not what he would later design as "a Palace worthy of the Grandeur of the King."[93]

---

[88] J. Summerson, *Architecture*, 143. For a detailed study of Wren's problems with Vanbrugh and other Whig architects and craftsmen, see Marsha Schuchard, "Jacobite vs. Hanoverian Claims for Masonic 'Antiquity' and 'Authenticity,'" *Heredom*, 18 (2010), 225-58. A French version, "La revue *The Post Man* et les *Constitutions de Roberts* (1722), appeared in *La Règle d'Abraham*, 30 (2010), 3-62.

[89] Bryan Little, *The Life and Work of James Gibbs, 1682-1754* (London, 1955), 20, 29-32.

[90] J. Anderson, Constitutions (1738), 121.

[91] Terry Friedman, "'A 'Palace worthy of the Grandeur of the King': Lord Mar's Designs for the Old Pretender, 1718-30," *Architectural History*, 29 (1986), 108-09.

[92] Eveline Cruickshanks and Howard Erskine-Hill, *The Atterbury Plot* (New York, 2004). 98.

[93] T. Friedman, "A Palace," 108.

When Harley and the Tories came back into power in August 1710, they determined to support Wren and to reinvigorate the stalled program of church building. On 7 October Swift presented a memorial to Harley, urging him to persuade the queen to raise the funds for church construction. Was it mere coincidence that three days later Wren and his son performed a public Masonic ceremony at St. Paul's? Wren *fils* placed the capstone on the now-completed cathedral, while his proud father and "other Free and Accepted Masons chiefly employed in the Execution of the work" performed the appropriate Masonic ceremonies.[94] Among the spectators was the twenty-two year-old Swedish scientist, Emanuel Swedenborg, who described St. Paul's as a "temple."[95] Swedenborg was allegedly initiated into craft Masonry in London, and Swedish Masons later claimed that Wren was re-elected Grand Master in 1710.[96] The report of this 1710 election was evidently part of a secretive Swedish Jacobite-Masonic tradition, for Anderson does not mention it in his Whig history of Masonry. Wren did regain his power within the fraternity, for within a year Harley's ministry commissioned the building of "fifty new churches of stone," in an ambitious revival of Stuart architectural-Masonic policy.[97]

This revival was also celebrated in Rome, where John Talman – son of the Williamite country house architect, William Talman – was presented to the Pope in April 1711 and allowed to make drawings in the Vatican Treasury, "an almost unheard of favor to a foreigner."[98] In June John repaid this papal honour by hosting a lavish "Entertainment" for his fellow members of the Accademia dell' Arcadia and other virtuosos, in which the major theme was "the rise of the arts in Britain." Pictures of Inigo Jones, Isaac Fuller, and Edward Pierce were juxtaposed with those of Palladio, Raphael, and Michelangelo. On the dinner table there were "three large Triumphs in praise of England," and Queen Anne's health was drunk to the sound of a trumpet. Graham Parry and Lindsay Boynton argue that William and John Talman were Freemasons and that their devotion to ecclesiastical architecture and Italian art led both to secretly convert to Catholicism.[99] John Ingamells agrees that John was a covert Catholic, but a conversion by his father, formerly a strong Williamite Whig, seems unlikely.[100]

News of this Roman celebration of Tory architectural revival spread through Italy and England, which provoked a Whig counter-attack on the whole Tory program of church building. It was led by Shaftesbury, currently living in Naples, where his asthmatic lungs continued to deteriorate. On 6 March 1712 he dedicated to Lord Somers his draft of "A Letter Concerning the Art, or Science of Design," in which he formulated a Protestant-Whig theory of art to replace the so-called Papist-Tory agenda of the Stuarts and Harley's ministry. Though Shaftesbury drew on Evelyn's translation of Roland Fréart's royalist treatise, *An Idea of the Perfection of Painting* (1668), he scorned Fréart's theories as "insolent"

---

[94] C. Wren, *Parentalia*, 293.

[95] Alfred Acton, *Letters and Memorials of Emanuel Swedenborg* (Bryn Athyn, 1955), I, 13.

[96] Marsha Keith Schuchard, "Swedenborg, Jacobitism, and Freemasonry," in *Swedenborg and His Influence*, ed. Erland Brock (Bryn Athyn, 1988), 359-79; M. Jacob, *Living the Enlightenment*, 92.

[97] Summerson, *Architecture*, 185.

[98] Graham Parry, "John Talman: A Life in Art," *The Walpole Society*, 59 (1997), 20-22.

[99] *Ibid.*, 35-36, 253.

[100] John Ingamells, *A Dictionary of British and Irish Travellers in Italy, 1701-1800* (New Haven, 1997), 924-26. Plus on-line edition.

and his criticism as "impertinent."[101] Paul Monod notes that Shaftesbury "blithely ignored the facts of recent history," while he disparaged the "foreign" influence of Charles II on English art and praised William III for enabling English taste to break "free of Gallic tyranny."[102] Arguing that "it is not the nature of a court (as courts generally are) to improve, but rather corrupt a taste," Shaftesbury claimed that what is set wrong by their example "is hardly ever afterwards recoverable in the genius of a nation." Instead, he advocated an oligarchy of Whig aristocrats who would lead the liberated "people" towards a new national taste.

Shaftesbury then launched a bitter attack on Christopher Wren, who was (according to the Swedes) the current Grand Master:

> As for architecture, it is no wonder if so many noble designs of this kind have miscarried amongst us; since the genius of our nation has hitherto been so little turned this way, that through several reigns we have patiently seen the noblest public buildings perish (if I may say so) under the hand of one single court-architect; who, if he had been able to profit by experience, would long since, at our expense, have proved the greatest master in the world. But I question whether our patience is like to hold much longer.[103]

As Wren and Harley struggled to finance their church-building program, Shaftesbury lamented the prospect of "many spires arising in our great city, with such hasty and sudden growth" that we may be "hereafter censured, as retaining much of what artists call the Gothic kind." For Wren and his operative Masons, Gothic was still an honored architectural tradition, which was often preserved within their classical renovation work.

From 1711 to 1713 Swift and Dr. Arbuthnot led meetings of the "Brothers' Club," which included their high Tory and Jacobite colleagues, who gathered for literary and occasionally political discussions. Several of the brothers were or became Freemasons, which may have influenced the Masonic-like rules of the club. John Collins observes that "In its meetings all those artificial distinctions which separate caste from caste and man from man were ignored. Its members met and mingled on terms of fraternal equality."[104] Like Ormonde (a Mason), Charles Boyle, 4th Earl of Orrery, was an Anglo-Irish Protestant; his family had been involved in Irish architectural projects and Masonry for decades, and he was reportedly an initiate.[105] When political differences intensified, the club disbanded but was followed by the much more influential Scriblerians' club, which focused more exclusively on literary matters.

*

* *

---

[101] The essay was not published until 1732; reprinted in Anthony Ashley Cooper, Third Earl of Shaftesbury, *Second Characters or the Language of Forms*, ed. Benjamin Rand (1914; rpt. New York, 1969), 8, 32.

[102] Paul Monod, "Painters and Party Politics in England, 1714-1760," *Eighteenth Century Studies*, 26 (1993), 378-79.

[103] Shaftesbury, *SecondCharacters*, 21.

[104] John Churton Collins, *Jonathan Swift: A Critical Biography* (London, 1893), 89-90.

[105] See M. Schuchard, *Restoring the Temple*, 678-80, 689; André Kervella, *Le Chevalier Ramsay, Une Fierté Écossaise* (Paris, 2009), 173-74.

During the period when political power shifted from Whig to Tory (1709-1712), the spread of imitative quasi-Masonic societies provoked concern about Judaizing, Rosicrucian, and heretical trends among them. In 1709 a Whig pamphleteer accused the English Anglican Henry Sacheverell and the Irish Anglican Charles Leslie, high-Tory polemicists, of being "false brethren" who maintain "Jacobite synagogues" in the interest of the Pretender.[106] In the same year, the Hebrew scholar and Jacobite George Hickes asked "Rabbi" Francis Lee to anonymously contribute his "History of Montanism" to the fourth revised edition of Hickes's *Spirit of Enthusiasm Exorcised*, written originally as a diatribe against pseudo-prophets who served radical republican ends. As noted earlier, Hickes had served as chaplain to the Earl of Lauderdale, and he made notes on the Jewish symbolism within Scottish Freemasonry. He now shared Lee's concern that the radical Huguenot sect known as the French Prophets or Camisards portended more sedition and schism within the British church. Thus, he wanted Lee to draw on his studies of ancient heretical and schismatic groups to expose the current threat.

In his "History," Lee described the secret fraternity of Montanists (second century A.D.), whose occult rituals were eventually exploited for political ends. In their "Magical College or Society," there was a hierarchy of members, in which the elite initiates called themselves "the Illuminati."[107] Like the Jewish Manichees, they were addicted to astrology, believed in the eternity of matter, and allegorized the Mosaic book of Genesis. Moreover, "they had a mysterious *Cabala* among them concerning the Longitude and Latitude, and the Local Diffusion of Christ and the Spirit." Though Montanus was initially sincere, his enthusiasm and zeal for reform "rendered him a most proper subject to be managed by invisible Springs, for such ends as he little surmized." To reinforce Lee's warnings, Hickes included Nathaniel Spincke's essay, "The New Pretenders to Prophecy Examined." Spinckes compared the French Prophets to followers of Sabbatai Zevi, the seventeenth-century Jewish "false messiah," and he accused the Papists of sneaking in Jesuits amongst the London group in order to stir up trouble and divide the Anglican church. In sum, Hickes's volume of essays provided an eerie foreshadowing of the charges of Jesuit and Jewish manipulation of Rosicrucianism and Freemasonry that proliferated later in the century.

This collective exposé would remind some readers of Toland's efforts to establish Brunonian fraternities to spread his radical political and philosophical views. In fact, some Freemasons may have feared that Toland was using their fraternity like the "Invisible" managers of the Montanists and French Prophets. In 1710, when the eccentric scientist John Woodward – an active Mason – wrote "Of the Wisdom of the Ancient Egyptians," he determined to counter Toland's Brunonian influence with a defence of the ancient Jews. Woodward was currently giving lectures on "The Bible and Its Uses," but he may have intended the essay – which touched on many Masonic themes – for his fraternal associates. Woodward referred directly to the circulation of Bruno's *Spaccio*, for which Toland was responsible:

---

[106] C.J. Abbey and J.H. Overton, *The English Church in the Eighteenth Century* (London, 1878), 66.

[107] George Hickes, *The Spirit of Enthusiasm Exorcized* , 4th rev. ed. (London, 1709), 167, 205-227, 312-43.

> That famous Atheist Jordano Bruno [*] Nolano, and others of like libertine principles, who bear no good will to Christianity, knowing how much this is built upon Moses, do not care to have thought his writings came from God, but from Egypt. These therefore extoll Egyptians beyond measure, and decry the Jews and vilify that nation, their archives, and laws, as merely of Egyptian extract...
>
> [*] *Spaccio della Bestia triumphante.*[108]

Woodward drew on his extensive knowledge of Egyptian and Jewish lore to dispute Toland's charge that the Sinaitic revelation was merely derivative. Countering Toland's argument that circumcision was not unique to the Jews, Woodward argued that the Egyptians used circumcision "as a charm...carrying with it some magical property," while "Everybody knows the Jews used it all along from the very beginning, wholly upon a religious account as an *initiation*, and in token of *covenant*. He then defended the Mosaic revelation with those Biblical accounts that were the central themes of Freemasonry. He pointed out that the Hebrews did not even know how to cast metals for images, so Solomon had to send for Hiram, son of a Jewish widow bred in Tyre, to cast figures for adorning the Temple. But in every other art and skill involved in temple construction, the Jews were inspired experts:

> the very designs and descriptions, and much more the building of that wonderfully noble and stately pile the Temple of Solomon, to say nothing now of the several royal palaces, could never have been performed in that manner without a very great, exquisite knowledge and mastery in carpentry, smithery, masonry, architecture, mechanicks, and all the better and more useful arts... The whole was, indeed, vastly superior to any thing to be met with in history then in being...and yet *it was built of stone made ready before it was brought hither,* as likewise the cedar....*so that there was neither hammer, nor axe, nor any tool of iron, heard in the house while it was building.*[109]

The italicized statements were central to the craft lore of operative Masonry. Woodward may have sensed that he revealed too much in the essay, which he never published – or, he may have intended it for use within the fraternity. It was later published in 1776 by a circle of Masonic antiquarians. Perhaps Woodward's attack on Bruno influenced Toland to anonymously publish his English translation of the *Spaccio* in late 1712-13.

---

[108] See [John Woodward], "Of the Wisdom of the Ancient Egyptians," *Archaeologia*, 4 (1776), 225, 246-47, 253, 294.
[109] *Ibid.*, 247.

CHAPTER FIVE

BUILDING CASTLES IN THE AIR, AT HOME AND ABROAD
(1710-1716)

> Free Masons beware Brother Bacon advises
> Interlopers break in & Spoil your Divices
> Your Giblin & Squares are all Out of Door
> And Jachin & Boaz shall bee Secretts no more.
>
> "The Prophecy of Brother Roger Bacon" (ca.1713).

> When the common people take notice of the secret managing of public af-
> fairs, They...suspect it to be a plot upon them...for treacheries and wick-
> edness deserve the night and darkness to cover and conceal them...the
> Brethren are thought guilty of concealing themselves...but let us consider
> that they travel and they, as all wise men, acknowledge no particular country
> but the whole world
>
> "The Rosie Crucian Secrets," Harleian MS. 6485 (1713).

While the Whigs Toland and Steele trailed a shadowy reputation as former students of Rosicrucianism, debates over the reality and purpose of the seventeenth-century German fraternity filled the pages of learned journals – which
often grappled with the claim that Descartes was an initiate. Samuel Parker, an embattled
Jacobite, published a journal, *History of the Works of the Learned* (1699-1711), which summarized the Continental controversies about the Rosicrucians. Because Leibniz and his
partisans supported the pansophic aims of the fraternity, their antagonists in England –
led by Newton – hoped to undermine their whole conceptual and historical basis.[1]
Throughout Parker's journal ran articles sympathetic to Rosicrucian science and alchemy,
which various authors claimed to be important influences on the development of modern
experimental science.[2] At the same time, Parker published many articles on the importance of knowledge of Cabala to the defense of revealed religion, as well as the

---

[1] *History of the Works of the Learned*, I, 140.
[2] *Ibid.*, VII, 630; VIII, 588; XII, 732-34.

importance of Christianizing the Cabala to the defense of "the true Church." Like its offspring, Rosicrucian science, Cabala could provide keys to natural science.

Opposing these "esoteric" Jacobite interests, Steele and his Whig network used *The Spectator* to reveal their own familiarity with and eventual scorn for the occult sciences and for non-operative Freemasonry. That Steele was now hostile to Harley, who was made First Earl of Oxford, meant that the Tory prime minister (and his suspected Jacobite cronies) became a frequent but oblique target in *The Spectator*. In the issue for 6 November 1711, when a correspondent named "Vitruvius" lamented his addiction to building castles in the air, he seemed to hint at the spread of speculative Jacobite Freemasonry into France:

> I am unhappily far gone in Building, and am one of that Species of Men who are properly denominated Castle-Builders, who scorn to be beholden to the Earth for a Foundation… but erect their Structures in the most unstable of Elements, the Air; Fancy alone laying the Line, marking the Extent, and shaping the Model…
>
> A Castle-Builder is even just what he pleases, and as such I have grasped imaginary Sceptres, and delivered uncontrollable Edicts from a Throne… I have made I know not how many inroads into France, and ravaged the very heart of that Kingdom… But alas I must tell you, the least Breath of Wind has often demolished my magnificent Edifices… I have been pulled by the sleeve, my Crown has fallen from my Head… Add to this the pensive Drudgery in Building, and constant grasping Aerial Trowels…[3]

The allusions to the Stuart king James VI and I (whose sleeve was pulled by a radical Presbyterian), to Charles I (whose crown fell from his head), and to James "III" (who grasps an imaginary sceptre) make clear that speculative Jacobite "builders" were the satiric target.

Toland, who bitterly resented Harley's political apostasy, returned to England and joined the anti-Tory propaganda campaign. However, Toland was also lampooned in *The Spectator*, for Steele was determined to distance the Whigs from the free-thinkers.[4] Nevertheless, the journal announced on 27 May 1712 the sale of an English edition of Bruno's *Spaccio*, whose anonymous translator was Toland. This backdoor support of Toland by Steele perhaps provoked Swift, whose friendship with Steele was cooling, to publish on 26 June a broadside, *Toland's Invitation to Dismal to Dine with the Calves' Head Club*. Swift gleefully accused the Whigs of cozying up to the radical republican Toland, who initiates them into the regicidal fraternity. Irwin Ehrenpreis argues that Swift based his description of Toland's club on his own experience in the Society of Brothers.[5] Thus, Swift's inclusion of Masonic-style practices is suggestive. When Toland invites the Whig leader Daniel Finch, 2nd Earl of Nottingham ("Dismal") to "eat the Calves' Head," he urges him to,

> Suspend a while your vain ambitious hopes,
> Leave hunting after bribes, forget your tropes;
> Tomorrow we our mystic feast prepare,

---

[3] *The Spectator*, ed. Donald Bond (Oxford, 1965), II, 158-60.
[4] See oblique mockery of Toland in volumes II, 155-56, 411-12.
[5] I. Ehrenpreis, *Swift*, II, 567.

> Where thou, our latest proselyte, shalt share;
> When we, by proper signs and symbols tell,
> How, by brave hands, the royal traitor fell;
> ....
> My province is, to see that all be right,
> Glasses and linen clean, and pewter bright;
> From our mysterious club to keep out spies,
> And Tories (dressed like waiters) in disguise.[6]

In Masonic lodges selected brothers served as stewards of the "mystic feast" and as tylers who kept out intruders or eavesdroppers, while lodge members enacted their Solomonic traditions through "signs and symbols."

While Toland published Bruno's praise of the Hermetic religion of Egypt and denigrated the religion of the Jews, the *Spectator* discussed Cabalistic codes that transmit secret messages, which are "not mysteries for ordinary Readers to be let into."[7] Vowing to "lay open the Arcana," Eustace Budgell recounted "the Story of Rosicrucius's Sepulcher," noting that "this man was the Founder of the *Rosicrucian Sect*, and that his Disciples still pretend to new Discoveries, which they never Communicate to the rest of Mankind."[8] When the tomb was opened, the country people learned that the allegedly supernatural effects were produced by mechanical trickery and that Rosicrucius "was resolved no one should reap any Advantage from the Discovery" of the ever-burning lamp. This, of course, was an inversion of the original account. On 2 June Steele described his own earlier dabblings in alchemy, making clear they were a past folly.[9]

In the midst of the Tory-Whig debates about Rosicrucianism, an advertisement appeared in the Whig newspaper, *The Post Man* (5-7 June 1712), which sought contact with the fraternity:

> Anonymous a Lover of the Fraternity of R.C. who Published their Fame and Confession in 1652, desires personally to converse with one of that Fraternity (if it may be) otherwise by Letters. He is to be heard of at Mr. Tompsons a Chymist in Cock Lane near Shore Ditch London. But to be Enquired after by no other Persons.

"Anonymous" was evidently Robert Samber, a Rome-educated Jacobite, who in 1698 (and 1722) called himself "Eugenius Philalethes Jun'r," the pseudonym used by Thomas Vaughan for his translation of the 1614 Rosicrucian *Fame and Confession* in 1652. Samber called on "all the true Sons of Hermes," members of "the Brotherhood mighty in Deed and Word, to stand up for or against the cause."[10] As we shall see, Samber would later publish a panegyric to a Rosicrucian branch of Freemasonry.

During the months when Robert Harley, Lord Oxford, carried on a secret correspondence with the Stuart court, he acquired a set of Rosicrucian manuscripts allegedly

---

[6] J. Swift, *Poems*, 125-26.

[7] *Ibid.*, II

, 360-61.

[8] *Ibid.*, III, 424-25.

[9] *Ibid.*, III, 479.

[10] The Bodleian Library lists Samber as the author of Eugenius Philalethes Jun'r, *Some Reflections on a late Book called the Golden Age* (London, 1698).

compiled by Dr. Rudd.[11] Much of the collection was copied by Peter Smart, "M.A. of London," in 1712-14. The manuscripts drew on earlier writings by John Dee, Thomas Vaughan, and John Heydon, and they included complex explications of Enochian magic, Metatron mysticism, and Cabalistic sexual cosmology. Of greatest interest to Oxford would surely be "The Rosie Crucian Secrets," attributed to Dee, which included keys to his angelic-Enochian code and probably drew on the same Dee manuscripts analyzed by Robert Hooke in a lecture to the Royal Society in 1690 (which was published in Hooke's posthumous works in 1703). Hooke argued that Dee's angelic conversations were an ingenious diplomatic code which could be deciphered through his system of Enochian Cabala.

In March 1713 Smart copied for Oxford "The Rosie Crucian Secrets" (501 folio pages), which gave special significance to the "sixth and last Law which is That the Fraternity of the R.C. shall be concealed an hundred years" – i.e., until 1714. The reason for the concealment was appropriate to Oxford's own dissembling practices and obsessive secrecy:

> When the common people take notice of the secret managing of public affairs, they, because of their ignorance, suspect it to be a plot upon them and openly censure it as not fitting to see the Sun; for treacheries and wickedness desire the night and darkness to cover and conceal them and therefore actions are bad because they are private... The Brethren are thought guilty of concealing themselves...but let us consider that they travel and they, as all wise men, acknowledge no particular country but the whole world to them is as their own native soil... Their actions are such as becomes those who hope to appear and shine in heaven, though they are obscure below.[12]

It was perhaps through Oxford's interest in Rosicrucianism that his confidant, Charles Boyle, 4th Earl of Orrery, began to accumulate his amazing, enormous collection of Rosicrucian and alchemical works, now housed in Christ Church Library in Oxford. While a member of Swift's Society of Brothers, he acquired *Themis Aurora, or Laws of the Rose Cross* (1656), as well as rare works by Paracelsus, Agrippa, Guillaume Postel, Robert Fludd, Van Helmont (father and son), John Heydon, George Ripley, George Starkey, Thomas Vaughan, Sendivogius, Elias Ashmole, Comte de Gabalis, and dozens of other Rosicrucian and Hermetic treatises.[13] Most interesting, given Orrery's current work in Tory diplomacy, was his acquisition of Dee's *Works* (1659) and Hooke's *Posthumous Works* (1705), which included Hooke's argument that Dee's angelic communications were a sophisticated diplomatic code and most useful in espionage.[14]

That Lord Oxford manipulated Masonic and/or Rosicrucian networks was suggested by a poem appended to a 1677 copy of the Old Charges of Freemasonry. Titled "The Prophecy of Brother Roger Bacon/ Disciple of Balaam w'ch Hee writt on ye/ N:E:

---

[11] British Library: Harleian MSS. 6481-86; see Arthur Edward Waite, *The Brotherhood of the Rosy Cross* (1924; New York, 1993), 398-401.

[12] British Library: Harleian MS. 6485; see John Dee, *The Rosie Crucian Secrets*, ed. E.J. Langford Garstin (Wellingborough, l985), 254-55. The attribution to Dee is probably spurious.

[13] Christ Church, Oxford: "A Catalogue of the Library of Charles late Earl of Orrery" (MS. Dated 1732).

[14] For a discussion of Hooke's analysis of Dee and its influence on diplomatic coding techniques, see M. Schuchard, *Emanuel Swedenborg*, 88-91.

Square of ye Pyramids of Egypt/ In Capital letters," the poem was composed after the Peace of Utrecht on 11 April 1713 and before the death of Queen Anne on 12 August 1714:

> When a Martyrs Grand Daughter
> In ye Throne of great Brittain
> makes Capets Proud Son look,
> You'd Think him beshitten
> when ye Midway and Mais Piss together In a Quill
> and Tayus & Rhine of ye Sein have their will,
> when ye Thames has ye Tay taen for better for worse
> and to purchase ye Doxy has well drained his purse,
> whyn by Roasting a Priest ye Church has her wishes
> Loyall Torys in Places, Whiggs Silent as ffishes
> when Europe grows Quiet, & a man y'ts right wily
> Setts up a woodbridge from ye Lands End to Chili
>
> ffree Masons beware Brother Bacon advises
> Interlopers break in & Spoil Your Divices
> Your Giblin & Squares are all Out of Door
> And Jachin & Boaz shall bee Secretts no more.[15]

G.W. Speth explicates the allusions to Queen Anne, Marlborough's victories over Louis XIV, the bribery that led to the Union of England and Scotland, the burning of Dr. Sacheverell's Jacobite sermon, the signing of peace between England and France, and Oxford's establishment of the South Sea Company (which created a wooden bridge of ships from England to South America). The author was a Tory, who warned his fellow Freemasons that the ousted Whigs were currently infiltrating the Jacobite lodges.

The Whigs had good reason to fear increasing Jacobite influence on the operative Masons and architects involved in royalist construction projects. Swift and his Jacobite friend, Bishop Francis Atterbury, had persuaded Queen Anne and Oxford to undertake a massive church building agenda, which many Tories and Jacobites praised as a rebirth of Stuart culture. Alexander Pope linked the architectural agenda with the Tory-achieved Peace of Utrecht, which he eulogized in the poem, *Windsor Forest*, published on 7 March 1713, a few weeks before the final signing of the peace treaty on 11 April. Pope dedicated the poem to George Granville, Lord Lansdowne, who was a member of the Society of Brothers and who was currently involved in Jacobite plotting. With references to Charles I, "the Martyr-King," Pope recalled the "dreadful Series of Intestine Wars," and then praised Queen Anne: "Rich Industry sits smiling on the Plains,/ And Peace and Plenty tell, a STUART reigns."[16] He gave the ailing queen full credit for achieving the peace: "At length great ANNA said let Discord Cease!/ She said, the World obey'd, and all was *Peace*!" As a visible expression of Stuart culture, Pope lauded the new architectural efforts in both domestic and ecclesiastical projects:

> Behold! Th' ascending *Villa's* on my Side

---

[15] G.W. Speth, "Two New Versions of the 'Old Charges,'" *AQC*, 1 (1888), 128-29.

[16] Alexander Pope, *Windsor Forest* (London, 1713), 2, 14, 16.

Project long Shadows o'er the Chrystal Tyde.
Behold! *Augusta's* glitt'ring Spires increase,
And Temples rise, the beauteous Works of Peace.

Like Wren, Swift, and Mar, he envisioned the rebuilding of White-Hall palace: "I see, I see where Two fair Cities bend/ Their ample Bow, a new *White-Hall* ascend!"

Pope's poem reflected the high hopes of various Jacobite Masons about a renewal of Stuart priorities, not only architecturally but politically. On 13 August 1713 Christopher Wren, Jr., presented to the Commission for Building New Churches an ambitious design by James Gibbs for a church, St. Mary le Strand, which would include a grand statue of Queen Anne.[17] On 18 November, on the recommendations of Oxford, Wren, Mar, and Arbuthnot, Gibbs secured the coveted co-surveyorship, with Nicholas Hawksmoor, a fellow Mason, to the commission.[18] Given the fraternal affiliation and Tory-Jacobite sympathies of these members, it is not surprising that they wanted the church to stand near the ancient Maypole in the Strand, which for decades had been interpreted as a symbol of earlier carefree and pleasure-seeking Stuart reigns. Damaged by the Puritans and neglected by recent ministries, the towering Maypole needed major reconstruction. As we shall see, after Anne's death and the advent of the Hanoverians, the Whigs would exact their revenge on the Jacobite-Masonic architects, sculptors, and supporters of this tribute to the Stuarts.

In the meantime, the Tory-Jacobite cause received more Cabalistic-Hermetic reinforcement when Pope added Rosicrucian "machinery" to an enlarged second edition of *The Rape of the Lock* (first two cantos published in May 1712, revised version in March 1714). In late 1713 Pope was advised by Oxford, St. John (now Viscount Bolingbroke), and other political "men of sense" about the revisions, which reflected their crypto-Jacobite preoccupations in late 1713, as Queen Anne's health deteriorated.[19] Brooks-Davies argues that the lovely "Belinda" represented Queen Anne, who was limited by the constitutional settlement inherited from William III.[20] Her Tory advisors (Pope's helpers) were then secretly negotiating with James III, the Stuart Pretender, about his possible conversion to Anglicanism and repeal of the Act of Settlement. Thus, "Catholic Union is the clue to the poem's larger meaning which embraces adverse criticism of the Whig settlement and, by implication, some kind of support for the Jacobite cause."[21] Pope's decision to add the Rosicrucian machinery was probably influenced by Oxford's, Orrery's, and Swift's knowledge of Rosicrucian lore and its subsequent usage in political codes. Oxford's Masonic link with the Duke of Hamilton has already been noted, and it may be relevant that the names of Pope and Swift would later appear on a lodge list, cumulative to 1730.[22] At the time of *The Rape of the Lock*, Pope may already have had access to Masonic lore through his "fraternal" friends, Arbuthnot, Swift, and Gibbs. Pat

---

[17] Pat Rogers, *Documenting Eighteenth Century Satire: Pope, Swift, Gay, and Arbuthnot in Historical Context* (Newcastle, 2012), 233-34, 238; Ingamells, *Dictionary*, 91-92.

[18] "James Gibbs," *ODNB*.

[19] Alexander Pope, *The Correspondence of Alexander Pope*, ed. George Sherburn (Oxford, 1934), I, 207.

[20] Douglas Brooks-Davies, *The Mercurian Monarch: Magical Politics from Spenser to Pope* (Manchester, 1983), 181-96.

[21] *Ibid.*, 182.

[22] Maynard Mack, *Alexander Pope: A Life* (New Haven, 1985), 437-40.

Rogers goes further to describe Pope "as a freemason, who knew a good deal about Rosicrucianism and other branches of 'ancient knowledge.'"[23]

In the dedication to the 1714 edition, Pope explained the Rosicrucian machinery he added to the mock-heroic poem:

> These Machines I determined to raise on a very new and odd foundation, the Rosicrucian doctrine of Spirits... The Rosicrucians are a people I must bring you acquainted with. The best account I know of them is in a French book call'd *Le Comte de Gabalis*... According to these Gentlemen, the four Elements are inhabited by Spirits, which they call Sylphs, Gnomes, Nymphs, and Salamanders. The Gnomes or Daemons of Earth delight in mischief; but the Sylphs, whose habitation is in the Air, are the best condition'd creatures imaginable. For they say, any mortals may enjoy the most intimate familiarities with these gentle Spirits, upon a condition very easy to all true Adepts, an inviolate preservation of Chastity.[24]

Swift had earlier drawn on *Le Comte de Gabalis* (1670), a Rosicrucian novella by the Abbé de Villars, for his satirical attack on religious schism in *Tale of a Tub*. But, as Brooks-Davies argues, Pope's decision to use *Gabalis* had definite political overtones. The French original "is a strange work...which Pope's critics have, by and large, been shy of. And yet here perhaps more than anywhere else the Jacobite heart of the poem lies."[25]

In *The Rape of the Lock*, Pope hinted at mystical rites and the possibilities of spiritual regeneration through a secret society. While his female characters negotiate their way through complex politics, "The Sylphs thro' mystic mazes guide their way." Belinda's *toilette* becomes "Each silver Vase in mystic order laid." The red cross suggests not only the hallmark of the Knights of St. George and the Knights Templar but also Rosicrucian efforts at ecumenical reform. The card game of Ombre and the tea table both point to the political intrigue and polarization that produced a Britain divided in religion and politics. By implication, James III offered the alternative of Catholic unity, in which all religions would be protected under the universal love advocated by Archbishop Fenelon, the spiritual mentor of the Stuart claimant. The revised *Rape of the Lock* was immediately perceived by the Whigs as a Jacobite work, and they commissioned John Ozell to rapidly publish an English translation of *The Count of Gabalis* (1714). Ozell, who worked as a Whig decipherer of intercepted correspondence, noted that the translation was done in response to Pope's poem, and he referred the reader to the exposé about Rosicrucius that appeared in *The Spectator*, #379.

*

* *

During the early months of 1714, the Jacobites found encouraging support from the Swedish ambassador Count Carl Gyllenborg, who had married into an English Jacobite family and who labored to gain the support of Carl XII and Louis XIV for a Stuart

---

[23] P. Rogers, *Documenting*, 241-42.
[24] Alexander Pope, *The Works of Alexander Pope*, eds. Whitwell Elwin and J.W. Courthope (London: John Murray, 1871-89), II, 143-44.
[25] D. Brooks-Davies, *Mercurian Monarch*, 192.

restoration. Gyllenborg became an intimate friend of Oxford, Bolingbroke, Arbuthnot, and Swift (who maintained a lifelong admiration for the audacious diplomat and his warrior king).[26] In October 1709, when Swift learned that the Swedish king had been defeated at Poltava and then imprisoned in Turkey, he wrote, "My Heart is absolutely broken with the Misfortunes of K. of Sueden, nothing pleased me more in the Thoughts I had of going abroad than some hopes I had of being sent to that Court."[27] Since September 1711, Gyllenborg had been secretly working with a Jewish Jacobite agent, whom he housed in "une maison circomcise" in London.[28] The Jew was Francis Francia, who would later emerge as the major financial agent in the Swedish-Jacobite plot of 1715-18. Francia used his contacts in France to develop links between Stuart partisans in Britain, France, and Sweden, and he utilized complex numerical codes, different handwritings, and several languages in his secret correspondence.[29]

Gyllenborg and Francia worked closely with Louis Marie, Duc d'Aumont, French ambassador in London who, like the Jew, was allegedly a Freemason. According to J.C. Carr, d'Aumont collaborated with Jacques Vergier, the reputed master of a shadowy Masonic lodge at Dunkirk.[30] This lodge later boasted of its historic ties with Freemasons who accompanied James II into exile. Though these claims remain questionable, given the lack of early documentation, Gyllenborg's coded correspondence with d'Aumont and his Jacobite and Swedish collaborators included Masonic-style symbols (cross, circle with dot, rectangle, triangle, etc.), and like Swedenborg – whom he recruited as an intelligence agent – Gyllenborg was possibly initiated in a Jacobite lodge in London.[31] At this time Swift was also friendly with d'Aumont, and he and the "Brothers" had worried about the Whig mobs who threatened the ambassador and then set his house on fire in January 1713.[32] An angry Queen Anne offered d'Aumont a palace on the Thames, which provoked mob cries that the ambassador was actually hiding the Pretender.[33]

John Shaftesbury claims that d'Aumont's collaborator Francia was a Freemason; thus, Francia's references to his "noble society" or "club" of royalist Jews who supported his Jacobite efforts was possibly a Masonic lodge.[34] The activities of these Jewish Jacobites perhaps provoked Toland to produce an atypical pro-Jewish tract. When he anonymously published *Reasons for Naturalizing the Jews in Great Britain and Ireland, On the Same Foot with All Other Nations*, probably in October 1714, Toland elaborated his earlier argument for the naturalization of foreign Protestants "by exploiting the extreme example of the

---

[26] See F.P. Lock, *Swift's Tory Politics* (Newark, 1983), 125-27.

[27] J. Swift, *Correspondence*, I, 268.

[28] Stockholm. Riksarkiv: Anglica, #212. Gyllenborg to Palmquist (21 September 1711).

[29] *Historical MSS. Commission: Calendar of the Stuart Papers* (London, 1902-23), IV, 499, 519. [Henceforth cited as *HMC: Stuart*].

[30] *Ibid.*, I, 249, 253, 322; J.C. Carr, "Gorgons, Gomorgons, Medusists, and Masons," *Modern Language Review*, 58 (1963), 73-78.

[31] J. Shaftesley, "Jews," 150-209; Stockholm Riksarkiv: Anglica #211. Gyllenborg to Palmquist (17 December 1710). Gyllenborg was friendly with the Masons Wren, Sloane, and Woodward, as well as Oxford's circle, and his family would later be active in *Écossais* Freemasonry in Sweden. For Gyllenborg's and Swedenborg's possible initiation in London, see M. Schuchard, *Emanuel Swedenborg*, Chapters Two and Three.

[32] J. Swift, *Journal to Stella*, 488-90.

[33] M. Schuchard, Emanuel Swedenborg, 74.

[34] J. Shaftesley, "Jews," 159.

Jews."[35] Disappointed at the repeal in 1710 of a naturalization bill passed the year before, he seemed to believe that a rational case for the Jews would make the foreign Protestants look more desirable by comparison. After years of denigrating Israel as the excrement of Egypt, Toland now presented the Jews as potentially useful citizens, whose addiction to usury would be cured by allowing them to work in fields where they anciently excelled – such as building. He was possibly aware of Francia's appeal to royalist Jews who were Masons, or he hoped to strike a blow at the Judaized Jacobites of Scotland, who appealed to Old Testament traditions of god-anointed kings.

Consistent with Toland's anti-clericalism was his claim that the banishment of Jews from England and Spain was "procur'd by the incessant bawling of the Priests in each Nation." Addressing the archbishops of Great Britain (whom he had long castigated), Toland reminded them, "you further know how considerable a part of the British inhabitants are the undoubted offspring of the Jews (to which the old Irish can lay no claim)." To support this claim, he asserted: "A great number of 'em fled to Scotland, which is the reason so many in that part of the Island, have such a remarkable aversion to pork and black-puddings to this day, not to insist on some other resemblances easily observable."[36] This hint that the Scottish Jacobites were circumcised would later be stated explicitly in Henry Fielding's pro-Hanoverian propaganda.[37]

Since spring 1714, the Tory commission for church building had employed the Masonic virtuoso John Talman in Rome to find the best sculptor to produce a magnificent bronze statue of Queen Anne.[38] As a private Catholic, he may have believed that she would name her half-brother James as her successor. On 1 July Arbuthnot was appointed by the commissioners to consider a model for a monumental stone pillar (250 feet high), dedicated to Anne, and to be situated near the Maypole and Gibbs's new church in the Strand. Working with Bishop Philip Bisse (a Jacobite and friend of Swift), Arbuthnot presented the plan to the queen, and a distinguished committee, including Arbuthnot and Wren was formed to "direct laying of the pillar's foundation," which was approved on 21 July.[39] At this time, they dreamed that their architectural homage to Anne as the representative of Stuart culture would usher in a new political reality.

During these summer months, while Oxford, Bolingbroke, Ormonde, and Arbuthnot attended the bed-ridden queen, they were secretly planning the peaceful restoration of James III. Though it is unclear how much Swift knew of their Jacobite intrigues, he was so distressed by the destructive rivalry between Oxford and Bolingbroke that in June he retired into the country, from where he wrote "Brother" Arbuthnot, "I have already half lost the ideas of Courts and Ministers."[40] However, on 11 July, Pope reported to Arbuthnot that Swift hinted at his inside knowledge of Jacobite overtures to Russia and Sweden:

> He talked of Politicks over Coffee, with the Air and Stile of an old Statesman,
> who had known something formerly; but was shamefully ignorant of the

[35] D. Katz, *Jews in History*, 234-36.

[36] John Toland, *Reasons for Naturalizing the Jews in Great Britain* (London, 1714), 37.

[37] H. Fielding, *Jacobite's Journal*, 283.

[38] G. Parry, "John Talman,"26.

[39] P. Rogers, *Documenting*, 234. For Bisses's Jacobitism, see Paul Monod, *Jacobitism and the English People, 1688-1788* (Cambridge, 1988) 148, 172.

[40] G. Aitken, *Arbuthnot*, 62.

Three last weekes. When we mentioned the welfare of England he laughd at us, & said Muscovy would become a flourishing Empire very shortly. He seems to have wrong notions of the British Court, but gave us a hint as if he had a Correspondence with the King of Sueden.[41]

David Wooley observes that through Swift's friendship with Gyllenborg, he planned a possible flight from England to Sweden in 1714: "A contingency arrangement seems on the cards."[42] As a current friend of Lord Mar, he could have learned of the Scottish Jacobites at the Russian court. He had just attended Mar's wedding at Acton in July, where Mar may have confided in him about "Muscovy."[43] Also through Gyllenborg, who was now collaborating with Mar, Swift could have learned more about the projected secret alliance between Russia, Sweden, and the Jacobites, which Gyllenborg's diplomatic colleague Baron von Görtz was then contemplating. Claude Nordmann argues that this "curious alliance" included a significant Masonic component.[44]

In the same letter to Arbuthnot, Pope cautiously joked about Swift's experiments with an orbicular glass, which made the sun's rays burn holes and figures on paper: "There was a large Gapp at ye edge of the Bill of Schisme, and several Specks upon the Proclamation for the Pretender. I doubt not but these marks of his are mysticall, and that the Figures he makes this way are a significant Cypher to those who have the skill to explain 'em." Ian Higgins notes that Swift was suspected of Jacobitism at this time and cautiously concealed his real views.[45] When Queen Anne suddenly died on 12 August, the polarized Tory-Jacobite party was unprepared for forceful action. A disappointed Arbuthnot wrote cautiously to Swift on that day to lament that Anne had not made a will and that the Elector of Hanover was pronounced King George I of Britain: "I can assure you the peaceable scene that now appears, is a disappointment to more than one set of people."[46] Swift had informed Arbuthnot that he would return to Ireland, and the Scottish doctor subsequently slipped out of England in order to visit his brother Robert, the Jacobite banker and arms supplier, in France.

Four days after the queen's death, the directions for laying the monumental pillar were rescinded, "with immodest haste"; orders were sent to the operative Masons that "No more stone to be laid in for foundation of the pillar intended to be erected in the Strand until further notice."[47] With the Hanoverian succession accomplished and the Whigs gaining ascendancy in the government, they began a campaign to dismantle the Tory commission for building fifty new churches, and they steadily undermined Gibbs's position as surveyor. As George I made clear that he scorned such ambitious projects of ecclesiastical construction, Mar shared in the disappointment of those who dreamed of a Tory-Stuart architectural revival. Like other Scottish and "ancient" Freemasons, he began to look abroad for both architectural and political support.

---

[41] J. Swift, *Correspondence*, I, 646.

[42] *Ibid.*, 647n3.

[43] Margaret Stewart, *The Architectural, Landscape and Constitutional Plans of the Earl of Mar, 1700-1732* (Dublin, 2016), 110.

[44] C. Nordmann, *Crise du Nord*, 10.

[45] I. Higgins, *Swift's Politics*, 80-83.

[46] G. Aitken, *Arbuthnot*, 78.

[47] P. Rogers, *Documenting*, 234-35.

Mar became increasingly angry and alienated when the new king ousted the Tories from all positions and appointed an all-Whig ministry. While continuing to attend court, he undertook secret negotiations with Gyllenborg, who hoped to shift the Czar's aggressions away from Carl XII and towards George I. While fighting each other, the Swedish and Russian monarchs both resented George's territorial aggrandizements on the North Sea and Baltic. Mar's first cousin Robert Erskine served as physician to the Czar, and – following Mar's own strategy – he appealed to Peter's Masonic associations. On 29 October o.s. 1714, in a letter from St. Petersburg, Erskine's colleague George Mackenzie hinted to Mar about the Masonic ties between himself, Erskine, Mar, and the Czar's trusted agent, Semen Grigor'evich Naryshkin. Dr. Erskine provided the Russian with a letter of recommendation to Mar, noting that he will carry the Czar's answer to a letter that George I sent him from Hanover. He will also have "several other matters given him in charge, whereof

> wthout breaking throw the Masson Word, I hope, as to a Bro'r Mechanick of his Czarian Maty, it will as yet be allow'd me to acquaint you so far, that he is to carry, say they, a sea Compass to our King: the value of that present is that 'tis of this Prince's own gradation, and the box of his own turning. What the other things may be? Are also Joyner's work; but not being so compleat a Carpenter as to let out all the cunning, without being seen, your Lordp, have so long ago pass't the Essay Master will enough be apprised of it there, before the whole is come to a walding...[48]

Robert Collis observes that the letter is "suitably cryptic, but it contains plentiful examples of Masonic phraseology." As noted earlier, the Czar's alleged initiation by Wren was connected with his study of naval architecture. The letter also revealed Mar's earlier Masonic initiation, for the "Essay Master" was a test given to Scottish operative Masons who had to construct an architectural model to be "pass'd" to the next degree. To come to a "walding" apparently meant to completion and final control.

In November 1714 these international schemes received new vigor when the Swedish king made a sensational escape from his Turkish prison and undertook a marathon horseback ride to the Baltic port of Stralsund, where he was determined to recover Sweden's lost German territories. Jacobite agents labored to link Carl XII, Czar Peter, and Louis XIV in an ambitious assault against George I. Soon Spain was recruited, and substantial funds were raised to fund the Swedish troops. Claude Nordmann argues that the curious alliance that developed between Sweden, Russia, and Spain against Hanoverian England was the outgrowth of Jacobite politics: "The partisans of the Stuarts, dispersed throughout Europe…formed as a secret society with multiple antennas outlined (ébauche), without doubt, by Freemasonry."[49]

Staying at the center of affairs in London, Mar contacted potential supporters in the British Isles. While he clandestinely plotted, he continued to design buildings for Scottish and English patrons.[50] Thus, Mar was probably aware of and outraged by George I's

---

[48] Robert Collis, *The Petrine Instauration: Religion, Esotericism, and Science at the Court of Peter the Great* (Leiden, 2011), 132-33.

[49] C. Nordmann, *Crise du Nord*, 10.

[50] T. Friedman, "Palace worthy," 102-03.

moves against Wren and the operative Masons. In November 1714 the king knighted Vanbrugh, whose Whiggish political intrigues had led the Tory ministry in 1713 to dismiss him as Comptroller of the Works. Now re-employed, the architect was asked by Lord Halifax, the new Lord Treasurer, to submit his recommendations for reorganization of the Office of Works. Halifax was aware of the Masons' oath of secrecy, and he apparently worried about their continuing Jacobite sympathies.[51] Vanbrugh had worked closely with the operative Masons at Blenheim, but the Master Mason Strong and his men continued their complaints about the arrears of payments due to them, and there were reports of their secretly organizing to improve their financial situation. Though Vanbrugh resisted the pressure to immediately oust Wren, "out of tenderness" for his age and long service, he made sure that Wren no longer had effective influence. On 29 November he determined to limit the power of "many Useless and Mischievous officers," and ordered "the abolition of the offices of Master Mason, Master Carpenter, and all the other Master Workmen" – thus diminishing Wren's base of support in the operative fraternity.[52] As further purges of Tory officials took place, many operative Masons resented the diminishment of the traditional practices maintained by Wren, his son, and their supporters.

It was perhaps in reaction to this Hanoverian policy that Mar, Wren, Oxford, Ormonde, and the operative Masons Strong and Prichard subscribed in 1714 to the proposed *Vitruvius Britannicus*, an ambitious illustrated treatise undertaken by a group of booksellers, with contributions by the Scottish architect Colen Campbell, who called for a revival of Inigo Jones's royalist style.[53] They were listed as subscribers before March 1715 and thus before Campbell switched his loyalty to the Hanoverian regime. Michael Gibbons argues that "the bulk of Campbell's material" had been prepared before Queen Anne died, and "the seeds of all the ideas which Campbell was to proclaim had been sown in the Stuart era."[54]

As many Scottish unionists moved south and hoped to gain positions under the new Hanoverian regime, their critics accused them of maintaining seditious Presbyterian principles. In February 1715 James Anderson, a native of Aberdeen and Presbyterian minister in the Swallow Street chapel, published *No King-Killers*, the sermon he preached on 30 January, the date of Charles I's execution. Anderson's father was a member of an Aberdeen Masonic lodge, and most scholars assume that his son was also familiar with or an initiate of Scottish "craft" Masonry.[55] In his sermon, in which he claimed to have connections with the new Whig ministry, he argued that Scottish Presbyterians were not anti-monarchical and were not implicated in the execution of Charles I. In the process, he drew upon the tradition of Scots-as-Jews, who were hindered from "the Rebuilding of the City and Temple of Jerusalem, by weakening the Hands of the People of Judah, troubling them in building, and hiring Counsellors against them."[56] But Jerusalem was "true and loyal to her Kings," and no one could "boast of greater Marks of Loyalty" to the

---

[51] For Halifax on Masonic oaths of secrecy, see C.N. Batham, "The Grand Lodge of England (1717) and its Founding Lodges," *AQC*, 103 (1990), 44.

[52] H. Colvin, *History*, V, 51.

[53] Colin Campbell, *Vitruvius Britannicus* (London, 1715), vol. I.

[54] Michael Gibbon, "The Making of 'Vitruvius Britannicus," *Architectural History*, 20 (1977), 14-30

[55] David Stevenson, "James Anderson: Man and Master," *Heredom*, 10 (2002), 94-95.

[56] James Anderson, M.A., *No King-Killers. A Sermon Preach'd in Swallow Street, St. James's, on January 30, 1714/15* (London, 1715), 1-3, 11, 40.

"Royal Family of David." It was other "sectaries" who brought about Charles I's death, and Presbyterians were justified in "resisting the late King James," to avoid "being swallowed up by a Deluge of Popery, or new molded, to be made as like to Popery as possible." He concluded with a call for loyalty to King George and an end to sectarian divisions in the nation.

Given Anderson's later important role in Hanoverian Freemasonry, it is curious that a furious opponent hinted at his connection with "craft" Masonry in his pamphlet, *No King-Sellers: Or, A Brief Detection of the Vanity and Villainy in a Sermon, entitutl'd No King-Killers. Preach'd by the Scotch-Presbyterian of Swallow-Street, Picadilly* (London, 1715). The anonymous author attacked Anderson as a "Diminutive in Divinity," a "little white-liver'd, red-headed Scot," and a "Pimp of a Presbyter."[57] While analyzing the allegedly dishonest points in Anderson's sermon ("the Excrement of his dull Brain"), which commits injustices against both Independents and Jacobites, the critic repeated puns upon the Scot's "craft" as part of "a Native stock of impudence." Anderson's claim to have an M.A. should denote "Mungrel of Aberdeen," rather than Master of any Arts, for he is actually "a Crafts Master," a "fraudulent Brother," whose "Journey-men ply for Jobs," as much as "Taylors at their Houses of Call." Though these hints were certainly broad, they do suggest an early recognition by a sympathizer with James III (a king whom the Presbyterians made "a sort of Vagabond, which, to a generous Spirit, is worse than Death itself"), of a link between Anderson's Masonry and his Hanoverian loyalty. Over the next years, this link would emerge more publicly.

*

* *

From the time of the accession of George I, the non-English speaking Elector of Hanover, the Jacobite Masons determined to remove him from the throne. In the process, they provoked a Whig counter-reaction that launched a new form of "speculative" Freemasonry, which became increasingly detached from its operative roots and Stuart traditions. While Jacobite refugees, exiles, and agents sought foreign support (in France, Italy, Spain, Sweden, and Russia), they extended their Masonic networks into those countries. The misleading claim by many historians that Freemasonry came from London to Europe includes the assumption that these traveling Masons were supporters of the Hanoverian government in London and transmitted Whiggish-Newtonian philosophy to their Continental brethren. In fact, most were opponents, dissidents, even traitors to that government. By moving beyond the Anglo-centric perspective that long dominated English Masonic histories, we can fill many gaps in Masonic and Jacobite history – especially the little-known support of Lutheran Sweden and Orthodox Russia for the Catholic Stuarts. In the process, we will gain new insight into the literary responses of Swift, Pope, Arbuthnot, Orrery, Defoe, Wharton, and a host of minor writers, who expressed their own familiarity with these complicated international political and Masonic intrigues.

The Jacobites were determined to gain Swedish support for a rising, and in February 1715 a syndicate of forty English "Tory/Jacobites" pledged to Gyllenborg that they would raise £200,000 to support the Swedish war effort, "on the understanding that Carl

---

[57] Anon., *No King-Sellers* (London, 1715), 3-5, 10, 14, 17.

XII would invade Britain as soon as he could spare the necessary resources."[58] During the early months of 1715, Mar communicated with Bolingbroke, Berwick, Gyllenborg, Görtz, and Francia, as they planned a Jacobite-Swedish landing near Newcastle.[59] However, by late spring the government got wind of the plot, and in March Bolingbroke fled to France, which provoked a Hanoverian propagandist to mount an attack on him and Swift. In *A Letter from the Lord Vi---t B------e, to the Rev'nd R. S---t, D--n of St. P-----k's: Written at Calais, on Tuesday the 29th of March. OS.* (London, 1715), the anonymous writer claimed to be Bolingbroke, who affirms that Swift is privy to and supports the Jacobite plotting. He urges Swift to join him in wonderful France, where he can "Renounce your poor Preferment, in an Apostate, abandon'd Island," and experience the generosity of Louis XIV, who "will Settle our Banish'd Monarch on the Rightful Throne of his Ancestors."[60] The *faux* Bolingbroke then urges Swift to burn "the Copies of those Papers which I gave you, either bury, or burn; I have transmitted the Originals, long since, to Versailles."

In another Whig satire, *Dr. Sw--'s Real Diary…containing his entire Journal, from the time he left London, to his Settling in Dublin* (London, 1715), the author quoted Swift's supposed diary, in which he recorded his preparation of a poem on the Pretender's landing and his subsequent decision to burn it, as well as his "Proposals for his speedy coming to England, and for Methods of making him easier here."[61] He also instructed his printer to burn a sheet "that was printed off," before proceeding to Jacobite-supporting Oxford, where the town was all up and the scholars frightened, but they neverless drank "Success to the University. To the Recovery of the old, or the speedy Arrival of the Lord's new STUART." At this time, the Duke of Ormonde, a Jacobite Mason, was Chancellor of the university. When news came of Queen Anne's death, Swift fled to Dublin. The Whig author, posing as Swift, published a poem lampooning his political opportunism:

> Nay, I did swear I was for Brunswick,
> With Conscience scrupulous and tender,
> But Wrote and Rode till I was Bumm-sick,
> In hopes to forward the Pretender.[62]

As further "hues and cries after Swift" appeared, his letters were confiscated and threats were made to arrest him. Further accusations of his seditious activities were relayed by Charles Delafaye, who subsequently became the government's chief spy-master on the Jacobites. On 25 May Delafaye reported that Isaac Manley, the Irish postmaster general, had seized a parcel of treasonable papers directed to Dr. Swift, and the Lord Lieutenant Sunderland hopes that "if there appears enough against the Doctor to justify it, he is kept in confinement."[63] Delafaye then flattered his Whig superior by boasting that "If anything can add to your grace's character, this application to the public service," i.e. the arrest of Swift, "will undoubtedly heighten it in the esteem of all good men."

---

[58] D. Szechi, *1715*, 48, 93.

[59] L. Gooch, *Desperate Faction*, 34-38, 43, 61.

[60] Anon., *A Letter Letter from the Lord Vi---t B-----ke, to the Rev.nd Dr. S---t, d – n of St. P-----k's* (London, 1715), 3 – 7. For the dangerous political context of the fake Bolingbroke pamphlet, see J. Swift, *Correspondence*, II, 121-28.

[61] Anon., *Dr. S----s Real Diary* (London, 1715), 4, 18-19.

[62] *Ibid.*, 24.

[63] *HMC: Second Report of the Historical Manuscripts Commission* (London, 1871), Appendix, 249.

Delafaye's diligent intelligence work led to promotion under subsequent secretaries of state, and he later became an important Hanoverian Mason.[64]

A month earlier, in April, Defoe had contributed to the Hanoverian propaganda with a pamphlet, *The Second-Sighted Highlander: Being Four Visions of the Eclipse, and something of what may follow* (1715). Drawing on his knowledge of Scottish Freemasonry and its links with second sight, he took advantage of various astronomers' predictions of a complete eclipse on 22 April to mock the Jacobites' superstitions and alliance between Louis XIV and Charles XII. Published two days before the actual eclipse (on 20 April), he spoke in the persona of Archibald Macdonald of Inverlochy, who boasts of

> being possest of the sublime Illumination, hereditary from many Ancestors, the bright Ray of Secret Knowledge, conveying to me a true Intelligence in things hidden from mortal View; that superior Gift, by which a more intense Sight of things to come is communicated, and whereby, in sacred Raptures, such Vision is convey'd.[65]

Worried by intelligence reports of French-Swedish-Jacobite collaboration, the Highlander envisions evil agents "raising Commotions, forming black and hellish Designs, laying the Foundations of Treason, Conspiracy, ambitious Struggles of Great Men one against another."[66] The French king, "Infatuate in the Opinion of his commanding Power," lays the foundation of his own ruin by "Espousing the Ambitious and Revengeful Swede." But Louis's delivery of "the Gothick Heroe" leads to his own "ECLYPSE." But the most important prediction from "the exalted Sight" reveals "the Destruction of all Party-Administrations" and the blowing up of "Faction, Cabal, cemented Parties, and all the secret little Knots, and Setts of Politicians, State-Disturbers" by "a wise Governour" (the Elector of Hanover). This was Defoe's last prophecy, and its message backfired, for the Jacobites interpreted the eclipse as a sign of heavenly approval for their cause.

In the meantime, Bolingbroke left Paris and moved on to James III's court at Bar-le-Duc, where in June he was made Jacobite secretary of state. He then collaborated with Robert Arbuthnot to raise money and procure ships for a projected invasion.[67] He intensified pressure on the Swedish king to contribute his seasoned troops to an invasion of Britain. Görtz now worked tirelessly to build an international coalition, which included the Polish "Pretender" Stanislas Leszcyzynski, the half-Jewish General Stanislas Poniatowski, the German spy and alchemist Theodore von Neuhof, the Russian *frères* of the Scottish Masons, and the Swedish members of the Sparre regiment of the French army. All of these foreign Jacobite-supporters developed secret Masonic associations that would become more public in the following decades.[68]

---

[64] For Delafaye's political and Masonic career, see R. Berman, *Espionage*, 38-58.

[65] [Defoe, Daniel], *The Second-Sighted Highlander* (London, 1715), 3-4.

[66] *Ibid.*, 12-19, 32. For his earlier pamphlets on Scottish second sight, see Rodney Baine, *Defoe and the Supernatural* (Athens, 1968), 109-28.

[67] *HMC: Stuart*, I, 395, 404, 446.

[68] See C. Nordmann, *Crise du Nord*, 153, and *Grandeur et Liberté de la Suède*, 1660-1792 (Paris, 1971), 199, 424, for the international associations of the Jacobite Masons.

Acting as a courier between Bolingbroke, Gyllenborg, and their agents was Robert Leslie, son of the Irish-Anglican polemicist Charles Leslie, now exiled in France. Robert later informed Thomas Carte, the Jacobite historian, about the Swedish invasion plans:

> In June 1715, King of Sweden would have come to England with an army, provided if K [James] would come to Stralsund, that he had a scruple at first of leaving Stralsund which was threatened with a siege but in case of K's coming he would have waived that and set sail immediately. That Lord Bolingbroke was entirely for K's going. Urged it in earnest and offered to go with him. King of France was at the time ready to advance any sum to King of Sweden to make that expedition.[69]

Robert Leslie wrote Carl XII, proposing seven thousand Swedish troops, and "the King of Sweden desired Mr L be sent to him, but it was not allowed at Avignon," where James now resided. Baron Eric Sparre, Swedish ambassador in Paris, urged Leslie to go to Stralsund "without the knowledge of the people there [Avignon], but he would not thrust himself into an important negotiation without orders." However, Leslie continued to correspond with the Swedish king, and by 7 July Sparre reported to the Duke of Berwick that Carl XII would put the plan into execution immediately by shipping a Swedish army to England, but that he must have funds to carry it out. That Robert Leslie became the admired friend of Swift and Pope suggests their own private sympathy for the Swedish-Jacobite cause. [70]

Delays in the funds and difficulties of communication with the embattled Stralsund gained time for George I, who ordered his Hanoverian troops to seize the Swedish city of Bremen and the English fleet to assist the siege of Stralsund. In July Ormonde fled to France, where he was named commander of the Jacobite troops in England. As noted earlier, Ormonde was a Freemason, and he linked up with his brothers abroad.[71] In the same month, Lord Oxford was arrested and committed to the Tower, but he managed to carry on secret communications with the Jacobites. On 1 August, when Mar audaciously attended a royal levee, George I publicly snubbed him. Sensing danger, Mar disguised himself as an artisan and set off secretly for Scotland.

En route Mar made an incognito visit to Newcastle for a final briefing of the principal Northumbrian Jacobites. He had established an extensive network of spies and couriers, disguised as scientific travellers, to link the northern magnates with their southern and Scottish allies.[72] He hoped to recruit colliers and craftsmen employed by Derwentwater, Crowley, and other Jacobite mine owners and industrialists. For the past two years, Derwentwater had undertaken extensive building projects, centered on his great stone mansion, Dilston Hall, and thus had contacts with operative Masons. One important recruit was James Robson, a Catholic stonemason, musician, and ballad-maker. He was joined by six Northumbrian operative Masons, who would fight with the Jacobite rebels at Preston.[73]

---

[69] Bodleian Library: Carte MS. 231, ff.22-23. Notes on Robert Leslie's conversation with Carte on 19 April 1725.

[70] I. Ehrenpreis, *Swift*, III, 623, 652, 656; I. Higgins, *Swift's Politics*, 22.

[71] F. McLynn, *Charles Edward Stuart*, 532.

[72] L. Gooch, *Desperate Faction*, 33-44, 61.

[73] P. Monod, *Jacobitism*, 300.

Moving on to the Highlands, Mar appealed to clan chieftains and disaffected Episco-palians; the latter would provide the publicly Protestant leadership for the campaign. Mystical inspiration was contributed by George Garden; James Cunningham; Alexander Forbes, 4th Lord Pitsligo; and other devotees of the French Boehmenists and Quietists (Bourignon, Guyon, Poiret, and Fenelon).[74] Pitsligo came from an old Scottish Masonic family; his grandfather, 2nd Lord Pitsligo, was a member of the Aberdeen lodge in the 1670s, which included an unusual number of Quakers.[75] The Quaker Masons' stress on stillness and the inner light was similar to that of the 1715 "mystics of the north-east." The 4th Lord Pitsligo evidently followed family tradition, for later Masons claimed that he presided over a private lodge at Rosehearty on his estate.[76] It is possible that the Masonic membership overlapped with George Garden's ecumenical religious community at Rosehearty, where "persons of different religious persuasions lived together in the love of God and the practice of self-abnegation".[77]

One of Pitsligo's protégés who wanted to join the community was the twenty-one year old Andrew Michael Ramsay, who characterized Pitsligo as "his most dear and hon-oured friend."[78] Ramsay would later become a major influence on mystical, chivalric de-velopments within Franco-Jacobite (*Écossais*) Freemasonry – developments which may have been rooted in the religious community and lodge at Rosearty.[79] However, in 1708 Ramsay moved to London, where he was employed as tutor to the two sons of David Wemyss, 4th Earl of Wemyss, a family long involved in Jacobite and Masonic affairs. James Wemyss, the 5th Earl, would become the Jacobite Grand Master of Scotland in 1743-44.[80] In 1710 Ramsay moved to France, where he became the secretary of Arch-bishop Fenelon, who had long been in contact with Pitsligo and the Scottish mystics.

When the French Prophets made recruiting trips to Edinburgh in 1709, James Cun-ningham and Pitsligo's sister joined them; Pitsligo met with them and "remained cau-tiously optimistic about their claims to divine inspiration."[81] The Scots then contributed to the Prophets their concept of the *novitiate*, which they elaborated in a process "almost as formal as a mystic's apprenticeship to an alchemist in seventeenth-century literature."[82] In the Prophets' *Orders* of 1714, a "hierarchy of spiritual growth" was outlined which provided a "key to hidden mysteries." This process would strikingly pre-figure the med-itation rituals developed in the higher degrees of *Écossais* Masonry. In 1715 Cunningham utilized the Prophets' graduated process of meditation and illumination to gain consent from "the spirit" to join the Jacobite rising in Edinburgh. He was followed by Pitsligo, first cousin of the Earl of Mar, with whom he may have shared the "Mason Word." Other members of old Masonic families joined Mar's campaign, such as Balcarres, Bruce,

---

[74] George David Henderson, *Mystics of the North-East* (Aberdeen, 1934), 16-55.

[75] D. Stevenson, *First Freemasons*, 138, 143.

[76] http://www.lodgeforbes67.com.history.

[77] David E. Shuttleton, "Jacobitism and Millennial Enlightenment: Alexander, Lord Forbes of Pitsligo's 'Remarks on the Mystics,'" in *Enlightenment and Dissent*, 15 (1996), 33-51.

[78] G. Henderson, *Mystics*, 45.

[79] D. Shuttleton, "Jacobitism," 45; "Alexander Forbes, 4th Lord Forbes of Pitsligo," *ODNB*.

[80] See ahead, Chapter Nineteen.

[81] D. Shuttleton, "Jacobitism," 43.

[82] H. Schwartz, *French Prophets*, 164-67.

Drummond, St. Clair, Keith, Cameron of Lochiel, and Seton.[83] George Seton, Fifth Earl of Winton, hosted Mar's party at Seton Palace, and he would later serve as Master of the Jacobite lodge at Rome.

In Ireland supporters of the Stuarts heard from their countrymen in Spain that Irish officers in the Spanish army were headed to Scotland to support Mar's campaign.[84] With reports abounding about these international Irish Jacobite projects, Swift tried to lay low, despite his private, disaffected attitude, and he confided to his Tory friend Dr. Patrick Delany,

> I do not see how a civil war can be avoided because the bulk of the people will never endure to see themselves entirely cut out and rendered incapable of all employments of trust or profit, and the whole power versed in the hands of a minority, whose interest it must of necessity be to alter the constitution, and oppress their fellow subjects.[85]

Swift's position became even more vulnerable after 12 November, when the first Irish parliament of George I met, "during an epidemic of panic and mistrust." They soon busied themselves not with law-making but "with revenge, intimidation, and blackmail."

Meanwhile in France, Bolingbroke lamented the death of Louis XIV in September 1715, but he believed that the regent Orléans (appointed for the minority of Louis XV) would continue the late king's support for the restoration project. However, Bolingbroke persuaded Ormonde to discard Mar's plan for the Newcastle landing and to aim instead for "a more theatrical invasion from the south," which (Leo Gooch argues) was "a calamitous decision because it caused confusion and delay in the north."[86] Despite his frustration with Bolingbroke, Mar determined to act, so he raised the Stuart standard at Braemar on 6 September and launched the "Rising of 1715." The government moved quickly against suspected Jacobites in England, including James Gibbs, who was deprived of his surveyorship in December, a move he blamed "on a false report...that misrepresented me as a papist and a disaffected person, which...is intirly false and scandalous." [87] It was not entirely false, as his later correspondence with Mar revealed.[88]

But the government's major catch was Francia, who had been arrested on 18 September and confined in Newgate Prison. A team of Whig decipherers, led by John Ozell (who earlier exposed the Rosicrucian-Jacobite codes of Pope's *Rape of the Lock*), worked on Francia's complex cipher and learned more about the international dimensions of the plot. Francia, who was kept informed about the Swedish king's activities, was aware that a party of Turkish Jews had joined Carl XII at Stralsund, drawn by the king's plan to open Sweden to Jewish immigration.[89] The Hanoverian government responded with a renewal of Jacobites-as-Jews propaganda. Probably commissioned by the ministry, the Whig preacher Simon Browne published a widely-distributed sermon, *Jewish and Popish*

---

[83] For their families' Masonic associations, see M. Schuchard, *Restoring the Temple*, passim; R.F. Gould, *Military Lodges: The Apron and the Sword* (London, 1899), 22, 24-25.

[84] Oscar Recio Morales, *Ireland and the Spanish Empire, 1600-1825* (Dublin, 2010), 174, 180.

[85] I. Ehrenpreis, *Swift*, III, 20-21.

[86] L. Gooch, *Desperate Faction*, 86.

[87] Terry Friedman, *James Gibbs* (New Haven, 1984), 10.

[88] M. Stewart, *Architectural... Mar*, 229-30.

[89] Hugo Valentin, *Judarnas Historia i Sverige* (Stockholm, 1924), 28.

Zeal Described and Compared (November 1715), in which he blamed the Jacobite rising on the Jewish "Spirit of fierce Zeal," which was copied by the Church of Rome in their "Zeal for God."[90] The Jacobites' campaign repeated the "Jews' persecution of Christ." Even worse was the fact that Protestants have joined Catholics in this "Jewish" rebellion.

In Scotland Mar's forces had some initial success, which inspired his fighting colleague (and possible "brother") Alexander Robertson of Struan to compose a song that circulated among the rebels:

> Since loyalty is still the same,
> Whether it win or lose the Game,
> To flinch it were a burning Shame,
> Since MAR has gain'd a Battle;
> Let each brave true-hearted Scot,
> Improve the Vict'ry he has got,
> Resolving all shall go to Pot,
> Or JAMES the Eighth to settle.
> ....
> Can poor Low-Country Water-Rats,
> Withstand our furious Mountain Cats,
> ....
> Come, here's to the victorious MAR,
> Who bravely first conceiv'd the War,
> And to all those who sent so far,
> To shake off Union's Slavery;
> Whose Fighting for so noble a Cause,
> As King, and Liberty, and Laws...[91]

In England another poet, the eighteen year-old Richard Savage, anonymously published poems full of hope for the Jacobite uprising. In "An Ironical Panegyrick on his Pretended Majesty G----- by the Curse of G----- Usurper of Great-Brittan France and Ireland, Non-defender of the Faith," Savage mocked George I as "drest up in borrow'd Plumes," and urged him to resign the throne to "Royal James what is his right,/ Learn to be Just; lest thou art forc'ed in Fight,/...Strip'ed of thy Vanities, then turn'd away."[92] In "The Pretender," he mocked George as the real pretender, for his right does not spring from birth, while James "is our Native Prince, /And Born a British King." Savage would follow the rebellion and its aftermath closely, and then publish politically dangerous poems in praise of its heroes and martyrs. He would subsequently become an important opposition Mason.

On 13-14 November the tide turned against the Jacobites, as the government's forces won at Preston and Sheriffmuir. At the latter battlefield, the nineteen-year-old John Lyon, 5th Earl of Strathmore, was killed, which set off widespread mourning, especially since he was shot by a dragoon whose life he had saved.[93] His ancestor, Patrick Lyon, the 3rd Earl, was a talented architect and Freemason, and the family had long royalist, Jacobite, and

---

[90] Simon Browne, *Jewish and Popish Zeal Described and Compared* (London, 1715), 4-5, 45-47.

[91] Alexander Robertson of Struan, *Poems, on Various Subjects and Occasions* (Edinburgh, 1749), 48-49.

[92] Richard Savage, *The Poetical Works of Richard Savage*, ed. Clarence Tracy (Cambridge, 1962), 16-19,

[93] F. Skeet, *Life of... James Radcliffe*, 63.

Masonic connections. The young 5th Earl had joined the Masons Mar, Pitsligo, Meston, and the Keith brothers in the rebellion, and he was reportedly an initiate. In December, when James III arrived at Peterhead, he was welcomed by George Keith, Earl Marischal, whose family would play a significant role in the fraternity over the next decades.[94] Accompanied by Mar and Keith, James moved on to Scone, where plans were made for his coronation on 23 January 1716. From his ancient royal city, James sent an eloquent appeal to Carl XII, but the Swedish king could not help him, given his bare escape from the siege of Stralsund. On 4 February Mar and James realized their cause was hopeless and boarded ships for France.

After the final defeat of the rebellion, Pitsligo hid out in the Highlands and in London, before making his way to the Continent in December 1716. During those months, his friend William Meston, tutor to the Keith family, "skulked in the heather," where he wrote poems lamenting the deaths of fallen heroes and praising traditional Scottish Freemasonry. Meston was especially grieved by the loss of the 5th Earl of Strathmore:

> For his lov'd Prince and Country's Cause
> He scorns to quit the bloody Field,
> While many fly whom Danger Awes,
> And many overpow'red yield.
> ....
> Thy Gratitude his Actions claim,
>   His Fate does thy Compassion crave;
> Still must STATHMORE remain a Name,
> Dear to the Loyal and to the Brave.
> ....
> If Corrupt Times your Courage try,
> When Honesty is judged Offence,
> Keep his Example in your Eye,
> And learn the worth of Innocence.

John Lyon's younger brother, James, later became the 7th Earl of Strathmore and a prominent Freemason, serving as Grand Master in London in 1733.

After the Earl of Derwentwater joined Mar's forces, his younger brother Charles Radcliffe led his men on the Scottish border, from where he opposed the march into England, declaring that he wanted "to take his fortune along with the Highlanders."[95] However, he followed his brother until the Jacobites were defeated at Preston. When their commander capitulated to the English, Charles defiantly protested, saying "he would rather die with sword in hand, than be dragged like a felon to the gallows." Before the brothers were shackled and taken to London, James Radcliffe managed to save his favorite iron-gray horse, which was used to secure and hide the Derwentwater family papers.[96] As we shall see, Pope would later refer to the sad fate of this horse and its proud owner in a melancholic poem.

The capture of Derwentwater was a bitter blow to the Jacobites, for George I and his ministers were determined to make an example of him, "fearing that his Stuart blood, his

---

[94] George Henderson, *Mystics of the North-east* (Aberdeen, 1934), 29; F. McLynn, *Charles Edward Stuart*, 532.
[95] F. Skeet, *Life of... James Radcliffe*, 155-56.
[96] *Ibid.*, 72.

wealth, and his popularity would make further rebellion a continuing threat."[97] The earl's pregnant wife approached the king in person and made such an impassioned appeal for mercy that she created a wave of sympathy for her husband, and most observers expected him to be released. Two of Derwentwater's Stuart relations – the 1st Duke of Richmond and James Waldegrave – also tried to help him.[98] Richmond carried an appeal from the House of Lords to save his cousin, but the king rejected it. Though George had made Richmond Lord of the Bedchamber and Privy Councillor of Ireland, he was still suspicious about his loyalty (especially because of his friendship with the French ambassador, d'Aumont).[99] Waldegrave, a grandson of James II and Arabella Churchill, was raised as a Catholic in France and married Derwentwater's sister Mary.[100] He visited his brother-in-law on the night before his execution, when he urged him to convert to the Anglican church, accept the Hanoverian succession, and thus be saved. But Derwentwater "spoke home to him upon the delusions he lay under in forsaking his religion and his principles," and asked that an inscription on his coffin read, "He died a sacrifice for his lawful Sovereign."[101] (Waldegrave himself would convert in January 1719, after the death of his Catholic wife, which allowed him to enter the House of Lords in 1722). He also became an important Hanoverian Mason.[102]

Intensifying Protestant pressure was put on Derwentwater, for the government believed that if he, the most prominent Catholic layman in the north of England, could be persuaded "to renounce his Catholic faith and to acknowledge the Hanoverian title to the throne, it would be a resounding blow to the Jacobite cause and a signal victory for the Whigs."[103] He was even pressured to convert while on the scaffold, but his steadfast refusal gained sympathy from some Whigs, such as Richard Steele (a Hanoverian Mason), who sponsored a petition in the Commons on his behalf. Lord Nottingham, lord president of the council, declared that he hoped the king "would pardon the prisoners if they confessed, nay, he hoped he would pardon them though they did not confess." Though most members of parliament and the prisoners themselves expected the king to exercise clemency, he was pushed by the aggressive Whig chancellor of the exchequer, Robert Walpole, to carry out the executions, even though the government had found no evidence of preliminary plotting by the prisoners (which was the main charge).

In order to counter the pro-Derwentwater popular sentiment, Walpole's supporters urged their fellow Whig, Charles Johnson, to write and quickly produce a play, *The Cobler of Preston*, to ridicule the Jacobites of Scotland and Northumberland as bumbling traitors and drunken fools. As Johnson planned for a large, sympathetic Whig audience, his plans were thwarted by a political and theatrical rival. In early January 1716, a draft of his play was stolen by an actor from the Lincoln's Inn Theatre, and on 20 January Christopher Bullock hurriedly wrote a new version with an opposite political view. His Lincoln's Inn

---

[97] "James Radcliffe," *ODNB*.
[98] L. Gooch, *Desperate Faction*, 91-95.
[99] John Doran, *London in the Jacobite Times* (Boston, 1877), 26, 42; Charles Lennox, Earl of March, *A Duke and His Friends: The Life and Letters of the Second Duke of Richmond* (London, 1911), I, 20, 24.
[100] Ralph Arnold, *Northern Lights: The Story of Lord Derwentwater* (London, 1959), 143.
[101] F. Skeet, *Life of… James Radcliffe*, 102, 111, 114.
[102] "James Waldegrave, First Earl Waldegrave," *DNB*.
[103] R. Arnold, *Northern Lights*, 143-46.

company then produced it a week before Johnson's version appeared on the Drury Lane stage.[104] According to a contemporary dramatic critic,

> Mr. Bullock, who always prided himself upon his Attachment to the Principles of *Toryism*, not only robb'd...Mr. Charles Johnson of a great Part of the large Profits he expected from the Run of a *Farce*, which was wrote, so much to the Support, and the Defence of the H-----r [Hanover] *Succession*, but wrote his own Farce, call'd *The Cobler of Preston*, likewise in quite another Manner, turning into Burlesque and Ridicule all Mr. Johnson's Thoughts and Designs, and giving Spirit to that Party [Jacobites] which Mr. Johnson had rendered contemptible and Spiritless.[105]

Johnson deliberately set his play in Preston, site of the first battle between George I's army and the Jacobite rebels and, more importantly, site of the arrest of Derwentwater, who was currently imprisoned in the Tower on charges of treason. To counter the widespread stories of the earl's reputation for generous hospitality, "leadership and courage in action at Preston," Johnson satirized his northeastern, Northumberland followers as credulous and cowardly tools of their foreign-based party. In the character of Kit Sly the cobbler, "a Comick Rebel" and "drinking, noisy Fool," he set up a political foil to Sir Charles Briton, a country gentleman and Hanoverian loyalist, who rejected "the worst Plot that ever was," concocted by impoverished Scotsmen from "those Hills of Snow,/ Where Traitors breathe, and North-Winds blow."[106] Johnson expressed astonishment that

> ...an English Cudden
> Should quarrel with his honest Beef and Pudden;
> And yet 'tis so; – And we contend with Knaves,
> That only wish to Conquer, – to be Slaves.

Fuelled by "Popish Liquor," Kit blusters his support "for Passive Obedience and Non-Resistance" and hints at his Catholic leanings: "I pronounce my self a Doxy Member of that Church which can forgive all my Sins, past, present, and to come."[107] Given the leadership role of artisans, such as the stonemason James Robson, among Derwentwater's troops, the cobbler boasts of "my Briskness, when I Randy my fine Speeches at the Head of the Mobility," for this lowly-born Jacobite can make "Men Plot without Brains, Fight without Courage, and Rebel without Reason," turn "Libertines into Zealots, and Fox-hunters into Statesmen." When threatened by troops who will charge him with treason, Kit admits to drinking "Jacobite Papish Healths," but in the future he will "mix Loyalty with my Liquor." Bidding farewell to "his mad Politicks," he will never "Rail against the Crown" nor "sham Pretences of Religion forge,/ but with true Protestants cry, Long live King George." Johnson would later become a Masonic propagandist for the newly-formed loyalist Grand Lodge of London.

---

[104] Katherine West Schiel, "Early Georgian Politics and Shakespeare: the Black Act and Charles Johnson's *Love in a Forest* (1723), *Shakespeare Survey Online@* Cambridge University Press, 2007), 46-48.

[105] George Akerby, *The Life of Mr. James Spiller, the Late Famous Comedian, in which is interspers'd much of the Political History of His own Times* (London, 1729), 24.

[106] Charles Johnson, *The Cobler of Preston* (London, 1716), Prologue.

[107] *Ibid.*, 23, 34, 44, 47.

While Johnson's actors were still rehearsing, Christopher Bullock struck a pre-emptive blow with his similarly named play, which he described as "intercepting of Ammunition going to the Enemy, and afterwards employing it against them."[108] In the first performance on 24 January, he lampooned "Some Heads, brim-full of Politicks," who produced a play "penn'd for the particular Service of a Party." He scorned Johnson, for a "Writer's Wit must sure be at a low Ebb, which can be supported by one Party railing at another," which is "beneath the Dignity of a Theatre." After reducing *The Cobler of Preston* to an apolitical farce, Bullock's actors concluded with a song in which the vices of the city are pitted against the virtues of the country (i.e., Northumberland). Echoing Jacobite and Non-juring polemicists, they sung of the mercenary, hypocritical, promiscuous behavior of the Hanoverian court and Whig aristocracy, without actually naming king or courtiers.

Despite Bullock's pro-Jacobite theatrics, Johnson's pro-Hanoverian polemics a week later strengthened the government's position on Derwentwater, and he was sentenced to a traitor's death. At the site of their execution, the prisoners put up a brave front and vowed their loyalty to their personal religion and rightful Stuart king. The Anglican Parson William Paul affirmed, "I die a dignified and faithful member of the non-juring Church... The Revolution, instead of keeping out Popery, has let in atheism."[109] When the handsome and popular Derwentwater went to the scaffold on 24 February 1716, a huge crowd gathered, with many weeping and cursing the government. After kneeling some time in prayer, he read aloud from his written statement:

> Being in a few minutes to appear before the tribunal of God, where though most unworthy, I hope to find mercy, which I have not found from men now in power: I have endeavoured to make my peace with his Divine Majesty...
>
> After this I am to ask pardon of those whom I might have scandalized by pleading guilty at my trial. Such as were permitted to come to me, told me, that having been undeniably in arms, pleading guilty was but the consequence of having submitted to mercy...
>
> But I am sensible that in this I have made bold with my loyalty, having never any other but King James the Third for my rightful and lawful sovereign; him I had an inclination to serve from my infancy, and was moved thereto by a natural love I had to his person, knowing him to be capable of making his people happy: and though he had been of a different religion from mine, I should have done for him all that lay in my power, as my ancestors have done for his predecessors...
>
> I die a Roman Catholic: I am in charity with all the world; I thank God for it, even with those of the present government, who are most instrumental in my death...
>
> P.S. If that prince who now governs had given me my life, I should have thought myself obliged never more to have taken up arms against him.[110]

---

[108] Christopher Bullock, The *Cobler of Preston* (London, 1716), Preface, vii.
[109] *Ibid.*, 270.
[110] J. Browne, *History*, II, 347-48.

Copies of Derwentwater's speech soon circulated widely at home and abroad. On 28 February Captain Straton wrote Mar that the earl made "a noble, gentlemanly and most Christian speech," and "it is said Nottingham and all the mercy men…are to be turned out."[111] A transcript of the speech was sent to James III, who wept over it and called Derwentwater "a true Christian hero."

A few days after the execution, citizens all over England were startled by a strange phenomenon of flashing lights and turbulent clouds, which culminated in an aurora borealis which broke through the clouds. John Doran describes the popular reaction:

> Superstition sharpened or deceived the eyes of beholders in all parts of the country. The Jacobites hailed this aurora as a message from heaven to cheer them after the depression caused by the execution of the sentence on the Jacobite leaders. The London Whigs did not know what to make of it, but men of both parties…agreed in seeing in the field of the sky armies fiercely engaged, giants flying through ether with bright flaming swords, and fire-breathing dragons flaring from swift and wrathful comets… The Jacobites had taken courage at the eclipse the preceding year. To them it was a sign that the temporary adumbration of the sun of Stuart would be followed by its triumphant effulgency…The aurora is still popularly called "The Earl of Derwentwater's Lights."[112]

As Derwentwater's decapitated body was secretly carried in a hearse to Dilston Hall, spectators along the road reported "a most Beautifull Glory" that hovered over it, "sending forth resplendant streams of all sorts of colours to ye east & west," and this occurred just when the "most dreadfull signs appear'd in London."

Popular anger at Derwentwater's execution worried the loyalist John Campbell, 2nd Duke of Argyle, who sensed that the government's brutal retaliation on the Jacobites would fuel even more rebellions. On 13 April 1716 Hugh Thomas wrote to David Nairne in Paris that Argyle "gains ground amongst both Whigs and Tories by his generosity to the prisoners," some of whom were spared from execution:

> All this goodness, it's thought, proceeds entirely from Argyle who met Lord Derwentwater's body on the road, and both heard and saw the great murmurs of the people, what honours they paid his dead body, and what vast concourses went to meet it in all the towns it was carried through, and what wonders they reported of him… Argyle using all his interest…[to get] the Triennnial Bill suspended for 10 years…Yet all this does not satisfy the people; they have nothing but the Pretender in their brains, and their common cry is, they shall never forgive them Lord Derwentwater's death[113]

On 27 April Thomas reported reported further: "Argyle every day gains ground…, nor do the people yet give over their lampoons even against the King himself and cry out mightily for the Lord Derwentwater, a noted Papist."[114]

---

111 *HMC: Stuart*, II, 10, 35.
112 J. Doran, *London*, I, 152-53.
113 *Ibid.*, II, 84.
114 *Ibid.*, II, 124.

For Swift, Argyle's military campaign against the Jacobites but subsequent political campaign for more lenient treatment of the rebels must have been puzzling. He later recorded, "The D. of Argyle was allways a Scot, and yet he deceived me for some time; and I once loved him much."[115] For Pope, who moved in Derwentwater's Catholic circles and who appreciated the earl's subscription to his translation of *The Iliad*, the Catholic nobleman's execution portended increasing persecution of himself, his family, and neighbors. Thus, he was slightly relieved when it appeared that through Argyle's efforts, "the bill for seizing two thirds of the Roman Catholics' estates is also like to sink."[116] Over the next years, Jacobite Freemasons would attempt to woo Argyle, an ambitious but ambiguous Whig, to their side – with often confusing and disappointing results.

Among the prisoners captured at Preston were the six stonemasons and their fraternal master James Robson, who had led the musical band in his regiment and regaled the troops with his ballads. Carrying on the poetic traditions of the seventeenth-century Cavaliers, Robson spent his time in prison writing witty and defiant poems against the reality of marital imprisonment, as well as military imprisonment.[117] Robson was eventually released, but he continued his Jacobite and Masonic activities over the next decades, which led the government to consider him "a political criminal." Robson shared his "Cavalier" poetic attitude with the initiates of the quasi-Masonic mock Corporation of Walton-le-Dale. The Yorkshire Catholic poet William Tunstall served as poet laureate of the Corporation, and he would issue similarly defiant poems after his capture at Preston.

Tunstall was joined by the Irish Catholic brothers Charles and Nicholas Wogan, and the three captives were taken to London on horseback, in an elaborate pageant staged by the government in order to show them humiliated and bound in chains. As they were forced to walk into the city, Whig-paid mobs greeted the prisoners' entrance with jeers and clattering of warming pans, thus endorsing the canard that the Pretender had been a substitute child.[118] Edward Harley (brother of Lord Oxford) witnessed the procession and reported to Mrs. Caesar that the rope-bound prisoners elicited "the compassion of the common people," who "kissd their garments as they past."[119] Charles Wogan had left Ireland around 1712 to reside in England, where he became a close friend of Alexander Pope.[120] Mrs. Caesar probably passed on this report to Pope, who would have shared her sympathy.

Wogan later wrote Swift about "my friend Mr. Pope, whom I had the honour to bring up to London, from our retreat in the forest of Windsor, to dress à la mode, and introduce at Will's coffee-house."[121] He added that "Mr. Pope and I lived in perfect union and familiarity, for two or three summers, before he ended up on the stage of the world, where he has since gained so great and so just an applause." According to Andrew Lang, Pope was also friendly with Charles's younger brother Nicholas, who was fifteen at the

---

[115] J. Swift, *Correspondence*, I, 346.

[116] *Ibid.*, II, 124.

[117] *Ibid.*, 250.

[118] Nicholas Rogers, "Popular Protest in Early Hanoverian London," *Past and Present*, 70 (1978), 80.

[119] Mary Caesar, *The Journal of Mary Freman Caesar, 1724-1741*, ed. Dorothy Potter (Lewiston, 2002), 18.

[120] "Charles Wogan," *ODNB*.

[121] J. Swift, *Correspondence*, III, 591-93.

time of the rebellion.[122] Travelling from their London base, Charles and Nicholas worked with Mar, the Keith brothers, and other Jacobite planners of the 1715 rebellion, "carrying Intelligence, discoursing with Persons, and appointing their Business… They kept always moving, and travelled from Place to Place, till Things ripened for Action."[123] Arriving in Northumberland, they linked up with Derwentwater, Tunstall, and the "knights" of the Corporation of Walton-le-Dale, which "directed the operations" of the emerging rebellion.[124] They were evidently initiated into the fraternity, and Charles especially developed a self-image of himself as the leader of "my little troop of Knights-errant," engaged in a chivalrous Jacobite crusade. Over the next decades, his close collaboration with known Freemasons suggests his fraternal affiliation.

The Anglican minister Robert Patten, who initially followed Derwentwater, subsequently turned king's evidence against the rebels. When he published a loyalist history of the rising, he admitted that Charles Wogan "behav'd very well at Preston."[125] But it was the teen-aged Nicholas Wogan who elicited the most praise from Patten:

> The Fifth Troop was commanded by Captain Nicholas Wogan, an Irish Gentleman…[who] joined the Rebels at their first Meeting. He is a Gentleman of a most generous Mind, and a great deal of Bravery, unwearied to forward the good of his Cause: His Bravery was made known by several Instances in the Action at Preston: His Generosity, as well as Courage, was most remarkable in bringing off the Prisoner Capt. Preston…who was mortally wounded… [Nicholas] hazarded his Life among his own Men, if possible, to save that Gentleman, though an Enemy, and was wounded in doing it…[126]

While in captivity in London, Charles Wogan and William Tunstall composed bantering and defiant poems, similar to those of James Robson. In fact, they probably shared their works between their Preston and London prisons. Wogan and Tunstall mocked the staged procession to London and praised their lady-loves, who supported them during their confinement. Tunstall had served as Paymaster and Quartermaster of the Jacobite forces, and the latter office was traditionally associated with military Masonry. The publication of *Poems of Love and Gallantry. Written in the Marshalsea and Newgate, by several of the Prisoners taken at Preston* (London, 1716) angered the government but won the poets many admirers. One wonders if Wogan's close friend Pope was among them. The sixty year-old Tunstall started the poetic enterprise with an appeal from the Marshalsea prison to Charles Wogan in Newgate, "Tune, *To all ye Ladies*":

> From me, Dear Charles, inspir'd by Ale,
> To Thee this Letter comes.
> To try if Scribling can prevail
> To moderate our Dooms:

[122] Andrew Lang and A.E.W. Mason, *Parson Kelly* (London, Green, 1900). In this historical novel, Lang described Nick Wogan's role in the Atterbury Plot, and he drew upon Wogan family papers for his information.
[123] Robert Patten, *The History of the Rebellion*, 2nd rev. ed. (London, 1717), 22.
[124] F. Wright, "Layburnes," 275.
[125] R. Patten, *History*, 141.
[126] *Ibid.*, 64.

> Tho' pent in Cage the Black-Bird swings,
> Yet still he hops, and struts, and sings.
> *With a fa, la, la, etc.*[127]

Jacobites used the blackbird as a symbol for James III and Stuart loyalists.

When Tunstall mocked the "hir'd shouts of wide-mouth'd Cits" of the government-paid mobs who greeted the prisoners at Barnet and Highgate-Hill, he was answered by Charles Wogan, who was amazed at his cheerful spirit, even after they were "Halter'd and pinion'd astride the Barnet Steed,/ In Triumph thro' the city to the Prison led,/ The Noise of Chains within the Iron Gate."[128] Identifying himself with the crusaders in Israel, he lamented, "If I with Captive Salem [Jerusalem] could forget/ My native Freedom, and my former State,/ With thee I'd sing, but now to sing's too late." However, Wogan soon regained his "Cavalier" spirit, and composed, "The Preston Prisoners to the Ladies about Court and Town," in which he called upon "You Fair Ones all at Liberty,/ We Captive Lovers greet," even though "pack'd up in Prison's base,/ With Bolts and Bars restrain'd,/ Think not our Bodies love you less,/ Or Souls are more confin'd." Having been charged with treason but still hoping for a reprieve, Wogan appealed to his female admirers:

> Nay, shou'd we Victims be design'd
> By those that Rule the State,
> Shou'd Mercy no Admittance find,
> To Hearts that shou'd be Great;
> What Dread can Gaols or Gibbets shew
> To Men who've died so oft for you.
> *With a fa, la, la, etc.*
> If Fate must fix th' unworthy Doom,
> We'll leave you fresh Supplies,
> And from our Ashes, in our Room,
> Some Phoenixes shall arise,
> Whose Vows will more successful prove
> In happier Days to win your Love.[129]

Sixteen years later, Wogan wrote Swift that he had lost his cheerfulness of temper, "sunk under a long and hopeless exile," but in his younger days he was "one of the merriest fellows in Europe."[130] Certainly, his witty, romantic, and defiant poetry – written with the spirit of the imprisoned knights of Walton-le-Dale – confirms this self-portrait.

Tunstall was eventually released on account of his age, and his prison poems would frequently be reprinted. In April 1716 his former companions Brigadier Mackintosh, Charles Wogan, and thirteen others managed to escape Newgate. Charles Wogan would later inform Swift about his many adventures while hiding in England and his ultimate flight to France. In May Nicholas Wogan was tried and condemned, but the pleadings of Captain Preston before his death that the young Irishman should be mercifully treated led to his reprieve. Removed to the custody of a messenger, Nicholas continued to visit

---

[127] [William Tunstall, Charles Wogan, etc.], *Poems of Love and Gallantry. Written in the Marshalsea and Newgate, by several of the Prisoners taken at Preston* (London, 1716), 5-6.
[128] *Ibid.,* 9-10.
[129] *Ibid.,* 12-13.
[130] J. Swift, *Correspondence*, III, 592.

the prisoners throughout the next twelve months before also escaping to France, where he and his brother joined Mar, the Keiths, and Ormonde, members of the Jacobite Masonic network. Many others of their fellow campaigners were not so fortunate, for the government continued to execute or transport them as traitors.

The executions of the rebels provoked more defiant poems from Richard Savage, who in autumn 1716 published "Brittania's Miseries," in which he called on his muse to grieve that Britain's king has been made a "Royal Exile," while the victors have "Proscrib'd her Patriots, and her Church betray'd."[131] Referring to "Derwentwater's Lights," he vowed that "The Skies in Prodigies foretell each Year/ New Cruelties for England's Soil to bear." He then praised the exiles and martyrs, and referred again to "Derwentwater's Lights":

> See how the Patriots of the Land become
> Martyrs, if here, or Exiles from their Home.
> Ormond, that once Preserver of our State,
> Like Hannibal, finds Banishment is his Fate;
> ....
> Great St. John, who in Youthful Glory shone,
> Nip't in his Bloom (like Ormond) was undone;
> While Mar, who sought his Monarch to restore,
> Whilst all in Exile their Land's Ills deplore.
> Here Derwentwater's Fate Britannia Morns,
> The first and greatest of her Martyr'd Sons.
> He from the Royal Martyr did proceed,
> And in his fall a Noble Stuart bled.
> ....
> O George, thy Councels are the Nation's Bane,
> Vile Regicides by thy Pernitions reign,
> They Murder'd Royal Charles in his great Race again.
> But may Blind fortune to the Right incline,
> And Derwentwater's Fate be justly thine.

In "A Littany for the Year," Savage ritualistically called for Heaven to preserve us "in this approaching Year./ From Civil Wars, and from uncivil Things,/That hate the Race of all our Queens and Kings." He concluded,

> Defend us Heaven, and to the Throne restore
> The Rightfull Heir and we will ask no more.
> ....
> And last from Whigs deliver us, who bring
> Userping Rulers and Abjure their King.[132]

Despite his attempted anonymity, a government spy identified Savage as the author of "Several treasonable and Seditious Pamphlets," and he was arrested in November 1716. He then boldly announced that he was the "natural son to the Late Earl Rivers,"

---

[131] R. Savage, *Poetical Works*, 19-25.
[132] *Ibid.*, 26.

who had been a good friend of Swift.[133] Because the intelligence file against Savage was not strong, he was soon pardoned. As he explored what he believed was his ancestry, he could have learned that his grandfather, Thomas Savage, 3rd Earl of Rivers, had allegedly served as Grand Master of the English Freemasons in 1666 (according to Anderson's official history in 1738).[134] Richard Savage too became a Mason, though the date of his initiation is unknown.[135] His interest in the fraternity was probably prompted by his family history as well as sympathy for the Jacobite Masons Mar, Derwentwater, and Ormonde.

After Mar's arrival in France, criticism of Bolingbroke's failure to provide support troops and arms for the rising led in March to his dismissal as James's secretary of state, a position then given to Mar. He immediately made contact with Robert Arbuthnot, who had continued to arrange shipments of arms and money to Scotland until the final defeat of the Jacobites. On 17 March Arbuthnot wrote from Rouen to Mar and urged him to remind James "III" of his family's long loyalty to the Stuarts, despite the danger this brings upon them:

> I have done my small endeavours since ever I was a child for his service and his father's. My brother, the Doctor, is always what he professed to be to your Grace, but Stanhope has frightened him damnably on my account, and has threatened that, if he finds he corresponds with me, he will ruin him and all my relations who shall do so. Stanhope caused one to write to the Duke of Norfolk here that he should have no converse with me, or else that he should repent it. However, I am out of reach, and shall give them, if ever I can, as little quarter as they would me.[136]

Given Swift's and Pope's close friendship with Dr. John Arbuthnot and later with Robert, these threats from the government reinforced their need for cautious and even secret communication. This would eventually be facilitated by the Masonic associations of Mar, the Arbuthnots, Norfolk, and Swift.

Back in Scotland, the Earl Marischal and his brother James Keith had planned to accompany James and Mar to France, but they missed the ship and hid out in the Highlands for several months, until they got away in May. While the Keiths, Pitsligo, Alexander Robertson, and others skulked in the heather, their companion William Meston composed poems to entertain and inspire them and other refugees.[137] When Meston finally emerged from hiding, he refused to comply with the Act of Indemnity and thus lost his position as Regent of Marischal College and governor of Dunnotar Castle. Protected by the Countess of Marischal, Meston wrote a poem, "To the Freemasons," which contrasted his rural skulking under Hanoverian persecution to his present protection among Masonic brethren. With Hudibrastic gusto, he satirized the iconoclastic Presbyterians and radical Whigs who destroy images of beauty, in sad contrast to the Freemasons who patronize art and letters while constructing "sacred buildings," schools and colleges.

---

[133] Many references to him in J. Swift, *Journal to Stella.*

[134] J. Anderson, *Constitutions* (1738), 102.

[135] Clarence Tracy, *The Artificial Bastard: A Biography of Richard Savage* (Cambridge, 1953, 124.

[136] *HMC: Stuart*, II, 23

[137] Biographical information in *The Poetical Works of William Meston*, 6th ed., (Edinburgh, 1767), v. Also, "William Meston," *ODNB.*

Praising the fraternity as sustainers of artistic tradition, religious tolerance, and civil behavior, he reminded readers of their great accomplishments:

> No more, my Muse, in doggerel rhime delight,
> The present theme requires a higher flight;
> Too long thou'st liv'd 'mongst shrubs and heath; too long
> Pleas'd rural ears with thy more rural song;
> Imploy thy vigour now, thy force exert,
> To celebrate the Mason's useful art.
> ....
> 'Tis only owing to the Mason's hand,
> That they [the Gods] have chapels now in every land.
> Ye sacred buildings, you alone can shew
> Th' immortal works which mortal hands can do;
> Through all the earth you loudly do proclaim,
> And trumpet forth the pious Mason's fame.
> ....
> Then let the Mason also have his praise;
> These are the men whose wonder-working hand
> Make arches over rapid rivers stand,
> Where men can walk on water as on land.
> Still may they flourish, may they still decore
> The earth with glorious structures, more and more;
> For if their art no longer should remain,
> The earth must needs turn *chaos* once again.[138]

---

[138] [William Meston], *Old Mother Grim's Tales* (Edinburgh, 1737), 195-96.

CHAPTER SIX

THE SWEDISH-JACOBITE PLOT
AND THE GRAND LODGE OF LONDON
(1716-1719)

King George I enter'd London most magnificently on 20 Sept. 1714. After the Rebellion was over A.D. 1716. The few Lodges at London finding themselves neglected by Sir Christopher Wren, thought fit to cement under a Grand Master as the Center of Union and Harmony....

James Anderson, *Constitutions of the Free Masons* (1738).

But this brave prince, in whose exalted mind
The martial valour of Gustavus shin'd
....
With bleeding heart bewail him, Britain's isle,
He would have brought thy Prince from his exile...

William Meston, "On the Death of Charles XII,
King of Sweden" (1719).

As Hanoverian forces swept through Scotland, many Jacobites fled by sea to Sweden, where Carl XII enraged George I by welcoming them and assisting them in their further journey to France. Before leaving Scotland, Kenneth Sutherland, Lord Duffus, wrote a Jacobite song that optimistically surveyed the European prospects of the cause:

Hard fate that I should banisht be
    And Rebell called with Scorn,
For scrving of a Lovely Prince,
    As e'er yet was Born,
....
But since the *French* doth take our part
    My fears Dispelled be
I hope few months will end our smart

And we our Friends shall see

....

The Noble *Sweed* our Friend appears…[1]

Duffus entered Swedish military service and married a Swedish woman, as Jacobite hopes for Carl XII's support intensified. In February 1716 the Swedish king led his revitalized army on a march to Danish-held Norway, where he planned to capture the port of Bergen to use as the launch-point for an invasion of Britain. On 2 March James III met with Ambassador Sparre in Paris and gave him a letter for Carl XII in which he requested asylum in Sweden. Sparre believed it was too risky to send the letter, but he did send a courier with an oral report to Carl about the request. In June a furious George I demanded assurances from the Swedish king that he would give no assistance to the Pretender nor "any Protection to Lord Duffus, and others, who are lately fled into Sweden from Scotland." Reports from the refugee Jacobites were so encouraging that in August Mar was able to recruit Bishop Francis Atterbury, an admired friend of Swift, to act as liaison with Gyllenborg and to raise £100,000 pounds in England to fund the Swedish troops.[2] However, in September Carl XII's frustration with the winter weather and the Danes' stubborn resistance led him to return to Lund, where he worked to revitalize his troops and prepare for another campaign. In October the Irish Jacobite Charles Ford wrote to Swift from Paris, inferring that he had been briefed about the efforts of the exiled Stuart court to recruit the intervention of Charles XII; unfortunately, Ford's enclosed message has disappeared.[3]

Meanwhile in Lund, the Swedish king gave Baron Görtz full powers to reorganize Sweden's government and to negotiate a more effective Jacobite plan. Worried by the bevy of Hanoverian spies who moved between Sweden and her embassies abroad and by Swedish opponents and informers, Görtz was determined to find a means of tightening security and ensuring loyalty to the king's agenda. According to Elis Schröderheim, who was initiated in a Swedish *Écossais* lodge in 1765, Görtz and his party introduced Freemasonry into Sweden in order to further their political designs.[4] Claude Nordmann argues further that in 1716-18 Jacobites introduced Masonry into their French regiments, which included many Swedish soldiers, especially the Sparre Regiment.[5]

One possible new recruit to Jacobite Masonry was Philip Wharton, rebellious son of the Whig politician, Thomas, Earl of Wharton, former Lord Lieutenant of Ireland and Swift's special *bête noire*. In 1715 the sixteen year-old Philip infuriated his father by marrying Martha, the daughter of Major-General Richard Holmes, who was dismissed from the army as a suspected Jacobite after the 1715 rebellion.[6] Philip's angry father died soon

---

[1] William Donaldson, *The Jacobite Song* (Aberdeen, 1988), 34-35.

[2] G. V. Bennett, *The Tory Crisis in Church and State, 1688-1730* (Oxford, 1975), 208.

[3] J. Swift, *Correspondence*, II, 185-86n.1.

[4] Elis Schröderheim, *Anteckningar till konung Gustav IIIs historia* (Örebro, 1851), 81. For further support of Görtz's Masonic strategy, see C. Nordmann, *Grandeur*, 424, and Andreas Önnerfors,"From Jacobite Support to a part of the State Apparatus – Swedish Freemasonry between Reform and Revolution," in Cécile Révauger, ed., *Franc-maçonnerie et Politique au Siècle des Lumières* (Pessac, 2006). 205-06.

[5] C. Nordmann, *Grandeur*, 199, 424.

[6] Eveline Cruickshanks, "Lord Cowper, Lord Orrery, the Duke of Wharton, and Jacobitism," *Albion* (1994), 37.

after, but he got his revenge by an injunction in his will that Philip must travel to Geneva with a Huguenot tutor, in order to be educated in the strictest Calvinist principles. Chafing at his father's posthumous Whig bit, Philip fled Geneva and arrived in Paris in August 1716. He wrote to Mar, reminding him that they had met earlier in England and vowing loyalty to James III.[7] Mar was delighted and invited him to come to Avignon to meet the king. James, in turn, wrote Wharton to assure him that he would always protect the Protestant religion. When Wharton arrived in Avignon, James warmly welcomed him and offered to make him Duke of Northumberland in the Jacobite peerage.[8] The impulsive youth then pledged to serve the cause his father had tried to destroy.[9]

From the beginning of their correspondence, Mar urged Wharton to "keep his good intentions to himself."[10] The usually indiscreet adolescent promised to "disguise his sentiments" if it would help James--a strategy that has confused many historians about his subsequent activities. It is quite possible that Mar initiated him into Masonry in order to insure his secrecy and loyalty. Wharton would soon develop Masonic contacts in Ireland and England before emerging five years later as a Jacobite-Masonic leader. When the young man returned to Paris, he "kept on the mask," frequenting Whig as well as Jacobite circles, while he gathered intelligence from the former to give to the latter. Returning to London, he wrote Mar that "I smile on the faces of the Whigs in order to cut their throats. I will always stand to what I have promised, and am ready to make one of twenty proclaim James in Cheapside."[11] In October 1716 he issued a circular letter to English freeholders which protested George I's sending a Baltic fleet against the Swedes, "who have committed no hostilities."[12] He would continue to be privy to Swedish affairs and Masonic intrigues in the years ahead.

Throughout 1716, as Mar directed negotiations with Sweden, Masonic encampments were allegedly formed in Carl XII's army at Lund.[13] Görtz may have learned from Mar and his Scottish associates about the effectiveness of Masonry for secret communication, spiritual inspiration, and morale-building. Moreover, a kind of ecumenical mysticism would bind together the disparate Protestant, Catholic, Russian Orthodox, Jewish, and Turkish supporters of the Swedish-Jacobite cause. Carl XII believed in the sincerity of Stuart declarations of religious toleration, and he determined to implement a similar policy in Sweden. In May 1716 the French traveler Aubrey de La Motraye wrote excitedly to Eric Benzelius, Swedenborg's brother-in-law, from Carl's camp in Norway that the king declared "liberty of conscience in his lands to all kinds of nationalities."[14] Curiously, his toleration policy has been generally ignored by historians, and few in modern Sweden are even aware of it.

---

[7] *HMC: Stuart*, II, 360-61, 390-91, 486.

[8] "Philip Wharton, Duke of Wharton," *ODNB*; E. Cruickshanks and H. Erskine-Hill, *Atterbury Plot*, 71. He was formally installed as Duke of Northumberland by James in 1726.

[9] Robert F. Gould, "Masonic Celebrities: the Duke of Wharton, G.M., 1722-23," *AQC*, 18 (1895), 115-55.

[10] *HMC: Stuart*, V, 396, 471. Adolescents were occasionally initiated by the Jacobites.

[11] Ibid., III, 312

[12] Ibid., III, 655.

[13] Claim made by Samuel Beswick, *The Swedenborg Rite* (New York, l870), 183-92.

[14] Linköpings Stiftsbibliothek MSS. "Bref til A.B. Eric Benzelius den Yngre," V, f.40. De la Motraye to Benzelius (Gothenburg, 21 May 1716).

Carl XII was also interested in architecture and operative masonry. In November 1716 he invited Nicodemus Tessin to his camp in Lund to discuss their long-delayed construction projects. Nicodemus's kinsman Edouart Tessin, a military architect, had been initiated in an Edinburgh lodge in 1652, and Nicodemus's services had been solicited by the "Mason King" Charles II and Christopher Wren in London in 1678.[15] Nicodemus had recently worked for Louis XIV at Versailles, where he designed a magnificent Temple of Apollo, which expressed his belief that architecture should express symbolically the reconciliation of contraries in the building of the Temple of Wisdom.[16] Carl XII shared this belief and, as Martin Olin observes,

> Seldom if ever has an architect, in any country, enjoyed such a combination of almost absolute authority in the arts with political influence and administrative power... Tessin not only directed all royal building projects; the cultural policy of the Swedish realm was increasingly perceived as his responsibility.[17]

The king was also aware that Nicodemus was always proud to call himself "a Master Mason," as his son Carl Gustaf later reported.[18] However, like those of the earlier Stuarts, the architectural plans of Carl XII and Tessin met resistance from political enemies – opponents now allied with the Hanoverians. Casten Feif, the Scottish-descended chancellor of Lund University, wrote Tessin that he must keep the king's building plans secret in order to avoid resistance from critics of royal economic and military policies. King and architect nevertheless carried on a private correspondence about their planned royal edifices.

Meanwhile in London, Ambassador Gyllenborg clandestinely recruited artisans (Masons?) to the cause, leading an indignant Defoe to attack him in a pamphlet: "The count's Agent in his libel pretends a Saint like Zeal and regard to Men of handicraft Callings, well knowing...how easily they may become additional Troops in aid of the *Swedes* when landed."[19] Gyllenborg, who corresponded regularly with Mar, was undoubtedly aware of Mar's continuing architectural activity, as the latter sent designs for buildings to old friends in London and Scotland.[20] As Carl XII rebuilt his army and received foreign loans, Gyllenborg continued his long-distance collaboration with Mar, while both made overtures to disaffected Whigs and to Tories who formerly supported the Hanoverian succession.

Gyllenborg's and Görtz's most ambitious design was the development of a secret alliance between Sweden and Russia, which could deal a final blow to the hated Hanoverians. While Sweden publicly braced for a Russian invasion and George I anticipated the collapse of Carl XII, Görtz met privately in Holland with Dr. Robert Erskine, Mar's cousin and fellow Mason, who represented the Czar. At The Hague Erskine garnered the

---

[15] M. Schuchard, *Restoring the Temple*, 513, 717; also, *Emanuel Swedenborg*, 110-14

[16] Ragnar Josephson, *L'Architect de Charles XII: Nicodéme Tessin a la Cour de Louis XIV* (Paris, 1930), 90, 121, 102-16.

[17] Martin Olin, *Nicodemus Tessin the Younger* (Stockholm, 2004), 9.

[18] Duc de Luynes, *Mémoires du Duc de Luynes sur la Cour de Louis XV* (Paris, 1930), XII, 113-14.

[19] [Daniel Defoe], *The Plot Discovered: or, Some Observations upon a late Vile Jesuitical Pamphlet, Written and Published by the desperate Agents and Understrappers of Count Gyllenborg* (London, 1717), 15.

[20] B. Little, *Gibbs*, 40-42.

support of various British naval officers and sailors, including Thomas Gordon, recently dismissed from English service. Gordon had allowed Jacobite sympthizers free access to areas that he patrolled for the British government, and he devised specific codes for foreign ships.

According to the diary of Mrs. Charles Caesar, whose husband served as naval secretary under Queen Anne and who was the close friend of Swift and Pope, it was Harley (Lord Oxford) who saved Sweden by sending Gordon to Erskine, who then recruited him for Russian service.[21] Mrs. Caesar further revealed that these men "managed to bring about a truce between Russia and Sweden." Gyllenborg, who was related by marriage to Caesar, often stayed at the latter's home.[22] He took advantage of his host's naval connections, which led Defoe to later charge that Gyllenborg also "undertook to furnish the Swedes with good Sea Officers," by recruiting disaffected sailors from the British navy.[23] Persuaded by Görtz of the aggressive intentions of George I and of the feasibility of a Russo-Swedish-Jacobite victory, Czar Peter cancelled his planned invasion of Sweden and travelled to France, where Dr. Erskine acted as an intermediary during further negotiations between the Czar and Mar.[24]

Encouraged by these promising international initiatives, Gyllenborg anonymously published a series of pamphlets in London aimed at winning over popular opinion to the Swedish-Jacobite cause. From his earlier friendship with Steele and Swift, and from his familiarity with Defoe's dissembling propaganda techniques, Gyllenborg cleverly employed a variety of pseudonyms and false personae. In *An English Merchant's Remarks upon a Scandalous Jacobite Paper* (1716), he posed as an Englishman who was hostile to the Jacobites. In the process of denying "scandalous" Jacobite charges against George I, Gyllenborg laid out a powerful indictment of the Hanoverian monarch, who hoped "to increase his dominions in Germany, at the expense of British blood and treasure, by involving these nations in foreign quarrels."[25] Gyllenborg exploited the English people's genuine aversion to a standing army and evoked much sympathy for Sweden. Despite Abel Boyer's charge that the anonymous pamphlet was published "by the Jacobite faction," it gained a widespread readership.[26]

Working with his agents in Holland and France, Gyllenborg sent out a bevy of pro-Swedish, anti-Hanoverian pamphlets that made such inroads on popular opinion in Britain and Europe that the Whigs mounted a furious counter-offensive. Whereas Gyllenborg's "English Merchant" praised the "noble and undaunted spirit of Charles XII," a Whig pamphleteer scorned the haughtiness, obstinacy, and brutality of the absolutist monarch who stole his people's freedom.[27] The Hanoverian author conceded that "there was scarce a *Jacobite* School-Boy, or poor Tradesman's Wife about the Streets," who was not "eagerly watching the [Swedish] King's enterprise." Moreover, he warned that Carl XII's campaign in Norway was the prelude to his invasion of Scotland.

---

21 M. Caesar, *Journal*, 20, 116.

22 E. Cruickshanks and H. Erskine-Hill, *Atterbury Plot*, 30.

23 [Daniel Defoe], *An Account of the Swedish and Jacobite Plot* (London, 1717), 11.

24 Steve Murdoch, "Soldiers, Sailors, Jacobite Spy: Russo-Jacobite Relations, 1688-1750," *Slavonica*, 3 (1996-97), 10-11.

25 See John Simpson, "Arresting a Diplomat, 1717," *History Today*, 35 (1985), 32-37.

26 Abel Boyer, *The Political State of Great Britain* (London, 1717), XII, 305-11.

27 Herbert G. Wright, "Some English Writers and Charles XII," *Studia Neophilogia*, 15 (1943), 115-17.

In June 1716 Mar and his collaborators worried that Francia might succumb to the bribe of £500 offered to him if he would testify against Harvey of Combe, but they were pleased at his steadfast refusal.[28] Because Francia handled the financial fund-raising for the Swedish-Jacobite plot, Gyllenborg was especially relieved. In October he wrote Görtz, "In short, it will be a glorious enterprise, which will put an end to all our misfortunes, by ruining those that are the authors of them."[29] Gyllenborg then informed Carl XII of the revitalized Jacobite plan, but in keeping with Görtz's admonishments for absolute secrecy, he put nothing in writing to the king and relied on oral transmission.[30] Görtz, who was not burdened with the Swedish king's absolute refusal to lie, blithely denied in public all connections between him and the Jacobites. In fact, he was so successful that, as Claude Nordmann observes, "the diplomatic fiction of Charles XII's ignorance of these intrigues" survives even today.[31] By the end of the month, Gyllenborg boasted to Görtz that his argument that the Swedes and Jacobites would maintain English liberties against Germanic oppression was shifting the sympathies of the people: "The greatest part of the nation being at present inflamed with Jacobitism."[32]

On 6 November 1716 Mar received news that Robert Walpole was so determined to break Francia that he recalled his brother Horatio Walpole from his diplomatic post in Paris in order "to be witness against Mr. Pen," code-name for Francia.[33] However, Francia held firm and shared Gyllenborg's ebullient confidence in the eventual success of their campaign. From his Newgate cell, the "Jacobite Jew," as he was called in the press, wrote happily to his wife:

> the Company here is much better than I expected. They are all Tories... You know on what Account I am here, which cannot disgrace me. Be therefore comforted, and do not grieve, God will assist us... [Harvey of Combe] may only be suspected of being a Friend to the *Pretender*, but that was well known before; and if all who are so were to be punished, above Three Fourths of the Nation would suffer. Therefore I laugh at anything they can do to me.[34]

Francia's cellmate and new collaborator George Flint even managed to write a popular Jacobite newspaper, *The Shift Shifted*, which his wife smuggled out of Newgate for publication. However, Francia was not aware that the government had been steadily intercepting Gyllenborg's correspondence and that Walpole was now determined to expose the international plot.

On 22 January 1717, when Francia was finally brought to trial, he was accused of "being moved and seduced by the Instigation of the Devil, as a false Traytor against our said Lord the King," and "conspired with others to raise rebellion and war."[35] However,

[28] *HMC: Stuart*, II, 227.
[29] Carl Gyllenborg, et al., *Letters which Passed between Count Carl Gyllenborg, the Barons Goertz, sparre, and Others Relating to the Design of Raising a Rebellion in His Majesty's Dominions to Be Supported by a Force from Sweden* (London, 1717), 9; also, C. Nordmann, *Grandeur*, 193-205.
[30] John Murray, *George I, the Baltic, and the Whig Split of 1717* (London, 1969), 307.
[31] C. Nordmann, *Grandeur*, 193-205.
[32] C. Gyllenborg, *Letters*, 10.
[33] *HMC: Stuart*, III, 187.
[34] Cecil Roth, *Anglo-Jewish Letters* (London, 1938), 96.
[35] *The Tryal of Francis Francia, for High Treason* (London, 1717), 4.

Francia's clever challenging of potential jurors produced a largely Tory jury, who believed his charge that the corrupt Lord Townshend first threatened and then tried to bribe him to "sign Harvey's life away." He argued that Boyer and Ozell, the government decipherers, had mistranslated his letters and misinterpreted other's handwriting as his own. The Solicitor General bullied the jury and proclaimed that if Francia was not convicted, "no man will be for holding a traiterous correspondence." To the shock of the government, the jury returned a verdict of Not Guilty. Though some historians assume that Francia must have been bribed and agreed to become a double agent, letters in the unpublished Stuart Papers make clear that he remained a faithful supporter of James III.[36]

Mar was delighted to learn of Francia's acquittal, and when the famous "Jacobite Jew" arrived in France, he was put in touch with Dillon, Ormonde, and other Jacobite Masons. It was probably at this time that he was initiated into the fraternity, for Mar used "the Mason Word" to ensure loyalty and discretion among his partisans.[37] Moreover, Francia may have formed a cross-channel network of sympathetic Jewish-Masonic financiers to support the cause. On 3 August 1717 Dillon wrote Mar about the progress of the Swedish plot:

> Francia assures by a letter of 28 July that the 60,000*l*.is already lodged and gives hopes the remaining part will be furnished in case of need and when required. This piece of news is not uncomfortable. Francia intends to settle his family at Calais, and says his noble society intends to send one of their trusties to compliment Peter (James) and assure him of their fidelity, zeal and efficacious assistance. I am sure Martell (Mar) will be highly pleased with this royal club.[38]

Mar would indeed have been pleased if Francia had established a "noble society" or "royal club" of Jewish Masons, for in the same letter, Dillon referred to the ongoing secret negotiations with Mar's cousin, Dr. Erskine, with whom he shared "the Mason Word."

Despite the initial euphoria over Francia's victory, Walpole was determined to get revenge. His agents learned that the Tory *Post Boy* did not dare print the material offered by Gyllenborg, who determined to use the press to stir up opposition to Britain's Baltic policy.[39] Despite the journal's caution, in February the ministry ordered the arrest of the editor, John Morphew, for publishing an item on Anglo-Swedish relations. Then, a week after Francia's acquittal, the government shocked the diplomatic world by arresting Gyllenborg at the Swedish embassy, where they searched his belongings and confiscated his papers (a clear violation of international law). But Gyllenborg had been warned and was able to destroy the most incriminating documents and burn the complex cipher. Arrested with the ambassador were Charles Caesar and Sir Jacob Bancks, a Swedish-born former Tory M.P., who now functioned as a Jacobite financier. A furious George I put heavy pressure on the Dutch government to arrest Görtz in Amsterdam, where he had been

---

[36] M. Lipton, "Francis Francia," 201-02. L. Gooch, *Desperate Faction*, 148-52. For evidence of his loyalty, see *Stuart Papers:* 191/149; 227/164; 247/178, which cover his continuing service to the Stuart court in 1736-43.
[37] John Shaftesley, "Jews in Regular English Freemasonry," *TJHSE*, 25 (1977), 159.
[38] *HMC: Stuart*, IV, 490.
[39] Jeremy Black, *The English Press in the Eighteenth Century* (1987; London, 2010), 108.

meeting with the Czar's agent Erskine and James's agent Jerningham to finalize Russian support for the Swedish invasion of Scotland.

The arrest of the diplomats reinforced Carl XII's hostility to the "Elector of Hanover" and hardened his resolution to support a Stuart restoration. Despite the outcries of the diplomatic community, the Whig government ordered the publication of selected letters from Gyllenborg's international correspondence. John Robethon, secretary to George I, edited the letters in order to gain popular support for British involvement in the Great Northern War.[40] Czar Peter was incensed that Dr. Erskine's name was published, and he cavalierly denied any involvement in the plot.[41] In London the Spanish ambassador, the Marques de Monteleon, (a friend of Swift) vehemently protested Gyllenborg's arrest and the publication of his correspondence, because all diplomats would now be at the mercy of spies, informers, and police.

To justify its unprecedented action, the government mounted a propaganda campaign against Sweden, led anonymously by Defoe, who had long followed Swedish affairs and now acquired the government's exposé of Gyllenborg's correspondence.[42] In his anonymous *Account of the Swedish and Jacobite Plot...Occasioned by the Publishing of Count Gyllenborg's Letters* (1717), Defoe outlined Sweden's negotiations with Russia and various bankers, and he condemned the English Tories who collaborated with Gyllenborg. In an unholy alliance, the Jacobites will "bring in the Pretender by Goths and Vandals, Muscovites, Turks, Tartars, Italian and French Papists."[43] Defoe's vilification of the Swedish king and people, which was repeated by other Whig polemicists, was so intense that it contributed to a poisoning of Anglo-Swedish relations that persisted for decades. Carl XII treats his people "like brute beasts," while the Swedes are "slavish and barbarous." In conclusion, Defoe ranted that "no Man who has any bowels of compassion, can think of seeing his native Country become a prey to Swedes, Laplanders, Finlanders, and the rest of the Northern Mohocks." Aware of overtures made to Non-juring Anglicans by Gyllenborg and Swedish clergymen, Defoe lashed out at the Swedes as "intolerant High Church Lutherans," whom the gullible Anglicans pitched upon "to bring in the Popish Pretender." In a follow-up pamphlet, *What if the Swedes Should Come?*, Defoe warned that English virgins would be ravished, while he invoked the threat of "Iron-Fac'd" Swedes to argue for a standing army in England.[44]

Undermining Defoe's effort was the continuing circulation of a popular poem that praised the simplicity, chastity, honesty and fidelity of Carl XII. Entitled *A Character of Charles XII of Sweden by a Polish Nobleman*, the poem appeared in successive multi-lingual editions in 1706-09, and Swift cherished his Latin manuscript copy.[45] To counter this pro-Swedish poem, the Hanoverians published a poem by the Whig dramatist Susanna Centlivre, who turned all Carl XII's virtues into vices – simplicity of dress became slovenliness, chastity became perversion, bravery became recklessness. Eveline Cruickshanks

---

[40] Matthew Kilburn, "John Robethon," *ODNB*.

[41] Guillaume de Lamberty, *Memoires pour server a l'histoire du XVIIIe siécle* (La Haye, 1727-31), X, 41-42; C. Nordmann, *Crise du Nord*, 92.

[42] Helmut Heidenreich, *The Libraries of Daniel Defoe and Philip Farewell* (Berlin, 1970), 112

[43] [D. Defoe], *Swedish and Jacobite Plot*, 21, 32.

[44] [Daniel Defoe], *What if the Swedes Should Come?* (London, 1717), 8, 10, 31.

[45] Eveline Cruickshanks, *Charles XII of Sweden: A Character and Two Poems* (Brisbane, 1983), endnote [29].

wryly observes that, according to Susanna, "any Swedish attempt would be easily crushed by George I, leading, it would seem, an army of dandies!"[46]

In April 1717 Defoe himself admitted that "things growing ripe for a breach with Sweden, everything was done both publick and private that might provoke the public against the King of Sweden."[47] George I's secretary Robethon denounced Carl XII as "a fury let loose out of hell," but when the king pressured Parliament to prohibit *all* trade with Sweden, in an attempt to starve the Swedes into submission, many of his British subjects were disgusted.[48] The French government finally persuaded England and Sweden to free their mutually arrested diplomats, and in July Gyllenborg learned of his impending release and exile from England, which greatly relieved his many friends (especially Swift, who was shaken by the count's arrest).[49]

Mrs. Caesar left a badly-spelled but colorful account of Gyllenborg's impact on Jacobite affairs in England:

> The King of Sweden's Minnister Count Gyllenborg who they seiz'd the same Night [as Mr. Caesar] continu'd still a Prisoner in his Own House, and some time after was carry'd to Plymouth, and then sent to Sweden. Mr. Caesar saw him before he went, which was a great Pleasure to Both, their Haveing been a Long and Intimate Friendship between them. The Count gave Mr. Caesar his Picture and wrote to him as He tuck shiping, Adieu my Dearest Friend Haven Bless you and make you as Happy as you deserve. I am to the Last Moments of My Life Yours. And has since sent him a picture of that Great King of Sweden Charles the 12.[50]

Gyllenborg made good on his life-long loyalty to Charles Caesar and his Jacobite friends in England; moreover, that loyalty was reciprocated by Swift, who would draw on Gyllenborg's traumatic experience in his description of the mad government decipherers in *Gulliver's Travels*.[51] Swift greatly admired Mary Caesar, and he would stay in touch with her over the next decades.

Gyllenborg left England convinced that a Jacobite restoration was the only hope for English national redemption. Soon joined by Görtz, Poniatowski, and Neuhof in Sweden, they renewed their overtures to the Czar, who sent General James Bruce and Prince Andrei Ivanovich Ostermann to the Åland Islands for further negotiations. Bruce's Masonic affiliation has already been noted, and Ostermann's family maintained shadowy ties with Masonry over the next decades.[52] Poniatowski interpreted their agenda in millenarian and Masonic terms – i.e., maintenance or restoration of the "legitimate" kings of Europe (Philip V in Spain and France, James III in Britain, and Stanislaus Leszczynski in Poland) would establish government according to "the maxims of the reign of

---

[46] *Ibid.*, iv.

[47] G. Murray, *George I*, 334, 346.

[48] E. Cruickshanks, *Charles XII*, iv; on the resultant political polarization, see John Murray, *George I*, passim.

[49] F.P. Lock, *Swift's Tory Politics* (Wilmington, 1983), 126.

[50] M. Caesar, *Journal*, 20.

[51] See F.P. Lock, *The Politics of Gulliver's Travels* (Oxford, 1980), 57-58, 155.

[52] T. Bakounine, *Répertoire Biographique*, 384-85.

Solomon."[53] The necessary restoration of the Jews to Palestine would follow in due course. Supporting this Solomonic agenda was Francia in Calais, who collaborated with Baron Eric Sparre and General Dillon in Paris. Though contemporary documentation is lacking, the three were allegedly now affiliated with *Écossais* Freemasonry.

In summer 1717 Mar wrote to Lord Pitsligo, then in Brussels, urging him to join him in Paris in order to discuss the negotiations with Sweden, but Pitsligo wanted to go to Blois, where in June Andrew Michael Ramsay and other Scottish devotees were attending the dying Madame Guyon.[54] It seems certain that Pitsligo met with Ramsay during the next months, before travelling to Vienna in September 1718, where he worked to get the Swedish envoy at the Hapsburg court to support Jacobite-Swedish initiatives. Buoyed by his belief in Carl XII's military invincibility, Mar urged the shipment of Scottish oatmeal to impoverished Sweden, and he suggested that agents in London approach Lord Oxford to raise money for Swedish troops through Mar's brother Edward Erskine and son Robert.[55] He planned to send James Keith, a fellow Mason, to Sweden to coordinate Scottish and Swedish planning.

In October 1717 Mar joined James III at Urbino and subsequently moved with the court to Rome. He confidently offered to design a palace for the king's anticipated restoration in London.[56] Confessing that he was "infected with the disease of building," Mar continued to send drafting instruments and drawings to Gibbs and other allies in Britain, whom he expected to join the next Jacobite rising. Defoe, who knew how Oxford earlier used Masonry, was made privy to the government's intelligence on Mar's foreign contacts, especially with Gyllenborg, who now joined Erskine and Ostermann on the island of Åland to plan Swedish-Russian strategy. As Defoe would later report, the Jacobite coalition maintained extraordinary secrecy:

> That this Treaty [between Sweden and Russia] was carry'd further than has ever yet been made publick, will not be doubted... There was nothing of this nature ever carried out with more art, or concealed with more care, than the negotiations at this place [Åland]; the whole world, and the most penetrating people in it, were at a loss about it, all the public accounts proved empty and frivolous...so exactly did the Czar and the King of Sweden preserve the Secret among themselves, and amuse the world.[57]

Thus, as Mar, Erskine, and Mackenzie collaborated earlier, "without breaking through the Mason Word," clandestine bonds now held the fragile coalition together. In late 1718 Mar would be joined in Rome by Pitsligo and the Wogan brothers, who extended the Jacobite Masonic links with Scotland and Ireland.

*
* *

[53] Stanisalus Mnemon, *La Conspiration du Cardinal Alberoni, La Franc-Maçonnerie et Stanislaus Poniatowski* (Cracovie, 1909), 62.

[54] G. Henderson, *Mystics*, 53; Henrietta Tayler, *The Jacobite Court at Rome in 1719* (Edinburgh, 1938), 49, 51.

[55] *HMC: Stuart*, V, 455-56; Romney Sedgwick, ed., *History of Parliament* (London, 1970), I, 455.

[56] T. Friedman, "A Palace Worthy," 103.

[57] [Daniel Defoe], *Some Account of the Life and Most Remarkable Actions of Georg Henry, Baron de Goertz* (London, 1719), 34-35.

These complex international intrigues provide the necessary context for deciphering the motives and methods behind the formation of the Grand Lodge of London in June 1717. According to James Anderson, the first move to develop a loyal Hanoverian system of Masonry came in the wake of the Jacobite rebellion:

> King George I. entered London most magnificently on 20 Sept.1714. and after the Rebellion was over A.D. 1716 the few Lodges at London finding themselves neglected by Sir Christopher Wren, thought fit to cement under a Grand Master as the Centre of Union and Harmony.[58]

A key player in these efforts was John Theophilus Desaguliers, who collaborated with Anderson, and whose career has been treated with often hagiographical reverence by Grand Lodge historians in England. However, recent research has revealed a more complex and controversial figure than the so-called "father of Masonic enlightenment."[59]

Son of a refugee Huguenot schoolmaster, Desaguliers developed unusual mechanical and mathematical skills which earned him a B.A. at Oxford in 1709. He then replaced his mentor John Keill as lecturer in mathematics and experimental science at Hart Hall. According to Swift, Keill's career was blocked by Whig-Low Church interference, for "Party reaches even to Lines and Circles, and he [Keill] will hardly carry it [a promotion] being reputed a Tory, which yet he utterly denies."[60] Desaguliers recognized his vulnerablility as a Huguenot, so in 1710 he took deacon's orders from Henry Compton, Bishop of London, in order to "hedge his bets."[61] The Whiggish Bishop Compton was deeply disrespected by Swift.[62]

In July 1713 Hans Sloane proposed Desaguliers as an FRS and suggested that he be made operator for the society, but the fellows did not act on Sloane's proposal. Perhaps the Tory members associated him with the blockage of Keill. Over the next year, Newton recognized that Desaguliers could be useful as his propagandist and demonstrator of experiments; thus, on 8 July 1714 he nominated his protégé to the Royal Society, where the Frenchman was promptly accepted. As Larry Stewart notes, Newton's nomination took place in the atmosphere of crisis created by the impending Hanoverian succession and "the possible descent of Leibniz on London."[63] At some time in 1714, while working closely with Newton, Desaguliers joined a Masonic lodge, #4, which met at the Rummer and Grapes in Channel Row, Westminster. Through the lodge and Royal Society, he gained access to Whig and Jacobite Masons, and it was perhaps his perception of Jacobite intrigues within the fraternity that motivated him to take on a Whig political role.

Interested in architecture and operative masonry, Desaguliers was friendly with William Talman, the Williamite-Whig architect, who in 1714 was working for James Brydges,

---

[58] J. Anderson, *Constitutions (1738)*, 109.

[59] For a sometimes negative and revisionist view of Desaguliers, see Larry Stewart, *The Rise of Public Science: Rhetoric, Technology, and Natural Philosophy in Newtonian Britain* (Cambridge, 1992). For a more positive and traditional view, see Audrey Carpenter, *John Theophilus Desaguliers: A Natural Philosopher, Engineer and Freemason* (London, 2011).

[60] J. Swift, *Correspondence*, I, 230.

[61] L. Stewart, *Rise*, 130.

[62] J. Swift, *Correspondence*, I, 469n.6, 520n.

[63] L. Stewart, *Rise*, 120.

recently made 9th Baron Chandos, on the latter's splendid mansion at Canons.[64] Though Chandos dismissed Talman because of his "ridiculous and extravagant charges of designing the offices at Canons," Desaguliers remained close to the architect and later housed Talman's great collection of pictures, sculptures, and architectural *objets* at his residence in Channel Row.[65] An FRS, Chandos was an energetic if mercenary "projector," and he utilized Desaguliers's mechanical talents for a host of entrepreneurial schemes. Though no documentation has emerged to prove Chandos a Mason, his long working relationship with architects and operative Masons suggests his affiliation; his son would later serve as a "modern" Grand Master.[66]

Chandos gained his fortune as "the most successful war profiteer" during the Anglo-French wars, and he was described by Edward Harley as "at the bottom of all the cheating."[67] A political opportunist, he introduced Desaguliers to a shadowy world of ambiguous loyalties, in which disaffected Whigs took out "insurance policies" with Jacobites. It was a world readily exploited by Mar and his Masonic collaborators in Britain. Chandos had been friendly with Swift during Queen Anne's reign, and subsequently became a cautious supporter of the Jacobites, secretly sending funds to St. Germain in 1715. Just before his friend Bolingbroke fled to France, Chandos loaned him £20,000 to protect his estates in England. In the meantime, Chandos employed Gibbs – Mar's agent – to rebuild his house and chapel at Canons. Gibbs had recently (January 1716) been dismissed from his post of surveyor of churches by the Whig commissioners, who also stripped Wren of his surveyorship of Greenwich Hospital and controllership at Windsor.[68] Led by Vanbrugh, the commission steadily undermined Wren, Gibbs, and their allies – a process that Anderson, in his Whig Masonic history, distorted into Wren's "neglect" of the few London lodges.

Gibbs believed that his dismissal was the result of the machinations of Colen Campbell, who had formerly been supported by Mar.[69] During the Jacobite rebellion, Campbell published the first volume of *Vitruvius Brittannicus*, in which he emphasized that the many Jacobite subscribers had signed on "before 25 March 1715." He studiously ignored the work of his rival Gibbs, who was criticized "by implication" as the chief British exponent of "the affected and licentious" forms of Italian baroque that Campbell condemned.[70] Calling himself George I's "most faithfull and obedient servant," Campbell dedicated the volume to the king; he now determined to become the Hanoverian architect *par excellence*.

After the failure of the Jacobite rising, Chandos publicly professed Hanoverian loyalty and began his career as "the quintessential trimmer."[71] Swift would later describe him as

---

[64] Brydges was made 9th Baron Chandos in October 1714, Earl of Carnarvon in 1714, and Duke of Chandos in April 1719. For convenience, he will henceforth be called Chandos.

[65] H. Colvin, *Biographical Dictionary*, 949-51.

[66] J. Anderson praised Chandos's architectural feat at Canons and flattered his son as Grand Master in the revised *Constitutions* (1738); see pp. iv, 121.

[67] C.H. Collins Baker and Muriel Baker, *The Life and Circumstances of James Brydges, First Duke of Chandos, Patron of the Liberal Arts* (Oxford, 1949), xi, xviii.

[68] H. Colvin, *Biographical Dictionary*, 399, 403, 1086.

[69] *Ibid.*, 399, 403.

[70] *Ibid.*, 209-10.

[71] L. Stewart, *Rise*, 214-16, 267.

"a great complier with every Court."[72] Possibly to counter the work of the privately Catholic Gibbs on the chapel, Chandos appointed Desaguliers as chaplain – in recompense for his engineering work. However, as Larry Stewart observes, "The last thing Desaguliers wanted was to be expected to provide much in the way of religious service."[73] His subsequent non-attendance and neglect of parish duties would earn him the mockery of Jacobites and make him the satirical target of his fellow Mason, William Hogarth.[74] Swift would later seem to target Desaguliers among the "slavish prostitute Chaplains to some Nobleman" in *Gulliver's Travels*.[75]

While Desaguliers and Gibbs worked for Chandos, the Scottish architect also served Richard Boyle, 3rd Earl of Burlington, allegedly a crypto-Jacobite with Masonic connections. Since 1712 Burlington, though a public Whig, was listed as a Jacobite supporter ("Mr. Buck") on Skelton's cipher at St. Germain.[76] In May 1714 he left suddenly for a continental tour, in which his architectural studies supposedly served as a cover for his Jacobite activities. While Burlington was abroad, Gibbs supervised renovations on the earl's house in Piccadilly – receiving advice from Mar in the process.[77] After Burlington's return in April 1715, Gibbs designed an unusual "Domed Temple" on the earl's estate at Chiswick, which would later be given a provocative Masonic significance.[78] A year later, Burlington gave refuge to Alexander Pope and his family, who were driven out of their home by the severe implementation of anti-Catholic laws.[79] As we shall see, Pope would also develop Jacobite and Masonic associations.

Suspicions about Masonic involvement in the Scottish rebellion and Swedish-Jacobite plot provide a context for an unusual Masonic allusion in a theatrical farce, anonymously co-written by John Gay, Alexander Pope, and John Arbuthnot, members of the Scriblerian Club. In *Three Hours After Marriage*, first performed on 16 January 1717, the authors targeted Dr. John Woodward in the character of Dr. Fossile, a zany, paranoid, and impractical virtuoso. Arbuthnot, who had earlier attacked Woodward's mineralogical (fossil) claims, evidently knew about the scientist's Masonic affiliation and supplied the oblique allusion:

> *Fossile.* Your Haft of an Antediluvian Trowel, unquestionably
> the Tool of one of the *Babel* Masons!
> *Nautilus.* What's that to your Fragment of *Seth's* Pillar?[80]

Arbuthnot was aware of the lodge traditions that referred to the Masons who built the Tower of Babel and to Seth's Pillars which preserved the esoteric secrets of the

[72] J. Swift, *Correspondence*, III, 755 n.

[73] L. Stewart, *Rise*, 130.

[74] Jenny Uglow, *Hogarth: A Life and a World* (London, 1977), 347-48.

[75] Jonathan Swift, *Gulliver's Travels*, ed. Paul Turner (Oxford, 1998), 117.

[76] J. Clark, "Lord Burlington," 252-57.

[77] John Harris, *The Palladian Revival: Lord Burlington, His Villa and Garden at Chiswick* (New Haven, 1994), 40, 43, 49n.2; T. Friedman, "A Palace," 103.

[78] J. Clark, "Lord Burlington," 298.

[79] Howard Erskine-Hill, "'Avowed Friend and Patron': The Third Earl of Burlington and Alexander Pope," in T. Barnard and J.Clark, *Burlington*, 218-19.

[80] [John Gay], *Three Hours After Marriage* (London, 1717), 61.

fraternity.[81] The play ran for seven tumultuous nights, initially with strong support from Tories and Jacobites, "a successful run but troubled by partisan catcalls and near-riot."[82] Woodward's friends rallied to his cause, and a hostile response was soon published by Edward Parker, the scientist's Whig friend. In *A Complete Key to the New Farce, call'd Three Hours After Marriage* (1717), Parker explicitly linked Arbuthnot with the Masonic allusion, noting "This is according to our *Scotch* Author's Chronology," and mocked "our *Highlander's* Skill in *Surgery*, the Art to which he was bred at *Glasgow*."[83]

The play provoked a storm of Whig reaction and further performances were cancelled. Parker's linking of Arbuthnot to Scottish Freemasonry occurred within a context of increasing concern among some Hanoverian Masons about the Jacobite sympathies of various Fellows of the Royal Society. Some older members, such as Arbuthnot, Halley, Orrery, and the Wrens, maintained their private support for the Stuarts. Among moderate Whigs, there were earlier, disturbing signs of nostalgic sympathy for Stuart traditions. In June 1711 Hans Sloane presented to the society a bust of Charles II, with praise of his beneficent role as patron of virtuosos.[84] Over the next few years, Sloane encouraged various Jacobite sympathizers to become Fellows – such as Oxford, Bolingbroke, Thomas and Richard Rawlinson, Gyllenborg, and d'Aumont.

During the last days of the Jacobite rebellion, the society had seemed split in its loyalties. On 8 March 1716 the Fellows excitedly discussed the aurora borealis that appeared after Derwentwater's execution, with Sloane reading a letter from John Keill, a private Tory, who described "the Lucid Crown that was near the Zenith."[85] For Jacobites, this was a sign of heavenly approval for James III. On 10 March, under pressure from Whig members, the society asked George I and the Prince of Wales to subscribe as Patron and Fellow (respectively) "in the Blank leaf as King Charles II and King James II and other Princes have done." Neither did so. On 15 March Sloane proposed for membership the Spanish ambassador Monteleon, who was well-known as a Jacobite supporter and friend of Swift. Even more suspiciously, Sloane organized a petition from the Royal College of Physicians to save from execution the Scottish physician Patrick Blair, who had been captured with the rebels at Preston.[86]

After Francia, Gyllenborg, d'Aumont, and Monteleon were implicated in the Swedish plot in early 1717, George I's excessively harsh policy towards Sweden contributed to a Whig split, in which some Whigs and Hanoverian Tories now seemed vaguely sympathetic to Jacobite intrigues. The dissidents blamed the rising naval debt on the king's Hanoverian motives in using the royal navy to seize Sweden's possessions in Bremen and Verden.[87] The king's ministers especially worried about the puzzling behavior of Philip Wharton, the 1st Duke of Richmond, and the Duchess of Portsmouth (the latter's

---

[81] Art DeHoyos, S. Brent Morris, eds., *Freemasonry in Context: History, Ritual, Controversy* (Lanham, 2004), 135-36, 142, 212.

[82] George Sherburn, "The Fortunes and Misfortunes of 'Three Hours After Marriage,'" *Modern Philology*, 24 (1926), 127.

[83] E. Parker, Philomath, *A Complete Key to the New Farce, call'd Three Hours After Marriage* (London, 1717).

[84] British Library: Sloane MS. 3342. "Minutes of the Royal Society, 1699-1712."

[85] Royal Society: Journal Book, XI (1714-20), ff.108-10, 116, 122.

[86] Bruce Lenman, "Physicians and Politics in the Jacobite Era," in Evelyn Cruickshanks and Jeremy Black, eds., *The Jacobite Challenge* (Edinburgh, 1988), 79.

[87] E. Cruickshanks and H. Erskine-Hill, *Atterbury Plot*, 72.

mother), and they attempted to woo them to the Hanoverian cause. After Wharton left the Jacobite circles in France, he briefly appeared in London in December 1716 and then served in the Irish House of Lords, where he publicly supported the government, while privately earning the admiration of Swift and other Tories. His boon companion was the rakish Richard Parsons, 1st Earl of Rosse, and the two young men took seats in the Irish House of Lords on the same day in August 1717. Rosse, whose family had Masonic connections, would become the succeeding "Great Master of Masons in Ireland" in 1725.[88] Wharton employed as his Latin secretary the poet Edward Young, whose name would later appear on Masonic lodge lists.

At the same time, George I determined to secure Richmond and his mother to the court. During Queen Anne's reign, the duke abandoned his Whiggism and supported the Tory ministry. He knew Swift, who however recorded in December 1710 that he would not speak to Richmond at court, and "I believe we are fallen out."[89] The duke visited Paris in May 1713 and July 1714, when he was mysteriously wounded near the Pont Neuf.[90] After his return to London and George I's accession, he was appointed Lord of the Bedchamber in October, but a loyalist mob – believing he was still a Jacobite – attacked him in November. The king continued to woo Richmond and his powerful mother, and in March 1715 the duke gave a supper at which the Duchess of Portsmouth ("this painted abomination of a woman") sat next to a triumphant George I.[91] Swift subsequently called Richmond "a shallow coxcomb."[92] Despite George I's patronage, the duke's effort to save his cousin Derwentwater in 1716 revived the old suspicions, and the government may have learned of his earlier connections with traditional Freemasonry in Chichester.

In February 1717 Charles Burman published the *Memoirs of the Life of that Learned Antiquary, Elias Ashmole*, which revealed the Masonic initiation and Rosicrucian adoption of a founding member of the Royal Society. Burman was the stepson (or son-in-law) of Robert Plot, a Catholic alchemist and Stuart supporter, who published an important account of English Freemasonry in 1686.[93] Burman now claimed that Ashmole's royalist diary reveals "the secret History of the Affairs" and "Discovers the springs" of political motion.[94] Ashmole's seventeenth-century collaboration with visiting Swedish virtuosos must have seemed oddly relevant to current diplomatic affairs. Ethel Seaton observes that Ashmole's gift of his history of the Order of the Garter to Swedish diplomats had the effect of creating Masonic-style bonds between its knights, at home and abroad.[95] It was probably no coincidence that Ashmole planned to follow his history of the Garter with a history of Freemasonry.[96]

---

88 Speth's note in R. Gould, "Wharton," 145; S. Murphy, "Irish Jacobitism," 78.
89 J. Swift, *Journal to Stella*, 85.
90 "Charles Lennox, 1st Duke of Richmond," *ODNB*.
91 J. Doran, *London*, I, 28, 44.
92 J. Swift, *Journal to Stella*, 643.
93 R. Plot, *Natural History of Staffordshire*, 11-13, 82-83. For Burman's relation to Plot, see B. Jones, *Freemason's Guide*, 99.
94 Charles Burman, *Memoirs of the Life of that Learned Antiquary, Elias Ashmole* (London, 1717), 15-16, 25, 37.
95 Ethel Seaton, *Literary Relations between England and Scandinavia in the Seventeenth Century* (Oxford, 1935), 111.
96 John Campbell, *Biographica Brittanica* (London, 1747), I, 224 n.E.

Thus, in summer 1717, when Desaguliers undertook new Masonic initiatives, his motives should be interpreted within the complex British, Swedish, and international political context. On 4 June Desaguliers attended a meeting of four London lodges that joined together to form the Grand Lodge of London and Westminster, a new organization that was clearly dedicated to the Hanoverian succession. To implement their loyalist agenda, the lodge masters planned a regularizing of festival days. The Masonic scholar Douglas Vieler argues that "the emphasis in organizing Grand Lodge on the Annual Feast with a public procession" was a response to the perceived linkage of Freemasonry to the Jacobite rebellion: "in an atmosphere of divided loyalty...masons in London, which was the center of much of the diplomatic intrigue of the time, felt the need...to demonstrate semi-publicly their loyalty."[97] J.R. Clarke goes further and states that the Jacobite agitation, especially the Gyllenborg plot, provoked the Hanoverian Masons to attempt a take-over of the fraternity.[98]

Before this Whig move, Jacobite Masons in the Royal Society had followed Desaguliers's scientific career with non-partisan interest, and the scientific-minded Earl of Orrery, a Fellow since 1706, acquired Desaguliers's publications on improving chimneys (1715) and lectures on experimental science (1717).[99] As noted earlier, he also collected Ashmolean and Rosicrucian works. For the Newtonian Whigs, the Ashmolean-Rosicrucian tradition seemed linked with Leibniz's pansophic agenda, which they were determined to suppress. Thus, as Desaguliers assumed a leadership role in the Grand Lodge, he also emerged as a propagandist in the Newton-Leibniz dispute. Since 1715 Desaguliers had performed Newtonian experiments for visiting French and Dutch scientists in order to spread Newton's philosophy to the Continent.[100] In 1717 he published *Leçons Physico-Mecaniques*, in which he defended Newton and discredited Leibniz, who was painted as a Cartesian (Rosicrucian?) enthusiast. George I, who despised Leibniz and ordered him to remain in Hanover to finish a trivial scholarly commission, appreciated Desaguliers's efforts and invited him to lecture on experimental philosophy to the royal family.[101]

Swift, who would later satirize the Newton-Leibniz quarrel, also lampooned Desagulier's mathematical lectures and demonstrations before the king and prince as examples of "Laputan" or prostituted, politicized (Whig) science.[102] On 27 September, when Desaguliers preached before the king at Hampton Court, he warned about the dangers of credulous scientific "projecting" (*à la* William Benson), while he presented Newtonianism as the proper religion for the Whig state. Some weeks later, Desaguliers received the orders of an Anglican priest and was given a living by William Cowper, Lord Chancellor and a fellow Grand Lodge Mason. Margaret Jacob observes that "In Hanoverian England, Whiggery provided the beliefs and values, while Freemasonry supplied one temple wherein some of its most devoted followers worshiped the God of Newtonian science."[103]

---

[97] Douglas Vieler, "As It Was Seen--and As It Was," *AQC*, 96 (1983), 83.

[98] J.R. Clarke, "The Establishment of the Premier Grand Lodge: Why in London and Why in 1717," *AQC*, 76 (1963), 5.

[99] Christ Church, Oxford: MS. Orrery Library Catalogue, 22, 24.

[100] L. Stewart, *Rise*, 120.

[101] *Ibid.*, 67, 130.

[102] J. Swift, *Gulliver*, 91, 150, 154, 177.

[103] M. Jacob, *Radical*, 121.

For Desaguliers and the Whig Masons, it was important to move operative as well as speculative Masonry into the Hanoverian camp. By 1717 the decreasing use of stone for building material in England had caused a serious "decline in the Mason trade," which led to widespread disaffection from Hanoverian building policies.[104] In his apologia for Newton, *Leçons Physico-Mecaniques*, Desaguliers included puffs for Chandos's construction and technological projects, thus linking them with Newton's Whig agenda. That Desaguliers's career was connected with Chandos's architectural (and Masonic?) activities was suggested by the Whig poet Charles Gildon in his poem *Canons: or, the Vision* (1717), dedicated to the baron. Gildon praised the great "teacher" Desaguliers as a man of "consummate learning and profound parts," whose services to construction of "Canons Noble Pile" elevated him to a Hiramic role in the earl's Solomonic career:

> What David wish'd in vain, to him [Chandos] is given,
> His favourite Hands have rais'd a *PILE to Heavens,
> Hands pure of Guilt, like that Wise Hebrew King
> With the large Heart; fit for such Offerings

> *[Note]. Has at his own Expence rebuilt the Parish Church
> in a most Beautiful manner.[105]

Gildon appealed to Chandos to extend his patronage of architecture to poetry, and he obviously hoped that Desaguliers would support his bid. Comparing bad poetry to bad architecture, in which the orders are clumsily mixed, he declared: "Nobody makes a Building without an *Ichnography* or Plan of the whole Design, else nothing could be regular in any Art, where there is a whole and Parts." But the poet, through loyalist propaganda, could imitate Amphyon's "Instructive Lyre": "I saw what Stones obey'd his Pow'rful Call/ And mov'd in Measures to the Theban Wall."[106] Because "immortal *George* now rules the Favour'd State," after defeating the "Rebels vile, with Infamy renown'd," Britain will no longer know "home-bred Tumults" and will be "secure from foreign foes." Chandos's building of Canons thus imitates the building of the Hanoverian state, which Gildon offered to immortalize. One wonders about the reaction of Chandos's chief architect – the crypto-Jacobite Gibbs – to this Hanoverian panegyric.

In June 1717, evidently influenced by Desaguliers, the otherwise obscure Anthony Sayer, "Gent.," was elected Grand Master by the four lodges, with a carpenter and soldier to serve as Grand Wardens. One year later, George Payne, a loyalist employee of the Tax Office and Whig Justice of Peace, replaced Sayer. Ric Berman suggests that Payne was familiar with the Freemasonry of his native Chester and that he was close to Desaguliers.[107] He observes further that Payne's rise in the Whig tax office and Westminster judiciary was assisted by Charles Delafaye, who joined the Grand Lodge and became the government's major anti-Jacobite intelligencer and decipherer. George Payne was

---

[104] G. Draffen, "Freemasonry," 366; for details on the problems within English operative Masonry, see M. Schuchard, "Jacobite versus Hanoverian Claims,'" 121-63.
[105] [Charles Gildon], *Canons: or, the Vision. A Poem addressed to the Right Honourable James Brydges, Earl of Caernarvon* (London, 1717), 9.
[106] *Ibid.*, 15-17.
[107] R. Berman, *Foundations*, 70-75.

possibly related to John Payne, a timber merchant and inventor who acted as Chandos's agent in various speculative building schemes.[108]

In the wake of the Swedish-Jacobite plot, the Hanoverian Masons worried about the Tory and Jacobite influence of Bishop Atterbury, who was suspected of collaborating with Gyllenborg. Though the government was unable to prove his involvement, they feared that he was continuing his Jacobite intrigues. An intimate friend of Wren, Atterbury was currently supervising the architectural renovations at Westminster Abbey, a project which employed many operative Masons who were loyal to Wren and traditional Masonry.[109] Once again, Walpole and his partisans would call upon their Whig theatrical polemicists to deliver a blow against the Non-juring and Jacobite admirers of Atterbury, who were identified with Wren's Masonic partisans.

On 6 December 1717 Colley Cibber, who became a loyalist member of the Grand Lodge, wrote and acted in *The Non-juror, a Comedy*, produced by the Drury Lane company. Taking off from Moliere's satire of religious hypocrisy in *Tartuffe*, Cibber also drew upon the Hanoverian propaganda of Charles Johnson's *Cobler of Preston* to ridicule the Jacobites. Some critics believed that Johnson, a friend and subsequent Masonic brother of Cibber, contributed to the script, especially in the references to "Sir Preston Rebel," "Humphrey Staunch the Cobler," and the cowardly retreat of Jacobites from "the King's forces marching towards Preston."[110] In what seems a hint at the Northumberland supporters of the late Derwentwater, the character Sir Charles, whose uncle was "a Gentleman of an ancient Family in the North" was bred in Non-juring principles that made him almost a Roman Catholic. The northern rebels are in touch with Scottish Jacobites, such as "Colonel Perth," who corresponds with the Stuart court at Avignon, and who was in arms in 1715 with the Non-juring Dr. Wolf, a crypto-Jesuit who is scorned as a "*Jewish* cormorant" (a hint at the Jacobites-as-Jews trope).

Atterbury and his supporters among the Non-juring churchmen were under increasing government surveillance. Thus, in Cibber's dedication to George I, he boasted that the true purpose of theater is to "divert the sullen and disaffected from busying their brains to disturb the happiness of a Government, which (for want of proper amusements) they often enter into wild and seditious schemes to reform."[111] Pleading for government financial support of theatrical comedies, he attacked "the blinded Proselytes of our few Non-juring Clergy...those *lurking* enemies of our Constitution." With Whigs and Grand Lodge Masons packing his theater, he would soon boast that the audience produced "no opposition from our publick Malcontents," which proves "the strength and number of the *Misguided* to be much less, than may have been artfully insinuated." Comparing the "stiff Non-juring separation-saints" to Satan, the Pope, madmen, and bawds, he urged them to leave England, "a land of Liberty they hate," and move to Italy, where their tyrannical "transalpine Master" rules at his court in Urbino. George I attended the play and, though he could not understand the language, rewarded Cibber with £200.

---

[108] L. Stewart, *Rise*, 355.

[109] See "Sir Christopher Wren's Report on the Abbey in 1713, to Dean Atterbury," *Wren Society*, 11 (1934), 15-20.

[110] Colly Cibber, *The Non-juror. A Comedy* (London, 1718), 37-49. Nathaniel Mist published an attack on Cibber and the play in his pro-Jacobite *Original Weekly Journal* (28 December 1718), which he claimed was a letter from Charles Johnson. However, the attribution was almost certainly false and an attempt to cause ill will between the two Whig playwrights.

[111] C. Cibber, *Non-juror*, 4-6.

As with the earlier duel of rival cobblers of Preston, the work of Cibber (and John-son?) provoked an immediate counter-blast from Christopher Bullock, who wrote and produced *The Per-juror* at the Lincoln's Inn Theatre. Though Bullock disingenuously de-nied that his play was Party-Wit" or that he lashed "a Whig or Tory," his satire upon the dishonest, money-grubbing, spying, informing aristocrats and politicians clearly targeted the Walpolean dictum that every man has his price: "the Commonwealth is a great Ma-chine, composed of many great and small Wheels, and every one must be greased." For what is life, without money: "That's the *Axis* on which the whole World turns, the Deity to which all Men sacrifice... and what signifies a little Perjury?" Much to the government's chagrin, despite the huge, loyalist audiences at Cibber's *Non-Juror*, Bullock's *Per-juror* also pulled in full houses, attracted by the comic performance of his chief actor, James Spiller (a staunch Tory). As a contemporary noted,

> No Body will wonder if this *Farce* had a considerable Run, to very large au-diences of Persons who went under the Censure of being disaffected to the Government, since Mr. Spiller was the Comedian, who, next to the *Party-Jokes* in it, gave, by his Performance, a Life and Spirit to it.[112]

Among those who enjoyed the success of *The Per-juror* was Pope, who issued his own satirical attack on Cibber's *Non-juror*. In an anonymous pamphlet, *The Plot Discover'd: or A clue to the Non-juror* (1718), Pope pretended that the play actually poked fun at the Whigs, claiming that Dr. Wolf was secretly a Presbyterian and that the characters spoke bad English, "a foreign jargon," implying they were German.[113] Bullock and Spiller became friendly with Pope and his circle and, more importantly, with the Duke of Wharton, who would soon become involved in Masonic intrigues. As Cibber and Drury Lane became more closely associated with the loyalist Grand Lodge, dissident actors collaborated with Tory and Jacobite Masons. The emerging political-Masonic rivalries in the public theat-rical world would soon overlap with those in the secret world of the lodges—both opera-tive and speculative.

While Pope pretended that Cibber's anti-Jacobite play was actually aimed at the Whigs, another master of literary dissimulation, Daniel Defoe, infiltrated various Tory-Jacobite journals in order to "manage" (censor, distort, euphemize) their articles before publica-tion. In a remarkable series of letters to Charles Delafaye in April-June 1718, he begged the government's main spymaster to explain to his new chief, James, 1st Earl Stanhope, why he had posed as a Jacobite during earlier secret service assignments (including his espionage work in Scotland). Defoe may have counted on Masonic bonds with Delafaye, as he justified his earlier deceptive activities. When working for Charles Spencer, 3rd Earl of Sunderland, until March 1718, he was ordered to "appear as if I were, as before, under the displeasure of the Government, and separated from the Whigs; and that I might be more serviceable in a kind of Disguise, than if I appeared openly."[114]

As the "secret Censor of Journals," Defoe was first commissioned "to write, in op-position to a scandalous Paper called the *Shift Shifted* (composed by George Flint while

---

[112] G. Akerby, *James Spiller*, 25.
[113] [Alexander Pope], *The Plot Discover'd; or a Clue to the Non-juror*, 2nd ed. (London, 1718), 8, 23; Helene Koon, *Colley Cibber: A Biography* (Lexington, 1986), 86-87.
[114] William Lee, *Daniel Defoe: His Life and Recently Discovered Letters* (London, 1969), xi.

imprisoned in the Tower), but instead he posed as a Tory and wrote for the anti-government journals, *Mercurius Politicus, Dormer's News Letter*, and *Mist's Weekly Journal*. At the latter paper, the most important Jacobite journal, he explained:

> I introduced myself, in the Disguise of a Translator of the Foreign News, to be so far concerned in this weekly paper of [Nathaniel] Mist's, as to be able to keep it within the Circle of a secret Management, also prevent the mischievous Part of it; and yet neither Mist, or any of those concerned with him, have the least Guess or Suspicion by whose Direction I do it.
>
> By this Management…the *Journal* will be always kept…to pass as Tory papers, and yet be disabled and enervated, so as to do no Mischief, or give any Offence to the government.[115]

Though Delafaye appreciated his work, Defoe worried about his own safety, especially because he may "one Time or other, run the Risk of Fatal Misconstructions":

> I am, Sir, for this Service, posted among Papists, Jacobites, and enraged High Tories – a Generation who, I profess, my very Soul Abhors; I am obliged to hear traitorous Expressions and outrageous Words against his Majesty's Person and Government, and his most faithful Servants, and smile at it all, as if I approved it; I am obliged to take all the scandalous and, indeed, villainous Papers that come, and keep them by as if I would gather Materials from them to put them into the News, nay, I often venture to let Things pass which are a little Shocking, that I may not render myself suspected.[116]

Defoe was especially anxious to stop the publication of *The Character of Sultan GALGA, the present Cham of Tartary*, "a villainous Paper," and he sent to Delafaye a copy of the manuscript received by Mist. The satire mocked the appearance and behavior of George I, noting that he was so little "formed by Nature for a Throne, that he seems conscious of it himself, and never makes a worse Figure than when he appears with the Ensigns of Royalty."[117] Galga/George I was cowardly, cruel, stingy, and ignorant: "In the Management of State Affairs he is a perfect Cypher," and "accordingly he is served by his Ministers, who seldom consult him in any thing." But Defoe was unable to stop the publication, and on 5 April 1718 Anne Oglethorpe wrote James III: "I send to you The Character of Galga, your opposite in everything, just come out."[118]

According to William Lee, who discovered Defoe's letters to Delafaye, his efforts were countered by the "profligate" Duke of Wharton and "a knot of his associates," who began to "frequent Mist's printing office, and to write sedition and treason for his *Journal*."[119] Defoe warned Delafaye that Mist was as disloyal as any of them and was a willing tool, except when he took Defoe's warnings against imminent prosecution seriously and toned down his anti-government writings. As we shall see, Lee further suggests that Wharton later collaborated with Mist in an attempt to use Defoe's *faux* Jacobite writings

---

[115] *Ibid.* xii.

[116] *Ibid.*, xiii.

[117] Anon., *The Character of Sultan GALGA* (London, 1718), 1-2.

[118] *HMC. Stuart*, VI, 280, 471.

[119] W. Lee, *Daniel Defoe*, 461

against him and even to assassinate him. Delafaye and the Grand Lodge would eventually see Wharton as a dangerous Masonic rival.[120]

In August 1718 the Jacobite Masons in France were pleased by the arrival of their "brother" Dr. Arbuthnot, though some were worried that he planned to meet with "Bolingbroke and others there on some scheme they have afoot."[121] Both John and Robert Arbuthnot had maintained contact with the exiled Mar, who relayed thanks through Robert for the assistance and care that the doctor was giving to Mar's son and daughter in London.[122] Robert wrote Mar to reassure him of John's loyalty to his old Scottish friend, stressing "the unchangeable respect my brother has for you," but "He is the object of the all the hatred of the Marlborough faction and is forced to live among them with great circumspection, for they would be well pleased to find a hole in his coat." In October the Stuart court received word that Dr. Arbuthnot planned to visit Urbino, and Secretary Edgar wrote Mar that his friend would be most welcome. Instead, the physician returned to London, from where he wrote Swift on the 14th:

> I cannot tell whither you care to hear from any of your friends on this side... I have been in france six weeks at paris and as much at Rowen wher I can assure yow I hardly heard a word of newes or politics... I was asked for Mon'sr Swift by many people I can assure yow, & particularly by the Duke D'aumont. I was respectfully & kindly treated by many folks & even by the great Mr Lawes...I saw your old friend Ld Bolingbroke who asked for yow he looks just as he did...[123]

An enclosed letter has disappeared and, despite Arbuthnot's claim of an apolitical role in France, Swift would have recognized that the Duc d'Aumont, a supporter of Gyllenborg and the Stuart cause, and John Law, the Scottish financier and Jacobite, were politically dangerous contacts for the cautious doctor. And certainly Bolingbroke was still distrusted and under surveillance by the Whig government.

As Mar continued his negotiations with the Swedes, his plan was supported by an Irish officer in Spain, Patrick Lawless O'Brien, who was sent by the Spanish court to Sweden to negotiate with Charles XII "a joint Hispano-Swedish landing in Scotland."[124] The necessity for secrecy meant that Mar's Masonic networks became increasingly important, as additional Jacobite Masons became active in France and Flanders. An important new actor was Charles Radcliffe, brother of the executed Derwentwater, who in December 1716 had escaped from Newgate and made his way to the Continent. On 26 October 1718, Tom Bruce wrote Mar that the younger Radcliffe is on his way from Paris to Italy. He had been in great familiarity with George Keith, the Earl Marischal, in Louvain, and he is "a pretty gentleman & full of good sense, but I fear somewhat proud and jealous...& ready to quarrel."[125] Bruce cautioned Mar about Radcliffe's temper, and he must have hoped that Marischal did not reveal to the young nobleman his increasing hostility to Mar. On 6 November Mar received a letter from James Malone, who had

---

[120] See ahead, Chapter Eleven.
[121] *HMC: Stuart*, VII, 187, 236, 413, 592.
[122] *Ibid.*, III, 505.
[123] J. Swift, *Correspondence*, II, 278.
[124] O. Morales, *Ireland and the Spanish Empire*, 174.
[125] *HMV: Stuart*, VII, 443.

served with the Radcliffe brothers until the defeat at Preston: "I lost my dear Lord Derwentwater, who was a father to me."[126] He had served as lieutenant in Derwentwater's troop, and was sentenced to transportation and sold as a slave, but friends bought his reprieve. Having "quitted my slavery," he now offered his services to Mar.

However, Mar was in an increasingly vulnerable position, as Bolingbroke and Atterbury publicly expressed their hostile attitude toward him. The Scot became the target of rumors in England, which especially worried his Irish Masonic brother, Lord Orrery. Throughout 1717 Mar had corresponded with Orrery, encouraging him to stay optimistic, despite the factions among the English Jacobites: "People in a ditch, who do not understand how to get out, must perish. You have more understanding as well as spirit, than to be one of those." [127] Orrery also sent Mar some of his poems, which Mar deemed "very pretty" and promised to send them on to James III. However, Orrery continued to press Mar to get James to change his religion, for his Catholicism worried many of his potential supporters. By December 1718 Anne Oglethorpe felt the need to reassure Mar: "Lord Orrery bids me tell you…that it is absolutely necessary for the King's affairs you should not be disgusted by foolish clamours that are below your minding, for justice is done to your merit, where they are."[128] For Mar, the loyalty and security achieved through the "Mason Word" must have become increasingly important for the Jacobites, especially as the Hanoverian Masons mounted their own counter-movement.

*

* *

Parallel with the Whig moves within the developing "speculative" system of Freemasonry was the effort to suppress Wren's influence on the operative craftsmen. The point man for the Hanoverians was the Whig politician William Benson, who had earlier engaged in a pamphlet war with Gyllenborg in which Benson accused Anglican high churchmen and Non-jurors of collaborating with the Swedes and Jacobites.[129] Benson himself was of Swedish descent and had visited Stockholm, and he gleaned his information from Carl XII's enemies. His portrayal of the "tyrannical absolutist king" and his "Satanical Lutheran Priests" earned him the lasting hatred of royalist Swedes, but it made him "a favourite of the Germans" at the English court.[130] In *The Examiner* (1711), Swift had characterized Benson's anti-Swedish pamphlet as "a libel."[131] An amateur architect with some talent but little experience, Benson collaborated in Colen Campbell's intrigues against Gibbs. In March Benson and Campbell launched a campaign to take over the Office of Works, in which Whig appointees would replace Wren's Master Masons and

---

[126] *Ibid.*, V, 80.

[127] *Ibid.*, V, 122-23, 205.

[128] *Ibid.*, VII, 648.

[129] See William Benson, *A Letter to Sir J[acob] B[anks], by Birth a Swede, but Naturaliz'd, and now a M[iniste]r of the Present Parliament, concerning the late Minehead Doctrine, which was Established by a certain Free Parliament in Sweden to the utter Enslaving of that Kingdom* (London, 1711); *A Second Letter to Sir Jacob Banks* (London, 1711). Gyllenborg was reportedly the author of *Reason and Gospel against Matter of Fact: or, Reflections upon two Letters to Sir Jacob Banks* (London, 1711).

[130] H. Colvin, *History*, V, 57.

[131] J. Swift, *Correspondence*, I, 335-36 n.5.

veteran craftsmen. By April Benson had persuaded the Building Commission to remove Wren, who went into bitter retirement at Hampton Court.[132]

Benson's position was to be temporary, lasting only until he received more lucrative posts from the government. However, in August he managed to replace Nicholas Hawksmoor, secretary to the board and Wren's protégé, with his brother Benjamin Benson ("lately come from a merchant in Holland"), and in September he appointed Campbell as deputy surveyor.[133] Determined to place his own partisans in all positions, Benson laid formal charges of corruption and mismanagement against Wren, Vanbrugh, and all the master craftsmen in the Office of Works. An indignant Wren replied with an eloquent appeal, which was seconded by the craftsmen, many of whom refused to work for Benson. Gibbs found employment with Alexander Pope, who shared his Jacobite sympathies and who asked him to design a new house at Twickenham. On 12 December 1718 Pope wrote wryly that he has been degraded "thro' meer dulness" from poet to translator to architect: "You know Martial's censure: *Praeconem facito, vel Architectum.*"[134] In Martial's epigram, he advises a father on how to educate his son: "If he makes verses, give him no encouragement to be a poet; if he wishes to study lucrative arts, make him learn to play on the guitar or flute. If he seems to be of a dull disposition, make him an auctioneer or an architect."[135] His sardonic quotation was more a dig at Benson than the embattled Gibbs.

Benson and his Whig allies were soon overjoyed to learn of the death of Carl XII in November 1718, while on campaign in Norway.[136] Having won his position of Surveyor as a reward for his anti-Swedish propaganda, Benson must have looked upon the current suppression of Jacobite influence in operative Masonry as providentially linked with the death of the Swedish king, who was perceived as James III's most powerful supporter. The Jacobites had provided Carl with the *Revolution*, the ship in which he was to take the Stuart king to Britain.[137] Edward Harley especially lamented the loss of the Swedish king, which "plunged the Jacobites into deepest gloom."[138] Many of the king's partisans, subsequently known as the "Carolinians," believed that he was murdered by a Hanoverian agent. Over the next months, Sweden was polarized by a disputed succession, while Hanoverians and Jacobites struggled for influence on the new regime.[139]

For Scottish Jacobites especially, Carl XII's death was a bitter blow, because they expected him to sail from Norway to Scotland in a major assault upon George I. The Masonic poet Meston, who knew that his patron James Keith had planned to join the Swedish king, contrasted the heroic Carl to the debased Elector of Hanover:

[132] H. Colvin, *Biographical Dictionary*, 122-23, 210, 1086. For a detailed discussion of Wren's problems and the Whig-Jacobite rivalries within operative Masonry at this time, see M. Schuchard, "Jacobite vs. Hanoverian Claims," 121-86.

[133] H. Colvin, *History*, V, 59-64.

[134] A. Pope, *Correspondence*, II, 4, 23.

[135] The Epigrams of Martial, Book 5.56. I am grateful to Robert Shaw-Smith for the translation.

[136] E. Cruickshanks, *Charles XII*, iv.

[137] E. Cruickshanks and H. Erskine-Hill, *Atterbury Plot*, 151.

[138] E. Cruickshanks, *Charles XII*, iv.

[139] For the unsavory behind-the-scenes intrigues concerning the Swedish queen's abdication and the subsequent disputed succession, see M. Schuchard, *Emanuel Swedenborg*, 136-39, 145-46. For suspicions about the "murder" of Carl XII, see Michael Roberts, "The Dubious Hand: the History of a Controversy," in his *From Oxenstierna to Charles XII* (Cambridge: Cambridge UP, 1991), 144-203.

...this brave PRINCE, in whose exalted Mind
The martial valour of GUSTAVUS shin'd,
Augmented with his own superior Fame,
Was Heir to his great Father's Crown and Name;
No petty Duke, brought o'er from foreign Lands,
To sway a Sceptre with unwieldy Hands;
No tributary Prince, no menial Thing;
The SWEDE was born an independent King,
And ne'er was Prince more fit than he to reign.
HE for his subjects good the Sceptre sway'd,
And him they lov'd, and out of Love obey'd.
From servile Fear unwilling Homage springs,
The Hearts of Subjects are the Strength of Kings.[140]

Meston concluded with an emotional appeal to all true Britons to lament the death of Carl XII with "bleeding heart," for "he would have brought thy Prince from his Exile,/ Wip'd off thy Tears, and made thee gladly smile."

One Anglo-Irishman who shared Meston's grief was Swift. On 6 January 1719 he wrote Charles Ford, who had earlier been privy to Swedish-Jacobite planning:

I am personally concerned for the death of the King of Sweden, because I intended to have begged my Bread at his Court, whenever our good Friends in Power thought fit to put me and my Brethren under the necessity of begging. Besides I intended him an honour and a compliment, which I never yet thought a crowned head worth, I mean dedicating a book to him. Pray let me know how I can write to the Count of Gyllenborg.[141]

Was Swift's reference to his "Brethren" a Masonic allusion? In March 1719 the new Swedish government executed Baron Görtz, but his colleague Georg Eckleff managed to flee Sweden. According to an eighteenth-century Swedish tradition, Eckleff took with him Masonic documents that his son would later bring back to Sweden and utilize in a revived *Écossais* system.[142]

---

[140] Published later in W. Meston, *Old Mother Grim's Tale*, 156-57.

[141] J. Swift, *Correspondence*, II, 289.

[142] E. Schröderheim, *Anteckningar*, 81; A. Önnerfors, "From Jacobite Support," 205.

CHAPTER SEVEN

SCOTTISH-SWEDISH MASONIC TRADITIONS
AND ENGLISH INNOVATIONS
(1719-1722)

You are hereby authorized, when you are in Scotland, to institute
A new Military Order of Knighthood, consisting of [blank space]
Persons, to be call'd the Restoration Order...

James III to the Earl of Mar (16 May 1722).

To the Grand Master... and Brethren...

Those of you who are not far illuminated, who stand in the Outward
Place... the Brotherhood begins to revive again in this our Isle... Ye Are
Living Stones, built up a Spiritual House, who believe and rely on the chief
Lapis Angularis, which the refractory and disobedient Builders disallowed...
We are exiled Children from our country, when shall we return?

Brother Eugenius Philalethes, *Long Livers* (1722).

In the early stages of the emerging power struggle in Stockholm, the Jacobite Masons were not aware of the threat to their sympathizers in Sweden. In January 1719 the Duke of Holstein argued for the continuation of Carl XII's Norwegian campaign, and the new queen, Ulrica Eleonora, ordered Gyllenborg to continue his negotiations with the Jacobites and Russians at Åland.[1] In February Lord George Murray wrote to Mar about the situation in Sweden:

> Another speculation is that, upon the meeting of the States of Sweden, the said estates, finding there was likely to be a contest between the Prince of Hesse and the Duke of Holstein about the succession to the Crown, had with their consent sent an ambassador to the Chevalier de St. George to invite him to reign over them till his own people should call him home, after

---

[1] Charles Petrie, *The Jacobite Movement: The First Phase, 1688-1736* (London, 1948-50), 20; C. Nordmann, *Crise du Nord*, 201.

which he would take care of the interests of Sweden and do justice to the contending parties.[2]

Also in February, as Cardinal Alberoni in Spain planned the Pretender's naval expedition to England, Ormonde advised him to seek Swedish support: "Would it not be well to try to get the Swedish government to join our enterprise?... If it is true that the Baron de Goertz was arrested, he will be sure to inform the successor of the late king's intentions."[3]

Though their "speculation" would prove to be wishful thinking, the Jacobites continued to solicit support from the new Swedish queen, and in late April 1719 George I learned about her correspondence with Mar. George thus ordered Baron John Carteret, who was preparing to leave as British envoy to Sweden, that he must "use your utmost endeavours to defeat and destroy anything" that supports the Jacobites.[4] In June Alberoni's small Spanish-Jacobite force was defeated in Scotland, and the British government learned that two Swedish ships were included in the expedition. Thus, when Carteret arrived in July, he implemented his orders to freely bribe the Swedish senators, "whose pressing poverty made the inducement irresistible." He was determined to bind Sweden into a Hanoverian alliance. Under intense military and financial pressure, Sweden ceded Verden and Bremen to Hanover for the price of one million crowns. But the Swedes would soon learn that George I had no intention of honoring his promises to protect them from foreign attacks.

Britain now backed the effort of Prince Fredrik of Hesse to become co-ruler with his wife, Queen Ulrika Eleonora, who was then "pressed to resign the crown to her husband, and she was threatened that he would desert her and retire" if she did not.[5] Fredrik I and his chief minister, Count Arvid Horn, tried to suppress and disenfranchise the supporters of Carl XII's nephew and favorite, Duke Carl Fredrik of Holstein, whose supporters (the Holstein party) would play the role of Jacobites in Swedish politics over the next three decades. As we shall see, the rivalries within Swedish politics would later emerge in Swedish Freemasonry, with significant ramifications in Britain. Similar rivalries were soon acted out among the operative craftsmen in London, and they were even given literary expression.

For the earlier participants in the Swedish-Jacobite plot, the replacement of Christopher Wren by William Benson as Surveyor of Works became even more galling, for it portended a dismantling of their Masonic networks. Sir Jacob Bancks, the Swedish-born M.P. who had been arrested with Gyllenborg, now published *A Letter from Sir J. B—ks to W.B.—, Esq.: S.O. By Birth an Englishman: but Unnaturaliz'd and turn'd Swede, Architect, Hydrographer, and Gardiner... concerning a late Contract to the utter Undoing of the Board of Works* (1719), a blistering satire on Benson's architectural incompetence and corruption that read like a manifesto of Stuart Freemasonry. Lamenting the death of Carl XII, Bancks reminded readers of Benson's scurrilous propaganda against Sweden and accused him of "restless Bustling and undermining."[6] Revealing his inside knowledge of the refusal of Benjamin Jackson, Wren's longtime Master Mason, to submit to Benson's corrupt

[2] H. Tayler, *Jacobite Court*, 148-49.
[3] M.K. Dickson, *The Jacobite Attempt of 1719*. Scottish History Society, 19 (Edinburgh, 1895), 52-53.
[4] J. Chance, *British Diplomatic Instructions, 1689-1789. Volume I: Sweden, I, 1689-1727* (London, 1922), 106.
[5] National Archives; SP 95/23, f.21. Henceforth cited as NA.
[6] Jacob Banks [Bancks], *A Letter from Sir. J.B – ks to W.B---n* (London, 1719), 6-13.

practices, Benson described the "secret history" of "Vitruvius Nothus" and "Benjius Brothers," the Master Mason and Master Carpenter employed by "Count Suderkoping," a Swedish version of George I.

Suderkoping had originally employed "Proper Artificers and Workmen," especially a Chief Mason, a Chief Carpenter, and a Layer of Bricks. However, "Cnute Torkel" (Benson), "who carries Masons and Carpenters, and most other Trades in his Belly," tried to entice them into a scheme to defraud the king and Office of Works. In collaboration with Colen Campbell, Benson had declared the House of Lords unsafe and insisted that it be demolished and a new one rebuilt. The alarmed lords cancelled the king's visit and removed to another edifice. Despite Benson-Torkel's offers of "Hush Money" to the master craftsmen, they refused to go along and exposed Benson's fraud to the government. The Master Mason Jackson-Vitruvius reported that the only damage in the Lords was caused by Benson's unnecessary roof-props. In his satire, Bancks pointed out the sad contrast with earlier days, when "Swercher Wrecken" (Wren), the "Old Inspector of Labourers," performed his office efficiently: "Old Swercher did not understand the Play of Booty; and there was peace among the Count's workmen in those days."

Bancks's attack placed Desaguliers and Chandos in an uncomfortable position. Many of Desaguliers's old admirers now viewed him as an abject puppet of Chandos's mercenary schemes, with the Jacobite librarian Thomas Hearne noting in March 1719 that he was mocked as "Chimney Desaguliers," who publishes projecting trifles and spends his time on "mechanical things."[7] Now patron and employee were tainted by Benson's corruption, for Chandos had become entangled in the surveyor's profiteering when he illegally bought Portland stone and Scotland Yard property from Benson. The over-reaching architect had made a crucial mistake by laying claim to the quarries on the Isle of Portland, which since Charles II's time had been crown properties. When he high-handedly fired more royal workers, even Lord Sunderland, the Whig treasurer, was irritated by Benson's insubordination and warned that his actions were "highly resented."[8] By spring Benson himself admitted that "the Office of His Majesty's Works is in very great Disorder," that "some of the best workmen are absented from the King's business, others refuse to goe on with it, and some are unable for want of the money that is due to them from His Majesty." On 16 April, responding to the Lords' complaints, George I reluctantly suspended Benson from his surveyorship. But the stubborn architect refused to leave and resorted to legal disputes and hard bargaining to retain his pecuniary advantages.

Thus, on 30 April 1719, when George I ("for no apparent reason") named Baron Chandos as the 1st Duke of Chandos, the "quintessential trimmer" realized that he must distance himself from Benson.[9] For Desaguliers, who was in charge of various water-supply schemes sponsored by Chandos, Benson seemed an impertinent rival, whose claims to expertise in "hydrography" were fraudulent (and a target of Bancks's Jacobite satire). Since 1716, when Benson gained the favor of George I by presenting a design for "a curious waterwork" for the Hanoverian palace at Herrenhausen, Desaguliers kept a critical eye on his activities. When the waterwork was finally built in 1718 by Joseph

---

[7] T. Hearne, *Remarks*, VI, 321.
[8] H. Colvin, *History*, V, 59-64, 446.
[9] M. Baker and C. Baker, *Brydges*, xv, 140, 373.

Andrews, an English mechanic, Desaguliers gave full credit to the artisan and denigrated Benson's contribution.[10] This rivalry between two Whig "hydrographers" inspired Swift's later satire (in *Gulliver's Travels*) on a club of "Projectors" who accuse each other of constructing faulty water supply machines.[11]

By June 1719 Benson was in such bad odor with Whigs as well as Tories that the protest of Wren's former Master Mason won popular as well as political support. Thus, in June, when Desaguliers became Grand Master of the Grand Lodge, he determined to improve the Masons' political as well as technological image. On 17 July Benson finally relinquished his post, illegally taking with him a number of plans and designs for palace building, stone quarrying, and water supply. Benson's critics were nonplussed when the king, still grateful for his anti-Swedish propaganda, rewarded him with Irish funds and appointed his ejected deputy Campbell as architect to the Prince of Wales. A disgusted Hawksmoor remarked that Benson "got more in one year (for confusing the King's Works) than Sr. Chris. Wren did in 40 years for his honest endeavours."[12]

However, Wren's partisans were still out of pocket, for Benson was replaced by Thomas Hewett, a strong Whig, who despised religious and royalist architecture. He became known as "One who neither feared God, nor regarded man," and his "atheism" was part of his Whiggery.[13] Proclaiming that "no great public work can succeed under the worst of tyrannies, I mean Church Tyranny for life," he represented the polar opposite to Stuart ideals of architecture. Hewett was apparently close to Desaguliers, and his wife later became godmother to one of the scientist's sons.[14] Indications of disaffection among operative Masons soon appeared in the press, such as the following in the *Daily Courant* (5 September 1719): "The Master Masons in and about London, are desired to meet some of their Brethren, and a Gentleman who hath a proposal to make them which will be beneficial to the Trade."[15]

Evidently sensing widespread Masonic opposition to Benson and Hewett, Desaguliers and his Whig colleagues determined to move the Grand Lodge firmly and publicly into the Hanoverian camp. They thus revived "the old regular and peculiar Toasts or Healths of the Freemasons," in order to make the annual Feast a demonstration of loyalty to the government.[16] In September Chandos improved his own loyalist image by removing Gibbs from his architectural post at Canons – a move probably advised by Desaguliers. As Grand Master, Desaguliers worked with his deputy Sayer to persuade the brethren to "bring to the Grand Lodge any old Writings and Records" to show "the usages of antient Times."[17]

Their effort was possibly provoked by Richard Rawlinson's publication of Ashmole's *Natural History of Berkshire* (1719), which included his biography of Ashmole. Since 1716 the Jacobite Rawlinson had secretly served as a bishop among the Non-jurors, and he

---

[10] L. Stewart, *Rise*, 239.

[11] Jonathan Swift, *Gulliver's Travels*, ed. Paul Turner (Oxford, 1998), 169-70. In part III, written in 1724-25, Swift says the water project occurred "seven Years ago," or in 1717-18.

[12] H. Colvin, *Biographical Dictionary*, 122.

[13] H. Colvin, *History*, V, 71-73.

[14] R. Berman, *Foundations*, 48.

[15] Quoted in Alfred Robbins, "The Earliest Years of English Organized Freemasonry," *AQC*, 22 (1909), 68.

[16] Vieler, "As It Was," 88.

[17] J. Anderson, *Constitutions (1738)*, 110.

now linked his party with royalist Stuart Freemasonry.[18] He reported Ashmole's initiation and added a sneer at contemporary oath-breakers and false brethren:

> On October 16 he [Ashmole] was elected a Brother of the Company of Free Masons...a Favour esteemed so singular by the members, that Kings themselves have not disdain'd to enter themselves into this Society... They have several Lodges in different Counties for their Reception... The manner of their Adoption, or Admission, is very formal and solemn, and with the Administration of an Oath of Secrecy, which has had better Fate than all other Oaths, and has been ever most religiously observed, nor has the World been yet able, by the inadvertency, surprise, or folly of any of its Members to dive into this Mystery, or make the least discovery.[19]

The defeat on 10 June of the Jacobite-Spanish fleet in route to Scotland (an expedition organized by the Masons Ormonde, Dillon, and the Keith brothers) influenced Rawlinson's decision to leave for France and Holland, where he made surreptitious Jacobite contacts while visiting universities. When he learned of the impending birth of a Stuart heir, he travelled to Rome in order to be present at the delivery (Charles Edward Stuart would be born in December 1720).

Meanwhile, in summer 1719, in the midst of the serious Jacobite threat, Delafaye was most disturbed on 13 June to receive from an informer a bundle of "libellous pamphlets, including an anonymous tract, *Vox Populi, Vox Dei* (1719), which had been circulating for over a month. The author called upon "Old Whigs" to become Jacobites, if they were true to their original principles.[20] Characterizing George I as an "Impostor on the Nation," he argued that "no written Law justified the sending KING JAMES the Second and his Royal Family a Begging; NO, it was the Voice of the People, the Law of Necessity and Nature."[21] Since the majority of the people now support James III, the Whig supporters of the Williamite Revolution should implement their earlier beliefs and now join the Jacobites. In the final incendiary lines, he proclaimed.

> I hope some Patriot will rouze up the People to shake off this *Arbitrary Government*,
> And Animate them with the Saying of the *Noble Roman* who defended the Capitol...
> – HOW LONG WILL YOU BE IGNORANT OF YOUR STRENGTH COUNT YOUR NUMBERS...
> Sure you ought to fight with more Resolution for Liberty than your Oppressors do for Dominion.
> COUNT YOUR NUMBERS.[22]

---

[18] For his secret ordination by Jeremy Collier, see William Macray, *Annals of the Bodleian Library at Oxford*, 2nd rev. ed. (Oxford, 1890), 231-32.

[19] Elias Ashmole, *The Antiquities of Berkshire* (London, 1719), biography of Ashmole by Richard Rawlinson, vi-vii.

[20] R.J. Goulden, "*VOX POPULI, VOX DEI*: Charles Delafaye's Paper Chase," *The Book Collector*, 28 (1979), 368-90.

[21] *Vox Populi, Vox Dei* [London, 1719], 1-7.

[22] *Ibid.*, 7.

When he received the pamphlet, Delafaye already was on high alert for seditious publications, because he had received orders in late 1718 to implement "fierce prosecution" of the perpetrators.[23] As an undersecretary of state, he was in charge of investigations of seditious tendencies in the publishing and printing trades. He immediately began arresting and interrogating printers and sellers, while urging their colleagues to come forward and betray them for a financial reward. On 6 July he arrested John Matthews, an eighteen year-old printer, who had already been in trouble for printing anti-government libels. On 6 November the audacious young printer was hanged – "the first and last execution of a printer for seditious and treasonable material." Many of the printers would never forgive their fellows who informed on Matthews, crying after one of them in the streets, "there he goes who sold Johnny Matthews' blood."[24] For the next three years, Delafaye kept up "his extraordinary paper chase" in a desperate attempt to identify the author of *Vox Populi*, and he did not hesitate to call upon Hanoverian Masons in official positions to assist him in his investigations. Though he ultimately failed to find the author, his surveillance drove Jacobite writers and printers even further underground, as they continued their campaign against the Hanoverian government. For Jacobite Masons such as Richard Rawlinson, who early acquired a rare copy of *Vox Populi*, it became necessary to be extremely cautious in their writings and correspondence.

Meanwhile in Sweden, with the execution and banishment respectively of the alleged Masonic organizers Görtz and Eckleff, George I's agents aided the attempted suppression of the Carolinian party in Sweden. In defiance of these political realities, Swift paid daring tribute to Carl XII and his faithful ambassador Gyllenborg, whose cause he still admired. On 2 November 1719, when he dedicated his proposed *History of England* to Gyllenborg, Swift was unusually explicit in his political sympathies:

> It is now ten years since I first entertained the design of writing a history of *England*... My intention was to inscribe it to the king your late master, for whose great virtues I had ever the highest veneration,... when I looked round on all the princes of *Europe*, I could think of none who might deserve that distinction from me, besides the king your master; (for I can say nothing of his present *Brittanick* majesty, to whose person and character I am an utter stranger, and like to continue so... I publish them [papers] now...to have an opportunity of declaring the ...sincere regard and friendship I bear to yourself; for I must bring to your mind how proud I was to distinguish you among all the foreign ministers, with whom I had the honour to be acquainted... We all loved you, as possessed of every quality that could adorn an *English* gentleman, and esteemed you as a faithful subject of your prince, and an able negotiator; neither shall any reverse of fortune have power to lessen you either in my friendship or esteem... my affection towards persons hath not been at all diminished by the frown of Power upon them. Those whom you and I once thought great and good men, continue still so in my eyes and my heart...[25]

---

[23] R. Goulden, "*VOX POPULI*," 371.

[24] *Ibid.*, 381, 388.

[25] J. Swift, *Prose*, V, 11-12.

This was fulsome praise indeed from the embittered Swift, who five years later would again try to contact Gyllenborg, "if he has not lost his head."[26]

In 1720, in the wake of the failed Spanish-Jacobite expedition, there was increasing worry among Jacobite Masons about government penetration of their networks. According to Anderson, in that year, "at some private lodges, several very valuable manuscripts...were too hastily burnt by some scrupulous Brothers, that those Papers might not fall into strange Hands."[27] Though Anderson does not make clear whose "strange hands" were a threat, his enemies soon made him a target of abuse. In *Anti-Priapeia: or, an Answer to Priapeia Presbyterianian, or the Presbyterian Peezle* (1720), the anonymous author responded to a Tory song or pamphlet (now lost) that charged Anderson with contracting venereal disease.[28] Claiming to possess an intercepted letter from the Presbyterian General Assembly of Scotland to its "Missionary in London," the narrator "paraphrased" its contents in a mercilessly bawdy poem. Accusing Anderson of promiscuity, hypocrisy, and stupidity ("for thy want of Circumspection,/ In not preventing the Detection"), he suggested the Presbytery's serious concern, linking it with "*Newgate Birds*, at their last Exit:/ When to the People they Harangue it,/ A little Space before they're hanged."[29] Anderson's arrogant role as "The *Patriarch of Picadilly*" was undermined by his sexual carelessness (he "rashly ventur'd out at random/ In unknown Depths without a C-nd-m" [condom]. His silly attempt to clear himself by claiming he caught the Clap by his "Engagement with a *Post*" was scorned in oblique sexual-building imagery. His "*Tool*," "*Augre*," and "doughty *Driller*" was used to "proselyte a *Post* or *Pillar*" and to "proselyte a *Stone* or *Stock.*"

Were these allusions to his Whiggish role in Masonry? If so, other lines hinted at the rumors about Masonic homosexuality, for the Tories sing that Presbyterians "convert more with our *Tails* than *Tongues*," with the "unnatural Fire,/ That has been kindled in *Kintire*,/ Whose *Synagogue's* become a *Sodom.*" Unless Anderson changes his ways, the Tories will make a new Ballad, with charges of Witchcraft and Black Necromancy. His Tory critic seemed aware of the historical link between Presbyterianism and Scottish Freemasonry, which had produced political turmoil:

> He knows our Mysteries and Maxims,
> Our secret Cabala, and Axioms,
> Our Politicks, and Artifices,
> Our deep Intrigues, and hidden Vices...[30]

Despite its obscure language, the *Anti-Priapeia* was obviously part of a Tory effort to blacken Anderson's reputation, just as he hoped to play a significant role in the emerging Hanoverian Freemasonry.

Perhaps inspired by the attack on the priapic Anderson, "A Gentleman," published another satire on the alleged homosexual practices of the Whiggish Freemasons. In the anonymous *Love's Last Shift: or, the Mason Disappointed. To which is annex'd, a Song on the Free*

---

[26] J. Swift, *Correspondence*, II, 557.
[27] J. Anderson, *Constitutions (1738)*, 88, 11.
[28] D. Stevenson, "Anderson," 204, 236 n.15.
[29] Anon., *Anti-Priapeia* (London and Edinburgh, 1720), 1-24.
[30] *Ibid.*, 14-16.

Masons (1720), the author drew on the popular play, *Love's Last Shift; or, the Fool in Fashion*, by Colley Cibber, now a well-known loyalist Mason. Originally printed in 1696, the play was frequently republished, and the 1720 edition provided a jumping off point for Cibber's critic. A typical Restoration comedy, it featured Loveless, a "debauched rake," and Amanda, his virtuous wife, who is abandoned by her husband, whose "sole Religion" is "drinking,/ Whoring, roaring, without the pain of thinking," rather than embracing "a dull chaste Wife;/ Such out of fashion stuff!"[31] Cibber got in a brief jab at Stuart sympathizers, when he portrayed a belching rogue, who gets drunk "as a *Jacobite* upon a day of ill news." The satirist took the lines about "my raking brother-hood" to draw a parallel with the Freemasons, for Cibber had described one "raking brother" as a hypocritical sinner who protests "against Fornication, when the Rogue was himself just crawling out of a flux" (symptom of venereal disease).

In the satire's Preface, "A Gentleman" refers to "the Folly and Baseness of a scandalous Book lately come out; which informs the World, that the ancient, and Laudable Society of Free-Masons, are no better than S-------s" [Sodomites].[32] He vows to "clear the Reputation of so Honourable a Society, from the brutish Aspersions of so infamous a Grub-street Scribler." Then with pornographic glee, he describes a Masonic brother who determines to lay siege to the beautiful Lesbia, who refuses to have intercourse with him, because of her venereal disease: "Fires fierce as Aetna, or the Flames of Hell,/ Rage in that Grott where Raptures use to dwell,/ Nor can the Streams that through the Cavern pass,/ Rebate the Conflagration of Myne A---s." He must not let his erect Pego, "Swoln big with Passion, and with anger red," come near her "scorching Womb," but he "condescended to accept from her fair Hands, the Satisfaction of a Manual Operation." After a stream of salacious details, the satire concluded with "A Song, on the Free-Masons":

> Ye Fools!... lend your Attention to my merry Song,
> And you shall a *Free Mason* be, e're it be long,
> *Which no body can deny, etc.*
> We make for five Guineas, the Price is but small,
> And then Lords and Dukes, you your Brothers may call,
> Have Gloves, a white Apron, get Drunk, and that's all.
> ....
> So welcome dear Brother to our Company.[33]

The Tory critic seemed aware of the current effort to recruit Whig aristocrats as well as fee-paying lesser mortals to the Grand Lodge. Cibber, in turn, deleted or euphemized some of his more vulgar expressions in his revised edition of the play in 1721.[34]

While the pamphlet and newspaper war raged, the Grand Master Desaguliers and his officers in the Grand Lodge determined to consolidate its power. In June 1720 George Payne was re-elected Grand Master, and he cooperated with Desaguliers in making the appointment of his successor the prerogative of the presiding Grand Master in advance of the Grand Festival (a measure to avoid debate or challenges by political opponents).

---

31 Colley Cibber, *Love's Last Shift; or, the Fool in Fashion* (London [The Hague], 1720), 13-15.

32 Anon., *Love's Last Shift: or, the Mason Disappointed* (London,1720), Preface, 1-4.

33 *Ibid.* 31-32.

34 Maureen Sullivan, ed., *Colley Cibber: Three Sentimental Comedies* (New Haven: Yale UP, 1973), 298099.

However, Grand Lodge did not yet control Freemasonry, and other lodges were maintained or organized with different political and philosophical interests.

*

* *

Since 1714, when John Toland returned to England from Holland, he had joined the Whig polemicists against Non-juring churchmen and Jacobites. His fascination with secret societies had been reinforced by his association with "The Knights of Jubilation" in Holland, and he now shared his radical, libertine ideas with John Woodward, an increasingly erratic Mason, and with other free-thinkers.[35] In 1720 Toland published anonymously two unusual descriptions of radical secret societies. In *Tetradymus* (1720), he argued for a "Mosaic theocracy," while he lampooned students of the Jewish Cabala: "No other Creature, but an enthusiastical Christian Father, or his more credulous modern disciple, instructed by a fabulous Jewish Cabalist, could be capable of conceiving... such absurdities" as Menasseh ben Israel's explanations of miracles.[36]

The volume included an essay with the title, "Clidophorus, or the Exoteric and Esoteric Philosophy; that is, of the External and Internal Doctrine of the Ancients; the One open and public, according to popular prejudices and the Religions established by Law; the other private and secret, wherein, to the few capable and discrete was taught the real *Truth* stript of all Disguises." After tracing the secret religion of nature through the ancient Egyptians, Pythagoras, Iamblichus, Apuleius, Proclus, and Porphyry, Toland concluded: "I have more than once hinted, that the *External and Internal Doctrine*, are as much now in use as ever; though the distinction is not so openly and professedly approved as among the Ancients."

Toland followed this with a privately printed work in Latin, *Pantheisticon* (1720), which he published at the request of Woodward's circle and distributed only to a few friends.[37] In this credo of a radical pantheist, he described a secret "Socratic Society," which challenged Rosicrucians and Cabalists on their own clandestine ground.[38] Toland's "Brethren" steadfastly assert liberty of thought and action, and they are sworn enemies of all tyrants, "whether despotick Monarcks, or domineering Nobles, or factious Mob-leaders." At their ceremonial banquets, no restraint is laid upon the tongue. He boasted that many Brethren can be found in Paris, Venice, Amsterdam, London, and "the very Court of Rome." He boasted that "the Pantheists can deservedly be stiled the *Mysts* and *Hierophants* of Nature."[39] Evidently aware of the current struggles within Freemasonry, Toland distanced his society from the craft fraternity. He stressed that "the Companies of Artificers," that were "often restrained and prohibited by the Laws," are "vastly different from ours."[40] The editor of the 1751 English translation added a marginal note for this passage: "It may be that the Author alludes here to the Company of Freemasons." Though

---

[35] M. Jacob, *Radical*, 127, 133, 157-62; R. Sullivan, *Toland*, 34-35.

[36] [John Toland], *Tetradymus* (London, 1720), 61, 94, 131-32.

[37] *Some Memoirs of the Life and Writings of John Toland* (London, 1722), lxxviii.

[38] Quoted from the first English translation, *Pantheisticon; or the Form of Celebrating the Socratic Society* (London, 1751), 55-58.

[39] *Ibid.*, 95.

[40] *Ibid.*, 11.

Margaret Jacob interprets this comment to demonstrate a mid-century perception that Toland's society was Masonic, Toland's own statement seems a defensive measure against any linkage of his "Socratic Society" with Freemasonry, for he recalled Henry VI's punitive restrictions on the craft organization and then claimed, "That misfortune never or seldom befel learned fraternities," such as the Greek *Symposia*.[41]

It was perhaps Toland's distancing himself from the Masonic fraternity that provoked his hostile annotations on Martin Martin's descriptions of Scottish second sight, still popularly associated with traditional Stuart Masonry. In September 1720 Toland scrupulously wrote his critical comments in the margins of the 1716 revised edition of Martin's *Description of the Western Islands*, and in October he had his Irish patron Robert Molesworth, 1st Viscount Molesworth, add his annotations to the volume. Though historians have seemed puzzled by their obsessive determination to expose the credulity, charlatanry, and deviousness of clairvoyant Scots, their concern was perhaps rooted in their awareness of the role of second sight in "ancient" Jacobite Masonry and Gaelic poetry. Molesworth, a staunch anti-clerical Whig, was "a key member of the so-called 'new junta for architecture,' which brought Palladian innovation to both England and Ireland."[42] He was aware of – and possibly participated in – the rival political factions within Freemasonry. Thus, it was perhaps through Masonic connections that the Duke of Wharton assumed that he and Swift could solicit the support of Molesworth in October for their defense of the Dublin printer Edward Waters, who was arrested for publishing Swift's anonymous pamphlet, *A Proposal for the Universal Use of Irish Manufacture* (1720).[43] Waters would later print a defense of Freemasonry in answer to the anti-Masonic Papal Bull in 1738.[44]

In Toland's annotations to *Description of the Western Islands*, he revealed his earlier familiarity with operative Masonry in Scotland, as he scorned Martin's un-Masonic technical terms in descriptions of Scottish stone construction. When Martin described a castle with a wall "two Stories high," Toland commented, "What means a wall two stories high? No Mason, that ever I could find, us'd any such language, or understood it."[45] He further objected to Martin's terminology, "Stories in a building is Sense, but in a wall I never heard," and even worse was "a square Stone-wall, about two Story high." But his and Molesworth's greatest scorn was aimed at Martin's detailed accounts of second sight. Toland dismissed the Jacobite Dr. Garden as "a divine altogether as credulous as Dr. Martin," and he promised to "speak particularly on this subject," but he did not accomplish this before his death in March 1722.[46] In the annotations, his Whig friend Molesworth was even angrier at the accounts of Second Sight, dismissing them as "a meer invention of Popish priests" and arguing that "Ye pretenders to such storyes ought immediately to be taken up & whipped at a carts tayle for cheates & impostors in a well

---

[41] M. Jacob, *Living the Enlightenment*, 61.

[42] "Robert Molesworth,1st Viscount Moleworth," *ODNB*; J.A.I. Champion, "Enlightened Erudition and the Politics of Reading in John Toland's Circle," *The Historical Journal*, 49 (2006), 111-41.

[43] J. Swift, *Correspondence*,II, 334-35, 346.

[44] R. Péter, *British Freemasonry*, IV, 5-10.

[45] Martin Martin, *A Description of the Western Islands of Scotland*, 2nd rev. ed. (London, 1716), 222, 227, 247; the annotated volume is in the British Library: shelfmark c.45.c.1.

[46] *Ibid.*, 300, 312.

policed government."[47] His last remark reveals the political motivation behind his and Toland's hostility.

Despite Toland's apparent rejection of the Masonic craft fraternity in the *Pantheisticon*, his hints at Druidic mysteries ironically provoked the curiosity of some Masonic readers. On 6 January 1721 the "Druidist" antiquarian William Stukeley--close friend of Newton and Desaguliers--recorded his desire to join Freemasonry, "suspecting it to be the remains of the mysterys of the antients, when with difficulty a number sufficient was to be found in all London."[48] At this time, the fraternity was polarized by anger in the wake of the South Sea scandal, and at least one lodge took action over one of its implicated brothers.[49] The bursting of the "bubble," which caused widespread financial losses, provided the Jacobites with new opportunities to attack the Whig ministry and its partisans – including those in the Grand Lodge.

After Stukeley's initial disappointment at his "modern" Masonic experience, he was encouraged by the meeting he attended on 24 June, when the Grand Master Payne "produc'd an old MS. of the Constitutions which he got in the West of England, 500 years old," and Desaguliers "pronounc'd an oration." He was further pleased by the increased social prominence brought to the fraternity by the election of John, 2nd Duke of Montagu, to the Grand Mastership, and he noted that Lord Herbert, Lord Stanhope, and Sir Andrew Fountaine accompanied Montagu and his deputy Dr. John Beale. Henry Herbert was the son of Thomas Herbert, 8th Earl of Pembroke, the recipient of the Masonic letter allegedly written by John Locke in 1696, and in 1733 he became the 9th Earl of Pembroke. James Anderson claimed that the family had long Masonic ties, and Henry was possibly introduced to military Masonry while serving with the Coldstream Guards. He now indulged his virtuoso interest in building, eventually earning the epithet, "the architect earl."[50] Phillip, Second Earl of Stanhope, had recently inherited the title from his father James, who had died of an apoplectic fit reportedly provoked by the Duke of Wharton's violent harangue against him in parliament. Stanhope was probably recruited by Desaguliers, with whom he shared a passion and talent for mathematics.[51] Sir Andrew Fountaine was a Whig virtuoso and art collector who maintained eclectic friendships – including Leibniz and Toland at Hanover in 1701 and Swift in Ireland in 1702 and London in 1710-12. He evidently shared their interest in Rosicrucian traditions and secret fraternities, and he conferred with Swift about the illustrations to *A Tale of a Tub*.[52] According to the *Post Boy*, the prestigious new members helped the growth in membership of the Grand Lodge to reach "two to three hundred" brothers.[53]

However, one "ancient" member who attended Montagu's installation – Christopher Wren *fils* – did not share Stukeley's enthusiasm for these new developments.[54] For Jacobite Masons the election of Montagu, a resolute Whig, was an abomination, for they would never forgive his insults to their martyrs. Five years earlier, on the night of

---

47 *Ibid.*, 313, 335.

48 Robert F. Gould, "Masonic Celebrities: William Stukeley, M.D.," *AQC*, 6 (1893), 127-38.

49 On the Hampstead lodge, A. Robbins, "Earliest Years," 68.

50 "Henry Herbert, Ninth Earl of Pembroke," *ODNB*.

51 "Phillip, second Earl of Stanhope," *ODNB*.

52 "Sir Andrew Fountaine," *ODNB*; J. Swift, *Correspondence*, I, 283-84.

53 Knoop, Jones, Hamer, *EMP*, 3.

54 "A Note on the Place of Sir Chr. Wren's Death and His Funeral in 1723," *Wren Society*, 18 (1941), 181n.1.

Derwentwater's execution, Montagu gave a masquerade ball for George I and three hundred of his "confederates in bad taste and overaffected loyalty."[55] Probably in reaction to Montagu's election, the crypto-Jacobite Duke of Wharton "was admitted into the Society of Free-Masons; the Ceremonies being perform'd at the King's Arm Tavern in St. Paul's Church-Yard" (in late July).[56] The lodge had twenty-nine members, with at least nine being "of the gentry or of superior rank," who were all "Tories or even almost Jacobites."[57] The flamboyant Wharton then drew public attention to his initiation by wearing his white leather Masonic apron while he walked home from the ceremony.[58] (As noted earlier, Wharton was possibly initiated by Mar at Avignon in 1716 and then developed Masonic support in Dublin and London).

The Hanoverians did not delay in mounting a counter-move to Wharton's initiatives. The duke had apparently tried to gain influence among loyalist Masons, and he acquired Desaguliers's *Physico-Mechanical Lectures* (1717), probably in an attempt to understand the thinking of his rival.[59] Supported by the Whig Grand Master, Desaguliers determined to expand the membership of the Grand Lodge and to bolster its claims to antiquity and authenticity. Thus, on 24 August 1721, while Desaguliers was visiting Edinburgh to consult on a water-supply project, he attended the ancient lodge of Mary's Chapel. Among the long-time members (since 1681) was William Mylne, architect, whose ancestors had served as Master Masons to the Stuart kings for generations. It was perhaps from him that Desaguliers heard that James VI and I, Charles I, and Charles II were all "Mason Kings," for those claims would soon be approved to appear in Anderson's history.[60]

He also met the poet Allan Ramsay, a convivial Jacobite, who was reportedly a Mason.[61] His son, the portrait painter Allan Ramsay, would later join the Jacobite lodge in Rome. Among the hundreds of subscribers to the senior Ramsay's recently published *Poems* (Edinburgh, 1721), printed by his fellow Jacobite Thomas Ruddiman, were many present or future Freemasons – such as Pope, Arbuthnot, Savage, Steele, James Arbuckle, and Andrew Michael Ramsay (identified as secretary to Fenelon). On 25 August Allan Ramsay gave Desaguliers a copy of *Poems*, which included his manuscript offering, "To Dr. John Theophilus Desaguliers on Presenting him with my Book."

> Is then, the famous Desagulier's son
> To learn the dialect of our Caledon?
> Wiel, Doctor, since you think it worth your while
> Sometimes on my laigh landart [Lowland] shrine to smile,
> Accept the haleware [whole work],and, when ye gae hame,

---

[55] J. Doran, *London*, 163.

[56] *Appleby's Original Weekly Journal* (5 August 1721);in A. Robbins, "Earliest Years," 68.

[57] Aubrey Newman, "Politics and Freemasonry in the Eighteenth Century," *AQC*, 104 (1991), 36.

[58] D. Stevenson, "Anderson," 211.

[59] *Bibliothecarum...ducis de Wharton...de Dr. Robert South* (London, sold at Thomas Osborne's Shop, 27 November 1733), #4871. South died in 1716, so it can be assumed that books published and purchased after that year were owned by Wharton.

[60] Edward Macbeen, "The Master Masons to the Crown of Scotland," *AQC*, 7 (1894), 106.

[61] Joe Rock, "A New Allan Ramsay [Junior] Self Portrait," https:sites.google.com/site/researchpages2/home/a-new-allan-ramsay-self-portrait, p.6.

Stand by your poet, and haud [hold] up his fame.[62]

A staunch opponent of the Union, Ramsay determined to write much of his poetry in vernacular Scots, in order to preserve the nation's heritage and literary traditions. But he also tried to reconcile Whigs and Tories in the egalitarian, bibulous meetings of the Easy Club, and he possibly viewed Masonry as serving a similar purpose. Thus, he praised the London Mason Desaguliers as a scientist: "O worthy wight [man], whase genius great refines,/ And puts in practice Euclid's unko [extraordinary] lines," which are "Sae beneficial to the common weal." He urged the London visitor to face down "surly bigots," while he himself will make Arthur's Seat his Parnassus, in the face of critics.

In the volume he presented to Desaguliers, Ramsay revealed his own, previous interest in the water project, praising "The spacious leaden Conduits," which first flow'd up the Castle-hill."[63] But he then gently mocked the pretensions of Isaac Newton and the Royal Society in London, in the context of praising the Scottish plaid and tartan:

> The Plaid itself gives Pleasure to the Sight,
> To see how all its Setts imbibe the Light;
> Forming some Way, which even to me lies hid,
> White, Black, Blew, Yellow, Purple, Green and Red,
> Let *Newton's* Royal Club through Prisms stare,
> To view Celestial Dyes with curious Care,
> I'll please my Self, nor shall my Sight ask Aid
> Of Cristal Gimcracks to survey the Plaid.[64]

Ramsay hoped to see the day when great architecture would again thrive in Edinburgh: "New stately Structures on new Streets shall rise,/ And new-built Churches tow'ring to the Skies."[65]

In January 1715 the Easy Club had addressed an anti-Union manifesto to George I, but it was evidently never sent.[66] In April Ramsay wrote a poem on the club, in which he urged greater toleration for differing points of view – a theme that would later emerge in Masonic meetings:

> From different Ways of Thinking comes Debate,
> This we despise, and That we over-rate,
> Just as the Fancy takes, we love or hate.
> Hence *Whig* and *Tory* live in endless Jarr,
> And most of Families in Civil War;
> Hence 'mongst the easiest Men beneath the Skies,
> Even in their easy Dome, Debates arise...[67]

But, as his note explains, the Easy Club was established "from the general Antipathy we all seem'd to have at the ill Humour and Contradictions which arise from Trifles,

---

[62] D. Stevenson, *First Freemasons*, 210.

[63] Allan Ramsay, *Poems* (Edinburgh, 1721), 380.

[64] *Ibid.*, 50.

[65] *Ibid.*, 91.

[66] "Allan Ramsay, poet," *ODNB*.

[67] A. Ramsay, *Poems*, 311.

especially those which constitute *Whig* and *Tory*, without having the grand Reason for it." The outbreak of the Jacobite rebellion five months later in September revealed just how difficult it would become to maintain this political neutrality, and the Easy Club was dissolved.

Though Desaguliers would not have had time to read much of Ramsay's volume on 25 August, he may have recognized the Jacobite faction in Scottish Masonry. On the same evening and later on the 28th, he returned to Mary's Chapel Lodge with a group of his acquaintances, who were all public officials and loyalist Whigs.[68] Trevor Stewart notes that "most, if not all of them, had shown themselves devoted to the Hanoverian cause," and "it is very likely that these men owed their entry into the lodge membership entirely to Desaguliers's recommendation."[69] Over the next years, Desaguliers was probably unaware of Ramsay's increasing Jacobite commitments, for he subscribed to the 1728 edition of his poems.

David Stevenson points out that it was just one month after Desaguliers's introduction to Scottish Freemasonry that the Grand Lodge in London commissioned James Anderson to provide revised constitutions for English Freemasonry: "It is very tempting to conclude that the two events are linked, that Desaguliers hastened back to London and persuaded the Grand Lodge that Scottish expertise was needed."[70] Grand Master Montagu then ordered Anderson to "peruse, correct, and digest, into a new and better Method, the History, Charges, and Regulations, of the ancient Fraternity."[71] Anderson "accordingly examined several Copies from Italy and Scotland, and sundry Parts of England," and "other ancient Records of Masons," in order to write a new history and constitution for the Grand Lodge. However, as Stevenson observes, Anderson's real agenda was the creation of "a mythology for the English," which would "fill past centuries with eminent English freemasons and thus create a much more acceptable and respectable past than a Scottish dominated masonic one could ever have been."[72]

Montagu and Desaguliers then sought royal patronage, as reported by *Appleby's* (23 December 1721): "We hear that a Lodge is shortly to be held in St. Paul's Church-Yard, for admitting his Royal Highness the Prince [of Wales] into the ancient Society of Accepted Masons."[73] Despite Prince George's employment of the Whig architect Campbell at this time, his bitter quarrels with his father must have placed obstacles in the way of his initiation, which did not take place. On 17 February the *London Journal* reported opposition to the claims of the Grand Lodge: "We hear that a Treatise is likely soon to appear Abroad, wherein the Author undertakes to prove, that the Gypsies are a Society of much longer standing than that of the Free-Masons."[74] The author possibly planned to draw upon the Scottish tradition that the Masonic family of St. Clair protected the gypsies and that the late George Faa, member of the royal family of the gypsy tribe, had

---

[68] Trevor Stewart, "'It is of a Service to the Public to shew where the Error is': A Re-examination of the Visit to Edinburgh by the Reverend Dr. John Theophilus Desaguliers," *AQC*, 119 (2006), 202, 211, 216-17, 223.

[69] *Ibid.*, 224.

[70] D. Stevenson, "James Anderson," 207.

[71] J. Anderson, *Constitutions (1723)*, 73.

[72] D. Stevenson, *First Freemasons*, 149.

[73] A. Robbins, "Earliest Years," 69.

[74] *Ibid.*, 69.

served as Master of a Scottish lodge.[75] With increasing press coverage and public curiosity about Freemasonry, it became important to get Anderson's "official" Grand Lodge history published. Thus, in early 1722 Montagu sent copies of the manuscript to various lodge officers for evaluation and criticism.

In the meantime, on 1 March 1722 a dissident Mason dedicated to "the Grand Master, Masters, Wardens and Brethren...of Great Britain and Ireland" an exhortation on what *should* be the aims and ideals of the fraternity. Aimed at Jacobite Masons with Rosicrucian interests, "Brother Eugenius Philalethes, F.R.S." issued a peculiar challenge to the emerging Hanoverian version of Masonry. Expropriating Thomas Vaughan's pseudonym, Robert Samber – a hack writer who had attended a Jesuit college in Rome – celebrated the Cabalistic and Rosicrucian traditions of "illuminated" Masonry. He was possibly spurred to produce this by Richard Rawlinson, who collected his papers and later donated them to the Bodleian. It was attached, as a fifty page introduction, to Samber's translation of Harcouet de Longeville's *Long Livers* (1715) and addressed to his Masonic brethren. Samber claimed that the Brotherhood had existed, in "an uninterrupted Tradition," since the time of the ancient Jews and primitive Christians and that some higher-degree Masons now possess its secrets:

> those of you who are not far illuminated, who stand in the outward Place, and are not worthy to look behind the Veil...will discover under these Shadows somewhat truly great and noble, and worthy the serious Attention of a Genius the most elevated and sublime... it hath pleased the Almighty...to send out his Light, and his Truth, and his vivifying Spirit, whereby the Brotherhood begins to revive again in this our Isle, and Princes seek to be of this sacred Society...
>
> Ye are living Stones, built up a spiritual Home, who believe and rely on the chief *Lapis Angularis*, which the refractory and disobedient Builders disallowed, you are called from Darkness to Light, you are chosen Generation, a royal Priesthood...
>
> This makes you, my dearest Brethren, fit Companions for the greatest Kings.[76]

Samber maintained a sincere though gushing tone in the first section, which culminated in his paean to the Grand Architect:

> But alas! my Brethren, what are we and our little Globe below, to that stupendous Celestial Masonry above! where the Almighty Architect has stretch'd out the Heavens as a Curtain, which he has richly embroidered with Stars, and with his immortal Compasses, as from a *Punctum*, circumscribed the mighty ALL....

With an oblique allusion to John Dee's *Monas Hieroglyphica*, which was featured in early Rosicrucian treatises, he compared the Brotherhood to the exiled Jews – a comparison resonant with Jacobite longing:

---

[75] M. Schuchard, *Restoring the Temple*, 236; R. Gould, *History*, III, 63.

[76] Quoted from reprint in Knoop, Jones, Hamer, *EMP*, 43-45.

O thou Eternal One! thou Immortal UNITE! thou Incomprehensible MO-
NAS! …Send out thy Light and thy Truth, that they may lead and bring us
to thy holy Hill and thy Tabernacle… We are exiled Children from our country, when shall we return? Here thou hast placed us as Novices and Proba-
tioners, when shall we be professed amongst those blessed Fraternities
above, and be made free Denizons of the celestial Jerusalem, not built with
Hands, and be re-instated in our Innocence?[77]

Samber apologized for his "digression," brought on by "my Meditation on this divine
Science," and he gave behavioral advice to the brethren. First, "avoid as much as possible
the Court, where a Man must indispensably be obliged to wear the Mask." Second, "avoid
Politicks and Religion." Third, "avoid all Companies where ridiculing of Religion is
thought witty." The great danger now lies in the number of false brethren who create
political schisms within Masonry:

> defend us from these Liars, these Brother-haters, these Sowers of Discord
> amongst Brethren…and if any such have crept in amongst us, thro' the Neg-
> ligence or Ignorance of the Watchmen upon the Walls, hard is our Lot in-
> deed…for most dangerous are a Man's enemies, when they are of his own
> House…. let their Names be erased for ever out the Book *M*, and be buried
> in eternal Oblivion…
>
> And now, my Brethren, you of the highest Class, permit me a few words,
> since you are but few; and these Words I shall speak to you in Riddles, be-
> cause to you it is given to know those Mysteries which are hidden from the
> Unworthy.[78]

The Book *M* was mentioned several times in the *Fama Fraternitatis* and other Rosicrucian
texts, and Samber concluded with an alchemical vision culminating in the "Mystical Union" and "admirable Commerce" of "our Mighty King and Queen." He further implied
that the Mason Word was an alchemical-Cabalistic secret – "the Square of wise Men"
and "the transparent Pyramid." The ultimate goal of Samber's translation was Rosicrucian regeneration, and the work concludes with recipes for the universal medicine culled
from Basil Valentine and Jan Baptiste Van Helmont.

Undercutting the apparent seriousness of Samber's peroration, however, was his long
burlesque history of the Jewish and Christian churches, which mocked their violence,
cruelty, and superstition in terms strikingly similar to Toland and the Knights of Jubilation. Years earlier, Samber had been disturbed by reading Toland's *Christianity Not Mysterious*, and he would later erratically echo his satirical and anti-clerical writings, while also
publishing religious works.[79] In fact, Samber seemed a strange amalgam of Toland's early
Rosicrucianism and later pantheism. Like Toland's knights, Samber's brotherhood professes the Religion of Nature but is willing to include universalist trinitarian doctrine. The
only Jewish era that was worthy was the Commonwealth, which was governed by the
priests, the nobility, and popular magistrates, without a king. Even Moses recognized that
the Jews, "a leprous, itchy Race," would benefit from exile (forty years in the desert):

---

[77] *Ibid.*, 47-48.
[78] *Ibid.*, 65.
[79] J.M. Blom, "The Life and Works of Robert Samber (1682-1745?)," *English Studies*, 70 (1989), 511.

> he knew that a Company of raw undisciplined People, trained up for the
> most part in keeping of Sheep, would not be a Match for those warlike Peo-
> ple, whose Cities and Kingdoms they were to take from them; besides they
> might be in Danger of falling into Idolatry, to which by their long Residence
> in *Egypt*, and their being acquainted with their Flesh-pots, Ragous, or made
> Dishes... he had learned they were too much addicted.[80]

With these bantering remarks, Samber conjured up the bedraggled Judaized Scots,
who passed their time in exile eating French *ragoûts* and converting to Catholicism. Samber thus made the Masonic peroration seem a *jeu d'esprit* – perhaps as a protective measure
against Whig decipherers and false brethren. Among the Rawlinson papers is Samber's
manuscript "Treatise on the Apparition of Spirits," which shows how such appearances
often happen before the death of great persons or signify changes in government.[81]
Whether he was serious or satirical in his Masonic introduction to *Long Livers*, he certainly
revealed that Desaguliers and the Grand Lodge would have to contend with Rosicrucian
dissidents in older lodges.

*
* *

The Grand Lodge Masons soon received encouragement from the reconstituted
Commission on Building, when the new Surveyor Hewett and commission member
Richard Willis, Bishop of Salisbury, persuaded George I to pay tribute to the operative
Masons working on the parish church of St. Martin's in the Fields. During Benson's
tenure as Surveyor, he was forced to admit that many workmen were "absented from the
king's business, others refuse to go on with it, and some are unable for want of the money
that is due them from His Majesty."[82] Recognizing this disaffection among the operative
Masons, Hewett and Willis (both strong Whigs) determined to undermine Wren's influence on the craftsmen and gain their loyalty to the government. Thus, on 19 March 1722
they organized a public Masonic ceremony that demonstrated Hanoverian loyalty. According to Anderson,

> The Bishop of Salisbury went in an orderly Procession, duly attended, and
> having levell'd the first Stone, gave it two or three knocks with a Mallet, upon
> which the Trumpets sounded, and a vast Multitude made loud acclamations
> of Joy; when his Lordship laid upon the Stone a Purse of 100 Guineas, as a
> Present from his Majesty for the use of the Craftsmen.[83]

Anderson tried to enhance the king's role by claiming that the ceremony took place

> by the Order, Countenance, and Encouragement of his present Majesty King
> George, who was also graciously pleased to lay the first Stone in the Foun-
> dation of his Parish Church of St. Martin *in Campis*, on the South-East Cor-
> ner (by his Majesty's Proxy for the time, the present Bishop of Salisbury)

---

[80] *EMP* 52-53.
[81] Bodleian: Rawlinson MSS. Poet.133.ff.162-96.
[82] H. Colvin, *History*, V, 63.
[83] J. Anderson, *Constitutions (1723)*, 44-45.

which is now rebuilding, strong, large, and beautiful, at the Cost of the Parishioners.

He also tried to enhance Hewett's position with the king, noting that a commemorative plaque recorded that Willis had been "Assisted (At his Majesty's Command) By Sir Thomas Hewet Knight Of His Majesty's Royal Buildings Principal Surveyor." However, Anderson vaguely conceded that the king's gift was too little too late, and that the church was being built "at the Cost of the Parishioners." Lack of government funding forced Hewett to cancel Gibbs's design for the church (drawn in 1720), which aimed at antique monumentality, and to substitute a scaled-down model in the interest of economy. A frustrated Hewett would soon complain to Vanbrugh that in the reign of George I architecture was "not a trade...for any body to recommend themselves by at Court."[84]

In the same month (March 1722) when surveyor and bishop tried to win over the disaffected operatives, Montagu's fourteen-man committee approved the manuscript of Anderson's *Constitutions*, and negotiations were undertaken to print it. Though Anderson included selected Scottish material (white-washed of recent political realities), his volume presented an Anglo-centric, Whig version of Masonic history. This official distancing of the Grand Lodge from the Jacobites was timely, for government intelligence agents were gathering information on an ambitious new plot, orchestrated by Bishop Atterbury. On 30 April the Whig minister Lord Sunderland, suddenly died, and papers found upon him suggested his complicity in the Jacobite plot.[85] He had earlier collaborated with Delafaye in reading Swift's intercepted letters, but he subsequently hedged his political bets by cozying up to the Jacobites.[86] On the same day, 30 April, the French foreign minister, Abbé Dubois, who secretly received English bribes, persuaded the Regent Orléans to alert George I's government about the planned coup.

In May the Whig prime minister, Robert Walpole, ordered the arrest of the Reverend George Kelly, a Non-juring Irish clergyman, who acted as amanuensis for Atterbury in the latter's correspondence with Mar and James III (which was transmitted from Calais by Francia). In July his brother Captain Dennis Kelly was also arrested, which prompted Swift to write sardonically to his Jacobite friend Robert Cope:

> It is said that Kelly the parson is admitted to Kelly the squire, and that they are cooking up a discovery between them, for the manufacture of the hempen manufacture. It is reckoned that the best trade in London this winter will be that of an evidence.... It is a wonderful thing to see the Tories provoking his present majesty, whose clemency, mercy, and forgiving temper, have been so signal, so extraordinary, so more than humane..., which appears also from a most ingenious pamphlet just come over, relating to the wicked Bishop of Rochester.[87]

---

[84] H. Colvin, *History*, V, 73.

[85] Eveline Cruickshanks, "Lord North, Christopher Layer and the Atterbury Plot," in Eveline. Cruickshanks and Jeremy Black, eds., *The Jacobite Challenge* (Edinburgh, 1988). 99.

[86] J. Swift, *Correspondence*, II, 122.

[87] *Ibid.*, II, 432.

Swift's ironic tone was a necessary protective measure, for he knew that his letters were being intercepted. However, his reference to the "hempen manufacture" (the hangman's noose) was still risky.

Walpole's punitive actions must have aroused alarm among Jacobite operative Masons, for Atterbury was currently supervising various architectural projects, especially renovation work on Westminster Abbey, where he had a loyal following of craftsmen. On 6 April he wrote Pope about the great stone vault that the Masons were building for "me and mine" in the Abbey.[88] As Dean of Westminster, Atterbury had consulted Wren--who retained his position as surveyor of the Abbey – about the renovation, which included construction of "the noble north window."[89] In 1722 he commissioned Lord Burlington to design a new dormitory for Westminster School. Atterbury had received from Wren a plan to site the dormitory in the chapter garden, which provoked a hostile response from the bishop's clerical enemies. Some of their unease was provoked by Atterbury's choice of architect.

Burlington publicly played the role of a Whig, but the Stuart Papers suggest his private Jacobitism.[90] In 1716-17 he employed Gibbs and then visited Mar, with whom he maintained architectural communications. According to Jane Clark, Burlington now included Masonic symbolism in the unusual three-storied, Solomonic temple he built at Chiswick.[91] On 5 February 1719 Mar wrote James III to recommend Burlington's uncle, Henry Boyle:

> When yr Majestie comes to be restored, alow me to informe you of one who in my humble opinion is one of the most proper to serve you as of yr principal ministers. It is Mr Henry Boyle, unckle to the present Earle of Burlingtone and who is now call'd Ld Carleton... he is well worth gaining to yr interest wch I believe will be no difficult work.[92]

Jane Clark suggests that Mar received this information from Burlington, whom he met in France during the earl's secretive travels in 1717-18, and that it indicated both Boyles' private Jacobite sympathies.

On 20 August 1721 Robert "Philalethes" Samber dedicated to Burlington his edition of *Roma Illustrata* (1722), in appreciation for the earl's hospitality at Chiswick and encouragement of Samber's publication of engravings of Roman sculpture and edifices.[93] When Atterbury gave Burlington his first commission in 1722, the earl had just returned from Italy, where he secretly contacted the Stuart court while studying Palladio's architecture.[94] Anderson, who believed that Burlington was a loyalist Whig, implied that he was a Freemason who "bids fair to be the best Architect of Britain, (if he is not so already)."[95]

While Atterbury and Burlington struggled to implement their projects in London, Mar continued his architectural career in Paris, where he designed future constructions for

---

[88] F. Williams, *Memoirs and Correspondence of Francis Atterbury, D.D., Bishop of Rochester* (London, 1869), I, 373.
[89] *Ibid.*, I, 427.
[90] H. Colvin, *Biographical Dictionary*, 147-48; J. Clark, "Lord Burlington," 257, 268, 273.
[91] *Ibid.*, 298.
[92] *Ibid.*, 272.
[93] [Robert Samber], *Roma Illustrata* (London, 1722).
[94] H. Erskine-Hill, "'Avowed Friend and Patron,'", 17-29.
[95] J. Anderson, *Constititutions (1723)*, 48.9

Edinburgh – including a three-story arched bridge, imposing stone houses for the gentry, and repairs to Holyrood Palace and the citadel at Leith.[96] Probably alerted to the Hanoverian penetration of Freemasonry in Edinburgh as well as London, Mar sent to James a proposal for a new "Royall Military Order of Knighthood to be erected and confer'd by His Majesty or the Commander in Chife from him," with the purpose of "Restoring Scotland to its ancient Military Spirit."[97] On 6 May 1722 James wrote Mar, "you are hereby authorised, when you are in Scotland, to institute a New Military Order of Knighthood...to be called the Restoration Order." He also sent Mar a warrant to erect "a Royall Academie," which would train Scottish youth in military and technological arts (in the spirit of earlier Stuart-proposed, Masonic-styled academies).[98] Mar was assisted in these proposals by his protégé, Andrew Michael Ramsay, who would later infuse chivalric traditions into *Écossais* Masonry.

Meanwhile in England, Mar's allies realized they were losing control of Freemasonry, which had earlier provided them with secure networks of communication. On 26 May Nathaniel Mist's *Weekly Journal*, organ of the Jacobite party, reported a move four days earlier by sympathizers among operative Masons to regain influence from the Hanoverian Whigs:

> As the first Stone of the Foundation of the church of St. Martin's in the Fields, under Ground was sometime ago laid on the Behalf, and by the Command of his Majesty, by the Bishop of Salisbury, Lord Almoner; so the first Stone of the Foundation at the same Corner above Ground, being 12 Foot above the other, was laid with a great deal of Ceremony by the Society of Free-Masons, who on that Occasion were very generous to the Workmen.[99]

As noted earlier, the royal benefaction in 1721 was considered paltry, and the parishioners had to finance the construction of the scaled-down church.

David Stevenson stresses the boldness of the Masons' second ceremony, in which they presumed to have a role in the dedication of public buildings:

> The fact that a foundation stone had been laid two months previously by the bishop of Salisbury, in the name of the king, made the matter potentially even more controversial. Laying a new stone, without permission, could be seen as an insult not only to the bishop and his church but to the king himself. That the new stone lay exactly over the original one, but twelve feet above it, might seem to suggest symbolically that the first stone was superseded. The masons had trumped the king.[100]

Thus, in Mist's report of 1722, the "Society of Free-Masons" represented the Jacobite-Tory faction. Anderson would later write a falsified account of the incident, reducing the two ceremonies to one and omitting the Masons' new foundation stone.

---

[96] S. Erskine, "Mar's Legacies," 197-203.

[97] *Ibid.*, 206-15.

[98] For James VI and I's desire to establish a Baconian "Royal Academy" in 1621 and 1624, see Schuchard, *Restoring the Temple*, 384-85.

[99] A. Robbins, "Earliest Years," 69.

[100] D. Stevenson, "James Anderson," 210.

In that same year appeared a pamphlet with the bold title, *By a Member of the Antient Society of Free-Masons, a Vindication of the Reverend Dr. Snape and Dr. Sherlock; Against Mr. Meadowcourt's Attempts to Calumniate and Defame those Gentlemen* (1722). Thomas Sherlock and Andrew Snape were both friends of Swift, and they shared his political and ecclesiastic concerns.[101] The anonymous Masonic-Jacobite author defended the two high Anglicans, who led the Tory faction at Cambridge, after they had been condemned by the Whig bishop Benjamin Hoadly, leader of the low-church party of the Hanoverian church.[102] Richard Meadowcourt, a friend of Newton, also attacked them and led a campaign against the Tory faculty and students at Oxford for their alleged "treasonous attitudes."[103] He now defended Hoadly by portraying his Anglican opponents as Judaized Jacobites. But the "Antient" Mason was not intimidated by the Whigs' attacks.

These Jacobite moves roused government suspicions about the whole fraternity, and Meadowcourt's friend Charles Delafaye was evidently instructed by Walpole to use his Masonic affiliation to keep his eyes on suspicious brethren.[104] Ric Berman suggests that Delafaye shared Hanoverian Masonic bonds with Meadowcourt.[105] The increasing government surveillance prompted a party of Whig Masons to call upon the secretary of state, Charles, 2nd Viscount Townshend, to profess their Hanoverian loyalty. On 16 June 1722 the *London Journal* reported:

> A few days ago, a select Body of the Society of Free Masons waited on…Townshend… to signify to his Lordship, that being obliged by their Constitutions, to hold a General Meeting now at Midsummer, according to annual custom, they hoped the Administration would take no Umbrage at that Convocation, as they were all zealously affected to his Majesty's Person and Government. His Lordship received this Intimation in a very affable Manner; telling them, he believ'd they need not be apprehensive of any Molestation from the Government, so long as they went on doing nothing more dangerous than the ancient Secrets of the Society; which must be of a very harmless Nature, because, as much as Mankind love Mischief, no Body ever betray'd them.

Berman notes that Townshend had a "close relationship" with Freemasonry, for his eldest son Charles and his under-secretary Delafaye were both members.[106] He suggests that the press account was designed to "reflect the Craft's Whiggist credentials to the public." Alfred Robbins observes that "a threat obviously underlay this sneer from the brother-in-law of Sir Robert Walpole, a Prime Minister then in the first flush of his long possession of power."[107]

Over the next two weeks, rival newspapers hinted at the emerging power struggle for control of the Grand Lodge, with one faction claiming to be "the most Ancient Branch

---

[101] J. Swift, *Correspondence*, I, 532; II, 420.

[102] Anon., *By a Member of the Antient Society of Freemasons, A Vindication of the Reverend Dr. Snape and Dr.Sherlock* (London, 1722), 1-2.

[103] "Richard Meadowcourt," ODNB.

[104] M. Jacob, *Radical*, 133-36; P. Fritz, *English Ministers*, 117.

[105] R. Berman, *Espionage*, 53n.66.

[106] R. Berman, *Foundations*, 142,

[107] A. Robbins, "Earliest Years," 71.

of this Society in Town" and warning about "false Brothers."[108] Having recruited their supporters to the annual feast, the Jacobites pulled off a surprising coup and defeated the Whig candidate for Grand Master. According to the later, official Whig history, the Duke of Wharton, "lately made a Brother, tho' not the Master of a Lodge, being ambitious of the Chair, got a Number of Others to meet him at Stationers-hall on 24 June 1722," when he was irregularly proclaimed Grand Master. "But," the report proceeds, "his Grace appointed no Deputy, nor was the Lodge opened and closed in due Form. Therefore the noble Brothers and all those that would not countenance Irregularities, disown'd Wharton's Authority."[109] However, the contemporary newspapers in London and Dublin reported Wharton's election as unanimous and gave no hint of irregularities.

Wharton's coup was distressing to the Hanoverian Masons, for he had recently earned the king's wrath by his blistering campaign against the corruption of Lord Stanhope, a Grand Lodge member, and the Whig ministry. Even worse, he had served as president of the Hell Fire Club, where forty aristocratic men and women staged rituals that satirized the deficiencies of the contemporary latitudinarian church. Suspecting a Jacobite element in the club's "subversive" mockeries, George I banned all "profligate clubs" on 28 April 1721. From his surveillance over Atterbury's network, Walpole learned that in May 1722 Wharton was listed as a member of "Burford's Club," a Tory fraternity that supported the Atterbury plot.[110] The masterminds of the plot assigned Wharton the task of recruiting and organizing the Thames bargemen, who were to seize the powder magazines at Greenwich. However, when Walpole published the names on the list, he omitted Wharton, possibly because "the Government hoped he had not entirely burned his boats," or because Walpole hoped to learn from his Masonic spies about Wharton's intentions within the Grand Lodge. Wharton continued to act the Whig in public, while he tried to organize a Jacobite take-over of the "modern" lodges.

Robert Samber was present when Wharton was installed as Grand Master on 24 June 1722, and he later described the barely suppressed political tensions at the banquet:

> whether, after a very disedifying manner their demolishing huge walls of Venison Pasty, be building up a spiritual house, I leave the brother *Eugenius Philalethes* to determine. However, to do them Justice, I must own, there was no mention made of politics or religion, so well do they seem to follow the advice of that Author [Philalethes in *Long Livers*]. And when the music began to play, *Let the King enjoy his own again*, they were immediately reprimanded by a person of great gravity and science…
>
> …the following healths were begun by a great man, the King, the Prince and Princess, and the Royal Family; the Church by law established; Prosperity to old *England* under the present Administration; and Love, Liberty, and Science, which were unanimously pledged in full Bumpers, attended with loud huzzas![111]

---

108 *Daily Post* (20 June 1722); *Daily Journal* (20-21 June).
109 A. Robbins, "Earliest Years," 76-77.
110 E. Cruickshanks, "Lord North," 96, 99, 105n.28.
111 Boniface Oenophilius [Henri Albert de Sallengre], *Ebrietatis Encomimum: or the Praise of Drunkenness*, [introd. and trans. Robert Samber] (London, 1723; facs. rpt. New York, 1910), 82.

That the musicians assumed the members wanted a Jacobite song is suggestive. It was evidently Desaguliers, a person of "science," who reprimanded their seditious performance, and a Whig noble (Montagu?) who commanded the pledging of loyalist toasts. However, none of the newspapers reported this incident, which remained an in-house controversy.

In the midst of these political rivalries within Masonry, a booklet appeared in London which greatly lifted the Jacobites' spirits. Charles Wogan, the old friend of Pope, published *Female Fortitude, Exemplify'd in an Impartial Narrative of the Seizure, Escape, and Marriage of the Princess Clementina Sobieski, As it was particularly set down by Mr. Charles Wogan (formerly one of the Preston prisoners),who was a chief Manager in the Whole Affair* (1722). Since his escape from Newgate, Wogan had served in the French regiment of his cousin Colonel Arthur Dillon, collaborated with Mar, and accompanied Ormonde on a journey to Russia to forge an alliance between Czar Peter and Carl XII, a plan sabotaged by the death of the Swedish king.[112] He then worked with Dillon and Ormonde on a mission to find a bride for James III. He finally selected the Polish princess Maria Clementina Sobieski and prepared for her to join James. However, after the English ministry pressured the Hapsburg government to arrest her at Innsbruck, Wogan and three Irish kinsmen from Dillon's regiment carried out a dangerous but romantic plan to rescue her in April 1719. In gratitude for their successful mission, James ennobled Wogan and the Pope made him a senator of Rome.

While in Italy, Wogan befriended Lord Pitsligo, who came to Rome in 1719, where he struggled to defend his first cousin Mar from James Murray's vendetta against him.[113] Pitsligo participated in "the discontented Club," whose members tried to warn James about Murray's arrogant and mendacious behavior. Unfortunately for Pitsligo, his frank letter to James irritated the king, who wrote Mar that it was a Club of "Grumbletonians." Given Mar's usage of Masonry to ensure loyalty and discretion, it is tempting to view the Club as a version of Pitsligo's lodge and religious community in Scotland. Charles Wogan helped Pitsligo regain James's good opinion, and the grateful Scot left Italy with Nicholas Wogan to travel to Paris. Before returning to Scotland in June 1720, Pitsligo spent time with General Dillon, a staunch supporter of Mar, and almost certainly with his former protégé Andrew Michael Ramsay, a confidant of Mar. Thus, he may have informed them of his views on spiritual initiation and regeneration that he had earlier practiced with his fellow "Mystics of the Northeast." Similar themes and rituals would later emerge in *Écossais* Freemasonry. Once back in Scotland, Pitsligo corresponded with Ramsay, who sent him books by their mutually admired Quietists and Pietists.[114] Unfortunately, some of their correspondence was destroyed; in November 1720 Pitsligo referred to the necessary burning of certain of his letters.[115]

Meanwhile, in 1722 Wogan's published narrative became a popular success, and he painted Clementina as the ideal bride for the legitimate Stuart king. His work soon

---

[112] Eamonn O'Ciardha, "Sir Charles Wogan," in J.I. McGuire and James Quinn,eds, *Dictionary of Irish Biography* (Cambridge, 2009), online ed.

[113] H. Tayler, *Jacobite Court*, 70, 74, 82, 95, 148, 151, 181.

[114] D. Henderson, *Mystics*, 168.

[115] For Pitsligo's political thoughts in the 1720s, see Murray Pittock, "Jacobitism in the North East: the Pitsligo Papers in Aberdeen University Library," in J. Carter and J. Pittock, *Aberdeen*, 69-76.

provoked a furious counter-blast from an anonymous Hanoverian loyalist. In *Remarks upon a Jacobite Pamphlet, privately handed about, entitled Female Fortitude* (1722), the author scorned Wogan as "a Preston rebel" who indulges in typical "Irish Rhetorick" and exaggeration. He rejected the importance of the account, which has "been handed about as a mighty Valuable choice Piece…as if dangerous to be seen," while "the Jacobites made a great stir with it."[116] He claimed that Dillon, an Irish officer in French service, was the chief manager of the affair, which Wogan stressed in order to impress his English readers with the great support that the Pretender had among French notables and especially the French army. The whole marriage of a "Mock-King to a Mock-Princess" was a farce, and the new bride will soon realize that her husband's status depends upon "a restless faction" who will "precipitate him into a new Enterprise" and "put him upon building new Castles in the Air," which will only result in misery and blood. This anti-Jacobite attack on Wogan must have pleased Daniel Defoe, who acquired a copy of the pamphlet.[117]

In his narrative, Wogan described his fellow adventurers as "my little troop of Knights-errant," a chivalric self-image he earlier assumed with the Knights of Walton-le-Dale. His crusader image was enhanced when he moved to Spain, where he became the companion of the Masons Ormonde, the Keith brothers, and eventually Wharton.[118] Over the next months, they did indeed try to build "Castles in the Air." Wogan and his brother Nicholas worked with Ormonde on planning an invasion of England, the project subsequently known as the Atterbury Plot. Nicholas Wogan and his cousin, also named Nicholas, worked with a group of Jacobite pirates based on the island of Madagascar, made up of sailors ejected from the British navy. In summer 1718 Captains Jaspar Morgan and John Monnery travelled from Madagascar to Sweden and got the support of Carl XII, who promised them protection when they attacked British shipping. After the Swedish king's death, Count Gyllenborg continued to collaborate with the Jacobite pirates, who acquired several Swedish ships, which would be commanded by Nicholas Wogan and his namesake cousin.[119]

Operating on behalf of Atterbury, Rev. George Kelly coordinated the far-flung, multi-national negotiations. When news of the project reached Ireland, hundreds of Irish recruits travelled to Spain to join the expedition.[120] From Paris Colonel Dillon collaborated with Sir Henry Goring in Sussex to gain the support of a network of smugglers called the Waltham Blacks, an affair which would subsequently bring great danger to Alexander Pope. The Keith brothers in Spain reported that 20,000 Scots would rise in support, and they planned to travel to Rouen, where Robert Arbuthnot promised to provide two ships for them. From the rash young Wogans to the aristocratic Ormonde and Orrery, "Parson Kelly" recruited the "great and small," who "were all in the network of the shifting and kaleidoscopic Jacobite plot."[121] As rumors about the plot reached the British government, increased surveillance was mounted over Swift, Pope, Dr. Arbuthnot, and other friends

---

[116] Anon.,*Remarks upon a Jacobite Pamphlet…entituled Female Fortitude* (London, 1722), "To the Reader," 9, 11, 20, 54.

[117] D. Defoe, *Librorum, #1451.*

[118] H. Tayler, *Jacobite Epilogue*, 281.

[119] M. Schuchard, *Emanuel Swedenborg*, 148-58, 164-67 Andrew Lang, *A History of Scotland from the Roman Occupation* (Edinburgh, 1907), IV, 337-38.

[120] Eveline Cruickshanks and Howard Erskine-Hill,*The Atterbury Plot* (New York, 2004), 150-51.

[121] A. Lang, *History*, IV, 338.

of Atterbury. According to Claude Nordmann, the Masonic ties of many of the participants helped initially to maintain secrecy and security during the planning.[122]

In summer 1722 a dispirited Swift left the rancorous politics of Dublin and visited Robert Cope in Loughgall, county Armagh. Cope had been arrested as a suspected Jacobite in 1715, and Swift made a risky visit to him when he was held in custody.[123] While at Cope's home in Armagh, Swift observed the Masons who were building a new Presbyterian meeting house, and he was amused by their using stones taken from a ruined abbey: "these lunatic Puritans are chiseling the very Popery out of the stones."[124] Swift quizzed the craftsmen about their pay, which was a shilling a day, and he told them that a good Mason could be got in Dublin for nine pence, which provoked one workman to reply, "We got a good Dean for £200 a year." On return trips to Armagh, Swift enjoyed his many conversations with stonemasons and builders, whom he would immortalize in light-hearted poems.[125] It is significant that he maintained his interest in the Masonic fraternity, which began at Trinity College in 1688 and was reinforced at Kilroot in 1695. However, he would soon learn that his rural retreat provided little protection from "ugly politics," for in August his friend Atterbury was arrested and charged with high treason.

[122] C. Nordmann, *Crise*, 109-10,153, 217-21.

[123] J.G. Simms, "Dean Swift in County Armagh," *Seanchas Ard Mhacha*, 6 (1971), 131-32.

[124] D.R.M. Weatherup, "Swift in County Armagh," *Review: Journal of Craigavon Historical Society*, vol.7, no. 3.

[125] J. Simms, "Dean Swift," 137-38.

CHAPTER EIGHT

ATTERBURY, WHARTON,
AND "COMBINATIONS OF WORKMEN"
(1722-1723)

From hence they've been for Traitors taken,
But still have Masons sav'd their Bacon;
....
And since they've been, at times, suspected,
They never once have been detected:
As Plotters and Confederates,
Whose Heads are plac'd on Poles and Gates.

The Freemasons: An Hudibrastick Poem (1723).

A Mason is a peaceable subject to the Civil Powers…[but] if a Brother
should be a rebel against the State,… the loyal Brotherhood must and ought
to disown his rebellion…[but] they cannot expel him from the Lodge, and
his relation remains indefeasible.

James Anderson, *Constitutions of the Freemasons* (1723).

While the political rivalries simmered within the London lodges, a letter was published in the government-supporting paper, *The Post Man* (7-10 July 1722), which criticized "the Building Gentry...who pretend to such great Things" and who foolishly rush to join the Freemasons.[1] Warning that "Combinations of Workmen" are dangerous to the trade of a nation, he pointed to the Late Act of Parliament against the Journeymen Taylors and urged a similar regulation of the "impudent" Masons. He issued an admonition to

> a Set of Low Gentry among our Artificers, who lately make a great Bluster
> among us, and call themselves FREE MASONS, pretending to great Mat-
> ters, and giving themselves Titles which Nature, or the Laws of the

---

[1] Reprint in *EMP*, 68-71.

> Constitution in England, never gave them… To support themselves in these Things, they have impudently pretended to bring Persons of Honour into their Fraternity, scandalously tying the Leather Apron, the Badge of their Mechanism, to the sides of Persons of Noble and Ancient Families; joyning the Robes of the Peer with the Ensigns of a Labourer: Incongruous Nonsense! As if the Apron-Strings of a Mechanick were to rank with the Blue Ribbon, and the Knight of the Garter be incorporated with the Mortar and Trowel.

The critic then quoted Henry VI's repressive regulations of the Masons and urged the newly recruited noble members to promptly abandon the fraternity before the upstart Masons cause serious trouble.

In August an "ancient" replied to the critic, and *The Post Man* published his comments and his version of the Old Charges. In answer to the "Piece of Ribaldry" and "Scurillity" of the anti-Masonic writer, the defender of the fraternity revealed:

> I have in my keeping, as a most valuable Piece of Antiquity, and what perhaps very few, if any of the Members of the Society, have had the Honour to see the Original Draught of the Sacred Foundations on which the Brotherly Fidelity of the said Society so many Hundred Years ago was first founded and has been to this Day preserved… I shall here give you a Specimen of this Piece of Antiquity, which was preserv'd for several hundred Years in the Archives of the Society, deposited for their service in an ancient Monastick Library, from whence it was taken in the late Rebellion, and by which it will now be shown to the World from whence this Worthy Society is deriv'd, how ancient they are, and of how great Esteem they were in those Days.[2]

The "ancient" Mason then gave a traditional Stuart history, which included "Orders and Constitutions made and agreed upon at a General Assembly held at ------ the 8th Day of December, 1663," complete with oaths of loyalty to the king, his heirs, and lawful successors.

The *Post Man* articles were subsequently published as a pamphlet entitled *The Old Constitutions Belonging to the Ancient and Honourable Society of Free and Accepted Masons* (1722), with a revised introduction that appealed to "the Persons of Honour who have lately grac'd the Society with their Presence" to remember "what mighty Fabricks they have erected, what glorious Buildings they have rais'd, from the Temple of Solomon to the magnificent Pile of St. Peter's at Rome." Douglas Knoop suggests that the letter and pamphlet were produced by "a conservative element in the Fraternity" determined to "steal a march" on Anderson, whose Whiggish *Constitutions* was still not published.

While the "ancient" Masons defended Stuart traditions in August, the government made a bold move against the Jacobites on the 23rd by arresting Bishop Atterbury, who had just written an appeal to Walpole for the funds owed to the operative Masons working on the Abbey.[3] The bishop joined George and Dennis Kelly and another plotter, Christopher Layer, in the Tower. Among the Kelly brothers' papers were letters from the

---

[2] *Ibid.*, 71-72.
[3] F. Williams, *Atterbury*, I, 384.

Irish merchant Christopher Glascock, Dillon's agent, to Nicholas Wogan, which revealed Wogan's plans to command a ship and to help Ormonde land Irish officers in England. These were reported to the government investigating committee, which reported ominously on "the evident footsteps of this treasonable correspondence from Ireland."[4]

Small wonder that Swift became anxious about the proceedings in London. He expressed to his Jacobite friend Robert Cope his concern for Orrery, who was also committed to the Tower on suspicion of complicity in the Atterbury plot: "Pray God keep all honest men out of the hands of the lions and bears and uncircumcised Philistines. I hoped my brother Orrery had loved his land too much to hazard it on Revolution principles."[5] Swift's language with its use of the Jacobite cant word "honest" and its implication that political allies are "circumcised" (Judaized) and fraternally bonded "brothers," had suggestive Jacobite-Masonic connotations. According to André Kervella, Orrery and Swift were indeed Masonic brothers.[6]

While Swift lamented that "the best trade in London this winter will be that of evidence," he probably remembered his own experience in May-June 1715 when Delafaye had confiscated letters to Swift and tried to implicate him (along with "brother" Ormonde and Atterbury) in Jacobite plotting.[7] Now Delafaye was examining Atterbury's papers, which had been "ransacked" from his deanery at Westminster and residence at Bromley.[8] Swift was probably aware that Delafaye was a member of the Grand Lodge and thus privy to Wharton's intrigues within the fraternity.[9] When Wharton was in Ireland, he befriended Swift and supported his ecclesiastical and political efforts.[10] The Dublin press had proudly reported the "unanimous" election of Wharton to the Grand Mastership in June 1722, so that Swift must have been aware of his friend's continuing Masonic activities.[11] On the very day, 9 October, when Swift wrote Cope, the government suspended *Habeas Corpus*. Still posing as a Whig, Wharton went along with the measure.

Though historians today acknowledge the reality of Atterbury's participation in the plot, the government at the time did not have enough evidence to convict him of treason. Thus, the decipherers stretched the limits of legal evidence to read sinister interpretations into otherwise innocent signs and language. As we shall see, this soon produced a satirical "Hudibrastick" response from an "ancient" Freemason. Swift, who was kept informed about the evidence being amassed by the government, wrote a poem, "Upon the horrid *Plot* discovered by *Harlequin* the B[ishop] of R[ochester]s *French* Dog" (1722), which was not published until 1735. The dog, which had a lame paw, had been a gift from Mar to Mrs. Atterbury, and references to it were used to link the bishop to Jacobite conspirators. A bitter Swift wrote that the dog's correspondence was "all decypher'd and translated," while his fore-foot "set his Mark."[12] Despite the fact that none of the intercepted letters

---

[4] T. B. Howell, ed., *A Complete Collection of State Trials and Proceedings for High Treason* (London, 1828), XVI, 439-42.

[5] J. Swift, *Correspondence*, II, 432.

[6] A. Kervella, *Chevalier Ramsay*, 173-74.

[7] J. Swift, *Correspondence*, II, 122.

[8] G. Bennett, *Tory Crisis*, 262-65.

[9] "Brother" Delafaye contributed a loyalist song to Anderson's *Constitutions (1723)*, 83-84.

[10] J. Swift, *Correspondence*, II, 335-36, 346.

[11] P. Crossle and H. Lepper, *History*, 43.

[12] J. Swift, *Poems*, I, 297-301.

were in Atterbury's handwriting and that all were in almost impenetrable code, Walpole and Delafaye determined to skewer their man on concocted evidence. Eveline Cruickshanks argues that Atterbury's purported correspondence was forged and that Walpole put out rumors that Mar had "made discoveries" in order to discredit him and split the Jacobites.[13] Though Mar's alleged betrayal seems dubious, Atterbury fell for the ploy and became the inveterate enemy of his former Jacobite colleague.

Though Swift had hoped that the caution of his "brother Orrery" would protect him, the earl's close association with Atterbury meant that he was imprisoned for six months in the Tower. The desperate appeals of his family, medical testimonies claiming that his life was in danger, and a £50,000 bond paid by his kinsman Burlington led to his release in March 1723.[14] A debilitated Orrery laid low during his protracted convalescence, but he subsequently resumed his Jacobite collaboration with Wharton. Though Orrery slipped his net, Walpole did develop a substantial case against the earl's co-conspirator, the eccentric lawyer Christopher Layer, who had visited James in Rome in 1721 and presented an ambitious, wide-ranging, and violent plan to seize George I and his family and take over crucial institutions in the city.[15] After being tortured and kept in heavy shackles for months, Layer was brought to trial in October 1722, when the painful lacerations produced by his iron fetters shocked even the judge. Condemned to be hung, drawn, and quartered, he was respited from time to time in the hope of further discoveries. Finally, in May 1723 he was executed at Tyburn, and his unusually harsh treatment provoked both sympathy and fear in Swift. In September Swift wrote Pope and obliquely identified himself with Layer, noting that "I...am everyday perswading myself that a Dagger is at my Throat, a halter about my Neck, or Chains at my Feet, all prepared by those in Power."[16] Dr. Arbuthnot wrote Swift that he had read these lines, but they were prudently suppressed by Pope.

During the months of the government's dragnet for suspected plotters and friends of Atterbury, the Grand Master Wharton boldly protested the illegality of Walpole's procedures. Wharton also recruited more Jacobites to the Grand Lodge, which must have distressed Montagu and Desaguliers. Government suspicions about Jacobite intrigues jeopardized the efforts of Whig Masons to gain control of the fraternity, for a general ban loomed as a possibility. Probably encouraged by Montagu, Desaguliers, and their allies, the Whig dramatist Charles Johnson produced a pro-Masonic prologue to his comedy, *Love in a Forest*, performed at the Theatre Royal, Drury Lane, on 9-15 January 1723. Newspapers had recently revealed that many actors in the Drury Lane company were Freemasons, including Colley Cibber, the manager and government propagandist.[17] Cibber and Johnson had earlier earned the Jacobites' wrath by their production of *The Non-juror*, still a popular favorite with Hanoverians.[18] As a loyalist member of Grand Lodge, Johnson dedicated the play to his brethren and praised their civil and international role:

---

[13] E. Cruickshanks and H. Erskine-Hill, *Atterbury*, 127, 208-09.

[14] "Charles Boyle, 4th Earl of Orrery," *ODNB*; Eveline Cruickshanks, "The Political Career of the Third Earl of Burlington," in T. Barnard and J. Clark, *Lord Burlington*, 206.

[15] Eveline Cruickshanks, "Lord North, Christopher Layer, and the Atterbury Plot: 1720-23," in E. Cruickshanks and J. Black, *Jacobite Challenge*, 92-106.

[16] J. Swift, *Correspondence*, II, 469, 476n.2.

[17] A. Robbins, "Earliest Years," 73-74.

[18] Richard Barker, *Mr. Cibber of Drury Lane* (New York, 1939), 106-08.

> If encouraging and being instructed in useful Arts, Charity, Humility, in a Word, if all those social Virtues which raise and improve the Mind of Man are Praiseworthy, your Society have a Right to demand the Applause of Mankind.
>
> You have taught all Nations one Idiom, which, at the same time that it gives a mutual Understanding, inspires a mutual Benevolence, removes every Prejudice of a distant Sun and Soil, and no Man can be a Foreigner who is a Brother.
>
> If it were not below the Dignity of the Brotherhood to boast what the Vulgar call Honours and Distinctions, you cou'd give a list of Royal Names, not only the first in Britain, but in Europe, have been proud to wear the Badge of your Order...
>
> It must be own'd your Society hath Enemies...yet our very Enemies, who have the least Candor, confess the Secrets of Masonry have been kept inviolable, and that too, during the Course of many Ages, among People of all Distinctions, Religions, and Nations in the known World.[19]

This benign, apolitical image was exactly what Desaguliers hoped to create for the Grand Lodge.

Thus, on 17 January 1723 Montagu summoned the Grand Lodge to meet in order to heal "the Breach of Harmony."[20] He extracted from Wharton a promise "to be True and Faithful" and then proclaimed him Grand Master. Under pressure, Wharton appointed Desaguliers to be his Deputy. At the same meeting, Anderson's manuscript of the new *Constitutions* was approved and commissioned for printing. In a note apparently added later, Anderson stressed that the work was undertaken at the command of Montagu, our late Grand Master" and was "not quite ready for the Press during his Mastership."[21] In the dedication, Desaguliers reiterated his loyalty to Montagu. It is possible that Wharton and his partisans were then able to delay publication of Anderson's work, and, in the meantime, to issue a scatological satire upon the modern speculative Masons.

On 15 February the opposition-supporting *Daily Post* advertised the publication of *The Free-Masons: An Hudibrastick Poem. Illustrating the whole History of the Ancient Free-Masons, from the Building of the Tower of Babel to this Time, with their Laws, Ordinances, Signs, Marks, Messages, etc. so long kept Secret Faithfully discover'd and made known, and the Manner of their Installation particularly describ'd. By a Free-Mason* (1723), and then printed it as an Appendix. The proprietor of the paper, Richard Nutt, was the son of the late John Nutt, a Tory "High Flyer," and his wife Elizabeth; mother and son would be prosecuted for publishing Tory, Jacobite, and opposition material.[22] Recent commentators on *An Hudibrastick Poem* have attributed the satire to Wharton, one of his friends, or less likely Robert Samber (who attended Wharton's installation).[23] (For convenience, the author will henceforth be called Hudibras). Alfred Robbins notes that "the brochure was launched with an amount of

---

[19] Reprint in *EMP*, 90-91.
[20] A. Robbins, "Earliest Years," 76-77.
[21] J. Anderson, *Constitutions (1723)*, 73, 91.
[22] Michael Harris, *Newspapers in the Age of Walpole* (London, 1987), 88; "Richard Nutt" and "Elizabeth Nutt," *ODNB*.
[23] Wallace McLeod, "The Hudibrastic Poem of 1723," *AQC*, 107 (1994), 9-50.

enterprise unusual in those days," with heavy advertising in the press.[24] From a reference to "Old Drury," it seems that the poem was provoked by Johnson's loyalist-Masonic prologue at Drury Lane:

> A MASON, holding up his Finger,
> Shews he has got below a Swinger;
> That he's a Member of Old Drury,
> And dares attack with manful Fury.[25]

Johnson, who was scorned by Pope as a prolific plagiarist, now became the peg on which to hang a satire about the Whig effort to develop a modern Masonry largely detached from its ancient operative roots.

Hudibras's obscene interpretation of the finger-sign was part of the "bogus" signs and tokens given by the author, who observed that they are no longer associated with the Mason trade. When the Masons were dispersed after the failed building of the Tower of Babel,

> …first they Signs and Marks did frame,
> To signify from whence they came;
> ………………………………………..
> Their sev'ral Rules and Orders made, Relating to the Mason Trade,
> Shou'd be observ'd as long as time,
> As Records writ in Prose or Rhyme:
> And by a solemn Oath enjoin'd,
> The only Tye upon the Mind.
>
> But since, 'tis found, the Masons-Free,
> Which in our modern Times we see,
> Workmen are of *another kind*,
> To Sport they're more than Toil inclin'd,
> They have no Trowels, nor yet Lines,
> But still retain their Marks and Signs…[26]

Hudibras trotted out bawdy analogies between the Masons' tools and labor with the sexual organs and intercourse. After describing rituals of arse-kissing, hot poker-prodding, floggings, and brandings, he conceded that not all Masons participate in such proceedings. Some lords and dukes are excused, while the non-aristocratic, speculative Masons indulge themselves:

> 'Tis only vulgar, common Masons,
> (That build no Churches, Walls, nor Bastions)
> Who feel the Whipping and the Marking,
> Are treated with such Strokes and Jirking…

---

[24] A. Robbins, "Earliest Years," 75.

[25] *The Free Masons: An Hudibrastick Poem* (London, 1723), 18.

[26] *Ibid.*, 9, 21-24, for the following quotes.

Hudibras hinted at older Scots-Irish traditions, such as the "antient custom" of branding an "M" on the buttocks (a practice mentioned in the Trinity College Tripos of 1688). Hudibras also admitted the importance of Jewish traditions:

> Some likewise say our Masons now
> Do Circumcision undergo,
> For Masonry's a Jewish Custom.

This comment throws a revealing light on Swift's earlier concern about his "brothers": "Pray God keep all honest men out of the hands of...uncircumcised Philistines."[27]

Pope shared Swift's and Hudibras's indignation at the dishonest "deciphering" undertaken by Walpole's agents. In a message to Dr. Arbuthnot, Pope warned that "even pigeon-pies and hogs' puddings are thought dangerous by our governors, for those that have been sent to the B. of Rochester are opened, and profanely pried into at the Tower."[28] Hudibras gave misleading interpretations of "bogus" Masonic signs and then lampooned the government's claim to see seditious evidence even on blank paper:

> Their [Masons'] Messages, and Scraps of Paper,
> Which are not seal'd with Wax or Wafer,
> Nor Writ upon, and yet make known
> The greatest Secrets of the Town.
>
> A Mason, when he needs must drink,
> Sends Letter, without Pen and Ink,
> Unto some Brother, who's at hand,
> And does the Message understand;
> The Paper's of the Shape that's square,
> Thrice-folded with the nicest Care...
> ....
> And he that can interpret these
> Unwritten Scrolls and Messages,
> He alone is welcome Guest,
> And fit to be at Mason's Feast.

This seems a direct attack on Delafaye, member of the Grand Lodge and song-writer for their banquets, whose current work on the deciphering of Atterbury's papers went beyond the bounds of legal evidence.

Remembering a golden age when Masonic signs provided international communication between traveling stonemasons ("Rovers"), Hudibras implied that certain modern Masons used their insiders' knowledge while collaborating with government decipherers to concoct false charges of sedition:

> But as where Paper has no Writing,
> So when 'tis of these Mens inditing,
> None but their mighty selves cou'd read,
> Or Myst'ries know of Mason's Trade;

---

[27] J. Swift, *Correspondence*, II, 432; see I. Higgins, *Swift's Politics*, 86.
[28] G. Bennett, *Tory Crisis*, 259.

And Dashes, and no Scribbling, mean
The self same Thing as Paper clean,
To him who knows not one or t'other,
Is not install'd a Mason's Brother.
From hence they've been for Traitors taken,
But still have Masons sav'd their Bacon;
....
And since they've been, at times, suspected,
They never once have been detected:
As Plotters and Confederates,
Whose Heads are plac'd on Poles and Gates,
....
Yet are they very harmless Creatures,
Have nothing plotting in their Natures,
But what's against Hoop-Petticoats;
For they've more Wit than risk their Throats,
Their valuable Lives expose...

When Hudibras dedicated the work to a "Worshipful Warden," he evidently targeted Anderson, a Grand Warden, as he ridiculed the loyalist toasts and political toadying introduced by the new Masons:

> Having had the Honour, not long since, when I was admitted into the Society of Masons, of Kissing your Posteriors, (an Honour superior to Kissing the Pope's Toe)...[You the Warden] can Vouch it to be True to a tittle... I may presage, if Examples are to be regarded, that in time you will be advanc'd to the Dignity of a Courtier...
> And I take it Court Politicians and Free Masons are oftentimes ally'd; for it is possible the one may build Castles in the Air as well as the other...so that it will not be a Wonderful Wonder of Wonders if you in time become a State-Politician, and arrive at Immortal Fame.[29]

Hudibras argued that besides the political corruption of the modern Masons, there was intellectual corruption, which degraded the earlier ideals of Masonic virtuosos who developed the New Science. Though "This Fellowship has Lodges many" and "Each Lodge with Library is grac'd," the moderns do not study "the Secrets of their Mother Nature" but instead read erotic, pornographic, and gynecologic works. They are supplied with this filth by Edmund Curll, "Bookseller to the Society." While getting drunk, they give endless toasts to local prostitutes and mistresses, "Down to the Royal Sovereign." The latter toast was a bold allusion to the hypocrisy and promiscuity of George I, who divorced his wife for infidelity in 1694 but then kept a string of mistresses. Widespread disgust at the Hanoverian government helped *The Free Masons: An Hudibrastick Poem* achieve popular success; a second edition appeared on 18 February, with third and fourth editions appearing within a year.

The delays in getting out the new *Constitutions* must have irked the moderns who received such merciless mockery. The ancient Masons soon received more positive press attention when the ninety-two year-old Christopher Wren died on 25 February 1723. His

---

[29] *The Free Masons*, 2-3.

supporters in the operative fraternity immediately began planning a grand funeral to honor their patron and protector.[30] It was perhaps this historic event that pushed Anderson days later to advertise the publication of his *Constitutions* in the government-supporting *Post-Boy* (26-28 February). That Anderson's work received little notice was probably a result of press and public preoccupation with the approaching ceremony for Wren. On 2 March Nathaniel Mist's *Weekly Journal*, a Jacobite paper, reminded readers of the shabby treatment Wren received in his last years:

> He was near 5 years ago removed from the Surveyor General of HM Works, which Post he had enjoyed for above 50 years upon Account of his known Abilities, notwithstanding the Changes of Ministry and Government till the time above mentioned. He was justly esteemed a great Mathematician and the best Architect of his time.[31]

Wren's son, who had also lost his position through Benson's machinations, worked with the operative Masons to produce "great funeral State and Solemnity" for his burial on 5 March. "Many persons of honour and distinction" accompanied the procession from Wren's house in Westminster to St. Paul's, where he was interred under the dome. Both the *Post Boy* and the *British Journal* called Wren "that worthy Free Mason." In the *Constitutions*, Anderson praised Wren, among others, as an "ingenious architect," but he did not mention Wren's Masonic affiliation or his various tenures as Grand Master. On the day after the architect's death, Wren's Grand Lodge enemies evidently presumed that they could get away with this glaring omission from their now "official" Masonic history. Certainly, Anderson's treatment of Wren suggests his complicity in the earlier Whig effort to strip Wren of influence in the fraternity.

Despite the ejection of Colen Campbell, Benson's deputy, from the Office of Works, Anderson puffed "Mr. Campbell the Architect's ingenious book, call'd *Vitruvius Brittanicus*, and associated him with the emerging "Disposition for true ancient Masonry."[32] David Stevenson notes that Anderson's "grandiose name-dropping sketch of the 'history' of Masonry has much to say about supposed English royal masons and very little about their Scottish royal counterparts."[33] Furthermore, "to admit that much of freemasonry, which the *Constitutions* sought to popularize in England, was derived from her despised northern neighbor would have discredited it." Anderson acknowledged the affiliation of James I, Charles I, and Charles II with the fraternity; he ambiguously suggested William III's association ("that glorious Prince, who by most is reckon'd a Free-Mason") and claimed that George I gave "Order, Countenance, and Encouragement" for the Building Commission's "grand design."[34]

In the new *Constitutions*, an apolitical "charge" made it clear that the Scottish-English, Jacobite-Hanoverian "truce" maintained in the Grand Lodge was at best shaky:

> A Mason is a peaceable subject to the Civil Powers, wherever he resides or works, and is never to be concern'd in plots and conspiracies against the

---

[30] "Note on Wren's Death," 181.
[31] Newspaper quotes in "Note on...Wren's Death," 181-82.
[32] J. Anderson, *Constitutions (1723)* 48.
[33] D. Stevenson, *First Freemasons*, 149.
[34] J. Anderson, *Constitutions (1723)*, 43-44.

peace and welfare of the nation... So that if a Brother should be a rebel against the State, he is not to be countenanc'd in his rebellion, however, he may be pitied as an unhappy man; and, if convicted of no other crime, though the loyal Brotherhood must and ought to disown his rebellion, and give no umbrage or ground of political jealousy to the government for the time being; they cannot expel him from the Lodge, and his relation remains indefeasible.[35]

Given the circumstances of government alarm at the Atterbury Plot, this charge suggests the continuing influence of Jacobites, who not only provided the current Grand Master but evidently supplied a majority of members to British lodges. Frank McLynn observes that "The primary impetus for the rise of freemasonry in the first quarter of the eighteenth century came from Jacobitism. The great names of early freemasonry were all partisans of the House of Stuart."[36]

It was probably Desaguliers, who was largely indifferent to religious matters, rather than the polemical Anderson, who composed the charge "Concerning God and Religion":

> A mason is oblig'd, by his Tenure, to obey the moral Law; and if he rightly understands the Art, will never be a stupid Atheist, nor an irreligious Libertine. But though in ancient Times Masons were charg'd in every Country to be of the Religion in which all men agree, leaving their particular opinions to themselves; that is, to be good Men and true, or men of honour and honesty, by whatever denominations or persuasions they may be distinguish'd; whereby Masonry becomes the centre of union, and the means of conciliating true friendship among persons that must have remain'd at a perpetual distance.[37]

In this idealized format, Grand Lodge Freemasonry would become a kind of utilitarian church which would have increasing appeal as the forces of Enlightenment rationalism gathered momentum in the later 18th century.

Anderson concluded the *Constitutions* with four Masonic songs, including two lengthy ones written by himself and later the target of Swift's satire. Drawing on Scottish traditions as well as the Old Charges, his virtually un-singable doggerel emphasized the Hebrew lore and Stuart role in Masonic history:

> For Father Abram brought from Ur
>   Geometry, the Science good;
> Which he reveal'd, without demur,
>   To all descending from his Blood.
>
> Nay Jacob's Race at length were taught,
>   To lay aside the Shepherd's Crook,
> To use Geometry were brought,
>   Whilst under Phar'oh's cruel Yoke;
> 'Till Moses Master-Mason rose,

---

[35] *Ibid.*, 50.
[36] F. McLynn, *Charles Edward Stuart*, 532.
[37] J. Anderson, *Constitutions (1723)*, 49-50.

> And led the Holy Lodge from thence,
> All Masons train'd, to whom he chose,
>   His curious Learning to dispense.
>
> Aholiab and Bezaleel
>   Inspired Men, the Tent uprear'd;
> Where the Scheckinah chose to dwell,
>   And Geometrick Skill appear'd:
> And when these valiant Masons fill'd
>   Canaan, the learn'd Phenicians knew
> The Tribes of Isra'l better skill'd
>   In Architecture firm and true.[38]

After describing the 40,000 craftsmen and 3,600 masters who worked under the "Gen'ral Master Mason" Hiram Abif on Solomon's Temple, Anderson proclaimed Free-masonry as "the Royal Art" and gave three Stuart kings credit for reviving it in England:

> Till British Crowns united were:
> The Monarch First of this whole Isle
>   Was learned James, a Mason King,
> Who First of Kings reviv'd the Style
>   Of Great Augustus: Therefore sing.
> ....
> King Charles the First, a Mason too,
>   With several Peers, and Wealthy Men,
> Employ'd him [Inigo Jones] and his Craftsmen true,
>   'Till wretched Civil Wars began.
> But after Peace and Crown restor'd,
> Tho' London was in Ashes laid,
>   By Masons Art and good Accord,
> A finer London rear'd its Head.
> King Charles the Second raised then
>   The finest Column upon Earth,
> Founded St. Paul's, that stately Fane,
>   And Royal Change, with Joy and Mirth:
> But afterwards the Lodges fail'd,
> Till Great Nassau the Tast[e] reviv'd,
> Whose bright Example so prevail'd,
>   That ever since the Art has thriv'd.

This song, which eliminated James II and the Jacobites from Masonic history, was dedicated to the former Grand Master Montagu. In a second "Warden's Song," Anderson called on the current Grand Master Wharton to "ever sing/ The Craftsman and the King." The third "Fellow-Craft's Song" was written by "Brother Charles Delafaye," who was presently employed in examining Atterbury's correspondence. In his song, Delafaye included Burlington, who was assumed to be a Whig, among the brethren "who have enrich'd the Art." Paul Monod argues that Burlington was "almost certainly a

---

38 *Ibid.*, 74-78.

Freemason"; though not included on London Grand Lodge lists, he may have been a member of "the rival York Lodge, based in northern England."[39]

Despite Charles Johnson's benign portrayal of Masonic ecumenicism and tolerance, the fraternity was increasingly polarized by political and religious differences. Christopher Layer's severed head was stolen and sold to Rawlinson, who had met Layer in Italy when the lawyer tried to persuade James of the feasibility of his plot. The skull became a Jacobite relic, which was later buried with Rawlinson. In June, a month after Layer's execution, Curll published Samber's description of Wharton's installation as Grand Master, when his Jacobite partisans sang a toast to the Pretender. Samber had inserted the passage in his translation of Albert de Sallengre's *Ebrietatis Encomium; or, the Praise of Drinking* (1723), which was based on the Frenchman's experiences at meetings of the "Knights of Jubilation." The publication was sweet revenge for Curll, who had recently been lampooned as the smutty bookseller to the modern Masons.[40] Publicized as "Written by a Person of Honour (who is a Free Mason")" and signed by Samber as "F. Sans-Terre" ("Frère" without land), the work served to link the exiled Jews and Jacobites with the "ancient" Masons. Samber dedicated the book to the Duke of Montagu, the former Grand Master, to whom he claimed to be a stranger, in an attempt to ingratiate himself with a potentially powerful patron. He subsequently shifted his politics to Whiggism and showered Montagu with eulogies, "in which the flattery rises to a shrill note of near hysteria."[41]

During Atterbury's trial, the bishop presented a vigorous defense, arguing that he was too busy "carrying on public buildings of various kinds at Westminster and Bromley" to engage in plotting.[42] However, one of his most implacable opponents was Bishop Willes, whose earlier effort to pacify discontent among the operative Masons was praised by Anderson but denigrated by the craftsmen. Willes scorned Atterbury's appeal to the precedent of Jewish law regarding witnesses, and he urged Parliament to crush him and all suspicious "Papists."[43] Against Walpole's charge that Atterbury raised £200,000 for the Pretender, the defendant claimed that the only funds raised were for the dormitory at Westminster (to be built according to Burlington's design). Walpole did not yet suspect Burlington, and it seems likely that the earl collaborated with the bishop in using architecture as a "cover" for Jacobite fund-raising.[44]

On 22 May in the House of Lords, Wharton (now publicly identified as the Grand Master) defended Atterbury in an eloquent speech that was subsequently published and widely distributed. Swift admired the speech, obtained a copy, and praised Wharton's virtuous action.[45] On 3 June Wharton anonymously launched a journal, *The True Briton*, which scorned "the Ambition and Avarice of Evil Ministers," who brand all "honest" critics of the government with the "odious names of Jacobites and Disaffected Persons."

---

[39] P. Monod, *Solomon's Secret Arts*, 182, 387n.109.

[40] Ralph Straus, *The Unspeakable Curll* (1927; New York, 1973), 273.

[41] J. Blom, "Life...Samber," *515*.

[42] F. Williams, *Atterbury*, I, 415.

[43] [Richard Willes], *The Bishop of Salisbury's Speech in the House of Lords upon the Third Reading of the Bill to inflict Pains and Penalities on Francis (late) Bishop of Rochester. 15 May 1723* (London, 1723), 3.

[44] E. Cruickshanks, "Political Career," 206, and J. Clark, "Burlington," in T. Barnard and J. Clark, *Burlington*, 268-73.

[45] J. Swift, *Correspondence*, II, 494-95 n. 11.

Posing as an "Old Whig," he flung his father's principles in the face of the New Whigs, who violated them. Most effectively, he examined and countered every charge against Atterbury and the plotters, demonstrating the illegality of the proceedings. Swift was pleased to receive the full run of *The True Briton* in 1723.[46] The Whig Mason Defoe followed the trials carefully, and he obtained copies of Wharton's speech, the report on Layer, and George Kelly's courtroom defense.[47] In the latter, Kelly defiantly rejected any role for the Earl Marischal, Earl of Mar, and General Dillon in the Atterbury plot, and he may have known that they were Jacobite Masons.[48]

Atterbury's innocence was long maintained by Swift, Arbuthnot, and Pope, whose awareness of his actual guilt is still a matter of debate among scholars.[49] However, in a secret letter to Pope, Atterbury expressed his worry that Pope and Arbuthnot might come under government suspicion and added a prayer: "God bless you both! And may no part of the Ill fortune that attends me, ever pursue either of you."[50] Pope subsequently suppressed the bishop's postscript ("I need not tell you that I must not be known to have written to you"), which the editor Sherburn suggests, "adds rather sinister implications to the prayer."

Atterbury was right to be concerned about Pope's vulnerability, because Delafaye had recently interrogated Pope's Catholic brother-in-law, Charles Rackett, whom he accused of being a Jacobite member of the "Waltham Blacks," deer poachers with blackened faces, who were accused of violence, robbery, and treasonous activities.[51] In May several newspapers linked Rackett with "the famous Mr. P---[Pope]," and revealed that "great application is making to men in power in his favour."[52] E.P. Thompson suggests that Pope appealed to Simon, Viscount Harcourt, on Rackett's behalf, while Colonel James Butler, a cousin of Ormonde, helped provide a financial "suretie." Thompson further speculates that Pope made some kind of financial contribution to Robert Walpole, who "was overseeing, and in detail, the case against the Blacks."[53] Their efforts paid off, for Charles was eventually released, while his brother Michael escaped to France, where "he might well have burnt his fingers further in the Jacobite cause." Though the "deeply disaffected" Pope was moving towards open criticism of the Walpole regime in the early months of 1723, from June of that year until 1728, when Charles Rackett died, he "had to tread very warily" in his political satires.

While Pope struggled to save his brothers-in-law, Delafaye, now well-known as a Grand Lodge Mason, advocated harsh treatment of the other Blacks, writing to Newcastle in June:

> The proceedings against the Blacks will, it is to be hoped, cure that Distemper which possibly might have proved an Epidemical one, the Infection

---

[46] Jonathan Swift, *Catalogue of Books, the Library of the late Rev. Dr. Swift* (Dublin, 1745), 22.

[47] D. Defoe, *Librorum*, part 2, #24, 25, 45.

[48] George Kelly, *The Speech of Mr. George Kelly. Spoke at the Bar of the House of Lords, on…2nd May 1723* (London, 1723), 4-7.

[49] See I. Higgins, *Swift's Politics*, 145-46.

[50] A. Pope, *Correspondence*, II, 165-66n.1.

[51] Pat Rogers, "The Waltham Blacks and the Black Act," *The Historical Journal*, 17 (1974), 472, 477.

[52] E. P. Thompson, *Whigs and Hunters: The Origin of the Black Act* (New York, 1975), 280-81..

[53] *Ibid.*, 287.

having begun to spread into more Countys. Some of the Malefactors at Reading for the Murder will be hanged in Chains.[54]

Thompson notes that "to be hung in chains, with one's body left to rot within sight of the relatives and neighbours, was a penalty worse feared than death." However despite Delafaye's efforts to discover a Jacobite "under every bed," the Blacks continued to operate, while the "special and most sanguinary law" continued to be used against them. It is clear that Pope and Swift were lucky to escape Delafaye's dragnet, and Swift would later scorn the Reverend Thomas Power, "a certain animal called a Walsh Black," as an informer who sent a half dozen men to be hanged.[55] Indeed, Power had acted as an *agent provocateur*, employed by Delafaye and Walpole, and Swift was appalled when he was given an Irish church position in 1726.

In December 1723, another Whig-Masonic colleague of Delafaye, Daniel Defoe, anonymously published *The Blacks of Waltham in Hampshire; and Those under the Like Denomination in Berkshire*. He stressed the Jacobite significance of the Blacks, noting that the nation was in the midst of political turmoil because of the South Sea scandal and the Atterbury plot ("the late horrid Conspiracy").[56] He reported that "this Gang of Banditti" formed themselves into a numerous band and took an oath to stand by one another "to the last Extremity," and "under these Anarchical and confus'd Principles they chose to be under a mock Kingly Government, and therefore elected a very robust, enterprising, and substantial Gentleman, yet unknown, for their King." Some who were in the "Secret of Affairs" believed that the Blacks were "in the Pretender's Interest, and went about thus Arm'd to be prepar'd for a general Insurrection." But their leader "King John" issued a Manifesto in London proclaiming, disingenuously, his Hanoverian loyalty.

While Pope backed away from overt disaffection, many Stuart sympathizers believed that he had been a supporter of their cause. The Non-juring historian Thomas Carte, a Jacobite Mason who served as Atterbury's secretary, believed that Pope was the author of the anonymous anti-Hanoverian broadside, "A New Ballad," which Carte copied from a manuscript in 1722.[57] Intended to be sung, with choruses of "Which No Body can deny," the ballad attacked Walpole and his decipherers:

> Come listen ye Tories and Jacobites now,
> Your Plot Mr. P----- as plainly will shew
> As your Friend 'Squire W----- did Eight Years ago.
> The Report and Appendix are both come to hand,
> Which wou'd cover, if spread, half an Acre of Land;
> So that few Folks can read 'em, and none understand.
> But Reader from hence, if so minded, may draw
> The most delicate Treason that ever Man saw,
> Provided he judge not according to Law.
>
> ....
>
> Whether guilty or guiltless, it signifies not,
> Tho' they cannot convict, they can punish by V---[Vote];

---

[54] *Ibid.*, 76.
[55] *Ibid.*, 221.
[56] [Daniel Defoe], *The History of the Blacks of Waltham in Hampshire* (London, 1723), 3-6.
[57] Bodleian.: Carte MS. 230, ff. 24, 246.

And who'er disbelieves it, is one of the Plot.

Carte also copied a version which added the lines: "Tho' Kelly and Layer to discover were loth,/ The Dog was more frank and a Person of Truth/ So they did not Examine him upon oath." In 1722 Carte fled to France, after he was accused of treason and a £1,000 reward offered for his capture. Thus, he did not learn that the ballad was actually written by Atterbury's confidant Samuel Wesley the Younger, who was indeed a Jacobite friend of Pope.[58] Wesley would later satirize James Anderson and his Masonic *Constitutions*.

Despite the flimsy evidence (characterized as "all hearsay," "uncertain ciphers," and "a French dog") and illegal proceedings, the bishop was convicted and banished for life from England.[59] Atterbury asked permission to revisit Westminster Abbey, in order to check on the renovation work, but Walpole feared an uprising among his Westminster supporters and rejected the request. On 18 June, when Atterbury embarked from the Tower, Wharton gave him a sword engraved with the mottoes, "Draw me not without Reason" and "Put me not up without Honour." Wharton's watermen and many other small ships then escorted him down the Thames.[60] A relieved Walpole, who had feared "a popular commotion," wrote Townshend:

> The Bishop of Rochester went away on Tuesday. The crowd that attended him before his embarkation, was not more than was expected; but great numbers of boats attended him to the ship's side. Nothing very extraordinary, but the Duke of Wharton's behavior, who went on board the vessel with him; and a free conversation betwixt his holiness and Williamson [Governor of the Tower]; with menaces of a day of vengeance.[61]

To Walpole's dismay, Wharton then published a poem in praise of Atterbury, which was widely acclaimed:

> Farewell! Renowned in arts farewell!
> Thus conquered by thy foe;
> Of honours and of friends deprived,
> In exile must thou go.
> Yet go content; thy look, thy will sedate,
> Thy soul superior to the shocks of state.
>
> Thy wisdom was thy only guilt,
> Thy virtue thy offence;
> With god-like zeal thou didst espouse
> Thy country's just defence;
> Nor sordid hopes could charm thy steady soul,
> Nor fears no guilty numbers could control.[62]

---

[58] The ballad was published anonymously in 1723.
[59] R. Sedgwick, *House of Commons*, I, 65-67.
[60] E. Cruickshanks, "Lord North," 105n.28.
[61] John Heneage Jesse, *Memoirs of the Court of England from the Revolution in 1688 to the Death of George II* (London, 1843), II, 236-37.
[62] *Ibid.*, II, 237.

Six days after Atterbury's departure, Wharton appeared at the Guildhall, where he encouraged the partisans of two Jacobite candidates for the shrievalty of the city of London, "at the same time organizing his Masonic adherents for the struggle the same evening in Grand Lodge."[63] That night, at the 24 June annual meeting, his enemies determined to subvert his influence on the fraternity. Wharton had earlier approved the choice of a Scottish Whig, Francis Scott, Earl of Dalkeith, to succeed him as Grand Master. The earl was the grandson of the Duke of Monmouth, who was the eldest illegitimate son of Charles II and who was executed by James II. Probably initiated in Scotland, he shared with his grandmother an interest in architecture and operative Masonry.[64] Wharton possibly believed that he could win over Dalkeith, but he was infuriated when the absent earl's proxy announced in Grand Lodge that Desaguliers would again serve as Deputy Grand Master. As Alfred Robbins notes, "that re-appointment, indeed, was ratified only by a single vote."[65]

> When Wharton challenged the accuracy of the division, Brother Robinson, producing a written Authority from the Earl of Dalkeith, for that Purpose, did declare in his name, that his Worship…did Appoint Dr. Desaguliers his Deputy…And also Brother Robinson did…protest against the above proceedings of the late Grand Master…as unacceptable, unwarrantable, and irregular… Then the said Grand Master and those who withdrew with him went away from the Hall without ceremony.[66]

Ric Berman argues that Dalkeith was influenced strongly by Desaguliers and supported his efforts to stabilize the Grand Lodge and distance it from Wharton's politically-suspect leadership.[67] Wharton subsequently severed his connection with the Hanoverian Masonry of the London Grand Lodge; he would later take Masonic documents abroad with him and use them when he became Grand Master of *Écossais* Masonry in France.[68]

On 24 June when the City contest was "waxing fierce," Wharton headed a party of Liverymen who marched to the poll in the Jacobite interest. These developments distressed Anderson, who wrote Montagu an account of the Masonic controversy and added a significant political report:

> May it please your Grace to accept the thanks of our Brethren for your good buck [venison] and your generous payment for the ticket; but your Grace's company would have been useful, because…W-----n [Wharton] endeavoured to divide us against Dr. Desaguliers…W-----n has been deeply engaged all this week among the Liverymen of London in the Election of Sheriffs, though not entirely to his satisfaction, which I'm sorry for, but none can help it except Mr. Wallpool [Walpole] who, they say, thinks it not worth while to advise him.[69]

---

[63] A. Robbins, "Earliest Years," 177.

[64] M. Clendinning, *History*, 88-89.

[65] A. Robbins, "Earliest Years," 77.

[66] *Ibid.*, 77.

[67] R. Berman, *Foundations*, 146-48.

[68] See ahead, Chapter Eleven.

[69] A. Robbins, "Earliest Years," 78.

Walpole realized that he had exhausted his political capital in his proceedings against Atterbury, for the blatant illegality even disgusted many Whigs.

After Wharton's candidates were all defeated in the City elections, he received a letter from a "West-Saxon," who criticized his recruitment efforts among the lower classes. He replied in *The True Briton* (5 July 1723) that it did not deserve an answer, for he was "determined to despise all the mean Reflections of mercenary Scribblers." However, he would write a letter to another Person in the style and words of "West-Saxon":

> To the False Briton...
>
> I hope the noble Push you lately made for the Rights and Privileges of the Citizens, when you abandon'd the Ease and Grandeur appendent to your Patrician Order, and descended from your High Rank, to sweat among the Crowds of Plebeians and Mechanicks, and to stretch your Throat with Leather-Apron'd Stentors, will never be forgot as long as Gog and Magog stand in the Hall. And pray give me leave to congratulate your L------p [Lordship] upon the success.
>
> – Without Admiration or Astonishment, the True Briton.[70]

In this ironic reversal, Wharton's characterization of the "Leather-Apron'd" operative Masons as "Stentors" (warriors whose powerful voices can move armies) was politically risky. He also distanced himself from the Whig Masons who attacked Atterbury. Wharton followed the letter to "The False Briton" with one from Dennis Kelly, who had defended George Kelly from the government's inaccurate interpretations of his brother's handwriting. Referring to Delafaye and Townshend, Dennis characterized "Brittanicus," the Whig decipherer as "this abominable Sycophant," who "perverted the whole Scope of my Evidence."[71]

Wharton obviously knew that Delafaye's activities went beyond writing songs for the Grand Lodge and that he was a well-known as a Hanoverian Mason. On 19 July he criticized Delafaye's interpretation of innocent mathematical and geometrical signs as evidence of sedition. Turning the decipherer's rationale back on him, Wharton ironically implied that Atterbury, Mar, the Earl Marischal George Keith, and other plotters had utilized Masonic-style codes in their correspondence. In a mock analysis, he compared the government decipherers' work to that of the Spanish Inquisition, when it deciphered Martin Luther's "code" by allegedly using Cabalistic methods of number-letter transposition:

> The *Magi* were then ordered to...explain a certain paper, which, it was pretended, the Bishop had formerly dropt out of his pocket; and though he had, it contained nothing but some rough Schemes of Geometry and Mathematicks; however, it was easy Matter to explain it into Heresy... The next Figure that occurs, is a Triangle...[which] must signify, according to the Rules of our occult Science, three thousand Heretical Pamphlets.[72]

---

[70] *True Briton* (5 July 1723), 85
[71] *Ibid.*, 86.
[72] A. Robbins, "Earliest Years," 117.

A triangle composed of three dots was currently used by Jacobite Masons to identify themselves, while the "schemes of Geometry" suggest the architectural codes used by Mar and Burlington. As noted earlier, Gyllenborg also used Masonic-style geometrical emblems in his ciphers.

Wharton probably learned that Delafaye in 1723 was compiling a catalogue of seditious passages issued by the printer of his journal, Thomas Payne, and the articles became slightly more cautious, which resulted in Delafaye being congratulated on the subsequent "dullness of the *True Briton*."[73] Wharton also recognized that his domestic Masonic networks were now penetrated and defeated, which made him increasingly desperate, to the point of recklessness, to serve the Stuart cause. In late August 1723 he entertained threescore "country people" at his residence, where he and Sir Christopher Musgrave drunkenly pulled off their coats, fell upon their knees to drink to King James, and compelled all their guests to do the same.[74] This made a great stir, wrote Lord Lonsdale, but "the magistrate would not meddle with so great a noise."

Wharton's defense of Atterbury and his Masonic effort received some oblique and bizarre support from a Jacobite writer, "Harry Wildair," who published *The Sermon Taster, or Church Rambler* (1723), with the subtitle, *A Pleasant Account of the Humours, Management and Principles of the Great Pontif Machiavel, his Scarfians, Pickl'd Herrrings, and other Fashionable Broachers of Religion, and Politicks*. The anonymous author attacked Bishop Benjamin Hoadly, who had vehemently opposed Atterbury and now served as the chief low-church supporter of the Whig party.[75] Wildair portrayed Hoadly as the "Great Pontif," who repeatedly visited dissenters' churches in order to pick up their language and promote their cause. Claiming that they possessed some great mystery, he placed Hoadly's church rambling in a Masonic context:

> I know that I have said enough already to give you strong Suspicions either of the turn of my Brains, or the ill Fortune of my Dice. But as there is not Mystery sufficient in the whole of my Narrative, to furnish out one Branch of the Occult Science, nor make even so much as a Free-Mason; you may expect immediately to see the whole of the seeming Obscurity dawn into Light, and the Clouds you are under dispell'd, and dispers'd.[76]

Wildair quoted "our Friend" Jonathan Swift on "Dedicators of an inferior Class": "whenever they give their Patrons a most bountiful Heart, you may be sure the Author has a most empty stomach."[77] He then exposed the "mystery" of Hoadly's and the dissenters' sermons, in which they charged anyone who opposed them with sedition: "To this end Defamation and Slander is dealt about by them as thick as Hail. One is a Papist, another a Jacobite, a third High Church." They then bawl out five or six words to which every thing else must give way: Protestant, Briton, Liberty, Constitution, Arbitrary, Tyranny, etc." At the bare sound of these, without reason or justice, they provoke their audience to "Cry out TREASON and POPERY." It is amusing to watch them, who "talk

---

[73] J. Black, *English Press*, 110-12.

[74] Alice Shield, *Henry Stuart, Cardinal of York and His Times* (London, 1908), 8.

[75] "Benjamin Hoadly," ODNB.

[76] Harry Wildair, *The Serman Taster, or Church Rambler* (London, 1723), 4.

[77] *Ibid.*, 12-13, 20, 28.

so much of Moderation very often foam in the Mouth." In their zeal against Popery, they determine that their audience will see how formidable and dangerous it is:

> After this comes a long Story of raw Head and bloody Bones about Queen Mary, and Fires and Fagotts in Smithfield; then all the Foam and Spittle comes out, the Word Succession ...and Jesuites, and Mines, and Gunpowder, and wishing to be Cardinals, and the Pope and the Devil, and---[78]

Even worse than their mob-provoking sermons, they determine to write parliamentary bills "in order to their Recommendation." They then send out their hundreds of packets by government-supporting *Flying Posts* and *Gazetteers*, and all join "in one Cry for our GREAT PONTIF." Atterbury and Wharton would certainly be amused by Wildair's contribution to their cause.

In the meantime, Wharton did not just give up on the potential usefulness of Freemasonry beyond England. In order to revive the international reach of Jacobitism, a new version of the fraternity was required that could link up the eclectic participants. He utilized *The True Briton* to signal his interest in a revived Swedish-Jacobite alliance. He got his inside information on Swedish politics from Charles Caesar, who assisted him on the journal and who maintained contact with Gyllenborg and the Holstein party in Sweden. On 14 July Wharton defended Sweden's policies of 1715 and charged that George I had used them as a pretense to interfere in the Northern War. On 15 July he praised the efforts of the Holstein partisans who were working to undermine the legitimacy of the Hessian claimant, King Fredrik I:

> In Sweden, the present King must have different views from the inclination of his people, and he must esteem his title to that Crown precarious. Such a thought will prompt him to make the best use of his time, to improve the advantages he has at present, to the private benefit of his hereditary dominions.
>
> The glorious stand lately by the States [Swedish Diet], deserves to be recorded to their eternal honour; who, not withstanding the King's and Queen's letters, resolved to give the title of Royal-Highness to the Duke of Holstein, whose right they seem inclined to defend...[79]

This linkage of Stuart and Holstein "legitimists" would endure over the next decades and play a major role in Masonic developments.

On 2 August Wharton hinted at a new Masonic strategy in his outreach to Sweden. He published a prophecy taken from Francis Bacon's *Essays*, which the former Lord Chancellor was unable to decipher:

> There shall be seen upon a Day,
> Between the Baugh and May,
> The Black Fleet of Norway:
> When that is come and gone
> England build houses of Lime and Stone

---

[78] *Ibid.*, 21.
[79] *True Briton* (15 July 1723).

For after, Wars you shall have none.[80]

Among "illuminated" readers, the Norwegian fleet would be interpreted as the Swedish fleet, which like Carl XII's, would invade Britain from Norway, while Masonic construction in lime and stone would usher in a peaceful Stuart reign.

---

[80] *Ibid.*, (2 August 1723).

CHAPTER NINE

CHINESE AND CABALISTIC THREATS TO THE GRAND LODGE
(1723-1724)

> Our Guardian is of Opinion, that the present Masonry is so tarnish'd
> By the Ignorance of the working…that very many, even whole Lodges
> Fall under the censure of the venerable Chinese Brachman, whose
> History of the Rise, Progress, and Decay of Free-Masonry, writ in the
> Chinese Tongue, is lately translated into a Certain European language.
>
> Jonathan Swift, *Letter from the Grand Mistress
> Of the Female Freemasons* (Dublin, 1724).

> Whereas the truly ANTIENT NOBLE ORDER of the Gormogons…have
> determined to hold a Chapter…This is to inform the Public…that no Ma-
> son will be receiv'd as a Member till he has renounced his Novel Order and
> been properly degraded.
>
> *Daily Post* (3 September 1724).

Wharton's recognition of the need for new international strategies was shared by Mar and his circle in Paris. The failure of the Atterbury plot convinced them that there was no hope for an imminent restoration in England. When the pro-Hanoverian, French foreign minister Cardinal Dubois died in August 1723, Mar determined to appeal to the Regent Orléans, who had earlier sympathized with the Jacobites, despite his acquiescence in Dubois's betrayal of Atterbury. In September Mar composed a "Memorial" advocating a Franco-Scottish alliance that would support the independence of Scotland and Ireland under a shared Stuart king.[1] He employed Andrew Michael Ramsay to translate it into French and Arthur Dillon to present it to the Regent.[2] While Scots would serve in the French army, French troops would be maintained in Scotland "to overawe England." When Mar sent the Memorial to the Stuart court, James approved

---

[1] Stuart Erskine, "The Earl of Mar's Legacy to Scotland, and to his Son, Lord Erskine," *Publications of Scottish Historical Society*, 26 (1896), 141-247. 151-56.
[2] George D. Henderson, *Chevalier Ramsay* (London, 1952). 102.

parts of it while waiting for the Regent's response. Unfortunately, Orléans died on 2 December, before he could meet with Dillon to give his reply.

Historians continue to argue about Mar's role in these intrigues, with interpretations largely determined by Anglo- or Scoto-centric perceptions. Thus, Edward Gregg accuses Mar of deliberately exposing Atterbury and using the Memorial to sabotage a Jacobite restoration in England, while Stuart Erskine and Maurice Bruce argue that Mar cleared all his actions and proposals with James and remained loyal to the Stuart cause.[3] From emerging evidence in the unpublished Stuart Papers and Swedish diplomatic archives, the latter opinion seems to be gaining ground.[4] Mar expressed concern about the bishop's anti-Scottish and anti-Catholic prejudices, which undermined the exiles' efforts in France. For six years John Menzies, a Scottish Jacobite agent, tried to palliate Atterbury's prejudices; when he would disprove the charges against Mar, "the Bishop would be soothed for a few days," but "then the fit would return."[5] Atterbury would declare that "the men of Scotland, which he mortally hated, were always addicted to their own countrymen," and there was a report that he "was resolved to break the neck of the Scotch interest, as he called it."

But it was not just Scots who worried about Atterbury's irascibility and suspiciousness, and Menzies claimed that "several of his own colleagues would long ago have gone over to the Jacobite side, but that they could not bear the thought of being yoked with him in anything." In May 1722 Thomas Wentworth, 3rd Earl of Strafford, had warned James about the bishop's "autocratic temper," for he is "so full of his own abilitys that if he can't have things go his own way, he would rather they did not go on at all."[6] Strafford, who had been impeached during the Jacobite scare of 1716, was an old friend of Swift.[7] In July 1722 Lord Lansdowne, one of Swift's "brothers," wrote James to defend Mar from the bishop's accusations that Mar's "coming to terms with the government" was treacherous, for despite threats and pressure, he had not provided them with any information. Lansdowne lamented that "it is a very hard case that a man must be either starv'd or hang'd to be believed honest." Even the Earl of Orrery began to distance himself from Atterbury, his old mentor, and he was privately relieved that the bishop was now on the "other side of the water."

As criticisms of Atterbury's behavior reached France, the embittered bishop determined to make a scapegoat of Mar. In summer 1723 he asked Mar to deliver his papers for examination, which an unsuspecting Mar agreed to do – much to his subsequent regret. As Eveline Cruickshanks observes, "it beggars belief" that Mar would hand over to Atterbury "anything incriminating that he did not think he could explain as having

---

[3] See Edwart Gregg, "The Jacobite Career of John Earl of Mar," in E. Cruickshanks, ed., *Ideology and Conspiracy: Aspects of Jacobitism in 1688-1759* (London, 1982), 179-200; versus S. Erskine, "Mar's Legacies," 151-56, and Maurice Bruce, "The Duke of Mar in Exile, 1716-32," *Transactions of the Royal Historical Society*, 4th s., 20 (1937), 61-82.

[4] E. Cruickshanks and Erskine-Hill, *Atterbury*, 128-29, 224-26, 284; Marsha Keith Schuchard, "Les Rivalités Maçonniques et la *Bulle in Eminenti*," *La Règle d'Abraham*, 25 (Juin 2008), 9-10, 14-19; revised English version, "The Political-Masonic Background to the 1738 Papal Bull *In Eminenti*," *Heredom*, 23 (2015), 55-106.

[5] *HMC. Stuart Papers*, VI, xxii. The following views were expressed by the editor, F.H. Daniell, in the Introduction.

[6] M. Bruce, "Duke of Mar," 65, 69.

[7] J. Swift, *Correspondence*, II, 122, 130, 132.

been accepted by James."[8] Despite the conventional wisdom that "Bobbing John" was a double agent, she concludes that the case against him is less clear than previously claimed. Moreover, Margaret Stewart reveals that the nickname "requires additional comment":

> Mar was known affectionately in Scotland as "Bobbing John" without any political connotation because he had a spinal deformity that caused his head to bob when he walked: the Whig mob in London gave it a pejorative political slant probably just after the Hanoverian succession to denigrate Mar's sympathy for a pro-Jacobite rising.[9]

Swift seemed to know the earlier physical significance of the adjective "Bobbing," for he would later record that Mar was "Crooked' (had a crooked back), adding that "he seemed to me to be a gentleman of good sense, and good nature."[10] That Mar remained a loyal Jacobite would be significant, as he, Ramsay, and their supporters played important roles in the development of *Écossais* Freemasonry – a movement independent of Atterbury.

While the impoverished refugees in France suffered in an atmosphere of mutual re-crimination, Swift was laying low in Ireland but planning new methods of attacking the government in London. Bolingbroke, who had broken from the Jacobites but still opposed Walpole, sent Swift veiled advice on how to safely proceed. In August 1723 he wrote to Swift from La Source in France:

> The hoarse voice of Party was never heard in this quiet place. Gazettes and pamphletts are banish'd from it, and if the Lucubrations of Isaack Bickerstaff are admitted, this Distinction is owing to some strokes by wch it is judg'd that this illustrious Philosopher had (like the Indian Foe, the Graecian Pythagoras, the Persian Zoroaster, & others his Praecursors among the Zabians, the Magians, and the Egyptian Seers) both his outward & his Inward Doctrine, & that he was of no side at the Bottom...[11]

Though Swift despised Toland, Bolingbroke coyly advised him to use techniques similar to those of the radical pantheist. Thus, the inclusion of esoteric meaning within exoteric writing, the technique advocated by the secret fraternity of the *Pantheisticon*, could also serve the Tory cause of Swift's "brothers."

Swift claimed to live an isolated life in Irish country houses, but he managed to keep up with the international ramifications of Jacobite intrigues. In a poem entitled "The Journal," published in London in January 1723, he recounted his visit to the Tory household of Baron George Rochfort.[12] In a bantering tone, Swift reported the baron's conversation:

> A word or two of Lord chief Baron;
> And tell how little weight he sets,
> On all Whig Papers, and Gazets:

---

[8] E. Cruickshanks and H. Erskine-Hill, *Atterbury*, 226.
[9] M. Stewart, *Archaeological...Mar*, xxi.
[10] J. Swift, *Prose Works*, V, 262. According to the *Oxford English Dictionary*, in the 18th century "crooked" referred to a physical deformity ("crook-back"), not to dishonesty.
[11] J. Swift, *Correspondence*, II, 465.
[12] I. Higgins, *Swift's Politics*, 147-48.

But for the Politicks of Pue,
Thinks ev'ry Syllable is true;
And since he owns the King of *Sweden*
Is dead at last without evading.
Now all his hopes are in the *Czar*,
Why *Muscovy* is not so far,
Down the black Sea, and up the Streights,
And in a Month he's at your Gates:
Perhaps from what the Packet brings,
By *Christmas* we shall see Strange things.[13]

The Tory printer Richard Pue was arrested for seditious publishing and accused of Jacobitism, which provoked a doggerel verse: "Ye Quidnuncs who frequently come to Pue's/ To live on politics, coffee and news."[14] Rochfort's remarks revealed his own access to international Jacobite initiatives, as Wharton and Mar tried to recruit Sweden and Russia to their cause.

In Mar's Memorial of September 1723, he urged the French Regent to join the Jacobite effort to rebuild the alliance achieved six years earlier by Gyllenborg and Görtz.[15] Given this context of renewed Swedish-Russian-Jacobite intrigues, a Hudibrastic poem published by the Scottish Mason William Meston suggests his awareness of these secretive international affairs and their Masonic component. Under the pseudonym "Quidal," Meston published *The Knight* at Edinburgh in 1723. Like Samuel Butler, Meston satirized a Presbyterian knight who destroys great architecture:

...his roving Roysters,
Demolished many Kirks and Cloysters,
Where nought but Ruins now appears,
Of what was built in many years.[16]

He seemed to target the Presbyterian Whig Anderson, whose efforts in the Grand Lodge threatened to divorce Masonry from its "ancient" operative and Stuart roots. Thus, Meston exploited all the claims about the Presbyterians' Jewish origins ("descended from *Ahiram*") and occultist credulities ("in the Rosi-crucian Trade"). However, these radical Scots sometimes provide magical services to architectural craftsmen:

A charm for masons and slaters,
That should be writ in golden letters,
Would keep them from all harm by falling;
In coming down make no more haste,
Than going up, *probatum est.*[17]

---

[13] J. Swift, *Poems*, I, 282.
[14] E. O'Ciarhda, *Ireland*, 165, 169, 231
[15] S. Erskine, "Mar's Legacies," 226.
[16] Quidal [William Meston], *The Knight* (Edinburgh, 1723), 4.
[17] *Ibid.*, 39.

While alluding to the brothers' signs that call an operative Mason down from the highest steeple, Meston also referred to a new initiatory ritual (probation) that involved climbing a ladder in a darkened room.[18]

Though Atterbury, after examining Mar's papers, accused him of being a double agent, the Scot was supported by Dillon and Lansdowne and continued to play a leading role among the Jacobites in Paris. In order to restore his credibility, Mar determined to send his confidant Ramsay to Rome, where he would act as tutor to the three year-old prince Charles Edward Stuart. When Wharton learned of Ramsay's appointment, he wryly remarked that he hoped the new tutor "might inoculate the royal charge with a taste for pleasurable vice."[19] Given Wharton's leadership role in Jacobite Freemasonry, his interest in and support of Ramsay is suggestive, for Bernard Fay argues that Ramsay also had a Masonic mission – to reveal to the Pretender and Pope "the true religion and its teaching within Freemasonry."[20] Though this claim remains controversial, Pierre Chevallier notes that Fay had consulted the Stuart Papers at Windsor and that "Le question reste posée."[21]

For some months, Ramsay had been working on his French biography of Fenelon and planned to edit the archbishop's works. In December 1722 Lansdowne wrote James, recommending these works by Ramsay, now his close friend: "The Situation & Adventures of Telemachus in search of his native kingdom [afford] so near a resemblance with your own…that one would imagine the Author…had no other Prince in his View but your self, when he wrote it."[22] He concluded that "In all Events of Life, your Majesty may have recourse to these Books as to an Oracle, either for consolation, or advice." In 1723, when Ramsay's *Histoire de la Vie de Fénelon* was published in Paris, it did not include the dedication that he had written to James III, who felt it might be too controversial "for both ecclesiastical and political reasons."[23] Ramsay wrote to James that he had extracted the lessons of Fenelon's works "only to maintain your rights and endeavor to undeceive my countrymen of your errors," and he explained that when a man had "seen the world in all its shapes," there could be nothing more useful "to forewarn [him] against an ambition of absolute government."[24] He would present "a model to future Princes of moderation in their Grandeur." Despite the flattery, James sensed that the work would insult his supporters at the French court.

Sans the dedication, the book was immediately translated into English by Pope's friend Nathaniel Hooke, a Catholic Jacobite. Hooke had tried (unsuccessfully) to dedicate it to Lord Oxford. Walpole's government insisted that two pages in the French edition be omitted from the English translation.[25] These contained a statement that James III professed full acceptance of the constitutional political theories of Fénelon's *Telemaque* and

---

[18] The recent introduction of a ladder ritual was mentioned in *The Plain Dealer* (14 September 1724).

[19] Alice Shield and Andrew Lang, *The King Over the Water* (London, 1907), 368

[20] Bernard Fay, "Les Origines et l'Esprit de la Franc-Maçonnerie," *La Revue Universelle*, 66 (1936). 175.

[21] Pierre Chevallier, *Histoire de la Franc-Maçonnerie en France* (Paris, 1974), I, 16.

[22] Stuart Papers: 59/100; quoted in Gabriel Glickman, "Andrew Michael Ramsay (1686-1743), the Jacobite Court, and the English Catholic Enlightenment," *Eighteenth-Century Thought*, 3 (2009), 401-02.

[23] G. Henderson, *Ramsay*, 88.

[24] Bodleian: Rawlinson MS.D1198/247. Undated "To the King of Great Britain"; in G. Glickman, "Ramsay," 402, 410.

[25] G. Henderson, *Ramsay*, 76-77.

an extremely flattering letter which Fénelon wrote about James in 1709, praising his character and religion. The biography soon became the target of Delafaye's espionage work, for he was warned on 3 September that it expressed seditious Jacobite views. Writing from Hanover, at the behest of Secretary Townshend, Stephen Poyntz informed Delafaye about Ramsay's publications:

> You will see in the advertisements a Book printed for Vaillant and published by one Ramsey in Eng. and French which pretends to give an account of the life of the late Archbishop of Cambray, and last year the same author published another piece entitled Maxims of Government on the principles of ye archbishop of Cambray or to that effect. You will find the drift of both these pieces is to lend the name and authority of that great man towards recommending the person and cause of the Pret----r [Pretender] which I think deserves your animadversion.[26]

Neither Ramsay nor Mar was aware that Delafaye, the government's chief anti-Jacobite spymaster, would soon make them targets, with the powerful Hanoverian Mason now pitted against two vulnerable Jacobite Masons.

Despite his rejection of the dedication, James III was grateful for the book and, aware of Ramsay's interest in chivalric traditions, urged the regent Orléans to make him a Knight of the Order of St. Lazarus of Jerusalem, an ancient military order which provided protection to pilgrims during the Crusades.[27] Orléans himself served as Grand Master of St. Lazarus, while his natural son Jean-Philippe d'Orléans served as Grand Prior of the Knights of Malta in Paris. Infused with chivalric enthusiasm, "Chevalier" Ramsay contributed to Mar's plan for a restorationist order of military knights. Though Ramsay's acceptance of *bontés* from Orléans and Dubois was approved by James, Atterbury interpreted the gifts as "proof" of Ramsay's collaboration with Mar and the French ministers when they betrayed the bishop's plot to George I. One wonders if Delafaye and his agents were spreading such reports, as they continued to provide disinformation in order to provoke divisions among Mar's and Atterbury's supporters.

On 17 October an Atterbury supporter in Paris wrote a colleague in Rome to warn him about Mar and Ramsay:

> A more certain voucher of his [Mar's] integrity is preparing to set out and you will soon see him, it is one Ramsay, a man of witt and learning of whose honesty and good intentions all that know him are persuaded to discern true merit, he is full of pretty notions of virtue which he learnt from a great master [Fenelon], but he has not practised men and easily imagines his hero [Mar] really is what he knows he should be. Such an one Scavenger [Mar] judg'd proper for his purpose, he has used him these three years past with all the art he is master of and now that he is well assur'd of his sentiments and inclinations, he ventures him in all affairs. Ramsay's reputation of a probity man contributes to supply the loss of his [Mar's] own. This is not to give you an ill impression of Ramsay who does not want merit (and may prove a good

[26] Jeremy Black, "A Failed Attempt at Censorship: the British Diplomatic Service and Pöllnitz's *Histoire secrète de la Duchesse d'Hanover,*" *Quaerendo,* 18 (1988), 212.

[27] *Ibid.,* 91; Pauline McLynn, *Factionalism among the Exiles in France: The Case of Chevalier Ramsay and Bishop Atterbury.* Royal Stuart Papers, #33 (Huntingdon, 1989), 3.

preceptor: *rayé*) and become capable of anything to the Prince, if the solidity of his judgment be equal to the vivacity of his imagination; what I have hinted is only to give you an idea of Scavenger's managment, his cunning and activity are really surprising…[28]

If Ramsay indeed planned to reveal to James his belief in a mystical and universalist Freemasonry, he would find the times unpropitious. During his tenure in Rome, on-going developments in the Grand Lodge in London would reinforce James's distrust of Masonry. In the wake of Wharton's defeat and withdrawal, the new Grand Master Dalkeith--now solidly Hanoverian – and his deputy Desaguliers consolidated their power. A rule was passed that no new lodge, "in or near London," would be countenanced by Grand Lodge, "without it be Regularly Constituted," and no Master or Warden from an irregular lodge would be admitted to the Grand Lodge.[29]

Meanwhile in Ireland, Swift admired Wharton's surreptitious attacks on the Whigs in *The True Briton* and hoped to find a way to safely contribute to the cause. On 20 September 1723 he complained to Pope of "my Infelicity in being so strongly attached to Tray-tors (as they call them) and Exiles, and State Criminals."[30] He corresponded with the Duchess of Ormonde, who had been named in the proceedings against Atterbury, de-spite his awareness of the government's interception of their letters. At this time, the duchess sent her chaplain, Mr. Creake, to serve George Kelly in the Tower.[31] Perhaps worried about Swift's vulnerability, Bolingbroke sent him a strangely worded letter from Aix-la-Chapelle on 25 December. At this time, Bolingbroke was trying to ingratiate him-self with Walpole by supplying information from France. Despite his shifting political loyalties, Bolingbroke was always personally loyal to Swift and evidently wanted to warn him about Walpole's internationally expanding intelligence system.

Writing in a jocular, veiled style, Bolingbroke revealed that someone in his company had read a letter by Swift and concluded that he was an initiate of a mystical society:

> A learned Rosycrucian of my acquaintance, who is a fool of as much knowledge and as much wit as I ever knew in my life…said a great many extravagant things about the natural and theurgick magick, and inform'd us, that tho' the sages who deal in the occult Sciences have been laugh'd out of some countrys, & driven out of others, yet there are to his knowledge many of them in Ireland. I stopped these guessers, & others who were perhaps ready, by assuring them my correspondent [Swift] was neither a Saint or Conjuror …I defended you the best I could… I depend on the fidelity of your friendship that it [his verse epistle] shall fall under no eye but your own.[32]

If Bolingbroke had learned of Swift's intent to publish an anti-Whig Masonic satire, he may have worried that Swift's burlesque style would be subjected to the same kind of "Cabalistic" deciphering that led to Atterbury's arrest. Nine months later, he would use explicitly Masonic language in another veiled warning to Swift.[33]

---

[28] Pierre Chevallier, *La Première Profanation du Temple Maçonnique* (Paris, 1968), 139.

[29] R. Gould, *History*, III, 125-31.

[30] J. Swift, *Correspondence*, II, 468.

[31] *Memoirs of the Life, Travels and Transactions of the Revd. Mr. George Kelly* (London, 1736), 21.

[32] J. Swift, *Correspondence.*, II, 478.

[33] *Ibid.*, II, 514.

Wharton continued to defend Atterbury in *The True Briton* and, on 18 October 1723 he published an especially risky poem. Comparing Atterbury to the Roman hero Tully and Walpole to Clodius, he stressed that Clodius, "a Lewd Roman Senator," who banished Tully, was eventually killed by Milo, "a person of Consular Dignity."[34] The last lines proclaimed, "Blest be the man, who does his [Clodius's] Pow'r defy,/ And dares or truly speaks, or bravely Die." Wharton knew that he was sailing close to the wind, and he worried about the similar vulnerability of Pope, who had publicly defended Atterbury. On 13 January 1724 he published a warning about the profusion of informers and maniacal decipherers unleashed by the Whig ministers. "I remember some years ago," that a gentleman published a treatise that "laid down many very important Arguments to demonstrate that Mr. Pope's Poem, intituled, *The Rape of the Lock*, was a sly and subtle Scheme, contrived by the said Mr. Pope to introduce Popery, Tyranny, Arbitrary Power," etc.[35] This reminder suggests that Wharton's description of government decipherers as occultist "Magi" was rooted in their earlier interpretation of Pope's Rosicrucian machinery as a Jacobite code. Sensing that he was the next target, Wharton announced his intention to leave England (in the last issue of the *True Briton* on 17 February 1724). Seven days later, his printer Payne was arrested and charged with libel upon "every Branch of the Legislature" which "manifestly tended to make the Constitution itself odious to the People."[36]

While Wharton undertook serious and dangerous political initiatives, he could not resist continuing his rakish behavior. In February 1724 Lady Mary Wortley Montagu, who had become temporarily friendly with him, wrote her sister, the exiled Lady Mar:

> Twenty very pretty fellows (the Duke of Wharton being president and chief director) have formed themselves into a committee of gallantry. They call themselves the *Schemers*; and meet regularly three times a week, to consult on gallant schemes for the advantage and advancement of that branch of happiness which the vulgar call whoring... 'tis true they have the envy and curses of the old and ugly of both sexes, and a general persecution from all old women; but this is no more than all reformations must expect in their beginning.[37]

Despite her amused and ironic tone, Lady Mary actually approved of the reforming philosophy of Wharton's secret society, whose young members determined to bring fresh air into the stuffy rooms of establishment England.

Rumors about the Schemers soon called forth an attack upon them in *The Universal Journal* (6 June 1724), a short-lived paper which aimed at a reformation of manners.[38] Aware of Wharton's recent role as Grand Master, the pious author compared the Schemers to the Masons, who use certain signs "not very unlike those used by the Free Mason," but they laugh to scorn that Society, "which they are resolved to excel in Secrecy":

[34] *True Briton* (28 October 1723), 1-2.

[35] *Ibid.* (13 January 1724), 525.

[36] R. Gould, "Wharton," 122.

[37] Lady Mary Wortley Montagu, *The Complete Letters of Lady Mary Wortley Montagu*, ed. Robert Halsband (Oxford, 1966), II, 38-39.

[38] Robert Collis, "Jolly Jades, Lewd Ladies and Moral Muses: Women and Clubs in Early Eighteenth-Century Britain," *Journal for Research into Freemasonry and Fraternalism,*" Equinoxonline (2012),15-24.

> It was once feared by them, that the Free Masons would be justly deem'd the most Ancient Society, they having, in a very learned Treatise, lately published, proved themselves as old as Adam; but they have been delivered from this Fear, by the promise of a worthy Member, who has engaged himself shortly, in a very elaborate discourse, to prove their Order is of longer standing than the World, and that Lucifer, with the rest of the fallen Angels, were a Society of Gallant Schemers.[39]

The author complained that they "put on an Appearance of distinguished Knighthood, with this Difference, that the Ribbons of their Order are to be concealed beneath their Shirts." His reference to the Masons' "very learned Treatise" – Anderson's *Consitutions* (1723) – and the Schemer's plan to issue a discourse proving their more ancient origin suggests that Wharton was already planning his attacks upon the Grand Lodge. In the minutes of a Schemers' meeting, the "Knights" had planned a dangerous prank, in which they would release the unfed lions from the Tower and then raise a panic in the city. The author's promise to eventually reveal the names of eighteen members who signed the minutes perhaps intimidated them, for several were politically ambitious Whigs, while the Earl of Strafford was a Jacobite collaborator with Wharton. It would not be until September 1724 that Wharton would issue his "very elaborate discourse," under the name of a new secret society, the Gormogons, organized to challenge the Hanoverian Masons (to be discussed later).

When not "whoring," Wharton undertook a clandestine correspondence with James III and awaited his orders to depart to the Continent. His exit from the Grand Lodge enabled the Hanoverians to accelerate their effort to take over the whole system. Their exclusion of Jacobites and suspicious Tories steadily detached Freemasonry from its Stuart roots. At the same time, their development of a modern "speculative" system increasingly distanced Grand Lodge Masonry from its operative roots. In the process, the operative trade declined so precipitously that even Thomas Hewett, staunch Whig and George I's surveyor of works, complained in December 1723:

> we have no prospect of fine new buildings and, if there were monys to build a palace...there are so many weak pretenders, and wrong-headed mules that it is impossible to have anything good and of a fine taste... I assure you, Arts, Geometry, Mathematics etc. are out of fashion here...[40]

In February 1724 the Grand Lodge passed stringent rules against admitting "Strange Brothers," and every Master or Warden was ordered to bring lists of the members in his lodge to the next meeting. By June the Hanoverians seemed to gain full control, and a Walpolean Whig, Charles Lennox, Second Duke of Richmond, was installed as Grand Master, with the free-thinker Martin Folkes as his deputy. His friend William Stukeley later expressed his disapproval of Folkes, recording that in 1720 "he set up an infidel club at his house," where "others of the heathen stamp assembled: "From that time he has been propagating the infidel System With great assiduity, & made it even fashionable in

---

[39] *The Universal Journal*, 26 (6 June 1724), 2.
[40] H. Colvin, *History*, V, 71.

the Royal Society, so that when any mention is made of Moses, the deluge, of religion, Scriptures, &c, it is generally received with a loud laugh."[41]

Under the leadership of Richmond and Folkes, the Grand Lodge continued its efforts to maintain Whig-Hanoverian dominance of the fraternity. In November a "Brother Huddleston" was expelled for "laying aspersions" on Desaguliers.[42] However, in predominantly Jacobite Wales, the Masons refused to go along with the London Grand Lodge. Led by Sir Watkin Williams Wynn, they founded "The Cycle of the White Rose," which like Derwentwater's "Corporation of Walton-le-Dale" used Masonic-style secret meetings and oath-bound initiations to support the Stuart cause.[43] Philip Jenkins argues that in Wales, a center of Toryism, "it was virtually impossible to distinguish between Jacobite secret societies and masonic lodges, for both had common origins and very similar membership."[44] It is almost certain that Wynn himself, like his future son, was a Mason – an affiliation that would become significant to his later political activities.[45]

Meanwhile in Rome, Ramsay attempted to spread his Fenelonian message in the faction-ridden, rumor-plagued court. From his mentor Fenelon, Ramsay had learned that a good ruler must go through certain stages of religious development. Fenelon had attempted to influence the Regent Orléans and James III to undergo this training. In his *Lettres sur divers sujets de religion et métaphysique*, Fenelon used the first letter to make Orléans a good Jew, the second a good Christian, and the third a good Catholic. As R.B. Kanter observes, "All three would attempt to make him a good Fenelonian."[46] Though James revered Fenelon, he apparently thought Ramsay interpreted the first stage – to become a good Jew – too literally. In conversation with Joseph Spence, Ramsay later described his contact with a heterodox Jew in Italy in 1724:

> The (outward) Rabbi Mr. R. met with, his elegant study, etc. – What do you think of Moses? He was a great juggler. – What of Mahomet? Un *scelerato*. – What of Spinosa? Un *sceleratissimo*. What of Jesus? -Un *grande philosopho*. – (Jews in Italy not punished for speaking against Jesus, but punishable for speaking against Moses).[47]

Among known heterodox Jews, whom Ramsay could have met in Italy was Dr. Giuseppe Athias, a learned physician, whose "elegant study" (library) at Leghorn contained many tic works and who became a Freemason.[48] Ramsay could have seen him again in 1725, when the physician visited Paris. The cosmopolitan Athias later befriended the philosophers Vico and Montesquieu, who both developed Masonic associations.

---

[41] Quoted in R. Berman, *Foundations*, 133.

[42] D. Vieler, "As it Was," 88.

[43] F. Skeet, *Life of...James Radcliffe*, 42.

[44] Philip Jenkins, "Jacobites and Freemasons in Eighteenth-century Wales," *Welsh History Review*, 9 (1978-79), 392.

[45] P. Monod, *Jacobitism*, 303.

[46] Sanford B. Kanter, "Archbishop Fenelon's Political Activity: the Focal Point of Power in Dynasticism," *French Historical Studies*, 4 (1965-66), 331.

[47] Joseph Spence, *Observations, Anecdotes, and Characters of Books and Men*, ed. James Osborn (Oxford, 1966), I, 52.

[48] Carlo Francovich, *Storia del la Massoneria in Italia* (Firenze: La Nuova Italia, 1974), 73; "Giuseppe Athias," *Dictionario Biographico de l'Italiani* (Roma, 1962), IV, 525-26; Francesca Bregoli, "Jewish Scholarship, Science, and the Republic of Letters: Joseph Attias in Eighteenth-century Livorno," *Alef*, 7 (2007), 96-181.

Within a few years, Dr. Athias would be instrumental in opening a lodge at Florence, and he and other Jews would become active in a lodge at Leghorn. Ramsay later wrote his friend Thomas Carte, a Jacobite Mason, "I am curious in everything that regards the Jewish Antiquities. I look upon the Rabbinical Cabbala as the Jewish mythology, which is not to be despised."[49]

Ramsay's investigations into Jewish lore were shared by Richard Rawlinson, who arrived in Rome in March 1724. He had read Ramsay's *Vie de Fenelon* (1723) and would continue to collect his writings (including an MS. letter "To the King of Great Britain").[50] Rawlinson had recently visited with various Jews, whom he interviewed about their beliefs, and then attended a Jewish wedding and circumcision ceremony.[51] He also shared Ramsay's interest in chivalric orders, having just visited Malta, where he was thrilled by a meeting with the Grand Master of the Knights of Malta. He was further gratified when one of the knights showed him volumes on Cabalism and the philosopher's stone. When Rawlinson returned to England in 1726, he pursued his studies in Jewish and Crusader lore, while he became active in oppositional Freemasonry.

For Ramsay the true spirit of religion lay hidden in the Cabalistic and Hermetic myths of Stuart Freemasonry, as refined in Fenelon's universalist Catholicism. He evidently tried to persuade the Pope as well as James of the relevance and importance of this eclectic mystical tradition. However, he later recalled to Spence that Pope Benedict XIII was "a good weak man, who delights in the trifles of religion, and has no notion of the true spirit of it."[52] While he tutored the young prince and conversed with James, Ramsay soon learned that Mar's enemies Atterbury and James Murray were determined to undermine his mission in Rome. In spring 1724 they wrote to James to warn him about Ramsay's intrigues, which provoked the following reply from James on 3 April:

> I shall make the proper use of the lights you give me and I hope soon matters
> will be put on a better footing, but there must be time for everything. Ramsay
> is not to be anyways concerned in writing or politics. I know him well enough
> and shall be able to employ him according to his talents.[53]

James later recalled his response to Ramsay's proposals: "Ramsay is an odd body. He exposed himself strangely here to myself and others, but as yet I will be charitable enough to think him a mad man."[54] Ramsay's strange "madness" probably consisted of his theosophical beliefs, based on his studies in Jewish mystical traditions. When he discussed these beliefs with John Hay (later Earl of Inverness), the skeptical Scot chided him, "For God's sake don't think there is a thing existent as true religion. Mankind is not capable of it. If we were, perhaps at length we might work ourselves up an independency on celestial powers."[55]

---

[49] Bodleian: Carte MS. 226.f.419. Ramsay to Thomas Carte (22 November 1736).

[50] *Bibliotheca Rawlinsoniana* (London, 1756), 39, 131, 213.

[51] Brian Enright, "Richard Rawlinson" Collector, Antiquary, and Topographer" (Ph.D. Dissertation: Oxford University, 1956), 146-49.

[52] J. Spence, *Observations*, I, 52.

[53] H. Tayler, *Jacobite Court*, 229.

[54] James to Dunbar (December 1727); quoted in Alec Mellor, "The Mystery of the Jacobites and the Craft," *Transactions of the Phoenix Lodge, No.30*, 3 (1971-72), 76.

[55] P. McLynn, *Factionalism*, 14 n. 35.

On 21 November Baron von Stosch, a paid spy for the British government who operated under the code-name "Walton," reported to London that Ramsay's free-thinking version of Catholicism was regarded as subversive by the powerful and influential Cardinal Gualterio of the ultramontane *Zelati* party in the Vatican. Stosch observed that Ramsay was an intellectual, "an owl among lesser birds," but James considered his unbigoted approach to theological questions symptoms of superficiality and insincerity.[56] James cited Ramsay's silly attempt to "obtain a sort of an approbation of connivance that a child, born at Rome, whose father was a Catholic and mother Protestant, might be christened there by a Protestant parson." Believing Atterbury's reports that Ramsay was not concerned about the young prince's education but only about advancing Mar's position, James concluded that Ramsay's "conduct did not match the sublime thoughts he uttered."

Despite discouragement from James and the Pope, Ramsay may have had some success with his Masonic initiative, for a commemorative medal, dated 1724, asserts that a lodge was established in Rome that year.[57] If true, it seems likely that Charles Radcliffe, who visited Rome in 1724 would have been instrumental in the founding. In June of that year Radcliffe emerged from his state of precarious poverty when he married at Brussels Charlotte Livingston, Countess of Newburgh and widow of Thomas Clifford, son of the 2nd Lord Clifford of Chudleigh.[58] The Jacobite Cliffords would later emerge in *Écossais* Masonic history.[59] Radcliffe's impulsive yet persistent nature was reflected in his repeated proposals to the countess, who finally accepted him when he descended through her chimney and went on his knees to make a final plea. After his marriage, Radcliffe travelled back and forth from Paris to Italy, where he visited Rome and Turin. In 1725 he would help found a Masonic lodge in Paris. According to some Masonic scholars, the alleged Roman lodge of 1724 – under a Chinese cover – was linked with Wharton's new Masonic initiative in London.[60] Radcliffe would later collaborate with Ramsay in reviving the Cabalistic and chivalric themes of earlier Stuart Freemasonry.

As Jacobite Masons on the Continent continued their intrigues, Bolingbroke wrote from France to Swift a letter with suggestive Masonic-style language. On 12 September he responded to a letter from Swift (now lost) in which the dean evidently implied that Bolingbroke was a "free thinker" or "esprit fort" and compared him to the Jewish rationalist Benedict de Spinosa. Characterizing some free thinkers as "the pests of society" because they tear down the structures of society, Bolingbroke contrasted them to religious believers:

> Reveal'd Religion is a lofty & pompous structure erected close to the humble & plain building of Natural Religion. Some have objected to you, who are the Architects...of the former, to you who built, or att least repair the house, & shew the rooms, that strengthen some parts of yr own building, you shake & even sap the foundations of the other, and between you and I, Mr Dean, this charge may be justify'd in several instances. But still your intention is not

---

[56] *Ibid.*, 5-7.
[57] According to Ulisse Bacci; see Silvio Gratton, *Trieste Segreta* (Trieste, 1987), 55.
[58] R. Arnold, *Northern Lights*, 185.
[59] A. Kervella, *Chevalier Ramsay*, 351.
[60] G. Henderson, *Ramsay*, 166.

to demolish, whereas the Esprit fort, or the free thinker, is…set upon pulling down yr house about yr Ears…

I make no doubt that you are by this time abundantly convinc'd of my orthodoxy, & and that you will name me no more in the same breath with Spinosa…[61]

It is curious that in 1724, when Swift was writing his *Letter from the Grand Mistress*, that Bolingbroke addressed him in Rosicrucian and Masonic terms.

In the meantime in England, the Hanoverian Mason Daniel Defoe worked to sabotage the efforts of Nathaniel Mist, whose *Weekly Journal* had become the main Jacobite organ.[62] Paula Backsheider observes that Defoe's chief government work was "to infiltrate Tory newspapers in order to weaken the effectiveness of their opposition to the Whigs."[63] His government controller was Delafaye, his Masonic brother. When Defoe anonymously published volume I of *A Tour Through the Whole Island of Great Britain* on 23 May 1724, he may have drawn on architectural and Masonic material he gleaned from Mist and his correspondents. Though his criticism of Cromwell and the seventeenth-century iconoclasts who destroyed architecture and his praise of Wren's achievement at St. Paul's seemed sincere, he hoped to retain Mist's trust by appealing to Stuart traditions. His practical architectural experiences may also have mellowed his attitude, for in 1724 he built for himself a substantial new house at Stoke Newington, where he also participated in a Masonic lodge.[64]

Defoe lamented that there was no city planning for London, which sprawled and festered chaotically, and he reminded readers of the earlier noble buildings that fronted the Strand.[65] He praised the "wise architect" of St. Paul's, despite its detractors, noting that Wren was "often baulked" in his efforts. Wren wanted the dome covered in copper, but "he was over-ruled by Party, and the city thereby deprived of the most glorious sight that the world ever saw, the temple of Solomon." Commenting that the king's palace at St. James was "too mean," he nevertheless praised its "living furniture," George I, who deserved a "more magnificent fabrick" at Whitehall: "The ruins of that old palace seem to predict that the time will come, when that Phoenix shall revive, and when a building shall be erected there, suiting the majesty and magnificence of the British princes."[66] Defoe then made a provocative statement: "I once saw a model of the palace itself, know its author, and when it was proposed." He gave a lengthy summary of "A Scheme for a Royal Palace in the Place of White-Hall," that eerily foreshadowed Mar's ambitious plan of 1726.

Defoe had worked with Mar during the union campaign and visited his residences in Scotland and England, where he admired the earl's architectural talents.[67] In 1710-12 Mar had lived in the ruined precincts of Whitehall and may have made a model for a new

---

[61] J. Swift, *Correspondence*, II, *514-15.*

[62] Jeremy Black, "An Underrated Journalist: Nathaniel Mist and the Opposition Press during the Whig Ascendancy," *Journal for Eighteenth-Century Studies*, 10 (2008),27-41.

[63] Paula Backsheider, *Daniel Defoe: Ambition and Innovation* (Lexington, 1986), 64.

[64] John Robert Moore, *A Checklist of the Writings of Daniel Defoe* (Hamden, 1971), 227.

[65] [Daniel Defoe], *A Tour Through the Whole Island of Great Britain*, ed. G.D.H. Cole and D.C. Browning (New York, 1962), I, 314, 326, 332-335.

[66] *Ibid.*, I, 355.

[67] M. Stewart, "Lord Mar's Gardens," 37.

palace as well as designs for canals and gardens. Like Mar's known plan, Defoe's architect called for extensive use of Portland stone, Palladian arches and columns, intricate canals, and the acquisition of Buckingham House to be incorporated into the new design. The ambitious stone work would supply employment and profit to British craftsmen, which would benefit the nation. Defoe also referred to Benson's "ignorance and vanity," which had a deleterious effect on architecture and the building trade.[68] If Mar was "the author" to whom Defoe referred, it would explain the latter's coyness about his source, for Defoe subsequently excoriated Mar for his role in the 1715 rebellion. Dr. Arbuthnot, who had been close to Mar and familiar with his architectural projects, acquired volume I of Defoe's *Tour*, and perhaps sensed that Defoe, now posing as a Jacobite sympathizer, was sincere in his praise of Scottish and Stuart architectural traditions.[69]

However, Defoe's employment by Mist ended soon after publication of *A Tour*, and his deceptive role was evidently exposed. William Lee suggests that Mist and Wharton "had discovered Defoe's connection with the government, while also in the management of the Journal." [70] Lee argues further that they ruined his reputation with other journal publishers and were probably behind the assassination attempt against a frightened Defoe in late 1724. While Defoe complained that his efforts to find intelligence work were "baffled and disheartened by Journalists," the government implemented intensified surveillance throughout the British Isles. Walpole was worried about a new Swedish-Jacobite plot, which included an Irish dimension.

In July 1724 Walpole's agents confiscated letters from Charles and Nicholas Wogan to their Dublin solicitor Francis Glascock, who was arrested and sent to Newgate.[71] The authorities charged Glascock with high treason for possessing three letters from the attainted Charles Wogan. Swift's friend Archbishop King was informed about Glascock's activities, which he considered "very foolish if not downright treasonable." Recognizing that his political correspondence with Dublin and London had become too risky, Charles Wogan consoled himself with plans for his marriage in Spain. He wrote to John Hay in Rome that his wealthy father in Ireland would send him "handsome furniture for a house" but nothing more, even though he was the eldest son, because "he is entirely govern'd by his present third wife" and is still "an able man in his generation, having been at ye trouble of getting 32 children, and 'tis odd enough to see me at forty have a brother of scarce one year old."[72] This enormous family would later prove a challenge to Swift when he tried to learn the identity of his anonymous correspondent, Charles Wogan. Wogan now honed his military skills in service to the Spanish king, in the hope that he would soon utilize them for the Stuart king.

In the meantime in London, Wharton took advantage of the new international opportunities to develop the "Gormogons" into an alternative fraternity to the Grand Lodge system, and he hinted at its links with the Stuart court in Rome. On 3 September 1724 the Tory-supporting *Daily Post* carried an odd announcement:

---

[68] *Ibid.*, 361-62.

[69] *Catalogue...Arbuthnot*, #15.

[70] W. Lee, *Daniel Defoe*, 462-65.

[71] Eamonn O'Ciardha, "Jacobite Jail-Breakers, Jail-Birds: the Irish Fugitive and Prisoner in the Early Modern Period," *Immigrants and Minorities* (2013), 17.

[72] H. Tayler, *Jacobite Epilogue*, 292-93.

Whereas the truly ANTIENT NOBLE ORDER of the Gormogons, instituted by Chin-Quaw Ky-Po, the first Emperor of China...many thousand
years before Adam, and of which the great philosopher Confucius was Oecumenical Volgee, has lately been brought into England by a Mandarin, and
he having admitted several Gentlemen of Honour into the Mystery of that
most illustrious order, they have determined to hold a Chapter at the Castle
Tavern in Fleet Street... This is to inform the public, that there will be no
drawn Sword at the Door, nor Ladder in a dark Room, nor will any Mason
be receiv'd as a Member till he has renounced his Novel Order and been
properly degraded. N.B. – The Grand Mogol, the Czar of Muscovy, and
Prince Tochmas are enter'd into this Hon. Society; but it has been refused
to the Rebel Meriweys, to his great Mortification. The Mandarin will shortly
set out for Rome, having a particular Commission to make a Present of this
Antient Order to his Holiness, and it is believ'd the whole Sacred College of
Cardinals will commence Gormogons.[73]

George Kloss, the able German Masonic historian, argued in the 1840s that the "Oe-
cumenical Volgee" referred to Ramsay, who summoned the "Mandarin" Wharton to
Rome.[74] Wharton later used the term "the Usurper Merryweis" (a variant of "the rebel
Meriweys") as a code name for George I, when he recklessly praised the Pretender in
"The Persian Letter" in 1728.[75] The inclusion of Czar Peter in the Gormogons, at a time
of renewed Jacobite and Swedish-Holstein overtures to Russia, suggests that "Prince
Tochmas" was perhaps Duke Carl Fredrik of Holstein.

Though R.F. Gould rejected Kloss's argument that Ramsay was connected with the
Gormogons, the German's claim has gained credibility from more recent archival scholarship, which reveals Ramsay's close friendship with Bishop Jean-François Fouquet, who
arrived in Rome in June 1723, after twenty-two years' service as a Jesuit missionary in
China. Ramsay was introduced to Fouquet by the Jesuit Edouard de Vitry, and he was
delighted to learn that Fouquet's "Figurist" beliefs reinforced his own studies in Jewish
mysticism, especially in its development into Christian Cabalism.[76] Ramsay elicited from
the Sinophile missionary an exposition of his belief that the ancient Chinese mystical
books pre-dated Moses, "having come from Adam through Seth and Enoch," and pre-
figured Christianity.[77]

If Ramsay was already a Freemason, he would be intrigued by the themes in Fouquet's
unpublished treatise, *Propylaeum templi veteris sapientiae* ("An entrance of the temple of ancient wisdom"), which drew on his interest in Chinese architecture as well as mysticism.

---

[73] Summarized in R. Gould, *History*, III, 129-30.

[74] *Ibid.*, III, 129.

[75] P. Monod, *Jacobitism*, 179. R. Gould analyses the analogies between contemporary political affairs in
Persia with Wharton's Gomorgon terminology: "The situation...of the Persian Crown Prince, with a
usurper in possession of his capital (Ispahan), seems to have afforded the Jacobite faction in England..with
some of the texture for an allegory"; see his "Wharton," 122-23.

[76] G. Henderson briefly noted the influence of Fouquet on Ramsay, but he did not know that the two
actually met and were friendly in Rome; see his *Ramsay*, 113. Later scholars drew upon Fouquet's unpublished diary and correspondence in the Biblioteca Apostolica Vaticana, Fondo Borgia, Lat MS 565. See
especially John W. Witek, S.J., *Controversial Ideas in China and in Europe: A Biography of Jean-François Fouquet,
S.J. (1665-1741)* (Rome, 1982), 203, 219-20, 310, 314.

[77] *Ibid.*, 311.

Like the more spiritual Masons, Fouquet envisioned the construction of the Temple of Wisdom. He argued that multi-level, esoteric interpretations of the Hebrew scriptures revealed their similarities to those of Chinese theosophical works, and he warned his critics "that the Kabbala could support his view and that even more modern authors as Kircher and Cornelius à Lapide who were acquainted with the works of the Kabbala could be cited."[78] Like Ramsay and the Christian Cabalists, Fouquet believed that Figurism could serve as a *via media* between religions. When Fouquet's opponents charged him with heresy, Ramsay defended him before important personages in Rome, such as the cardinals Gualterio and Polignac.[79] Surprisingly, though Gualterio and James III disapproved of Ramsay's eclectic, "free-thinking" theosophy, the Pretender admired and accepted that of Fouquet, who became his intimate friend and constant companion. The old Jesuit even instructed James in Chinese languages, and the two conversed together in Mandarin.[80]

After Ramsay returned to Paris in November 1724, Fouquet wrote him on 4 December and noted with excitement that they shared the same ideas about "the ancient traditions":

> Your discoveries enchant me and I see with extreme joy that you proceed to the summit of the divine philosophy... Continue to search the great and unique object of your researches and be assured that you will find it everywhere: in the sky, in the earth, in all nature which is its image, in the sciences and in the arts, in the antique monuments, in the traditions of the peoples, in the fables themselves, which are the immutable and incorruptible truth. Also, never cease communicating to me your views.[81]

Bruno Neveu suggests that Ramsay now merged Figurist and Masonic notions and that he was received in a "gallican lodge" formed by Jacobite and Catholic Masons.[82] D.P. Walker notes Ramsay's continuing correspondence with Fouquet and affirms his belief that Ramsay assimilated his interest in Chinese, Jewish, and neo-Platonic mysticism – the "Ancient Theology" – into his Masonic philosophy.[83]

Thus, it is certainly possible that, as Georg Kloss argued, Ramsay was associated with the Chinese-themed Gormogons and with Wharton's efforts in London to distance Jacobite Masonry from the Hanoverian Grand Lodge. Kloss suggests further that the Jesuits hoped to utilize the Gormogons to further their own and the Stuarts' cause. Given Ramsay's important friendship with Fouquet and Jesuit support for Ramsay's subsequent publications, Kloss's previously discounted argument becomes more plausible. As we shall see, around 1740 a Masonic degree of "Irish Master" would utilize Jesuit and Chinese symbols, at a time when Ramsay was writing his "Chinese Letters" (now lost) and

[78] *Ibid.*, 215.

[79] Bruno Neveu, "La 'Science Divine' du Chevalier Ramsay," in Denise Leduc-Fayette, ed., *Fénelon: Philosophie et Spiritualité* (Genève, 1996), 188.

[80] Edward Corp, *The Stuarts in Italy, 1719-1766* (Cambridge, 2011), 69-70, 75, 166, 248.

[81] B. Neveu, "La 'Science Divine,'" 188.

[82] Bruno Neveu, "Un Roman de Spiritualité: *Les Voyages de Cyrus* du Chevalier Ramsay," in *Ecriture de la religion, Ecriture du roman. Mélanges de la littérature et de critique offerts à Joseph Tans* (Lille, 1979), 17-18.

[83] D.P. Walker, *The Ancient Theology: Studies in Christian Platonism from the Fifteenth to the Eighteenth Century* (Ithaca, 1972), 239-40, 248.

influencing the development of "higher degrees" in the *Écossasis* system.[84] In June 1745 the unusual degree would be administered in the Clermont lodge in Paris, a bastion of Jacobite support.

*

* *

During this period in London, a high-church Tory took advantage of the exposures of Masonry to mock the fraternity's alleged links with black magic – an oblique way of tarnishing the Whiggish Grand Lodge. Edward Ward, a prolific satirist, had gained Swift's admiration, especially for his attack in 1715 on the recently deceased Thomas, Lord Wharton: "Farewell, Old Bully of these Impious Times,/ True Patron of the Whigs, and of their Crimes."[85] Ward now published *The Dancing Devils: or, the Roaring Dragon. A Dumb Farce* (1724), in which he portrayed the magician Dr. Faustus as a Freemason, who uses secret signs to seduce innocent maids:

> The Doctor thus salutes the Lasses,
> But not a Word between 'em passes;
> For Scholars vers'd in magick Art,
> By Signs, their Sentiments impart,
> And can another's meaning reach,
> By gaping, better than by Speech.
> *So the Free-Masons have a way,*
> *By private Signals, to convey*
> *Their Secret Minds to one another,*
> *And can at once command a Brother,*
> *To quit his Scaffold and descend*
> *The Ladder, to salute his Friend;*
> *Without the needless sound of Words,*
> *Which makes th' illnatur'd World conjecture,*
> *(Instead of useful Architecture)*
> *They, in* ARS MAGIC, *have some dealing,*
> *And with the Dev'l a fellow-feeling;*
> *For Secrets by such numbers held,*
> *Must be suspected, whilst coneal'd,*
> *Because, if good, they'd be reveal'd.*[86]

He showed how "Faustus, who is, among the rest,/ As free a Mason as the best," gulls and seduces the ladies with the same kind of artifice that appears on the dramatic stage in low-level, corrupting performances. In conclusion, Ward revealed his true agenda, which was to expose "the screeks of the Machine" which lead to theatrical and political deceptions:

---

84 For the Irish degree, see René Désaguliers and Roger Dachez, "Chinese Thought and Freemasonry in the Eighteenth Century," in Arturo de Hoyos and Brent Morris, eds., *Freemasonry in Context: History, Ritual, and Controversy* (Lanham, 2004), 145-61. For Ramsay's possible influence, see ahead, Chapter Nineteen.
85 [Edward Ward], *The Lord Whiglove's Elegy* (London, 1715), 1; J. Swift, *Correspondence*, II, 126n.15; I, 113n.9.
86 [Edward Ward], *The Dancing Devils: or, the Roaring Dragon* (London, 1724), 36-37.

So, when an injur'd Peer is brought;
To die for some new Party-Plot,
Lest Truth the Peoples Ears should reach,
With Noise they drown his dying speech.[87]

As we shall see, Ward would later become a Freemason, on the high-church Tory side.

Another Tory took further aim at a well-known Whig Mason, John Heidegger, the Swiss-born sponsor of rowdy and profitable masquerades, in *A Seasonable Apology for Mr. Heidegger. Proving the Usefulness and Antiquity of Masquerading from Scripture, and prophane History, with Observations on the several Species of masks now in Use* (1724). Posing as a supporter of Heidegger, the ironic author dedicated the pamphlet to "Mother N---M," a brothel madam, who uses "the Mask of Sanctity" to "cover the Lewdness you get a Livelihood by." He rejected the xenophobic charge that Heidegger "designs by these Entertainments of his, to introduce Popery, and the Pretender," because he "has necessarily taken the Oaths to the Government, and abjur'd the Pretender."[88] He mocked the credulous history given in Anderson's *Constitutions* by noting that the brothers claim, without any proof, a tradition older than that of masquerades. "Some of them claimed their Original from Solomon, and say, they were instituted at the Building of the first Temple of Jerusalem," while another has fathered "the Follies of his Society on the All-wise Creator of all Things, and calls him their first Grand Master, as he created the Structure of the Universe; which Madness, I shall not think worth my Trouble of answering."[89]

The rumors circulating about black magic, seductive secrecy, and political subversion (whether by Jacobites, Whigs, or free-thinkers) provoked a warning in *The Plain Dealer* (14 September 1724). Christine Gerrard argues that the editor, Aaron Hill, was stimulated to launch this journal by his previous links with Wharton's *True Briton*, which was terminated in February 1724.[90] Hill, as "Verus Commodus," claimed to be a Mason and responded to the *Daily Post* story on the Gormogons.[91] He rebuked "my own Brotherhood, I mean the Worshipful Society of Free and accepted MASONS," for "the unaccountable Pother and Noise they have lately made in the World" and for their admission of "empty Coxcombs," "weak Heads," and lowly workmen:

> 'Tis my opinion that the late Prostitution of our Order is next to betraying it... I'm afraid some of the Brotherhood too, may stop here, and stare, as if I had blabb'd out the Mystery ... But I must... assure my guilty Brethren, that they have promoted Superstition and Babbling, contrary to the Peace of our Sovereign Lord the King, by their late Practices and Condescentions. Alarming Reports, and Stories of raising the DEVIL, of WITCHES, LADDERS, HALTERS, DRAWN SWORDS, and DARK ROOMS, have spread Confusion and Terror... If the Government does not put the Laws against us in Execution, it will be an extraordinary Favour, or Oversight... I have resolv'd never to countenance a Lodge again, unless the Grand Master puts

---

[87] *Ibid.*, 70

[88] Anon., *A Seasonable Apology for Mr. Heidegger* (London, 1724), 21.

[89] *Ibid.*, 18-19.

[90] Christine Gerrard, *Aaron Hill: The Muses' Projector, 1685-1756* (Oxford, 2003), 102.

[91] Marie Mulvey Roberts, "Hogarth on the Square: Framing the Freemasons," *British Journal for Eighteenth-Century Studies*, 26 (2003), 255-56.

a Stop to these Proceedings, by a speedy and peremptory Charge to all the Brotherhood.[92]

Praising the Gormogons for being "better establish'd, and regulated," Verus Commodus then revealed two letters from "Hang Chi" and "Shin Shaw," emissaries of the new fraternity, who urge interested brothers to abandon "the Society of Masons" and join the more dignified and merit-based Gormogons. Hoping to send the name of the *Plain Dealer* essayist to "the OECUMENICAL VOLGEE in China," Hang Chi receives a letter from Shin Shaw in Rome:

> I congratulate you on the speedy Progress you have made from the Court of the Young SOPHY, in Persia, and your safe Arrival in the Isle of Britain. Your Presence is earnestly expected at Rome. His Holiness is fond of our Order, and the Cardinals have an Emulation to be first distinguish'd.

The author then proposed "the good Conduct, and Regularity, of the GORMOGONS, as a Pattern to the Free and Accepted Masons for the Future."

On 2 October the *Daily Journal* advertised the publication of a new attack on the Grand Lodge, its official *Constitutions*, and its credulous and inaccurate authors. In *The Secret History of the Free-Masons: Being an Accidental Discovery of the Ceremonies Made Use of in Several Lodges* (1724), the anonymous author presented a genuine copy of the Old Charges, which he claimed was a three hundred year-old translation of an ancient original:

> some curious Talmudists among the Jews, and the Chaldean Magi, do assert the Original of this Copy was found by Moses in search after the Burial Place of Adam, in whose Monumental Stone-Coffin is suppos'd he met with other invaluable Materials which enabled him to compile that Part of the History of the World, before the Deluge, which some Infidels are apt to cavil at...[93]

The author criticized Anderson and Desaguliers for not consulting a Bodleian manuscript of the *Arabick Catena*, which describes Adam's "Monumental Stone" which was covered with hieroglyphics and preserved the secrets of Seth and Enoch.

He then quibbled with Desaguliers's misreadings and misinterpretations of Hebrew scriptures, as well as Anderson's undocumented claims about English history (especially the alleged initiations of Charles II and William III). He posited instead an alternative history, stressing that "the Rosy-Crucians and Adepts" are "Brothers of the same Fraternity, or Order." Alchemical masters such as Trismegistus, Paracelsus, and Sendivogius all contributed to Masonry, but the Grand Lodge went too far in claiming every variety of "Jack of all Trades" as Masons. Though *The Secret History of the Freemasons* avoided any Jacobite associations, it seemed to target the Grand Lodge Whigs. Or, did it reflect the government's concern about the fraternity as a whole? Some Masons feared that a full ban might be implemented.

On 17 October the "ancient" Masons followed up the Gormogon story in the *Plain Dealer* by using *Mist's Weekly Journal* to puff the antiquity and current expansion of the new "Chinese" fraternity:

---

[92] Reprint in Knoop, Jones, Hamer, *EMC*, 130-35.
[93] *EMP*, 111-30.

We hear another ancient Society is started up, in Town, of GORMOGONS, of much greater Antiquity and Reputation than the FREE MASONS; for whereas the latter can deduce their Original but from the Building of Babel, the former derive theirs some thousand years before Adam. The Order was lately brought over from China by a Mandarin, who is now departed for Rome, to establish a Lodge in that City, as he has done in London. We are informed a great many eminent Free Masons have degraded themselves, and come over to this Society, and several others rejected for want of Qualifications.[94]

Given the heavy press coverage of the Gormogons, the young artist William Hogarth sensed the opportunity to market a print depicting the controversy. According to Jenny Uglow, he issued "The Mystery of Masonry Brought to Light by the Gormogons" in late 1724, at a time when his teacher and future father-in-law James Thornhill was active in the Grand Lodge. Uglow observes that Hogarth's print, showing a ridiculous Gormogon procession, "Would please the Whig speculatives, to which Thornhill belonged."[95] Drawing on recent pamphlets, especially *An Hudibrastick Poem*, Hogarth showed a quixotic leader (Wharton) and his Chinese partisans, whose antics bring disgrace upon the ancient Masons as well as Gormogons. In the caption, Hogarth mocked their pretensions:

> The GORMAGONS, a Venerable Race,
> Appear Distinguish'd with peculiar Grace,
> What Honour! Wisdom! Truth! & Social Love!
> Sure such an Order had its Birth above.
> But Mark *Free Masons*! What a farce is this?
> How wild their Myst'ry! What a *Bum* they kiss.
> Who would not Laugh when such Occasion's had?
> Who would not Weep, to think ye World so Mad.[96]

Hogarth's mockery of Wharton and his cronies evidently paid off, for he was invited to join a "modern" lodge in autumn 1725.

On 12 December the Tory-supporting *British Journal* hinted further at Wharton's role in these bizarre intrigues, when it reported that "a Peer of the first Rank, a noted Member of the Society of Free-Masons, hath suffer'd himself to be degraded as a member of that Society" and thereupon "enter'd himself a Member of the Society of Gormogons." R.F. Gould comments that "the number of renegade Gormogons must, I think, have been very large."[97] The embattled Wharton longed to leave England, and he waited impatiently for orders from James. In the meantime, Wharton's alleged collaborator Ramsay had left Rome and was back in Paris, where his Jacobite colleagues would launch another Masonic initiative in the following year.

*

* *

---

[94] Reprinted in A. Robbins, "Earliest Years," 79.
[95] Jenny Uglow, *Hogarth: a Life and a World* (London, 1977), 108-11.
[96] *Ibid.*, 110.
[97] R. Gould, *History*, III, 130.

These Masonic-Gormogon squabbles provide a revealing context for Swift's anonymous publication of *A Letter from the Grand Mistress of the Female Free-Masons to Mr. Harding the Printer*, published by John Harding in Dublin, probably in late 1724, and again anonymously by Harding's widow in 1730. John Harding's *Dublin Impartial News* had reported on Masonic affairs in London and Dublin since 1721, the year when Swift first worked with him.[98] A daring critic of the English government, Harding had printed a Jacobite proclamation, and he spent much of 1723 in prison, during a period when *no* Masonic news appeared in the Dublin press.[99] The newspapers were preoccupied with the turbulent Irish protests against William Wood's copper coinage, which was seen as the product of Hanoverian greed and a direct attack on Irish national interests. Isaac Newton, the Whig director of the London Mint, assayed Wood's coins and issued a report defending his cause, which particularly irked Swift, who thought Newton had no right to intervene in the Irish case.[100]

By early 1724 Swift determined to publish an anonymous attack on Wood, Newton, and the Whig government in London, and he solicited Harding's collaboration as printer for *The Drapier's Letters* (issued anonymously by Swift from March to October 1724). It was evidently after the last letter appeared that Swift wrote his attack upon the modern Masonry of the London Grand Lodge, now dominated by Newton's partisans. Harding published the Masonic satire under the same imprint used for the *Drapier's Letters*, and in a Postscript, the Grand Mistress addresses Harding: "Our Lodge unanimously desire you will give our Sincere Regrets to your Ingenious DRAPIER, to whose Pen we, as well as the Rest of the Nation, own our selves oblig'd. If he be not already a Free-Mason, he shall be welcome to be our Deputy."[101] Irish academic and Masonic historians have long identifed Swift as the author, with credible contextual arguments.[102]

As Swift's pamphlets against Wood's coins steadily appeared, he became a patriotic hero to Irish nationalists, who organized the artisan guilds to demonstrate their support for him. The Irish Masonic historians Lepper and Crossle argue that the Freemasons of Dublin joined the other Trade Gilds to support Swift's campaign: "at this period we find the natural leaders of the new school of Freemasonry also heading the patriotic party in politics... Jonathan Swift himself was, in the opinion of many masonic scholars, a Fellow

---

[98] P. Crossle, and J.Lepper, *History*, 41-48; Jonathan Swift, *The Drapier's Letters*, ed. Herbert Davis (Oxford, 1935), xxii-lxviii, 201.

[99] I. Higgins, "Jonathan Swift," 95.

[100] J. Swift, *Drapier's*, 21, 205.

[101] J. Swift, *Prose Works*, V, 333.

[102] In Chapter Two, I presented the 18th-century publishing history of *Letter from the Grand Mistress*, in which Swift was repeatedly identified as the author. The Irish Masonic historian Chetwode Crawley argued for Swift's authorship in "Early Irish Freemasonry and Dean Swift's Connection with the Craft," in Henry Sadler, ed., *Masonic Reprints and Historical Revlations* (London, 1898), vii-xxxv. In 1910 the Irish editor Elrington F. Ball noted that Swift, Pope, and Arbuthnot were Freemasons and that it was "tolerably certain" that the *Letter from the Grand Mistress* was "a genuine production of Swift's pen"; *Correspondence*, I, xxxi-xxxii. The Irish Masonic historians J.H. Lepper and Philip Crossle discussed his authorship in *History of the Grand Lodge of Free and Accepted Masons of Ireland* (1925), I, 445-62; which was reinforced by Crossle in "Freemasonry in Ireland, circa 1725-31," *The Lodge of Research, No. CC. Ireland. Transactions for the Year 1924* (Dublin, 1931). In 1962 the English editor Herbert Davis included it as *possibly* by Swift in the Appendix of *Prose Works*, V, 323-33. In 2013 the American historian Paul Monod wrote in *Solomon's Secret Arts*, 381n16,that "Swift is now acknowledged to have been the author"

of the Craft.[103] At the Truck Street Club, which was formed to agitate against Wood's halfpence, members composed tunes in honor of the patriotic "Drapier." One was published as a Masonic song – i.e. *A New Song Sung at the Club at Mr. Taplin's the Sign of the Drapier's Head in Tuck Street* – to be sung "To the Tune of the Apprentice's Song in Massonary." The song became so popular in Dublin that Faulkner printed it as a broadsheet.[104]

Lepper and Crossle note further that "For some years to come we shall find the Speculative Craft not wholly divorced from their operative Brethren in Ireland."[105] From June to December 1724, Swift was in close contact with operative Masons, while he supervised the construction of an ambitious and expensive stone wall for "Naboth's Vineyard," south of his deanery.[106] He became increasingly interested in building projects and would later record his pleasure in "levelling mountains" and "raising stones" while acting as "overseer" to stonecutters and craftsmen. He was also in contact with "gentleman" Masons, such as Richard Parsons, 1st Earl of Rosse, who had earlier been friendly with Wharton, when both attended the Irish House of Lords in August 1717, and Wharton especially earned Swift's admiration. David Ryan notes that Rosse and Wharton must have recognized one another as kindred spirits: "They were of a similar age and shared a liking for drink and dissipation, an underlying Jacobitism, and a strong disregard for orthodox religion."[107] On 14 October 1724 Rosse signed the legal protest against Wood's halfpence and supported Swift's campaign.[108] From about 1723 or 1724, Rosse was evidently involved in a secret Grand Lodge in Dublin, which became public in June 1725 when he was elected Grand Master, in succession to the previous (un-named) Grand Master.[109] Thus, when Swift wrote his Masonic pamphlet, he had access to traditional and contemporary Irish and English Masonic lore and a readership who could easily decipher his allusions.

In Chapter Two of this book, I quoted from Swift's long Scots-Irish version of Masonic history (from Solomon through Fergus, the Druids, Cabalists, Lullists, and Rosicrucians to the Stuarts), so I will not repeat it here. I placed his account in the context of his experiences in Ulster in 1695-96. But in the 1724 context of *A Letter from the Grand Mistress*, Swift revealed his insider's knowledge about the struggles within the London Grand Lodge system, which involved Wharton (who had planned to return to Ireland in 1723 and may have been in secret communication with Swift, Rosse, and their friends). Swift responded to specific items published in rival pamphlets about Masonry (including *An Hudibrastick Poem*), which were often reprinted in Dublin or circulated through local lodges.[110] In *The Plain Dealer* (14 September), the anonymous Masonic author (Aaron Hill) criticized the indiscriminate recruitment of unworthy brethren (Wigmakers, Weavers, etc.) and reported that he had heard it asked, "Why we don't admit Women, as well as

---

[103] J. Lepper and P. Crossle, *History*, 47-48.
[104] P. Crossle, "Freemasonry," 125.
[105] *Ibid.*, 125.
[106] J. Swift, *Correspondence*, II, 500.
[107] David Ryan, *Blasphemers & Blackguards: The Irish Hellfire Clubs* (Dublin, 2012), 25.
[108] P. Crossle and J. Lepper, *History*, 46.
[109] *Ibid.*, 53-54; S. Murphy, "Irish Jacobitism," 78.
[110] Swift collected and read a huge number of political pamphlets, which are listed only as "many bundles of pamphlets," without titles, in his 1745 library catalogue.

Taylors, into our Lodges?"[111] This jibe may have contributed to Swift's decision to assume a female personae in *Letter from the Grand Mistress*.[112] Drawing on the story of Elizabeth St. Leger's initiation in an Irish lodge, Swift's Grand Mistress boasts that "our Female Lodge has the whole Mistery as well as any Lodge in Europe" – a hint at Swift's awareness of the expansion of Jacobite Freemasonry on the Continent.

Swift also made clear the Scottish origins of the fraternity, which was brought to England by James VI and I, who "reviv'd Masonry, of which he was Grand-Master," because it had been entirely suppressed by Queen Elizabeth. Like the Scottish monarchs, the French kings were "always eminent Free-Masons." Stressing that "Marine Architecture" was the "most useful Branch of the Sacred Art," Swift called those Masons "workers in Oak" – thus hinting at the development of naval Masonry under Wren and its association with the royalist oak tree of Stuart iconography. (Wharton had recently protested that an intercepted letter from the "Royal Oak" was used against Atterbury).[113] Swift pointed to the current polarization within the fraternity in London, noting that "when a Dissention happens in a Lodge the going off and forming other Lodges is...call'd Swarming." He then praised the efforts of "the Chinese Sage" to develop an alternative Masonry (i.e., the Gormogons):

> Our Guardian is of Opinion, that the present Masonry is so tarnish'd by the Ignorance of the working, and some other illiterate Masons, that very many, even whole Lodges fall under the censure of the venerable Chinese Brachman, whose History of the Rise, Progress, and Decay of Free-Masonry, writ in the Chinese Tongue, is lately translated into a Certain European language.[114]

This certainly suggests his awareness of the Sinophile Figurists' influence on Jacobite Freemasons such as Wharton and Ramsay.[115]

However, Swift also addressed the current dangers that ancient Masons faced from government informers and spies. Under the guise of explaining the origins of Masonic signs in the shapes of Hebrew letters, he hinted at the Cabalistic techniques now used by government spies to decipher Masonic-style communication:

> Now as to the Secret Words and Signals used among Free- Masons, 'tis to be observ'd that in the Hebrew Alphabet...there are Four Pairs of Letters, of which each Pair is so like, that at first View they seem to be the same, *Beth* and *Caph*, *Gimel* and *Nun*, *Cheth* and *Thau*, *Daleth* and *Resch*, and on these Depend all their Signals and Grips. *Cheth* and *Thau* are shap'd like Two standing Gallowses (of Two Legs each) when Two Masons accost each other, one cries *Cheth*, the other answers *Thau*, signifying that they wou'd be Hang'd on the Gallows rather than Divulge the Secret.

---

[111] *The Plain Dealer*, no. 51 (14 September 1724).

[112] *EMP*, 132.

[113] *True Briton* (5 July 1723), 78.

[114] J. Swift, *Prose*, 328.

[115] For more on the relationship of Swift and Ramsay, see my article, "Swift, Ramsay, and the Jacobite-Masonic Version of the Stuart Restoration," in Richard Caron, ed., *Ésoterisme, Gnoses & Imaginaire Symbolique: Mélanges offerts à Antoine Faivre* (Leuven, 2001), 491-505.

> Then again *Beth* and *Caph* are each like a Gallows lying on one of the Side-Posts, and when used as above, imply this Pious Prayer: *May all who Reveal the Secret hang upon the Gallows till it falls down.* This is their Master Secret, generally call'd the Great Word.[116]

His repeated references to the Hebrew letters as shaped like gallows suggested the political dangers faced by opposition, Jacobite, or oath-breaking Freemasons. He further interpreted patterns of posture and walking as rooted in Hebrew: "when one Brother orders another to walk like a Mason," he must walk backwards "because the Hebrew is Writ and Read Backwards." The Masons' secret body language of certain handshakes, gestures, embraces, and postures enabled intiated brothers to identify each other.

It is relevant that his Tory friend Thomas Sheridan owned a rare copy of *Liber Jezira*, translated and edited by Rittangel (Amsterdam, 1642), a work that revealed the architectural imagery of hewing and setting stone used in the Cabalists' manipulation of Hebrew letters and numbers.[117] Swift frequently drew on books in Sheridan's library, and Rittangel's Latin translation of the Hebrew *Sepher Yetzirah* would become an important influence on Ramsay's Cabalistic-Masonic notions.[118] Moshe Idel explains that the mystical language of the *Sepher Yetzirah* has a "masonic" function, for the letters and words serve as building blocks:

> Letters are regarded as stones, as full-fledged entities, as components intended to build up an edifice of words to serve as a temple for God and a place of encountering Him for the mystic. After the Temple was destroyed…man is supposed to rebuild the Temple in his ritual use of language…The "masonic" aspects of the divine and human activity reveal a hidden and mighty dimension of the Hebrew letters…[which enable] operations that can bridge the gap between the human – or the material – and the divine.[119]

Thus, the Jewish adept meditates upon and chants these "masonic" lines, which enables him to visualize the rebuilding of the Temple:

> Two stones build two houses,
> Three stones build six houses,
> Four stones build twenty-four hosues,
> Six stones build one hundred and twenty houses,
> Seven stones build five thousand and forty hosues.
>   From here on go out and think what the mouth is unable to speak, and
> the ear is unable to hear.[120]

---

[116] J. Swift, *Prose*, V. 325.

[117] Thomas Sheridan, *Catalogue of Books in the Library of the Rev. Dr. Thomas Sheridan* (Dublin, 1739),40.For Sheridan's and Swift's interest in the *Sepher Yetzirah*, see M.K. Schuchard, "Swift, Ramsay, and 'the Cabala, as *Masonry* was call'd in those Days,'" *English Language Notes*, 42 (August 2018).

[118] Andrew Michael Ramsay, *The Travels of Cyrus* (London, 1727), II, 134-37.

[119] Moshe Idel, "The Reification of Language," in Steven T. Katz, *Mysticism and Language* (New York, 1992), 43.

[120] David Blumenthal, *Understanding Jewish Mysticism: The Merkabah Tradition and the Zoharic Tradition* (Leiden, 1980), 37.

Swift certainly seemed familiar with this meditation technique from the *Sepher Yetzirah*, which had influenced the Art of Memory required of early Scottish Masons, and he scorned the modern Masons who were unaware of the ancient Hebrew traditions of "Celtic" operative Masonry:

> I believe there are even some Masons who know nothing of it [the *Manabo-leth*], viz. that it has been an Antient Practice among the Cabalistic Philoso-phers to make every Hebrew Letter a Hieroglyphick Misterious in its Figure above all other Letters, as being thus Shap'd and Form'd by the immediate Directions of the Almighty, whereas all other LETTERS are of Humane Invention.
>
> Secondly, that the *Manaboleth* has a very close and unconstrain'd Analogy with Masonry or Architecture...and I think it pretty plain, that Timber and Stone are as much the Elements of Masonry as the Alphabet is of Books.[121]

Katsumi Hashinuma suggests that the word Manaboleth "is apparently derived by anal-ogy with 'shibboleth,' a word of Hebrew origin,...used as a kind of testword by Gileadites in order to detect Ephraimites, their contending faction, who could not pronounce the sound *sh*."[122]

Like Pope's earlier *Key to the Lock*, in which he made such outrageous Jacobite inter-pretations of his own poem that it rendered them ridiculous and incredible, Swift's Ma-sonic "Key" aimed to render absurd and legally un-actionable the deciphering of Delafaye and other Whig-Masonic spies. Swift concluded the Grand Mistress's letter with a song from the *Constitutions*, which "is of as little Signification as the Rest of their Secrets." It was written by "one Anderson," just "to put a Good Gloss on the Mistery." As noted earlier, Anderson's songs were demonstrations of loyalty to George I and his Whig min-istry. Despite the burlesque style, Swift's pamphlet was not merely a "tease" or *jeu d'esprit*, for he was in real danger because of the government's suspicion that he wrote the *Drapier's Letters*. The unfortunate Harding, printer of those and the Masonic letter, was charged with seditious publishing and sent to prison, where he soon died. In 1730 his widow boldly republished the *Letter from the Grand Mistress*, while maintaining the ano-nymity of the author.

*

* *

For several months in 1724, Thomas Carte consulted with Mar, Dillon, and Lans-downe about Atterbury's charges against Mar. Dillon assured him that James had ap-proved of all Mar's dealings with the British ambassador Lord Stair and believed that their contact could be useful to the Stuart cause.[123] He showed Carte the letter from James which justified all of Mar's actions. Though Atterbury claimaed that Mar received an English pension and provided information to Walpole, Dillon reported that Mar never wrote anything nor received the pension. Carte apparently met Ramsay at this time, who

---

[121] J. Swift, *Prose*, V, 331.
[122] K. Hashinuma, "Jonathan Swift and Freemasonry," 21.
[123] Bodleian: Carte MS. 231,ff.51-52,102,122.

returned to Paris in November and began to work closely with Mar. Unfortunately, for the Paris "Triumvirate" and Ramsay, by the end of the year, Atterbury's campaign to blacken their reputations had so disturbed James that he acquiesced in the bishop's policy of eliminating their influence on the court at Rome. In the process, James and Atterbury's party lost the benefit of their Masonic networks of communication and recruitment. In December the Scottish exile George Lockhart lamented that the old "detexerity" and "secresie" had gone from Jacobite affairs.[124] However, most of the Jacobites in Paris remained loyal to Mar and, under the leadership of Radcliffe (and possibly Mar and Ramsay), they soon established a new lodge in the city that would become an important vehicle for preserving and expanding the ideals of Stuart Freemasonry. In the process, they eventually developed "la maçonnerie nouvelle" of *Écossaisme*, which merged "ancient" Cabalistic traditions with chivalric ideals and international ambitions.

---

[124] M. Bruce, "Mar in Exile," 81.

CHAPTER TEN

MASONIC RIVALRIES AND INTERNATIONAL RAMIFICATIONS
(1725-1726)

If ever you hear from me…it will be in a few REMARKS on that
Empty Book called, The Constitutions, &c. of the Free-Masons,
Written, as I am told, by a Presbyterian Teacher, and pompously
Recommended by a certain Orthodox, tho' Mathematical Divine.

Verus Commodus, *Two Letters to a Friend* (1725).

She might easily have sought
To sound the Bottom of a Plot;
Or, though a Woman, ta'en Occasion
T'enquire the Secret of *Free Mason*,
Or how, as Mystic Lodge supposes,
Duke *Wharton* can succeed to *Moses*.

Samuel Wesley, *The Pig and the Mastiff* (1725).

In the wake of Swift's *Letter from the Grand Mistress*, with its Cabalistic macaronics and gallows humor, the Jacobite Masons entered 1725 with new strategies to protect their networks, recruit sympathizers, and expand their influence internationally. After returning to Paris in February, Ramsay cooperated with Charles Radcliffe, Sir Hector Maclean, and Dominic O'Heguerty, during the period when they established a new lodge at the premises of "Huré," an English caterer, on rue de Boucheries, faubourg St. Germain.[1] The lodge drew members from the Irish regiments in French service and from descendants of the original Stuart court at St. Germain-en-Laye. The initiates (a majority in their twenties) had been brought up at St. Germain in the 1690s and early 1700s, and most still lived there (ten of them in the château itself). The seventeen known or suggested members of the lodge were the cream of the Jacobite crop, in terms of their political, military, and Masonic significance. Their names and titles (past, present, and future) are here given:

---

[1] P. Chevallier, *Ducs*, 27-29, 141; P. Morbach, "Les régiments," 144.

Charles Radcliffe (later 5th Earl of Derwentwater); Francis Heguerty (a cadet in the Dillon regiment); Hector, 1st Jacobite Baron Maclean; James Drummond, 3rd Jacobite Duke of Perth; Charles (later 2nd Jacobite Earl) Dillon; John, 3rd Earl of Middleton; George Douglas, 2nd Earl of Dumbarton; Thomas Sackville (previously Groom of the Bedchamber to James III); Daniel O'Brien (later 1st Jacobite Earl of Lismore); Clement MacDermott (son of Terence MacDermott, Lord Mayor of Dublin); Charles Hamilton (illegitimate son of the 4th Duke of Hamilton); William Sheldon (son of Ralph Sheldon, late Equerry to James III); Richard Talbot, 3rd Earl of Tyrconnell; Charles FitzJames (son of the 1st Duke of Berwick, and later 2nd Duc de FitzJames); Charles Hyde (son of William Hyde, late Groom of the Privy Chamber to Mary of Modena); Daniel Macdonnell (previously Groom of the Bedchamber to James III); Sir Gerard Lally, 1st Jacobite Baronet (Lieutenant-Colonel in the Dillon regiment) or possibly his son Thomas Lally (later Comte de Lally, lieutenant in the Dillon regiment).[2]

Crossle and Lepper note that in Scotland and Ireland, Freemasonry was "hereditary in some families."[3] The family affiliation was so important that some heirs were initiated at very young ages, such as the thirteen year-old Duke of Perth and sixteen year-old Earl of Tyrconnell.[4] These Scottish and Irish *frères* represent the continuity of Stuart Masonic traditions from the seventeenth into the eighteenth centuries.

Though Ramsay's name does not appear on the list, he had probably been initiated earlier; he would definitely influence the developments in *Écossais* Masonry that emanated from the lodge. Mar's name was not on the list, but he was living at St. Germain during the summer of 1725, when so many of his fellow residents joined the new lodge.[5] He was probably involved behind the scenes, while he worked on architectural projects in Paris and spent much time with Ramsay, Maclean, and Dillon.[6] In March 1726 Mar would advise his son Thomas Erskine to get "our friend Mr. Ramsay" to edit his memoirs and historical papers: "I name Mr. Ramsay because of the trust I have in him, founded on the experience of his uprightness and honesty"; moreover, he has been a good friend to both of us.[7] Though Mar recommended that his son enjoy and perform music, he warned against getting "bewitched" by it, "as perhaps I did to my architecture and designing." In 1716, with his father in exile, the twelve year-old Thomas had been a student at Westminster School, where the Jacobite headmaster, Dr. Robert Freind (a friend of Swift), urged him to head the Stuart party among his schoolmates.[8] Thomas joined his attainted

---

[2] This list of members, with their signatures, was originally published by Gustave Bord in 1909 from documents that are now lost; see his *Les Franc-Maçonnerie en France de Origines á 1815* (Paris, 1909), 117-20. More accurate and detailed identifications have since been made by Pierre Chevallier in *Première Profanation*, 18-23, and Edward Corp, *Lord Burlington*, 20-21, whose list I use here.

[3] P. Crossle and J. Lepper, *History*, 117, 128. I discuss some of these families in *Restoring the Temple*, 540-46, 751-68, 783-84, 792.

[4] E. Corp, *L'autre exil*, 17; G. Bord, *Franc-Maçonnerie*, 118.

[5] *Ninth Report of the Historical Manuscripts Commission, Part II: Appendix* (London, 1884), 217-18. (Atterbury to James Keith, 7 November 1725).

[6] M. Bruce, "Mar in Exile," 161-62, 182.

[7] *Ibid.*, 161-62.

[8] P. Monod, *Jacobitism, 274.* In 1715-16 Freind corresponded with his good friend Swift and hinted that he had "inside knowledge of Jacobite intentions"; see J. Swift, *Correspondence*, II, 146-47, 159-61.

father in 1724, when he obtained a company in one of the Irish regiments in French service.[9] Four years later, he would return to Britain and collaborate with the Duke of Argyll and his brother Lord Ilay, who promised him the restoration of the family estate (which they failed to accomplish).

Many of the Jacobites resented Atterbury's vendetta against Mar, who still had a strong following in Scotland and France. They thus refused to work with the imperious bishop, who replaced Mar as James's minister in Paris.[10] James himself did not fully trust Atterbury and assigned Daniel O'Brien, a French-educated Irishman, to act as secretary to the bishop while reporting secretly to James. As a moderate and a Mason, O'Brien provided a bridge between the rival camps.[11] Because Atterbury's barely-constrained hostility to Catholicism insulted the Catholic Jacobites and their French supporters (especially Bishop Fleury, governor of the young Louis XV), the new lodge provided a way to bring Protestants and Catholics together. Mar also considered Atterbury "the most prejudiced against Scotland"; he further noted "how necessary it is for the Scots and Irish to be well together," for they share common bloodlines and traditions and "ought to look on one another as *brothers.*"[12]

Despite Atterbury's growing sense of isolation and paranoia, he determined to revive the Swedish-Russian project of Gyllenborg and Görtz. But his hopes were dashed when Czar Peter died in February 1725, which the Jacobites considered to be a loss comparable to that of Carl XII. James's agents in Russia assured him that Peter's widow, now Czarina Catherine I, would continue her late husband's support for the Jacobite-Holstein cause. He got word to Wharton of plans for a new Russian and Swedish-Holstein expedition, and Wharton wrote enthusiastically to James to offer his diplomatic services.[13] In May Atterbury met secretly with Hector Maclean, Cameron of Lochiel, the Marquess of Seaforth, and other Scottish Jacobites to plan the international expedition. He brought letters and funds from James, and he tried to mend fences with the Scots.

Meanwhile in London, John Byrom, a private Jacobite, used his expertise in shorthand to gain friends among the Hanoverian Masons in the Royal Society. In summer 1717 Byrom had moved to France, where he claimed to study medicine at Montpellier. However, there remains a mystery about his movements, and "politics had much to do with his concealment."[14] His extensive diaries were censored and truncated by his executors before publication and the original manuscript destroyed, but the surviving material makes clear his activities as a secret agent and code-maker for the Jacobites. He later told William Law that he visited Avignon in winter 1717, when he kissed the hands of James III.[15]

After Byrom's return and marriage, his wife remained in Manchester, while he tried to make a living in London by teaching shorthand to select pupils. Genuinely interested in science, he was elected to the Royal Society in March 1724 and recruited many of his

[9] R. Sedgwick, *History*, II, 17.

[10] G. Bennett, *Tory Crisis*, 282-87.

[11] G. Bord, *Franc-Maçonnerie*, 118.

[12] M. Bruce, "Mar in Exile," 169, 171.

[13] F. Williams, *Memoirs*, II, 66; R. Gould, "Wharton," 126.

[14] John Byrom, *The Private Journal and Literary Remains of John Byrom*, ed. Richard Parkinson (Manchester, 1855), I, part 1, 34-35.

[15] *Ibid.*, II, part 1, 259 (1 August 1739).

students from its ranks. He sought contact with the Duke of Richmond, Grand Master of the Grand Lodge, and in March 1725 he recorded his friendship with Richmond, Hans Sloane, and Martin Folkes, all Whig Masons, when "we talked about masonry and short-hand."[16] In April Sloane and Folkes tried to recruit him to the lodge which met above their Sun Club in St. Paul's Churchyard, and they were evidently successful, though the first surviving record of his membership (in the French Lodge) dates from 1730.[17] At this time, Byrom formed a Cabala Club among his students which adopted some features of Masonry; they took an oath not to reveal the secrets of his system and they called him Grand Master.

While he taught his method to various Masonic Whigs and Tories, Byrom also received a report from a fellow Jacobite, Mr. Lounds, his earlier companion at Montpellier, about a shorthand code that baffled Walpole's decipherers.[18] In April 1725 Byrom was pleased that Alexander Pope is "a subscriber to me," and in July a friend promised to introduce him to the poet and urged him to write some verses that could be presented to Pope.[19] While Byrom and Pope consorted with both Jacobite and Hanoverian Masons, Swift in Ireland claimed to live in monkish isolation. But he too consorted with Masons at the operative level, while he supervised the rebuilding of the country house of his Tory friend, Thomas Sheridan, at Quilca.[20]

Keeping discretely in touch with his Jacobite contacts, Swift was evidently informed about Atterbury's effort to revive collaboration with Sweden and Russia, for he sought to renew contact with the pro-Stuart diplomats Monteleon and Gyllenborg. On 19 June Swift wrote to James Stopford, who was planning a trip abroad, to recommend people to contact: "If the Marquis de Monteleon be in any Ambassy," he will "be kind to any one who knew me," and "the Count de Gillinberg, if he has not lost his Head, may perhaps be an Ambassador somewhere on your way."[21] Swift wanted to communicate with Gyllenborg "upon an affair wherein he promised to inform me" (apparently the earlier Swedish-Jacobite plots, in which various Freemasons were involved). These were risky contacts, for Walpole suspected Gyllenborg of planning a Holstein coup in Sweden and then joining Spain and Russia in support of a Jacobite invasion.

As an impatient Wharton waited for orders from James to leave England, he received a witty but oblique tribute from Samuel Wesley the Younger, who had admired the duke's support of Atterbury during the trial. In 1723 his anonymous broadside, "A New Ballad," which Carte had read in manuscript and attributed to Pope, was published in London. In 1725 Wesley enjoyed Wharton's attacks on the ministry, and in *The Pig and the Mastiff, Two Tales*, he referred obliquely to the "True Britons," to "Passive Obedience," and to Wharton's earlier role as Grand Master. In the comic skit, a faithful wife who wants to find the source of her jealous husband's unfounded suspicions is told:

---

[16] *Ibid.*, I, part 1, 92, 109, 121.

[17] Joy Hancox, *The Queen's Chameleon: The Story of John Byrom, A Study of Conflicting Loyalties* (London, 1994), 100, 217. Though Hancox's argument that Byrom had an affair with Queen Caroline and was the father of the Duke of Cumberland is implausible, her study of Byrom is still the most substantial to date.

[18] J. Byrom, *Private Journal*, I, part 1, 96.

[19] *Ibid.*, I, part 1, 122, 167.

[20] J. Swift, *Correspondence*, II, 555-56, 559. On Sheridan's Jacobitism, see E. O'Ciardha, *Ireland*, 215-16, 232, 234, 377.

[21] J. Swift, *Correspondence*, II, 557.

> She might as easily have sought
> To sound the Bottom of a Plot;
> Or, though a Woman, ta'en Occasion
> T'enquire the Secret of *Free Mason*,
> And how, as Mystic Lodge supposes,
> Duke *Wharton* can succeed to *Moses*.[22]

It is unknown if Wesley was an initiate, but he followed Masonic affairs and referred to them in his future writings.

At this time, Wharton received support from George Kelly, who had been convicted of conspiracy in the Atterbury plot and who was still imprisoned in the Tower. In 1725 Kelly anonymously published his translation from the French of Jacques Morabin's *History of Cicero's Banishment*, which included a fulsome dedication to Wharton. He praised the duke for his defense of Atterbury, "our English Cicero," and for being the "incomparable Orator" in the British Senate, "the Noblest School of Eloquence and Nursery of Liberty the World ever knew."[23] According to a contemporary German critic, Morabin's work was "said to have been written in Allusion to, (or by Way of Parallel of) the Case of Dr. Atterbury, Bishop of Rochester, exil'd from England."[24] Moreover, "the vile Behaviour of Clodius," who abused Cicero, "will be found very nearly to resemble that of a certain European Prime Minister," Robert Walpole. Swift must have enjoyed this work, for he knew and admired Kelly, Wharton, and Atterbury.

In the early months of 1725, Wharton worked with Orrery to raise money among City merchants and bankers, where the duke's influence was viewed as potentially "a chief instrument" in a restoration attempt.[25] He sent to James a list of "Jacobite support among the peerage," which included sixty-seven names, many of whom were or became Freemasons.[26] While he and Orerry canvassed potential supporters, they utilized their Masonic and Gormogon contacts. On 3 May they protested a bill for the disarmament of the Scottish Highlanders, but their failure to stop it exemplified the opposition's weakness. Orrery bitterly informed James: "in this indolent & careless manner are most of our affairs manag'd." He was so discouraged by the disarming of the Highlanders and the timidity of the English Jacobites that he wrote James on 7 May, urging him to consider Ireland as a suitable target for a Jacobite invasion.[27] Orrery and Wharton would find that this view was not shared by Atterbury, who distrusted the Irish Catholics at home and abroad.

Though the bishop admired Wharton, he worried about his recklessness, for the duke continued to publicly drink the Pretender's health. Finally, in late June 1725 Wharton received orders from James that it was time to move to the Continent. Orrery was charged with supervising Wharton's affairs, but he warned James that Wharton should not meet with Atterbury, because in a fit of drunken loquaciousness he might reveal the

---

[22] [Samuel Wesley], *The Pig and the Mastiff. Two Tales* (London, 1725).

[23] Jacques Morabin, *The History of Cicero's Banishment*, trans.[George Kelly] (London, 1725), vii-viii.

[24] *Acta Eruditorum Lipsae* (1723); cited in *Memoirs of the Life, Travels and Transactions of the Revd. G.K. [George Kelly]* (London, 1736), 24.

[25] Lawrence Smith, "Charles Boyle, Fourth Earl of Orrery" (Ph.D. Dissertation: Edinburgh University, 1994), 393.

[26] P. Fritz, *English Ministers*, 160-61.

[27] E. O'Ciardha, "Jacobite Jail-Breakers," 21.

English Jacobites' cant names to the bishop and provoke a "fatal jealousy" in Atterbury.[28] As Wharton prepared to depart, he left his will with Orrery, who along with Charles Caesar and Sir Christopher Musgrave served as his executors.[29] Mary Caesar, who like Swift greatly admired the eloquent and exuberant duke, recorded John Clavering's story about Wharton's stamina even after excessive drinking: "After sitting up all Night, [he] Lay Him self on the ground and Wrote a *True Briton*, sending it from thence to the Press, and It came out that Day."[30] She also recorded her last meeting with him:

> The Duke of Wharton took Leave of Mr Caesar saying, they [Whigs] carry All before them but We have the satisfaction of Doing Our Duty. He Reprinted the "True Britons" that Were of His Own Wrighting to Give His Friends. He Honord me with them. So Discontent'd So Had He Been att the Proceedings of the two Last sessions [of Parliament] that He took Leave of me, Saying, I leave my Country with Pleasure.[31]

Wharton had written that "he would rather carry a musket in an odd named Muscovite regiment than wallow in riches by favour of the usurper."[32] Instead of ordering him to Russia, James planned to send him to Vienna to negotiate a treaty between the Hapsburg Empire and Spain that would support the international scheme. On 16 July Atterbury wrote James to praise Wharton's diplomatic skills:

> He has all the talent requisite to dive into the intentions of those he deals with; and an extraordinary degree of application, when he pleases, and is intent upon compassing any point. He will be at a distance from all that company which misled him sometimes into frolics at home; and will, I hope, have no starts of that kind in a foreign country and a grave court.[33]

On 25 July John Hay wrote Atterbury to advise sending a minder, who "can take a cup with the Duke, and perhaps divert him from excess, which I take to be the Duke of Wharton's greatest failing."

When he left London, Wharton carried with him his copy of *The Constitutions of the Free Masons* (1723) and other Masonic documents, which he would subsequently make available for initiations on the Continent.[34] Advised by Orrery, he avoided going to Paris because of the bitter feud between supporters of Mar and Atterbury. When he arrived in Vienna he told George I's representative Saint-Saphorin "that I was of no party and had devoted the remainder of my life to pleasure, that I was weary of politicks and should intermeddle no more in public business."[35] This kind of claim, plus his often erratic and drunken behavior, has led many historians to believe that Wharton was not a sincere Jacobite, but his "putting on the mask" was always approved by James.[36]

---

[28] L. Smith, "Charles Boyle," 407.

[29] M. Caesar, *Journal*, 51, 59.

[30] *Ibid.*, 58.

[31] *Ibid.*, 51-52.

[32] A. Shield, *Henry Stuart*, 8.

[33] R. Gould, "Wharton," 126.

[34] *Biblothecarum…de Philippi ducis Wharton and Robert South* (London, 1733). #2548.

[35] Stuart Papers: 84/104 (24 July 1725).

[36] On Wharton's consistent Jacobite loyalties, see E. Cruickshanks, "Lord Orrery," 37-40.

Among the diplomats whose support he sought was Count Carl Gustaf Tessin, son of the Swedish architect and "master mason," Nicodemus Tessin. Both Swedes were leaders of the Holstein party and strong supporters of the Stuarts. The young Tessin recorded the efforts of the English diplomat Stephen Poyntz to bribe him into spying on the Jacobites at Vienna, which the count indignantly refused.[37] Tessin's links with the Jacobite Masons would become increasingly important in the coming decades. For the next seven months, Wharton skillfully bamboozled the English diplomats, who thought he might still be a Whig at heart, while he carried out serious, secret negotiations with the Austrian ministers.

These complex intrigues provide an international context for the continuing rivalries and struggles within Freemasonry in Britain. A profusion of newspaper stories and pamphlets made clear the competing claims of Hanoverians, Jacobites, Rosicrucians, and Gormogons to "authentic" Masonry. On 8 June 1725 Defoe anonymously issued volume II of his *Tour Through the Whole Island of Great Britain*, in which he no longer lamented the decline of royalist architecture and the Masons' craft; instead, he praised the accomplishments of private Whig builders. Though the great palaces of Italy were the work of sovereign princes and took ages to complete, England should be proud that the Duke of Chandos's mansion at Canons took only three years to complete.[38] As we shall see, this "quickie" style of building would soon provoke Swift to satire. Defoe portrayed his revered William III as "an allowed judge of fine buildings," and he noted that the great Walpole would soon complete his "fine house" in Norfolk (designed by Colen Campbell). Most of volume II dealt with trade, which Defoe admitted was "the Whore I really doted on," and the *Tour* took on an increasingly anti-Jacobite tone.

In Dublin, while most of the press reported favorably on Wharton's activities, the Masons made an unprecedented march through the city. On 26 June 1725 the *Dublin Weekly Journal* featured a long, detailed description of the public procession of one hundred Masons, wearing leather aprons and white gloves and carrying "Mistical White Wands," which concluded with a lavish banquet at the "Mistical Table."[39] The *Journal* revealed to the public the existence of an Irish Grand Lodge, which was already several years old and which included "Six Lodges of Gentlemen Freemasons" as well as "Private Brothers." The six lodges accepted the jurisdiction of the Grand Master of the Grand Lodge, while the "Private" Masons apparently maintained their independence. In fact, most Masonic lodges in Ireland operated independently of the Grand Lodge in Dublin, while the "hedge or bush" Masons did not seek or receive warrants from Dublin.[40]

In the June 26 ceremony, after all the brothers marched around the Great Hall, the Grand Lodge members separated and held a secret meeting, "where after performing the Mystical Ceremonies of the Grand Lodge which are held so sacred, that they must not be discover'd to a Private Brother; they proceeded to the Election of a new Grand Master, etc." They then rejoined the rest of the Masons and announced that they "had chosen the Rt Hon. Earl of Ross, Grand Master for the Year ensuing, and Sir Thomas Prendergrass [*sic*], and Mark Morgan Esq. Grand Wardens; and that the Grand Master had

---

[37] Sigrid Leijonhufud, ed., *Carl Gustaf Tessins Dagbok, 1748-1752* (Stockholm, 1915), 58.

[38] [D. Defoe], *Tour*, II, 5-8, 13, 134.

[39] *Dublin Weekly Journal* (26 June 1725).

[40] R. Péter, *British Freemasonry*, IV, 423n.6.

appointed the Hon. Humphrey Butler Esq., Deputy Grand Master." After Ross gave a deliberately short speech, noting that dinner was ready and he believed they were hungry, the company again separated into "private Brothers who were seated at three tables at the lower end of the hall, "for the Grand Lodge only sat at the Mystical Table." After the dinner of 120 dishes of meat, they all went to the Play, where the private brothers sat in the pit, while the Grand Lodge officers sat "in the Governments Box."

This description raises questions about the political motivations behind the elections, for Richard Parsons, Earl of Rosse, was suspected by the government of Jacobite leanings. He had earlier befriended Wharton and supported Swift's campaign against Wood's coinage. Sean Murphy notes that Rosse was the great-great-grandson of Sir William Parsons, who held the office of surveyor-general of Ireland, in which capacity he was involved in the plantation of Ulster:

> Though documentary evidence is wanting, it is quite possible that the second Earl of Rosse was appointed Irish grand master in 1725 as a result of his family's prior association with Freemasonry, rather in the way that Sir William Sinclair of Roslin was to be appointed first grand master of Scotland in 1736, because of his family's intimate connection with Freemasonry in that country.[41]

As we shall see, a year later, Rosse would be accused of publicly supporting the Pretender.

Perhaps Rosse, at this time, hoped to clear his name with the government, for he was surrounded with loyalist Whigs as his co-officers. His Grand Warden, Sir Thomas Prendergast, was a Hanoverian Whig, whose family was despised by Swift. In 1696 Prendergast's father, a Catholic Jacobite, had initially participated in a Jacobite assassination plot against William III, but he then betrayed his collaborators to the government. He was amply rewarded and converted to Protestantism.[42] Swift detested both father and son, whom he scorned in later poems, as "the spawn of him who shamed our isle,/ The traitor, assassin, informer vile."[43] First cousin of the Duchess of Richmond and confidant of her husband, the 2nd Duke of Richmond, Prendergast had been initiated in the Horn Lodge in London. A second Grand Warden was Marcus Anthony Morgan, and both were "staunch supporters of the Hanoverian succession."[44] Morgan would later try to befriend Swift, but they parted ways over political differences.[45] The Grand Master appointed the Deputy Grand Master, the Hon. Humphrey Butler, who served in the Irish Parliament with his co-MP for Belturbet, Charles Delafaye. Swift had satirized Brinsley Butler, Humphrey's father, in *The Public Spirit of the Whigs* (1714), as "Prince Butler, a splenetic madman, whom everybody may remember about the town."[46]

The new Grand Secretary was Thomas Griffith, a leading actor, whose comic skills were admired by Swift. In April 1721 he had spoken Swift's epilogue for a charity performance of *Hamlet*, which raised funds from all political factions to help thousands of

---

[41] Sean Murphy, "Irish Jacobitism and Freemasonry," *Eighteenth-Century Ireland*, 9 (1994), 78.

[42] I. Higgins, "Jonathan Swift," 91; "Sir Thomas Prendergast," *ODNB*.

[43] J. Swift, *Complete Poems* [ed. Rogers], 550.

[44] S. Murphy, "Irish Jacobitism," 78.

[45] J. Swift, *Correspondence*, IV, 150, 298.

[46] Jonathan Swift, *The Public Spirit of the Whigs* (London, 1714), 35.

starving Irish citizens.[47] At the 1725 Masonic gathering, Griffith sang "the Free Mason's Apprentices Song," with the whole body joining in. One wonders if they also sang Delafaye's "Fellowcraft's Song." Griffith would probably have been sympathetic to Delafaye's espionage activities, for he doubled as tide waiter to the port of Dublin, where he ordered the arrests of those recruiting for or seeking to enlist in the service of the Pretender. A year after his Masonic election, *Hume's Courant* (8 June 1726) reported that he and Mr. Hamilton, "belonging to his Majesty's Revenue," apprehended a group of Jacobites , who were "conducted up to the Castle, in order to be examined, it seems they have already confessed they were going to the Pretender, and had arms and other necessaries for that purpose."[48] Though Griffith's intelligence post could prove dangerous for Swift and his crypto-Jacobite friends, Swift knew that the actor had received this "lucrative post in the revenue" in 1710 from Edward Southwell, a friend and moderate Tory MP, who then served as chief secretary to Ormonde; he evidently considered Griffith to be no threat.[49] Over the next years, because Griffith was "esteemed by the Brotherhood, his benefits were in consequence bespoke by the Grand Master, who accompanied by the brethren, always walked in procession to the theatre."[50] As we shall see, he would later appeal to Swift for financial support, promising to repay it with his next benefit performance.[51]

The writer of the Masonic report in *The Dublin Weekly Journal* was James Arbuckle, who according to Lepper and Crossle, was a Mason who "enjoyed the friendship of Swift, by whom, being lame and sprightly, he was nicknamed 'Wit upon Crutches.'"[52] They further believed that Swift contributed to Arbuckle's journal. However, more recent scholarship has revealed that Swift's relationship with Arbuckle was mutually hostile in the 1720s and '30s.[53] As a member of the Irish Grand Lodge and not a "Private Brother," Arbuckle would have sided with the Hanoverian Whigs in Masonic affairs. Born in Belfast, raised as a Presbyterian, and educated in Glasgow, Arbuckle started his journal as part of a Whig program to refine the manners and tastes of his Irish readers and to defuse the sectarian hatreds that spoiled Irish civil discourse. Taking Addison's essays as his model, he contributed as "Hibernicus" hundreds of articles, in which he wrote in rather abstract terms about literature, beauty, and taste. However, his steady criticism of satirical and comical writers, which targeted Swift by implication, roused the enmity of the dean and his supporters. Moreover, Arbuckle may have known that Swift was the author of the *Letter from the Grand Mistress of the Female Freemasons* (1724), which challenged the official history of the English Grand Lodge, when he wrote his detailed praise of the Irish Grand Lodge in 1725.

In *Wit upon Crutches, or, the Biter Bitten. Most Humbly Dedicated to the Ingenious Mr. Arbuckle Author of the Dublin Weekly Journal* (1725), a work attributed to Swift but probably written

---

[47] J. Swift, *Correspondence*, II, 370; IV, 261.

[48] R. Berman, *Schism*, 223-24.

[49] "Notes on the Early History of the Irish Stage," *The Irish Builder*, 18 (15 April 1876), 101; (1 May 1876), 121.

[50] *Ibid.*, 101.

[51] J. Swift, *Correspondence*, IV, 261.

[52] P. Crossle and J. Lepper, *History*, 46, 53-58, 70.

[53] Richard Holmes, "James Arbuckle and Dean Swift: Cultural Politics in the Irish Confessional State," *Irish Studies Review*, 16 (2008), 431-44; "James Arbuckle," *ODNB*.

by his friends at Trinity College, the authors mercilessly mocked Arbuckle for presuming to have expertise in poetry when he was so boring and lame in prose:

> A writer held in great Renown,
> By all News-Boys of the Town
> Who ne're (as I imagine) rose
> Above the Vulgar turn of Prose,
> Seeing so many Younkers Dabble
> In Poetry to please the Rabble.
> ………………………………..
> Sir, Phoebus made a Declaration
> 'gainst all Lame Members of the Nation;
> Nor do's he ever think that those
> Should run in Rhime, who Limp in Prose.[54]

The Swiftian author concluded with a note "To Mr. Arbuckle," that despite "much Studdy," he could find "little humour," so he sends him "this comical Ditty" just to liven up his dull journal. Though Arbuckle initially vowed to keep his journal apolitical, such opposition from Tories and Jacobites led him to write more stridently in support of the Hanoverian succession and the present Whig government.[55]

The Irish Masons had published *The Free-Masons Vindication* (Dublin, 1725) in response to *The Grand Mystery of the Free-Masons Discover'd* (London, 1724 and 1725), which revealed the catechistical questioning and "signs and tokens" found in the papers of a dead brother. Hinting at "Differences in Speculative Matters," the Irish claimed that "Mr. Informer" would disappoint his employers with his inaccurate information.[56] As noted earlier, the Irish press had covered Wharton's election as Grand Master in London, and Arbuckle now covered his political activities in his journal. He initially seemed sympathetic to Wharton's actions in the English parliament, and on 15 May 1725 he described how Wharton and Orrery protested against the government's plan to disarm the Highlanders. They argued that the Highlanders had not committed in recent times any of the crimes attributed to them by the government and such repressive measures would only rouse them again to violent opposition: "We think it would become us better as true Patriots to endeavor to keep them quiet, than to make them unruly." However, after Wharton's exodus from England in June, Arbuckle's attitude changed and he portrayed the duke as a traitorous Jacobite.

By September, when news reached London of Wharton's negotiations for a Jacobite alliance with Austria and Spain, his partisans published another answer to the *Grand Mystery*, which was appended to a second edition of the work. In *Two Letters to a Friend* (1725) "Verus Commodus" attacked the modern Masons as well as those Rosicrucian Masons who were not loyal to the Gormogons. The first letter targeted Robert Samber, "a certain *Renegado Papist*," who was currently trying to curry favor with the Duke of Montagu.[57] Ridiculing Samber's type of Masonry for its occult pretensions and heretical fantasies,

---

[54] *Wit upon Crutches, or, the Biter Bitten* (Dublin, 1725), broadside.
[55] Bryan Coleborne, "James Arbuckle and Jonathan Swift: New Light on Swift's Biography," *Eighteenth-Century Life*, 11 (1987), 170-80.
[56] *Ibid.*, 51; Knoop, Jones, Hamer, EMC, 76-80.
[57] Armitage, "Samber," 107.

the author noted that "they assume to themselves the August title of Kabalists," but they are really "Cabal-ists: i.e., a Knot of whimsical, delirious Wretches, who are caballing together, to extirpate all manner of Science, Reason, and Religion out of the World."[58] As we shall see, Swift would also satirize Samber's Rosicrucian fantasies, when he completed the section on the "Struldbrugs or Immortals" in *Gulliver's Travels* in autumn 1725.[59]

In *Two Letters to a Friend*, Verus Commodus also claimed that Samber maintained links with contemporary virtuosos, especially those physicians and great men who were really "Gnosticks, who took their original from Simon Magus":

> These were a Set of Men, which ridicul'd not only *Christianity*, but even *Rational Morality*; teaching that they should be sav'd by their *capacious Knowledge*, and *Understanding* of no Mortal Man could tell what. They babbled of an *amazing intelligence* they had, from no-body knows whence. They amus'd, and puzzled the hare-brained, unwary Crowd that follow'd 'em, with *Superstitious Interpretations, of extravagant Talismanical Characters Characters*, and *abstruse Significations*, of uncommon *Kabalistick Words*; which exactly agrees with the proceedings of our *Modern Free Masons*.[60]

One of the doctors "makes wonderful Brags of being of the *Fifth Order*" of Masonry and that he possesses "a Mysterious Hocus-Pocus Word." It is possible that the author referred to Dr. John Woodward, who shared Samber's enthusiasm for magical lore, collected talismans, and earlier collaborated with Toland's free-thinking circle. Arbuthnot and the Scriblerians had earlier targeted Woodward as a crack-pot virtuoso, and Swift would continue the attack in *Gulliver's Travels*.[61]

Verus Commodus used his second letter to praise "the Most Ancient Order of Gormogons." The Chinese Mandarin who brought the order into England claimed that the Chinese "have Accounts of Time and Transactions, many Thousand Years before Adam."[62] This Masonic notion of a pre-Adamic, pre-Hebraic illumination that secretly survived in China would later be utilized by Ramsay and Swedenborg.[63] The Gormogons complained of the prostitution of Freemasonry by drunks, illiterates, and mercenaries, which contrasted sadly with their own cultivation of arts and sciences and egalitarian recognition of individual merit. While claiming that their order makes great progress at Rome, the Gormogons accused the modern Masons of promoting heterodoxy, free-thinking, and sedition. The "good Order and Regulations" of the Gormogons "have so alarm'd the Masons," that many brothers were now determined to reform their fraternity. Thus, on 29 September a new lodge would be opened "for regulating the Modern Abuses, which crept into the Ancient Fraternity of Free-Masons; where 'tis desired, that all the old real Masons will be present."

Verus Commodus then vowed to publish "a few Remarks on that empty Book called, The Constitutions, etc. of the Free-Masons, written, as I am told, by a Presbyterian

[58] Knoop, Jones, Hamer, *EMP*, 137.
[59] J. Swift, *Gulliver*, xi-xii, 202, 347.
[60] *Ibid.*, 139.
[61] J. Swift, *Gulliver*, 245-46, 359.
[62] Knoop, Jones, and Hamer, *EMP*, 140-50.
[63] B. Neveu, "La 'Science Divine,'" 177-96; M. Schuchard, *Emanuel Swedenborg*, 257, 599.

Teacher, and pompously recommended by a certain reverend Orthodox, tho' Mathematical Divine."[64] At this time, Desaguliers was an easy target, for he was accused of neglecting his Anglican, Royal Society, and Masonic duties, while he indulged in mercenary "projecting" schemes with Chandos. Anderson, who had experienced serious financial losses from the South Sea and other "bubbles," turned his attention to translating and expanding a vast German genealogical history, which he hoped would prove profitable in an English edition.[65]

Nevertheless, the "modern" system, under its aristocratic leadership, had expanded dramatically. On 27 November 1725 the Quarterly Communication of the Grand Lodge was attended by the officers of forty-nine lodges. In order to facilitate further expansion, the rule limiting the election of new Masters to the Quarterly Court was changed to allow each lodge, with the consent of the Wardens and the majority of brethren, being Masters, to make Masters at their discretion.[66] This change was evidently pushed by dissident Masons, who resented the attempt at Grand Lodge to control all elections. When the "Regular Constituted Lodges" turned in their membership lists, it was clear that some remained loyal to Wharton and previous Jacobite leaders.

Perhaps concerned about Samber's overture to Montagu and certain "modern" Masons, a dissident brother (and possible Gormogon) reported an increasing Rosicrucian influence. Writing to the Tory-supporting *Daily Journal* (24 December), he complained that

> there is a Society abroad from whom the English Freemasons (asham'd of their true origin...) have copied a few Ceremonies and take great Pains to persuade the World that they are derived from them, and are the same with them. These are called *Rosicrucians* from their Prime Officers being distinguished on their High Days with Red Crosses...On this Society have our Moderns...endeavour'd to graft themselves, and are acquainted only with some of their signs of Probation and Entrance...[67]

This letter provoked an immediate satirical response in *The Daily Journal* (27 December 1725):

> The Brethren of the Shears and Shopboard are hereby Informed that their Whimsical kinsmen of the Hod and Trowel, having (on new Light received from some worthy Rosicrucians) thought fit to change both their Patron and Day, and unexpectedly taken up our usual Place of Meeting: the Worshipful Society of Free and Accepted TAYLORS are desired to meet...in order to Chuse a Grand Master... You are desired to come Cloathed, and Armed, with Bodkin and Thimble.[68]

This mock advertisement seemed to draw on the early threat that the Freemasons should be regulated by the government in the same way as the tailors.

---

[64] Knoop, Jones, and Hamer, *EMP*, 149.
[65] A. Robbins, "Dr. Anderson,"15.
[66] R. Gould, "Wharton," 127.
[67] A.C.F. Jackson, "Rosicrucianism and Its Influence on Masonry," *AQC*, 97 (1984), 129.
[68] D. Knoop, G. Jones, D. Hamer, *EMP*, 156.

A month earlier, on 25 November, Swift had written to James Stopford (then in Italy) about the scandalous appointment of the Reverend Thomas Power to an Irish church post. Power was especially hated by Tories and Jacobites because he had served Walpole as an *agent provocateur* among the Waltham Blacks and informed on them to Delafaye, whose investigations led to the execution of several of them.[69] Swift was probably aware that one of Delafaye's victims was Charles Rackett, Pope's brother-in-law, for whom the anxious poet worked to gain a reprieve. Swift also knew that Delafaye had earlier hoped to prosecute him as a Jacobite. Thus, Swift complained to Stopford about Power, "a certain Animal called a Walth[am] black," which is "a Cant word for a Deer stealer." [70] This fellow was "Leader of a Gang, and had the Honor to hang half a dozen of his Fellows, in Quality of Informer, which was his merit." One wonders if this letter was intercepted in Italy, for the British-paid spy Baron Stosch reported on Stopford's presence in Rome.[71]

While Swift scorned Delafaye and his informers, James Arbuckle expressed his concern about the attacks upon Freemasonry, for they led to a defensive shutting of minds among the members, who closed ranks in self-defense and became impervious to constructive criticism. On 26 February 1726 he wrote in *The Dublin Weekly Journal*: "I might mention in this place the Antient and Worshipful Society of Free-Masons, where every private Brother thinks himself obliged to support the Honour, and fight the Battels of the whole Order." He would soon have to defend the Grand Master Rosse, who was publicly accused of flaunting his Jacobite sympathies. The charges against Rosse came in the wake of government concern about new initiatives undertaken by some Jacobite Masons.

The odd charges that Freemasons were caballing Cabalists and subversive Rosicrucians were provoked by rumors of renewed Jewish support for Jacobite schemes – schemes which possibly involved Ramsay. Walpole was aware that Francia had worked for Atterbury, when they planned the Russian-Swedish-Spanish enterprise, and that he accompanied the bishop to Calais.[72] Thus, when he learned about a daring Jewish-Jacobite plan of financial sabotage, he determined to act forcefully. On 18 November 1725 William Erskine, Jacobite agent at The Hague, wrote to John Hay at Rome:

> Two Jews, one here whose name is Costa and his brother, Baron Schwartze at London, have proposed to me that if the King [James] will...act in concert with them for a few days only they'l make the stocks fall 20% and thereby gain 40% on a capital of , 200,000 and are willing his Majesty have half thereof. I am particularly acquainted with the brother that lives here and it is at his desire that I doe address myself to your Lordship on this occasion... Those people, the Jews, have a fair character in the world as to morals and 'tis known they can, when they please purchase for much more than the sum mentioned in the Stocks. They pretend to be well affected to his Majesty but I won't say that what they propose proceeds more from the motive of serving him than for that of private interest, whatever may be in that... If your

---

[69] P. Rogers, "Waltham Blacks," 484; I. Ehrenpreis, *Swift*, III, 285, 356.

[70] J. Swift, *Correspondence*, 621 and n.10.

[71] "James Stopford," in Ingamells, *Dictionary*.

[72] P. Fritz, *English Ministers*, 118

Lop [Lordship] thinks proper to acquaint the King with this proposal and that his Majesty orders me to go to Italy I will with great pleasure obey.[73]

Given the current Jewish-Jacobite context, it is suggestive that Ramsay had recently contacted a heterodox Jew in Italy. Moreover, Ramsay had travelled with Hay when he journeyed to Rome. Hay, in turn, spent much time in Rome with Rawlinson, who had also made overtures to certain Jews. Though nothing more is known of James's reaction to this Jewish-Jacobite financial scheme, it was apparently set in action by early 1726. On 25 January Dr. William Stratford, former opponent of Atterbury, wrote, "It is said that Walpole has sent to the Jews to let them know that if they continue to sell out stock with a design of retiring they shall find that, notwithstanding the laws lately made in their favour, there are enough left to keep them in England."[74] That Walpole suspected Wharton's involvement in this scheme was suggested by Edmund Curll, who some months later referred to the time "When to buy Stock the cunning Jew repairs" in *Whartoniana* (1727), a collection of piracies and libels on Wharton, Pope, Swift, and the Irish in general.[75] Walpole's ability to crush this plot was based on his proliferating intelligence system in Europe, where his agents learned of the expansion of Jacobite Freemasonry abroad.

While Wharton negotiated in Vienna, Orrery and his nineteen year-old son John, Lord Boyle, visited Paris, under the pretense of furthering John's education. Wharton had written James that he possessed "an intire friendship" with Orrery, whom he had named to handle his financial affairs in England.[76] As noted earlier, Orrery was allegedly a Mason, and it is not surprising that he secretly met with his "brothers" Mar, Ramsay, and Dillon in Paris. As Mar had written earlier, because of Atterbury's prejudices, the Scots and Irish must act together as "Brothers." Lord Boyd may have been initiated in Paris, as suggested by his later letter to Mr. Salkeld (a Jacobite friend of Ramsay in Paris), about his acquaintances in the French city: "If I may speak as a Citizen of the Universe," a term reflecting Ramsay's universalist Masonic creed.[77] Three years later, he and his father would host Ramsay in England, when Ramsay joined an English lodge, under the Grand Mastership of the crypto-Jacobite Duke of Norfolk (who appeared on Wharton's list of Stuart supporters).[78]

In May Orrery's strong incognito and obsessive secrecy means that there is little surviving evidence about his intelligence work or the claims and counter-claims about his contact with either Mar or Atterbury. In 1726 John Sempill (Sample), Horatio Walpole's spy on Atterbury, reported that Wharton was to become secretary of state to the Pretender, while Orrery "is the man that directs all; and you may depend upon it that nothing is done but what comes from his channel."[79] The bishop seemed desperate to keep Orrery away from Mar and to affirm the earl's loyalty to himself. However, Sempill reported

---

[73] A. and H. Taylor, *Stuart Papers*, I, 76-77.

[74] *HMC: Report on the Manuscripts of His Grace the Duke of Portland* (1901), VII, 416.

[75] Edmund Curll, ed., *Whartoniana* (London, 1727), 175.

[76] For their time in Paris, see L. Smith, "Charles Boyle," 403-22.

[77] Harvard. Houghton: Eng. MS. 218.2, vol. 1, f.32. (Lord Boyle to Salkeld, 13 December 1726).

[78] See ahead, Chapter Eleven.

[79] Francis Atterbury, *The Miscellaneous Works of Bishop Atterbury*, ed. John Nichols (London: John Nichols, 1798), V, 332.

to Walpole that "Orrery and the Bishop is not well together."[80] In the meantime, the ministry in London was sure that Orrery was collaborating with Wharton's negotiations in Vienna, and they tried to maintain intense surveillance over him. Horatio Walpole employed as one of his most "diligent" agents Mr. La Roche, a Huguenot and Hanoverian Mason, who reported on the Jacobites in France and Holland over the next years.[81] Orrery wrote to his friend William Byrd in Virginia about their visit, which prompted a reply on 13 December 1726 that Byrd was pleased to read that Lord Boyle had learned French to perfection: "I wish every Secretary of State could write it as perfectly...that their performances might not be subject to the corrections of Mr. De La Fay."[82] Obviously, they knew that their intercepted correspondence was read by Delafaye, which increased the necessity of oblique writing and oral communications.

Back in Dublin, Arbuckle continued to publish news on Jacobite activities abroad, especially focused on the marital troubles of James III and his wife. In order to maintain Irish Protestant alarm, he also reported rumors spread by Whig agents. For example, on 11 June 1726 he reported that Henry Somerset, 3rd Duke of Beaufort, met with the Pretender in Rome, who arranged for him to receive a "remittance of 20,000 pistols by way of Amsterdam."[83] Swift had known the 2nd Duke of Beaufort during Queen Anne's days, when he was head of the quasi-Masonic "Loyal Brotherhood." In 1714 Swift received news about the 2nd duke's death, which greatly concerned the Duchess of Ormonde, Beaufort's friend and correspondent.[84] The Somerset/Beaufort family would maintain shadowy Masonic ties over the next decades. Arbuckle immediately followed his report on the 3rd Duke by an inaccurate notice that "the late Bishop of Rochester was on his Journey to Rome, to take upon him the Education of the Pretender's Children, and to instruct them in the principles of the Church of England." This certainly would have interested Swift and his supporters at Trinity College, who were great admirers of Atterbury, but it would alarm Arbuckle's pro-Hanoverian readers.

Throughout 1726 pamphlets were issued attacking and defending Masonry, with the Jacobites getting in the most telling blows against the modern Grand Lodge. Arbuckle had complained that every private brother felt obliged to "fight the Battels of the whole Order," and Philip Crossle argues that Swift joined the battles by issuing an anonymous pamphlet, probably first published in Dublin.[85] No copy has been found of the first edition but a second Dublin edition, dated 1726, exists. A revised version of the Dublin edition was then published in London, bearing the title, *The Grand Mystery, or Art of Meditating over an House of Offices, Restor'd and Unveil'd; after the Manner of the Ingenious Dr. S[wif]t, with Observations Historical, Political, and Moral; Shewing the Derivation of this Science from the Chaldees and Aegyptians... Dedicated to the profound Dr. W------d* [Woodward] (1726).[86] In the early months of 1726 Swift was preparing to take to London his manuscript of *Gulliver's Travels*, in which he satirized Woodward, Desaguliers, and other speculative Masons and

---

80 L. Smith, "Charles Boyle," 418.

81 *Ibid.*, 420; M. Jacob, *Radical Enlightenment*, 101

82 Harvard. Houghton: Eng. MS. 218.2, vol. 1, f. 27 (Byrd to Orrery, 5 July 1726).

83 *Dublin Weekly Journal* (11 June 1726).

84 J. Swift, *Correspondence*, I, 604-05 n.4.

85 P. Crossle, "Freemasonry," 139.

86 *EMP*, 194-95. The editors prudishly rejected Crossle's attribution of "this coarse and unsavoury pamphlet" to Swift, but they gave no counter-argument. It is attributed to Swift in the British Library catalogue.

virtuosos as "Laputan" projectors and political meddlers. Moreover, the scatological Masonic themes of *The Grand Mystery* echoed many passages in *Gulliver*.

Mocking the Whig establishment for their speculative entrepreneurial projects – such as the York Buildings Company in which Desaguliers and Chandos were heavily invested – the Swiftian author proposed a corporation to erect "Necessary Houses" (public toilets) throughout London. With gleeful jokes on flatulence and excrement, the author portrayed a "Protocaccographer," who boasts of his virtuoso standing as an FRS, an adept in "this noble art of Turd-conjuring."[87] For the benefit of the public, he will publish a work "in the same Volume, Paper and Letter, as the *Constitutions of the Free-Masons* was some time ago published, in which are laid down...all the Principles and Rules of this great Science." More important for the Whig "Fertuosi" who sponsor such schemes, "a timely search of Close Stools will reveal Plots and Conspiracies against the government."

In *Gulliver* Swift harked back to the Atterbury plot, when Whig agents discovered some of the bishop's correspondence in his close stool (toilet). Among the "political Projectors" on the island of Laputa (whore, in Spanish) were similar turd-conjurors:

> Another Professor shewed me a large Paper of Instructions for discovering Plots and Conspiracies against the Government. He advised great Statesmen to examine into the Dyet of all suspected Persons ; their Times of eating; upon which Side they lay in Bed; with which Hand they wiped their Posteriors; to take a strict View of their Excrements, and from the Colour, the Odour, the Taste, the Consistencie, the Crudeness, or Maturity of Digestion, form a Judgment of their Thoughts and Designs: Because Men are never so serious, thoughtful, and intent, as when they are at Stool; which he found by frequent Experiment: For in such Conjunctions, when he used merely as a Trial to consider which was the best way of murdering the King, his Ordure would have a Tincture of Green; but quite different when he thought only of raising an Insurrection, or burning the Metropolis.[88]

That the Whig Mason Delafaye had helped "ransack" Atterbury's house in the search for papers and then led the team of decipherers reinforces the Masonic associations of the two Swiftian satires.

In *The Grand Mystery*, the author echoed Swift's earlier tribute to Stuart architectural ideals in "The Burning of Whitehall Palace," while he scorned the selfish individualism of arrogant and extravagant Whig builders: "London is now the largest city in the Universe, and would be the most beautiful, if its publick Buildings were answerable to the private, and our People were animated to erect stately and convenient Edifices for the common Benefit.[89] However, given the present corruption, the only public offices that Whig "Fertuosi" will erect – with huge bureaucracies maintained at public expense – will be toilets for turd-decipherers. In *Gulliver* Swift similarly contrasted speculative Whig building projects with noble structures, "built according to the best Rules of ancient

---

[87] [Jonathan Swift, attrib.], *The Grand Mystery, or Art of Meditating*, 2nd rev. ed. (London, 1726), 9-12.
[88] J. Swift, *Gulliver*, 182, 339.
[89] J. Swift, *Grand Mystery*, 15.

Architecture."[90] Crossle notes that the scatological pamphlet marked the temporary end of press coverage and publicity about the Grand Lodge of Ireland."[91]

In the London edition of *The Grand Mystery*, evidently revised after Swift's arrival in the city in March 1726, the author added six pages of burlesque proposals for the implementation of the toilet scheme. That Swift was interested in architectural affairs in London is suggested by his letter to Thomas Tickell on 16 April, informing him that "Mr. Arundel is made Surveyor of Works" (in succession to the recently deceased Whig architect Thomas Hewett).[92] The architectural historian Howard Colvin notes that Hewett was mourned neither by Wren's surviving colleagues nor by the new Palladians, while Walpole was presented with "a convenient vacancy."[93] The prime minister appointed Richard Arundell of Yorkshire, whom Colvin describes as "a rather frivolous aesthete" and "a placeman with architectural connections rather than an architect in his own right." He would subsequently earn much ridicule when he disfigured the Wilton marbles "by marking their torsos with pubic hair."

Arundell had served as a page to Queen Anne from 1707 to 1714, when Swift knew him.[94] Through shared architectural interests, he became the lifelong friend of Burlington, who used his influence to get Arundell elected to parliament in 1720, while Walpole secured his appointment as surveyor in 1726.[95] Despite Arundell's friendship with Whig Masons such as Newcastle, Richmond, and Walpole, Burlington continued to value his Palladian taste in architecture. It is unclear what Swift thought of Arundell's architectural appointment in 1726, when he would have much influence over the operative craft in London. But, if Swift was aware that Burlington was a secret Jacobite, he may have viewed sympathetically the effort of the earl's Palladian faction to take over the Office of Works. Though English historians long described Palladianism as a Whig ideology, Colvin argues that its origins were actually Scottish and Tory, its development crypto-Jacobite: "his [Burlington's] cult of Palladianism, far from reflecting Whig ideology, could be seen as a conscious reversion to the architectural ideals of the early Stuart court during the surveyorship of Inigo Jones."[96] In 1744 the government would receive a report that Arundell "had been present at one of the meetings of Jacobite conspirators," and in 1745 he, like Burlington, would be suspected of Jacobite sympathies.[97]

The Whig furor over Swift's anonymous satires seemed to intimidate the Dublin press from further coverage of Irish Masonic activities; nevertheless, hints at the political polarization within the fraternity occasionally surfaced. Sean Murphy notes that "in 1726 the Dublin press featured accounts of Jacobite activities, as well as the espousal of the Jacobite cause by the leading English Freemason, the Duke of Wharton."[98] But the anti-Jacobite Masons gained an important supporter when, in early June 1726, Thomas

[90] J. Swift, *Gulliver*, 152, 168.

[91] P. Crossle, "Freemasonry," 144.

[92] J. Swift, *Correspondence*, II, 637.

[93] Howard Colvin, *The History of the King's Works* (London, 1963), V, 73-74.

[94] J. Swift, *Journal to Stella*, 158.

[95] R. Sedgwick, *History of Parliament*, I, 421.

[96] Howard Colvin, "A Scottish Origin for English Palladianism," *Architectural History*, 17 (1979), 5-12, and *Biographical Dictionary*, 147.

[97] J. Clarke, "Lord Burlington," 306-07.

[98] S. Murphy, "Irish Jacobitism," 78.

Prendergast arrived in Dublin, and new "bones of contention" were thrown into the "silenced" Irish Grand Lodge. On 10 June there was a serious riot on the Pretender's birthday, with rival factions fighting in the streets.[99] Two days later, there was an effort to blacken the reputation of the Earl of Rosse, without mentioning his role as Irish Grand Master. In *Dickson's Dublin Intelligencer*, the rumor was reported that Rosse appeared at the government barracks in "Jacobite Dress" (white suit and white roses in his hat), acted "Unmannerly" when questioned by an officer, and was then killed in a sword fight.[100]

Though the story of Rosses's death was apocryphal, it revived the specter of Rosse's suspected Jacobitism. Evidently worried by this smear upon his Grand Master, Arbuckle published a rebuttal in which he rejected the story about "a certain Noble Lord" (not naming Rosse) who was accused of celebrating 10 June and wearing white roses, and, even worse, for passing an order "for Disarming all persons under his Jurisdiction, that do not carry Crosses and Beads by way of Reprizals…for several Acts of Parliament in Force against those of his Religion in this Kingdom."[101] Arbuckle angrily argued that the account was "False, Groundless, and Malicious, and invented by some Anonimous Person, without any sort of Foundation, but in revenge for some private Pique, or some other evil intent." Tory and Jacobite Masons suspected that Thomas Prendergast and his English-Whig cronies were behind the charges against Rosse, and on 9 August the nationalist Masons seemed to reply with an oblique story published by Swift's friend Faulkner in his *Dublin Journal*, a rival to Arbuckle's *Weekly Journal*. The narrator is approached by a guilt-stricken acquaintance, who confesses that "I have bred Discord and strife between 500 honest Brethren, and I fear they will never be reconciled… I must be gone, for Darkness best becomes those whose deeds are evil." Was this a veiled threat to Prendergast to stop meddling in Masonic matters and return to London? Chetwode Crawley argues that Faulkner was "an active Freemason in his early days," and the printer would later identify Swift as the author of *Letter from the Grand Mistress*.[102]

During the same period, Wharton advanced the cause of the Jacobite Masons in Italy and Spain. Arriving in Rome in February 1726, Wharton seemed to refer to his interest in or affiliation with the mock-chivalric, quasi-Masonic "Order of Toboso," which had been established by the Keith brothers in Spain. George Keith, the Earl Marischal, merged his fondness for Don Quixote and Spanish romances with his knowledge of Masonic rituals to develop the fraternity, which subsequently established links with Jacobite Masons in Russia.[103] One probable member was Sir Charles Wogan, now a colonel in the Spanish army and close to the Keith brothers. In April 1725 he wrote from Madrid to Lord Inverness: "My life has ever been a sort of Romance, and as tis but fit in this country to follow in ye steppes of my renown'd predecessor, Don Quixote, I give yr Lordship this scene of it, as to a friend heartily interested in wt regards me."[104] Meanwhile in Rome, Wharton similarly described himself as "full of the Spirit of Knight Errantry,"

[99] *Ibid.*, 78.

[100] P. Crossle and J. Lepper, *History*, 71.

[101] *Dublin Weekly Journal* (23 July 1726).

[102] Chetwode Crawley, "Early Irish Freemasonry," xxix, xxxii.

[103] Robert Collis, "The Order of Toboso: A Pan-European Jacobite Fraternal Network, c. 1726-1739," in Pierre-Yves Beaurepaire, Kenneth Loiselle, Jean-Marie Mercier, and Thierry Zarcone, eds., *Diffusions et Circulations des Pratiques Maçonniques, XVIIIe-XXe Siècles* (Paris, 2013), 141-56.

[104] H. Tayler, *Jacobite Epilogue*, 298.

while he emulates his "famous predecessor Don Quixot" and ruminates "on all my Books of Chivalry."[105] The restless duke repeatedly urged James to send him to Spain or Russia, and certainly any Tobosan links would be helpful in both places.

By March James was so impressed by Wharton that he installed him as a Knight of the Garter, despite his previous reluctance to make chivalric appointments until he recovered his throne. Perhaps encouraged by Wharton's interest in chivalric fraternities, James also revived the British order of Knights of Malta, appointing the Irish exile Nicholas Gerardin as Grand Prior in 1726. Because Wharton allegedly participated in a Gormogon lodge in Rome, these chivalric initiatives may be relevant to Ramsay's later development of knightly degrees in *Écossais* Masonry. Cyril Batham states that Wharton met Ramsay in Rome "in 1724/25," but the meeting, if it took place, would have occurred after Wharton's arrival in February 1726.[106] Batham suggests further that Ramsay was involved in Freemasonry through his contact with Wharton, before going to England in 1729. Stosch reported that Ramsay was indeed in Rome at this time, acting as governor to Richard Hales (scion of a Jacobite family).[107] It is unknown if Wharton now shared Atterbury's hostility to Ramsay and his mentor Mar.

In March James sent Wharton on a mission to Madrid, where he worked closely with Ormonde, the Keith brothers, and the Irish Anglican parson Ezekiel Hamilton, all fellow Masons.[108] "Zecky" Hamilton wrote to the Stuart court to praise Wharton; he is "delighted with the honour of his conversation, so great vivacity and sprightliness of wit mix'd with so clear and sound a judgment is very rarely to be met with. His talents are entirely devoted to the service of the King."[109] Wharton probably participated in the Order of Toboso, for which the Grand Master Hamilton made restorationist toasts "to a fair meeting on the green," the ritual gesture of the "quixotic" order.[110] Under its playful pose, Toboso concealed a serious political agenda, and Hamilton worked with Wharton to compile a military cypher, "contriv'd chiefly for an Invasion."[111] He stressed that the "Meeting at Home is the end of all negotiations and correspondence abroad." He would later describe Toboso as "a military order of knighthood."[112]

Wharton sent a letter from Madrid to the Irish bishop John Stearne in which he praised "our common friend, honest Jonathan Swift" (thus deliberately using the Jacobite cant word, "honest").[113] Like Swift, Sterne was accused by his enemies of being not just a Tory but a Jacobite.[114] Emboldened by the fawning "Zeckie" Hamilton, Wharton

---

[105] Stuart Papers, 90/illeg. (10 February 1726).

[106] C. Batham, "Ramsay," 286; C. Francovich, 39.

[107] C. Batham, "Ramsay," 283: NA: SP, 85/19 (19 December 1725); J. Ingamells, *Dictionary*, 443. Ramsay was still in Italy on 3 July 1726.

[108] According to Frank McLynn, Ormonde, Marischal, and Hamilton were all Freemasons; see his *Charles Edward Stuart*, 532.

[109] Stuart Papers: 92/136 (13 April 1726).

[110] NA: SP, 93/111 (July 1726).

[111] Stuart Papers: 93/111a (May 1726); 93/111 (July 1726). See Robert Collis, "'To a Fair Meeting on the Green': The Order of Toboso and Jacobite Fraternal Networks," unabridged version online www.academic.edu.

[112] Stuart Papers: 192/98; quoted in Patrick Fagan, *An Irish Bishop in Penal Times: The Chequered Career of Sylvester Lloyd, OFM* (Dublin, 1993), 145.

[113] Patrick Fagan, ed., *Ireland in the Stuart Papers* (Dublin, 1995), I, 76.

[114] I. Ehrenpreis, *Swift*, III, 53-54.

boasted to Benjamin Keene, the British Resident at Madrid, that he was James's "Prime Minister" and "mentioned great things from Muscovy."[115] In April 1726 Keene reported that he met Wharton at the house of the Duc de Liria, son of Marshal Berwick, where Wharton drunkenly proclaimed to the Whig diplomat:

> It is in my power to make your stocks fall as I see fit... Hitherto my master's interest has been managed by the Duchess of Perth and three or four old women who meet under the portal of Saint Germains; he [James] wanted a Whig, and a brisk one, to put them in train, and I am the man. You may look upon me, Sir Philip Wharton, Knight of the Garter, and Sir Robert Walpole, Knight of the Bath, running a course, and, by God! he shall be hard pressed.[116]

As Wharton flaunted his Garter ribbon, Walpole soon received reports about "the receiving and caressing" of him, which seemed to determine the prime minister to retrieve Masonic and Garter prestige for the Hanoverians.[117] He persuaded George I to install him, as the legitimate Prime Minister, and the Duke of Richmond, as the legitimate Grand Master, in the Order of the Garter on 16 June.

Wharton's enemy Curll wrote a poem of praise, "On Sir Robert Walpole's being created a Knight of the Garter," which he wickedly published in *Whartoniana*.[118] Wharton's former protégé Edward Young issued a panegyric to Walpole's achievement, entitled *The Instalment, 1726*.[119] Young was desperately seeking a position at court, and he subsequently became a member of the modern Grand Lodge.[120] His tribute to Walpole provoked "honest" William Shippen, a Jacobite M.P., to denounce the poet as showing "the most abject spirit of flattery and prostitution...that perhaps ever appeared in any writer, even of the same stamp."[121] Pope shared Shippen's disgust, and he would later refer to the corruption of the Order of the Garter and the increasing "taciturnity" of Freemasonry under the Walpolean regime.[122] In Dublin the loyalist Mason Arbuckle responded on 23 July with a positive report about Young's receiving a pension of £220 from George II and then quoted Young's praise of Walpole in *The Instalment*:

> My Breast, O Walpole, glows with grateful Fire.
> The Streams of Royal Bounty, turnd' by Thee,
> Refresh the dry Domains of Poesy.
> My Fortune shews, when Arts are Walpole's Care,
> What slender Worth forbids us to despair
> Be this... I smile from Censure free:

---

[115] A. Lang, *History*, IV, 423.

[116] R. Coxe, *Walpole*, II, 598.

[117] In 1726 Richmond named James Hamilton, Lord Paisley, as Grand Master, but because Paisley was away in the country, Richmond acted as his proxy and "continued in his chair"; see J. Anderson, *Constitutions (1738)*, 119-20.

[118] Edmund Curll, ed., *Whartoniana* (London, 1727), 146.

[119] Harold Foster, *Edward Young: The Poet of "Night Thoughts," 1683-1765* (alburgh, 1986), 98.

[120] *General Evening Post* (23 November 1732).

[121] H. Foster, *Edward Young*, 99.

[122] A Pope, *Dunciad*, 392-99.

'Twas meant for Merit, tho' it fell on me.[123]

Swift's supporters did not let Arbuckle get away with his praise of Walpole and Young, and they published *The Printers' Petition to the Poetical Senate Assembled in Grub-Street* (Dublin, 1726), in which they mocked his poetic and journalist skills:

> Arbuckle writes in's Weekly Journal
> How Phoebus rose and set diurnal,
> A motto takes from Rome or Greece,
> A venerable Frontispiece,
> He tells how forty Thousand Men
> Arose, and went to Bed again,
> And mixed true News with what's Spurious,
> To please the Ignorant, and Curious.
> Yet after all this Stir and Pother,
> The Journal soon becomes Bum Fodder.[124]

At this time Swift was staying with Pope at Twickenham, and he added to the *Gulliver* manuscript a passage on the current political manipulation of the Orders of the Garter, Thistle, and Bath. George I had made the Earl of Dalkeith a Knight of the Thistle in February 1725 and then, pushed by Walpole, the king revived the Order of the Bath in May, when he installed Montagu and Richmond.[125] Thus, three Whig Grand Masters were given chivalric prestige to counter the Garter and Masonic claims of Wharton. Swift accordingly portrayed the petty-minded Lilliputian emperor (George I) holding out a stick, while

> the Candidates advancing one by one, sometimes leap over the Stick, sometimes creep under it backwards and forwards several times... Whoever performs his Part with most Agility, and holds out the longest in *leaping* and *creeping*, is rewarded with Blue-coloured Silk; the Red is given to the next, and the Green to the third...[126]

When Benjamin Motte, the Tory-supporting printer, received the manuscript in August, he perceived this passage as too dangerous and changed the colors of Garter blue, Bath red, and Thistle green to purple, yellow, and white.

From June 1726 onwards, hints at the growing rivalry in chivalric and Masonic developments appeared in the English press. In "a skit, written by some well-informed person upon Dr. Desaguliers and his friends," another critic of the London Grand Lodge advertised a meeting on 26 June of "Antediluvian" Masons.[127] A Gormogon would guard the door against "the Cowin and Eves-droppers," while a lecturer on "Ancient Masonry" would expose "what Innovations have lately been introduced by the Doctor and some other of the Moderns, with their Tape, Jacks, Moveable Letters, Blazing Stars, etc., to the great indignity of the Mop and Pail." In response to George I's praise of a model of the

---

[123] *Dublin Weekly Journal* (23 July 1726).
[124] [Anon.], *The Printers' Petition to the Poetical Senate Assembled in Grub-Street* (Dublin, 1726).
[125] W. Fraser, *Scotts*, 486; J. Swift, *Gulliver*, 287.
[126] *Ibid.*, 26, 297.
[127] *EMP*, 193-94.

Temple of Solomon constructed in Hanover and now exhibited in the Haymarket, the lecturer would give "a particular Description of the Temple of Solomon, shewing which way the Fellow Crafts got into the Middle Chamber to receive their Wages," showing "that neither the Honorary, Apollonian, or Free and Accepted Masons know anything of the matter." Various newspapers reported that the king's Hanoverian Temple spurred Mr. Winston, evidently an "ancient" Mason, to construct a rival model of Solomon's Temple, "to shew in opposition to that in the Hay-Market; both of which are pretended to be true Models yet are different. I fear if Virtuosi can't agree upon Corporeals, *no Wonder there is such Difference in Speculative Matters.*"[128]

Another "ancient" Mason attacked the legendary history presented in Anderson's *Constitutions*. In *An Ode to the Grand Khaibar* (1726), the Masonic Khaibarites boast of more ancient and accurate traditions, noting that the authors of the *Constitutions* "Sir Christopher [Wren] forget,/ And pass unnam'd Sir Isaac by."[129] The modern Masons' claims to enlightenment are as unfounded as the possibility of a mechanic becoming greater than Isaac Newton or William Benson greater than Jabal. The Antediluvian also referred to the seventeenth-century tradition that "Mason Lairds in Scotland" were "skill'd in the second Sight." As we shall see, the hope that second sight, clairvoyance, and Cabalistic vision could serve Jacobite political needs would eventually influence *Écossais* rituals.

Meanwhile, Prime Minister Walpole took seriously Wharton's boasts of international support, and he feared that Russian, Swedish, and Spanish arms were already landed in Scotland and Ireland.[130] These rumors of seditious political intrigue, as well as charges of drunkenness and debauchery, were creating a negative public image for Masonry in general. In *The Free-Masons Accusation and Defence* (London, 1726), a father tries to dissuade his son from joining the fraternity by warning him of government concern about "these Meetings and Combinations" and about the unsavoury character of "Sir Thomas ----" [Prendergast] who was trying to recruit the son.[131] Though the Masons give lectures on mathematics and the useful arts, Sir Thomas "is a great Sensualist, a Man of Indolence and Pleasure." The son refers to Anderson's *Constitutions* as proof of the fraternity's moral purposes and sends a copy to his father, who concludes that it is a "miserable Performance," especially the author's "execrable Ballads."

The son then argues that Masonic affiliation aids social mobility at home and abroad, for it gives "Access to the greatest Men in all Courts by the *Signs of Masonry*, who are obliged to receive you as a Brother." At this time, the only known Masonic enclaves abroad were Jacobite or, possibly, deist-Tolandian fraternities. Thus, the father pooh-poohs the son's claim of international brotherhood:

> As for your Story of the Universality of Masonry, it's all a Juggle. You are deceived to the last Degree. I have been in France, Spain, and Italy, yet never heard a Word of this Stuff before. You would be laughed to scorn in any of those Countries, to mention any Thing so compleatly ridiculous.

---

[128] P. Crossle and J. Lepper, *History*, 48.
[129] *EMP*, 185-92.
[130] M. Blackett-Ord, *Hell-Fire*, *161*.
[131] *EMP*, *156-72*.

In response to the father's argument, a Grand Lodge Mason published *A Full Vindica-tion...of the Free and Accepted Masons, from the Malicious Aspersions* (London, 1726), dedicated to the Grand Master "Lenogius" (Charles Lennox, 2nd Duke of Richmond). Claiming that forty thousand "Gentlemen of Honour, Integrity, and Substance" in London are Masons, he boasted that there are "besides many Lodges in Holland, Flanders, France, Spain, Italy, etc. nay in the East and West Indies there are many worthy Brethren."[132]

It is unknown if there were indeed lodges in Spain, but the most prominent Mason in the country – Wharton – would soon be involved in controversy caused by his precipi-tous conversion to Catholicism, undertaken in order to marry an Irish maid-in-waiting to the Spanish queen. His first, estranged wife died in London in April 1726, and three months later in July, Wharton astonished and dismayed his Protestant Jacobite support-ers by his conversion and marriage. He also hoped to gain favor with the Irish exiles serving in the Spanish army. His fellow Mason Ezekiel Hamilton, who had admired Wharton as a genius, now worried that he was too reckless to be trusted with any im-portant role. He wrote to John Hay, now titular Earl of Inverness, that Wharton was determined to become tutor to Prince Charles Edward Stuart, but he feared that "as an illustrious member of the Hell-Fire Club," the duke will "attempt to Bamboozle or Whar-tonize the King," and change "the mild and merciful temper of the Stuarts into that of a Caligula or Nero."[133]

When news of Wharton's conversion reached England, the Whigs rejoiced and un-leashed a flood of satires. In *A Letter from a Quaker at Aylesbury in Buckinghamshire, to Philip, Duke of Wh----n, at Madrid in Spain* (1726), the author "Obadiah Sorrow" used scriptural language to hint at his betrayal of Freemasonry: "Friend *Adoniram* still cherish'd and com-forted thee, but thou did'st with him deal craftily, returning Evil for Good," and "thou wentest forth into *Jerusalem*, and did'st there join thyself…to mean *Craftsmen*, saying, *Let us take Counsel together against the Rulers of the Land.*"[134] Even worse he did not "cherish the Wife of thy Bosom" and "revell'd in the Embraces of the Scarlet whore." He rejected the English government's invitation to return, and instead joined himself "unto the Vag-abonds and Fugitives of the Earth." The Quaker acknowledged Wharton's intellectual gifts:

> It is reported that thou vain-glorieth mightily because of thy human Learn-ing, and can'st speak the Language of the Beast [Latin]; and Men moreover say, thou has Wisdom in abundance; but, friend *Philip*, remember that all thy Wisdom hath hitherto been Foolishness, and that the true Wisdom restest not in thee.[135]

In an odd reply to the Quaker, doubtfully attributed to Wharton, the author mocked Sorrow's text as "a Rhapsody of Nonsense," which trifles with "the Holy Text, and bur-lesques the Stile of the Divine Writ."[136] He then argued that he acts only out of self-interest and may one day return to his original religion and hinted at his ambiguous

---

[132] *Ibid.*, 177.
[133] Stuart Papers: 95/110 (20 July 1726).
[134] Obadiah Sorrow, *A Letter from a Quaker…to Philip, Duke of Wh----n, at Madrid in Spain* (London, 1726), 4.
[135] *Ibid.*, 6.
[136] *Philip Duke of Wh----n's Answer to Obadiah Sorrow* (Dublin, 1727), 1-2.

loyalties to "a Prince of the Royal Blood," who could be George I or James III. It is curious that George Faulkner, a friend of Swift who admired Wharton, printed this strange text in Dublin. Perhaps Wharton's Protestant and Masonic supporters in Ireland hoped that his conversion was temporary.

On 9 August 1726, in the midst of these Masonic and Jacobite controversies, Defoe published volume three of his *Tour through the Whole Island of Great Britain*, which featured important descriptions of Scottish architecture. David Sperry notes that though "the tone of the *Tour* is unmistakably, if rather mildly, anti-Jacobite," Defoe expressed surprising admiration and fairness towards individual Jacobites, such as James III, Pitsligo, and even Mar.[137] Defoe admitted that the union, for which he worked so hard, had not brought the expected advantages to Scotland, but he hoped that Providence would eventually improve the situation. He drew extensively on *A Journey Through Scotland* (1723) by John Macky, a native Scot and fellow Whig intelligencer, who described the former glories of Scottish architecture and lamented the deterioration caused by the exile and impoverishment of so many talented but foolish Jacobites. To appeal to his English audience, Defoe omitted Macky's patriotic tributes to Scottish history and added his own concerns about trade.

Defoe had visited many of the palaces and stately homes described by Macky during his earlier residences in Scotland, and his descriptions made clear that contacts with architects and builders were important to him while he carried out intelligence work for Robert Harley. He praised the monumental style and stonework of Scottish edifices — arts now out of fashion in England. The Royal Mile in Edinburgh is "perhaps the largest, longest, and finest street of buildings...not in Britain only, but in the world."[138] The finely-built bridges, with their great stone arches, also deserve notice. Among the many private estates, Defoe especially praised Kinross, "the most beautiful and regular piece of architecture, (for a private gentleman's seat) in all Scotland, perhaps, in all Britain":

> The house is a picture, 'tis all beauty; the stone is white and fine, the order regular, the contrivance elegant, the workmanship exquisite. Dryden's lines, intended for a compliment on his friend's poetry...are literally of the house of Kinross.
>
> > Strong dorick columns form the base,
> > Corinthian fills the upper space;
> > So all below is strenth, and all above is grace.
>
> Sir William Bruce, the skilful builder, was the Surveyor General of the Works, as we call it in England, or the Royal Architect, as in Scotland. In a word, he was the Kit Wren of North Britain, and his skill in the perfect decoration of buildings has many testimonials left upon record for it...[139]

As noted earlier, Bruce was a committed Jacobite who suffered for the cause. Defoe also described Hamilton Palace as "fit rather for the court of a prince than the palace of a

---

[137] David Sperry, "A Study of Daniel Defoe's *Tour Through Great Britain*" (Illinois University: Ph.D. Thesis, 1950), 229-32.

[138] D.Defoe, *Tour*, 299, 302, 341.

[139] *Ibid.*, 367.

subject," and Dalkeith Palace as "a magnificent building, and the inside answerable to the grandeur of the family."[140] He was pleased that the heirs were continuing the grand style of building in stone.

Among the great Jacobite builders, Defoe pointed to "the antient and noble house of Seaton and Winton," whose "houses are now in a state of ruin." Winton, who was currently living in Rome where he later became Master of the Jacobite lodge, was described almost sympathetically: "the late Earl of Winton, who did so many weak and rash things, to say no worse of him, in the affair of the late rebellion; and the kindest thing can be said of him now is, to leave it upon record, that he seem'd to be turn'd in his head." The estates of the Dysarts and St. Clairs were now "in the full perfection of decay and "indeed, a most lamentable object of a miserable, dying corporation," while the "very noble seat belonging to the Bruces, Earls of Kincairn [Kincardine]" at Culross suffered from the exploitation of the mines by the York Buildings Company, which expropriated many Jacobite properties.[141]

Defoe was probably not aware that the current Earl of Kincardine was on Wharton's list of Jacobite peers.[142] But it was the Earl of Mar who most provoked Defoe's admiration and exasperation, both for his architectural talents and his political recklessness. When Defoe described Stirling Castle, he noted that the "Earl of Mar, of the name of Ereskine," claimed to be hereditary keeper of the king's children and of the castle. He especially admired the castle for its great stonework and sense of permanence: "They who built the castle, without doubt built it, as the Scots express it, to continue aye, and till somebody else should build another there, which, in our language, would be for ever and a day after... the castle seems as firm and fair, as it had been but lately built."[143] He further praised "the great bridge at Sterling to Alloway [Alloa], the seat of the present or rather late Earl of Marr, the present Earl being attainted for treason, and so dead, as a peer or earl, though alive in exile." Defoe knew that Mar had designed the castellated residence, gardens, canals, harbor, and streets at Alloa, which he acknowledged were among the finest in Britain.

The memory of Mar's achievements at Alloa led Defoe to ponder the folly of the Jacobites in giving up everything for their cause:

> It is a strange testimony of the power of envy and ambition, that mankind, bless'd with such advantages, for an easy and happy retreat in the world, should hazard it all in faction and party, and throw it all away in view, and even without a view, of getting more: But I must not phylosophize...[144]

Though Defoe was disillusioned with Walpolean corruption and Whig profiteering (exemplified by the York Buildings Company), his intense anti-Catholicism made him place the current Jacobites beyond the pale.

However, in another unexpected tribute from a veteran Hanoverian propagandist, Defoe praised the architectural ideals of the Scottish kings:

---

[140] *Ibid.*, 339, 360.
[141] *Ibid.*, 371, 391.
[142] P. Fritz, *English Ministers*, 160.
[143] D. Defoe, *Tour*, 343.
[144] *Ibid.*, 390.

however mean our thoughts in England have been of the Scots court in those times, the kings of Scotland had more fine palaces than most princes in Europe, and, in particular many more than the Crown of England has now; for example, we see nothing in England now of any notice but Hampton-Court, Windsor, Kensington and St James's.

Greenwich and Nonsuch are demolished.

Richmond quite out of use, and not able to receive a Court.

Winchester never inhabited, or half finished.

Whitehall burnt, and lying in ruins, or, as we may say let out into tenements.

Westminster, long since abandon'd...

Whereas the kings of Scotland had in King James the VI's time all in good repair, and in use, the several royal palaces of

Haly-rood House,

The Castle, at Edinburgh.

The royal palace in the castle at Sterling.

Linlithgow.

Dumfermling.

Falkland.

Scoon...[145]

Defoe's work with operative stonemasons and participation in a lodge at Stoke-Newington seemed to give him renewed access to and respect for "ancient" Masonic traditions, with their strong Stuart heritage.

When volume three of Defoe's *Tour* came out, Swift was still in London, where he stayed from mid-March until 15 August 1726. He was perhaps informed about Defoe's praise of Scottish architecture and stonemasonry, especially the works of the attainted Mar at Alloa, through Dr. Arbuthnot, who acquired the successive volumes of the *Tour*. During this period, when Arbuthnot was active in a London lodge, Swift and Pope also (allegedly) participated in Masonry, and their names appear on the membership list (cumulative to 1730) of the lodge that met in the Goat Tavern at the foot of the Haymarket.[146] The Master of the lodge was Isaac Dubois, possibly a kinsman of Nicholas Dubois, who now served as Master Mason to the Office of Works under Richard Arundell, whose appointment Swift had noted.[147]

In March Dr. Arbuthnot introduced Swift to Philip Dormer Stanhope, 4th Earl of Chesterfield, a Grand Lodge Mason, who was then collaborating with Bolingbroke in the Whig-Tory opposition to Walpole. In April and May Swift had two meetings with Walpole, in which he tried to present Ireland's grievances to a very close-minded and prejudiced Prime Minister. Chesterfield later claimed that "Swift made an offer of his pen to Sir Robert Walpole: that the terms were, his getting a preferment in England, equal to what he had in Ireland; and that Sir Robert rejected the offer."[148] As rumors of Swift's alleged offer swirled, he vehemently denied them and claimed that "I absolutely broke with the first minister, and have never seen him since." He wrote an Irish Tory friend

---

[145] *Ibid.*, 366.

[146] Facsimile of lodge list in M. Mack, *Pope*, 437-39.

[147] On Nicholas Dubois, see H. Colvin, *Biographical Dictionary*, 185, 761.

[148] I. Ehrenpreis, *Swift*, III, 484-88.

that the affair made him for the first time weary of England and long to be in Ireland, though "you all live in a wretched dirty Dog-hole and Prison, but it is a place good enough to die in."[149]

As "all the Walpoleans and the whole Party of the Whigs" accused Swift of venality and hypocrisy, he may have turned a more sympathetic eye to the Jacobites and their Masonic supporters. On 27 June Burlington gave him a copy of Fréart's *Parallele del'Architecture antique et de la moderne*, with the inscription: "I give this book to Dr. Jonathan Swift...in order to constitute him Director of Architecture in Ireland, especially on my own estate in that Kingdom," signed by his "Witness Alexander Pope."[150] Burlington learned that Swift left for Ireland on 15 August, and on the 23rd, the earl, his wife, and Catholic brother-in-law left for Paris, on what was allegedly a Jacobite-Masonic mission. Jane Clark argues that the earl's two-month stay was connected with secret fund-raising for the proposed Jacobite invasion, expected within the next months.[151] At this time, Burlington's code-name in Ezekiel Hamilton's cipher was "Lamb" or "2376," and Hamilton was serving as Ormonde's secretary in Spain.

Thus, Burlington may be the shadowy visitor who flits in and out of Atterbury's letters at this time. Writing to James from Paris on 16 September, the bishop referred to "They that know Robert Walpole well, and came lately from England." Howard Colvin acknowledges that Jane Clark's "shocking" case is "carefully argued" when she explains Burlington's notorious debts as the result of his lavish contributions to the Jacobite cause rather than his architectural extravagance. Burlington was "in other words an eighteenth-century Anthony Blunt, masquerading as a loyal courtier while concealing a record of treasonable activity."[152] On the earl's return to England, he infused mystical Masonic themes into the design and decoration of the villa at Chiswick, which – according to Clark – was built as a Masonic Temple to welcome home the restored James III.

Throughout Swift's stay in England, the manuscript of *Gulliver* passed among his friends, who made suggestions and revisions. It was sent to the publisher in August, but Motte the printer omitted some of the more politically dangerous passages. After the work appeared on 28 October, Swift was furious that his work had been "mangled and murdered."[153] His Jacobite friend Charles Ford, who had seen the original manuscript, wrote to Motte and protested the alterations, but the "prudential changes in the text were retained until 1735." Despite the bowdlerization, it seems certain that Swift's "brothers" would have perceived many allusions in *Gulliver* as Masonic. He merged into one target the modern Freemasons, Royal Society virtuosos, and religious latitudinarians – who had all contributed to the current Masonic pamphlet wars. In the Laputan "Island in the Air," with its "Academy of Projectors," he attacked the whole Whig enterprise of speculative Masonry, secular science, and heterodox theology.

Marie Roberts argues that Swift drew on Theophilus Schweigardt's *Speculum Sophicum Rhodo-Stauroticum* (1618), with its bizarre engraving of the winged "Invisible College of

---

[149] J. Swift, Correspondence, II, 651-52.

[150] M. Mack, *Pope*, 440.

[151] J. Clark, "Burlington," 275.

[152] H. Colvin, Introd., *Burlington*, xxv.

[153] J. Swift, *Gulliver*, xiv.

the Rose Cross Fraternity."[154] Various Scottish Freemasons acquired this work in the seventeenth-century, and its imagery may have been carried to Ireland by immigrant Scottish Masons.[155] In Swift's portrayal of the Struldbruggs, who achieve immortal life, he seemed also to draw on Robert Samber's translation of *Long Livers*, which described a Rosicrucian style of Masonry and concluded with detailed instructions on "How to Prepare the Universal Medicine."[156] Swift's allusions to "those Reverend Sages," their "immortal Brotherhood," and the "universal Medicine" echoed Samber's perorations, which the "renegado Papist" now attempted to link with modern Whig Masonry.

In *Gulliver*, when Swift described how the island of Laputa "is made to rise and fall" by means of a gigantic magnetic loadstone, he seemed to target James Hamilton, Lord Paisley, current Grand Master of the English Grand Lodge, who had donated a huge and powerful lodestone to the Royal Society. J.L. Heilbron notes that the society had long made a "fetish" of studying magnetic phenomena, an obsession carried by William Stephens, FRS, to Trinity College, Dublin.[157] Paisley was also fascinated by mathematical music composition – another subject mocked in *Gulliver*.[158] Desaguliers served as Paisley's deputy Grand Master, and Prendergast--Swift's *bête noir* – served as Grand Warden (while still holding office in the Irish Grand Lodge).[159] Paisley and Desaguliers were members of the "Philomat" faction in the society, which was so devoted to Newtonian, abstract mathematics that other areas of scientific inquiry (natural history, chemistry, experimental physics) were neglected.[160] Swift had already mocked Desaguliers's hydrographical projects and mathematical lectures before George I, and he now dismissed Newton's theories of attraction and gravity as ephemeral scientific fads (and, by implication, Desaguliers's public lectures on Newtonianism).[161]

According to Swift, the virtuosos' preoccupation with abstract, theoretical mathematics has led to disastrous practical results, especially in the detachment of speculative Masonry from its operative roots. Thus, the Laputans produce corrupted architecture:

> Their Houses are very ill built, the Walls bevil, without one right Angle in any Apartment; and this Defect ariseth from the Contempt they bear for practical Geometry; which they despise as vulgar and mechanick, those instructions they give being too refined for the Intellectuals of their Workmen; which occasions perpetual Mistakes. And although they are dextrous enough upon a Piece of Paper in the Management of the Rule, the Pencil, and the Divider, yet in the common Actions and Behaviour of Life, I have not seen a more clumsy, awkward, unhandy People...[162]

Moreover, these architectural and Masonic faults stem from their Whiggism:

[154] Marie Mulvey Roberts, "Science, Magic, and Masonry: Swift's Secret Texts," in *Secret Texts: The Literature of Secret Societies* (New York, 1993), 99-104.
[155] M. Schuchard, *Restoring*, 361, 422.
[156] J. Swift, *Gulliver*, 202, 347.
[157] J. Heilbron, *Physics at the Royal Society during Newton's Presidency* (Los Angeles, 1983), 19, 73, 75; "James Hamilton, 7th Earl of Abercorn," *DNB*.
[158] J. Swift, *Gulliver*, 152, 158.
[159] J. Anderson, *Constitutions (1738)*, 119.
[160] J. Heilbron, *Physics*, 37-41.
[161] J. Swift, *Gulliver*, 190.
[162] *Ibid.*, 153.

> the strong Disposition I observed in them towards News and Politicks; perpetually enquiring into publick Affairs, giving their Judgements in Matters of State; and passionately disputing every Inch of a Party Opinion. I have indeed observed the same Disposition among most of the Mathematicians I have known in Europe, although I could never discover the least Analogy between the two Sciences...[163]

In contrast to the defective Whiggish architecture, Swift portrayed "Lord Munodi," who had lost his position through a "Cabal of Ministers" but who adhered to traditional norms of architecture:

> We came at length to the House, which was indeed a Noble Structure, built according to the best Rules of ancient Architecture... I gave due Praises to every Thing I saw... after supper, when there being no third Companion, he told me with a very melancholy air, that he doubted he must throw down his Houses in Town and Country, to rebuild them after the present Mode; destroy all his Plantations, and cast others into such a Form as modern Usage required...unless he would... increase his Majesty's displeasure.[164]

Munodi blames the current problem on the influence of the Royal Society, which for forty years has encouraged virtuosos "with a very little Smattering in Mathematicks," to fall "into Schemes of putting all Arts, Sciences, Languages, and Mechanicks upon a new Foot." The Laputan projectors claim that "a Palace may be built in a Week," while one "ingenious Architect" contributed a new method of building houses, "by beginning at the Roof and working downwards to the Foundation." However, Munodi "was content to go on in the old Forms; to live in the Houses his Ancestors had built, and act as they did in every Part of Life without Innovation."

Swift may have been aware of Mar's "Description of the Designe for a New Royall Palace for the King of Great Britain at London," a treatise with drawings composed in 1726. Gibbs, who corresponded with Mar about their mutual architectural projects, probably informed his friends Pope, Arbuthnot, and Burlington about it.[165] Mar's designs were intended to produce a "palace worthy of the grandeur of the king" – that is, the restored James III. His eloquent proposal to "restore the true ancient simple taste" paralleled Swift's architectural and civic themes in *Gulliver*, for Mar observed that

> Fine and magnificent things cannot be had without Expence and Cost. The Building of a Palace for the King at London, has always been Lookt on as a publick work, and to be done by Parliament... A King of England who is well with his people, by showing in Conduct that he has no seperat Interest from theirs, and makes no attempts on their Rights and Liberties, would find no Dificulty of getting the Parl to come to such a project, which would be as much for their and for the Nations honour as for his, and their makeing a yearly fund for purchasing the ground necessary, and for putting it all in execution, as was done for St Pauls Church, the Designe might be Compleated in a few years, without being grivous to the People, or making them

---

[163] *Ibid.*, 154.
[164] *Ibid.*, 168.
[165] Gibbs worked for Burlington in 1725-26; see H. Colvin, *Biographical Dictionary*, 404.

any ways repine, and indeed the moneys not going out of the Nation that would be Bestowed but Circulat amongst the people, would make the expence of no charge of Consequence and answer almost what Sir Christopher Wren said of St Pauls that it had Cost the Nation Nothing but the Charge of the Scaffolding which was the only foraigne Comodity employ'd in the Building.[166]

Terry Friedman concludes that Mar's extraordinary plans and drawings for this and other palaces and buildings in France and Britain make clear that he was one of the most "remarkable and visionary" architects of the age.[167]

In 1726 the Irish Jacobite exile and hero, Sir Charles Wogan, sent all of Swift's previously printed works to the Stuart court in Rome, which was eager to get copies of *Gulliver's Travels*.[168] Wogan would later establish an important correspondence with Swift. James Edgar, the Protestant secretary to James III, made sure that Michael McDonough, Catholic bishop of Kilmore, would send a copy of *Gulliver* directly to the king. Two years later, these Irish Jacobites assured James of "Dean Swift's eagerness to see him and his zeal in satirizing the [Whig] government."[169] Throughout the British Isles, *Gulliver* was an immediate best seller, with new editions and a French translation appearing rapidly. While Swift's friends were delighted by the reception, they also worried about the infuriated response of Walpole and George I.

The Whigs immediately branded it a Jacobite work, and Walpole determined to identify the anonymous author. Swift's satire on the merciless spies who deciphered Gyllenborg's and Atterbury's correspondence implicated the ministers in perjury, fraud, bribery, and self-serving inventions of Jacobite plots. In a passage that echoed the Cabalistic decipherers of the *Letter from the Grand Mistress of the Female Free Masons*, Swift charged:

> When this Method fails [false witnesses], they have two others more effectual; which the Learned among them call Acrosticks, and Anagrams. First, they can decypher all initial Letters into Political Meanings: thus, *N* shall signify a Plot; *B*, a Regiment of Horse: *L*, a Fleet at Sea. Or Secondly, by transposing the Letters of the Alphabet, in any suspected Paper, they can lay open the deepest Designs of a discontented Party.[170]

Even more worrisome to the prime minister would have been Swift's reference to the Madagascar pirates, for Walpole's spies reported that they were a Jacobite enclave currently linked with the Holstein party in Sweden.[171] This arcane allusion reinforces the case for Swift's access to extremely secret, international Jacobite intrigues. Perhaps he learned about the Madagascar pirates from Robert Arbuthnot, who had access to Swedish-Jacobite affairs and who spent much time with Swift in London, before returning to his

---

[166] T. Friedman, "Palace," 115.

[167] *Ibid.*, 110.

[168] I. Higgins, "Jonathan Swift," 90.

[169] E. O'Ciardha, *Ireland*, 216-17.

[170] J. Swift, *Gulliver*,

[171] For more on the Swedish Jacobites' earlier use of the Madagascar Company as a cover for their military contributions, see M. Schuchard, *Emanuel Swedenborg*, 150-52, 166-67, 185.

Jacobite financial activities in Rouen and Paris. Pope was much impressed with Robert, noting that he was "a more extraordinary man than Dr. John, 'a Philosopher all of Fire.'"[172]

Defoe, who had earlier written on pirates at Madagascar, reacted to the simmering Masonic controversies by adding his own warnings to those Whig scientists and Masons who dabble in magical studies.[173] In *A System of Magick; or, a History of the Black Art*, published on 24 November 1726, he granted that the earliest magicians of Chaldea, Egypt, and Israel were honest seers and natural philosophers. He then satirized William Whiston, an eccentric Newtonian, as a profiteering modern magician, who paralleled the exiled Scottish Jacobites in his credulous heterodoxy and implicit sedition.[174] Defoe made clear that he believed the Scottish capacity for second sight was real and "not inconsistent with Reason or the Nature of Things." Thus, it was especially dangerous for superficial wits and virtuosos to dabble in visionary and occult studies. Portraying an Arabian magus in the desert, Defoe wrote:

> Here was a great deal of Ceremony, before his Worship would be spoken with; and I cannot but think of our Friend *Roger C---* (Accepted Free Mason, etc.) speaks with him [the devil] upon much easier terms... I doubt not the *Arabian* would have made no more Scruple of it, than our Brother of the Trowel, who adorns so often his blue Ribband with the most honourable Badge of the Leather Apron; being first incorporated, as above, in the Ancient Society of free *Th-gs* [Thugs] may, for ought we know, build two or three Churches abroad, seeing the Devil and he are known to be upon their Travels together.[175]

In that obscurely worded passage, Defoe seemed to point at Wharton, whose flaunting of his Jacobite-bestowed Garter ribbon was making news in England. He further suggested that Wharton had established "two or three" churches (lodges?) on the Continent. Or, Defoe possibly wanted to warn Whig Masons like the Duke of Richmond, a Garter knight, that his dabbling in scientific "conjuring" experiments could be linked with the seditious heterodoxy of Wharton. Richmond often boasted of his unusual scientific experiments, in which he collaborated with French friends while abroad. For example, while staying with the Duke of Bourbon at Chantilly, he wrote to his fellow Mason Folkes that "Wee hatch chickens, without hens, make burning glasses of a piece of concave ice & in short a thousand more conjuring tricks."[176] He further praised Folkes for being "of the first class of conjurors."

Defoe then targeted Robert Samber's entrée into Whig scientific circles, where the self-proclaimed Rosicrucian hoped to interest Fellows of the Royal Society in his version of natural magic. Defoe admitted that he risked the charge of being unfashionable by criticizing the current craze for "illumination":

---

[172] J. Swift, *Correspondence*, II, 661n.2. A full biography of Robert Arbuthnot is a scholarly desideradatum.
[173] Daniel Defoe, *The King of Pirates* (London, 1720).
[174] Daniel Defoe, *A System of Magick* (London, 1727), 55, 87, 324030.
[175] *Ibid.*, 177-78.
[176] William Wonnacott, "Charles, Duke of Richmond, GM 1724-25," *AQC*, 30 (1917), 178.

Tho' it should...draw me in again to the Sin of Gravity, which the Town hates; yet venturing the general Displeasure, I say 'Tis necessary to take Notice, here that these religious *Effluvia* of Hell, which at present make such confusion of Principles among us, are so demonstrably embrac'd by the present *Magi*, the Sages, the Conversers with good Spirits, the other Pretenders to Supernaturals, and secret Illuminations; that they leave us no more room to doubt but they are all Natives of the same Climate, bred up in the same Country, carrying on the same Interest, and will share at last in the same Destruction; when the Tares and Wheat shall be skillfully and critically separated, as we are well assur'd they will be.

This indeed stands fair against all the modern Teachers of the *Rosicrucian* whimsies, and the Doctrine of Spirits, *viz.* that None of them apply to the Establishment of the true Religion.[177]

Defoe soon learned about the role of Swift, Pope, and Arbuthnot in the publication of *Gulliver's Travels*, for he obtained a copy of *Gulliver Decypher'd*, published in early December 1726, which was followed by a second edition with "a complete Key" identifying the characters.[178] The author disingenuously argued that the pious Dean Swift could not be the author because he would never publish such obscene, blasphemous, and seditious remarks. He then claimed that Pope, Arbuthnot, and the Scriberlians' were co-authors, assisted by Ormonde from Madrid. They were all hypocritical accusers of the government, because they were desperate to get places and pensions for themselves. While Gulliver's criticisms have long been "a common Jacobite insinuation," he now echoes radical republicans, as well as Orator Henley's "admirable Burlesque upon Preaching and Praying."[179] Defoe would certainly approve of the decipherer's explication of his trade as a way of uncovering political plots, for he had participated in the exposure of not only Gyllenborg's but Atterbury's coded correspondence:

Our author [Swift] here shews how these Artists may if they fancy, interpret a Sieve to signify a Court Lady, a lame Dog as an Invader, the Plague a standing Army, a Buzzard a great Statesman, the Gout a High Priest, a Chamberpot a Committee of Grandees, a Broom a Revolution,...a Bottomless-pit a Treasury,...a running Sore an Administration.[180]

Pope, who also acquired *Gulliver Decypher'd*, would not appreciate the accusation that he supplied the "obscene" touches in the Brobdingnag section.[181]

While Defoe worried about occultist, "conjuring" interests among some modern Masons, many ancient Masons worried about the moderns' Whiggish presumptions. The resistance in Dublin and London to attempts at domination by the modern Grand Lodge ramified into Edinburgh, where on 27 December 1726 a majority of members in Mary's Chapel Lodge defeated a Whig attempt at initiating more merchants in order to achieve a "deeper infusion of the Theoretical element into its membership."[182] The "anti-

---

[177] D. Defoe, *System*, 354-55.
[178] D. Defoe, *Librorum*, #1434.
[179] Anon., *Gulliver Decypher'd*, 2nd ed. (London, 1726), 43.
[180] *Ibid.*, vi.
[181] I. Ehrenpreis, *Swift*, 505.
[182] D. Murray Lyon, *History of the Lodge of Edinburgh, Mary's Chapel, No. 1* (London, 1900), 167-68.

Operative party" then "matured measures secretly for the accomplishment of their design," which launched a "struggle for supremacy." The long Scottish tradition of cooperation between operative and gentleman Freemasons must have made Mar's 1726 recommendations for improving Edinburgh by building new bridges and streets, thereby transforming the town "from a bad and incommodious situation to a very beneficial and convenient one," seem a feasible and authentic project for traditionalist Masons.[183] Many Scots looked to Mar's protégé Gibbs, whose works in London seemed the prototype of what could and should be achieved in Edinburgh.

On 27 December 1726 another resistance movement was launched in York, where the physician and antiquary Francis Drake delivered to the York Grand Lodge a speech which was subsequently published.[184] Though Drake and Charles Bathurst, the Grand Master, were private Jacobites, Drake carefully praised Masonry as a non-partisan brotherhood that brought men of different beliefs together for rational sociability. Noting humorously that the lodge would not hear "a Cicero, a Demosthenes, or even – a *Henly*" in his discourse, he suggested his awareness of the Orator's speeches on Masonic topics.[185] He lamented the drunkenness that often unleashed quarrels over politics and religion and thus blighted lodge meetings. He also worried about the increasing detachment of modern Masonry from its operative roots. Calling upon "My Brethren, the Working-Masons" and "You that are of other Trades and Occupations," he urged them to remember their ancient traditions of great architecture. Quoting an essay by Joseph Addison, he affirmed:

> We are oblig'd to Devotion for the noblest Buildings that have Adorn'd the several countries of the World. It is this which has set Men at Work on Temples and publick Places of Worship, not only that they might by the Magnificence of the Building invite the Deity to reside there; but that such Stupendous Works might at the same Time open the Mind to vast Conceptions, and fit it to converse with Divinity of the Place...[186]

After giving polite praise to Anderson's *Constitutions*, Drake claimed that the York Grand Lodge was the oldest in England. Arguing that Edwin, the first Christian king of Northumberland, laid the foundation stone of York Cathedral and sat as Grand Master, he observed: 'This is sufficient to make us dispute the Superiority of the Lodges at *London*: But as nought of that Kind ought to be amongst so amicable a Fraternity, we are content they enjoy the title of Grand-Master of *England*, but the *Totius Angliæ* we claim as our undoubted Right." In a footnote, Drake stressed that "Edwin's Chief Seat of Residence was at Derventio, now call'd Auldby," a subtle reference to Derwentwater, ancestral home of Charles Radcliffe, current member of the Jacobite lodge in Paris. By maintaining civil discourse, the York Masons "can be in no Danger from the Malice of our Enemies without the Lodge, nor in *Perils amongst False Brethren* within," for "even at this critical Time all Parties are buried in Masonry." Noting that most lodges in London feature "a Lecture on some Point of Geometry or Architecture," he asked "why the *Mother Lodge* of

---

[183] T. Friedman, "Palace," 109.
[184] *EMP*, 196-207.
[185] *Ibid.*, 201.
[186] *Ibid.*, 203.

them all shou'd so far forget her own Institutions," which cannot be accounted for "but from her exteam old Age."

On the same day, 27 December 1726, Irish Masons in Munster elected James O'Brien as Grand Master, with the Quaker Springett Penn as his Deputy. Penn was the grandson of William Penn, founder of the colony of Pennsylvania, who had been a close friend of Swift in 1710-12.[187] At that time, the elder Penn was a strong supporter of James "III," for he appreciated the Stuarts' promise of liberty of conscience.[188] In 1712, like Swift, he became friendly with the Swedish diplomat Carl Gyllenborg, with whom he collaborated on negotiations for a marriage between James II's daughter to the Swedish king Carl XII (her death aborted the plan).[189] He was undoubtedly aware that during the reigns of Charles II and James II Quakers in Scotland had joined Masonic lodges, and that some of them carried their fraternal association to Pennsylvania.[190] In 1726, when Springett Penn, became Deputy Grand Master in Munster, the local fraternity was Tory and "tolerant of passive Jacobitism."[191] Given Swift's admiration for William Penn and the Quakers, it its certainly possible that he knew Springett Penn, who from his Irish residence in Munster served as governor of Pennsylvania.[192] This might explain the letter that Swift would receive in 1729 from a Quaker in Pennsylvania, expressing admiration for his writings and sending him a salted ham, "the Product of the Wilds of America."[193]

---

[187] J. Swift, *Journal to Stella*, 30, 369.

[188] Vincent Buranelli, *The King and the Quaker: A Study of William Penn and James II* (Philadelphia, 1962).

[189] M. Schuchard, *Emanuel Swedenborg*, 52.

[190] D. Stevenson, *First Freemasons*, 139-43.

[191] D. Dickson, *Old World Colony*, 275.

[192] R. Berman, *Schism*, 251-52.

[193] J. Swift, *Correspondence*, III, 227-28.

CHAPTER ELEVEN

A NEW KING, YET OLD CORRUPTION
(1727-1730)

Great Changes were now talked of; Sir Robert Walpole was to be
Demolished; the Duke of Newcastle's Head taken off; the Duke of
Ormonde recalled; and…all the Whigs and Tories to be mixed in the
Administration; but as yet, Things stand as they did.

John Lord Boyle, to William Byrd (3 September 1727).

Say from what cause, in vain decry'd and curst,
Still Dunce the second reigns like Dunce the first?

Alexander Pope, *The Dunciad* (1728).

While many Masons in Dublin and York resisted the domination of the Grand
Lodge of London, two exiled Masons launched their ambitious Jacobite agendas on the Continent. In January 1727 Charles Radcliffe left Paris for Turin,
where he solicited funding from James to bring his family to Italy, adding that he hoped
to see the king "this year with Sword in Hand."[1] In July Walpole's spy Stosch reported
that Radcliffe, his rich wife, and her beautiful daughters had arrived in Rome, bringing
with them "much merchandise of gallantry."[2] Describing him as "brother of the decapitated Lord Derwentwater," Stosch became convinced over the next two years that Radcliffe was the most dangerous enemy to England's Hanoverian government, for his charismatic personality, generous entertaining, and attractive family gained adherents among
English as well as Italian visitors to their home.[3] He was especially worried by Radcliffe's
occasional disappearances, when he could not track him in Italy.[4] As we shall see, these
were occasions when Radcliffe secretly visited France and England, where he utilized his
Masonic contacts.

---

[1] Stuart Papers: 101/137 (8 January 1727; 102/84 (30 January 1727).
[2] NA:SP 105/124 (9 July 1727).
[3] *Ibid.*, 85/16 (12 May 1729).
[4] *Ibid.*, 105/235, 238, 241 (October-November 1727).

Throughout 1727 Zecky Hamilton's fears that the Stuart court would be "Whar-tonized" and Caligula-ized by the new Catholic convert were echoed gleefully by Whig writers in England. Wharton's former protégé Edward Young drew on the duke's Hell Fire and Masonic notoriety in satire IV, published in *The Universal Passion: The Love of Fame* (1727). After chastising freethinkers like Anthony Collins, he mocked "Narcissus," member of "the Tartarian Club," whom Horace Walpole later identified as Sir William Stanhope, brother of Lord Chesterfield, and alleged member of the Hell Fire club.[5] Young then made an obscure allusion to Freemasonry:

> Narcissus the Tartarian club disclaims,
> Nay, a Free-mason with some Terror names,
> Omits no duty, nor can *Envy* say
> He miss'd these many Years the Church, or Play;
> He makes no noise in Parliament,'tis true,
>
> ....
>
> *Narcissus* is the Glory of his Race:
> For who does nothing with a better Grace?[6]

Young implied that William Stanhope, like his brother Chesterfield, was a Grand Lodge Mason. Elected as a Whig M.P. in January 1727, Stanhope seemed an appropriate model for Young's "Proper Idler," for he cast no votes in parliament during the next five years.[7]

While Whigs like Young and Jacobites like Hamilton worried that Masons like Stanhope and Wharton could "bamboozle" their fellows into useless or reckless activities, the continuing Masonic rivalries spilled over onto the Royal Society, which underwent a power-struggle in the wake of Isaac Newton's death in March 1727. After the decease of George I in June, the new president Hans Sloane tried to revive the invitation drafted for the late king and to request that George II become a patron of the society. Led by John Byrom, "the Tory interest at the Society" opposed the resurrection of the address to a Hanoverian king.[8] In May Sloane spread rumors that Byrom was a Jacobite and tried to pressure the Tories into acquiescence. Rallying around Byrom, his partisans put up Folkes for president, though Sloane managed to prevail. From later evidence, it is clear that Folkes, a moderate Whig, knew about Byrom's Jacobite activities, which were real and serious.[9] Byrom was then supplying codes for a "network of espionage," especially between Manchester and Scotland, and on 14 May he was addressed by his northern partisans as "Dear Grand Master." The genial, free-thinking Folkes seemed more amused than appalled by his friend's Jacobite loyalties.

The Tories and Jacobites were so successful in their satirical campaign against the modern Masons and Walpolean Whigs that Defoe, armed with inside knowledge from his work on Mist's *Weekly Journal*, issued his own counterblasts in 1727. Like Swift, he couched his attacks in a Rosicrucian-Masonic context. In *An Essay on the History and Reality of Apparitions*, published on 21 March, Defoe revealed his worry about the collusion of

---

[5] Antony Coman, "Walpole's Annotations in a Copy of 'Love of Fame, the Universal Passion," *Notes & Queries*" (December 1979), 552.

[6] [Edward Young], *Love of Fame, The Universal Passion* (1727; Dublin, 1728), 4-5.

[7] R. Sedgwick, *History*, II, 437-38.

[8] J. Heilbron, *Physics*, 36-38; J. Hancox, *Queen's Chameleon*, 77-81.

[9] J. Hancox, *Queen's Chameleon*, 99.

various virtuosos with crypto-Jacobite occultists. Referring to "a new suppos'd Class of Spirits," he remarked "upon the general Indolence, which...has so fatally possess'd our Men of Wit in this Age":

> To see a Fool, a Fop, believe himself inspir'd... To this unscrew'd Engine talk of Spirits, and of the invisible World, and of his conversing with unembodied Soul... I don't wonder such as these meanest of mad Things call'd *Free-Masons*; such rought Cheats and confess'd Delusions...are the fittest things to amuse them...[10]

Perhaps referring to Byrom, who was immersed in Jacob Boehme's theosophical works, Defoe described "a late Visionist," who attacked me with "a strange hypothesis" that he would prove from Boehme "that a Man's soul was capable of comprehending God, Futurity, Eternity, and all occult and retir'd things."[11] While Byrom attracted various virtuosos and Masons to his Cabala Club by teaching them his new method of shorthand, he also hinted at his access to the visionary traditions of the Jewish Cabala. As Byrom later remarked, "If thou consultest the Rosicrucians and Freemasons, thou wilt find in them certain remains of the ancient Cabala, of which they have retained the secret without the understanding."[12] Defoe warned the Whig dilettantes that such studies were linked with Jacobite traditions. Referring to the Scots' political utilization of second sight in "the late Preston and Dumblaine affairs," he reminded them and their gullible new cronies of the fate of Derwentwater and the sufferings of many families, who had lost their estates because of the 1715 rebellion.[13]

In Dublin Arbuckle continued his coverage of Jacobite activities in Spain, noting on 11 March that Wharton has gone to the Spanish camp before Gibraltar to serve as a volunteer in the siege designed to oust the British troops.[14] On 25 March he reported that the attainted Earl Marischal, George Keith, also serves as a volunteer in the Spanish camp. Arbuckle was almost certainly aware that both men were Masons and that they gained many recruits from Ireland for the planned campaign against the English troops at Gibraltar. His fellow Mason Thomas Griffith was on high alert to catch these recruits, and Arbuckle reported that "10 persons were seiz'd on the North Bull, as they were going on Board, being (as 'tis said) Inlisted for Foreign Service, and were committed to Newgate."[15] The issue of 25 March 1727 was the final one under Arbuckle's editorship, for he broke with John Carson, his publisher, who then continued the journal in a style opposite to that of Arbuckle. Known as the "facetious Jemmy Carson," he reveled in humor and satire, which he directed against the Scots and Presbyterians.[16] It was under his aegis that Swift allegedly contributed to *The Dublin Weekly Journal*. Arbuckle subsequently launched a bitter campaign against Swift.

In England the defiant actions of Wharton and Marischal intensified Hanoverian alarms. In September 1727 Edmund Curll published *Whartoniana*, for which he employed

---

[10] Daniel Defoe, *An Essay on the History and Reality of Apparitions* (London, 1727), 43.

[11] *Ibid.*, 309.

[12] J. Hancox, *Queen's Chameleon*, 74.

[13] D. Defoe, *Essay*, 119.

[14] *Dublin Weekly Journal* (11 March 1727); on Marischal (25 March 1727).

[15] *Ibid.*, (3 December 1726).

[16] John T. Gilbert, *History of Dublin* (Dublin, 1903), 170-72.

John Morgan, a Grand Lodge Mason, to translate French manuscripts supposedly found among Wharton's family papers. Curll prefaced the book with rival epigrams featuring Walpole and Wharton. In "On Sir Robert Walpole's being created a Knight of the Garter," Curll wrote that the "The True Blue as worn by you can never stain," followed by "On the Duke of Wharton's Renouncing the Protestant Religion," noting that "A Whig he was bred, but at length is turn'd Papist,/ Pray God the Next Remove be not an Atheist. N.B. –To believe every Thing and Nothing is much the same."[17] He included a long poem, written in collaboration with Morgan and titled "A Vindication of the Duke of Wh----n's Answer to the Quaker's Letter":

> Pray isn't it queer
> That a wild Peer,
> So known for rakish Tricks,
> That Wharton shou'd
> At last be Good,
> And kiss a Crucifix?
> ……………………………..
> What less cou'd He
> Than thus agree,
> With Chevalier divino?
> Who gave Him Two
> Brave Titles New,
> Tho' he cou'dn't make Him dine, Oh.
>
> This Duke is then
> Duk'd o're again,
> And Glorious shines his Garter!
> What Honours more
> Has Fate in store,
> E're Tyburn dubbs him Martyr.[18]

Curll and Morgan included contemporary poems that linked architectural pretensions, Jewish financial plots, and Masonic initiatives to the seditious activities of Wharton, "a late perverted Peer." In William Selbey's poem, "The Temple of Venus," a diabolical agent serves Wharton and his Masonic craftsmen:

> To raise for you, my Son, immortal Fame:
> You, my chief Fav'rite of the Pimping Train,
> Shall have the Glory of this darling Fane;
> To Earth I came, and summon'd to my aid
> Each useful Artist of the Building Trade.[19]

Curll also portrayed Wharton as a spent force and warned his supporters in Ireland that King George and his council would prevent the fulfillment of their international intrigues with Spain, Russia, and Turkey.[20]

---

[17] Edmund Curll, *Whartoniana, 146.*

[18] L. Melville, *Life…Wharton*, 198-99.

[19] Curll, *Whartoniana*, 179.

[20] *Ibid.*, 8-12.

Since early 1727 Walpole's agents had been determined to identify the author of *Gulliver*. On 22 January Atterbury's son-in-law William Morice wrote him that the "reputed author" was Swift, who had inquired about Atterbury while staying with Pope.[21] This report was dangerous for Swift, because Morice's correspondence was regularly intercepted and read by Walpole.[22] Even worse, Atterbury's employee and confidant John Sempill (Sample) secretly sent regular reports to Horatio Walpole, Robert's brother and ambassador in Paris. Swift, who spent seven cautious months in Ireland, returned to London from April to September. In May Bolingbroke warned him that Walpole's spies had reported on the dean's authorship of various anonymous works. In early June Swift sensed his increasing vulnerability, and he prepared to leave for France, where Ramsay planned to host him.

However, after Swift learned of George I's death, he cancelled the journey and decided to remain in London. Many Tories and Jacobites now hoped that George II, who reportedly hated his father and Walpole, would implement a new reign of fairness and cooperation to replace the corruption of Walpolean politics. The former Princess of Wales (now Queen Caroline) was a philosophical bluestocking, whom Swift had obliquely praised in *Gulliver* ("this Princess, who hath an infinite deal of Wit and Humour").[23] Thus, on 24 June Swift wrote enthusiastically to Thomas Sheridan: "The talk now is for a moderating scheme, wherein nobody shall be used worse or better for being called Whig or Tory, and the King [George II] hath received both with great equality... It is agreed the ministry will be changed, but the others will have a soft fall."[24]

In Paris Ramsay had not heard of Swift's cancelled travel plans, and he expected to welcome him to France. He soon shared Swift's hope that England was entering a new era, one in which a more moderate government (and, possibly, ecumenical Freemasonry) would bring together honest Whigs and Tories. On 1 August Ramsay wrote Swift:

> Mr. Hooke having acquainted me with what Goodness and Patience, you have been pleas'd to examine a performance of mine, I take this occasion to make my acknowledgments. Nothing could flatter me more sensibly than your approbation... I should be proud of receiving your commands, if I could be anyway useful to you in this part of the world, where I assure you, your Reputation is as well established as in your own country.[25]

Ramsay had sent to Swift a copy of his allegorical novel, *Les Voyages de Cyrus* (1727), which Hooke immediately translated into English, with the assistance of Swift's Jacobite friend, Dr. William King.[26] Swift eventually owned two copies of the 1727 English edition and one of the 1730 fourth edition.[27] Soon *Gulliver* and *Cyrus* were linked in the Whig press as "popular literary works of disaffection."[28]

---

[21] F. Williams, *Memoirs...Atterbury*, II, 101.

[22] P. Fritz, *English Ministers*, 113, 122.

[23] J. Swift, *Gulliver*, 91, 313.

[24] J. Swift, *Correspondence*, III, 100-01.

[25] *Ibid.*, III, 108.

[26] G. Henderson, *Ramsay*, 135.

[27] Harold Williams, *Dean Swift's Library* (Cambridge, 1972), nos. 496, 535.

[28] *Senator*, ii (13 February 1728); iii (16 February 1728); see I. Higgins, "Jonathan Swift," 91.

Ramsay dedicated *The Travels of Cyrus* to Lord Lansdowne, who had joined with Mar and Dillon to form the "Triumvirate" of Jacobite supporters in Paris – a trio despised by Atterbury. Woven through the tale of the spiritual education of an ideal philosophical prince is a subtle political allegory, which traces the Hanoverian dethronement of the Stuarts. As Albert Cherel observes, the character "Astyage" represents the French Regent Orléans, while the dethroned "Apries" refers to James III.[29] "Prince Cyrus" embodies Ramsay's dreams for the future role of Prince Charles Edward Stuart. The Egyptians (devoted to materialistic science) are the English, while the Athenians (curious about the "sublime sciences") are the French. Ramsay argued that the ancient theosophical traditions, up-dated with Cartesian and Newtonian science, could reunite men of good will in a universal religion.

Besides his heavy debt to Fenelon's *Telemachus*, Ramsay was influenced by Swift's satire on religious extremism in *A Tale of a Tub* and by the Abbé Jean-Paul Bignon's Rosicrucian allegory *Les Aventures d'Abdallah* (1712). Drawing on his long experience in tutoring young aristocrats (especially his ten months with Charles Edward Stuart), Ramsay described the education of Prince Cyrus by a series of ancient Eastern and Greek philosophers, but the penultimate and most impressive was Eleazar, a Jewish "allegorist." Through Eleazar's voice, Ramsay affirmed that "the Religion of the Jews was not only the most ancient, but the most conformable to Reason."[30] He explained that "the Hebrew Traditions were often folded up in Allegories, according to the Eastern Custom; …This was what gave Rise afterwards to the famous Sect among the Hebrews, called the Allegorists." He drew on their tradition of Adam Kadmon, the Grand Man, noting that "Adam does not represent one single Man, but all Mankind." In the narrative, Eleazar paves the way for the ultimately Christian resolution of the primeval Hebrew tradition: "In the End, the great Prophet, whom we call the *Messiah*, will come and renew the Face of the Earth… The Deity has united himself to him in an intimate manner from the Beginning of the World… It is He, who is call'd everywhere *The Desire of Nations*.[31]

But Ramsay differed from Christian orthodoxy when he affirmed that "God has no need of a bloody Victim to appease his Wrath… This is what the Messiah will do. The great EMANUEL, God-Man, will descend upon Earth, to shew by his Sufferings the infinite Aversion of The Most High, for the Violation of Order.' [32] In the subsequent "Discourse," Ramsay drew more explicitly on the Cabalistic notion of *Tikkun*, the reintegration and restoration of all things, thus rejecting the Christian notion of eternal punishment. The novel ends with Cyrus's call for rebuilding the Temple of Jerusalem: "The Lord God of Heaven hath given me all the Kingdoms of the Earth; and he hath charg'd me to build him a House at Jerusalem… Whoever among you is of his People, his god be with him: and let him go up to Jerusalem, and build the House of the Lord God of Israel.[33] For his Masonic readers, these words would resonate with their own rituals of Temple building, within the individual and society. Thus, it is significant that Ramsay

---

[29] Albert Cherel, *Un Aventurier Religieux, Andrew Michael Ramsay* (Paris, 1925), 145-46.
[30] Chevalier [Andrew Michael] Ramsay, *The Travels of Cyrus. To which is annex'd A Discourse upon the Theology and Mythology of the Ancients* (London, 1727), I, 142-48.
[31] *Ibid.*, I, 148-49.
[32] *Ibid.*, I, 181.
[33] *Ibid.*, I, 186.

intensified and elaborated his Masonic allusions in the appended "Discourse upon the Theology and Mythology of the Ancients." He repeatedly referred to "the Architect of the World," the "wise Architect of the Universe," "God the supreme Architect," explaining that "This Architect of the World had a Model by which he produced every thing, and this Model is himself."[34]

Articulating his own universalist-Masonic philosophy, he made clear that the Indian Gymnosophists, Pythagoreans, Egyptians, and Greeks all had a tradition of the God-Man, who embodies the cosmos and unifies its exoteric and esoteric manifestations. He then noted that "the discovery of these uniform and agreeing Sentiments" in different cultures made him "carry my Searches as far as China."[35] Describing his conversations with Fouquet, without naming him, he discussed the ancient Chinese works, especially "the book Yking, ie. the Book of Changes," which continually speaks of "a double Heaven; a primitive Heaven, and a posterior Heaven." The same books "speak of a time when every thing is to be restored to its first Splendour, by the coming of a Hero called Kiuntse...the most Holy, the Universal Teacher, and the Supreme Truth." The Hero will suffer but "rise again to make Men happy." Thus, all religions speak of "a Nature exalted, fallen, and to be repaired again by a Divine Hero." Bruno Neveu argues that in Ramsay's discussions of rites of regeneration and restoration, he assimilated the Chinese Figurists' theosophy into his Masonic philosophy.[36]

But, for Ramsay, the penultimate vision of truth still came from "the Jewish Mythology," despite some if its extravagances, and his version of Cabbalism would influence the development of some *Écossais* higher degrees. Noting that it was "the universal Taste of the Orientals to make use of corporeal Images to represent the Properties and Operations of Spirits," he explained:

> The Creation, according to them, is a Picture of the Divine Perfections. All created Beings are consequently Images of the Supreme Being... Hence it follows that all Creatures are in some respect like one another, and that Man, or the Microcosm, resembles the great World or Macrocosm, the material World resembles the intelligible World, as the intelligible World does the Archetype, which is God.
>
> These are the Principles upon which the allegorical Expressions of the Cabbalists are founded. If we strip their Mythology of this mysterious Language, we shall find in it sublime Notions... Now these are the four principal ones which I find clearly enough set forth in the Works of the Rabbins Irira, Moschech, and Jitzack, which Rittangelius has translated in his *Cabbala denudata*.[37]

Though Ramsay had learned much about Cabala from his recent readings, he also drew upon earlier Scottish Masonic traditions – the same ones described by Jonathan Swift in his *Letter from the Grand Mistress*. As quoted earlier, Swift claimed that

---

[34] *Ibid.*, II, 30, 49,55,93.

[35] *Ibid.*, II, 126-33.

[36] B. Neveu, "Un Roman," 17-18.

[37] A. Ramsay, *Travels of Cyrus*, II, 134-37.

> all the Kings of Scotland have been from Time to Time Grand Masters without Interruption from the Days of Fergus...[who] was carefully instructed in all the Arts and Sciences, especially in the natural Magick, and the Cabalistical Philosophy... Speaking of the *Cabala*, as *Masonry* was call'd in those Days.[38]

No wonder that Ramsay was so eager to meet with Swift, for he evidently believed that they shared the same Masonic philosophy. Lepper and Crossle note that Swift and Pope are named as attendees at a London lodge held "at the Goat at the foot of the Haymarket," on a list cumulative to 1730.[39] Chewode Crawley goes further to suggest that Swift's publisher, George Faulkner, also attended that lodge in 1727: "He was in London at the time of Swift's last visit, and, if the Register of 1730 were complete, we should expect to find his name in it. For he is stated to have been an active Freemason in his early days, though his zeal could not stand against political pressure in his old age."[40] Faulkner would later identify Swift as the author of the *Letter from the Grand Mistress.*[41]

After completing *Cyrus*, Ramsay spent three months in Avignon, where he worked on "An Answer to Spinoza." His English Jacobite colleague Salkeld wrote from Montpellier to Carte that Ramsay planned to publish it "in the Latin tongue."[42] Ramsay also worked on "an high philosophical work" which, according to his friend Joseph Spence, would have made him appear "an Heretic in our Church, as well as his own."[43] He withheld publication of these treatises after the Sorbonne condemned *Cyrus* as heretical. But *Cyrus* received a wide readership and was especially well-received in Masonic circles, in England as well as France and Sweden. One English sympathizer – Lord Burlington--may even have infused Ramsay's Masonic allegories into the decorations at Chiswick. According to Jane Clark, Burlington included Jacobite-Masonic allusions to *Cyrus* in the designs and decorations.[44]

At this time, while Ramsay planned even more Masonic allusions in a second edition of *Cyrus*, he was also collaborating with Mar on a controversial "Memorial." Mar proposed that Hanover be substantially enlarged for George II, if he would agree to James III's return to the British throne.[45] Ramsay assisted Mar on the memorial, which enraged Atterbury. Mar and Ramsay possibly learned from Burlington that George I had revised his will in order "to provide for the dissolution of the personal union of Britain and Hanover after his son's death."[46] Jane Clark suggests that Burlington pursued the agenda of their "Memorial" after his return from Paris: "Possibly...Burlington hoped to persuade the usurper to invite the exiled Israelites to return and go back to his own lawful lands in Germany."[47] If "Chiswick was a symbolic Second Temple" to welcome home his exiled king, then its unusual design made perfect sense. The hopes of Mar, Ramsay, and perhaps Burlington would remain wishful thinking, for Earl Waldegrave assisted George II in

---

[38] J. Swift, *Prose*, V, 324-33.

[39] J. Lepper and P. Crossle, *History*, I, 446.

[40] Chetwode Crawley, "*Early Irish Freemasonry*," xxix. They were also both in London in 1726.

[41] *Ibid.*, xxxii.

[42] Bodleian. Carte MS. 100, f. 131 (29 January 1729).

[43] J. Spence, *Anecdotes*, 50-51.

[44] *Ibid.*, 293.

[45] S. Erskine, "Mar's Legacies," 241.

[46] Jonathan C.D. Clark, *Memoirs of James*, 2nd *Earl Waldegrave* (Cambridge, 2002), 25.

[47] J. Clark, "Burlington," 293.

destroying the will, whose sensational contents remained a well-kept secret. As a reward, Waldegrave was again sent as Envoy Extraordinary to Paris in December 1727, where he took advantage of his own Masonic affiliation to gather intelligence on his Jacobite relatives and friends.

On 3 September 1727 Burlington's cousin Lord Boyle wrote from his country home at Brittwell to William Byrd about the wild rumors and airy hopes that a major political change would occur after the death of George I. In the first weeks after the royal demise,

> Our future Prospect was so delightfull that we even despised Ourselves. Each Man had fixed upon a Place of Profet and Honour, and was to be awarded to his great Deserts! Bribery and Corruption were to be destroyed; Piety was to fill the Bishop's Sees, Justice the Judge's Bench. Foreigners were to be banished, and even Scotch-men confined to their own Country. These were the Schemes, these the Chimaeras of our noble true-born Britons. But to begin methodically – His Majesty departed this Life the 11th of June (the Jacobites will have it the 10th...).[48]

Orrery and his son travelled to London to be received at court, where the new queen remarked on how much Boyle had grown, which he realized was "a Reproof," since "it carries with it a sort of Reprimand for not having been at Court before in many years." He continued to Byrd,

> Great Changes were now talked of; Sir Robert Walpole was to be demolished; the Duke of Newcastle's Head taken off; the Duke of Ormonde recalled; and what was the greatest News of All, the Whigs and Tries to be mixed in the Administration; but as yet, Things stand as they did...[49]

The hope for political change led many of the Tories, Jacobites, and disaffected Masons to envision better times ahead, and they accordingly made accomodationist plans.

It was perhaps this confidence that encouraged John Gay to write *The Beggars' Opera*, which opened on 29 January 1728 at the Lincoln's Inn Theatre, after being turned down by Colley Cibber for Drury Lane. Swift and Arbuthnot urged Gay to satirize not only the craze for Italian opera but the corruption of the Whig government. Though Gay was evidently not a Freemason, he included a prominent Whig Mason – Delafaye – among his satirical targets. The character "Peachum," who supported thieves while also informing on them for government rewards, was viewed as a caricature of Robert Walpole, with "Lockit," who not only informed but got adversaries locked up, was aimed at Lord Townshend. But the most egregious was the character "Filch," who filched through or forged papers to serve "Peachum" (also called "Bob Booty"). Folkestone Williams, referring to Delafaye's earlier and posthumous "fingering" of Atterbury's papers, remarked: "If the author of *The Beggars' Opera* made Sir Robert Walpole and Lord Townshend the originals of the characters of Peachum and Lockit, he must certainly have found his Filch in Mr. Delafaye."[50] Though *The Beggars' Opera* was a popular success, Walpole was so

---

[48] Orrery, E.C. Boyle, Countess of Orrery, *The Orrery Papers* (London, 1903), I, 53.
[49] *Ibid.*, I, 56.
[50] F. Williams, *Memoirs*, 460.

angry that he banned the production of Gay's next work, *Polly*, which nevertheless gained a substantial body of subscribers for the printed text.

Swift was thrilled with the success of *The Beggars' Opera*, and he shared the hopes of the Tories and Jacobites that the political scene would change for the better. Early in 1728 he heard from Burlington that he intended to visit his Irish estates, where the dean – whom he named his "Director of Architecture in Ireland" – would certainly have welcomed him (though Burlington eventually cancelled the trip). At this time, the always cautious Burlington was widely believed to be a Freemason, with Grand Lodge Masons assuming he was one of them. If he had made the Irish visit, he undoubtedly would have attended a public Masonic ceremony on 3 February. It seems certain that Swift did witness it, when his friend John, Lord Carteret, a moderate Whig and new Viceroy of Ireland, joined "with many Freemasons" to lay the foundation stone of the new Houses of Parliament in College Green.[51]

However, Swift probably shared the Tories' resentment that the parliamentary commission went to Edward Lovett Pearce, a former army officer, who gained his architectural employment through his father's connection as first cousin of Vanbrugh.[52] Even worse, he had been supported by Thomas Hewett, whom the Tories and Jacobites considered an atheistical Whig. After studying Palladio's designs in Italy in 1723-24, Pearce returned to Dublin in 1725, where he became a loyalist member of the Irish parliament. After much political maneuvering, he was surprisingly selected as the architect for the Parliament House, over the head of the more experienced architect, Thomas Burgh. The older architect had designed the famous library at Trinity College and was supported by Swift's friend, Archbishop King but Pearce was a Whig and won out over "that dull Tory, Thomas Burgh."[53] Not only a Tory but a traditionalist Freemason, Burgh was "forced to surrender" his position as surveyor-general to Pearce. As we shall see, Pearce's controversial role would later provoke a "scurrilous" satire against him by Swift's Oxford ally, Dr. William King.

For the Whig Masons, Pearce's success was the occasion for celebration. Henry Nelson, a bricklayer and Freemason, published a poem which praised Captain Pearce, "the great Architect" of the work, whose craftsmen raise and polish the rough stone to serve as the foundation stone of the new parliament building.[54] Nelson eulogized "Glorious George," "beauteous Caroline," and Carteret, and made clear that the narrator is "a Loyal Stone." Before the stone sleeps, he wishes "Great Briton's Foes' Designs may perish." Though the Masonic nature of the occasion was not mentioned in the "silenced" Dublin press, it was later described in Edward Spratt's *New Book of Constitutions* (Dublin, 1751).

In June 1728 Swift travelled to Armagh, where he stayed for the next eight months with his friend Sir Arthur Acheson at Market Hill. Acheson was proud of his Scottish descent, which he shared with the majority of Protestants in Ulster, but he was an

---

[51] P. Crossle, "Freemasonry," 148-49.

[52] Edward McParland, "Edward Lovett Pearce and the New Junta for Architecture," in T. Barnard and J. Clark, *Lord Burlington*, 151-65.

[53] "Thomas Burgh," on-line Dictionary of Irish Architects.

[54] Henry Nelson, *The Speech of the first Stone laid in the Parliament-House to the Government, February 3d, 1728* (Dublin, 1728).

Episcopalian, and the government regarded him as "a professed Jacobite."[55] Swift admired Acheson and especially enjoyed his neighbors Robert and Henry Leslie, who had long been active Jacobites. Robert had collaborated in Jacobite plans with Charles Wogan in France and Spain, and he returned to Ulster with a Spanish wife. During his earlier visit to Armagh in 1722, Swift was interested in the work of local operative Masons, with whom he conversed, and it was perhaps significant that Acheson was a Freemason and probably privy to the Scottish Masonic traditions brought to Ulster.[56] Despite both men's staunch Anglicanism, they worried about the mass emigration of Presbyterians from Ulster in 1728-29, caused by crop failures and terrible weather.[57] Recently elected an Irish M.P., Acheson evidently encouraged Swift to write pamphlets in protest at the English government's disastrous policies. Such attitudes led their Whig critics to look upon all the Tories in Ireland as Jacobites.[58]

Over the next months, under Carteret's more tolerant regime, the Dublin press renewed its coverage of Irish Masonic activity. On 3 August *Dickson's Old Dublin Intelligence* reported a parade to honor "his late Majesty of Happy Memory...as usual," in which "several Societies of Different Occupations, march'd thro' the City, as the Bricklayers and Masons, a great many in Number, in handsome Order, with King Solomon's Figure at their Front, and the Famous Temple of Jerusalem finely adorn'd in Miniature carried before him."[59] This account reveals the continuing Stuart-Scottish traditions of mixed artisan and gentleman members in lodges, as well as their strong Solomonic visual and ritual symbolism. Moreover, hints of an emergence (or revival) of Jewish mystical themes began to appear in Swift's writings.

J.H. Lepper argues that Swift adopted a Masonic phrase, taken from Irish references to a royal arch: "And let the *Cement* of the *Brotherhood* be so well preserv'd, that the whole *Body* may remain as a *well-built* Arch."[60] On 21 September 1728, while staying with Acheson, Swift published "Two Letters of a Projector" in the *Dublin Weekly Journal*, which was now under the more sympathetic editorship of "facetious Jemmy Carson." Swift wrote "that Mathematics resemble a well-built Arch," words that became famous in the Royal Arch ritual that later reached England from Ireland. The original dates of the Royal Arch degrees are hotly debated by Masonic scholars, but they may well have developed in the Franco-Irish context of 1727-28. Certainly, the infusion of Cabalistic symbolism and Jewish lore into these degrees was consistent with Ramsay's interests at that time, for the rite drew upon Cyrus's liberation of the Jews in Babylonian exile and Zerubbabel's role in rebuilding the Temple of Jerusalem. The narrative expanded into the middle ages, when certain crusaders discovered the lost "Name of God" in a cave (vault) under a stone arch in the ruins of the Temple. Through ritualized meditation upon the Hebrew letters and symbols, the chivalric initiate could envision "the 'old Master-word,' i.e., the Name of God," and attain "felicity/bliss."[61]

[55] J.G.Simms, "Dean Swift and County Armagh," *Seanchas Ardmhacha. Armagh Diocesan Historical Society*, 6 (1971), 134.

[56] R. Berman, *Foundations*, 254-55.

[57] I. Ehrenpreis, *Swift*, III, 609-19.

[58] D. Weatherup, "Swift," 1.

[59] P. Crossle and J. Lepper, *History*, 72.

[60] *Ibid.*, 60.

[61] J. Snoek, *British Freemasonry*, III, xx.

A vague perception that some branches of Freemasonry were becoming increasingly mystical was expressed in Ephraim Chamber's *Cyclopedia: or, an Universal Dictionary of Arts and Sciences*, which was completed in 1727 before the death of George I but published in 1728. Chambers had written a dedication to the late king, whom he urged to become a great promoter of science and knowledge. Chambers was reportedly a member of the Richmond Lodge, and the *Cyclopedia* was considered a Masonic undertaking.[62] Although he was a freethinker, Chambers believed in natural magic, which he differentiated from superstitious magic. Natural magic included alchemy, which he discussed learnedly. He also referred to the current controversies about Freemasonry, in which charges of Rosicrucianism (and Jacobitism) circulated in the press. Chambers claimed that the "Free and Accepted Masons" are a "very ancient body...now found in every country of Europe."[63] He praised them as a benevolent and charitable group, and then went on to describe the Rosicrucians, whom he believed to be a real society:

> Because they [Rosicrucians] pretended to protract the Period of Human Life, by means of a certain *Nostrum*, and even to restore Youth, they were called *Immortals*. As they pretended to know all things, they have been called *Illuminati*, and because they have kept altogether *incognito*, they have been called the *Invisible Brothers...*
>
> Some, who are no friends to Free-Masonry, make the present flourishing Society of Free-Masons a branch of *Rosicrucians*; or, rather the *Rosicrucians* t'selves under a new name, or Relation; *viz.*, as Retainers to Building. – and 'tis certain there are some Free-Masons who have all the characters of *Rosicrucians*; but how the Aera and Original of Masonry, as traced by Mr. Anderson, and that of *Rosicrucianism*, here fixed from *Naudaeus*, who has wrote expressly on the subject, consist, we leave others to judge.[64]

As we shall see, Ramsay would later seek out Chambers as a potential recruit to his Masonic agenda. Moreover, the *Cyclopedia* was the forerunner of the great French *Encyclopédie*, which would also have a significant Masonic component.

Though 1727 had seemed so full of promise for the Jacobites' international alliances, the far-flung schemes eventually unraveled. Spain declared war against England, and Wharton boldly took part in the siege of British-held Gibraltar. In May he drunkenly taunted the British soldiers with obscenities and huzzahs for the Pretender, until he was wounded in the foot. But the fall of the Spanish foreign minister Ripperda – Wharton's collaborator – effectively cancelled the prospect of Spanish funding for a Jacobite invasion. Since the participation of Austria and Russia was dependent on that funding, they now withdrew from the plot. After Wharton's conversion to Catholicism became public, his enemies in London were delighted and determined to outlaw him as a traitor for taking up arms against British forces.[65] Atterbury was mortified and angry at Wharton's conversion, which reinforced Whig charges in England that the Jacobite cause was entirely a Papist plot. At the same time, Atterbury's negotiations with the Lutheran court at Holstein came to nothing. In Sweden the success of the Holstein party (led by Gyllenborg

---

[62] M. Jacob, *Radical*, 125-26.

[63] Ephraim Chambers, *Cyclopedia* (London, 1728), I, 506.

[64] *Ibid.*, II, 1032.

[65] Mark Blackett-Ord, *The Hell-Fire Duke: Life of the Duke of Wharton* (London, 1982),, 173, 181.

and Nikodemus Tessin) in weaning King Fredrik away from Hanoverian dependence was reversed, when England secretly paid the avaricious monarch £50,000 to ensure a Hessian succession and Swedish accession to the Anglo-French Treaty of Hanover.[66]

In late 1727 or early 1728, Wharton founded in Madrid a Masonic lodge, which met in a French hotel in a neighborhood popular with exiled Stuart sympathizers. Two of his co-founders, Eldridge Dinsdale and Andrew Galloway, were Irish Jacobites. In 1723 Galloway was captain of the *Revolution*, a ship purchased earlier by Carl XII to support the Jacobites, and he attempted to transport Irish and Scottish recruits to England during the Atterbury Plot.[67] By February 1728 they were joined by the hydraulic engineer Charles de Labelye, a Swiss Huguenot, who had worked closely with Desaguliers in London and joined a loyalist lodge. Employed by the British navy, he worked on an engineering project in Spain. Ric Berman suggests that he was instructed "to seek out Wharton" and to gather intelligence on his activities and those of other Jacobite sympathizers.[68]

Labeyle's timing was propitious, for in the early weeks of 1728, Tories and Jacobites in England continued to hope for relief under the new regime of George II. Rumors circulated that Wharton would make his peace with the government in order to recover his vast estates. Perhaps motivated by such hopes, on 15 February Wharton directed the lodge officers in Madrid to write to the Grand Lodge in London to praise his actions as "a second Deputy" to Henry Hare, 3rd Baron Colerane, current English Grand Master. Colerane, who inherited an Irish peerage, was an antiquary and collector of prints and drawings.[69] Wharton may have been aware of his private Tory sympathies, which emerged publicly when he became an anti-Walpolean M.P. in 1730. The officers claimed that Wharton approved their sending to London the lodge proceedings, bye-laws, and membership list, as well as a request to be listed as a regularly constituted lodge in the London records – a request granted on 17 April. However, the records were not sent, and after Labeyle returned to London some months later, he complained that the Madrid lodge was never "regularly constituted" by authority of the Grand Lodge, and he requested a "Delegation" to carry this out himself.[70] But he then remained in London, where he continued his collaboration with Desaguliers.[71]

Wharton's overture to the English Grand Lodge reflected the Tory and Jacobite hopes (naïve, as it proved) that the Walpolean-Whig hegemony ended with the death of George I. According to Ramsay, the new king George II invited him to return to England and to assume a position as tutor to his second son, William Augustus, Duke of Cumberland.[72] Ramsay politely refused the job, noting that his Catholic beliefs would present awkward difficulties in England. It was possibly in response to Ramsay's current celebrity that Desaguliers issued a poetic challenge to the philosophy of *Cyrus*, with its Jacobite-Masonic themes. In 1728 Desaguliers issued his own Masonic appeal to George II in the poem, *The Newtonian System of the World, the Best Method of Government*. Though Audrey

---

[66] M. Schuchard, *Emanuel Swedenborg*, 174.

[67] José Ferrer Benimeli, "La Présence de la Franc-Maçonnerie Stuartiste à Madrid et à Rome," *Politica Hermetica*, 24 (2010), 74-75.

[68] R. Berman, *Espionage*, 198-99.

[69] R. Sedgwick, *History*, I, 109-10.

[70] J. Benimeli, "La Présence," 74-75.2.

[71] H. Colvin, *Biographical Dictionary*, 590-92.

[72] G. Henderson, *Ramsay*, 130.

Carpenter observes that the poem was "overtly Hanoverian and sycophantic," Desaguliers declared disingenuously, "I never made *Politicks* my Study," and then vowed his constant obedience to the new king's government.[73] He dedicated the poem to Archibald Campbell, 1st Earl of Ilay, a loyalist Whig, who served as godfather to one of Desaguliers's sons and who was allegedly a fellow Mason.[74] Brother of the powerful John Campbell, 2nd Duke of Argyll, Ilay became Walpole's manager of Scottish affairs.

Representing the philosophy of the Hanoverian Grand Lodge, Desaguliers argued that the limited monarchy in Britain mirrored the universal gravity of Newton: "I have considered Government as a Phenomenon, and looked upon that Form of it to be most perfect, which did most clearly resemble the Natural Government of our System, according to the Laws settled by the All-Wise and Almighty Architect of the Universe."[75] George II's government "makes us sensible that Attraction is now as universal in the Political, as the Philosophical World." He praised Pythagoras, whose system of the universe leads to harmony of government, versus the "usurping Ptolemy" and whimsical Descartes, who are linked with tyranny in government.[76] Desaguliers then gloated over the failure of the Stuarts to re-establish their Cartesian-Jacobite dominance – "So when a Minor King, the Scepter Sways/ Some Kings, alas! are Minors all their Days." With the Hanoverian George II now firmly in power, the Jacobite prince can only sulk "in his own vortex/ Suffering each Globe a vortex of his own."

By spring 1728 it became clear that Walpole had prevailed with the royal couple, first gaining the support of the domineering Queen Caroline and, through her, the acquiescence of George II. Thus, in May a disillusioned Pope issued anonymously a satire on literary and architectural dullness under the Hanoverians, entitled *The Dunciad: an Heroick Poem*. Initially planned in collaboration with Swift, the volume carried a false Dublin imprint. Richard Savage, a Jacobite Mason and friend of Pope, helped the secret publishing arrangements. The anti-hero of the poem was Lewis Theobald, a Grand Lodge Mason, who had earned Pope's hatred by his criticism of the poet's edition of Shakespeare.[77] Frustrated by the disappointing results of George II's accession, Pope asked plaintively, "Say from what cause, in vain decry'd and curst/ Still Dunce the second reigns like Dunce the first?"[78] In mock-epic style he announced:

> This, this is he, foretold by ancient rhymes,
> Th' *Augustus*, born to bring *Saturnian* times!
> ....
> B[enson] sole judge of Architecture sit,
> And Namby Pamby be prefer'd for Wit,
> I see the unfinish'd *Dormitory wall*.
> I see the *Savoy* totter to her fall![79]

---

[73] A. Carpenter, *Desaguliers*, 206; J.T. Desaguliers, *The Newtonian System of the World* (London, 1728), preface.

[74] R Berman, *Espionage*, 49, 252 n. 76; A. Carpenter, *Desaguliers*, 230.

[75] J. Desaguliers, *Newtonian System*, iii.

[76] *Ibid.*, 2-3, 11, 19, 32.

[77] W. Williams, "Alexander Pope," 120.

[78] A. Pope, *Poetical Works*, 725.

[79] *Ibid.*, 749.

The allusion to Atterbury's aborted project of building a dormitory at Westminster school was politically risky. Like Swift, Pope blamed the decline in architecture on secular, abstract, projecting mathematicians, who had no sense of religious tradition or spiritual revelation: "See Mystery to Mathematicks fly!"

Pope also attacked a series of Whig Freemasons, starting with John Ozell, "who had "Less human genius than God gives an Ape."[80] As noted earlier, Ozell worked as a government decipherer and had charged Pope with Jacobitism for writing *The Rape of the Lock.* Pope next satirized James Moore, who in 1728 took an additional surname of Smythe and whom Pope charged with plagiarizing some of his lines: "A fool, so just a copy of a wit;/ So like, that criticks said and courtiers swore,/ A wit it was, and call'd the phantom M----[Moore]." He inaccurately claimed that Daniel Defoe was arrested and placed in a pillory: "Ear-less on high, stood pillor'd D----[Defoe]." He not only scorned Colley Cibber, the playwright, but his actor son Theophilus, who were both loyalist Masons: "With all thy Father's virtues blest, be born!/ And a new C-----[Cibber] shall the stage adorn."[81] The bookseller William Mears, a long-time Mason, represents "delusive thought," while he issues anonymous works "in Calf's array."[82] John Dennis, poet and critic, was included among the "chatt-ring, grinning, mouthing, jabb'ring" critics, as "D[ennis} and dissonance" and "ill-starred rage."[83] It would later be claimed (inaccurately?) that Dennis was a Gormogon for many years but renounced that fraternity and became a Freemason in April 1730. Pope skewered "H" for sinking in the poetic mud and then bobbing up into the lights, and contemporaries identified "H" as Aaron Hill, who had earlier written about his"brother" Grand Lodge Masons and the Gormogons.[84]

Curiously, Pope included one Mason who was a high-church Tory, when he scorned Edward (Ned) Ward for the popularity in America of his satirical works: "Or shipp'd with W[ard] to ape and monkey lands."[85] Ward had earlier portrayed Dr. Faustus as a magician and Freemason, and he recently served as Warden in a London lodge.[86] He admired Pope's intelligence and talent but lamented that the great poet had sunk so low in his unfair attacks on minor writers. He expressed his criticism in *Durgen. Or, a Plain Satyr upon a Pompous Satyrist* (1728), in which he portrayed Pope as a "durgen" or dwarf, who betrayed his friends and made false claims against his targets:

> 'Tis strange a Bard of such exalted wit,
> For Sacred Hymns and heav'nly Anthems fit,
> Should in his anger lavishly bestow
> A Style so lofty on a Theme so low.[87]

Ward subtitled the poem as "Amicably Inscrib'd, by the Author, to those Worthy and Ingenious Gentlemen misrepresented in a late invective Poem, call'd *The Dunciad*," but

---

[80] *Ibid.*, 731, 733, 735, 742,746; for the Masonic affiliation of the following writers, see W. Williams, "Alexander Pope," 117-24.

[81] A. Pope, *Poetical Works*, 745.

[82] *Ibid.*, 735, 743.

[83] *Ibid.*, 737, 746.

[84] C. Gerrard, *Aaron Hill*, 125.

[85] A. Pope, *Poetical Works*, 730; "Edward Ward," *ODNB*.

[86] E. Ward, *Dancing Devils*, 36-37; W. Williams, "Alexander Pope," 124.

[87] [Edward Ward], *Durgen. Or, a Plain Satyr upon a Pompous Satyrist* (London: T. Warner, 1728), 40-41.

his relationship with Pope did not become amicable, as both poets continued their attacks upon each other.[88]

More seriously than his minor scuffles with Ward, Pope's satire in *The Dunciad* made a life-long enemy of John Oliver Cromwell Henley, known as the "Orator," who claimed that he confronted "Mr. Pope, pale and trembling," about his unflattering portrayal.[89] An eccentric, erudite, and disaffected clergyman, Henley gave bizarre lectures at his Oratory, which attracted large, fee-paying crowds. In a satirical pamphlet, *Antediluvian Masonry* (1726), he was included in a satire directed at Desaguliers and his friends. The lodge will sponsor "an Oration in the Henleyan Style, on the Antiquity of Signs, Tokens,…Compasses, Squares," etc., concluding with a "genuine Account of Penalties, Throats, Tongues, Hearts," etc., all part of the "solemn Obligations" of the Masonic oath."[90] On 5 April 1727 he gave a lecture, "To the Memory of Inigo Jones, the Rise and Progress of Masonry, the Vindication of it, from its old Unpublish'd Constitutions, and proving Masonry in all Arts, Sciences, and Professions."[91]

His large audiences evidently gained the attention of Delafaye, who ordered his arrest in February 1728 and then intimidated him into producing Walpolean propaganda, in which he defended the Grand Lodge and attacked Jacobite and opposition Masonry. However, Delafaye would soon learn that he could not really control the incorrigible Henley, who in April 1728 included "Plots and Masonry" in his "Dissertation Upon Nonsense," as part of "the Kingdom of Darkness, or, the History and Philosophy of Unintelligibles," along with "the Cabbala, Mysticks, and Rosycrucians…&the Art of Decyphering a Deciphyrer."[92] In *The Dunciad*, Pope was amused that Henley's zany and florid sermons attracted bigger congregations than the established and more boring Whig clergymen:

> …Lo H-----[Henley] stands
> Tuning his voice, and balancing his hands,
> How honey'd nonsense trickles from his tongue!
> How sweet the periods, neither said nor sung!
> Still break the benches, H-----with thy strain,
> While K------, Br------, W----- preach in vain.[93]

The less exuberant and less effective preachers were Bishop White Kennett, Reverend James Bramston, and possibly Dr. Robert Warren.

While Pope seemed aware of developments in Hanoverian Masonry, he may also have been privy to the mystical and chivalric developments in the *Écossais* system in France. His planned but cancelled epigraph for *The Dunciad* was a stanza from Spenser's *Faerie Queene*, in which "the Red Cross Knight battling Error's viperous offspring is compared to a 'gentle Shephearde'… brushing away a cloud of stinging gnats." As Maynard Mack points out, this was a dangerous pose for a vulnerable Catholic poet suspected of Jacobite

---

[88] Howard W. Troyer, *Ned Ward of Grubstreet* (Cambridge, 1946), 196-202.

[89] Graham Midgley, *The Life of Orator Henley* (Oxford, 1973), 1770-71.

[90] *EMP*, 194. The "Henlean" oration may have occurred later; the advertisement was reprinted in the *Daily Post* (20 June 1729. See R. Péter, *British Freemasonry*, V, 302.

[91] J. Henley, *Oratory Transactions. No. II*, 3rd ed. (London, 1728), 3-4.

[92] *Ibid.*, 13-14, 25-26.

[93] A. Pope, *Poetical Works*, 746.

sympathies.[94] Two years earlier, the wearing of red crosses had been publicly condemned as a Rosicrucian development within Freemasonry.[95] With the exiled Masons Mar and Ramsay attempting to revive a military order of knights in Scotland, Pope's self-identification as a Red Cross Knight was indiscrete though timely. At this time, Pope was approached by an old friend, the Abbé Thomas Southcott, who asked him to help secure an income for Ramsay by persuading Walpole to not protest the appointment of Southcott, "a known Jacobite," to the abbey of St. André in Avignon, where he would be an absentee and pass on his pension to Ramsay.[96] He probably also informed Pope of Ramsay's intention to visit England.

Southcott was the principle revenue raiser for the Stuarts in 1715-18, when he promised James III that he could raise funds from the 8th Duke of Norfolk for the Swedish-Gyllenborg plot.[97] In May 1728 he was evidently in touch with Norfolk and wrote James to inform him that the English Catholics wanted Ramsay to travel to London and "act for them." They hoped Ramsay could persuade Walpole to relax the severe restrictions imposed in the wake of the Atterbury Plot.[98] Southcott then helped Ramsay plan his journey to England. However, other Jacobites thought this initiative would be harmful to the cause. In June Father Sylvester Lloyd wrote Colonel O'Brien that Norfolk, the chief Catholic in England, seemed inclined to take the oath of allegiance in order to get relief from the penal laws. They want to employ "one Mr. Ramsey now at Paris, as their agent, being as was given out a person very much in the esteem of the Cardinal" (Fleury).[99] The Jacobite activist William Howard-Stafford, Earl of Stafford (a kinsman of Norfolk), was the man who recommended Ramsay and wrote into England that he had accepted the commission.

Lloyd warned that the move would be "injurious" to James's cause, especially because some of the agents previously involved were "despised and hated by all honest men in London." He worried that Christopher Nugent, Lord Delvin, an Irish Catholic, "is very obsequious to the English Court, and was recently introduced to the Elector" by the Duke of Richmond. Lloyd worried that Delvin would sell out the Catholics in order to gain lands and leases in Ireland. That Richmond was a staunch Whig and recently served as Grand Master of the Grand Lodge was alarming to Jacobite Masons. Moreover, Richmond would soon preside over Norfolk's and Delvin's initiation into the Whig-dominated Horn Lodge, in a ceremony attended by the Irish Masons Kingston and Inchiquin.[100] Lloyd also suspected (accurately) that one of the "agents," Thomas Strickland, Catholic bishop of Namur, secretly served as an anti-Jacobite spy for the British government.[101] His nephew, Walter Strickland, would later be initiated by Richmond in

[94] M. Mack, *Pope*, 473-74.
[95] *Daily Journal* (24 December 1725).
[96] J. Spence, *Observations*, I, 456; II, 615.
[97] Abbot Geoffrey Scott, "Thomas Southcott," *English Benedictine Congregation History Commission Symposium* (2202), 1-5; P. Monod, *Jacobitism*, 286.
[98] D. Henderson, *Ramsay*, 131.
[99] P. Fagan, *Irish Bishop*, 95-111; *Ireland in Stuart Papers*, 69.
[100] *London Evening Post* (6-8 February 1729), *York Courant* (6 January 1730); in R. Péter, *British Freemasonry*, V, 12-13.
[101] "Thomas Strickland," *ODNB*.

Paris.[102] Ramsay must have been warned, for Lewis Innes soon wrote James that Ramsay would now "scarcely venture to meddle in that matter, unless very privately."[103]

However, Ramsay still determined to visit England and, as we shall see, he and Norfolk would undertake an effort to supplement Wharton's Masonic efforts in Spain and France. That month in Italy, Wharton met secretly with James, who urged him to move to northern France, where he could handle his and the Jacobites' affairs more conveniently. Evidently with James's connivance, Wharton wrote to Horatio Walpole in June that "Since his present Majesty's [George II's] accession to the throne," he has withdrawn from Jacobite affairs and seeks reconciliation with the English regime.[104] In July, worried by the charges of treason against him, which could cut off the annuity from his English estate, Wharton called on the ambassador in Paris, claiming that he had become an entirely new man. Horatio reported to Newcastle that the duke spoke with "that eloquence so natural to him" and with his "usual Gaiety of Temper," but he was surprised when Wharton then announced that he was going to dine with Atterbury, "because he must know that such a Correspondence was made Felony by the same Law that sent that Prelate abroad."

The biographer William Lee, who discovered Daniel Defoe's correspondence with Delafaye, suggests that Wharton had a secret plan, concerted with the now exiled printer Nathaniel Mist, to provide copies of Defoe's pro-Jacobite writings when he worked on Mist's journal as a government spy. Lee speculates,

> If they possessed manuscript documents, obnoxious to the English government, but containing Defoe's editorial hand-writing, – what would appear more feasible than that his ruin might be effected by placing such papers in the hands of Mr. Walpole, the British Ambassador in France, with whom it is known that the Duke of Wharton obtained a long interview, shortly after Mr. Mist's arrival in France?[105]

That Wharton planned to join Mist at Rouen gives some plausibility to Lee's conjecture, but no substantiating documents have been found.

After his controversial meeting with Ambassador Walpole, Wharton called on Atterbury at his country retreat, but the bishop was distressed by his Catholic conversion and alcohol-fueled, erratic behavior. He later reported that Wharton claimed he was "no Catholic" and laughed that "We might as well think he was Turk."[106] Even worse, wrote the bishop, when Wharton found that his application for pardon was not accepted, "he made another sudden turn, and is now as true a Catholic and Jacobite as ever he was.... I keep my distance from him." In July Wharton had written James about his meeting with Walpole and about "the steps I have taken to avoid attainder pursuant to your Majesty's directions," but this "has drawn upon me ill opinion"; nevertheless, "I scorn the venom of their impotent spleen."[107] He begged James to send word to his friends in England that he was still in good standing with him. Atterbury was so disillusioned with

---

[102] For the Parisian initiation in September 1734, see R. Berman, *Foundations*, 149.
[103] G. Henderson, *Ramsay*, 131.
[104] L. Melville, *Life...of Wharton*, 215-25; R. Gould, "Wharton," 129.
[105] W. Lee, *Life...of Defoe*, 463.
[106] L. Melville, *Life...of Wharton*, 224025.
[107] Stuart Papers: 118/54,105.

not only Wharton but James that in August he hoped for a pardon and return to England.[108] When that was not forthcoming, he left the Jacobite circles in Paris and moved to Montpellier in October.

In the meantime, Wharton determined to enhance his Jacobite reputation, and he worked on plans for a rising in Ireland, where the old Swiftian agitation against Wood's half-pence had re-emerged, along with anti-English sentiment "even among the Presbyterians in Ulster."[109] Wharton further expected his negotiators in London to organize a simultaneous rising. To counter Atterbury's criticism of his drinking, he informed James in August that he now realized that wine had often "robbed my brains of common sense" and now limits himself to "no more but a pint of burgundy at dinner and a bottle at supper."[110] He rejected Atterbury's jealous and hostile attitude towards Daniel O'Brien, "who is a Gentleman. That must please everybody that knows him except some few who can be pleased with nobody." In September O'Brien wrote James that Wharton "has passed his former follies and has a resolution to serve you and re-establish his reputation"; moreover, he has now "completely quit drinking."[111] O'Brien, who had never believed Atterbury's slanders against Mar, determined to reconcile Wharton with Mar, who was eager to heal the old division.

In 1728 Mar and his close friend Ramsay were living on Rue de Boucheries, meeting place of the Jacobite lodge. Wharton may well have met with Ramsay, for he acquired *Les Voyages de Cyrus* (1727), as well as his earlier works on Fenelon.[112] He seemed to share Ramsay's interest in chivalric fraternities, and he bought Vertot's *History of the Knights of Malta* (1728) and *The Book of the Order of Chivalry, or Knighthode*, "black letter."[113] Like Ramsay, he was most interested in the history of General Monk, as published in the biographies by Skinner and Webster in 1723 and 1724.[114] As noted earlier, Ramsay believed that Monk had utilized Masonic networks to organize the Restoration of Charles II. Wharton was probably aware of Mar's support of James Gibbs, a crypto-Jacobite Mason, and he acquired Gibbs's *Architecture* (1728), a publication encouraged by Mar.[115] Indicating his revived interest in architecture, he also obtained *The Designs of Inigo Jones*, published by William Kent in 1727, at a time when Kent was painting the Masonic images on the ceilings in Burlington's Chiswick house.[116] He purchased further architectural and scientific works by Whig Masons, such as Batty Langley's *Sure Guide to Builders* (1729) and Desaguliers' *Leçons Physico-Mechanique* (1727).[117] These interests evidently convinced O'Brien that Wharton was ready for a reconciliation with the party of Mar and Ramsay.

O'Brien decided to use James, 6th Lord Cranstoun, a Scottish friend of Mar, as an intermediary in the outreach. Cranstoun had recently spent seven months in Rome, where Stosch reported that he had shocked all well-intentioned Englishmen by throwing

---

[108] Rex Barrell, *Francis Atterbury (1662-1732), Bishop of Rochester, and his French Correspondents* (Lewiston, 1990). 12.

[109] Stuart Papers: 114/136,; 118/66; 119/56.

[110] *Ibid.*, 119/56.

[111] *Ibid.*, 120/16, 31.

[112] *Bibliothecarum…Ducis de Wharton*, #3917, 1358.

[113] *Ibid.*, #1001,2545.

[114] *Ibid.*, #2879, 2910.

[115] *Ibid.*, #451.

[116] *Ibid.*, 452,1973, 3953.

[117] *Ibid.*, #1973, 3953.

himself into the arms of the Pretender for love of Lord Nithsdale's daughter.[118] In December 1728 Cranstoun arranged a meeting between Wharton and Mar, which led the now teetotalling Wharton to report piously to James that Mar arrived drunk, got worse, and had to be carried home.[119] Unfortunately, there is no record of the substance of their discussions. Cranstoun was a Freemason, who in 1745-47 would serve as Grand Master of the Grand Lodge of England. The group of Masons – Cranstoun, O'Brien, Mar, and Ramsay – may have collaborated in getting Wharton elected as the first Grand Master of Freemasonry in France.[120] His election was kept so secret that it was unknown in England, though surviving documents in French and Swedish Masonic archives provide proof of his new role.

These moves by the Jacobite Masons were undertaken without Atterbury's knowledge, and he became more isolated from their Masonic political agendas and networks. Despite the bishop's disapproval of Ramsay's heterodox notions in *Cyrus*, O'Brien had defended Ramsay from the bishop's charges, including an absurd one that Ramsay gave the French police memorials against Atterbury.[121] Though the bishop hoped *Cyrus* would "sink," the Masonic allegory was widely admired and new multi-lingual editions were planned. With Ramsay's eloquent appeals and Wharton's flamboyant leadership, the Jacobite Masons were becoming a force to be reckoned with.

On 14 August a worried Ambassador Walpole reported from Paris that the Jacobites had "a design of printing a manifesto here in favour of the Pretender," but that it was seized and prohibited.[122] With the French government tied uneasily to the Hanoverian regime in England and Hessian regime in Sweden by the Treaty of Hanover, the cautious Fleury (now chief minister) acquiesced with increasing frequency to Walpolean pressure. Despite the official French ban on the manifesto, Walpole observed that Wharton (who "has renewed commerce with the Jacobites") has gone to Dieppe, where he is meeting with Nathaniel Mist, the Jacobite printer. "They may be planning to print the manifesto there or at Rouen." James approved the plan, but James reported to O'Brien that Atterbury wrote him "a peevish letter about the Manifesto" and seemed to be "picking a quarrel with me."[123]

After the seizure of the manifesto, Wharton came up with another plan. On 24 August *Mist's Weekly Journal* in London published the anonymous "Persian Letter," written by Wharton at Rouen. It contained an unusually explicit panegyric to James III:

> He is a Prince whose gracious Behaviour is sufficient to win, his Majesty to awe, and his Courage to face the most inveterate of his Enemies. His Sufferings have added Experience and Patience to those endearing Qualities, in order to compleat the greatest Character that ever Eastern Monarch bore. The Misfortunes of his Subjects grieve him more than his own, such is his Public Spirit.[124]

---

[118] J. Ingamells, *Dictionary*, "Cranstoun."

[119] Stuart Papers: 122/110.

[120] P. Chevallier, *Histoire*, I, 7.

[121] Stuart Papers: 115/47.

[122] W. Coxe, *Walpole*, II, 636-37.

[123] Stuart Papers: 120/100.

[124] Quoted in P. Monod, *Jacobitism*, 37.

According to the new Grand Master in France, the usurper "Meryweis" (George I) and his son "Esreff" (George II) were by contrast mercenary and tyrannical. Embedded in the letter were allusions to the Chinese king ("Eastern Monarch") and code-names ("Meryweis") used earlier by the Gormogons.

The "Persian Letter" created a sensation; the whole issue of the *Journal* was soon sold out and hand-written copies were issued at half a guinea apiece.[125] Walpole and Queen Caroline were outraged, and retaliatory measures were promptly unleashed. Mist's printing press was smashed, and searches were made for the printer, John Wolfe, who escaped to Rouen. An exhilarated Wharton issued more inflammatory articles from his French base, and Jacobite hopes rose again in London. It may have been these Jacobite-Masonic stirrings that provoked Pope's meditation on the martyrdom of James Radcliffe, Third Earl of Derwentwater, whose exiled brother Charles was now recruiting *frères* in Italy to join the hazardous enterprise. On 4 September Pope wrote from Bath,

> as I travelled all alone, [one circumstance] made me contemplative. I was drawn by a horse now employed by Lord C. [Cobham] in rolling the gardens, which was the same in former days on which the Earl of Derwentwater rid at Preston. It made me reflect, that man himself is as blind and unknowing of his fate, as the beast he bestrides; equally proud and prancing in his glory, and equally ignorant whither or to what he is running.[126]

As noted earlier, James Radcliffe had used his beloved gray mare to carry family papers to safety. Thus, the horse's current lowly employment was especially poignant. Pope often visited Sir William Temple, Viscount Cobham, and admired his lavish, allegorical gardens at Stowe, which featured statues of Whig heroes. At this time, Cobham was a loyal Walpolean and Grand Lodge Mason, and he evidently influenced Pope's wistful disillusionment with the Jacobite attempt of the executed Derwentwater.[127]

In late 1728, with England and Spain at war, the issue began to emerge of Masonic fraternity between brothers serving in rival armies – an issue which reflected differences within the British fraternity. Though Richmond and the Whig Masons may not have known that Lord Colerane was privately a Tory when he was elected Grand Master in London, the next Grand Master also had an ambiguous political background. James King, 4th Baron Kingston, was born in France, where his father, the 3rd Baron Kingston, resided after fleeing Ireland to serve James II at Saint-Germain. Kingston *père* had converted from Protestantism to Catholicism, and he remained privately Catholic after he was pardoned and allowed to return to Ireland in 1694. Over the next years, father and son were suspected of Jacobitism, and in July 1714 Swift hinted at his awareness of their intrigues: "Lord Kingston's Affairs are all Chimeraes; besides I hope I have done with Courts forever."[128] In June 1722, the year of the Atterbury plot, Kingston *père* was arrested in Cork on suspicion that his son "was concerned in enlisting men" for a Jacobite plot.[129] When the father appealed to Swift's friend Archbishop King for help, King

---

[125] Blackett-Ord, *Hell Fire Duke*, 205.

[126] A. Pope, *Correspondence*, II, 513.

[127] M. Mack, *Alexander Pope*, 596; R. Berman, "Architects," 265.

[128] J. Swift, *Correspondence*, I, 633.

[129] S. Murphy, "Irish Jacobitism," 79-80.

observed pointedly that Ireland has been "disturbed by a sort of people called the 'Wild Geese,' and that thousands have been listed for service to the Pretender." He also chided Kingston that "it is much observed that your family is altogether Papists [*sic*], and that you live as much after the old Irish manner as the merest Irishman in the Kingdom, which brings you into many inconveniences."

While his father's case was still pending, King *fils* fled to England, and his father was eventually released from jail "upon entering into recognizances of forty thousand pounds." In April 1724 the Lord Lieutenant Grafton wrote Carteret that the witnesses against Lord Kingston made false accusations and gross prevarications, but he still believed that father and son "are not so free as might be wished of having favoured these treasonable practices."[130] On 22 September 1727 Daniel O'Brien wrote from Paris to James III that "My [cipher] Kingston is here with his family and tells me to assure you of his loyalty."[131] After the death of Lord Kingston in February 1728, his son James became 4th Baron Kingston, and he took seriously the warnings (threats) of Irish and English authorities. He converted to Anglicanism, took the oaths, and joined the House of Lords in 1728. On 9 March Father Sylvester Lloyd wrote from Dublin to James that the Stuart interest was strong even among the Protestants: "besides the majority of Tories I already hinted at in the House of Commons, those they call Converts are almost to a man your friend, as are seven in ten of old Protestants."[132] Like Wharton and Colerane earlier, Kingston evidently "kept on the mask," but the government continued to suspect him of Jacobitism. As Eamonn Ó Ciardha notes, "sympathy for the Stuart cause survived among members of the old Tory interest," especially among Protestant converts such as the 4th Baron Kingston.[133]

Thus, the rather surprising election of the 4th Baron Kingston as Grand Master in London suggests that crypto-Jacobite and Tory Masons were stealthily building influence within the fraternity. On 28 December 1728 Kingston presided over an important lodge meeting:

> 'Tis remarkable that there were present the Master of the Lodge at Madrid in Spain, and the Wardens belonging to the Lodge at Caermarthen in South Wales…
> And at the same Time, The Grand Master and Wardens, and most of the Gentlemen present took Tickets to appear in White Gloves at the Theatre-Royal in Drury Lane, where…a Prologue and Epilogue [were] spoken suitable to the Occasion and in Honour of that Society.[134]

In the Prologue, the actor spoke passages prepared by Kingston, to affirm the social benevolence and political loyalty of Freemasonry:

> If due Regard to Liberty and Laws,
> Zeal for our King, and [for] our Country's Cause;
> If these are Principles deserving Fame,

---

[130] E. Ó Ciardha, *Ireland*, 200.

[131] Stuart Papers: 110/85.

[132] P. Fagan, *Ireland*, 108.

[133] E. Ó'Ciardha, *Ireland*, 232.

[134] P. Crossle and J. Lepper, *History*, 73.

> Let MASONS then enjoy the Praise they claim,
> Nay, more, tho' War destroys what MASONS build,
> E'er to a Peace inglorious we would yield,
> Our Squares and Trowels into Swords we'll turn,
> And make our Foes, – the Wars they menace – mourn,
> For their Contempt, we'll no vain Boaster spare,
> Unless, by Chance, we meet a MASON there.[135]

Kingston's ambiguous statement – affirming military loyalty while admitting possible fraternal bonds with opposing soldiers – was made in the presence of the Hanoverian Labeyle, master of the Madrid lodge, and of several Welsh Masons, whose lodges were predominantly Jacobite.[136]

Three days later, on 31 December Edward Oakley, "Architect, M.M. late Provincial, Senior Grand Warden in Carmarthen, South Wales," seemed to reply to Kingston's words, when he delivered an oration in a London lodge that reaffirmed his brothers' "ancient" operative and Rosicrucian traditions. Oakley pointed out that in former times, "each Master was then chosen according to real Merit, so that the Craft was not only instructed in our inestimable Constitutions, but also in the Liberal Arts and Sciences."[137] He stressed the fraternity's roots in operative Masonry and praised "the great Restorers of Architecture" – Serlio, Scamozzi, Vignola, Palladio, Jones, and Wren. Unlike Swift, who mocked virtuoso culture, Oakley praised the Royal Society's contributions to the study of architecture. He then warned the lodge about the intrusion of unworthy brothers and spies:

> And if any such have already crept in amongst us, through the Negligence
> or Ignorance of the Watchmen upon the Walls, hard is our Lot indeed. –
> For most dangerous are a Man's enemies, when they are of his own House.
> These, my dearest Brethren, are Thieves and robbers, and never enter'd into
> the Sheep-Fold by the Door, but climbed up some other Way: These make
> their Belly their God, and their little sordid Interest their Idol...[138]

According to Oakley, the increasing detachment of the fraternity from operative Masonry made it vulnerable to unscrupulous brethren and political placemen. The basic qualifications to become a Freemason should continue to be connected with architecture

> by studying Architecture, working in the Craft, or Building Trades, ingenious
> Sculptors, Painters, or well skill'd in Arithmetick or Geometry, or other wise
> qualified by real Merits, such as may redound to the Encouragement, Pro-
> motion, Honour of sound Masonry.
> Those of the Brotherhood, whose Genius is not adapted to Building, I hope
> will be industrious to improve in, or at least to love and encourage some Part
> of the seven Liberal Sciences, – "which in some Sort depend on each other,
> Musick, Harmony, and Proportion run through all."[139]

---

[135] *EMP*, 208-09.
[136] J. Jenkins, "Jacobites and Freemasons," 392.
[137] *EMP*, 210.
[138] *Ibid.*, 212.
[139] *Ibid.*, 212.

Without this limitation on membership, the fraternity becomes plagued by "False Brethren," who "not having the Fear of God before their Eyes, value no sacred Obligations, turn Rebels, and endeavour to defame the Craft, by their vilanous pretended Discoveries."

Then, in rather startling statements, Oakley asserted passionately the Rosicrucian traditions of his Welsh brethren.[140] Of the interlopers, "Let these be ever excluded from the Congregation of the Faithful; let their Names be razed for ever out of the Book *M.* and be buried in eternal oblivion." Quoting Samber's mystical peroration in *Long Livers*, he affirmed:

> the Brotherhood begins to revive again in this our Isle, and Princes seek to be of this sacred Society… "Ye are living Stones, built up a spiritual House, who believe and rely on the chief *Lapis Angularis*, which the refractory and disobedient Builders disallow'd; you are call'd from Darkness to Light; you are a chosen Generation, a royal Priesthood."[141]

These mystical themes – especially the Jewish tradition of Masons as royal priests of the Temple – would emerge in the *Écossais* system encouraged by Ramsay over the next decade.

On 16 January 1729 Ramsay wrote Thomas Carte that he planned to visit London to attend the opening of parliament and to publish an enlarged English edition of *Cyrus*. He hoped to get assistance from "nos beaux esprits" – Pope, Swift, and Congreve – whose disgust with George II was now well known. In March Ramsay wrote the Marquis de Caumont, a friend at Avignon, to complain about the lack of support he received from the overly-cautious Fleury, his former mentor, who despised Atterbury, distrusted the English Jacobites, and opposed new restorationist initiatives. Ramsay thus determined to try his luck in England. He warned Caumont that he would not be able to write from London to his French friends, because James frowned on correspondence that could rouse suspicions. He especially must avoid writing to his friends at Avignon, "a city famous for its laudable attachment to the rightful king… You understand me, 'A word to the wise is sufficient.'"[142]

That Ramsay had a Masonic mission to England is further suggested by the activities of the Duke of Norfolk, who had earlier sought Ramsay's help to alleviate Catholic conditions in England. A relieved Father Lloyd reported to James that the efforts of Norfolk had come to nothing:

> that the Duke of Norfolk and others had communicated their thoughts to Sir Robert Walpole, that he had given them fair promises, that the duke had been drawn to kiss the Elector's hand, and that some others were preparing to follow his example, when Sir Robert all of a sudden sent them express orders at their peril not to apply either to the Congress [of Soissons] or to any foreign power whatsoever… they were thunderstruck at this and found

---

[140] On 17th-century Welsh Rosicrucianism and Freemasonry, see M. Schuchard, *Restoring the Temple*, 495-504.
[141] *EMP*, 214.
[142] Françoise Weil, "Ramsay et la Franc-Maçonnerie," *Revue d'Historie Littéraire de la France*, no. 2 (1963), 27.

they had been duped but still...they were resolved to proceed in a private manner.[143]

That "private manner" evidently included an attempt by Norfolk and other Catholic Masons to increase the Tory and Jacobite influence within the English fraternity.

According to James Anderson, Norfolk came from an ancient Masonic family; his progenitor was Thomas Howard, Earl of Arundel, who allegedly served as Grand Master in 1635.[144] In 1747, when the "Duke of Norfolk's Mason Lodge" was placed on the Scottish roll, members claimed that it was founded in 1685.[145] As discussed earlier, the 8th duke served as "Mayor" of the Jacobite secret society, the Corporation of Walton-le-Dale, in 1709-11, when he was succeeded by his close friend, the Third Earl of Derwentwater.[146] W.E. Moss suggests that the Corporation was a Masonic society and that Norfolk and the Radcliffe brothers were initiates.[147]

In 1715 Norfolk sent £2,000 to James III to support the rising. His younger brother Edward joined Mar's campaign, was taken in arms at Preston, and charged with high treason.[148] Norfolk appealed to George I to acquit Edward, and it was rumored that he vowed his personal loyalty to the regime. His ardently Jacobite wife then left him for "truckling to the usurper," and moved in with a lover, Peregrine Widdrington, who had been "out" in the 1715. Paul Monod reveals that Norfolk wrote "a cringing letter" to James, defending his conduct: "I have always aimed in all my actions to serve you... I flatter myself that if my enemys should asperse me that you would not believe me capable of anything prejudicial to your interest."[149] In 1722 Norfolk was arrested in Bath and charged with complicity in the Atterbury plot; he was imprisoned in the Tower until May 1723, when he was released because of lack of evidence. Though he subsequently played a neutral role in public, he privately remained loyal to the cause. In 1725 he was listed by Wharton as a Stuart supporter, and his Jacobitism was documented in French diplomatic archives. It was rumored that he melted down the ducal plate to send funds to James, and as late as 1731 the Jacobites still expected financial contributions from him.

This secretive Jacobite context makes Norfolk's Masonic actions in 1729-30 especially provocative. Probably encouraged by Wharton and Ramsay, Norfolk steadily increased his influence in the Grand Lodge system. On 27 February 1729 he was initiated in the Horn Lodge, Westminster, which included many members of Parliament, government placemen, and two former Grand Masters (Desaguliers and Richmond).[150] Ironically, it was Richmond, a staunch Whig, who served as Master of the lodge and presided over Norfolk's initiation.[151] Like Wharton and Kingston, Norfolk seemed to "keep on the mask" in his dealings with the Hanoverians, while he quietly built support among the "brothers."

---

[143] P. Fagan, *Irish Bishop*, 114.

[144] J. Anderson, *Constitutions (1738)*, 99.

[145] Robert Freke Gould, *Military Lodges* (London, 1899), 40.

[146] F. Skeet, *Life of...James Radcliffe*, 42.

[147] W.E. Moss, "Freemasonry in France in 1725-1735," *AQC*, 47 (1934), 105.

[148] P. Monod, *Jacobitism*, 133-34; John M. Robinson, *The Dukes of Norfolk* (Oxford, 149-54.

[149] Stuart Papers: 47/79; quoted in Monod, *Jacobitism*, 134.

[150] Fisher, "Cavalcade," 53.

[151] R. Berman, *Foundations*, 157.

Norfolk was an old friend of Pope, who must have followed his Masonic activities with interest.[152] On 12 March, when Pope published the *Dunciad Variorum* (1729), with mock-pedantic notes, his own "Masonic" agenda became clearer – an agenda understood by Wharton, who acquired the enlarged *Dunciad*.[153] To Pope's mocking commentary on Benson's architectural incompetency and Atterbury's aborted plans for the Westminster dormitory, he added the line, "And Jones' and Boyle's united labours fall," with the following footnotes:

> * W-----m B----n [William Benson] (late Surveyor of the Buildings to his Majesty King George I). gave in a report to the Lords, that their House and the Painted Chamber adjoining were in immediate danger of falling... In favour of this man, the famous Sir Christopher Wren, who had been Architect to the Crown for above fifty years, who laid the first stone of St. Paul's, and lived to finish it, had been displac'd from his employment at the age of near ninety years.

> * The Dormitory in Westminster was a building intended for the lodging of the King's Scholars; toward which a sum...was raised by contributions procured...by the interest of Francis late Bishop of Rochester, and Dean of Westminster. He requested the Earl of Burlington to be the Architect, who carry'd on the work till the Bill against that learned Prelate was brought in, which ended in his banishment. The shell being finished according to his Lordship's design, the succeeding Dean and Chapter employ'd a common builder to do the inside, which was perform'd *accordingly*.

> * At the time when this Poem was written, the Banquetting-house of White-hall, the Church and Piazza of Covent-Garden, and the Palace and Chappel of Somerset-house, the works of the famous Inigo Jones, had been for many years so neglected, as to be in danger of ruin. The Portico of Covent-garden had been just then restored and beautify'd at the expence of Richard Earl of Burlington; who, at the same time, by his publication of the designs of that great Master and Palladio, as well as by many noble buildings of his own, revived the true Taste of Architecture in this Kingdom.[154]

In the revised *Dunciad*, Pope added to his criticism of Orator Henley, mocking his "gilt Tub," covered "with velvet and adorned with gold," while "Henley's periods...conduce to sooth the soul in slumbers."[155] He then expanded his earlier description of the flamboyant preacher:

> But, where each Science lifts its modern Type,
> Hist'ry her Pot, Divinity his Pipe,
> While proud Philosophy repines to show
> Dishonest sight! His breeches rent below;
> Imbrown'd with native Bronze, lo Henley stands,
> Tuning his voice, and balancing his hands.

---

[152] A. Pope, *Correspondence*, III, 346.

[153] *Biblothecarum...de Ducis Wharton*, 3876.

[154] Alexander Pope, *The Dunciad Variorum, with the Prolegomena of Scriblerus* (London, 1729), 76-77.

[155] *Ibid.*, 23, 49.

How fluent nonsense trickles from his tongue!
How sweet the *periods*, neither said nor sung!
Still break the benches, Henley!, with thy strain,
While K**, B**, W**,preach in vain.
O great Restorer of the good old Stage,
Preacher at once, and Zany of thy Age!
O worthy thou of Aegypt's wise abodes,
A decent Priest, where monkeys were the Gods!
But Fate with Butchers plac'd thy priestly Stall,
Meek modern faith to murder, hack, and mawl...[156]

In a long footnote, Pope repeated Leonard Welsted's biographical account of Henley, adding that the Orator "had an ambition" to be a writer "for Ministers of State." Moreover, he "offer'd the service of his pen, in one morning, to two great men of opinions and interests directly opposite; by both of whom being rejected, he set up a new Project" – his Oratory in Butcher Row. In the index, Pope identified the great men as Sir Robert Walpole and William Pulteney, but it is not clear if he knew that Delafaye was indeed subsidizing Henley. A month after publication of *The Dunciad Variorum*, Henley counterattacked with *Tom O'Bedlam's Dunciad: Or Pope, Alexander the Pig* (1729), in which he charged that Pope drew his low language from watermen and Billingsgate, was malicious and mercenary, and was terrified by Henley's criticism of him: "But see! he hears me, grins, and wildly stares,/ And deep in Wrath hangs down his Midas'd Ears."[157] Despite his "Zany" posturing, Henley would prove a persistent and dangerous enemy to Pope – and to his Tory and Jacobite Masonic friends.

While Wharton enjoyed Pope's newest satire, his reckless behavior increased his vulnerability. He had defiantly worn the regalia of the Garter in Paris, which provoked Atterbury to warn that the duke "should have care of appearing in his star and garter...if he intends to continue in Paris; complaint from W[alpole] on that head, may easily procure an order that will grieve him" (i.e., the confiscation of his estates). In spring 1729 the Duke of Richmond--a rival Garter knight and former Grand Master – visited Paris, where he met twice with Wharton. On 4 May he wrote to Folkes and described a deteriorating Wharton, whose shabby appearance and dirty Star and Ribbon suggested that he was no longer serious competition.[158] It was probably Richmond who instigated the founding in Paris of a new lodge, "St. Thomas au Louis d'Argent," affiliated with the Grand Lodge of London, which allegedly dated from 1729.[159]

In the meantime, Ramsay arrived in London in March 1729, when he must have been welcomed by Norfolk, who had earlier solicited his help for their fellow Catholics. According to some historians, Ramsay had a secret Jacobite mission, while he quietly sought out potential recruits to "une Maçonnerie nouvelle," which drew upon his interest in Jewish-Oriental mysticism and chivalric traditions.[160] However, his publicly stated purpose was the solicitation of subscribers for an expanded English edition of *The Travels of*

---

[156] *Ibid.*, 67-68.

[157] J.V. Guerinot, *Pamphlet Attacks on Pope, 1711-1744* (London, 1969), 170-71.

[158] March, *Duke*, I, 178.

[159] P. Chevallier, *Ducs*, 2; *Histoire*, I, 8.

[160] A. Cherel, *Aventurier*, 163-64; G. Henderson, *Ramsay*, 167; Claude Thory, *Acta Latamorum*, (Paris, 1815), I, 23; Nicolas de Bonneville, *Maçonnerie Écossosie compare avec des...Templieres* (Hamburg, 1788), II, 74.

Cyrus, to be published by the Non-juring, Jacobite printer James Bettenham (whom he later proposed as the publisher of his famous Masonic oration).

His project had already received opposition from loyalist Whig writers, such as Stephen Whatley, who in early 1729 published *A Criticism of Mr. Ramsay's Travels of Cyrus, wherein the Character of Cyrus is clear'd up, and the many Absurdities, Inconsistencies, Trifling Sentiments, Affected Expressions, Obscurities, Injudicious Reflections, False Quotations, and Notorious Plagiarisms of Mr. Ramsay, are Expos'd and Rectify'd*. Whatley drew upon and translated French critics who charged Ramsay with plagiarizing Bossuet and Fenelon, but he was especially scornful of his universalist and theosophical themes: "how can one, with Patience, hear all the Childish Things that are told you? The Egg of the World; the old She-Goat of Hermes; the Entrance of our Souls into the Bodies of a Cat, an Ape, etc."[161] Though some may find "Sublime Mysterys" in these traditions, they are actually nothing but "Chimeras and Absurdities." He then attacked Ramsay as a Scotsman, a native of the barren rocks and empty minds of Caledonia. Whatley, who had earlier published support of the "warming pan" conspiracy, appealed to the Lord Mayor of London and Whig politicians to now subsidize his writings.

Ramsay apparently brushed off such attacks, and he determined to spread his ecumenical message. Hoping to bridge the distrust between French and English scientists, Ramsay called on Newton's apologist Samuel Clarke, with whom he held long discussions on the master's scientific and religious beliefs.[162] Ramsay was aware of Newton's earlier collaboration with Fatio de Duilliers (alchemist, Cabalist, and French Prophet) and Newton's privately heterodox opinions. After Clarke's sudden death on 17 May, Ramsay continued his effort to find common ground with English scientists. As he wrote Caumont, he was working towards an alliance between the Royal Society of London and the Academy of Sciences at Paris.[163] He discussed with certain Fellows his "ether theory," which he believed Newton shared, and revealed "a high idea of the Geometry of the Grand and Sovereign Architect." He thus merged his scientific notions into his Masonic philosophy.

As Ramsay worked with Nathaniel Hooke on an enlarged edition of *Cyrus*, he was disappointed to learn that Swift was back in Ireland, with no plans to return to London. Ramsay may have learned that Swift still considered the Earl of Mar, Ramsay's mentor and confidant, among the "Men of Distinction and my Friends who are yet alive," for he included the exiled earl on this list, composed by the dean on 19 February 1729.[164] On 10 April Ramsay sent a message to Swift through "our Common Friend Mr. Lesley" (Robert Leslie), whose Jacobite activities were well-known to both men. Leslie had been close to Sir Charles Wogan, who admired Leslie's "stirring spirit," despite the opinion of James that his audacious proposals were "mad."[165] In Ramsay's letter to Swift, he acknowledged his debt to *A Tale of a Tub* in the development of his universalist theosophy: "It is now many years since I had the highest esteem for your writings, and when I was very young, I found in some of them certain ideas, that prepared me for relishing those principles of universal religion, which I have since endeavoured to unfold in

---

[161] Stephen Whatley, *A Criticism Upon Mr. Ramsay's Travels of Cyrus* (London, 1729), 63,142-43, 190.

[162] G. Henderson, *Ramsay*, 140.

[163] Wellcome Medical Library: MS 5744. Ramsay, Letter #6.

[164] Eugene Hammond, *Jonathan Swift: Our Dean* (Newark, 2016), 478.

[165] E. O'Ciardha, *Ireland*, 220.

Cyrus.[166] A Dublin edition of *Cyrus*, published in April 1728, "was much talked about," and Ramsay thanked Swift for making his work esteemed. He now supplied Leslie with one hundred copies of proposals for the revised edition of *Cyrus*, in order to solicit subscribers in Ireland.

Ian Higgins suggests that Swift was influenced by Ramsay's *Essay upon Civil Government* (1721), when he composed *A Modest Proposal for Preventing the Children of Poor People from being a Burthen to their Parents or Country, and For Making them Beneficial to the Publick* (1729), his most bitter attack upon Whig policies towards Ireland.[167] Ramsay had argued that subjects should never take up arms against a lawful sovereign. However, in extreme cases, such as the king forbidding his people to cultivate the ground and thus forcing them through starvation to cannibalism, then the "Body of the Nation" should bind the hands of the mad king and hand him over to the physicians. In Swift's satire, the narrator proposes the selling, cooking, and eating of poor children, so they will not be forced to "leave their dear Native Country, to fight for the Pretender in Spain."[168] He blithely affirms that "a young healthy child well Nursed is at a year Old, a most delicious nourishing and wholesome Food, whether Stewed, Roasted, Baked, or Boiled, and I make no doubt that it will equally serve in a Fricasee, or a Ragout."[169]

In a thrust at Ireland's notorious absentee Protestant landlords, Swift gives the "collateral advantage" of decreasing the number of Papists, who are not only "the principal Breeders of our Nation" but also "our most dangerous Enemies":

> who stay at home on purpose with a Design to deliver the Kingdom to the Pretender, hoping to take their Advantage by the Absence of so many good Protestants, who have chosen rather to leave their Country, than stay at home, and pay Tithes against their conscience, to an Episcopal Curate.[170]

He ironically dismisses "other Expedients" that would actually solve the problems of Ireland's misery and poverty under England's Whig government:

> Let no Man talk to me... Of taxing our Absentees at five shillings a pound: Of using neither Cloaths, nor Household Furniture, except what is our own Growth and Manufacture: Of utterly rejecting the Materials and Instruments that promote Foreign Luxury:...Of learning to love our Country...; Of quitting our Animosities, and Factions..: Of being a little cautious not to sell our Country and Consciences for nothing: Of teaching Landlords to have at least one Degree of Mercy towards their Tenants...[171]

Swift's blistering satire was judged to be dangerously seditious by Anthony Collins, the Whig freethinker, who wrote in 1729 that Swift was inciting a new Jacobite "Revolution,

---

[166] J. Swift, *Correspondence*, III, 233.

[167] I. Higgins, "Jonathan Swift," 99.

[168] Jonathan Swift, *A Modest Proposal for Preventing the Children of Poor People from being a Burthen to Their Parents or Country, and for Making them Beneficial to the Publick* (Dublin, 1729), 6.

[169] *Ibid.*, 9.

[170] *Ibid.*, 14.

[171] *Ibid.*, 17.

as far as choosing the most proper Topicks of Invective, and treating them in the way of *Drollery*, can do."[172]

Swift's sentiments about the role of greed in creating national corruption and misery were shared by Ramsay, who wrote in *Cyrus:*

> Where-ever a People carry on Commerce only to increase their Wealth, the State is no longer a Republic, but a Society of Merchants, who have no other Bond of Union, but the desire of Gain. The generous Love of their Country is no longer thought of, and they imagine they may renounce it, when the publick Good interferes with their private Interest.[173]

Ramsay believed that his universalist and mystical notions of Masonic brotherhood provided an antidote to the role of greed and factionalism in society, and he assumed that Swift shared this perspective.

The Jacobite Masons in England and Ireland were distressed when they learned that on 3 April 1729 the English parliament declared Wharton an outlaw and began the confiscation of his estates. Though he retained his title as Grand Master in France, he plunged deeper into debt and alcoholism, until he was forced to move to Spain in May – a return that seemed to him "as if I were doom'd to be buried alive."[174] However, when he arrived in Spain, he could have learned from his new friend Charles Wogan about the Wogan brothers' ambitious plan to send a Spanish expeditionary force to Ireland in support of an invasion of England. In May Wogan wrote from Spain to James III that he learned from "gentlemen of good sense lately returned from Ireland" that the Irish Catholics were ready to rise and that even the Protestant converts "would shake off the yoke from their consciences" by embracing the Jacobite cause.[175] Did he include Lord Kingston, current Grand Master in England, among those converts who would break their yokes? Kingston had many Masonic supporters in Munster, where Wogan argued that the expeditionary force should land. Lisa Meaney discusses the Tory, Jacobite, and Anglican sentiments of most Masons in Munster.[176] However, Wogan feared that "England is sick at heart, as France is rotten," and he lamented the futile sacrifices made by Irish Jacobites in French military service:

> I speak as a private man. It may appear bold of me to look on France with such indignation. I cannot help but when I see the exile of the royal family sacrificed for her and graves of one hundred thousand of our countrymen who died bravely without having been of any use in the cause that banished themselves and designed to fight for.[177]

Three years later, he would share these thoughts with Swift.

---

[172] I. Higgins, "Jonathan Swift," 87; see [Anthony Collins], *A Discourse Concerning Ridicule and Irony in Writing* (London, 1729), 40.

[173] A. Ramsay, *Travels of Cyrus* (1727), I, 286.

[174] Stuart Papers: 117/85 (20 June 1726).

[175] E. O'Ciardha, "Jacobite Jail-Breakers," 17-19, 32n.33-37.

[176] Lisa Meaney,"Freemasonry in Munster, 1726-1789" (MA Thesis: Mary Immaculate College, Limerick, 2005), 35,90,183.

[178] E. O'Ciardha, "Jacobite Jail-Breakers, 19.

Despite the disappointment at Wharton's outlawry, the spirits of Norfolk and Ramsay must have been lifted by the secret arrival of Norfolk's Masonic collaborator Charles Radcliffe in London in June 1729. While Radcliffe tried to maintain secrecy about his contacts, he was known to meet frequently with John Byrom, Grand Master of the Cabala Club and director of the Jacobite "network of espionage" between Manchester and Scotland.[178] Byrom was a member of the French lodge, which in 1730 was meeting at the Swan in Long Acre.[179] He utilized his Masonic contacts to not only recruit Whigs to his shorthand course but also to keep an eye on their political activities. In July he spent much time with his Jacobite friend Henry Salkeld, member of a Northumberland family long loyal to the Stuarts. The two Jacobite Masons spent an unexpectedly convivial evening with Desaguliers, when the fraternity's ideal of sociability sometimes led to cross-party friendliness.[180] In August Desaguliers attended a dinner at the home of Alderman Sir Humphrey Parsons, a wealthy brewer, Freemason, and staunch Jacobite.[181] Another guest, John Grano, a Mason and Handel's trumpeter, wrote about the gathering, in which "the spirit of toleration...prevailing among members of the fraternity" allowed them to pass beyond party and religious differences.[182]

Because Radcliffe was still attainted and subject to arrest, he remained incognito, while Byrom surreptitiously arranged meetings with him and fellow Jacobites. But Byrom's activities soon aroused suspicions, and he was teased by Martin Folkes, his Whig Masonic friend, that it was rumored that he "had gone to Rome afoot to see the Pretender." In a later pamphlet, a Whig author claimed that Radcliffe began to frequently visit England in disguise, using the name "Johns," while he sowed seeds of rebellion; even worse, "the secrets of government" were thus "betrayed to the enemy."[183]

During this period, Ramsay became friendly with Joseph Spence, professor of poetry at Oxford, who recorded in detail their many conversations. James Osborne, editor of Spence's journals, argues that Ramsay hoped "to convince the English Grand Lodge of Masons to alter the legend of their origin to make membership more palatable to the French aristocracy"; unfortunately, he gives no documentation for this claim, which he perhaps found in Spence's unpublished papers.[184] Spence reported Ramsay's conversations with the heterodox Jew in Italy and his belief in the shared trinitarian traditions of the Jewish Cabala and Christianity, especially as expressed in Knorr von Rosenroth's *Kabbala Denudata* (1677).[185] Ramsay further discussed Fouquet's "Figurist" beliefs, which he and the old Jesuit believed were similar to the Cabalists'. As noted earlier, the historians Bruno Neveu and D.P. Walker argue that Ramsay assimilated Figurist and Cabalistic themes into his Masonic philosophy, before his journey to London.[186]

The stolid Spence was sometimes confused by Ramsay's erudite and eclectic beliefs, such as the pre-existence of souls and the universal restoration. He noted that Hooke, a

---

[178] Joy Hancox, *Queen's Chameleon*, 79, 81, 98.
[179] *Ibid.*, 255n.15. Information sent to Hancox by the librarian of the Grand Lodge of England.
[180] A. Carpenter, *Desaguliers*, 221.
[181] "Humphrey Parsons," *ODNB*.
[182] A. Carpenter, *Desaguliers*, 219.
[183] Anon., *A sketch of the Life and Character of Mr. Radcliffe* (London, 1746), 19.
[184] J. Spence, *Observations*, I, 441.
[185] *Ibid.*, I, 470.
[186] B. Neveu, "Un Roman," 17-18; D. Walker, *Ancient Theology*, 239-40, 248.

devout Catholic, "said of some of [Ramsay's] most elevated notions – 'Like stars, when of too great a height,/ That neither give us heat nor light' – seemed to be very well grounded."[187] Nevertheless, Spence and Hooke admired Ramsay, and they took him to Oxfordshire in June, where Ramsay was not impressed by the "Whiggish" architecture of Blenheim palace. Like Swift, he scorned Vanbrugh's designs, and he found "the relative austerity" of the chapel depressing; he commented to Hooke that the altar "was veritably Republican."[188] However, the critics of Vanbrugh soon had better news in July, when Christopher Wren *fils* was installed as Master of the Lodge of Antiquity, #1 which seemed to reflect a revival of Stuart architectural-Masonic traditions.[189]

In July 1729 Ramsay wrote to old friends in Scotland, soliciting subscriptions, while noting that "tho my notions be sometimes eccentricat and projectile, yet I hope the great principle of attraction prevails."[190] He affirmed that "if I had either money or time I would have certainly gone to Scotland to embrace your Lo. Feet, and those of some other friends whose tender regard I look upon as the principal happiness of this mortal state." In London he asked the Scottish twin brothers, Hugh Hume-Campbell, 3rd Earl of Polwarth, and Alexander Hume-Campbell, to solicit subscribers. The former succeeded and sent Ramsay his list, but the latter was too busy and did not carry out his commission. In an embarrassing case of mistaken identity, Ramsay "overwhelmed" Alexander "with a profusion of thanks and compliments" which should have been made to his brother.[191] The brothers came from an old Masonic family in Scotland, where their grandfather, Sir Patrick Hume of Polwarth, 1st Earl of Marchmont, had joined the Edinburgh lodge in 1667.[192] The twins were dissident, anti-Walpolean Whigs, who began to support Tory measures, and Ramsay perhaps hoped to win them over to more Jacobite support.

Despite (or because of) Ramsay's heterodox opinions, he made many friends, and he eventually solicited over five hundred subscribers. Spence's friend John Fanshawe reported that he is "so vastly caressed by everybody that he has not time to publish his *Cyrus*."[193] In November Ramsay wrote Caumont that he was receiving much support for his expanded edition, in which he developed "several dogmas of antiquity and several points of theology which have a rapport with our sacred mysteries."[194] By those mysteries, he meant the esoteric themes of *Écossais* Freemasonry. In *Cyrus* Ramsay's portrayal of the exile of a legitimate king (an obvious reference to James III) provided an opportunity for moral reflection and universalist education.[195] He quoted a "famous Passage" from Hermes Trismegistus: "When the Gods love Princes, they pour into the Cup of Fate, a Mixture of Good and Ill, that they may not forget that they are Men."[196] In an equally obvious

---

[187] J. Spence, *Observations*, I, 468-69.

[188] *Ibid.*, I, 455.

[189] "Note on...Wren's Death," 182.

[190] G. Henderson, *Ramsay*, 137-38.

[191] Marchmont, Earls of, *A Selection from the Papers of the Earls of Marchmont* ed. G.H. Rose (London, 1831), I, xiv.

[192] D. Stevenson, *First Freemasons*, 31.

[193] J. Spence, *Observations*, I, 454.

[194] Wellcome Medical Library: Ramsay, #7. The manuscript letter is dated London, 21 November, which places it in 1729, not 1730 as stated in F. Weil, "Ramsay," 275.

[195] A. Ramsay, *Cyrus* (1727), 137.

[196] *Ibid.*, 137.

reference to his former pupil, Prince Charles Edward Stuart, Cyrus receives the following advice:

> Go, Prince, go render yourself worthy to accomplish the oracles; and never forget in the midst of your successes, that you have seen a Monarch, who was heretofore triumphant and glorious, driven on a sudden from his throne, and become the sport of fortune... Cyrus left Egypt without seeing Amasis, whose character and usurpation he abhorred.[197]

These were stirring words for Stuart supporters, many of whom were probably aware of his Jacobite mission. However, this was kept so secret that there are only shreds of evidence for his contacts in England. It seems likely that he met Richard Rawlinson and John Arbuthnot, who were fellow Masons and Jacobites and who subscribed to his new edition. Ramsay almost certainly knew Robert Arbuthnot in France, and his brother (the doctor) acquired multiple copies of French and English editions of *Cyrus*, as well as those of Ramsay's mentor Fenelon.[198] Ramsay was definitely welcomed by Thomas Carte, also a Mason, who had been exiled for six years, until he was allowed to return to England in 1728. Ramsay later thanked Carte for his many civilities when they met in London, but there is no other record of their meetings in England.[199] This is unfortunate because Carte's extensive studies of chivalric and crusader orders were relevant to Ramsay's subsequent influence on the development of such themes in *Écossais* Masonic rituals.[200] They continued to correspond after Ramsay's return to France.

There is brief but tantalizing evidence of Ramsay's contact with the Earl of Orrery and his son Lord Boyle, with whom he spent much time in autumn 1729. Ramsay and Radcliffe had met them during their visit in 1725-26 to Paris, where the earl carried out secret negotiations with Jacobite supporters and managed Wharton's negotiations with the Austrians. Orrery was currently corresponding with the Stuart court about new initiatives. Working with Henry Hyde, Lord Cornbury, he made lists of potential supporters for a restoration. They hoped to attract various disaffected Whigs, and the Masonic lodges would provide potential recruiting grounds.

From references in Lord Boyle's correspondence, it is clear that he kept company with various Freemasons, both Whig and Tory. On 23 November Boyle wrote from London to his Tory-Masonic friend, the lawyer John Kempe, a comical letter about a political dust-up in their rural parish. A curate of Hornsey preached a sermon which offended one "Pendulum," who reported him to the government, charging that the clergyman had been "bred at Westminster School when Atterbury was dean of that College."[201] Orrery's neighbor Jackson turned it all into "Laughter and Mockery":

> Jackson is an errant Wag, Sneers at all Plots and Politicks, and even thinks Government itself is a Farce. He sleeps without any fear of Popery, and he curses the Fanaticks and Dissenters for Knaves and Hypocrites. He frequently puts a merry Paragraph in the News-Papers... He is a Bachelor and

---

[197] A. Ramsay, *Cyrus* (1730), 143.
[198] *Catalogue of...Dr. Arbuthnot*, #27,70,133,188,278,-79,295.
[199] Bodleian: Carte MS.227, f. 56 (12 July 1732).
[200] *Ibid.*, MSS. 100, f. 336; 106, f. 481; 225, f. 162; 226, f.186; and many more on chivalric orders.
[201] Harvard. Houghton: Eng.218.2, vol. 1, f. 100.

a Free Mason, and was never conquered by liquor but twice in his Life, once
at High-Borlase at Oxford, and once at a Lodge in Southwark.

Jackson made peace between the curate and Pendulum, and thus saved the former from
prosecution. Boyle, who often mocked the heavy drinking of the local Hanoverian gentry,
also associated such drunkenness with lodge meetings. He would later lament that "Wine
and Free-Masonry have brought poor old Kempe to his grave." [202]

In December 1729 Ramsay was elected to the Royal Society, which provided a further
venue for recruitment to his and Orrery's political and Masonic cause. On 25 December
Boyle wrote to his Jacobite friend Salkeld and reported that his father, Orrery, was visiting
him at their country home in Britwell:

> This Christmas has likewise brought down hither the Chevalier Ramsay, who
> was born in Scotland and educated in France. Methinks *Un Ecossois François*
> appears like a Tulip engrafted upon a Thistle. One is afraid to venture near
> the Scotch Root, but one is allured toward it by the gaudy Colours of the
> prominent Flower. I look upon this doughty Knight as the true Representa-
> tive of the Book He is going to publish, a pious Romance at once fictitious
> and improving.[203]

Boyle then added a long, peculiar diatribe against the Scots, while noting that "Many
Men there are amongst them to my Knowledge of Probity":

> The Highlanders are indeed a dreadfull People, and upon the whole may not
> the Scotch Nation be aptly compared to a Yew Tree? It naturally grows
> rough from the Bottom to the Top, but may easily be cut into what shape
> you please. It is a Screen to other Trees, and it sets at Defiance, the bleakness
> of the Wind, and the severity of the Winter, nor can a more excellent De-
> fence be divised either for an old Wall or a New Castle.

The word "dreadfull" currently meant "inspiring dread or fear," and Orrery and his son
would view that quality of the Highlanders positively. In May 1725 Orrery and Wharton
had voted in parliament against the disarming of the Highlanders (they lost).[204] Months
later in Paris, Orrery almost certainly met with Sir Hector Maclean, Cameron of Lochiel,
and other Highland chiefs, whom Atterbury was consulting about Scottish unrest.

Orrery and Boyle knew that they were under surveillance by the Walpolean regime,
and they were extremely cautious about their communications, often using pseudonyms
for persons they discussed. Thus, Boyle's further disquisition on "two Brothers in Iniq-
uity, Empson and Dudley," who were caught up in a controversial treason case in Henry
VII's time, when the legal charges and process were confused and corrupted, seemed a
cover for current concerns. J.H. Lepper suggests that the various names given in the
letter were in Jacobite code to communicate secret intelligence, while J.E.S. Tuckett observes that the letter conveyed "an intimation of the different degree of readiness of the
Highlander as compared the Lowlander – readiness to take active steps for the cause.

---

[202] *Ibid.*, Eng.218.2, vol.4, f.7.
[203] Orrery, *Orrery Papers*, I, 75-77.
[204] L. Smith, *Charles Boyle*, 393, 408.

Whether readiness means a state of preparation or good will to the cause is not clear."[205] Orrery's modern biographer L.B. Smith speculates that Ramsay, "the mysterious Jacobite Freemason," supplied French intelligence to Orrery, who was currently being urged by James to travel to Paris to make new approaches to the French court.[206] Boyle concluded his letter to Salkeld with a jovial send-off: "I hear Chevalier Ramsay at this moment singing in the Hall *Oh! la Vertue, qu'elle est aimable!* and must go and joine in the Chorus."

Ramsay's friendship with Orrery and his son, who were cousins and confidants of Lord Burlington, raises the question of whether he met the architect of Chiswick while he was in England. As noted earlier, Jane Clark suggests that Burlington was influenced by the Masonic symbolism of *The Travels of Cyrus*, a thesis reinforced by Ricky Pound, modern curator of Chiswick. Pound argues that in 1729-30 Burlington included the Hiramic legend of the "The Master Mason Slain" in the artistic decorations of the Red Velvet Room. The paintings were produced by William Kent, a Freemason, and drew upon the Solomonic identification of James I and VI and the murder of his son Charles I. From his careful study of Kent's designs, which portray Inigo Jones in a context of Masonic and Hiramic symbols, Pound concludes:

> In recent years historians have suggested that Lord Burlington was a secret Jacobite supporter, covertly plotting the return of the exiled House of Stuart. Read in such terms, the advertisement of the Hiramic legend in the Red Velvet Room takes on a more subversive role. It is know from Masonic ritual in France, for example, that the murder of Hiram Abiff was equated with the beheading of the Stuart martyr, Charles I. Many Jacobite Freemasons perceived the exile of the Stuarts to be comparable to the 70-year exile of the Israelites to Babylon after the destruction of the original Temple of Jerusalem by King Nebuchadnezzar II in 587 B.C... the supine bust of Jones/Hiram could also be a reference to the unlawful murder of Charles I, exemplified by the architects Inigo Jones and Hiram Abiff. This being the case, the presence of Hermes is a fitting symbol for the envisaged second restoration of Stuart kingship...[207]

Given Burlington's extreme caution about his Jacobite activities and the many gaps in our knowledge about Ramsay's contacts in England, the question of their possible meeting remains open – and tantalizing.

During this period, various anti-Walpolean Masons made a public show of non-partisanship and conciliation. Henry Carey, a witty and whimsical friend of Burlington and Pope, seemed to express this new strategy in 1729. In a revised edition of his *Poems on Several Occasions*, dedicated to the Countess of Burlington, Carey echoed Swift's and Pope's criticism of George I's reign but hoped for reconciliation and non-partisan government under George II. In "The Moderator Between the Free-Masons and Gormogons," he posed as a genial peace-maker between the factions, observing that

The Masons and Gormogons

---

[205] John Heron Lepper, "The Earl of Orrery, Chevalier Ramsay, John Kempe," *AQC*, 35 (1922), 77-78.

[206] L. Smith, *Charles Boyle*, 444.

[207] Ricky Pound, "The Master Mason Slain: the Hiramic Legend in the Red Velvet Room at Chiswick House," *English Heritage Historical Review*, 4 (2009), 161.

Are laughing at one another;
While all mankind are laughing at them;
Then why do you make such a pother.

They bait their hook for simple Gulls
And Truth with Bam they smother;
And when they've taken in their Culls,
Why then t'is... Welcome Brother.[208]

The ecumenical Lord Kingston, Grand Master of the English Grand Lodge, was in Ireland, when he received some kind of alarming news. As an Irish patriot who was suspected of Jacobite sympathies, he backed the steady rise of Norfolk within the Grand Lodge system. In early November he heard from his Deputy Grand Master that his presence was urgently needed for the upcoming Quarterly Communication of 25 November 1729. Kingston then "rode post from Holyhead in two days and a half," in order to preside over the meeting.[209] He apparently headed off an attempt to prevent Norfolk's selection as succeeding Grand Master, and he soon built nearly unanimous support for his choice. On 27 December 1729, at a meeting of the Grand Lodge, the deputy Grand Master Nathaniel Blackerby read a letter from Kingston, proposing Norfolk as his successor in the top office.[210]

Two days later, Kingston copied the Irish practice of leading a public procession of Masons to a grand feast. All former Grand Masters, except the exiled Wharton, marched in the splendidly attired parade. At the feast, Kingston invested and installed Norfolk in Solomon's Chair. Norfolk then appointed Blackerby to continue as deputy Grand Master. A tone of reconciliation prevailed at the meetings, and Norfolk invited the brothers to attend a performance of *Henry IV, the Sequel*, on 12 February at Drury Lane. Norfolk and Blackerby then wrote a Prologue to be spoken by John Mills, the actor and Mason, at the gala performance. Mills was evidently a Jacobite, for his name appears among the confidants of Radcliffe and Byrom in 1729-30.[211] Chastising the many critics who "curse the Centry with the flaming Sword,/ Who keep Eves-droppers from the *Masons Word*," Mills praised two Presbyterian ministers from Scotland who fairly and objectively investigated the fraternity's secrets:

Not so th' Assembly of the *Scottish* Kirk;
their Wisdoms went a better Way to work;
When they were told the Masons practic'd Charms,
Invok'd the De'il, and rais'd tempestuous Storms,
Two of their Body, prudently they sent,
To learn what could by MASONRY be meant.
Admitted to the Lodge and treated well,
At their Return, th' Assembly hop'd they'd tell:
We say nea mare nor this, they both reply'd,

---

[208] *EMP*, 329.
[209] R. Gould, *History*, III, 136.
[210] J. Anderson, *Constitutions (1738)*, 124-25.
[211] J. Hancox, *Queen's Chameleon*, 99.

Do what we've dune, and ye'll be satisfied.[212]

Despite the public effort to reconcile factions within Masonry, political and literary rivals continued to vent their mutual opposition. In Ireland supporters of Swift had continued their attacks on the loyalist Mason Arbuckle. In *The Dublin Scuffle, or, the Hungry Poets Petition, Humbly Dedicated to a Certain Great Man. By a Well-wisher of the Society* (1729), the poet linked Arbuckle with William Connolly, M.P., who had earlier purchased Wharton's castle at Rathfarnham and who served effectively as "the undertaker" to the English Whig government. Known as "the great man of the North," he earned Swift's wrath by his authorization of the government's *Proclamation* against the Drapier"[213] The author then mocked Arbuckle's Presbyterianism, Scottishisms, and lameness, both poetical and physical. Scorning him as a loyalist Dissenter who hoped to demolish Episcopacy, the poet unashamedly called him "a Frog, that drags along/ Its wounded Limbs."[214]

This was cruel stuff, even by Swiftian standards, and Arbuckle fought back with the anonymously published *A Panegyric on the Reverend Dean Swift. In Answer to A Libel on Dr. Delany, and a certain Great Lord*, published in Dublin in February or March 1730 and then in London. He voiced a scathing criticism of Swift's alleged arrogance and hypocrisy:

> Could all we little Folks that wait,
> And dance Attendance on the Great,
> Obtain such Privilege as You,
> To rail, and go unpunish'd too;
> To treat our Betters like our Slaves,
> And all Mankind as Fools, or Knaves.
> ....
> A Deanery you got, when in;
> And now you're out, enjoy your Grin.
> ....
> No Wonder 'tis, you think it little
> To lick a Rascal States-mans' Spittle.[215]

Ironically, *A Panegyric* was long believed to be a "Scrub Libel," written by Swift himself, though Arbuckle's authorship was subsequently documented.[216]

While Lord Kingston called for Masonic ecumenicism and good will, Edward Young joined the chorus calling for writers to abstain from partisan politics. As noted earlier, Arbuckle had praised Young for his Walpolean loyalty, after the poet had earlier been the protégé of Wharton. He now published ambiguous praise of Alexander Pope in *Two Epistles to Mr. Pope, Concerning the Authors of the Present Age* (1730). He regretted the petty and venomous pamphlets and poems that poured forth in London, and he urged Pope to "Let Satire less engage you, than Applause," for "It shews a generous mind to wink at

---

[212] *EMP*, 230-31.

[213] J. Swift, *Correspondence*, III, 428 and n.5.

[214] Anon., *The Dublin Scuffle* (Dublin, 1730), 25-30.

[215] Anon.[James Arbuckle], *A Panegyric on the Reverend Dean Swift* (London, 1730), 3 – 7.

[216] James Wooley, "Arbuckle's 'Panegyric' and Swift's Scrub Libel: The Documentary Evidence," in John I. Fischer and Donald C. Mell, eds., *Contemporary Studies of Swift's Poetry* (Newark, 1981), 191-209.

Flaws."[217] Rather than attacking minor writers in *The Dunciad*, Pope should aim for a more "glorious End,/ Be your King's, Country's, Truth's, Religion's friend."

Young's ambiguous stance provoked a furious counter-blast from James Moore Smythe, the Grand Lodge Mason, and Leonard Welsted, who in *One Epistle to Mr. A. Pope, Occasion'ed by Two Epistles Lately Published* (1730), suggested Pope's petty malice and secret Jacobitism. They attacked the Catholic poet's continuing admiration for Atterbury, "The Prelate! Next, exil'd by cruel Fates,/ Who plagues all Churches, and confounds all States;/ With Treasons past perplex'd, and present Cares."[218] Even worse was Pope's friendship with the Jacobite Mason, Dr. Arbuthnot, a "quack," described as "That puzzling, plodding, prating, pedant Scot!," whose medicine and writing are "two Arts to kill." Finally, in an extremely low blow, the authors alluded to Swift's secret marriage to Stella (the first published reference to it):

> So when Vanessa [Stella] yielded up her Charms,
> The blest Cadenus [Swift] languish'd in her Arms;
> High, on a Peg, his unbrush'd Beaver hung,
> His Vest unbutton'd, and his God unsung;
> Raptur'd he lies; Deans, Authors are forgot,
> Wood's Copper Pence, and Atterbury's Plot;
> For he quits the Tythes of Patrick's Fields,
> And all the Levite to the Lover yields.[219]

Pope would continue his own attacks on Moore Smythe, whom he publicly linked with Hanoverian Masonry. And an intimidated Young would soon become a loyalist Freemason.

Despite the literary wars, the Grand Master Kingston maintained a public non-partisan stance, while his Jacobite friends made secret overtures to potential sympathizers among the Masons. Ramsay's decision to join the Horn Lodge in March 1730 suggests the increasing Jacobite presence within the Grand Lodge system, under the leadership of Norfolk, the Grand Master elect. Surprisingly, Norfolk attended no more meetings of the Grand Lodge, but he "personally constituted several lodges" in March before leaving for the continent.[220] The most important of these met at the Bear and Harrow, with the Grand Master Norfolk, previous Grand Master Kingston, and Deputy Grand Master Blackerby in attendance. A significant number of Jacobites became members, including John Webb, whose sister Anna Maria was the widow of James Radcliffe, the executed Third Earl of Derwentwater.[221] He was joined by Charles Radcliffe's friend, Sir David Threipland, who was "out" in 1715, escaped to France, but was advised by James III to return to England, since he is "firm as a rock in his principles" and should "accept a license to go home," even if offered by a Whig, because "One man there is worth ten here." Also joining the lodge was Sir Henry Goring, who would later become Prince Charles Edward Stuart's most trusted companion.

---

[217] Edward Young, *Two Epistles to Mr. Pope* (London, 1730), 36.

[218] [James Moore Smythe and Leonard Welsted], *One Epistle to Mr. A. Pope* (London, 1730), 11, 16-17.

[219] *Ibid*, 20.

[220] R. Gould, *History*, III, 137.

[221] For the many Jacobite members, see W. Firminger, "Members," 104-13.

Though there were a few Whigs and independents, the lodge provided a cautiously convenient meeting place for the Norfolk-Ramsay-Radcliffe partisans. Given the names of Swift and Pope on a lodge list "cumulative to 1730," it seems that Pope may have met Ramsay at a Masonic gathering. Scholars have long puzzled that there is no surviving evidence that Ramsay met the poet, whom he later described as "my friend," but it could well have occurred in a secret fraternal context.[222] In March Ramsay extended his Masonic network, when he was elected to the Gentleman's Society of Spalding, which included many prominent Masons, from both sides of the partisan divide.[223] Some of these were targets of Orrery's recruitment efforts.

In April 1730 Ramsay's Jacobite contacts paid off, when Charles Butler, 2nd Earl of Arran, chancellor of the University of Oxford and brother of the exiled Ormonde, proposed him for an honorary doctorate of law.[224] It is presently unknown if Arran was a Mason, but it seems likely since his revered older brother was an initiate. When an undergraduate strongly opposed Ramsay, on the grounds of his Catholicism and Jacobitism, Dr. William King, head of St. Mary's Hall, came to his defense. King had earlier participated in the Swedish and Atterbury plots and continued to serve the cause. As noted earlier, he had helped Hooke translate Ramsay's *Cyrus*, when he and Hooke were staying at Dr. Cheyne's house in Bath.[225] King was allegedly a Freemason, and he would later stay with Ramsay in Paris at the time of the chevalier's most important Masonic activities.[226]

King was also a friend and correspondent of Swift, whom he visited in Ireland in 1727. He may have informed Ramsay about Swift's recent allusion to Freemasonry in *A Vindication of His Excellency John, Lord Carteret, from the Charge of Favouring none but Tories, High-Churchmen, and Jacobites*, published by Faulkner in Dublin in April 1729. Though Carteret was a staunch Hanoverian, he hated Walpole and enjoyed Swift's diatribes against the prime minister. As Lieutenant-Governor of Ireland, his relatively benign administration earned the friendship of Swift, who persuaded him to grant small benefices to Tory friends like Dr. Patrick Delany. The Whigs then accused Carteret of Jacobitism, and Swift rushed to his and Delany's defense:

> since the Doctor hath not, in any of his Writings, his Sermons, his Actions, his Discourse, or his Company, discovered one single Principle of either *Whig* or *Tory*; and that the Lord Lieutenant continues to admit him; I shall boldly pronounce him ONE OF US: but, like a new *Free-Mason*, who hath not yet learned all the Dialect of the Mystery, neither can he justly be accused of any *Tory* doctrines.[227]

---

[222] For "Pope's friend Ramsay," see Maynard Mack, *Collected in Himself*, 203.

[223] C. Batham, "Chevalier Ramsay," 284.

[224] G. Henderson, *Ramsay*, 141-43.

[225] J. Spence, *Observations*, I, 455.

[226] King would stay with Ramsay in Paris in late 1736, when Ramsay was preparing his famous Masonic oration.

[227] Jonathan Swift, *Irish Tracts, 1728-1733*, ed. Herbert Davis (Oxford, 1955), 166.

Carteret left Ireland that month and refused to take further office under Walpole, leaving Swift to comment wryly that he "had a genteeler manner of binding the chains of the kingdom than most of his predecessors."[228]

When Ramsay brought out his enlarged English edition of *Cyrus*, he produced an impressive list of Jacobite and Masonic subscribers, but he had become increasingly disillusioned with the England of George II and the "Robinocracy." He made many friends and received surprising honors, but he missed France and realized it was now his home. In August 1730 he wrote to Caumont about the misuse of British liberty of speech: "They vomit here injuries against the Church and State without fear of anathemas or prisons. They say whatever they think whenever they want. This liberty furnishes a variety of characters and the spectacle is diverting enough for the imagination, but it desolates reason and virtue."[229] As he planned his return to France, Ramsay must have been pleased by a report that was currently circulating about the English Grand Master. On 20 August the *Norwich Gazette*, a Jacobite paper that had steadily covered Norfolk's rise within Freemasonry, published a startling claim:

> We hear that some Gentlemen returned lately from France among other things say, That His Most Christian Majesty had been made a FREE-MA-SON, in the usual Forms, by the Duke of Norfolk, Grand Master of the Society; and that His Majesty hardly ever appeared more merry, that he did at that Ceremony.[230]

This Jacobite report probably represented wishful thinking, but Ramsay definitely harbored ambitions to initiate the French king. However, this is the only known report of Louis XV's affiliation taking place before 1737. Probably in late August, Ramsay slipped quietly out of England, leaving behind him a wave of controversies about Masonry.

---

[228] Swift to Gay (19 November 1730); quoted in "John Carteret, 1st Earl Granville," *DNB*.

[229] F. Weil, "Ramsay," 275.

[230] Gilbert Daynes, "The Duke of Norfolk, 1730-1731," *AQC*, 29 (1926), 109-10. Henry Cossgrove, editor of the *Norwich Gazette*, used the paper as an organ of the Jacobite party; see P. Monod, *Jacobitism*, 30.

CHAPTER TWELVE

CHIVALRIC MASONRY EXPANDS INTERNATIONALLY
(1730-1732)

> If this mighty Aenigma of the Free Masons be a Fraud...it ought to be detected and exposed...so we seem bound in Duty to those Knights of the Leather Apron, to let them know that the Secret has reached our more important Ears...
>
> Daniel Defoe, "Of the Ridiculous Fraud of Free Masonry" (1730).

> I have...two rings of the Order of Toboso, such as all the knights wear... We knights daily after drinking the healths of the Royal Family, a fair meeting on the green follows; our two young Princes are protectors of the order...
>
> William Hay to Admiral Gordon (Rome, 1732).

Immediately after Ramsay's arrival in Paris, he sent a note to the Abbé Jerome Bignon, the royal librarian, that he planned to deliver a packet from Ephraim Chambers.[1] It was possibly at this time that Ramsay, inspired by Chambers and Bignon, began to contemplate a new universal encyclopedia, to be produced by Freemasons in several countries.[2] He probably also met with Norfolk, who visited Paris on his way to Italy. They could have learned about the important initiations of two Swedish nobles in the *Écossais* lodge in late 1729.[3] Counts Nils Bielke and Johan Sack were members of the Holstein party, and their families had earlier Jacobite contacts.[4] Though Sack returned to Sweden, Bielke converted to Catholicism and became a naturalized citizen of France, before moving to Rome, where he became a family friend of the Stuarts. He separated amicably from his wife, who returned to Stockholm, and he maintained cordial relations and correspondence with his brothers-in-law, Axel Wrede Sparre, who would also be

---

[1] P. Chevallier, *Ducs*, 136.
[2] M. Jacob, *Radical*, 257-58.
[3] Eero Ekman, *Highlights of Masonic Life in Nordic Countries* (Helsinki, 1994), 27-29.
[4] M. Schuchard, *Emanuel Swedenborg*, 183, 293.

initiated in Paris, and Carl Gustaf Tessin, who later became a confidential friend of Ramsay and infused the chevalier's mysticism into Swedish Freemasonry.

Thomas Carte would be most interested in the Swedish initiations in Paris, for he had collected much material on the earlier Swedish-Jacobite plot. In 1728, while still exiled in Paris, Carte wrote James that he wanted to return to England in order to print a defense of his right to the throne, which he had intended to publish "at the landing of the King of Sweden" in 1717.[5] In 1730, when back in England, he fueled renewed Jacobite interest in Sweden, when he circulated a manuscript copy of a speech given by Carl XII which expressed his sympathy for the Stuart cause.[6] At this time, the Swedish opposition "Holstein" party, led by Gyllenborg and Tessin, was gaining power and sending signals to the Jacobites of their support.[7] It was perhaps through Swedish-Masonic contacts in Paris and Italy that Norfolk acquired a famous sword of King Gustavus Adolphus, which, according to Swedish tradition, conferred magical powers on the seventeenth-century warrior king. Nils Bielke, who was an expert on the archives and treasures of Queen Christina, may have informed Norfolk about her father's sword, which was acquired in Italy, during the duke's six-month visit there.[8] Norfolk would subsequently send the sword to London, where it was used as the Sword of State in Grand Lodge ceremonies.[9]

While in Italy, Norfolk was watched carefully by British agents, who were on the alert to discover if he made any Jacobite contacts. On 14 December 1730 Stosch reported that the duke "will have a difficult role to play here, where his name is known to so many."[10] On 13 January 1731 Eliezer Burges, English consul in Venice, reported that Norfolk, with "young Mr. Southcott," was in the city but did not plan to go to Rome, "which he may fear would give some umbrage at home, which he has too much prudence, and I hope, too much duty for his Majesty to do at any time."[11] Young Southcott was a relative of the Abbé Thomas Southcott, who had helped plan Ramsay's journey to England. Back in France, Ramsay wrote to Carte on 16 January 1731, describing his correspondence with "the English Benedictine" (i.e., Southcott), which increases the probability of his contact with Norfolk, the travelling companion of "young Mr. Southcott," when the duke was in France.[12]

Despite Norfolk's caution, his link with the Southcott family would certainly rouse suspicion among Walpole's many spies in Italy. Though it is unknown if Norfolk contacted supporters of James III in Italy, the Jacobites in England and France hoped to gain his financial support. On 15 January 1731 "Mr. B.," a Jacobite in London, wrote Mist the printer, now in Boulogne, that Norfolk should be approached "by proper persons" on "your side of the water" to contribute a large sum to a planned rising, but

---

[5] Stuart Papers: 116/104.

[6] Bodleian: Carte MS. 226, f.40 (Notes made in March 1730).

[7] M. Schuchard, *Emanuel Swedenborg*, 181-84.

[8] J. Ingamells, *Dictionary*, 711.

[9] R. Gould, *History*, III, 137; Algernon Tudor-Craig, ed., *Catalogue of the Contents of the Museum at Freemasons' Hall in the Possession of the United Grand Lodge* (London, 1938), I, 65; "Note," *AQC*, 29 (1916), 72.

[10] NA: SP 98/32.

[11] *Ibid.*, 99/63.

[12] Bodleian. Calendar of Carte MSS: vol. 72, f.276. The name Southwell and date 1730 seem errors of transcription.

"Norfolk is very covetous and proud, and must be promised large interest."[13] He noted that Carte is in London and could be sent to France for instructions on who should approach Norfolk. On 8 February Mist wrote to James about Mr. B.'s letter, noting that Norfolk "must needs have a great sum by" from leases he "obtained, I won't say bought, from an Act of Parliament" that allows him to make huge sums from fines.[14] The Jacobites expected him to contribute to a regular remittance system, which may have alerted the government.[15] When the duke returned to England in June, he was placed under surveillance by Walpole.

During the period (1729-31) when Norfolk and the Jacobites were gaining power in the Grand Lodge system, the Hanoverian Masons were not passive in the face of this power shift. In June 1730 Orator Henley received a secret subsidy from Walpole to mount a campaign against the opposition Masons. Since his arrest by Delafaye, Henley had produced pro-government propaganda, and Walpole now wanted to exploit his insider's knowledge of Freemasonry to counter the Jacobites' ongoing publications. Thus, the press reported that Orator Henley was initiated on 11 June 1730 into the Prince William Lodge, Charing Cross, where "several Noblemen and Persons of Distinction" attended.[16] On 13 June he advertised that, in the absence of Grand Master Norfolk, he would entertain the Deputy Grand Master Blackerby and the society of Freemasons with an "Eulogium of Masonry, and a Gentleman will be ready to dispute on Gormogonism."[17] In his eccentric, rollicking sermons and publications, Henley would attack Walpole's enemies within and without the fraternity. He greatly admired the satirical techniques of Swift, his Tory rival, and he later explained his similar methods: "Our Advertisements...ought to be incomprehensible, Abracadabra, Jargon, Chimaera; to have Riddles; and we only the Key; be incog, Masquerade;...Cryptical...have their Arcana, Secrets, Mysteries, …and be Masonry, Cabals, Rosycrucian Lore, Alchymist…"[18]

In August Defoe, who had anonymously taken over the late Abel Boyer's position as Whig editor of *The Public State of Great-Britain*, joined the attack on the opposition Masons in his article, "Of the ridiculous Fraud of Free Masonry, and their pretended Secret detected and exposed." Working from his own inside knowledge, he asked rhetorically, "If this mighty Aenigma of the Freemasons be a Fraud, not withstanding it hath been so cried up in the World, as to have drawn in some persons of Distinction, to link themselves with Mechanicks, and sometimes with Worse People," then they should know the truth about "those Knights of the Leather-Apron," who utilize a rainbow "from the Pattern of an Arch."[19] Defoe seemed to hint at the Jacobite development of chivalric and Royal Arch themes.

On 20 August the playwright William Rufus Chetwood produced at Bartholomew Fair his Tragi-Comi-Farcical Ballad Opera, *The Generous Free-Mason: or, The Constant Lady. With the Humours of Squire Noodle and his Man Doodle.* The work was dedicated to the Grand Master (Norfolk) and top officers of "the Ancient and Honourable Society of Free and

---

[13] Stuart Papers: 142/141 (15 January 1731).

[14] *Ibid.*, 142/141-42 (8 February 1731).

[15] P. Monod, *Jacobitism*, 286.

[16] G. Midgley, *Life*, 131, 260-61.

[17] W.B. Hextall, "Orator Henley, M.A., 1692-1756," *AQC*, 29 (1916), 369.

[18] G. Midgley, *Life*, 89, 169.

[19] [Daniel Defoe], *The Political State of Great Britain* (London, 1730), XL, 210-19.

Accepted Masons," by "the author, a Free-Mason." Carol Howard gives a useful summary of the complicated and often zany plot:

> The drama centers on two genuine Masons who discover each other amidst a stock orientalist captivity plot set in Tunisia. The humorous subplot involves an elaborate ruse in which Squire Noodle, accompanied by his man-servant Doodle, submits unwillingly to a mock initiation into Freemasonry that results in a scene of comic humiliation as well as the comic substitution of appropriate marriages for inappropriate ones.[20]

In keeping with Norfolk's ecumenical agenda, Chetwood portrayed the universal brotherhood maintained by the fraternity, while still poking fun at some members' credulity.

In order to win the hand of his beloved Maria, who is betrothed to another, Sebastian plans to flee with her to Spain. His only regret at leaving England is that "from my noble Brethren I must part":

> Those Men, whose Lustre spreads from Pole to Pole,
> Possessing every Virtue of the Soul.
> But yet all Climes the Brotherhood adorn,
> As smiling Phoebus gilds the rosy morn.[21]

After they are captured by Tunisian pirates, Sebastian affirms to Mirza, the High Admiral, that he wears a glorious Masonic "badge," which leads Mirza to reveal that he too is a brother Mason. Sebastian asks, "Can it be possible!":

> In this barbarous Clime,
> Where Arts and Sciences are hardly known
> Our antient, noble, and most glorious Craft,
> (Which even Kings and Heroes have adorn'd)

Mirza assures him that "so Divine an Art/ Can not subsist but with Humanity," and then confesses that he was British-born but raised in Tunisia, where he was pressured to "forsake my Christian faith." But the succeeding king forgot this and promoted him to the Admiralty. Some English Masons residing in Tunisia recruited him and he was "made a Mason in most perfect Form."

In the meantime, Noodle is made a Mason in most imperfect form. In a comical satire on the credulous early history and chronology in Anderson's *Constitutions*, the initiator Davy claims that a shaving basin "was made out of half the Queen of Egypt's great Pearl, when she treated Marc Antony in the Highlands of Scotland."[22] This very basin was "given to our Honourable Society by Alexander the Great, when he turn'd Protestant after conquering North Wales." A common penknife was "made of Eve's Spanish Needle that she sew'd Adam's fig breeches with – when they were strip't by the Turks at the Siege of Namur." When Noodle dons a petticoat (substitute for the leather apron), he

---

[20] Carol Howard, "A Female Freemason on Stage?: Eliza Haywood's Patriotism at Henry Fielding's Haymarket Theatre," in Laura Engel, ed., *The Publics Open to Us All: Essays on Women in Performance in Eighteenth-Century England* (Newcastle, 2009), 142.

[21] William Rufus Chetwood, *The Generous Free-Mason* (London, 1731).

[22] *Ibid.*, 27.

will gain prophetic vision and second sight. The whalebone stay was made of "one of the Hairs of King Brobdingnagian's Beard, brought over by Captain Lemuel Gulliver."

Despite Chetwood's mockery of Anderson's credulous history, the comic opera made only slight hints at political partisanship. Thus, Noodle parrots the usual cries of anti-Jacobite mobs, "Murder! Fire! Popery, and Sedition!" and "Fire! Brimstone and Gunpowder!" Chetwood employed Henry Carey to set some songs, and he must have been aware that Carey had earlier been blacklisted because of his publications in support of Robert Harley, Lord Oxford. More recently, Carey published an anti-Walpolean satire, *A Learned Dissertation on Dumpling* (1726). In the concluding song to *The Generous Freemason*, Carey praised the Masons as international architects and builders, thus voicing the view of traditionalist brothers:

> By Masons' Art th' aspiring dome
> In various Columns shall arise:
> All Climates are their Native Home,
> Their God-like Actions reach the Skies.

The Generous Free-Mason was a popular success and continued to be performed at the fairs and the Haymarket Theatre.

The comical exposures and Tory-Jacobite inroads may have spurred Desaguliers to argue in Grand Lodge on 28 August that various protective measures must be taken to prevent "irregular" Masons from visiting "regular Lodges" and to provide "security against all open and Secret Enemies to the Craft."[23] His move was timely, for on 5 September "A.Z." wrote to the *Daily Journal* to attack Freemasonry in general. He reminded the public that Henry VI had repressed the fraternity because "the *Discontented* herded together in the same Manner, and the Gentry also underhand" supported the "malcontents."[24] He further connected seventeenth-century Masons with party faction: "From the like infamous Origin commenced those pernicious Names of Distinction, WHIG and TORY," spawn of "Field Conventiclers in Scotland" and "Irish Rapperies and Robbers." Repeating the charge of 1725 that the Freemasons claim Rosicrucian origins, A.Z. scoffed at the whole Solomonic-Hiramic tradition of Masonry.

Defoe, who in August published the Masons' oath of secrecy and affirmed that "Masonry is a mere Nothing," reprinted in September A.Z.'s diatribe, adding that "After this, we recommend to those Gentlemen and Persons of Distinction...to throw away the Apron and Gloves, to be ashamed of the scoundrel Society, and for the Future to treat the Introducers of the Fraud as they deserve."[25] Responding to these public controversies, the Whig officers of the Grand Lodge on 15 September admonished Anthony Sayer, first Grand Master in 1717, for taking part in illegal assemblies of dissatisfied Masons, "who were seeking to undermine the authority of the society they and others had so recently constituted."[26]

Worse was to come, for in October 1730 a renegade Mason from the Grand Lodge published an exposure, *Masonry Dissected*, that angered Hanoverians and Jacobites alike.

---

[23] R. Gould, *History*, III, 138.
[24] *EMP*, 233-36.
[25] [Defoe], *Political State*, 328-82.
[26] W.J. Hughan, *Memorials of the Masonic Union of A.D. 1813* (London, 1874), 4.

The author, Samuel Prichard, was disappointed that he got so little for his money after he joined "a Constituted and Regular Lodge," because the increasing expenses made it impossible for him to advance and to learn "the Mystery for which he has already paid."[27] Prichard disputed the claims to antiquity of the Grand Lodge, noting that "the Terms of Free and Accepted Masonry (as it now is) has not been heard of till within these Few Years." Even less credible was the claim that the Grand Lodge "Badge of Honour" is "more ancient and honourable than is the Star and Garter." Prichard argued that "Accepted Masons" were artificers (operatives), from whom "sprang the real Masons" (speculatives): "from both sprang the *Gormogons*, whose Grand-Master the *Volgi* deduces his Original from the *Chinese*, whose Writings, if to be credited, maintain the *Hypotheses* of the *Pre-Adamites*, and consequently must be more antique than Masonry."[28] Prichard predicted that the additional initiation fees demanded of visitors to new lodges "will be expended towards the forming another system of Masonry, the old Fabrick being so ruinous, that unless repair'd by some occult Mystery, will soon be annihilated."[29]

Prichard gave a crude version of the catechisms used in the first three degrees, which seemed to draw on the older Scottish traditions plus the newer master's degree. He also revealed the luridly frightening vow of secrecy that was so effective in maintaining silence outside the brotherhood. *Masonry Dissected* set off a furor in the Grand Lodge, while it ran into multiple editions. On 20 October Orator Henley advertised

> a new Oration in reply to Masonry Dissected, or the Freemasons Triumph, or hod and trowel, beat the whole field, for wager, against Prichard's jaw bone of an ass; being a defense of Masonry against yelping, braying, burring, snapping, snarling…and petulant chatter of late about it in papers and pamphlets.[30]

On 30 November Defoe responded with his anonymous pamphlet, *The Perjur'd Freemason Detected; and yet the Honour and Antiquity of the Society of Freemasons Preserv'd and Detected* (1730). Calling himself "A Freemason," he scorned Prichard for breaking his oath of secrecy and then defended the Grand Lodge system as the authentic core of Masonry.

In the meantime, "Masons of the Old Order" took advantage of Prichard's exposure and Henley's defense to ironically propose a Cromwellian "new modelizing" of the system. In November "Peter Farmer" dedicated to Henley his pamphlet, *New Model for the Rebuilding Masonry on a Stronger Basis than the Former* (1730).[31] He attributed to Henley "a curious dissertation," *The Free Masons Trimph; or Hod and Trowel beat the Whole Field*, though it is unknown if it was published or just delivered at the Oratory. In a parody of the question and answer format used during initiation into each degree, the questioner seems to draw on the ancient traditions of operative Masonry, which have been lost as newer members build only castles in the air, while they "attend/ On the Place-insuring Friend." The questioner asks, "Did you not belong to those/That Sam Prichard did expose?" To reform the fraternity, the high initiation fees must be abolished, but "some antick

---

27 Samuel Prichard, *Masonry Dissected*, 3rd ed. (London, 1730), 6-8.
28 *Ibid.*, 7.
29 *Ibid.*, 30.
30 Albert Mackey, "Orator Henley and Masonry," *The Freemason and Masonic Illustrated*, 8 (2 October 1875), 428.
31 EMP, 237-58.

Gestures and Grimaces" will be allowed, as confirmed by "the Orator," who proves it "by the tale of Jews,/ who held some Rites of ancient Use/ Amongst the Egyptians, after they/ From Pharaoh's Host had run away." In a series of songs, Peter Farmer defended the Masons' exuberant drinking and rejected the charges of sodomy, political and religious factionalism, and treason. One song "at a Bacchanalian Banquet of Freemasons" gained the approbation of "the late D. of W. [Wharton]." The rather bizarre pamphlet concluded with a poem on "the Downfall of Masonry," and accused Prichard of being worse than "crooked Richard [III]" who only took a crown and slew women and children, while Prichard

> In publick makes his wild Brevada.
> Of overturning a Community;
> The greatest that e'er held in Unity.
> All round the Globe our Arts diffus'd
> Emp'rors and Kings our Friendship chus'd;
> And thought it not the least Disgrac'd
> In Masons Lodge to take a Place...[32]

On 15 December another critic of Prichard published *A Defense of Masonry, Occasion'd by a Pamphlet called Masonry Dissected*, in which he discussed the similarity of beliefs and rituals among the Pythagoreans, Essenes, Cabalists, Druids, and Freemasons. In the process, he reinforced the claims to Jewish origins maintained by Ramsay:

> The Essenes among the Jews were a sort of Pythagoreans, and corresponded in many Particulars with the Practice of the Fraternity... For Example: When a Person desired to be admitted into their Society, he was to pass through two Degrees of Probation before he could be perfect Master of their Mysteries. When he was received into the Class of Novices, he was presented with a white Garment...
>
> The Cabalists, another Sect, dealt in hidden and mysterious ceremonies. The Jews had a great Regard for this Science, and thought they made uncommon Discoveries by means of it. They divided their Knowledge into Speculative and Operative. David and Solomon, they say, were exquisitely skilled in it, and no body at first presumed to commit it to Writing; ...the Perfection of their Skill consisted in what the *Dissector* calls Lettering of it, or by ordering the Letters of a Word in a particular manner.[33]

With the opposition and Jacobite Masons apparently winning their public relations campaign, Walpole embarked on one of the most bizarre of his many projects to discredit the opposition. He paid "Orator" Henley £100 annually to publish *The Hyp Doctor*, in which Henley posed as "Sir Isaac Ratcliffe," a Jacobite physician who travelled three years in Europe, supported by money from Stuart symphathizers at Oxford. By linking the fictitious narrator to the Radcliffe family, who included the late Jacobite physician John Radcliffe, the Jacobite martyr James Radcliffe, 3rd Earl of Derwentwater, and

---

[32] *Ibid.*, 257.
[33] Anon., *A Defense of Masonry* (London, 1731); reprinted in D. Knoop, G. Jones, D. Hamer, *EMC*, 217-18.

Charles Radcliffe, current Jacobite-Masonic plotter, Henley made clear his Whig agenda. Moreover, Walpole may have informed him about Charles's secret visits to England.

In the first issue (15 December 1730), Henley hinted that certain English politicians – especially a "treasurer" – had succumbed to blandishments from the Jacobite Masons. This reminder of the 3rd Earl of Sunderland's secret collaboration in the Atterbury plot, perhaps frightened off his son, Charles Spencer, 5th Earl of Sunderland, who refused the invitation to serve as Grand Master of the Grand Lodge. Though Sunderland was a Whig, Norfolk's Jacobite allies favored him because of his opposition to Walpole and George II (who despised him). The Grand Lodge next proposed the rakish Charles Colyear, 2nd Earl of Portmore, because he was the grandson of James II's mistress, and his father had earlier dabbled in Jacobite politics.[34] But he too refused the office. Bowing to Hanoverian pressure, the Grand Mastership finally went to the ineffectual but properly Whiggish Thomas Cook, Lord Lovell, member of the Duke of Richmond's social set. More importantly, Lovell was the wealthy neighbor and strong supporter of Walpole.[35] The prime minister had rewarded him with the sinecure of joint-Postmaster General in England in 1725. On 15 December 1730, the Desaguliers party complained that the former Grand Master Anthony Sayer was making "clandestine" and "irregular" initiations, and he was warned to "do nothing so irregular for the future!"[36]

In January 1731 two Hanoverian Masons collaborated in an attack on the opposition journal, *The Craftsman*, which had recently published the "Hague Letter," revealing Walpole's secret negotiations toward the Treaty of Vienna, which infuriated his supposed ally, Cardinal Fleury. John, Lord Hervey, and Sir William Yonge, Grand Lodge members, published *Sedition and Defamation Display'd: In a Letter to the Author of the Craftsman* (1731). In the introduction, Hervey targeted Bolingbroke's "Baseness, Ingratitude, and Treachery," and William Pulteney's determination "to destress and disturb that Prince and that Family to which he owed the highest Obligations."[37] They accused the "pretended Patriots" of encouraging the Jacobites:

> their drooping Spirits are again revived; those who were before despised, and almost forgotten, who were in their own Country as Strangers and Vagabonds in a foreign Land, after many years of fruitless Struggles to subject their County to a strange and vagabond Prince... The Jacobites refused to receive those Indendiaries or their Patrons, as their new Allies, till they had given convincing Proofs...that they are not so far Germanized, as to submit any longer to that Family, whom they treat as Tyrants and Usurpers.[38]

The publication deliberately paved the way for the arrest of Richard Francklin, printer of the *Craftsman*, a few days later.

The perception that Jacobites were gaining ground in both politics and Masonry provoked further countermoves. In January 1731 Joseph Morgan, who had worked with

---

[34] See "Charles Spencer, Fifth Earl of Sunderland," and "Charles Colyear, Second Earl of Portmore," in *ODNB*.

[35] R. Berman, *Schism*, , 2, 147, 233.

[36] R. Gould, *History*, III, 138.

[37] John, Lord Hervey, and Pulteney, William, *Sedition and and Defamation Display'd*, ed. Alexander Pettit (1731; New York, 1997), 1v.

[38] *Ibid.*, 35-36.

Curll on the *Whartonia*, was so worried by the problems in the Grand Lodge that he published a defense in *Phoenix Britannicus*.[39] A member of the loyalist Horn lodge, Morgan dedicated the work to Richmond, praising the duke's earlier service as Grand Master, when the Grand Lodge won "universal applause":

> If all the social Virtues of the Mind;
> If an extensive Love to all Mankind;
> If hospitable welcome to a Guest;
> If speedy Charity to the Distress'd;
> If due Regard to Liberty and Laws;
> Zeal for our King, and for our Country's cause;
> If these are Principles deserving Fame,
> Let MASONS then enjoy the Praise they claim.[40]

Morgan then lamented that despite their benevolent role, the Grand Lodge Masons continued to receive vicious criticism from their rivals:

> Should fifty mercenary Wretches, for a miserable Pittance, nefariously, not to say perjuriously, attempt to bespatter those who would only answer them with the Scorn they deserve, they would be-mire themselves with their own Filth. And what mighty Feats of Chivalry have they done, who, thro' Excess of Gormogonian Smartness, exquisitely insinuate, in the News Papers, That they are glad at not finding any thing greatly Indecent in MA-SONRY! Have they done more than turn the Tables upon their own inconsiderable Selves!
>
> Are not the MASONS, obviously in the eye of the Sun, a very numerous, a respectable Body of MEN? Would a MONTAGUE, a NORFOLK, a RICHMOND, a BEDFORD, a LOVEL connive at indecencies! Would a DALKEITH, a INCHIQUIN, a PAISLEY, a KINGSTON, a COL-ERAINE, a SUNDERLAND, a PORTMORE, and abundance more of our right worthy Chieftains, Countenance Immoralities! Barbarous Nonsense!

Morgan's praise of all previous Grand Masters – English, Irish, and Scottish – had one telling omission, the Duke of Wharton. Though Wharton's death in May 1731 diminished the influence of the Gormogons, Henley continued to use *The Hyp Doctor* to mock the "Chinese" fraternity, its claim to Hebrew illumination, its connections with York and the northern Jacobites, and its subversive spread into foreign countries. Pope added a note to *The Dunciad*, in which he scorned Henley's Whiggish propaganda: "This man had an hundred pounds a year given him for the secret service of a weekly paper of unintelligible nonsense, called the Hyp-Doctor."[41] Until its last sputtering out on 20 January 1741, Henley's journal remained the most peculiar of Walpole's weapons against the Jacobite Masons.

---

[39] Harry Sirr, "J. Morgan and his *Phoenix Britannicus*, with Notes on his Other Works," *AQC*, 19 (1906), 127-36; for his forename Joseph, see J.E.S. Tuckett, "Some Further Light on J. Morgan of the *Phoenix Britannicus*," *AQC*, 26 (1913), 71-82.

[40] J. Morgan, *Phoenix Britannicus* (London, 1731), Dedication.

[41] A. Pope, *Dunciad*, 247.

In February 1731 two opposition Masons, Aaron Hill and Alexander Pope, helped to arrange the production at Drury Lane of David Mallet's drama, *Eurydice*, with Prologue and Epilogue by Hill. The play was a popular success, running for thirteen performances through April, which alarmed the government. Mallet, who came from the Scottish Malloch family, was careful in London to shield his Catholic family's Jacobitism, for members had been "out" in 1715 and would be again in 1745.[42] Though it is unknown if Mallet was a Freemason, his close associates such as Hill, Pope, Allan Ramsay, and James Thomson were "brothers." Thus, when the play was attacked as Jacobite propaganda, his circle of Masonic friends was indirectly targeted.

In *Remarks on the Tragedy of Eurydice. In which It is endeavoured to prove the said Tragedy is wrote in favour of the Pretender, and is a scurrilous Libel against the present Establishement* (1731), the anonymous critic argued "that it was written with a View to serve the Pretender, and to revive among us the failing spirit of Jacobitism. Insolent attempt!"[43] The critic admitted that he had not read the play, but he was sure that it was an "audacious, temeracious Insult upon our present happy Constitution," and that it was planned by "an eminent Hand, remarkable for great Parts and great ones, who made use of the [author] as a Tool" (an apparent allusion to Bolingbroke or Pope). He further mocked Sir Charles Wogan for his rescue of Princess Clementina, claiming that he was portrayed in the character of Talbot, who with another (the "two Irish Traytors"), were "both desperate Fellows, and as bigoted to Popery as the Pretender." But fortunately, her proxy marriage failed, and she and James are estranged. It was perhaps no coincidence that Mallet soon left the employment of the Whig Duke of Montrose and subsequently enrolled at St. Mary's Hall, which was under the leadership of the Jacobite Dr. King.

With such charges of Jacobite subversion in the air, Walpole intensified his surveillance, and his vigilance was actually justified by events. In November 1730 the twenty year-old Henry Hyde, Viscount Cornbury, had arrived in Rome, where he resided with the Jacobite Patrick Darcy and renewed his friendship with Charles Radcliffe.[44] It is unknown if Cornbury shared Masonic ties with Radcliffe, but given the fraternal affiliation of Orrery, his close collaborator, it seems likely. After consulting with Radcliffe, he and the Duchess of Buckingham made secret visits to the Pretender in January 1731, when he presented his and Orrery's restoration plan to James. The duchess was the illegitimate daughter of James II and thus James III's half-sister. An immensely wealthy lady, she was described by contemporaries as half-mad with pride and by Whig historians as "mad *tout court.*"[45] Cornbury was the great-grandson of Edward Hyde, the famous Lord Chancellor Clarendon, and during one meeting, James wept when he recalled the loyalty of the Hydes to the Stuarts.

The plan agreed upon "was to win over leaders of both sides of the Opposition with offers of places and favours and to appeal to France to mount an expedition to restore the Stuarts. Whigs such as William Pulteney, Earl of Berkeley, and the dukes of Dorset,

---

[42] Sandro Jung, *David Mallet, Anglo-Scot: Poetry, Patronage, and Politics in the Age of Union* (Newark, 2008), 20-29.

[43] Anon., *Remarks on the Tragedy of Eurydice* (London, 1731), 7-8, 14, 18.

[44] J. Ingamells, *Dictionary*, "Lord Cornbury."

[45] E. Cruickshanks, *Lord Cornbury, Bolingbroke and a Plan to Restore the Stuarts, 173-1732*. Royal Stuart Papers, 27 (1986), 2-3. The following information comes from her study.

Somerset, and Argyll would have places, while Tories such as William Shippen, William Wyndham, and lords Bathurst, Gower, and Bolingbroke (the latter reluctantly accepted by James) would lead the new ministry. During their meetings, James promised Cornbury that he would deliver his country from "tyranny and oppression" and solemnly undertook "to preserve the Church of England and the English Constitution." Cornbury was greatly impressed not only by James but by his Scottish favorite, James Murray, titular Earl of Dunbar, whom he believed to have been maligned in England. He accepted the place of lord of the bedchamber at the Stuart court, before leaving Rome in April and returning to England in August. Stosch, who had difficulty penetrating Cornbury's secrecy, reported to Newcastle that he was a "man of spirit, very phlegmatic and sober, and therefore very dangerous, if it is true that he has thrown himself into the Jacobite party."[46]

After Cornbury's departure, on 2 May 1731 James sent Orrery his support of their plan and gave him full powers to negotiate with the court of Versailles. When the vigilant Walpole threatened to send Orrery to the Tower if he tried to go to France, the earl then recommended to James that Captain Charles Hardy, a former naval officer, should go instead. Wharton had earlier recommended Hardy to James as "an honest English gentleman," who was "removed from the Navy for his zeal for the common cause."[47] Though Orrery's health was deteriorating, he continued to collaborate with Cornbury and Bolingbroke on the plot, and in July 1731 he spent a month in Dublin, where he called on his old friend Swift. The dean wrote Lord Bathurst, who was privy to the Orrery-Cornbury plan, that Orrery "gives a very indifferent account of affairs on your side. You stick together like sand, and cannot agree in any single *point de veue*."[48] Unfortunately, there is no further record of their Dublin conversations, so that we do not know if Orrery confided the plan to Swift. On 17 July Lord Boyle wrote to his father, expressing his relief that he arrived safely in Dublin and promising to attend him when he returns to England and then "as far as Calais, to see you safe on the Gallick shore."[49] He hoped that "a better Clymate and a happier Country may restore you to that degree of Health which I beseech God to grant you."

Janetta Guite claims that Orrery actually accompanied Hardy to Paris in late July 1731, where they learned that their plotting with Dillon and negotiations with France and Spain had become "a complete fiasco."[50] If true, their journey was shrouded in secrecy, while Lord Boyle collaborated in covering it up by sending disinformation to his correspondents. On 3 August Boyle wrote Kempe that his father plans to leave in September and to stay in Paris all winter. He then apologized for not being able to recommend Kempe to the Duke of Dorset, who "must prefer Friends of the Ministry to those who are not." And he must suspect that "as I have been bred at the Feet of Gamaliel, my intimacies run in an anti-ministerial Channel. I believe they will ever flow in the same Course, for I look upon a Chief Minister to be another denomination for a Chief Tyrant.[51] Unfortunately for the plot, Orrery suddenly died on 28 August in London and was buried on 11

[46] J. Ingamells, "Lord Cornbury." on-line *Dictionary.*
[47] L. Melville, *Life and Writings*, 50.
[48] J. Swift, *Corresondence*, III, 406 and n.8.
[49] Orrery, *Orrery Papers*, I, 91.
[50] Janetta Guite, "The Jacobite Cause, 1730-1740: The International Dimension" (Ph.D. Dissertation: McMaster University, 1987), 134.
[51] Orrery, *Orrery Papers*, I, 92.

September in Westminster Abbey. Bolingbroke, who had secretly collaborated with Orrery, sent his condolences to Boyle, and the Jacobites were encouraged that the new 5th Earl of Orrery maintained his Stuart sympathies, though he would act much more cautiously than his father.

The 5th Earl would subsequently become a frequent visitor to Swift, and he probably learned that Swift was the ghost writer for the *Memoirs of Capt. John Creichton, Written by Himself* (1731), privately printed in Dublin, almost certainly by Faulkner. Swift had met the octogenarian Creichton in 1728, when staying with Sir Arthur Acheson in Armagh, where he and the Jacobite Leslie brothers enjoyed the old soldier's accounts of his experiences as a royalist Irish officer in Scotland in the 1680s. In 1729, working with Creichton in Dublin, Swift assembled and edited the memoirs, interjecting much of his own political and religious bias, in order to produce "a pro-Stuart Episcopalian polemical history of Presbyterian sedition."[52] In his anonymous "Advertisement to the Reader," Swift coyly distanced himself from Creichton's beliefs:

> The Author of these Memoirs, Capt. John Creichton, is still alive, and resides in the Northern Part of this Kingdom. He is a very worthy Man; but of the old Stamp: And it is probable, that some of his Principles will not relish very well, in the present Disposition of the World. His Memoirs are therefore to be received like a Posthumous Work, and as containing Facts, which very few alive, except himself, can remember: Upon which Account, none of his generous Subscribers are, in the Least answerable for many Opinions, relating to the Publick, both in Church and State, which he seems to justify, and in the Vindication of which, to the Hazard of his Life, and the Loss of his Fortune, he spent the most useful Part of his Days.[53]

The eighty-three year-old Creichton wanted to clear his reputation from the charges by radical Presbyterians, "a Fanatick Rebellious Party," that he was "a Persecutor of Saints, and a Man of Blood."[54] Swift wanted to counter the anti-Episcopalian propaganda of Whig historians like Gilbert Burnet and Robert Wodrow. In the process, the two collaborators were vulnerable to government prosecution, as Creichton declared:

> The [Williamite] Revolution was then an Event altogether new, and put many Men, much wiser than myself, at a loss how to proceed. I had taken the Oath of Allegiance to King James; and, having been bred up under the strictest Principles of Loyalty, could not force my Conscience to dispense with that Oath, during his Majesty's Life... And lastly, the established Religion in Scotland, which was Episcopal, under which I had been educated, and to which I had always the highest Veneration, was now utterly destroyed in that Kingdom; (although preserved in the other Two) and the Presbyterian Kirk, which had ever been my greatest Aversion, exalted in its Stead.[55]

---

[52] Ian Higgins, "Jonathan Swift's Memoirs of a Jacobite," in A. Macinnes, K. German, L.Graham, eds., *Living with Jacobitism*, 71-84..

[53] [Jonathan Swift], *Memoirs of Capt. John Creichton, Written by Himself* (1731), Advertisement.

[54] *Ibid.*, 10.

[55] *Ibid.*, 134.

Avoiding explicit support of the Stuart Pretenders, Swift portrayed William of Orange as willing to be tolerant but manipulated by the radical Covenanters in Scotland. Though Orrery and the Leslie brothers knew that Swift was the ghost-writer, Faulkner did not reveal Swift's role until 1762. Swift's sympathy for the "almost posthumous" Creichton foreshadowed his support of a more dangerous, current Jacobite activist, Sir Charles Wogan, in 1732.

*
* *

While participants in the Cornbury-Orrery-Bolingbroke plot negotiated with sympathetic French diplomats, their actions were monitored by Earl Waldegrave, current British ambassador in Paris. On his appointment in August 1730, Waldegrave had been instructed by Newcastle, Walpole's foreign minister, "to keep a vigilant eye" on the Duke of Berwick and the Jacobites in Paris, and not to spare expenses "in subsisting Gambarini and other effective spies."[56] Despite his conversion to Protestantism and submission to George II, Waldegrave maintained friendly relations with Berwick, his uncle, and he was undoubtedly aware of the Masonic activities of his cousin, Charles Radcliffe. The ambassador also befriended Ramsay, who sought his help in obtaining copies of manuscripts in French libraries.[57] When Waldegrave joined the second Parisian lodge, "Louis d'Argent," which included members loyal to Walpole and the Hanoverian Alliance, he gained a base for infiltration of *Écossais* meetings.[58] On 1 April 1731 Newcastle sent a private letter to the ambassador, alerting him to new plots: "It is certain the Jacobites begin to conceive hopes of France, & therefore the greatest Attention imaginable should be given to that. You have *a way* of knowing what Foundation there is for it, and whether France is playing us any such Trick or no."[59] Through his Jacobite kinship and Masonic connections, he did indeed have "*a way*" of learning about emerging Jacobite plots.

In 1731 the international situation became more promising for the Jacobites and their Masonic supporters, as the Hanoverian Alliance between Britain, France, and Sweden began to unravel. In each country, the reigning ministries had become increasingly unpopular. For Walpole and Newcastle, an especially worrisome development was the revival of Swedish-Jacobite links, as the Holstein opposition gained ground against the Hessian regime. It is unknown if Waldegrave learned about the initiation of Counts Bielke and Sack in Paris in late 1729, but he probably did report on the initiation of Count Axel Eric Wrede Sparre on 4 May 1731 into the Jacobite lodge in Paris.[60] Since his arrival in April 1730, Wrede Sparre had been welcomed by the Jacobite admirers of his father, Eric Sparre, the former Swedish ambassador in Paris, who had collaborated with Wharton and Mar in developing the Gyllenborg-Swedish plot, which had a significant Masonic component. Wrede Sparre had worked with Tessin at Vienna in 1726, when the Swedes

---

[56] Wilfrid G. Fisher, AA Cavalcade of Freemasons as Recorded in *The Gentleman's Magazine* for 1732,@ *AQC*, 76 (1963), 57.

[57] Bodleian: Carte MS. 227.f.54 (Ramsay to Carte, 20 April 1732).

[58] P. Chevallier, *Ducs*, 31, 34,182

[59] J.C.D. Clark, *The Memoirs and Speeches of James, Second Earl Waldegrave, 1742-1763* (Cambridge, 1988), 26.

[60] B.J.. Bergquist, *St. Johanneslogen den Nordiska Första* (Stockholm, 1999), 33.

reassured the Jacobites of their continuing support, and Tessin reinforced those vows in 1728 when he visited Paris with his new wife Ulla, the sister of Wrede Sparre. Tessin informed Daniel O'Brien that he had persuaded a majority of the Swedish Diet to begin repayment of the "Debt of Görtz" to James III.[61]

Meanwhile in France, the Jacobites received news that Wharton had died of a fever in a Spanish monastery on 31 May 1731. During the last two years of his life, the duke intermittently struggled to maintain sobriety and to seriously consider spiritual and philosophical questions. In spring 1729 he went on a religious retreat in a convent outside Paris and, for a while, considered taking monastic vows.[62] He studied the works of Fenelon and Ramsay and began a poetic translation of *Telemachus*. Though the monks greatly admired him and believed his conversion sincere, he fell into his old ways after leaving the monastery. When he returned to Spain, he rejoined his Irish regiment at Lerida and reportedly lived a regular life. Wharton was encouraged in his attempt at personal reformation by his new friend and probable Masonic brother, Sir Charles Wogan, and the two discussed each other's religious and historical writings (their collaboration will be discussed later, when Wogan sends his and Wharton's writings to Swift in 1732).[63]

Determined to reclaim his literary reputation, Wharton worked on a manuscript about the Stuart martyr, Mary Queen of Scots. He sketched out a plan to write "A History of My Times," and completed a first, well-written section on Lady Masham, the Duchess of Marlborough, and Sacheverell, up to 1714.[64] Thomas Carte obtained this manuscript and noted that Wharton observed that both political parties hated him, so he could now be objective as an historian. In spring 1731, his body weakened by years of dissipation, he was taken into a Franciscan convent, where he wrote "The Fear of Death. An Ode," which was later sent from Spain and published in London in 1739.[65] The dying Wharton described his "lab'ring Frame," which "dire Convulsions rend," but he rejected "the threat'nd Terrours" of death's reign. To die is "but to slumber into Immortality," leaving behind "Seditious Tumults," the "Feuds" of zealots, and "Debated Empires." According to the monks, he "made a very penitent and Christian end."[66] He had signed his will, Philip *James* Wharton, "the second forename presumably assumed to indicate his Jacobitism."[67]

In London, when Mary Caesar learned of Wharton's death, she grieved over the loss of a friend whom she had long defended against his detractors

> He was Not Onely the Finest Writer but the Finest Orator, and Had a most Happy Adress and Delivery Even in His Common discourse. The Duke was Him self so senceable of His Errors Often to say He Wanted No sence but common sence. Tis said Just before he Dy'd He Repeated these Lines:
> When you shall my Unhappy Deeds Relate
> Speak of me As I Am – Nothing Extenuate

---

[61] Stuart Papers, 234/138. O'Brien's memoir to Tessin in 1741.
[62] L. Melville, *Life*, 237-39.
[63] See ahead, Chapter 13.
[64] Bodleian: Carte MS. 125, ff. 96-100.
[65] Duke of Wharton, *The Fear of Death. An Ode by the Late Duke of Wharton* (London, 1739), 1-4.
[66] L. Melville, *Life*, 252.
[67] "Philip, Duke of Wharton," *ODNB*.

But set me Down Nought in Malice.[68]

With Lord Strafford, Mrs. Caesar reminisced about the recent deaths of Lord Orrery and his close friend Wharton:

> Lord Orrery Liv'd Not to Hear of the Death of His Great Friend and Tuter the Depriv'd Bishop of Rochester, but Did of the Death of the Duke of Wharton, Whose Will When He last Left England He plac'd in that Lord's Hands, Who Found Him self, and Mr Caesar Executors, With Sr. Christopher Musgrave Interlind. The Duke was as all Agreed Of the Best Natural and Acquird Parts, and He could nither tire Nor Drownd them. For Mr Clavering told me Who saw Him, After sitting Up all Night, Lay Him self on the ground and Wrote a True Britton, Sending it from thence to the Press, and it came Out that Day.[69]

James III lamented the destitution of Wharton's widow and employed Orrery to help secure her jointure, but the earl's death in August placed that burden on his son John, Lord Boyle.[70]

As the 5th Earl of Orrery, John acquired *The Life and Writings of Philip Late Duke of Wharton* (London, 1732), which reprinted and expanded the *Memoirs of the Life of His Grace Philip late Duke of Wharton. By an Impartial Hand* (1731), written by an acquaintance of Wharton.[71] In the 1732 preface, the editor observed:

> As few Persons could equal the Duke of Wharton in Extensiveness of Wit, Liveliness of Imagination, all the Graces of a most persuasive Oratory, and an exceeding Frankness of Temper and good Nature that shone out in all his Actions and Conversation; so it must be confess'd, that hardly any Person ever made a worse Use of those amiable Qualities, or took more Pains than his Grace seem'd to do, to turn to his own Disadvantage those fine Talents, that, rightly improv'd, and apply'd, might have made him, not only an Honour to his Country, but an ornament to human Nature.[72]

None of the contemporary English critics recognized Wharton's popularity and respect among the Irish exiles in Spain, who did not agree with the current image of him as a drunken and cowardly wastrel. His friendship with Sir Charles Wogan in his last years, to be discussed later, provides a new perspective on his attempt at personal rehabilitation.

Alexander Pope, who was a good friend of the Caesars, did not share their sympathy for Wharton – reportedly because of jealousy over the duke's earlier relation with Martha Blount. But he also knew of Atterbury's disillusionment with Wharton after his Catholic conversion. Three years later, Pope would publish a harsh portrait of the late Jacobite Grand Master. In his "Epistle to Cobham" (1734), he used Wharton as an example of "the Ruling Passion":

---

[68] M. Caesar, *Journal*, 59.

[69] *Ibid.*, 58.

[70] "Philip, Duke of Wharton," *ODNB*.

[71] Bodleian: MS. 2591.d.6 [7]. *The Library and Collection of Autograph Letters of the Right Honourable The Earl of Cork and Orrery* (London: Christie, 21 November 1905), #11.

[72] *The Life and Writings of Philip Late Duke of Wharton* (London, 1732) I, Preface.

Wharton, the scorn and wonder of our days,
Whose ruling Passion was the Lust of Praise;
Women and Fools must like him or he dies;
Tho' wond'ring Senates hung on all he spoke,
The Club must hail him master of the joke.
Shall parts so various aim at nothing new?
He'll shine a Tully and a Wilmot too.
Then turns repentant, and his God adores
With the same spirit that he drinks and whores;

....

A Tyrant to the wife his heart approves;
A Rebel to the very king he loves;
He dies, sad out-cast of each church and state,
And harder still! Flagitious, yet not great.
Ask you why Wharton broke thro' ev'ry rule?
'Twas all for fear the Knaves should call him Fool.
Nature well known, no prodigies remain,
Comets are regular and Wharton plain.[73]

After Wharton's death, the *Écossais* Grand Mastership was passed on to Sir Hector Maclean, a Scottish protégé of Mar and current collaborator with Ramsay. Since the seventeen year-old Maclean's arrival in France in 1721, Mar had pressed James to fund his education, for he believed the young Highlander was intellectually gifted. Despite the often niggardly response of James, Maclean became "well versed in Divinity, History, Politics, Civil Law, and Mathematics," while "he spoke English, Irish, Gaelic, French, and Italian, and understood Latin well."[74] Maclean was aware of the factions in Rome and, like Derwentwater, he hoped to conciliate Marischal, Ormonde, O'Brien, Dillon, Ramsay, and others who had been divided by the feud between Atterbury and Mar.[75] With the deaths of the two antagonists (Atterbury in February and Mar in May 1732), Maclean and Derwentwater perhaps envisioned a revitalized Freemasonry as a secret vehicle for unifying the Jacobites (they would later collaborate on Masonic affairs in France).

The German Masonic historian Hugo Ball argues that Ramsay had unfolded to James, Maclean, Radcliffe, and others a grand design for "securing the support of French noblemen for the Jacobites...by making them Masons in a British mould."[76] Bernard Fay adds that Ramsay hoped to form a Masonic "syndicate" of great but fallen aristocratic families in Europe, including the Stuarts, Sobieskis, Rohans, and Bouillons, who were essentially hostile to the reigning ministries.[77] His new employment gave him ample opportunity to undertake this agenda – as well as new chivalric developments within Freemasonry.

---

[73] Alexander Pope, *The Poetical Works*, ed. Herbert Davis (London, 1966), 288-89.
[74] J.P. Maclean, *A History of the Clan Maclean* (Cincinnati, 1889), 223; quoted in J.E.S. Tuckett, "The Early History of Freemasonry in France," *AQC*, 31 (1918), 20.
[75] NA: SP 78/203 (April 1732 through December 1733).
[76] Quoted in P. Chevallier, *Ducs*, 134.
[77] B. Fay, "Origines," 175.

Appointed tutor to the four year-old Prince of Turenne, Ramsay became the close friend and confidant of the boy's father, Charles Godefroi, Duc de Bouillon. Despite his family's earlier disaffection from the court, Bouillon served as "grand chambellan" to Louis XV from 1728 onwards. Taking advantage of his new position with the Prince de Turenne but aiming further at the young Stuart princes, Ramsay prepared *A Plan of Education for a Young Prince*, which was published in London in 1732. The treatise presented an odd amalgam of mysticism, mathematics, and science, with a non-partisan political appeal that would further the Jacobite-opposition agenda of Orrery, Cornbury, and Bolingbroke.

Ramsay opened with an unusual affirmation for an educator of children: "True Education is the Art of curing the Diseases of the Mind, so as to restore our decay'd Faculties to their primitive Vigour... Thus we re-install in their different Functions the Philosopher, the Painter and the Lover, of which our Spiritual Nature seems to be composed."[78] He then presented a very non-Hanoverian, non-Walpolean vision of a future monarch: "The following Plan is what I would propose for the Education of a Prince, who may one Day govern a Nation whose Genius is equally proper for Learning and War, and who loves a King that can direct its Councils by his Wisdom, as well as defend its Interests by his Courage."[79] After strong training in the Classics, the prince will advance in mathematics until he is 'initiated into these Mysteries of the sublimer Geometry.'[80] This will lead him to a perception of 'the first and soveraign Geometer, who created and dispos'd all Things with Order, Measure, and Proportion," a Masonic-sounding allusion. The first laws of motion are the "voluntary Establishments of an Intelligent Cause, and not the necessary Effects of a blind Force." Then, in a startling combination of Newton's ether theory and Pythgorean-Egyptian-Cabalistic esoteric theory, Ramsay proclaimed:

> That the Creation is but an Image or Picture of the divine Perfections, and therefore bears a Character of his Infinity and Immensity...
>
> That the Cause of Attraction, and all the other wonderful Phenomena of Nature depend upon the Action of an ethereal Fluid that pervades all Things: That as the infinite Spirit, present everywhere, acts upon all intelligent Natures, and gives them at once both Being and Well-Being, so this ethereal Fluid is like the Sensorium of the Deity, by which he acts upon all material Beings, as our Body is the Medium, by which our Soul acts on all objects that surround us. This seems to be the true Meaning of the Orientals, the Egyptians and Pythagoricians, when they consider'd the Divinity as the Soul of the World, and this ethereal Fluid, purer than Light itself, as the Body of God.[81]

Though Ramsay so far presented a model of a mystical Masonic prince, he added the role of a "patriot prince," such as Orrery, Cornbury, and Bolingbroke currently advocated. Notions of absolute monarchy and hereditary succession should be "concealed from a young Prince, and especially an English one":

---

[78] Andrew Michael Ramsay, *A Plan of Education for a Young Prince* (London, 1732), i.

[79] *Ibid.*, ii.

[80] *Ibid.*, iii, viii.

[81] *Ibid.*, v.

He should be taught on the contrary, that the universal, free, unbrib'd Consent of the States of a Kingdom, is what gives in each Generation the true Right to Crowns: The Hereditary Right was never exactly observ'd in England for many Generations together...

The constitution of England seems to be the most adapted to prevent these Inconveniencies [Anarchical and Monarchical Frenzy]. The States of the Nation, assembled in Parliament, seem to be the best Bridles of the Multitude and Kings; but because Human Nature is weak and imperfect, this excellent Constitution may be spoil'd and corrupted by Bribery, Faction, and Prejudices.[82]

James III must have approved of this message, for he was currently encouraging his supporters to work with Tories and Whigs to overcome Walpole and bring about a restoration. At the urging of Daniel O'Brien, James now placed Ramsay on a colonel's list, making him eligible for a pension, and Ramsay welcomed his revived favor with the Stuart court. However, he was unable to implement his educational plan with his young ward, for the Prince of Turenne died in March 1732. Ramsay now turned his attention to researching and writing a history of the Bouillons, who believed that they were direct descendants of the Knights Templar. Godfrey of Bouillon, Crusader King of Jerusalem, who died in 1100, was "the totem of the family."[83] The duchesses of Bouillon participated in an effort to "revive in part the ancient crusades...however, without the view of conquering the Holy Land."[84] The pious female members of the household called themselves "chevalières de la Croix." In addition, the mother of Ramsay's late pupil was a Sobieski and kinned to the Polish wife of James III.

Thus, as Ramsay worked on his *Histoire de Turenne* and studied the history of the Templars, his plan to encourage a form of chivalric (Templar?) Masonry had strikingly contemporary relevance. Moreover, the controversial tradition that he implemented a Masonic "Rite of Ramsay," also called the "Rite Ancien de Bouillon," may have some historical foundation.[85] A London lodge, constituted in 1732, was reported to be working the Bouillon rite circa 1740.[86] Gustave Bord grants that it is not known exactly when the "Rite of Bouillon," which officially emerged in 1774, was established, but he cautiously observes: "that the Duc de Boullion founded a special regime, and that at his side Ramsay wanted to revive the Masonry of Godefroy de Bouilllon, that is to say at the epoch of the Crusades, one is right to suppose that this new rite was the work of collaboration between the two persons."[87] In the Bouillon MS., allegedly from 1740, the Crusaders under Godefroy de Bouillon discovered the lost word, the Hebrew name of God, and learned the original traditions of masonry, which had been distorted in the centuries after Solomon: "so that the return of the Crusaders introduced once more into Europe the pure and simple mysteries of Jerusalem, and they are those which have been preserved even until now."[88] When the initiate receives the master's degree, he is shown a gold medal,

---

[82] *Ibid.*, xiv.

[83] G. Henderson, *Ramsay*, 152-53.

[84] P. Chevallier, *Profanation*, 137-38.

[85] J.T. Thorpe, "Rite Ancien de Bouillon," *Masonic Reprints*, IX (Leicester, 1926), 22-31.

[86] Jan Snoek's commentary in R. Péter, *British Freemasonry*, III, 41-44.

[87] G. Bord, "Franc-Maçonnerie," 236.

[88] R. Péter, J. Snoek, *British Freemasonry*, III, 45, 66-67.

"whereon is engraved a double triangle, enclosed within a circle, and in the midst of which are the Hebrew letters" (the sacred Tetragrammaton). He is also given "the Caballistick interpretation" of the emblem on the medal. The use of three knocks and the identification of a brother by a triangle composed of three dots repeats earlier references to such Masonic practices.

As discussed previously, hints at Jacobite interest in higher Masonic degrees of Crusader and Cabalistic mysticism had emerged for decades, and Ramsay was perhaps the elaborator rather than the originator of them. Certainly, his current employment gave him motivation to develop a rite of Freemasonry devoted to not only Stuart but Bouillon traditions. In November 1733 he wrote Thomas Carte that he hoped to visit England to print *Turenne* there, for he feared that there will be matters in the book "that will not digest with a French monarch."[89] In 1735-36, when he published *The History of Henri de La Tour, Viscount de Turenne, Marshal-General of France*, in French and English editions, he made clear that Turenne had been a close friend of James Stuart, Duke of York, who became James VII and II. He also included "Memoirs of the Duke of York," based on a manuscript source.

The political agenda behind the *Écossais* Masonic agenda was veiled in increasingly mystical and allegorical terms, which found their way into Jacobite Masonic drinking songs in Britain. In the Jacobite stronghold of Caermarthen, South Wales, "The New Fairies" was sung at a lodge in which the brothers were instructed in the hidden mystical meanings of the lyrics. When the Welsh song was included in *A Curious Collection of the Most Celebrated Songs in Honour of Masonry* (London, 1731), it was introduced by an epigraph from Pope: "Science in gay attractive Fable lies,/ And veil'd, the more invites the Lover's Eyes."[90] The appended footnotes explained the symbolic interpretations of the explicitly simple lines, which suggest that Ramsay-style allegorization was practiced in some Welsh lodges. Thus, "every *Idea* points out *four several Ways, viz.* To Things *Celestial* and *Angelical, Terrestrial* and *Human,* etc."

For example, the Elves represent "the five *external Senses,* and Ideas of the Soul"; the Fairies "the *internal Senses* or Faculties of the Soul; the Sylphs "the seven *Influences,* both natural and divine, of the Heart, or *gradual Successions* and Acquirements." The last phrase, hinting at a hierarchical process of illumination, foreshadows the series of higher degrees of "regeneration" that emerged in later *Écossais* Masonry. Though these arcane mysteries flowed from the sacred Temple ("Solomon's Temple") and were practiced by John the Baptist ("the first Restorer of Masonry, who fed on the Tops of wild Herbs and wild Honey, etc."), they were first taught in the East ("alluding to the natural Light of the *Chinese*"). With that hint at Gormogonism, the traditional Masonic fairies' song foreshadowed Ramsay's developing "illuminist" system, which fused Cabalistic with Chinese theosophy.

The Masons remained a target for both low- and high-brow humorists, and they were soon lumped with other "pretenders" to elite knowledge, such as the universities and Royal Society. In early autumn 1731, reference to the fraternity was made in a collection of "Bog-house" poems – i.e., graffiti written on the walls of privies. In *The Merry-Thought,*

---

[89] Bodleian. Calendar of Carte Papers: vol. 73, f. 170.
[90] *A Curious Collection of the Most Celebrated Songs in Honour of Masonry* (London, 1731); reprint in D. Knoop, R. Jones, D. Hamer, *EMP*, 265-73.

or, the Glass-Window and Bog-House Miscellany, someone inscribed "The Wish" on a privy wall near Lincoln's Inn Field.[91] The author called for Colley Cibber and Orator Henley (loyalist Masons), and other "learned Sophis" to "join their Puns,/ To make the Bog-house shine":

> Each learn'd Society would try all
> (From lowest Club, to that call'd Royal),
> To furnish something might improve
> Religion, Politicks, or Love:
> Grand Keyber, Gormogons, Free Masons,
> And Heydeger, with all his gay Sons,
> Would find to suit, with Lectures there,
> Their Intellectuals to a Hair.

J.E.S. Tuckett notes that the poem "aspires to be an imitation of *The Dunciad"* and that the poet was familiar with Gormogonist literature.[92]

Another author who was familiar with Gormogonist literature was the Manchester satirist John Collier (pseudonym "Tim Bobbin"). The appointment of the Hanoverian Mason Colley Cibber as Poet Laureate in December 1730 provoked Collier to scorn him as a groveling sycophant who shall never want a Quill to celebrate" his Whig patrons.[93] In *The Goose: A Poem*, Collier wrote that he was often on "the Point of changing the title of my Poem from *The Goose*, to *The Gander*. But reflecting, that the Geese, who gave warning of the Enemy's Approach, were called *Servatores Romae* I chose to retain my former Title in Honour of them, and such like illustrious Patriots." In this attack on Cibber and his Hanoverian Masonic supporters, Collier posed as a Gormogon, who under Wharton's leadership had presented a more honourable fraternity than the Grand Lodge: "Sir, as I have the Honour to be a Member of the ancient and venerable Order of the Gormogons, I am obliged by the Laws of the great *Chin Quaw-Ki-Po*, Emperor of China, to read yearly some Part of the ancient Records of that country." Collier then praised the magistrate's "consummate Wisdom, and prodigious Virtues," for had all Britain such Justices as your Worship, we might sing, or say, with one accord, *Our Country is finely Govern'd!"*

While humorists mocked or praised Gormogons and Freemasons, the more politically-minded Whig brothers undertook more serious agendas. Determined to counter the inroads of Jacobitism at home and *Écossaisme* abroad, the Grand Lodge took advantage of Desaguliers's presence at The Hague in late September 1731, when he participated in a special Masonic meeting arranged by Lord Chesterfield, the British ambassador. The purpose was the initiation of Francis, Duke of Lorraine, who was expected to marry the designated Hapsburg heiress, Maria Theresa. Walpole determined to gain the duke's support as the Hanoverian Alliance began to unravel"[94] George II hoped to strengthen England's ties with Austria, the arch-enemy of France. Desaguliers initiated Lorraine into the first two degrees, while Chesterfield's brother Charles Stanhope, the embassy secretary Charles Holzendorf, and a nephew of Thomas Strickland, Bishop of Namur, looked on.[95]

---

[91] Hurlo Thrumbo, *The Merry-Thought: or, the Glass-Window and Bog-House Miscellany* (London, 1731), Part IV, 4.

[92] J.E.S. Tuckett, "The Royal Society and Freemasonry," *AQC*, 28 (1915), 57.

[93] John Collier, *The Miscellaneous Works of Tim Bobbin* ((Manchester, 1778), 122-24.

[94] M. Jacob, *Radical*, 111; E.E. Stolper, "The Initiation of the Duke of Lorraine," *AQC*, 95 (1982), 170-79.

[95] A. Carpenter, *Desaguliers*, 47, 103.

The Masonic connection of the nephew is suggestive, because Strickland was supplying intelligence on the continental Jacobites to the English ministry.

After the Duke of Lorraine received the first two degrees at The Hague, he visited "the famous Bro. Boerhave" at Leyden.[96] Moving on to England in October, the duke was invited to a house party at Houghton-Hall, Walpole's ostentatious "great house" in Norfolk. There, at an occasional lodge called by Grand Master Lovell in November, Lorraine was given the third Master's degree. Also participating in the ceremony were Walpole, the foreign minister Newcastle, the Earl of Essex, and Major-General Churchill. James Anderson, who would later fudge the political motivation behind the meeting, did not mention Walpole's initiation, while he implied that Newcastle was already a Mason and now received the Master's degree.[97]

Probably at the urging of his government paymasters, Orator Henley determined to mock a rival to the Grand Lodge, and on 13 November he advertised that his new oration "will be on ALL SIGNS IN THE WORLD, or a Learned Charge to the HONORARY FREE-MASONS, jocose; the first Attempt of the Kind."[98] Henry Sadler notes that they were "rather an important body," and had been mentioned in Grand Lodge minutes of 28 August 1730:

> Dr Desaguliers stood up and (taking notice of a printed paper lately published and dispersed about the Town…) recommended several things to the consideration of the Grand Lodge, particularly the Resolution…for Preventing any false Brethren being admitted into regular Lodges and such as calling themselves *Honorary Masons*.[99]

Henley's satire on the Honorary Masons was evidently provoked by a newspaper announcement of their defiantly public procession in 1731: "the Fraternity of Honorary Free Masons will set out from Whitehall, and proceed to Richmond, in two Barges, with a very fine Concert of Musick, by most of the best Hands, and return in the Evening." Though little more is known about this group, they were "a schismatick body which arose soon after the revival," when the members rejected "the established formula of an obligation, and bound themselves to secrecy and obedience by a pledge of honour only." The Honorary Masons were still meeting in 1739.

Meanwhile in Dublin, George Faulkner continued to print Masonic news in his *Dublin Journal*, and in the volume for 7-11 December 1731 he advertised the forthcoming publication of *A Letter from the Grand Mistress of the Female Freemasons, to George Faulkner, Printer*, with a reprint of the opening poem, and on 18-21 he announced that on "this Day" it is published.[100] Though Faulkner, who was currently working closely with Swift, maintained the anonymity of the pamphlet, he allowed his London agents to identify him as the author in 1746, and he would include the Masonic pamphlet in his great edition of the dean's works in 1762. Meanwhile, on 14 December 1731 a writer in his journal appealed to "several lodges of FREE MASONS," spread throughout Ireland, "without a Warrant"

---

[96] This is a little-known reference to Boerhaave's Masonic affiliation.
[97] J. Anderson, *Constitutions (1738)*, 129.
[98] W. Hextall, "Orator Henley," 369.
[99] Henry Sadler, "Inaugural Address," *AQC*, 23 (1910), 327.
[100] C. Crawley, *Caementaria Hibernica*, 2.

from the Grand Master Kingston, to send in their fees and receive authentic warrants. The Grand Master had no control over the many provincial lodges, especially those called "hedge or bush Masons," rural lodges without warrants from the Grand Lodge.[101]

In the same volume (18-21 December) in which he announced the publication of *Letter from the Grand Mistress*, Faulkner reported a Masonic meeting in Dublin, called by Nicholas, 5th Viscount Netterville, the Deputy Grand Master.[102] Netterville was close to Lord Kingston and succeeded him in 1732 as Grand Master. Kingston had recently broken all ties between the Irish and English Grand Lodges. Netterville was a member of a prominent Catholic family and nephew of the 1st Earl of Rosse. Though his ancestors had fought for the Jacobites, Netterville took his seat in the Irish House of Lords in 1730, "without refusing the oaths, usually a sign of at least outward religious as well as political conformity."[103] However, like Kingston, he kept on the mask while supporting the Irish patriotic party. Two years later, an Irish bishop would recommend him to the Pretender as "a man of good fortune and wishes our affairs very much." The bishop urged James to assist the 5th Viscount in the purchase of Austrian military companies for "two young gentlemen of the Nettervilles."[104]

During this period, John Boyle, 5th Earl of Orrery, was in Ireland, working on his late father's tangled financial affairs, and he associated with various Irish Masons. David Dickson observes that Masonic membership in Munster and Cork, center of Orrery's negotiations, was "socially, more than confessionally, determined, and the order helped in the construction of social networks that transcended county and province."[105] Moreover, there was "a distinct political aura surrounding its early sponsors – the Kingstons, St. Legers, Inchiquin O'Briens, Callagans...and Matthews." Munster Masonry was "Tory, tolerant of passive Jacobitism, and...avoided association with ostentatious Whig and Hanoverian symbols."

During his residence, Orrery dealt with his father's land agent, Walter Gould, who was a member of the Grand Lodge of Munster.[106] On 4 July 1732 he wrote to his Masonic friend Kempe about his relationship with William O'Brien, 4th Earl of Inchiquin, who had served as Grand Master in England in 1727 and who, with his brother James (Grand Master in Munster), continued to play a significant role in Irish Masonry.[107] Formerly a loyalist Whig M.P., Inchiquin went into opposition in 1730, when he represented Irish interests in parliament and continuously voted against the ministry.[108] Orrery was thrilled by his politics and personality, writing from Cork that Inchiquin is "the lawful Sovereign who is adored."[109] "He smiles on the Men, and kisses the Women. It would be happy if every Monarch were equally beloved in his Dominions, with this merry-hearted Earl." After the tragic death of Orrery's first wife in August, he left Cork and moved to Dublin,

---

[101] R. Péter, *British Freemasonry*, V, 423 n.6.

[102] *Ibid.*, V, 16.

[103] S. Murphy, "Irish Jacobitism," 81.

[104] P. Fagan, *Ireland*, I, 199, 201, 220.

[105] David Dickson, *Old World Colony: Cork and South Munster, 1630-1830* (Cork, 2005), 275.

[106] R. Berman, *Schism*, 178.

[107] *Ibid.*, 38, 252.

[108] R. Sedgwick, *History*, II, 303-04.

[109] Harvard, Hougton: Eng. MS.218.2, vol. 1, part 2, f. 49.

where Swift welcomed him as "an honest man, & of good dispositions."[110] Swift knew Inchiquin, and it seems likely that he and Orrery would discuss the earl's political and Masonic "dispositions."

Back in England, the initiation of the Earl of Essex at Walpole's lodge meeting was fraught with irony, for Essex had recently been snubbed by his brother-in-law, Lord Cornbury, whose integrity was proof against Walpole's attempted mercenary pressure. Though Cornbury was "badly off" financially, he refused a pension of £400 a year which Essex had obtained for him from George II. Turning this down contemptuously, Cornbury replied, "How could you tell, my Lord, that I was to be sold? Or at least, how could you know my price so exactly?"[111] This courageous act greatly impressed Pope, who later advised all clamoring pursuers of government pensions: "Would ye be blest? Despise low Joys, low Gains;/ Disdain whatever CORNBURY disdains."[112] In February 1732 Cornbury was unanimously elected M.P. for Oxford University, which inspired Gay to write Swift:

> Lord Cornbury refus'd the Pension that was offer'd him. He is chosen to represent the University of Oxford without opposition. I know him and I think he deserves it. He is a young Nobleman of Learning & Morals which is so particular that I know you will respect and value him & to my great comfort he lives with us in our family. Mr. Pope is in town and in good health.[113]

While Cornbury continued to work on the restoration plot, in collaboration with Arran at Oxford, it seems implausible that Gay, Pope, and Swift knew nothing about it.

Another guest of Walpole at the Masonic ceremony for the Duke of Lorraine, though not mentioned by James Anderson, was Burlington, whose presence at the house party is revealed in his wife's unpublished letters.[114] Jane Clark suggests that Burlington secretly shared the Jacobites' hope of gaining Austria to their side. He may have informed Pope about the lodge meeting, which forms a suggestive backdrop to Pope's architectural-political tribute to Burlington, which he published on 13 December 1731. In "An Epistle to the Right Honorable Richard, Earl of Burlington. Occasion'd by his Publishing Palladio's Designs," Pope satirized the dreadful taste of extravagant Whig builders, epitomized in the Brobdignagian monumentality of "Timon." Critics charged that Timon was a caricature of the Duke of Chandos, but Pope denied this and pointed out the differences in the decoration of Canons and his "fictional" estate. In the concluding lines, Pope called on Burlington to revive the traditions of Palladio and Inigo Jones and – in a suggestive echo of Mar--to create architecture worthy of the grandeur of some future sympathetic king:

> You to proceed! make falling Arts your care,
> Erect new wonders and the old repair,
> Jones and Palladio to themselves restore,

---

[110] J. Swift, *Correspondence*, III, 547-48.

[111] E. Cruickshanks, *Lord Cornbury*, 3.

[112] M. Mack, *Pope*, 688.

[113] J. Swift, *Correspondence*, III, 461-62.

[114] BL: Althorp MSS, box B8 (2, 4, 6 November 1731); noted in J. Clark, "Burlington," 308.

And be whate'er Vitruvius was before;
Till Kings call forth th' Ideas of your mind,
Proud to accomplish what such hands design'd,
Bid Harbors open, public Ways extend,
Bid Temples, worthier of the God, ascend;
Bid the broad Arch the dang'rous Flood contain,
The Mole projected break the roaring Main;

....

These Honours, Peace to happy Britain brings,
These are Imperial Works, and worthy Kings.[115]

Pope thus catalogued the great architectural achievements under earlier Stuart kings – especially the arched stone bridges, fortified harbors, and great Mole at Tangier.[116] Small wonder that he soon had to defend himself against charges that the epistle reeked of Jacobitism.

On 14 December, one day after the "Epistle to Burlington" was published in London, Faulkner reported Walpole's lodge meeting in the *Dublin Journal*. He did not mention Burlington's presence, which would have dismayed the earl's Irish admirers as well as Swift, Burlington's designated "Architect in Ireland": "We hear that during the Stay of the Duke of Lorain at Houghton in Norfolk, a Lodge of Free and Accepted Masons was held before Lord Lovell, Grand Master, in which Sir Robert Walpole and Count Kinski were admitted Brethren."[117] Phillipus Josephus, Count Kinski, was the Emperor's ambassador to George II. Though Lord Hervey described Kinski as possessing "the two Imperial characteristics of dullness and pride," Walpole hoped the Masonic initiation would gain the count's support for his Hapsburg agenda.[118]

Smarting under Whig charges of Jacobitism, Pope reverted to his old tactic of writing an ironic "Master Key to Popery," which Burlington's wife copied in February 1732.[119] Denying that he targeted Chandos, he jauntily argued that he might as well have aimed at Walpole, whose architectural pretensions at Houghton paralleled those of Timon. He coyly referred to Walpole's splendid entertainment of the Duke of Lorraine, though he did not mention the lodge meeting. Then he cleared himself of the Walpolean attribution by asserting that the prime minister could not be Timon because "The Author never saw Houghton." However, Pope was aware of the many satires against Walpole's extravagant construction project which had earlier been published by Tories and Jacobites. If Chiswick really was planned as a Masonic lodge to welcome home an architecturally-ambitious Stuart king, then Pope's *jeu d'esprit* must have amused Burlington, allegedly a crypto-Jacobite witness to Walpole's recent Masonic power play.

Despite Pope's denial that his poem targeted Chandos, many readers found his denial unconvincing. In early 1732 William Hogarth, a Grand Lodge Mason, engraved a satirical print, "The Man of Taste, or Burlington Gate," which had a large print sale. The diminutive figure of Pope on a scaffolding is seen "vigorously whitewashing the gate, and

[115] A. Pope, *Poems*, III, ii, 155.
[116] For the Stuart-Masonic significance of the great mole (sea-wall) at Tangier, built under Charles II and destroyed because of a hostile Whig Parliament , see M. Schuchard, *Restoring*, 639-46, 733-36.
[117] P. Crossle, "Freemasonry," 148.
[118] Hervey, *Memoirs*, II, 347.
[119] A. Pope, *Poems*, III, ii, 186.

bespattering the passers-by, among others the duke of Chandos, while Lord Burlington brings the whitewash, and his architect William Kent looks on in dismay.[120] Hogarth also drew a satirical frontispiece for *Mr. Taste, the Poetical Fop, a Comedy* (1732), written by James Miller, which when finally performed in 1735 included a dialogue between Martin (Lord Apemode) and Reynard (Colonel Cockade):

> Martin: "As soon as I had finished settling with these polite accomplishments, I resolved to crown all with a Smattering of Philosophy: and for that purpose am now Fellow of the Royal Society."
> Reynard: "And I am a Free-Mason, which is the same thing, you know."[121]

Miller's mocking linkage of the "foppish" scientific Fellows and the Masonic brothers would later be echoed by Pope in his 1742 version of *The Dunciad*.

*
* *

With "Brother" Walpole's spies now infiltrating Jacobite lodges at home and abroad, Ramsay's chivalric ambitions provided a means of outflanking the enemy, and he would soon have a new collaborator in his Masonic agenda, Charles Radcliffe. In December 1731 the latter inherited his family's title from his deceased nephew John and thus became 5th Earl of Derwentwater, though his attainted status meant his title was not recognized by the British government. Escaping Stosch's spies, the new earl managed to secretly travel to Paris, where he arrived in mid-January 1732. A worried Waldegrave reported on 31 January that Radcliffe, "who goes by the name of Lord Derwentwater, has been about a week in Paris, and is I hear set out within this day or two for Rome, from whence they say he is to remove his family, in hopes of adjusting his affairs in England."[122]

In March an inventory was made of the Derwentwater library at Dilston Hall, which revealed the Radcliffe family's commitment to the cultivation of non-Catholic English opinion in favor of a Stuart restoration. Leo Gooch notes that not only the works of Fenelon and Ramsay were prominent in the library but also Catholic advocates of the Gallican critique of papal supremacy: 'The Radcliffes were reading the contemporary authors who espoused political and ecclesiastical reform… far from being unyielding defenders of the papacy and absolutist government, they had moved into the more progressive circles of the early English Catholic Enlightenment."[123]

Once in Paris, Derwentwater must have contacted his old friends Ramsay and the current *Écossais* Grand Master, Hector Maclean. He may also have met some of the Swedes recently initiated in Jacobite lodges in Paris.[124] One of these, Axel Wrede Sparre, had recently travelled to Italy, where he evidently learned about a quasi-Masonic society formed by the Keith brothers and their allies in Spain, Italy, Prussia, Russia, and France.

---

[120] W. Hexall, "Man of Taste," 23-31.

[121] *Ibid.*, 234.

[122] NA: SP 78/204.

[123] Leo Gooch, "The Derwentwater Library," *Recusant History*, 30 (2010), 122.

[124] Some Swedish Masonic historians assert that Wrede-Sparre was initiated by Derwentwater.

When George Keith moved to Rome in 1730, he brought with him the rituals of the "Order of Toboso," a chivalric fraternity, which he and Ezekiel Hamilton had organized in Spain in 1726.[125] Though the order drew playfully on Keith's love of Don Quixote and Spanish romances, it also included a strong Masonic element and definite political-military aims.

Among the Stuart Papers is a draft of sixteen closely-written pages, in which the "true Knights" of the chivalric order are instructed by the Grand Master, meet in a lodge, and study physiognomy and other occult sciences.[126] Hamilton later described Toboso as "a military order of knighthood," of which he was Grand Master.[127] Marischal initiated the Stuart princes, and over the next years, it drew its members from the action-minded Jacobites, who would try to influence Prince Charles to convert to Anglicanism and to pursue a more independent and aggressive policy than that of his cautious father.[128] According to "Zecky" Hamilton, the "Great Prelate of the Order" was Bishop Atterbury, who supported the faction led by Marischal, Ormonde, and Hamilton in the on-going power struggles within the Stuart entourage.[129]

Wrede Sparre must have sent descriptions of Toboso to Stockholm, for on 25 January 1732 Carl Gustaf Tessin and his political allies organized the secret fraternity of *Awazu och Wallasis*, which replicated many of the themes and rituals of Toboso. The Knights of Awazu claimed to inherit the mystical secrets of their fathers and aimed to revive the golden age of chivalry. They utilized geometric symbolism and maintained rules that were strikingly similar to those of Freemasonry, and the fraternity would soon emerge as a powerful but secretive force in Swedish politics.[130] Both fraternities also looked towards a Jacobite-Holstein alliance with Russia, where they hoped the old Görtzian alliance could be revived. Since 1728 James Keith had served in Russia, where he became the agent of his brother's Tobosan innovations.[131]

On 2 February 1732 William Hay wrote from Rome to Admiral Gordon in St. Petersburg:

> I have putt up a small wooden box containing 2 rings of the order of Toboso, such as all the knights wear; one for your-self, the other for my dear sir Henry [Stirling]... We knights daily after drinking the healths of the Royal Family, a fair meeting on the green follows; our two young Princes are protectors of the order and wear the rings... They are the most lively and engaging two boys this day on earth... I made your compliments to Sir George Keith... [who] may justly be stiled the hero of our cause. He with Sir William

---

[125] On 22 April 1734 Ezekiel Hamilton claimed to have served as a Grand Master of Toboso since 1726; RA Stuart: 169/180.

[126] Stuart Papers: 144/126.

[127] P. Fagan, *Irish Bishop*, 145.

[128] *HMC. Report on the Manuscripts of the Earl of Eglinton*, ed. Sir John Stirling Maxwell, et al., (London, 1885), 178-84.

[129] Stuart Papers: 173/37; quoted in Robert Collis, "'To a Fair Meeting on the Green'": The Order of Toboso and Jacobite Fraternalism, c. 1726-1739," in Allan Macinnes, Kieran German, Lesley Graham, eds., *Living with Jacobitism, 1690-1788* (London, 2014), 134

[130] B. Bergquist, *St. Johanneslogen*, 35; Martin Lamm, *Olof von Dalin* (Uppsala, 1908), 124-45.

[131] S. Murdoch, "Soldiers," 13-14.

> Maxwell, Sir William Livingston the Grand Master...join in their hearty service to all our brother knights with you.[132]

The initiations of the twelve year-old Prince Charles and seven year-old Prince Henry were consistent with those of children and adolescents in the Jacobite lodge in Paris in 1725.[133] The Order of Toboso thus served as a kind of pre-Masonic training camp for the princes – one that would not unduly alarm their father. Given James III's negative reaction to Ramsay's earlier proposals, perhaps Marischal hoped to disguise their Masonic strategies under the façade of the seemingly light-hearted Order of Toboso.

Meanwhile in Dublin, Swift responded to the government's intensified surveillance and published his *Examination of Certain Abuses, Corruptions, and Enormities in the City of Dublin*, published by Faulkner in March 1732. Ridiculing "the absurdity of some of the suspicions entertained by the Court against the Tories and Jacobites," Swift comically interpreted the various cries of street vendors as Jacobite codes. He ironically described Robert Harley, the late Earl of Oxford, as a corrupt and mercenary Papist, attributing to his former mentor Walpolean traits that were opposite to his true character. Like Walpole, the reinvented Harley was "grievously suspected" of selling places at court to the highest bidder:

> Certain women were employed by his emissaries to carry *fish* in baskets on their heads, and bawl through the streets, *buy my fresh places* [plaices, a type of fish]... Although they carried *fish* in their sieves or baskets to save appearances, yet they had likewise a certain sign, somewhat resembling that of the *free-masons*, which the purchasers of *places* knew well enough, and were directed by the women whither they were to resort and make their purchase.[134]

Swift was evidently aware of Walpolean infiltration of Irish as well as French and English Freemasonry. In March 1732 Bishop Atterbury died in southern France, and his own role as "Great Prelate" of the Order of Toboso and his earlier collaboration with Tory and Jacobite Masons made both fraternities vulnerable to Walpole's espionage network. Richard Rawlinson wrote Thomas Carte that he hoped Atterbury had made cautious arrangements for the disposal of his papers.[135] Newcastle ordered Delafaye, now a secretary of state, to seize the bishop's papers, and Delafaye accordingly wrote Waldegrave:

> it will be difficult to compass but well worth the while if it can be brought about. I remember that as cautious as he was, and careful to put everything out of the way when he was seized here, I found among his loose papers a letter he had written to the Pretender... he had laid it by and forgot to destroy it.
>
> As he might not be under the same apprehensions now that he was then, and his death was sudden, probably there are some curiosities to be met with in his *scrutore*, if one knew how to come at them. I return you one that shows

---

[132] 59. *HMC. Eglinton*, 178.
[133] On such "precocious" Masonic initiations, see E. Corp, *Burlington*, 10-12, 20-21; A. Kervella, *Maçonnerie*, 321, and *La Passion Écossaise* (Paris, 2002), 247.
[134] J. Swift, *Irish Tracts*, xxxv, 227.
[135] Bodleian. Calendar of Carte Papers: vol. 73, f. 71.

his spirit and ill-nature held out to the last. What a pity it is that so good parts should have been in such bad hands![136]

When Atterbury's papers were brought from southern France to Paris, Cardinal Fleury and the French lieutenant of police, who would later confiscate Masonic documents, placed a seal on them. Many papers were burned, with some returned to the authors. But Fleury made sure that neither the Jacobite O'Brien nor the Whig Waldegrave (members of rival lodges) got to see any of them. When the bishop's corpse arrived in England, Delafaye was determined that the government should have "the fingering of his papers"; thus, his coffin was broken open, searched, and what survived of "the much-coveted papers" taken away.[137] Atterbury's son-in-law Morice was arrested and grilled by Delafaye and his agents, but he was eventually released.

Despite his difficult personality and paranoid jealousies, Atterbury continued to have many admirers in England, especially among his old literary friends. Pope wrote an epitaph in the form of a dialogue between the bishop and his late daughter:

> Dear shade, I will
> Then mix this dust with thine, O spotless ghost,
> O more than fortune, friends, or country lost!
> Is there on earth one care, one wish beside?
> Yes, save my country, Heaven!
> He said, and died.[138]

Samuel Wesley the Younger wrote a scathing indictment of the Delafayes and Walpoles who persecuted Atterbury, while they ruled by corruption, spy-networks, and hypocrisy:

> He who to gold perpetual worship gave,
> Secret as night, unsated as the grave,
> To friendship bland, sharp-sighted to a bribe,
> ....
> Rav'nous for gain, yet loud for common weal,
> With party madness and inverted zeal...[139]

As the "fingering" went on, all of Atterbury's former colleagues feared the government dragnet. Marischal was so worried about his own incriminating letters in the bishop's correspondence that he planned to escape to Russia ("to get away with the least noise"), where he would join his brother James Keith, but he could not manage it.[140] Given the international reach of Walpole's spies, the Jacobites' secret Masonic networks became even more important. It was no coincidence that in 1732 James Keith became head of a Masonic lodge in St. Petersburg where, according to Russian tradition, he took up Peter the Great's role as leader of Freemasonry, for which he was immortalized in a Russian song:

---

[136] F. Atterbury, *Memoir*, II, 459-60.

[137] *Ibid.*, II, 464.

[138] *Ibid.*, II, 466

[139] *Ibid*, II, 468-69.

[140] R. Wills, *Jacobites*, 183.

> After him [Czar Peter], Keith, full of light, came to the Russians; and, exalted by zeal, lit up the sacred fire. He erected the temple of wisdom, corrected our thoughts and hearts, and confirmed us in brotherhood.[141]

Though no list of the lodge members survives, they were surely part of the large Scottish Jacobite contingent in the city and linked with the Knights of Toboso.[142]

In May 1732, two months after Atterbury's death, the target of his obsessive vendetta, the Earl of Mar, also died. After Mar's exclusion from James's affairs, he had continued his friendship with his Masonic brothers Ramsay and Maclean, while he found solace in architectural designing and consulting (he designed the first green houses in France and supervised their construction). He also maintained contact with his many admirers in Scotland, who never believed the charges against him. His former comrade in battle, the attainted Alexander Robertson of Struan, wrote "An Epitaph on the Earl of Mar":

> Here Loyalty supine with Valour lyes,
> And much, 'tis fear'd, will never, never rise,
> Since great Mar has clos'd his wakeful Eyes:
> With him alive they rested and they toil'd,
> Advanc'd with Prudence, or with Art recoil'd.
> Alas! That Love of Friends, or Hate of Foes,
> No more can rouse them from their dull Repose.
> Tho' Envy strives, at her inglorious Rate,
> To soil the Virtuous and debase the Great,
> Mar's Worth shall endless, in those grateful Lays,
> Shine thro' the longest Stretch of future Days.
> Farewel, who couldst our Doubts and Fears expel,
> Thou great in Faith and Fortitude, farewell![143]

For his Scottish supporters, Mar was not the "Bobbin' John" of Whig propaganda and Atterbury's slanders. In Ireland Jonathan Swift had long admired Atterbury, but he also continued to respect Mar, writing in 1733 that Mar was "crooked," a reference to his deformed crook-back: "He seemed to me a Gentleman of good sense & good nature."[144]

Given the growing disaffection among opposition Masons in southern England, Ireland, and Scotland, rumors about Jacobite intrigues and *Écossais* developments soon reached the Whig Masons in London. Probably spurred by Waldegrave's reports from Paris, the London Grand Lodge granted a constitution to a new Parisian lodge, St. Thomas, on 3 April 1732. In the next month, reports of Masonic "irregularities" surfaced in southern England. On 20 May, in a letter to the editor of the *Universal Spectator and Weekly Journal*, a Mason in Canterbury defended the "Royal Craft" from slanderers who misrepresented Masonry "not only as Unnatural but Seditious, nay Traiterous and Magical in their Practices."[145] He then mocked the efforts of the chief magistrate to penetrate

---

[141] James Billington, *The Icon and the Axe* (New York, 1966), 245.

[142] Atina L.K. Nihtinen, "Field-Marshal James Keith: Governor of the Ukraine and Finland, 1740-1743," in A. Mackillop and Steve Murdoch, eds., *Military Governors and Imperial Frontiers c.1600-1800: A Study of Scotland and Empires* (Leiden, 2003), 103-04.

[143] A. Robertson, *Poems*, 10-11.

[144] J. Swift, *Prose Works*, V, 262.

[145] *EMP*, 286-87.

and disrupt a lodge meeting, "wherein he suspected Practices against the Peace of our Sovereign Lord the King, his Crown and Dignity, as well as Breaches on Morality." That "certain mighty Dons" were sent down from London to recruit Masons in Canterbury convinced the magistrate (and Walpole) that they had a "Plot against the State." This article was obtained by the Jacobite Rawlinson for his Masonic collection.[146] By late 1733 Walpole would use Henley's renamed *Free-Mason/Hyp Doctor* to condemn the Jacobite takeover of certain lodges in Kent.[147] In the meantime, Henley continued his support of the government, as reported on 7 August 1732 in the *Daily Journal:*

> We hear from Sir Isaac Ratcliffe's Under Door-Keeper's Friend's Friend, that he will, in his Tomorrow's Hyp-Doctor, vindicate, unanswerably, the Justices of the Peace against the last Craftsman; and will shew that the Crafts-man has stole his Title from the Free Masons; and he desires his Enemies not to fret because he laughs at them.[148]

At this time, Burlington, Pope, and their friends responded indignantly to the exposure of scandals committed by the York Buildings Company and the Charitable Corporation. These two "projecting" companies had handled the expropriation of forfeited Jacobite estates, because the hostility of the local populations had prevented private individuals from buying them.[149] Since 1727 John Thompson, George Robinson, and three other managers of the Charitable Corporation had embezzled funds earmarked for the "Industrious Poor" to line their own pockets. Despite the enormous sums they siphoned off, their gambling and other debts led them into a desperate attempt to collaborate with the Jacobites. In late 1730 they approached Orrery, Cecil, and Hardy with a plan to raise money by lowering and then raising the stocks in London. Robinson gained the Jacobites' and Fleury's confidence by revealing Walpole's secret negotiations with Austria. Claiming to have access to Walpole's clandestine activities, Robinson posed as a Whig and was elected an M.P. in May 1731. When a parliamentary inquiry was opened upon the scandal of the Charitable Corporation, he and Thomson fled to France in October 1731. After some months, Robinson utilized the spy Sempill to spread rumors that Thomson "had run off with large amounts of the Company money to offer it to the Pretender."[150]

By this time, Dillon and Hardy suspected that Robinson was Walpole's *agent provocateur*, and James accordingly had the Pope arrest Thomson in Rome. In Paris Waldegrave pressured the French court to force Robert Arbuthnot to deliver up Thomson's papers, and then added that "The Doctor his Brother writes to him to this purpose, which, it is to be hoped will have some effect."[151] With sly amusement, the papal authority sent Thomson's papers to Waldegrave, accompanied by a letter from the Stuart banker Belloni, "explaining that all this was done at the instance of the king-in-exile, as an act of justice to his defrauded and victimized subjects."[152] James's action provoked a furor in

---

146 Bodleian: Rawlinson MSS. C.136.f.147. Masonic Miscellanies.

147 *Free-Mason/Hyp-Doctor* (11 December 1733).

148 R. Péter, *British Freemasonry*, V, 150.

149 E. Cruickshanks, "Burlington's Political Career," 208-09.

150 For the complicated plot, see J. Guite, "Jacobite Cause," 152-82.

151 John Arbuthnot, *The Correspondence of John Arbuthnot*, ed. Angus Ross (München, 2006), 326-27.

152 J. Guite, "Jacobite Cause," 159-60.

London, where Belloni's letter was burned by the common hangman, and threats were muttered of bombarding the papal coasts.

The complicated scandal took on an odd Masonic significance when two skits were added to a performance of *The Blazing Comet*, a rollicking farce by Samuel Johnson of Cheshire. On April 19 1732 the skits were performed at the Haymarket Theater, on the same day that Anthony Browne, 6th Viscount Montagu, was named as Grand Master of the Grand Lodge, in succession to the loyalist Whig, Lord Lovell. Montagu, member of a Catholic Jacobite family, was a friend of Norfolk and privately shared his Stuart sympathies. His father, the 5th Viscount, had served as secretary of state to the exiled James II. He himself had married Barbara Webb, sister of Anna Marie Webb, wife of the executed 3rd Earl of Derwentwater. The sisters' father, Sir John Webb, was a Jacobite member of Norfolk's lodge at the Bear and Harrow. Though Montagu served as the second Catholic Grand Master of the Grand Lodge, his religious affiliation led to his being deprived of his hereditary seat in the House of Lords. In 1743 he would be included on a list of Jacobite supporters sent to Louis XV, and his wife would continue to support Charles Edward Stuart into the 1750s. [153]

On 13 April, a week before the theatrical performance, Montagu had hosted at Hampstead a lodge dinner for one hundred guests, which included brothers from both political sides.[154] With Norfolk and Richmond in attendance, Desaguliers initiated Henry Pelham, brother of Thomas Pelham, Duke of Newcastle, who had earlier been initiated at Walpole's Houghton House.[155] Montagu then resigned his role as Master of the Hampstead lodge to Henry Roper, 10th Baron Teynham, a fellow Catholic. In 1730 Teynham had visited the Pretender's court in Rome, and his Jacobite contacts in Italy were reported to Newcastle.[156] Despite the presence of major Hanoverian Masons, the unusual lodge meeting at Hampstead portended the increasing Jacobite influence within Freemasonry.

Within this context, a bold public display of satire on the Whig Masons by Eliza Haywood becomes provocative. A popular actress and author of anti-Walpolean works, Haywood extended her leading role in *The Blazing Comet* to act the initiate in an "Additional Scene of the Ceremony of Lady Flame's being made a Free Mason, wherein the Grand Mystery is discover'd."[157] In an interlude added to this performance, a satire on the embezzlers at the Charitable Corporation was performed: "A Song on the Privileges and Happiness of Free-Masonry. A Very Humorous Song on the Charitable Corporation, sent by George Robinson, Esq. Late Treasurer, from Italy to his Friends in London."[158] Robinson had been expelled from the House of Commons two weeks before the performance, and Haywood perhaps shared Dillon's and Hardy's belief that he acted as an *agent provocateur* for Walpole, while posing as a Whig, sending intelligence to the Jacobites, and exploiting his Masonic connections.

[153] E. Cruickshanks, *Political Untouchables*, 135; Andrew Lang, *Pickle the Spy, or the Incognito of Charles Edward*, rev. ed. (London, 1897), 129, 306.

[154] R. Gould, *History*, III, 140n.2.

[155] *London Evening Post* (27-9 April 1732); in R. Péter, *British Freemasonry*, V, 17.

[156] "Teynham, Henry Roper," J. Ingamells, *Dictionary*.

[157] Carol Howard, "A Female Freemason on Stage? Eliza Haywood's Patriotism at Henry Fielding's Haymarket Theatre," in Laura Engel, ed., *The Public's Open to Us All: Essays on Women and Performance in Eighteenth-Century England* (Newcastle, 136-37).

[158] *Ibid.*, 145.

During this period, the fraudulent sale of the Derwentwater estates provoked more public outrage at Whig corruption. In April-May 1732 Burlington attended every day in the House of Lords when the Derwentwater sale was considered. Vast lands worth over £200,000 had been sold to a jobber in London for £1,060, "for the benefit of prominent supporters in Parliament." On 17 May Swift wrote sardonically to Charles Ford about the Derwentwater case, noting that "We must own with shame that England exceeds us in villainy, as to its greatness; but ours is more epidemick."[159] In Paris an enraged Derwentwater began planning a secret journey to England, in order to contact his many supporters in the north and to reclaim something of his forfeited patrimony.

Over the next months, Derwentwater's Masonic "brother" Norfolk began to suffer from a long, mysterious illness that led to his death on 23 December 1732. His friend, Sir Thomas Robinson, wrote that "It is currently reported that he was poisoned...his case entirely puzzled the doctors."[160] Mrs. Caesar, who had observed his declining health and called on their Jacobite friend Dr. Mead to treat him, recorded her concern and her admiration for the late Catholic Grand Master. She noted that she and Mr. Caesar lost a great and pleasant friend in the Duke of Norfolk, who had been in excellent health until it "soon Vanish'd," and he looked fifty years older than at their previous meeting.[161] She and their Jacobite friends blamed the illness on his "close confinement in the Tower [1722-23], when they tryd'd all way's to frighten and perswaid Him to a Confession." She praised Norfolk for "a great Magnifiscence in His Temper, Void of Pride and full of Good Nature, which Made Him Much Lamented by all," especially his younger brother, "who was a True Mourner for His Death, knowing him self Not Equel to the filling that Station."

Norfolk was succeeded by his younger brother Edward Howard, who had been arrested for treason in 1715 and was now excluded from official and government positions. Possibly fearing a similar fate to his brother's, the 9th Duke of Norfolk played a loyal role in public but quietly maintained his Jacobite ties.[162] His "accomodationist" wife personally vowed loyalty to George II, but her husband would later host a secret assembly of Jacobite Masons and Catholics at his London residence.[163] As we shall see, the 9th duke kept up his clandestine Jacobite and Masonic intrigues into the 1770s.[164]

---

[159] J. Swift, *Correspondence*, IV, 25.

[160] J. Robinson, *Dukes of Norfolk*, 154.

[161] M.Caesar, *Journal*, 85.

[162] P. Monod, *Jacobitism*, 134.

[163] Stuart Papers: 194/159 (15 March 1737).

[164] P. Monod, *Jacobitism*, 125, 134,304, 332; R. Gould, *Military Lodges*, 40.

CHAPTER THIRTEEN

MASONIC POLITICS AND "A BABEL OF RELIGIONS"
(1732-1733)

As I have been long dealing in Cypher and other Intricacyes of negotiation, my mind was warping itself insensibly into Politicks…Uranius allways shook his head and shew'd a constant aversion to subjects of that nature.

Charles Wogan, MS. "Uranius or the Epistle Dedicatory
to Jonathan Swift" (1732).

The Catholicks, in such a Babel of Religions, chose to adhere to their own Faith left by their Ancestors, rather than seek for a better among a Rabble of Hypocritical, rebellious, deluding Knaves, or deluded Enthusiasts.

Jonathan Swift, *Reasons Humbly Offered to the Parliament
Of Ireland for Repealing the Sacramental Test, in Favour of
The Roman Catholicks* (1733)

It was probably through his conversations with Ramsay in London that Joseph Spence became interested in Freemasonry, and he would soon participate in an important Masonic affair in Italy. One of his students at Oxford was Charles Sackville, Earl of Middlesex, whom he greatly admired: "He is a young gentleman of fine parts, of a very polite turn, and extremely good-natured."[1] Pope shared his admiration and recommended that Spence travel with Lord Middlesex when he made his Grand Tour. Though Middlesex's father, Lionel Cranfield Sackville, 1st Duke of Dorset, was a staunch Hanoverian Whig, his son and his travelling companion were more open-minded towards Tories and Jacobites. A friend described Spence as the perfect tutor, because he was "a man of letters, without pedantry, no bigot, nor violently attached to any party, but of a catholic spirit, and not unacquainted with natural philosophy and the mathematics." This attitude would provide an important context for their Jacobite contacts and Masonic experiences in Italy.

---

[1] Joseph Spence, *Letters from the Grand Tour*, ed. Slava Klima (Montreal, 1975), 2-5.

As Spence and Middlesex made their way from Calais to Rome, they enjoyed friendly conversations with exiled Jacobites and with Ramsay's Jesuit friends, while enjoying "bibulous" and merry evenings, which gained Middlesex a reputation as "a budding Lord of Misrule."[2] From Dijon, Spence wrote his mother about his correspondence with Ramsay but warned her,

> Not one word of any kind relating either to religion or politics ought to be in any letter sent me into Italy... As I never quarreled with anybody in my life about being of a different religion from me and never pretended to be anything like a politician, I can be absolutely reserved on both those heads without any balk to my inclinations. One of my best acquaintance here was a Jesuit, and a very agreeable man he is, and I am recommended to another at Rome by Mr. Ramsay who wrote *The Travels of Cyrus* that I left with you. I have had several letters from him (Mr. Ramsay) of late; he is particularly obliging to me. He lives at Paris, and is lately made governor to a young French Duke there and has a good pension settled on him for life.[3]

When they arrived in Rome in March 1732, Spence sought out Father Fouquet, and he sent to Ramsay accounts of his conversations with him over the next three months.[4] Spence was familiar with Ramsay's assimilation of Chinese "Figurist" and Jewish Cabalistic themes into his Masonic philosophy, so his notes on Fouquet's description of "The Temple of the Most Ancient Wisdom" would certainly interest Ramsay. Fouquet revealed

> (1) that Adam was informed of the doctrine of the Trinity and that of the future redemption, (2) that this knowledge was delivered down to Moses and revived by him, (3) that it was preserved in other mystic books, and (4) that several of these books are still Preserved in China.[5]

Fouquet showed Spence a letter from a brother missionary which showed how the Chinese sacred books "exactly agreed with ours, even in the highest mysteries":

> It says the Y KING is the oldest of these sacred writings, that in it are contained most of the great truths and mysteries of the Christian religion, and that the Y KING and the rest of them teach, in particular, the doctrine of the fallen angels, the creation of the world, the state in paradise, the fall from thence, the incarnation of the great hero, his birth, by a virgin, his low estate, his teaching for three years, his suffering for the sins of the whole world, his resurrection, ascent into heaven, and coming in judgment, the eternal happiness of the good and eternal misery of the wicked.
> He supposes all this knowledge to have come by tradition from Adam to the antediluvian patriarchs, and by Noah to his children, in whose time some of these books were written.[6]

---

[2] J. Spence, *Observations*, I, 45n. 1, 102-03, 474.; *Letters*, 3,

[3] *Ibid.*, 66.

[4] J. Spence, *Observations*, I, 520.

[5] *Ibid.*, I, 519.

[6] *Ibid.*, I, 523.

Unfortunately, we do not know if Fouquet discussed with Spence his (Fouquet's) confidential relation with James III, whom the old Jesuit was instructing in the Mandarin language and Chinese lore, or Fouquet's close friendship with Derwentwater, who would later collaborate with Ramsay when he infused chivalric and "Figurist" themes into *Écossais* Freemasonry.[7]

After Middlesex and Spence arrived in Florence on 11 July 1732, the young earl and evidently his tutor were welcomed by the members of a Florentine Masonic lodge. Their new friend Dr. Cocchi recorded in his diary on 4 August, "Last evening I was received among the 'Free Masons,'" and "Their Master was Mr. Shirly, others were Capt. Spens, Mr. Clarke, Capt. Clarke, Mild. Middlesex, Milord Robert Montaigu, Mr. Frolik, Mr. Collings, Baron Stosch; initiates were Sr. Archer and Mr. Harris."[8] Horace Walpole would later write Horace Mann that Sewallis Shirley was no great genius: but a noted lady-killer, and he would later play a temporarily oppositionist role in parliament.[9] In May 1733 Shirley was succeeded as Master by the twenty year-old Sir Hugh Smithson, who was raised in a Catholic Jacobite family, but who converted to the Anglican church on becoming heir to his grand-father.[10] Throughout the 1740s, he served as a Tory M.P., but in 1745 opposed the Jacobite rebellion.

Ric Berman suggests that Middlesex had already been initiated in Ireland.[11] For many decades, Masonic historians claimed that he was the founder of the Florentine lodge in 1733, a claim disproved by Cocchi's diary. Slava Klima, editor of Joseph Spence's travel journal, observes that "It seems probable that a lodge of a sort existed before, but that in 1733 its status was either raised or made 'official'; that Lord Middlesex became its Master is clear, for he appears on Natter's Masonic medal, struck in his honor in 1733, as 'Magister Florentiae.'"[12] Klima further notes that it is not surprising that Spence does not explicitly refer to Freemasonry in his letters at this time, though a later letter shows his familiarity with Masonic lore.[13] Moreover, he must have attended the Saturday meetings with Middlesex and his Italian friends, who were all but one Masons. Spence's biographer, Austin Wright, notes that his intimacy with Ramsay, "an ardent Freemason," suggests that Spence had "ties with Freemasonry," and he would soon visit Ramsay in Paris in 1733.[14] Over the next years, the Florentine lodge attracted Italian intellectuals, Whig diplomats, and English visitors who were predominantly Hanoverian loyalists.[15] It would also provoke the hostility of the Pope and the Pretender.

In the meantime, in September 1731 Middlesex's father, the Duke of Dorset, had taken up his position as Lord Lieutenant of Ireland, where he soon made clear that he had no time for Swift, despite his wife's liking for the dean. Dorset "took it for granted that preferments should be reserved for camp followers and the English interest," and

---

[7] NA: SP 98/32, f.318; 98/36, f.45. Stosch's report on Fouquet and Derwentwater.

[8] C. Matteo Pellizzi, "The English Lodge in Florence in the Eighteenth Century," *AQC*, 105 (1992), 129-36.

[9] R. Sedgwick, *History*, II, 424.

[10] *Ibid.*, II, 428.

[11] R. Berman, *Schism*, 38.

[12] J. Spence, *Letters*, 5-6.

[13] *Ibid.*, 292-94.

[14] Austin Wright, *Joseph Spence: A Critical Biography* (Chicago, 1950), 213n.112.

[15] Nicholas Hans, "The Masonic Lodge in Florence in the Eighteenth-Century," *AQC*, 71 (1958), 109-12.

Swift was no longer prepared to fight.[16] When he first met Dorset, he promised that he would not write any "state-scribble," because he looked "upon this kingdom's condition as absolutely desperate, [and] I would not prescribe a dose for the dead." However, by early 1732 he was so depressed that he wrote "Verses on the Death of Dr. Swift," which he circulated in manuscript. In couplets and notes, he mocked Robert Walpole, who "hath a Set of Party Scriblers, who do nothing else but write in his Defence," especially his subsidized hack Orator Henley.[17] Faulkner had published reports in his Dublin newspaper on the affiliation of Walpole and Henley with the London Grand Lodge system.

Swift may also have learned that in October 1731 Henley gave a lecture on "Scripture-Masonry," with learned and detailed Biblical allusions to architecture and the operative craft.[18] Coming from a defrocked, Walpolean churchman, this would have seemed impudent to Swift, who wrote:

> Then, here's a Letter finely penn'd
> Against the *Craftsman* and his Friend,
> It clearly shows that all Reflection
> On Ministers, is Disaffection.
> Next, here's sir R[obert]'s Vindication,
> And Mr. Henley's last Oration.

Swift then explained in a note:

> Henley is a Clergyman who wanting both Merit and Luck to get Preferment, or even to keep his Curacy in the Established church, formed a new Conventicle, which he calls an Oratory. There, at set Times, he delivereth strange Speeches compiled by himself and his Associates, who share the Profit with him: Every Hearer pays a Shilling each Day for Admittance. He is an absolute Dunce, but generally reputed crazy.

Swift looked back to the days of Queen Anne, when Bolingbroke's skill in state affairs, Ormonde's valor, and Oxford's care could have saved their sinking country. Though it is still unknown if Bolingbroke was a Mason, Swift surely knew that Ormonde and Oxford were affiliated with traditional Masonry. He made clear that he sided with "His Friends in Exile, or the Tower,/ Himself within the Frown of Power," and he was proud of his Drapier's role in the Wood's copper coinage furor: "The Dean did by his Pen defeat/ An infamous destructive Cheat." As noted earlier, the patriotic party among Dublin Masons had supported his campaign.

It was perhaps Swift's praise of Bolingbroke and scorn for Henley that provoked a counter-attack by the Orator, who used his Walpolean journal, *The Hyp-Doctor*, to attack Bolingbroke's opposition journal, *The Craftsman*, in Masonic terms. On 8 August 1732 Henley headlined the issue, "A False Brother: or the Craftsman no Free-Mason." He

---

[16] I. Ehrenpreis, *Swift*, III, 714.

[17] Jonathan Swift, *Verses on the Death of Dr. Swift, D.S.PD., Occasioned by Reading a Maxim in Rochefoucault... Written by Himself, November 1731* (London, 1739), 25-26, 33-36. I am grateful to Shawn Eyer for sending me his transcript of "Scripture Masonry," which he will publish in facsimile.

[18] Daniel Lysons, *Collectanea. Advertisements and Paragraphs, relating to the Celebrated Orator Henley* (Strawberry Hill, n.d.), f. 47.

accused the editor of stealing the name "Craftsman (the)" from the Masons, for stealing "is assuming and using what does not belong to him, injuriously":

> The Popularity of that name in the Worshipful Society of Free-Masons may create a Persuasion that the Craftsman is their Friend, because they are called Craftsmen, but the Deceit and Fallacy of the Pretense will appear by the following Considerations.
>
> The Craftsman is extremely Free, but no Free-Mason, for he is not accepted, which is the Mason's Title; he is always writing disrespectfully of the Deputy Grand-Master, and sometimes I think , he is not overly dutiful to the Grand-Master himself, which is inconsistent with Masonry.[19]

Henley rather daringly implied that Walpole served as Deputy to George II, the virtual Grand Master of Britain (though certainly the king was not a Mason). After long, detailed analogies between the Masons and their enemy, the journalistic *Craftsman*, he charged that the latter "is better for pulling down, than building," and stressed that "The Ministry are *Accepted*; I exhort all Accepted Masons to reverence them." He concluded with a jolly Masonic drinking song.

Henley's concern about disaffected and opposition "brothers" was shared by the Hanoverian Masonic officials, who worried about the expansion of Jacobite Freemasonry in France. On 3 April 1732 the Grand Lodge granted a constitution to a new Parisian lodge, St. Thomas, and on 24 June the Duke of Montagu, former opponent to Wharton's Grand Mastership, sent a loyalist Masonic delegation to Paris, where they competed with the Jacobite lodge for French members.[20] From Stosch in Florence and from Waldegrave in Paris, Walpole received reports that the Jacobites were planning a major expedition to Scotland.[21] Thus, in August, when Stosch and Waldegrave wrote that Derwentwater was in France and was headed to Louvain, the English spy network went on high alert. Stosch, who was a member of the Florentine lodge, and Waldegrave, affiliated with the Whig Grand Lodge, determined to penetrate Derwentwater's secret plans.

On 26 September the English Consul Eliezer Burges in Venice reported to Delafaye that Derwentwater "is gone from Rome to Brussels upon ye wildest project in nature. The poor man, who was in ye Rebellion and is ye fiercest Jacobite alive, has taken it into his head, that being so near England, he shall find friends there, to get his Brother's attainder reversed and himself put in possession of ye Estate of ye Family."[22] Burges argued that George II should show no mercy to Derwentwater: "He sets up at Rome as ye Bully of the Party, and when he is drunk which is often he goes into ye Coffee Houses, which our young people frequent, to proclaim his Disaffection to His Majesty's Person and Government." While Delafaye's agents kept watch over him, Derwentwater spent several months in England in 1733, but the government decided not to publicize his presence: "the Ministry did not think proper to take Notice of him, so long as he behaved quietly and gave no Disturbance to the Government."[23] With James's permission, he

---

[19] *The Hyp-Doctor*, #88 (8 August 1732).

[20] P. Chevallier, *Ducs*, 34.

[21] NA:SP 98/32 (19 July 1732).

[22] *Ibid.*, 99/63 (26 September 1732).

[23] Gerard Penrice, *A Genuine and Impartial Account of the Remarkable Life and Vicissitudes of Fortune of Charles Radcliffe, Esquire* (London, 1747), 91.

visited his family's forfeited estate in the north of England, where he was accompanied by Marmaduke Constable, his kinsman and fellow Mason.[24] The two undoubtedly contacted sympathizers among the traditionally Jacobite Masons in their home area.

During this period, when Swift was so depressed at English oppression and Irish misery that he promised to write no more "state scribbles," he received a politically dangerous, anonymous letter from Spain, written by Sir Charles Wogan. Unfortunately, Wogan's letter is lost, but Swift's reply on 2 August 1732 revealed his intense interest in the author, whose identity he was determined to learn.[25] As noted earlier, Swift had recently published anonymously the memoirs of the octogenarian Jacobite soldier, Captain John Creichton, whose Episcopalian loyalty he greatly admired. When first writing to Swift, Wogan was determined to maintain his incognito, and his letter was enclosed in a green velvet bag which included more of his writings, along with a cask of Spanish wine, which arrived in Dublin in May. His letter, poems, and prose touched a responsive chord in Swift and seemed to increase his sympathy for Jacobitism, at a time when he was thoroughly disgusted with English governance. Swift's reply is worth quoting at length:

> I received your Packet at least two months ago, and took all this Time not only to consider it maturely myself, but to shew it to a few judicious Friends I have in this Kingdom. We all allowed that the Writer was a Scholar, a Man of Genius, and of Honour. We guessed him to have been born in this Country from some Passages, but not from the Style, which we wondered to find so correct in an Exile, a Soldier, and a Native of Ireland. However, altho' I am utterly ignorant of present Persons and Things, I have made a Shift, by talking in general with some Persons, to find out your Name, your Employments, and some of your Actions.
>
> [I was] little expecting a History, a Dedication, a poetical Translation of the Penitential Psalms, Latin Poems, and the like, and all from a Soldier. In these Kingdoms you would be a most unfashionable military Man, among Troops without the least Pretension to Learning or Piety, or common Morals. Although I have no great Regard for your Trade, from the Judgment I make of those who profess it in these Kingdoms, yet I cannot but highly esteem those Gentlemen of Ireland, who, with all the Disadvantages of being Exiles and Strangers, have been able to distinguish themselves by their Valour and Conduct in so many Parts of Europe, I think, above all other Nations; which ought to make the English ashamed of the Reproaches they cast on the Ignorance, the Dulness, the Want of Courage in the Irish Natives; those Defects, wherever they happen, arising only from the Poverty and Slavery they suffer from their inhuman Neighbours, and the base corrupt Spirits of too many of the chief Gentry, etc. I have found the poor Cottagers here, who could speak our Language, to have much better natural Taste for good Sense, Humour and Raillery, than ever I observed among People of the like Sort in England. But the Millions of Oppressions they lye under, the Tyranny of their Landlords, the ridiculous Zeal of their Priests, and the

---

[24] State Papers: 98/35 (May 1734); Ingamells, *Dictionary*, 234-35.
[25] "Charles Wogan," *ODNB*.

general Misery of the whole Nation, have been enough to damp the best Spirits under the Sun.[26]

David Wooley suggests that Swift contacted Nicholas Wogan, who later subscribed to the dean's works, but it is not clear if he was in Ireland at the time, for he continued his service in the Berwick regiment in France.[27] Given the fact that their thrice-married father had thirty-two children, any one of them could have been Swift's source for the letter writer's identification. Charles Wogan replied that "the gentleman of my family" mentioned by Swift, "is the honestest, but the idlest fellow breathing. I cannot even get a letter from him. Thus my reliance for the revising and publishing these pieces is entirely upon Mentor."[28] As noted earlier, "honest" was the Jacobites' cant word for Stuart loyalty (a word earlier applied to Swift by the Duke of Wharton). Despite the serious risk of corresponding with such a known Jacobite activist, Swift agreed to help Wogan get his works published, and even to place his name and acknowledgment "in the next Page after your Epistle; but giving you no Name, nor confessing my Conjecture of it. This Scheme I am still upon, as soon as my Health permits me to return to England."

Swift disagreed with Wogan's dislike of the low comedy of *The Beggar's Opera*, and chided him that he is "in Danger of quarrelling with the Sentiments of Mr. Pope, Gay the author, Dr. Arbuthnot, and myself, Dr. Young, and all the Brethren whom we own." Curiously, except for Gay (as far as is known), all "the Brethren" were Masons, though Edward Young had abandoned his loyalty to Wharton, joined the London Grand Lodge, and generally supported the government. Swift justified their satirical, personal attacks on the political "scoundrels," in order "to lash the Vices out of Practice." But he recognized that Wogan's "Genius runs wholly into the Grave and Sublime"; he thanked him for "the Distinction you please to show me," and promised to send him works by Gay, Pope, Young, and, interestingly, James Bramston, who would soon publish some suggestive Masonic lines.

Copies of the papers Wogan sent to Swift were made later in the eighteenth century by the Bishop of Ossory and are now preserved in the Dioscesan Archives in Galway, Ireland.[29] The following quotes come from those unpublished documents. In Swift's August letter, he responded to Wogan's long manuscript, "URANIUS or the Epistle Dedicatory to the Reverend Doctor JONATHAN SWIFT, DEAN OF St.PATRICK'S, DUBLIN." In a critique that would certainly please Swift, Wogan began:

> Authors of the present, mercenary Age are very often at a loss in the choice of a Patron, as their addresses are not meant, in fact to his real Excellencyes, but merely to his wealth or his influence… Where Classical Learning is to become only a wretched HAND-MAID to POLITICKS; where the PRESS is grown a common PROSTITUTE, and chief purpose of writing rather a means to procure a PLACE, or gain a livelihood, than to instruct Mankind, or improve its Taste… In this case, the DISTINCTION of appearing in

---

[26] J. Swift, *Correspondence*, III 514-15.

[27] J. Ingamells, *Dictionary*, "Nicholas Wogan."

[28] J. Swift, *Correspondence*, III, 593.

[29] I am grateful to the diocesan archivist, Tom Gilgariff, for sending me scanned copies of the English-language documents. A publication and study of the Latin documents is a scholarly *desideratum*. The following quotes are from the archived transcripts.

PRINT becomes entirely PLEBEIAN... The GRAVE, the INSTRUC-
TIVE, the SUBLIME, are utterly abandon'd to the DULLNESS of vulgar
Geniuses.

In a further critique that was not as pleasing to Swift, Wogan compared the superior
Stuart literature produced "during the reigns of our two CHARLESES," when there was
"a LUCID INTERVALL among Men of the best figure in our Nations":

> Those Princes were neither of the HIGH, nor the LOW-DUTCH-CAST:
> they had a Taste of Witt, Learning and Politeness, that gave persons of the
> first Distinction...a necessary Invitation to excell. The Press was not aban-
> don'd to vulgar HIRE-LINGS, nor the Stage to such TRULL-PERSON-
> AGES, as that of POLLY PEACHUM... But, since the CONSULAR Dig-
> nity of the Republick of WITT is entirely subjected to the Tribunes of the
> People, 'tis no wonder the MOBB shou'd make a PROPERTY of PARNAS-
> SUS, and the Theatre be Defiled by the Lowest and most Scandalous of all
> caracters... the Buskins are only fitted for common CHEATS, WHORES
> and ROBBERS... the absurd VILLANYES of MACHEATH [are] attended
> with more concourse and applause, than the staunch HONOUR and
> SENSE of MANLY.

For Wogan, the character of Manly in William Wycherley's *The Plain Dealer* (1676) was
the ideal contrast to John Gay's anti-hero, the thieving Macheath, for Manly expressed
an honest sailor's creed: "I weigh the man, not his title; 'tis not the king's stamp can make
the metal better or heavier."

In his determination to find a worthy patron, Wogan was enlightened by a mystical
vision of his guardian angel, Uranius, who revealed to him that he should send his more
serious works to Jonathan Swift, but he should not presume to send his Hudibrastic
satires and burlesques, because he could never imitate the inimitable Swift. He explained
that his "Angelicall Friend" was his "better Genius," with whom he communicated when
in deep contemplation. It was Uranius who persuaded him to stop obsessing over politics
and government affairs:

> As I have been long dealing in Cypher and the other Intricacyes of negotia-
> tion, my mind was warping itself insensibly into Politicks. Every turn in Af-
> fairs of State, every change of Ministry and Alliance; every Session of Parlia-
> ment or controverted Election, made me either cheerfull or uneasy... [Ura-
> nius] allways shook his head and shew'd a constant aversion to subjects of
> that nature...[He explained] that all those Evills are inflicted by Heaven as
> Scourges on Mankind for having subjected themselves, by their own fault,
> to a train of Calamytes, for which they were not designed.... Thus all your
> HOPES and FEARS arising from the vanity of Politicks and of public oc-
> currences are perfectly idle. Your business is to act with integrity and honour
> in all those scenes of Life, to which you are called. Leave the rest to God.

Wogan assured Swift that he has "enter'd into inviolable Articles with my self to conceal
nothing from you, that may be told with safety to us both (for I here protest against
Politicks, and absolutely forbid the most ingenious and conceited Dullness to spin out
any Inferences from what I say relating to any party or Government)." It is suggestive

that an attainted Jacobite activist believed that Swift shared equally his vulnerability to government prosecution. Unfortunately for posterity, Uranius also advised Wogan to burn his many comical, rhymed, and political writings, before he set off for a military campaign in Italy. In the event of his death or capture, they could provide information dangerous to the Jacobite cause.

Among the mass of papers sent to Swift, Wogan revealed his close friendship and collaboration with Wharton during the duke's last years in Spain. He also hinted at his own Masonic affiliation, noting in "URANIUS" that "All men in their own interior take themselves to be, at least, upon a level" (a well-known Masonic phrase), which again raises the question of whether he was a lodge brother of Wharton, the current Écossais Grand Master, as well as a Tobosan brother of the Masons Ormonde, James Keith, and Marischal Keith. Wogan defended Wharton and Bolingbroke in "An Answer short and pithy to some hireling Poetasters, Authors of the late Pieces in Doggrell and Heroick Viz; The Petition of the Duke of WHARTON, and the Epistle of the Lord Bolingbroke to his Grace. In Imitation of Lord Rochester's sketch upon Rhimers in Generall." He had assured Swift that he kept up with current British and Continental literature, despite his isolation in Spain, and he proved it by responding to *The Humble Petition of His Grace Ph---p D. of Wh----n to a Great Man*, published in London in November 1730 and subsequently in Dublin with "Sir R----t W----e" identified in the title.

The anonymous "hireling Poetaster" attacked Wharton as a political opportunist and drunken rake, who hypocritically changed religions but was no more converted to Catholicism "than Pigs were by St. Anthony."[30] The duke was not even a good Jacobite, for he "beg'd an Alms as a poor Peer,/ And nicked the credulous Chevalier:/ What better Service could I render/ Than out-pretending the Pretender?" He claimed that Wharton tried to gain Walpole's support by promising to reveal "useful Secrets" and providing "a List of Persons disaffected." If George II will forgive his "Writing, Speeching and Protesting," he actually, for the first time, "Shall Pray." In *An Epistle from the Lord Bo----ke to the Duke of W----n*, published in May 1730, another of Walpole's "hirelings" (probably William Arnall) pretended to be Bolingbroke, who advised Wharton to continue their treasonous and Jacobite activities, which he linked with Radcliffe's rebellious troops, Henley's whimsies, Swift's falsehoods, Fog's gloomy fears, and D'Anvers's sneaking *Craftsman*, but all their Jacobite propaganda cannot dislodge Walpole from victory or from George II's love.[31]

Wogan countered the Hanoverian propaganda and the attacks upon his current confidant Wharton by referring to Swift's *Gulliver's Travels*:

> Have you not seen the Dwarfs in LILIPUT
> attempt by swarms, the sleeping Gyant's Foot?
> Or Pygmyes skip for ladders to and fro,
> to scale, secure, ALCIDES' mighty Toe;
> while he, supinely resting on his dub,
> deigns not to crush the wretches with a drub?

---

[30] Anon., *The Humble Petition of his Grace Ph---p D. of Wh---n to a Great Man* (London, 1730), 5-12.
[31] Anon., *An Epistle from the Lord B---ke to the Duke of W----n* (London, 1730), 7-12.

After describing other cowardly, hypocritical attacks, he concluded, "if you have seen all this, to crown the Farce,/ you and your Pay-master, come kiss my A-se." He then quoted Monsieur de Thou's preface to his memoirs to affirm that Virtue, "congeniall to th' eternal Being, shall ever stand secure," while Vice "Loaden with its ever-growing Guilt," sinks the deeper. Wogan knew that his brother Nicholas had helped Thomas Carte in collecting the papers of Jacques Auguste de Thou, whose history and biography were greatly admired by the Jacobites. Swift had earlier referred to Carte as "a Jacobite Parson" and co-editor of the "Edition of Thuanus," at the time when Carte was collaborating with Nicholas Wogan in the collection of materials in France.[32]

Though it may seem surprising that Wogan would praise Wharton as a paragon of virtue, he was then closely collaborating with the duke on his historical and religious writings, and he believed that Wharton was sincere in his Catholic conversion and effort at personal reformation. Some of Wogan's most eloquent writings were his commentaries on seven penitential psalms, which seemed targeted at Wharton's state of physical deterioration and spiritual yearning (a yearning vouched for by various monks who counselled the duke, both in France and Spain). In "A Comment on the 37th. Psalm, Third of the Penitential," Wogan introduced his theme of repentance and salvation, written in an up-side-down pyramidal form which ended with "GOD" at its apex (which I will not duplicate):

> Shewing the habituall sinner reclaim'd by the Dint of all Worldly Miseryes and Misfortunes, Still render'd more feeling by the sharp stings of Worldly shame, Reproach, Loss and contempt of Friends; inveteracy, Perfidy and Triumph of Enemyes: all which he patiently bears by way of atonement for his sins, while in the very act of Resignation and Humiliation, he craves pardon of All-mighty God.

Then, in the blank verse that he preferred to rhyme, Wogan described a Wharton-like figure, to whom an instructive God has "blasted all the Beauty of this clay,/ that wrapps my soul, withere'd of all its Health,/ late so robust for sin." Wharton, with Wogan's encouragement, had joined Hainalt's regiment composed of Irish exiles, and he tried to fulfill his military duties. But his years of alcoholism had so weakened him that he was vulnerable to fevers and infections. He and Wogan knew that the once-famous duke was being mocked, ridiculed, and scorned in England – even by former Jacobite colleagues. Thus, Wogan wrote lines that were directly relevant to Wharton's situation:

> Great God! (for sure there's Room yet left for Grace)
> Behold thy Suppliant prostrate at Thy Feet,
> ....
> Behold my troubled Heart and all my Limbs
> Spoyl'd of their wonted Vigour; my poor Eyes
> Shorn of their Beams; their Gloryes, once so glad
> And glad'ning to my soul, all drown'd in Tears,
> ....
> Behold those , late my Friends, my nearest Kin
> Partners in Dearest Amity and Blood,

---

[32] J. Swift, *Correspondence*, III, 268 and n. 7.

All frown upon me, nor frequent my Door,
But to provoke feel [?] war, and vex my soul
With bitter Curses and opprobrious Taunts.

Behold my Flatt'ers (Parasites and Knaves)
Friends once in shew, Adorers of my Pow'r,
That fawn'd on me in Crowds, still on the Watch
To pay their Court, and lived upon my smiles;
Now at my Mishaps scared, All stand aloof,
And as a baleful Omen, shun my sight.
While my fierce Foes, still thirsting for my Blood,
Insatiate, not with all my Woes asswaged…
……………………………………………………….
Nor are these, Ills enough. My covert Foes
Backward to wage fair Warr and open strifte,
Inglorious, sett their Aspic Tongues on Edge
dipp'd in the deadly Gall of Calumny,
sarcasm and keen Reproach, to blast my Fame,
And sink it with my Fortune, in vile Hope
To leave me a meer By-word to the World…

In *Écossais* Masonic rituals, the initiate's gradual spiritual regeneration was expressed in terms of rebuilding the Temple in Jerusalem, and Wharton – still a Grand Master and founder of a Madrid lodge – was certainly familiar with these themes. Thus, in "A Comment on the 50th. Psalm Fourth of the Penitential," Wogan portrayed the repentant sinner "in true Remorse/ mourning its sins, and humbled in the dust," who cries out:

Grant Thou, O Lord! In thy paternal Love
For Zion, that the walls and lofty Tow'rs
Of thy Jerusalem may quickly rise
Awfull, impenetrable to all her Foes,
Sure guard and Harbour of her Chosen Race.
Then shall thy Votaryes their Homage Pay
Secure, and fearless crowd thy Holy Place.

That Wogan's reformist efforts fared better with Wharton than the poetic hectoring of Edward Young is revealed in the duke's poem of tribute to "MY FRIEND SIR CHARLES WOGAN, BARONET, on his excellent Poeticall Comment on the Seaven PENITENTIAL PSALMS":

With thoughts sublime of true Devotion fired,
YOU sing those Themes, which GOD alone inspired.
Ev'n SATYR shall grow dumb, and owne it true;
That MILTONS Spirit still survives in YOU.
……………………………………………………….
The World's CREATOR who from nought did raise,
This nether Globe is PATRON of your Lays:
He bids YOU write; in ev'ry matchless Line
I feel the force of ENERGY DIVINE.

Wharton agreed with Wogan's disparagement of rhymed verse: "VERSE should be free as AIR. Each thought SUBLIME/ or RAPID, lives in NUMBERS, not in RHIME," for "Blank Verse is a SONATA; RHIME a JIGG." Ironically, Wharton's tribute to blank verse as more suitable for epic and heroic poetry was written in rhymed couplets, of which he was a master. He then mildly criticized Pope for his failure to use Miltonic blank verse, which did a disservice to Homer in Pope's translations:

> O POPE! Hadst THOU lay'd out thy matchless strain
> In EPICKS free and copious, as THY vein;
> In all THY lights HOMER had shone alike
> Glorious in ENGLISH, as in Native Greek.
> The MOBB, 'tis true, had loath'd the Work Divine,
> Baulk'd of the ECCHO in each second line.
> ……………………………………………………..
> BRITONS! Henceforth, in works of EPICK Height,
> free as your SPEECH and GENIUS by your WITT.
> Leave RHIME for LOVE-TALES, SONNETTS and BURLESQUE,
> There let YOUR STRINGS of ECCHO'S NEIGH and frisk:
> ……………………………………………………..
> Play not with childs UNISONS, the badge
> Of DULLNESS, that gives leading-strings to RAGE,
> Loads the SUBLIME, or casts a friv'lous air
> ON GREAT RESOLVES, and triffles with DESPAIR.

The duke concluded with praise of his new and valued friendship with Wogan:

> These lines, MY FRIEND (LATE and IN EXILE found)
> Test of our Union, must with yours be bound:
> that both may share a happier Fate than ours,
> Wellcome at home, whoever guard the doors.
> ……………………………………………………..
> GREAT in your VERSE, as on the MARTIALL SCENE,
> WHOSE ESSAY WAS TO FREE A CAPTIVE QUEEN.
>
> WHARTON.

That Wharton's poem was bound with Wogan's commentaries on the psalms means that they were in the packet sent to Swift, who had earlier greatly admired Wharton and had wryly hoped that the duke intended to take his "Advice of fancying to have Virtue." [33] We will return to Wogan's correspondence with Swift, in the years after Wharton's death.

In 1732, although Swift lamented that he was exiled "Far to the Land of Slaves and Fens," he kept up with his political allies and enemies in England, while praise and criticism of the Masons continued in the popular press and theater. On 24 February 1732 the *Grub Street Journal* described a sham Masonic ceremony, in which an initiate wears "Hiram's mask," which is painted inside with "an ointment of faecal matter of a citron hue," and other indignities, which "Ceremonies are...as significant as those of the Original Free

---

[33] *Ibid.*, II, 494.

Masons, and much more diverting."[34] On 27 April an actress delivered an Epilogue at the Drury Lane Theatre in which she addressed charges of sodomy against the Masons by portraying them as virile impregnators:

> They're Lovers of our Sex, as I can witness;
> Nor e'er act contrary to Moral Fitness!
> They'll not deceive your largest – Expectations;
> They're able Workmen, and compleatly skill'd in
> The deepest – Arts and Mysteries of Building;
> They'll build up Families, and, as most fit is,
> Not only will erect – but people Cities.
> They'll fill, as well as fabricate, your Houses,
> And found a lasting Race of strong built Spouses.[35]

In May the *Gentleman's Magazine* featured a satire on extravagant Whig builders, which echoed Pope's criticism of the ostentatious but vulgar Timon. "Jenny Downcastle" gives "Mr. Stonecastle" her thoughts on modern architecture and defies him to produce in all his inventory of female extravagancies "any thing so enormous, so expensive, so exposing, as your modern Vanity of Buildings, Gardening, Vistas, and Avenues," etc., and adds, "All these fall among your own Sex; you have no Vitruvius, no Palladio in Petticoats."[36] She mocks "those designing Virtuosos," who signalize themselves for "this Grand Gusto of distorting and disguising nature," from their "renown'd Exemplars Mr Inigo Pilaster and Sir Christopher Cupolo, down to that incomparable Engineer, Mr Alderman Pantile, who has spent thirty years building himself "a Palace in the Country," while ignoring the education of his children or the good of his fellow citizens. In a final jab at the Whig builders, she asserts, "How ridiculous will he be, if a noble Body of Buildings should be found animated with a Plebeian Soul!" Swift and Pope would certainly share this jaundiced view.

In September Henley obtruded himself into a Masonic controversy over whether a Jew can be made a Mason. He responded to an article in the *Daily Post* (22 September 1732), which described a lodge meeting at the Rose Tavern in Cheapside, where "in the presence of several Brethren of Distinction, as well Jews as Christians, Mr. Ed. Rose was admitted of the Fraternity by Dr. Dan'l Delvalle, an eminent Jew snuff-merchant, the Master, Capt. Willmott, who were entertained very handsomely…in a manner not infringing on the Christian morality of the Christian Sabbath."[37] On 30 September Henley advertised an oration on "Another question, – whether a Jew can be a Mason; or a Mason can be made on a Sunday, caused by a Letter on a late Making in Cheapside." Seven Jewish members of Bricklayer's Lodge at the Barbican moved to the Rose, apparently to support the new Jewish initiates, after some dissention about the "making."[38] Henley then advertised in *Fog's Journal* (7 October 1732) that he would lecture on "the cause of the Jew-Masons fully clear'd, and the Affair of the Bricklayers Lodge from the Barbican to the Rose in Cheapside disclos'd."

[34] D. Knoop, G. Jones, D. Hamer, *EMP*, 289.
[35] *Ibid.*, 285.
[36] "Of Extravagance in Building," *Gentleman's Magazine*, 17 (May 1732), 765-66.
[37] *Daily Post* (22 September 1732); quoted in C. Crawley, "Masonic MSS.," 30.
[38] For the Jewish Masons' names, see J. Shaftesley, "Jews," 190.

While these obscure Masonic skirmishes took place in London, Dr. William King, Ramsay's sponsor at Oxford, launched his own attack on Whig Masonry and architecture. He sent to Swift a hundred, pre-publication copies of his bizarre attack on King's financial and political enemies in Dublin, entitled *The Toast, An Epic Poem, in Four Books. Written in Latin by Frederick Scheffer, Done into English by Peregrine O'Donald.* King had long admired Swift's satirical methods, and he may have met him during his periodical visits to Dublin when he tried to win a tangled lawsuit. On 14 October 1732 Swift wrote Charles Ford that a printer brought to him copies of "a most bitter satyr," which is "very malicious, and worth reading. It is called *the Toast.*"[39] He claimed (disingenuously?) not to know the author "one Dr. King the Head of a Hall" in England, who "I presume employd some young Oxonians to write it." Both Swift and King knew that their correspondence was regularly opened by government agents, so they were cautious about revealing the identities of anonymous authors.

One of King's targets was the Dublin architect, Captain Edward Lovett Pearce, who in 1730 gave Swift an inscribed copy of Cicero's *de Officiis* (1517).[40] As noted earlier, Pearce was eulogized by Henry Nelson in *The Speech of the First Stone laid in the Parliament-House to the Government, February 3d, 1729*, a loyalist Masonic broadside, which implied Pearce's own affiliation:

> Next let me First to this great Honour bring:
> Let ev'ry Tongue in softest Notes Rehearse,
> Time after Time, the worth of Captain Pierce;
> All hail to thee! who only is the Man,
> That by your Art has form'd this Noble PLAN,
> And as the Structure on my Shoulders rise,
> So shall your Praise Exalted to the Skies;
> The Pile Majestick shall its Beauty show,
> And all its Glory to your Judgment owe;
> To future Ages celebrate the Name
> Of its Projector, and Record your Fame.

Reports that Pearce was not really the sole architect and craftsman of the project were believed by Dr. King, who "having a personal grudge against him, alleged that Pearce, among other colourful vices and misdemeanours, had relied on Richard Castle's advice, skills and labour in the construction of the Parliament House but had denied Castle both credit and payment for his work."[41] Castle was the son of an English-born Jew who served as Director of Munitions and Mines in Saxony, and he travelled widely in Europe before coming to England in 1725, where he was in contact with Lord Burlington's circle.[42] In 1728 he moved to Ireland, where Pearce employed him as a draughtsman on the plans for the new Parliament House. Known as a man of integrity and convivial but eccentric manners, Castle evidently met King in Ireland and confided the ill treatment by Pearce; King would subsequently accuse Pearce of forgery.

---

[39] J. Swift, *Correspondence*, III, 546-47.
[40] J. Swift, *Prose*, V, xxxi.
[41] "Edward Lovett Pearce," On-line Dictionary of Irish Architects.
[42] "Richard Castle," On-line Dictionary of Irish Architects.

In *The Toast*, which was published in London and Dublin in November 1732, King satirized Pearce as "Sir Piercy," and in a note he condemned his constructions:

> At that time the old Theatre was standing. But a new Play-House hath since been built in Dublin under the Direction of that wise and honest Architect, who built the new Parliament House. In the latter you cannot hear, and in the new Theatre you can neither see nor hear.[43]

King also targeted Pearce's friend and benefactor, Joshua Allen, 2nd Viscount Allen, whom Swift had scorned as "Traulus," the "corrupt spawn of a line of Masons." King suggested that his mythological villains, "Sir Mars and old Vol" (Sir Thomas Smith and Captain John Pratt) were similarly corrupt Freemasons, for "by Contact one God can distinguish another;/ As a learned Free Mason discovers his Brother."[44]

King boldly included praise of Swift as the Drapier and author of *Gulliver*. The dean's "Brob-dig-nag Giants...repell'd the Brass Thunder," and "preserv'd the poor Town," followed by the explanatory note:

> The Poet here insinuates the Attempt which was made about the Year 1723, by Wood and his Patrons to carry off the Gold and Silver, the current Coin of this Country, in exchange for Brass Halfpence, and which was defeated by some excellent Pieces written on that Occasion by Dr. S---t, the present Dean of St. P-----k's, than whom no Country can boast a better Patriot and no Age has produced a greater Genius.[45]

He subsequently commented that Swift was "chiefly pleased with the notes." As we shall see, Swift would later go even further than King in attacking Pearce's architecture and Allen's Masonry in *The Legion Club* (1736).

On 8 February 1733 the *Grub Street Journal* ran a humorous criticism of the modern Freemasons' claim to architectural expertise. Confessing that he is not an "accepted" brother, the author argued that "the fraternity might as well be called the society of carpenters, joiners, chimney-sweepers, or rat-catchers, as Masons."[46] Reflecting the distancing of Grand Lodge Masonry from the traditional operative craft, he scorned their claim of special secrets, for Archimedes, Vitruvius, and other ancients, "as well as the architects and mathematicians of the later ages, have delivered their knowledge in this science freely, generally, and publicly." Moreover, in the modern lodges, there are "a very great number of brethren, who are not quite *Euclidical* enough to comprehend an intricate mathematical demonstration, or even a geometrical definition." In these non-craftsman, non-architectural Masons, he could not "perceive the least tincture of *Vitruvism, Euclidism,* or *Burlingtonism.*" The "brethren build no better than some of the moneyed gentry among the Grubs." The critic then referred to "their cabalistical doctrines," and rejected the charge that their ceremonies derive from "the popish mass," because so many "zealous Protestants, nay even Jews, the constant enemies of transubstantiation, are accepted

---

[43] David Greenwood, *William King, Tory and Jacobite* (Oxford, 1969). 59, 66.

[44] [William King], *The Toast, An Epic Poem in Four Books* (Dublin, 1732), I, 32.

[45] *Ibid.,*I, 71.

[46] *EMP*, 292-95.

Marsha Keith Schuchard

brethren." One wonders if the critic had heard Orator Henley discourse on "Whether a Jew can be a Mason."[47]

In March 1733 the Anglican minister James Bramston published *The Man of Taste*, a genial, positive response to Pope's *Epistle to Burlington* (1731), which was re-issued with the title "On Taste."[48] In *The Dunciad* (1728), Pope had contrasted Bramston's subdued preaching to Henley's bombastic sermons, and he praised his mildly oppositionist poem, *The Art of Politicks* (1729).[49] Swift sent the latter work to Charles Wogan, and he would undoubtedly share Bramston's mockery of the intellectual pretensions of Whig Freemasons, builders, and scientists, in his new poem. The narrator in *The Man of Taste* is a vain and vapid *poseur*, who praises *The Boghouse-Miscellany*, as "well design'd/ To ease the body, and improve the mind," but "Swift's whims and jokes for my resentment call,/ For he displeases me, that pleases all."[50] He then scorns the splendid architectural achievements of the Stuart architects versus the supposedly "great" works of Vanbrugh and current Whig builders:

> I know the town, all houses I have seen,
> From High-Park corner down to Bednal-Green.
> Sure wretched Wren was taught by bungling Jones,
> To murder mortar, and disfigure stones!
> Who in Whitehall can symmetry discern?
> I reckon Convent-garden Church a Barn.
> Nor hate I less thy vile Cathedral, Paul!
> The choir's too big, the cupola's too small:
> 'Thus Vanbrug's structures that my fancy strike:
> ....
> Building so happily I understand,
> That for one house I'd mortgage all my land.
> Dorick, Ionick, shall not there be found,
> But it shall cost me threescore thousand pound.
> From out my honest workmen, I'll select
> A Bricklay'r, and proclaim him architect.[51]

Like Swift in *Gulliver's Travels*, Bramston associated Whig architecture with Whig science and modern Masonry:

> Bears, Lyons, Wolves, and Elephants I breed,
> And *Philosophical Transactions* read.
> Next Lodge I'll be Free-Mason, nothing less,
> Unless I happen to be *F.R.S.*[52]

Bramston's praise of Pope and mockery of Whig Masonry prompted an indignant response from Orator Henley in *The Hyp-Doctor* (10 April 1733):

[47] D. Lysons, *Collectanea*, f. 65 (*Fog's Journal*, 30 September 1732).
[48] W.B. Hextall, "'The Man of Taste,' a Satire of 1733," *AQC* (1908), 230-37.
[49] "James Bramston," *ODNB*.
[50] James Bramston, *The Man of Taste. Occasion'd by an Epistle of Mr. Pope's on that Subject* (London, 1733), 7.
[51] *Ibid.*, 10.
[52] *Ibid.*, 14.

348

> A New Sect has lately appear'd, consisting of Philosophers of both Sexes call'd the TASTERS; they took their Origin from a Poem intitul'd OF TASTE; in the title the author complimented a Brother Poet, lodging at a Pastry-cook's…to be sent after them, particularly large Reams of the late Craftsman, Fog's, Instructions from the Country, and other Profundities upon Excises…These TASTERS form'd into a Regular Society; the Pastry-Cook aforesaid is President, Mr. POPE is Vice-President, Mr. BEE is Secretary, Mr. Craftsman, and Mr. Fog are the two Writing-Clerks, Mr. Grub is Shoe-cleaner, and the Other Officers and Members are rang'd in a decent Subordination.

Henley's rejoinder must have pleased Delafaye and Walpole, for in the coming weeks he would step up his defense of Hanoverian Masonry and ridicule of opposition brothers.

The Orator's propaganda was especially needed from October 1732 onward, when *The Craftsman* began a sustained attack on Walpole's proposed bill to transform the customs duties on wine and tobacco into a centralized excise tax. On 19 February the prime minister anonymously published *A Letter from a Member of Parliament to his Friends in the Country, Concerning the Duties on Wine and Tobacco* (1733), in which he dismissed "this chimaera of a General Excise," in which a "standing army" of excise collectors could arbitrarily enter private homes to search for infractions, as the seditious fantasy of Jacobites and republicans. He then characterized their "unnatural union" as a "sacred mystery," concocted by secret enemies to the Royal Family and happy constitution.[53] Their groundless imaginings are "as little necessary, as I have to expatiate upon the absurdity of the popish religion under a Protestant King."

The pamphlet provoked an angry reply, *A Candid Answer to a Letter from a Member of Parliament* (1733), in which the author jumped upon Walpole's reference to "a sacred mystery" to charge that he was not really a representative of the people but in fact a common Freemason:

> It is hardly possible for him to mistake a well-known Right for a wrong Bias on his Judgment. If, therefore, Conjectures are allowable, I should think him a Free-Mason of the lowest Order, for two Reasons: The first, because he seems to write not so much for Bread, as for good Drink: My other Reason for thinking him one of that antient Order, is, that he lays Colouring and Varnish on the Excise, as if he did it with a Trowel.[54]

Moreover, his Masonic-style mystery will largely consist of great sums of public money applied to "Secret Services," which enable the government to spy on their suspected rebellious subjects.

The disaffected Whig, William Pulteney, also jumped on Walpole's phrase, the "sacred mystery," noting that "The grand Mystery, which was long deemed too sacred for the unhallow'd Eyes of the People," was used by "hireling Writers" who tried shamelessly to persuade "the People, that it was only the chimerical Offspring of disaffected and

---

[53] [Robert Walpole], *A Letter from a Member of Parliament to his Friends in the Country, concerning the Duties on Wine and Tobacco* (London, 1733), 7-11, 18.

[54] Anon., *A Candid Answer to a Letter from a Member of Parliament to his Friends in the Country, Concerning the Duties on Wine and Tobacco* (London, 1733), 1v-v, 17.

seditious Brains." In his anonymous pamphlet, *The Budget Opened* (1733), Pulteney mocked the call of "the great man" for "Days of Reformation": "Methinks I see you in your Closet, while you are writing this elegant Passage, knitting your Brows, and muttering to yourself – CHARITABLE CORPORATION! – DERWENTWATER! – YORK BUILDINGS! – Where the Devil will this Reformation end?"[55] All of these scandals, whose perpetrators were allegedly shielded by Walpole, involved injustices to Jacobite and opposition Masons. Noting that the author dropped his "smooth, cajoling style, and, losing all your Temper at once," you call "every Body about you, Jacobites and Republicans." The opposition eventually became so strong that Walpole was forced to drop the excise bill.

Meanwhile in Dublin, Swift received in March a fifty-page letter from Wogan, who sent it from Spain on 27 February 1733. Though Swift's modern editors reprint only four paragraphs (David Wooley dismisses it as a mere "screed"), Wogan's eloquent letter deserves fuller consideration, for it apparently influenced Swift's increasing hostility to the English government and Scottish Presbyterians and, more importantly, sympathy for the Irish Catholics.[56] Though Wogan had planned to maintain his incognito, Swift's discovery of his identity led Wogan to grant permission for Swift to share his writings, but only with "those whom he judges worthy of his intimacy."[57] He addressed Swift as "Mentor," thus recalling the relationship of Mentor and Telemachus as described by Fenelon and Ramsay. He stressed that his caution was necessary because "the arms of whiggism are extremely long, and reach them to their remotest haunts."[58] He appreciated Swift's praise of the "Wild Geese," the exiled Irish Jacobites, and he responded:

> Those who have chosen a voluntary exile, to get rid of oppression, have given themselves up, with great gayety of spirit, to the number of above 120,000 men, within these forty years. The rest, who have been content to stay at home, are reduced to the wretched condition of the Spartan helots. They are under a double slavery.[59]

Though Mentor certainly does the exiles "that justice which cannot be denied them by any of those nations among whom they have served, it is seldom or ever allowed them by those who can write or speak English correctly." Moreover, "all the honour the protestant Irish have acquired by their pen or their swords, passes generally for English":

> Thus England...is allowed a right to all those who have either written or fought in English with any distinction, as Scotland impudently whips away from Ireland all her old saints and her sophists, on account of having shared with her the name of Scotia. The Ushers, Boyles, Congreves, Garths, Denhams, Swifts, Ormonds, Cadogans, Aylmers, etc. are taken for English

---

[55] [William Pulteney], *The Budget Opened. Or, an Answer to a Pamphlet intitled, A Letter from a Member of Parliament* (London, 1733), 18, 26-27.

[56] J. Swift, *Correspondence*, III, 518, 592.

[57] Jonathan Swift, *The Works of Jonathan Swift, D.D....Arranged by Thomas Sheridan, A.M* (rev. ed. John Nichols (London, 1803), XVIII, 172-217. Reproduces the full text of the letter.

[58] *Ibid.*, XVIII, 181.

[59] *Ibid.*, XVIII,173.

in foreign countries... In short, what can Ireland have left her, but her bogs and stupidity, since England and Scotland have swept away the stakes.[60]

Swift took these words to heart, for he had recently turned down an offer from Bolingbroke to move to England and take up a church living near his old friend. According to Irvin Ehrenpreis, he now had "a tie with the common, industrious, and productive people of Ireland that he did not wish to break."[61]

Wogan responded to Swift's chiding him for his negative reaction to the satires of Pope, Gay, and their circle, which seemed preoccupied with petty people and petty matters (a judgment shared by the late Atterbury):

> I should be very sorry to make enemies of those whom, of all mankind, I would choose to make my friends. Mr. Pope and I lived in perfect union and familiarity, for two or three summers, before he ended up on the stage of the world... The other geniuses have a right to all my regard... They are at home, and endeavour to give the world a sense of its follies with great humour and gaiety. The cheerfulness of my temper is in great measure sunk under a long and hopeless exile, which has given it a serious, or, if you will, a supercilious turn. I lash the world with indignation and grief, in the strain of Jeremy... However, if there be any room for a grave, sullen fellow, that has been one of the merriest fellows in Europe, in Mentor's academy, I offer myself...[62]

Wogan then unleashed a learned and blistering attack on Edward Hyde, 1st Earl of Clarendon, whom he blamed for undermining the national Anglican church and monarchy. Though Swift admired Clarendon as a historian, especially compared to the Whiggish Gilbert Burnet, he must have been disturbed by some of Wogan's charges: "the proceedings of Clarendon, upon the restoration, only laid in seed for a larger crop of rebellion. How could the church and monarchy thrive, by fostering their covert foes in their very bosom, and obliging their only friends to become their inveterate enemies?"[63] For Swift, whose attitude toward the Williamite revolution had become increasingly negative, Wogan's charge against "the unthinking tories" would sting:

> King James the second had given a liberty of conscience in general. This, as it was shocking to the established church, was exchanged, by the prevalence of calvinistical and free-thinking interlopers, for the softer title of toleration, which has been improved....into actual domination. A great cry was kept up on all sides, about the dangers that threatened the church. The unthinking tories, or church of England men, joined in it along with the whigs, with a view to keeping out popery. The whigs heightened it at every turn, not to keep out popery, which they made use of as a bugbear, but to oblige the church to suppress her true doctrine and discipline, and let in presbytery. The tories were all along the dupes of this farce...[64]

---

[60] *Ibid.*, XVIII, 182.
[61] I. Ehrenpreis, *Swift*, III, 730.
[62] J. Swift, *Works...Thomas Sheridan*, XVIII, 216.
[63] *Ibid.*, XVIII, 197.
[64] *Ibid.*, XVIII, 209.

But Swift appreciated Wogan's judgment that "It is true, the tories had a lucid interval in the last years of Queen Anne; but it could not last, because they never can have spirit enough to play all their game, and fix their fortune."[65] Swift would be reminded of his unsuccessful attempt to heal the rivalries between the Tories Oxford and Bolingbroke, which led to George I's succession and the victory of the Whigs. He would be further frustrated that his manuscript *History of the Last Four Years of the Queen* was still considered too dangerous to publish. In an argument that Swift would subsequently echo, Wogan charged that the English people

> flatter themselves with a notion of being free, because they have an air of being represented, and yet it is that very representation makes them slaves. They have no real liberty left but that of the press... Clarendon's antimonarchical scheme is like to continue for ever the surest support of tyranny. The whigs must be the majority in parliament. They alone can be bribed to sell and subdue the people.[66]

In a statement that still puzzles many Swift scholars, the dean predicted that England would soon be ruled by an absolute monarch, thus repeating Wogan's conclusion that the corruption and power of the prime minister and his Whig placemen would render the king the equivalent of an absolute tyrant.[67]

Wogan devoted many pages to the oppression and miseries of the Irish Catholics, whose only crime was being loyal to their traditional religion and legitimate kings. Despite his own criticism of Charles II and James II, Swift recognized that the Irish Catholic position had become much worse after the "Glorious" revolution. Thus, he was evidently sympathetic to Wogan's description of a truly catholic Catholicism which, like that of Ramsay, was tolerant of other religions. Echoing Ramsay's statements of universal brotherhood, Wogan affirmed that "We are all brethren in fact."[68]

> Dear Mentor, excuse me for having finished as folks do generally in their drink, with a dispute about religion; I love religion, with all my soul, where it is sincere; but abhor, above all things, the pretence or abuse of it, to advance any purpose but those that regard the other world. As I have a soul (I hope) to be saved, I have studied all the present religions with care: and if my creed did not determine me to be a catholic, I freely own I should be troubled with none of them, because of all the vile and cruel rogueries I have seen them misapplied to. Most of them, for want of authority, are lost in free-thinking; others for want of authority, vanish into superstition. ... The catholic may be free from either, if he pleases... The same may be said of a national church, guarded by the civil, and fenced by her own ecclesiastical authority. She may be very catholic, without being enslaved to the decretals and extravagancies of popery; or overlaid by the heavier weight of presbytery; or made the jest and handmaid of free-thinking![69]

---

[65] *Ibid.*, XVIII, 210.

[66] *Ibid.*, XVIII, 212.

[67] J. Swift, *Correspondence*, IV, 173.

[68] J. Swift, *Works...Thomas Sheridan*, XVIII, 216.

[69] *Ibid.*, XVIII, 215.

For Swift, who was engaged in a bitter pamphlet battle against Whig efforts to remove the Test Act, Wogan's words would be tonic. Moreover, he must have been touched by the personal tolerance of a once wealthy and privileged Irishman who had sacrificed and would continue to sacrifice everything for the Jacobite and Irish national cause:

> with all my spleen and vexation of spirit, I am the most inoffensive creature in the world in regard of religion.. I would not shed one ounce of blood in anger or enmity, or wrong any man living of a cracked sixpence, to make all the world catholic; yet I am as staunch a one myself as any pope in the universe....I laugh, with great contempt, at those who will force others to Heaven their way, in spite of charity.[70]

Unfortunately, Swift did not live up to his promise to publish Wogan's works, with his own imprimatur. As Ian Higgins observes, it would be "presumably too dangerously provocative an act, even for the Dean of St. Patrick's and his risk-taking printers to contemplate."[71]

Though Swift claimed to indulge in no "state-scribbles," he plunged headfirst into "church-scribbles." In November 1733 he continued his battle against English and Presbyterian attempts to repeal the Test Act, which protected the established Anglican church.[72] Evidently influenced by Wogan, Swift posed as a Catholic and gave an ironic review of Irish history, "showing how innocent and oppressed the Roman Catholics have been," when compared to the rebellious and murderous Presbyterian and Puritan dissenters. In his anonymous tract, *Reasons Humbly Offered to the Parliament of Ireland for Repealing the Sacramental Test, in Favour of the Catholicks, Otherwise Called Roman Catholicks, and By their Ill-Willers, Papists, Drawn Partly from their Arguments as they are Catholicks, and Partly from Argument common to their Brethren the* Common Dissenters (1733), Swift portrayed the original English settlers of Ireland as Catholics, who were "always Defenders of Monarchy, as constituted in these Kingdoms, whereas our Brethren the Dissenters, were always Republicans both in Principle and Practice."[73]

He further argued that Catholics only rebelled when there was severe oppression: "They had no Intention to introduce a new Religion, but to enjoy the Liberty of preserving the *old*; the very same which their Ancestors professed from the Time that Christianity was first introduced into this Island, which was by Catholicks." When the Puritans murdered their King and turned the Monarchy into a Republic, it is not to be wondered at "if the Catholicks, in such a Babel of Religions, chose to adhere to their own Faith left by their Ancestors, rather than seek for a better among a Rabble of hypocritical, rebellious, deluding Knaves, or deluded Enthusiasts." Though Swift was not explicitly supporting the Jacobite cause, the pamphlet was later considered so dangerous that the subtitle – "Written in the Style of a Roman Catholic" – was omitted from the 1746 edition, when Britain was still in the throes of the 1745 Jacobite rebellion.[74]

---

[70] *Ibid.*, XVIII, 217.
[71] I. Higgins, "Jonathan Swift's Memoirs of a Jacobite," 84.
[72] I. Ehrenpreis, *Swift*, III, 762-65.
[73] J. Swift, *Prose*, XII, 286-87, 290.
[74] *Ibid.*, XII, 347.

Despite his ironic stance when defending the Irish Catholics (versus those he considered much worse, the Scottish Presbyterians), Swift had been deeply moved by Wogan's eloquent defense of a tolerant Catholicism. Thus, he must have been pleased that an Irish Catholic became Grand Master in Dublin. In 1733-34 the Irish Grand Mastership was held by Henry Benedict Barnewall, 4th Viscount Kingsland, who came from an Anglo-Catholic family long settled in Ireland.[75] His father was a captain in James II's army and was attainted by William III. In December 1716 Swift had called upon "old Barnwell," kinsman of the Viscounts Kingsland, to help him collect tithes in county Meath.[76] Henry Benedict's mother was from the Rosse family; thus, Lord Kingsland (as he was called) was related to the first Irish Grand Master, and he carried on that family's private Stuart sympathies. He became a Mason in Dublin in the late 1720s, and he and his family would play a significant role in the fraternity in Ireland and France.[77] He appointed his brother Richard Barnewall as his Deputy Grand Master in 1733 and another Catholic, the physician James Brennan, as DGM in 1734.

In 1740 Kingsland presented himself to the House of Lords and refused to sign the English act of allegiance, "declaring it was not agreeable to his conscience he being a Roman Catholic, and in consequence never took his seat as an Irish peer." Recently widowed, he took his brother Richard and two sons to St. Germain-en-Laye, where he befriended Derwentwater and Ramsay. He must have been pleased with their emphasis on the chivalric traditions of ancient Freemasonry, for the Barnewalls' revered ancestor, Roger de Barneville, participated in the First Crusade and was beheaded during the siege of Antioch.[78] In 1741 his brother moved to Toulouse where he founded the first lodge, which had strong Jacobite ties. He was probably the donor of the two manuscript copies of Ramsay's Masonic "Discours" deposited in the Museum of Toulouse.

But back in 1733, the rise of Irish Catholic officers, with suspected Jacobite sympathies, was opposed by the Whig Masons, such as John Allen and Thomas Prendergast (despised targets of Swift's satires). Prendergast had become M.P. for Clonmel in Ireland in 1730 and for Chichester in England in 1733, both achieved through the political pressure of his in-law, the Duke of Richmond.[79] At this time, Swift characterized Richmond's late father as "a shallow Coxcomb."[80] Despite the dean's scorn for the family, Richmond's almost obsessive campaign to advance the unsavory Prendergast worked better in Ireland than in England, where Walpole disliked him and George II called him "an Irish blockhead."[81]

Swift continued to gain information on Masonic affairs from Faulkner, his confidant and publisher, who knew of Swift's authorship of *A Letter from the Grand Mistress of the Female Freemasons*. For years Faulkner's *Dublin Journal* steadily reported on Masonic

---

[75] J. Lepper and P. Crossle, *History*, 150-51.

[76] J. Swift, *Correspondence*, II, 201-02.

[77] Edward Corp, "The Jacobite Presence in Toulouse in the Eighteenth Century," in Sophie Dulucq, ed., *Genealogies Rêvées* (Toulouse, 2004), 124-55.

[78] C. Krey August, *The First Crusade: The Accounts of Eyewitnesses and Participants* (Princeton, 1921), 101-03. I am grateful to John Barnwell for sending me this information.

[79] J. Lepper and P. Crossle, *History*, 133-34; Richmond, Charles Lennox, Duke of, *The Correspondence of the Dukes of Richmond and Newcastle, 1724-1750*, ed. Timothy J. McCann (Lewes, 1984), 4-6.

[80] Scottish National Library: Advocates MSS. 32.4.2: Swift's annotations to Macky's *Memoirs* (1733), 36.

[81] J. Lepper and P. Crossle, *History*, 90.

meetings and members and, as noted earlier, he was allegedly "an active Freemason in his early days."[82] On 20-24 November 1733 he reported a session of the Irish Grand Lodge, attended by the Grand Master Lord Kingsland and Lord Kingston, who would regain the Grand Mastership in 1735. [83] They represented the patriotic party who always supported Swift. However, the Whigs were also present, for John Allen and Thomas Griffith, who often opened Swift's correspondence, continued their membership. The Earl of Middlesex, son of the Lord Lieutenant Dorset and home from his Masonic adventures in Florence, attended as a new member. His brother, Lord George Sackville, also became an Irish Mason, but Swift resented the repeated appeals that he help the young man, who eventually reported to his father that "the Dean has shown himself more mad and absurd than ever."[84]

Faulkner published another pamphlet, *A Prologue, and an Epilogue, and Songs, spoken and sung To the Antient and Rt. Worshipful Society of Free-Masons, at the Theatre Royal, on Thursday November 29th, 1733, being Mr. Griffith's Benefit* (Dublin, 1734). Interestingly, given Giffith's government job as a tide waiter, the benefit performance was bespoke by the Grand Master Barnewall, whose fellow Jacobites would come under Griffith's surveillance at the port of Dublin. The Prologue and Epilogue had been spoken earlier at the New Theatre in Goodman's Fields in London, and the first praised the fraternity "where kings, and a long shining train/ Of garter'd heroes wait upon thy reign."[85] In the finale, the actress fears that her husband will be castrated by his initiators, but he returns home intact and more potent than ever. Faulkner added three songs not published elsewhere. In lines that would have appealed to the embittered Swift, who now saw friendship as the last bastion of truth and honor, the Masons sang:

> To state Disputes we ne'er give Birth,
> Our Motto Friendship is and Mirth.
> ....
> By Friendship's strict Tyes we Brothers are join'd,
> With Mirth in each Heart, and Content in each Mind,
> And this is a difficult Secret to find.[86]

One of Swift's new friends was John Boyle, 5th Earl of Orrery, who came to Ireland to bring order into a mismanaged estate. Swift had long been a friend and confidant of John's father, Charles, the 4th Earl, who had visited the dean in Dublin in August 1731, one month before his death.[87] As noted earlier, the senior Orrery was then collaborating with Cornbury and Bolingbroke on an ambitious restoration plan. Orrery *fils* was privy to that plot and continued to support it, though not with his father's activism. The 4th and 5th earls were allegedly Freemasons, and father and son had hosted Ramsay in England; they subsequently kept up with developments in English and Continental Freemasonry. Thus, it seems likely that young Orrery privately shared with Swift information on Jacobite and Masonic developments at home and abroad. The two met in autumn 1732,

---

82 Chetwode Crawley, in H. Sadler, *Masonic Reprints*, xxiv/
83 J. Lepper and P. Crossle, *History*, 90.
84 J. Swift, *Correspondence*, IV, n.4.
85 Knoop, Jones, Hamer, *EMP*, 290-91.
86 *Ibid.*, 297-98.
87 I. Ehrenpreis, *Swift*, III, 731

and during Orrery's repeated visits to Dublin, their friendship ripened through common literary and political interests.

At this time, Orrery risked provoking Pope's wrath by supporting Lewis Theobald in his effort to bring out a scholarly edition of Shakespeare's works. Orrery's father had been an early patron of Theobald, and despite Pope's making Theobald chief of the Dunces, the 5th Earl continued to respect his critical abilities. Orrery placed his late father's papers in Theobald's hands in order to have them "regulated." [88] In 1732 Theobald published a poem in praise of Orrery, while he rather desperately sought financial support from Walpole. Feeling keenly "the pinch of poverty," he appealed to his fellow Freemasons in the Grand Lodge to support the production of his much-delayed play, *The Fatal Secret*, and the Masonic officials in December 1733 urged the brethren to help their brother get the play performed in spring 1734. [89] When the script was published in 1735, Theobald's dedication to Walpole, who never granted him any funds, must have annoyed Orrery, who had rewarded Theobald with £100 for dedicating to him the Shakespeare edition of 1733.

In that year, while he was in Ireland, Orrery counted on Thomas Carte to send him political news from England, so that he "may not be totally ignorant of what they are doing at a certain obscure corner of the world named Westminster." [90] Carte, who communicated by courier, may have informed him of Derwentwater's incognito presence in England in 1733. Though the ministry decided not to act publicly against the attainted earl, Walpole evidently ordered Orator Henley to change the title of the *The Hyp-Doctor* to *The Free-Mason* in November 1733, in order to counter not only the opposition journal, *The Craftsman*, but the opposition craftsmen among the Masons. Supported by Walpole's secret subsidy, Henley had already risen within the fraternity, for it was reported on 9 June 1733 that the Freemasons "made Choice of the Rev. Mr. Orator Henley for their Chaplain for the ensuing year." [91]

At that lodge meeting, James Lyon, 7th Lord Strathmore, was chosen Grand Master, but he remained in Scotland and was installed by proxy. Though he descended from a Jacobite family and was on Wharton's list of Stuart supporters in 1725, he was apparently acceptable to the Whigs in the Grand Lodge. [92] The members came from both political sides, including John Ward, a crypto-Jacobite, and James Moor Smythe, a Whig target of Pope's and Swift's satire. In August Strathmore presided in Mary's Chapel Lodge in Edinburgh, in which he served not only as Grand Master of England but also was "chosen Grand Master for the present meeting." [93] Several important noblemen were initiated, including John Lindsay, 20th Earl of Crawford, and John Keith, 3rd Earl of Kintore, who both appeared on Wharton's list and who would later serve as Grand Masters of England. Kintore was a cousin of the attainted Jacobites, George and James Keith, and in 1746 he would be reported to the government as "in his heart" a Jacobite. [94] At Strathmore's

[88] Richard F. Jones, *Lewis Theobald: His Contribution to English Scholarship* (London, 1966), 153-59.
[89] A. Carpenter, *Desaguliers*, 99-100.
[90] Bodleian: Calendar of Carte MSS: vol. 73, ff.128, 137, 147, 151.
[91] *Read's Journal* (9 June 1733).
[92] P. Fritz, *English Ministers*, 160-61.
[93] R. Gould, *History*, III, 141.
[94] See ahead, Chapter 18.

meeting, the initiation of two Lord Provosts of Edinburgh suggests his effort to appear politically neutral.

A week later, on 16 June, Henley published an ad in *Fog's Weekly Journal*, which now "represented the high tide of Tory accommodation with Whiggery," announcing that he would soon deliver "the First Oration on Free-Masonry, by Command of the Right Worshipful the Grand Master; the Brethren are desir'd to come cloath'd. It will be fully adverstised."[95] He must have drawn a sufficient audience, for on 30 June he again advertised, "There will be a Second Oration on Masonry, address'd to the Ladies." In the first issue of *The Free-Mason* (13 November), Henley posed as "Tyle Stonehouse," and claimed to be a member of the operative craft who hopes to become an "Accepted" Mason, which allows him to ironically criticize Tory architects and builders, while praising Whig ones. He opened with an epigraph from Dr. Young:

> Thus a fair Model of the World design'd,
> First takes a Copy of the Builder's Mind;
> Before the Structure, firm with lasting Oak,
> And Marble Bowels of the solid Rock,
> Turns the strong Arch, and bids the Column rise,
> And bear the lofty Palace to the Skies. [96]

For Swift and his political allies, Edward Young was a troubling apostate. Swift had known and liked him when he was in Dublin, serving as Latin tutor to the Duke of Wharton, to whom Young dedicated *The Revenge* (1721). The epigraph above came from Young's *Poem on the Last Day* (1713), which he had dedicated to Queen Anne. But after the Atterbury Plot and Wharton's rebellious Grand Mastership, Young became a Grand Lodge Mason and servilely sought patronage from Walpole and the Whig ministry. Though Swift admired his satires on "the vicious manners of English society" in *The Universal Passion* (1725-28), he believed that Young undercut his moral position when he praised "the supposed virtues of the royal family, of Walpole (to whom the seventh satire is fulsomely dedicated), and a sad number of peers, courtiers, and politicians."[97] For Henley to feature Young's Masonic-sounding verses as his epigraph reflected his and Walpole's Whig-Masonic agenda.

Swift had earlier blasted Young's hypocrisy and fawning in the poem, "On Reading Dr. Young's Satires, called the Universal Passion" (1726), and he had recently renewed the attack in "On Poetry: A Rhapsody" (1733). He described the flattering court poets, including the Whig Masons Cibber and Moore Smythe, and placed Young among those who write obsequious birthday odes to the royal family: "The Court...where Young must torture his Invention,/ To flatter Knaves, or lose his Pension."[98] He further condemned all the writers subsidized by Walpole and the ministry:

> Lay now aside all Thoughts of Fame,
> To spring more profitable Game.
> From Party-Merit seek Support;

---

[95] P. Monod, *Jacobitism*, 33.
[96] *The Free-Mason*, #1 (13 November 1733).
[97] I. Ehrenpreis, *Swift*, III, 772.
[98] Jonathan Swift, *The Poetical Works of Jonathan Swift*, ed. Herbert Davis (London, 1967), 577, 580.

A Pamphlet in Sir *Bob's* Defence
Will never fail to bring in Pence;
Nor be concern'd about the Sale,
He pays his Workmen on the Nail.[99]

Many of Swift's lines were so incendiary that they were cut from the published version, but they were treasured by Orrery, who kept a copy of the omissions among his papers.[100]

---

[99] *Ibid.*, 574.
[100] *Ibid.*, 583-84.

CHAPTER FOURTEEN

OUTBREAKS OF THE "HYP" AT HOME AND ABROAD
(1734)

> The Duke of Wharton bore an honourable Relation to our Fraternity and
> would have been acknowledg'd as a Compleat Master of Masonry, if he had
> not put too much Spanish dirt in his Bricks and Tiles…and left some dan-
> gerous Trap-Doors in his flooring Work, unknown to the Craft…
>
> Orator Henley, *The Free-Mason/ Hyp Doctor* (4 December 1733).

> Whom have I hurt? Has Poet yet, or Peer,
> Lost the arch'd eye-brow, or Parnassian sneer?
> And has not Colley still his lord, and whore?
> His butchers Henley, his free-masons Moor?
>
> Alexander Pope, "Epistle to Dr. Arbuthnot" (January 1735).

As the Hyp-Doctor, Orator Henley not only served the political needs of the Hanoverian Masons but also responded to developments in France, where Derwentwater and his Masonic collaborators Maclean and Ramsay were attracting prominent members to the *Écossais* system – news undoubtedly sent to Delafaye and Newcastle
by Ambassador Waldegrave. In Henley's *Free-Mason*, Tyle Stonehouse's uncle, Sir Isaac
Ratcliffe, has been invited by persons of the first rank in the court of France to consult
with physicians about a species of the Hyp, or spleen, which has broken out in violent
symptoms called there "a Manifesto and a Declaration of War."[1] As noted earlier, the
name Sir Isaac Ratcliffe suggested Dr. John Radcliffe, the late Jacobite physician, as well
as Charles Radcliffe, the attainted 5th Earl of Derwentwater.

At this time, prime minister Walpole was concerned about Louis XV's support for
Stanislaus Leszczynski, his father-in-law and an *Écossais* Mason, who was elected King of
Poland by a mass assembly of nobles, but whose claim was challenged by August "III,"
Duke of Saxony, with the military support of Russia and Austria. The ensuing War of the
Polish Succession led to the final unraveling of the Alliance of Hanover, with France and

---

[1] *The Free-Mason, #1* (13 November 1733).

Sweden backing Stanislaus and Britain backing his rival, while pretending to neutrality. Rumors circulated that many Poles wanted James Stuart, married to a Polish princess, to become king, but James instead gave his whole-hearted support to Stanislaus. In Sweden the Knights of Awazu utilized their secret networks to support Stanislaus, and they were soon joined by Swedes who had been initiated into *Écossais* Freemasonry in France.[2]

Henley made clear that his attack upon dissident Masons was provoked by "this Physical Crisis of foreign affairs," which made him transition from a "Hyp- to a House-doctor":

> I shall make no Scruple of calling any Ingenious Connoisseur in Building, Brother, whether he be a Member of a Regular Lodge, or not. ... my good Brother, the City-Critic... assures us, that the Pope and French King have got Money by shewing their Buildings to Strangers, an Example properly hinted at to a Trading Nation...
>
> ...it calls to my Mind a peculiar Refinement on Masonry contriv'd by a Noble Lord in his House at Chiswick, to which none are Introduc'd without a Ticket: this is certainly in Taste on the Raree-shew System of Architecture, which might constitute a new Order of Building call'd the Pecuniary, in the Lucrative Style, though not thought of by Vitruvius, any more than the Composite.[3]

By criticizing Lord Burlington as a "peculiar" (irregular) Mason and as the architect and owner of Chiswick, Henley served Walpole's agenda, for Burlington had finally taken off the mask and resigned all his government positions on 3 May 1733, when he immediately went into opposition. He was angry that the king lied and did not give him the cabinet position ("a white staff") he had promised. But he was also provoked by his disgust at the fraudulent sale of the Derwentwater estates, which had gone at a pittance "for the benefit of prominent court supporters in Parliament."[4] As noted earlier, Burlington had attended every day of the Derwentwater sale in April and May. Jane Clark's argument that Chiswick featured Masonic designs for the restoration of James III suggests that Burlington's requirement of a ticket to visit Chiswick was possibly a way of vetting potential viewers.[5]

On 20 November in issue #2, Henley gave a contorted argument about many pretenders to architectural and Masonic skills, in which he scorned Wharton's old supporters, "the Chairmen plying near St. James's Palace," who are "Male-content and Ripe for an Insurrection," because "they cannot all get Places there: And they are promis'd a Change of Ministry, that there is not a Man amongst them but shall ply in the Ball-Room."[6] In a further dig at the opposition journal, *The Craftsman*, he asserted:

> A man may assume the Title from the CRAFT, and be no CRAFTSMAN: Something more is requisite to the skill of raising a Column or House than

[2] M. Schuchard, *Emanuel Swedenborg*, 192-94.

[3] *The Free-Mason*, #1 (13 November 1733).

[4] E. Cruickshanks, "Political Career," 209-11.

[5] *Ibid.*, 293.

[6] *The Free-Mason*, #2 (20 November 1733).

> a Boldness and Vivacity in pulling them down: Imagination is not Judgment,
> nor is firing a whole Town the most natural Method of Building.

He then claimed to have built for the Duke of Rutland (a staunch Whig), the castle of Belvoir, and from its hillside position he has "observ'd Mists and Fogs over-spreading the whole Country for an Hour or two, then vanishing, and never reaching the second story of the Castle." Thus, the opposition papers, *Mist's Weekly Journal* and its more cautious successor *Fog's Weekly Journal*, will never rise enough to envelope or topple the Whig castle.

Henley further defended Grand Lodge Masonry and attacked its opponents who were trying to undermine it. In a pretended letter from Inigo Jones to Tyle Stonehouse, the late architect complains that "False Brethren" charge that our attempt to clear the rubbish from the foundation is "aim'd at disrespect to Masonry," but we will rescue it from "the Hands of false Workers, and assert it in its full Purity and Lustre." Attacking the opposition journals published by "Tom Foggy and Caleb Dandiprat" for supporting defective masonry, Henley argued that the Tory-Jacobite "Harry Oldcastle's "most renown'd Works are Castles in the Air":

> They are imaginary Structures, that never were nor can be Establish'd...
> There is not a more sanguine or Enterprising Pretender to Masonry than Mr.
> Oldcastle; and, indeed, if Boldness and Railing at the truest Masons were
> sufficient to constitute a Mason, no Person would be more entirely accom-
> plish'd for it.

The government also received reports from its agents in Italy, and Henley could have learned about the Jacobite Order of Toboso, which invited aristocratic ladies to become members and patronesses.[7] Under Derwentwater's leadership, the *Écossais* Masons in France and Sweden would later invite female supporters to participate in "androgynous" or female lodges. Thus, Henley promised to soon publish an address to his "beloved Sisters, the Ladies who are Masons, particularly to such of them as have the good Fortune to be Empresses, Queens, Princesses, Dutchesses...and all other esses, except Foolish-nesses and Wickednesses."

On 15 November, two days after the launch of *The Free Mason/ Hyp Doctor*, opposition writers at *The Grub Street Journal* were quick to respond. In line with their criticism of Grand Lodge Masonry, the author mocked Henley's depiction of Isaac Ratcliffe, noting that he is merely the voice of the "Father of the Oratory":

> Because it is well known, that Sir Isaac Ratcliffe of Elbow Lane has been a
> long time out of order, and out at the elbows, and in a consumption both of
> mind and body... I am well informed, that at this very instant he lies in a
> very deplorable condition, in a garret at the Sign of the Oratory; where he
> has been often denied, and has lately taken upon the name of Tyle
> Stonehouse, Esq., who is a Freemason just as his brother Walsingham is a
> Free Briton.[8]

---

[7] M. Schuchard, *Emanuel Swedenborg*, 231, 416; R. Collis, "Order of Toboso," 125-38.
[8] *Grub Street Journal*, #203 (15 November 1733).

The Grubean knew that Francis Walsingham, editor of *The Free-Briton*, was in the pay of the government and was no more "free" than Henley himself.[9]

On 20 November Henley counter-attacked in *The Free-Mason*, # 3, using the pseudonym "Inigo Jones":

> All Prejudices are a sort of Rubbish, which ought to be clear'd before the Foundation of a Pile can be settled. Some well-intention'd and False Brethren who have scarcely a Pretension in Merit to be Carriers of Hods or Shovers of Wheel-barrows have yet been applying their kind Endeavours to lay in my Way a large heap of that Rubbish, by insinuating to my Brother Crafts that our Attempt is aim'd a Disrespect to Masonry. I am sensible that the Matter and Declaration of my Brother Stonecastle in his First address…will obviate that envious Court; but to Disarm it in the most incontestable Manner, I am directed to avow further that the Glory and Interest of Free-masonry is our leading Design, which we shall study, to remove from the Hands of false Warders and assert in its full Purity and Lustre.

In a note he added that he was prepared to open a ladies' lodge to improve upon the comic sections published long ago by "a reverend Mason."

Henley was a great admirer of the satires by Dean Swift ("a reverend Mason"), and he was evidently familiar with *A Letter from the Grand Mistress of the Female Freemasons*, which had been reprinted in 1730 and 1731. On 26 November he advertised in the *Daily Journal* that "There will be a particular Account of the LADY'S LODGE, by Sister Christophera Wren, with two Prints of the masons Salutation, and one shewing the Plan of a Building to another, in the Free-Mason of Tomorrow."[10] On 27 November, posing as "Sister Wren," Henley announced the opening of an Academy by "our Brother Inigo Jones, for the Advancement of Female Masonry, call'd the LADIES LODGES," of which she will serve as "the Grand-Mistress Elect of the Female Masons." He then unleashed a bawdy barrage of comparisons between technical-architectural-Masonic terms and physical features of the female body:

> Every Lady belongs to one of the five Orders, and if she appears too full or scanty behind or before, too broad at bottom, or narrow at the Top of her Person, it is owing to one single and deplorable Defect, that she is not a Free-mason… when we declare a Person is well-made, we call it well-built…
> My Lady Squat never made an advantageous Appearance, till she was a Graduate Mason, then on finding by Square and Compass that she was of the Tuscan Order, she adjusted her Habiliments according to that Discovery, and no Woman in the World is more agreeable. Miss Tall-boy, a Hoyden, poked her Chin out before and her ---- behind in an acute Angle: I admitted her a Mason; I found out that she is an Ionic Pillar…

The opposition editors fought back by spreading reports that Henley's *Free-Mason/Hyp-Doctor* was secretly subsidized by Walpole. On 4 December in issue #4, the

---

[9] Alexander Pettit, "Packaging Heterodoxy: Orator Henley's Free-mason-oratorial Puffs," paper presented at Annual Meeting of American Society for Eighteenth-Century Studies, Pittsburgh, April 1991), 5. I am grateful to Professor Pettit for sending me a copy of his paper.
[10] R. Péter, *British Freemasonry*, V, 258.

Orator (in the guise of "Palladio") defended his Masonic writings against his critics at *Fog's Weekly Journal* and *the Craftsman*. Justifying the Masons' right to secrecy, he attacked the exiled Nathaniel Mist of *Fog's* and Caleb d'Anvers of *The Craftsman*, implying that they were both affiliated with foreign powers (Italy and France):

> I can by no means indulge Signor Foggio and Monsieur Caleb Dandus, a Grotesque Architect, in their Objections that my Mysteries are Secret Services [to Walpole], that I ought to be plain whether I ridicule their false Orders of Architecture, or no, that my Plans for Building which are describ'd according to the Antient Receiv'd Constitutions of Masonry are in their modest Opinion, destitute of Wit and Genius, and either mere Puns or sheer Blunders... There are two principal Objects of a Free-mason's Study, Architecture and Society; Both are reducible to the same Principle; to direct and govern a House requires at least equal Skill as to build One. A Kingdom is a larger House, a more extensive Society.
>
> Architecture is called a Royal Art; Caleb Dandus, the Grotesque Mason, is for making it not Royal, but Plebeian; he is debasing a Palace to a Cottage... [He has] an unhappy Talent for sowing Discord and Disobedience among Members of the Grand Lodge... [He is] for erecting every Prentice into a Master-Mason, and though out of the Craft, calls himself the Craftsman.
>
> Foggio, whose manner is retarded by the Gothic Taste introduc'd by Barbarians in Ignorant ages, is one of the most insipid Pretenders to the Craft; his natural Principles are Slavish, inconsistent with those of a Free-Mason, yet he puts on a chimerical Air of Liberty... The lights are narrow, the Buttresses and Supports clumsy; he builds in a dark, heavy Method, and is very tedious in finishing his Models, depending altogether on the dictates of Foreign Correspondents.

As Alexander Pettit observes, Henley's central metaphor in *The Free-Mason* is that "the extant government is a great architect and the opposition are the destroyers of 'the Royal Art' of architecture."[11]

Then, emphasizing his insinuations of Jacobitism (Pretenderism), Henley featured a letter written by "Lucinda Locke, from the Lodge in Triangular Square," in which she announces that the Duchess of Wharton is making a claim on her lodge and is on her way from Spain to England:

> Her deceas'd Consort the D---- [of Wharton] bore an honourable Relation to our Fraternity and would have been acknowledg'd as a Compleat Master of Masonry, if he had not put too much Spanish dirt in his Bricks and Tiles, contrary to an Act of Parliament, and left some dangerous Trap-Doors in his flooring Work, unknown to the Craft, which might have been fatal to the steps of the Workmen and Prentices.

Palladio replies to Lucinda that there is "no free Hereditary Right in Masonry" and warns her that she is connected with the "treacherous, false Masons at Vienna, France, and Sardinia." The day before, 3 December, Henley had advertised in the *Daily Journal* that he would answer "whether the Dutchess of Wharton is to be made a mason, etc.," which

---

[11] A. Pettit, "Packaging Heterodoxy," 5.

will be in the Free Mason of Tomorrow, Numbers of which are sent for in all Parts of England.[12] The duchess had apparently arranged the shipment of her husband's books to London, for his library was sold by Thomas Osborne on 27 November 1733.[13] As noted earlier, the catalogue revealed his interest in works by Ramsay, Gibbs, Kent, Arbuthnot, and other Freemasons in the later 1720s. One wonders if Henley attended the sale.

On 11 December 1733 Henley honored the presence in London of Lord Strathmore by publishing an unusual tribute to the Scottish origins of Freemasonry. Using the pseudonym "Vitruvius Brittanicus," he dedicated the issue to the Scottish Grand Master, whose patronage he sought:

> The united Body of Scottish and English Masons, the most considerable in the World, is honour'd with bright Distinction in your Lordship's Superintendency over them. On the Sun-set of Masonry to the Southern and Western Parts of the Globe, the antient Masons of Scotland, Stars of the North, preserv'd its Light, and return'd it to Mankind.[14]

The editors Knoop and Jones remark that here "in 1733, before the establishment of the Grand Lodge of Scotland, we have the interesting suggestion that modern or speculative masonry is descended from ancient or operative masonry through a Scottish line of transmission."[15] However, this line of Scottish transmission had already been suggested by Swift and would soon be repeated by Ramsay. Henley claimed to have extensively studied old manuscript constitutions, and he may have recognized that organized Freemasonry originally developed in Scotland rather than in England. Also, countering the trend in Whig Masonry to detach the "craft" from its operative roots, he gave a traditionalist history of the fraternity as rooted and developed in architecture and practical construction skills.[16]

On 25 December in *The Free-Mason*, #7, he renewed his attacks upon Pope, *The Grub Street Journal*, and *The Craftsman*. Using the personae of Sir Henry Wotton, author of *The Elements of Architecture* (1624), Henley made the opposition Tyler speak to Master Parallel:

> Master Parallel indeed observ'd that GRUBS are destructive to MASONRY, but I think that a Free-mason is free to contradict his Master; for that reason only I would be an Advocate for GRUBS: Worms are as serviceable to Masons as they were to Mr. Pope, when he wrote verses on Dr. More [Moore Smythe]. GRUBS make work for Masons, therefore I not only acknowledge but glory in MY GRUBS… By virtue of those…my Houses are soon rotten, and are literally tumblers, falling almost as soon as they rise. Now in this Oeconomy I serve my Brethren, he that builds in the most precarious and inconvenient Manner is the most excellent Craftsman.

"Wotton" further charges that "Wat Tyler," the radical Puritan, "protests that if he is not elected, the freedom of Masonry must be sacrificed." Tyler claims that "Freemasonry

---

[12] R. Péter, *British Freemasonry*, V, 258.

[13] *Bibliothecarum…ducis de Wharton*, title-page.

[14] *The Free-Mason*, #5 (11 December 1733).

[15] *EMP*, 311.

[16] *The Free-Mason*, #5 (11 December 1733).

consists in an unlimited Freedom of abusing the Grand-Master and Grand-Warden."[17] Wotton warns that this disaffection will countenance "the Interest of the Pretender to the Mastership of the Grand-lodge, and his Church-mason, Dr. Corsini [the Pope]."

On 1 January 1734 Henley published a pretended letter from Paris, sent by "Monsieur Colbert," reporting a great Masonic feast, attended by men and women, in which the costumes, utensils, and food were described in architectural and Masonic terms.[18] He followed this with a letter from Dublin calling for implementation of the strict laws against Popery, because the Papists and Non-jurors support Grub Street and the Craftsman: "Whether L--- B----- is a Papist, the L---d only knows," but "Fog is known to be written by a Papist." The implication that Lord Bolingbroke was a Catholic Jacobite was especially provocative and must have pleased Walpole. On 7 January Henley abandoned his Masonic personae and explicitly attacked *The Craftsman* and all the opposition press as enemies to the Protestant Succession and Interest: "I conclude with this Clincher, that had the Laws against Popery been timely executed there could have been no such paper as a Craftsman, and I wish the Ministry may consider that Matter before it is too late." By 19 February with #15, he changed the title back to *The Hyp-Doctor*. Perhaps Delafaye and Walpole realized that his bizarre defenses of Hanoverian Masonry and their ministry made them look ridiculous.

The changed title of *The Free-Mason* did not mean that Walpole became less determined to use Grand Lodge Masonry as a vehicle for his political policies. From Italy British agents reported that the Whig-Hanoverian agenda of certain members of the Florentine lodge was causing consternation at the Vatican and Stuart court. The concerns of the latter were undoubtedly increased by the arrival in Rome on 31 October 1733 of Martin Folkes, former deputy Grand Master of the London Grand Lodge and close friend of Richmond, former Grand Master and ardent Hanoverian Whig. In an intriguing but controversial study, William Eisler argues that a principle objective of Folkes's Grand Tour was "the establishment of a Roman chapter to consolidate the Craft's foothold in central Italy, on the heels of the contemporaneous creation of the Florentine lodge."[19] This may be true, but Eisler's argument that Folkes was a secret Jacobite who instigated "the creation of a Masonic lodge, under covert Stuart protection," lacks credibility, given Folkes's constant loyalty to and correspondence with Richmond during his Italian visit. Moreover, it was Richmond who wrote letters of introduction for Folkes to various Italian savants, whom the duke had earlier met during his own Grand Tour in the 1720s.[20] The genial, free-thinking Folkes was indeed friendly with at least one Jacobite Mason in London, John Byrom, and he met with several Jacobite antiquarians and scientists in Italy.

Eisler's argument centers on Folkes's attendance at a dinner in the Roman residence of Sir Thomas Dereham, a Catholic Jacobite, which was also attended by George Seton, 5th Earl of Winton, a Scottish exile who would later serve as Master of the Jacobite lodge in Rome; Abbate Antonio Niccolini, former friend of Ramsay and a member of the

---

[17] *Ibid.*, #7 (25 December 1733).
[18] *Ibid.*, #8 (1 January 1734).
[19] William Eisler, "The Construction of the Image of Martin Folkes (1690-1754): Art, Science and Masonic Sociability in the Age of the Grand Tour," *The Medal*, 58 (2011), 6, 11-12.
[20] March, *Duke and His Friends*, 252-61.

Florentine lodge; Luigi Guido Grandi, mathematician and FRS; and Antonio Leprotti, scientific tutor to Prince Charles Edward and physician to Pope Clement XII. Dereham was a devout Catholic and Stuart supporter, who also served as an advocate of Newtonian science to enlightened Catholics in Italy. He translated into Italian the *Transactions of the Royal Society* and frequently corresponded with Hans Sloane. According to Eisler, "It appears certain that this meeting constituted the prelude to the creation of the new lodge, with Folkes as its guiding spirit." But Dereham had been a youthful friend of Richmond, with whom he travelled in Italy in 1724, and he had written the duke in 1731 hoping that he would return to Italy; thus, it was probably at Richmond's urging that Dereham invited Folkes to dinner. [21] A few years later, the Whig Mason and diplomat Sir Charles Fane reported from Florence that Dereham "had a great correspondence in England and by means of the French Ambassador made a very regular report to the Pretender."[22]

It was Dereham's choice to include the guests who were associated with the Stuart court, when he hosted Folkes. Drawing on Eisler's work, Edward Corp goes further to declare that Folkes was "a secret Jacobite," and that at the luncheon "the decision was taken to found a lodge in Rome for Jacobite Freemasons."[23] However, it seems unlikely that Folkes, who was an important member of the Whig-dominated Grand Lodge in London, would have participated in founding a Jacobite lodge. He was the close friend of two Hanoverian Grand Masters, Montagu and Richmond. According to William Stukeley, FRS and Grand Lodge member, Folkes in matters of religion was "an errant infidel & loud scoffer. Professes himself a godf[athe]r to all monkeys, believes nothing of a future state, of the Scriptures, of revelation."[24] Even worse, "He perverted Duke of Montagu, Richmond, Lo'd Pembroke, & very many of the nobility" to "throw off the mask, & openly deride & discountenance even the appearance of religion." In his unpublished Italian journal, Folkes made clear his antipathy to Roman Catholicism, but he was surprised at the radical free-thinking of many Italian intellectuals. In Venice he noted that there is much less real religion in Italy than in England:

> It often inclines to direct disbelief of the very first cause itself, but in general revealed religion is in no vogue among those that have any degree of learning, nor is it at all wonderfull when we consider how very irrational that religion [Catholicism] is. They are taught by rote, which it cannot be the first consequence of any knowledge or free conversation to shake off... They are greedy for any free-thinking book.[25]

Like other English visitors to Italy, Folkes mixed with Jacobites, Hanoverians, foreigners, and Italian savants who shared his scientific and antiquarian interests. One frequent companion in Venice was the Swedish count, Nils Bielke, who had been initiated by the Jacobites in Paris before converting to Catholicism and moving to Italy.[26] Bielke assiduously sought out Folkes, and he possibly sent reports on his activities to Louis XV, who employed Bielke as his personal intelligencer on Italian affairs, and to the Stuart

---

[21] *Ibid.*, 40, 199.

[22] L. Lewis, *Connoisseurs*, 109.

[23] E. Corp, *Stuarts in Italy*, 327.

[24] William Stukeley, *The Commentarys, Diary, & Common-place Book of William Stukeley* (London, 1980), 87-88.

[25] Bodleian: MS. Eng. Misc. C. 444, ff. 23-24.

[26] *Ibid.*, ff.7, 39-41, 45.

court, with which he was intimate. Could Dereham and Winton have had a similar motive in their overture to Folkes, who was known as the confidant of powerful Whig nobles and Masons in England? Or, was the dinner just a convivial gathering of "ex-pats" and Italian intellectuals with no Masonic or political agenda at all?

Because an Italian-made Masonic medal was later struck for Folkes, Eisler believes he definitely participated in Masonry in Rome. If true, it seems more likely that he joined with other Hanoverian-English visitors to participate in an occasional lodge affiliated with the Grand Lodge of England and the Whig-influenced lodge in Florence. Moreover, Stosch later reported that the loyalist English Masons in Rome refused to initiate Dereham, who wanted to be admitted, because they would not accept any Jacobites.[27] Italian scholars suggest that it was not Folkes but Henry Fox, 1st Baron Holland, a "political figure close to Robert Walpole, unrelenting opponent of Jacobitism," who founded the "mysterious lodge" in Rome in 1733.[28] Pushed by Lord Hervey, his fellow Whig and Mason, Fox would be appointed Surveyor General of the Office of Works in 1737, which required an interest in architecture and operative Masonry (if not competence). His subsequent failure to accomplish much would lead even Hervey to describe him as the "Neglector of His Majesty's Works."[29]

Some clues to the puzzle about the mysterious lodge in Rome emerge in British diplomatic correspondence and Stosch's spy reports. Thus, on 26 December 1733, a week after Dereham's luncheon, Consul Brinsley Skinner reported that on Christmas Eve a guard was placed at the Pretender's house and next to the Muti Palace because of a "sudden panick" occasioned "by a lodge of Free Masons, which the English travelling Gentlemen at Rome held that night."[30] Some say "a numerous Lodge of Free Masons" went to midnight Mass "a little gay, and were somewhat noisy in the Pretender's neighborhood." Others say he feared the English "intend to destroy him." On 2 January 1734 the spy Stosch, member of the Florentine lodge, reported:

> There are actually in Rome more than fifty English gentlemen, all affectionate towards the government of His Majesty [George II], who never want to have any liaison with the Jacobites nor admit them in their Masonic lodge. According to all appearances, these mysterious assemblies have given occasion to fears in the Pretender that they plot something against his person, even though there is not the least appearance of such a thing.[31]

Stosch later reported that "it is well known that at Rome the Masonic assemblies ceased, for lack of English travelers, before the Bull of Excommunication, because they would not admit the servants nor declared adherents of the Pretender."[32] Furthermore, "The refusal they made some years ago to Sir Thomas Dereham who wanted to be admitted to the Society, greatly irritated the Pope against the members."[33] Since 1731 Stosch had spied on Dereham, whom he despised, and reported that he translated the anti-

---

[27] NA:SP 98/41 (9 February 1739).

[28] W. Eisler, "Construction," 12.

[29] H. Colvin, *History*, 75

[30] NA:SP 98/35 (26 December 1733).

[31] *Ibid.*, 98/37 (1 January 1734).

[32] *Ibid.*, 98/41 (2 February 1739)

[33] *Ibid.*, 98/41 (9 February 1739).

Walpolean journal, *The Craftsman*, for the Pope and made him think that these opposition statements represented the sentiments of the whole British nation.[34] In Stosch's voluminous intelligence reports, no reference has *yet* been found to a Jacobite lodge in Rome, despite his many comments on the Hanoverian Masons in Rome and Florence. As we shall see, the later identification of Folkes as the author of a Masonic pamphlet burned by the Inquisition in Rome may also be a case of mistaken identity.

Joseph Spence, whose visit did not overlap with Folkes, had earlier reported that he met "forty English travelers" in Florence, many of whom visited the lodge where Spence's student Lord Middlesex was elected Master in 1733.[35] One of these lodge members was Captain Spence, whom Joseph described as "a namesake of ours," who came from Gibraltar and who "is the only son of that Mr. Spense of Scotland, who was so cruelly tortured by King James in the Duke of Monmouth's time."[36] King William gave him a place soon after the Revolution, "which saved us all from any such barbarities in the future." It is curious that both Spences shared their lodging with Edward Holdsworth, a learned Jacobite who abhorred that Revolution but whom Joseph Spence nevertheless greatly admired and whose frequent company he enjoyed. Holdsworth also hosted Folkes, as the English of all political stripes socialized together abroad, leaving behind temporarily the political factionalism of their homeland. Of course, it was still considered treason for them to visit the Stuart court or contact James III and his sons, despite their mingling with local Jacobites.

Meanwhile in Dublin, in January 1734 Swift provoked (or pretended to provoke) a quarrel between the Freemasons and Richard Bettesworth, Seargeant-at-law and M.P., who had supported a bill to reduce the tithe on hemp- and flax-growers which would largely benefit the northern Irish Presbyterians and reduce Anglican church revenues. As part of his ongoing campaign against the Dissenters, Swift ridiculed Bettesworth's claim that he was a "brother sergeant" to Swift's good friend Henry Singleton, for there was no more kinship than between Hebrews and Philistines. Even worse, he called him "Booby Bettesworth" and compared him and his brethren to "a Swarm of Lice."[37] An enraged Booby confronted Swift at his home, and a report circulated that he had threatened to stab or maim the dean, which then inspired crowds of Swift's supporters to surround his house to defend him. Swift then "went after the loudmouthed M.P. with a series of ferocious attacks in verse."[38] As we shall see, over the next year, Swift's stormy relationship with Booby would take on a Masonic significance.[39]

While Swift and his supporters battled against Bettesworth, their colleague Faulkner published *A Prologue and an Epilogue and Songs* (1734), which had been performed by Thomas Griffith at a benefit given him by the Freemasons. Responding to critics of the fraternity, Griffith answered, "No Matter what they Say:/ Still may thy Mystick Secrets be conceal'd/ And only to a Brother be reveal'd."[40] In the Epilogue, Mrs. Bellamy comically addressed the rumor that Masons undergo a "dreadful Operation" (circumcision). She assured the

---

[34] *Ibid.*, 98/32 (23 November 1731).

[35] J. Spence, *Letters*, 152.

[36] *Ibid.*, 122.

[37] J. Swift, *Poetical Works*, 588.

[38] I. Ehrenpreis, *Swift*, 770.

[39] See ahead, Chapter Fifteen.

[40] *A Prologue…Spoken and Sung to the Rt. Worshipful Society of Free-Masons…being Mr. Griffith's Benefit* (Dublin: George Faulkner, 1734), 4, 11-12.

audience that after her husband's initiation, he"brought Home every Thing he carry'd out," and even became much more amorous: "That to increase our mutual Dear Delight,/ Wou'd he were made a Mason every night." This inside Masonic joke recalls Swift's earlier reference to the enemies of his "brother Orrery," a Jacobite Mason, as "uncircumcised Philistines."[41]

Faulkner also published *The Poetical Works of the Reverend James Sterling* (1734), which included "The Master-Mason's Ballad," an expression of the traditionalists' view of Freemasonry as closely tied to architecture. Sterling's praise of the church building commission appointed by Queen Anne, who had responded positively to Swift's architectural proposal, must have pleased the old dean:

> On, on, my brave boys, and pursue my great lecture:
> Refine on the models* of old Architecture:
> To masons high honour such diligence brings;
> Those brothers of princes, and fellows of kings!
>
> We'll drive the rude Vandals and goths off the stage;
> Reviving the arts of Augusts' fam'd age!
> Lo! Titus destroy'd the vast temple in vain,
> Some fifty more rose in fair Anna's blest reign!
>
> Of Jones, Wren, and Angelo, mark the great names:
> Immortal they live as their Tiber and Thames!
>
> _____
>
> *Shewing a plan of a building.[42]

Sterling called for an end to "all the contention 'mong masons," and bumpers of beer to be raised to "free social masons."

Sterling's ecumenicism had been expressed some months earlier, when he anonymously published a poem, "To the Honourable Miss Peggy B------l, a young lady of the Church of Rome," in *Faulkner's Dublin Journal* (3-7 July 1733). Patrick Fagan identifies the young lady as Margaret (Peggy) Barnewall, a sister of the Jacobite-Masonic Barnewall brothers.[43] Like Swift, whose sympathy for Irish Catholics was influenced by Wogan's eloquence, Sterling's tolerance for them was won by Miss Barnewall's beauty:

> I yield, I yield, all-conquering maid!
> Your charms triumphantly prevail;
> Such wondrous beauty must persuade
> Though Fathers, Popes and Council's fail.
> ....
> Against thy innocence and bloom,
> What fool of reason can dispute?
> Ye serious triflers, foes of Rome,
> Can you that air and shape refute?[44]

[41] J. Swift, *Correspondence*, II, 432.

[42] *EMP*, 232-33.

[43] Patrick Fagan, *A Georgian Miscellany: Irish Poets of the Eighteenth Century* (Dublin, 1989), 88.

[44] *Ibid.*, 86-87.

Swift probably knew Sterling, a recently-ordained Anglican minister, whose wife acted the part of Polly Peachum in Gay's *Beggar's Opera* in Dublin, and he had long been friendly with the Barnewall family.[45] While praising Peggy Barnewall , Sterling supported Lord Kingston's patriotic party, which had broken all contact with the Grand Lodge of London, when they re-elected Kingston as Grand Master in 1735, to succeed Henry Benedict Barnewall, Viscount Kingsland[46] The new Grand Master kept Dr. Brennan, a Catholic, as his Deputy. While Sterling advocated religious toleration, he was evidently not a Jacobite, and he served as chaplain to the king's "own Royal Regiment of Foot."

During this period in Scotland, when nationalist feelings were increasingly heated, the Whigs determined to maintain control of Freemasonry. As Ric Berman reveals, at least a quarter of Scotland's representative peers were loyalist Masons.[47] In England the elections for a new parliament in early 1734 were hotly contested, as the government historian recounted:

> The whole nation was in a ferment about chusing a new one; which notwithstanding all the arts of the opposition, went greatly in favour of the court. But the great object of the nation at this time was the election of the Scotch peers... In the courtyard of the palace of Holyrood-house a battalion of foot was drawn up. This was a very idle precaution, but was meant to prevent any tumults, some being apprehended from the disposition of the populace, and the importance of the occasion. It was, however, improved by the anti-ministerial party into a kind of over-awing of the election.[48]

The Scottish opposition petitioned for redress, charging that Walpole had bribed and threatened the peers and forced through the election of his list of sixteen. Among these Walpolean loyalists were the following Freemasons. The main target of the petitioners' wrath was James Murray, 2nd Duke of Atholl, whose accession as a duke resulted from his brother's attainder for supporting the Jacobites. When Wharton included Atholl on his list of Stuart supporters in 1725, he referred to the exiled William Murray, Marquess of Tullibardine, who was still called the Duke of Atholl in the Jacobite peerage. Tullibardine allegedly served as regent of the Masonic Order of the Temple, in succession to the late Earl of Mar.[49] In March 1734 in London, the Hanoverian Atholl was admitted a member of the Old King's Arms lodge, which maintained close connections with the Grand Lodge.[50] The other government-approved Masons included William Kerr, 3rd Marquess of Lothian; Alexander Lindsay, 4th Earl of Balcarres; James Douglas, 14th Earl of Morton; and John Campbell, 4th Earl of Loudoun. Among the petitioners who protested at the illegal proceedings were the Earl of Orrery, Lord Strathmore (the recent Grand Master), and the Earl of Marchmont, a disaffected Whig Mason and friend of Ramsay and Pope. Strathmore's opposition evidently led to the unusual early conclusion of his tenure as Grand Master, for the Earl of Crawford – an apostate from Wharton's

---

[45] "James Sterling," *ODNB*.

[46] W.J. Chetwode Crawley, *Caementaria Hibernica* (Dublin, 1895), 15.

[47] R. Berman, *Foundations*, 160-61.

[48] William Cobbett, *Parliamentary History of England...1733-1737* (London, 1811), Ix, 607-09.

[49] J.E.S. Tuckett, "The Origin of Additional Degrees," *AQC*, **32** (1919), 5-31; and "Dr. Begemann and the Alleged Templar Chapter in Edinburgh in 1745," *AQC*, 33 (1940), 40-62.

[50] R. Berman, *Schism*, 155.

list and now a loyalist – was installed as his replacement on 30 March 1734 (he had come to London and joined the Bear and Harrow lodge in December 1733).

The Scottish petitioners' personal courage and eloquent arguments gained much public sympathy, not only in Scotland but in England. In a tribute to Marchmont and other Scottish patriots, the poet William Hamilton of Bangour, a staunch Jacobite, published anonymously *The Faithful Few. An Ode, Inscribed to all Lovers of their Country* (Edinburgh, 1734). Echoing the opposition criticism of Walpolean corruption, he praised those Scots who resist the bribes and places:

> While Pow'r triumphant bears unrival'd Sway,
> Propt by the Aid of all-prevailing Gold;
> While bold Corruption blasts the face of Day,
> And Men, in Herds, are offer'd to be sold;
> Select, *Urania*, from the venal Throng,
> The FAITHFUL FEW, to grace the deathless Song![51]

Among his Scottish heroes, he especially lauded Marchmont:

> Marchmont, whose Wisdom different Courts have found,
> Whose freeborn Soul has never chang'd its State;
> For Knowledge fam'd, and Eloquence renown'd,
> In whom the honest Statesman shines compleat!
> Accept this Homage, which the Muses pay,
> And still deserve Applause the PATRIOT-WAY![52]

Linking the nationalist Scots with England's opposition, he called upon more "Patriot Names" to oppose the powerful flood of corruption and to "risque themselves to save a sinking Land." Though it is unknown if Hamilton was a Freemason at this time, he would later be associated with important Jacobite Masonic developments.

Meanwhile in London, Marchmont was in close contact with Pope, and he undoubtedly informed him about the bribing of the Scottish represenrive peers, which added to the poet's sense of frustration with politics.[53] In April 1734, determined to create his image as an artist above the fray, but still committed to the opposition, Pope published anonymously in one volume his *Essay on Man*, which had appeared in installments throughout 1733. Dedicated to Bolingbroke, it drew upon his friend's "Dissertation upon Parties" and his deistic views, while maintaining a non-sectarian religious attitude:

> Awake! My St. John! leave all meaner things
> To low Ambition and the Pride of Kings.
> Let Us (since Life can little more supply
> Than just to look about us, and to die)
> Expatiate free, o'er all this *Scene of Man*,
> A mighty Maze! but not without a Plan.[54]

---

[51] [William Hamilton of Bangour], *The Faithful Few* (Edinburgh: W, 1734), 3.

[52] *Ibid.*, 6.

[53] M. Mack, *Alexander Pope*, 610-11.

[54] [Alexander Pope], *An Essay on Man. Being the First Book of Ethic Epistles. To Henry St. John, L. Bolingbroke* (London, 1734), Epistle I, ll. 1-5.

Writing in accessible couplets, Pope aimed to find order in the apparent chaos of human life by building upon the Renaissance notion of the "Chain of Being":

> Vast Chain of Being! Which from God began,
> Natures Ethereal, human, Angel, Man,
> Beast, bird, fish, insect; which no Eye can see,
> No Glass can reach: from Infinite to thee,
> From thee to Nothing!...
> ....
> And if each System in gradation roll,
> Alike essential to th' amazing Whole;
> The least confusion but in one, not all
> That System only, but the whole must fall.
> All Discord, Harmony not understood;
> All partial Evil, universal Good:
> And spight of Pride, in erring Reason's spight,
> One truth is clear; "Whatever Is, is RIGHT."[55]

Pope's bland conclusion was initially immensely popular, both in Britain and abroad, but it would later be subjected to more sophisticated philosophical and theological analysis, which provoked a defense of Pope by Chevalier Ramsay.[56] Many later Freemasons believed that the poem's call for universal charity and ecumenical religious conciliation was influenced by his association with the fraternity, and lines from the *Essay on Man* would frequently be quoted in Masonic publications.[57]

In mid-summer 1734 in Paris, Ramsay received a Scottish guest, the budding philosopher David Hume, whom he received with great kindness and hospitality. During his studies at Edinburgh University, Hume associated with many Jacobites, including the artist Allan Ramsay and the poet William Hamilton of Bangour. His most intimate friend since childhood was a distant cousin of Chevalier Ramsay, Michael Ramsay of Mungale, who was also in Paris. As we shall see, Michael Ramsay was a Mason, and he became close to Derwentwater.[58] Chevalier Ramsay and Hume soon discovered their opposite views in philosophy, but the former supplied letters of recommendation for his fellow Scot when Hume moved to Rheims and then La Flèche. Three years later, as Hume prepared to return to Paris, he complained to Michael that,

> I shall be oblig'd to put all my Papers into the Chevalier Ramsay's hand when I come to Paris; which I am really sorry for. For tho' he be Free-thinker enough not to be shockt with my Liberty, yet he is so wielded to whimsical Systems, & and is so little of a Philosopher, that I expect nothing but Cavilling from him. I even fortify myself against his Dis-approbation & am

---

[55] *Ibid.*, 19-20.
[56] See ahead, Chapter Sixteen.
[57] W.J. Williams, "Alexander Pope and Freemsonry," *AQC, 38 (1925), 111-48*.113-14.
[58] Ernest C. Mossner, *The Life of David Home*, rev.ed (1954; Oxford, 1980), 60, 93-96. For Michael Ramsay's friendship with Derwentwater and attendance at Chevalier Ramsay's funeral, see ahead Chapter 19.

resolv'd not to be in the least discouraged by it, if I should chance to meet with it.[59]

Hume's papers included the manuscript of his *Treatise of Human Nature* (1739-40), in which he expressed his skepticism about many of the "mystical" ideas so important to Ramsay. However, Richard Popkin argues that they had "strikingly similar and strikingly divergent views" and that "the very curious Ramsay," who was "a strange metaphysician," was "a major influence on Hume.[60] We will return to their relationship when it becomes relevant to Hume's negative attitude toward Freemasonry.

In summer 1734 Hume was not the only important visitor to Ramsay. The Earl of Orrery made a mysterious journey to France, which remained so secretive that no correspondence survives about it. It seems certain that he contacted his old friend Ramsay, for he made a kind of pilgrimage to sites connected with their mutual hero, Archbishop Fenelon. Twenty years later, in his *Letters from Italy, in the Years 1754 and 1755* (published posthumously in 1773), he revealed that he visited Cambray for the *third* time and expressed his continuing admiration for Fenelon, noting that his memory "is still held in the highest veneration," versus the current decadent and absentee archbishop.[61] He noted that the French peasants are still loyal to the government, but not as much as in 1734, when they adored Louis XV. In that year, he was evidently sent by the Jacobites to deal with their supporters in the French king's ministry, who hoped to take advantage of the War of the Polish Succession to mount a Jacobite initiative. It is also probable that he contacted the *Écossais* Grand Master, Hector Maclean, for Orrery was currently collaborating with various Scottish Masons in London in opposition efforts against Walpole.[62]

At this time, Orrery's old friend, the banker Robert Arbuthnot, was facilitating Jacobite contacts between England and France, but he was dismayed to learn of his brother's deteriorating health. The long-time Mason John Arbuthnot was seriously depressed by Walpole's success in May 1734, when the prime minister managed to bring in the "King's List" of loyalist Scottish peers. Pulteney later wrote Swift that "Poor Arbuthnot" grieved to see "the wickedness of mankind, and was particularly ashamed of his own countrymen."[63] In July 1734 Pope heard from the physician that he was suffering from a terminal illness, which prompted Pope to reply in August that he intended to produce "a new satiric onslaught."[64] He finished his "Epistle to Dr. Arbuthnot" eight weeks before the doctor's death on 27 February 1735.

Calling the poem "a Sort of Complaint" against authors who had attacked his "Person, Morals, and Family," he acquiesced to Arbuthnot's advice to not name them. Thanking his friend, whose medical care helped him "thro' this long disease, my Life," he praised Swift, Bolingbroke and Atterbury, who loved him and made his studies happy.[65] He then

---

[59] Richard Popkin, "So, Hume Did Read Berkeley," *Journal of Philosophy*, 61 (1964), 775.

[60] *Ibid.*, 776-77.

[61] John Boyle, Earl of Orrery, *Letters from Italy, in the Years 1754 and 1755*, ed. William Duncombe (London, 1773), 3, 9.

[62] *Ibid.*, xiv-xvi.

[63] J. Swift, *Correspondence*, IV, 70-71.

[64] Pat Rogers, *Alexander Pope* (Oxford, 1993), 110.

[65] A. Pope, *Poetical Works*, 327-32.

scorned several Whig Masons – Cibber, Henley, and Moore Smythe – who claimed to be innocent victims of his malicious satire in *The Dunciad:*

> Whom have I hurt? Has Poet yet, or Peer,
> Lost the arch'd eye-brow, or Parnassian sneer?
> And has not Colley still his lord, and whore?
> His butchers Henley, his free-masons Moor?

In the months before Pope wrote "Epistle to Arbuthnot," Moore Smythe had reached a high position in loyalist Masonry, serving as Grand Warden with James Anderson, and urging the Grand Lodge to restrict membership to those who would pay five guineas into the General Charity Fund.[66] When he died in "reduced circumstances" in October 1734, Pope did not change his hostile view of him. He retained the lines which criticized the Whig poet for defaming Pope's blameless parents:

> Yet why? That Father held it for a rule,
> It was a sin to call our neighbour fool:
> That harmless Mother thought no wife a whore:
> Hear this, and spare his family, James Moore![67]

In an epitaph, he kept up his attack upon the recently deceased Moore:

> Here lies what had nor birth nor shape nor fame
> No gentleman! no man! no-thing! no name!
> For Jamie ne'er grew James; and what they call
> More shrunk to Smith – and Smith's no name at all.
> Yet die thou canst not, phantom oddly fated:
> For how can no-thing be annihilated?
> Ex nihil nihil fit.[68]

His harshest criticism went to Lord Hervey, the Walpolean Mason, waspish wit, and bisexual courtier:

> Let Sporus tremble – 'What? That thing of silk,
> Sporus, that mere white curd of Ass's milk?
> Satire or sense, alas! Can Sporus feel?
> Who breaks a butterfly upon a wheel?
> . . . .
> Now high, now low, now Master, now Miss,
> And he himself one vile Antithesis.
> Amphibious thing! That acting either part,
> The trifling head, or the corrupted heart,
> Fop at the toilet, flatt'rer at the board,
> Now trips a Lady, and now struts a Lord.[69]

---

[66] W. Williams, "Alexander Pope," 117 – 18.

[67] A. Pope, *Poetical Works*, 339.

[68] W. Williams, "Alexander Pope," 118.

[69] A. Pope, *Poetical Works*, 337.

Though Pope's philosophical *Essay on Man* took the high ground on the current political context, Bolingbroke's *Dissertation on Parties*, which was serially published in *The Craftsman*, was targeted at the forthcoming septennial election of 1734.[70] Worried by Bolingbroke's increasing influence on the opposition, Orator Henley intensified his attacks on Walpole's critics in his re-named journal, *The Hyp-Doctor; or the Free-Mason*, published by Tyle Stonehouse of Berkshire. On 4 June 1734 he lampooned the opposition "Patriots," while praising the great Whig prime minister.[71] Walpole evidently called upon his staunch supporter, the Duke of Richmond, to counter the moves by the opposition Masons and their allies in France. Waldegrave in Paris reported his fears that the Jacobite Masons were renewing their plots against the "Elector of Hanover." Thus, in September 1734 he welcomed the arrival in Paris of Richmond, his good friend and former Grand Master. The duke and Desaguliers "called" a lodge at the Hotel de Bussy, attended not only by Waldegrave but by Montesquieu and St. Florentin, secretary of state to Louis XV.

Richmond determined to renew his relationship with Montesquieu, for he may have learned that the French *philosophe* was friendly with many Jacobite Masons and often expressed his admiration for the Stuart princes, whom he had met in Italy.[72] Though Montesquieu had been initiated by Grand Lodge Masons in England in 1730, he was also privy to developments in *Écossais* Masonry. In June 1734 he wrote to Madame de Renel, sister of the Jacobite Abbé François de Fitzjames, that he had spent an hour in Fitzjames's chamber where he was shown a special ritual.[73] André Kervella argues that this was a secret ritual, invented by the Jacobites and reserved for an elite.[74] He suggests further that the ritual later emerged in England as the "Royal Arch." As we shall see, Richmond would continue to press Montesquieu to renew their fraternal bonds.

While in France, Richmond established a lodge at his family's estate in Aubigny, and in August he heard from his Masonic friend Tom Hill that he had communicated to the right worshipful Dr. Desaguliers the duke's "command relating to the brotherhood of Aubigny sur Nere":

> I need not tell you how pleased he is with the further propagation of masonry... When I mentioned the diploma [warrant], he immediately asked me if I had not *Amadis de Gaula*, or some of the other romances. I was something surprised at his question, and began to think, as the house was tiled [lodge was closed and guarded], our brother had a mind to crack a joke. But it turned out quite otherwise. He only wanted to have a little of the vieux Gaulois in order to give his style the greater air of antiquity and consequently make it more venerable to the new lodge. He went from me fully intent on getting that or some other such book. What the production will be you may expect to see soon.[75]

---

[70] M. Mack, *Alexander Pope*, 601.

[71] *The Hyp-Doctor; or the Free-Mason*, #187 (4 June 1734).

[72] F. McLynn, *Charles Edward Stuart*, 30, 345.

[73] « Une Correspondance Inédit de Montesqueiu," *Revue d'Histoire Littérraire de la France*, 2 (1982), 189.

[74] André Kervella, *Le Mystère de la Rose Blanche: Franc-Maçons et Templiers en XVIIIe Siècle* (Paris, 2009), 105.

[75] Letter quoted in Ric Berman, "Architects," 236.

Amadis de Gaula was a sixteenth-century tale of knight errantry, and Desaguliers's determination to insert chivalric material in the new lodge warrant suggests that he was aware of such themes emerging in *Écossais* rites in France. He further expressed to Hill his hope to join Richmond in Holland, where they could recruit Hanoverian Masons and then form a lodge on "one of his Majesty's yachts" during the voyage home.

For the Jacobite Masons, Richmond's presence in France was worrisome, and he had recently written recommendations for English visitors to the British lodge in Florence.[76] Richard Towneley, a wealthy Lancashire landowner and Catholic Jacobite, visited Italy in 1732-34, when he was considered for the position of tutor to Prince Charles.[77] He later observed that Richmond "is our hottest enemy, which makes me tremble for Prince Charles, because he is a man excessively devoted to the House of Hanover."[78] Stosch reported that Towneley met frequently with Derwentwater and Marmaduke Constable, and he was sure that Towneley was carrying out a serious Jacobite mission, but he was frustrated by the high level of secrecy maintained over their activities.[79] Given James's worry about the activities of the Hanoverian Masons in Rome, it seems certain that the Jacobite Masons discussed the increasingly volatile situation. In July 1734, in a "Most Private" letter, Newcastle wrote to Charles Fane, newly appointed "minister plenipotentiary" to Florence, with instructions on how to spy on the Jacobites and set up intelligencers in Rome.[80] Fane was ordered to "insinuate yourself" with Cardinal Corsini and offer him a large annual bribe. He must also complain to the Stuart court about the ill treatment of Stosch, while sending his secret intelligence to Lord Essex at Turin. Significantly, Newcastle, Fane, and Essex were Hanoverian Masons, and Richmond encouraged their political usage of Masonry in Italy.

The activities of the Whig Masons and Italian free-thinkers provoked further suspicion in the Vatican, which led the British press to report in September 1734 that a society, "after the model of the famous Free-Masons in England, under the name of *La Cucchiara*" (Society of the Trowel), has lately been erected in Rome, where the Inquisition is "diving into the Mysteries of the Fraternity." Stosch would later send to Newcastle a copy of an Italian pamphlet against "La Cucchiara," which he said was made up of some high personages, "Altra-montani Eretici."[81] He still seemed unaware of a Jacobite lodge in Rome, for the Inquisition's concern was about the English Hanoverians and Italian free-thinkers.

In Scotland, despite Walpole's successful packing of the representative peers with loyalist Masons, Jacobite sympathies became even stronger in various lodges, and many families were split in their political allegiances. One example of such division was personified in William Boyd, 4th Earl of Kilmarnock. On 14 November 1734 he and his supporters petitioned to form a lodge in his home district of Kilmarnock.[82] As a "country Whig," whose father had fought against the Jacobites in 1715, Kilmarnock supported

76 J. Ingamells, *Dictionary*, 640.

77 NA:SP 8/32 (20 December 1732, 28 February 1733).

78 *Ibid.*, 98/56 (9 December 1748).

79 *Ibid.*, 98/37 (6 February 1734).

80 *Ibid.*, 98/84 (20 July 1734).

81 *Ibid.*, 98/36, f. 470 (20 December 1732); 98/37 (11 February 1736).

82 Stephen Drury, "Lodge St. John Kilwinning Kilmarnock, no. 22: An Historical Sketch 1734-1992," *Yearbook of the Grand Lodge of Antient Free and Accepted Masons of Scotland* (Edinburgh, 1993), 87.

Walpole, and in the disputed elections of 1734, the opposition reported that he had been brought from France at government expense, and that he and his wife each received pensions of £200.[83] Apparently in order to appeal to traditionalist Masons, the charter for Kilmarnock's new lodge was issued "under the ordinances of the Schaw Statutes," which were formulated by William Schaw, a Catholic architect, who had reorganized Scottish Masonry under the direction of King James VI in 1598-99.[84] Kilmarnock would assume the leadership of many Scottish lodges, which initially were dominated by Whigs. However, he would later switch sides, and reports surfaced that he participated in *Écossais* lodges in France.[85]

While Whig aristocrats in Scotland utilized Scotland's "ancient" Masonic traditions to attract members, Grand Lodge aristocrats in England increased the sociability and frivolity of many of their meetings. In December 1734 Richmond received an amusing letter from his convivial chaplain, Mick Broughton, who was visiting the Duke of Montagu at his country house of Ditton. He mentioned that "Some great Mason is wanting to initiate Bob Webber," a minor canon of Winchester cathedral. Broughton subsequently wrote about the arrival of Desaguliers, who joined the houseguests in acting out various plays before participating in a private lodge meeting. Desaguliers had recently published volume one of *A Course of Experimental Philosophy* (1734), which supported the Whigs' Newtonian agenda to counter French critics of some of Newton's theories. As Patricia Fara observes, Desaguliers used his preface to attack the French critics as ignoramuses: "In a characteristically chauvinistic assault on René Descartes's 'Philosophical Romances,'" he stressed that it was through Newton's experimental and observational approach that "we owe the routing out of the army of Goths and Vandals in the Philosophical World."[86]

Relying on aristocratic patronage to pursue his experimental career, Desaguliers was willing to entertain his sponsors and hosts in the lab and in their homes, while at the same time collaborating in their private Masonic ceremonies. As Broughton reported to Richmond,

> On Sunday night at a Lodge in the Library, St. John, Albemarle, and Russell made chapters; and Bob admitted Apprentice; the Dr. being very hardly perswaded to the Latter, by reason of Bob's tender years and want of Aprons. My being out of this farce likewise, excludes me the Honour of styling myself Brother…
>
> P.S. Russell left us on Monday; Ld. Albemarle yesterday; and this day Ld. Pem[broke], Hollis, Stanhope, and the Dr, in the Earl's coach…[87]

Audrey Carpenter identifies "St. John" as Henry St. John, Viscount Bolingbroke, but he was more commonly identified as "Bolingbroke" at this time. She also writes that he "had renounced his Jacobite affiliation." However, Bolingbroke was currently involved with Cornbury, Orrery, and sympathetic French diplomats in plotting a new restoration

---

[83] "William Boyd, 4th Earl of Kilmarnock," *ODNB*.

[84] D. Stevenson, *Origins*, 26-51.

[85] René Le Forestier, *La Franc-Maçonnerie Templière et Occultiste au XVIIIe et XIX Siécles*, ed. Antoine Faivre (Paris, 1970), 244, 536-38.

[86] "John Theophilus Desaguliers," *ODNB*.

[87] A. Carpenter, *Desaguliers*, 220.

effort.[88] In exchange for promised information, he received from France an initial payment of £10,000, and a projected annual pension of £3,000. For those Jacobites who still distrusted Bolingbroke, Walpole's savage denunciation of him in parliament seemed apt, when he described his witty opponent as a man "void of all faith and honour, and betraying every master he has ever served." A few months after the Ditton house party, Bolingbroke would flee England for prolonged residence in France. The Masonic house guest was possibly Bolingbroke's half-brother, John 2nd Viscount St. John (d. 1748), Tory M.P. for Wooten Basset, who voted with the opposition except on the repeal of the Septennial Act in 1734.[89] Perhaps Montagu hoped to win him over on future votes. However, it is more likely that the Mason was Paulet St. John, Whig M.P. for Winchester, who was a strong government supporter.

In 1734 a significant extension of Grand Lodge Masonry occurred in the new American colony of Georgia, when the governor, General James Edward Oglethorpe, opened Solomon's Lodge in Savannah. Two years earlier, the Irish-born politician John Perceval, 1st Earl of Egmont, was named as first president of the trustees for the colony. Egmont had become interested in the Americas through his friendship with the Irish philosopher George Berkeley, a good friend of Swift.[90] Though Berkeley's project to found a colony and Anglican college in Bermuda foundered, Egmont transferred his interest to Oglethorpe's colony of Georgia. Though Walpole disliked Egmont, the earl had enough friends among the moderate Whigs and Masons to gain financial support from the English Grand Lodge, which was granted to the colony in December 1733. Over the next years, political storm clouds would hover over the colony, sometimes provoked by the political views of General Oglethorpe.

Oglethorpe came from a staunch Jacobite family, and his Irish Catholic mother, Eleanor, was a good friend of Swift during Queen Anne's reign.[91] Lady Oglethorpe was known as "Old Fury" because of her temperament, while her eldest daughter Anne was known as "Young Fury." Both became "increasingly influential with king and court when in France" and "at the epicenter of Jacobite conspiracy when in England."[92] It seems certain that Swift was aware of their Jacobite activities. Eleanor's son, James Edward, served in Anne's army but left his regiment on the eve of the 1715 rebellion; for three months his whereabouts are unknown.[93] After the failure of the rebellion, he attended a military academy in Paris, where he formed a lifelong friendship with James Keith, the exiled Scottish Mason. Though it is unknown when he was initiated into Masonry, it may have been during his association with the exiled Keith, Ormonde, and Mar. He next served as a military aide to Prince Eugene of Savoy. In October 1717 he visited his brother Theophilus in Italy. When the two met with Mar in Urbino, the duke introduced James to the Pretender, and Mar reported that the king "was well pleased with him, and

---

[88] E. Cruickshanks, "Lord Cornbury," 6.

[89] R. Sedgwick, *History*, II, 403-04.

[90] "John Perceval, 1st Earl of Egmont," *ODNB*.

[91] J. Swift, *Journal to Stella*, 290-95, 321, 326, 345, 376, 655.

[92] Thomas Wilson, *The Oglethorpe Plan: Enlightenment Design in Savannah and Beyond* (Charlottesville, 2012), 9-10.

[93] *Ibid.*, 11; Eveline Cruickshanks, *The Oglethorpes: A Jacobite Family, 1689-1760*. Royal Stuart Society, Paper XLV (1995), 1-11.

I believe Jamie no less with him."[94] Young Oglethorpe swore fealty to James, and his friend Mar would subsequently collaborate with Anne Oglethorpe in Jacobite plotting.

Returning to England, Oglethorpe won a seat in parliament as a high Tory, and he courageously defended Atterbury. He remained in opposition until 1727, when his interest turned to prison reform, especially the hard plight of debtors. His successful campaign gained the admiration of Lord Egmont and the poetic praise of Samuel Wesley the Younger. In Wesley's *The Prisons Open'd. A Poem* (1729), he interpreted Oglethorpe's accomplishment as a blow to Walpole's ability to "screen" wrongdoers and buy off opponents through bribes:

> When Villains first beheld the Tempest lour,
> They sneer'd and trusted to the Screen of Pow'r;
> Numbers t'avoid the dire Example bent,
> Lest righteous Vengeance grow to Precedent:
> And Gifts which fiercest Anger oft' appease
> And secret Friends and secret Services:
> No Pangs of Conscience struck the hardn'd Mind,
> To God's right Hand and heav'nly Justice blind.[95]

Walpole believed that not only Oglethorpe but Wesley were Jacobites, and he stubbornly opposed the general's next great philanthropic mission – the founding and maintenance of the colony of Georgia. Influenced by Masonic notions and James III's promise of toleration, Oglethorpe advocated a policy of liberty of conscience, but the Whigs on the committee refused admission to Catholics. Nevertheless, the colony welcomed Jews, Moravians, Quakers, Methodists, and various dissident sects, while refusing to permit slavery. Thomas Wilson argues that Oglethorpe's Masonic philosophy also influenced his design and city plan for Savannah, which expressed Masonic mathematical imagery.[96] A serious student of architecture, ever since his meeting with Mar in Italy, Oglethorpe acquired Palladio's works and William Kent's edition of Inigo Jones's designs.[97] He read Robert Plot's descriptions of English Freemasonry (1685-86), and he acquired Chevalier Ramsay's Masonic-influenced treatise on Civil Government (1732). He also acquired the works of Swift, Arbuthnot, Pope, and a complete run of the opposition journals, *The True Briton* and *The Craftsman*.[98] David Shields notes that "a literary cult of personality" developed around Oglethorpe, which "erupted into ecstatic praise" when he determined to go to Georgia in 1731.[99] By 1734 Pope sensed that Oglethorpe was a kindred spirit, and he praised him in a Horatian epistle as the model of a good "brother": "One, Driven by strong Benevolence of Soul,/ Shall fly like OGLETHORPE, from Pole to Pole."[100]

Unfortunately, the Jacobite-Hanoverian rivalries within Masonry ramified into the colony, where complaints were made that the Scottish members of Solomon's Lodge in

---

[94] T. Wilson, *Oglethorpe Plan*, 13.

[95] [Samuel Wesley], *The Prisons Open'd. A Poem* (London, 1729), 19.

[96] T. Wilson, *Oglethorpe Plan*, 64.

[97] Sotheby's Sales Catalogue: Library of General James Edward Oglethorpe (5 May 1788), #440, 1084, 1179, 1664. 1884, 2341.

[98] *Ibid.*, #314, 345, 347, 496, 523, 563,609, 1026, 1084.

[99] David Shields, *Oracles of Empire: Poetry, Politics, and Commerce in British America* (Chicago, 1990), 47-50.

[100] Henry Bruce, *Life of General Oglethorpe* (New York, 1890), 140.

Savannah were Jacobites, who opposed the Hanoverian succession.[101] In the same year, Walpole engineered the defeat of Lord Egmont's son John at the Harwich election, and the father never forgave the prime minister. He intensified his support for the Georgia colony, turning to opposition Whigs and moderate Masons for assistance. Over the next ten years, Oglethorpe would struggle to maintain a difficult balance between his private Jacobite sympathies and the necessity of support from the Whig ministry if the colony was to survive.

---

[101] Ricard Berman, *Loyalists and Malcontents: Freemasonry and Revolution in the American Deep South* (Goring Heath, 2015).

CHAPTER FIFTEEN

RIOTS IN BRITAIN, WARS IN EUROPE, CHARGES OF MASONIC CONSPIRACY (1735-1736)

Our Brother Axel runs in his head a plan to establish in Stockholm after the French model a lodge of Freemasonry... Our friends in Awazu are enchanted... All this is between you and me.

> Carl Gustaf Tessin to Ulla Tessin (5 January 1735).

The old approved Master Masons...were replaced by some Day-Labourers who deceived the Architect...to sap and undermine the Foundation and level the English palace, and from its ruins build a French one in the place.

> Ambassador William Finch to Secretary Newcastle
> (Stockholm, 5 March 1735).

Perhaps he [Swift] may be safe in Poland during the time of these troubles. I can assure him by the name of a Polish lady...that Dr. Swift is perfectly known there.

> Lord Bathurst to Jonathan Swift (September 1735).

In early 1735 Swift continued his duel with "Booby" Bettesworth, in an affair that took on Masonic significance. His action was provoked by a letter of appeal sent to him on 8 February by Thomas Giffith, whose benefit performances continued to be supported by his Masonic brothers. Griffith's project of opening Dublin's Aungier Street Playhouse burdened him with increasing debts, and he was now hounded by Bettesworth, whose prosecutions threatened the actor with bankruptcy. With fulsome praise for Swift's previous patriotic efforts, he explained his precarious situation:

> Nothing but the last extremity and your Humanity can plead my excuse for troubling you, with the many Misfortunes, that at present attend me – Having defended my self from my merciless Creditors, as long as my

381

Circumstances, cou'd possibly protect me. But now they all fall upon me with determin'd cruelty, and resolve to undo me, tho' I am willing to divide the last shilling of my late Benefit Play amongst 'em, but that is not sufficient...to answer their Demands – my good friend Councill'r B – [Bettesworth] having pursu'd me with implacable Malice...[1]

Griffith appealed to Swift, "who sav'd a whole unhappy Nation from Destruction," to lend his supporting hand "to defend me and my little State from Misery and Misfortune." He promised to repay Swift "at my next Benefit." His appeal raises a question about his possible protection of Swift, while his government employers expected him to be on the lookout for Jacobites.

Possibly with Swift's support, the patriotic Masons, under their current Grand Master Kingston, sponsored Griffith in a benefit performance of *The Provoked Wife* on 4 March 1735. However, he was subsequently attacked by a loyalist newspaper:

His brethren in the Grand Lodge attended in force, as usual, but the Dublin *Evening Post* on 8 March deplored the choice of the play and hoped the Masons would in future discourage Griffith from producing such a vile and obscene work: "Griffifth ought never to have any Recommendation from the Grand Lodge; and we hope the future Grand Officers will never encourage him."[2]

Philip Crossle argues that Swift entered the lists with a broadside, printed in 1735, in which he requested the "Worshipful the free and accepted Masons" to impeach "Grimaldo Sergeant Kite" (Bettesworth, Sergeant-at-law) for illegal profiteering in the Dublin Theatre, and, among other accusations:

the said incorrigible Kite doth refuse absolutely to consent that the Right Worshipful Fraternity of Free Masons shall have admittance to the Stage to see a Play they have themselves bespoke, and which they intend to Honour in their Dresses proper to the Order. – Unheard of Presumption![3]

For loyalist Masons in Ireland and England, the skirmishes with home-grown opposition must have seemed trivial in the context of mounting international problems, which increasingly occupied prime minister Walpole. By summer 1735 he and Delafaye evidently decided that it was time for Henley to revise the explicit title of *The Free-Mason*, which on 17 June was re-named *The Hyp-Doctor, or The Free-Mason*. The journal made a final attack on the opposition by singling out the Orator's *bête noire*, Alexander Pope, who was linked with the Patriot opposition: "The Country Party now is for Popery... Alexander Pope is known to be an odd kind of Monster, a republican Papist, and that he has written *Fogs* and *Craftsmen* is not to be doubted."[4]

---

[1] J. Swift, *Correspondence*, IV, 261-62.
[2] *Dublin Evening Post* (4-8 March 1734); Philip Highfill, K.A. Burnim. E.A. Langhans, eds., *Biographical Dictionary of Actors* (Carbondale, 1973), VI, 382-83.
[3] J. Lepper and P. Crossle, *History*, I, 124-25. The broadside is in the Thorp Collection in the National Library of Ireland.
[4] *The Hyp-Doctor, or, The Free-Mason*, #299 (17 June 1735).

With the outbreak of the War of the Polish Succession and the collapse of the Hanoverian Alliance between Britain, France, and Sweden, Walpole feared the growing collaboration between the Jacobites and the emerging "Hat" party in Sweden. The Hats and France supported the claim of the exiled king and *Écossais* Mason, Stanislas Leszczynski, for the Polish throne, while Russia and Austria supported the anti-Mason, Augustus "III" of Saxony. To the disgust of the Tories and opposition Whigs, the English government claimed neutrality but favored Augustus and kept the English fleet on alert in order to intimidate Cardinal Fleury. The Jacobites saw the split between England and France as an opening for their cause, and they were sure Louis XV would mobilize massive support for Stanislaus, his father-in-law, believed to be a future "philosopher king."

Ireland was "awash with rumors" of French-Jacobite-Polish collaboration, and the outpouring of Irish-language poetry alarmed the government, leading the Church of Ireland bishop Hugh Boulter to warn about the Papists' "increasing insolence" concerning their international prospects.[5] Swift despised Boulter, who had opposed him during the Wood's half-pence controversy, and the feeling was mutual. Thus, it is curious that Lord Bathurst worried that the Polish crisis might lead to increased government surveillance over Swift and his associates. In September 1735 he wrote Swift a veiled letter in which he expressed concern for the dean's safety:

> Perhaps he [Swift] may be safe in Poland during the time of these troubles. I can assure him by the mouth of a Polish lady, who was late in London, by name Madam de Monmorancy (for she was married to a French gentleman of that great family) that Dr. Swift is perfectly known there; and she was very solicitous to know whether he was a Stanislaist or not, she being a zealous partisan for that cause.[6]

Bathurst's Polish friend was Emerentia Warszycka, wife of Comte Joseph-Alexandre de Montmorency de Bours, who served in the Polish military; he was a kinsman of Chrétien de Montmorency, Prince de Tingry, an important French Freemason and Jacobite sympathizer.[7]

In both Poland and Sweden, *Écossasis* Freemasonry was used by supporters of the Polish "Pretender" and the Swedish opposition leader Tessin to further their political and military goals.[8] Working with Tessin was Gyllenborg, Swift's old friend, with whom he had tried to renew contact. While Walpole packed the Scottish government with Hanoverian Masons, Jacobite Masons in many countries undertook a counter-movement that intensified the rivalries within the supposedly apolitical fraternity. This international Masonic context spurred many of the literary satires and debates that emerged in the British Isles over the next decade.

Developments in far-away Sweden would thus have an important influence on affairs in Hanoverian Britain. In January 1735 Axel Wrede Sparre, who had been initiated by the Jacobites in Paris, worked with his brother-in-law Tessin to recruit the "Knights of

---

[5] E. O'Ciardha, *Ireland*, 250.

[6] J. Swift, *Correspondence*, IV, 183 (13 September 1735).

[7] I am grateful to André Kervella for this indentification.; also, see his *Chevalier Ramsay*, 123, and *Francs-Maçons au Duché de Bouillon* (Neufchâteau, 2006), 55-56, 75, 80, 122, 187.

[8] For detailed discussion of the context, see M. Schuchard, *Emanuel Swedenborg*, Chapter 7.

Awazu" to a more effective secret society, a Masonic lodge, "after the French model."[9] Over the next two months, many of their political allies and sympathetic diplomats were initiated, and on 5 March the worried British ambassador, Edward Finch, sent to his fellow-Mason Newcastle a long metaphorical account of the replacement of English Masonry by new builders. He described an English palace built in Stockholm by an architect and "the old approved Master Masons," who by accident were replaced by "some Day-Labourers," who deceived the architect and contrary to his design planned "to sap and undermine the foundation and level the English palace, and from its ruins build a French one in the place."[10] The architect finally opens his eyes, dismisses these labourers and "desires the old Masons to think of the properest and speediest methods to repair the disorders."

Tessin and the Swedish Masons would soon develop contacts with their Jacobite *frères* in France and Italy. They maintained contact with Sir Hector Maclean, current *Écossais* Grand Master; General Arthur Dillon, collaborator with the late Earl of Mar; and Daniel O'Brien, the Pretender's main agent in Paris. Tessin's brother-in-law Nils Bielke had been initiated by Jacobites in Paris, was friendly with Chevalier Ramsay, and was close to the Stuart family. He was undoubtedly aware of the Jacobite lodge that had been meeting for some time in Rome, though its surviving minute book begins on 16 August 1735.[11] The lodge included Protestants and Catholics from Scotland, England, France, Italy and, surprisingly, Sweden. Tessin had sent the young architect Carl Johan Cronstedt from Paris to Rome to study designs for a new Swedish palace, and Cronstedt not only joined the lodge but carried messages from the French court to the Stuart family.[12] While Nils Bielke welcomed him, the spy Stosch sent worried reports to London about the Swedish architect's contacts with the Jacobites.

In Ireland Jacobite agents received news about the Swedish Hats' support of Stanislas and James III from a network of correspondents established by the Catholic bishop Sylvester Lloyd, who sent Swedish information through Bordeaux to a "a Mr Pine in Dublin."[13] News of these Swedish developments probably reached Swift, for his current Jacobite friends Robert Leslie and Dr. William King had long been involved in negotiations with Swedish sympathizers.[14] In King's satire, *The Toast*, which Swift greatly admired, he had drawn on his Swedish contacts to portray the supposed author, Frederick Scheffer, as a Swede. When King was in Dublin in summer 1735, Swift entrusted him with his manuscript of "The Four Last Years of the Queen," which he was determined to have published in London, despite its politically-risky material.

King then made a secret journey to Scotland, where he contacted Stuart supporters and prepared a report for the Pretender on their readiness.[15] From Scotland he travelled to northern France to consult with Jacobite colleagues, before returning to London, from where he wrote Swift on 20 September: "Soon after I came into England I was obliged to cross the seas again and go into France, upon a business of consequence to my private

[9] B.J. Bergquist, *St. Johanneslogen den Nordiska Första* (Stockholmt, 1935), 37-38.

[10] NA: SP 95/69, ff. 150-51.

[11] William James Hughan, *The Jacobite Lodge at Rome, 1735-7* (Torquay, 1910).

[12] M. Schuchard, *Emanuel Swedenborg*, 253-54.

[13] E. O'Ciardha, *Ireland*, 239.

[14] For Robert Leslie's Swedish negotiations, see Bodleian: Carte MS. 231, ff. 22-23.

[15] J. Swift, *Correspondence*, IV,187-88; D. Greenwood, *William King*, 74-75.

affairs. I am but just returned to this place, where I met with your letter of 21st of last month."[16] Swift's letter is lost, but he was likely aware of King's mission, for he would maintain a confidential relationship with the outspoken Jacobite over the next years.

During King's returns to Oxford, he participated in a Tory-Jacobite fraternal society, the High Borlace, whose members met annually in a tavern to celebrate their Stuart sympathies: "The members, both ladies and gentlemen, wore jewels... Like those of the Freemasons they [the jewels] differed according to the rank or office held by the member."[17] On 4 September 1735 the *Grub Street Journal* reported from Oxford that "at the high Borlace, there was a very great appearance of Borlacians, and...Miss Kitty Dashwood was unanimously chosen patroness for the ensuing year."[18] Like the Knights of Toboso and some *Écossais* lodges, the Borlacians invited female "protectresses." Catherine Dashwood was the muse and lover of the poet James Hammond, confidant of Chesterfield and equerry to the Prince of Wales, and she became a heroine to her Jacobite admirers. In 1736 Dr. King published *The Toast. An Heroick Poem in Four Books*, an expansion of the 1732 version, which he dedicated to Swift and the late Stella. In new lines, he praised "the bright Patroness of the *Oxford Borlace*," the beauteous Kitty.[19]

Meanwhile in 1735, while Dr. King carried on a secret correspondence with James III, he also stayed in touch with Ramsay, who in June married Marie Nairne, daughter of Sir David Nairne, under secretary to James III. The wedding took place in the church of St. Sulpice, where Ramsay was friendly with the Curé, Languet de Gergy, who oversaw the continuing construction of the great Baroque edifice, which put him in close touch with architects and operative Masons. Ramsay was probably aware that De Gergy had approved of a Masonic ceremony in 1733, when the Papal Nuncio, "being a Free Mason," laid "the first Stone toward the building of the Altar in the Church of St. Sulpice."[20] The Nuncio, Ranier d'Elci, served as papal ambassador and was busy "making visits to the Princes and Princesses of the Blood, in paying and receiving Compliments to and fro among the Cardinals, Ministers, and prime Nobility."[21] At this time, a Masonic Nuncio was acceptable to the Papacy and to French churchmen, and Ramsay was on good terms with d'Elci, who would later be accused of serving as Master of a secret lodge within the church in Rome.[22]

Ramsay's current prominence provoked criticism from various French literary men, who accused him of shallow philosophical notions and sycophantic social climbing. The poet Claude Roy published a pamphlet, titled the *Ramsajde* (1735), in which he hinted at the Scot's political intrigues and eroticized "illumination": "Simple charlatan à la Cour,/ Chez les Femmes grand Politique,/ Methaphysicien d'Amour,/...Vray caméléon in Intrigue,/ Ce ténébreux illuminé."[23] The hostility did not bother Ramsay, and he confidently continued his historical researches and correspondence with Jacobite friends in

[16] *Ibid.*, IV, 187-88.

[17] William Copeland Borlase, *The Descent, Name and Arms of Borlase of Borlase* (London, 1888), 69.

[18] R. Péter, *British Freemasonry*, V, 305, and Robert Collis's comments in V, 292 n. 16.

[19] William King, *The Toast. An Heroick Poem in Four Books* (London and Dublin, 1736), 116.

[20] Reported in *The Boston Weekly Rehearsal* (19 February 1733); quoted in Melvin M. Johnson, *Freemasonry in America prior to 1750* (Cambridge, 1917), 37.

[21] I am grateful to Edward Corp for identifying the Nuncio.

[22] W. Eisler, "Construction," part 1, p. 15.

[23] Quoted in P. Chevallier, *Ducs*,

the British Isles. In October 1735 he honored Swift's letter (now lost) recommending a young Irish medical student John Sican, and treated him with great hospitality in Paris. Sican wrote Swift that the Chevalier Ramsay "sends you his best respects."[24] Swift also recommended Sican to Robert Arbuthnot, another well-known Jacobite friend of Ramsay, in Paris.[25] Ian Higgins suggests that Robert Leslie facilitated Swift's correspondence with Ramsay (and Wogan), some of which has disappeared.[26]

At this time, Ramsay was collaborating with the Grand Master Maclean in Masonic affairs, while he completed his *Histoire du Vicomte de Turenne, Maréchal General des Armées du Roy* (1735), which was soon published in London in Hooke's English translation. As noted earlier, the second volume included the memoirs of James, Duke of York, who became James VII and II, and was infused with Jacobite themes. After Swift sent him copies of his own works, Ramsay shipped volumes of the *Histoire* to the dean, whose opinion he was eager to learn.[27] Ramsay's next writings would change the development of *Écossais* Freemasonry in important ways, as the partisan and international rivalries of the divergent systems emerged more publicly.

Meanwhile in London, at the Grand Feast of Grand Lodge in April 1735, there was a large turnout of Whigs – both loyalist and opposition – when the Grand Master Crawford chose Thomas Thynne, 2nd Viscount Weymouth, as his successor. Weymouth was the son-in-law of Carteret, with whom he collaborated in trying to defeat Henry Fox, a decadent Whig then in the middle of a sex scandal, who was supported by Walpole.[28] The Duke of Richmond represented the pro-government members, and he was accompanied by the Hanoverian James Murray, 2nd Duke of Atholl. One month earlier, the loyalist supporters of Atholl had welcomed the birth of his male heir: "Dunkeld was illuminated, and a Procession of Freemasons had celebrated the event, 'the fraternity in their aprons made a circle about the Bonfire, crosst arms, shook hands, repeated healths, and a Marquess forever.'"[29]

Unfortunately, the baby died a few months later, and the Jacobites continued to consider William Murray, Marquis of Tullibardine, the legitimate heir – and, reportedly, the secret regent of the late Mar's military order of knighthood.[30] Tullibardine and his *Écossais* brothers would surely have scorned the presence at the Grand Feast of Alexander Brodie, a Walpolean Mason and the first Hanoverian to be named as Lord Lyon King of Arms in Scotland. In 1727 Brodie had been appointed by the government to this traditional Scottish post, which regulated heraldry, in the place of Sir Alexander Erskine, who had been "deep in Jacobite intrigues" and made the office "a centre of Jacobite sympathies."[31] Brodie gave himself airs "of being my Lord Ilay's minister in the north," and also served as a government informer, receiving a secret-service pension of £300 a year.

---

[24] J. Swift, *Correspondence*, IV, 221.

[25] I. Ehrenpreis, *Swift*, III, 637.

[26] Ian Higgins, "Jonathan Swift and Charles Leslie," in P. Monod, M. Pittock, and D. Szechi, *Loyalty and Identity*, 150.

[27] J. Swift, *Correspondence*, IV, 474.

[28] R. Berman, *Foundations*, 161; R. Sedgwick, *History*, II, 48-50.

[29] Margaret Nairne, "A Bundle of Jacobite Letters," *Scottish Historical Review*, 4 (1906), 20.

[30] See ahead, Chapter 20.

[31] "Alexander Brodie," *ODNB*.

One wonders if Brodie's presence at the Grand Lodge feast worried another attendee, the Irish M.P., Sir Arthur Acheson, close friend of Swift, who had been regarded by the Irish government as "a professed Jacobite."[32] During this period in Ireland, under Lord Kingston's leadership, the Irish Masons determined to play a more significant role on a larger British stage. In January and May 1735, William Smith, a Dublin-based bookseller, published in Dublin and London *A Pocket Companion for Free-Masons*, produced by the Irish printer Ebenezer Rider. Smith argued that younger Masons could not afford Anderson's *Constitutions* and needed a smaller, more portable handbook of Masonic history, regulations, and songs. He also affirmed the Irish Masons' traditional belief about the connection between operative and speculative Masonry, between architecture and ritual:

> Let it never be said, that as our Numbers increase the Sciences decrease…
> No Man ought to attain to any Dignity in Masonry who has not, at least, a
> competent Knowledge of Geometry and Architecture; and if the Sciences
> were more Follow'd in the Lodges, what is unhappily substituted in their
> Places would not prevail as it does.[33]

Smith then gave a condensed version of the traditional history in Anderson's *Constitutions*, and praised Lord Burlington, William Kent, and Henry Flitcroft for maintaining the great architectural traditions of the Masons.[34] Going beyond Anderson, he described the many fine buildings in Dublin, especially the Parliament House designed by "the ingenious Captain Pierce, Successor to the famous Architect Bourk, under whose direction most of the fine Buildings of Dublin were erected." Though this description would have annoyed Dr. William King, who despised Pierce, Smith managed to gloss over the controversy about the replacement of Burgh, "the dull Tory," by the upstart Whig, Pearce. Quoting from Irish songs, he rejected political partisanship as unwelcome in Dublin's lodges:

> The Lodge excludes the Fop and Fool,
> The plodding Knave and party Tool
> That Liberty would sell.
> ……………………………………
> We have no idle Prating,
> Of either Whig or Tory;
> But each agree
> To live at Ease
> And sing or tell a Story.
> ………………………………..
> If any are so foolish
> To whine for Courtiers Favour
> We'll bind him o'er
> To drink no more…[35]

---

[32] J. Simms, "Dean Swift and County Armagh," 134.'

[33] William Smith, *A Pocket Companion for Free-Masons* (London, 1735), Preface.

[34] *Ibid.*, 11.

[35] *Ibid.*, 80-81.

As noted before, Lord Kingston and his supporters had little contact with the Grand Lodge in London, which made William Smith's *Pocket Companion*, targeted at Irish and English Masons, seem a threat to London's attempted Whig monopoly. In February James Anderson accused Smith of plagiarism, and the English Grand Lodge ordered its members not to buy the book.[36] However, it was sanctioned and adopted by the Grand Lodge of Ireland, and it was acquired by Jacobite Masons in England, such as Richard Rawlinson and General Oglethorpe.[37] English antagonism towards the Irish Masons was further expressed on 11 December 1735, when the English Grand Lodge rejected the request of "the Master and Wardens of a lodge from Ireland," who had a Deputation from Lord Kingston, to visit a lodge at the Devil Tavern, in central London.[38] In the absence of higher officers, George Payne, the Whig tax official and magistrate, acted as Grand Master, and he peremptorily refused the visit, "unless they would accept of a new Constitution here," and the Irish were effectively "snubbed."

While Smith and the Irish tried to play a bigger role on the British Masonic stage, the Duke of Richmond continued his efforts to gain French support for the Whigs' Grand Lodge system. Throughout the summer of 1735 he wooed Montesquieu, urging him to visit his lodge at Aubigny. On 2 July Montesquieu replied that he could not make the journey, but he was pleased to learn that Dr. Desaguliers, "la première colonne de la maçonnerie," was in Paris, and he was sure that this news would lead many French men of merit to become Masons.[39] On 31 July Richmond replied that it was not only himself but Madames Richmond and Hervey who want to see him, but he has another reason why the baron should take advantage of such a visit:

> Know, therefore, my most venerable brother, that Masonry is very flourish-
> ing at Aubigny. We have a lodge with more than twenty brothers. And that
> is not all: know also that the great Beelzebub of all the Masons, who is Dr.
> Desaguliers, is actually at Paris, and he will come to Aubigny to hold the
> lodge. Come, therefore, my dear brother, at least to receive the benediction.
> But to speak more seriously and Masonry consequently a part, you will oblige
> me infinitely if you will come to see us.[40]

Desaguliers would not have appreciated Richmond's wry characterization of him as the Devil (or one of Milton's fallen angels), but the duke was always a bit snobbish about his non-aristocratic "brothers."

The lodge at Aubigny was definitely a speculative entity, with no connection to the fraternity's operative roots, which reflected trends in the London Grand Lodge system. The efforts of traditionalist Masons like William Smith in Dublin and Francis Drake in York to maintain the architectural themes of Masonry were a response to the increasing detachment of English Whig Masonry from its origins in the architectural "craft" of design and construction. On 11 December 1735, at the same Grand Lodge meeting where the Irish were barred from attending, the Whig mathematician Martin Clare delivered a

---

[36] Cecil Adams, "The Freemasons' Pocket Companions," *AQC*, 45 (1932), 166, 169, 176.

[37] Oglethorpe Library Catalogue, #31.

[38] R. Berman, *Schism*,13.

[39] Robert Shckeleton, "Montesquieu's Correspondence: Additions and Corrections," *French Studies*, 12 (1958), 328.

[40] "Une Correspondence inedit," 217. My translation from the French.

discourse on "the inward Civility of the Mind," which aimed to curb the unruly behavior that evidently erupted at many lodge meetings (which Orrery attributed to the heavy drinking). Clare seemed to associate Freemasonry mainly with sociability and "good conversation."[41] In order to maintain the support of "the Great, the Noble and the Honoured of the Land," Masons must avoid natural roughness, censoriousness, raillery, contradiction, and captiousness at their meetings. They must follow the example of the aristocratic and politically-powerful "Great" men, persons "who esteem it neither Condescencion or Dishonour to patronize and encourage the Professors of our Craft." For "Great" Masons like Walpole, Newcastle, and Richmond, such loyalist taming of the brothers' behavior would indeed maintain their support of the increasingly speculative Masonry – especially as opposition and Jacobite Masons were gaining ground against the unpopular ministry.

There was strife even among the Hanoverian Masons, as Richmond continued his efforts to gain profitable places for Sir Thomas Prendergast. In March 1736 Egmont recorded an ugly scene when the duke insisted that Walpole appoint Prendergast as Postmaster General of Ireland, "a coveted and lucrative post."[42] Lord Lovell, former Grand Master in 1731, argued that it should go to his brother-in-law Sir Marmaduke Wyvil. Walpole told Richmond that he asked Lovell to waive his pretensions and when he refused, the prime minister responded that "if his Grace would have a little patience, he should get it for Sir Thomas." This infuriated Richmond, who replied in a passion that Walpole "did but trifle with him, and that he found there was no dependence on him, nor would he ever depend on what he said. Sir Robert was stunned" and had "too much spirit to be bullied into the affair." However, he prudently delayed the appointment until tempers had cooled , and then Lovell named Wyvil to the Irish post. Nevertheless, Richmond continued to push for an Irish "job" for Prendergast, who in August 1736 was made an Irish privy councillor.

Swift may well have heard about this contentious dispute among three important Whig Masons, which would increase his scorn for Prendergast. Moreover, the Tory and Jacobite Masons had other causes for complaint. The hostile reception of the Grand Lodge in London to Smith's *Pocket Companion*, coupled with Swift's grief over the death of the old Jacobite Mason Arbuthnot, may have encouraged the dean to renew his attacks upon Prendergast, who represented to him all that was wrong in politics, religion, and Masonry. He expressed his revived animus about not only Thomas Prendergast but his father in the poem, "On Noisy Tom" (1736):

> If noisy Tom should in the Senate prate,
> That he would answer both for Church and State;
> And, further to demonstrate his Affection,
> Would take the Kingdom into his Protection:
> All Mortals should be curious to enquire,
> Who would this Coxcomb be, and his Sire?
> What! thou the Spawn of him who sham'd our Isle,
> That Traitor, Assassin, Informer vile...[43]

---

[41] *EMP*, 327-32; Shawn Eyer, "The Inward Civility of the Mind," *Philalethes*, 69 (2016), 58-67.

[42] *HMC: Report on the Manuscripts of the Earl of Egmont* (London, 1920)., II, 247-48; R. Berman, *Schism*, 221.

[43] J. Swift, *Poetical Works*, 600.

As in *Gulliver's Travels*, Swift linked corrupt politicians with corrupt architects and Masons, who constructed "The Legion Club," the Irish Parliament House where, as in the Gospel of Mark, the spirit named Legion is exorcized by Jesus and becomes a crowd of devils that rushes into a herd of swine, who then drown themselves in the sea. As Ehrenpreis observes, "Madness, damnation, and bestiality are thus joined in opposition to Christ. This, for Swift, is the condition of the House of Commons."[44] Swift began drafting the poem in January 1736 and then made changes over the next months, as he circulated the manuscript among his closest friends. He began with a description of Captain Pearce's controversial construction of Parliament House, which had been praised by loyalist Whig Masons but scorned by Swift's friend, the Jacobite Mason William King:

> As I strole the City, oft I
> Spy a Building large and lofty,
> Not a Bow-shot from the College,
> Half the globe from Sense and Knowledge.
> Plac'd against the Church direct;
> Making good my Grandames Jest,
> *Near the Church* – you know the rest.[45]

The complete proverb was "Near the church and far from God." Pearce had sited the Parliament House close to St. Andrew's Church, which stood for values opposite to the majority of Irish Members of Parliament:

> Tell us, what this Pile contains?
> Many a Head that holds not Brains.
> These Demoniacs let me dub
> With the Name of *Legion Club*.
> Could I from the Building's Top
> Hear the rattling Thunder drop,
> While the Devil upon the Roof,
> If the Devil be Thunder Proof,
> Should with Poker fiery-red
> Crack the Stones and melt the Lead;
> Drive them down on every Scull,
> While the Den of Thieves is full,
> Quite destroy that Harpies Nest,
> How might then our Isle be blest?[46]

Swift reluctantly accepted that "the Pile may stand" and "the House is like to last," so he poetically put the placemen in cells where they grovel in straw, dabble in their own dung, and "form a grand Committee/ How to plague and starve the City." He then turned his wrath on Prendergast, who was arrogantly enjoying his new position:

> Let Sir *Tom*, that rampant Ass,
> Stuff his Guts with Flax and Grass;

---

[44] I. Ehrenpreis, *Swift*, III, 829.
[45] J. Swift, *Poetical Works*, 601-02.
[46] *Ibid.*, 606.

But before the Priest he fleeces
Tear the Bible all to Pieces.
As the Parsons, *Tom*, Hello boy,
Worthy Offspring of a Shoeboy,
Footman, Traytor, vile Seducer,
Perjur'd Rebel, brib'd Accuser;
Lay the paltry Privilege aside,
Sprung from Papists and a Regicide;
Falls a Working like a Mole,
Raise the Dirt about your Hole.

At this time "The Legion Club" circulated only in manuscript, but Prendergast heard about it, which renewed his anger at Swift's earlier attack upon his father published in Faulkner's 1735 edition. The enmity between Swift and the Whig M.P. and Grand Lodge Mason would continue.

Swift also attacked Mark Anthony Morgan, who in 1725 served as a fellow Grand Warden with "Sir Tom, the rampant Ass," in the Irish Grand Lodge.[47] In 1735 Morgan, a loyalist Mason and M.P., subscribed to Swift's *Works*, invited him to visit his fine library, and initially won his friendship.[48] However, in 1736 Swift turned on him, "more in sorrow than anger," when Morgan chaired a parliamentary committee that voted for a tax levied on cattle and pasturage, which claimed to benefit the church but which the dean and others opposed:

Bless us, *Morgan!* Art thou there Man?
Bless mine Eyes! Art thou the Chairman?
Yet I look on thee with Pity.
Dreadful Sight! What, learned *Morgan*
Metamorphos'd to a Gorgan!
For thy horrid Looks, I own,
Half convert me to a Stone.
Hast thou been so long at School,
Now to turn a factious Tool!
....
When you walk among your Books,
They reproach you with their Looks;
....
While you in your Faction's Phrase
Send the Clergy all to graze;
And to make your Project pass,
Leave them not a Blade of Grass.[49]

Swift renewed his attacks upon Joshua, 2nd Viscount Allen, whose Elizabethan ancestor was a famous architect and operative Mason, while he, his brother, and son were currently prominent Whig Freemasons:

Those are Allens, Jack and Bob,

[47] R. Berman, *Schism*, 223.
[48] J. Swift, *Correspondence*, IV, 15051.
[49] J. Swift, *Poetical Works*, 607.

First in every wicked Jobb,
Son and brother to a Queer,
Brainsick Brute, they call a Peer.
We must give them better Quarter,
For their Ancestor trod Mortar'
And at Hoath to boast his Fame,
On a Chimney cut his Name.[50]

As Swift continued to lambaste the corrupt Irish politicians, he finally called on another Mason, William Hogarth who, though affiliated with the London Grand Lodge, shot his satire against a variety of targets, including Desaguliers, Henley, Pope, and Burlington:

How I want thee, humourous *Hogart*?
Thou I hear, a pleasant Rogue art;
Were but you and I acquainted,
Every Monster should be painted;
You should try your graving Tools
On this odious Group of Fools...[51]

The Legion Club was the last important work written by Swift, but his friend and publisher Faulkner considered it too inflammatory to print in Dublin; thus, he sent it to his London counterpart William Bowyer, who later published it in *Political Tracts*, *Vol. II* (1738). The danger was real, and Faulkner was imprisoned in March 1736 for publishing in another work two paragraphs that mildly disparaged Bettesworth, the recent target of Swift and his Masonic sympathizers.

While drafting "The Legion Club," Swift in early 1736 wrote a belated reply to Charles Wogan in Spain, and he reaffirmed his admiration for and sense of shared fate with the Jacobite exile:

I think you are the only person alive who can justly charge me with ingratitude: because, although I were utterly unknown to you, and become an obscure exile in a most obscure and enslaved country; you were at the pains to find me out, and send me your most agreeable writings, with which I have often entertained some very ingenious friends, as well as myself: I mean not only your poetry, in Latin and English, but your poetical history in prose of your own life and actions, inscribed to me; which I often wished it were safe to print here, or in England, under the madness of universal party now reigning...[52]

Swift explained that he had tried to locate Wogan's brother and kinsmen, employing his friends to learn when any of them came to Dublin, but in vain:

But, I suppose on account of their religion, they are so prudent to live in privacy: although the Court hath thought it better in point of politicks (and, to keep the good will of Cardinal Fleury), hath thought it proper to make the

---

[50] *Ibid.*, 606.
[51] *Ibid.*, 608.
[52] J. Swift, *Correspondence*, IV, 272-73.

> Catholicks here much more easy than their ill-willers, of no religion, approve
> of in their hearts. And I can assure you, that those wretches here, who call
> themselves a Parliament, abhor the clergy of our church more than those of
> yours, and have made an universal association to defraud us of our un-
> doubted dues.

Swift also made clear that he was friendly with Irish wine merchants who dealt with Spain (a trade dominated by Jacobites), and he promised to ask "Mr. Hall, an honest Catholick merchant here," to bring him a cargo of whatever wines Wogan recommended. Thomas Hall was one of the few Catholics bold enough to sign his name in support of Swift in the Wood's Halfpence controversy.[53] Swift also heard from a merchant who knew Wogan in Spain that the Irish knight wanted no recompense from the dean but only desired his recently published works. Given Wogan's current participation in emerging plots among the Jacobite exiles in Spain, France, and Italy, one wonders if Swift was informed by his contacts in the Spanish wine trade about these international intrigues – which were supported by the networks of *Écossais* and Tobosan Masons.

Reports of Swift's increasing sympathy for the Jacobites reached the Whig ministry, who may have learned about his correspondence with Wogan. Henley soon used his Walpolean journal, once again titled *The Hyp-Doctor*, to attack Swift as a Stuart supporter and a has-been. On 11 May 1736 he published a long, scurrilous poem, in which he denounced Swift as "once a courtly Fop," but now "you hourly more malicious grow/ You squeal in Verse and Yell in Satire/ And not one Mortal minds the Matter."[54] He echoed Swift's critics in the Irish government, charging "Then Doctor, your ordain'd to feed,/ And oft with J[a]mes's doleful Breed." Finally, he boasted, "See, Screech Owl, if thou canst, from far/ Where shines great W[ALPOL]E's glittring Star."

The Whig attacks on Swift provoked his Irish friend the Reverend William Dunkin to come to his defense. In *A Curry-Comb of Truth for a certain Dean: or, the Grub Street Tribunal*, published in Dublin soon after Henley's May attack, Dunkin lambasted the many hireling writers who accused Swift of Jacobitism, including the loyalist, Walpole-subsidized Freemason, James Arbuckle: "Arbuckle rise upon thy Sticks,/ And stifle him with Politicks."[55] With high spirits, Dunton mocked the outlandish charges of Jacobitism, ironically addressing Swift: "Culprit, You'll not deny, we hope,/ Your strong Attachment to a Pope," and then revealing that Swift not only had white roses in his garden, which "Prove it is Jacobitism ground," but on June 10 (James III's birthday) he actually ate, drank, and excreted.[56] Even worse, on May 29 (Restoration Day) he sat upon "an Oaken Chair;/ And 'tis observ'd he will not Smoak,/ without a Stopper of Royal Oak."

Such ironic and comical defenses of Swift only prodded Henley to more attacks. He further linked Swift with the Jacobites in his all-out attack on Pope in *Why How Now, Gossip Pope? Or, The Sweet Singing-Bird of Parnassus Taken out of its Pretty Cage to be Roasted* (1736). He scorned the satirical wit of Swift, Arbuthnot, Bolingbroke, and Pope, who should have his verses sung "at St. Patrick's," though his "Catholick Epistles on Man"

---

[53] Patrick Fagan, *Catholics in a Protestant County: The Papist Constituency in Eighteenth-Century Dublin* (Dublin, 1998), 165.

[54] *The Hyp-Doctor*, #293 (11 May 1736).

[55] [William Dunkin], *A Curry-Comb of Truth for a certain Dean* (Dublin, 1736), 7.

[56] *Ibid.*, 4-5.

would be a musical challenge.[57] He linked Swift's *Tale of a Tub* to Papists and Mass-Houses, and then argued that execution of the Penal Laws against Papists would prevent his and Pope's scurrilities from appearing. He railed further against Richard Savage, a Jacobite Mason, for furnishing Pope with vicious, unsubstantiated gossip ("Tittle-tattle for Bread"), and against Richard Russell, the Non-juring editor of *The Grub street Journal*. Walpole must have thought that Henley well-earned his subsidy with this free-wheeling attack, for the government in London and Dublin increasingly considered Swift and his opposition supporters, both Masonic and non-Masonic, a real danger.

Swift's communications with Jacobite Masons in Spain, France, and England were bad enough, but the Hanoverian Masons were also concerned about a looming crack-down on their allies in Italy. Stosch continued to send reports to Newcastle and Walpole about the Inquisition's determination to penetrate the secret of the English Masonic lodges, especially the Whig-dominated one in Florence. He claimed that James III seemed threatened by these Hanoverian Masons but, surprisingly, he never mentioned the Jaco-bite lodge in Rome. In fact, he seemed unaware of its existence, which was kept so secret that it was only briefly made public in 1853, while the lodge journal was not published until 1910.[58]

On 28 January 1736 Stosch reported that the Inquisition had arrested a servant of Dr. James Irvin, the Pretender's chief physician, but he did not connect it with the Jacobite lodge.[59] Despite Irvin's staunch loyalty to James, he often hosted visiting Englishmen, whatever their political sympathies. Robert Adam later commented that "the best Whigs go to see him, so that it is no stain and he is so sensible as not to say or do anything to offend them."[60] Thus, it is possible that the Inquisitors thought Irvin was affiliated with the Masonry of the "English travelers" (organized by Fox or Folkes?). In February Stosch reported that the Inquisition would not touch the masters but hoped to learn the mystery from the domestic servants. He also sent to Newcastle an article published in the Gazette of Rome, designed "to interrupt the course of this assembly so odious to the Pretender and spiritual Government of Rome."

On 11 March the *Old Whig; or, the Consistent Protestant*, published a report from Flor-ence: "the Tribunal of the Inquisition at Rome, has received Information of a Soci-ety....called *La Cucchiara*,...[an] Imitation of the famous Society of the Free Masons at London...The Tribunal has even caused several Domesticks to be taken up belonging to Persons suspected to be of that Cabal.; but all Endeavours have hitherto proved ineffec-tual."[61] On 3 September the diplomat Charles Fane reported to London that the Pre-tender was "extremely apprehensive" about the Masonic meetings organized by Stosch in his home (in Florence).[62] Newcastle would soon write Richmond to praise Fane as "Our Great Friend & Brother Mason."[63]

The summer of 1736 was filled with widespread disaffection to Walpole and George II, as riots broke out all over the British Isles. The widespread publicity given to Masonic

---

[57] John Henley, *How Now Gossip Pope?* (1736; reprinted London: J. Roberts, 1743), 1-4.

[58] W. Hughan, *Jacobite Lodge*, 11.

[59] NA: SP 98/37 (28 January , 4 and 11 February 1737).

[60] "James Irvin," Ingamells, *Dictionary*.

[61] R. Péter, *British Freemasonry*, V, 151.

[62] Lesley Lewis, *Connoisseurs and Secret Agents in Eighteenth-Century Rome* (London, 1961), 110-11.

[63] C. Richmond, *Correspondence*, 18.

controversies provoked lurid and bizarre rumors among the Irish populace. On 27-30 March the *Dublin Evening Post* reported that,

> A sudden *Stupor*, seiz'd the Brains of several hundred Persons, both Males and Females,…which in a few Moments, turn'd to a most deplorable *Frenzy*; occasioned, it is thought, by puzzling their Heads about the meaning of the FREE-MASON-SOCIETY; several Masons being made on that Day, in order to constitute a Lodge… Some said it was a *Plot* against the Government; others, that it was a *New Religion*; that they had abolished all the *Christian Precepts*, and were about to introduce the Jewish Rites of *Circumcision*; others averr'd, that everyone, at his *Initiation*, was first to be *Castrated* and made *Eunuchs*, not for Heaven's Sake, but solely for the Glory of *Free-Masonry*…[64]

As gullible readers swallowed such Irish "blarney," many Protestant Hanoverian Masons were so fearful of the brazen behavior of Jacobites that they drowned more than ever their fears in drunken loyalist toasts. In May Orrery wrote from Dublin to Salkeld in France about their alcoholic and oafish behavior:

> Drunkenness is the Touch Stone by which they try every Man. He is abus'd behind his Back, He is hurt in his Property, and He is persecuted as far as the Power of Malice and Intemperance can go. A right jolly glorious-memory Hibernian never rolls into Bed without having taken a sober Gallon of Claret to his own Share. You wonder perhaps what this glorious animal is? It is a Yahoo that toasts the glorious and immortal Memory of King William in a Bumper without any other Joy in the Revolution, than that it has given him a Pretence to drink so many more daily Quarts of Wine. The Person who refuses a Goblet to this prevailing Toast is deemed a Jacobite, a Papist, and a Knave. It is well if he escapes with his life…[65]

In London in July, the Whig ministry was especially disturbed by a serious riot in Spitalfields, when rivalries between Irish and English weavers erupted in violence. Lord Hervey whom Pope had scorned as "Sporus, that mere white curd of Ass's milk," recognized the seriousness of popular discontent, noting that "the people showed a licentious, riotous, seditious, and almost ungovernable spirit":

> Those who wish ill to a Government may turn a flame they had no hand in kindling to annoy such persons it was at first not intended to touch nor thought likely to reach. This was the case of the Spitalfields weavers, who began with railing against Irishmen, but came in twenty-four hours to cursing the Germans, reviling the King and the Queen, huzzaing for James III.[66]

He also reported an explosion of gunpowder in Westminster Hall, set off by a radical Non-juror, that frightened government officials into believing a plot was underway.

---

[64] R. Péter, *British Freemasonry*, V, 259.

[65] Orrery, *Orrery Papers*, I, 157.

[66] J. Hervey, *Some Materials*, 565-66.

Throughout the summer, there were riots in Cornwall, Worcestershire, Edinburgh, and Dublin, and between "Irish, Welsh, and English haymakers."[67] Pope and Swift were attuned to the unrest, which heightened their own scorn for the regime. In that summer Pope began writing lines on Swift that so angered the government that their Jacobite friend John Barber feared that the arrest of Pope was imminent.[68] With sedition becoming more public in Ireland, Pope reminded his readers of Swift's nationalistic role as the Drapier:

> Let Ireland tell, how Wit upheld her cause,
> Her Trade supported, and supplied her Laws;
> And leave on SWIFT this grateful verse ingrav'd,
> The Rights a Court attack'd, a Poet sav'd.
> Behold the hand that wrought a Nation's cure,
> Stretch'd to relieve the Idiot and the Poor,
> Proud Vice to brand, or injur'd Worth adorn,
> And stretch the Ray to Ages yet unborn.[69]

Like Swift, Pope linked political corruption to architectural corruption, and he once again attacked Walpole's favored architect, Thomas Ripley, who repeatedly submitted inferior designs for a bridge over the Thames. Pope scorned Ripley for his lack of architectural training: "Who builds a Bridge that never drove a pile?/ (Should Ripley venture, all the world would smile)."[70] Not surprisingly, Henley had earlier praised Ripley in one of the last issues of *The Free-Mason*.[71]

During this summer of discontent, Hervey, a Whig Mason, also distrusted Lord Burlington and was suspicious about the purpose of Chiswick House. To entertain Queen Caroline, he wrote the following epigram on Burlington's unusual edifice:

> Possess'd of one great hall for state
> Without a place to sleep or eat;
> How well you build let flattery tell,
> And all mankind how ill you dwell![72]

In more verses meant to amuse the bored queen, he mocked Lady Burlington and her "mason- husband," suggesting that she had made him a cuckold (with horns):

> And Dame Palladio, insolent and bold,
> Like her own chairman, whistle, stamp, and scold;
> Her quiet still preserv'd, though lost her fame,
> As free from ev'ry punishment as shame;
> Her worn-out huntsman frequent may she hold;
> Nor to her mason-husband be it told

---

[67] Ian Gilmour, *Risings, Riots, and Revolution: Governance and Violence in Eighteenth-Century England* (London, 1993), 93,102, 154, 253.

[68] M. Mack, *Alexander Pope*, 683.

[69] A. Pope, *Poetical Works*, 367.

[70] *Ibid.*, 367; H. Colvin, *Biographical Dictionary*, 818-20.

[71] *The Free-Mason* (16 January 1734); he calls him Jack Ripley.

[72] John, Lord Hervey, *Some Materials towards Memoirs of the Reign of King George II*, ed. Romney Sedgwick (London, 1931). , 574.

> That she, with capital Corinthian grac'd,
> Has finish'd his in the Ionic taste.[73]

The editor notes that "Corinthian" means "brazen-faced" and that the volutes of Ionic capitals were sometimes called "horns."

It is possible that Hervey had learned from Walpole's intelligencers about Swift's still unpublished "Verses upon the Death of Dr. Swift," which had been circulating among the dean's friends since 1731, for he further entertained the queen with "The Death of Lord Hervey, or, a Morning at Court: A Drama." In the script, when Caroline is told that Hervey was murdered by a highwayman, her first concern is to have "a little breakfast," with some chocolate, sour cream, and fruit. She then turns to Lady Burlington and asks her reaction to Hervey's death, which provokes the sardonic answer, "I am just as sorry as I believe he would have been for me."[74] The queen replies, "I am sure you have not forgiven him his jokes upon Chiswick. I used to scold him for that too, for Chiswick is the prettiest thing I ever saw in my life. But I must say, poor my Lord Hervey, he was very pretty too." Lady Burlington colors and takes snuff before answering, "I can't think Your Majesty does Chiswick any great honour by the comparison." When Caroline defends Hervey for being "very well bred," Lady Burlington insolently replies, "Where it was his interest, perhaps; he was very well bred to your Majesty, I dare say."

This odd bit of "drama," in which Hervey makes fun of his own foppishness and fawning, contains hints at his anger at Lord Burlington, a "mason-husband," for deserting Walpole and apparently Grand Lodge Masonry. Hervey's repeated criticisms of the earl and his wife provoked a retort from Pope in "To the Earl of Burlington, asking who writ the Libels against him":

> You wonder Who this Thing has writ,
> So full of Fibs, so void of Wit?
> Lord! Never ask who thus could serve ye?
> Who can It be but Fibster H[erve]y.[75]

The Whig courtier's attacks on Burlington were followed by those of another Grand Lodge Mason, Batty Langley, a mediocre architect but prolific author of practical treatises on the art and science of building. From July 1734 to March 1735, he issued his English patriotic versions of good architecture in *The Grub Street Journal*. As Eileen Harris observes,

> Shielded by the pseudonym Hiram, Langley viciously attacked the foreign, Palladian taste imposed by Lord Burlington, praising Gothic architecture (or native Saxon, as he preferred to call it) and the works of Hawksmoor, who was married to the daughter of his patron, Nathaniel Blackerby.[76]

As noted earlier, Blackerby was a Whig justice of the peace and Deputy Grand Master of the Grand Lodge, and in 1735 he employed his close neighbor Langley to design and erect "a curious grotesque temple *in a taste entirely new*, finely decorated with busts of King

---

[73] *Ibid.*, 584.
[74] *Ibid.*, 587-88.
[75] A. Pope, *Poetical Works*, 702.
[76] Eileen Harris, "Batty Langley," *ODNB*.

William III, George I, and five gentlemen of the club of liberty;…which without prejudice doth very greatly exceed every artificial hermitage, grotto, and cave, that has been
yet made or begun in this kingdom."[77] Langley apparently determined to outdo Pope,
whose elaborate grotto had become famous.[78]

Langley was so devoted to Grand Lodge Masonry that he gave his four sons the Masonic names of Euclid, Vitruvius, Archimedes, and Hiram.[79] He further identified himself
with the Masonic Whigs when he published *Ancient Masonry* (London, 1736). This enormous, unwieldy book with over five hundred engraved plates, was dedicated to Francis,
Duke of Lorraine, and then all the British Grand Masters from the Duke of Montagu in
1722 to the Earl of Loudoun in 1736. John Campbell, 4th Earl of Loudoun, was a Scottish
Whig and army officer, who was a part of Walpole's packing of "representative peers"
that caused so much outrage in Scotland.[80] His election as Grand Master in London was
aimed at consolidating the government's power in the Grand Lodge system as well as in
parliament.

In a final patriotic outburst, Langley pledged to overcome "the censorious Part of
Mankind" and to bring "this most Noble Art" to the "service of my Country." In the
process, he managed to get in more digs against Burlington, whom he earlier admired,
but after the earl's desertion of the Whig ministry he turned against him with "xenophobic" anger.[81] He railed against "all the iniquities imposed by Burlington's Rule of Taste,"
which brought in foreign (i.e., Italian and French) artists and styles, and praised the native
English Gothic in nationalistic terms.[82] Harris suggests that Langley shared the agenda of
Orator Henley in *The Free Mason/ Hyp-Doctor*, as both loyalist Masons used architectural
arguments to defend the government's policies.

The efforts of the Grand Lodge Masons to solicit subscriptions for a new version of
Anderson's *Constitutions* greatly annoyed Samuel Wesley, who mentioned it in "The
Bonds-man: A Satyr" (1736), in which he attacked an agreement (a "bond") by a group
who determined to stop the tradition of subscribing funds for works to be published in
the future. Admitting that there were many abuses, he criticized those "scrubby penceless
Rascals" who list the names of subscribers who never agreed to lend their names, but the
"bonds-men" want to punish the guiltless with the guilty. They should confine their protest to works which defend "Party-Rage and Vice":

> Or Slander false, or Treason mean and base?
> Or Reams of Chit-chat 'gainst the STUARTS' Race?
> No! let such Wretches meet your Scorn or Hate;
> Let NEWGATE or BEDLAM be their Fate.
> ....
> Or is their Thrift confin'd to this alone?
> ....
> Have they e'er wasted idle Sums of Gold,

---

[77] *St. James Evening Post*, quoted in James Peller Malcolm, *Londinium Redivivum* (London, 1802-07), IV, 172.
[78] Eileen Harris, "Batty Langley: A Tutor to Freemasons (1696-1751), *Burlington Magazine*, 119 (May 1977), 328.
[79] E. Harris, "Batty Langley," *ODNB*.
[80] "John Campbell, 4th Earl of Loudoun," *ODNB*.
[81] Batty Langley, *Ancient Masonry* (Londonr, 1736), 220, 333.
[82] E. Harris, "Batty Langley," 330-31.

> The Craft of sage FREE-MASONS to uphold?
> No matter whether Arts and Letters live,
> If Gloves they buy and Aprons they can give:
> No printed Volume they desire to see,
> But *the Grand History of Masonry.*[83]

Pope and Orrery must have appreciated this critique of Anderson and Grand Lodge Masonry, which they read in Wesley's *Poems on Several Occasions* (1736), to which they both subscribed.[84]

Meanwhile on the Continent, whatever fear that James III had about the Hanoverian Freemasons, his faithful supporter Derwentwater continued to work to increase the political usefulness of Jacobite Masonry. In summer 1736 he arrived secretly in Paris, where he collaborated with Ramsay on reforms and reinvigoration of the *Écossais* lodges. In the process, they drew on the older Scottish and Irish themes of Christian chivalry and Jewish mysticism that Swift had revealed in *Letter from the Grand Mistress* – themes that would soon emerge in Ramsay's famous Masonic oration. In July Dr. King was with Swift in Ireland and perhaps passed on Ramsay's current interest in Hebrew mysticism and allegorization.[85]

In August King made another secret journey to Scotland, from where he wrote Mrs. Whiteway, Swift's cousin and constant companion, that if Swift approves of it, he "will prevail upon Ramsay the author of Cyrus to translate the whole work ["The Four Last Years of the Queen"] into French, so that it may be published at the same time in both languages."[86] King did not mention his Jacobite mission, for he knew that his and Swift's letters were intercepted by the government; he thus used Mrs. Whiteway as an intermediary. But he subsequently made an important intelligence report to James III on the readiness of Stuart sympathizers to rise against the Hanoverian regime.[87]

From Scotland King travelled to Paris, where he stayed with Ramsay, who was working on his oration for the Jacobite Grand Lodge. In September and November Ramsay again wrote to Carte, requesting that he send him books on Jewish mysticism and its Christianization by various scholars. Noting that Dr. King was with him, he asked for Henry More's works on the Jewish Cabala, explaining that

> I am curious in everything that regards the Jewish antiquities. I look upon the Rabbinical Cabbala as the Jewish mythology which is not to be despised… the other mythologys, of which I have made a collection founded upon the great principle, and followed with very important consequences against deists, socinians, and freethinkers. I received lately the Chinese mythology from Canton which is a most curious piece, but I have no permission to give it to the world so soon… But say nothing about me on this head, for

---

[83] Samuel Wesley, *Poems on Several Occasions* (London, 1736), 256-58

[84] A. Pope, *Correspondence*, III, 504; Bodleian. MS. 2591.d.6 [7]. *The Library and Collection of Autograph Letters of the Rt. Hon. the Earl of Cork and Orrery* (London, 1905), #604.

[85] J. Swift, *Correspondence*, IV, 336.

[86] *Ibid.*, IV, 346.

[87] D. Greenwood, *William King*, 74-75.

I live in a country where true noble Christian freethinking (dramatically opposite to skepticism…) is not allowed, nor even tolerated.[88]

In August 1736 the internationalization of the Jacobite-Masonic efforts was made evident at the fashionable watering-place of Spa. The center of the social world was the Duchess of Buckingham, the Pretender's half-sister, who was still mourning the death of her nineteen year-old son Edmund Sheffield, at Rome on 30 October 1735. On 3 February 1736 the *Daily Journal* reported that "the late Duke of Buckingham, having been made a Free Mason when abroad, several fine Favours of Gold and Silver have been presented to all the Members of the Grand Lodges, to be worn in Memory of him."[89] The report did not mention that his death occurred while he was visiting his uncle, the Pretender, or that he joined a Jacobite lodge (probably in Paris or Rome). From Dublin, Orrery sent a consolatory poem to the duchess, and he shared her Jacobite ambitions.[90] At her request, Pope composed an epitaph which praised the youth as a patriot and saint. One wonders if they knew about his recent *Écossais* initiation.

At Spa the Irish Jacobite agent Sylvester Lloyd kept his eye on both Jacobites and Whigs, and he was particularly concerned about the activities of the Duchess of Buckingham and her constant companion Lord Cornbury. As noted earlier, the duchess had accompanied Cornbury to Rome in 1731 to plan an invasion and restoration. Despite her strong Jacobitism, the duchess could not stand the irritating Ezekiel Hamilton, who was trying to recruit new members to the Order of Toboso. Lloyd reported that,

> Mr Zachy Hamilton…took it very ill that he was not the person employed to perform that service [read prayers for the Protestants with the duchess], and that the reason…was because it was presumed he would not pray for [King] George and his family… . I have observed him narrowly. He seems to be angry with everybody and not pleased with himself. He travels like a fencer with a Scotch sword and target which he shows to everybody. He says he is Grand Master of a military order of knighthood, and shows to all sorts of people a ring as a badge of that honour, which he can confer. In a word he talks a little too freely of things past and present and does not spare the most Sacred Persons. He has something in his looks and ways that make me fear his head is turned.[91]

Cornbury evidently shared the duchess's distaste for Zecky's outlandish Jacobitism, and on his return to London, he joined the party of the Prince of Wales.

From Spa Hamilton moved on to Leiden, where he maintained an extensive correspondence with Ormonde, Marischal, and the Jacobite network. This correspondence was steadily intercepted by the spy, "Le Connu," who sent copies to the English foreign office and then forwarded the originals to Hamilton's correspondents.[92] Unaware of the danger, Hamilton continued to recruit not only brother knights but sisters for Toboso — a practice that would subsequently emerge in *Écossais* Freemasonry. In November he

---

[88] Bodleian: Carte MS. 226, ff. 415-16, 419 (15 September, 22 November 1736). He was also interested in Pierre Allix's work "upon the Trinity known to the Jews," a key theme among Christian Cabalists.

[89] R. Péter, *British Freemasonry*, V, 21.

[90] Harvard. Houghton: Eng.MS.218 F, vol. 7, f.27 (17 March 1736).

[91] P. Fagan, *Irish Bishop*, 145-46.

[92] *HMC. Reports on MSS. Eglinton*, 452.

wrote Lady Elizabeth Caryll, "Protectrice of the most Noble order of Tobosco," that "her brother My Lord Sempill and Mr Sempill will do a particular Honour to the most Nobel order by the acceptance of the Stalls in it."[93] The new Tobosan knight was the loyal Jacobite, Francis, Lord Sempill, not the John Sempill (Sample) who served as Horatio Walpole's spy on Atterbury. Hamilton also reported to Ormonde that George Kelly, co-conspirator in the Atterbury plot, has escaped from the Tower: "I hope in God he will get safe out of the hands of those whose tender mercys are cruel and I long impatiently to hear that he is safe on this side of the water." Hamilton continued to imply that all the old partisans of Atterbury were affiliated with Toboso, which made his further news seem ominous to the Jacobite Tobosans and Masons – i.e., the Duke of Richmond, politically powerful Hanoverian Mason, was in Leiden with the Princess of Orange (both incognito).

The opposition and Jacobites spread salacious rumors that the princess, daughter of George II, was not really pregnant, because her physically mis-shapened Dutch husband was impotent. Egmont recorded that the Prince of Orange was "greatly deformed…by an excessive rounding of his right shoulder; waist short, legs long and without calves; very short."[94] The gossip followed her and Richmond to The Hague, where they caused a slight Masonic scandal. In December 1736 Hamilton reported to Ormonde:

> A Ridiculous Quarrel hap'n'd lately at ye Hague between the Duke of Richmond and a Phisician in that Place at a Club of the Knights of St George as it is Call'd, whc by what I can learn of ye Nature of that Club is a sort of Society like the free Masons, the Phisician has said that he was sure the Prince of Orange could have no Succession for he had known him from a child; It was at ye Close of the Night after they had drunk Very plentifully, and the Duke of Richmond immediately seiz'd the Doctor by the Throat and would have strangled him if he had not been prevented; This adventure as made a good deal of Noise in this Country And is the subject of all most every Conversation.[95]

Given the recent Dutch prohibition of Freemasonry, on the grounds of its alleged Orangist political intrigues, Richmond may have participated in a secret lodge which met under a different name.

While Hamilton in Spa and Leiden recruited for Toboso, two visiting Scots were inititated into the Jacobite lodge in Rome on 2 January 1737. The artist Allan Ramsay, son of the poet of the same name, and his companion, Dr. Alexander Cunningham, "were received as freemasons by the Earl of Wintoun, as Grand Master of the Roman Lodge."[96] Like his father, the young Ramsay was a Jacobite, and he and Cunningham frequently met James III and his sons, as well as other members of the Stuart entourage. The painter was very close to his father, who on 15 October 1736 dedicated *A Collection of Scots Proverbs* (1737) to the tenantry, farmers, and "Store Masters of the Hills," with a call to them to "serve their King and Country by Sea and Land, with the Spirit of their auld Forbears, wha never fail'd to prove as a brazen Dike, in Defence of their Nation's independent

---

[93] *Ibid.*,462-63.
[94] *Ibid.*, 417.
[95] *HMC. Reports on MSS. Eglinton,*, 466.
[96] "A Visit to Rome in 1736," *Gentleman's Magazine*, 33, n.s. (June 1853), 580.

Honours and ancient Renown."[97] Given the heated nationalist tensions in Scotland, these were almost fighting words, and "their King" was interpreted by Jacobites to mean James III.

While in Rome, Cunningham noted that he "chatted about politics with the Earl of Wintoun and Mr. Campbell." Campbell, a Scot who earlier was employed as tutor to the son of Lord Egremont, had been friendly in Italy with Richard Rawlinson, the Duchess of Buckingham, and Martin Folkes.[98] Stosch reported that he was a zealous Jacobite. Cunningham's political discussion with Wintoun and Campbell must have included the current international situation, as the Jacobites hoped for assistance from the Swedish Hats. As noted earlier, the Swedish architect Carl Johan Cronstedt had joined Wintoun's lodge in February 1736, and he carried messages from the French court to the Pretender. He was welcomed by Count Nils Bielke, who had been initiated by the Jacobites in Paris.[99] Thus, it is provocative that on 13 February Cunningham noted in his diary that he and Ramsay observed the Pope's appointment of "a Swede, called Count Bielki, of a noble family," as a new Roman senator: "They made rejoicings on his account that day, and in the night there were fine fireworks."[100] It is unknown if the Scottish visitors conversed with Bielke, but Stosch would soon alert the British government that the Swedish convert was the main "channel" for Scottish-Swedish intrigues and restoration plans.[101]

In Georgia the rise of Scottish nationalism was noticed by Oglethorpe, who had welcomed a contingent of Highlanders to the colony. In 1736 he honored them by sometimes wearing Highland dress.[102] An enemy of Oglethorpe would later report to London that the Scottish Freemasons in Savannah always expressed "an Inveteracy to the present government finding fault with all measures since the Revolution (excepting during the few years of Bolingbroke's Ministry.)"[103] He scorned them because "they dressed Gay, set up a Free Mason's Clubb, a St. Andrews Clubb and other Tipling Societies," but "from what Fund they are supported in this expensive way of living is yet a Secret, and only Guessed at." This hint that Jacobite-Masonic sedition was funded from abroad would intensify the problems of the struggling colony and provoke attacks on Oglethorpe.

In 1736 two British poets – James Thomson and Samuel Wesley – came to the general's defence. In February Thomson, an opposition Whig and Freemason, praised Oglethorpe in *The Prospect; being the Fifth Part of Liberty*, for providing in Georgia an anti-slavery refuge for debtors and victims of persecution:

> Lo! Swarming southward on rejoicing suns,
> Gay colonies extend; the calm retreat
> Of undeserv'd distress, the better home
> Of those whom bigots chase from foreign lands.

[97] Allan Ramsay, *A Collection of Scots Proverbs* (Edinburgh and London, 1737), Dedication.
[98] J. Ingamells, "Campbell," *Dictionary.*
[99] M. Schuchard, *Emanuel Swedenborg*, 253-55, 271-73, 276.
[100] "A Visit," 582.
[101] NA: SP 98/4, ff.334-35.
[102] Egmont, HMC: *Egmont*, II, 268.
[103] Egmont Papers, vol. 14205, #126. http://djued.libs.uga.edu/egmont/. I am grateful to Richard Berman for this reference.

> Not built on rapine, servitude, and woe,
> And in their turn some petty tyrant's prey;
> But bound by social Freedom, firm they rise;
> Such as, of late, an Oglethorpe has form'd...[104]

In March Wesley, who closely followed Masonic affairs, anonymously published *Georgia. A Poem*, in which he lauded Oglethorpe's courage for crossing the tempestuous sea in order to grant deliverance to the oppressed, who now "long to build the Town, and clear the Land."[105] He and co-author Thomas Fitzgerald in another poem praised the native American chief Tomochachi, whom the general brought to London, for reviving "the old gen'rous Strain/ So fam'd amongst us once for Patriot Zeal," but "Alas! few such as These, few OGLETHORPES are here." Unfortunately, their poetry did not influence Walpole, who continued to oppose the colony.

Meanwhile, in January 1737 Marischal wrote from Madrid to "Grand Master" Hamilton that he was concerned about reports that Atterbury had converted to Catholicism on his deathbed. He had read in an old issue of *Fog's Journal* (19 July 1735) an article against Pope, which concluded with an advertisement:

> Last Monday I published the second Volume of your Litterary Correspondence and am ready to produce the Originals (under your hand & seal) therein contain'd – Bishop Atterbury's letters to you [Pope], you will know are genuine and some other Pieces of that Great Man wch I had of his son etc. together with his last will, wch Fully Proves he did not die a Papist.[106]

Marischal worried that by Fog's advertisement "it would appear that Pope had said the Bishop dyed a Papist wch I can not believe of Pope without better Authority – Let me know what you can learn of this matter." He recalled that while he was in Italy, he was told that Pope planned to publish a collection of "familiar letters particularly of ye Bishop," and "as I was honoured with Many I sent copys of a part and parts to Pope," but now he is concerned about the allegations in *Fog's*. This letter is the only known evidence of Marischal's correspondence with Pope, at a time when the Whigs publicly accused the poet of Jacobitism – an accusation that this letter, sent by Le Connu to the ministry, would strengthen.

In March Ezekiel Hamilton replied that he had never heard what Marischal mentioned out of Fog:

> Curl a Bookseller Who is a very impudent Fellow publish'd a great many Letters to and from Mr Pope, He got those Letters from a Servant of Mr Pope's without his Master's Knowledge, which I believe was the Occasion of that Advertisement, I have writ to England to be more fully informed of this Matter, and also to Mr. Holds[worth] concerning the Letters & Extracts You send to be perused by him.[107]

---

[104] James Thomson, *The Prospect: Being the Fifth Part of Liberty. A Poem* (London, 1736), 153.

[105] [Samuel Wesley and Thomas Fitzgerald], *Georgia. A Poem. Tomochichi. An Ode* (London. 1736), 7, 14.

[106] *HMC. Reports on MSS. Eglinton.*, 474-75.

[107] *Ibid.*, 477.

For Atterbury's partisans, any tainting of his reputation would damage their cause, especially in their campaign for the removal of Dunbar and Inverness from the Pretender's court. Moreover, any lessening of his prestige would hamper Hamilton's efforts to continue recruiting for Toboso, for the late bishop had served as "Grand Prelate" of the order.

Hamilton continued Atterbury's hatred of the late Mar and his supporters, and the nationalistic distrust between many Irish, Scottish, and English Jacobites made the *Écossais* Masons' efforts to unify the scattered Stuart supporters even more important.[108] Thus, there was increasing collaboration between Tobosans and Masons, with Lord Andover (recent Master of the Jacobite lodge in Rome) now working with the Tobosans.[109] On 4 December 1736 Andover wrote from England to Hamilton that the Chancellor of the Order of Toboso "has been with me & desired that I would make his complements wherever due"; Andover then offered his services in London to Hamilton in Leiden.[110] Unfortunately, the identification of the Chancellor, resident in England, is still unknown. Andover continued reporting to Hamilton on the plans of George II "to take a trip to Lilliput [Hanover] which occasions great Uneasiness not withstanding that *Sic volo sic jubeo stat pro ratione Voluntas*" [Thus I want. Thus I order. My wish stands in place of reason].[111]

While Dr. King was in France, Ezekiel Hamilton evidently planned to travel from Leiden to meet him and recruit him to Toboso. On 4 December 1736 Sir Redmond Everard, a Tobosan, wrote Hamilton that he assumed that King gave him "a particular account of the state of your friends" in England, but he hoped that Hamilton had not revealed to him their criticism of Dunbar and Inverness, because of the negative consequences for James III: "I am sure you said nothing on that head."[112] Hamilton responded, "I am sorry I did not see Dr Ki – tho if I had seen him I should not have given him the darkest hint of what Binet [James] had to fear from the two brothers."[113] It is unclear if Hamilton managed to meet King, but Everard would later write "Zecky" that he heard that [Dr.] King had returned to England, and "I hope he parted in friendship."[114] Thus, even within Toboso, Hamilton's obsessive vendetta against Dunbar and Inverness, the *par ignobile*, seemed divisive to the Stuart cause.

The issue of nationalistic differences that often divided the Jacobites also surfaced in Dr. King's relationship with Swift. In November 1736, while he was in Paris with Ramsay, King wrote Mrs. Whiteway a veiled letter, in which he hinted at his work in Scotland and promised to get Swift's satiric and politically volatile "verses on his own death" published when he returned to London.[115] He also responded to a letter (now lost) from Mrs. Whiteway in which she apparently echoed Swift's scorn for Scottish Presbyterians, whom King now defended: "I hope you are not in earnest, when you throw out such horrible reflections against my friends in Scotland. Will you believe me, when I tell you upon my

---

[108] *Ibid.*, 468. He worried that Charles Forbes had arrived in Leiden, for "he was a great friend of Lord Mar's and was with him at his death."

[109] E. Corp, *Stuarts in Italy*, 328-29.

[110] *HMC: MSS. of Eglinton*, 466, 479.

[111] I am grateful to Robert Shaw-Smith for the Latin translation.

[112] *HMC: Tenth Report*, 465-66.

[113] British Library: Add. MS. 73,999.

[114] *HMC: Tenth Report*, 508.

[115] J. Swift, *Correspondence*, IV, 361-62.

word, that I was entertained with the greatest politeness and delicacy during my short stay in that country?" Many of King's Scottish contacts were Jacobite Presbyterians and Episcopalians, and he believed that even the Scottish Whigs were ready to support James III. As we shall see, he became the confidant of Ramsay's Scottish friend, Lord Marchmont, a Presbyterian Whig and Mason, who joined the opposition to Walpole.

At this time, King and Ramsay were encouraged by the riots in Scotland over the Porteous affair, in which an unpopular captain of the city guard had ordered his troops to fire into a protesting mob in Edinburgh in April 1736. When Dr. King reported to James III that "The King's Friends in Scotland" are "grown very rich," he drew on these recent events, which had aroused fierce nationalist feelings. Chetwode Crawley notes that in Scotland "smuggling was considered a gentlemanly occupation, and the collection of the Excise an intolerable outrage."[116] When Andrew Wilson, a condemned smuggler, was executed, a huge protesting crowd stoned the city guard, and Captain Porteous ordered them to fire into the crowd, hitting many bystanders. Porteous was arrested by Edinburgh officials, charged with murder, and sentenced by a narrow jury vote of eight to seven to be hung on 8 September.

In London the verdict provoked anger among the Whig ministers; the Earl of Ilay, Walpole's manager in Scotland, then "made a grave miscalculation when he sought to appease his political masters with little consideration as to the depth of feeling in Scotland."[117] An appeal was made to parliament on behalf of Porteous and an order for deferment of six weeks arrived in Edinburgh on 2 September. Leaders of the Scottish "popular party" believed he would be reprieved by Queen Caroline, regent while George II was in Hanover, and the Whig ministry, so they broke him out of his jail cell and hung him on a makeshift gallows.

The wave of anger against England shook the Scottish government to its foundations, and Henley entered the fray with a defense of Porteous in *The Hyp-Doctor* (21 September 1736). In "Seasonable Reflections on the Tryal of Captain John Porteous, the Cause and Consequences," he gave a relatively sober summary of the charge ("libel") pronounced by "the King's Advocate, Duncan Forbes," who should have supported "his Highness's Interest," and of the jury's verdict.[118] Forbes had surprised the government by indicting Porteous, who was supported by the queen and ministry. Henley defended the captain, arguing that "he was exercising his Duty and attending his Office, and the Aggressors were answerable for the Event." Noting that Porteous had seventy men under his command, Henley agreed that he ordered them to shoot, but that he was then illegally "assassinated." Queen Caroline was right to have given him a reprieve.

Over the next months, the Whig agents searched for the perpetrators, whose secrecy and careful organization led to charges of Jacobite and Masonic conspiracy. In October the Jacobite intriguer Simon Fraser, Lord Lovat, wrote to Lord Grange (James Erskine, brother of the late Mar), that Porteous deserved a thousand deaths for shedding so much innocent blood. He then hinted at the conspiracy theories circulating in Scotland: "That riot was carried on with so much secrecy, dexterity, and good conduct that some people

---

[116] W.J. Chetwode Crawley, "Contemporary Comments on the Freemasonry of the Eighteenth Century," *AQC.* 18 (1905), 205-06.
[117] "John Porteous," *ODNB.*
[118] *The Hyp-Doctor*, #303 (21 September 1736).

in this country said that my Lord Grange was at the bottom of it; but I told them that it was too mean a game for that gentleman."[119] Grange and Lovat's oldest son Simon were indeed Masons, which lent credibility to the rumors.

Though Lovat insincerely shielded Grange from the charge, he definitely saw advantage to the Jacobites from the Porteous affair. He informed Grange that he wants to educate his son as a Scot and Frenchman, not an Englishman. Moreover, he believes that the Union will be broken, and "then Scots men must be Scots men, whither they will or not; whereas we are now but poor, mean, servile, and mercenary English slaves." From Paris a worried Waldegrave reported to Newcastle that Fleury referred pointedly to "the joy the Jacobites had at the disturbances in Scotland."[120] In Rome reports about the effective organization of the Porteous "mob" convinced the Pretender that the time was ripe to solicit foreign assistance for a Jacobite rebellion.[121] As we shall see, a profusion of rival literary responses to the riots and the government's harsh response would emerge in the coming months.

In November 1736 in Scotland, as Jacobites and Hanoverians competed for Masonic influence, pressure was put on William St. Clair of Roslin, to renounce his family's traditional role as head of Scottish Masonry. Beset by debts and without a male heir, in 1735 William had sold Roslin castle and chapel to his kinsman, General James St. Clair, a Hanoverian loyalist from a strong Jacobite family. James's older brother John had been attainted in 1715 but allowed to return to Scotland in 1726, when his brother turned over to him the family estate (as they had earlier agreed). In early 1736 James St. Clair began the restoration of the ruined Roslin Chapel, long considered the historical home of Stuart Freemasonry. It is unknown if James himself was a Mason.

In circumstances that still puzzle historians, William St. Clair joined the Canongate-Kilwinning lodge in June 1736 and on 22 November was elected Grand Master of the new Grand Lodge of Scotland. Just five days earlier, William Home, 8th Earl of Home, had been endorsed by Mary's Chapel Lodge to become Grand Master. Home was a loyalist military officer, a supporter of the Argyll faction, and a friend of Lord Loudoun, elected Grand Master of England in November.[122] In a surprising move, St. Clair advanced "with remarkable alacrity through a series of offices to qualify as master," and the subsequent election meeting was dramatic. Lord Home was not in attendance when William St Clair renounced and discharged his *hereditary* grand mastership, whereupon he was appointed grand master.[123] However, only thirty three of some one hundred lodges joined the new Grand Lodge, and political divisions within Scottish Masonry and within Scottish Masonic families – often reflected in literature – would intensify over the next few years.[124]

---

[119] *HMC. MSS. Mar and Kellie*, 546.

[120] BL: Add MS. 32,793, f. 64. Waldegrave to Newcastle (28 October 1736).

[121] Stuart Papers: 192, passim – entries in November-December 1736.

[122] "William Home, 8th Earl of Home," *ODNB*; R. Berman, *Schism*, 127, 151, 201.

[123] "William St. Clair of Roslin," *ODNB*.

[124] According to David Stevenson, in Henrik Bogdan and Jan Snoek, eds., *Handbook of Freemasonry* (Leiden, 2014), 59.

CHAPTER SIXTEEN

RIVAL CLAIMANTS TO THE "HIGHER ORDER" AND "ANCIENT FOOTING" (1737)

Who knows whether they [Freemasons] have an higher Order of Cabalists, who keep the grand secret of all intirely to Themselves?... I cannot help thinking them at the bottom of one Affair, I mean the late tumult at Edinburgh, and the murder of Captain Porteous...

"Jachin" to Caleb D'Anvers, *The Craftsman* (6 April 1737).

Mylord Earl of Derwentwater, martyr of Royalty and Catholicism, wanted to bring everything here back to its origin and to restore everything on its ancient footing... Our assemblies at the head of which Louis XV intended to declare himself chief have been suspended for a while.

Chevalier Ramsay to Marquis de Caumont (Paris, 16 April 1737).

On 30 November and 12 December 1736, Waldegrave reported (belatedly) to London that Derwentwater is in Paris, where he "is very busy in the Pretender's behalf," and something is brewing between the French and Stuart courts.[1] He added that "I knew him formerly a very shadowy Gent. I do not know whether the air of Rome has brightened his Parts. I will enquire further about him." At this time, Derwentwater was working closely with Ramsay on Masonic affairs, and Walpole, Delafaye, and their Whig-Masonic intelligencers learned of the two Jacobites' Masonic agenda. It seems likely that the vigilant Delafaye turned to one of his agents in Paris to counter their efforts in Paris by establishing a loyalist Whig lodge in Paris.[2] He thus employed an obscure Mason from London, John Coustos, who worked as a lapidary in the galleries of the Louvre. Son of a physician from southern France, Coustos was allegedly a Marrano,

---

[1] NA: SP 78/212 (30 November and 12 December 1736).
[2] For Newcastle's later payment to Coustos, see British Library: Add. MS. 33,054, f. 313.

who converted to Protestantism and moved to Switzerland.[3] He next resided in London, where in 1730-32 he joined two French-affiliated lodges, which included many placemen in the Hanoverian regime. At least one of these, M. De la Roche, also reported to Walpole on the Jacobites in Paris.[4] On 17/18 December Coustos opened his lodge and began official meetings on 28 December.

In between those dates, Ramsay delivered his eloquent oration to the Grand Lodge on 26 December, and on the 27th Derwentwater was elected Grand Master, in succession to Hector Maclean, who "had served for several years to the contentment of the society."[5] In his lecture, Ramsay opened with a universalist vision of Freemasonry, which stressed its moral and educational value:

> The noble ardour that you show to enter into the ancient and very illustrious Order of Freemasons, is a certain proof that you already possess all the qualities necessary to become members. These qualities are philanthropy, inviolable secrecy and a taste for the fine arts… The whole world is nothing but a huge republic, of which each nation is a family and each individual a child… We wish to unite all men of good taste and agreeable manners, by a love of the fine arts, whence ambition becomes a virtue, whence the interests of the Brotherhood are those of mankind as a whole, whence all the different Nations can draw valuable information and whence the subjects of all the different Nations can conspire together without arousing jealousy and live without discord… [6]

So far, this does not differ much from standard English Grand Lodge material. But Ramsay drew upon his studies in Jewish mysticism to go further than Anderson's *Constitutions*. Noting that mathematics and architecture are the basic sciences of Freemasonry, he differentiated the non-Masonic content and uses of these sciences from those of his ancient fraternity:

> The difference between ours and those of all other human Societies is that ours are founded on the annals of the most ancient race in the world, the only one still in existence with the same name as of old and not intermingled with other nations and also the only one that preserved its ancient books, whereas those of almost all other races are lost…

Ramsay then recounted the Jewish history of Freemasonry, drawing on those traditions revealed in seventeenth-century Stuart, Scottish, and Irish manuscripts and reported by Swift in *Letter from the Grand Mistress*. God, the Grand Geometrician and Grand Architect, infused symmetry into the universe and architectural skills to the patriarchs, with Noah, the inventor of naval architecture, serving as the first Grand Master:

> The secret science was handed down by oral tradition from him to Abraham and the Patriarchs… The secret science can be preserved pure only amongst

---

[3] Wallace McLeod, "More Light on John Coustos," *AQC*, 95 (1982), 117-18.
[4] M. Jacob, *Radical Enlightenment*, 131.
[5] Recorded by Bertin de Rocheret; see Louis Trebuchet, *De l'Écosse à l'Écossisme; Les deux siècles fondateurs, 1598-1804* (Marseilles, 2015), 124-25.
[6] C. Batham, "Chevalier Ramsay," 299—303.

> God's people… King Solomon wrote in hieroglyphic characters, our stat-
> utes, our maxims and our mysteries and this ancient book is the original
> Code of our Order. After the destruction of the First Temple…the great
> Cyrus who had been initiated into all our mysteries, appointed Zerubbabel
> as Grand Master of the Lodge of Jerusalem and instructed him to lay the
> foundations of the Second Temple, where the mysterious book of Solomon
> was deposited. This book was preserved for twelve centuries in the Temple
> of the Israelites, but after the destruction of the Second Temple…this au-
> thentic record was lost until the time of the Crusades, when a part of it was
> rediscovered after the relief of Jerusalem.

Claiming that "here now is our true history," Ramsay revealed the Crusader and chivalric transmission of Freemasonry from medieval to modern times:

> At the time of the holy wars in Palestine, many Princes, Lords and Artists,
> entering into association, made a vow to restore the Christian Temples in
> the Holy Land, and engaged themselves by solemn oath to employ their
> knowledge and their possessions in reviving architecture in its original form
> and in bringing back all the ancient signs and symbolic words of Solomon
> so as to recognize themselves and distinguish themselves from the Infi-
> dels…This union was after the manner of the Israelites when they built the
> Second Temple, while some handled the trowel and compasses, others de-
> fended them with the Sword and Buckler.

The editor of the Epernay manuscript of Ramsay's December oration notes that "This
idea forms the groundwork of all subsequent Scots grades: Knightly Scots Masons who,
in the old Temple, rediscovered the Sacred Name, the trowel in one hand, the sword in
the other." In March 1737 Ramsay would elaborate further on these Jewish and chivalric
themes, which he and Derwentwater considered to be the ancient and authentic ones of
the order. One wonders if the Jacobite Mason Thomas Carte, who had helped Ramsay
in his studies of Cabalistic mysticism and chivalric orders and who visited him in Paris,
reported any of this to Swift, with whom Carte was currently corresponding.[7]

One day after Derwentwater's election, Coustos began holding meetings of what soon
became a rival lodge. He initially sought out Jacobites and foreign visitors to Paris, and
he kept written records and lists of most (but not all) members. It was soon easy pickings
for Fleury's police, in what seems a set-up job. The establishment of a new lodge with
no ties to Derwentwater, who was on good terms with Louis XV, evidently caused concern in the French court, for the king asked Coustos to initiate the Duc de Villeroy, the
royal favorite, who on 17 February replaced Coustos as Venerable of the lodge.[8] But
Coustos was allowed to continue performing many of the ceremonial tasks at lodge meetings. Villeroy was joined by Louis Alexandre Bontemps, the king's valet-de-chambre and
personal secret agent, who became an important *frére*. At this time, the king and his newly-
initiated confidants were becoming more sympathetic to the Jacobites, and despite the
opposition of Fleury, they seemed to privately approve of the rapid expansion of *Écossais*
Masonry that soon took place.

---

[7] J. Swift, *Correspondence*, IV, 337-40.
[8] P. Chevallier, *Ducs*, 31, 37, 72-97.

On 9 March the Duc de Luynes recorded the "frequent talk" about the Freemasons, who have attracted many "young men of good family."[9] At their reception, there is a big supper and a speech by Ramsay, the "Chancellor of the Order." Over the next months, rumors about Ramsay's oration and the recruitment of "nouveaux chevaliers" to the *Écossais* lodges spread in Paris. Barbier recorded in his journal that the Masons' rule of secrecy makes them dangerous to the state; thus, it is believed that Fleury will "suffocate this Order of Chivalry at its birth."[10] On 16 March a gazette reported that the Parisian Freemasons are like the Order of Templars and that Villeroy is a leading figure.[11]

In London the *Gentleman's Magazine* reported that it was expected that the French government, like the Dutch, would soon move against the lodges.[12] Nevertheless, prominent aristocrats flocked to the lodges, as reported in a letter from Paris published in *The Leeds Mercury* (22 March 1737):

> The Order of the Free Masons increases so fast, that it now takes up nine lodges; amongst the new members are the Prince of Conti, all our young Dukes, and even the Count of Maurepas, Secretary of State. The Ladies we hear design to set up a new Order in imitation of it; but as none but those who can keep a Secret are to be admitted, 'tis thought their Society will be very thin.[13]

Encouraged by this expansion, on 20 March Ramsay wrote a flattering letter to Fleury. He sent a draft of his oration and added a eulogy to Louis XV, "that most amiable of Kings," and to the cardinal, his "Mentor," whom he hopes will become the new patrons of the Royal Art:

> Deign, Monsieur, to support the Society of Freemasons in the large views which they entertain and your Excellency will render your name more illustrious by this protection than Richelieu did by his founding the French Academy. To encourage a society which tends only to reunite all nations by a love of truth and of the fine arts, is an action of a great Minister, of a Father of the Church and of a Holy Pontiff... As I am to read my discourse tomorrow in a General Assembly of the Order... I pray your Excellency to return it to me tomorrow by express messenger...[14]

Fleury's reply is lost, but he rejected Ramsay's appeal. He wrote in the margin of Ramsay's letter, "It is not the King's wish," but as subsequent events showed, it was the cardinal – not the king – who feared Masonic subversion of his power

In the Epernay manuscript, Ramsay traced the order back to the Old Testament, claiming that the early history of Masonry was closely tied up with the history of God's chosen people. Charles Batham notes that in the General Assembly version sent to Fleury,

---

[9] C. Batham, "Chevalier Ramsay," 304.

[10] E.J.F. Barbier, *Chronique de la Regence et Regne de Louis XV, 1718-1763* (Paris, 1885), III, 80-81.

[11] José Ferrer.Benimeli, *La Masonería, Iglesia e Illustracion* (Madrid, 1976-77), 252.

[12] "From Paris," *Gentleman's Magazine* (March 1737), 191.

[13] Quoted in P. Tunbridge, "Climate," 109.

[14] C. Batham, "Chevalier Ramsay," 290.

> Ramsay discards the suggestion that the histories of the Jewish race and of early Masonry are bound up together at least until the year 70 A.D. when the Second Temple was destroyed by the Emperor Titus. He dismisses the idea with these words: "Some ascribe our institution to Solomon, or to Moses, some to Abraham, others to Noah, even to Enoch, who built the first city, or to Adam. Without any pretence of denying those origins, I pass on to matters less ancient."[15]

He then expanded the Crusader history and made Masonic development much more Christian but still ecumenical:

> Our ancestors, the Crusaders, gathered together from all parts of Christendom in the Holy Land, desired thus to reunite into one sole Fraternity the individuals of all nations. …to form in the course of ages a spiritual empire where…a new people shall be created, composed of many nations…
> We have amongst us three kinds of brothers… To the first are explained the moral virtues; to the second the heroic virtues; to the last the Christian virtues.[16]

Ramsay then traced the "auld alliance" between France and Scotland, which allowed the ancient traditions of the fraternity to be preserved. He made clear that he and Grand Master Derwentwater believed that their version of Masonic history would lead to "the renewal of the Order":

> At the time of the last Crusades many lodges were already erected in Germany, Italy, Spain, France and from thence, to Scotland, because of the close alliance between the French and Scots. James, Lord Steward of Scotland, was Grand Master of a Lodge established at Kilwinning in the West of Scotland 1286…This lord received into his Lodge, the Earls of Gloucester and Ulster, the one English, the other Irish…
> …The fatal religious discords which embarrassed and tore Europe in the sixteenth century caused our Order to degenerate from the nobility of its origin… The beginnings of a remedy have already been made. It is necessary only to continue and, at last, to bring everything back to its original institution.[17]

Ramsay also called for an international effort to develop a universal encyclopedia of the arts and sciences, an agenda far beyond that of traditional "craft" Masonry:

> All the Grand Masters in Germany, England, Italy and elsewhere exhort all the learned men and all the artisans of the fraternity to unite to furnish the materials for a Universal Dictionary for the liberal arts and useful sciences, excepting only Theology and Politics. The work has already been commenced in London and, by means of the Union of our Brothers, it may be carried to a conclusion in a few years…[18]

---

[15] *Ibid.*, 287-88.
[16] *Ibid.*, 299.
[17] *Ibid.*, 303.
[18] *Ibid.*, 301.

He referred to Ephraim Chambers's *Cyclopedia: or, an Universal Dictionary of Arts and Sciences* (London, 1728), and he stayed in touch with the English Mason over the next few years.

In early 1737 Jacobite hopes were running high, and in Dublin where Orrery was visiting Swift, they both paid tribute to Mary Caesar, the staunch Jacobite, whose husband had helped organize the earlier Swedish-Jacobite plot, with its Masonic connections. Charles Caesar, along with Orrery's father had been entrusted with Wharton's will and estate when the duke left England in 1725. On 24 February Orrery wrote to Mrs. Caesar and begged her to send political news from London, adding that, "The Dean [Swift], Madam, toasted You Yesterday. You reign absolute Sovereign in his Heart. By the by, He owes his Peace and Safety to his Gown..."[19]

Encouraged by reports from Ireland, Scotland, and England, Derwentwater made a secretive visit to the latter, where he tried to garner support to reclaim his confiscated estate. Walpole took advantage of the Tories' sympathy for the attainted Jacobite and his family, and he tried to use it to gain Tory votes against the opposition's motion to increase the allowance of the Prince of Wales, whom Walpole despised. He approached Sir Watkins Williams Wynn, leader of the Welsh Jacobites, with a tempting offer. He knew that Derwentwater's wife, the Countess of Newburgh, had visited England in 1736, when she tried to prevent the sale of the family's estates.[20] As a member of the quasi-Masonic White Rose Society, Wynn had contacts with Derwentwater's Masonic supporters in northern England and Wales. Walpole offered to "get £20,000 to be given to Lady Derwentwater," if he would vote against the Prince of Wales's allowance, but Wynn refused , telling Walpole that "though he should be very glad that poor lady might have something of her husband's forefeited estate, yet he could neither apply for her or anyone else in so mean a manner."[21]

In June 1737 a worried Waldegrave wrote Newcastle about reports that the Abbé Fitzjames would "go minister to Rome," in succession to the Duc de St. Aignan.[22] Both men were staunch supporters of the Stuarts and, more provocatively, Fitzjames possessed a secret Jacobite Masonic ritual which he had revealed to Montesquieu. Bowing to English pressure, Fleury blocked the appointment, to the great relief of the Whig ministry. However, they were soon alarmed by the actions of another French Mason, the Comte de Froulay, ambassador to Venice, who welcomed the seventeen year-old Charles Edward Stuart to the city. The English consul Brown protested to Newcastle that Froulay entertained the prince like a royal personage and that Charles Edward went without a mask, "as if he affected to shew himself, and thereby satisfy the curiosity of the people, that crowded about him, to see him."[23] George II was so angry at the enthusiastic welcome to the Stuart prince that he expelled the Venetian representative from England. Froulay had been a close friend of Chevalier Ramsay, and he eventually became the secret channel of communication between Stuart supporters in Italy and the Masonic Hats in Sweden.[24]

---

[19] Orrery, *Orrery Papers*, I, 200.

[20] L. Gooch, *Desperate Faction*, 112-13.

[21] R. Sedgwick, *History*, II, 543.

[22] British Library. Add. MS. 32,703, ff. 102, 114.

[23] *Ibid.*, ff. 151, 153, 157, 300.

[24] M. Schuchard, *Emanuel Swedenborg*, 264.

Waldegrave was disappointed that Fleury did not punish Froulay, for he sensed that the old cardinal was shifting towards the Jacobites. Even worse was the rapturous welcome Charles Edward received as he toured more of northern Italy. In Bologna and Florence, he was welcomed and entertained by the Abbé Niccolini, member of the Florentine lodge and a close friend of Ramsay in the 1720s.[25] In Tuscany the price was lavishly entertained by Prince Corsini and local aristocrats, while at the same time the Inquisition tried to get Stosch expelled on the grounds that he encouraged meetings of Freemasons.[26] Newcastle sent Fane's account of the attempted expulsion of Stosch to Walpole, and the two responded to Fane that unless Stosch committed a proven crime, it would be disrespectful to George II, who employs him.[27] Newcastle then ordered Fane, his brother Mason, to prevent a meeting between Charles Edward and Gian Gascone de Medici, Grand Duke of Tuscany. Stosch managed to stay on, but he would long resent the attempt to persecute him as a heretical Freemason.

In London the Irish peer Egmont was now allied with Frederick, Prince of Wales, the estranged son of George II. With some worry, he recorded that "several gentry begin to whisper that the Pretender's son is a fine accomplished Prince, and that a person of quality, now returned to England has been in conference with the Pretender."[28] These developments provoked a combined effort by the Hanoverian government and Fleury to suppress not only the Jacobites but their international lodges. According to "les frey-massons politiques," the police measures were solicited by Waldegrave on the orders of George II, because the Grand Master Derwentwater was a "catholique jacobite outré," who used all his associations in favor of the Pretender.[29] However, Derwentwater and his Grand Lodge sensed the danger, and they tried to deflect Fleury's anger onto Coustos and his "heretical" cronies. Earlier, on 12 March Coustos and his partisans had protested the chivalric changes made by Derwentwater and Ramsay in the *Écossais* Grand Lodge.[30] Suspicious of the Hanoverian ties of the Coustos faction, the Jacobites subsequently tried to blacken their reputations.

Several anonymous members of the "Villeroy" lodge wrote to Derwentwater to affirm their "own innocence and obedience" to the Grand Master and his Grand Lodge. They then accused "Jean *Meyers* Coustos," Thomas Le Breton (member of the London Grand Lodge), and their "Confederation" of serious religious and civil irregularities. The use of the middle name "Meyers," which suggested his Jewish origin, was deliberate, for Coustos himself kept the name secret. According to his Masonic enemies,

> Thomas Le Breton, with his kindred spirits (*La Confederation*), as well as the man called Jean Meyers Coustos, and others, in defiance of the laws of God and man, held a meeting in the rue du Four, and another at Passy, both absolute orgies – and that too during Lent, in fact during Passion Week. The whole progeny of turpitude and excess evidently ran riot in the streets;

---

[25] NA: SP 98/41, ff. 59, 62.
[26] L. Lewis, *Connossieurs*, 111.
[27] British Library. Add. MS. 32, 793, ff. 155-56.
[28] Egmont, *MSS. Egmont*, II, 311.
[29] J. Benimeli, *Masoneria*, I, 260.
[30] P. Chevallier, *Ducs*, 80.

drunkenness, gluttony, fireworks, revelry; the entire village of Passy turned out. And all this on the pretence of holding a Masonic meeting.[31]

The accusers of Coustos further claimed that he and Le Breton defiantly recruited members who had been rejected by the Parisian Grand Lodge and secretly sought out new members who were unknown to the ancient officers of the Grand Lodge.[32] Coustos planned to open a "Loge de Maître" without the license or permission of Derwentwater. The accusers reminded Derwentwater of their known loyalty and assured him that they were not members of "cette séditieuse caballe." In the Villeroy lodge, the Jacobites inked out various sections in the record books which dealt with the Coustos "scandal," noting that they were "cancelled by the advice (and order) of the brethren…considering certain reasons known to the brethren." The implication that Coustos was a crypto-Jewish heretic and anti-Jacobite was accompanied by a warning (also inked out) to other Villeroy members that they should be respectful to the Catholic sensibilities of the French government.

Ramsay's appeal to Fleury was fruitless, and the cardinal soon unleashed a crack-down on the Masons. On 29 March a Parisian correspondent wrote to *The Leeds Mercury*,

> All the Taverns and Eating Houses are forbid, by an Order of the Lieut. De Police, to entertain the Free-Masons, which has baulked a great Feast that was lately bespoke, but the Gentlemen generously paid the Charges of it; however they meet in private Houses without the least disguise of secrecy, and as the high Rank of several of `em puts them above minding the ordinary Magistrates, `tis thought the King will exert his whole Authority to stop their further Meetings in any Place or Shape whatsoever.[33]

As rumors about Ramsay's oration circulated, his friend Caumont asked him for information about it, which drew an interesting reply on 16 April 1737. He explained the different degrees, giving the names novices to apprentices; professed to the companions; and adepts to the masters.[34] He stressed the ancient Jewish mystical sources of the Order, and named Jean Lord Stuart as the Grand Master of the Royal House of Scotland. He denounced Queen Elizabeth as "la parricide usurpatrice," who regarded our lodges as nests of Catholicism, which it was necessary to suppress. The Protestants altered, disguised, and degraded our hieroglyphs, changed our love feasts (*agapes*) into Bacchanals, and profaned our sacred assemblies. Derwentwater, martyr of royalism and Catholicism, determined to bring the Order back to its origin and restore it on its ancient footing. The ambassadors of Holland and of George, "duke of Hanover," argued that we want to launch a new crusade to restore the true monarch of Great Britain. The British and Dutch ambassadors influenced Fleury, by angrily blaspheming against what they were ignorant of, and imagining that "the Catholic, royalist, and Jacobite Freemasons" resemble the "heretical, apostate, and republican Freemasons." He lamented that Fleury suspended our assemblies, "of which Louis XV wanted to be declared chief."

---

[31] W. McLeod, "More Light," 118.
[32] J. Benimeli, *Masoneria*, IV, 222.
[33] P. Tunbridge, "Climate," 109.
[34] F. Weil, "Ramsay," 276-78.

Waldegrave and Richmond supported the extension of Hanoverian Masonry into France, and they were perhaps responsible for "an apologizing letter," sent from Paris to *The Gentleman's Magazine* on 6 April 1737, alleging,

> That the views the Free-Masons propose to themselves are the most pure and inoffensive, and tend only to promote such Qualities in them as may form good Citizens, and zealous Subjects… He assures the Fair, that the whole Brotherhood is full of Respect and Veneration for them; but that these Sentiments are not exempt from Fear; and that this Fear obliges the Free-masons to exclude the Sex from their Assemblies; Which, he concludes, ought not to provoke the Indignation of those who are the Objects of it; To prevent such an Effect, they need only recollect from whom Adam received the Apple: Sad Present! Since had it not been for that fatal Apple, Adam would have remained the first Free-Mason.

Despite such virtuous (and amusing) justifications of Freemasonry, concerns about the political agenda of Jacobite Masons emerged not only in France and England but in Scotland. As rumors about Masonic conspiracy in the Porteous Riots continued to circulate, Jacobite Masons and Tobosans worried about the government's efforts to penetrate their secrets. On 10 March 1737 Ezekiel Hamilton reported to Ormonde:

> The House of Lords has begun an Inquiry into the Execution of Capt Porteous who was [the] Captain of the Militia [who was killed] by the Mob of Edinburgh. Lord Carteret spake with great Vehemence against them and made some Reflections on the Scotch in general, Lord Bathurst said they were a brave People and had been provoked by ill usage.[35]

Reports of Bathurst's bold defense of the rebellious Scots, in the face of Whig attacks, undoubtedly reached his friends Pope, Swift, Orrery, and King.

On 27 March 1737 John Byrom recorded his conversation about the execution of Porteous with a clergyman, who informed him that "somebody from Scotland" had told his friends in England "the day after it was done, that it was done" (suggesting that the Scot had pre-knowledge of the plans).[36] Over the next few days, Byrom met with his Scottish pupil Charles Erskine and the Jacobite Mason Corbet Kynaston, as they studied Porteous's trial, "whose affair was agitating in the Hall [of parliament], and, as they say, a bill of pains and penalties ordered by a vast majority." Charles's father, Charles Aerskine, M.P. for Dumfrieshire, had earlier worked with his cousin Lord Mar on the Swedish-Jacobite plot but later joined Lord Ilay in the management of Scotland. However, Aerskine recognized that "nine out of ten" Scots were for the execution of Porteous and thus argued vigorously against the proposed penalties to be inflicted on Edinburgh.[37]

Among the "nine out of ten" Scots who opposed the government's harsh policy was the poet James Thomson, a Presbyterian and pro-Unionist, who had previously supported Walpole's policies. Now a permanent resident of London, Thomson published his five-part poem, *Liberty* (1735-1736), in which he drew upon his visit to Italy in 1731

---

[35] *HMC: MSS of Eglinton*, 479.
[36] J. Byrom, *Private Journal*, II, part 2, 83, 95, 102.
[37] R. Sedgwick, *History*, I, 420

to disparage the decadence of contemporary Catholic culture and its current Stuart residents. James Sambrook observes that "In Thomson's case, travel had the not uncommon effect of confirming the traveller's insularity, and reinforcing his British chauvinism."[38] In the final part of *Liberty*, published in February 1736, he denounced the Stuart kings from Charles I to James II as bigots and tyrants, who led Britain to ruin until "Immortal Nassau came" to save the nation and restore liberty.

But Thomson now joined the opposition Whigs in opposing Walpolean corruption and praised the architectural accomplishments of Bathurst, Cobham, Pope, and Burlington. A year later, when the government determined to implement draconian punishment on Edinburgh, which hurt loyal as well as disaffected Scots, Thomson – previously a strident anti-Jacobite – became more radical in his opposition to Walpole, and he collaborated with not only dissident Whigs but crypto-Jacobites who began to gather around the Prince of Wales. Thomson would subsequently join a Masonic lodge that supported the prince's oppositionist agenda – a move that would bring the wrath of the government down on him.[39]

As the debates about the penalties proposed against Edinburgh raged in parliament, with some English speakers insulting and denouncing the whole Scottish nation, rumors about Masonic complicity in the Porteous affair took an unusual and puzzling turn. Since February 1737 two Irish Jacobites, John Kelly and Charles Molloy, who had earlier worked with Nathaniel Mist, published in London *Common Sense, or the Englishman's Journal*, which received secret funds from James III, Colonel Cecil, and the Duchess of Buckingham.[40] George Kelly told O'Brien that Alexander Pope, Lord Chesterfield, and Lord Grange (Mar's brother) would contribute to it, but their names must be kept hidden.[41] Kelly had received their support before he escaped from the Tower and made his way to France, and he noted that Pope has "avoided entering any party affairs," but nevertheless offered his private support

On 27 February *Common Sense* published a report that George Kelly, "lately escaped from the Tower, appears publicly at Boulogne," and that "William McLaughlin, late footman to the Countess of Wemyss and now a prisoner in the Castle" has been indicted "as accessory to the hanging of John Porteous last 7 September." The long association of the Wemyss family with Jacobitism and Freemasonry reinforced Whig suspicions of Masonic complicity in the Porteous Riots. Given the emergence of Jacobite Masonry as an increasingly significant international force, as well as the accusations against the Porteous mob, it is curious that the opposition newspaper, *The Craftsman*, suggested that the Freemasons concealed a seditious agenda under their supposedly apolitical façade. After accusations targeted especially at Jacobite Masons, the journal would make a provocative charge about Masonic complicity in the Porteous riots.

Certainly, Bolingbroke and his partisans who contributed to *the Craftsman* wanted to distance themselves from the Jacobites, and they may have viewed *Common Sense* as an

---

[38] James Sambrook, *James Thomson, 1700-1748. A Life* (Oxford, 1991), 117.

[39] *Ibid.*, 160, 167.

[40] Paul Chapman, "Jacobite Political Argument in England, 1714-1766" (Ph.D. Dissertation, Cambridge University, 1983), 90-92.

[41] George Hilton Jones, "The Jacobites, Charles Molloy, and *Common Sense*," *Review of English Studies*, 14 (1953), 144-47.

unwelcome competitor. On 16 April 1737 a letter from "Jachin" to Caleb D'Anvers appeared in *The Craftsman*:

> Amongst all the various Instances of our Advantages over other Nations in Point of Liberty, there is one so very remarkable that it deserves your most serious Consideration; I mean the Toleration of that mysterious Society call'd Free Masons, who have been lately suppressed not only in France, but in Holland, as a dangerous Race of Men; whereas here they are permitted to hold their private meetings in every Part of the Town, and even to appear in Publick Procession, with the Ensigns of their Order.
>
> Indeed, I have often wonder'd that they have not been laid under some Restraints even in England; for tho' our present most excellent Ministers have always preserved a sacred Regard to Liberty, I think no Government ought to suffer such clandestine Assemblies, where Plots against the State may be carried on, under the Pretence of Brotherly Love and good Fellowship.

Obviously, Bolingbroke and the editors did not consider "our present ministers" as excellent lovers of liberty, so Jachin's subsequent comments were tinged with irony. While criticizing the Masons' secrecy, ecumenicism, and "nocturnal Rites and Ceremonies," Jachin claimed that the Masons are a "military order," similar to the Knights of Malta, and the Grand Master carries a Sword of State which was presented by "a great Roman Catholick Peer." Even worse,

> There seems to be something emblematical in the Gloves and Aprons; a Glove is only another Word for a Gauntlet, which is a Piece of Armour for the Hands. An Apron, indeed, is a proper Badge of Masonry, in the literal sense, but is likewise a Term in Gunnery for a flat Piece of Lead to cover the Touch-hole of a Cannon, when it is loaded...

Though many Masons (and later historians) considered this analysis far fetched, "Jachin" was evidently aware of the military symbolism of the rituals practiced in some *Écossais* lodges in France. In an English exposure of such rituals, the author reported that all the terms which they make use of in drinking are borrowed from artillery:

> When they drink in ceremony, they use this expression, Give us powder; they hereupon fill their bowls [which they call cannons], and the Grand Master says, Handle your arms – present fire: thus are the three different actions they observe... In the first, they lay their hands on their bowls; in the second, they hold them out as it were to present arms; and in the third they all drink....they all keep their eyes on the Grand Master, in order to perform the exercise together...it must be said, to the praise of the Free-Masons, that there is no military school in which the exercise is performed with greater exactness.[42]

In *The Craftsman* article, Jachin suggests that the Masons conceal seditious purposes under their supposedly apolitical façade:

---

[42] J. Snoek, *British Freemasonry*, II, 53, quoting from *A Master-Key to Freemasonry* (London, 1760).

Notice how artfully they have dispersed themselves, in different Lodges through all Parts of the Kingdom; and particularly in this great Metropolis; as if it were on Purpose to beat up for Volunteers, in which they not only admit Turks, Jews, Infidels, but even Jacobites, Nonjurors, and Papists themselves.... .

But the most material Argument is, that there are so many of the Nobility, Gentry, and even the Clergy, of the most undoubted Affection to his Majesty's Person, Family and Government, in this Society; ... [but] how can We be sure that those Persons, who are known to be well-affected, are let into all their Mysteries? They make no Scruple to acknowledge that there is a Distinction between Prentices and Master-Masons; and who knows whether They may not have an higher Order of Cabalists, who keep the grand secret of all intirely to Themselves?...

It may be ask'd, perhaps, in what Plots, or ill Designs of any Sort, they have been engag'd... I cannot help thinking them at the Bottom of one Affair, I mean the late Tumult at Edinburgh, and the murder of Captain Porteous; which was concerted and executed with so much Unanimity and Secrecy, that none but a Mob of Free Masons could be guilty of it, without the Discovery of one Person in so numerous a Multitude as were concern'd in the Perpetration of that atrocious Fact.

Jachin then urged the passage of a law "in the nature of the Black-Act," which targeted Jacobite smugglers and poachers, for preventing such riots, and he hoped to see the Freemasons included in the same bill. If a total suppression seems unconstitutional, then the government should lay a double tax "upon all Free Masons, as there hath been so many years upon the Papists." Though the letter was meant to be ironic and tongue-in-cheek, it was too subtle for most readers, and three days later Orator Henley issued an indignant response headlined "For the Free-Masons":

What kind of Drollery it is in which Mr. *Craft* indulges his vain imagination on the *Masons*, is a deeper Secret than any of their Mysteries; for into those the Initiated may be admitted; but his, no Mortal, not even himself, can explore... [He writes] The wise governments of France and Holland have suppress'd them, and a double Tax on the Masons would be as useful as on the Papists... But how Caleb who loves Liberty and hates Excise, calls a French and Dutch government Wise, the former which is an enemy to Liberty, and the Latter abounds with Excises, would puzzle a *Master-Mason* to discover. It is a Proof of the greatest Liberty in this Government that the Masons enjoy an Immunity, which the polite French, and even the free Commonwealth of Holland disallow.[43]

Henley attacked the hypocrisy of Caleb, who has always railed against taxes but now calls for "a Quadruple Tax on some Masons," who are Catholics and already double-taxed. He then went after the coalition work of Bolingbroke and the Patriots:

The author of the Dissertation on Parties [Bolingbroke], a Craftsman, ought to admire the Fraternity of the Masons, for his intention is to dissolve all Parties into one Coalition, and he tells us, that Jews, Infidels, Turks,

---

[43] *The Hyp-Doctor*, #327 (19 April 1737).

Jacobites, Nonjurors, Papists, are admitted into the Fraternity. This is a Comprehension which cannot displease the Author of a Scheme to unite all Parties. On this Footing, the Friends of the *Craftsman* ought to be double-taxed as pretended Promoters of the very Principles, which the Masons, more really, and on juster Grounds contend for.

In what became a series of articles on the Porteous Riots, Henley denied the *Craftsman's* charge of Masonic complicity:

> As to that Piece of his Banter, in which he would cast the Mock-execution of Captain Porteous on the Masons, I would beg this Arch-Gent. to read the 50th page of the printed Constitutions of the Free-Masons, where he will find that a mason is "a peaceable Subject to the Civil Powers, and is never to be concern'd in Plots and Conspiracies."

In the May volumes Henley explained the laws of Scotland and argued that the government was justified in its determination to impose draconian penalties on officials in Edinburgh.[44] What most aroused Scottish anger was the order to all Presbyterian preachers to denounce the rioters and to solicit informers to report to the government.

Jacobite Masons like Orrery, a steady reader of *The Craftsman*, were puzzled by the apparent attack on the fraternity by an opposition journal. They worried about the ferocity of the parliamentary debates concerning the proposed penalties on Scotland. On 9 June Orrery's friend and former Jacobite plotter, Lord Cornbury, warned in parliament that, though the murder of Porteous was reprehensible, the government should not punish the Lord Provost and the city of Edinburgh. He argued that there was so much disaffection in Scotland that passage of the bill "may shake the Pillars of this House," for "a people who think themselves oppressed will always find pretensions to rebel, and despair will furnish them with arms."[45]

Cornbury's appeal that mercy should be shown to the Scots provoked a furious response from Henry Fox, 1st Baron Holland, a Walpolean Mason. He sneeringly rejected the Scots' defense that the rioters had spontaneously come to Edinburgh from their rural homes, for people living "at a distance from one another in the country" could not find the means to lay down "so regular, so artful a plan of murder and rebellion, and afterwards execute it in so cool and so determined a manner, in the heart of a populous, well-affected city, and that too in the view of the magistrates and citizens of the same city."[46] He boasted that "I don't fear the resentment of Scots," for "I believe that nation smarted sufficiently for their rebellion in the year 1715, and will not be very forward to renew the same behavior, lest they meet with the same fate." He called for an immediate government crack-down to check the spread of disloyalty. Fox's biographer notes that "the tone of his remarks had a far-reaching effect upon his future career. The Scots never forgave his words; and to his dying day he had to reckon with the hatred and suspicion of those who belonged to the northern nation."[47]

[44] *Ibid.*, #3331, 333 (17 and 31 May 1737).
[45] Cobbett, *Parliamentary History*, X, 295-302.
[46] *Ibid.*, X, 302-06.
[47] 6th Earl of Ilchester, *Henry Fox, First Lord Holland: His Family and Relations* (London, 1920), I, 67.

"Jackin's" letter suggesting Masonic complicity in the Porteous Riots provoked a defense of Scottish Freemasonry from James Anderson, who was drafting an expanded edition of the Grand Lodge *Constitutions*, which included his new work, "The Secretary's Song":

> In vain would *Danvers* with his Wit *
>   Our slow Resentment raise;
> What He and all Mankind have writ,
>   But celebrates our Praise.
> His Wit this only *Truth* imparts,
>   That Masons have firm *faithful Hearts*.
> With a Fa, la, etc.[48]

In the margin by the asterisk, Anderson wrote "That those who hang'd Capt: Porteous at Edinburgh were all Free Masons, because they kept their own Secret. See *Craftsman*, 16 April, 1736 [*sic*]. No. 563." The tradition of Masonic complicity in the riots persisted for decades, and in 1764 the Irish head of the dissident "Antients" Grand Lodge added to Anderson's marginal note a claim that the Porteous rioters "all wore white leather aprons," while disingenuously and ironically dismissing the Masonic significance of such apparel.[49]

Jackin's letter to Caleb d'Anvers also called forth a response from the Abbé de Prévost, a French Jesuit- soldier, who took advantage of his exile in London to publish twice a week a journal, *Le Pour et Contre*, which also appeared at The Hague and Paris. Given Fleury's attempt to suppress Freemasonry in France, Prévost's rejection of the charges of Masonic complicity in the Porteous riots and his defense of English Freemasonry meant that the controversy became public knowledge in Paris. In May 1737 appeared "The Freemasons' Defence Against *The Craftsman*."

> The author of *The Craftsman*, of 16th April last (No. 563) …takes upon himself to show up the Free Masons as a dangerous faction, against which he even advises to take the field for reasons and motives which are hardly consistent with the politeness of which he has ever made profession… Again, what is the object of *The Craftsman* in trying to make them objects of fear and hate by explanations of their symbols that had never occurred to any one else?[50]

The editor Crawley observes that the Abbé Prévost, like the Rev. Dr. Anderson, "failed to appreciate *The Craftsman's* ironical humour. So, too, did the Secretary of State who arrested Nicholas Amhurst (Caleb D'Anvers), and suppressed his paper on July 2nd, 1737."

Prévost also described the feast and procession of the Grand Lodge Masons, which was undertaken with full public hoop-la on 28 April 1737, twelve days after D'Anvers charges of Masonic sedition during the Porteous affair. Led by the Grand Master Loudoun, accompanied by the Duke of Richmond and the Earl of Crawford, the Whigs

---

[48] W. Crawley, "Contemporary Comments," 206.
[49] Laurence Dermott, *Ahiman Rezon*, 2nd ed. (London: Robert Black, 1764), 109.
[50] W. Crawley, "Contemporary Comments," 208-10.

determined to show who was in charge of not only English but Scottish Masonry. The tenure of the autocratic Loudoun and his unpopular appointed officers exacerbated frictions and divisions within London Freemasonry, for their creation of a Stewards' Lodge with special privileges antagonized many members, whose protesting petition was arrogantly dismissed. As the Grand Masters heard complaints about "irregular" initiations, "Expulsions and secessions rapidly succeeded one another, and for a time the lofty principles of Freemasonry were forgotten in unseemly recriminations fostered by the rebellion."[51]

On the Continent the Jacobite Tobosans and Masons were eager to learn more about the Porteous affair. Ezekiel Hamilton requested more information from Thomas Carte, who replied on 17 April:

> [You] will have seen in the Publick Papers the Proceedings of the House of Lords in the case of Capt'n Porteous: The Bill brought into that House is for dissolving the Town Guard of Edinburgh, appointing a Watch in its stead and demolishing the Nether Bow Gate. The House of Commons are to add a Fine of 2,000 *l.* upon the City to be given to Porteous Widdow who having got rid of a brutal Husband will now have the fortune to marry a better. The Kirk in the meantime from the Pulpit exhorts every body to stand up in the defence of their Liberties and extol [the] Porteous Execution as an heroic Act of Justice and Vengeance on a Wretch that had imbrued his hands in the Blood of the People of the Lord.[52]

Hamilton then asked for "the most remarkable Particulars of ye Debate concerning the Affair of Porteous," which will "oblige a Scotch Gentleman" [Marischal] whom you greatly admire. He copied Carte's information and sent it on to Ormonde and Marischal, which led the latter to reply on 20 June: "It's certain that Porteous was a most brutal Fellow, his last Works at the head of his Guards was not the first time he had ordered his Men to fire on the People. I will not call them a Mobb, who made so orderly an Execution."[53] Marischal seemed to hint at the secret organization carried out (allegedly) by Scottish Masons.

Throughout the summer of 1737, the harsh penalties proposed against Edinburgh were heatedly debated in the English parliament. The provost of the city was skillfully defended by William Murray, a Scottish lawyer and close friend of Pope, who must have followed the proceedings with interest. Murrays' complicated and often ambiguous political attitude provides an interesting perspective on Pope's. In 1737 the young lawyer was a "patriot" supporter of the Prince of Wales, but in his earlier years he followed the Jacobite traditions of his family. His older brother was James Murray, Earl of Dunbar, currently secretary of state to the Pretender, who from his exiled position in 1719 sent the fourteen year-old William to Westminster School in London, where he was under the supervision of Atterbury.[54] In 1723 he matriculated at Christ Church, Oxford, where there were many fellow Jacobites. On 6 August 1725 he visited his brother in Paris, from

[51] William James Hughan, *Memorials of the Masonic Union of A.D. 1813* (London, 1874), 4-5; R. Gould, *History*, III, 143-45.

[52] *Ibid.*, 486.

[53] *Ibid.*,489, 491, 498

[54] Cecil Herbert. Fifoot, *Lord Mansfield* (Oxford, 1936), 27-35.

where he wrote to John Hay, Earl of Inverness, his brother-in-law and then secretary of state to James III:

> I flatter myself you will excuse the ambition of a young man, if I make use of the freedom I am at present to have, to desire you to make a tender of my loyalty to the King; a very small present, but all I have to offer... The chief end I would propose from my studies and education, and the greatest glory I can aim at is to be able to serve his Majesty in any way that he pleases to command me.[55]

From Oxford Murray entered Lincoln's Inn to study law, taking his degree in 1727. His biographer Fifoot suggests that he met Pope while he was a student, but it is not clear at which school or whether Pope knew about his Stuart sympathies.

By the time of the Porteous affair, the two were close friends, and Murray had left behind his Jacobitism but not his Scottish patriotism. In July 1737 his eloquent defense of the provost of Edinburgh against the harsh bill proposed by the Hanoverian Whigs led to the weakening of the bill, which was finally reduced to a fine and not much else. Murray was eulogized as a hero in Scotland, and Pope dedicated one of his Horatian imitations to him, as

> One whom Nature, Learning, Birth, conspir'd
> To form, not to admire but be admir'd."
> ....
> Grac'd as thou art, with all the Pow'r of Words,
> So known, so honour'd, at the House of Lords:
> Conspicuous Scene! another yet is nigh,
> (More silent far) where Kings and Poets lie;
> Where MURRAY (long enough his Country's pride)
> Shall be no more than TULLY, or than HYDE!
> ....
> Would ye be blest? Despise low Joys, low Gains;
> Disdain whatever CORNBURY disdains;
> Be virtuous, and be happy for your pains.[56]

In the 1730s Murray had no contact with his exiled Jacobite brother and brother-in-law, so we do not know if he was aware of the controversies and scandals that erupted about their relationship with the Order of Toboso. It is curious that in the same letter that Thomas Carte wrote to Ezekiel Hamilton (on 17 March 1737), the historian revealed his own connection with Toboso, for he tried to deliver one of the engraved rings of the order to Corbet Kynaston, which again suggests the overlapping membership in Toboso and Jacobite Masonry. As we shall see, Carte would later deny his link with Toboso when being interrogated by Robert Walpole. He now described to Hamilton his current dealings with Swift and Orrery:

> I know the Dean of St Patricks Very well as he is much my friend. He labored all he could with the Dublin Booksellers to prevail with them to lay aside

---

[55] RA. Stuart Papers: 85/21; quoted in R. Sedgwick, *History*, II, 285.
[56] A. Pope, *Poetical Works*, 357. Published 23 January 1738.

> their design of Pirating my Book [*Life of James, Duke of Ormonde*]; Lord Or-
> rery, Dr de Long, Dr Helsham and others did the same....[57]

He praised Orrery for persuading Faulkner to publish a legal defense against the pirating, when other printers were afraid to issue it. Despite his Irish friends' efforts to maintain secrecy, the interception of this letter by "le Connu" meant that the involvement of Swift and Orrery in Carte's Jacobite, publishing, and perhaps Masonic activities was well-known to the government. Carte's further revelation to Hamilton that his friends want him to write a history of England put the ministry on further alert about the expected Jacobite nature of such a history. Carte concluded with his hope to see Hamilton in Paris in July 1737.

For some months, "Zeckie" Hamilton had sent information to Ormonde and Maris-chal about their "old Acquaintance," King Theodore I, whose rebellious campaign and briefly successful reign in Corsica became emblematic for Jacobite Masonic ambitions.[58] Dr. William King determined to exploit the widespread sympathy for his cause by con-tributing an anonymous article to *Common Sense*, the Pretender's subsidized journal. Charles Molloy, the editor, published it on 28 May, the same day that Abbé Prévost de-fended the Masons against complicity in the Porteous riots. King drew on his inside knowledge of the colorful career of Baron Theodore von Neuhof, a German adventurer, who had earlier participated in the Swedish-Jacobite plot.[59] When the flamboyant Theo-dore was elected king of Corsica by the nationalist rebels, he was supported by the Jaco-bites but opposed by Fleury, who sent troops to drive him out of his new kingdom. Contemporary journals found French policy puzzling and "all Europe was indignant" that France did not help the Corsican struggle for "liberation from tyranny."[60] In his article, King made the Corsican rebellion an allegory for a future Jacobite rebellion and Stuart restoration:

> If I were a Corsican, I should certainly be a Rebel; that is, I should hazard
> my Life and Estate to recover my Liberty... The Corsican Chiefs, if they
> would be advised by me, should form the Plan of their future Government
> even while their Affairs are low, and the Event uncertain; lest, hereafter, they
> suffer greater Evils than ever yet they have felt, by intestine Divisions; and
> are prompted by a Spirit of Jealousy or Ambition to destroy one another,
> when they have no other Enemies left to consider... I would preserve the
> Rank and Dignity of my Country, by restoring the ancient Form of Govern-
> ment, which was *Kingly* or *Monarchical*... But my King should not be a Tyrant.
> He should be even incapable of committing any Act of Violence, or Oppres-
> sion... My Prince should be made of the Heart of Oak....[61]

King then targeted the coarse manners, lecherous behavior, and hot temper of the non-oak (i.e., foreign) George II, and urged the Corsicans to reject standing armies, cor-rupt parliamentary placemen, and irresponsible charges of treason. He concluded with

---

[57] *HMC. MSS of Eglinton*, 485-86.

[58] *Ibid.*, 488.

[59] For Theodore's career, see M. Schuchard, *Emanuel Swedenborg*, 128, 278, 450-58.

[60] Anon., *The History of Theodore I, King of Corsica* (London, 1743), 97, 110.

[61] *Common Sense*, no. 17 (28 May 1737).

regret that he has recently learned that King Theodore has abdicated his Crown and was now imprisoned at Amsterdam, but he expected the revolution undertaken by "this enterprising Monarch" to open the door to his King of Oak. Though he did not mention Theodore I's establishment of the quasi-Masonic "Order of Deliverance," in which the royal Grand Master initiated his loyal followers and oversaw symbolic rituals, he was undoubtedly aware of it.[62] However, it is unclear if King knew that Theodore utilized his skills in Cabala and alchemy to subsidize his campaign.[63]

Dr. King sent the article to Swift, and it was welcomed by the Jacobites abroad, for they followed Theodore's affairs with great interest. In May 1737 Hamilton wrote Ormonde about the arrest of Theodore for debt in Amsterdam, adding that he will find out more about his situation.[64] He soon wrote another Tobosan that "my old Acquaintance King Theodore" has been released and will return to Corsica, where his subjects are impatient for his return:

> Some people here Are so ill bred as to call him Baron de Neuhoff *tout court*…
> he was Ellected by all the Estates of ye Realm of Corsica And the General
> Assembly of Scotland with their famous Moderator Mr Andrew Cant have
> long ago determin'd that Vox populi is Vox dei…[65]

Hamilton's letter, which included his experiments with new weaponry, was intercepted by Le Connu.

Despite Zecky's scorn for the Scottish kirk, Dr. King's belief that many Presbyterians would now join the Jacobites in the name of Scottish nationalism was shared by Ramsay, who was pleased that the Scottish Attorney General, Duncan Forbes, a staunch Presbyterian and Hanoverian, issued vigorous protests against the English government for their attempt to impose severe penalties on Edinburgh.[66] In May 1737 Ramsay wrote Carte that he was excited by reading Forbes's *Letter to a Bishop, Concerning Some Important Discoveries in Philosophy and Theology* (1732; 1736), in which Forbes praised and summarized the "scientific" theories about ancient Hebrew published by John Hutchinson in *Moses' Principia: Of the Invisible Parts of Matter, of Motion, of Visible Forms, and of their Dissolution and Reformation* (1724). David Katz observes that in a sense, the disciples of Hutchinson

> were Hebraic alchemists, trapped somewhere between superstition and science. Their theology was based on the notion that only the consonants in the Hebrew Bible were divinely ordained, and that the vowels were a Jewish invention designed to pervert the original meaning of Scripture… the consonants themselves could be constituted into words by the use of any vowels that happened to fit, so as to give the text a variety of meanings….[producing] the multi-layered message of the Bible. The Old Testament became a sort of code-book containing all the secrets of the universe, which now became available to the creative Hebraist. In many ways, the Hutchinsonians

---

[62] Julia Gaspar, *Theodore von Neuhoff, King of Corsica* (Newark, 2013).

[63] Cecil Roth, "The King and the Kabbalist," in his *Essays and Portraits in Anglo-Jewish History* (Philadelphia, 1962), 139-64; M. Schuchard, *Emanuel Swedenborg*, 450-54.

[64] *HMC: MSS of Eglinton*, 488.

[65] *Ibid.*, 488.

[66] "Duncan Forbes," *ODNB*.

were merely a variety of the Christian kabbalist school which sought gentile messages within the Jewish Holy Writ.[67]

Forbes's simplified summary of Huchinson's theories was much more comprehensible and benevolent than the author's complicated and strident texts, and it had an enormous influence among Non-jurors and High Tories, especially in the Jacobite enclaves of Oxford and Aberdeen. Like Ramsay, Forbes was interested in the universal role of "Hieroglyphicks, or Emblems" in both concealing and revealing spiritual truths, with the ancient Hebrews the greatest masters of the esoteric art. Ramsay evidently saw similarities with Masonic teachings in Forbes's summary that all the utensils and decorations in the Jewish Temple were "an hieroglyphical description of the Powers of this System."[68] Forbes conceded that Hutchinson was "bitter and severe" in his arguments against Newton and Clarke but concluded benignly that "he only wants to honor religion."[69] Probably through the medium of Ramsay and Carte, Hutchinson's theories initially impressed Alexander Pope, who wrote Swift that he hoped to meet the dean in heaven, along with Atterbury, "Mr Hutchenson," and other old friends.[70] In 1736 Pope told Spence that "Hutchinson is a very odd man and a very bad writer, but he has struck out very great lights and made very considerable discoveries by the way, as I have heard from people who know ten times more of those matters than I do."[71]

Duncan Forbes was a powerful figure in Scottish politics, and Ramsay hoped that his sympathy for the Porteous rioters and interest in ancient Hebrew emblematics and linguistics would gain him a positive hearing for both causes. In June 1737 he instructed Carte to ask Forbes to send to him in Paris all Hutchinson's works "under cover to Lord Waldegrave."[72] As a former Catholic Jacobite and current Hanoverian Freemason, Ambassador Waldegrave maintained cordial relations with Ramsay, whom he undoubtedly pumped for indiscreet revelations about Jacobite activities.

In that same month, Richard Savage drew on his Masonic interests to publish a revised version of his poem, *Of Public Spirit in Regard to Public Works* (1737), which he dedicated to Frederick, Prince of Wales. Calling for construction of great public architectural works, beyond the Walpolean-Whig obsession with grandiose private edifices, Savage echoed the earlier architectural pleas of Swift, Mar, Arbuthnot, and other Tory-Jacobite Masons. His heroine, "Publick Spirit," welcomes all, "but most the Poor":

> She turns the Pillar, or the Arch she bends;
> The Quire she lengthens, or the Quire extends;
> She rears the Tow'r, whose Height the Heavens admire;
> She rears, she rounds, she points the less'ning Spire;
> At her Command the College-roofs ascend;
> For Publick Spirit still is Learning's Friends.

---

[67] David S. Katz, *God's Last Words: Reading the English Bible from the Reformation to Fundamentalism* (New Haven, 2004), 159.

[68] [Duncan Forbes], *Letter to a Bishop, Concerning Some Important Discoveries in Philosophy and Theology* (London, 1732), 45-46.

[69] *Ibid.*, 64.

[70] A. Pope, *Correspondence*, III, 273 and n. 12.

[71] J. Spence, *Observations*, I, 214.

[72] Bodleian: Carte MSS. 226, ff. 395-97.

Stupendous Piles, which useful Pomp compleats,
Thus rise Religion's, and thus Learning's Seats.

....

Now grant, ye Pow'rs, one great, one fond Desire,
And, granting, bid a new White-Hall aspire!
Far let it lead, by well pleas'd Thames survey'd,
That swelling Arch and stately Colonnade;
Bid Courts of Justice, Senate-chambers join,
Till various All in one proud Work combine![73]

In his quest for the prince's patronage, Savage appealed to his interest in royalist architecture and, as we shall see, in Freemasonry.

Another poet appealed to the Freemasons to support his unlikely venture into publication. John Bancks, a former Spittlefields weaver, issued his *Proposals for Printing by Subscription, Miscellaneous Works in Verse and Prose* in September 1737. Prominent among his sample poems was "Of Masonry: An Ode," in which he revealed that he wrote poems for delivery in lodge meetings in which he stressed the "the mystic numbers" of the fraternity. In a bizarre exercise in esoteric linguistics, he made Hiram/Liram, the Biblical architect, equivalent to "Loudon (the Right Honourable the Earl of) our late Right Worshipful Grand Master, at the Sound of whose voice, the Masons would rise, join, and rejoice."[74] One wonders if Pope knew Bancks in a Masonic context, for he subscribed for two sets of the proposed edition, and his patronage increased the artisan's reputation. However, he must have been dismayed when two years later Bancks published a very sympathetic biography of Oliver Cromwell, which revealed the weaver's strong anti-Catholic biases.[75]

During this tumultuous spring and summer, as the *Écossais* lodges continued to recruit new members, Fleury intensified his crackdown, for which he claimed the support of Louis XV. The suppression not only obstructed Ramsay's ambitious agenda but intimidated some of his Jesuit and priestly friends. On 9 June 1737 *The Boston Weekly News Letter* reported from Paris :

> The Humour of entering into the Society call'd Free Masons, runs so high in France that there are no less than nine Lodges constituted in Paris, a vast many young Noblemen are become Members of the Order, particularly the Prince of Conti, and even the Minister of Marine Affairs, as well as several General Officers and two Bishops. The Ladies push forward for an institution of this Kind, in order for an engraftment... Several other Men of Science and Poets of all Sizes were admitted Members, but as the old Curée of St. Sulpice the Great Protector, and Father Tournemin the celebrated Preacher and Jesuit, were going to initiate themselves, out comes an Order from the King, like a Thunderbolt, and throws down the Babel Building.[76]

---

[73] R. Savage, *Poetical Works*, 229.

[74] John Bancks, *Proposals for Printing by Subscription, Miscellaneous Works in Verse and Prose* (London, 1737), 33, 36-37.

[75] "John Banks," *ODNB*.

[76] Melvin Johnson, *Freemasonry in America Prior to 1750* (Cambridge, MA., 1917), 97.

As noted earlier, the Curé Languet de Gergy was associated with both operative and speculative Masons. Father René-Joseph Tournemine was an old friend of Ramsay, with whom he earlier collaborated in defenses of Fenelon; he also encouraged Ramsay's contributions to the *Mémoires de Trévoux*, the learned Jesuit journal he founded. If the Boston report was true, it suggests that Ramsay's Masonic agenda was supported by influential French churchmen.

At the same time in Italy, the Inquisition persecution of Whig and free-thinking Masons raised concerns in both Jacobite and Hanoverian camps. The Inquisitors pressured the dying Grand Duke to close the Florentine lodge, on grounds of "quietism, Molinism, and Epicureanism," and several brothers were arrested.[77] One wonders if Charles Fane sent this accusation to his fellow Masons, Newcastle and Richmond. Their fraternal colleague, William Capel, 3rd Earl of Essex, faced similar problems during his embassy in Turin. The Inquisition accused the Masons in Turin of following perverse principles – that sexual relations with women were not sinful, that confession to priests was not necessary, and that meat could be eaten on Fridays. As noted earlier, Essex had been initiated with the Duke of Lorraine at the occasional lodge held by Walpole at Houghton in 1731.

On 2 July 1737 Count Thomas Tyrrell, an Irish Jacobite, wrote from Florence to James Edgar, Protestant secretary to James III, about the rumors concerning the Florentine lodge. He reported a "tale that there is a new sect here, but it is nothing but a lodge of Freemasons."[78] It is significant that Tyrrell and presumably Edgar did not consider Masonry itself a threat. Tyrrell then pointed out the Inquisition's concern about "certain sentiments among the young" and their alarm that over thirty thousand members of "this sect" existed in Italy. He further noted the Inquisition's hostility to Stosch, who played a role in spreading the heresy. These rumors reached England where on 7 July the *Old Whig; or, The Consistent Protestant*, reported that "Count Tirel" (Tyrrell), the Grand Duke's "first Gentleman of the Chamber," was "gone to meet the eldest Son of the Pretender, and to conduct him into this City":

> The Count, who is an Irishman, has not taken this Step by order of the Duke. And that the Grand Duke being inform'd that the Society of Free Masons grew numerous here, recommended to the inquisitor to put a stop to the Progress of this new Fraternity, whereupon several of them have been taken up: From whence, and from what has been told us from France concerning this Society; we may conclude them Enemies to Popery and arbitrary Power, and of consequence, that they are, as Gratitude and every other Virtue require them to be, Friends to the present Establishment, in which Country only they are permitted without Interruption to subsist.[79]

On 9 July Fane reported to Newcastle that the newspapers of Italy are filled with accounts of "a Sect of Hereticks, spread at Florence, and that it was begun, and encouraged by some Free Masons."[80] On 17 July, just after the Duke of Lorraine was named as the new Grand Duke of Tuscany, Richmond wrote to a fellow lodge member: "Will our

---

[77] J, Benimeli, *Masoneria*, I, 156, 174.
[78] Stuart Papers: 198/130 (2 July 1737).
[79] R. Péter, *British Freemasonry*, V, 152.
[80] NA: SP 98/40 (9 July 1737).

brother the Grand Duke keep quiet possession of his Grand Dukedom? I fear the Pope wont approve of a Free Mason so near the Holy See. If there should be any disputes, all wee of the Brotherhood must attend the Holy Warr."[81] On 21 July Newcastle wrote Richmond about Fane, "Our Great Friend & Brother Mason will, I hope, have little or no Difficulty in Tuscany. If he has we must call a Lodge & send our Succours."[82] On 9 August *The Leeds Mercury* reported that "a Deputation from the Society of Free and accepted Masons of this Kingdom is to be sent to Germany, to congratulate (a Royal Brother) the Duke of Lorain, on his Accession to the Dutchy of Tuscany."[83] Despite Richmond's support, the Florentine lodge stopped meeting in summer 1737, according to Fane's colleague Horace Mann, who later recounted that "at that time," Freemasonry "was not even deemed a fault by the Court of Rome."[84]

In England, as opposition to Walpole and the Hanoverian court intensified, the Grand Lodge official James Anderson showed his support for the regime by publishing *The Lord Looseth the Prisoners*, a sermon he preached on 3 July in Prujean Court, Old Bailey, on occasion of the late bill in Parliament to relieve insolvent debtors. He dedicated the work to Sir Robert Walpole, Knight of the Garter, and praised his "long and wise Administration of Publick Affairs," which is the envy of your enemies and the joy of your friends. In a rather bizarre peroration, drawing on endless quotes from the Old Testament, Anderson painted Walpole and George II as the most humane and merciful of all public servants. Noting that "To manifest his Love, God sometimes sends his People into Gaol," he assured the prisoners that it is all for their own spiritual good.[85] In an oblique reference to the Porteous riots, when Scottish nationalists helped one smuggler escape and broke Porteous out of jail in order to hang him, Anderson observed:

> Sometimes Prisons have been opened, and the Prisoners loosed, by Riots, Tumults, Rebellions and the Confusion of Wars. But though this is an extraordinary Case, not to be wish'd for, yet It is under the Conduct of the over-ruling Providence of God, who out of such Evils or Disorders, often brings Good to Particular Persons.[86]

He thus supported the extreme penalties that the government tried to inflict on Edinburgh, which were vehemently opposed in parliament by the Hume-Campbell brothers (earls of Polwarth and Marchmont), Scottish Masons, who were friends of Ramsay, Pope, and Dr. King.[87]

Anderson argued further that "our King, both Just and Merciful," has supported our constitution and exercised clemency for thousands of prisoners:

> Therefore, whatever may be suggested, insinuated and mutter'd by foolish, little and lying People, ignorant of publick Affairs, utter Strangers to the Cabinets of Princes, and below the Notice of a Wise Administration, impos'd

---

[81] P. Tunbridge, "Climate," 95.

[82] Richmond, *Correspondence*, 18.

[83] Quoted in P. Tunbridge, "Climate," 109.

[84] NA: SP 98/42 (25 May 1739).

[85] James Anderson, *The Lord Looseth the Prisoners* (London, 1737), 18.

[86] *Ibid.*, 24.

[87] R. Sedgwick, *History*, II, 159-60.

upon, and perhaps suborn'd, by the irreconcileable Enemies of the Protestant Succession to the Crown in the present Royal Family… I hope All Prisoners now to be loosed, will ever acknowledge this Great Benefit, by rebuking and avoiding all such abominable Mutterings; and will gratefully shew their Love and Loyalty to the King, by yielding due Subjection to his good and legal Government, as Examples to others.[88]

With his hints at access to the inner sanctums of the Whig government, Anderson continued his role as an advocate of loyalist, Hanoverian Masonry.

Serving an opposite agenda in Paris, Ramsay circulated manuscripts of his oration among various lodges and planned to publish an English translation. On 2 August he wrote Thomas Carte:

> You have no doubt heard of the rumours our French free masons made. I was the orator and had great views if the Card. [Fleury] had not wrote to me to forebade. I sent my discourse made at the acception at different times of eight dukes and peers, two hundred officers of the first rank and highest nobility, to his Grace the Duke of Ormonde. George Kelly is to translate it and send it to Mr. Bettenham to be printed. You'll see there my general views for learning, but my particular views for the good of our country I'll tell you when at meeting. If the Cardinal had deferred one month longer, I was to have gone to the "merite" to harangue the King of France, as head of the confraternity and to have initiated his majesty into our Sacred mysterys.[89]

Ramsay's choice of Kelly as translator was apt, for the Irish Anglican was well-versed in the Hermetic, Cabalistic, Rosicrucian, and chivalric themes of "ancient" Stuart Freemasonry, and he was almost certainly an initiate himself. He had left behind in London most of his books, which were sold on 8 February 1737 to settle his debts. Among them were all of Swift's works, most of Pope's, and many suggesting his shared interests with Ramsay – such as Robert Fludd's *Mosaical Philosophy* (1659); *The Fame and Confession of the Rosy Cross* (1652); Tasso's *Gerusalemme Liberata* (1628); Vertot's *History of the Knights of Malta* (English and French editions of 1726 and 1728); Fenelon's *Adventures of Telemachus* (1735); and *A Description of the Temple of Solomon* (1735).[90] Not only Ramsay but Swift admired Kelly, and they were pleased that he was now working with Ormonde. At this time, Ramsay and Swift were sending each other copies of their works, as both corresponded with Thomas Carte and Dr. King; thus, it seems likely that Swift was aware of their Jacobite and Masonic efforts.[91]

During these months, Pope was encouraged by an energetic group of young politicians, including disaffected Whigs, Tories, and crypto-Jacobites, who clustered around Frederick, Prince of Wales, and campaigned against Walpole. He had reported to Swift, "Here are a race sprung up of young Patriots, who would animate you"; they are young men who "look rather to the past age than the present,"

---

[88] *Ibid.*, 31.
[89] Bodleian: Carte MS. 226, f. 398.
[90] *A Catalogue of Books in Several Languages and Faculties; being the Library of Mr. George Kelly, Lately a State-Prisoner in the Tower* (London, 1737).
[91] J. Swift, *Correspondence*, IV, 474-75,.

and therefore the future may have some hopes of them. If I love them, it is because they honour some of those whom I, and the world, have lost, or are losing. Two or three of them have distinguish'd themselves in Parliament, and you will own in a very uncommon manner, when I tell you it is by their asserting of Independency, and contempt of Corruption.[92]

The prince welcomed their support, for his parents had long despised and mistreated him. George II said, "I always hated the rascal, false lying, cowardly, nauseous puppy"; Queen Caroline went further, "My dear first-born is the greatest ass, and the greatest liar, and the greatest canaille [scum], and the greatest beast in the whole world, and…I most heartlily wish he was out of it."[93] Ironically, what disgusted them most was the prince's campaign to become "popular." Frederick reached out to the disaffected in all parties and religions, and his pose as a Bolingbrokian "Patriot Prince" attracted former supporters of Walpole's regime, including many Grand Lodge Masons.

The rift in the royal family was intensified when Frederick secretly took his wife from Hampton Court, where his parents resided, to St. James Palace for the birth of their first child. The impulsive move enraged the king and queen, who believed he was encouraged in his defiance by the Patriots. George II formally expelled him from St. James, and ordered him to stop consorting with those advisors who encouraged him in "unwarrantable behavior to me and the queen."[94] He further ordered all foreign diplomats and aristocratic courtiers to have no contact with the prince. On 10 September 1737 the king sent the Duke of Richmond with two other officials to deliver his message – which placed the former Whig Grand Master and still powerful Freemason in a public position of opposition to the prince. As we shall see, this background makes Frederick's initiation three weeks later politically provocative.

On 13 September 1737 the *Daily Gazetteer*, well-known as "the principal Walpole organ," reported a significant Masonic meeting in Charing Cross:

> The Hon. William Hawley, Esq; Gentleman Usher to the Prince of Wales, James Thomson, Esquire; Author of the Seasons, Dr. Armstrong, Author of the synopsis of the Venereal Disease (abridg'd from Astruc) and of several beautiful Poems, Mr. Paterson,…Author of a tragedy not yet published, and Mr. Sargent, Linnen Draper near Mercers' Chapel, were admitted Free and Accepted Masons. Richard Savage, Esq; Son of the Late Earl Rivers, officiated as Master, and Mr. Cha[u]vine, and Dr. Schomberg, Jun. as Wardens; after which the new-made Brethren gave an elegant Entertainment.[95]

Savage, a private Jacobite, had attracted three Scottish Presbyterian Whigs (Thomson, Armstrong, and Paterson); a prosperous London merchant, John Sargent; and William Hawley, a prominent member of Prince Frederick's entourage. They were aware of Frederick's interest in opposition Freemasonry as a vehicle for his political agenda, and they definitely hoped to receive his patronage. The role of Isaac Schomberg, a Jewish physician, as an officer in the lodge was consistent with the close friendships with Jewish

---

[92] *Ibid.*, IV, 277, 380.
[93] M. Mack, *Alexander Pope*, 696.
[94] J. Walters, *Royal Griffin*, 156-57.
[95] J. Sambrook, *James Thomson*, 167.

Masons (such as Solomon and Moses Mendes) maintained by Savage, Thomson, and their circle.

On the very day, 13 September, that Thomson's initiation was reported in the Walpolean *Gazetteer*, three other newspapers printed the poet's lines, "To his Royal Highness the Prince of Wales: An Ode on the Birth of Princess Augusta." Thomson proclaimed more vociferously than ever his adherence to the prince's cause. His biographer Sambrook notes that

> He laments Walpole's pacific foreign policy, which allows Spain and France to take every advantage by their cunning diplomacy, and the corruption at home, which "eats our Soul away"; he hails the birth of Frederick's first child…; finally he prophesies the recovery of Britain and the happy age "When *France insults* and *Spain* shall rob no more."[96]

The Scottish printer Andrew Millar worried about the stridency and toned it down a bit, which elicited a disappointed response from Thomson: "I thank you for getting my Ode printed. In the meantime, who was so very cautious as to advise France & Spain being printed with a Dash? You, I dare say, it was not – You have a superior Spirit to That. I wish you got or would get it into The Craftsman or Common Sense."[97] That Thomson, a staunch anti-Jacobite, was willing to publish in *Common Sense*, reveals his participation in the current effort to unite opposition Whigs, Tories, and Jacobites in the prince's Patriot party.

Because of the king's recent expulsion of the prince, Thomson's ode seemed a defiant gesture to the government, which soon mounted a counter-attack. On 6 October the *Daily Gazetteer* devoted a full issue to criticize the poem and advised Thomson "to attempt no more to appear in Characters so very unsuitable to him, as those of a Poet and a Courtier."[98] Though the *Gazetteer* had ignored Thomson's more important poem, *Liberty*, the simultaneous publication of his Masonic initiation and his pro-Frederick ode, apparently provoked the Walpolean journal to expand its attack on Thomson. On 31 October it branded the poet as "Manyweathers," alluding to him as the writer of the *Seasons* as well as his "political turnabout," which stimulated Lord Hervey, a rival Mason, to denigrate him as "an obscure, bombast, laborious, *Diseur des riens* [idle talker]."[99]

Despite (or because of) the Duke of Richmond's role in the punishment of the prince, Frederick continued to consort with the opposition Masons. His interest in the fraternity allegedly began earlier in 1731, when *The Daily Post* reported on 4 December that he and the Duke of Lorraine "were at a Lodge of Free-Masons at the Devil Tavern near Temple-Bar, where they were handsomely entertained by the Brethren."[100] If the account is correct, the visit was probably arranged by the recent Grand Master, the 8th Duke of Norfolk, with whom Lorraine dined on 2 December. The prince apparently attended as an observer, not an initiate, but his curiosity was certainly piqued. Over the next few years, he became intimate with Burlington and his architect, William Kent, currently serving as

---

[96] *Ibid.*, 168.
[97] *Ibid.*, 169.
[98] A. McKillop, *James Thomson*, 115.
[99] J. Sambrook, *James Thomson*, 170.
[100] Alfred Robbins, "Frederick, Prince of Wales, as a Freemason," *AQC*, 29 (196), 326-29.

Master Mason in the Office of Works, and he took an active interest in architecture and operative Masonry.[101] However, definite evidence of his formal Masonic initiation did not emerge until 1737.

According to James Anderson, on 5 November 1737 Desaguliers presided as Master at an occasional lodge in the prince's residence at Kew, in which Frederick "was in the usual Manner introduced, and Made an Enter'd Prentice and Fellow Craft."[102] At a subsequent lodge meeting, he was made a Master Mason and, according to Anderson, "ever since, both in the Grand Lodge and in particular Lodges, the Fraternity joyfully remembered his Royal Highness and his Son, in the proper Manner." Desaguliers's move to the prince's party was influenced by his frustration with the government's failure to support his scientific and entrepreneurial projects. Frederick's initiation was not welcomed by his father, and the split in the royal family made news abroad. A Swedish physician wrote from Leiden to a *frère* in Falun, Sweden, about the initiations of the Prince of Orange and Prince of Wales, adding that King George II tried to force the disclosure of the Masonic secrets held by his own courtiers but was stymied by his favorite (Brother Walpole), who said the king's desire was as impossible to fulfill as the desire to fly.[103]

The death of Queen Caroline on 20 November seemed to release Frederick into more energetic opposition. He acquired from his old friends the 9th Duke and Duchess of Norfolk the lease of their town residence, Norfolk House, which he extensively refurbished.[104] While Charles Edward Stuart developed a popular following on the Continent, Frederick transformed himself into an alternative heir to the Stuarts, surrounding himself with "actual, suspected or erstwhile tory jacobites: cultivating as his hosts, his champions and his political protectors the men his father accused of 'weakening the common interest' of the Hanoverian dynasty."[105] An indignant Walpole remarked that the British state under George II was confronted by two "Pretenders to the King's crown…one at Rome, the other at Norfolk House." Gabriel Glickman observes that the identification of "a second Pretender" in English politics carried a particular sting, because Frederick rejected many politically acceptable offers of a residence and entered the London household of Norfolk, "a catholic former rebel of 1715, who had resided in the Tower for a year under threat of execution."[106]

Since the suspicious death of his brother, the 8th Duke of Norfolk and former Grand Master, the 9th Duke had kept a low political and Masonic profile, but on 15 May 1737 his exiled cousin Lord John Drummond wrote James III from Boulogne that he had recently spent twelve months in Scotland and three in England, where he saw many faithful subjects: "there was to be an assembly of all the Catholics in town where there appeared a vast deal of zeal"; it was at the Duke of Norfolk's house, "where I lived most of the time in London." [107] Drummond planned to return to England and Scotland, and

---

[101] On Kent as "Master Mason," see H. Colvin, *Biographical Dictionary*, 581.

[102] A. Robbins "Frederick," 328.

[103] R. Robelin, "Johannis-Freimaurerei," 43-44. The date given (22 January 1736) is wrong, for the Masonic events recounted by the Swede took place in 1737-38.

[104] "Frederick Lewis, Prince of Wales," *ODNB*.

[105] Gabriel Glickman, "Parliament, the Tories and Frederick, Prince of Wales," *Parliamentary History*, 30 (2011), 120-21.

[106] *Ibid.* 123.

[107] Stuart Papers: 194/159 (15 March 1737).

he intended to spend more time at Norfolk's London residence. One wonders if the Prince of Wales met him there. Though little more is known of the prince's Masonic activities, which he determined to keep private, it is suggestive that both Norfolk and Drummond were "brothers."

In Ireland, where the loyalist Whigs had regained temporary control of the Dublin Grand Lodge, Swift was soon pleased to receive support from a prominent Mason, William Stewart, 3rd Viscount Mountjoy. Swift had been friendly with his father William, 2nd Viscount, a distinguished army officer who had served on Queen Anne's Privy Council. In 1725 the Duke of Wharton included "Lord Mountjoy" on a list of Jacobite supporters that he sent to the Stuart court.[108] After the 2nd Viscount's death in January 1728, Swift maintained a connection with the family. The 3rd Viscount was a supporter of the Hanoverian succession but not necessarily of the Whig ministry, especially when it tried to implement measures detrimental to Ireland.[109] He had joined the Bear and Harrow lodge in London in 1731, when the 8th Duke of Norfolk was Grand Master and a founder of the lodge. Since then, he had been active in Irish Masonry. In 1734 Mountjoy had joined Orrery and Inchiquin in refusing to walk as English barons, insisting instead on having their traditional precedence as Irish noblemen, in the procession for the wedding of the Prince of Orange.[110] Ric Berman observes that the government's disrespect for these members of the Irish elite led to their alienation , which was reflected in "a changed relationship" between Irish and English Freemasonry.[111]

On 17 November 1737 Mountjoy wrote Swift, promising his support for the dean's effort to gain an exemption from the bill of mortmain, then pending in the Irish parliament.[112] In his will, Swift had bequeathed his entire fortune to build and endow a hospital for lunaticks and idiots, and the bill would prohibit all legacies to the church or any public charity. He appealed to Mountjoy to support his petition for exemption, and he received a generous reply with advice on how to improve the legal terminology and a promise to present it (the bill was eventually defeated). At this time, Swift was despised by the Irish governors, who accused him of Jacobitism and inciting seditious mobs. Thus, it is suggestive that Mountjoy signed his letter as the dean's "most obedient and most humble servant." Soon after writing Swift, Mountjoy was elected Grand Master, and served in 1738-40 with great popular support. His Masonic activities were frequently reported by Faulkner in his *Dublin Journal*. Though he was sometimes criticized as a wealthy, absentee landlord, he established the first Masonic charitable fund and was noted for his hands-on philanthropy and generosity to the Irish poor.[113] Though Mountjoy publicly appeared as a loyalist, in 1743 his name would be included on a list of Jacobite supporters sent to the French government.[114]

News of Swift's continuing defiance of the Hanoverian government had been reported by Lord George Sackville, a Whig Mason, to his father, the Duke of Dorset. In

[108] P. Fritz, *English Ministers*, 161.
[109] For Mountjoy's Masonic career, see R. Berman, *Schism*, 40-41, 230-31,
[110] Egmont, *MSS.Egmont*, II, 60.
[111] R. Berman, *Schism*, 41.
[112] J. Swift, *Correspondence*, IV, 473-74.
[113] J. Lepper and P. Crossle, *History, I, 165-66.*
[114] J. Colin, *Louis XV et les Jacobites: Le Projet de Débrquement en Angleterre de 1743-1744* (Paris, 1901), 31.

October 1737 Sackville wrote from Dublin that "the coinage has made a great rout here and the Dean [Swift] has shewn himself more mad and absurd than ever":

> The poor Primate [Archbishop Boulter] has been greatly threatened by anonymous letters, so that he has been obliged to have a corporal and six men lye in his house very night…to secure him from any insult. The other day at the Lord Mayor's feast the Dean before all the company talked against low[e]ring the gold, and told the Primate that had it not been for him he would have been torn to pieces by the mob, and that if he had held up his finger he could make them to do it that instant…[115]

Reports about Swift's defiant and dangerous behavior were welcomed by Jacobite Masons and Tobosans on the Continent. On 5 December Ezekiel Hamilton wrote to Ormonde:

> The Irish Parliament have passed an Act to confirm the Order of Council for lowering the Gold. At a feast, given by the Lord Mayor of Dublin to the Duke of Devonshire Dr Swift was present, and the Primate who is a very weak Man, bluntly tax'd the Dr before the whole Company for endeavouring to raise the Mob and to begin a Rebellion on account of the lessening of the Value of Gold, the Dr answer'd that he lov'd his Country and thought ye Diminution of the Coin was a Prejudice to it, that he could by lifting up a Finger have influenced the Mob to tear him to pieces, But he deferr'd doing it, because it would make an odd Figure in History that a Primate was destroy'd by the People for doing an odd Jobb, he would not at present give an Other Name: The Dr. immediately left ye room; the next Day the Duke of Devonshire sent to the Dr to come to the Castle, and he made his Excuse that he had got the Country Disease, alluding to what had pass'd the Day before in his Presence.[116]

Orrery was pleased that his neighbors and relations in Cork, who included many nationalist Protestant Masons, backed Swift and sent in a petition against the gold measure, which led Middlesex to complain that "the people at Cork are still more outrageous" and "have sent to their members to desire they would oppose giving the necessary supplies till the King should think fit to recall his proclamation."[117]

As hostile authorities in England and France determined to penetrate, infiltrate, and suppress the opposition and Jacobite Masons, their brothers in Scotland managed to elect a Jacobite as Grand Master of the Scottish Grand Lodge. George Mackenzie, 3rd Earl of Cromarty, was made head of the fraternity on 30 November 1737.[118] Cromarty came from a line of architecturally-engaged noblemen, who since the Restoration had worked closely with operative Masons.[119] When he became Grand Master, a majority of his "brothers" expressed their nationalist feelings by refusing to conform to the London Grand Lodge regulation that elections should be held on 24 June, St. John's Day. They

---

[115] *HMC: Report on the Manuscripts of Mrs. Stopford-Sackville* (London, 1904), I, 166.

[116] *HMC: MSS. of Eglinton*, 508-09.

[117] *HMC: Stopford-Sackville*, I, 166-67.

[118] R. Gould, *History*, III, 306.

[119] R. Mylne, *Master Masons*, 236; M. Glendinning, *History*, 92.

voted instead for St. Andrew's Day, 30 November, birthday of the tutelary saint of Scotland. As we shall see, Cromarty and his son, Lord McLeod, would develop important relationships with *Écossais* Freemasonry in Sweden.[120]

In the month of Cromarty's election, an important Swedish statesman, Count Carl Frederick Scheffer, was in Paris, where he received from Derwentwater a patent to establish Jacobite-French affiliated lodges in Sweden.[121] Scheffer had recently visited England, where he met with Dr. King and other Jacobite Masons, who urged him to found new lodges in Sweden. The patent listed the previous *Écossais* Grand Masters as the Duke of Wharton and Sir Hector Maclean, one of the rare references to Wharton's role in France. Scheffer asked Derwentwater to also prepare a revised version which would make Swedish Freemasonry exclusively Christian. He worried that recent ordinances implemented by Count Horn's government against Jews and Pietists might be used against the ecumenical Masons, so Derwentwater rewrote the patent, and the revision was sent to Sweden in November.[122] When Scheffer arrived in Stockholm, he found the lodges in such a flourishing condition that he had no use for the patent and thus gave it to "Frère Posse, comme mon ancien." According to Samuel Beswick, Count Posse had been a Mason in the camp of the late Carl XII.[123]

Derwentwater managed to keep his Masonic outreach to the Swedes so secret that Waldegrave – despite his extensive spy network in Paris – was unaware of it. In late September, when Scheffer set out for Sweden with Derwentwater's original patent, he was accompanied by the Comte de St. Severin, newly appointed ambassador to Sweden and an *Écossais* Mason. Waldegrave reported to Newcastle that St. Severin's appointment was not significant, but he did not know that the diplomat carried Masonic documents and a secret briefing from Louis XV that he should counter all efforts by Hanoverian England to increase her influence in Sweden.[124] This was the beginning of a major turn of the political tide in Sweden, as France and the Jacobites worked to bring the Masonic Hats to power.

Thus, by the end of 1737 the old Gyllenborg-Görtz-Tessin alliance between Stuart sympathizers in England, Scotland, France, and Sweden was revived. Once again, *Écossais* Freemasonry would provide a critical secret network of communication and effective oaths of loyalty that helped the new *chevaliers* in their struggle to outsmart the Hanoverian intelligence system.[125] The operations of these networks and oaths would provoke even more intense rivalries among the literary factions in the British Isles.

---

[120] M. Schuchard, *Emanuel Swedenborg*, 464-65, 489, 492.

[121] *Ibid.*, 234-35, 247; J. Bergquist, *St. Johannislogen*, 11; P. Chevallier, *Histoire*, I, 119.

[122] M. Schuchard, *Emanuel Swedenborg*, 247, 250.

[123] S. Beswick, *Swedenborg Rite*, 188.

[124] British Library. Add. MS. 32,793, f. 398.

[125] M. Schuchard, *Emanuel Swedenborg*, 129.

CHAPTER SEVENTEEN

TWO YOUNG PRETENDERS TO THE BRITISH THRONE
(1738-1739)

[Ramsay's] history of the secret of the Freemasons is incidentally Pleasant, and I hope that you will definitely not forget to send me a copy of the deposition, because our Princes have a great curiosity to learn the secret.

Lord Dunbar to Daniel O'Brien (Rome, 8 January 1738).

The [Opposition] spirit you saw decline here is now extinct, and that of Jacobitism rises anew among the Tories, and that of the narrow, interested party, knaves and fools, among the Whigs.

Lord Bolingbroke to Lord Denbigh (London, 20 November 1738).

Walpole's observation that there were now two "Pretenders to the King's crown" pointed to the politics and ideology "behind the Jacobite self-fashioning of Frederick, Prince of Wales."[1] Gabriel Glickman argues that Frederick and his supporters became engaged "with an idea of kingship extracted from *avant-garde* circles in the Jacobite diaspora." It was less the remnant of belief in a divine right prince than a "civic humanist creed," influenced by Fenelon and Ramsay, who advocated "an anti-Machiavellian idea of princely rule.[2] In September 1729 a blank-verse translation of Fenelon's *Adventures of Telemachus* was dedicated to Frederick, with an appeal for him to emulate the ideal prince described by the noble author.[3] Fenelon had personally instructed James III in these moral themes twenty years earlier.

As opposition Masons now supported the "Fenelonian" Frederick, the 5th Earl of Orrery knew that his friend Ramsay had virtually created the archbishop's universalist image in England. Thomas Carte, another Masonic friend of Ramsay, closely followed the activities of Frederick's supporters and reported to O'Brien and his *frères* in Paris on

---

[1] G. Glickman, "Parliament," 121.

[2] *Ibid.*, 123-26.

[3] Anon., *The Adventures of Telemachus. Attempted in Blank Verse, from the Archbishop of Cambray* (London, 1729), Dedication.

the developments. Carte was both pleased at the opposition's increasing influence in parliament and worried about this rival to the true "Pretender," James III.[4] The opposition agitation worried Waldegrave, who spent three months in London in early 1738, which led him to write that the people in England are "very warm" and "barely restrained from outbreaks."[5] On his return to Paris, he determined to ingratiate himself with his cousin Derwentwater, currently serving as Grand Master of the *Écossais* lodges, and with Derwentwater's confidant, Ramsay.[6]

As Ramsay's Masonic oration circulated in manuscript, reports about its contents spread to England, where Grand Lodge officials must have realized that it was time to issue an up-dated and expanded version of the *Constitutions*. In January 1738 the Grand Master Darnley ordered James Anderson to produce a new version, which would be twice as long and include "the principal Transactions of the Grand Lodge ever since" the 1723 edition. Darnley, 2nd Earl of Bligh, was an Irish peer and opposition Whig who disliked Walpole and supported the Prince of Wales, but he was not anti-Hanoverian. The new *Constitutions*, when they appeared in late 1738, would stress Grand Lodge loyalty to the prince *and* George II. Despite Frederick's wooing of Stuart supporters, the taint of Jacobitism was still a dangerous position for the increasingly eclectic opposition. Ramsay's Scottish friend, the 2nd Earl of Marchmont, worried that he and his fellow supporters of Frederick "are called Jacobites by some."[7] As we shall see, in the literary wars that ensued in 1738-39, the often confusingly blurred lines between the opposition Whigs, loyalist Tories, and crypto-Jacobites would find expression in the poets' publications and in Masonic rivalries.

Meanwhile in Italy, the Inquisition crackdown took its toll on Jacobite and Hanoverian Masons. Horace Mann recorded that the Florentine lodge stopped meeting in summer 1737, and the last surviving minute of the Jacobite lodge in Rome dates from August of that year. However, the Jacobites in Rome apparently kept meeting privately, and Ramsay's oration continued to circulate. In December 1737 O'Brien wrote to Lord Dunbar about recent Masonic developments in Paris and referred to Ramsay's history of the fraternity. In January 1738 Dunbar replied that "the history of the secret of the Freemasons is incidentally pleasant, and I hope that you will definitely not forget to send me a copy of the deposition, because our Princes have a great curiosity to learn the secret."[8] Charles Edward's interest in Ramsay's discourse was reinforced by his current studies of military architecture, fortification, and mathematics, including the acquisition of the mathematical instruments (compass, square, etc.) so important in operative, military, and symbolic Masonry.[9]

In the meantime, Ezekiel Hamilton continued to report on the new "Pretender," Prince Frederick, whose increasing popularity worried the Jacobites abroad. On 17 March 1738 Hamilton wrote to George Kelly at Avignon, expressing his fear that his letters

---

[4] Stuart Papers: 201/40 (6 October 1737).

[5] BL: Add. MS. 32,797, f. 309.

[6] *Ibid.*, f. 97. He assisted Ramsay with access to French library materials.

[7] G. Glickman, "Parliament," 124.

[8] Stuart Papers: 203/163 (8 January 1738).

[9] *Ibid.*, 183/62 (20 October 1735); 186/82 (12 October 1735); 189/110 (5 September 1736).

from Marischal had been intercepted, but also his hope that the defection of some Tories and crypto- Jacobites to the Prince of Wales had ended:

> I have heard that the Difference between the Elector and his Son, is accommodated, that the Son is accommodated, and he will have £80,000 a year, and He will probably sacrifice all those who have attached themselves to him during his Disgrace as far as it is in his Power to sacrifice them. It is not believed however that the Father will leave him Regent, and it is certain that his [George II's] Journey to Hanover this summer is resolved on.[10]

Hamilton determined to counter any shift from James to Frederick by recruiting new "knights" and protectresses to the Order of Toboso. In spring 1736 he had secretly visited London, where he claimed that his recruitment efforts were "thwarted by Lord Dunbar's minions," whom he accused of consorting with James's enemies in England.[11] On 26 March 1738 he wrote Patrick Briscow, asking for Jacobite prints to send to Ireland and noting the expansion of Toboso:

> Remember me to all my Friends in Surry Street and elsewhere: Last Year the Order was much enlarged by making Necklaces with the Motto on them, I sent a few of them to England, as many as could be made during the time I stayed at Spa. I plan to get more done the next season and I will not forget the lady in Surry Street. I sent one to Sir William ---- for his Lady which I hope he has received.
> Dr. Hawley a very honest and a very ingenious Physician is lately established in London… He was chosen Physician to the Order at a Chapter held at Spa… I hope you provided yourself with Rings for yourself and Friends in England…[12]

James Hawley, M.D., had studied under Dr. King at St. Mary's Hall, and subsequently became a Fellow of the Royal College of Physicians; he was thus an important recruit to Toboso. Hamilton took advantage of the many Jacobites visiting or studying at Leiden (under "Brother" Boerhaave) and wrote to Kelly that "there are a great many honest Gentlemen here" who will celebrate Ormonde's birthday: "They are all Members of Oxford and Cambridge."[13] Despite the Tobosans' efforts at secrecy, Le Connu sent copies of all this material to the foreign office in London.

On 25 March the Grand Lodge Masons in London got some unwelcome publicity, when William Hogarth published an engraving of "Night," which, as Marie Roberts argues, served "as a metaphor for the state to which Freemasonry had deteriorated."[14] The main target of the complex satire was Sir Thomas DeVeil, a member of Hogarth's early lodge and now a powerful Whig magistrate. He was portrayed as a lodge Master in Masonic attire (white apron, emblematic square on a necklace), staggering drunkenly along, with the aid of his lodge Tyler, Sir Andrew Montgomery. De Veil, who had a reputation as a whore-monger and self-righteous hypocrite, is hit with the contents of a chamber

---

[10] *HMC: Eglinton*, 516.
[11] Stuart Papers: 186/140.
[12] *HMC: Eglinton,.*, 517.
[13] *Ibid.*, 517.
[14] M. Roberts, "Hogarth," 259-62. The engraved print was based on a painting, produced ca. 1736.

pot emptied from a window. In the background is a statue of Charles I, while a small individual wears Jacobite oak leaves in his hat and brandishes a wooden sword shaped like a cross.

Hogarth drew on Henry Fielding's earlier satire on De Veil in *The Coffee-House Politician; or, the Justice Caught in his own Trap* (1730), in which the author portrayed the venal and corrupt magistrate as "Justice Squeezum." At that time, Fielding wrote for the opposition and was a reformer; thus, he criticized the class divisions in judicial punishments: "the Laws are Turnpikes, only made to stop People who walk on Foot, and not to interrupt those who drive through them in their Coaches."[15] Justice Squeezum's wife threatens to expose him if he does not let her buy anything she wants: "I'll be reveng'd, I'll blow you up, I'll discover all your midnight Intrigues, your protecting Ill Houses, your bribing Juries, your snacking fees, your whole train of Rogueries." Fielding did not refer to De Veil's Masonic role, but he did make an oblique reference to Chevalier Ramsay, when the virtuous heroine says to her politically-obsessed father, "I do not understand one Word of your Politicks," and he answers, "I am sorry you do not – a News-Paper would be a more profitable Entertainment for you than a Romance. You would find more in one half sheet, than in the grand *Cyrus*."[16] In late 1730, when *The Coffee-House Politician* was published, Ramsay's *Travels of Cyrus* was a virtual best seller and popular with the ladies.

While Jacobite Masons and Tobosans recruited in Britain and Europe, the Masons in Ireland also received much unwanted publicity, as the former Grand Master Rosse and his "brother" Colonel Jack St. Leger, nephew of the famous "lady Freemason," joined with two visitors from London to establish the Dublin Hellfire Club, also known as "The Blasters."[17] The artists James Worsdale and Bernard Lens encouraged the reportedly Satanic blasphemies of the hard-drinking fraternity, whose group portrait hangs today in the National Gallery of Ireland. On 9 March 1738 Swift wrote to his Jacobite friend John Barber, former Lord Mayor of London, first reassuring him that we share "the same Principles in Church and State," and then chiding him: "We thank your good City for the Present it sent us of a Brace of Monsters called Blasters, or Blasphemers, or Bacchanalians (as they are here called in Print) whereof Worsdaile the Painter and one Lints, (a Painter too, as I hear) are the Leaders."[18] Swift had known Lens's father, Bernard, who illustrated *The Tale of a Tub* in 1710, and he had recently tried to reform the wild behavior of young Henry Barry, Lord Santry, another member, who would soon be found guilty of a reckless murder.[19] The Blasters were currently the subject of an inquiry in the Irish House of Lords, and the Masonic affiliation of some members would taint the reputation of the whole fraternity over the next years.

Meanwhile in Italy, the Inquisition surveillance over suspected Masons reached its fruition on 28 April 1738, when Pope Clement XII issued the Bull *In Eminenti*, which condemned Freemasonry and threatened punishments to Catholics who joined the fraternity. Edward Corp argues that James instigated the Papal action which was targeted at

---

[15] Henry Fielding, *The Coffee-House Politician; or, the Justice Caught in his own Trap* (London, 1730), 16, 18.
[16] *Ibid.*, 3.
[17] "James Worsdale" and "Bernard Lens," *ODNB*; Geoffrey Ashe, *Do What You Will* (London, 1974), 60-62.
[18] J. Swift, *Correspondence*, IV, 503-04.
[19] *Ibid.*, IV, 390n.

the Hanoverian Masons, not the Jacobites, but his role in the affair is not clear.[20] James certainly knew that many of his most loyal supporters were Masons, including Derwentwater, the current Grand Master in France, so if he backed the Pope's total ban on the fraternity, he was virtually shooting himself in the foot. In Rome the Swedish convert and senator, Nils Bielke, who had been initiated by Jacobites in Paris and was close to the Stuart family, seemed more amused than worried by the Bull. On 3 May he wrote to his wife in Stockholm to congratulate the Hat party on their political gains. He then asked about his brother-in-law and Hat leader, Count Tessin: "Will the Marshall of the Diet fall into the hands of Tessin?... It will be most interesting since he is the Grand Master of the Freemasons."[21] Once in power, Tessin and the Hats launched a decades-long campaign to support Franco-Jacobite enterprises – a campaign that utilized Masonic networks and reached into the British Isles.

In London the Whig newspapers boasted that the Inquisition could not touch the Florentine Masons, because the city was now under the rule of England's Austrian ally, Duke Francis of Lorraine. On 24 May 1738 the *St. James Evening Post* published a letter from Florence:

> The Freemasons' Lodges which have been interdicted during the life of the Grand Duke [of Tuscany] are now held again with all the liberty and freedom imaginable, and without any dread of the Inquisition, which has no right to attack a society of which the new sovereign is a member. The Freemasons of Leghorn have also reopened their lodges.

Two days later, Stosch wrote to London that his agents in Rome report that the Pope has excommunicated "all the Freemasons and their abettors and adherents. The Jesuits are put in charge of the destruction of this Society at all cost, and they invent strange impostures to achieve their goal."[22]

On 2 June Stosch sent a copy of the Bull to London, accompanied by his explanation of the affair:

> The government of Florence will not permit the publication in the states subject to the Grand Duke the Papal Bull...because no one hears in Italy about any disorder caused by this society since it was established. It is believed that the principal aim of the Court of Rome in the Condemnation is to displease indirectly the Duke of Lorraine, Grand Duke of Tuscany, since they dare not display their extreme chagrin that this [Austrian] occupation of the country causes them.[23]

On the same day, Stosch's colleague Charles Fane also sent a copy of the Bull and similarly explained that it seemed an affront to the Grand Duke, a member of the Society of Freemasons; moreover, the Florentine Council will not agree to publish it.[24] On 9 June he added that the Edict is greatly disapproved by many Cardinals in Rome, and "in

[20] Edward Corp, *The Stuarts in Italy, 1719-1766: A Royal Court in Permanent Exile* (Cambridge, 2011), 330-32.
[21] Stockholm, Riksarkiv.: Bergshammer Samlingen. Nils Bielke Brev, f. 20 (3 May 1738). Bielke's letter is the only known evidence for Tessin's role as Grand Master at this time.
[22] NA:SP 98/41 (26 May 1738).
[23] *Ibid.*, 98/41 (2 June 1738).
[24] *Ibid.*, 98/40 (2 June 1738).

Florence nobody scruples publicly to express great indignation for the affront offered thereby to the Great Duke."[25] Stosch added that,

> It is said also that Cardinal Riviera and several Cardinals here were strongly opposed when the Pope proposed it [the Bull] to the Consistory. But His Holiness, prejudiced by Sir Thomas Dereham and the Jesuits against the Society, never wanted to give up his prized resolution to condemn it, believing to thus alienate the Grand Duke from the affection of the peoples of Tuscany.[26]

One Cardinal who opposed the ban as Clement XII's "worst political error" was Prospero Lambertini, who was rumored to have been initiated himself; two years later, he would become the enlightened Pope Benedict XIV.[27] Lambertini was greatly admired by Ramsay, who later sent him copies of his works, and he knew that many priests as well as Jacobites were Freemasons and not anti-Catholic. Moreover, there was an obscure, secret tradition that Lambertini not only tolerated but participated in the fraternity after the papal ban. In 1786 a visiting Danish Mason, Friedrich Münter, was told by a Neapolitan abbot that the Florentine priest, Ranieri d'Elci, who was made a cardinal in 1738, served as the secret Master of a lodge within the Roman church. Among its alleged members was Cardinal Domenico Passionei, Vatican librarian and intimate friend of Benedict XIV: "The pope himself was said to be a member."[28] As noted earlier, d'Elci had been initiated while serving as Papal Nuncio in Paris in 1733.

Given the unpopularity of the Bull, it is not surprising that Charles Edward still wanted to join the fraternity, especially since he was close to Derwentwater and had many friends in the Roman lodge. He later recalled that he repeatedly asked his father to allow him to be initiated but that James replied "each time that, not being himself a Mason, he could not give his son permission to become one."[29] Charles did not share his father's respect for papal authority, and his liberal attitude was recognized by British intelligencers. Mann reported that the "eldest son" was "very far from being so much attached to his Religion, as the Pretender, that he made very light of it, and would at least allow liberty of conscience."[30] Thus, the ecumenical ideals of Freemasonry would have appealed to Charles; according to some Scottish traditions, the rebellious adolescent defied his father and secretly became "Worshipful Master" in the Roman lodge.[31]

Though no documentation has yet been found for this claim, the editor of the lodge journal (Hughan) pointed out that it could have been recorded on the torn-out, missing leaf (between the later-numbered pages 10 and 11) in the lodge register, and "One naturally wonders what was the Object of such abstraction."[32] Charles Edward would later

---

[25] *Ibid.*, 98/40 (9 June 1738).

[26] *Ibid.*, 98/41 (9 June 1738).

[27] F. McLynn, *Charles Edward Stuart*, 533; also, NA:SP 98/43 (3 May 1741); 98/46 (6 April 1743). For Lambertini's alleged initiation, see Johann August Starck, *Apologie des Francs-Maçons* (Philadelphie, 1779), 69-70; C. Francovich, *Storia*, 121.

[28] Eisler, "Construction," part 1, p. 15-16.

[29] R. LeForestier, *La Franc-Maçonnerie*, 537.

[30] NA:SP 98/42 (25 May 1739).

[31] David Murray Lyon, *History of the Lodge of Edinburgh (Mary's Chapel), Number 1* (London, 1900), 350-51.

[32] Hughan, *Jacobite Lodge*, 10.

assert that "the secret Grand Mastership of the Masons *was* hereditary in the house of Stuart, and that papers hidden at St. Germain would affirm it."[33] In 1988 his biographer Frank McLynn wrote that Prince Charles did not advance "beyond simple curiosity" about Freemasonry, but by 2004 he changed his opinion and referred to the Prince and "his fellow Freemasons," adding that Charles Edward became "a leading light of eighteenth-century freemasonry."[34] Since then, much new documentation has emerged from international archives that supports the secret role that the Stuart prince played in *Écossais* Freemasonry.[35]

In France Waldegrave was receiving reports from John Sempill (Sample) who continued to pretend to be a Jacobite sympathizer and even expected to get a pension from Lord Inverness. Sempill flattered Waldegrave that he and the ambassdor had effectively neutralized Derwentwater: "Your Exc will wonder to be assured that the lenity of the government, and your good nature, have even deprived Ld. Derwentwater of words to ray'l more and he is become much changed in his behavior."[36] He tried to cause a break between Sir Hector Maclean and Colonel O'Brien, by falsely claiming that the latter was hatching secret projects, which led Maclean to declare that, if true, O'Brien and "the favorite should be sent to the Devil…and have the Bastille for his lot." A smug Sempill concluded, "In short, I came at my point both ways; first to be almost concerned that there had been such projects given in to their court, and second to give him a distrust that the favourite and O'Brien had advised the Chevalier to render them abortive." Despite his boastings, his targeted Jacobite Masons continued their serious negotiations and plottings throughout 1738, with the private encouragement of Louis XV and the *frères* in his inner circle.[37]

At this time, Derwentwater's wife wrote from Paris to James seeking permission to visit England in order to investigate a possible reversal of her husband's attainder and restoration of his estates. Some critics evidently questioned her proposed visit, which led Derwentwater to write James that he should not suspect disloyalty in "my lady's visit," for she goes with my consent; moreover, if she takes any steps "not suitable to my maxims," he will never see her again.[38] James then sanctioned her visit, but it proved unsuccessful, and she returned to Paris empty-handed. Though Fleury continued his effort to suppress the French lodges, the *parlement* refused to implement the Papal Bull in France. Nevertheless, the English newspapers kept up their coverage of the French and Italian repressive measures. The *Daily Post* (26 June 1738) reported that "His Holiness has hurled his Thunder" at the Freemasons, while the *Leeds Mercury* (4 July 1738) mocked the Pope with a tongue-in-cheek article:

> We learn by private Letters from Rome, that the Pope, upon his having a Sum of Money collected from several Lodges of Masons in London to be dispos'd of in Charity in *his Way*, has issued Order to have his Bull recalled,

---

[33] P. Monod, *Jacobitism*, 303.

[34] See McLynn's, *Charles Edward Stuart*, 533; and *1759: The Year Britain Became Master of the World* (2004; New York, 2007), 79, 223.

[35] M. Schuchard, *Emanuel Swedenborg*, 396-97, 590, 634, 689, 696, 737,753-54; and *Masonic Esotericism*, 43-50.

[36] BL: Add. MS. 32,798 .ff.95-96.

[37] M. Schuchard, *Emanuel Swedenborg*, 240, 248, 251.

[38] Stuart Papers: 205/123 (Paris, 17 March 1738); L Gooch, *Desperate Faction*,

and has sent several Messengers to stop its appearing before the Grand Duke; `tis futher said, that he and several of the Cardinals have been proposed in different Lodges in Europe, according to their *Jesuitical* Desire, and are in a manner accepted of; so that `tis not doubted, but he'll soon issue an Order to excommunicate those who are not of the ancient and Honourable Society of *Free and Accepted Masons*.[39]

The Pope's Bull, Fleury's pressure, and the British press coverage perhaps influenced the decision by Derwentwater, a devout Catholic, to resign the Grand Mastership in July.[40] He was succeeded by the Duc d'Antin, who enjoyed the king's favor and who sympathized with the Stuart cause. Though Derwentwater now kept a lower Masonic profile, he would later join d'Antin at an important lodge meeting.[41] Pierre Chevallier speculates that those invited for "le reception d'un monsieur distingué" would attend a meeting of the "Loge du Roi," the French king's private lodge.[42] He argues further that there is convincing evidence that Louis XV was privately initiated by Villeroy in a special "Loge du Roi," held in the "Petites Appartements" at Versailles.[43] Since mid-1737 Louis had withdrawn from the governance of Fleury and asserted a more active role in foreign policy, especially in consultation with his Masonic courtiers. A British agent reported to Newcastle that the French king "is quite another man. He has thrown off his natural bashfulness…and is certainly Master, and has a great share of Dissimulation."[44] Even worse, "No man living keeps his own Designs more close," for "he is remarkable for secrecy"; he begins to "shake off by Degrees the Prejudices of his Bigotted Education." Thus, it would not be surprising if Louis was willing to utilize secret Masonic networks, as he planned a more aggressive foreign policy against "the Elector of Hanover."

But Louis did not have complete control over the Lieutenant-General of Police, René Herault, a supporter of Fleury, who in 1737 ordered the publication of *La réception d'un frey-maçon*, an exposure of Masonic rituals. He received the information from "le fameuse Carton," a dancer with the Paris Opera, who allegedly seduced an un-named "English" Mason and pried the secrets out of him.[45] William Parker argues that the seductee was actually the Irish Lord Kingston, who was in Paris at that time, attended French lodge meetings, and was set up by the French police.[46] In January 1738 a partial English translation, "The Secret of the Order of Free-Masons and the Ceremonies observed at the Reception of Members into It," was published in *The Gentleman's Magazine*, which made clear that the rituals aimed at moral improvement and spiritual enlightenment, followed by wine-fueled conviviality. The blind-folded candidate will eventually hear the words, "shew him the Light, he has been long deprived of," and in that instant, they take off the

---

[39] R. Péter, *British Freemasonry*, V, 152-53.

[40] P. Chevallier discusses several possible motives for his resignation; see his *Ducs*, 120.

[41] J. Benimeli, *Archives Sècretes*, 146 n.218.

[42] P. Chevallier, *Histoire*, I, 42.

[43] P. Chevallier, *Ducs*, 72, and *Première*, 43-44; also, Pierre-Yves Beaurepaire, *L'Autre et le Frère: L'Étranger et Franc-Maçonnerie en France au XVIII Siècle* (Paris, 1998), 298; André Kervella, *La Maçonnerie Écossaise dans la France de l'Ancien Régime: Les Annés Obscures, 1720-1755* (Paris, 1999), 262.

[44] NA:SP 78/215 (5 June 1737); 78/218 (1 August 1738); 78/219 (8 December 1738).

[45] For other versions of Carton's revelations, see R. Péter, *British Freemasonry*, V, 262-63.

[46] William Parker, "The Church and the Craft," *Philalethes*, 5 (June 1994).

cloth from before his eyes, and "all the Brothers standing in a Circle draw their Swords." The Brother Orator then addresses him:

> You are going to embrace a respectable Order, which is more serious than you imagine: There is nothing in it against the Law, against Religion, against the State, against the King, nor against Manners… The Ceremony being performed and explained, the Recependiary is called Brother, after which they…drink the Brother's Health. Every Body has his Bottle… they say, Give some Powder, viz. Fill the Glass. The Grand Master says, Lay your Hands to your Firelocks…they clap their Hands three times, and cry three times Vivat.[47]

Herault's exposure provoked another anonymous publication, *Masonry Farther Dissected; or, More Secrets of that Mysterious Society Reveal'd. Faithfully English'd from the French Original just publish'd at Paris, by the Permission and Privilege of M. De Harraut, Lieutenant-General of Police* (London, 1738). In copious notes the author stressed that the French rituals differ from the English, especially in using blindfolds and gun powder, and even from the Scots, "who are Schismaticks in this, as well as other Points," and he hinted at the un-English practice of "branding the letter M on the buttocks.[48] He further sneered at the French misunderstanding of the words Jachin and Boaz, and "indeed one need not wonder at finding such Ignorance of Scripture among *Papists*, more especially those of the laity." In an Appendix, the author reprinted the article, "Free Masons a Dangerous Society," from *The Craftsman* (16 April 1737), which brought the accusation of Masonic conspiracy by the Porteous rioters back into the public spotlight.

Masonry Farther Dissected triggered a counterblast, entitled *Relation Apologique et Historique de la Sociéte des Franc-Maçons, par J.G.D.M.F.M.* (Dublin: chez Patrice Odonoko, 1738). Actually printed in Paris, with an odd version of the Irish name Patrick O'Donoghugh, the anonymous author has been variously identified as Chevalier Ramsay, Martin Folkes, and J. Gautier de Faget.[49] Ramsay was definitely not the author and, despite W.E. Moss's ingenious argument for Folkes, it is more credible that the Frenchman was the writer. Faget was a Protestant refugee who lived in London in 1727-28, where he practiced medicine and joined a Masonic lodge. In 1728 he published a critique of Voltaire's *The Henriade*, in which he defended deism, the spirit of toleration, and expressed "violently anti-papist" sentiments.[50]

In the *Relation Apologique*, the author described English Freemasonry as harmless and partronised by the most honorable members of society, who march in public processions.[51] He rejected charges that they use magical material from "Grimoires Cabalistique" and practice the infidelities and disorders of the Templars. The credulous believe this just as they believe in the "Vampires de Hongrie." Though he distinguished the Grand Lodge Masons from simple operative mechanics, he noted that some of the stonemasons

[47] *Gentleman's Magazine*, 8 (1738), 54-55.

[48] Anon., *Masonry Farther Dissected* (London, 1738), 5, 9, 11, 16.

[49] W.E. Moss, "A Note on the Relation Apologique et Historique de la Societe des Franc-Macons," *AQC*, 51 (1940), 226-31.

[50] J. Sgard, *Dictionaire des Journalistes (1600-1789)* (Grenoble, 1976), 149.

[51] Anon. [J. Faget de Gautier?], *Relation Apologique et Historique de la Société des Franc-Maçons* (Dublin, 1738), 5, 14-15, 63, 76, 84.

propose subjects that tend toward the perfection of their art, including very curious debates between the chemists and alchemists. He was apparently aware of the Rosicrucian and Jacobite themes of some lodges, for he praised the Freemasons of Rome, who are charmed with the" high degree of perfection," and he quoted a ceremonial toast, "Fiat, fiat," used by Jacobites.[52] In February 1739 the Inquisition stated that the work was "Small in Size, but most wicked in Regard to its bad Subject," and ordered its public burning. In April the *Gentleman's Magazine* published a report from Rome about the burning, which was carried out "with great Solemnity," and described the work as

> a Piece in French wrote by the Chevalier Ramsay (Author of the *Travels of Cyrus*, etc.) entitled *An Apologetical and Historical Relation of the Secret of the Freemasons*, printed at *Dublin* by *Patrick Odonoko*. This was published at Paris, in answer to a pretended Catechism printed there by Order of the Lieutenant de Police, (see Vol. VIII, p. 54) much like Pritchard's in English.[53]

Though the charge against Ramsay was inaccurate, it would gain him sympathy from anti-Inquisition readers.

In Ireland, where there were many Catholic Masons, their priests did not implement the Bull; nevertheless, it roused the fury of a Protestant brother, who took advantage of it to disparage the Roman church. The anonymous author, "Philo-Lapidarius," dedicated *An Answer to the Pope's Bull* (Dublin, 1738) to Lord Mountjoy, Grand Master of Ireland and current friend of Swift.[54] The pamphlet was printed and sold by Edward Waters, who had earlier served as Swift's "Tory Dublin printer" and who spent time in prison for refusing to name Swift as the author in 1720. In 1736 Waters printed Swift's diatribe against lowering the gold coins.[55] The author began with an address to Mountjoy:

> My LORD,
> As the Fraternity of Free Masons have made such a Noise in the World, and have not only became dreadful to the Ignorant part of Mankind, but even suspicious to *some certain Powers*; I hope…to paint their *Folly*, who blame that with which they cannot possibly be acquainted. And I must imagine, that it will appear as ridiculous in any of them, as it wou'd in a Man, (altho' he had never been in *China*, and an entire Stranger to its Inhabitants, Laws, Constitutions, and Government;) who would confidently report, *That the People of that Nation were the most Disloyal, Rebellious, and wicked Subjects throughout the World*: and that this is the Case with the Enemies of Masonry will plainly appear…[56]

On the title-page, the white horse of Hanover was featured as a sign of government loyalty. The author reacted to rumors about the Irish Masons that were not mentioned in the Papal Bull, which did not portray the initiates as "Disloyal, Rebellious, and wicked

[52] W. Moss, "A Note," 231.

[53] *Gentleman's Magazine*, 9 (April 1739), 219).

[54] The pamphlet has sometimes been attributed to Fifield D'Assigny; for his later publications, see ahead, Chapter 18.

[55] J. Swift, *Correspondence*, II, 346, 354; IV, 288.

[56] Pamphlet reproduced in R.E. Parkinson, "*An Answer to the Pope's Bull*, 1738, and *An Impartial Answer to the Enemies of Freemasonry*, 1741," *AQC*, 77 (1964), 151-55; also in R. Péter, *British Freemasonry*, IV, 1-8.

Subjects." But in Ireland, many disaffected Masons were indeed Jacobites. Nor did the Bull mention accusations of black magic, which the Irish brother reported and rejected. Thus, the "enemies of Masonry" inform the world, "that Masons in their *private Assemblies* draw such Circles, and other strange Lines, that causes the Devil to pop up, and take his Place amongst Them, which some say is under the Table, and others as a Door-keeper." This charge was evidently provoked by the activities of Lord Rosse, former Grand Master, who founded a year earlier the Dublin Hell Fire Club. "Philo-Lapidarius" then took on the Pope, the "most formidable" enemy, who some reckon "*Infallible*," and who forbids any Catholic "to enter into, Countenance, or Defend" the Masons. He accused the Pope of disapproving of the fraternity only because it does not provide an annual financial stipend to him. This was even more hypocritical, because the Pope tolerates brothels and gains a valuable yearly income from them. A true Mason is "one who pays a due Reverence to his Great Creator, free from the gross errors of Superstition, or blind Arrogance of Atheism and Deism," and one who "is very true and loyal to his Prince."

Though the Bull was ineffective in France and the British Isles, many Catholic Masons were put in an uncomfortable position. For Alexander Pope, a tolerant Catholic Mason, who was currently collaborating with opposition Protestant Whigs as well as Tories, the fueling of anti-papist attitudes seemed part of the general hypocrisy and venality of the Walpolean government. On 6 May the government-supporting *Daily Gazetteer* published an attack on Pope, mocking him for his credulous reverence for Bolingbroke as "a true Briton."[57] Maynard Mack comments that for the poet, "these were fighting words," which drove him to compose "two of the most eloquent poems of his career." On 16 May he published *One Thousand Seven Hundred and Thirty Eight. A Dialogue Something like Horace*. His supposed friend, "A," was portrayed as a "typical ministerial time-server," whose advice represents "both the establishment and the cautionary or Sancho Panza side of the poet's own heroic quixoticism." Pope recklessly scorned Walpole, "an artful Manager, that crept between/ His Friends and Shame, and was a kind of Screen," for his protection of the corrupt and criminal.[58] He then included Walpole's fellow Whig Masons in his targets – such as "Lord Fanny" (Hervey), "Cibber's son" (Theophilus Cibber), and, as usual, "Henley's Oratory." The character "Vice" triumphantly proclaims,

> That "Not to be corrupted is the Shame."
> In Soldier, Churchman, Patriot, Man in Pow'r.
> `Tis Av'rice all, Ambition is no More!
> See, all our Nobles begging to be Slaves!
> See, all our Fools aspiring to be Knaves!
> The Wit of Cheats, the Courage of a Whore,
> Are what ten thousand envy and adore.
> All, all look up, with reverential Awe,
> On Crimes that `scape, or Triumph over Law:
> While Truth, Worth, Wisdom, daily we decry –
> "Nothing is Sacred now but Villany."
> Yet may this Verse (if such a Verse remain)

---

[57] M. Mack, *Alexander Pope*, 705-06.
[58] Alexander Pope, *One Thousand and Thirty Eight. A Dialogue* (London, 1738), 2, 4, 7.

Show there was one who held it in disdain.[59]

Walpole was so angered by the poem that he summoned Pope to a meeting, and he apparently attempted to frighten him out of publishing more.[60] However, Pope was emboldened by the return of Bolingbroke on 8 July, who became his guest at Twickenham, where he stayed for the next nine months while trying to sell his farm at Dawley. One night a government supporter broke Pope's windows, while he was dining with Bolingbroke and Bathurst. On 18 July Pope boldly published *One Thousand Seven Hundred and Thirty Eight. Dialogue II*, in which he mocked Walpole's official censor and his lackeys:

> What? Shall each spur-gall'd [hired] Hackney of the Day,
> When Paxton gives him double Pots and Pay,
> Or each new-pension'd Sycophant, pretend
> To break my Windows, if I treat a Friend;
> Then wisely plead, to me they meant not hurt,
> But `twas my Guest at whom they threw the dirt?[61]

He then launched an even stronger attack on Walpolean dishonesty. His intimidated friend, "A," begs him to issue only general satire without names. "A" warns that Nicholas Paxton, Walpole's official censor of dissident opinion, will argue that Pope's satire "is all a Libel" – i.e., punishable by law.[62] Compared to the flatterers and hypocrites he lashed, Pope referred to those men he admired – especially the late Bishop of Rochester: "How pleasing ATTERBURY's softer hour!/ How shin'd the Soul, unconquer'd in the Tower." He included the current opponents to Walpole – Pulteney, Chesterfield, Argyle, Wyndham, but claimed he is "No Follower, but a Friend!" "A" challenges him that his admired opposition and Patriots are mere opportunists:

> A. Faith, the thought's no Sin,
> I think your Friends are out, and would be in.
> B. If merely to be in, Sir, they go out,
> The way they take is strangely round about.
> A. They too may be corrupted, you'll allow?
> B. I only call those Knaves who are so now.
> Is that too little? Come then, I'll comply –
> Spirit of Arnall! Aid me while I lye.
> Cobham's a Coward, Polwarth is a Slave,
> And Lyttleton a dark, designing Knave,
> St. John has ever been a wealthy Fool –
> But let me add, Sir Robert's mighty dull,
> Had never made a Friend in private life,
> And was, besides, a Tyrant to his Wife.
> ....
> Why rail they then, if but a Wreath of mine,

---

[59] *Ibid.*, 10.

[60] M. Mack, *Alexander Pope*, 715.

[61] Alexander Pope, *One Thousand Thirty Eight: Dialogue II* (London, 1738), 10,

[62] *Ibid.*, 1, 7, 10, 11.

Oh All-accomplish'd St. John! deck thy Shrine?[63]

"A" then asks why the poet wastes his time on such political targets: "What's that to you, who ne'er was out nor in?" Moreover, "You're strangely proud," which provokes Pope's eloquent rejoinder:

> So proud, I am no Slave:
> So impudent, I own myself no Knave:
> So odd, my Country's ruin makes me grave.
> Yes, I am proud; I must be proud to see
> Men not afraid of God, afraid of me:
> Safe from the Bar, the Pulpit, and the Throne,
> Yet touch'd and sham'd by *Ridicule* alone.[64]

On 8 August 1738 Swift wrote a letter to Pope and Bolingbroke to express his admiration for the scathing poems: "I take your second Dialogue that you lately sent me, to equal almost anything you ever writ," but he also warned that "I have an ill-name in the Post-Office of both Kingdoms, which makes the Letters addressed to me not seldom miscarry, or be opened and read, and then sealed in a bungling manner before they come to my hands."[65] His warning was timely, for Pope was frightened enough by Walpole to drop his plan to write a third installment. According to Bishop Warburton, "his enemies agreed to drop the prosecution, and he promised to leave the third Dialogue unfinished and suppressed."[66] After this Pope published no more major poems and, as Maynard Mack observes, "in some sense, Pope was silenced."

Curiously, Pope seemed to draw on Ramsay's biography of Turenne, with its strong Jacobite themes, when he described Turenne, "the prudent Gen'ral," as a man who admirably turned an insult that could lead to violence into "a jest."[67] In early 1738 Ramsay had sent Swift the biography and "a small box of books."[68] Did these include a copy of his Masonic oration, which drew on similar "Celtic" traditions of Freemasonry as in Swift's *Letter from the Grand Mistress?* As noted earlier, Ramsay had commissioned George Kelly to make an English translation of the oration, and from March to August, Swift's correspondents sent him news about Kelly and Ormonde, including rumors that the latter planned to return to England "from his banishment."[69] When the Jacobite John Barber wrote Swift that unfortunately the rumor was false, he also relayed the good news from Avignon that Ormonde was in good health and spirits, along with Kelly, to which Swift replied that he was pleased that the duke had "so valuable a companion." It was an unnamed mutual friend of Barber and Swift who visited with the two exiles, at the time when Kelly was working on his translation of Ramsay's Masonic oration.

While Pope may have been silenced by Walpole's threats, another powerful voice had emerged to challenge the regime, Samuel Johnson, described by Howard Erskine-Hill as

---

[63] *Ibid.*, 9-11, 13.

[64] *Ibid.*, 14.

[65] J. Swift, *Correspondence*, IV, 535.

[66] M. Mack, *Alexander Pope*, 735.

[67] A. Pope, *One Thousand and Thirty Eight*, 14.

[68] J. Swift, *Correspondence*, IV, 496-97.

[69] *Ibid.*, IV, 510, 529, 533.

"a Jacobite-inclined non-juring Tory."[70] Johnson was working for Edward Cave, who as "Sylvanus Urban" published *The Gentleman's Magazine*. His writing for the magazine gave him access to parliamentary debates, foreign relations, and reports on Masonic affairs. There is a vague, undocumented tradition that Johnson was affiliated with Freemasonry or, at the least, a close friend to certain "brothers." Arthur Heiron observes that "it does seem fairly certain that at some time or other, Dr. Johnson (1709-1784) was a member of the Craft, it being quite clear now that several of his most intimate friends and associates were themselves Freemasons."[71] Though his Masonic affiliation seems unlikely, he later told his confidant and biographer James Boswell, an activist Scottish Mason, that he was intimately acquainted with Wapping, and it is perhaps relevant that in 1767 a lodge in Wapping recorded Samuel Johnson, "made a Mason" and "Raised a Master."

However, Johnson's night-time prowlings and carousings through the seedy neighborhood of Wapping occurred much earlier, during his close friendship with Richard Savage, whom he met soon after arriving in London, when Savage contributed to *The Gentleman's Magazine*. Savage's role as Master of a Masonic lodge had been publicized in the press and was undoubtedly known to Johnson, who also was aware of his early Jacobite publications and resumed Stuart sympathies. Perhaps the obscure tradition of Johnson's Masonic association was rooted in those early, secretive visits to taverns in Wapping. Savage was allegedly the prototype for "injur'd Thales," the embittered hero of Johnson's anonymous satire, *London: A Poem, in Imitation of the Third Satire of Juvenal*, published on 13 May, a week after Pope's first 1738 dialogue. Johnson and Savage admired and discussed Pope's dialogues, and Johnson later noted Savage's "critical attention" to their political content.[72]

After the death of Queen Caroline, who had promised Savage a pension, George II refused to honor her commitment, so the impoverished poet's friends, especially Pope, planned for him to move to less-expensive Wales, where they would contribute to his upkeep. Johnson thus made *London* a poem of double-leavings, Thales to Wales and George II to Hanover, to the company of his German mistresses. As Howard Erskine-Hill notes, "The idea of Jacobite exile…lurks within the printing of Johnson's lines."[73]

> Tho' Grief and Fondness in my Breast rebel,
> When injur'd Thales bids the Town farewell,
> Yet still my calmer Thoughts his Choice commend,
> I praise the Hermit, but regret the Friend,
> Who now resolves, from Vice and London far,
> To breathe in distant Fields a purer Air,
> And, fix'd on Cambria's solitary Shore,
> Give to St. David one *true Briton* more.[74]

---

[70] Howard Erskine-Hill, "The Political Character of Samuel Johnson," in Isabel Grundy, ed., *Samuel Johnson: New Critical Essays* (Totowa, 1984), 117.

[71] Arthur Heiron, "Was Dr. Johnson a Freemason? Some Phases of His Life," *The Builder Magazine* (January, February, and March 1923) [on-line].

[72] J. Clark, *Samuel Johnson*, 43.

[73] H. Erskine-Hill, "Political Character," 126.

[74] Samuel Johnson, *London* (London, 1738), 1.

In his italicized emphasis on "*true Briton*," Johnson recalled the exile of the late Duke of Wharton, supporter of Bishop Atterbury and publisher of the Jacobite journal, *The True Briton*. Thales/Savage knew that Wharton had also served as the dissident Grand Master of the English Grand Lodge. A further Jacobite resonance is given in lines suggesting exile from Ireland and Scotland:

> For who would leave, unbrib'd, *Hibernia's* Land,
> Or change the Rocks of *Scotland* for the Strand?
> There none are swept by sudden Fate away,
> But all whom Hunger spares, with Age decay:
> Here Malice, Rapine, Accident, conspire,
> And now a Rabble rages, now a Fire.[75]

According to Boswell, Johnson believed that George II was "unrelenting and barbarous," a king of executions, a view expressed indignantly in *London*:

> Scarce can our Fields, such Crowds at *Tyburn die*,
> With Hemp the Gallows and the Fleet supply.
> Propose your Schemes, ye Senatorian Band,
> Whose *Ways and Means* support the sinking Land:
> Lest Ropes be wanting in the tempting Spring,
> To rig another Convoy for the K – ng.

Unlike the honorable exiles from Ireland and Scotland, the king will depart by convoy to Hanover, while Thales leaves for "internal exile" in Wales. Among the admirers of the poem was General Oglethorpe, supporter of the Jacobite Masons in Georgia, who immediately became "one of the warmest patrons" of *London* and a close friend of Johnson. J.C.D. Clark suggests that their affinity was from shared Stuart sympathies.[76] In 1738 Oglethorpe also contributed ten guineas to Thomas Carte for his proposed history of England. It is not surprising that the Hanoverian Mason Henley would attack *London* as a seditious publication.[77] When Thales/Savage scorned those who "laugh at H---y's Jest," he targeted the Whig Mason Hervey, who agreed with the king in omitting Savage from the deceased queen's pension list. It was perhaps Hervey's suspicions about Savage's Jacobite background and questionable loyalty that led to Thales's self-description, "Spurn'd as a Beggar, dreaded as a Spy."

Among Savage's friends were not only the opposition Masons Thomson and Armstrong but their Jewish "brothers," Solomon and Moses Mendes, who both served as Grand Stewards and helped organize the annual processions and Grand Feasts held by the Masons. Solomon contributed to the fund for Savage's support in Wales, and his actual brother Moses admired his poetry and shared his political views. The Mendes families had long connections with the royal Stuart family, and Moses continued the tradition of "Jewish Jacobites" epitomized by Francis Francia (whose family was still receiving a

---

[75] *Ibid.* 4.

[76] J.C.D. Clark, *Samuel Johnson: Literature, Religion and English Cultural Politics from the Restoration to Romanticism* (Cambridge, 1994), 200-01.

[77] *Hyp-Doctor*, #471 (13 November 1739).

pension from James III).[78] Moses's paternal grandfather, the physician Fernando Mendes, served Charles II's queen, Catherine of Braganza, and attended Charles on his deathbed.[79] He was still living in 1724, and his grandson (b. 1690) was familiar with his Stuart loyalties. Moses had earlier studied under Dr. William King at St. Mary Hall, Oxford, and the two remained friends. Moses was nominated for his Masonic stewardship by Sir Bouchier Wrey, Sixth Baronet, who was described by a political opponent as "born and bred a Jacobite."[80] A talented poet and genial companion, Moses valued his friendships with opposition writers, while his closest friend was John Ellis, a fellow Mason. An erudite scrivener, Ellis had earlier assisted Sacheverell and worked on Mist's Jacobite journal.[81]

In the Library of the Grand Lodge of London there is a curious MS. Notebook, comprised of 326 pages, which was initially believed to belong to Moses Mendes but later to be a compilation by his friend Ellis.[82] A large majority of the poems were by Mendes, while others were by his friends and fellow Masons Savage, Thomson, King, Byrom, and Bramston. Percy Simson notes that "Masonic interest is centred mostly in a Poem by Philip Duke of Wharton," dated 1726, while there are also "three or four most treasonable Jacobite songs. Many of Mendes's poems lamented Walpolean corruption and called for a return of the Stuart claimant, who had promised liberty of conscience to Jews, Catholics, and other religions. In one, "To Mr. Pope," he urged, "Oh Pope arise and weed the encumbered land." Mendes apparently knew Pope, for he collaborated with him in contributing funds to enable Savage to move to Wales (Pope would later chastise the ungrateful Savage for mistreating Mendes).[83]

Moses's brother Solomon arranged for their friends Savage, Thomson, Armstrong, and Thomas Birch to visit Lord Burlington's controversial villa at Chiswick in September 1738.[84] Solomon had procured the tickets, which the earl apparently used to select his visitors and keep out unwanted critics. If Chiswick was indeed planned as a Masonic temple to welcome home James III, Solomon's group of opposition Masons would have an opportunity to interpret its carved and painted symbolism. Over the next years, the poems of Moses Mendes and his initiated "brothers" became more radically Jacobite, and they would support the cause of "Bonnie Prince Charlie" in the 1745 rebellion.

In autumn 1738 Moses Mendes's friend Dr. King anonymously published *Miltonis Epistola ad Pollionem*, a Latin satire upon the decadence of the Hanoverian government. With a dedication to Pope, he utilized ironically the republican Milton's praise of liberty to chastise the current ministry. David Greenwood identifies "Pollio" as Sir Patrick Hume, 1st Earl of Marchmont and Baron Polwarth (d. 1724), a Presbyterian Whig who supported the Williamite Revolution and union of Scotland and England.[85] He does not

---

[78] Marsha Keith Schuchard, "Stuart Policies of Liberty of Conscience and the Jacobite Jews," paper presented at South-Central Society for Eighteenth-century Studies (25 February 2005); also, Leon Zeldis, "Some Sephardic Jews in Freemasonry," *Pietre-Stones Review of Freemasonry*. <http://www.freemasons-free-masonry.com/zeldis14html.

[79] Vivian Lipman, "Moses Mendes," *Encyclopaedia Judaica*, 2nd ed. (London, 2007), XIV, 41-42.

[80] R. Sedgwick, *History*, II, 558.

[81] "John Ellis," *ODNB*.

[82] UGLE: MS. 1860 Men.

[83] A. Pope, *Correspondence*, IV, 418.

[84] J. Thomson, *Letters and Documents*, 123-24.

[85] D. Greenwood, *William King*, 89-90.

mention that the first earl was also a Freemason and participated in the Covenanters' Masonic networks.[86] According to J.C.D. Clark, "King shielded himself behind the persona of a republican poet writing to a Presbyterian Whig in order to encourage the second Earl of Marchmont in his support for the Tory-inspired opposition to Sir Robert Walpole."[87] Alexander Hume-Campbell became Lord Polwarth in 1709 and 2nd Earl of Marchmont in 1724, serving as an anti-Jacobite supporter of the government.[88] As noted earlier, his twin sons were friends of Ramsay in 1730 and carried on their father's Masonic affiliation. Since 1733 Marchmont *père* had joined the "patriot" opposition to Walpole's excise scheme and spoke out strongly against the proposed penalties on Edinburgh during the Porteous affair. He was one of the Scottish Presbyterians that Dr. King hoped to recruit to the Jacobite cause, and the two had become good friends.

King's cautious shielding of himself was significant, for his soliciting of disaffected Scottish Whigs and Jacobites had been noticed at court. In March 1738 Lady Binning wrote to Marchmont's son Hugh Hume, Lord Polwarth, that a noble lord had told George II that "St Mary Hall was a nest of all the Scots Jacobites who came there on purpose to support it."[89] One of them was James Menteath, "the Tall Scot," whose long legs and physical strength won him the admiration of his fellow students. He greatly admired Dr. King, whose political sympathies he shared. King's other protégé, Sanderson Miller, wrote a biography of Menteath, in which he noted that "Jacobus Montaltus Scotus" introduced himself to the best company at Oxford "by clinging fast to a Knot of Scotsmen well known for their great abilities in the Mathematics Algebra," etc. Miller respected Menteath's Jacobite loyalty, joked about his second sight, and hinted that he later joined "Kilmarnock's People" in Scotland during the 1745 Jacobite rebellion.[90] At St. Mary's, Sanderson Miller joined Dr. King in studying medieval architecture and contemporary stonemasonry, and he would gain fame as an architect and progenitor of the Gothic Revival, in which he worked closely with his master mason, William Hitchcox, who also served as his personal valet.[91] It seems certain that both Miller and Menteath had Masonic affiliations.

Another member of Dr. King's "nest of Scots Jacobites" was Alexander Forbes, Lord Pitsligo, who earned King's great admiration. After Pitsligo's participation with his first cousin Lord Mar in the 1715 rebellion, he fled to the Continent, where he joined Mar at the Stuart court in Rome in 1719.[92] He returned to Scotland in 1720 and lived "in retreat" at Pitsligo Castle, from where he corresponded with Pietists in Europe while writing philosophical treatises, including *Thoughts Concerning Man's Condition and Duties in this Life* (MS. 1732), and *Essays Moral and Philosophical* (1734). King met him either in Scotland or during the Scot's secret visit to Oxford, and he later praised him as "my acquaintance"

[86] D. Stevenson, *First Freemasons*, 31.

[87] J. Clark, *Samuel Johnson*, 37.

[88] "Alexander Hume Campbell, 2nd Earl of Marchmont and Lord Polwarth," *ODNB*.

[89] *HMC: Report on the Manuscripts of Lord Polwarth* (London, 1961), V, 213.

[90] William Hawes, ed., *The Diaries of Sanderson Miller of Radway* (Bristol, 2005), 334,-45, 351.

[91] Lillian Dickins and Mary Stanton, eds., *An Eighteenth-Century Correspondence, being the Letters…to Sanderson Miller, Esqu., of Radway* (London, 1910), 6, 82, 111-115, 127-28.

[92] "Alexander Forbes, 4th Lord Forbes of Pitsligo," *ODNB*. Henrietta Tayler published his diary of his experiences, *The Jacobite Court at Rome in 1719* (Edinburgh, 1938).

and "an excellent man, who, besides, is a polite scholar."[93] Pitsligo shared with his earlier protégé Chevalier Ramsay a belief in Fenelonian ecumenicism, writing that "Everybody knows 'tis accident, for the most part, that makes us of one Religion, rather than another." Like Ramsay's, this theme infused his Masonic philosophy, while he reportedly presided over a lodge at Roseharty on his estate.[94] As an old man, Pitsligo would earn fame for his heroic role in the 1745 Jacobite rebellion.

In King's "Miltonic" poem, he echoed the opposition call for war against Spain, a cause that Polwarth heatedly supported in parliament.[95] The Jacobites hoped to exploit the tension, for the war would make Britain vulnerable to a foreign invasion. Though "Milton"/King admits that he does not have the eloquence of "Cadenus"/Swift in his appeal to "true Britons" to throw off the yoke of oppression imposed by "Pallas"/Walpole and his foreign king/George II, his passionate indictment took Latin to new heights, an achievement still admired today. His friend John Ellis translated the intricate Latin into English in a version published two years later. In contrast to the mercenary and lecherous George II, who is "by lust impair'ed," Milton would choose a Sovereign, who first

> Should with consummate Prudence rule himself;
> Be Temp'rate, Just, free from Excess of Passion;
> Should all his Pow'r and Policy employ
> T'advance the Publick Good, not uninform'd
> In aught that might conduce to its Improvement;
> Humane, Pacifick…[96]

Evidently influenced by Ramsay's praise of Chinese religion and governance and aware of James III's studies of Mandarin with Fouquet, King portrayed his ideal king in Chinese and Confucian terms. He then issued a resounding Jacobite call to bring "the imperial Lion Home,/To guard the Subject from oppressive Power." On 23 January 1739 King wrote to Swift to explain his censoring of certain political lines in *Verses on the Death of Dr. Swift*:

> I am in truth more cautious than I used to be, well knowing that my superiors look on me at present with a very evil eye, as I am the reputed author of the Latin poem I have sent you… for although that piece hath escaped the state inquisition, by being written in a language that is not at present very well understood at court, and might perhaps puzzle the attorney-general to explain, yet the scope of the poem and principal characters being well understood, the author must therefore expect no mercy, if he give his enemies any grounds or colour to attack him.[97]

King's praise of Lord Polwarth, a Scottish Whig, who now seemed open to Jacobite recruitment, was shared by Ramsay and his colleagues abroad, who viewed the

93 W. King, *Political and Literary Anecdotes*, 144-45.
94 www.lodgeforbes67.com.history.
95 Cobbett, *Parliamentary History*, X, 598-99.
96 [William King], *Milton's Epistle to Pollio. Translated from the Latin, and Illustrated with Explanatory Notes* (London, 1740). Translation attributed to John Ellis.
97 J. Swift, *Correspondence*, IV, 557.

intensification of Scottish nationalism in the wake of the Porteous affair as encouragement for the Stuart cause. On 29 September 1738 Thomas Innes, head of the Scots College in Paris, wrote to James Edgar, the Pretender's Protestant secretary, about the visit to Paris of two young Glaswegians, Robert and Andrew Foulis. On the way, they had stopped over in Oxford, where they evidently met Dr. King and received letters of introduction to Ramsay from King as well as from friends in Glasgow. Father Innes wrote Secretary Edgar in Rome that "the chief person they keep in, and were recommended to…is Chevalier Ramsay," who supervised their examination of the early records of Glasgow University, preserved in the Scots College.[98] Innes was pleased that they shared Ramsay's reverence for Fenelon and universalist religious opinions. They told him that "all moderate thinking people begin to have a contempt and aversion to the old canting way of formal whiggism in religion, and that even the Knoxian way of Reformation, the Covenant, and wild doings of these times, was looked upon as a kind of madness."[99] Even the formerly Hanoverian Glaswegians "have a particular pick at the usurper, for having used them so ill upon the tumult that happened some years ago about the Malt Tax, since which they have a guard over them that they were never used to."

Like Dr. King, who assured Mrs. Whiteway that the Scottish Presbyterians were not as Whiggish as she and Swift thought, Innes saw the rising Scottish nationalism as important to the Stuarts' cause. On 27 October Innes wrote again to Edgar that the Foulis brothers compared "their project of education and tolerantisme to the indulgence published by the late B. King A.D. 1687," referring to James II's declaration of "liberty of conscience," which led to the anti-Catholic, Williamite revolution. Referring again to the Glasgow riots of 1725, Innes concluded that the brothers "seem to be for monarchy, but a limited one; but have, no kindness for the present usurping family." On their return to Glasgow, the Foulis brothers began the book-selling and publishing business that made them famous, and Robert would later be noted for "something sublime in his conceptions, darkened by a slight dash of mysticism, caught perhaps from some French writers, he was said to be fond of." The influence of their Masonic friend Ramsay continued, as they published and sold his works, with Robert later lecturing on Ramsay's "Principles of Universal Religion" to the Glasgow literary society.[100]

Throughout 1738 the other "Pretender" to the British throne, Prince Frederick, increased the influence of his "Patriot" supporters within the Grand Lodge, especially with the installation of Henry Brydges, Marquess of Carnarvon (later 2nd Duke of Chandos), as Grand Master in April 1738. Carnarvon served as Gentleman of the Bedchamber to Frederick. Carnarvon reportedly "showed every attention to the society," and contributed a valuable ceremonial jewel, but his granting of the office of Provincial Grand Master to the West Riding of Yorkshire was considered an encroachment by the York Masons and widened their disaffection from the London Grand Lodge.[101] As noted earlier, the majority of York Masons were Jacobites, loyal to the other "Pretender." The prince's favor to Carnarvon was probably increased by George II's scorn for the marquess, whom the king described as "a hot-headed, passionate, half-witted coxcomb, with no more

---

[98] The following quotes are from David Murray, *Some Letters of Robert Foulis* (Glasgow, 1917), 63-68.
[99] *Ibid.*, 64.
[100] David Murray, *Robert and Andrew Foulis and the Glasgow Press* (Glasgow, 1913), 38, 105.
[101] *The American Freemason*, ser. 2, vol. II (New York, 1858), 448.

sense than his master."[102] As heir to a vast fortune, Carnarvon was "an irresponsible spendthrift," whose great debts later led to the sale and demolishment of his father's magnificent mansion of Canons.[103]

With the Grand Master virtually in his pocket, Prince Frederick continued to consolidate his Masonic associations. In October 1738, during his lavish "royal" progress to Bath and Bristol, he was accompanied by his chaplain Desaguliers. Both men attended an "Extraordinary Meeting" of a Masonic lodge in Bath, called to celebrate the birthday of George II. The *St. James' Evening Post* (30 October 1738) reported that not only Desaguliers but the late Grand Master Darnley, Deputy Grand Master John Ward, Sir Edwin Mansell, and other brothers attended. They were joined by Richard "Beau" Nash, member of a Bath lodge, who asked Pope to compose an inscription for the obelisk that Nash wanted to erect in Queen's Square in honor of the prince's visit.[104] Pope had known Nash for years, but he found the request distasteful, for unlike Nash he had "received so few favours from the great myself, that I am utterly unacquainted with what kind of thanks they like best."[105] He finally demurred and composed such a bland inscription that it inspired the scornful lines: "But then that Square – within whose centre railed/ Lies taste upon an Obelisk impaled." Pope's reluctance was perhaps influenced by Nash's reputation for reckless Jacobitism, as described by Lord Egmont in 1736: "[At] the coffee house, where Nash of the Bath, a perfect Jacobite, but one that for his jests and humour is received everywhere.".[106]

Another possible reason for Pope's reluctance to publicly honor Nash's request was the secret political agenda behind Frederick's visit to Bath. The prince and Bolingbroke had planned "a secret conference of opposition members to work out strategy for ensuring Walpole's early downfall."[107] They decided to meet in Bath in order to avoid Walpole's omnipresent spies in London; as Chesterfield later explained, "An event so interesting to the nation afforded a favourable opportunity of assembling the prince's friends, and concealing business under the appearances of festivity of joy." Though the Jacobite Nash was in charge of the lavish entertainments, Bolingbroke was determined to distance his Patriot party from the Jacobites, and he may have warned Pope about collaborating too closely with Nash. In the same month, Pope also tried to resist the blandishment of Lord Lyttleton, leader of the Patriot party, who wrote from Bath urging the poet "to animate" the prince to virtue, to "love of the public," noting that "the morals, the liberty, the whole happiness of the country depends on your success." There could not be "a better morning spent by you; no, not in conversing with Lord Bolingbroke":

> In short if you had any spirit in you, you would come to Bath, and let the
> Prince hear every day from the man of this age who is the greatest dispenser
> of fame, and will best be heard by posterity, that, if he would immortalize

---

[102] R. Sedgwick, *History*, I, 500.

[103] "James Brydges, 1st Duke of Chandos," *ODNB*.

[104] W. Williams, "Alexander Pope," 126.

[105] A. Pope, *Correspondence*, IV, 170, 176.

[106] Egmont, *HMC: MSS.Egmont*, II, 254-55.

[107] J. Walters, *Royal Griffin*, 176-77.

himself, the only way he can take is to deserve a place by his conduct, in some writing where he will never be only for his rank.[108]

If Pope had accepted the charge, he would have joined the Masonic party in Bath, but he was wary of an explicit commitment to the prince, who had asked him during a meeting at Kew in 1738, "how shall we reconcile your love to a Prince with your professed indisposition to Kings, since Princes will be Kings in time?"[109] Pope replied, "Sir, I consider royalty under that noble and authorized type of the Lion; while he is young, and before his nails are grown, he may be approached and caressed with safety and pleasure." Within weeks of the Bath meeting, Bolingbroke feared that the opposition around Frederick "had shot its bolt," and on 20 November he told Lord Denbigh, "The spirit you saw decline here is now extinct, and that of Jacobitism rises anew among the Tories, and that of the narrow, interested party, knaves and fools, among the Whigs."[110]

Meanwhile, the prince's party moved on to Bristol, where Desaguliers organized an extravagant fireworks display, which he watched with the prince. Then, in November, Anderson's *New Book of Constitutions* was finally published, with a fulsome dedication to Frederick, Prince of Wales, "A Master Mason, and Master of a Lodge," who was praised not only as 'Prince Royal of Great Britain' but as "Prince and *Stewart* of Scotland" (thus reinforcing his self-fashioning as a legitimate heir of the Stuarts). Anderson wrote that Frederick "well knows, that our Fraternity has often been patronized by Royal Persons in former Ages; whereby Architecture early obtain'd the Title of the Royal Art." In the text, he reiterated the Masonic membership of the former Stuart kings (except James VII and II), who were royal brothers and Grand Masters "by Prerogative." Anderson stressed that "we meddle not with Affairs of State in our Lodges," and when we peacefully assemble, we do so happily "in these Islands under your royal Father, and our Sovereign Lord," George II.

In the historical section, he pointed out that the late Grand Master, the 8th Duke of Norfolk, came from a Masonic family dating back to the 1630's, which gave new prestige to Norfolk's successor, the 9th Duke (who was currently collaborating with Prince Frederick and the Jacobites).[111] Samuel Johnson and other friends of Richard Savage would be interested to learn that his purported ancestor, Thomas Savage, Earl of Rivers, served as Grand Master in 1666. In an effort to distance the Grand Lodge from the Jacobites, Anderson claimed that the Duke of Wharton's initiation into the fraternity was irregular and his election as Grand Master in 1722 was performed "without the usual Decent Ceremonials."[112] The lodge was not opened or closed "in due form," so "the noble Brothers and all those that would not countenance irregularities, disown'd Wharton's authority," until the "worthy Brother Montagu heal'd the Breach of Harmony" and got Wharton to promise to be "True and Faithful." Anderson did not reveal the dissention over the appointment of Desaguliers as Deputy Grand Master, which led to the walk out by Wharton

---

[108] W. Williams, "Alexander Pope," 127.

[109] M. Mack, *Alexander Pope*, 757.

[110] Simon Varey, "Hanover, Stuart, and the *Patriot King*," in *British Journal for Eighteenth-Century Studies*, 6 (1983), 164-65.

[111] James Anderson, *The New Book of Constitutions of the Antient and Honourable Fraternity of Free and Accepted Masons* (York, 1738), 99, 102, 210, 199.

[112] *Ibid.*, 114-15.

and his supporters (a controversy recorded in the unpublished lodge minutes). Defending his publishing territory against possible competitors, Anderson gained a recommendation from the Grand Lodge officers that his will be "the only Book of Constitutions, for the use of the Lodges, of the Free and Accepted Masons."

At the end of the volume, Anderson included a reprint of *A Defence of Masonry*, published in 1730 in reaction to *Masonry Dissected*. The author claimed to not be a Mason, but he added some interesting speculation on the similarities of Masonry to the ancient Pythagorean, Essenean, and Cabalistic fraternities – similarities which emerged more in *Écossais* lodges abroad. This in turn provoked a response from "Euclid," member of "our old Lodge, the Horn," on 9 November 1738. Euclid argued that if the previous author had indeed been a Mason, he would know that such esoteric and mystical secrets would become available to interested Masons who passed through the proper probation – a hint at emerging higher degrees even in Britain. He then rejected the silly charges against the Masons – such as raising the devil in a circle, an old woman between the rounds of a ladder, and the hot-iron branding on the buttocks. Finally, he praised the rise in great architecture since Freemasonry had expanded in Britain and predicted the success of "the English Masons Grand Design of rivaling fair Italy in Architecture." However, the next year – 1739 – would witness increasing turbulence and a decline in Masonry's prestige in England, while the reverse occurred in Scotland.

In the same month as the *New Constitutions* appeared, the Scots elected John Keith, 3rd Earl of Kintore, as Grand Master in Edinburgh. Though Kintore appeared publicly as a loyal Whig and had attended meetings of the London Grand Lodge, his background raised suspicions in the government. His father was a Jacobite who was out in 1715, and he himself married a niece of the late Earl of Mar. Wharton included him in his 1725 list of Jacobite peers. Throughout 1738 Kintore was in communication with his Jacobite cousin, General James Keith, in an attempt to protect the attainted George Keith's inheritance, which had been transferred to Kintore.[113] He commissioned "a very fine mahogany spoon-back chair" in tribute to his role as protector of the Earl Marischal's estate. The motto painted on the chair was *Quae Amissa Salva* ("what has been lost is safe").[114] James Keith now wanted Kintore to petition parliament to make himself the heir of the childless Kintore, instead of his brother George (to which George agreed).

In January 1738 James Keith had gained the assistance of the Russian ambassador Antiokh Kantemir, and, in February, on the advice of Duncan Forbes, President of the Court of Session in Scotland, he got the Empress Anna to personally intercede with George II on his behalf. She wrote in praise of Keith's military service and loyalty and asked for his due rights of inheritance, but the king replied that the Scot had behaved "obnoxiously" to his government and that he must "abstain from all farther misconduct towards us." George left open the door if Keith abjured the Pretender and swore loyalty to the Hanoverian succession. There was much talk in parliament about his past and continuing Jacobitism. When the petition was presented to parliament on 8 March, it was rejected, and Lord Grange told Kantemir that the letters between himself and Keith had gone missing (evidently intercepted). Grange also wrote Keith that "the peevishness of a

[113] For this complicated affair, 1740, see R. Wills, *Jacobites*, 155-61.
[114] "Very fine George II Mahogany Spoon-Back Hall Chair for the Earls of Kintore," http://www.michaelpashby antiques.dom/antique _furniture_details.

minister" (Walpole) led to the petition's defeat. In the meantime, doctors in Russia told James that his unhealing leg wound required amputation, but his brother George, who had joined him at Poltava, persuaded the Empress to let him travel to Paris for treatment in November. As we shall see, James Keith was in contact with Ramsay during the next eleven months of treatment in France.

Kintore received the poetic support of Charles Leslie, a disaffected Scottish Whig and Freemason, who anonymously published *The Fall of Virtue, or the Iron Age* (1738), in which he praised the Duke of Argyll and John Cockburn, M.P., who collaborated with Lord Marchmont in backing the Prince of Wales in his struggle against his father.[115] Despite Cockburn's fighting for the government in 1715, he was neglected by the Whig ministry and joined the opposition in 1733. Leslie noted that "he suffers without the Sting of Resentment. How little can the Frowns of a Court discompose the steady Mind?"[116] In another anonymous poem, *On the Scarcity of the Copper Coin. A Satyr* (1739), he scorned the Scottish placemen who served Walpole's agenda:

> Hence Gaugers, Waiters, Custom-Officers,
> Well-fed Collectors, and Commissioners,
> Clerks, Supervisors, a tremendous Band,
> Like Egypt's Locusts eat up all the Land.
> ....
> What various Ills, *O Scotia*, hast thou seen?
> And what Misfortune has the U[nio]n been?
> Enslav'd, excis'd by a corrupted Crew,
> A curs'd, a brib'd, a damn'd abandon'd few;
> Who set their Conscience and their Votes to Sell;
> And trudge to London for their private Weal.[117]

Leslie implied that Kintore shared his political sentiments, and would help Scotland recover "Its pristine Age, when happy, great and free,/ Above Corruption, and deserv'dly great, "when there was "Much Virtue, small Estates, and no Excise."[118] He was thus delighted when Kintore was elected Grand Master, and he dedicated his long poem *Masonry* (1739) to the new head of Scottish Masonry. Signing himself "A Freemason," he praised Kintore: "The Free Masons are distinguished by an universal good-will to mankind; and while they are happy in having your Lordship at their head, may despise the little censures of ridiculous men, who, ignorant of the beauty of the Science, lose themselves to all the good and the wise, by railing at what they can never know."[119] Leslie then drew on the "ancient" Scottish and Stuart traditions of Masonry as intimately linked with royalist architecture, stressing the importance of Solomon's Temple and the "Great work of Kings." He lamented the destruction caused by iconoclastic radicals, "The spite and fury of hot zeal run mad," and praised the accomplishments of the Gothic designers and operative Masons who created the great cathedrals (thus countering Anderson's denigration of the Gothic in the *New Constitutions*). However, he was pleased that those great

---

[115] R. Sedgwick, *History*, I, 562.
[116] [Charles Leslie], *The Fall of Virtue, or the Iron-Age* (Edinburgh, 1738), [ii-iii].
[117] [Charles Leslie], *On the Scarcity of the Copper Coin. A Satyr* (Edinburgh, 1739), 14-15.
[118] *Ibid.*, 14.
[119] [Charles Leslie], *Masonry: A Poem. To which are added several Songs* (Edinburgh, 1739), Dedication.

medieval architects were now surpassed by the even worthier Palladians, such as their "generous modern sons…a Kent, a Flitcroft, and a Burlington."[120]

In politically risky lines, Leslie praised the patriotic role of the Keith family, which Kintore was expected to continue:

> Behold Kintore, by merit call'd to reign,
> Great Sov'reign of the Virtuoso Train,
> ………………………………………..
> He from a race of noble Chiefs, who won,
> By glorious deeds, their honours and renown,
> Who oft in fields of death undaunted stood,
> And sought their Country's glory with their blood,
> By true descent derives the Patriot-flame,
> And rises to hereditary fame.
> With low pursuit let others seek to gain
> A place, a garter, or a splendid train,
> And glitter in the pageantry of state,
> Rais'd by their country's spoils, ignobly great;
> Illustrious KEITH demands a nobler praise,
> A place to which desert alone can raise;
> And, lifted to the height of human pride,
> O'er Arts and Masons chuses to preside.[121]

The poet's praise of the Keiths' long tradition of royalism, nationalism, militarism, and Masonry would not help James Keith's cause in London. He taunted the monarchs who run mad after riches and power, the dull "fat Gown-men," and "Philosophers sour," while also lambasting the "slavish nations, servile tools of Rome," whose governments attempted to ban Freemasonry.

With Kintore now serving as Grand Master in Scotland and his cousins George and James Keith now in France, the Jacobite Masons were encouraged by the changing national and international situation. The former Grand Master, Hector Maclean, wrote to the Stuart court about the Keiths' arrival in Paris, adding that the trouble between England and Spain can be "turned to good account."[122] He enclosed a memorial from their fellow Mason, Lord John Drummond, who assured James that Scotland will rise, and many Whigs and Patriots in England will join them. Provocatively, Maclean added that Lord Aberdour wants him to speak to Cardinal Fleury, flattering him, "since he seems to be willing." If Maclean referred to James Douglas, who until 1738 was known as Lord Aberdour, this report of Douglas's Jacobite sympathies is provocative. After the death of his father, the 13th Earl of Morton, on 4 January 1738, Aberdour became the 14th Earl of Morton, but his oldest son and future Lord Aberdour was only six years old. It seems likely that Maclean, away in France, still referred to his old friend Douglas as Lord Aberdour. Douglas was an eminent scientist, who had developed good relations with French scientists during his Grand Tour, and he now served as President of the Philosophical Society of Edinburgh. Anita Guerrini observes that the 14th Earl of Morton's "politics

---

[120] *Ibid.*, 9-13.
[121] *Ibid.*, 18-19.
[122] Stuart Papers: 213/119 (9 February 1739); 214/50 (February 1738); 214/174 (30 March 1739).

are unclear," but he played a public role as a representative peer of Scotland and government loyalist.[123] He would succeed Kintore as Grand Master of Scotland in 1740. As we shall see, he would later be accused of Hanoverian and/or Jacobite complicity in 1746 and imprisoned in the Bastille.

While the *Écossais* Masons flourished in France, despite Fleury's attempted suppression, the Inquisition crackdown in Italy intensified, as a worried Stosch reported to the government in London. Since August 1738 Richmond had consulted with Newcastle about the situation, because he heard that their "brother Mason," Charles Fane, would be succeeded by someone other than his choice, Burrington Goldsworthy, to the consular position in Florence and Leghorn.[124] Richmond counted on Fane and his allies to defend the Hanoverian Masons in Italy, whom he viewed as a counterforce to the Jacobites. A problem for Fane was the trust that Newcastle maintained in Stosch, whom Fane and Mann despised and wanted expelled from Florence. To protect himself, Stosch intensified and exaggerated his anti-Jacobite reports, which the ministers in London evidently believed and thus kept him on the payroll.

In December 1738 Stosch reported that the Nuncio received precise orders from Rome to move heaven and earth to get him expelled from the country before the Duke of Lorraine arrives in Tuscany.[125] The Nuncio and his satellites used the same maneuver against him "under the frivolous pretext of Freemasonry a little before the arrival in Florence at another time [1737] of the pretended Comte d'Albanie [Prince Charles]." It is urgent that George II give orders to Horace Mann to protect him against his formidable enemies, especially "since the Pretender has thrown himself into the arms of the Jesuits, his authority and his adherents are much augmented throughout Italy." On 2 February 1739 Stosch wrote that Clement XII wants the Papal historian to give him materials to compare himself to his predecessors, *Pontifes Zelés*, in order to merit the title of "Persecutor of Heresies" at the expense of the Freemasons:

> It is well known at Rome that the assemblies ceased, for lack of English travelers, before the Bull of Excommunication, because they would not admit the servants or declared adherents of the Pretender. Nevertheless, his Holiness issued a few days ago a new Edict promising a considerable sum of money to those who will reveal the secrets of the Freemasons, and who will reveal to the government the locations of their clandestine meetings.[126]

A week later, Stosch sent another report, enclosing the "terrible" Edict of the Pope against the Freemasons, whose members are condemned to death and large sums promised to those who will reveal the secrets of the Society:

> Since none of the subjects of the Pope are Freemasons, all the threats concern rather the English travelers and no one else. The refusal they made some years ago to Sir Thomas Dereham who wanted to be admitted to the Society greatly irritated the Pope against the members. The said Chevalier,

---

[123] "James Douglas, 14th Earl of Morton," *ODNB*.

[124] Richmond, *Correspondence*, 19.

[125] NA:SP 98/41 (8 December 1738).

[126] *Ibid.*, 98/41 (2 February 1739).

against the expectations of his physicians, is almost completely cured of his dangerous malady.[127]

Clement XII and James were "deeply grieved" by Dereham's illness, but Stosch was able to report happily on 16 February that Dereham had died after all, and he was relieved that his persecutor was gone.[128]

In the meantime, reports were published in England that implied (not directly charged) that James III collaborated with the papal crackdown. On 6-8 February the *London Evening Post* printed a letter from Rome, dated 24 January:

> The Chevalier de St. George had lately an audience of, and a long conversation with the Pope. A Decree has been published renewing the Condemnation of the Fraternity of Free Masons, with a Promise or a Reward of a Hundred Crowns of Gold to any one that shall discover any or [*sic*] the Heads or Members of that society, and the same for those who shall point out the Place where they assemble in this City.[129]

In Italy, despite widespread opposition to the Bull, the pope's witch-hunt continued.

The British representative Horace Mann sent reports from Florence on the arrest of his lodge brother Thomas Crudeli in May 1739.[130] The Stuart agent Tyrrell in Florence also reported the arrest to James Edgar, noting that he is "a partisan of the sect" and it seems that the Inquisition will carry this affair as far as possible."[131] During months of intense interrogation, Crudeli was forced to explain various Masonic symbols and rituals, which (provocatively) included swearing over a volume of *Don Quijote*.[132] Could there have been an influence from the Order of Toboso on Italian Masonry? As Crudeli's health declined and his supporters continued to protest his imprisonment, the Austrian minister Richecourt, himself a Mason, wrote Duke Francis that "the affair of Crudeli becomes everyday more embarrassing."[133] He added that it is surprising that they have attacked Crudeli when their real target is Stosch. Crudeli was frequently with Fane and Mann, who wanted Stosch expelled, and Fane even chased Stosch out of his house. Stosch then sent reports to Newcastle in which he attacked Fane. Mann told Richecourt that the English court regards Rome's persecution against the English and Stosch as "an affair of Cardinal Corsini in favor of the Chevalier de Saint Georges."

Stosch continued to claim that the Pretender hated Freemasonry "to the extremity," because he believed it was "destructive to good morals and the Roman Catholic religion." However, it is provocative that James's close ally, Cardinal Lambertini, did not share that belief (if Stosch was accurate in his report about James's attitude), for he was the admiring friend of Derwentwater, Ramsay, and other Catholic "brothers." The Inquisition crackdown may have proved counter-productive, for the Jacobite Masons seemed to go even further underground. Mann soon complained about "the art of secrecy" practiced by

---

[127] *Ibid.*, 98/41 (9 February 1739).

[128] *Ibid.*, 98/42 (16 February 1739).

[129] R. Péter, *British Freemasonry*, V, 155.

[130] NA:SP 105/281 (18 May 1739).

[131] Stuart Papers: 215/147 (12 May 1739).

[132] F. Benimeli, *Masoneria*, II, 45.

[133] Maria Timpanaro, *Tommaso Crudeli*, (Firenzei, 2003), 297.

Stuart supporters, especially concerning Prince Charles, which made it "almost impossible to dive into their secrets."[134]

Mann further warned Newcastle that the Jacobites were launching a major new plot, involving France's alliance with Sweden, which neither he nor his spies in Rome could penetrate. Stosch also feared secret maneuvers from Sweden, charging that the new "Hat" regime (led by Gyllenborg, Tessin, and Scheffer) maintains connections with conspirators in Rome and Scotland against George II's government, and he identified Count Nils Bielke, now a Roman senator, as the "channel" for this dangerous intrigue.[135] Surprisingly, Stosch seemed unaware of the Masonic affiliation of Bielke, as the Swedish Catholic collaborated with his Protestant in-laws Tessin and Wrede-Sparre to make *Écossais* Freemasonry in Sweden part of an international network of support for the Franco-Stuart cause. In Paris Waldegrave worried about reports of the close collaboration in Stockholm between St. Severin and Count Tessin, both Masons, who worked to develop a Franco-Swedish-Spanish project to support the Jacobites.[136]

As the international situation heated up, the opposition writers in England came under increasing scrutiny and persecution. In February 1739 the Anglo-Irish playwright Henry Brooke was refused a license for his play, *Gustavus Vasa*, which was already in rehearsal in Drury Lane. The punitive Stage Licensing Act, enacted earlier in June 1737, was rumored to be a reaction to a new play, *The Golden Rump*, which "took its cue" from Dr. King's allegory published in March in *Common Sense*. J.C.D. Clark suggests that the "indecent" script of *The Golden Rump*, for which no text survives, was possibly written at the instigation of Walpole, who read the most vulgar passages to an astonished parliament in order to gain support for the licensing bill.[137] Pope and other opposition writers determined "to test the mettle of the new Licensing Act" and collaborated on the composition of a series of defiant plays.[138] The first victim of the act was the Anglicized Scot, David Mallet, who had studied under Dr. King at St. Mary Hall and subsequently joined Pope and the "Patriots" in support of the Prince of Wales.[139] In January 1738 part of Mallet's prologue to James Thomson's contentious opposition play *Agamemnon* was censored by the Lord Chancellor, whom Mallet had deliberately provoked:

> …we hope to see
> Our judges, – here at least, – from Influence free;
> One Place, – unbias'd yet by Party-Rage, –
> Where only Honour votes, – the British Stage.
> We ask for Justice, for Indulgence sue:
> Our last best License must proceed from you.[140]

Thomson had dedicated the play to his Masonic brother, the Prince of Wales, and his supporters determined to continue their campaign on the stage.

---

[134] NA:SP 105/281 (24 August 1739).

[135] *Ibid.*, 98/41 (24 August 1739).

[136] British Library. Add. MS. 32,798, f. 114.

[137] J. Clarke, *Samuel Johnson*, 165-66.

[138] M. Mack, *Alexander Pope*, 758-60.

[139] "David Mallet," *ODNB*.

[140] James Thomson, *Agamemnon. A Tragedy* (London, 1738), Prologue.

Over the next months, Walpole waited to fully impose the law until he had a sure target, and Brooke's paean to a Swedish hero who withstood a Danish enemy to ensure his kingdom's liberties seemed to be a vulnerable and timely victim. Brooke had been tutored by Swift's Tory friend, Dr. Thomas Sheridan, and he became friendly with the dean, before moving to London in 1724, where he was welcomed by Pope and his circle. Though it is unknown if he was a Freemason, many of his kinsmen were associated with Irish Masonry.[141] It is also unknown if Brooke was aware of the Swedish Masons' current collaboration with Derwentwater and the Jacobites in an ambitious plan to overthrow George II and restore James III.[142] Unfortunately for him, Walpole was aware of the Swedish-Jacobite intrigues, and Brookes' play thus seemed especially seditious.

Gustavus Vasa portrayed a "Deliverer of his Country" from foreign oppression, with some interpreting Gustavus as Prince Frederick and others as James Stuart. The Danish usurper Christiern represented George II and his evil minister Walpole. Sixteenth-century Sweden was "Queen of the North," home of a "Race of hardy, northern Sons," whose "Hands scorn'd Bondage, for their Hearts were free."[143] With contemporary Sweden plotting to support a Jacobite invasion of Scotland, and with Scotland's "hardy, northern Sons" bristling with nationalistic antagonism to England, Brooke had entered a political minefield. Samuel Johnson's Whig friend, Sir John Hawkesworth, remembered that the implementation of the Licensing Act was looked upon by Brooke's friends, in which number were included all the Jacobites in the kingdom, as an infraction of natural right, and as affecting the cause of liberty."[144] Though the play was banned from performance in England, Brooke was able to print an edition, which gained over nine hundred subscribers and became a best seller. The subscribers included a large number of Jacobites, disaffected Whigs, and opposition Freemasons, including Dr. King, John Ellis, Solomon Mendes; the Scots Murray of Broughton, Polwarth, and Marchmont.

In Ireland not only the opposition Mason Inchiquin subscribed to Brooke's drama, but Swift ordered ten copies of the work, which revived charges of Jacobitism against him. On 10 April 1739 James Arbuckle, his old Whig-Masonic antagonist, wrote to the Presbyterian minister Thomas Drennan that Swift had praised an article by Arbuckle (published in Faulkner's journal) and announced an intention to call on him.[145] Arbuckle treated this as a joke: "So you see, it is more than one and a half to a hundred and fifty thousand, that I may be a great man, whenever I shall either turn Tory, or the Pret[ender] …be king of G[reat] B[ritain], both which are likely to happen the same year."[146] Swift's motive in trying to visit "Wit upon Crutches" is unclear, for he was aware that in 1734 Arbuckle received from Walpole a permanent government position in Ireland.[147] Though a loyal Hanoverian, Arbuckle did complain against the often unjust treatment of Ireland

---

[141] Denis McLoughlin, *Grand Masters of the Grand Lodge of Ireland, 1725 to 2010* (Dublin, 2013?), Brooke family.

[142] M. Schuchard, *Emanuel Swedenborg*, 249-50, 271-76, 279.

[143] Quoted in Christine Gerrard, *The Patriot Opposition to Walpole: Politics, Poetry, and National Myth* (Oxford, 1994), 114.

[144] Quoted in J. Clark, *Samuel Johnson*, 166.

[145] Rev. Thomas Drennan was the father of Dr. William Drennan, who later utilized Freemasonry in organizing the United Irishmen; however, it is unknown if Thomas was a Masonic brother of Arbuckle.

[146] R. Homes, "James Arbuckle," 431

[147] B. Coleborne, "James Arbuckle," 180n.22.

by the English government. Perhaps Swift hoped to gain sympathy for the Anglo-Irish Brooke's work, which the author planned to publish in Dublin. Moreover, it may have been Faulkner, who published Arbuckle's article and then a reprint of *Gustavus Vasa*, who arranged a meeting between the two political rivals and who later claimed that Arbuckle "was acquainted with the Dean many years."[148] Irish nationalists interpreted Brooke's play as the struggle between Ireland and England; when it was later produced in Dublin, it was re-named *The Patriot*.

On 27 March Walpole struck again, this time banning Thomson's *Edward and Eleonora*, dedicated to the Princess of Wales, two days before it was due to open at Covent Garden. The play glorified the loving relationship between the medieval king and his wife, in pointed contrast to the adulterous reality of George II, his late queen, and his German mistresses. Like Brooke, Thomson made up for his lost stage profits by printing subscription and trade editions. Samuel Johnson, who was indignant at the banning of the plays, contributed an anonymous attack upon the government in *Marmor Norfolciense*, first advertised on 11 May. His author's pose as *Probus Britannicus* ("True Briton") once again harkened back to the Jacobite publications of Wharton. The work pretended to be a commentary on an ancient Latin inscription, discovered near the town of Lynn in Norfolk, "for which borough Sir Robert Walpole was the sitting MP."[149] Posing as a Whig antiquarian who tries to interpret the prophecy, Johnson commented ironically on the declining state of the nation and joined the opposition cry for war against Spain. His image of the Hanoverian horse sucking the blood of the British lion roused immediate charges of Jacobite sedition. Two weeks later he issued another defiant work, *A Compleat Vindication of the Licensers of the Stage, From the Malicious and Scandalous Aspersions of Mr. Brooke, Author of Gustavus Vasa* (London, 1739). Johnson's Whig friend Hawkins remembered that these publications were so inflammatory and Jacobitical that warrants were issued for his arrest, leading him to take "an obscure lodging in Lambeth-marsh, and lay there concealed till the scent after him was grown cold."[150]

These opposition attacks were too much for Henley and his patron Walpole, so the Orator launched a series of counter-attacks in *The Hyp-Doctor*. On 5 June, under the headline "A Spy upon the Times, or the whole Plot of the Play, Edward and Eleonora, discovered," he vowed (threateningly) that the Lord Chancellor can "make a better Tragedy" than all the Gustavus Vasas, the Eleonoras, the Mustaphas put together – the products of "Pigmy Pamphleteers."[151] Commenting on the portrayal of Edward II, he noted that "the Kings of England, of the Denominations of, – THE SECOND – were doomed to be unfortunate: and here a Resignation of the Crown is the Plot, from a weak Pusillanimous Prince to his eldest born Son: Less than this has been interpreted to carry the Sense of Constructive Tr----n [Treason]." He was amazed that no friend of the government has been so vigilant as "to smoke this Paragraph: – It is the Key to the whole Cabinet of Patriotism." He then linked the author, an opposition Mason, to the Porteous rioters: "I should be apt to suspect that Mr. T[homso]n was a Scot, for the Scots killed most of their Kings; and Captain Porteous was a pretty Fellow in his Time": I daresay

---

[148] Faulkner's note in Jonathan Swift, *The Works of Jonathan Swift*, ed. Deane Swift (Dublin, 1762), iii n.
[149] J. Clark, *Samuel Johnson*, 159-60.
[150] *Ibid.*, 168.
[151] *Hyp-Doctor*, #447 (5 June 1739).

another Dunblain Battle will be loyally fought by one brave and honest Commander, – myself, I mean: – a second Preston may answer Edward the Second..." He got in a final blow at Brooke by pointing out that the historical Gustavus Vasa was originally a Papist.

On 31 May-2 June the *London Evening Post* reported the burial of Dr. James Anderson, whose Pall was supported by five dissenting teachers and Dr. Desaguliers: "It was fol-low'd by about a Dozen of Free Masons, who encircled the Grave...the Brethen, in a most solemn dismal Posture, lifted up their Hands, sigh'd and struck their Aprons three Times in Honour to the Deceased."[152] On 3 July Henley praised the late James Anderson, author of the Grand Lodge *Constitutions*, in "A Supplement to Dr. Anderson's Genealo-gies, containing a new and true Account of the Pedigree of the Opposition," with an epigraph, "Etcaetera, the elder, begat Etcaetera the Younger," from Swift's *Tale of a Tub*.[153] Henley praised "the ingenious, facetious Dr. Anderson, lately deceased," for trac-ing "the Pedigrees of all the great Families of the World," which proves that Opposition leads to the earth bringing forth Thistles, "a Prophecy about Scotland," and the "Seces-sion of the North." He quoted "our Poet, Cleveland," though his verse is trite, for writ-ing, "Had Cain been Scot, God would have changed his Doom/ Not sent him to wander, but confined to Home," because "It is well known that all People in Scotland are willing to run away from it." Moreover, "the History of hanging Captain Porteous perfectly agrees with Cain's rising slily against Abel and killing him. And Porteous was a Brother of the same Country."

The opposition to Walpole was becoming so strong that the wily Prime Minister made secret overtures to James III, as a kind of insurance policy against possible dismissal by the king. In late summer 1739 he sent Mr. Avery, a London merchant and supposed Jacobite, to Calais with a message for Thomas Carte that he was to take to Rome, but Carte was to say nothing that would bring Walpole in danger of the law.[154] Since 1733 Avery had carried letters between Ramsay and Carte, and they had no reason to suspect him of deception.[155] On 11 September Carte left Paris and travelled to London, where Avery informed Walpole of the Jacobite's arrival. When they met secretly, Walpole said that he believed Carte was "averse to the shedding of blood, abundance of which must be spilt in an invasion" and that he "was zealous for the Protestant religion." Carte rec-orded, "I never was so surprised in all my life...or indeed in so much confusion...at the hearing such an unexpected proposal." He feared that he was betrayed and "all that had passed was an artifice to trepan me into England and into the power of the government." Walpole warned that the warrant against me could still be used and two witnesses would swear that "I knew there were ten thousand armes concealed and ready to use in an insurrection." It was no coincidence that Lord Egmont recorded on 13 September, "I heard that in...Carte's papers when seized were found some notices of arms disposed of in England.[156]

---

152 R. Péter, *British Freemasonry*, V, 26.

153 *Hyp-Doctor*, #451 (3 July 1739).

154 British Library: Add. MSS. 34, 522: Mackintosh Collections, vol. 36, ff. 1-14. Thomas Carte, "Journal of My Journey into England in September 1739, until 23 October."

155 Bodleian. Carte MS. 227, ff. 163-64.

156 *HMC.MSS. of Earl of Egmont* (London, 1923), III, 33.

Walpole continued that Carte "was linked with an ungrateful party [which] never served its friends but cut them in pieces." He offered Carte a large bribe, which only he and George II would know about, "not even Avery himself to whom he gave small sums from time to time." He then asked Carte why he had come over, and Carte replied that Avery said you had sent for me and I could return with safety. He then asked why Carte went to Rome, and got the reply "to see and evaluate James." He asked if James would consent for the princes to be educated as Protestants. Then he queried how Bolingbroke and his friends stood with James, and Carte answered, "in the worst light, because James objected to their treatment of his ancestors in the *Dissertation on Parties* and in the *Craftsman*. Moreover, James considered that set of people his inveterate enemies, which seemed to please Walpole. At their next meeting, Carte gave Walpole a message from James about restoring him, noting that the long-time Whig could make his own name as great as General Monk.

During their conversations, Walpole also revealed that he was aware of the role of the Order of Toboso, and he tried to glean information from the uneasy Carte on the quasi-Masonic society. He told him of "a new health or manner of drinking used by gentlemen, among which Corbet Kynaston was one and it was by putting a ring into the glass." Carte lied and said it was new to him but conceded that the ring may be of the Knights of Toboso, which has the inscription to "a Fair Meeting on the Green"; but "not having the honour to be of that Order, nor having been ever at the said ceremony of drinking," he knew nothing more about it. At their final meeting, Walpole denied that he gave Avery this mission and only wanted to win Carte over to his party: "who should I employ else, how can I learn the Jacobite designs but from the Jacobites themselves," all said with great merriment and humor. When a shaken Carte reported this bizarre encounter to James, the king praised him for his effort and made clear that he had never and would never trust Walpole.

In September 1739 Swift enjoyed the company of Robert Nugent, Earl Nugent, an Irish poet and politician who lived much of the year in London and could inform him about the activities of the opposition Masons.[157] As noted earlier, Nugent came from an old Irish Catholic family but converted to Anglicanism and then served as Deputy Grand Warden of the Grand Lodge of Ireland. He "worked relentlessly for the advancement of the Masonic order" in Ireland and continued his work with opposition Masons in England.[158] He became a good friend of Pope, who frequently visited him at Gosfield, where he supervised the expansion and reconstruction of the great house. Using his poetry as a propaganda vehicle for the Patriot party, he published eulogies to its leaders. In *Political Justice* (London, 1736), dedicated to Lord Cornbury, he praised him as one of the "chosen Few," who "with gen'rous Warmth your Country's good pursue."[159] Perhaps aware of Cornbury's former Jacobitism and subsequent disillusionment with the Stuarts' cause, he seemed to worry that the independent-minded M.P. might desert the opposition cause. Thus, he warned him about the "slipp'ry Paths" and temptations that lead the best of men into corruption.

---

[157] Claud Nugent, *Memoir of Robert Nugent, Earl Nugent* (Chicago and New York, 1898), 242; J. Swift, *Correspondence*, IV, 463, 614.

[158] L. Conlon, "Freemasonry in Meath and Westmeath"<meath.org./lodge/lodge_131.html.>

[159] Robert Nugent, *Political Justice* (London, 1736), 3-4, 22.

In 1739, among his eulogies to the Prince of Wales, Cobham, and other Patriots, his 'Ode to William Pulteney" included the rationale behind his conversion from Irish Catholicism to the Church of England, which made his poem a popular success among the Anglo-Irish elite and in England:

> Remote from Liberty and Truth,
> By Fortune's Crime, my early Youth
> Drank Error's poison'd Spring.
> Taught by dark Creeds and Mystic Law,
> Wrapt up in reverential Awe,
> I bow'd to Priests and Kings.[160]

With the help of Hooker, Locke, Sidney, More, and Harrington, he was able to break free from Rome, and turn his attention to fighting Walpolean evil.

One of his oddest poems was his anonymous *Epistle to the Right Honourable, Sir Robert Walpole* (London, 1739), in which he attempted to convince the prime minister to resign in the name of healthy change, with of course the Patriot hero Cobham waiting in the wings to take over when Walpole happily retires into blissful calm.[161] He had dedicated *An Essay on Happiness* (London, 1738) to Chesterfield, whom he praised for enjoying the loss of courtly favor, for in "glorious Exile" he can cheerfully rove, "And, far from Courts, fresh bloom in Cobham's Grove," while "Too mean the Wealth, the Smiles, the Crowns of Kings."[162] Faulkner reprinted the poem in Dublin, and Swift was obviously familiar with it. On 20 September 1739 Chesterfield wrote to Nugent, who had urged him to visit Ireland, that he was tempted, especially because "I hear you are often with the Dean of St. Patrick's, which I am glad for both of your sakes, and wish for my own that I could make a third."[163]

In October, despite Walpole's reluctance, England declared war on Spain, and Jacobite hopes soared that the kingdom's increasing vulnerability opened the door for their more aggressive initiatives. From their posts in Paris and Stockholm, the *Écossais* Masons Tessin and Scheffer pressured Spain to fund a contingent of Swedish troops to support a Jacobite invasion.[164] As word of Jacobite-Masonic plotting reached the government in England, Henley in November renewed his attacks on Samuel Johnson's *London* and on Richard Glover's opposition play, *Leonidas*. On 4 December Henley announced the he would present "The Utopians, or No-Place but give Place, Being a Scheme for an excellent new Droll."[165] In one scene, he will "exhibit an old House of C-----s [Commons] falling, and the People seceding, in fear of a new Scrue-plot, then let a new House rise, like Milton's Pandemonium, and none sit there but Patriots and Free-masons."

Though Henley and Walpole may have worried about the opposition Masons among Prince Frederick's party, loyalist Grand Lodge Masonry was in increasingly sad shape. In 1739 Robert Raymond, 2nd Lord Raymond, was elected Grand Master. Two years earlier,

---

[160] Robert Nugent, *Odes and Epistles* (London, 1739), 5-7.

[161] [Robert Nugent], *An Epistle to the Right Honourable, Sir Robert Walpole* (London, 1739), 9.

[162] Robert Nugent, *An Essay on Happiness* (London; Dublin: Re-printed by George Faulkner, 1738), 16.

[163] C. Nugent, *Memoir*, 242.

[164] Tessin became Swedish ambassador in Paris in July 1739; he became a confidant of Louis XV. For details on Swedish-Spanish negotiations, see M. Schuchard, *Emanuel Swedenborg*, 275-80, 286.

[165] *Hyp-Doctor*, #474 (4 December 1739).

the twenty-two year-old Raymond had been the boon companion of Lord Middlesex in Florence, where he was an active member of the lodge. In August 1737 he witnessed the murder in a drunken brawl of Stosch's colleague Denys Wright, the anti-Jacobite spy, by John Fotheringham, a visiting Scot.[166] Though the quarrel erupted over a card game, there may have been a political context, for Fotheringham's family "was predominantly Jacobite at this time."[167] His father was exiled after the 1745 rebellion and died in Rome, and John later lived at Saint- Germain with a fellow-resident, the widow of Chevalier Ramsay.[168] Reports about the drunken fracas "were more or less suppressed in London," but Raymond's continuing Masonic activities and reputation as a deist and un-believer aroused the ire of Cardinal Corsini, who on 16 April 1739 asked the Grand Duke of Tuscany, Francis of Lorraine, to expel Raymond and Stosch from Florence.[169]

Despite the Papal Bull, Corsini still feared the Whiggish, free-thinking Masons and urged the duke to arrest a few in order to root out members of the sect. Ambassador Mann was able to forestall Stosch's expulsion, and Duke Francis wrote to Newcastle, his fellow Mason, to apologize for his action against Stosch. By 3 May Raymond was back in England, where he was immediately elected Grand Master and staunchly supported the Walpolean ministry. During his tenure, many disaffected lodges rejected affiliation with the Grand Lodge, and the loyalist officials determined to exclude "irregular" Masons from their meetings. Small changes were made in the wording of certain rituals, in order "to detect these imposters."[170] Many Masonic historians view this "momentous period" as the beginning of the split ("schism") that eventually led to the development of the independent "Antients" system, which ran counter to the "Modern" Grand Lodge system.[171]

On 27 December 1739, "A.Z" wrote from Edinburgh to *The Gentleman's Magazine*, with a dire diagnosis for the English Masons: "Free Masonry, now little regarded in your Metropolis, like a worn-out Fashion, is now become the Vogue here: I desire, therefore, you will, for the Sake of your North British readers, insert the following true account of the Antiquity and Institution of Free Masons."[172] A.Z. then described the actions of operative Masons in Edward III's and Henry VI's times, when they banded together to protect their secrets and their wages. He sarcastically says that "from such a reputable Beginning has this worthy Fraternity derived their boasted Glories," and this is why they keep the secret, "since at first their Necks were in danger by the discovering it." Moreover,

> From the like infamous origin commenced those pernicious Names of Distinction, *Whig and Tory*, which we have heard gloried in, tho' at first the Nicknames of enemies, and Terms extremely opprobrious; the first signifying, from the supposed narrow Principles, and crude and indigested Notions of

---

[166] "Raymond, 2nd Lord," J. Ingamells; P. Tunbridge, "Climate," 95.
[167] H. Walpole, *Correspondence*, XXXVII. 33-34/
[168] Edward Corp, "The Scottish Community at Saint-Germain after the Departure of the Stuart Court," in A. Macinnes, *Living with Jacobitism*, 36.
[169] F. Benimeli, *Masoneria*, II, 17, 240-41.
[170] *Pennsylvania Gazetteer*, #458 (7-14 June 1739).
[171] See R. Berman, *Schism*, 4-6.
[172] *Gentleman's Magazine*, 10 (January 1740), 17-18.

the Field Conventicles in Scotland, Sour Milk; the last, Irish Repparees and Robbers.

Then, in an apparent recognition of the mystical, chivalric "high degrees" being developed by Jacobite masons abroad, A.Z. pointed to rites that strongly diverged from the basic craft degrees of the English Grand Lodge:

> It must be confessed, that there is a Society abroad, from the English Free-Masons (ashamed of their true origin, as above) have copied a few Ceremonies, and taken great Pains to persuade the World that they are derived from them, and are the same with them: These are call'd *Rosecrusians*, from their Prime Officers (such as our Brethren call Grand Master, Wardens, etc.) being distinguished on their High Days with red crosses… they affect to be thought of as a mystical Society, and promote cheerfully one another's Benefit in a very extraordinary Manner, they meeting for better Purposes than Eating…

One wonders what Samuel Johnson thought of this odd missive as he worked on *The Gentleman's Magazine*, though it is clear that Orator Henley would happily believe that it was a response to his "excellent new Droll" in *The Hyp-Doctor* three weeks earlier. As the turbulent year of 1739 ended, the Orator would turn his wrath on the Jacobite Masons abroad (and in Ireland and Scotland), who threatened to bring down the Hanoverians' "House of Commons" and fill it with "nothing but Patriots and Free-masons" – a linkage which increasingly operated outside of the official Grand Lodge of England.

CHAPTER EIGHTEEN

MASONIC CABALISTS AND THE OPPOSITION CABAL
(1740-1742)

> The Jewish Cabalists had a great Veneration for the Mysteries supposed to be contained in certain numbers… Our Heroes and Demi-gods of the Patriot Set… are… for turning out and turning in, they are doing this Cabalistically, by a Numerical Cabala, or, as the English has it, Cabal: To augment the Number of the Minority, and dislike a Majority anywhere, but of their own Making.
>
> Orator Henley, *The Hyp-Doctor* (8 April 1740).

> The re-establishment of King Charles II had first been spoken and decided in a conference of Freemasons because General Monk had been a member and able to bring it to fruition without incurring the least suspicion about his secret plot.
>
> Chevalier Ramsay to Herr von Geusau (Paris, 1741).

While the Keith brothers were in France, they were in touch with Chevalier Ramsay, who was kept informed about James Keith's provocative visit to London in January 1740.[1] James was sent by the Czarina on an espionage mission to determine England's attitude toward the expected rupture between Russia and Sweden.[2] Throughout his brother's visit, Marischal corresponded with the Stuart court about his activities in London. On 15 January he wrote to the Pretender about James's meeting with the Duke of Argyll, whose collaboration with the opposition made him seem susceptible to Jacobite recruitment:

> Mr Keith did what he could for your Service, he had more civility from the Duke of Argyle than from any one, but Argyle never would give him any encouragement to converse of your Majesty's affairs; they were together

---

[1] Stuart Papers: 222/13 (21 May 1740).
[2] R. Wills, *Jacobites*, 158-61.

when Argyle got a message which vexed him, he said on reading it, Mr Keith, fall flat, fall edge, we must get rid of these people, which might imply both man and master, or only the man. However, Mr Keith resolved on this to speak freely to him…[3]

According to Ramsay, who wrote to Edgar about it, James Keith continued to talk with Argyll over the next months.[4]

On 25 January General Keith, splendidly attired in his Russian officer's uniform, was introduced to George II by the Russian ambassador Scherbatov. He was accompanied by his cousin, the Earl of Kintore, recent Grand Master of Scottish Freemasonry. The press reported that he was welcomed politely by the king, who had lately expressed his hostility to the Jacobite rebel. He was also "caressed by the principal nobility," including James Erskine, Lord Grange, who had corresponded with Keith and continued to support his petition.[5] Grange was currently communicating with the Pretender on a restoration plan negotiated by his intimate friend and Masonic brother, William Macgregor of Balhaldy.[6] On 2 February Marischal received a commission from James as commander-in-chief of all the Jacobite forces in Scotland during the planned rising. When Walpole's intelligencers reported that Marischal had left for Spain on a Jacobite mission, he complained," Is Mr Keith come to plague us with his damned [inheritance] bill while his brother is going into Galicia against us?"

The Franco-Swedish overture to Spain was to solicit funding for Swedish troops to join the Jacobites in an invasion, with the Stuart princes sailing from Spain to Ireland for an invasion from the west and with Swedish help coming from the east. Within this context, General Keith's attendance at a Masonic meeting in London on 24 March, when his cousin Kintore was installed as Grand Master of the Grand Lodge of England, was fraught with political significance.[7] Though Keith had long been associated with the Order of Toboso and *Écossais* Masonry in Russia, Kintore now linked him with the "regular" or English Grand Lodge system by naming him Provincial Grand master for Russia. Another Scottish Mason, the artist Allan Ramsay, painted Keith's portrait while he was in London. As noted earlier, Ramsay was introduced to James III and Charles Edward in Rome, where he joined the Jacobite lodge in January 1737.

While in England, James Keith met with Dr. King, and discussed his brother George's situation. In March 1740 King anonymously published *Scanmum, Ecloga* (The Bench, an Eclogue), a Latin political satire, dedicated to "the Illustrious G.K.M.S." In 1741 the English translator identified him as "George Keith, Marshal of Scotland, General to the Czarina."[8] This seems to be a conflation of the brothers, for James was the Russian general and George was the Marshal. In a letter to Orrery on 25 March, King made clear that he meant George Keith and praised the "Marischal of Scotland" for doing so much

---

[3] *Ibid.*, 160.

[4] Stuart Papers: 222/13 (21 May 1740).

[5] *The Scots Magazine* (1740), 43; *The London Magazine and Monthly Chronologer* (1740), 48.

[6] R. Sedgwick, *History*, II, 16.

[7] N. Paton, *Jacobites*, 38; R. Robelin, "Johannis-Maurerei," 45.

[8] William King, *The Bench. An Eclogue. Occasion's by the War between England and Spain* (London, 1741), Dedication.

honour to himself and his country "in the greatest courts of Europe."[9] He explained that in his panegyric and satire, "I have drawn my characters by my personal knowledge of the men, their virtues and vices." He assumed that Orrery would not mind his name appearing in the same work with Marischal's. However, "the Ministers of the Post-Office…have ever had an evil eye to my epistolary correspondence and for the last month my letters have all been opened; he added disingenuously, "Yet I never deal in politicks."

King promised to praise Orrery by name in a second edition, which did not appear, and then allowed Josiah Graham to point to him in a note to the English translation: "Earl O*****, in whom (when he retires to his distant Seat) what a Friend do I lose! What a Loss to the Publick!" After praising Orrery, the character "Tityrus" laments the state of England and expresses "barely disguised hopes…for a golden age under the restored House of Stuart."[10] King defended himself against charges of obscurity by noting that if he identified his Latin-named characters, he and his poem might be "banished to a most distant Island of the West" (i.e. Ireland). He defiantly boasted that he valued George Keith's approbation more than the denunciation of his critics – "Court-Prelates, who have nothing Holy but their Denomination, and Orators of the HALL, who have nothing of the Place but the Impudence; who sitting in Judgment-Seats, or supported by the Great, surely despise my Bench." Worried about the continued interception of his letters, King informed Orrery that he would use the Irish Jacobite Henry Leslie as a courier to his Irish correspondents.[11]

With Dr. King praising a Scottish rebel and fearing exile to Ireland, and with Orrery actually moving to the "western island," Orator Henley launched new attacks on Scotland and Ireland – especially targeting the Tory and Jacobite Masons who collaborated with opposition Whigs. On 29 January he charged that "Swift has coalesced with Pope, a Protestant and a Popish Rabbet, and often imports from Dublin a Remnant of Irish Manufacture, to mend and patch the Old Suit of the Patriot Cause."[12] On 19 February he lambasted the hypocrisy of the Patriots' calling for war with Spain, for earlier Spain, Russia, and Sweden collaborated with the Pretender: "The Duke of Ormonde and the Duke of Wharton, had a Commission, and one of them a Garter, from the Pretender, to pursue this Attempt. This is a Matter of Fact, and let them gloss or grin it away, as they please, this Opposition is not Whiggish, but carry'd on by Under-Tools of the Pretender."[13]

One import from Dublin was Swift's friend Robert Nugent, who shared Pope's distress over the loss of two Scottish Masonic allies, one by death and another by political change. In February 1739 the 2nd Lord Marchmont died, and his son Hugh Hume, Lord Polwarth, succeeded him as the 3rd Earl of Marchmont. Unfortunately for the opposition, his elevation nullified any political role that he could play in parliament. In March Nugent sent Pope an "Ode to Lord Marchmont," in which he expressed his concern for Hugh's political frustration. The editors Croker and Elwin explain that "as a Scotch peer he was disqualified from remaining in the House of Commons, and, not being elected a Scotch

---

[9] Bodleian: MS. Eng. Hist.d.103, f. 11.
[10] D. Greenwood, *William King*, 113-14.
[11] Bodleian: MS. Eng. Hist. d.103 (13).
[12] *Hyp-Doctor*, #482 (29 January 1740).
[13] *Ibid.*, #485 (19 February 1740).

representative peer, he had no seat in the House of Lords."[14] Nugent's ode is "a commemoration of the wonders he performed in the lower house, and an entreaty that his exclusion from Parliament would not induce him to retire from "his sinking country's cause." On 26 March Pope replied and thanked Nugent for his "Ode to Lord Marchmont," which he considered worthy of the celebrated Greek lyric poet Alcaeus. Christine Gerrard argues that Pope was so infatuated with the thirty-two year-old Marchmont that he overvalued not only the Scot's political skill but Nugent's poetical talent.[15] Bolingbroke shared Pope's high opinion, and he lamented "Marchmont disabled!" and then hosted him in France in April and May.

This "disabling" of the disaffected Scot was grist to the propaganda mill of Orator Henley, who intensified his attacks upon the opposition. On 8 April, in an especially convoluted argument, he accused the opposition of employing Cabalistic techniques to augment their followers and ultimately bring in the Pretender:

> I have met with a learned Book, called, the *Cabala*, or *Secrets of State*, The Word is originally Hebrew, and means peculiar Doctrines delivered to one another by Tradition; The Jewish Cabalists had a great Veneration for the Mysteries supposed to be contained in certain Numbers... Our Heroes and Demi-gods of the Patriot Set...are...for turning out and turning in, they are for doing this Cabalistically, by a numerical Cabala, or, as the English has it, Cabal: To Augment the Number of the Minority, and dislike a Majority anywhere, but of their own Making... these Cabalists are as profound in Physiognomy, as in Numbers, and can count Noses... Six appears to represent the Coalition, which is reducing at least half a dozen Parties to an Unit, and that, perhaps to a Cypher: Non-jurors, Republicans, Tories, Old Whigs, Court Whigs and Testy Dissenters' add a seventh string to this Melody of the Political Spheres, and it will shew a new Scotch Lilt, for the Saints beyond Jordan and Tweed, to join their geud Brethren on this side Berwick: all which seven Notes will make the Octave the same still – To the tune of, *the King* shall enjoy his own again...[16]

He then made a direct linkage between the Patriot coalition and the opposition Masons, which included a jab at Desaguliers and the implication that Bolingbroke was an initiate:

> I cannot help observing that he who moved for the Six is reported to have lately been initiated in the Mysteries of the Free-masons, who belong to the Holy Lodge of St. John: Not St. John the Evangelist or Divine, but another St. John of the modern Calendar, who was once banished to Patmos, and is now waiting, till his Change come: Dr. D----s [Desaguliers] and the other Heads of the Masons are of his Opinion.

A frustrated Bolingbroke had returned to France in April 1739, but Henley had a bigger target closer to home, the Duke of Argyll, who had opposed not only Walpole but

---

[14] Alexander Pope, *The Works of Alexander Pope, New Edition*, ed. John Wilson Croker and Whitwell Elwin (London, 1871), VII, 378.

[15] C. Gerrard, *Patriot Opposition*, 38, 90-91.

[16] *Hyp-Doctor*, #493 (8 April 1740).

his own brother Ilay in the wake of the Porteous affair. Throughout 1740 Henley mocked the hypocrisy of Argyll and linked him with the increasing rebelliousness in Scotland. On 3 January 1740 he referred to an opposition pamphlet, *The D--- of A---e's Letter to the Right Honourable Sir----- ------, upon the Present Intended Expeditions* (London, 1740), in which the duke argued that Walpole's ministry was the enemy of the people; he "saps the Foundations of their Liberties, makes them Slaves imperceptibly, till with their own Substance, he bribes them to betray each other."[17] On 30 April Argyll resigned all his appointments under the government, and he subsequently returned to Edinburgh, where he received a rapturous welcome.

His Masonic supporter Charles Leslie anonymously published *Mum. A Political Ballad, for the Present Times: With Annotations Political, Critical, and Historical* (Edinburgh, 1740), in which he satirized the Walpolean government's punishment of Scotland in the wake of the Porteous affair:

> The Porteous-Act is too recent to be forgot yet in this Country; and every Article was so, weighty, that we may well remember it a great While to come. I am told we are, in great Measure, obliged for it to his Lordship of Islay and our present worthy Member; and that they designed to have done still more to us, had not Argyle very officiously interposed, and baulked their good Intentions...[18]

Leslie's attack on Lord Ilay and praise of his brother Argyll were followed by an insulting portrait of Walpole as "some overgrown *Norfolk* Scoundrel, some fat pilfering attorney, who...goes about plundering us of the Fruits of our Labour," which entitles him "to build magnificent Palaces and Villas; to fill them, tho' without Taste himself, with the finest Pictures and most curious Works of Art or Nature."[19] His "pilfering" of the citizenry, allows him "to support at once the Extravagance of a Wife, and the unsatiable Avarice of a Whore."

Some months later, Leslie delivered a discourse, *A Vindication of Masonry*, to the Lodge of Vernon Kilwinning, in which he was identified as a Master of Arts and a Master Mason. Given the weakened state of English Grand Lodge Masonry and the political divisions within Scottish Masonry, he urged his Scottish brethren to remember the traditional, ecumenical, and apolitical role within the global fraternity:

> Masonry flourishes...and by those secret and invisible signs which we preserve amongst our selves, and which are one and the same throughout the world, MASONRY becomes an universal language...We unite men of all religions and of all nations. Thus, the distant Chinese can embrace a brother Briton, thus they come to know that besides the common ties of humanity, there is a stronger still to engage them to friendly and kind actions; thus the spirit of the *damning priests* may be tamed, and a moral brother, tho of a different religion, engage his friendship.[20]

---

[17] Duke of Argyll, *The D--- of A----e's Letter to the Right Honourable Sir----- ------* (London, 1740), 10, 16, 29.
[18] [Charles Leslie], *Mum. A Political Ballad for the Present Times* (Edinburgh: 1740), 17-18.
[19] *Ibid.* 20.
[20] Reprinted in John Entick, *The Freemason's Pocket Companion* (Edinburgh, 1765), 158

Meanwhile in Ireland, Orrery was delighted at the honors heaped on Argyll, writing that "I am proud to see so great a Man as independent as myself."[21] For Henley the powerful Scotsman's apostasy from Walpole called for all-out attack. A supporter of Argyll anonymously published *The Conduct of His Grace the D-ke of Ar – le for the Four Last Years Review'd. Together with His Grace's Speech April 15th 1740. Upon the State of the Nation* (London, 1740). Henley identified the author as James Ralph, who collaborated with Henry Fielding in anti-Walpole writings in the journal, *The Champion*. In *The Hyp-Doctor* (3 June 1740), he published "One Epistle to Ralpho, the gentle Squire of the Scotch Hudibras," in which he mocked the author's praise of Argyll's opposition to the penalties imposed in the wake of the Porteous rioters."[22]

On 22 July Henley referred to Desaguliers, now an opposition Mason, and Arbuthnot, the late Jacobite Mason, to bolster his scatter-shot argument against Argyll and Scotland As he mocked the traditional notion of the Scots as God's covenanted people, he promised to compose "a Bag-pipe Opera":

> Dr Desaguliers might give an ingenious Explanation of this Procedure in a Course of Pneumatics, or Wind-Experiments… Dr Arbuthnot, a Scotch Wit, wrote several Craftsmen… Scotland is said to be the Back-side of the Nation, by its fundamental Union, and the Bag of Whustles may cause a Fistula in Ano…Both Kirk and Pope pretend to a Power over the Civil Magistrate…No People have been more rebellious than the Inhabitants of North Britain.[23]

A week later, he declared that "Scotland's refusing the Hanover Succession [in 1703] was rather worse than the Affair of Captain Porteous."[24]

The death of William Wyndham on 17 June greatly depressed Pope, Bolingbroke, and Marchmont, who were increasingly disillusioned by the self-seeking and hypocrisy of many so-called "Patriots." Over the next weeks, Pope drafted but did not finish a bitter poem, "1740," in which he castigated many former allies and friends, who now contributed to the further decline of the nation. The names were left blank but supplied by nineteenth-century editors:

> O Wretched B------[Britain]! Jealous now of all,
> What God, what mortal, shall prevent thy fall?
> Turn, turn thy eyes from wicked men in place,
> And see what succor from the patriot race.
> C-------[Carteret], his own proud dupe, thinks monarchs things
> Made just for him, as other fools for kings;
> Controls, decides, insults thee every hour,
> And antedates the hatred due to pow'r.[25]

---

[21] Harvard. Houghton: Eng.MS.218,2, vol. 4 (14 May 1740).
[22] *Hyp-Doctor*, #501 (3 January 1740).
[23] *Ibid.*, #508 (22 July 1740).
[24] *Ibid.*, #508 (29 July 1740).
[25] A. Pope, *Works*, ed. Croker and Courthope, III, 495.

Even "Good C-------[Cornbury]" just "hopes, and candidly sits," while Gower, Cobham, and Bathurst "pay thee due regards,/ Unless the ladies bid them mind their cards."[26] And Chesterfield's wit finds Britain just "at best, the butt to crack his joke on." In the meantime, "Hervey and Hervey's school," includes Fox, Hinton, and Henley (all officious Hanoverian Masons). With the death of "Good M--------[Marchmont]," which "tore P------[Polwarth] from thy side," the last sigh was heard, "when W--------[Wyndham] died."

Though disgusted with the fecklessness of the opposition, Pope rejected militaristic Jacobitism: "To purge and let thee blood, with fire and sword,/ Is all the help stern S------[Shippen] would afford." However, in concluding, he left ambiguous the identity of the ideal king who could save the sinking ship of state:

> Alas! on one alone our all relies,
> Let him be honest, and he must be wise;
> ……………………………………………..
> Be but a man! Unminister'd, alone,
> And free at once senate and the throne;
> Esteem the public love his best supply,
> A [astrological symbol for king]'s true glory his integrity;
> ……………………………………………
> Whatever his religion or his blood,
> His public virtue makes his title good.
> Europe's just balance and our own may stand,
> And one man's honesty redeem the land.[27]

The editors note that Pope could have meant Frederick, Prince of Wales, or more likely James Stuart: "It is evident that he meant an heir apparent, and 'whatever his religion or his blood,' would equally suit either the heir *de facto* or *de jure*." The unfinished manuscript was in the custody of Bolingbroke and Marchmont but ended up in Trinity College, Dublin, where the librarian who discovered it noted: "This poem I transcribed from a rough draft in Pope's own hand. He left many blanks for fear of the Argus eye of those who, if they cannot find, fabricate treason; yet spite of caution it fell into the hands of his enemies." Given the contacts of several of Pope's confidants with agents of James III at this time, he may well have looked toward a Stuart restoration as the last best hope for the corrupted nation. Pat Rogers's analysis of the alchemical and astrological symbols used by Pope as "hieroglyphics" in the manuscript ironically supports the charge by Orator Henley that the opposition utilized "Cabalistic" coding to hide their seditious messages.[28]

The second "Pretender" to the throne, Prince Frederick, was delighted by Argyll's withdrawal from the government, and he determined to employ him in a proposed coalition ministry. To bolster the opposition cause in July, the prince commissioned his fellow Mason James Thomson and David Mallet, both Scots, to compose a patriotic masque, *Alfred*, which was performed before the prince and his wife at Clifden on 1 August 1740. A dispossessed and wandering King Alfred is welcomed by a pious hermit,

---

[26] *Ibid.*, 496-500.

[27] *Ibid.*, 501.

[28] Pat Rogers, "The Symbols in Pope's One Thousand Seven Hundred and Forty," *Modern Philology*, 102 (2004), 90-94.

who recounts a dream-vision of the future, in which "guardian laws/ Are by the patriot, in the glowing senate,/ Won from corruption."[29] He assures the depressed Alfred about "the noble uses of affliction" (a theme often used by Jacobites in reference to the exiled James III). Alfred vows "To be the common father of my people/ Patron of honor, virtue and religion," in order to "raise our drooping *English name.*" He will heal "the divisions of her people," by saving "from the vermin of a court,/ Her treasure." Countering the government propagandists' charge that the Prince of Wales was surrounded and manipulated by Jacobites, the authors called up the "Spirit of William III, who saved Britain from ruin by James II, who was "the slave of dreaming monks."[30] Fortunately, "immortal William" responded to the desperate call from Albion, and defeated superstition and oppressive power – a feat that Alfred will repeat in the future.

Frederick determined to consolidate the gains he made from Argyll's action, and he flattered and solicited support from disaffected Scots, many of whom were Freemasons. On 13 September 1740 a satirical print, "design'd by several great Masters from the Original Plan laid down by the Champion" (i.e., Ralph and Fielding), was published and soon became a sensation. Titled "The State Pack-Horse," it showed Walpole preparing sackfuls of money, titles, and petitions to be carried by horseback to Edinburgh, where Argyll was waiting to refuse the bribes that other servile, loyalist Scots were eager to receive.[31] Countering the many emblems of corruption versus integrity was a quotation from Pope: "Argyll! A nation's Thunder born to Wield/ And Shake alike the Senate and the field."

The print, plus *The Champion's* recent anti-government writings, angered Walpole enough to pressure Fielding to change political sides in return for a sizeable pension. On 4 October Fielding (posing as "Captain Hercules Vinegar") published a provocative dialogue, in which "R.F." (Walpole) asks "H.V":

> WHAT is the Reason, Sir, that you write against me? Prithee, what dost mean by those cant Words of *Virtue* and *Publick Spirit?* Do'st think they will go to Market? Kiss my A--- I would not give a Fart for all the virtue in the Universe.
>
> They tell me you have some Wit and Humour, and have you no more Sense than to starve with them? To write on the Side of a Set of Rascals and sturdy [Beggars] D-mn them, I'll shew them who I am.
>
> If you will not come over and say some good Things of me, stay at Home and be quiet and neuter, and I'll give you a hundred Pills
>
> But if you will say a *single Word* in my Favour, I will give you two hundred Pills.[32]

Fielding went on to admit that he had taken money from Walpole in the past "to stop the Publication of a Book, which I had written against his Practice." Within two months, Fielding would indeed sell out to Walpole and become a pro-government propagandist, who would eventually mount blistering attacks upon Catholics, Jacobites, and their Masonic brothers.

---

[29] [James Thomson and David Mallet], *Alfred: A Masque* (London, 1740), 17-19, 25.

[30] *Ibid.*, 27.

[31] *Catalogue of Prints and Drawings in the British Museum*, ed. F.G. Stephens and E. Hawkins (London, 1877), III, part 1, pp.293-96.

[32] J. Downie, *Political Biography*, 100-01.

In the meantime, the Keith brothers were not sure where Argyll actually stood, as the arrogant and stubborn aristocrat thundered against Walpole. James Keith was not impressed by the cobbled-together opposition, and he wrote his brother from London: "as to the country here, I never was in one I like less…everything is in confusion, the one side crying out against arbitrary power; the other crying out that it is their mutinous proceedings which oblige them to act so."[33] Marischal sent to the Pretender his brother's account of his visit to George II's court, and James then urged General Keith to leave the Empress's service and enter more actively into his own. But Marischal and Ormonde reported the depressing news that the Spanish-Swedish project had fallen through, and James Keith returned to Russia, where the Empress promoted him to high military position and named him governor of Ukraine. He was welcomed by the Freemasons, who praised him in song as the successor to Peter the Great, traditional founder of the fraternity in Russia:

> Then Keith, enlightened, came to the Russian Empire
> And lit for us the sacred fire
> A Temple of Wisdom he erected, and its spark
> Showed Virtue, Brotherhood to Masons, still in dark.
> He was an image of the Sun whose rise so bright,
> Is message of the shining dawn of the Queen of Light.[34]

With Sweden threatening war against Russia, General Keith would soon be placed in a difficult situation, for many Swedish Jacobites and Masons considered him their ally and hoped to transfer his allegiance from Russia to their cause.

In France and Italy the Jacobite Masons shared the uncertainty about Argyll's agenda, as they watched the political turbulence in England for signs of their opportunity. In the meantime, they developed rituals that emphasized chivalric and mystical themes, designed to spiritually inspire and fraternally bond their initiated "knights" for the planned crusade against the "Elector of Hanover." In September 1739 Joseph Spence, in route to Italy, visited Ramsay in Paris, and their conversations increased Spence's interest in the esoteric themes of Freemasonry. On 13 April 1740 he wrote from Turin that Dr. Thomas Shaw, who travelled in Egypt, believed that "the freemasons in the heathen religion kept their secrets" in an inner chamber in the great pyramid.[35] On 22 June Spence wrote about the mysterious inscriptions found among heathen artifacts and even today in Italy:

> Among the heathens there were several companies of people, something like our freemasons at present. They kept several secrets, with inviolable secrecy, for several hundreds of years… These secrets were chiefly of a religious nature, and 'tis said that in those societies they laughed at idols and gave up all the heathen deities as false ones. 'Twas the great maxim in all those lodges

---

[33] R. Wills, *Jacobites*, 162.

[34] Boris Telepneff, note to H. Poole, "Masonic Song and Verse of the Eighteenth Century," *AQC*, 40 (1928), 28; for another song, see Atina L.K. Nihtinen, "Field-Marsha James Keith: Governor of the Ukraine and Finland, 1740-1743," in *Military Governors and Imperial Frontiers c. 1600-1800: A Study of Scotland and Empires*, ed. A. Mackillop and Steve Murdoch (Leiden, 2003), 104.

[35] J. Spence, *Letters*, 269.

that there were three great gods that governed the whole universe, and that these three were of one and the same mind...[36]

The editor Slava Kliwa notes that Spence seemed to hint "at secret information derived from Masonic sources," and his interest in the ancient mysteries was no doubt influenced by Ramsay's "semi-deistic" Masonic views of the Trinity.[37]

Ramsay may also have influenced Spence's interest in the Hermetic and Rosicrucian traditions that increasingly influenced some lodges in the *Écossais* system. The Masons at Turin developed a reputation for a peculiarly secretive form of Masonry, with an emphasis on alchemy and the occult sciences.[38] Swedish Masons would later claim to have special ties to a Rosicrucian lodge in Turin (ties possibly formed by Swedenborg when he visited Turin in 1738).[39] Thus, Spence's letter from Turin on 25 October 1740, which linked Rosicrucianism with Swedish politics and military prowess is provocative. Writing to his mother, who was always interested in these matters, Spence asked:

> Have you ever heard of the people called Adepts. They are a set of phi-
> losophers, superior to whatever appeared among the Greeks and Romans.
> The three great points they drive at is to be free from poverty, distempers,
> and death – and if you will believe them, they have found one secret that is
> capable of freeing them from all three. There are never more than twelve of
> these men in the whole world at a time, and we have the happiness of having
> one of the twelve at this time in Turin. I am very well acquainted with him,
> and have often talked with him of their secrets, as far as he is allowed to talk
> to a common mortal of them.
>
> His name is Andrey: a Frenchman… I asked him whether he had ever
> been in England and how he liked the country? He said that he had, and that
> he liked it more than any country he had ever been in. "The last time I was
> in England," added he," there were eleven philosophers there." I told him I
> hoped there might be more than eleven in England. He smiled a little and
> said, "Sir, I don't talk of common philosophers, I talk of Adepts [originally
> "Rosicrucians"], and of them I saw in England what I never saw any where
> else: there was eleven at table, I made the twelfth; and we came to compare
> our ages all together they made somewhat upward of four thousand years."[40]

Andrey claimed to be "not quite two hundred" years old but only looked forty; he noted that St. John and the Travelling Jew stayed on the earth "above seventeen hundred years." He said the Great Elixir, some of which he had in his pocket, would cure him of any illness and make as much gold as he pleased." Swedenborg would later (1744) describe his own entry into a society of immortals in London, his association with alchemists there, and his mystical rejuvenation.[41]

In 1740, as the opposition to Walpole intensified, his Grand Lodge supporters received some unflattering public notice. The Duke of Richmond was the inseparable

---

[36] *Ibid.*, 293.
[37] *Ibid.* 294 n. 7, 9.
[38] C.Francovich, *Storia*, 173-83.
[39] M. Schuchard, *Emanuel Swedenborg*, 259.
[40] J. Spence, *Letters*, 303.
[41] L. Bergquist, *Dream Diary*, #243-44, 260, 268.

companion of the Duke of Montagu, both former Grand Masters and still politically active Masons. Probably with Richmond's connivance, Montagu staged a silly prank in which they ridiculed John Heidegger, a fellow Mason and producer of the risqué masquerades enjoyed by the courtiers. Montagu was notorious for his childish love of practical jokes, and he got Heidegger drunk and had a wax mask made from his unconscious face. Then at court, with the royal family assembled for a masquerade, Heidegger ordered the musicians to sing, "God save the King!," but an impostor wearing the face mask commanded them to sing, "Charlie over the Water!"[42] George II and his mistress, who were in on the joke, laughed uproariously, but the Duke of Cumberland, who was not and "who could hardly contain himself interposed," and shouts of "Shame! Shame!" resounded from all parts. Cumberland ordered Heidegger and the "false Heidegger" to apologize, and the latter's role so shocked and shamed the impresario that he exploded in anger.

Hogarth immortalized the incident in a sketch, "Heidegger in a Rage," while Pope satirized him as a drunken "false Heidegger! who wert so wicked/ To let in the Devil."[43] At a time when the Grand Lodge was losing members and prestige, this widely-publicized incident did not help. Montagu's mother-in-law, the dowager Duchess of Marlborough, scorned his frivolity, noting that "all his talents lie in things natural in boys of fifteen, and he is almost two and fifty; to get people into his garden and wet them with squirts; and to invite people to his country houses, and put things into their beds to make them itch, and twenty such pretty fancies as these."[44]

As popular disaffection from the current English and French ministries increased, there emerged a shadowy linkage between some disaffected British Masons and *Écossais* Masons on the Continent. A newly energized and aggressive Louis XV moved further away from Fleury's pacific policies and was willing to listen to a project sent by the "Association," seven Scottish lords who were all Masons, vowing the willingness of Scotland to rise. In early spring James sent Colonel Arthur Brett to ascertain the intentions of his leading supporters in England, and Brett wanted to hear from Carte, but especially from Orrery and King, who became his close friends.[45] On 28 March Brett reported that the English supporters of James were "more timorous and backward than heretofore," but "as full of good intentions as ever," while the City of London is full of spirit and gives effectual proof of it."[46] The chief reason for the English backwardness was "the Duke of Hanover's vigilance," but they vow to rise if the French king sends military assistance.

The need for intensive secrecy perhaps prompted the Jacobite Masons to utilize their networks to glean more intelligence in England. In April 1740 they sent James Barry, 4th Earl of Barrymore, to Paris, to reinforce Brett's message. An Irish Protestant and old friend of Swift, the seventy-three year-old Barrymore was reportedly a Mason and close

---

[42] William Hogarth, *The Works of William Hogarth*, eds. John Nichols and George Steevens (London, 1810), II, 323-25.

[43] John Ireland, *A Supplement to Hogarth Illustrated* (London, 1798), 323-24.

[44] Martin Battestin, *A Henry Fielding Companion* (Westport, 2000), 104.

[45] J. Clark, *Samuel Johnson*, 178.

[46] E. Cruickshanks, *Political Untouchables*, 221-22.

to the members of the Corporation of Walton-le-Dale.[47] As a merely Irish peer, he was able to serve in the English House of Commons as a Tory M.P. for Wigan. An experienced military officer, Barrymore was expected to provide a hard-nosed assessment to Fleury about the feasibility of a Franco-Jacobite invasion. The old cardinal listened to him but only promised to send a personal agent to England to report on the situation there.[48]

In the event, the agent was chosen by Louis XV, and he would have a secret but significant influence on the development of *Écossais* Masonry in France and England. In June the king sent the Marquis de Clermont d'Amboise on a secret mission to England to evaluate the extent of opposition support for the Jacobites. When he returned to Paris in September, Clermont reported to the king that conditions in England "were favorable to the Jacobites' designs," even though he distrusted Argyll's change of allegiance.[49] He had met with Barrymore and various sympathetic Masons, who believed that they convinced him of the viability of their cause. However, to Barrymore's surprise and disappointment, Clermont met others who told him "lies" and undermined the Jacobites' case. He added that the supportive Jacobites would not submit to Fleury's request that they give written pledges, because of the risk involved.

But the Marquis de Clermont may have had an additional agenda, which he did not reveal to Fleury. He was the son-in-law of the Jacobite Duke of Berwick and affiliated with *Écossais* Masonry. According to André Kervella, Clermont was also the brother-in-law of the Abbé Fitzjames, who in 1734 possessed a secret Masonic ritual, invented by the Jacobites and reserved for the elite.[50] He suggests further that Clermont was privy to this degree, which later emerged in Ireland and England as the "Royal Arch." Coincidental with the secretive visit of Clermont to England was the introduction of the "Royal Order of Heredom of Kilwinning," a highly ritualistic Jacobite Masonic order, which drew on Ramsay's mystical teachings, and which eventually had clandestine lodges in London and several strategic port cities.[51] The order was brought to England by a French engraver, Lambert de Lintot, who had served in the regiment of Colonel MacMahon in Rouen.[52] In the Stuart Papers there is correspondence between Lambert and Macmahon at Rouen and James Edgar at Rome in 1738.[53]

It is also possible that Derwentwater was associated with Heredom of Kilwinning, for a 1750 document of the order was sealed with the armorial bearings of the Scottish family of Livingston of Parkhall. Sir Charles Livingston, 2nd Earl of Newburgh (d. 1755), was a Jacobite and father of Charlotte-Maria Livingston, Countess of Newburgh, who was married to Derwentwater.[54] Unaware of Clermont's clandestine visit, Fitzjames's secret ritual,

---

[47] J. Swift, *Correspondence*, II, 540; P. Monod, *Jacobitism*, 295,303. His son Richard Barry and grandson Richard, 6th Earl, evidently carried on a family tradition when they became Masons; See R.F. Gould, *History of Freemasonry throughout the World*, rev. ed. Dudley Wright (New York, 1936).

[48] "James Barry, 4th Earl of Barrymore," in R. Sedgwick, *History of Parliament Online*.

[49] Mahon, *History*, III, 31.

[50] André Kervella, *La Mystère de la Rose Blanche: Francs-Maçons et Templiers au XVIIIe Siècle* (Paris, 2009), 105.

[51] M. Schuchard, *Emanuel Swedenborg*, 304-05..

[52] William Wonnacott, "The Rite of Seven Degrees in London," *AQC*, 39 (1926), 63-98.

[53] Stuart Papers: 205/85,86 (February-March 1738).

[54] George Draffen, "Early Charters of the Royal Order of Scotland," *AQC*, 62 (1951), 325-26.

or the Livingston seal, the nineteenth-century Scottish Masonic historian Murray Lyon argued that

> The paternity of the Royal Order is now pretty generally attributed to a Jacobite knight named Andrew Ramsay, a devoted follower of the Pretender, and famous as the fabricator of certain rites, inaugurated in France about 1735-40, and through the propagation of which it was hoped the fallen fortunes of the Stuarts could be retrieved.[55]

The Royal Order of Heredom and Kilwinning would later claim Charles Edward Stuart as its Grand Master.[56]

In 1740, during this period of serious Jacobite Masonic activity, Orator Henley continued his propaganda for Hanoverian Masonry, and on 30 December he audaciously linked Bolingbroke with the former Grand Master Wharton, claiming that "my L--- B--, who, they say has turned Catholic, as the late D--- of W----- did, who neither before nor after had any Religion at all, …accuse the Ministry of Popery…to cover their own Crimes."[57] But the days of the Walpole-funded *Hyp-Doctor* were coming to a close, and the last issue was published on 20 January 1741.

While "Cobham's Cubs" and his Patriots continued their efforts to win places, Dr. King became disturbed by their distancing themselves from the Jacobites, as well as the deteriorating health of Swift and other sympathizers. On 15 January 1741 he wrote Orrery, who was in Ireland, that he received a letter from Henry Leslie, "whom you have probably seen," giving him "a very melancholy account of ye poor Dean."[58] Even worse, former supporters like Cornbury had given up the cause:

> We are all here full of Politicks – so full that we admit of no other conversation. Ld. C------y [Cornbury] they say has left us. I say he has betrayed us, for we chose him in confidence and fully persuaded that he would act on our principles: I think he has now gone round ye compass – perhaps – but I have room for no more news.

With postal interception increasing, King assured Orrery that this letter (and others) would be hand-carried to Ireland

The disarray in the English opposition was mirrored, ironically, in the Grand Lodge establishment. When "Jachin" wrote from Edinburgh that Freemasonry in England was on the decline while on the rise in Scotland, he was accurate. Ric Berman demonstrates that in the 1740s the "two decades of growth in mainstream English freemasonry came to a halt."[59] Bureaucratic incompetency was "taking over the English Grand Lodge. The organization became arrogant and self-obsessed. And disaffection grew." It seems likely that the election of the recent Grand Master of Scotland, James Douglas, 14th Earl of Morton, in February 1741, to the Grand Mastership in England reflected the disaffection of many Grand Lodge members from the Walpolean regime and its supporters in the

---

[55] David Murray Lyon, "The Royal Order of Scotland," *The Freemason* (4 September 1880), 393.
[56] W. Wonnacott, "Rite of Seven Degrees," 41.
[57] *Hyp-Doctor* , #531 (30 December 1740).
[58] Bodleian: MS. Eng. Hist. d.103, f.20.
[59] R. Berman, *Schism*, 4.

fraternity. As noted earlier, Morton, when known as Lord Aberdour, sympathized with the Jacobites and in 1738 urged them to persuade Fleury to support the cause. An eminent scientist and FRS, he publicly appeared as a moderate Whig, but his actions over the next decade would arouse government suspicions about his loyalty.[60]

Nevertheless, on 19 March "the Annual Assembly and Feast of the Freemasons was attended with more than customary pomp. The Procession of March, in particular, was swelled by the inclusion of "several representatives of the Continental Craft," including the Swedish ambassador, Carl Wasenberg, agent of the Masonic Hats.[61] Lord Kintore led a huge procession of Masons to Lord Morton's residence, where they were entertained at breakfast and then marched through the streets to Haberdasher's Hall, where Morton was installed in Solomon's Chair. Though Masonic historians have noted the large number of supporters of the Prince of Wales in the procession, on the very next day, a counter-procession of "mock Masons" was organized by Esquire Carey, surgeon to the prince, and Paul Whitehead, an anti-Walpolean poet. The mockers road on jackasses, banged pots and pans, and wore burlesque costumes representing lodge officers. *The London Daily Post* (20 March 1741) described the burlesque procession but warned "the witty contriver of this Mock-scene whose Misfortune is, that though he has some Wit his Subjects are generally so ill-chosen, that he loses by it as many Friends as other People of more Judgment gain."

A week later, a print entitled "Mock Masonry: or the Grand Procession," was sold by Mrs. Dodd and advertised in *The Daily Gazetteer* (28 March 1741), a government subsidized journal, which identified Carey and Whitehead as the organizers. The print was dedicated to "the Antient and Honourable Society of Free and Accepted Masons,"and was "most humbly inscribed by their very humble Servants, Esq. C----y, and P. W – --h – d, Directors," which implies that both men were initiates. In the doggerel verses below the print, written in a faux Irish accent, the "Modest Montgomery of Hiber – a [Hibernia]," the Tyler or Guard, is portrayed, who had earlier been featured by Hogarth in the act of escorting the drunken Sir Thomas De Veil when the lodge Master was soaked in urine. The poet mocked "the Flower of all the Nation,/ De Cavalcade of de Free Mason," and referred to the Stewards and Grand Masters in mocking tones. He then seemed to warn Carey and Whitehead about their risky prank: "Now C – r-y, Wh-t-ad, me intenda-/ For, Thanks dis sage Advice to lend-a,/ Ne'er break your Jest to loose your Friend-a. *Doodle, Doodle, etc.*"

Carey's collaborator, Paul Whitehead, had already come under government fire, for his poem, *Manners: A Satire*, published in February 1739. A friend of Pope and admirer of *The Dunciad*, Whitehead boldly attacked not only Walpole but George II for their corruption of the nation's churches. An ecclesiastical sycophant, who so desperately wants employment that

> ...he trim Chaplain, conscious of a See,
> Cries out: my King, `I have no God but Thee':
> Lifts to the Royal Seat the asking Eye,
> And pays to George the Tribute of the Sky;

---

[60] For some of his suspicious activities, see M. Schuchard, *Emanuel Swedenborg*, 364, 585-86, 616-18.
[61] W.J. Chetwode Crawley, "Mock Masonry in the Eighteenth Century," *AQC*, 18 (1905), 132-33.

> Proves Sin alone from humble Roofs must spring,
> Nor can one earthly Failing stain a King.
> ....
> If the lawned Levite's earthly vote be sold,
> And God's free Gift retail'd for Mammon Gold;
> No Rev'rence can the proud Cathedral claim,
> But Henley's shop, and Sherlock's are the same.[62]

Though it is not definitely known if Whitehead was an initiate, he would maintain confidential friendships with opposition and Jacobite Masons over the next decade. He certainly had inside information about Masonic affairs, and the characters in *Manners* were nearly all loyalist or opposition members of the fraternity. The jab at the Walpolean Mason Henley was followed by praise of the opposition Mason Chesterfield, whose diplomatic work serves "his Country's Cause," while at home he defends "her Laws" so well that "bold Corruption almost drops the Bribe."[63] He contrasted that with such Hanoverian Masons as Horatio Walpole, the prime minister's brother, whose diplomatic service at The Hague can never rival Chesterfield's. Even worse was Lord Essex, who was initiated by Robert Walpole, supported his policies, and thus earned a post at Turin: "Why E---- whispers, votes, and saw *Turin*." He further attacked "Laureat" Colley Cibber and "Fanny" Lord Hervey, who crawls and is "an Ear-wig on the King." Lavishing further praise on opposition Masons like Cobham and Pope, he eulogized the Patriots Pulteney, Carteret, and Pitt, and concluded with a call for the most prominent Mason, Frederick, Prince of Wales, to save the country.

Whitehead knew he was sailing close to the wind and practically invited government prosecution:

> I name not W-----e [Walpole]; You the Reason guess;
> Mark yon fell Harpy hov'ring o'er the Press.
> Secure the Muse may sport with Names of Kings,
> But Ministers, my Friend, are dang'rous Things.
> ....
> *Pope* writes unhurt – but know, `tis different quite
> To beard the Lion, and to crush the Mite.
> Safe may he dash the Statesman in each Line,
> Those dread his Satire, who dare punish mine.[64]

In March a government supporter, Thomas Odell, responded to this challenge by publishing *Characters: An Epistle to Alexander Pope Esq; and Mr. Whitehead* (London, 1739). Odell served as deputy to William Chetwynd, licenser of the stage.[65] He accused Pope of "Craft and Avarice," and of writing malicious slashing satire that becomes treasonous:

> Now drop with *St. John* to the deepest Hell,
> And unto Traitors there your Poems sell:
> There let your Hawkers cry `em on a String,

---

[62] Paul Whitehead, *Manners: A Satire* (London, 1739), 6.
[63] *Ibid.*, 9, 11, 15-17.
[64] *Ibid.*, 14.
[65] "Thomas Odell," *ODNB*.

And spread Sedition to dethrone your King.[66]

He scorned Whitehead as a mere follower of Pope in issuing a "full Torrent of abusive Song," and warned that "the Wasp, tho' but a little thing,/ Shall gaul you with the Poignance of its Sting." [67]As the ministry still hoped to win back Chesterfield, Odell agreed with Pope's and Whitehead's praise of him, but cautioned the opposition that "If George offends, sweet Fred'rick cannot hope/ To please a Whitehead, or to charm a Pope." The prince needs to scan "with an Eagle's Eye, the Patriot, ere you trust designing Man."

The warning was timely, for the House of Lords decreed Whitehead's *Manners* as scandalous and ordered the author and publisher (Robert Dodsley) into custody. "Whitehead decamped and Dodsley was not further prosecuted: `the whole process was probably intended rather to intimidate Pope than to punish Whitehead.'"[68] While in hiding, Whitehead began planning with Carey the parade of mock Masons. As a prominent member of the Grand Lodge, who had participated in Kintore's official parade in 1740, Carey's motives for organizing the burlesque on the fraternity are unclear, but a follow-up satirical print was published, entitled "What's all this! The Motley Team of State," which depicted Walpole and his political placemen riding on asses, and Desaguliers as "a broad-faced parson."

The bold actions of Carey and Whitehead were admired by John Perceval, son of the 1st Earl of Egmont, who participated with them in opposition agitation during the Middlesex election in May 1741. Perceval shared his father's resentment at the English "snubbing" of Irish peers; though he had held a seat in the Irish parliament, he was opposed by Walpole and failed to win a seat in England.[69] He joined a committee of tradesmen and merchants who opposed the court candidate William Clayton, Lord Sundon, who would have lost the election if the bailiff had not illegally closed the poll and sent armed guards to protect Sundon from the enraged "mob."[70] Encouraged behind the scenes by the Prince of Wales and disaffected noblemen, the angry citizens presented a petition to the Commons that resulted in the election being declared void. Perceval was then elected without opposition, which pleased the prince but enraged his brother, the Duke of Cumberland.

Though it was later claimed, possibly inaccurately, that Prince Frederick dismissed Esquire Carey after the Mock Masonry procession, Perceval – a supporter of the prince – praised Carey and Paul Whitehead for their role in the opposition protests. When he attended the committee, Perceval recorded:

> I found a surgeon of my acquaintance one Esquire Carey a man of admirable spirit and activity most eminently qualified for these undertakings, as likewise one Paul Whitehead an ingenious man, of parts, learning and republican spirit who I likewise knew well, both of them members of this committee…
> I found these men really my friends, from a kind of freedom which I had accustomed myself to in dealing with my inferiors which being different

---

[66] [Thomas Odell], *Characters: An Epistle to Alexander Pope Esq, and Mr. Whitehead* (London, 1739), 8.

[67] *Ibid.*, 14-15.

[68] "Paul Whitehead," *ODNB*.

[69] "John Peceval, 2nd Earl of Egmont," *ODNB*.

[70] Egmont, *Diary*, III, 219-20, 233.

> from the insolence generally practiced by persons of my rank to that class of men, has upon many occasions done good service.[71]

It is unknown if Perceval was a Mason, but he surely knew of Carey's affiliation, as well as his and Whitehead's collaboration in the mock-Masonry procession.

*

* *

Throughout 1740 and 1741, the Irish Grand Lodge underwent factional divisions, which had resulted in the election of two rival Grand Masters, as reported in Faulkner's *Dublin Journal* (1 July 1740).[72] On the same day, 24 June, Arthur St. Leger, Viscount Doneraile, was installed as Grand Master at the Masons' ancient hall in Smock Alley, while Richard Annesley, 6th Earl of Anglesey, was installed as the Grand Master at the Rose Tavern.[73] The causes of the dispute are obscure, but possibly arose from the political backgrounds of the rivals. Doneraile was the nephew of Elizabeth St. Leger, who had been initiated in 1710, and he was a friend and supporter of Frederick, Prince of Wales. Anglesey, who was nominated by the Grand Master Lord Mountjoy, had the support of the more aristocratic faction; he came from a Protestant Tory family, which "retained an affection for the exiled Stuarts."[74] His father, Arthur Annesley, 5th Earl of Anglesey, had been devoted to Atterbury and was a friend of Swift.[75] However, the 6th earl's unsavory reputation as a bigamist and kidnapper eventually led to the acceptance of Doneraile as the legitimate Grand Master.

By 1 April 1741 these troubles led Fifield d'Assigny to deliver a lecture to the Irish Grand Lodge, published as *An Impartial Answer to the Enemies of Free-Masonry* (Dublin, 1741). He was possibly "Philo-Lapidarius," the anonymous author of *An Answer to the Pope's Bull* (1738). D'Assigny came from a Protestant Walloon family, settled in Ireland and noted for its strident anti-Catholicism. As discussed in Chapter Two, his kinsman Marius d'Assigny had published a Protestant, word-oriented work on the Art of Memory to counter the image-oriented mnemonic technique so important to Catholics and Scottish Freemasons.[76] Fifield was a strong Whig and a public defender of the Walpolean regime. His earlier publications provide a provocative backdrop to his Irish Masonic publications. In his anonymous *Poems on Several Occasions* (London, 1730), he published the verses he presented to the King's Scholars at Westminster on 30 January 1730, their annual Feast on Queen Elizabeth's birthday:

> Our Fathers, gall'd with Rome's oppressive Yoke,
> Provok'd at length, their Iron Bondage broke;
> Bravely threw up the long usurp'd Command,
> And swept the Papal Locusts from our Land.

---

[71] Aubrey Newman, "Leicester House Politics, 1750-60," *Camden Miscellany*, 4th *s.* (1969), VII, 101.

[72] R. Péter, *British Freemasonry*, V, 27.

[73] R. Parkinson, "An Answer," 149; J. Lepper and P. Crossle, *History*, I, 226-28.

[74] E. O'Ciardha, *Ireland*, 215; "Arthur Annesley," *ODNB*.

[75] J. Swift, *Correspondence*, II, 161 n.1.

[76] On the architectural visualization techniques (Art of Memory) used by Scottish Masons, see D. Stevenson, *Origins*, 49, 82, 85-97.

Yet Jesuits, inch by inch, dispute their Ground,
And schools at Doway and St. Omers found;
In hopes once more our Island to enchain,
And what they lost by Men, by Boys regain.[77]

D'Assigny included in the volume his criticism of the Anglican minister Samuel Crox-all, who though a loyal Hanoverian, dared to preach a sermon against Walpole in the House of Commons on 30 January 1730. Taking Proverbs 25:5 as his text, Croxall "de-clared that kings should not screen wicked servants," giving many examples of how kings are badly served by maintaining corrupt ministers.[78] D'Assigny responded with a mocking poem, "To Dr. Croxall":

Prithee, Sammy, reflect, can there be such a Thing,
As taking the Wicked away from the King?"
....
Who would'st thou put there then, but those full as bad,
Till with chopping and changing the Court would run mad?.[79]

D'Assigny was not the only Walpolean Mason who attacked Croxall, for Orator Henley joined the fray in a bizarre pamphlet, *Light in a Candlestick* (London, 1730), which utilized Hebrew, Aramaic, and Arabic to attack Croxall's criticism of Walpole.

Thus, d'Assigny was no stranger to political controversy when he published *An Im-partial Answer to the Enemies of Free-Masonry* in Dublin in 1741. Giving a traditional history of ancient Masonry, including the fraternity's debts to the Pythagoreans, Essenes, Caba-lists, and Druids, he stressed the ethical and moral training it gave initiates, while admit-ting that not all brothers were so pure and holy (an oblique reminder of the recent scan-dals surrounding the Dublin Hell Fire club): "And how unequitable it is then to blame a whole Society for some few mistaken Men?"[80] He further rejected "the ridiculous Inven-tions of the Vulgar," who charge the Masons with "raising the Devil, Conversing with infernal Spirits, the wild Story of an old Woman between the rounds of a Ladder, the Cook's red hot Iron, or Salamander, and many more of the same idle Stamp." [81] He concluded with a warning to the Irish Grand Lodge to "Reject all PRETENDERS as Men of base and ignoble Principles," and from his later Masonic writing, it is clear that d'Assigny was worried about Jacobite infiltration and the importation of higher, *Écossais* degrees.

At this time in Ireland, Orrery became so disgusted with "the Rage of Party" among his fellow Protestants, which he called "the invincible stupidity of these Sons of Thun-der," that he returned to England, where from his rural retreat at Marston he maintained a lively and humorous correspondence with Dr. King. They both grieved for the death of the old Jacobite Charles Caesar, and Orrery sent his widow Mary a poem of consola-tion: "The Parts well acted both of Friend and Wife/ Thro' every Scene of all thy

---

[77] [Fifield D'Assigny], *Poems on Several Occasions* (London, 1730), 1.
[78] "Samuel Croxall," *ODNB*.
[79] F. D'Assigny, *Poems*, 31-32.
[80] Reproduced in R. Parkinson, "An Answer," 166.
[81] *Ibid.*, 165, 168.

blameless Life."[82] Remarking to King that his letters were seized by the government and were now "in the hands of a Bishop to decipher," Orrery indicated his knowledge of the role of Willes, recently made Bishop of St. Davids.[83] Thus, his comical accounts of the local, loyalist Freemasons seemed a cover for his own interest in the activities of Hanoverian and Jacobite brothers.

The hard-drinking local squire, John Whitchurch, a Grand Lodge Mason and staunch supporter of George II, constantly blustered with anti-Jacobite, anti-Non-juror invectives, which were so misinformed that they could only amuse Orrery. In summer 1741 Whitchurch hired a Masonic brother to build a stone bridge, but he refused to pay for a protective wall and then drunkenly fell into the stream and apparently drowned.[84] This roused Paul Stevens, the parish clerk, to proclaim a curse on the Masonic fraternity. Orrery wrote that the intoxicated squire had "floundered through Mire and Marshes to the other World," but after some therapeutic vomiting, he was resurrected. To escape from boredom and hangovers, Orrery and his second wife (Lady Henrietta Hamilton), concentrated on building and gardening projects, led by a talented designer and operative Mason, "that Prince of Architecture, Master James Scott," who came to Marston from London.[85] In July Dr. King wrote Orrery that "your Architect Scott" called on him in Oxford, on his way to Marston.[86]

While political factions and Grand Lodge controversies weakened the fraternity in England and Ireland, Ramsay believed that the Jacobite Masons were making progress in Europe, especially in France and Sweden. His Parisian oration received new publicity when it was published in the *Almanach des Cocus, ou amusements pour la beau sexe* (1741), though he would not approve of the obscene material in other sections of the cuckold's calendar. In that same year, he became the confidential friend of Carl Gustaf Tessin, Swedish ambassador in Paris. As noted earlier, Tessin had served as Grand Master in 1738 and was currently considered the chief of the *Écossais* Masons in Sweden.

According to a German visitor and diarist, Herr von Geusau, Ramsay often visited Tessin, and it was apparently at the ambassador's residence that Ramsay informed his Swedish host and German guests about Masonic history and his plans for its future.[87] Ramsay showed them his oration and explained that he wanted "to clear away from Masonic ceremonial a great deal that had become meaningless with a view to restoring the primitive ceremonial."[88] From his earlier letter about his collaboration with Derwentwater, he obviously meant to restore the chivalric and mystical themes of "ancient," Stuart Masonry. He hoped to establish regular suppers at which members of all classes of society "should sit side by side, in order that they might be suitably impressed with the fact that by nature all men are equal." He wanted to establish a fund "to further the main objects of Freemasonry," which would finance a "universal lexicon," an encyclopedic project he had mentioned in his oration.

---

[82] Harvard. Houghton: Eng.MS.2182, vol.4, f. 220.

[83] *Ibid.*, 249.

[84] *Ibid.*, 226.

[85] *Ibid.*, f. 240.

[86] Bodleian: MS. Eng. Hist.d.103, f.28.

[87] Extracts of Von Geusau's diary, which is now lost, were published by Anton F. Büsching, *Beiträge zu der Lebensgschichte denkwürdiger Personen* (Halle, 1783-89); for Ramsay and Tessin, see II, 115, 133-36, 147-48

[88] G. Henderson, *Chevalier Ramsay*, 171-72.

Ramsay then made his provocative claim about General Monk's strategy in the resto-ration of a Stuart king in 1660: "The re-establishment of King Charles II had first been spoken and decided in a conference of Freemasons because General Monk had been a member and able to bring it to fruition without incurring the least suspicion about his secret plot."[89] As discussed earlier, Ramsay may have learned this from Lord Lansdowne, whose father had served as Monk's personal emissary during the top secret planning and implementation of the restoration. Ramsay explained that he had not mentioned Monk's Masonic plan in the orations he delivered to Parisian lodges because the statutes forbade discussion of politics, and he wanted to avoid suspicion that the brotherhood participated in "matters of state." Tessin must have found the claim plausible, for his own ancestor, the Swedish military architect Edouart Tessin, had been initiated in Edinburgh in 1652 while working with Monk; he then marched with Monk to London and entered the ar-chitectural service of Charles II.[90] In April Ramsay was delighted to oversee the Masonic dedication of a house to be constructed for him by the Duc de Bouillon: "In laying the first stone, I consecrated the house as a Bethel and as a living temple of the Most High by the prayers of Solomon."[91] As noted earlier, Bouillon was kinned to the Stuarts, and he and Ramsay reportedly developed a special Jacobite rite of Masonry.[92]

Ramsay's revelation of this politicized Masonry was made at a crucial time, for in London his fellow Mason, Lord Grange (brother of the late Mar), wrote to Fleury on 27 March asking for French help in restoring the Stuarts.[93] At this time, Grange served as Prince Frederick's secretary of state for Scotland, while he carried on a secret correspond-ence with the Pretender. Like the seventeenth-century Masonic Covenanters, he main-tained since 1733 a clandestine network of Scottish Jacobites and Masons, by which "we have engaged to mutual assistance, in every place, and they to me in a particular manner, not only as to elections but other things, if Sir Robert tumbles."[94] From 1739 on, he was kept informed about the Scots' negotiations with the French government by his fellow Mason, Magregor of Balhaldy. In May James suggested that Grange should assure his friends among the opposition Whigs that if they "enter seriously and heartily into measures for bringing about my restoration…there is no reasonable demand they can make, either on behalf of themselves in particular, or of the country in general, that I shall not readily and heartily comply with." When Grange presented the letter to Pulteney, which included James's written pledge to safeguard English liberties and the Protestant religion, Pulteney cautiously returned it, saying "I do not love such papers."

Grange confided James's promises to Argyll, Cobham, and Chesterfield and according to Eveline Cruickshanks, "it would appear" that the three opposition Whigs were "either willing to pay, or appear willing to pay, the Tory price for bringing down Walpole: a restoration."[95] In August Chesterfield wrote about his disgust with Pulteney's "silly, half-witted, zealous Whigs" and vowed that "if the Duke of Argyll sounds to battle, I will

---

[89] A. Büsching, *Beiträge*, III, 329. For a detailed examination of the historical context of Monk's alleged Masonic strategy, see M. Schuchard, *Restoring the Temple*, 573-94.

[90] *Ibid.*, 582-83, 643.

[91] C. Batham, "Chevalier Ramsay," 285.

[92] André Kervella, *Francs-Maçons au Duché de Bouillon* (Neufchâteau, 2006), 7-12, 68-71.

[93] R. Sedgwick, "Hon. James Erskine," II, 16.

[94] *Ibid.*, 15.

[95] E. Cruickshanks, *Political Untouchables*, 27-28.

follow my leader." He then set out for France, claiming that because of ill health, he needed baking "by the sun of Provence and Languedoc."[96] In September Dr. King wrote Orrery about Chesterfield's "rambling in the south of France," and he eagerly awaited his expected return in November.[97]

Chesterfield spent three days at Argeville, consulting with Bolingbroke,"the oracle," about his apparent willingness to support the Jacobites. According to Daniel O'Brien, the frustrated Bolingbroke seemed "to dread that any business of the King's should be thought of" without him."[98] Chesterfield then travelled to Avignon, where he stayed with Ormonde, his distant relative, to whom he brought a message from the disaffected Whigs. According to Horace Walpole, they wanted Ormonde to obtain the Pretender's order to the Jacobites "to vote against Sir R.W. upon any question whatever."[99] Chesterfield had been authorized by Argyll and his Whig partisans to report that they would restore James III in return for the Jacobite vote. Shellabarger notes that Chesterfield's proceedings in France "required a rather elaborate camouflage, and by a legalist might technically be construed as treason."[100]

The sequel to Chesterfield's visit to Ormonde was a letter from the Pretender to his friends in England dated 27 September 1741 and sent through Colonel William Cecil. James urged them to cooperate with all opposers of "the present Government and ministry," regardless of their particular motives.[101] If "my friends" show a proper spirit, it will encourage Cardinal Fleury to declare for us. "I desire you will communicate this letter or the contents of it to as many as you can with safety and prudence." Robert Walpole later said that he had proof that one hundred copies of this letter had been distributed and that "it was procured by Chesterfield through Ormonde." Another letter, pre-dated 25 May, was then circulated, in which James expressed in detail the tolerant religious policies and political reforms he would implement when restored. In a bid to gain Whig and independent support, he promised "a general indemnity, without exception, for all that passed against me and my family." Grange made sure members of his Scottish network received the letters. Dr. King undoubtedly received copies and was privy to the negotiations; he wrote Orrery on 10 November that Chesterfield was back in London, and he designed to visit him the next day.[102]

Throughout 1741 Dr. King worked on the draft of an allegorical epic poem in Latin, *Templum Libertatis*, despite his gout-crippled fingers. On 20 May he wrote Orrery that he invented a wooden writing instrument which enabled him to "perform tolerably well and to be able to write so plainly, that any Clerk in the post-office may read my Letter without calling for a Decypherer."[103] His work was frequently interrupted by visitors, including Orrery, Pope, Marchmont, and Chesterfield, who was back from his mission to Ormonde. Orrery learned about those negotiations, and on 14 September he wrote King,

[96] Samuel Shellabarger, *Lord Chesterfield* (New York, 1935), 192.
[97] Bodleian: MS. Eng. Hist.d.103, f.33.
[98] E. Cruickshanks, *Political Untouchables*, 23.
[99] R. Sedgwick, *History*, I, 71.
[100] S. Shellabarger, *Chesterfield*, 192.
[101] E. Cruickshanks, *Political Untouchables*, 27-28.
[102] Bodleian: MS. Eng. Hist. d.103, f.46.
[103] D. Greenwood, *William King*, 120, 125-45.

"Long may the Earl of Chesterfield live! England may breathe whilst He, and such as He, continue amongst us," and he should join King's heroes in the Temple of Liberty. [104]

King also struggled to get Oxford University to grant Pope and his new editor, Rev. William Warburton, honorary degrees, but Warburton was opposed as unorthodox, and Pope thus withdrew. Writing to Orrery, Pope explained that "it was monstrously refused by the unaccountable Dissent of 2 or 3. Dr. King either has, or will acquaint you of the particulars." In January 1742 the first volume of *Templum Libertatis* was anonymously published, and a letter-writer to *The London Magazine* (February 1742) identified some of the allegorical characters as Orrery, Chesterfield, Cobham, and Gower. Orrery wrote King that he recognized that "Memmius" represented Chesterfield, one of the "Heroes of your Temple." "Scotus" was identified as John Dalrymple, 2nd Earl of Stair, a Scottish military officer and diplomat, who was earlier a staunch anti-Jacobite. From 1733 on, he broke with Walpole and went into opposition with the 2nd Earl of Marchmont, and King determined to gain their support for not only the Tory but the Jacobite cause.[105]

Or, according to the letter writer, "Scotus" referred to the Scots in general. David Greenwood observes, "Whatever his identity, his presence augurs well. He promises honours for those citizens who have merited them, peace for the farmers, and safe seas for the sailors. Already the future of Scotland looks brighter."[106] King's poem revealed his intimate knowledge of Scottish opposition and Jacobite activists. According to the Whig historian William Coxe,

> The duke of Argyle exerted himself with such effect in Scotland, that he baffled all the efforts of his brother, the earl of Ilay, who had long managed the interest of the crown in that quarter; and the majority of Scottish members, who had formed a strong phalanx in favour of the government, were now ranged on the contrary side. These acquisitions were considered by the opposition as a sure omen of success… the homogeneous parts [of the opposition] were consolidated, and the whole phalanx, however divided and discordant in other respects, moved on uniformly to one great object, the removal of the minister.[107]

In January 1742 King's close friend, Alexander Hume Campbell (twin brother of the 3rd Earl of Marchmont), won a hotly contested Scottish election at Berwick against the court candidate.[108] A disgusted Horace Walpole wrote of the opposition that

> their man was Hume Campbell, Lord Marchmont's brother, lately made solicitor to the Prince [of Wales] for being as troublesome, as violent, and almost as able as his brother. They made a great point of it, and gained so many of our votes that at ten at night we were forced to give it up without dividing.[109]

---

[104] Harvard. Houghton: Eng.MS.218.2, vol.4, f.241.
[105] "John Dalrymple, 2nd Earl of Stair," *ODNB*.
[106] D. Greenwood, *William King*, 143
[107] W. Coxe, *Memoirs…Walpole*, I, 684.
[108] *Ibid.*, I, 693.
[109] H. Walpole, *Correspondence*, XVII, 297.

The Prince of Wales was delighted to get the support of the 3rd Earl of Cromarty, former Grand Master of Scotland, whose elderly father-in-law, Sir William Gordon, was M.P. for Cromartyshire, and who was brought in from his sick-bed to vote with the opposition. Horace Walpole reported to Mann: "It was a most shocking sight, to see the sick and dead brought in, on both sides! And Sir William Gordon from his bed, with a blister on his head, and flannel hanging out from under his wig. I could scarce pity him for his ingratitude."[110] Both Cromarty and Gordon had earlier received government pensions, and Gordon's son had been named the captain of a government ship, so their loyalty was expected. The opposition determined to keep secret the news of the son's recent drowning, so that Gordon would not absent himself, but a Scottish Hanoverian revealed the death to him in the House: "The old man, who looked like Lazarus at his resuscitation, behaved with great resolution and said he knew why he was told of it, but when he thought his country in danger he would not go away." On 28 January he rose again from his bed on the critical Chippenham election petition, which Walpole lost by one vote. Six months later, the Scottish Lazarus was dead, but his support of the Prince of Wales and his party would eventually save the life of his son-in-law Cromarty in 1746.[111]

William Coxe sardonically observed that the Scottish campaign was "to produce a new aera, the revival of the golden age: a Junction of all parties was to take place, and the sovereign, instead of being chief of a sect, was to become at one the father of his people, and to reign in the hearts of his subjects."[112] In *Templum Libertatis* King boldly expressed these Scottish themes, as well as all the criticisms of the Walpolean ministry and Hanoverian regime that the opposition was currently voicing. He speculated on "the vice of conformism under tyranny" and warned that "citizens should be prepared to defend freedom with financial contributions and military intervention."[113] He admonished his readers against despair and urged that it is better "to die a thousand times than to be a slave." In the narrative, the Goddess of Liberty descends and is installed in the Temple of Liberty, "a building especially erected for her." A long, solemn procession is formed," which would remind readers of the recent, elaborate Masonic parades. King then provided a "gorgeous" description of the edifice and its decorations, which were equivalent to the Temple of Solomon. No wonder some readers considered the Temple of Liberty to be a Masonic construction.

In conclusion, a *dux magnus* eulogizes the Goddess of Liberty. The military hero calls on Liberty to "retouch the traces of your falling name,/ Lost arts recall, lost trade, and publick fame." In order to calm fears of rebellion and bloodshed, he reassures the audience that there is nothing to fear, for "Liberty is calm and kind," and "no high passions labour in her mind." Readers believed that King referred to Argyll, who at this time was secretly collaborating with supporters of the Stuarts. With an implicit allusion to Wharton's Jacobite journal, the letter-writer in *The London Magazine* appealed to "every *True Briton*" to appreciate the difficult task of creating a Latin epic poem that describes so fittingly the age's characters. A year later, King would publish volume two, which praised

---

[110] *Ibid.*, XVII, 298

[111] *Ibid.*, XIX, 302.

[112] W. Coxe, *Memoirs…Walpole*, I, 684.

[113] D. Greenwood, *William King*, 128-29, 136, 144.

James III as a phoenix, "Rex ipse." The anonymous translator of the extract was reportedly John Ellis, a close friend of King and Moses Mendes, his fellow Jacobite Masons.[114] With King's "entire approbation," Ellis translated the whole *Templum Libertatis*, which unfortunately remains unpublished.

King wrote Orrery that he would himself provide a key to the characters, because he was not "altogether inattentive to some threatening expressions, which have been thrown out," especially "if it be attacked by any old or new ministerial writers."[115] In February Robert Walpole succumbed to the opposition's attacks, and on 11 February he resigned as prime minister. However, several days earlier he had been created 1st Earl of Orford and granted a substantial pension (which caused a public outcry). King evidently felt the key to *Templum Libertatis* was no longer needed, and it was never published. However, Walpole did not go quietly and, according to Coxe, he worked behind the scenes with "three great objects in view: "1st. To disunite the heterogeneous parties which composed the opposition. 2d. To form an administration on a Whig basis. 3d. To save himself from a public prosecution."[116] He determined to lure the Duke of Argyll and the Tories, to conciliate the Prince of Wales, and to detach Pulteney from the Tories. To effect these views, "he had recourse to the grand engine of political jealousy."

On 12 February Argyll led a meeting of the whole opposition and proposed the formation of a government based on the principle of "the Broad Bottom." Eveline Cruickshanks explains that these were cant words, "which corresponding equally with the personal figure of some of their leaders and the nature of their pretensions" and "was understood to imply a party united to force the Tories into the Administration." [117] Wynn was doing his utmost to secure for Argyll the post of commander-in-chief of the army, "to act as the General Monk of a second Stuart restoration." Though Argyll refused to accept this office unless his Tory friends were given places, Wynn pressed him hard to accept his Majesty's offer to restore him to his posts. On 17 February Prince Frederick paid his personal respects to the king, and the next day "the whole party who had formed the opposition to the late minister, made their appearance at court." But it was soon apparent that many of the Tories and Jacobites who expected government employment would be disappointed.

It was in this context of hopes raised and then dashed that Pope composed an expanded *Dunciad*. In January 1742 he wrote Hugh Bethel, an opposition Whig, that he expected his new poem to draw "the whole polite world upon me": "An Army of Virtuosi, Medalists, Ciceronis, Royal-Society men, Schools, Universities, even Florists, Freethinkers, & Free masons, will incompass me with fury."[118] On 20 March he published *The New Dunciad. As it was Found in the Year 1741* (London, 1742). Pope's main target was Colley Cibber, Hanoverian Mason and "composer of inept laureate odes," who was now enthroned in the key role of king of the Dunces. Pat Rogers observes that "One aim is to strike at the court through its appointed public bard."[119] As the goddess of dullness

---

114 "John Ellis," *European Magazine*, 21 (January 1742), 4.

115 D. Greenwood, *William King*, 139-40.

116 W. Coxe, *Memoirs…Walpole*, I, 698-703.

117 E. Cruickshanks, *Political Untouchables*, 30-31.

118 A. Pope, *Correspondence*, IV, 377.

119 P. Rogers, *Alexander Pope Encyclopedia*, 62.

mounts the throne and holds a levee attended by mediocre, groveling sycophants, Pope remembered more worthy citizens, such as Atterbury and other Jacobites, whose tragic fates meant that "Wit dreads Exile, Penalties and Pains."[120]

He praised the opposition writers for their abilities, which would be lost under the reign of dullness. Still devoted to Bolingbroke, he distanced himself from Jacobitism by quoting in a note his friend's condemnation of the Stuart king, James I, who "first assumed the title of Sacred Majesty, which his loyal Clergy transferr'd from God to Him." In that "inglorious reign," the principles of passive obedience and nonresistance "were talk'd, written, and preach'd into vogue." In the poem, he mocked those who yearn for "some pedant Reign,/ Some gentle James to bless the land again!" The goddess urges Cambridge and Oxford to teach arbitrary rule: "May you, May Cam, and Isis preach it long!/ `The RIGHT DIVINE OF KINGS to govern wrong.'"

In a sweeping condemnation of the corruption of education, governance, arts, and science, Pope got in a jab at loyalist Freemasonry:

> Next, bidding all draw near on bended knees,
> The Queen confers her Titles and Degrees,
> Her Children first of more distinguish'd sort,
> Who study Shakespeare at the Innes of Court,
> Impale a Glow-worm, or Vertù profess,
> Shine in the dignity of F.R.S.
> Some, deep Free-Masons, join the silent race
> Worthy to fill Pythagoras's place:
> Some Botanists, or Florists at the least;
> Or issue Members of an Annual Feast.
> Nor past the meanest unregarded, one
> Rose a Gregorian, one a Gormogon.
> The last, not lest in honour or applause,
> Isis and Cam made Doctors of her Laws.[121]

In a note, he explained: "a Gregorian, or a Gormogon. A sort of Lay-brothers, slips from the root of the Free Masons." Pope had evidently read Aaron Hill's anonymous essay on the Gormogons, first published in *The Plain Dealer* (September 1724) and reprinted in the collected edition of 1730, which Hill presented to Pope in January 1731.[122]

In an expanded note, published in *The Dunciad, in Four Books* (1743), Pope and his new editor Warburton explained:

> The Poet all along expresses a very particular concern for this silent Race.
> He has here provided that in case they will not waken or open (as was before
> proposed) to a Humming bird or a Cockle yet at worst they may be made
> Free-Masons where Taciturnity is the only essential qualification as it was
> the chief of the disciples of Pythagoras.[123]

---

[120] Alexander Pope, *The New Dunciad: As it was Found in the Year 1741* (London, 1742), 3, 5, 11, 12, 16.

[121] *Ibid.*, 35-36.

[122] A. Pope, *Correspondence*, III, 164.

[123] [Alexander Pope], *The Dunciad, in Four Books. Printed According to the Complete Copy found in the Year 1742* (London, 1743), 201.

Like much of *The New Dunciad*, the expanded note only added to the obscurity and mystification of many lines and references, which was probably deliberate, as Pope and Warburton hoped to avoid government prosecution.

In May Pope's friend Whitehead encouraged a new satire on the Grand Lodge, when his opposition colleagues mocked the recent "Procession of March" in a print titled "The Free-Masons Downfall; or, The Restoration of the Scald Miserables." Published in *The Westminster Journal* (8 May 1742) by "Thomas Touchit," the accompanying text claimed to be the "Remonstrance" of the Grand Master and Brethren of the "most Ancient and Honourable Society of Scald-Miserable-Masons."[124] Touchit mocked the Freemasons for their credulous claims to antiquity while claiming to possess the real key to the mysteries and "many Things Emblematical, Mystical, Hieroglyphical, Comical, Satirical, Political, etc." In a key to the engraving of the procession, he identified many Masonic symbols and revealed the rituals employed in initiations. Like Wharton's Gormogons earlier, these new rivals to loyalist Masonry used parody and ridicule to irritate and embarrass the Hanoverian brothers.

Another friend of Pope, the poet and dramatist James Miller, collaborated with Whitehead in his satires on the loyalist Masons.[125] In a 1742 pamphlet, Miller took on the persona of "Dick Poney, Esq., Grand-master of the Right Black-guard Society of the Scald-Miserable-Masons," who attacked Nicholas Paxton, "Grand-Master of the Right Scoundrel Gazetteer Legion, at his Chambers in Newgate." Miller/Poney cruelly mocked Paxton, the solicitor of the treasury who had prosecuted many anti-Walpolean writers. When Paxton defiantly refused to testify before the secret committee investigating Walpole's distribution of secret service money, he was sent to Newgate in an attempt to break his silence. Equating Paxton's government-subsidized *Gazetteer*-journalists with Hanoverian Masons, Poney scorned the masters of "the most eminent Lodges belonging to that Bastard Fraternity, who stile themselves Free Masons."[126] In a supposed speech before his execution, the Walpolean urges the gazetteers to "enter into a strict Confederacy and Association with your Kindred Societies of the Scald-Miserables, and the Black-guards; but never have any thing to do…with the Worshipful the Frees [Freemasons], for they are a Species of Scoundrels by themselves."

In a postscript, Poney noted that "Colonel Ding-Dong" of the Post Office, "an eminent Brother of your Scoundrel Society, and the Publisher and Disperser of the Daily Memoirs of your Gazetteer Legion, is taken into keeping." Ding-Dong has been identified as John David Barbutt, brother-in-law of John Coustos, the Hanoverian Masonic opponent to Derwentwater's Grand Mastership.[127] Barbutt was removed as secretary of the Post Office in July 1742, as a result of the secret committee's investigation of Walpolean espionage. As an admirer of Whitehead and Miller, Pope followed these obscure Masonic and political intrigues, and he sent Swift additional lines to *The New Dunciad* (1742) in which he mocked Paxton: "And rueful Paxton* tells the world with tears,

---

[124] C. Crawley, "Mock Masonry," 128.

[125] For his friendship with Pope, see "James Miller," *ODNB*.

[126] James Miller, *An Epistle from Dick Poney, Esq., Grand-Master of the Right Black-Guard Society of Scald-Miserable-Masons… to Nick P----n, Esq., Grand-Master of the Right Scoundrel Gazeteer Legion, at his Chambers in Newgate* (London, 1742), 4, 15, 56..

[127] R. Berman, *Espionage*, 99-103..

`These are – ah, no! – These were, My *Gazettteers.*" His marginal note* identifies Paxton as "A Sollicitour who procur'd & payd these writers."[128] He also referred to Barbutt's removal from office and subsequent bankruptcy.

Despite Pope's deliberate obliqueness and obscurity in Book Four of *The New Dunciad*, many pro-government readers thought he had crossed the line with his smear attacks. Colley Cibber, who had long suffered quietly under the poet's satires, was finally provoked to respond in *A Letter from Mr. Cibber, to Mr. Pope, Inquiring into the Motives that might induce him in his Satyrical Works, to be so frequently fond of Mr. Cibber's Name* (London, 1742). Though Pope did not identify Cibber as a Freemason, the laureate suggested that Pope's malice was prompted by his sympathy for Non-jurors and Jacobites (who were popularly linked with the Gormogons). Like Wogan and Samber earlier, Cibber wondered why Pope wasted his time satirizing "a parcel of poor Wretches, that were not able to hurt or resist you, so weak, it was almost Cowardice to conquer them."[129]

He concluded that Pope still resented his early play, *The Non-juror* (1718), which was re-published in 1736: "What terrible Apprehensions it gave him!" Like many "Daily-Paper Criticks," who joined "in full Cry" against its popular success, Pope resented it for "so audaciously exposing the sacred Character of a lurking, treason-hatching Jesuit, and for inhumanly ridiculing the conscientious Cause of an honest deluded Jacobite Gentleman." If the play had not "so impudently fallen upon the poor Enemies of the Government, Mr. Pope, possibly, might have been less an Enemy to the Play." Implying that it was his Papist prejudices that drove the satirist, he observed that "surely those who are of a different Religion" should be excused for looking upon Pope "as their Enemy." Up to this point, Cibber had maintained a dignified restraint, but he could not resist recounting an incident when he and Pope as young men were taken to a whore house by the eighteen year-old, rakish Duke of Warwick, where Pope, "this little hasty Hero, like a terrible Tom-Tit," was seen "pertly perching upon the Mount of Love," until Cibber pulled him off and saved him from catching venereal disease.

Cibber's attack on Pope and the apostasy of so many opposition Masons and "Patriots" provoked Moses Mendes to satiric verse. He was evidently unaware of Swift's mental deterioration, for he addressed him in "The 13th Ode of the 4th Book of Horace Imitated":

> Swift, say woud'st thou then refuse with me
> To cross St. George's sea
> And visit well known regions?
> ……………………………………………….
> Say canst thou blame the spoon I chase?
> Where Pope first call'd the willing muse,
> There let me read his matchless lays,
> Together mingle grief and praise,
> While Cibber stands by snarling.[130]

Recalling pleasant days at Windsor, Mendes ironically scorned its degradation when Walpole was received as a Knight of the Garter and Pulteney was made Earl of Bath:

---

[128] J. Swift, *Correspondence*, IV, 581.
[129] Colley Cibber, *A Letter from Mr. Cibber to Mr. Pope* (London, 1742), 11, 21, 23, 26, 48.
[130] UGLE. MS 1860. Men., ff. 14-15.

> Yet be the place not slighter
> Where Walpole felt the circling blue,
> Alike belov'd by me and you,
> And Bath would fain be knighted.
> If the kind Pow'rs should grant my pray'r,
> And thou shoulst breath in British air,
> Fate can no more contribute.
> In honest ease we'll pass our time,
> And snatch the triplet crutch of rhyme
> To prop a falling gibbet.

Mendes's reference to "a falling gibbet" (the gallows used for public hanging) revealed his recognition of his own and Swift's political vulnerability, and the poem remained in manuscript.

As the War of Jenkin's Ear spluttered indecisively to an end, with no real gains by Britain, the country was soon drawn into even bigger European conflicts. Mendes voiced his disgust with the wars' ineffectual perpetrators and praised those exiles who would provide better leadership in Britain. In "Men and Measures Characterized from Horace," he scorned "the brib'd" and "venial train," who voted a shameful peace with Spain.[131] He praised Bolingbroke, now in France:

> St. John from Britain exil'd flies
> While Nations from his tongue grow wise.
> And pension'd Horace [Walpole] swells, while States
> Are smit with folly, as he prates.
> ....
> And soon Argyle, a beardless boy
> May wield the truncheon you enjoy.
> See Keith, the Russian vengeance pours
> On Ozakov's devoted Tow'rs!

The linking of the "beardless boy," the young Charles Edward Stuart, to the Scottish Jacobite General Keith, and the challenge to the now powerless Argyle were risky statements in the heated political context.

While Pope was attacked by a Hanoverian Mason, he was also defended by a Jacobite Mason – Chevalier Ramsay – who supported him against the criticism of Louis Racine, a French poet who scorned Pope as an "abstract reasoner, who complains of nothing in his phlegmatic Anglican answer that 'all is for the best.'"[132] Racine considered his *Essay on Man* to be "a nursery of heretical opinions."[133] Apparently at Pope's request, Ramsay wrote Racine on 28 April 1742 that the purpose of his letter was to render justice to his friend and countryman, who is a very good Catholic, who has always maintained the religion of his forefathers in a nation where he would find many temptations to abandon it.[134] In a long theological argument, Ramsay affirmed that Pope, "Our English Homer,"

---

[131] *Ibid.*, ff. 35-37.

[132] A. Pope, *Works*, eds. Croker and Elwin, II, 291-92.

[133] M. Mack, *Alexander Pope*, 739.

[134] For the correspondence between the three men, see Louis Racine, *Oeuvres de Louis Racine* (Paris, 1808), I, 435-49. My translation.

holds that man and nature have fallen but that they will be eventually regenerated. Milton was an extreme Calvinist and degraded his poem by the puerile and insensitive injuries he vomited against the Catholic church. Newton was a great mathematician but no metaphysician, who fell into Arianism, which his disciple Clarke repented of (in conversation with Ramsay) just before his death. Locke was a superficial Socinian. The man who saved Ramsay himself from his youthful scepticism was the sublime Fenelon, who helped him understand the beauty of Christian morality and the possibility of understanding its mysteries.

On 15 May Racine wrote Ramsay that he appreciated the defense of Pope, which was rendered more credible because Ramsay loves truth more than he does his countrymen, whose errors he does not dissimulate. In fact, he wants to publish Ramsay's letter. On 2 September Ramsay responded to Racine and enclosed Warburton's defense of Pope's orthodoxy and Pope's own reply to the Frenchman. Pope suffers from the attacks of enemies who are either jealous of his talent or angry at his opposition to the court. Ramsay then repeated an inaccurate story, apparently related to him by Pope, that Queen Anne had offered the poet a high position, without the need for him to change his religion or take the required oaths. His firm refusal was such a sacrifice that no non-believer nor deist would make.

In Pope's enclosed letter, he excused Racine for imputing principles to him that he never held, because Racine had read only a faulty French translation. He sincerely avowed that "all my opinions are intirely different from those of Spinosa, or even of Leibnitz; but on the contrary conformable to those of Mons. Pascal and Mons. Fenelon: the latter of whom I would most readily imitate, in submitting all my opinions to the decision of the Church."[135] Voltaire, who had known Pope in London when the poet was much influenced by Bolingbroke's deism, claimed that Pope's letter, which he did not read in the English original but in the French translation, was a forgery: "If Pope wrote this letter to Racine, God must have given him the gift of tongues," for Pope knew little French.[136] He further charged that "Ramsay alone was responsible for the sentiments expressed in the letter to Racine." Voltaire later had Ramsay in mind when he observed, "There is nothing to gain with an Enthusiast; one must never be so bold as to tell a man the faults of his mistress, nor a pleader the folly of his cause, nor must one talk reason to an *illuminé*."[137]

Ramsay was especially sensitive to the charges of deism and heterodoxy flung against himself and Pope, for he was laboring to complete what he called his "Great Work," an extensive and sophisticated analysis of science, mathematics, philosophy, and religion. On 14 August 1742 he wrote his old friend Dr. Stevenson in Edinburgh about his expectation that Francis Hutcheson will not be pleased with his dialogues and treatise, "because of the high opinion he has of the English genius and of the great Sir Isaac Newton, as also because of the great contempt he has for the French genius, the popish system, and metaphysical learning, which I look upon to be the source & mother of all the sublime sciences."[138] He worried about the chauvinism and xenophobia of many home-

---

[135] *Ibid.*, I, 445-46.
[136] A. Pope, *Works*, ed. Croker and Elwin, I, 291.
[137] M. Schuchard, *Emanuel Swedenborg*, 672.
[138] M. Baldi, *Verisimile*, 459.

bound Englishmen, for it is a great disadvantage "to the most exalted genii not to have travelled in foreign countries, seen and conversed with their nicest men":

> There are many fine spirits in this nation [France], who are disgusted with all religion, both natural and revealed, and that are become spinosists & incredulous scepticks by the abuses of Christianity & especially of the predestinarian scheme. I have these gentlemen in view in my Dialogues, but more especially in my great work… My Dialogues are levelled directly against deism, Socinianism & pharisaism, but in the great work I endeavor over and above to undermine spinosism.[139]

Despite his earlier admiration of Newtonian science, he now took on the English "idol":

> I am convinced that the world will at last be undeceived and even ashamed of the *doctrine of attraction*… Sir Isaac's imagination stuff'd & cramm'd-full of conicks & trajectorial theories, fancyed two real forces correspondent to these fictitious lines, one that razes the tangent & another that draws to wend toward the center… I should be very sorry to leap into the other world with my soul daubed and bescribbled with geometrical figures.

On 24 August he wrote again that he does not want to be branded as he was when *Cyrus* appeared, "with the idle odious names of a deistical freethinking, Socinian, latitudinarian despiser of all external ordinances."[140] He informed Stevenson that he will find in volume two of his great work "a true key to antiquity, a fine introduction to the mystical sense of Scripture & philanthropy… proper to reconcile the philosophical members of all communions, & thereby to diminish our discords and make us hiss & abhor priestcraft of every kind." He then hinted at the secret teachings that emerged in the higher degrees of *Écossais* Freemasonry, which became increasingly mystical and visionary, aiming at the spiritual and intellectual regeneration of the elite initiate:

> No theorys, nor speculations do harm but those that enslave the heart to passions of self idolatry, & turn off the mind & soul from the love & contemplation of the sovereign beauty. Many contemplative saints, pagan, Jewish & Christian, in the days of yore and at present, know nothing of the Christian schemes… *O!mihi si centum linguae sint oraque centum* [O! would that I had a hundred tongues, a hundred mouths] that I might preach this doctrine to all congenial minds endow'd and blest with the sixth sense; for to these only I speak & for all these only I work, and this is frenzy, madness & fanatical folly to think of converting those who have not this moral, divine, vital taste & relish of the sovereign beauty of the eternal order.[141]

His hint that those endowed with "the sixth sense" could achieve a visionary trance state through ritualized meditation became one of the most secret goals of certain *Écossais* rites.

Ramsay had completed his "Lettres Chinoises" (now lost) and hoped to publish them in English translation as well as French, but when Stevenson suggested that David Hume

---

[139] *Ibid.*, 460.
[140] *Ibid.*, 465-66.
[141] *Ibid.*, 467.

be solicited as the translator, the chevalier replied that Hume "is too full of himself, to humble his pregnant, active, protuberant Genius to drudge at a translation."[142] Given Ramsay's current influence on the developing higher degrees, it is provocative that a new ritual of "Irish Perfect Master" emerged circa 1740, which included the Chinese words for "the seat of the soul" and "the action of kneeling": "Reduced to its essential and most baffling elements, the degree is composed of: a solemn genuflection; two words *Civi* and *Ki*, associated with this genuflection; a password of alluring consonants, *Xin Schu.*"[143] The Irish Master degree preceded the Scottish Master in the series of initiatory ceremonies, and it "adapted the traditional Chinese ceremony of homage to the dead to the soul of Hiram," the architect of Solomon's temple. A surviving tracing board includes the Jesuit insignia "I H S," which certainly suggests the influence of Ramsay on the infusion of Fouquet's Jesuit-Chinese "Figurist" themes into the Irish and subsequent Scottish degrees.

This Irish combination of Cabalistic and Chinese symbolism also points back to Swift's *Letter from the Grand Mistress*, his satirical response to Anderson's Whiggish constitutions, in which the Masonic "Guardian" refers not only to ancient Jewish but Chinese contributions to authentic Scots-Irish-Stuart Masonry.[144] These Irish-Jewish-Chinese rituals would be practiced in the Parisian lodge "Saint-Jean de Jerusalem" in June 1745, one month after the Irish Brigade led the stunning defeat of the British army at Fontenoy in May. This lodge was headed by the Comte de Clermont, Grand Master, military leader, and strong supporter of Charles Edward Stuart's planned invasion of England, in which the Masons in the Irish Brigade were expected to play a leading part.

Meanwhile, back in 1742, Ramsay continued his criticism of David Hume in his correspondence with Dr. Stevenson:

> By the little I heard from & read of that young Gentleman [Hume], he seems to me to be far from being a True master of metaphysicks… That bright ingenious Spark does not seem to me to have acquir'd a sufficient Stock of solid Learning, nor to be born with a fund of noble Sentiments, not to have a genious capable of all that Geometrical attention, penetration and Justness necessary to make a True Metaphysician. I am affray'd his spirit is more lively than solid, his Imagination more luminous than profound, and his heart too dissipated with material objects & spiritual Self-Idolatry to pierce into the secret recesses of divine Truths… He seems to me one of those philosophers that think to spin out Systems, out of their own brain, without any regard to religion, antiquity or Tradition sacred or profane.[145]

As we shall see, though Hume did not accept Ramsay's Masonic theosophy, he learned enough about Freemasonry not only from Ramsay but from his initiated friends Allan

---

[142] E. Mossner, *Life*, 94.

[143] René Désaguliers and Roger Dachez, "Chinese Thought and Freemasonry in the Eighteenth Century: the Degree of Irish Master, Provost, and Judge," in Arturo de Hoyos and Brent Morris, eds., *Freemasonry in Context: History, Ritual, and Controversy* (Lanham, 2004), 145-61.

[144] J. Swift, *Prose Works*, V, 328.

[145] E. Mossner, *Life*, 94-95.

Ramsay, Lord Morton, and others to later satirize the fraternity's themes of Cyrus, Zerubbabel, and the rebuilding of the Temple.[146]

Ramsay expected a better response from an old friend in Rome, for he planned to send the first copies of his French dialogues to Pope Benedict XIV, for "he is a very clever, fine, jovial, agreeable freethinking man" – a description that raises the question of whether Benedict's alleged youthful Masonic initiation was influenced by Ramsay during his visits to Rome in the 1720s. Stosch had recently reported that Benedict was angry at the Inquisitor of Rome because of his scandalous conduct during the trial of the poet Crudeli, which reflected the pope's sympathy for the imprisoned Freemason.[147] Ramsay designed another to "Mahomet Effendi, the Turkish ambassador at this court, who understands well the French and our European learning." Ramsay concluded that "you see I am no partial admirer of any sect or party, since I wish the moral sense were awakened in all... *Universae religionis vindex & martyr* is the inscription I desire may be put upon my tomb, and on the frontispiece of my work *Si non verum, verisimile.*" In conclusion, he expressed his hope that he and his wife could visit Scotland, but he dared not absent himself from France for long, "without royal permission, as his pensionary. Such slaves are we to despotick power."

It was perhaps no coincidence that a version of his Masonic oration was now issued in a more respectable publication, when it was included by M. de la Tierce as "Discours prononcé a la reception des Free-Maçons, par m. de Ramsay, grand orateur de l'ordre," in *Histoire et Statuts de la tres venerable Confraternité des Francs-Maçons* (Frankfurt sur le Meyn, 1742). Though Ramsay's Dialogues were never published and have disappeared, his Great Work was completed before his death in May 1743 but not published until 1748-49. Because it drew upon and embellished the philosophical and esoteric themes of his oration, it will be appropriate to examine the beliefs and practices that the elite adept could access through initiation in the higher degrees. For several years, his friends in France and Scotland had read and commented on extracts from the manuscript, which was eventually published in two volumes as *The Philosophical Principles of Natural and Revealed Religion, Unfolded in a Geometrical Order* (Edinburgh: Robert and Andrew Foulis, 1748-49). Despite the loss of his "Chinese Letters," he included enough Chinese theosophical material to suggest what he probably had discussed at greater length in them.

In the Introduction, he appealed to "all serious Freethinkers" to study his "attempt to discover the original meaning of the symbols, fables, and obscure traditions of antiquity, particularly of the old canonical books of the Chinese."[148] However, most of the first volume contained an elaborate, sophisticated, and rational discussion of the mathematics and philosophy of Spinoza, Descartes, Newton, Leibniz, and other major thinkers. At one point, he observed that if we consider the "three principal sorts of men who shine upon the great theatre of life, warriors, statesmen, and mean of learning, what terrible scenes of vice present themselves to the mind."[149] Noting that "the most cruel wars are very oft produced by the most trifling disputes, and for as ridiculous subjects as we

---

[146] See ahead, Chapter Twenty-three.

[147] NA:SP 98/43 (3 May 1741).

[148] Andrew Michael Ramsay, *The Philosophical Principles of Natural and Revealed Religion, Unfolded in a Geometrical Order* (Edinburgh, 1748-49), I, iv, viii.

[149] *Ibid.*, I, 339.

know," he seemed to refer to the British "War of Jenkins's Ear" in 1739. He revealed that this section is "much borrowed from a modern Humourist, well versed in the darkest side of human nature, and of a very singular genius, DR. SWIFT."

Occasionally, in the midst of the abstract and often arid analytical philosophy and mathematics, he hinted at his Masonic beliefs – at the symbolism and rituals that led to illumination and regeneration:

> The material universe is an immense theatre with glorious paintings and dec-orations, by which God displays for ever and ever his power, wisdom and goodness. Spirits are living, lively images or actors upon this great theatre, that are capable of knowing, loving and enjoying the original. Wherefore in the following essay by the simple pictures we denote the material world; and by the living images, the intellectual universe of spirits.[150]

To perceive this great theatre, the individual must achieve "a state of pure and exalted nature" through ritualized meditation, in which "God can manifest his divine perfections to finite intelligences" in the contemplation of his divine essence and in the knowledge of "his created representations."[151]

The ancient Chinese wrote about the means of "re-uniting the soul to God by con-templation," and they meditated on their "hieroglyphical characters" to achieve their "sublime analogical philosophy."[152] This great principle was also the source of that "sym-bolic and hieroglyphical language," by which the first sages expressed all the mysteries of religion, and all the secrets of the invisible world":

> They looked upon the material universe and all its parts as shadows, em-blems, pictures of the intellectual world; and so made use of the properties, virtues, and qualities of the one to design, indicate and represent the powers and attributes and faculties of the other. These sacred symbols therefore were not at first veils and masks to hide sublime truths from vulgar minds; but types, and images to recall these great truths to our remembrance.[153]

Ramsay then merged his studies of Hermetic and Cabalistic traditions with his belief in Newton's ether theory:

> This ethereal fluid is…the instrument, image, and sensory of the Deity, to make use of Sir Isaac Newton's expression, upon which he [God] acts im-mediately, and by which he acts upon all other corporeal being. It is the physical spring of the universe that sets the great machine going. It is this universal agent that animates and enlightens, moves and penetrates, unites and separates, compresses or expands, forms and produces compound bod-ies of all kinds solid and liquid. Hence it is that in the Hebrew language, the plural word Schemim which expresses the different principles of the celestial fluid signifies in different places of the sacred text; agents, formers, dispos-ers… All the different forms, divisions and motions of solid, visible, tangible bodies, are produced by the action of this invisible, universal fluid, according

---

[150] *Ibid.*, I, 193.
[151] *Ibid.*, I, 283.
[152] *Ibid.*, II, 12, 408.
[153] *Ibid.*, I, 290.

to immutable laws known to God alone, and most proper to express his divine perfections, and accomplish his great designs.[154]

In the Appendix to volume one, Ramsay revealed more of his Cabalistic studies, which he used to discredit Spinoza's philosophy as a "monstrous chimera" of predestinarianism:

> Spinosa derived his great and fundamental principle that all flows from God by way of emanation and not creation, from the Cabbalists; who talk thus, "the first cause ENSOPH, produced immediately from his own substance the intelligible world called ADAM KADMON, which contains all the productions of the first cause. God expressed in this production all his holy names, yea all the eternal letters of these names, which are the innumerable forms of things... so all individuals, species and kinds are formed from the different composition of the holy names...
>
> From all this it appears that Spinosa's monstrous system is composed of Cabbalism, Cartesianism, and Predestinarianism differently conjoined and interwoven...It is possible that Spinosa did not think of himself as an Atheist; [but] his principles lead visibly to atheism and immorality.[155]

In volume two, he would draw upon the Christianization of Cabala to paint a more positive picture of the esoteric Jewish science.

That Ramsay believed his heterodox philosophy-theosophy could be taught within Freemasonry was revealed in his hints at a spiritual initiation process, which leads to "true conversion, and the beginning of wisdom."[156] Through meditation and self-examination, the soul becomes "elevated from self" and becomes "truly regenerated, and breathes a new life hid with Christ in God":

> It is then that it enters into the HOLY OF HOLIES, that it becomes a living temple of the most High, partakes of the royal priesthood ... The first of these three operations detaches us from terrestrial objects: the second disengages us from false self-love: the third transforms us into the divine image.

At this time, three higher degrees beyond the basic three craft and fourth Scottish Master's degrees emerged in certain *Écossais* rites, especially in the Rite of Seven Degrees, affiliated with the Royal Order of Heredom. Ramsay described "these three illuminating, purifying, and regenerating operations, "in which the soul becomes receptive to the divine inspirations." If the soul cooperates fully with this process, God will enlighten, purify "by degrees," and regenerate us at last – "and in these three operations consist all the degrees, the beginning, the progress and the consummation of the spiritual life." In conclusion, he promised to show in volume two that "all the mysteries, rites, and ceremonies of the Pagan initiations were originally symbols of these three purifications transmitted from the beginning of the world, to all successive generations." It is obvious that under Ramsay's influence, many *Écossais* rituals were moving far beyond the basic degrees of English Grand Lodge Freemasonry. Moreover, it was through Ramsay's close friendship with Count Tessin that Swedish Masonic ceremonies became especially elaborate.

---

[154] *Ibid.*, I, 317-18.
[155] *Ibid.*, I, 537-39.
[156] *Ibid.*, I, 406-07.

In volume two Ramsay drew upon the ancient writers of "the perennial tradition," such as Plotinus, Porphyry, Iamblichus, and especially Hermes Trismegistus, to reveal the myth of the two ante-diluvian pillars which preserved the ancient hieroglyphics – a tradition maintained within Freemasonry.[157] Arguing that "all religious and learned nations have by tradition the idea of a Great Man or Legislator, who was the first author of these sacred symbols and hieroglyphics, he referred to the Christian Cabalistic theories of Athanasius Kircher, Henry More, Ralph Cudworth, and Pierre Allix, who portrayed Jesus as the universal God-Man. The Jewish Cabalists believed that Adam Kadmon, the divine man, contained the whole "primitive world" and was all "luminous, transparent and beautiful." Quoting the Christian Cabalist Johann Rittangel's "*Visio. Ezekiel. Mercav.*" (Ezekiel's Vision of the Mercava, or Divine Chariot), he stressed that "the pre-existence of the sacred humanity of the Messiah is a doctrine yet believed and retained by the Rabbins, as an ancient tradition of their fore-fathers from the days of Noah and Moses."[158] Ramsay explained that the Cabalistical Jews "fix the number of three persons in the divine essence; they speak of the emanation of the two last from the first, and say, that third proceeds from the first by the second. They call the first person ENSOPH, the second MEMRA, and the third BINAH." He added that

> These cabbalists are properly the mythologists of the Hebrew nation and therefore their theology is very oft mixed with and disguised under many allegorical images and fables, that seem as impertinent as those of the Pagans, but still we may find among this heap of mudd, many precious pearls which seem to be emanations of the patriarchal, Noevian tradition.[159]

Though Ramsay was personally attracted to Jewish mysticism, he recognized reluctantly that "we have no longer any relish for this sublime analogical philosophy"; even worse, "the Cabbalists have lost all credit among the learned, because of the extravagant fictions mixed in their mythologies." Thus, it is fortunate that "Providence has opened a communication to China, "so we might find vestiges of our sacred religion in a nation which had no communication with the ancient Jews."[160] Despite his caveats about the unfashionableness of these traditions, Ramsay's theories about Cabalistic and Chinese theosophy would influence the esoteric themes of *Écossais*, Illuminist, and Swedenborgian Freemasonry.[161] They also contributed to the increasing divergence of Jacobite from Hanoverian Masonry – a divergence that would emerge in the literature and politics not only in the British Isles but in Europe, Scandinavia, and Russia.

In late 1742 Ramsay moved from Pontoise to St. Germain-en-Laye, which had long served as refuge and residence for exiled Jacobites. He and his wife appealed to the Pretender for financial support, because the Duc de Bouillon had not properly paid him for his services. As his health deteriorated and he determined to finish his "Great Work," he and his Scottish correspondents suggested that it should be dedicated to the Duke of Argyll, whom the Jacobites in Britain hoped would play the role of General Monk in a

---

[157] *Ibid.*, II, 9-10.
[158] *Ibid.*, II, 173.
[159] *Ibid.*, II, 117.
[160] *Ibid.*, II, 12, 304, 185.
[161] M. Schuchard, *Emanuel Swedenborg*, 599-600.

second Stuart restoration.[162] One wonders if Ramsay believed that Argyll would imitate Monk and utilize Masonic networks to fulfill this project. The Scots advised further that he enlist the support of Alexander Pope, who now owed Ramsay a favor. His more cautious friends worried about the heterodoxy of many passages and suggested that Dr. King should be called in to edit the work.

Despite Ramsay's immersion in finishing his Great Work, he kept up his political interests, especially in company with three *frères*, Charles Radcliffe, Earl of Derwentwater; George de Leslie, Baron de Blantyre; Alexander Montgomery, 10th Earl of Eglinton; and Michael Ramsay of Mungale (almost certainly a Mason). The twenty year-old Eglinton had recently been initiated by the Earl of Kilmarnock in the Kilwinning lodge in Edinburgh, and he was now travelling with his tutor, Michael Ramsay.[163] Eglinton's father, the 9th Earl, was included on Wharton's 1725 list of Jacobites. It was reported that he had been "a great under-hand supporter of the exiled family," and his mother, the famously beautiful Duchess of Eglinton, was known for her "thorough-paced Jacobitism."[164] While with the two Ramsays, Eglinton asked Michael to send, under Chevalier Ramsay's cover, a letter to arrange his meeting with James Edgar, the Pretender's secretary, when tutor and pupil arrived in Rome.[165] Edgar replied that he would be at their service. As we shall see, their behavior in Rome would lead Mann to report to Newcastle on their Jacobite proclivities.[166]

When the aged Fleury died on 19 February 1743, Chevalier Ramsay rejoiced that the cardinal's death "hath set me free from managing his false delicacy…and one of the principle parts of the ministry is now entrusted to a gentleman [Cardinal Tencin] who calls himself my most intimate friend, but I put no trust in princes or great men."[167] Tencin was close to James III, but he would not prove an effective minister. Ramsay did not live to see the emergence of one prince, his former pupil Charles Edward Stuart, as a Jacobite leader and hero, for he died on 6 May 1743 and was fittingly buried at St. Germain-en-Laye. Attending at his funeral were Michael Ramsay and his *Écossais* brothers Derwentwater, Blantyre, and Eglinton.

---

[162] G. Henderson, *Chevalier Ramsay*, 203.

[163] For Kilmarnock's role, see Alain Bernheim, "Ramsay's *Discours* Revisited." www.ordo-ab-chaos.org/ordo/Docs/Ramsay.PDF.

[164] Robert Chambers, *Traditions of Edinburgh* (Edinburgh, 1869), 211, 216.

[165] A. Kervella, *Chevalier Ramsay*, 339.

[166] See ahead, Chapter Nineteen.

[167] C. Batham, "Ramsay," 312.

CHAPTER NINETEEN

MOCK MASONS, ROYAL ARCH REBELS,
AND INVASION FEARS
(1743-1744)

Yesterday several of the mock-Masons were taken up by the Constable empowered to impress men for his Majesty's service, and confined till they can be examined by the Justices.

London Daily Post (3 May 1744).

...in this city lately hath appeared a number of mean and low spirited wretches, who... turned rebels to our well formed Government, and artfully brought into their iniquitous net several unguarded men... Some have been led away by ridiculous innovations... by a certain propagator of a false system... the Royal Arch...

Fifield d'Assigny, *A Serious and Impartial Inquiry into ...the Present Decay of Freemasonry* (Dublin, 1744).

In the months after Walpole's fall, the hopes of the Tories and Jacobites who had been attracted to the Prince of Wales were soon disappointed. Because of George II's "unconquerable aversion to the Tories," none of them were given offices, while many of the former opposition Whigs (the ministry's "New Friends") were won over with pensions, places, and bribes.[1] When the king refused to appoint John Hynde Cotton, a known Jacobite, to the Admiralty, Argyll resigned his new army post, and he with Watkins Williams Wynn reverted to opposition. During his political struggles, Wynn had been bolstered by his ardent Welsh supporter, David Thomas Morgan, the poetic lawyer, who anonymously published in 1741 a second canto to *The Country Bard: or, the Modern Courtiers*, dedicated to Wynn and the Prince of Wales.

---

[1] E.Cruickshanks, *Political Untouchables*, 32-35.

Morgan decried the government's anti-Jacobite, "hard push'd" propaganda campaign as an "expedient trite," in which "the Chevalier/ Invades the Junto with a panic Fear."[2] Though he and Wynn were indeed Jacobites, he argued that only "Marrall's Schemes at Home" (Walpole's policies) could raise the hopes of the Pretender, while this "Bugbear" of Jacobite threat, "this trifling Mean Appeal" will fill the "unguarded with mad wretched Zeal." He defended not only Wynn but Bolingbroke, Schippen, Orrery, Arran, Cobham, Stair, Chesterfield, and "Brilliant Swift in Wit." But "No virtuous Morals could advance," while "Henley foam'd an Orator in pay." In a final tribute to the late Atterbury, he lamented that "A banished Prelate was presum'd too Proud." Though it is unclear whether Morgan was a Mason, his poems were circulated by Wynn and his fellow Masons in the White Rose Society.

All the efforts to enlist Argyll as leader of the Jacobites came to a frustrated end in June 1742, when the news broke out that he had given his brother, Lord Ilay, to hand over to the king, two letters he had received from the Pretender:

> At first, Argyll said he had them from Col. Cecil, which Horace Walpole thought unlikely since Argyll had not seen Cecil for two years. Then Argyll admitted that "upon recollection he thought it right to say he had received those letters from Lord Barrymore." The first, in the Pretender's own hand, was "to thank Mr. Burnus [Argyll] for his services, and that he hopes he would answer *the assurances* given to him."[3]

The second letter had been distributed to the Jacobite network in England, and it congratulated them and the opposition for defeating Walpole; but now they must work to distress and overthrow "the present government and whoever shall be the chief ministers and directors of it, to the overthrowing all entirely at last." Given the loyalty of many Tories and opposition Whigs to the Prince of Wales, this challenge went too far for Argyll, who was more interested in personal power than in the Stuart cause.

Argyll's betrayal of the seventy-five year-old Barrymore, who was now scorned in London as "the Pretender's General," was the last straw for some of the opposition, who began to look toward the Stuart prince as a more worthy claimant than the Hanoverian Prince of Wales. Barrymore had earlier given loyal military service to Argyll, which provoked Lord Grange to write of the duke that "His conduct to Lord Barrymore is condemned by all on earth," for he had long lived in great friendship with him and should have given him notice of "the danger he was to bring him into." Barrymore left immediately for Ireland, where he would learn that his old friend Swift was institutionalized with dementia. Robert Walpole scorned Argyll's cowardice, claiming that when Cecil sent the letter to the duke, "he had not the courage to stand by his promise." After this, Argyll lived "retired, hardly seeing anybody" and "indolent and broken-hearted." Despite Pope's praise of his "thunder," Ramsay's hope for his patronage, Orrery's lauding him as "great" and "independent," and Dr. King's portrayal of him at the hero of the Temple of Liberty, Argyll ended his days as a spent force, dying in October 1743.

In Scotland, many of Argyll's supporters were unaware of his betrayal of Barrymore, and they continued to publicly praise him. Charles Leslie, the Edinburgh Freemason,

---

[2] [David Morgan], *The Country Bard: or, the Modern Courtiers.Canto the Second* (London, 1741), 2, 14, 17-19.
[3] The following quotes are from E. Cruickshanks, *Political Untouchables*, 32-34.

anonymously published a pseudo-masque, *The Masque of Patriotism and Truth: or, the Court Fool As it was presented before the **'s Majesty in Christmas Holiday at the Court of **** (1743). It was written in 1742 before the holidays but never performed. The female characters "Truth" and "Patriotism" argue with "Somebody" (George II) that he is being deceived by his courtiers, so Truth asks the king if she and her companion Patriotism can have "free Intercourse with you." An indignant king answers:

> *Some Body. Patriotism*! Is that *Patriotism?* Why, I don't know: I have heard dismal Stories of that Person, that she was a very Fiend, and a near Relation of one *Jacobitism*.
>
> *Truth.* You see how you are impos'd on: But, poor Maid, her Character, as well as mine, is prostituted and defam'd.
>
> *Patriotism:* And for the worst Purposes.
>
>   LILLEBULERO.
>
> *Of late ye have seen what Patriots we have,*
>   *For Freedom and Justice who strenuously call'd,*
> *From the Devil, from ruin their Country to save,*
>   *And loud against Places and Pensions they baul'd:*
>   *Premier* [Wapole] *turn'd out,*
>   *The righteous Rout,*
> *For Places and Pensions fell scrambling amain;*
> *And Patriots the greatest*
>   *Turn'd Rogues the compleatest,*
> *Their Faith all a Jest, and their Virtue mere Gain.*[4]

The king is not impressed by the exposure of the hypocritical Patriots, and replies that "While Somebody I am, and wear a Crown; No Wrong can I do – and no Wrong I'll own. (Struts off with his Courtiers)." However, *Patriotism* affirms that all is not lost, for there are "Friends left in the *Country* still: I could name many – The Duke of -----[Argyll]".

All the reform measures proposed by the anti-Walpoleans were defeated, which led Richmond to write a gloating letter to Newcastle on 6 December 1742: "You have heard by what Majorities, we have demolished Watkin Williams, flung out the Revival of the Secret Committee, & rejected the place Bill."[5] Richmond was sure that more opposition members would soon support the new ministry. Though Chesterfield was secretly collaborating with the Tories and Jacobites, some of their allies worried that his loyalties would shift if he gained a lucrative, new government post. On 4 February 1743 Lady Orrery wrote her husband that she was concerned "at any decay in Lord Chesterfield's health, yet in this corrupted Age, I doubt whether death to a man in his greatest Glory is not the greatest blessing, the Gods can bestow upon him."[6] She hinted that in future years Chesterfield may sully "his Honour, by adoring the Golden Image that Nebuchadnezzar hath set up." She then contrasted him to Dr. King and her husband, whose "hearts [are] so fixed so steady in supporting the cause of Liberty and Virtue, that length of Days will constantly add an increase of Fame to their Characters." Her concern about

---

[4] [Charles Leslie], *The Masque of Patriotism and Truth: or, the Court Fool* (London, 1743), 21-22, 27.

[5] Richmond, *Correspondence*, 94-95.

[6] Mildred Pierce, "The Literary Life….of John, Earl of Orrery" (Ph.D. Thesis: Smith College, 1948), 63.

Chesterfield's loyalty to the Stuart cause of King and Orrery would prove prophetic, when he later advocated merciless treatment of the Scottish rebels in 1745.

In 1743 Richmond suspected Chesterfield of sedition, and he despised his former Whig-Masonic brother. He thus continued to call upon his network of Hanoverian Masons (George Payne, Prendergast, Middlesex, Montagu, and Albemarle) for support, as the Walpolean Whigs clung to power.[7] Richmond also counted on Henry Fielding, a decade-long friend, to support the cause. In 1733 Fielding had dedicated to the duke his translation of Moliere's *The Miser*, in which he boasted of receiving the "Countenance" and "Honour," from such "High Rank," especially since Richmond knew so well the language, manners, and taste of the French.[8] In 1743, having received the duke's political support for his law career, Fielding outdid himself with praise in a poem, "Of Good Nature, To his Grace the Duke of Richmond." The duke's good nature is "A Flow'r so fine,/ It only grows in Soils almost divine."[9] Motivated by "the glorious Lust of doing Good," his heart "Can feel another's Pain, and taste his Ease." Other men, raised high on life's summit, little know "The Ills which blacken all the Vales below." "Swelt'ring with Wealth, where Men unmov'd can hear/ The Orphans sigh, and see the Widow's tear." Two years later, the Jacobite rebellion would test Richmond's supposed good nature, when he – like Chesterfield, his fraternal brother – called for draconian punishment of the rebels, their widows, and orphans.

The controversial new ministry received further literary backing from Edward Young, a loyalist Mason, in his long religious and philosophical poem, *Night Thoughts*, published anonymously and serially in 1742-44. With Jacobite Masonry emerging as a real threat, Young drew on his memories of the Duke of Wharton to portray "Lorenzo," a libertine and infidel, whom he tirelessly (and tediously) tries to reform: "Thou say'st I preach, Lorenzo! `tis confest/ What, if for once, I preach thee quite awake?"[10] As noted earlier, Young had revered Wharton when he served as the duke's Latin secretary in Ireland, but broke with him after Wharton became the defiant Jacobite Grand Master and defended Bishop Atterbury. The poet wore himself out with years of litigation trying to acquire the funds that Wharton had promised him, which the duke's attainder made impossible to achieve. Young now chastised Lorenzo/Wharton as a hedonist, libertine, and blasphemer:

> Vile laugher! At whom Pity cannot laugh;
> Scorner of All, but what deserves his Scorn!
> Who thinks it is Ingenious to be Mad,
> And is quite Fool enough to be a Wit.
> Wits spare not Heaven, O *Wilmington!* – nor Thee.
> FINIS.

This feeble conclusion revealed Young's continuing, almost servile effort to gain patronage from Whig politicians, as well as his naiveté and misjudgments about the constant shifting of power and places among the upstart, post-Walpolean ministers. He had

---

[7] Richmond, *Correspondence*, 71,92, 103, 182-83, 198, 201.

[8] Henry Fielding, *The Miser* (London and Dublin, 1733), Dedication.

[9] Henry Fielding, *Miscellanies* (London and Dublin, 1743), 10-13.

[10] [Edward Young]. *Night the Second. On Time,Death, and Friendship* (London, 1742), 8.

dedicated Night One to Arthur Onslow, Speaker of the House of Commons, who had earlier led the prosecution of Atterbury, generally supported the Whig ministry, and was mocked by both sides because of "his pretence to popularity."[11] He dedicated Night Two to Spencer Compton, Earl of Wilmington, who was close to George II but had an uneasy relationship with Walpole, who had "pandered to his avariciousness" in the 1720s. Walpole could not prevent him from joining Argyll in the Broad Bottom and then becoming a powerless prime minister for the few months before his death in July 1743.[12] Chesterfield despised Wilmington and could not believe that he was chosen to replace Walpole, but he recognized that Carteret, his own rival, was the real power behind the throne. In a letter to Marchmont, Pope also scorned the deceased Wilmington as "a worthless man of Quality," who lived without "one worthy Deed, public or private!"[13]

Young dedicated Night Three to Margaret Cavendish Bentinck, Duchess of Portland, an intellectual patron of the arts and sciences, who tried unsuccessfully to obtain from Newcastle a deanery for Young.[14] When these appeals got nowhere, he dedicated Nights Four and Five to "Mr. York" (Hon. Charles Yorke, a Whig) and to his brother-in-law and Masonic brother, the 2nd Earl of Lichfield, a Tory, who died in February 1743.[15] In Night Six he boldly appealed to Henry Pelham, younger brother of Newcastle and a Whig Mason, who became prime minister in August 1743. As *Night Thoughts* continued, with increasing philosophical aridity and rhetorical bombast, Young's criticism of Lorenzo/Wharton became harsher. In the sections called "The Infidel Reclaim'd," his scorn grew more contemptuous for "A celebrated Wretch":

> When I behold a Genius bright, and base,
> Of towering Talents, and terrestrial Aims;
> Methinks I see, as thrown from her high Sphere,
> The glorious Fragments of a Soul Immortal,
> With Rubbish mixt, and glittering in the dust.
> Struck at the splendid, melancholy Sight,
> At once Compassion soft, and Envy rise –
> But wherefore Envy? Talents Angel-bright,
> If wanting Worth, are shining instruments
> In false Ambition's Hand, to finish Faults
> Illustrious, and give Infamy renown.[16]

In comparison to the degenerate Jacobite Wharton, Young praised the morally upright Whig prime minister: "If wrong our Hearts, our Heads are right in vain;/ What is Pelham's Head, to Pelham's Heart?"

It is possible that Young's almost obsessive effort to posthumously reclaim the infidel Wharton was influenced by the increasing influence of Tory and Jacobite Masons within the Grand Lodge. Kintore and Morton, the Scottish Grand Masters who became Grand Masters of England, were both suspected of Jacobite sympathies, despite their public

[11] R. Sedgwick, *History*, II, 308-09.
[12] *Ibid.*,I, 568-69.
[13] A. Pope, *Correspondence*, IV, 458.
[14] Margaret Cavendish Bentinck, Duchess of Portland," *ODNB*.
[15] R. Berman, *Foundations*, 162.
[16] Edward Young, *Night the Sixth. The Infidel Reclaim'd* (London, 1744), 14-15.

loyalism. Their successor in England was John Ward, 1ˢᵗ Viscount Dudley and Ward, a Tory who consistently voted against the Walpolean ministry until he lost his parliamentary seat in 1734.[17] In 1743, during the Jacobites' negotiations with the French to plan an invasion, Ward's name was sent to the French government as one of their most wealthy and influential members. Having inherited in 1740 the potentially most valuable mineral estate in England, he used most of his wealth to construct a great Palladian mansion in Himley, where he employed the talented sculptor and Master Mason Charles Trubshaw. Ric Berman argues that Ward "epitomized the unreconstructed agricultural landed interest"; under his stewardship, "Grand Lodge became increasingly arrogant and self-obsessed," which led to increasing "Masonic disaffection."[18] One wonders if his private Jacobitism contributed to this decline in the Grand Lodge, which had earlier been dominated by government loyalists.

It was this decrease in Hanoverian-Whig influence in England and in Austria that led to a correspondence between Horace Mann in Florence and Horace Walpole in London concerning current Masonic problems in spring 1743. Mann wrote Walpole on 22 April, "Pray remember to inform me how the Queen's severity against freemasons is taken in England at the instigation of the Pope and the Devil."[19] Mann referred to the Hapsburg empress Maria Teresa's action against a Masonic lodge in Vienna, in which thirty brothers were arrested, including "several persons of distinction, who were soon released." The lodge had been founded in 1742 by her husband Francis, Grand Duke of Tuscany, who as Duke of Lorraine had been elevated in the fraternity in a lodge held by Walpole and Newcastle in England. It was reported that her husband escaped the raid by the back stairs. The affair was covered by *The Gentleman's Magazine* (1743), and Mann expected it to be taken seriously by Grand Lodge Masons. However, Walpole replied on 4 May:

> The Freemasons are in so low repute now in England, that one has scarce heard the proceedings against them in Vienna mentioned. I believe nothing but a persecution can bring them into vogue again here. You know how great our follies are, we even grow tired of them, and are always changing.[20]

For nearly ten years from June 1742, "no less than forty-five lodges, or about a third of the total of those meeting in the metropolis were struck out of the list" of the Grand Lodge of England.[21]

During the first half of 1743, Pope struggled with deteriorating health but managed to spend time with his friends King, Bolingbroke, Marchmont, Orrery, and George Arbuthnot, son of the Jacobite physician. His letters were very cautious, informing Orrery in January of his collaboration with Dr. King in their abortive effort to achieve an Oxford degree for Bishop Warburton, while he lamented the rejection of Tories and Jacobites from the new ministry. Using .the Jacobites' cant word "honest," he wrote that

[17] "John Ward," R. Sedgwick, *History*, II, 520; E. Cruickshanks, *Political Untouchables*, 134; H. Colvin, *Biographical Dictionary*, 990.
[18] Ric Berman, "Freemasonry, the London Irish, and the Antients Grand Lodge," in Christopher Murphy and Shawn Eyer, *Exploring Grand Lodge Freemasonry* (Washington, D.C., 2017), 256-59.
[19] H. Walpole, *Correspondence*, XVIII, 208.
[20] *Ibid.*, XVIII, 226.
[21] *Ibid.*, 226 n.15.

All honest Company is a rarity, but principally among Gentlemen. I think this one Sentence includes a General account of Publick affairs. I have seen and heard what makes me shut my Eyes, & Ears, and retire inward into my own Heart; where I find Something to comfort me, in knowing that it is possible some men may have some Principles.[22]

In February he wrote Orrery that he "*dare* not" send news of "some of your acquaintance," but it is unknown if he knew that Orrery was currently considered by James III and Louis XV as a key supporter for a Jacobite restoration.[23]

In March Pope wrote Hugh Bethel of his concern that the recently deceased Duchess of Buckingham, a life-long Jacobite intriguer, had named Robert Walpole as her Trustee and Lord Hervey as her executor. The eccentric duchess had tried to recruit Walpole and Hervey to support a Stuart restoration, and she was so gullible that she thought she had won them over.[24] Pope now worried that his letters to her might come out, but he was sure that "they make no part of her Treasonable Correspondence," which they say she expressly left to Hervey: "Sure this is Infamous Conduct towards any common acquaintance… I know you [Bethel] are one of those that will burn every Scrap I write you, at my desire."[25] As Hanoverian Whig Masons, Walpole and Hervey would certainly be interested in the duchess's contacts with opposition and Jacobite Masons (the latter had initiated her son before his untimely death). Colonel William Cecil shared Pope's concerns and complained that the late duchess had "appropriated to herself the part of Embassadress extraordinary to the King and Court of France," to whom she demanded such exorbitant funds and troops for a Jacobite invasion that it made the French believe that James III had "few friends ready to appear for him."[26]

On 11 May Lady Orrery teased her husband about his uncomfortable contacts with Lord Hervey, who will turn Orrery into "a charming Adonis," for "Lady Fanny" will instruct him in how to wear stays, make-up, etc.[27] A week later, she wrote a risky letter, in which she mocked George II for reviewing his Hanover troops, "paid by the poor people of England," and then compared them to her horse "King Nobby" and his activities.[28] In a high-spirited passage that evidently alarmed her husband, she wrote, "I have a mind to write a weekly Paper …filled with those innocent Politicks, I should only apprehend that Bishop Willes might decipher dangerous meaning out of the transactions of King Nobby's court."[29] From June to October 1743 Orrery, Barrymore, and Grange undertook risky negotiations with William Macgregor of Balhaldy, secretary of the associated Scottish lords, who was sent from France by the Pretender to evaluate Stuart support in England.[30] Balhaldy reported that he was satisfied with their positive responses.

The death of Cardinal Fleury in January 1743 had not only lifted the spirits of Chevalier Ramsay but also changed the whole European political and military situation. Fleury

---

[22] A. Pope, *Correspondence*, IV, 437.

[23] *Ibid.*, IV, 441.

[24] J. Jesse, *Memoirs*, II, 24-27.

[25] A. Pope, *Correspondence*, IV, 446.

[26] W. Murray, *Memoirs*, 48.

[27] Harvard, Houghton: Eng. MS. 218.26, letter 57.

[28] *Ibid.*, letter 59 (18 May 1743).

[29] *Ibid.*, letter 63 (30 May 1743).

[30] A Lang, *History*, IV, 441;E. Cruickshanks, *Political Untouchables*, 41.

was not replaced, while Louis XV and his closest advisors re-directed foreign policy towards greater support for the Stuarts. Encouraged by Balhaldy's reports, Louis XV sent James Butler, his Irish master of horse and cousin of Ormonde, to England under the pretext of buying horses. Arriving in August, he met with a vast number of supporters of the Stuarts and was given a list of the nobility in England and Wales "who could be relied upon."[31] He stressed that in Northumberland, most of the ancient families have never been perverted away from loyalty to the Stuarts, and they are united with "Mylord Derwentwater."

Included on Butler's list were the opposition Masons Orrery, Chesterfield, Burlington, Norfolk, Andover, Cobham, and Nugent. Two former Grand Masters of England – Viscount Montagu (1732) and Baron Ward (1742) were named. Lord Sempill added to the list Lord Mountjoy, former Grand Master in Ireland (1738-40).[32] Butler attended the Lichfield races with Barrymore, where they dined with "fourscore gentlemen," who, "Lord Barrymore told him, were all Jacobites except a few."[33] A surprising entry on Butler's list was James, 2nd Earl Waldegrave, son of the late Hanoverian minister and ambassador to France, who had been initiated in France. Perhaps James believed in the pious Catholic story that his father, on his deathbed, "put his hand to his tongue that had abjured his religion and cried: 'This bit of red rag has been my damnation.'"[34]

During these months in Paris, the Jacobite Masons initiated a German nobleman, Baron Carl Gotthelf von Hund, in a ceremony conducted by the masked "Knight of the Red Feather," who inducted him into the Masonic Order of the Knights Templar. Hund later claimed that Lords Clifford and Kilmarnock were present at his initiation and that he met Charles Edward Stuart, but the prince was still in Italy and definitely not in Paris in 1743. However, according to a Swedish Masonic document (written in French, dated 1788), Charles Edward succeeded ("succedit") as chief of the Order in 1743, with the ritual title "Eques a Sole Aureo" (Knight of the Golden Sun).[35] Because this document resulted from King Gustaf III's personal negotiations with Charles Edward in 1783, its claim should not be summarily rejected. Perhaps the *Écossais* Masons in France named him the successor, without his actually participating in a ceremony. As we shall see, two years later in Edinburgh, he would reportedly become the official but secret Grand Master of the Order of the Temple – in what some historians believe was a revival of Mar's Restoration Order of Military Knights.[36]

André Kervella suggests that Hund may have mistaken James Bartholomew Radcliffe, son of Derwentwater, for the prince.[37] The young Radcliffe so resembled Charles Edward that the two were sometimes mistaken for each other. Kervella further identifies Lord Clifford as Hugh Clifford, a seventeen year-old cousin of James Bartholomew Radcliffe. He argues that Kilmarnock was not William Boyd, 4th Earl of Kilmarnock, but his son

[31] *Ibid.*, 39-44, 123-38.
[32] J. Colin, *Louis XV*, 31.
[33] J. Murray, *Memorials*, 456.
[34] "James, 2nd Earl Waldegrave," *ODNB*.
[35] Pericle Maruzzi, *La Stretta Osservanza Templare e il Regime Scozzese Rettificato in Italia nel Secolo XVIII* (Atanòr, 2000), 100-01; Pierre Mollier, "Les Stuarts et la Franc-Maçonnerie: Le Dernier Épisode," *Renaissance Traditionnelle*, 177-78 (2015), 72.
[36] See ahead, Chapter Twenty.
[37] A. Kervella, *Ramsay*, 340, 349-51.

(evidently Charles Boyd, who was close to the Jacobite Mason, Lord Balmerino, and later served in his regiment during the 1745 rebellion). In 1778, when a Prussian Mason, Baron von Wächter, wrote Charles Edward to inquire about Hund's claims, the prince replied that "the elder Kilmarnock was decapitated after the affair of '45," but "the young Clifford and Kilmarnock…were in Paris" at the time of Hund's ceremony.[38] Kervella concludes that Hund's initiation was "an affair of the young men, with the blessing of their elders."

J.E.S. Tuckett argues, on the other hand, that Kilmarnock *père* may well have visited France in 1743, as he did in the early 1730s.[39] On the basis of a rather dubious source, Michael Baigent and Richard Leigh claim that the "Knight of the Red Feather" was Alexander Seton, also known as Alexander Montgomery, 10th Earl of Eglinton, who had been initiated by Kilmarnock and subsequently accompanied Derwentwater at Ramsay's funeral.[40] In 1750 Eglinton was still a Jacobite and became Grand Master of Scotland. In the meantime, Hund left Paris in September 1743 and returned to Germany, where in 1751 he would found the Rite of Strict Observance, which maintained Stuart traditions over the next decades.

For the Jacobites, the recruitment of a German nobleman in Paris was encouraging, and their hopes were raised even higher when the *Écossais* system gained an impressive, aristocratic Grand Master in December 1743. After the death of the Duc d'Antin, the Comte de Clermont (Bourbon-Condé) was named as his successor. Clermont, a prince of the blood, was close to Louis XV and may have assisted Villeroy in the reported initiation of the king in the "petite appartements" at Versailles."[41] Like his kinsman, the Marquis de Clermont d'Amboise, who earlier undertook an intelligence mission to England, the Comte de Clermont was a strong supporter of Charles Edward Stuart, and he would utilize a special *Rose-Croix* rite to serve the prince's cause.[42]

The Masonic Hats in Sweden were delighted with the election of Clermont, and they would collaborate closely with him in developing the chivalric and mystical rituals of the Swedish Rite. Also encouraging was the arrival in Stockholm of General James Keith in October 1743, as the commander of 12,000 Russian troops in Sweden. When the Hats declared war on Russia in July 1741, they hoped to recruit General Keith to their service, even collaborating with Louis XV in an attempt to kidnap him.[43] But the Empress refused to release him, and he oversaw Russia's humiliating defeat of Sweden. Nevertheless, his sympathies were with the Swedes, warmed by his love affair with a Swedish mistress, and he now played a romantic role in revitalizing the "Carolinian" dreams of the Hats, who considered him an "oracle." Though his public orders were to defend Sweden against Denmark, his private plans were to utilize Russian and Swedish troops in offense against Hanoverian England.[44] In November he learned from his brother that Louis XV had

---

[38] *Ibid.*, 351; Stuart Papers: 493,19.

[39] J.E.S. Tuckett, "Prince Charles Edward Stuart, G.M.," *The Builder Magazine*, 11 (1925), 53-66.

[40] Michael Baigent and Richard Leigh, *The Temple and the Lodge* (1988; London, 2013), 268.

[41] P. Chevallier, *Histoire*, I, 125.

[42] *Ibid.*, I, 47-57, 100-26.

[43] The following details with documentation on Keith's role in Sweden are given in M. Schuchard, *Emanuel Swedenborg*, 339-48.

[44] NA: SP 95/96, ff.71, 120, 144, 180.

made a firm commitment to the Jacobites and that the Stuart prince was preparing to leave Rome to lead the rebel forces in Scotland.[45]

General Keith, Tessin, Gyllenborg, and Scheffer then undertook a complex strategy of dissembling their Jacobite plans, which were organized in secret lodge meetings. Keith obtained from his cousin Kintore a warrant from the Grand Lodge of Scotland to establish a provincial lodge in Stockholm.[46] The Whig Mason Albermarle later scorned Kintore as in his heart a Jacobite.[47] Keith outwardly wooed the British ambassador, Melchior Guy Dickens, and convinced the rival "Cap" party that the lodge was affiliated with English Grand Lodge. But he used its meetings as a cover to recruit Masonic Hats who were willing to support the aggressive new plans of the Jacobites. Masons who had received degrees in Wrede Sparre's *Écossais* lodge could receive a special Scottish Master's degree in Keith's lodge. The Hats were also preparing Carl Scheffer to take over the Swedish embassy in Paris, from where he would utilize a Masonic network to coordinate the secret purchase and shipping of Swedish cannons and arms to the Jacobite army. These Swedish initiatives would subsequently lead international observers to comment on the similarities between the great warrior king Carl XII and Charles Edward Stuart, an identification which would be celebrated in Jacobite verse and song.[48]

On 23 December 1743 James III signed a declaration which was to be printed and distributed when the Jacobite landing in Britain took place. It was drawn up by six leading Tory-Jacobites in England and represented the points most likely to appeal to a broad segment of the population:

> We have seen our people, for many years, groaning under the weight of most heavy taxes, and bearing many of the calamities of war, while the rest of Europe enjoyed the blessings of peace. We have seen the treasures of the nation applied to satiate private avarice, and lavished for the support of German dominions...
>
> We see, with sensible satisfaction, the eyes of the greatest part of the people opened, to their present deplorable situation, and that they are convinced they can find no relief by by restoring their natural born Prince, whose undoubted title will of course put an end to the many calamities suffered during the Usurpation...[49]

To counter Hanoverian warnings about a papist tyranny, James promised to support the Church of England, allow a toleration of all Protestant dissenters, and declared himself "utterly averse to all persecution and animosity on account of conscience and religion." A manifesto of the Duke of Ormonde as commander-in-chief, also drawn up at the time, stated that the existence of a large standing army, many of them foreigners, was "contrary to the Constitution of the Kingdom." For the Jacobite Masons, these manifestos

---

[45] F. McLynn, *Charles Edward Stuart*, 77-81.

[46] C.H.I. Thulstrup, *Anteckningar till Svenska Frimuriets Historia* (1892), 14-18; Göran Behre, "Gothenburg in Stuart War Strategy, 1649-1760," in Grant Simpson, ed., *Scotland and Scandinavia, 800-1800* (Edinburgh, 1990), 113-14.

[47] William Anne, 2nd Earl of Albemarle, *The Albemarle Papers*, ed. Charles S. Terry (Aberdeen, 1902), 357-58.

[48] Niall Mackenzie, *Charles XII of Sweden and the Jacobites*. Royal Stuart Papers, LXII (London, 2002), 3-5, 17-27.

[49] E. Cruickshanks, *Political Untouchables*, 47-48.

represented the best thinking and most attractive recruiting tools for their potential supporters in the British Isles.

The Orrerys and their Jacobite friends determined to use couriers to deliver their letters, for they knew that their posted letters were intercepted and copied by government agents. Thus, their more secure Masonic communication networks became increasingly important, especially after Balhaldy returned to Paris and Rome, where in January 1744 he gained the approval of Louis XV and James III for a French-Jacobite invasion of England. Though Freemasonry in England was in decline, the situation in Scotland was quite different, as Jacobite sympathizers recruited new members to certain lodges, which developed closer relations with their brothers on the Continent. In 1742-43 John Murray of Broughton and Dr. Alexander Cunningham, members of the Jacobite lodge in Rome, visited the Canongate Kilwinning lodge in Edinburgh, which was predominantly Jacobite; the minute book records other "visiting Brethren from Rome."[50] Five years earlier, Murray had been greatly impressed by Charles Edward Stuart and reported that he had "an unspeakable majesty diffused through his whole mien," combined with an "excessive affability."[51] On St. Andrew's Day in 1743, Murray was named Junior Grand Warden in the Grand Lodge in Edinburgh.

On 30 November 1743 the Earl of Kilmarnock was succeeded as Grand Master of Scotland by James, 5th Earl of Wemyss, a long-time Stuart supporter. In 1709 in London the ten year-old Wemyss and his brother were tutored by Andrew Michael Ramsay, who described them as "two of the most innocent, sweet, sprightly little boys I ever knew."[52] In 1720 Wemyss became an Episcopalian, which prompted a Presbyterian minister to chastise him for leaving "the pure worship of God" in order to set up for Popery," which gave occasion to the Government to "look upon you as a Jacobite."[53] The minister argued further that "The Jacobites' common cant is that King George has not right, and the Pretender only has the blood right…and though King James VII had a blood right, yet he justly forefeited it to him selfishly by his tyrannies against the laws of God and Man." But Wemyss remained an Episcopalian and a Jacobite, and he acquired all of Ramsay's writings, which may have influenced his own Masonic ideas.

As noted earlier, in 1737 Lady Wemyss's steward was arrested for participating in the mob's "murder" of Porteous. The family was placed under government surveillance, which did not stop the 4th Earl from corresponding with James III.[54] From October 1740 to April 1741, he sponsored the visit of his nineteen year-old son David, known as Lord Elcho, to the Pretender in Rome, where he was hosted generously by the Jacobite Masons.[55] Elcho later described his meeting with James III, after he climbed a secret staircase that led him to a trap-door under a table in Edgar's room, who then sent him on to the king's chamber, where he also met the two princes.[56] Elcho returned to Scotland in

---

[50] D. Lyon, *History*, 352-53; Robert Strathern Lindsay, *History of the Mason Lodge of Holyrood House* (Edinburgh, 1935), I, 72.

[51] F. McLynn, *Charles Edward Stuart*, 73.

[52] William Fraser, *Memorials of the Family of Wemyss of Wemyss* (Edinburgh, 1888), I, 346-49.

[53] *Ibid.*, II, 196-98.

[54] Elcho, David Lord, *A Short Account of the Affairs of Scotland in the Years 1744, 1745, and 1746* , ed. Evan Charteris (Edinburgh, 1907), 5, 118, 44.

[55] "David Wemyss, known as Lord Elcho," *ODNB*.

[56] Alice Wemyss, *Elcho of the '45*, ed. John Gibson (Edinburgh, 2003), 5, 25-26.

October 1741, when he informed his father about these affairs. In spring 1743 Wemyss was sent by Lord John Drummond to the French court to solicit support for a Jacobite expedition, and he received a letter from James praising his son, Elcho, who returned to France from September 1743 to April 1744. [57] Elcho was joined by his brother Francis Charteris, and they and their *Écossais* brothers were delighted at his father's election as Grand Master of Scotland in November.

On 20 December 1743, three days before James signed his declaration, the Whig Mason and Hanoverian poet laureate, Colley Cibber, signed his new attack on Warburton, Pope's eulogistic editor, and on 9 January 1744, he added a long criticism of Pope himself. Given the context of Jacobite plotting and French military preparations, Cibber's initially innocuous response to the latest edition of *The Dunciad* took on more dangerous implications. In *Another Occasional Letter from Mr. Cibber to Mr. Pope* (London, 1744), Cibber mocked Warburton's hypocrisy for his earlier negative criticism of Pope during the controversy over Tibbald's Shakespeare ("Mr. Pope, whose Labours he had so unluckily disgrac'd!") versus his current fawning praise of him in the preface to the new *Dunciad*. The newly-crowned King of the Dunces could not resist recounting his rescue of the youthful Pope from the venereal whore:

> What now restrains him [Cibber] from once more reminding thee of the former friendly Office he did thee, when in thy dangerous Deed of Darkness, crawling on the Bosom of thy dear Damsel, he gently with a Finger and a Thumb, pick'd off thy small round Body, by thy long Legs, like a Spider, making Love in a Cobweb; why, I say might not such a human insect such a dismal of a *Dunce* in Love, make as proper a Figure on the Throne of Stupidity, as the more wholesome Sinner with *his Lady at Fourscore*?[58]

Scorning Pope's papist prejudices, Cibber asked, "Would not one think, by this Sort of Writing, that Mr. Pope had an Exemption from all the Laws of Morality, or Government?" Surely he knows that in countries where the Popish religion prevails, "People have been broil'd alive, for Words less criminal than the Poison contain'd in the above mention'd Verses!" But here under "the Lenity of a Protestant Faith, he will only have a Mark set upon his Morals, and, possibly, be but avoided, or detested for them." In a final warning (almost a threat), Cibber fulminated that "Satyr in so malevolent a Heart is Fire in a Madman's Hand, in a Powder Room!"[59]

On 23 December James wrote to Ormonde that Louis XV "is resolved to undertake in my favour," but he requires "so great and strict a secrecy in the affair, that I was not at liberty to mention anything of it to you before."[60] James assured the seventy-nine year-old Ormonde that the plan has the support of the duke's friends in England, and that he will serve as military commander, with Charles Edward as regent. He urged Ormonde, once across the channel, to consult Barrymore, Orrery, Wynne, Cotton, Westmoreland, and Cobham. This list made Pope even more vulnerable for he was especially close to Cobham, who had once been a hero to the Whigs. Ormonde should also engage

---

[57] J. Browne, *History*, II, 450.

[58] C. Cibber, *Occasional Letter*, 52.

[59] *Ibid.*, 38.

[60] J. Browne, *History*, II, 450

Derwentwater to follow him into England. On the same day, James wrote Marischal that the expedition was on and that he should proceed to Scotland, where he should link up with the Duke of Perth, Lord Lovat, and other Jacobites. The Masonic connections of Derwentwater and Marischal would thus become important.

On 9 January 1744, the day Cibber signed his new attack on Pope as a seditious papist, Charles Edward secretly set out from Rome on a dangerous journey to Avignon, where on 1 February he conferred with Ormonde, the senior statesman and idol of the English Jacobites, on the French invasion project. The prince finally arrived at Paris on 8 February, "like a thunderbolt from a clear sky."[61] His precipitous action forced the French to begin serious action, and he moved to Gravelines in anticipation of sailing with the invasion force. French and Swedish diplomats worried about the extent of support for the Stuarts in England, for the Jacobites expected support from both governments. Despite their efforts at secrecy, the English government was steadily intercepting their correspondence and employing "moles" in their embassies and courts

From the enormous amount of "Secret Intelligence" preserved in Lord Carteret's papers, the success of English espionage is clearly demonstrated, as in the following examples. [62] On 10 January from Stockholm, the French ambassador Lanmary reported that the behavior of General Keith is very puzzling, for he is friendly with the "Minister of England and his Cabal" and displays "a constant reserve with me."[63] On 23 February the French foreign minister Amelot wrote Lanmary that the time is ripe for an assault on George II, so he must convince the Swedish government that it is "a prime occasion to raise the glory and avantage of Sweden." Thus, it's crucial that Lanmary learn "the manner and thoughts of General Keith about the impression that the arrival of Charles Edward will make in Great Britain and the amount of favour the prince will find in that kingdom." On 24 February an English spy at the French court reported to Carteret that the French are sure they can draw Sweden into their measures. In Sweden the Masonic Hats – led by Tessin, Scheffer, and Gyllenborg--utilized their "secret interior organization" in a determined attempt to by-pass British intelligence.

Meawhile in England, the government rounded up Jacobite suspects and unleashed a loyalist propaganda campaign. On 14 February the Earl of Egmont recorded that George II announced in parliament that the Young Pretender is in France, "whereupon the House of Lords sent an address that they would stand by the king," but the Commons "were not so decent when the Address was moved."[64] Chesterfield and the opposition questioned it, "which the zealous men on the government side interpret to be done with design to shew the French what numbers in the House they might depend on." Though numbers of the opposition "went over to the court," the chief leaders spoke "with passion to inflame the House." Fortunately, "the king is full master of the French plan, and undoubtedly knows of several here at home who are engaged in it."

Sir Francis Dashwood, an opposition Mason, protested in parliament against the scare tactics, while Colonel Cecil and other suspects were arrested. A warrant was issued for Carte, but he managed to flee. Though Lord Morton told Egmont that "he had a letter

---

[61] F. McLynn, *Charles Edward Stuart*, 83-89.
[62] BL: Carteret Papers. Add. MSS.22,539-25,541.
[63] *Ibid.*, Add. MS. 22,541, ff. 28, 124, 136, 140.
[64] Egmont, *Diary*, I, 285-89. The following details are taken from his diary.

from Scotland taking no notice of any rising in Scotland," Walpole sent orders to Scotland to arrest Lord Elcho, son of the Grand Master, and fifteen others, most of whom were Masons. Was Morton trying to protect his Masonic brothers? Reports from Ireland claimed that 14,000 arms which belonged to Barrymore had been discovered in Cork, and in February he was arrested and interrogated. The government charged that the septuagenarian Barrymore was "to be General of all the invading troops and disaffected English who shall rise to favour the cause." When examined by the Cabinet, Barrymore brazenly responded," I have, my lords, a very good estate in Ireland, and, on that, I believe, fifteen hundred acres of very bad land; now by G-d, I would not risk the loss of the poorest acre of them to defend the title of any king in Europe, provided – it was not my interest."[65] However, the earl had already provided £12,000 from his own pocket to finance the rising, and he had sent his second son, Richard Barry, to France to accompany the invading force.

The arrest and seizure of the papers of Barrymore was especially alarming to Orrery, for the two had secretly worked together, and both were close to the Jacobite Masons in Cork, who were now vulnerable to prosecution. Orrery's land agent in Cork, the loyalist Richard Purcell, had reported that Lord Barrymore might "in ten days have 20,000 well-made strong young fellows at his heels."[66] Orrery and his network, who were certainly aware of the reality of the Jacobite invasions plan, launched a campaign of disinformation to avoid prosecution. On 4 February Orrery had written his wife that reports of the Pretender and French fleet near our shore were mere propaganda ploys from the government:

> It will be of use to the Ministry to have these apprehensions continued. It will hurry all anti-Courtiers (you may guess the Title we bear) into more immediate and more certain Slavery, Votes of Credit, Plots, Suspensions of the Habeas Corpus, and all sorts of Ministerial Devices will be plaid against us, and our Integrity will never be Shield sufficient to defend us against such powerful Machines… Were, however, these Reports true, wh. I cannot the least believe, I should not wonder if I were forc'd to write you from amidst the Lyons and Monsters of the Tower."[67]

Orrery worried that the "unaccountable imprudence of the M. as I have heard of late, has made my Name be call'd in question," and I "am probably mark'd in the Book of Treasons and Disloyalty."On 6 February the irrepressible Lady Orrery responded, "I know not whether the customs of the Tower and Newgate be the same," but I have sent you "a fine pheasant, an excellent turkey, and two hares to treat and sup your fellow Prisoners." Despite Lady Orrery's high-spirited defiance, her obviously frightened husband joined Pope and Dr. King for a confidential dinner with Burlington on 9 February.[68] They evidently decided to publicly (and in their intercepted correspondence) issue denials of the reality of the Jacobite plot, and on 18 February Orrery wrote his wife that "the Court seems in the highest Alarms, as you must observe by the King's Messages," but

---

[65] "Barrymore," R. Sedgwick, *History of Parliament Online.*

[66] E. O'Ciardha, *Ireland,* 304.

[67] Orerry, *Orrery Papers,* II, 181.

[68] *Ibid.,* II, 183.

"the City seems quiet, and most People laugh at Plots, Pretenders, Fleets, and the numerous mushroom Reports that rise and dye in a day":

> It is imagined a Plot is necessary for the Ministers, and therefore our Dangers (if any) are treated as proceeding from the Ministerial quarter rather than France. The account of the Young Pretender as publish'd in the Gazette is very romantick and I daresay false. Ye what is most absurd it seems to present him a kind of Hero, and this is published by Authority. All these Chimaeras only frighten People in regard to money.[69]

On 27 February Lady Orrery wrote that their close friend Colonel Cecil was taken up and imprisoned in the Tower, but she could not resist adding a comical account about her dog, comparing him to Harlequin in the Atterbury Plot: "I have written two letters to him, a gift of Irish whiskey, which could be considered putting arms into his hands, and a guinea fowl, which may be said was assisting the Pretender with a guinea."[70] She concluded, "I suppose the Post Master opens all Letters." Their letters must have crossed, because on 28 February Orrery sent her a worried letter about "our Friends":

> Poor Col: Cecil is sent to the Tower; many more are suspected: (would to God my real Sentiments were known as fully to the Privy Council as they are to you!) and from Suspicions all dangers are to be apprehended... Ld Barrimore is apprehended...and Tom Carte... In short, these are gloomy Times. Write to me accordingly; pray name no names...for Innocence airy and unguarded, is never so properly adorned and defended as when shielded by Caution and Prudence... I beg you will keep your Sentiments entirely to yourself. As to my own Part, I am so entirely innocent I have no Fears...yet Appearances may perhaps be against me. Old Habits, Old Friends, and my own invincible Shyness, may raise engines against me.[71]

On 9 March, after her husband warned her that not only the post master but the secretary of state had examined their letters, Lady Orrery replied that they only revealed the love of a husband and wife and concern for their country, "which we will never betray either to Popish Pretenders, or the Interest of Hanover."[72] Moreover, "now and then a little raillery on corrupt ministers, wrote in the integrity of two honest hearts," cannot be considered seditious: "And now, o ye Post Masters, ye Secretarys of State, and all your Discerning Eyes, who are to overlook these Lines..., we are innocent of subverting the laws and will stand so in Heaven." While her husband laid low in the country, a more cautious Lady Orrery recommended that "our wise men" follow the advice of Chevalier Ramsay, who in his *Cyrus* praised the life of solitude, as practiced by the Magi who spent their time in "Study, Music, and Conversation." She also urged Henry Salkeld, Jacobite friend of Ramsay and her children's tutor, to translate all of Dr. King's Latin works into English.

The government not only suspended Habeas Corpus but implemented the old penal laws against Catholics, proclaiming that they could not appear within ten miles of

---

[69] *Ibid.*, II, 184-85.
[70] Harvard: Orrery , Eng. MS. 218.2, letter 82 (27 February 1744).
[71] Orrery, *Orrery Papers*, II, 186-87.
[72] Harvard: Eng. MS. 218.2, letter 86 (12 March 1744).

London. John Bancks, the former Spittlefields weaver and loyalist Mason, contributed to the anti-Catholic campaign by publishing *The History of the Life and Reign of William III* (1744), in which he revived the warming-pan claims of the illegitimacy of the Pretender, while praising William as the bulwark against "the Encroachments of Popery and Arbitrary Power." He evidently forgot the important support he got from Alexander Pope, who had helped him launch his literary career. On 6 March a frightened Pope invited his Bath friend Ralph Allen to visit him at Twickenham, because "a decent Obedience to the Government has since oblig'd me to reside here, ten miles out of the Capital, & therefore I must see you here or nowhere":

> The utmost I can do, I will venture to tell you in your Ear. I may slide along the Surrey side (where no Middlesex Justice can pretend any Cognizance) to Battersea, & thence cross the Water for an hour or two, in a close Chair to dine with you, or so. But to be in Town, I fear, will be imprudent & thought insolent, at least hitherto, all comply with the Proclamation... It may possibly be, that I shall be taking the secret Flight I speak of to Battersea...to the only Great Man in Europe [Bolingbroke]...[73]

It is unknown what Pope thought of the Jacobite attempt, despite his lifelong disaffection from the Hanoverian regime, but his turning to Bolingbroke placed him in an even more ambiguous situation.

As Eveline Cruickshanks observes, "Bolingbroke, who was against any restoration of the Stuarts except on his own terms, had written in February: 'The crisis is terrible – much to be feared – little to be hoped. God help us!'"[74] Given his own recent negotiations with the Jacobites and his secret French subsidy, as well as his half-brother's inclusion on the list of expected supporters of an invasion, he was in a vulnerable position. Thus, he once again reversed his position and became an informer on the Jacobites, informing the Pelham ministry that he was "un honnete homme convaincu de son erreur," and determined to repent his recent Jacobitism."[75] However, he was still not trusted, and Hardwicke employed as many as eight spies to watch him.

In the meantime, on 29 February 1744 the Grand Lodge Masons lost one of their most valuable supporters, Dr. Desaguliers. Seven weeks earlier, as the scientist's health declined, Martin Folkes gained the imprimatur of the Royal Society on 17 November 1743 to publish the long-delayed second volume of *A Course of Experimental Philosophy*. The dedication to the Prince of Wales was repeated from volume one, but Desaguliers's association with the opposition had damaged his prospects with the Whig ministry, and he failed to get his plans for ventilating ships accepted by the Admiralty. Voicing his frustration in the Preface, he warned against incompetent and dishonest scientists and engineers, who unfortunately obtained government support: "Our Legislators may make Laws to govern us, repeal some, and enact others, and we must obey them; but they cannot alter the Laws of Nature; nor add or take away one iota from the Gravity of Bodies."[76]

---

[73] A. Pope, *Correspondence*, IV, 504-05.
[74] E. Cruickshanks, *Political Untouchables*, 60.
[75] S. Varey, "Hanover, Stuart, and the Patriot King," 172 n.34.
[76] J. T. Desaguliers, *A Course of Experimental Philosophy* (London, 1744), II, vii-viii.

In 1742 Desaguliers had been pleased to receive praise from France, when the Academy of Bordeaux awarded him a prize for his *Dissertation on Electricity*, and French historians claim that his last years were clouded by neglect and poverty.[77] Larry Stewart observes that his final portrait, painted shortly before his death, shows a man "tortured by gout and disappointment."[78] In 1749 the Whig poet and schoolmaster James Cawthorne published "The Vanity of Human Enjoyments," which portrayed Desaguliers as a disappointed and neglected scientist:

> And still permit the weeping muse to tell
> How poor neglected Desaguliers fell?
> How he, who taught two gracious kings to view
> All Boyle ennobled, and all Bacon knew,
> Died in a cell, without a friend to save,
> Without a guinea, and without a grave?
> Posterity, perhaps, may pay the debt
> That senates cancel, and that courts forget.[79]

In 1815 John Nichols, in his short biography of Desaguliers, remarked, "If credit be given to Mr. Cawthorne, Dr. Desaguliers was in very necessitous circumstances at the time of his death."[80] Though it is unknown if Cawthorne was a Mason, his tenure as assistant to the important Mason Martin Clare at the latter's Soho Academy in the late 1730s suggests the probability of his affiliation. Nevertheless, Desaguliers's modern biographers, Patricia Fara and Audrey Carpenter, reject Cawthorne's description, noting that the once eminent scientist left property in his will to his descendants.[81] Perhaps the publicly acknowledged decline in English Grand Lodge Freemasonry contributed to his reported disappointment.

Though Colley Cibber criticized Pope's recent satire on the English clerical profession as seditious and papist, Dr. King enjoyed it and launched his own attacks on "time-serving" English bishops. In December 1743 King had published his three Latin speeches, given at the granting of Oxford degrees to the eighteen year-old James Hamilton, Duke of Hamilton and Brandon; to the twenty-six year-old George Henry Lee, 3rd Earl of Lichfield; and to his old friend Lord Orrery. All three were Jacobites, and the publication provoked an attack on King by Dr. John Gilbert, Bishop of Llandaff, who had been characterized by Pope as "leaden," an adjective repeated by King.[82] In the preface to his Latin speeches, King noted that he has been attacked by "some anti-Jacobite canon" and that "other members of the New Interest [the new Whig ministry] are engaged in personal onslaughts against him." Gilbert called for the expulsion of King from the Convocation but was not successful. In spring 1744, in a bizarre series of pamphlets, written anonymously by King, he fought back with high-spirited defiance, noting "That it is a dangerous Thing/ Indeed to anger Dr. K---"; moreover, "The Dr. is not to be made a

---

[77] « Jean-Théophile Desaguliers, *Biographie Universelle*.

[78] L. Stewart, *Rise of Public Science*, 380.

[79] James Cawthorn, *Poems by the Rev. Mr. Cawthorn* (London, 1771), 180-81.

[80] J. Nichols, *Literary Anecdotes*, IX, 641.

[81] Patricia Fara, "J.T. Desaguliers," *ODNB*; A. Carpenter, *Desaguliers*, 238.

[82] "John Gilbert," *ODNB*; D. Greenwood, *William King*, 162-66.

Jest of, and he shan't be run down; He can make Reprisals, and will."[83] He argued that if the corrupt Whig churchmen are angry at being called fools, then they should stop meddling; if they are disgusted at being set out as time-servers, they should stop espousing principles "manifestly obnoxious."

At this time, King was working closely with the operative Masons who were rebuilding the east range of St. Mary's Hall, and he wrote a Latin tribute to his former Jacobite collaborator, Theodore von Neuhof, the short-lived king of Corsica. On 24 April he wrote Orrery,

> I have just now finished the Corsican Epistle. I think no party can be angry with it. And yet it may so happen, that as I have formerly been deemed a Jacobite, I may now be called a Republican. The Leaden Man [Bishop Gilbert], you may be sure, will criticize me with all his might – but not in Latin.[84]

The argument repeated that of King's article in *Common Sense* (1737), with the Corsicans representing Britons and Theodore representing James III. In the succeeding years, Theodore had been defeated by the Genoans with French help and driven into exile, but he was still attempting to return and achieve a restoration. He continued to exercise his Cabalistic and alchemical skills, while he initiated knights into his quasi-Masonic "Order of Deliverance."[85]

King's high spirits were based on the Jacobites' optimism that the French and Charles Edward Stuart would soon invade. During Barrymore's negotiations with the French, he had employed his second son, Richard Barry, as his secretary, and in January 1744 he sent him to France to join the proposed French invasion.[86] Barry was an officer in the British navy, and his military expertise was greatly appreciated. At Dunkirk, the proposed port of departure, Charles Edward heaped praise upon Barry, "une tres jolie figure," and the two developed a lifelong friendship[87] Richard was reportedly a Mason, and the prince's party was soon joined by Marischal and Derwentwater.[88]The Masonic bonding of these important Jacobites was relevant to the secrecy demanded of the plotters. Charles Edward's close relationship with Derwentwater – reviver of the chivalric traditions of Stuart Masonry – during these months in France would prove significant when the prince allegedly participated in a Templar Masonic ceremony in Edinburgh in September 1745.[89]

Unfortunately for the Jacobites, two huge storms in March damaged the French fleet and drove the ships back into port, leaving a frustrated Prince Charles high and dry on the Normandy coast. Though Louis XV declared war on England on 30 March, the planned expeditions stalled amidst French bickering and political factionalism. A week later, a gloating Baron Stosch claimed that the Jacobites are mortified that there is no

---

[83] William King, *A Chiding Letter to S.P.Y.B. in Defence of Epistola Objurgatoria* (London, 1744), 8, 15
[84] *Ibid.*, 170.
[85] Valerie Pirie, *His Majesty of Corsica: the True Story of the Adventurous Life of Theodore I* (London, 1939); C. Roth, "The King and the Kabbalist," 113-29.
[86] E. O'Ciardha, *Ireland*, 304n.126.
[87] J. Colin, *Louis XV*, 101. Henrietta Tayler, *A Jacobite Miscellany: Eight Original Papers on the Rising of 1745-1746* (Oxford, 1948), 133.
[88] On Barry's Masonic affiliation, see Monod, *Jacobitism*, 303n.172.
[89] See ahead Chapter 20.

support for the Stuart prince in England.[90] Sensing that the threat had diminished, the government released Lord Barrymore on bail, and he returned to Ireland, from where he secretly sent even more audacious plans to the French court. Like Orrery, with whom he collaborated, Barrymore was able to secretly work with the Jacobites and French while seeming to publicly acquiesce to the government.

Over the next sixteen months, Charles Edward would struggle to convince the French government and a reluctant Earl Marischal to mount a new expedition. An unfortunate and damaging personality conflict now emerged According to McLynn, Marischal had disliked Charles on sight when he saw him in Rome in 1732: "This kind of 'hate at first sight' is as difficult to explain as its existence is undeniable. The clash between the two men was now and later to yield bitter fruit."[91] To the prince, Marischal seemed "a hopeless pessimist," and his "monumental defeatism" had already scuttled the ambitious invasion plans of Nicholas Wogan, who was Charles Edward's second choice for his emissary to Scotland. Despite the prince's problems in France, his most effective pleading targeted the Swedish Hats. In these negotiations, the networks of *Écossais* Masons played a significant role – in a replay of the earlier Görtz-Gyllenborg plot in the glory days of Carl XII.

On 5 April 1744 a Swedish agent – Emanuel Swedenborg – began to play a secret role in the emerging Jacobite-Masonic plot. Stationed at The Hague, he recorded in the peculiar language of his dream diary his initiation into the *Écossais* high degrees:

> It seemed to me that the whole night I was first brought into association with others…Afterwards, that I was bandaged [blind-folded] and wrapped in wonderful and indescribable courses of circles; showing that during the whole night I was inaugurated [initiated] in a wonderful manner. And then it was said, "Can any Jacobite be more than honest?" So at last I was received with an embrace… it was a mystical series.[92]

At this time, the Swedish Masons worked with their Jacobite colleagues on Masonic rituals that reinforced secrecy and loyalty, while providing recognition signs and symbolic codes to manage their oral and written communications.

On 18 April in Amsterdam, while Swedenborg's close friend and diplomatic colleague, Ambassador Preis, facilitated plans to ship Swedish cannons to the Jacobites, Swedenborg referred obliquely to a secret military operation:

> It seemed to me that we worked long to bring in a chest, in which were contained precious things which had long lain there; just as it was a long work with Troy; at last, one went in underneath and eased it onwards; it was thus gotten as conquered; and we sawed and sawed…[93]

The editor Van Dusen observes that Swedenborg's reference to Troy is most curious, for the Trojan horse contained soldiers who opened the enemy gates and enabled the town

---

[90] BL: Carteret Papers. Add. MS. 25,541, f.244.
[91] F. McLynn, *Charles Edward Stuart*, 96-97.
[92] Emanuel Swedenborg, *Journal of Dreams*, #43; for the detailed Jacobite-Masonic context, see M. Schuchard, *Emanuel Swedenborg*, 349-55.
[93] E. Swedenborg, *Journal*, #141.

to be conquered: "It is the same here. The chest contains something precious that will allow the 'town' to be conquered." In early May Swedenborg moved to London, where he served as an anonymous intelligencer for his Hat-Masonic collaborators, who were planning to support the expected Franco-Jacobite invasion of Britain.

In the same month in Stockholm, General Keith continued to deceive the British ambassador, Guy Dickens, about his true loyalties, and he took part in a grand Jacobite-Masonic *fête* in which fourteen new *frères* were initiated, virtually under the ambassador's nose. The Hats determined to maintain secrecy about their political-Masonic activities, which meant that Count Tessin was distressed when he learned from the Swedish embassy in Paris that two exposés of Freemasonry were published – Gabriel Perau's *Le Secret des Francs-maçons* (1744) and Louis Travenol's *Le Cathéchisme des Francs-maçons* (1744). The authors not only revealed the rituals but the secret recognition signs, symbols, and codes of the fraternity. Tessin's diplomatic informant tried to reassure him that the "true brothers" mock the works, but the "prophanes" receive them like revelations.[94]

For Alexander Pope, this revival of a Swedish-Jacobite movement important in his youth came too late, for he died on 30 May 1744. According to Joseph Spence, who was at the deathbed, when Mr. Hooke asked him "Whether he wou'd not dye as his Father & Mother had done; & whether he should send for a Priest? He said, `He did not suppose that was essential; but it will look right: and I heartily thank you for putting me in mind of it."[95] Edward Pigott, a Benedictine priest, gave the dying poet the last sacraments and reported that "he had Pope's Directions to declare to every body, that Pope was sorry for every thing he had said or wrote, that was against the Catholick Faith." In the midst of his grief, Bolingbroke learned that Pope had secretly printed, but did not circulate, 1,500 copies of an early manuscript of *The Patriot King*, which evidently included material sympathetic to the Stuarts. A panicked Bolingbroke at once burned all the copies he could find, and only three copies of this clandestine text are known to have survived.[96] In 1749, in his personally revised and "authorized" edition, Bolingbroke would accuse Pope of treachery for his clandestine printing of the earlier (incriminating) version.

In the meantime, Cibber, who in his recent pamphlet had hinted happily that Pope was near death, was not the only Hanoverian Mason who did not grieve at the poet's demise. Orator Henley outdid himself with posthumous, gloating comments on Pope's alleged hypocrisy, malice, and disloyalty. In the Oratory advertisement for 28 April, he drew together the *Dunciad* collaborators in "Mr. P's Extreme Unction from Mr W-rb-n" [Warburton], and his death inevitably provoked Henley's funeral oration on 9 June:

> Friend Pope's funeral Sermon, the fifth Dunciad. Mr. P*pe's Obsequey, or a Farewell Lecture to the Arch-Poetist and Executioner General of his Age; who never dedicated one Poem to the 10th of June, nor an Epic to our Glorious Edward I or III or to the Black Prince, or Richard I, or Henry V. nor wrote one Satire on M*M; but was more fond of hanging up in Effigie little

94 Jan Heidner, *Carl Reinhold Berch* (Stockholm, 1997), 93-94.

95 A. Pope, *Correspondence*, IV, 526.

96 S. Varey, "Hanover, Stuart, and the Patriot King," 167.-

Fools than great R*s, and had been the woeful ruin of many a Pretty Gentleman's Judgment and Honesty.[97]

After constantly accusing Pope of papism, he now portrayed him as a free-thinking deist, who in his last will resigned his soul to God, "enquiring whether he did not die in – Tindals, Toland's, and Woolston's – Religion, etc." Graham Midgley notes that over the next months, Henley continued "to cast pebbles on the grave from the Oratory pulpit."

Since the death of his patron Walpole, Henley had declared his political independence, and in 1744 he began issuing inflammatory anti-Hanoverian and pro-Stuart sermons. In January, while still lecturing on Freemasonry, he mocked the physically unattractive (dumpy) Germans: "– our Royal Race is more exalted – lose none of their Stature – High German – Cock & Strut – a couple of them joyn'd at top, might go towards a Stuart."[98] At this time, the Jacobites issued boasting portrayals of Charles Edward Stuart as tall (nearly six feet), physically fit, and handsome. In April Henley preached that "to ye King our loyalty is due, but ye Elector is a stranger to our Constitution." In September he bewailed that "it is really a misfortune to Englishmen that they are obliged to go into these mean and beggarly Sovereignties of *Germany*, whose people are Slaves." As we shall see, the Orator's surprising swing to Jacobitism was undertaken to act as an *agent provocateur* for the government, but over the next months he would fool many observers into believing that his change of political and Masonic allegiance was sincere.

While Henley continued to disparage the deceased Pope, Paul Whitehead, who had helped the opposition Mason Esquire Carey organize the procession of Mock Masons, grieved for the poet and assured his readers that his recent satire on scribblers was not aimed at his beloved friend, noting that "Immediately on hearing the Report of Mr. Pope's Death, he [Whitehead] was heard to break forth in the following Exclamation. `Pope dead! – Hush, Hush Report, the slanderous Lye,/ Fame says he lives, – Immortals never die."[99] While many of Pope's friends among the opposition Masons had gone over to the government, Whitehead had kept up his mockery of the Grand Lodge. Thus, in April, when Grand Master Strathmore led the annual "Procession of March," the Mock-Masons staged their burlesque, counter-march, which the public greatly enjoyed. However, the government now took their defiance seriously, as reported by the *London Daily Post* on 3 May 1744: "Yesterday several of the mock-Masons were taken up by the Constable empowered to impress men for his Majesty's service, and confined till they can be examined by the Justices."[100]

The irrepressible Whitehead was not intimidated, and he carried on Pope's satirical campaign with a daring mock panegyric dedicated to the bare-fisted pugilist John Broughton. Appointed to George II's bodyguard, Broughton accompanied the king to Hanover when George took command of the army in 1743.[101] He also became a favorite of the king's younger son, the Duke of Cumberland, who took Broughton with him to a European battlefield, where the boxer boasted that he could beat every member of the "formidable foreign regiment, albeit with a breakfast between each contest." A Masonic

---

[97] G. Midgley, *Life*, 185.
[98] *Ibid.*, 233-34.
[99] Paul Whitehead, *The Gymnasiad, or Boxing Match* (London, 1744). Ix.
[100] C. Crawley, "Mock Masonry," 143.
[101] "John Broughton," *ODNB*.

writer in 1763 claimed that during Cumberland's service abroad in 1743, the duke was initiated into a military lodge.[102] If true, his pugilistic companion was probably also initiated, and Cumberland avoided his father's censure by maintaining a low Masonic profile, especially since his hated older brother, Prince Frederick, was publicly known as a Mason.

Whitehead was possibly aware of Cumberland's reputed affiliation, which would provoke his further scorn of the duke as a representative of the loyalist Masonry he continued to satirize. Writing as "Scriblerus Tertius," he published in June 1744 *The Gymnasiad, or Boxing Match. A Very Curious Epic Poem*, in which he mocked Broughton's role as "the Safe-Guard of Royalty itself" and one whose "puissant Arm" would make any Frenchman tremble.[103] As he ridiculed the "brutish" custom of boxing, he knew that the poem would offend Cumberland, who was a great encourager of the sport. Like the late Alexander Pope, Whitehead was depressed and disillusioned by the apostasy of so many opposition Whigs and Masons who scrambled for government places, and he would continue his satirical attacks upon them, bringing charges upon him that he was not only a Tory but a Jacobite.

Meanwhile in Sweden, the French Masonic exposés of June 1744 could not have appeared at a worse time for Tessin and Carl Scheffer, who utilized their Masonic "interior organization" to organize their planned Jacobite support. In July the Russian Czarina became so alarmed at reports of General Keith's "independent" actions that she ordered him to return to Russia. At the same time, Hanoverian agents tried to blacken the reputation of his brother by spreading scandalous stories about the young Turkish girl who had been "adopted" by the Earl Marischal. William Hamilton of Bangour, who had met Marischal and his "handmaiden" on the Continent, issued a poetic defense of the couple in "Horace, Book II, Ode IV, an Imitation: To the Earl Marshal of Scotland*" (the asterisk pointing to the footnote, "The Jacobite, forfeited Earl."[104] Written in 1744 but not published until later, Hamilton excused his friend's unconventional love life: "A vow, my noble friend, thy kind desires,/If Phillis' gentle form thy breast inspires,/Nor glory, nor can reason disapprove."[105] To those who disparage her as low-born, the poet speculates that she secretly springs from royal parentage, who gifted her with "Such a sincere and lovely mind," as well as "melting eyes and slender waste,/Fair tap'ring from the swelling breast." Finally, embarrassed at his own adulation, the recently-married Hamilton concluded, "Alas! such badinage but ill would suit/ A married man, and forty years to boot."

For the Swedish Hats, despite their disappointment at the removal of General Keith, there were encouraging signals for the Jacobites from France. The Masonic leader Scheffer set out for Paris, where he was to serve as Swedish ambassador and push the Hats' agenda for stronger action against England and an increasingly unfriendly Russia. He arrived at Metz, where a seriously ill Louis XV expected to die and was convinced by

---

[102] [Anonymous], *The Complete Free Mason, or Multa Paucis, for Lovers of Secrets* (1763), edited J.T. Thorp (London, 1924), 99. Later Masons claim that the initiation took place in Germany or Belgium. See *English Royal Freemasons*. United Grand Lodge of England, Library and Museum of Freemasonry. Information Leaflet No. 1 www.freemasonry.london.museum. David Barrett, "The Influence of Kings on Craft Freemasonry, with Especial Reference to Great Britain, *Pietre-Stones: Review of Freemasonry* http://www.freemasons-freemasonry.com/royal_family_freemasonry.html.

[103] [P. Whitehead], *Gymnasiad*, v-vi.

[104] N. Bushnell, *William Hamilton*, 66-67.

[105] W. Hamilton, *Poems*, 124-26.

François de Fitzjames, now Bishop of Soissons, that he had been unjust to Charles Edward Stuart and owed the Stuarts stronger support.[106] As noted earlier, Fitzjames possessed a special Masonic ritual, designed for the Jacobite elite. It was possibly at this time that Louis XV wrote to the prince those promises that Charles Edward would later claim to possess among his papers.[107]

When the king unexpectedly recovered, Scheffer boldly demanded a meeting, in which he assured him that Sweden and Prussia would collaborate with a French-Jacobite enterprise. He was the confidant of the Prussian king's representative, Count von Schmettau, who shared Masonic bonds with his Swedish *frère*. Schmettau had introduced the Templar degrees into Berlin in 1742 and established a "Scots Lodge" in Hamburg in 1744.[108] However, Scheffer's correspondence with Tessin about these negotiations was intercepted by the British, and a copy is preserved among Carteret's "Most Secret" intelligence files.[109] An English-employed French spy reported that a great council was held at Metz and pushed for a campaign against Britain and especially the former Swedish possessions of Bremen and Verden, which will recruit Sweden fully to the French cause. Though the French "are not capable of such a grand enterprise," the "enterprising spirit of Schmettau and Scheffer may supply the will to commence it." Louis XV was greatly impressed by Scheffer and made him a trusted member of his secretive inner circle, where the Swede utilized Masonic connections to build support for the expected Stuart restoration. From Florence, Stosch reported to Newcastle that the Pretender is happy with the news of Louis's recovery, for the French king sends new promises of powerful support, while the Jacobites in Italy say that Charles Edward Stuart will soon go to the court of Sweden.[110]

The almost obsessive secrecy maintained by the *Écossais* Masons means that the Swedish involvement in the preparations in the 1744-45 invasion plans did not become public knowledge (and, indeed, almost disappeared from the historical record). In Ireland, which was to be included in the Swedish plan, Jonathan Swift had long admired Gyllenborg and Carl XII, but his mind had deteriorated to the point that he was no longer aware of the public world, much less the revival of the Gyllenborg plot. However, in May-August 1744 he did receive a visit from an old friend, the Jewish Mason and poet Moses Mendes, the confidant of Dr. King and Orrery, who had been privy to many of the Jacobite negotiations with the Swedes. J. Percy Simpson, who claims that "Bro. Mendes" was "on intimate terms of friendship with Jonathan Swift," suggests that he may have" met Swift in Masonic circles, as he and Pope were members of the Goat , at the Foot of the Haymarket."[111] Mendes had earlier addressed to Swift a poem urging him "to cross the sea and visit; haste thee to thy paternal lands."[112] He lamented the death of Pope and scorned Cibber who "stands by snarling." In another poem to the deceased poet, he cried, "Oh Pope arise and weed the encumbered land."[113]

[106] F. McLynn, *Charles Edward Stuart*, 104.

[107] Marquis d'Argenson, *Journal and Memoirs of the Marquis d'Argenson*, trans. K.P Wormeley (Boston, 1902), II, 33.

[108] René Le Forestier, *Les Illuminés de Bavière et la Franc-maçonnerie Allemande* (Paris, 1914), 145.

[109] BL: Add. MS. 22,541, ff. 337, 358.

[110] NA:SP 98/49 (6 October 1744).

[111] J. Simpson, "Brother Moses Mendez," 105.

[112] UGLE: MS 1860. Men., f. 1.

[113] *Ibid.*, f. 4a.

In Dublin Mendes was welcomed by Deane Swift, Jonathan's cousin, and the two exchanged verses of welcome and appreciation.[114] Deane Swift apparently took him to see the ailing satirist, whom Mendes had visited during earlier trips to Ireland. On 5 July Mendes sent from Dublin to John Ellis "The Author's Account of his Journey to Ireland," in which he hoped that "the "Temple of Liberty" will "mount thee to fame" (referring to the planned publication of Ellis's translation of Dr. King's *Templum Libertatis*).[115] In Lichfield, where the famous cathedral had been damaged by Cromwellians but repaired by James II in 1687, he wrote, "Thy Gothic cathedral new homage still claims,/ Nor refuse I thy due, tho' repaired by King James." On arriving in Dublin, he rejected the stereotypical criticism of Ireland made by Englishmen,

> Who with taunts contumelious this island o'er load,
> As with bogs, and with blunders, and nonsense full stow'd,
> For believe me, they live not unbless'd with good air,
> And their daughters are beauteous, and sons debonair.
> Here tho' Bacchus too often displays his red face,
> Yet Minerva he holds in the strictest embrace...[116]

On 26 August Ellis responded with a hint at the trouble that his unpublished translation of *Templum Libertatis* was provoking, for Dr. King was under surveillance by the government and receiving attacks from loyalist churchmen. Apologizing for being incapable of sending a witty reply, he urged Mendes to continue his satires upon the corruption of the times:

> Then take, for all, a grateful heart.
> To business chain'd, as to an oar,
> My soul regrets she cannot soar,
> The charms of liberty to sing,
> And to her temple follow King,
> Who emulates great Maro's strain,
> But flatters no Augustus reign.
> ....
> In study pass an Attic night,
> Review the folly and the crimes,
> That scandalize the present times;
> And making Horace your bright rule,
> Reform the world with ridicule;
> Or, where vice more enormous urges,
> Like Juvenal your satire scourges.
> O double vengeance on them lay
> Who the land's liberty betray,
> Who prostitute their votes for price,
> And owe their greatness to their vice.[117]

---

[114] *Ibid.*, f. 1.

[115] Moses Mendez, *A Collection of the Most Esteemed Pieces of Poetry...with Variety of Originals by the Later Moses Mendez and other Contributors to Dodsley's Collection* (London, 1767), 257, 259.

[116] *Ibid.*, 263.

[117] *Ibid.*, 264-65.

The threat of prosecution was apparently effective, for Ellis's translation of King's masterwork was never published. Moreover, many of the strongly Jacobite poems by King, Mendes, Ellis, and their friend Byrom were preserved only in the manuscript note-book currently held in the Grand Lodge Library in London. Given Mendes's strong Jacobite sentiments, it seems certain that Deane Swift, Orrery, and probably Jonathan Swift were aware of them. But he must have been disheartened by Swift's mental deterioration, which eventually took away his speech.

In July 1744 Edward Young contributed to the government's anti-Jacobite campaign by publishing *The Complaint*, Night Seven and Part Two of "The Infidel Reclaim'd." In his preface, he targeted France, the late Wharton, and his fellow free-thinkers as the cause of the current military conflict:

> As we are at War with the Power, it were well if we were at War with the Manners, of France. A Land of Levity, is a Land of Guilt. A serious Mind is the native Soil of every Virtue… all our Infidels, whatever Scheme for Argument's Sake, and to keep themselves in Countenance, they patronize, are betray'd into their deplorable Error, by some Doubt of their Immortality, at the Bottom.[118]

He then addressed Lorenzo (Wharton), whose stubborn heart is still unsubdued: "For there/ The Traitor lurks, who doubts the Truth I sing":

> Ye curst by Blessings infinite! Because
> Most highly favour'd, most profoundly lost!
> Ye motly Mass of Contradictions strong!
> …………………………………………..
> Lorenzo! This black Brotherhood renounce;
> Renounce St. Evremont, and read St. Paul.[119]

Though Young seemed to refer to the "black Brotherhood" of free-thinkers, contemporary readers in Ireland perhaps remembered his friendship with Wharton during the young duke's Hell Fire club days and controversial tenure as Grand Master of the Grand Lodge.

The blasphemous activities of the Blasters or Dublin Hell Fire clubbers, who included several well-known Masons, plus the increasing boldness of British Jacobite and foreign *Écossais* Masons led the Protestant loyalist Fifield d'Assigny to issue a heart-felt plea for reform in the Irish fraternity. In *A Serious and Impartial Enquiry into the Cause of the Present Decay of Free-masonry in the Kingdom of Ireland* (1744), he did not, as in previous publications, dedicate it to the current Grand Master, John Allen, 3rd Viscount Allen, the old enemy of Swift. Instead, he dedicated his plea to the "Most Nobel and Puissant Prince, TRUTH." D'Assigny hoped the brothers would understand that he pointed out the problems in Masonry in order to save it; by distinguishing "the base and impure from the generous and brave," the fraternity can prevent the former from gaining admittance. It was not surprising that the "base and impure" were present, because in all sects of men, "some impious and turbulent spirits appear, whose unlawful actions ought rather to be exposed

---

[118] Edward Young, *The Complaint. Or, Night-Thoughts* (London: G. Hawkins, 1744), Preface.
[119] *Ibid.*, 17, 60.

than concealed."[120] D'Assigny then gave a traditional, "ancient" history of Masonry, in-cluding the role of the Scottish Stuarts as "Mason Kings." His reference to James II was more ambiguous than Anderson's, for he said that during his reign, "the Lodges of Free Masonry in *London*, dwindled into ignorance, for want of being duly frequented and properly cultivated."

Besides the "base and impure" (the Blasters), d'Assigny was disturbed by reports that in York there were meetings of an assembly of Masons under the title of the Royal Arch, who consider their qualities and excellencies superior to regular Masons.[121] On 14 January 1744 the earliest public reference to the Royal Arch appeared in *Faulkner's Dublin Journal*, in a description of a Masonic procession in County Cork in which "the Royal Arch" was carried by "two Excellent Masons." André Kervella argues that the ritual was developed by Jacobites in France, who drew on older Irish and Scottish traditions of Jewish mysti-cism.[122] It should be recalled that Swift referred to "Cabala, as Masonry was call'd in those Days." The additional degrees focused on the rebuilding of the Temple of Jerusalem, after the Jews were liberated by King Cyrus, when Haggai, Joshua, and Zerubbabel were clearing away the ruins of Solomon's temple and discovered under an arch a secret vault which contained the "lost word" (the Hebrew name of God). The rituals became elabo-rate and compelling and recalled the great mystical masques of the Stuart kings James I and Charles I, when Inigo Jones and the operative Masons often designed and partici-pated in the royalist dramas.[123] They also intensified the personal, emotional, and imagi-native experience of the aspiring adept. As Jan Snoek observes, "The rituals of Freema-sonry were devised to be performed. It is believed that by performing the rituals the symbols are internalized and thereby change the personality of the initiate."[124]

For d'Assigny, the importation of these "irregular" Masonic rituals undermined the Grand Lodge's authority and were politically seditious. He thus lamented:

> It is too well known that in this city lately hath appeared a number of mean and low spirited wretches, who, (if ever just) turned rebels to our well formed Government, and artfully brought into their iniquitous net several un-guarded men… These despicable traders or hucksters in pretended Masonry, every prudent Brother ought carefully to avoid holding any converse with them…[125]

After these rather oblique allusions to political disaffection, d'Assigny focused on the importation of the Royal Arch:

> Some have been led away with ridiculous innovations, an example of which, I shall prove by a certain propagator of a false system some few years ago in this city, who imposed upon some worthy men under a pretence of being Master of the Royal Arch, which he asserted he had brought with him from

---

[120] The whole pamphlet is reprinted in William James Hughan, ed., *Memorials of the Masonic Union of A.D. 1813*, rev. ed. John Thorpe (Leicester, 1913, Preface, 121.

[121] *Ibid.*, 119.

[122] A. Kervella, *Chevalier Ramsay*, 138-40, 209, 274.

[123] M. Schuchard, *Restoring the Temple*, 355-56, 407-08, 411-15, 424-27, 440-44.

[124] J. Snoek and H. Bogdan, *Handbook of Freemasonry*, 7.

[125] W. Hughan, *Memorials.*, 126.

the city of *York*; and that the beauty of the Craft did principally consist in the knowledge of this valuable piece of Masonry. However, he carried on his scheme for several months, and many of the learned and wise were his followers, till at length his fallacious art was discovered by a Brother of probity and wisdom, who had some small space before attained that excellent part of Masonry in *London*, and plainly proved that his doctrine was false...[126]

Even worse was the importation of "foreign schemes" from Italy – a hint at the emergence of Jacobite and *Écossais* higher degrees:

There is lately arrived in this city a certain itinerant Mason, whose judgment (as he declares) is so far illumin'd, and whose optics are so strong that they can bear the view of the most lucid rays of the sun at noon day, and altho' we have contented ourselves with three material steps to approach our *Summum Bonum*, the immortal God, yet he presumes to acquaint us that he can add three more, which when properly plac'd may advance us to the highest heavens.... I could never yet hear that there was any order in Masonry under that particular denomination of the *Italic* order, until this mighty Architect, or, I may rather say, extravagant climber, came to impart to his countrymen so valuable a production... I hope that no innocent and worthy Brother may at any time be misled by false insinuations, or foreign schemes.

His hope that no "foreign schemes" would emerge became wishful thinking, as Jacobite Masons in Britain and abroad undertook ambitious new initiatives.

---

[126] *Ibid.*, 127.

CHAPTER TWENTY

REBUILDING THE TEMPLE IN THE NORTH
(1745)

A vague rumour is circulating amongst Freemasons, concerning a certain Order which they call "les Ecossois," superior, as they claim, to ordinary Freemasons and having their own distinct ceremonies and secrets…they conceal it from even the *Masters* of Freemasonry.

Abbé Perau, L'Ordre de F.M. trahi (Amsterdam/Paris, 1745).

It is a proud thing to see our Prince in the palace of his Fathers… there was a solemn Chapter of the ancient chivalry of the Temple of Jerusalem… Our noble Prince looked most gallantly in the white robe of the Order, and… did vow that he would restore the Temple higher than it was in the days of William the Lyon.

Duke of Perth to Lord Ogilvy (Edinburgh, 30 September 1745).

As invasion fears intensified in England, many of the opposition Whigs and Masons drew back from their secret collaboration with the Jacobites. Pope's friend James Thomson, an Anglicized Scottish Mason, expressed his ambiguous reaction to the Jacobite threat in *Tancred and Sigismunda. A Tragedy*, which opened on 18 March 1745. Dedicated to the Prince of Wales, it cautiously made no explicit reference to the current Jacobite unrest, but his story of two rival families in a contest for the Sicilian throne led to differing interpretations of just which prince he favored – Frederick or Charles Edward. His main theme was reconciliation which would prevent the "dark intestine Broils, of Civil War,/ And all its dreadful Miseries and Crimes."[1] He praised "Siffredi," who rooted out "Division from the Land," and urged that citizens must exercise "impartial Care" to "watch o'er Prejudice and Passion,/ Nor trust too much the jandic'd Eye of party!"

---

[1] James Thomson, *Tancred and Sigismunda. A Tragedy* (London, 1745), 20, 23.

Despite Thomson's caution, loyalist critics denounced the play as pro-Jacobite, even though the poet was, according to James Sambrook, "a typical anti-Papist, lowland Scotch Whig" and "faithful to the spirit of 1688."[2] Thus, Thomson joined other opposition Masons who either accepted government positions or became propagandists for the new Whig ministry – a move that provoked attacks on them in the anti-government *Daily Post* (26 April 1745).[3] The paper condemned *Tancred* as a subsidized voice of the new Whig placemen, such as Pitt and Lyttleton, who were "all very lately most flaming Patriots!" It scorned Thomson's call for reconciliation and unity as an attempt to stop all opposition to the current government, but the play was so tedious and dull that in the audience, "we sigh, we nod, applause; some snore aloud; till partial Claps awake the sleepy crowd."

The political apostasy of so many members of the opposition prompted a Tory-Jacobite attack on them and on the Grand Lodge Freemasons. In *The Devil's Almanac: Being a Curious Sett of Hellish Predictions, Calculated for the British Meridian. From the Glorious First of April 1745. Printed at Pandaemonium* (1745), the anonymous author mocked the hypocrisy and venality of government officials, as well as the zealous Protestant bigotry of the laureate Colley Cibber, well-known as a Grand Lodge member.[4] He then targeted the planned "Procession of March" by the loyalist Freemasons:

> The Free-Masons will repeat their Anniversary Farce of a Cavalcade, in the Teeth of public Derision; but be not offended, at the triumphant Procession of one trifling Branch of Folly, thro a Capital where nothing else governs: Were all her *Ministers* as harmless, their Equipages would provoke more Mirth, and less Indignation.[5]

When the current Grand Master, James, 6th Lord Cranstoun, led the public parade on 18 April, he was mocked by a rowdy crowd of Mock Masons, who were not intimidated by the arrest of some mockers a year earlier.[6] However, the "public derision" led the Grand Lodge to terminate the public processions, and no more were performed. Cranstoun was a Scot and a supporter of the Prince of Wales, and he may have been targeted by the "Devil" as an apostate from the Jacobite cause. As discussed earlier, in the late 1720s he had associated with Jacobite Masons in Italy, and in 1728 he tried to reconcile Mar and Wharton.[7] By 1745 he had evidently left his Jacobitism behind him, and in October his brother would inform Newcastle about the activities of the rebels in Scotland.[8]

Though the Whig Mason James Thomson maintained some sympathy for his "deluded" fellow Scots, Pope's and Orerry's other Scottish-Masonic friend, Lord Marchmont, surely would have surprised them by his desperate effort to be recalled into the government in order to fight the Jacobites. Marchmont boasted in an interview with

---

[2] James Sambrook, *James Thomson: A Life* (Oxford, 1991), 240-42.

[3] A. McKillop, *James Thomson*, 179.

[4] Anon., *The Devil's Almanac* (London, 1745), 11-16.

[5] *Ibid.*, 19.

[6] C. Crawley, "Mock Masonry," 142-43.

[7] Murray Pittock, *Material Culture and Sedition: Treacherous Objects, Secret Places* (Houndsmill, 2013), 111; "Cranstoun," J. Ingamells, *Dictionary*.

[8] NA: SP, on-line: volume 71 [46], f.

George II that he and his brother Alexander were the first to propose "making it treason to correspond with the Pretender's son," when such a move was neglected by others.[9] He told the king that he desired to inform him about the state of Scotland and that all the South and Presbyterians were "zealous for him." George replied that he worried about Edinburgh, where there were a great many Jacobites, and Marchmont reassured him that even there he had four out of five supporters. The king then referred to Lord Kilmarnock, as a lowland Scot who was disloyal, and Marchmont explained that Kilmarnock (his former friend and Masonic brother) was "a man of desperate fortune, whose estate would go to his creditors, when his person was under forfeiture." Over the next months, despite Marchmont's pleadings to lead the government party in Scotland, the king and ministers did not trust his change of allegiance.

The Jacobite Masons tried to maintain a high level of secrecy, but their activities alerted suspicious authorities, and in January 1745 George II was so alarmed by reports of Masonic intrigues on the Continent that he published an Edict forbidding the clergy of the Electorate of Hanover from becoming Freemasons.[10] Charges emerged of a secret "forward movement" by elite initiates of the *Écossais* high degrees in support of a Stuart restoration. In a new edition of *L'Ordre de F.M. trahi* (Amsterdam, 1745), the editor added,

> I am not ignorant that a vague rumour is circulating amongst Freemasons, concerning a certain Order which they call "Les Ecossois," superior as they claim to ordinary Freemasons and having their own distinct ceremonies and Secrets… if they have any Secret peculiar to themselves they are so extremely jealous concerning it that they conceal it from even the *Masters* of Freemasonry.[11]

In London, the currently incognito Swedenborg began quoting scriptural passages in a Messianic treatise, in which he suggested his participation with the exiled Scottish Masters in rebuilding the temple: "They shall build a temple, not like the former, but one that shall endure as long as the world shall endure. And afterward, returning from the places of exile, they shall build up Jerusalem gloriously."[12] He quoted another suggestive passage: "That he hath redeemed the Jacobite, and will deliver him from prison; for thou wast precious to me. I will gather thee from the west and the east. I will command the north, that it give up; and the south, that it refuse not to bring my sons from afar."[13] It would not be beyond the paranoia (now justified) of the English government decipherers to read these Biblical lines as referring to an attempt to liberate the recently arrested Jacobite prisoners from the Tower, with Stuart forces coming from Ireland (west) and Sweden (east), with Charles Edward landing in Scotland (north) and the invasion coming from France (south). Moreover, British intelligence recognized that the Jacobites often resorted to Scriptural codes to conceal their messages.

At this time, the most important Jacobite prisoner was Sir Hector Maclean, former *Écossais* Grand Master and close collaborator with the Swedish Hats in planning their

---

[9] Marchmont, *A Selection of the Papers of the Earls of Marchmont*, ed. George Henry Rose (London, 1831), I, 162-63.
[10] *Monthly Review*, 25 (6 October 1798), 36; F. Benimeli, *Masoneria*, II, 214-16.
[11] [Abbé Perau?], *L'Ordre des Francs-Maçons Trahi* (Amsterdam, 1745).
[12] Emanuel Swedenborg, *Concerning the Messiah About to Come*, trans. Alfred Acton (Bryn Athyn, 1949), 67. The treatise remained unpublished until 1949.
[13] E. Swedenborg, *Concerning the Messiah*, 53.

joint expedition. Maclean had spent much time in France with Charles Edward, who sent him to Edinburgh to prepare the Maclean clansmen for his projected landing on Mull, their territory.[14] His orders were to not open his papers until he was in the presence of James Drummond, 3rd Duke of Perth, his fellow Mason. Perth had been initiated in Derwentwater's lodge in Paris in 1725-26, and he maintained close relations with Maclean and his *Écossais* brothers over the next seven years. After his return to Scotland in 1732, he was reportedly involved in chivalric Masonry in his "northern Convent."

Unfortunately for Maclean, Perth was absent from Edinburgh, and Maclean incautiously refused to hide in the county until they could meet, because he was waiting for a pair of specially-made boots to fit his misshapen feet.[15] In early June he was arrested, but the government agents, who had been intercepting his correspondence since April, could not decipher his codes. The Whig examiners reported that they could make nothing of "the cant names in letters," while his correspondents prevaricated and contradicted themselves "without blushing."[16] Much of the communication between Maclean and his supporters was in Gaelic, as in the ballad, "Maclean's Welcome," which called for the Stuart prince to come to Scotland to join Sir Hector and his clan: "Come o'er the stream brave Charlie, and dine with Maclean, and though you be weary, we'll make your heart cheery," while we'll "drink to your sire, and his friend the Maclean."[17]

In another anti-Jacobite exposé, the *Examen de la Société des Francs-Maçons* (1744; reprint 1745), the author charged that Freemasonry began very nearly when the Knights Templar ended and that contemporary Masons have revived all the vices and seditions of the Templars.[18] Swedenborg had recently written that "a broad foundation must be laid, yea, a temple must be built."[19] But his most provocative quotations seemed almost a prophecy of a Masonic ceremony that would allegedly take place two months after Charles Edward Stuart arrived in Scotland in early August. Swedenborg quoted the prophet Ezekiel who was set upon a high mountain, where he saw a man in the city below "having in his hand a measuring line":

> A wall surrounded the temple without, and he measured all the things…the chambers, the doors, the gates, the outer court, the upper chamber, the porch, etc., in short the holy city…The splendor of Jova came into the temple by way of the gate looking to the east – he showed the place of the throne…The prince he shall settle in the sanctuary. – The northern gate…[20]

Sensing that he was "on thin ice" in London, Swedenborg suddenly left and sailed to Sweden in late July, where he found his Hat "brothers" eagerly following the exploits of the Stuart prince, whom they constantly compared to their beloved Carl XII.[21]

On 3 August Charles Edward landed with a small party, "the seven men of Moidart," on a remote northern island, where he audaciously launched the rebellion of 1745. His

[14] F. McLynn, *Charles Edward Stuart*, 120.

[15] Elcho, *A Short Account*, 29.

[16] NA:SP 54/25, ff. 5, 21.

[17] James Hogg, *The Jacobite Relics of Scotland*, 2nd Series (Paisley, 1874), 90-91.

[18] J. Tuckett, "Origins," 22.

[19] Alfred Acton, *An Introduction to the Word Explained* (Bryn Athyn, 1927), 89-90.

[20] E. Swedenborg, *Concerning the Messiah*, 67.

[21] N. Mackenzie, *Charles XII*, 2-26.

companions included one Englishman, Colonel Francis Strickland; two Scots, Aeneas Macdonald and William Murray, Marquis of Tullibardine; and four Irishmen, Sir Thomas Sheridan, Sir John Macdonald, Colonel William O'Sullivan, and Rev. George Kelly. The prince immediately sent a stirring message to his father:

> The worst that can happen to me, if France does not succor me, is to die at the head of such a brave people as I find here… The French must now take off the mask, or have an eternal shame on them; for at present there is no medium, and we, whatever happens, shall gain an eternal honour by restoring our master, or perish with sword in hand.[22]

When the prince learned that the English government had put a price of £30,000 on his head, he laughed it off and "jokingly offered £30 for George II's capture in response."[23]

On 31 August Charles Edward arrived at Blair Atholl castle, the ancestral home of Tullibardine, the Jacobite 2nd Duke of Atholl. His younger brother James Murray was a loyalist who had assumed the title after William was attainted for following Mar into battle in 1715. While in exile, Tullibardine was supported by Mar and, as we shall see, he allegedly played a significant role in Mar's Restoration Order of Military Knighthood. After Mar's death, he spent much time with Chevalier Ramsay.[24] At Blair Atholl, Tullibardine taunted his brother, a Hanoverian Mason, who then fled to the government forces.

The prince's party was now joined by John Roy Stewart, a valuable recruit, who had served in the British and French armies and was an excellent swordsman and military tactician. He served as quarter-master general in Berwick's regiment, a position considered fundamental in military Masonry, and he was close to the former Grand Master Maclean and the Duc de Bouillon, the reputed co-founder with Ramsay of a special *Écossais* Masonic rite.[25] On 16 August, as Stewart prepared to sail to Scotland, he wrote from Ghent to secretary Edgar about a letter he was to deliver to the prince in which Bouillon appealed to Louis XV to support Charles Edward's enterprise:

> The Duke of Bouillon gave me the prettiest & most tender letter I ever saw to the Prince… There are not words enough to express his good heart to the cause. He went on his knees to the King with tears in his eyes to beg his assistance to the Prince, and the King most graciously desired him to assure the P. of it. He gave me a hundred kisses at parting and…desired me to tell his dear Prince that he would sacrifice all his fortune all his family and all his blood for him. I'll love him as long as I live for the force of love he so lively expresses for my K. & Prince.[26]

This letter to Charles Edward from Bouillon, heir to his family's Templar traditions, is unfortunately lost, but it and Stewart's intimate connection with Bouillon would soon become relevant to Masonic developments in Edinburgh. Much of the fame of *Ruadh*

---

[22] Fitzroy Maclean, *Bonnie Prince Charlie* (London, 1988), 43-44.
[23] F. McLynn, *Charles Edward Stuart*, 135,137.
[24] A. Kervella, *Chevalier Ramsay*, 211.
[25] *Ibid.*, 334-35; H. Tayler, *Jacobite Epilogue*, 246-58.
[26] *Ibid.*, 250.

(red) Stewart came from his excellent Gaelic poetry, which was chanted and sung for decades in Scotland and Ireland.

With bagpipes skirling and flags flying, Charles Edward made a triumphant entry on 17 September into Edinburgh, "the capital of his ancestors' ancient kingdom," and received a rapturous reception. McLynn notes that if the crowd wanted to see a fairy-tale prince, he would oblige them, and even his opponents grudgingly conceded that he made a very favorable impression: "Tall, handsome, with brown eyes and a fair complexion, clearly a magnificent horseman and at the peak of physical fitness, he seemed to combine the attributes of the perfect prince with the rougher qualities of a martial hero."[27] Splendidly attired, he proudly presented his rough-hewn Highlanders as heroes, and he even impressed the loyalist ladies. The eighteen year-old Magdalen Pringle, a staunch Whig, recorded that he was so handsome and charismatic that he could enchant his followers and carry people "to consent to their own Slavery in spite of themselves."[28]

His entourage included an impressive array of Scottish aristocrats and lairds, many of whom were Freemasons.[29] Among his supporters were five former Jacobite Grand Masters – Maclean, Derwentwater, Cromarty, Kilmarnock, and Balmerino, as well as the current cautious Grand Master Wemyss. (Balmerino's little-known Masonic role in France will be discussed later). Derwentwater, who was revered by the prince, had planned to sail with him in the aborted 1744 expedition, and he had received a letter (now lost) from Charles Edward just before the prince precipitously sailed for Scotland in 1745. Thus, Charles Edward was in close contact with two former Grand Masters (Maclean and Derwentwater), as he planned his journey to Scotland.[30] The activities and ultimate fates of these prominent Jacobite Masons will be discussed later.

The prince moved into Holyrood Palace, the traditional residence of the Stuart kings of Scotland, where a Masonic lodge occasionally held meetings. Ten years earlier, the lodge of Holyrood House had been founded by Robert Nucoll and his son, who were operative Masons and Jacobites.[31] Over the next years, the lodge maintained its independence from the Grand Lodge of Scotland, which did not invite it to its first Grand Election, and its membership remained predominantly Jacobite. On 18 May 1744 Robert Gordon, a merchant and Jacobite, occupied the Chair of King Solomon in the Holyrood lodge. On 27 August Robert Maxwell, a professional writer and fellow Jacobite, joined the lodge and began transcribing its records from 4 December 1734 to 4 February 1737, followed by a gap, and then from 7 June 1744 to 2 September 1745, when he abruptly stopped. The cessation was caused by Maxwell's joining Prince Charles's army, along with his lodge brothers Nucoll and Gordon. Though we do not know what rituals were performed in the Holyrood lodge, there is evidence from a Holyrood-affiliated lodge in Stirling that Royal Arch and Templar degrees were being worked by early 1745.[32]

---

[27] F. McLynn, *Charles Edward Stuart*, 148.

[28] H. Tayler, *Jacobite Miscellany*, 41.

[29] For the Jacobite Masons among his troops, see Robert Strathern Lindsay, *A History of the Mason Lodge of Holyrood House* (Edinburgh, 1935), I, 63-73; Allen Mackenzie, *History of the Lodge Canongate Kilwinning* (Edinburgh, 1888), 27, 57-66; D. Lyon, *History*, 165-77, 196-200. 350-53,

[30] H. Tayler, *Jacobite Epilogue*, 157.

[31] R. Lindsay, *History of the Mason Lodge*, I, 35-41, 57-59, 63-64, 72.

[32] W.J. Hughan, "The `Ancient' Stirling Lodge," *AQC*, 6 (1893), 108-11.

Thus, despite the loss of lodge records from early September 1745 to April 1746, there is a credible Scottish context for the report of Charles Edward's installation as Grand Master of the Order of the Temple within the sanctuary of Holyrood Palace. Accompanying the prince in Holyrood was George Kelly, who had been chosen by Ramsay to make an English translation of his Masonic oration, which Charles Edward had yearned to read in 1737. As noted earlier, the oration was infused with the chivalric mysticism of the crusaders who recaptured Jerusalem. Working with Ramsay at that time, the Grand Master Derwentwater was determined to restore the fraternity to its ancient chivalric roots. Kelly was thus familiar with these Masonic traditions of the Temple, and he was currently close to Charles Edward, with whom he may well have discussed them. However, on 26 September the prince ordered Kelly to return to France, where he should work to gain support from Louis XV and his courtiers, many of whom were *Écossais* Masons. Before Kelly's departure, he and the prince wrote an important letter "in the style of the ancient chivalry" to Charles Wogan in Spain (to be discussed later).

It is unknown if Kelly was still in Edinburgh, when a private ceremony was reportedly held in Holyrood that seemed to fulfill not only the ambition of Ramsay and Derwentwater to restore the Temple of Jerusalem but Swedenborg's vision of the prince, who from the northern gate, enters the sanctuary of the Temple. On 30 September 1745 the Duke of Perth wrote from Edinburgh to his kinsman David, Lord Ogilvy:

> It is truly a proud thing to see our Prince in the palace of his Fathers, with all the best blood of Scotland around him. He is much beloved of all sorts, and we cannot fail to make the pestilent England smoke for it. Upon Monday last, there was a great ball at the Palace, and on Tuesday, by appointment, there was a solemn Chapter of the ancient chivalry of the Temple of Jerusalem, held in the audience room – not more than ten Knights were present, for since my Lord of Mar demitted the Office of Grand Master, no general meeting has been called, save in your North Convent. Our noble Prince looked most gallantly in the white robe of the Order, and took his profession like a worthy night; and, after receiving congratulations from all present, did vow that he would restore the Temple higher than it was in the days of William the Lyon. Then my Lord Athol did demit as Regent, and his Rl Highness was elected G Master. I write you this knowing how you love the Order…[33]

Though some Whig-oriented historians of English Masonry rejected Perth's letter to Ogilvy as a forgery, others who were better informed about Scottish history and international Jacobite Freemasonry (such as J.E.S. Tuckett, André Kervella, and Edward Corp) have vouched for the credibility of the account (even if the letter, first published in 1843, was a partial translation or transcript of an original).[34] Kervella argues that the Order of the Temple was founded in 1722 by the Earl of Mar, with assistance from Ramsay. Approved by James III as the "Restoration Order," it was defined by Mar as "a new military order of knighthood" dedicated to reward "the chiefs of the clans" who "act heartily" in

---

[33] Transcript of full letter in Grand Lodge of Scotland; I am grateful to the librarian Robert Cooper for sending me a copy.

[34] J. Tuckett, "Origin," 5-31, and "Dr. Begemann and the Alleged Templar Chapter of Edinburgh in 1745," *AQC*, 33 (1920), 40-62.

the Stuart cause.[35] Mar would surely have included Maclean, his protégé, among those initiated "chiefs of the clans." Edward Corp affirms that Mar served as Grand Master, while his confidant Atholl/Tullibardine was his deputy.[36] When Mar fell into disfavor because of Atterbury's vendetta against him, the order went underground in Scotland and survived only among his strongest supporters in the north. After Mar's death, the "Regency" of the order was passed to Atholl/Tullibardine in France, but when he accompanied Charles Edward in Scotland, he "demitted" the regency, the prince was named Grand Master, and "the order was properly instituted."

Defenders of the credibility of Perth's account cite the subsequent publication of the letter in the *Memoirs of Sir Robert Strange, Knt…and of his Brother-in-Law Andrew Lumisden* (London, 1855), for the young artist Strange accompanied the prince in Holyrood and was commissioned to engrave the plates for the new Jacobite currency.[37] Strange had served his apprenticeship under Richard Cooper, a Jacobite and proselytizing Freemason, and lived in his home for six years. Thus, it seems likely that Strange was also a Mason. Perth's original letter was possibly found among the papers of the Lumisden family, for Strange's brother-in-law Andrew Lumisden served as secretary to the prince in Edinburgh and later joined the Stuart court in Rome in 1749. It was Lumisden who received the minute book of the Jacobite lodge in Rome, after the death of the Earl of Wintoun.[38] The nineteenth-century editor of the *Memoirs* lamented that many documents in the Lumisden family papers had disappeared, for they were important to shedding light on the Jacobite cause.[39] Tuckett, who was apparently unaware of Mar's establishment of "a new military order of knighthood," and of Perth's initiation in Derwentwater's lodge in Paris in 1725, responded (cautiously) to the skeptical arguments of Dr. Begemann that "some such letter" from Perth "did actually exist, was seen, got lost or destroyed, and was reconstructed later from memory and possibly with embellishments."[40] The Masonic historians Charles Cameron and W.J. Hughan agreed that Charles Edward's connection with a "Knight Templar Order," probably "introduced from France by the Pretender's partisans," was historically credible, and that Perth's letter "appears to be genuine."[41]

Despite the gap in the Scottish records and questions about the provenance of the letter, the most compelling and enduring belief in the Templar ceremony emerged in Sweden, where the story was brought to the Hats by Swedish soldiers who fought with Prince Charles and by Scottish Masons who later found refuge in Sweden. In early September the Swedish soldiers were secretly ordered to Scotland by the Masonic Hat, Count Scheffer, who recruited them from the French regiment of the *Royal Suédois*.[42] Robert

---

[35] A. Kervella, *Mystère*, 279-93; also, M. Schuchard,"Rivalités," 9-10.

[36] Edward Corp, "The Jacobite Community at Saint-Germain after the Departure of the Stuart Court," in A. Macinnes, K. German, L. Graham, *Living with Jacobitism*, 29-31.

[37] James Denistoun, *Memoirs of Sir Robert Strange, Kt., the Eminent Engraver, and His Brother-in-Law, Andrew Lumisden, Private Secretary to the Stuart Princes at Rome* (London, 1855), I, 79-82. It was also published in *Statutes of the Religious and Military Order of the Temple* (Edinburgh, 1843), I, 81-82; repeated in editions of 1877 and 1897. Also, in *The Edinburgh Advertiser* (1 December 1843), and *The Freemasons Magazine* (27 September 1862), 256.

[38] *Gentleman's Magazine*, 33, n.s., (June 1853), 580n.

[39] J. Denistoun, *Memoirs*, I, iv, 78.

[40] J. Tuckett, "Dr. Begemann," 55.

[41] Charles Cameron, "On the Origin and Progress of Chivalric Freemasonry in the British Isles," *AQC*, 13 (1900), 156; W. J. Hughan, "Origin of Masonic Knight Templary in the United Kingdom," *AQC*, 18 (1905), 91.

[42] Stockholm. Riksarkiv: Gallica, #330. Scheffer's journal (10 September 1745).

Strange possibly befriended the Swedes, because he had visited Gothenburg in 1734 when he served on board a ship, and he marched with them in the prince's army. After the defeat of the Jacobite army at Culloden in April 1746, Lord Ogilvy, the recipient of Perth's letter, fled to Bergen and then to Gothenburg, where he was assisted by local Masons, some of whom subsequently joined his regiment in France.[43] In 1763 "Brother" J.P. Pollet, a Swedish member of a French military lodge, referred to

> the Scotch Degree usual in England…is the same which resembles what the French call the Royal Arch. It was first known in France from the raising of the Scottish Regiment Ogilvy in 1746. The Collar of the French Royal Arch is red, the Apron green, with a St. Andrew's Cross… the clothing mentioned being more suggestive of the Royal Order of Scotland. [44]

Pollet added that his brother was Orator of the Gothenburg lodge and would seek information on the degree in London. Kervella argues that the Jacobite degree drew upon the Stuart-Templar ceremony in Holyrood Palace.[45] Tuckett notes that Ogilvy's regiment "was composed for the most part of destitute Scottish refugees willing to enter the French Service."[46] Many of these refugees had escaped to Gothenburg in route to France.

None of the skeptics who doubt the reality of the Holyrood ceremony were aware of the role of the Swedish officer, Magnus Wilhelm Armfelt, who marched with the rebel troops from Prestonpans until the terrible defeat at Culloden. Decades later in 1783, Armfelt's son, Gustaf Moritz Armfelt, would accompany his Masonic brother, King Gustaf III, to Italy, where the elderly Charles Edward made the Swedish king his successor as Grand Master of the Order of the Temple.[47] According to Gustaf's secretary and fellow Mason, Elis Schröderheim, the king in a series of secret and emotional ceremonies "worked on mysteries with the Pretender in order to raise the Temple of Jerusalem" and to achieve "the re-establishment of the sanctuary."[48] The aged English diplomat Horace Mann, former Whig member of the Florentine lodge, received a report from a suborned French member of Gustaf III's entourage. On 30 December 1783 Mann wrote scornfully to Consul John Udny at Leghorn:

> His Swedish Majesty…has taken other steps, which though they may appear ludicrous, are not less certain. It is supposed that when the Order of the Templars was suppressed and the individuals persecuted, some of them secreted themselves in the High Lands of Scotland and that from them, either arose, or that they united themselves to the Society of Free Masons, of which the Kings of Scotland were supposed to be the Hereditary Grand Masters. From this Principle the present Pretender [Charles Edward] has let himself

---

[43] Arne Odd Johnsen, "Jacobite Officers at Bergen, Norway, after the Battle of Culloden," *Scottish Historical Review*, 57 (1978), 189.

[44] J.F. Pollet to J.P. Gogel (25 April 1763); quoted in William James Hughan, *Origin of the English Rite of Freemasonry, Especially in Relation to the Royal Arch Degree* (London, 1847), 157, 160.

[45] A. Kervella, *Mystére*, 354-55.

[46] J. Tuckett, "Dr. Begemann," 59.

[47] R. Nisbet Bain, *Gustavus III and his Contemporaries* (London, 1894), I, 267; F. McLynn, *Charles Edward Stuart*, 534-57; M. Schuchard, *Emanuel Swedenborg*, 399, 752-54.

[48] Elis Schröderheim, *Anteckningar till Konung Gustaf IIIs Historia* (Örebro, 1851), 84; Claude Nordmann, *Gustave III*, 219-20.

be persuaded that the Grand Mastership devolved to him… the King of Sweden during his stay obtained a Patent from the Pretender in due form by which He has appointed his Swedish Majesty his Coadjutor and Successor to the Grand Mastership of the Lodges in the North, on obtaining which…the King expressed his greatest joy.[49]

In September 1746, among the Scottish escapees to Sweden was the poet William Hamilton of Bangour, who befriended Prince Charles in Rome in 1740, was made a member of the prince's lifeguard in September 1745, and was possibly privy to the Templar ceremony. In Sweden he was assisted by a network of Masonic Hats, who arranged the journey to France taken by him and other Scottish refugees.[50] He had earlier expressed an almost mystical reverence for Holyrood Palace, in a mock-epitaph on himself in which he "spoke what he thought":

> Courts he abhorred, their errors, their abuses,
> St. James', Versailles – all, all, but Sanctae Crucis*
> There, where no statesman buys, no bishop sells –
> A virtuous palace, where no monarch dwells.[51]

The footnote to the asterisk says "Holyrood House."

But Hamilton's most famous poem was his triumphant "Ode on the Battle of Gladsmuir," also known as Prestonpans, which was printed and distributed soon after the Jacobites' victory on 21 September 1745. Commanded by the Walpolean loyalist, Sir John Cope, the government forces bolted with barely a show of resistance when the Highlanders launched their broadsword charge. Cope struggled to rally his troops, exclaiming, "For Shame, Gentlemen; don't let us be beat by such a set of Banditti." [52] All over Scotland, the Jacobites sang a rousing taunt, "Hey, Johnnie Cope! Are ye waukin yet?" According to Sir Walter Scott, the rebels used the name Gladsmuir instead of Prestonpans in order "to reconcile the victory to some ancient metrical prophecies, which happen to fix on Gladsmuir as the field of battle in which the Scottish should be victorious: – On Gladsmuir shall the battle be, saith the Book of Prophecies – printed by Andro Hart, Edinburgh, 1615."[53] Hamilton accordingly linked the victory to ancient Scottish prophetic tradition:

> As over Gladsmuir's blood-stain'd field,
> Scota, imperial goddess flew,
> Her lifted spear and radiant shield
> Conspicuous and blazing to the view;
> Her visage lately clouded with despair,
> Now resum'd its first majestic air.
> …………………………………………...

---

[49] NA: FO 79/3. For a detailed account of Charles Edward's Masonic dealings with the Swedish royal family from 1776 to 1788, see M. Schuchard, *Emanuel Swedenborg*, 752-57; Pierre Mollier, "Les Stuarts et la Franc-Maçonnerie: le Dernier Épisode," *Renaissance Traditionnelle*, 177-178 (2015), 59-73.

[50] *Ibid.*, 406-08; N. Bushnell, *William Hamilton*, 81-83.

[51] *Ibid.*, xxxiv.

[52] "Sir John Cope," *ODNB*.

[53] Sir Walter Scott, *The Prose Works of Sir Walter Scott* (Paris, 1830), VII, 819.

> "'Tis done! My sons! 'tis nobly done!
> Victorious over tyrant pow'r;
> How quick the race of fame was run!
> The work of ages in one hour;
> Slow creeps th' oppressive weight of slavish reigns;
> One glorious moment rose and burst your chains.[54]

He went on to credit Scotland's deliverance to "the gallant youth," who was early nursed by Scotia; even when he was "ill detain'd on foreign shores," she "fill'd his mind with love of truth,/ With fortitude and widsom's stores." An optimistic Hamilton predicted peace and plenty, mercy and forgiveness when the prince wins not only Scotland but England.

Hamilton was overjoyed when Lord Pitsligo arrived in Edinburgh on 8 October with hundreds of Highland troops, for the philosopher and philanthropist was revered by the vast majority of Scots, including many Whigs. The poet wrote that when Pitsligo joined the prince, "It seemed as if Religion, Virtue and Justice were entering the camp under the appearance of the venerable old man; and what would have given sanction to a cause of the most dubious right, could not fail to render sacred the very best."[55] His fellow Mason Murray of Broughton described Pitsligo in 1745 as,

> A little thin fair man, a great scholar and fond of study. Of the primitive stamp and fitter to have been a martyr in the days of Nero, than to live in an age of villainy and corruption. He is the deservedly most popular man in the country, not beloved but adored, the best father, the best friend and the best subject in Britain.[56]

At age sixty-seven and severely asthmatic, Pitsligo had "weighed and weighed again" the prospect of joining the rising, but when he did he entered with enthusiasm: "Did you ever know me absent at the second day of a wedding," he asked his friends, reminding him of his participation in the "first day'" in 1715.[57] Forbes drew support from his Highland neighbors and Masonic brothers, and his charge to his troops became famous all over Scotland: "Oh Lord, Thou knowest our cause is just. Gentlemen, march."

Meanwhile in England, Orrery followed carefully the progress of the rebellion, but he made sure that almost nothing remained of his correspondence from July 1745 to May 1746. This would eventually prove life-saving for him, because on 20 August 1745 Marischal had presented a *Memoire* to the French court, based on the report of English supporters and brought over to France by the Earl of Clancarty, Orrery's reckless cousin.[58] In it he affirmed that the Irish land-holders Orrery, Barrymore, and Clancarty were prepared to raise the standard of King James in their respective parts of the kingdom.[59] Thomas Carte had chosen Clancarty to deliver an *oral* message that Irish and English Jacobite leaders would move immediately when the French landed. They had drafted

---

[54] N. Bushnell, *William Hamilton*, 62-63.

[55] H. Tayler, *Jacobite Court*, 33.

[56] *Ibid.*, 33.

[57] "Alexander Forbes, 4th Lord Forbes," *ODNB*.

[58] Andrew Lang, *The Companions of Pickle* (London, 1898), 36-37.

[59] E. O'Ciardha, *Ireland*, 304 n.126.

their message before they knew that the prince had landed in Scotland and, in an excess of caution, they refused to sign their names to the memorial, which led the French ministers to doubt their sincerity. At the same time, Marischal burned all his papers.

Among Orrery's few surviving manuscripts from that perilous time are his hand-written copies of Hamilton's "Ode on the Victory of Gladsmore, Sept. 21st, 1745," and a brief poem which mocked the defeated Cope. [60] In a note, he wrote that the following verses were made and spoken aloud, "by a Young Lady in her Sleep. Her Bed Fellow, who happened to be awake, wrote them down immediately, and heartily wishes they may be prophetical":

> Say what Reward shall be decreed
> For Deeds like those of Sir John Cope?
> Reason and Rhyme are both agreed,
> His Ribband should be made a Rope.[61]

Cope's "Ribband" referred to his installation as a Knight of the Bath, after he participated in George II's victory over the French at the Battle of Dettingen, but she believed he deserved the hangman's "Rope."

Orrery knew that he was under government surveillance, but he risked sending two letters (now missing) on 25 and 27 September to his Irish land-agent, Richard Purcell, a loyalist Protestant. As noted earlier, Purcell had warned a fellow Hanoverian that Lord Barrymore could easily rouse 20,000 stout followers in Cork for a Jacobite rising. He was evidently unaware of Orrery's collaboration with Barrymore in planning just such a rebellion. On 11 October Purcell thanked Orrery for sending news, noting that the account of Sir John Cope's defeat has created the greatest consternation and has so depressed trade that he will not be able to send Orrery his rents and arrears. He added that the papists continue quiet and will probably continue so, "if foreign Forces should not invade," but if that should happen, he was "confident that they would join them, and in such an Event the Protestants in this Province [Munster] must suffer exceedingly."[62] Purcell's further remarks provided significant intelligence to Orrery:

> Our Militia in this Country hath not been arrayed since the year 1715, but Orders arrived last week from our Government for their Array and Exercise, and many People fear that this Order would not have been given at this Time, notwithstanding our having but few regular Troops, if the Government had not suspected that there may be some Foundations for a Report here that a Descent is to be made by…the Irish Forces in the French Service.

At this time, a French police official reported that M. de Valette, an Irish officer, served as Grand Master of the "Loges Écossaises de Paris."[63] Pierre Chevallier observes that the new Scottish degrees provided a way to favor the Stuart cause, to augment their resources, and to sustain "la dynamique du secret."[64] Moreover, there was a strong

---

[60] Harvard: Orrery, Eng. MS. 218.2, ff. 349-52.

[61] *Ibid.*, f. 304.

[62] Harvard, Houghton. Orrery Papers: MS. Eng. 218.4F, f. 87.

[63] P. Chevallier, *Histoire*, I, 85.

[64] *Ibid.*, I, 86.

Jacobite Masonic presence in the Irish Brigade, many of whose members would join the rebel forces in Scotland.[65] From this date forward, there are no more surviving letters to or from Orrery during the months of the rebellion, as he and his fellow Jacobite Masons (Dr. King, Mendes, Byrom, etc.) maintained very low profiles.

Meanwhile in Scotland, the rebels' victory over Cope at Prestonpans/ Gladsmuir inspired the publication of *The Chronicle of Charles, the Young Man* (Edinburgh? 1745), attributed to the Earl of Kilmarnock. Recognizing the deep religious feelings (from Presbyterian to Episcopalian to Catholic) held by the majority of Scots (both Jacobite and Hanoverian), propagandists on both sides appealed to the Scots' traditional sense of being a covenanted nation and heirs of the ancient Jews. Thus, Kilmarnock adopted a Biblical tone which also drew upon the Jacobites' usage of scriptural codes in their correspondence and publications:

> And it came to pass in the eighth Month, even in the Month of August, in the Year 1745, that the Young Man landed at Moidart, in the Wilderness of Lochabar.
>
> That the Prophecies of John the Scribe might be fulfilled, who prophesied, saying, In the eighth Month, the young Man will come again, and many will go out after him.
>
> But the People laughed him to Scorn, and believed not the Words of John the Scribe; for they said, He is a false Prophet, and prophesieth for filthy Lucre, for their Hearts were hardened.
>
> [But] he reposed his Trust in the Affections of the Subjects of his Father, and many resorted to him…
>
> Now the young Man was a great Prince, and of a goodly Countenance, and all they that saw him loved him, and they called his name CHARLES.
>
> Moreover, he had been trained up in Arms, in Exercise, and in Studies, even from his Youth, in such as were becoming the Son of a great King, and the Heir apparent of the Crowns of Three Kingdoms.
>
> Yet he humbled himself in his Host, he did eat as his Soldiers did eat, and he lay as they did, he marched on Foot before them, saying, *I will not dwell in Ease, whilst they who fight for me suffer Hardships.* '[66]

Observers, both Jacobite and Hanoverian, noted the prince's "self-fashioning" in the image of the Swedish king Carl XII, who famously shared the full experiences and hardships of his troops.[67] In contrast, according to Kilmarnock, "George the Usurper," wallowed in his lewd love nest with his concubine, Wolmate, in Hanover.[68] Despite his attempts to "put a Bridle into the Mouth" of the English parliament, the Usurper was determined to take his Hanoverian troops "into British pay and use them to crush the rebellion, while keeping "the Troops of Britain abroad." On the Continent, the Hanoverian troops "joined not in the Fight," saying in themselves, "Let the English fight and be slain, there will fewer remain alive to oppose the Will of our Master."

---

[65] Charles Trevenix Trench, *Grace's Card: Irish Catholic Landlords, 1690-1800* (Cork, 1997), 34.

[66] William Boyd, 4th Earl of Kilmarnock, *The Chronicle of Charles, the Young Man* [Edinburgh, 1745], 1-3..

[67] Niall Mackenzie, "'A great affinity in many things': Further Evidence for the Jacobite Gloss on 'Swedish Charles," *The Age of Johnson*, 12 (2001), 255-72.

[68] Kilmarnock, *Chronicle.*, 3-5.

Kilmarnock then recounted the series of defeats of the English commanders, who had tried to frighten the local populace with charges that "CHARLES would take away their Wives, and their Children, and their Cattle, and all their Goods."[69] But the Stuart prince paid for everything the army took and treated all men kindly, "So the Fame of his Moderation reached to the outmost Corners, and he saved the enemy prisoners, "and would not allow them to be destroyed." He came "not as a conquering Enemy, but as a Deliverer, and Father to his People," and he proclaimed at Prestonpans that "This Day I will make my People a free and a happy People, or I will perish in the Attempt; and the whole Host shouted, and said 'We will follow thee, and we will deliver thine Enemies into thine Hand.'" But Charles saved the enemy prisoners, "and would not allow them to be destroyed."

Reports of the rebels' victories soon reached Spain, where Sir Charles Wogan was laboring to solicit funds and organize the shipping of Irish officers and arms to the prince's army. In his correspondence with James III, he seemed to draw upon not only Masonic but Tobosan themes that reinforce the possible reality of Charles Edward's initiation into the Order of the Temple. On 5 October 1745 Wogan wrote James that he had received "Mr Kelly's instructions and my noble Prince's billet to me," which had been written before Kelly left Edinburgh.[70] Wogan translated the letter into French to present to the Spanish majesties , "who then seem'd very well satisfied at the choice his R.H. was pleased to make of me for ye conductor and manager of ye enterprise and succours here." In the prince's letter, he seemed to allude to his and Wogan's knightly and fraternal bonds:

> Their MMs. laugh'd heartily at ye Prince's kind expressions to me, wch were all in the style of the ancient chivalry, as to ye successor of Don Quixote in ye Govermt. of his native country, etc. and ye Queen said it show'd the undaunted spirit of her nephew to be in so much gayety in ye midst of his troubles and ye perplexities attending so hazardous an adventure.

That Charles Edward used "the style of the ancient chivalry" is suggestive, because Perth described the prince's initiation into a chapter of "the ancient chivalry of the Order of the Temple of Jerusalem." As discussed earlier, Wogan was close to Wharton when the duke served as Grand Master of *Écossais* Freemasonry, and he was probably a Mason himself (given his earlier collaboration with James and Charles Radcliffe, Mar, the Keith brothers, Ormonde, and Ezekiel Hamilton). The fact that the young Stuart princes were honorary members of Toboso in Italy makes the many references to Don Quixote, Toboso, and La Mancha in Wogan's correspondence especially provocative. In the 1720s he referred to his career as a chivalric romance, in which he followed the steps of "my renown'd predecessor, Don Quixote."[71] In 1744, after he was appointed governor of Quixote's home territory, he wrote James on 8 December from "San Clemente de La Mancha":

---

[69] *Ibid.*, 8-11.
[70] H. Tayler, *Jacobite Epilogue*, 306.
[71] *Ibid.*, 298.

> For tho' I have, in a manner, laid down my sword by taking up with a civil
> employment (as Governor of this country, so celebrated for the life and la-
> bours of the famed Don Quixote) tis but to snatch it up again with the
> greater eagerness whenever yr Majesty shall be pleased to honour me with
> ye command. One might think that Providence designed me from my birth
> for a knight errant…and to have preferred me in my advanced age, to this
> post which lays the renowned Tobose itself and all the Dulcineas thereto
> belonging, as well as the ever famous La Mancha, under my jurisdiction…
> Thus I entreat yr Majesty not to forget me here whenever kind providence
> gives a call. I am but five and twenty when any occasion can offer to serve
> yr Majesty with that sprightly zeal and inviolable duty yt must ever distin-
> guish me.[72]

Over the next months Wogan continued to make Tobosan allusions, while he tire-lessly negotiated for Spanish support for the planned Jacobite invasion.[73] On 10 December 1745 he replied to Charles Edward's letter and related his appeals to the ministers in Madrid. He explained that the Spanish court felt jealous that the prince had entered an alliance with France, which "seemed a sort of neglect or contempt of them," so Charles should occasionally write to the king and ministers.[74] But, they were strong supporters of the prince, and their jealousy was that of lovers for a beloved. Wogan admitted that, given the parlous state of Spain's financial condition, he was surprised that they had earlier managed to ship substantial sums to the Jacobites. He was further pleased that over fifty Irish officers received licenses to leave Spain and join the Jacobites in Scotland.[75] Charles Edward would later refer to Wogan's letters, when in 1747 he secretly travelled to Spain to woo the jealous Spaniards, but he lamented that Wogan was then away from Madrid and he thus missed a meeting with his chivalric brother.

Wogan also determined to get backing from the French court for his Spanish efforts, and on 4 March 1745 he had dedicated an expanded French version of his rescue of Princess Clementina Sobieski to her cousin, Marie Leszczynski, Queen of France. In *Mémoire sur l'Entreprise d'Inspruck en 1719*, he praised both queens in fulsome, chivalric terms and concluded with a call to "Divine Justice and the union of Catholic Princes" to bring about "the reinstatement of the Royal House of Stuart."[76] He reminded her that the rescue and marriage of the Polish princess had "a happy issue, giving the world two beautiful Princes, who are as nephews to your Highness," and he predicted a successful restoration which will be universally applauded. Among those pressing for French support of the Stuarts was the queen's father, Stanislas Leszczynski, an activist *Écossais* Mason, whose own career had been stirred by mystical prophecies and fraternal bondings.

During these weeks in Scotland, the Hanoverians determined to counter the circulating reports about second sight, which some Scots believed to be achieved through Masonic initiation. They thus issued anti-Jacobite accounts of the phenomena. A loyalist "Clergyman in the Isle of Sky," published *The Young Pretender's Destiny Unfolded: Being an*

[72] *Ibid.*, 301.
[73] *Ibid.*, 302-19.
[74] Alexander C. Ewald, *The Life and Times of Prince Charles Stuart*, new ed. (London, 1883), 312-14.
[75] O. Morales, *Ireland and the Spanish Empire*, 176.
[76] Sir Charles Wogan, *The Rescue of Princess Clementina (Stuart): A 1719 Adventure of the Irish Brigades*, trans. Cathy Winch (Belfast, 2008), 33.

Account of Several Prodigies Seen in the Highlands Before the Breaking out of the Present Rebellion, *together with the Visions seen by John Ferguson, a Man endued with the Second Sight* (London, 1745). Many Scottish Masons would be familiar with Henry Adamson's poem, *The Muses Threnodie* (Edinburgh, 1638), in which he linked second sight, Freemasonry, and Rosicrucianism to the Stuart monarchy:

> For we be brethren of the *Rosie Crosse,*
> We have the *Mason word,* and second sight,
> Things for to come we can foretell aright.
> And shall we show what misterie we mean,
> In fair acrosticks *Carolus Rex* is seen...[77]

The loyalist clergyman at Sky wrote to a friend in London, noting that the post from his island to Edinburgh was disrupted by "this unnatural Rebellion," and that he was overjoyed that his friend was at London, "safe from the Troubles of this unhappy Country, where nothing but Confusion dwells; there is nothing but Plunder and Devastation everywhere; Divisions and Animosities reign among the Gentry, and the Common People are harras'd out of their Lives, and oppress'd on all Hands."[78] The author knew that his educated friend might laugh at superstition, but he himself was "now less an Infidel in these Matters than ever I was; since, for a Twelve-month before these Calamities broke out, many People have been alarmed by Prodigies, and unnatural Spectres, which they at the Time explain'd to foretell what has since happened." He warned about free-thinkers and materialists who do not believe in "Spiritual Beings, or the Possibility of their holding any Intelligence with us Mortals."

The clergyman pointed to the appearance of apparitions in the sky relating to rebels such as Cameron of Lochiel and Macdonald of Kinloch-Mudart, but more significantly to the second-sight visions of John Ferguson, whose case even interested Dr. Cromwell Mortimer, FRS, who published an investigation of it in the *Transactions of the Royal Society* in December 1740.[79] Ferguson saw several visions of persons now engaged in the rebellion, "which seem to prognosticate no Good to that Cause," but the most important one concerned "the young Chevalier," who appeared in "black Apparel, mournful and dejected, brought by several Persons to a Block whereon his Head was laid, and then chopp'd off with a Hatchet." The seer related these visions several weeks before the prince's landing and described "the Visionary Youth by such Marks as agreed very well with the young Chevalier's Person":

> As this Man has a great Reputation amongst the Vulgar, these Visions of his disheartened many of them, and hindered them from joining that mad Enterprize...Whatever is in it, the Man is in himself an extraordinary Fellow;

---

[77] H.Adamson, *Muses Threnody,* 31-32. For the Stuart Masonic context, see M. Schuchard, *Restoring the Temple,* 402-06.

[78] Clergyman in the Island of Sky, *The Young Pretender's Destiny Unfolded* (London, 1745), 3-7...

[79] I have discussed elsewhere Mortimer's friendship with Swedenborg, who claimed to use his second sight in revealing many secrets of state; moreover, both men were associated with Freemasonry and interested in Rosicrucian "science"; see M. Schuchard, *Emanuel Swedenborg,* 299, 363, 383, 386.

and his Visions have had some Effect upon many, who would be thought to condemn such Visionaries.[80]

In Scotland and Sweden, folk traditions of second sight were linked with the Rosicrucian interests of many *Écossais* Masons, who utilized Cabalistic meditation techniques to achieve states of trance and (supposedly) clairvoyance. In the months leading up to the Jacobite rebellion, an adept of such techniques was in London. A mysterious Rosicrucian Mason, the crypto-Jewish Comte de St. Germain, arrived in London in 1743, where he moved into the home of Dr. Philip De la Cour, a fashionable Jewish physician and Freemason.[81] He then ingratiated himself with the Prince and Princess of Wales, became the intimate friend of Lord and Lady Chesterfield, "Lady B.," and other members of the disaffected opposition.[82] A talented violinist, "upon his first arrival" he was "much in favour" with the music-loving Prince Frederick until the rebellion, when he was arrested on suspicion of being a French-Jacobite spy. It is possible that St. Germain was André, the Rosicrucian, whom Joseph Spence met in Italy in 1740 and who claimed to be affiliated with a Society of Immortals in London.

Decades later, a jaded and cynical St. Germain claimed that before coming to London he had received the fourth degree of Masonry (Scottish Master) and that in Paris he met with a group of about two hundred people, "led by the imbecile Duc de Bouillon and some women, followers of the Comte de Gabalis's system," who sought him out, "supposing him to be the Superior in Chief."[83] As noted earlier, Bouillon had patronized the late Ramsay, with whom he allegedly developed a special Jacobite Masonic rite. He was also the cousin and ardent supporter of Charles Edward Stuart, who in 1743 was planning the Jacobite assault on Britain. In autumn 1744 Lord Elcho, whose father, the Earl of Wemyss, was serving as Grand Master of Scotland, met St. Germain in Leiden, at a time when Elcho was collaborating in Holland with John Murray of Broughton, initiate of the Jacobite lodge in Rome, on plans for the invasion. Elcho later recorded (disingenuously?) his impression of the mysterious Rosicrucian, "No one knows where he comes from, and he passes himself off as being able to make gold and possessing the secret for prolonging life. All that I know about him is that he is a very good violinist."[84]

While St. Germain treated Louis XV's mistresses and gullible courtiers with his Rosicrucian rejuvenation powders, he gained the confidence of the French king, who employed him on various intelligence missions. Thus, when he was arrested in London in 1745, there was good reason to suspect him of espionage activities. Horace Walpole was intrigued by him and recounted the fantastic stories circulating about his musical talents, chemical expertise, and esoteric knowledge, as well as the large foreign remittances he received. On 9 December 1745 Walpole wrote Mann that

---

[80] Clergyman, *Young Pretender's Destiny*, 18-19.

[81] Jean Overton Fuller, *The Comte de Saint-Germain* (London, 1989), 72.

[82] H. Walpole, *Correspondence*, XXVI, 20-21; for his Jewish background, see Raphael Patai, *The Jewish Alchemists* (Princeton, 1994), 465-66.

[83] J. Fuller, *Comte de Saint-Germain*, 227. De la Cour often took visitors to meet Dr. Samuel Jacob Falk, a Cabalist and alchemist, known as the "Baal Shem" of London; see M.K. Schuchard, "Dr. Samuel Jacob Falk: A Sabbatian Adventurer in the Masonic Underground," in Matt Goldish and Richard Popkin, eds., *Millenarianism and and Messianism in Early Modern European Culture* (Dordrecht, 2001), 203-26.

[84] A.Wemyss and J. Gibson, *Elcho*, 57.

> We begin to take up people…and t'other day they seized an odd man, who goes by the name of Count St. Germain. He has been here these two years, will not tell who he is or whence, but professes two very wonderful things, the first that he does not go by his right name; and the second, that he never had any dealings with any woman – nor, with any succedaneum. He sings, plays on the violin wonderfully, composes, is mad, and not very sensible. He is called an Italian, a Spaniard, a Pole; a somebody that married a great fortune in Mexico, and ran way with her jewels to Constantinople; a priest, a fiddler, a vast nobleman. The Prince of Wales has a vast curiosity about him, but in vain. However, nothing has been made out against him; he is released; and what convinces me that he is not a gentleman, stays here, and talks of his being taken up as a spy.[85]

Mann replied on 21 December that "The contents of your letter are like sal volatile to my drooping spirits. You cannot think how the insolent Jacobites at Rome deject one. I have often made a resolution not to believe a word they say, but they come upon one so many ways that it is impossible to be quite indifferent to their reports.[86]

Though Walpole did not report it to Mann, Newcastle's interrogation of St. Germain was not successful. Fifteen years later, the newspapers published an account from an acquaintance of the count that in autumn 1745 one who was jealous of him with a lady, "slipt a letter into his pocket, as from the Young Pretender (thanking him for advices, and desiring him to continue them), and immediately had him taken up…His innocence being proved…he was discharged out of custody of the messenger, and asked to dinner by Lord H."[87] Horace Walpole, who distrusted him, was nevertheless amused by his witty reply to Newcastle, "who finding no evidence against him, made him many excuses: the Count piqued, and at the same time *au fait* of the Duke's capacity, replied, `My Lord, I easily excuse your Grace, I am persuaded you took me for St Germain en Laye."[88] His later espionage activities for Louis XV and Madame de Pompadour suggest that the Jacobite charges of 1745 were accurate.[89]

Three years after St. Germain's arrest, Lord Chesterfield seemed to refer to St. Germain, his former "intimate friend," in a letter to his natural son:

> I stumbled the other day, at a bookseller's upon *Comte de Gabalis*, in two very little volumes, which I had formerly read… Most of the extravagancies are taken from the Jewish Rabbins, who broached those wild notions, and delivered them in the unintelligible jargon which the Cabalists and Rosicrucians deal in to this day. Their number is, I believe, much lessened, but there are still some; and I myself have known two, who studied and firmly believed in that mystical nonsense.[90]

---

[85] H. Walpole, *Correspondence*, XIX, 181-82.

[86] *Ibid.*, XIX, 182.

[87] *Read's Weekly Journal or British Gazetteer*, 17 (May 1760); *The London Chronicle* (31 May-3 June 1760).

[88] H. Walpole, *Correspondence*, XIX, 21.

[89] See Giacomo Casanova, *History of My Life*, trans. Willard Trask (New York, 1966), 528-50.

[90] Earl of Chesterfield, *The Letters of Philip Dormer Stanhope, 4ᵗʰ Earl of Chesterfield*, ed. Bonamy Dobrée (London, 1932), IV, 1233.

When St. Germain returned to London in 1749, he sought out Lord Morton, former Grand Master, and carried out another intelligence mission for Louis XV.[91]

During the Stuart rebellion, while sympathetic poets, ballad singers, prophets, and seers praised the charismatic Charles Edward, an important artist and Freemason, Allan Ramsay, contributed to the campaign. On 26 October 1745, John Stuart (valet to the prince) wrote to Ramsay: "Sir, you are desired to come to the Palace of Holyrood House as soon as possible in order to take his Royal Highness' picture."[92] The painting was to be taken to England, reproduced in engravings, and used as "the basis for an official royal portrait" once Charles ascended the throne. After the defeat at Culloden, the painting ended up in the home of the Earl of Wemyss, Allan Ramsay's Masonic brother, where it virtually disappeared for 250 years. Its discovery and authentication in 2013 by the art historian Bendor Grosvenor provided the first proof of Ramsay's personal support of Charles Edward in Edinburgh, which had long been disputed by historians.

Despite the military support of so many Scottish, Irish, English, French, and Swedish Masons, the efforts of the six Jacobite Grand Masters were thwarted at various levels, as they struggled to support the rebels' campaign. Their actions were countered by four Hanoverian Grand Masters – Richmond, Montagu, Loudoun, and Crawfurd – who led military actions against them. As noted earlier, Hector Maclean was arrested in Edinburgh in June and then imprisoned in London, where he managed to maintain contact with his partisans. This especially angered his rival Grand Master, the Duke of Richmond, who wrote Newcastle on 21 October 1745:

> I don't know whether Sir Hector Macklean is your Grace's Prisoner or My Lord Tweedale's, butt the Messenger in whose hands he is, is very negligent, for a servant of myne is ready to make oath that last Saturday at eleven o'clock he saw a letter or piece of paper let down by a Pack thred from the garret window of the house where Sr Hector is kept; into the street, & there taken by three men, that had been walking up & down the street the whole day…. Would it not be best to seem to know nothing of this butt have a trusty person to watch, & take up these men if they return.[93]

Given the publicity surrounding Maclean's arrest, Edward Young was apparently aware of the significant role played by Jacobite and *Écossais* Masons in the rebellion. In October he completed the final, ninth night of *Night Thoughts*, titled *The Consolation*, to which "*are Annex'd, Some Thoughts, Occasion'd by the Present Juncture* (1745). Dedicated to Newcastle, his fellow Whig Mason, Young tried to utilize traditional Masonic architectural imagery to support the government (a strategy implemented earlier in Orator Henley's more zany compositions). In the first section, "A Moral Survey of the Heavens," Young praised "the glorious Architect" in "His Universal Temple," noting that "An undevout Astronomer is mad."[94] His target again was the "undevout" Lorenzo (Wharton),

---

[91] See ahead, Chapter Twenty-three.

[92] Maev Kennedy, "Bonnie Prince Charlie portrait found by art historian Bendor Rosvenor," *The Guardian* (23 February 2014). The discovery was the subject of a BBC documentary, "the Lost Portrait of Bonnie Prince Charlie," on BBC Two on 22 February 2014.

[93] Richmond, *Correspondence*, 185.

[94] Edward Young, *The Consolation* (London, 1745), 40.

noting that "this may seem Harangue to Thee." He then asked the late Jacobite Grand Master,

> Who dare pronounce it Madness, to *believe*?
> Why has the Mighty BUILDER thrown aside
> All Measure in His work; stretch'd out His Line
> So far, and spread Amazement o'er the Whole?[95]

Lorenzo's cramped vision is incapable of perceiving the vast heavenly architecture and thus "dwarfs the Whole/ And makes an Universe an *Orrery*" – a jab at Wharton's Jacobite collaborator, the 4th Earl of Orrery, who had commissioned a mechanical apparatus that illustrated with moving balls the motions of the stars and planets (henceforth called an "orrery"). Young argued that such small-minded men as Wharton and Orrery should mark

> The *Mathematic* Glories of the Skies:
> In Number, Weight, and Measure, All ordain'd;
> Lorenzo's boasted Builders, *Chance*, and *Fate*,
> Are left to finish his aerial Tow'rs.
> ....
> Say, at what Point of Space JEHOVAH dropp'd
> His slacken'd *Line*, and laid His *Balance* by;
> Weigh'd *Worlds*, and measur'd *Infinite*, no more?
> Where, rears His *terminating Pillar* high
> Its extra-mundane Head?[96]

Young presumed that his vision of architectural Whiggery would appeal to Newcastle, and he dedicated the annex to "Holles! Immortal in far more than Fame!" He pleaded that the minister, "Tho' station'd high, and press'd with public Cares," would "Disdain not to peruse my serious Song."[97] He hoped that Englishmen will suppress their vices and wake to "the noble Pulse of War," and "With all the Weight of British Wrath," cleave the "Papal Mitre" and the "Gallic Chain," and thus save "a sinking land":

> And shall a Pope-bred Princeling crawl ashore,
> Replete with Venom, Guiltless of a Sting,
> And whistle Cut-throats, with those Swords, that scrap'd
> Their barren Rocks, for wretched Sustenance,
> To cut his Passage to the British Throne?
> One that has suck'd in Malice with his Milk,
> Malice to Britain, Liberty, and Truth?

Young called on Newcastle to protect England, "This Temple, built by Heaven's peculiar Care,/ In a Recess from the contagious World," and "strengthen Britain's military Strength" to save it from "the Continent, that World of Slaves."[98] He then castigated

---

[95] *Ibid.*, 41- 42, 71.
[96] *Ibid.*, 75-76.
[97] *Ibid.*, 120, 126-27.
[98] *Ibid.*, 129-31.

Charles Edward as a traitor who was supported by French magicians, superstitious Catholics, and necromantic Swedes:

> A Foe, who (like a Wizard in his Cell),
> In his dark Cabinet of crooked Schemes,
> Resembling Cuma's gloomy grot, the Forge
> Of boasted Oracles, and real Lies,
> (Aided, perhaps, by second-sighted Scots,
> French Magi, Reliques riding Post from Rome,
> A Gothic Hero* rising from the Dead,
> And changing for spruce Plad his dirty Shroud,
> With Succour, suitable, from Lower still;)
> A Foe, who, These concurring to the Charm,
> Excites those Storms that shall o'erturn the State…[99]

The asterisk points to a footnote reading, "The Invader affects the Character of Charles the Twelfth of Sweden." Young asked, "Is Britain on her Death-bed?" "Will British profligates sell their country to "Daemons, by Holiness Ordain'd/ To propagate the Gospel – penn'd at Rome," and "Hawk'd, thro' the World, by consecrated Bulls?"[100] No, as long as "Religion crowns the Statesman," no "Highland Pole-ax" can deeply wound.

One Frenchman who enjoyed the comparisons between the Stuart prince and Carl XII was Voltaire, who had written a popular (but often inaccurate) biography of the Swedish warrior king. In November 1745 he was commissioned by Argenson to draft a manifesto expressing Louis XVs support for Charles Edward, as the French planned to launch an invasion of England, led by the Duc de Richelieu, Voltaire's friend and a prominent Freemason. Voltaire portrayed Louis XV as praising the prince for landing in Scotland, "with no support but his courage," by which "he gained the admiration of all Europe as well as "the hearts of all the true Englishmen."[101] The French king feels it is his duty to answer the appeal from the most sound party ("le plus saine partie") in Britain to restore the Stuart prince to his country, where he will maintain its liberties, laws, and welfare, which is the aim of his whole enterprise. Unfortunately for Voltaire, the English version of the draft was sent to François de Bussy, to check its content and linguistic accuracy, for the proof-reader was a paid spy (agent 101) for the English, and he nitpicked the phrasing while managing to stall its issuance.

While Newcastle received a flurry of intelligence reports from his many agents, he probably did not take the time to read Young's long, bombastic poem, with its Whiggish Masonic imagery. But he must have worried about Richelieu, a successful military leader, who was scheduled to lead the invasion. And he soon had another *Écossais* Grand Master to worry about. On 30 November Newcastle wrote Richmond about the capture of the French ship *Soleil*, which was transporting Jacobite troops to Scotland: "There is the greatest reason to think that the second son of the Pretender [Prince Henry], is taken in the Soleil & passes for your Cousin Ratcliff's son. We have sent a strong guard to bring

---

[99] *Ibid.*, 136.
[100] *Ibid.*, 139-40, 144.
[101] Laurence Bongie, "Voltaire's English, High Treason and a Manifesto for Bonnie Prince Charlie," *Studies on Voltaire and the Eighteenth Century*, 171 (1977), 7-29.

them up to London."[102] The prisoners were actually Derwentwater and his son, James Bartholomew Radcliffe, but there was confusion about their true identities, as reported by Horace Walpole to Horace Mann on 9 December:

> the greatest demonstration of loyalty appeared on the prisoners being brought to town from the Soleil prize – the younger man is certainly Mr. Radcliffe's son; but the mob, persuaded that it being the youngest Pretender, could scarcely be restrained from tearing him to pieces all the way along the road, and at his arrival. He said he had heard of English mobs, but could not conceive they were so dreadful, and wished he had been shot at the battle of Dettingen, where he had been engaged. The father, whom they call Lord Derwentwater, said, on entering the Tower, that he had never expected to arrive there alive. For the young man, he must only be treated as a French captive; for the father, it is sufficient to produce against him at the Old Baily, and prove that he is the individual person condemned for the last rebellion, and so to Tyburn.[103]

Unlike his father, the 1st Duke of Richmond, who pleaded with George I to have mercy on his cousin James Radcliffe, the 2nd Duke had no pity for Charles Radcliffe, and wished that he could immediately be executed rather than held prisoner.[104]

Ironically, Richmond was no admirer of George II, despite his strong support for his ministry. Over the past two years, Richmond had become increasingly disgusted with the king's stubbornness, and he raged to Newcastle about George's "cruel partiallitys" shown to his "damned Hanoverian troops," which led to disaffection among his English soldiers. But he nevertheless vowed that "I was bred up from a child in whig principles, & consequently my attachment to him & his family, is so fix'd in my mind & heart, that not even ill usage can efface it."[105] However, he warned the minister, that "there is not a general, nor a common soldier in the whole army that is not in some degree discontented; it is butt too true & it is with the most deep concern that I say it. Pray burn this letter." Richmond's hero was the king's favorite son, the Duke of Cumberland, whom he believed was the man to crush the Scottish rebellion. And crush is what Richmond meant, for he despised the Scots and was therefore delighted to be promoted to the rank of full general in November. He wrote Newcastle that he wanted

> to drive these rascals to Hell, which is little worse, butt a more proper place for them than their own Country they came from… You know I have not generally much bile or choler about me, butt upon this occasion my gall overflows, & I long to be revenged upon these Scotch Rascalls, that dare disturb such a nation as this, & I shall be excessively happy to have an opportunity of doing it, & you may be assured I will make good use of it.[106]

---

[102] Richmond, *Correspondence*, 192.
[103] H. Walpole, *Correspondence*, XIX, 180.
[104] Richmond, *Correspondence*, 237.
[105] *Ibid.*, 104.
[106] *Ibid.*, 191.

After the rebels began capturing towns in northern England and headed towards London, the English defeats and ensuing public panic provoked Richmond to write Newcastle on 5 December:

> I make no doubt but this [French] embarkation will go on at Dunkirk. Are we all mad? That you don't send for 10,000 more forces, be they Hessians, Hanoverians or devils if they will but fight for us... The whole kingdom is asleep. Our cavalry can't be here before February and the Pretender may be crowned in Westminster by that time.[107]

In London Henry Fielding spoke of "a panic scarcely to be credited," and Hanoverian propagandists unleashed a barrage of satires on the filthy, savage, almost sub-human Highlanders.[108]

The propaganda backfired in Manchester, where Dr. Byrom, his daughter Beppy, and other Stuart sympathizers welcomed the Highlanders and were enthusiastic about their meeting with Bonnie Prince Charlie.[109] Beppy described the arrival of Lord Pitsligo's horse troop, and her father was pleased when Pitsligo asked to meet with him at Mr. Sedgwick's. Byrom and the Scottish noble shared pietist and theosophical interests as well as Masonic bonding. However, their meeting would cause alarm among Byrom's enemies in the city. Loyalist suspicions were raised about the apparent collusion between Non-jurors and Freemasons in Manchester, which led a Hanoverian author to describe a Jacobite Non-juring Chapel:

> I don't know of what Body the Congregation consists, they not allowing any to come amongst them but such as are of their own Sort, who (like the more worshipful Society of Free Masons) are under an Oath not to divulge what is transacted there, except it be to a just and lawful *Jacobite*, as he or she shall appear to be upon Examination.[110]

J. E. S. Tuckett comments that "the wording suggests something more than mere badinage," for it is clearly the author's intention to imply that the religious services were "a pretext to cover up treasonable political activities" and to imply that "this was being done under the form of a pretended Jacobite Freemasonry," which is less "worshipful" than the ordinary kind.[111]As a Jacobite Mason and supporter of the Non-jurors, Byrom was politically vulnerable to such charges, but he continued to admire and support several of his close friends who joined the Manchester Regiment to fight for the Stuart cause (and who eventually paid a high price for their bold decision).

The combination of aloof Whig scorn at Scottish military expertise and Highland barbarism provoked William Hamilton of Bangour to write "On a Lion Enraged at Seeing a Lad in the Highland Dress":

> Calm and serene the imperial lion lay,

---

[107] E. Cruickshanks, *Political Untouchables*, 92-93.
[108] F. McLynn, *Charles Edward Stuart*, 191.
[109] J. Bryom, *Remains*, II, part ii, 385-98.
[110] John Ray, *A Compleat History of the Rebellion from its Rise, in 1745, to its Total Suppression, at the Glorious Battle of Culloden* (London, 1746), 207-08.
[111] J. Tuckett, "Origin," 23.

Mildly indulging in the solar ray;
On vulgar mortals with indifference gazed,
All unconcerned, nor angry, nor amazed;
But when the Caledonian lad appeared,
Sudden alarmed, his manly mane he feared,
Prepared in fierce encounter to engage,
The only object of his rage.[112]

On 4 December the rebel troops reached Derby, just 120 miles from London, from where Charles Edward expected to march towards the capitol. According to John Sleigh, the prince signed a warrant for the Masonic lodge of Derbyshire, whose head-quarters was at nearby Longnor.[113] Sleigh also published a list of officers who marched north with the prince, which included a large number of known Scottish Masons, which makes a Masonic initiative plausible.[114] John Jesse argues that the 9th Duke of Norfolk, "the premier peer of Great Britain," upon learning of the prince's arrival at Derby, was "on the very point of declaring himself in his favour."[115] As brother of the late Grand Master and a prominent Mason himself, Norfolk could exercise considerable influence on his Catholic brethren, who had been exercising extreme caution. Though he might have been "on the very point," Norfolk was intimidated when government agents searched his house for arms, and on 6 December he and his "accomodationist" wife went to court to explain away the fact that his chief steward had joined the rebel army. Nevertheless, it was later reported to the government that "there is scarce one Roman Catholic gentleman, the Duke of Norfolk not excepted, but what have made remittances to the Young Pretender during the rebellion."[116]

Norfolk's show of loyalty on 6 November was timely, for events had suddenly taken an unexpected turn. On 5 November at Derby the Jacobites held a council of war. After heated debates, a majority persuaded a reluctant Charles Edward to abandon the march to London and to retreat northward. The prince was supported by the Welsh poet David Morgan, who later revealed that the rebels planned to march to Oxford, where the students would join the prince, thereby attaching their families to him.[117] One wonders if Dr. King and his students were included in this plan. Morgan further argued that there were mainly "undisciplined troops" and few in number ordered to defend London (a judgment supported by both contemporary Hanoverian commentators and later historians). And, in fact, if the Jacobites had proceeded to the capitol, the French would indeed have sent a large force to support them. A confident Barrymore sent his son Richard from London to deliver a message to the prince, in which he and Wynn offered to join him "either in the capital or every one to rise in his own county," but Richard was

---

[112] W. Hamilton, *Poems*, 185.

[113] John Sleigh, "Prince Charles Edward Stuart at Leek in the '45," *Notes & Queries*, 4th s., vol. 3 (5 June 1869), 532; also, "The Stuarts and Freemasonry, *N & Q*, 4th s., vol. 4 (17 July 1869), 66. Sleigh's claim set off a long-running argument between John Yarker and various doubters in succeeding issues of *N & Q*.

[114] John Sleigh, "The '45," *N & Q*, 3rd s. 4 (14 November 1863), 392.

[115] John H. Jesse, *Memoirs of the Pretenders and Their Adherents* (London, 1858), II, 68.

[116] H. Walpole, *Correspondence*, XIX, 176 n. 27, 29.

[117] "David Thomas Morgan," *Dictionary of Welsh Biography* (National Library of Wales, on-line).

dismayed to learn that the prince had left two days before on his way back to Scotland.[118] Thus, the prince lost his contact with the Anglo-Irish and Welsh Masonic networks.

The controversial decision to retreat from Derby was a lucky break for the government, because "the defenders of London had a comic opera quality," which was later illustrated by William Hogarth, a Whig Mason, in "The March of the Guards to Finchley." On 6 December, when the Jacobites began their retreat, there was only "an ill-trained rabble of perhaps 4,000 at Finchley," where the King's Guards were to meet with the local defenders.[119] In 1750, four years after the defeat of the rebels, Hogarth presented George II with a painting of the comical scene at Finchley, in which drunken soldiers, ragged beggars, prostitutes, and robbers are expected to join the disciplined Guardsmen. A pregnant ballad singer carries copies of "God save the King," while an old woman wearing priest's robes and a crucifix holds a rolled Jacobite newspaper above her head. But George II was infuriated by the painting, which seemed to mock his most favored Guards, and he responded to Lord Harrington, the unfortunate deliverer of Hogarth's gift:

> "Pray, who is this Hogarth?"
> "A painter, my liege."
> "I hate painting and poetry too! Neither the one nor the other ever did any good.!"
> "The picture, please your majesty, must undoubtedly be considered a burlesque!"
> "What? A painter burlesque a soldier? He deserves to be picketed for his insolence! Take this trumpery out of my sight."[120]

Hogarth was mortified by the king's response to what he considered one of his finest works, and he re-inscribed it to "The King of Prussia" and sent it to Frederick II, a fellow Mason, who appreciated its artistry and enjoyed the mockery of English troops, for he had initially supported the Stuart prince and disliked George II.

From the beginning of the rebellion, the volatile military and political situation provoked an outpouring of propaganda from the rival camps. As Jacobite poems and songs celebrated the initially victorious forces in Scotland and northern England, the government in London launched a new propaganda campaign, led off by Thomas Herring, Archbishop of York, on 21 and 24 September. A "noisy Whig" and confidant of George II, Herring had earlier earned Swift's wrath by condemning Gay's *Beggar's Opera* as immoral and seditious.[121] Now, at the bequest of the government, the archbishop called for funds and arms to organize a militia to defend England from the northern barbarians, papist superstition, and tyrannous France and Spain. He even dressed in "a lay military habit" to inspire his diocese and countrymen.[122] His powerful speech in York was published in *The Gentleman's Magazine* in October, and was followed by "A Rhapsody," a eulogy to him by James Cawthorne, who claimed that the archbishop's courageous, militaristic stance will one day make men "mistake thee for Argyle*" (the asterisk pointing

---

118 "Barrymore," R. Sedgwick, *History of Parliament Online*.
119 F. McLynn, *Charles Edward Stuart*, 191.
120 W.M. Clark, *Tales of the Wars; Or, Naval and Military Chronicle* (1836), 144.
121 I. Ehrenpreis, *Swift*, III, 559.
122 Henry Fielding, *The True Patriot and Related Writings*, ed. W.B. Coley (Middletown, 1987), xxv.

to "the late Duke").[123] As noted earlier, Cawthorne had recently praised the late Desaguliers and lamented his ill treatment.

But the government needed an even stronger voice, and it brought Henry Fielding out of his nearly four-year withdrawal from political pamphleteering to publish anonymously on 3 October *A Serious Address to the People of Great Britain. In which the Certain Consequences of the Present Rebellion are fully Demonstrated* (1745). The author, who had recently entertained the public with the novels *Jonathan Wild* and *Joseph Andrews*, now embarked on a campaign of stinging attacks on the Jacobites, whom he would eventually accuse of being seditious Jews and Freemasons. Though there is no evidence that Fielding was a Mason, he was close to Richmond and other Whig Masons and familiar with the fraternity, to which he had recently referred in *Jonathan Wild:* "Men of great genius as easily discover one another as freemasons can."[124]

In *A Serious Address*, he drew heavily on Gilbert Burnet's Whig history of England, even repeating Burnet's claim that the baby who became James III was an impostor brought in a warming pan: "The suspicious Birth of the Pretender was attended with such glaring Evidence of Fraud and Imposture, that no Jury would have suffered him to succeeded, even to a private Right descended from James the Second."[125] Later, conceding "this Pretender to be the Son of James the Second, the stronger is the Reason for rejecting him. *Shall we return like a Dog to his Vomit?*" To counter the declarations of religious toleration made in the Pretender's recent manifesto to the people of England, Fielding claimed that "His Bigotry is so well known to the whole World, that it requires no Instances. His whole Life is one constant Act of Superstition." Moreover, his son, who pretends to open-mindedness in religion, is "but the Tool of the Father." He then gave gruesome, detailed descriptions of the torture inflicted by the Spanish Inquisition on its innocent victims and predicted similar outcomes in England if the rebels win.

The large printing of several thousand copies of *A Serious Address* encouraged Fielding to immediately issue, also anonymously, *The History of the Present Rebellion in Scotland. From the Departure of the Pretender's Son from Rome, down to the Present Time* (1745). While pretending to give accurate accounts of the military campaigns, he repeated his earlier anti-Jacobite charges and even invented characters and incidents to exaggerate the superstition and tyrannical intent of the Stuart prince and his supporters. He warned his readers, "your Religion, my Countrymen, your Laws, your Liberties, your Lives, the Safety of your Wives and Children, THE WHOLE, is in Danger, and for God Almighty's Sake! Lose not a Moment in ARMING YOURSELVES for their Preservation."[126] On 15 October he followed this with the anonymous *Dialogue Between the Devil, the Pope, and the Pretender* (1745), in which his charges became more lurid, with the Devil and Pope promising to impose the Inquisition on England, while carrying out immediate massacres of Protestants.[127] Fielding then attacked Orator Henley (without naming him), who was still drawing large audiences:

---

[123] *Gentleman's Magazine*, 15 (October, 1745), 471-72, 553.

[124] Henry Fielding, *The Life Story of Mr. Jonathan Wild, the Great* (1743; Dublin, 1754), 14.

[125] [Henry Fielding], *A Serious Address to the People of Great Britain*, 3rd rev. ed. (London, 1745), 4-5, 9-10.

[126] H. Fielding, *True Patriot*, 73.

[127] *Ibid.*, 89.

And to shew their [Jacobites'] Profligacy in the highest Light, one single impudent Buffoon hath for many years gone on with Impunity, in Defiance not only of Law but of common Decency, to vilify and ridicule every thing solemn, great and good amongst them; and, with a Mixture of Nonsense and Scurrility, Treason and Blasphemy, once a Week, in the public Papers, and once in a public Assembly (if any be so infamous to frequent it) to traduce the Persons and Characters of Nobles, Bishops, and even of the King himself.[128]

While still lecturing on Freemasonry, Henley also gave fiery sermons that seemed to express Jacobite sympathies.[129] On 24 August he advertised that he would remark on "the coming of Messiah the Prince," that is, "the Young Pretender, son of God."[130] In September he used bizarre allusions to mock the Whig generals who were defeated by the rebels. On 5 October he responded to Fielding's *Serious Address* by lecturing on "The Pr[etende]r annihilated by an Author," which suggests that "the two men had their eyes on each other's activities at this time." Graham Midgley argues that Henley used his inflammatory, pro-Jacobite orations as an *agent provocateur*, "spreading his provocative and near-seditious discourses only as a bait to draw out and expose those who might agree with him. If any unsuspecting listener rose to the bait he was noted and reported, and the Secret Service disbursed the rewarding guineas."[131] His ploy worked so well that the disturbances at the Oratory made him realize that he was pursuing a dangerous line, and he wrote Pelham to communicate to Newcastle, in great secrecy, that he was actually exposing Jacobites and expected compensation from the government. On 20 October he drafted a statement objecting to the clamour and to the claims that he was "inclin'd to Popery and the Pretender," for he was "humbly at the devotion of his most Gracious Majesty."[132] He must have been encouraged by the ministers to maintain his duplicitous role, for he continued his rantings over the next months.

Fielding evidently took Henley's outrageous orations at face value, and he would continue to mock him as a Jacobite sympathizer over the next year. He in turn launched a relatively more dignified journal, *The True Patriot: And the History of our Own Times*, which was published anonymously in weekly installments from 5 November 1745 to 10 June 1746.[133] In the first issue Fielding surprisingly published a eulogy to Jonathan Swift, who had recently died, noting his erudition, wit, and courageous "Defence of his Country, against several pernicious Schemes of wicked Politicians." Fielding's praise of Swift was the last echo of his role as an opposition writer, for the rest of the journal voiced exaggerated praise of the Hanoverian government and its beloved king, while excoriating the Jacobites, Non-jurors, his former opposition colleagues, and any current critic of government policies. He recruited James Thomson, a former opposition Whig and Mason,

---

128 *Ibid.*, 98.
129 W. Hextall, "Orator Henley," 369.
130 *Ibid.*, lviii.
131 G. Midgley, *Orator Henley*, 230.
132 H. Fielding. *True Patriot*, lix.
133 I quote from the full copies of the journal published on ECCO, rather than from Coley's edition, which reprints the main extracts.

to contribute to the journal, and the Scot may have provided him with information on the current factions within the fraternity.[134]

Reflecting his familiarity with the processions of Mock Masons, Fielding described an anti-Jacobite procession in Deptford and urged other towns to copy it.[135] The mock-procession featured a Highlander, carrying a pair of wooden shoes, with the motto, "The newest make from Paris"; a Jesuit, carrying a banner inscribed "Inquisition, Flames and Damnation"; two Capuchin friars, carrying a standard inscribed "INDULGENCIES cheap as Dirt," to buy forgiveness for the sins of murder, adultery, fornication, perjury, reading the Bible, and rebellion; the Pretender, with a green ribbon and nosegay of thistles, riding upon an ass, supported by a Frenchman and a Spaniard, "dressed to the Height of the newest Modes from Paris and Madrid; and finally, "The Pope riding upon his Bull," an apparent reference to the Papal Bull against Freemasonry in 1738. In a section on ghostly appearances, Fielding reported that there lately appeared in Scotland, "the Ghost of a Print called *A Hint to the Wise*, which so frightened the Pretender's Son, that he fainted, and was not seen for two days." In the print, sub-titled "the surest way with the Pretender, "The church militant is represented on one side offering but a weak resistance to the Pretender, while the standard of broad-bottom, set up by the Courtiers against the Jacobites, promises no great strength of resistance, but the mass of the people crowd together to fight successfully under the banner of liberty."[136] For Fielding, the implied weakness of the Anglican Tories and hypocritical opposition members, now part of the "broad-bottom" ministry, would be overcome by the Hanoverian, Whig loyalties of the majority of Englishmen. This prediction supposedly sent Charles Edward into a coma.

In the second issue of *True Patriot* (12 November), Fielding distanced himself from his former Patriot colleagues, who included many opposition Masons, noting that "this Word *Patriot* hath of late years been very scandalously abused by some Persons,…while they have pushed their own Preferment, and the Ruin of their Enemies, at the manifest Hazard of the Ruin of their Country."[137] Claiming that this paper is not written on the principles or with the purpose of "modern Patriotism," he excoriated those members of the opposition who sounded the alarm when there was no real danger, who misrepresented "the best of Men as Enemies to the Public, and the most wholesome Schemes of Government, as Snares for our Liberties; in order to animate the People to their Subversion." Without a trace of irony, he warned that "the Hypocrite finds it so easy to impose on Mankind." Worried by tales of the adoration of young women for the handsome Stuart prince, Fielding called upon "my fair Countrywomen" to support the government and thus avoid "Highland rapine, Italian bigotry, and French tyranny." He rejected a report that the Duke of Ormonde, commanding the Irish Brigade, had sailed from Dunkirk, arguing that it was "a Design to keep up the Spirits of the Pretender's Party." This time he was right, for Ormonde died four days later in Avignon.

In number 3 (19 November), Fielding outdid himself with sensationalist propaganda, as he recounted his dream in which barbarian Highlanders broke into his house, dashed

---

[134] *True Patriot*, #1 (5 November 1745).

[135] *True Patriot*, #1 (5 November 1745).

[136] Thomas Wright, *England Under the House of Hanover*, 3rd ed. (London, 1849), I, 220-21.

[137] *True Patriot*, #2 (12 November 1745).

his small son to the ground, arrested the father, led him through streets filled with burning houses and butchered corpses, and imprisoned him with other Hanoverian martyrs, such as Thomas Herring, the militaristic Archbishop of York, and Benjamin Hoadly, the strongly Whiggish Bishop of Winchester.[138] In Fielding's prophetic dream-vision, the victory of the tyrannical Stuarts led to rule by vicious, filthy, lecherous Highlanders, who destroyed English law and the Protestant religion. He not only saw his little boy "sprawling on the Floor, and weltering in his Blood," but his little girl "prostituted even in her Infancy to the brutal Lust of a Ruffian, and then sacrificed to his Cruelty." In prison he saw a distraught and insane Non-juror, "who had lent considerable assistance to the Pretender's cause, out of Principle; and was now lamenting the Consequences which the Success of it had brought on such honest Gentlemen" as himself.

After portraying the Non-jurors as seditious, Fielding got in a jab at the formerly Walpolean Freemason Orator Henley, portraying him as a Catholic priest, "whose Face I remember to have seen at a Place called an Oratory," who is now "preferred to be the Ordinary of Newgate." As chaplain of that prison, Henley would prepare condemned prisoners for death. Thus, the Jacobite executioner gets ready to decapitate Fielding, but he allows Henley to try to convert him to Rome:

> [He] began to revile me, saying I was the wickedest Heretic in the Kingdom, and had exerted myself with more Impudence against his Majesty and his Holiness than any other Person whatsoever; But he added, as I had the good Fortune to make some atonement for my Impiety by being hanged, if I would embrace his Religion, confess myself and receive Absolution, I might possibly, after some Expiation in Purgatory, receive a final Pardon.

In a future issue, "Mr. Mac-henly, the Ordinary," would attend three Anabaptists before their execution, but he would not allow their teacher, "Mr. Obadiah Washum" to counsel them.[139] Mac-henly also attended four heretics burnt at Smithfield, assisted by "Father O-Blaze." Fielding's nightmarish vision ended when his actual daughter woke him to say that his tailor had brought his new suit to wear to George II's birthday celebration.

In succeeding issues, Fielding continued to paint the Jacobites as ruthless, raping savages, and he tried to downplay their military successes while praising the heroics of the Whig commanders Loudoun, Montagu, Richmond, and others. He blamed the earlier criticism published by opposition spokesmen for deceiving the Stuart prince into believing he had widespread support in England.[140] And, in one of the first public revelations about Swedish support for the rebels, he reported that the French ambassador in Stockholm was offering huge sums to Swedish officers and soldiers to join the projected Franco-Swedish expedition from Gothenburg: "These Fellows who sell themselves as mercenary Tools, to effect the Mischief of Princes, or Slaves, which are no better than Cattle…to be purchased in a Market." He made no mention of George II's use of Hessian, Danish, and Dutch mercenaries in his campaign.

On 10 and 17 December 1745, Fielding was delighted to report (inaccurately) that a son and other relations of Lord Kilmarnock were run out of town by loyalist citizens and

---

[138] *Ibid.*, #3 (19 November 1745).
[139] *Ibid.*, #10 (14 December 745).
[140] *Ibid.*, #5 (3 December 1745).

(accurately) that Lord Derwentwater and his son were being brought as prisoners to London.[141] He praised the London mob for being "so zealous on the Right side," that the Guard could barely stop them from tearing Derwentwater to pieces. They even tried to burn the coach with the prisoners inside, for they supposed, "not without some Reason, that a Person of high Note was included" (Prince Henry Stuart). Though he claimed that Charles Edward was sick and depressed and his troops suffering from a massive bloody flux, he was surprised that despite the prince's "vehement" argument to march to London, his council of war at Derby voted for a retreat.

During this period, General Oglethorpe was put in the difficult position of chasing the retreating rebel troops. His surprise appointment in March 1744 to raise a regiment of Hussars to defend the English coasts was made to fill the gap created by "the absence on the Continent of the flower of the British army."[142] Oglethorpe's supporters were delighted, because he was currently under government attack and subjected to court martial proceedings for his alleged corruption and dereliction of duty in Georgia, but he was completely exonerated in June. In September 1744 a poetic tribute to his service, "On Envy and Slander. To Brigadier General Oglethorpe," was published in *The Gentleman's Magazine*, in which he was praised as "Th' illustrious Roman" who

> well could aid the state,
> And make in distant climes his country great,
> Could bid the infant colony succeed,
> And cherish industry in times of need;
> To blacken him yet satire took delight,
> And tho' it could not wound him, strove to bite;
> So in the race of virtue which you ran,
> And in the western world pursued the plan,
> While, with divine philanthropy inspir'd,
> You for the good of thousands toil'd untir'd.[143]

Oglethorpe had been ordered to Gravesend and the southern coast, and his activities there gained him a promotion to Major-General in March 1745. Over the next months, his sister Eleanor Oglethorpe de Mézières helped plan French support for a Jacobite invasion, while her son, Oglethorpe's nephew, served in a French regiment that was expected to sail. Despite these family ties, in September Oglethorpe was sent north to recruit and train loyalist volunteers. Over the next three months, his actions were controversial, and it seems certain that he retained his sympathy for the Jacobite Masons and Highlanders that he had developed in Georgia. Amos Ettinger notes that since his Georgia days, the general had been well known among the Scots who became the rebels of '45. In December Cumberland ordered Oglethorpe to follow and attack Charles Edward's army from Preston to Shap, but he allowed them to march just ahead, so that they retreated safely back to Scotland.[144] His failure to engage them infuriated Cumberland, and his critics charged him with "latent Jacobite sympathies." He would eventually be

---

141 *Ibid.*, #6 and 7 (10 and 17 December 1745).

142 Amos Ettinger, *James Edward Oglethorpe: Imperial Idealist* (Oxford, 1936), 258-65.

143 *Gentleman's Magazine* (September 1744), 501.

144 E. Cruickshanks, *Oglethorpes*, 6.

subjected to another trial by court martial and endure the hatred of Cumberland for years to come.

Watching from afar, an embittered Prince of Wales resented the role of his hated brother Cumberland, whose bravery and aggression were constantly praised by Hanoverian propagandists. Though Frederick had repeatedly petitioned George II for a military commission, the king refused and continued to distrust and humiliate his oldest son. His late mother, Queen Caroline, had accused him of "being ready and willing to sell his right of succession to the crown to the Pretender, for a few hundred thousand Pounds."[145] On 4 May 1745 Frederick indiscreetly rejoiced after he heard news of Cumberland's defeat at the Battle of Fontenoy, in which the Jacobite Irish Brigade daringly defeated the English. Horace Walpole wrote indignantly to Mann that Frederick "not only went to the play the night the news came, but in two days made a ballad."[146] It was perhaps no coincidence that the play, Congreve's *Old Bachelor* and a "ballad farce," was performed as a benefit "For the Entertainment of the Grand Master, and the rest of the Brethren of the Antient and Honourable Society of Free and Accepted MASONS," with "the usual Songs in Masonry."[147] As noted earlier, Grand Master Cranstoun was a former Jacobite who now supported Prince Frederick.

On 19 November Horace Walpole wrote even more indignantly that on the night of the christening of Frederick's new son, "he had the citadel of Carlisle in sugar at supper, and the company besieged it with sugar plums."[148] This mockery of his brother's military success made Walpole lament, "Alas! It would be needless to tell you all his *Caligulisms*" (a reference to Caligula who made his horse a consul). On 21 November, possibly influenced by Frederick, Lord Cranstoun summoned eight lodges to explain why they should not be sanctioned for non-attendance at the Grand Master's meetings, and first on the list was the Horn, "the duke of Richmond's lodge, *de facto*," but the threat of erasure was "a relatively empty gesture," for the Horn had sufficient stature to function without recognition by the Grand Lodge.[149] Was the gesture just a tossing of Masonic sugar plums at loyalist rivals like Richmond? Despite Frederick's sometimes silly and immature behavior, his disaffection from the ministry and alleged sympathy for the Jacobites would make him the figure-head of opposition Masonry. As we shall see, he would posthumously contribute to the split between "Modern" and "Antient" Freemasons, which emerged in the wake of his unexpected death in 1751.

---

[145] John Doran, *The Book of the Prince of Wales* (London, 1860), 490, 493.
[146] H. Walpole, *Correspondence*, XIX, 44 and n.20.
[147] *Daily Advertiser* (4 May 1745).
[148] H. Walpole, *Correspondence*, XIX, 174-75.
[149] R. Berman, *Schism*, 123-25

CHAPTER TWENTY-ONE

EARLY JACOBITE VICTORIES,
LATER HANOVERIAN TRIUMPH
(1745-1746)

God bless the King! (I mean our faith's defender!)
God bless! (No harm in blessing) the Pretender.
But who Pretender is, and who is King,
God bless us all! That's quite another thing!

John Byrom, "A Toast" (1745).

Arise, O George! Why sleepest thou? Awake,
Thy Fame, thy Crown, thy Kingdom lies at stake,
....
Insulted by a beardless Boy from Rome,
Bullied by baser Traytors still at home;
They who can Govern nothing Govern Thee,
A trifling, timid, treacherous Ministry..

London Grand Lodge MS. 1860. Mendes (1746).

While the Jacobite campaign continued in northern England and Scotland, Ireland remained quiet, leading Murray Pittock to characterize it as the big dog that failed to bark in the night.[1] However, Eamonn O'Ciardha argues that this view overlooks the suppressive measures taken by the government in the early days of invasion threat and the outpouring of Irish-language verse and song in support of the Stuarts.[2] The activities of the new Lord Lieutenant Chesterfield, from his arrival in Dublin on 31 August 1745 to his departure on 11 April 1746, shed light on this unexpected Irish quiescence – and the role that English-language literature played in maintaining it.

---

[1] Murray PIttock, *Poetry and Jacobite Politics in Eighteenth-Century Britain and Ireland* (Cambridge, 1994), 188.
[2] E. O'Ciardha, *Ireland*, 273-323.

His assignment to Ireland was a means of getting him away from George II, who despised him as a "tea-table scoundrel" and "dwarf baboon."[3]

For Orrery and his Tory-Jacobite friends in Ireland, the appointment of Chesterfield made them hope for a moderate regime, for they had long collaborated with him in opposition politics. On 1 July 1745 Orrery wrote from Marston to welcome Chesterfield back to England from his diplomatic appointment at The Hague; he promised that he would be loyal to him as Lord Lieutenant of Ireland, "but my loyalty may be misrepresented to my more exalted Master" (i.e., George II).[4] Orrery was aware of Chesterfield's earlier secret negotiations with Ormonde, and the Lord Lieutenant was aware of Orrery's current Jacobite sympathies. In the event, Chesterfield did not betray his old friend.

After his arrival in Dublin, Chesterfield publicly downplayed the threat of the Jacobites rebelling in Ireland, but he immediately raised regiments among the frightened Protestants in the north, and he continued the policies of disarmament of Catholics practiced by his predecessors. He warned a suspected Jacobite that "if the Irish behaved like faithful subjects, they would be treated as such. If they act in a different manner, I will be worse than Cromwell."[5] But he also believed that his predecessors' harsh treatment of the majority Catholics – closing mass houses, arresting priests, etc. – would backfire and fan the flames of rebellion. In one of the most unscrupulous but effective literary charades of the century, he took advantage of his old friend Swift's dotage and dementia to publish under his name a powerful appeal to the Irish to reject the Jacobite call to rebellion.

In September 1745 Chesterfield anonymously published *The Drapier's Letter to the Good People of Ireland* and pretended that it was written by Swift, thus exploiting the dean's popularity among the common people who were expected to be most sympathetic to the campaign of "Bonnie Prince Charlie":

> MY DEAR COUNTRYMEN,
>
> It is now some considerable time since I troubled you with my advice; and, as I am growing old and infirm, I was in good hopes to have quietly laid in my grave, before any occasion offering of addressing you again: but my affection for you, which does not decay, though my poor body does, obliges me once more to put you in mind of your true interests, that you may not unwarily run yourselves into danger and distress, for want of understanding or seriously considering it.
>
> I have many reasons to believe, that there are not a few among you, who secretly rejoice at the rebellion which is now raised in Scotland; and perhaps conceive hopes of some alteration for the better, in their circumstances and condition, if it should succeed. It is those mistaken people whom I design to talk to in this letter, and I desire not more of them than to give me a fair hearing...
>
> It is no Objection to my speaking to them, that they are generally *Papists*. I do not know how other People are disposed, but for my Part, I hate no

---

[3] Kevin Berland, "Chesterfield Demands the Muse: Dublin Print Culture, Poetry and the `Irish' Voice, 1745-6," *Eighteenth-Century Ireland*, 17 (2002), 122-23.

[4] Harvard. Hougton: Eng.MS. 218.2, vol. 2, f. 39.

[5] E. O'Ciardha, *Ireland*, 310.

Man for his Religion; I look upon a *Papist* as my Countryman and Neighbour, tho' I happen myself to be a *Protestant*.[6]

Chesterfield echoed Swift's disapproval of most of the landed gentry (predominantly Protestant) and targeted "the common People, the Labourers, Farmers, Artificers, and Tradesmen of this Nation, who are in Danger of being deluded by their Betters, and made Tools to serve their Purposes, without any Advantage to themselves." Only the wealthy and "perhaps the *French* and *Scotch* Friends of the *Pretender*" will benefit from rebellion. Thus, he cannot find why "he should think it worth his while to venture a Leg or an Arm, and the Gallows too into the Bargain, to be just where he set out." Indeed, let designing people say what they please, "you will all be ruined in the Struggle, let it end which Way it will." Is it worth it to beggar yourselves and your family "that the Man's Name upon the Throne may be *James* instead of *George*?"[7]

Lord Mahon noted that *The Drapier's Letter* "was so much in the dean's style, and was so greedily received, that it went through a variety of editions in a month's time."[8] As news reached Ireland of the Jacobites' continuing military victories, Chesterfield quickly issued *The Drapier's Second Letter to the Good People of Ireland* (1745), in which he took a harsher tone (again in Swift's name): "fighting for nothing against a superior Force, and with a Halter about one's Neck, which you must do, if you should be deluded to take Arms, is downright Stupidity or Madness."[9] Warning the Catholics that if they oblige the Protestants to take up arms for their defence, the latter will use them bravely rather than let papist priests execute them by "the Gibbet or the Stake," to be hung or burned alive. Venturing a more insulting tone, he wrote that he had taken some threatening words "out of a Book, which you are, many of you, not acquainted with; and that is the Bible. I can assure you, if you had read it, you would be very cautious of meddling with brave Protestants fighting for their Religion." He concluded with more predictions of disaster if the Catholics dare to support the Jacobites.

According to most British Protestant historians, Chesterfield was a model of religious toleration and benevolent reform. Publicly, he revoked his predecessor's policy by which the private papist chapels had been ordered to be shut up and proclamations issued to impel the priests to leave the capital: "He allowed the Catholics perfect religious freedom; intimated that he wished their places of worship to remain open, and took measures to prevent any molestation of those who resorted to them."[10] Privately, he wanted the chapels to remain open in order "to discover whether the Roman Catholics remained in the kingdom, or left it to join their co-religionists in Scotland; and to ascertain this, he employed persons to frequent the chapels and fairs for the purpose of reporting to him how they were intended."

On 8 October 1745 Chesterfield spoke to both houses of parliament and urged the stricter implementation of the anti-papal laws and suggested that they should be made even harsher. He stressed the great advantages to Ireland from the Protestant succession, which helped protect the country from the Catholics' "pernicious influence upon civil

---

[6] [Chesterfield.], *The Drapier's Letter to the Good People of Ireland* (Dublin, 1745), 3.

[7] *Ibid.*, 7.

[8] Lord Chesterfield, *The Works of Lord Chesterfield*, ed. Lord Mahon (New York, 1855), xxxv.

[9] [Chesterfield], *The Drapier's Second Letter to the Good People of Ireland* (Dublin, 1745), 3-5.

[10] W.H. Craig, *Life of Lord Chesterfield* (London, 1907)), 222-23, 228.

society." W. H. Craig, who reported these actions, commented wryly that "This eloquent tirade against …the national faith has almost comical significance, as issuing from a man who did not attach the slightest importance to creeds." While Chesterfield publicly played the role of a friend of all the people and an advocate of tolerance and peace, he sent blistering letters to Newcastle recommending the most severe and merciless treatment of the Scots.[11] As Samuel Shellabarger observes, Chesterfield, "like most Englishmen of his time, bitterly detested the Scots and Scotland," and he agreed with a policy of "fire and sword" to be used against them.[12]

When Swift died on 19 October 1745, he was unaware of the propaganda ploy published in his name by Chesterfield. He would have been dismayed to learn that Chesterfield told some of the dean's admirers in Dublin that "to his knowledge Swift made an offer of his pen to Sir Robert Walpole: and the terms were, his getting preferment in England, equal to what he had in Ireland; and that Sir Robert rejected it."[13] He thus repeated the charge spread by Swift's longtime enemies, the "Walpoleans." Because Chesterfield did not name the publisher of his Drapier letters, it is unknown if George Faulkner was aware of his secret authorship, despite his developing friendship with the new lord lieutenant. It is perhaps significant that Faulkner did not include them in volume eight of Swift's works that he published in early 1746.

In his fulsome dedication to Chesterfield, dated 27 January 1746, Faulkner eulogized Swift as "one of the greatest Patriots and Genius's, and most correct Writer of this or any other Age; and to whom no Person living bears a greater Resemblance than the Earl of Chesterfield."[14] As a moderate Episcopalian, with ancestral ties to the Catholic-Jacobite (and Masonic) Dillon family, Faulkner tried to avoid party factionalism while acting as an Irish patriot.[15] Perhaps Swift would have agreed with his praise of Chesterfield's political policies during the Jacobite rebellion, especially given their shared anti-Scottish prejudices, or perhaps not. In January 1746 Faulkner characterized the lord lieutenant as

> The truest Friend and Benefactor this Nation ever had, by the Care he hath taken of this Country, by preserving it in a profound State of Peace, when all Europe and particularly, his Majesty's Kingdom of Great-Britain, hath been embroiled in bloody and intestine Civil Wars, to the Ruin of Trade and Credit, and the Devastation of whole Countries… The name of LORD CHESTERFIELD will be mentioned by the People of Ireland to latest Posterity, and the best Friend this Nation ever was blessed with.[16]

The Masonic affiliation of Chesterfield was well known, which may have encouraged Faulkner to allow his London agents in 1746 to publish of *A Letter from the Grand Mistress of the Female Free-Masons to George Faulkner*, in *Miscellanies. By Dr. Swift*, volume XI of Swift's works.[17] However, Swift would have been dismayed to observe the welcome given to

---

[11] Chesterfield, *Private Correspondence between Chesterfield and Newcastle, 1744-1746* (London, 1930), 93, 122-23, 130.

[12] S. Shellabarger, *Lord Chesterfield*, 228-29.

[13] I. Ehrenpreis, *Swift*, III, 484.

[14] Jonathan Swift, *The Works of Jonathan Swift* (Dublin: George Faulkner, 1746), VIII, Dedication.

[15] Robert E. Ward, *Prince of Dublin Printers: The Letters of George Faulkner* (Lexington, 1972), 127n.12.

[16] J. Swift, *Works* (1746), VIII, Dedication.

[17] Jonathan Swift, *Miscellanies. By Dr. Swift* (London: C. Hitch, C. Davis, R. Dodsley, and M. Cooper, 1746), XI, 170-86. Hitch and Davis were Faulkner's London agents.

Chesterfield, upon his arrival in Dublin, by Sir Thomas Prendergast, the dean's *bête noir*, who continued his Whig-Masonic activities in Dublin.[18] Though it is unknown if the lord-lieutenant attended Masonic meetings in Ireland, he definitely met with two former Grand Masters, Sir William Stewart, 3rd Viscount Mountjoy, and Charles Moore, 2nd Lord Tullamore (according to Faulkner's *Dublin Journal*).[19] As noted earlier Mountjoy, who served as Grand Master in 1738-40, had supported Swift in the mortmain controversy, and he had been included on Sempill's list of Jacobite sympathizers in 1743. He would later (as Lord Blessington) serve as Grand Master of the schismatic Antient Masons in London. Tullamore served as Grand Master in 1741-42, and was the son of Swift's old enemy, the 3rd Viscount Allen, who served as Grand Master in 1744-45, until his death after a drunken brawl, which led to the rapid re-election of Lord Kingston in May 1745.[20] We do not know if Chesterfield met with Kingston, whom the ministry in London still distrusted as a Jacobite, though the Grand Master prudently remained quiet during the rebellion.

The Protestant establishment and press poured forth poems to flatter and praise Chesterfield, and he was soon courted by two poetic artisans, a bricklayer and a (pretended) cobbler, who carried on the tradition of Henry Nelson, the operative Mason who earlier dedicated poems to the Whig architect, Sir Edward Pearce. Henry Jones, a bricklayer and Freemason, gained access to Chesterfield when he worked on the repairs to the Parliament House in Dublin, part of the ambitious architectural agenda in which the lord lieutenant also devoted much public money to "completing the building of the castle."[21] For Irish nationalists and Jacobites, the castle was the architectural embodiment of English and Protestant domination of Ireland. On 9 October, ten days before Swift's death, Jones arranged for his panegyric, *The Bricklayer's Poem. Presented to his Excellency the Lord Lieutenant on His Arrival in this Kingdom*, to be hand delivered by the Chief Justice to Chesterfield, who loved the flattery and became Jones's patron.

The poet praised Chesterfield's literary gifts, support of the liberal arts, and conciliatory role in politics: "Thee even Factions with one Voice require,/And HEAV'N and GEORGE indulge the strong Desire."[22] Though Chesterfield as the Drapier had appealed to Catholic "artificers," Jones made clear his Hanoverian loyalties: "Tho' ne'er great BRUNSWICK to HIBERNIA rise," we still can view "His God-like Pow'r." Then, in an opportunistic move, Jones called upon Chesterfield to replace the mentally deteriorated Swift, especially since Lord Orrery (Boyle) was often away in England:

> Thrice happy Genius! In whose Soul conspire
> The Statesman's Wisdom, and the Poet's Fire:
> O Friend to Arts! Revive our drooping Isle,
> Ev'n here thy Presence shall their Strength restore,
> …………………………………………………..
> [Tho'] Britain's Senate noble BOYLE detains;
> Tho' Swift be DUMB, for Swift Ierne weeps,

---

[18] *Faulkner's Dublin Journal* (27-31 August 1745).
[19] W. Craig, *Life of Chesterfield*, 252.
[20] R. Berman, *Schism*, 230-32.
[21] Chesterfield, *Works*, xxxv.
[22] [Henry Jones], *The Bricklayer's Poem* (Dublin, 1745), 4-5.

The Pride, the Pillar, of his Country sleeps.
His clouded Soul emits no dazzling ray,
But faintly warms the animated Clay.
Not Rome's sad Ruins such impressions leave,
As Reason bury'd in the Body's Grave.
His living Lines shall mix their sacred Fire
In Nature's blaze, and with thy Works expire.[23]

The ambiguous (inept?) "thy" seemed to imply that Swift's works would die out with his body, a line that apparently offended another poet, James Eyre Weeks, a Trinity graduate and opposition Freemason, who responded to the artisan's panegyric with Masonic terminology. In *The Cobler's Poem. To a Certain Noble Peer. Occasioned by the Bricklayer's Poem. To which is added The Exception. After the Manner of Dean Swift* (1745), Weeks expressed his admiration for Swift and his mockery of Jones, who attempted to join the ranks of loyalist mediocrities like Stephen Duck, the self-educated farm laborer who became a protégé of the late Queen Caroline. But Jones is "like the Weather-cock assign'd/ The Sport of every puff of Wind":

His Brick work Rhimes and tuneful Lays,
Like Sand and Lime attempt thy Praise,
His Water cannot be outdone,
Brought all the way from Helicon,
Thus 'twist the Bricks and Verses too,
Poetic Mortar you may view,
And while the Rhimes and Mortar mix,
He builds as well in Verse as Bricks,
Orders appear, and Harmony,
In Building as in Poetry,
Tho' Muster very often some pass,
That are not fram'd by Rule and Compass,
In both, there's many a Projector,
That knows no Rule in Architecture,
As Gamesters still are held unfair,
That will not play upon the Square.[24]

Weeks then mocked Jones's "bold Ambition," as the brick-layer tried to reach Chesterfield by building a Babel Tower to heaven:

Oh! Wond'rous bard divinely Skill'd!
With Trowel, as with Pen to Build,
To Rule thy Verse how aptly Joyn
The Muse's and the Mason's Line!
While Bricks with Words and Words with Bricks,
In one Poetic Chaos mix,
With Language, as with Brick-work able,
To Build again the Tow'r of Babel.

---

[23] *Ibid.*, 6.
[24] [James Eyre Weeks], *The Cobler's Poem*, 2nd Ed. (Dublin, 1745), 4-5.

Unfortunately for Weeks, Chesterfield was more responsive to Jones's appeal for patronage, and he received accusations of disloyalty for his satire on Jones. He then defended himself by publishing *Rebellion. A Poem Humbly Inscribed to His Excellency Philip, Earl of Chesterfield* (1745). With a slight tone of his tail between his legs, he scorned Charles Edward as "the mock Prince [who] the titled Wreath assumes," while praising Chesterfield's early role as an opposition Patriot, "when Faction wore the masque of Public Good."[25] Lamenting the recent death of his revered Swift, he went beyond Jones's awkward implication that Swift's writings would die with him and urged:

> In time, my Lord, oh! save this sinking Isle,
> Place her within the Sunshine of thy Smile.
> The DRAPIER's dead – her future Guardian be,
> And let her find a Nobler Swift in thee.
> For now Rebellion rudely stalks abroad,
> And Idly menaces his feeble Rod;
> His distant threats Hibernia cannot fear,
> While George rules Britain, and while Stanhope's here.[26]

Though Weeks did not gain Chesterfield's patronage, he remained in good standing with many of the Irish Freemasons, who without supporting the Scottish rebellion continued their opposition to the repressive policies of the London ministry. Weeks would later write the words for *Solomon's Temple, an Oratorio*, which in 1753 was performed in Dublin for the benefit of sick and distressed Masons and was subsequently published by the "Antient" Masons in London, predominantly Irish immigrants who opposed the "modern" Grand Lodge of England.[27]

Swift did not live to learn of the determined attempt of his admired correspondent, Sir Charles Wogan, to join his brother Nicholas in the Jacobite army in Scotland. Charles planned to bring hundreds of Irish officers to join the Stuart "crusade." Inspired by the chivalric language of Charles Edward's letter to him, he determined to outdo his earlier knight errantry and recruit Irish Jacobites from regiments in Spain, Italy, France, and Morocco.[28] In November 1745 he wrote James, expressing his frustration at Spanish and French dilatoriness but full of enthusiasm at reports of Prince Charles's victories. The Stuart restoration is happening by "the most honourable and glorious Means… [by] the right hand of your Heroick son:"

> Here is no Monck; no Rebel become loyal, by seeing the Resources of Treason sinking in bad and insufficient hands; no tricks and Double-dealings between a General, yt finds all his honour and safety consists in returning to his Duty, and a Parliament upon its last legs… Here is all noble and fair; 'tis the right heir of the Crown, yt does justice to his Royal Father in the hearts of his People by the Charms of his Person… All this executed and your Majesty proclaim'd and Acknowledg'd…in less than two months time,

---

[25] [James Eyre Weeks], *Rebellion. A Poem* (Dublin, 1745), 3.
[26] *Ibid.*, 4.
[27] Laurence Dermott, *Ahiman Rezon: or, a Help to a Brother* (London, 1756), 203.
[28] H. Tayler, *Jacobite Epilogue*, 306-08.

without any foreign assistance, or any officer of note, out-does the Glory of your famous Ancestor, Robert Bruce, *"et est mirabile in oculis nostris."*[29]

Wogan finally left Spain for France, where he planned to bring members of the Irish Brigade to Dunkirk to depart for Wales, in order to recruit, train, and discipline local Jacobites and lowland Scots, but he thought it best to let "the honest Highlanders" continue their "own way of fighting and breaking ye enemy by pouring in upon `em with their usual Cry and impetuosity." However, the rebels' retreat from Derby made the French stall on their support, and Wogan never got further than Arras, where he spent much time with Charles Edward's brother. In January 1746 Father Flynn reported to the Stuart court about "the excess of joy shewn by ye Irish Brigade at the appearance of H.R.H," Henry Stuart.[30] As noted earlier, Jacobite Masonry was strong in the brigade, and Wogan may have learned that Arras hosted an important *Écossais* lodge, which later claimed (controversially) to have received a hand-signed warrant from Charles Edward.[31]

While the Jacobite Masons in Ireland laid low and their Irish brothers abroad tried to join the rebels in Scotland, a controversial *frère* from the days of Derwentwater's and Ramsay's *Écossais* leadership re-emerged on the Masonic stage in England. John Coustos, who in 1737 had opposed their efforts to transform the French lodges into an order of chivalry, returned to London after his release from an Inquisition prison in Portugal. His brother-in-law, John David Barbutt (the earlier target of Dick Poney and the Scald Miserble Masons) used his friendship with his earlier employer William Stanhope, 1st Earl of Harrington, to persuade Newcastle to pressure the Portuguese government to release Coustos, as a British citizen.[32]

After his return to London in December 1744, Coustos worked on his memoirs, and he sent a draft to Newcastle before the rebellion broke out in Scotland.[33] By August 1745 the minister realized the propaganda value of the memoirs, and he evidently ordered a government-agent to edit them and to add hundreds of pages of anti-Catholic polemics. The resultant book, *The Sufferings of John Coustos, for Free-Masonry, and for His Refusing to Turn Roman Catholic, in the Inquisition at Lisbon*, was published in early 1746. It was printed by William Strahan, printer to George II, and dedicated by Coustos to Harrington, secretary of state, who had earlier served as ambassador in Spain.[34] There is a controversial tradition that he was associated with Wharton's Masonic lodge in Madrid, which included the Hanoverian Labelye as well as Jacobites, and he was currently a Whig Mason.[35]

Coustos's *Sufferings* presented a searing indictment of Roman Catholicism and a lurid portrayal of Inquisition torture; its publication was timed to address "the unnatural

---

[29] *Ibid.*, 312-13.

[30] H. Tayler, *Jacobite Epilogue*, 159.

[31] C. Thory, *Annales*, 63; J. Tuckett,"Prince Charles Edward Stuart, G.M." Tuckett suggests that the prince passed through Arras when he travelled back and forth from the coast to Paris in 1745. He further notes that the prince could send a signed warrant without being present in the lodge. A. Kervella argues that the warrant should be dated April 1747, after the prince's return to France; see *Le Mystère*, 312-13. Other critics say the Arras claim was fraudulent.

[32] R. Berman, *Espionage*, 182-83.

[33] BL: Add. Newcastle Papers: MS. 33,054,f.313.

[34] R. Sedgwick, *History*, II, 437.

[35] Gustave Gottrand, "On the Antiquity of Lodge `La Parfaite Union,' at Mons, Belgium," *AQC*, 10 (1897), 50-58.

Rebellion now carrying on against His Majesty, whose Lenity ought to have secured him the Hearts of all but the most abandoned."[36] In the preface, the anonymous editor wrote on 15 October that he was "desired by a Person of Eminence" (probably Newcastle) to publish the papers as soon as possible. He urged all Englishmen to contribute to the defeat of the rebellion with "their Tongues, their Pens, their Purses, their Persons," in order to prevent "an universal Inundation," "the Flood of Popery and Tyranny now driving in." Among the subscribers were the well-known Freemasons, Lord Cranstoun (listed as Grand Master), the Whig Earl of Pembroke, the Hanoverian Duke of Atholl, and (surprisingly) the Jacobite Earl of Eglinton. The editor quoted lines from *Liberty*, by the former opposition Mason, James Thomson, to support his anti-Jacobite, anti-Catholic argument.

Curiously, while Coustos presented Freemasonry as a benign, charitable institution, he also gave credibility to the suspicion that he was an espionage agent, for he advised the Inquisitors to contact "Mr. Dogood, an Englishman, who was both a Roman Catholic and a Free-Mason," and who "settled a lodge in Lisbon" in 1738.[37] He referred to William Dugood, a Scottish jeweler, Hanoverian Mason, and anti-Jacobite spy, whom he believed would acquaint the Inquisitors "with the Nature and Secrets of Masonry," if "he thought proper." Coustos thus inadvertently revealed his collaboration with another government-paid spy, for Dugood had earlier served as Stosch's "primary source of information" on the Jacobites in Italy.[38]

In 1718 Dugood was recommended by the unsuspecting Duke of Mar to be jeweler to the Pretender and, as a recent Catholic convert, he gained detailed knowledge of the secrets of the Stuart court. In 1721, when Stosch became a spy for the Hanoverian regime, he recruited Dugood, who joined him and Denys Wright, also an ex-Jacobite, in reporting to the Whig ministry. In 1723 Dugood was driven out of Italy, and he eventually arrived in London, where in 1725 he joined a Whig lodge and in 1728 was nominated to the Royal Society by Desaguliers, Halley, and Folkes. In 1728 he was in Portugal, where he founded a Masonic lodge, and in 1731 he returned to Italy, where he continued reporting to Delafaye on the Jacobites. Driven out of Italy again, he returned to Lisbon, where he gained eminence as a jeweler and scientist.

Portugal had implemented the Papal Ban of 1738, so Dugood and Coustos held lodge meetings in private residences. When Coustos was arrested in March 1743, he defended Masonry as an ancient Scottish institution, in which the kings of Scotland had been Grand Masters, and affirmed that the fraternity was strongly royalist. He argued that Louis XV would not have asked him to initiate the Duc de Villeroy, the royal favorite, if he believed that the meetings were contrary "to the State, to Religion, and to the Church."[39] The editor of *The Sufferings* obviously perceived the story of Coustos as an opportunity to praise Hanoverian Freemasonry, while making Catholicism seem so appalling that no Mason could be a Catholic (perhaps aimed at the expanding Jacobite

---

[36] John Coustos, *The Sufferings of John Coustos, for Free-Masonry, and for His Refusing to Turn Roman Catholic in the Inquisition at Lisbon* (London, 1746), vii, xxix, xl.

[37] *Ibid.*, 42.

[38] David Connell, "The Collection of William Dugood FRS—Jeweller, Scientist, Freemason, and Spy," *Journal of the History of Collections*, 21 (2009), 33-36.

[39] *Ibid.*, 40-41, 70.

lodges in France). He added over three hundred pages of accounts of the horrors of the Inquisition, and Coustos's memoirs played a significant propaganda role in the heated context of the Scottish rebellion. The editor also included accounts of the persecution of Marranos, crypto-Jews in Portugal and Spain, and he may have been aware of claims that Coustos was a Marrano turned Protestant.[40]

The issue of Jews and Freemasonry, with both Hanoverians and Jacobites claiming their loyalty, was thus in the air on 3 January 1746 when the Hat government in Sweden, controlled by *Écossais* Masons, issued an invitation to Sephardi Jews in England to immigrate to Sweden. The Hats wanted the Jews to work with the Swedish East India Company, which employed a large contingent of Scottish Masons and which the English ministry considered "a nest of Jacobites."[41] The ministers knew that the Gothenburg company was instrumental in the Swedish effort to support the Jacobite rebels in Scotland. They thus called upon the wealthy Jewish merchant Joseph Salvador, a Hanoverian Mason, to reject the offer, and he and the financier Samson Gideon supported an effort by the British East India Company to offer employment to influential Scots in order to "deliberately weaken, dampen and finally suck the heart out of Scottish Jacobitism."[42] It is unknown if Gideon was a Mason, but his son became a major figure in the loyalist Grand Lodge system.

Though Gideon strongly supported the government during the rebellion and virtually saved the bank of England from a panicked flight of creditors, there were still concerns about the Jacobite Jews who sympathized with the rebels.[43] Thus, on 21 January 1746 Henry Fielding entered the lists, hinting at his awareness that some Jews supported the Stuart cause. He claimed in a faked letter from James III to Prince Charles that "Paul Regnier, the Jew, was here [Rome] for interest due on the last-advanced 40,000 Crowns, and we had nothing to content him with but civil words."[44] Fielding remembered the role of Francis Francia, the famous "Jacobite Jew," in the Swedish plot, an "unholy alliance" that seemed to be revived in the Swedish invitation to the Jews in England. Francia's family was still receiving a subsidy from James III, and over the next seven years his "orphans" prayed for the restoration of James III.[45] Fielding may also have been aware that Solomon and Moses Mendes were Stuart sympathizers. Since Francia, allegedly, and the Mendes brothers were Freemasons, this early claim points forward to Fielding's arguments in 1747 when he identified the Jacobites with Jews and Masons.[46]

In April Fielding would report the terminal illness of Swift's old friend, Count Gyllenborg, the Swedish Jacobite Mason who had worked closely with Francia.[47] Gyllenborg

---

[40] J. Shaftesley, "Jews in Regular English Freemasonry," 150-209; Wallace McLeod, "More Light on John Coustos," *AQC*, 95 (1982), 117-18.

[41] For this Swedish-Jewish project and its Masonic component, see M. Schuchard, *Emanuel Swedenborg*, 407-09, 420-23.

[42] George McGilvary, *East India Patronage and the British State: The Scottish Elite and Politics in the Eighteenth Century* (London, 2008), 67.

[43] Lucy Sutherland, "Samson Gideon: Eighteenth Century Jewish Financier," *TJHSE*, 17 (1951-52), 79-90.

[44] *True Patriot*, #12 (21 January 1746).

[45] Stuart Papers: 303/6 (Paris, 2 January 1750. Appeal from Peter and Elinor Francia, orphans of Francia; 343/22 (Paris, 30 December 1753. Appeal from Francia's children and prayer for James III's restoration.

[46] H. Fielding, *Jacobite's Journal*, 95, 97, 103, 281-87, 331-34.

[47] *True Patriot*, #26 (29 April 1746).

was a strong supporter of the Swedish effort to help Prince Charles in 1745-46, which was frustrated by confused orders from Paris and the confinement of the ice-bound ships in Gothenburg harbor.[48] The organizer of the Swedish effort was Baron de Blantyre, the Jacobite Mason who had accompanied Derwentwater at the funeral of Chevalier Ramsay. On 24 January the Swedish Jacobites were delighted by the birth of Prince Gustaf, and a Masonic medal was struck in his honor and presented to the Swedish crown princess, who sent a copy to her brother, Frederick II of Prussia. In Swedish Pomerania a German translation of Ramsay's *Travels of Cyrus* was dedicated to Gustaf, who later became a "Mason king" in 1771 and continued to support Charles Edward into the 1780s.

After the Jacobites retreated to Scotland, they experienced shifting victories and defeats, while the prince's counselors quarreled among themselves, often unable to overcome nationalistic distrust between the Irish, Scots, and English. But for the Duke of Richmond, it was the Scots who most deserved defeat and annihilation – possibly fueled by his anger at Masonic rivals. His vitriol against Scotland was so strong that it even shocked Newcastle, to whom he wrote in February 1746 that he wished "to have heard that these Villains were totally destroy'd," though "you used to scold me for despising them, but I allways did & allways shall despise them as the scum of Scotland which is certainly the sinke of the Earth."[49] Richmond was especially angry about the rebels' victory at Falkirk on 17 January, and he continued, "I was sure that they would never stand their ground":

> Butt indeed if our people run away at the sight of them, they must be beaten by the Westminster scholars; and what did that pannick come from, butt their hearing that these were desperate fellows with Broad Swords, Targetts, Lochaberax's, & the Devil knows what, that was eternally preach'd up by the Scotch Jacobites, even at White's & St. James's, stuff actually fit to *frighten* nothing but old women & children.

The rebels' victory over General Hawley at Falkirk provoked rival accounts, with the governmental *London Gazette* (23 January 1746) down-playing the ignominious retreat of the Hanoverian forces and loss of their cannon and weapons. Paul Whitehead, still linked with the opposition Masons, wrote an epilogue for the Irish actress Peg Woffington to be delivered at her Drury Lane benefit performance of *The Scornful Lady*. He knew that James Lacey, manager of the theater, was so worried by the dearth of audiences during the rebellion that he "applied for leave to raise a Regiment of Actors in defense of His Majesty's person against the Young Pretender."[50] Lacey also staged repeated performances of Cibber's play, *The Non-juror*, which was considered timely because of its "suggestive and patriotic hits." However, Woffington pleaded illness and someone else had to read her part in the play, leading to suspicions that "the large-hearted Irishwoman may have been a strong sympathizer with Prince Charley, and had little interest in local flings at his expense."

---

[48] For the Swedish efforts, see M. Schuchard, *Emanuel Swedenborg*, 338, 400, 403-08.
[49] Richmond, *Correspondence*, 204.
[50] Augustin Daly, *Woffington: A Tribute to the Actress and Woman*, 2nd ed. (1888; Troy, 1891), 69.

It was perhaps to counter that suspicion in the dangerous days after Falkirk that she agreed to perform Whitehead's epilogue with its "antipopish" verses. She entered dressed as a volunteer and reading the *Gazette*, "which gives an Account of the Battle of Falkirk":

> Curse on all Cowards! Say I – why – bless my Eyes –
> Our Men Retreat before a scrub Banditti,
> Who scarce could fright the Buff-coats of the City!
> Well – if 'tis so, and that our Men won't stand,
> 'Tis time we Women, take the thing in hand –
> Thus, in my Country's Cause, I now appear
> A bold, smart Khevenhuller [Hussar] Volunteer –
> ....
> They cry these Rebels are so stout and tall,
> Ah! Lard! I'd lower the proudest of them all.[51]

Woffington then coyly argued against "the Progress of this Popish Treason," because women do not want to go into convents or have men become celibate monks: "What gay Coquet would like a Nun's Profession,/ And I've some private Reasons 'gainst Confession."

Despite its slightly risqué, anti-Catholic tone, the epilogue's satire on the retreating Hanoverians was appreciated by Mendes, Ellis, Byrom, and their Masonic circle, who included a hand-written copy in their MS. notebook of Jacobite poems. Their friend Dr. King wrote a versified satire, "The Gazette of January 23, 1745" [1746], in which he mocked the defeated General Hawley and the white-washing account in the government journal:

> I'll tell you a Tale for a Groat,
> That highly advances our Glory,
> Of a Battel so gallantly fought,
> As not to be equall'd in Story.
> To Scotland repairs Chieftain Hawley,
> The fiercest of British Commanders.
> Had promis'd the King he would maul ye,
> O ye cowardly, rebel Highlanders.
> And now All so brave on the Green
> This Heroe his Army assembled;
> Were ever such Myrmidons seen?
> O how ye blue-bonnet Men trembled![52]

King went on to scorn the ludicrous retreat of Hawley's troops under the onslaught of rain and wind, and especially their abandonment of their weapons and cannons:

> The Gen'ral look'd sharply about,
> And swore that he miss'd all his Cannon.
> Some think in a Trap they were caught,
> The Highland-Men stole 'em we say:
> But Others more justly have thought,

[51] Quoted in William Rufus Chetwood, *A General History of the Stage* (Dublin, 1749), 258-59.
[52] Harvard, Houghton. Orrery Papers, MS. Eng. 218.

> By the Wind they were all blown away.
> And now he that rightly can ken
> My Tale, tho' the Truth may be doubted,
> Must own, by a Handful of Men,
> The whole [loyalist] Highland Army was routed.

In an MS. note, Mendes and Ellis attributed the poem to Dr. King, and Orrery included a full hand-written copy among his papers.

Unfortunately for the Jacobites, their officers did not take full advantage of the victory at Falkirk. When Prince Charles took up residence in Bannockburn house, he fell seriously ill from 5 to 16 January. He was nursed by Clementina Walkinshaw, whose father had collaborated with Charles Wogan in the rescue of the prince's mother, Clementina Sobieski.[53] Abandoning the celibate stance of his Swedish idol Carl XII, the prince became the lover of Clementina – a move that would later bring him and his followers great grief. However, the restless Highland troops were thrilled to be stationed at Bannockburn, and they circulated songs and prophecies about the historical significance of the site. A popular song from 1714 was revived, in which the bard called on the "brave loyal clans" to "Restore with sword in hand" their "ancient Stuart Race": "Like Bruce at Bannockburn, boys,/ The English home we'll chase."[54] Cromarty's son, Lord Macleod, who had become close to the prince, later recounted: "The Highlanders, who are very much addicted to superstition, were very desirous that the battle might be fought at Bannockburn, as they thought that they wou'd then certainly win it because their ancestors had won a great victory over the English at the same place some ages before."[55]

Many members of the Irish Brigade, who had joined the Highlanders, would sense an additional Masonic significance to the proposed field of battle. *Écossais* Masonry was strong in the brigade, and Bannockburn was often mentioned in the Templar degrees and those of the Royal Order of Scotland. In the latter, the "Rosy Cross" degree taught that it was first conferred on the field of Bannockburn in 1314 "as a reward for the valour displayed by a body of Templars who aided Bruce in that memorable victory."[56] However, Charles Edward was persuaded, against his will, by Lord George Murray to begin a retreat from Bannockburn to the Highlands, which eventually proved to be a disastrous decision.

In February 1746, as fears of a French invasion receded, George II turned on Newcastle and his ministers, which led to their resignation *en masse* and forced the king to reinstate them two days later. The political confusion prompted a member of Mendes's Masonic circle to write a satire on the unpopularity of the king and his opportunistic Whig ministers:

> Arise, O George, why sleepest thou? Awake,
> Thy Fame, thy Crown, thy Kingdom lies at stake.
> Why dost thou still the impoverish'd Country fleece,
> Yet shun a War, uncertain of a Peace.
> Content abroad to abandon thy Allies,

---

[53] F. McLynn, *Charles Edward Stuart*, 204.
[54] M. Pittock, *Poetry and Jacobite Politics*, 137-38.
[55] William Fraser, *The Earls of Cromartie* (Edinburgh, 1876), II, 391.
[56] D. Lyon, *History*, 342. For the fourteenth-century context, see M. Schuchard, *Restoring the Temple*, 89-94.

And fall to fools at home a sacrifice:
Insulted by a beardless Boy from Rome,
Bullied by baser Traytors still at home;
They who can Govern nothing Govern Thee,
A trifling, timid, treacherous Ministry.[57]

In a bold call for the king to turn to the Tories, widely condemned as crypto-Jacobites, the poet continued:

TORIES may still thy drooping cause revive,
They're friends at least to the Prerogative,
But should you fail at last in this design,
And find it hard to save th' illustrious line;
Take Heart and like your Ministers, resign.

Small wonder that this poem was not published and was preserved only in the notebook now in the Grand Lodge Library. In the notebook, the poem was immediately followed by a copy of John Byrom's famous Jacobite toast in which he wrote God bless the King and the Pretender, but "Who that Pretender is, and who that King is…is quite another Thing."

In the early months of 1746, the Duke of Richmond counted upon his loyalist Masonic brothers to support the military campaign against the rebels and he was especially assisted by two former Hanoverian Grand Masters, John, 2nd Duke of Montagu, and John Campbell, 4th Earl of Loudoun, as well as his lodge brother, William Keppel, 3rd Earl of Albemarle. As noted earlier, Montagu had earned the hatred of Jacobites in 1716, when he gave a grand ball for George I on the evening of James Radcliffe's execution, and he now had little sympathy for James's brother, Charles, Jacobite Earl of Derwentwater. Like his close friend Richmond, Montagu was made a general in 1745 and fought against the rebel forces. Loudoun was a Scottish Whig, from a staunch Presbyterian Covenanting family, who raised a regiment of loyal Highlanders. However, "a certain number" of his Highland recruits deserted and joined the prince's army.[58]

In February 1746 Loudoun sought to end the rebellion (and obtain the £30,000 reward) by attempting to capture Prince Charles at Moy Hall, near Ruthven, where the dowager Lady Mackintosh determined to protect him. Robert Forbes reported that "The night march terminated in farce after five quick-thinking Jacobites succeeded in panicking Loudoun's column of 1500 men by giving the impression, through much loud shouting, of being a large ambushing force. The "rout of Moy" prompted desertions among Loudoun's forces, leading to the abandoning of Inverness. Loudoun himself was forced to retreat to the Black Isle, and from there to Skye."[59] The Jacobites celebrated "the Rout of Moy" in mocking songs and poetry, and John Roy Stewart so admired the Scottish heroine that after her death he wrote "Lament for Lady Mackintosh," in which he praised her manly courage: "'Tis woman's meed for chieftain's deed,/ That bids our eyes to shower."[60] After Moy, it still seemed possible that the prince's forces might succeed. For

---

[57] London, Grand Lodge: MS. 1860. Men.
[58] Alistair and Henrietta Tayler, *Jacobite Letters to Lord Pitsligo, 1745-1746* (Aberdeen, 1930), 91n.3.
[59] "John Campbell, 4th Earl of Loudoun," *ODNB*.
[60] Charles Rogers, *The Modern Scottish Minstrel* (Edinburgh, 1846), II, 341-42.

the Jacobite Masons, the fact that Charles sent their former Grand Master Cromarty in pursuit of the former Hanoverian Grand Master Loudoun must have been piquant.[61] Even more encouraging, their chivalric brother Perth defeated Loudoun at Sutherland on 20 March.[62]

During these difficult weeks, the Whig Mason Albemarle worked closely with Cumberland in Aberdeen, and on 5 March 1746 he wrote Newcastle about their mutual hatred of the Scots:

> I make no doubt of beating them, a brush would put an end to this cursed and unnatural rebellion, and without such a thing this affair may be tedious and Lasting, for these villains will Lead us a dance from one bad country to a worse, and throw ye worse people I ever knew; for I protest I prefer ye soil to ye Inhabitants, for more malice, falsehood, cunning, and self interest was never met with in any country whatsoever; … [but] I would rather stay here (bad as I am) a twelve month longer, then leave it in ye power of these rascals of ever attempting to give trouble to their Lawfull King, or quiet neighbors…[63]

On 21 March Horace Walpole reported that Cumberland "complains extremely of the *loyal* Scots, says he can get no intelligence, and reckons himself more in an enemy's country than he was warring with the French in Flanders."[64] They publicly swear loyalty to him, but before he is out of sight, they "beat up for volunteers for the rebels." Albemarle would later face the challenge of making the reluctant, often hostile Scottish stonemasons work on the new army barracks at government-controlled Fort William.[65]

In early 1746, as the rebels stubbornly survived the assaults by the government's troops, Fielding in London became frustrated by the lack of popular and ministerial support for his journal. On 4 February he made a seemingly desperate appeal to the "great Man" Pelham, who so far had been indifferent to efforts of political writers to support or oppose him. Claiming that most opposition writers have been mere "scriblers" and "factious malcontents," Fielding distanced himself from them and pleaded "with Reluctance, of Myself, and endeavor to recommend *The True Patriot* to his Regard and serious Attention."[66] On 25 February he complained that someone was preventing the sale of his journal by "propagating Lies and Nonsense" about it, and he hinted that certain opposition members were behind the hostile campaign, which prompted him to declare: "It is now therefore, that Opposition is really and truly Faction; that the Names of a Patriot and Courtier are not only compatible, but necessarily conjoined; and that none can be any longer Enemies to the Ministry, without being so to the Public. All malicious and invidious Insinuations against such an Administration ought to be discouraged, and the Persons who forge or promote them, should be detested as the most dangerous Vermin to Society."[67]

---

[61] Robert Forbes, *The Lyon in Mourning*, ed. Henry Paton (Edinburgh, 1896), I, 355.

[62] A. and H. Tayler, *Jacobite Letters*, 91.

[63] Albermarle, *Albemarle Papers*, II, 2.

[64] H. Walpole, *Correspondence*, XIX, 228.

[65] Albemarle *Albemarle Papers.*, II, 22-23, 44.

[66] *True Patriot*, #14 (February 1746).

[67] *Ibid.*, #17 (25 February 1746).

One former opposition Mason, Chesterfield, made clear that he was no longer an opponent of the ministry. While his mixed policies of military suppression and religious moderation helped keep Ireland quiet, he urged Newcastle to implement harsh policies against the Scots, making no distinctions between Hanoverians and Jacobites. On 11 March he wrote from Dublin Castle, urging the government to treat all Scots like criminals: "I would starve the loyal with the disloyal" and "order all the *Loyall Highlanders* under your Loudouns and Campbells into garrison…in towns in England, and employ only English and Hessians in subduing the Highlands." [68]

When he learned that his diatribes were greatly appreciated by George II and Cumberland, he intensified his advocacy of "no mercy":

> Recall your Scotch heroes, starve the whole country indiscriminately by your ships, put a price upon the heads of all the chiefs, and let the Duke put all to fire and sword. Here is one of the rascals, a Maclaughlin, who, as I am informed, is come over to raise some men and carry them to Scotland. I intend to put a price of two hundred pounds upon him…[69]

Chesterfield, who knew that Loudoun had served as a Whig Grand Master, nevertheless distrusted all Scots, including their Masonic brother Marchmont, whose offers to help the government campaign were rejected. On 5 March Newcastle wrote Chesterfield, "I can't oblige Lord Marchmont. My politicks as to Scotland are exactly the same with yours… If the power of the Highlands is not absolutely reduced, France may play the Pretender upon us whenever she pleases."[70]

Charles Edward had issued strong orders that his men were not to pillage or damage the property of the locals, whose respect he needed when he would become king. However, in early April a rebel party plundered and destroyed Cullen House, the magnificent residence of James Ogilvy, 5th Earl of Findlater, a loyal Whig and Walpolean representative peer of Scotland, who was despised by the local Jacobites.[71] On 8 April a worried Pitsligo wrote to the elderly Sir Thomas Sheridan to lament the destruction, for "This no doubt will vex R.H. generous heart and it throws a great disparagement on his army."[72] He wanted the prince to make a public declaration of his disapproval of such proceedings, in order to maintain his reputation for compassion and lawfulness. On 11 April Findlater welcomed Cumberland, who shared his wrath at the plunder of Cullen House, and the earl then contributed substantial funds to the duke's army. Pitsligo's concern was shared by Charles Edward, who reiterated his opposition to pillaging of local property.

To undermine the success of Jacobite propaganda about Charles Edward's merciful attitude, John Anderson, a loyalist Scot, determined to counter Kilmarnock's scriptural panegyric to the Stuart prince by copying its style in praise of Cumberland. Son of a Presbyterian Whig preacher, Anderson drew on the ancient Jewish identification of the radical Covenanters when he issued in March *The Book of Chronicles of His Royal Highness William Duke of Cumberland; Being an Account of the Rise and Progress of the Present Rebellion*

---

[68] Chesterfield, *Private Correspondence*, 122-23.
[69] *Ibid.*, 130.
[70] Chesterfield, *Private Correspondence*, 119.
[71] William Cramond, *The Plundering of Cullen House by the Rebels* (Buckie, 1887).
[72] A. and H. Tayler, *Jacobite Letters*, 96n.2, 113-14.

(Edinburgh, 1746). Echoing Kilmarnock, he wrote, "And it came to pass," that an arrogant Prince Charles "did evil in the sight of the Lord, after the Abominations of the Heathens."[73] He had "a Vineyard at Holy-rood House," where he plied his five hundred concubines with drink until they brought him gold and silver. Despite the bravery of all the government commanders, the "uncircumcised" Highlanders with heretical glee somehow kept winning.

The Jacobites' hero, the Duke of Perth, was actually a murderer, who "swore and blasphemed," until the loyalist forces gave up Edinburgh to "the uncircumcised by Capitulation." Anderson contrasted Perth, who was well-known as a pious and serious Jacobite Mason, with Lord Loudoun, equally well-known as an unpopular and ineffective Grand Master in London, by reversing their reputations. Lord Albemarle, a Whig Mason, would soon destroy "the Children of Belial," the "uncircumcised Highlanders." All of this was foretold by "the Sign of the Blazing Star; are they not written in the Book of the Prophecy of John the Scribe." Ironically, Henry Fielding would later characterize the Jacobites as circumcised Jewish Masons.

Despite Chesterfield's urging that Loudoun be dismissed, the former Whig Grand Master got his revenge on 15 April when he defeated and captured Cromarty, just before Cumberland's army crushingly defeated Charles Edward's troops on 16 April at Culloden. When news reached Dublin of Cumberland's victory, Chesterfield lavished praise upon the conquering hero, "his young Marcellus." Irish Masons, even those with private Jacobite sympathies, felt compelled to join the celebrations. Lord Kingston, the Grand Master, celebrated the Hanoverian victory "by a Masonic banquet of such magnificence that it was chronicled in the public journals of the day."[74] On 6 May Faulkner's *Journal* reported that in Mitchelstown, where Kingston had earlier held private lodge meetings in his own house, he now gathered eminent Masons to honor "the victory of our arms over the rebels."[75]

Though the Whigs eulogized Cumberland, he was already receiving criticism for his cruelty to wounded soldiers and local civilians, as well as his refusal to maintain a cartel for exchange of prisoners. In February, when Prince Frederick of Hesse-Cassel, Cumberland's contracted ally, arrived with Hessian troops in Scotland, he was repelled by the duke's brutality and became sympathetic to the more merciful Stuart prince.[76] The Jacobite commander Lord George Murray sent a Swedish courier to Frederick asking him to implement a mutual cartel for humane treatment of prisoners, but Cumberland was enraged at the prince's willingness to meet with Murray. Annoyed by Frederick's opposition to his "irregular" treatment of prisoners, the duke allowed the Hessians no significant military role, and they would leave Scotland with the reputation of "a gentle race."

It seems likely that Murray appealed to Frederick's sense of Masonic fraternity, for they were both initiates of *Écossais* lodges, which may have provoked Richmond's scornful comment on the Hessian prince. On 4 June, when Frederick visited London, the

---

[73] John Anderson, *The Book of the Chronicles of His Royal Highness William Duke of Cumberland* (Edinburgh, 1746), 7-13, 23-24.

[74] William James Hughan, "The Three Degrees of Freemasonry," *AQC*, 10 (1897) 143.

[75] L. Meaney, "Freemasonry in Munster," 36.

[76] Christopher Duffy, "Hidden Sympathies: the Hessians in Scotland in 1746," in Monod, Pittock, and Szechi, *Loyalty and Identity*, 128-29.

Duke of Grafton asked Richmond to entertain him, but Richmond refused, noting that he could do nothing for him "butt attend him to Mother Douglass [a brothel] or to a Lodge of Freemasons, which I assure you are his two highest pleasures."[77]

Prince Frederick was the nephew of the ailing and corrupt Swedish king, Fredrik I of Hesse, who had received British bribes for decades. However, the king angered George II and Cumberland when, in the early stages of the rebellion, he "let drop in the Senate, that, considering how Affairs stood in Scotland, it appeared doubtful which Side would turn out to be Rebels."[78] The Hessian's reports about the savagery of "Butcher" Cumberland reached the Swedish court, where a scandal soon emerged that the English would pay the Swedish king £100,000 if he would abdicate in favor of the Duke of Cumberland.[79] The chancellor Tessin, chief of the *Écossais* lodges, learned of the plot and ordered the arrest and beheading of Dr. Alexander Blackwell, a Scottish physician resident in Sweden, who had collaborated in the bribery offer and who threatened to expose the Hats' support of the Scottish rebellion.

On 30 April 1746 Cumberland ordered Loudoun "to pursue & hunt these Vermin amongst their lurking holes," and government forces implemented a scorched earth policy in Scotland.[80] John Roy Stewart, who had fought in the front line at Culloden, escaped and hid in a Highland cave, where he composed poems of lamentation. In his Gaelic poem, "Culloden Day," he worried about the skulking Charles Edward: "Woe is me for handsome fair Charlie/At the mercy of George and his beasts," and he prayed, "O God, if thou'rt willing/ Give the kingdom back into your hands,/ Restore to us our rightful ruler/ To reign o'er us while we're alive."[81] In "Another Song on Culloden Day," he scorned the clans that had not risen, and he hinted at the suspected treachery of Lord George Murray, "Who played the turncoat/ for the heavier purse."[82] He prophesied infertility and barrenness to Butcher Cumberland, and by second-sight he predicted that "we'll yet see thy head/ Straightaway gibbeted,/ While the birds of the air flock to rend it."

In "John Roy's Prayer," he called up charms and incantations to heal his wounded ankles and then compared the Jacobite rebels to the Jews who followed Moses across the Red Sea, successfully escaping the evil Pharaoh.[83] He composed in English "John Roy's Psalm," which is still sung in Scotland and Ireland. A paraphrase of the 27th Psalm, he proclaimed:

> The Lord's my targe, I will be stout,
> With dirk and trusty blade,
> Though Campbells come in flocks about,
> I will not be afraid.
> The Lord's the same as heretofore,
> He's always good to me,

[77] Richmond, *Correspondence*, 224-25.

[78] NA: SP 95/98, f. 176.

[79] For this complicated affair, see M. Schuchard, *Emanuel Swedenborg*, 411-15.

[80] Doron Zimmerman, *The Jacobite Movement in Scotland and in Exile, 1746-1766* (London, 2003) 26-27.

[81] John Lorne Campbell, *Highland Songs of the Forty-Five* (1933; Edinburgh, 1984), 169-75.

[82] *Ibid.*, 181, 183.

[83] *Ibid.*, 187, 191.

Though red-coats come a thousand more,
Afraid I will not be.

....

Though hundreds guard each road and pass,
John Roy will not be found.[84]

Cumberland also determined to punish General Oglethorpe, who in December 1745 had incompetently or deliberately let the retreating Jacobite army get away. In March 1746 he stripped Oglethorpe of his command and in August ordered his court martial. Though Oglethorpe was acquitted in October, much to the dismay of Cumberland, his military reputation was ruined, for many believed with Lord Hardwicke that he was a private Jacobite.[85] Nevertheless, he was re-elected M.P. for Haslemere, maintaining the district's Tory affiliation. Many of his Masonic brothers in Georgia, England, Scotland, and France remained loyal to him, and he would eventually resume a secret but significant Jacobite role.[86]

Oglethorpe must have followed with interest the fate of Bonnie Prince Charlie, whom he had allowed to escape from Cumberland's troops. After the defeat at Culloden, the prince "skulked" in the Highlands and islands, evading arrest by government forces, until the bold Flora Macdonald dressed him in woman's clothes and helped arrange his flight to France in September. He was joined by John Roy Stewart, whom indeed the redcoats could not find.

---

[84] Donald Shore, *Highland Legends and Fugitive Pieces of Original Poetry* (Edinburgh, 1859), 166-67.

[85] A. Ettinger, *Oglethorpe*, 266-69.

[86] E. Cruickshanks, *Oglethorpes*, 6.

CHAPTER TWENTY-TWO

RIVAL GRAND MASTERS, BEHEADINGS AND BOASTINGS
(1746-1748)

Recall your Scotch heroes, starve the whole country indiscriminately by your ships, put a price upon the heads of all the chiefs, and let the Duke put all to fire and sword.

Lord Chesterfield to Duke of Newcastle (Dublin, March 1746).

I have divided the mysterious Doctrines of Jacobitism into Esoteric and Exoteric ...In this Instance we rather resemble the Free-Masons... I have often amused myself with comparing the People called Jacobites with the People called Jews ...in the Humour of Circumcision... The Original of the Practice was set on Foot, as I am told, soon after the Battle of Culloden... there is not a Jacobite now in England who is uncircumcised..

John Trott-Plaid [Henry Fielding], *The Jacobite's Journal*
(December 1747 and May 1748).

While Charles Edward managed to escape to France, many captured rebels were taken to London to await trial. Of the six Jacobite Grand Masters, Wemyss had worked behind the scenes and avoided prosecution despite his family's support of the prince. His estranged wife had given a ball for Charles Edward in Edinburgh, where she danced with the prince.[1] His younger son Francis Charteris did not publicly join the rebellion, but he privately provided funds for the prince. He would later serve as Grand Master of Scotland in 1747-48 and secretly participate in the international network of Jacobite Masons who organized the Elibank Plot.[2] His oldest son Lord Elcho, member of the prince's life guard, escaped to France, where the family continued to send him funds over the next years.[3] Kilmarnock, Cromarty, and Balmerino joined Maclean

---

[1] Elcho, *Short Account*, 82.
[2] Andrew Lang, *Pickle the Spy, or the Incognito of Prince Charles*, 3rd ed. (London, 1897), 177-78.
[3] Elcho, *Short Account*, 109. In late 1746 Elcho's attempt to gain a pardon and his published complaints about the conduct of the Scottish campaign earned the contempt of Charles Edward, who refused to meet

and Derwentwater as prisoners in London. Though Maclean's early arrest made him unable to join the rebellion, he was proud of his clansmen for fighting "like Spartans" at Culloden, where they displayed "desperate courage," until only fifty out of two hundred survived.[4]

In the same letter (4 June) in which Richmond scorned the Hessian prince, he also called for the prompt prosecution of the Jacobite peers, whom he knew were prominent Freemasons. Expressing his usual hatred of Scotland, he wrote Newcastle that nothing butt force will keep that stinking corner of the kingdom quiet:

> since I am upon that Toppick I wonder to hear nothing of the Tryals of those Peers or any of the rebels. I hope that untimely compassionate argument of their having still some of our people prisoners does not prevail, for if it did all these villains would escape unpunish'd which I am sure every honest English subject would have butt too much reason to cry out loudely upon.[5]

Cumberland agreed, and he wrote Newcastle that "Mild measures will not do."[6] When leaving the North in July, he observed bitterly, "all the good we have done is but a little blood-letting, which has only weakened the madness but not at all cured it, and I tremble that this vile spot may still be the ruin of this island, and of our family." In August the prisoners taken at Carlisle circulated papers before their execution in which they wrote that "they forgave all men but three, the Elector of Hanover, the *pretended* Duke of Cumberland, and the Duke of Richmond" (the latter signed the capitulation at Carlisle).[7]

Tales of Cumberland's cruelty circulated in London, where popular sympathy was aroused for the imprisoned rebels. Even Horace Walpole was dismayed by the duke's merciless policy, and he wrote Mann on 1 August:

> Great intercession is made for the Earls [Kilmarnock and Cromarty]; Duke Hamilton, who has never been at court, designs to kiss the King's hand and ask Lord Kilmarnock's life. The King is much inclined to some mercy; but the Duke, who has not so much of Caesar after a victory, as in gaining it, is for the utmost severity. It was lately proposed in the City, to present him with the freedom of some company; one of the aldermen said aloud, "Then let it be of the *Butchers*!"[8]

Caesar had written "That the chief enjoyment he had of his victory was, in saving every day one or other of his fellow-citizens who had borne arms against him."

Despite the sobriquet of "Butcher" now applied to Cumberland, he was eulogized as a national hero by Chesterfield, other Whigs, and Grand Lodge Masons. Thus, there was little chance for mercy for the Jacobite nobles, whose "irregular" form of Freemasonry made them even more despised by their Hanoverian brothers. During his trial in London,

---

with him. Elcho spent the next decade pressuring the prince and James III into repaying the money he and his brother contributed to the campaign.

[4] A. Lang, *History*, IV, 368, 512.

[5] Richmond, *Correspondence*, 224.

[6] A. Lang, *History*, IV, 519.

[7] H. Walpole, *Correspondence*, XIX, 296.

[8] *Ibid.*, XIX, 287-88.

Kilmarnock, who had served as Scottish Grand Master in 1743, while he or one of his sons initiated *Écossais* Masons in Paris, retracted his loyalty to the Stuarts. He pleaded bad judgment in being persuaded to join the rebellion after the battle of Preston-pans/Gladsmuir. Stressing that his oldest son, James, Lord Boyd, served as a loyalist officer in a government troop, he asserted that "he brought him up in the true principles of the revolution and an abhorrence of Popery and arbitrary power."[9] He did not mention that his second son, Charles Boyd, fought on the Jacobite side and after Culloden fled to France.[10]

From the Tower, Kilmarnock wrote to Lord Boyd, advising him to "continue in your loyalty to his present Majesty, and the succession as by law established."[11] Never let your regard for your family "drive you on the rock I split upon, when on that account I departed from my principles and brought the guilt of rebellion…on my head." He then urged him to "use all your interest to get your Brother pardoned and brought home as soon as possible, that his circumstances, and the bad influence of those he is among, may not induce him to accept of foreign Service and lose him both to his Country and Family." The effort to recall Charles Boyd to Hanoverian loyalty was unsuccessful, for he remained in France and continued to support Jacobite invasion plans into the 1750s.[12] Lord Boyd and two younger brothers would join the Stirling lodge in 1749, and Boyd would serve as Grand Master of Scotland in 1751-52. As we shall see, they may have been among "the Whiggers" who covertly supported the Elibank Plot.[13]

Kilmarnock's critics claimed that it was pressure from his Jacobite wife and an aunt, who threatened to disinherit him, that prompted his reluctant support of Prince Charles. He told his former Whig colleague, the 3rd Duke of Argyll, that he cared not a farthing which king prevailed: "but I was starving, and, by God, if Mahommed had set up his standard in the Highlands, I had been a good Mussulman for bread, and stuck close to the party, for I must eat."[14] This cynical comment makes the overly-pious account of Kilmarnock's last days by the Presbyterian minister James Foster seem more self-serving than accurate.

Kilmarnock pleaded guilty and appealed to George II, Cumberland, and the Prince of Wales for mercy, especially given the misery of his wife and many children. According to Reverend Foster, he claimed that his wife, "tho' bred in different sentiments," was "now more inclined to Whiggish than Jacobite principles."[15] Reports circulated that her maid had revealed to Lady Kilmarnock a horrifying vision by second sight, in which Kilmarnock's bloody head rolled towards her. Despite the emotional pleading of the countess, who threw herself at the king's feet and then fell unconscious, the earl was condemned for high treason. Horace Walpole reported that Cumberland "interposed for Ld Kilmarnock's execution," while the Prince of Wales advocated mercy for the rebel lords.[16] At the trial, Walpole noted that Kilmarnock looked younger than his forty-one years, "tall

---

[9] *Scots Magazine*, 8 (August-September 1746), 376-84, 420-27.

[10] H. Walpole, *Correspondence*, XIX, 285 n.41.

[11] James Allardyce, ed., *Historical Papers Relating to the Jacobite Period, 1699-1750* (Aberdeen, 1895), 326.

[12] D. Zimmerman, *Jacobite Movement*, 131-32.

[13] See ahead, the Epilogue.

[14] Murray Pittock, "William Boyd, 4th Earl of Kilmarnock," *ODNB*.

[15] *Scots Magazine*, 8, p. 384.

[16] H. Walpole, *Corrspondence*, XIX, 300.

and slender, with an extreme fine person," and that he behaved with a "most just mixture between dignity and submission."[17]

Despite his guilty plea, the earl would not accept the charge that the Young Pretender would have imposed popery, arbitrary government, and slavery on the British people. While Foster pressured him to condemn the prince's autocratic papism, Kilmarnock insisted that in all his conversations with Charles Edward, he never sensed anything but a practical desire to uphold the laws and constitution of England.[18] He vehemently denied that he had received or given orders to treat prisoners or the wounded with inhumanity, a canard that was spread by Cumberland to counter his own growing reputation as the "Butcher of Culloden." Though many prominent men petitioned for a reprieve, the high rank of Kilmarnock, his position as a lowland Scot, and his political apostasy meant there would be no mercy.

Also tried with Kilmarnock was George Mackenzie, 3rd Earl of Cromarty, Scottish Grand Master in 1737-38, who similarly pleaded guilty: "I was unhappily seduced from that loyalty [to George II], in an unguarded moment, by the arts of desperate and designing men," but no sooner did I awake from that delusion, "than I felt a remorse for my departure from my duty; but it was then too late."[19] This was disingenuous, for Cromarty had engaged to support Charles Edward in 1740. Cumberland was determined to destroy him, because of his role in pursuing General Loudoun after the humiliating "Route of Moy." But the pregnant Lady Cromarty's passionate appeals to the Prince and Princess of Wales won a reprieve for her husband, who was kept in prison for two years and then ordered to never leave the south of England. His son, the eighteen year-old John Mackenzie, Lord McLeod, who also fought against Loudoun, pleaded his youth and duty to his father, and he too was imprisoned for two years. After his release, McLeod traveled to Berlin, where Field Marshall James Keith wrote Chancellor Tessin, to recommend him to Swedish military service. McLeod then provided a valuable liaison between Jacobite-Prussian-Swedish military planning, while rising to a prominent position within Swedish Masonry.[20]

The third prisoner was Arthur Elphinstone, who inherited the title of 6th Lord Balmerino on 5 January 1746. After his arrest in 1716, he escaped to France, where he became close to Mar, who expressed his full trust in him.[21] He resided in France until 1734, when his dying father gained a pardon for him, without his own knowledge.[22] After receiving permission and financial support from James III, he returned to Scotland, where he maintained a low profile and periodically visited France. André Kervella affirms that Balmerino was "a Freemason of high rank," and some French historians claim that he served as a Grand Master and initiated Masons at Avignon in 1736.[23] As noted earlier, the term Grand Master was still sometimes used in France and Britain to address the Master of a lodge, a usage that probably pre-dates the Grand Lodge of England.[24]

---

[17] *Ibid.*, XIX, 281.

[18] *Ibid.*, XIX, 382.

[19] *Ibid.*, XIX, 377.

[20] M. Schuchard, *Emanuel Swedenborg*, 464.

[21] *HMC. Stuart Papers*, V, 366.

[22] "Arthur Elphinstone, 6th Lord Balmerino," *ODNB*.

[23] A. Kervella, *La Mystère*, 43; Joanny Bricaud, *Les Illuminés d'Avignon* (Paris, 1927); P. Chevallier, *Les Ducs*, 66.

[24] R. Péter, *British Freemasonry*, IV, 397n.7.

A Prussian Mason, Heinrich von Biberstein, recorded that he met Balmerino and Kilmarnock at St. Germain in 1738 and learned from them about a kind of Masonry quite different from what he had experienced in England.[25] In 1745 Kilmarnock's son Charles Boyd served in Balmerino's regiment in Scotland. After Culloden, Balmerino helped Prince Charles escape and then told his Masonic brother Elcho that if the prince's troops did not reassemble he would give himself up. He knew that he would lose his head, but he was too old to hide out, and he "could meet death with firmness," which "would gain reputation thereby."[26] In prison he calmly requested that his friends drink him "ain degrae ta haiven," which a later Masonic commentator interpreted as a reference to taking his "last degree" as a Master Mason.[27]

Unlike Kilmarnock and Cromarty, Balmerino did not plead guilty and defiantly defended his role in the rebellion as a just and honorable cause. He was so disturbed by the allegation that Kilmarnock and Prince Charles had ordered "no quarter" be given to government troops that he interrogated Kilmarnock and continued to reject the charge as "an invention" by the government "to justify their own murder, or murderous scheme."[28] He was probably correct, for no copy of the letter which supposedly contained the order has been found, and William Lowe notes that "doubts exist about the authenticity of the order that came into Cumberland's hands."[29]

Lieutenant-General Adam Williamson, keeper of the Tower, was infuriated at Balmerino's bold behavior, especially when he insisted on addressing the populace from his window, which Williamson then ordered to be boarded up.[30] He brought the warrant for execution to Balmerino while he was dining with his wife, who fainted at the news, leading the defiant Scot to remark, "Lieutenant, with your damned warrant you have spoiled my lady's stomach." On 12 August Williamson argued that Balmerino should not have the spiritual counsel of "one Gordon, a young fellow and a non-juring priest," who comes daily to "confirm him in his rebellious principles." Moreover, he should certainly not be allowed to console him on the scaffold

Balmerino's swaggering behavior and flow of witticisms greatly impressed Horace Walpole, who reported that

> Old Balmerino keeps up his spirits to the same pitch of gaiety. In the cell at Westminster he showed Lord Kilmarnock how he must lay his head – bid him not wince lest the stroke should cut his skull or his shoulders, and advised him to bite his lips. As they were to return he begged they might have another bottle together as they should never meet any more till – and then pointed to his neck. At getting into the coach he said to the gaoler: "Take care or you will break my shins with this damned axe."[31]

---

[25] Christian von Nettelbladt, *Geschichte Freimaurerischer Systeme in England, Frankreich und Deutschland* ((Berlin, 1878), 236; quoted in A. Kervella, *Chevalier Ramsay*, 275.

[26] H. Tayler, *Jacobite Miscellany*, 163.

[27] W.P.B., "Lord Balmerino's Last Degree," *Freemasons' Magazine and Masonic Mirror* (14 May 1870), 387.

[28] *Scots Magazine*, 8 (1746), 422.

[29] William Lowe, "Kilmarnock," *ODNB*.

[30] Adam Williamson, *The Official Diary of Lieutenant-General Adam Williamson, Deputy-Lieutenant of the Tower of London, 1722-1747*, ed. J.C. Fox (London, 1912), , 36, 216.

[31] *Ibid.*, 127n.2.

He informed Mann that Balmerino "was the most natural brave old fellow he had ever seen," who "behaved himself like a soldier and a man." After describing Kilmarnock's genteel behavior on the scaffold, he wrote:

> Then came old Balmerino, treading with the air of a general. As soon as he mounted the scaffold, he... surveyed the spectators, who were in amazing numbers, even upon masts of ships in the river; and pulling on his spectacles read a treasonable speech...and said, the young Pretender was so sweet a prince, that flesh and blood could not resist following him; and lying down to try the block, he said, "If I had a thousand lives, I would lay them all down in the same cause."[32]

Balmerino's "treasonable speech" was such an eloquent defense of the Stuart cause that T. Ford, who published an account of the execution, was afraid to print his words: "Whatever may be offered in excuse for his Lordship's making that speech in his last moments, nothing but the highest authority can justify the publishing it."[33] Nevertheless, manuscript copies circulated widely, and it was eventually published in full in 1750, when it confirmed the position of Balmerino as the ultimate Jacobite hero. In contrast to Kilmarnock's pleading his early loyalty to the Williamite revolution, Balmerino affirmed, "I was brought up in True, Loyal, ANTI-REVOLUTION Principles; and I hope the World is convinc'd that they stick to me."[34] He apologized for his youthful mistake in accepting a military commission under Princess Anne, "who I knew had no more Right to the Crown than her Predecessor the Prince of Orange, whom I always looked upon as a vile, unnatural Usurper." To make amends, he left his government troop in 1715 and joined James III when he was in Scotland; after his arrest he escaped to France and lived abroad until 1734.

Skipping over the next eleven years, when little is known about his activities, he described his immediate enthusiasm for Charles Edward Stuart:

> When his Royal Highness came to Edinburgh, as it was my bounden and indispensible Duty, I join'd him, tho' I might easily have excused myself from taking Arms on Account of my Age; but I never could have had Peace of Conscience, if I had stayed at Home when that Brave Prince was exposing himself to all Manner of Dangers and Fatigues, both Night and Day... the incomparable Sweetness of his Nature, His Affability, His Compassion, His Justice, His Temperance, His Patience, and His Courage, are Virtues, seldom All to be found in One Person. In short, He wants no Qualifications to make him a Great Man.[35]

He passionately defended the prince from Cumberland's accusation that he issued an order to give no quarter before the battle of Culloden, "for his Royal Highness abhorred all those who were capable of doing Injustice to any of the King his Father's Subjects, whatever Opinion they were of." He was convinced that "it is a malicious Report industriously spread to excuse themselves from the Murders they were guilty of in calm Blood

---

[32] H. Walpole, *Correspondence*, XIX, 301.
[33] *Scots Magazine*, 8 (September 1746), 425.
[34] *True Copies of the Dying Declarations of Arthur Lord Balmerino* (Edinburgh, 1750), 3.
[35] *Ibid.*, 4.

after the Battle." While forgiving others for his imprisonment, he scorned Williamson, who treated him barbarously in the Tower, "but not quite so ill as he did the Bishop of Rochester." He declared himself a member of the Church of England, "as in Union with the Episcopal Church of Scotland," and prayed for the Stuart royal family and "all the faithful Adherents of the Cause for which I am about to suffer." He then removed his wig to reveal a plaid cap and blindfold, which expressed his loyalty to Scotland. Laying his head on the block, he proclaimed, "God preserve my Friends, forgive my Enemies, Restore the King, and have Mercy upon my soul."[36]

Walpole conceded that the rough-hewn Balmerino "certainly died with the intrepidity of a hero," which evoked a universal admiration: The "gallant Arthur" was said to "go to Death as others go to Sleep."[37] In Scotland a song soon circulated in praise of his final heroics:

> Brave Balmerrony…in the midst of his foes
> Claps Tartan on his eyes…
> A Scots Man now I die…
> May all the Scots my footsteps trace. [38]

Among the more militant Hanoverians, Kilmarnock's submission was praised, while Balmerino's defiance was condemned. On 18 August Colonel Borland wrote Albemarle that today Kilmarnock and Balmerino were beheaded: "'tis said the former dyed very decently, and the latter as indecently."[39]

The most important Jacobite Grand Master, Derwentwater, had been in the Tower since November 1745. On 24 February 1746 his son James Bartholomew Radcliffe wrote from the Tower to Newcastle to petition for his own release as a French citizen: "he should be put upon the same footing as other officers born abroad and exchanged upon the new cartel."[40] After he was released on parole, Horace Walpole wrote indignantly to Mann on 15 April that "Mr Ratcliffe, who had been so long confined in the Tower, and supposed [to be] the Pretender's younger son, is not only suffered to return to France, but was entertained at a great dinner by the Duke of Richmond, as a relation."[41] In September Richmond received a letter from "my cousin the Countess of Newburgh, who is Ratcliffe's wife," seeking a reprieve for her servant named Vaugler, who was taken prisoner with her husband.[42] He sent her letter on to Newcastle. Richmond's display of polite acquiescence to Derwentwater's son and wife appeared to Horace Walpole as a rather vulgar remnant of snobbish "pride and Stuartism." But the duke's sympathy did not extend to the attainted earl.

The French government and many English supporters kept up the pressure on the government to reprieve Derwentwater, who had been captured before he could join the rebels in Scotland and therefore was not taken in arms. In September the French foreign minister Argenson made a bold move and arrested Lord Morton, former Grand Master

---

[36] *Ibid.*, 6.
[37] "Arthur Elphinstone, 6th Lord Balmerino," ODNB.
[38] *Ibid.*
[39] Albemarle, *Albemarle Papers*, I, 127.
[40] H. Tayler, *Jacobite Epilogue*, 159-60.
[41] H. Walpole, *Correspondence*, XIX, 241.
[42] Richmond, *Correspondence*, 233.

in Scotland and England, on the grounds of his expired passport. He and his family had been in France for some months, and they were now confined in the Bastille. Argenson hoped by this maneuver to arrange the prisoner exchange of Morton for Derwentwater. According to *The General Advertiser* (1 November 1746),

> it was reported that a private Alphabet and Cypher were found among Lord Morton's Papers, which have discovered the Part he had in the Descent upon Britany, and that which was to have been made upon the Coasts of Poitu and Aunis, where, we are told, he had concealed Arms for 4000 English Prisoners of War, who are now at Angiers, and the neighboring Places, which they were to burn, and then to join the landed Troops.

In the same month, the *Scots Magazine* reported:

> We are told, that there are upwards of forty British subjects of distinction now in the Bastile. The Lord of Moreton is still detained there; and it is wrote from thence, that it has been discovered, or at least suspected, that his Lordship has received very considerable sums from England, to distribute among the disaffected in that kingdom… The Earl's papers have been put into the hands of a learned Englishman, to be strictly examined.[43]

Hanoverian critics of Morton suspected that he was a crypto-Jacobite who collaborated in Argenson's plan, and rumors circulated that his papers revealed his Jacobite rather than Hanoverian collaboration. As Derwentwater languished in his Tower cell, the Jacobites hoped that Morton's confinement in a Bastille cell would alleviate the attainted earl's situation.

On 24 November 1746 Derwentwater was tried, but he defiantly refused to acknowledge any jurisdiction but that of the King of France, "in whose dominions he had lived about thirty years, and whose commission he had in his pocket."[44] On hearing his former indictment from the treason charge of 1716, he "said he was not Charles Ratcliffe, but the Earl of Derwentwater," in the vain hope that his long absence from England would mean that no one could positively identify him. After the government presented two ineffective witnesses against him, they called a third man, who had befriended him over a bottle of wine in the Tower and who claimed that Derwentwater confessed to being the same man. But the earl objected that the accuser had also confessed that he believed that there was neither God nor Devil, "and it would be an absurdity to swear a man upon the Bible, who had no belief in anything it contained." Despite the many petitions for mercy, George II and Cumberland were determined that he would follow his brother as a recipient of Hanoverian justice.

On hearing that his execution was scheduled for 8 December, Derwentwater told the court, "that he wished they had given him so long time as that he could have wrote to France, that so his brother the Earl of Moreton and he might have set out on their journey together." By calling Morton his brother, he seemed to refer to their Masonic bonds. On 5 December Horace Walpole reported to Mann that "Jacobitism seems to have gasped its last," and "Mr Ratcliffe, the last Derwentwater's brother, is actually named to

---

[43] *Scots Magazine*, 8 (November 1746), 540-41.
[44] W. Fraser, *Earls of Cromartie.*, 530-31.

the gallows for Monday, but the imprudence of Lord Morton, who has drawn himself into the Bastille, makes it doubtful whether the execution will be so quick." [45] Mann replied, "I think that I should vote for the execution of Ratcliff's sentence, let the consequence be what it will for Lord Moreton, whose imprudence seems inexcusable, but perhaps I am not acquainted with the whole affair." [46] On 6 December Morton was removed from the Bastille to his Parisian residence, where he remained a prisoner on parole. Charles Edward was furious that the release destroyed his hope of saving Derwentwater, whom he revered.

On 16 December Richmond wrote Newcastle to praise the execution of the attainted earl, adding that Scotland is still "a nest of rogues" and needs harsh treatment:

> The execution of Ratcliffe I am sure must be approved of by every friend to this government. I wish the Att Genll had not forgot him & that it had been done immediately upon the receipt of Van Hoey's letter, however better late than never. I hear old Pitt and the master [Prince of Wales] are in mourning for him, surely that's ridiculous. I fancy my relations would not mourn for me if I was to be hanged which I am vain enough to thinke I certainly should be if the Pretender came in. [47]

In June Van Hoey, the Dutch minister at Paris, had joined Argenson in urging the British government to show clemency to the rebels, which infuriated Richmond. Richmond's harsh attitude made the former Hanoverian Grand Master an object of detestation to the Jacobites. On 24 December an intercepted Jacobite poem was sent to Newcastle that vowed "Behold this blood that Cries This Day on Tower Hill/ For Vengeance it doth Cry the Lord on high." [48] André Kervella argues that this theme of vengeance was subsequently expressed in new "Kadosh" degrees in some *Écossais* lodges. [49]

The execution of three former Jacobite Grand Masters in this tragic drama points to the continuing rivalries and complexities within international Freemasonry. The Swedish ambassador in London, Caspar Ringwicht, sent encrypted, detailed notes on the trials to the Masonic leaders Tessin and Scheffer, and followed them with miniature portraits of Derwentwater, Kilmarnock, Cromarty, and the other executed "martyrs." [50] In December 1746 in Stockholm, the British ambassador Guy Dickens, a Hanoverian Mason, protested to the Swedish king about the Hats' attempt to send troops to Scotland, "during the heat of the rebellion there"; even worse, were the ministry's actions against England, "a free and Protestant Nation, in concurring in Measures, the success of which would have been the introducing of Popery and Slavery into another free and Protestant Nation, and sooner or later the ruin of Sweden." [51] He urged George II to send troops into Finland to terrorize the Swedes and, if that didn't work, to implement even harsher reprisals against Sweden, because "there is nothing but Force that can bring the French Slaves to

---

[45] H. Walpole, *Correspondence*, XIX, 341.

[46] *Ibid.*, XIX, 353.

[47] Richmond, *Correspondence*, 237.

[48] D. Zimmerman, *Jacobite Movement*, 49, 197n.2.

[49] A. Kervella, *La Mystère*, 352-55.

[50] Stockholm, Riksarkivet: Anglica, #333 (Februrary-December 1746).

[51] NA: SP 95/100, ff. 23, 28, 72.

reason." But the Masonic Hats continued to support new restoration plans, for they admired "Scottish Charles" as the courageous successor to "Swedish Charles."

Though Russian politics had kept General James Keith from implementing his secret plan to bring Swedish and Russian troops to support the rebels in Scotland in 1744-45, he continued to call on his cousin Kintore to help him in his political (and Masonic?) plans. On 27 October 1746 Kintore replied to Keith's letter of 14 July, sent from Riga, in which he reported his intention to return to Scotland and run for a parliamentary seat. Kintore was relieved to receive Keith's letter, because

> the confusions in the country occasioned by the late rebellion had for so long a time interrupted our correspondence. And although peace is now in some manner restored I'm much afraid the unhappy consequences will not be soone att ane end. The part which I myelfe acted seem'd to me most prudent and reasonable, and I'm mighty glad it meetis with your approbation.[52]

Though the Keith clan had supported the rebels, Kintore apparently laid low, and he now warned the general that his estate had been sequestrated for debt, and he only survived by "bounty of the Crown." Thus, "if I should acte aney part that might give offence to the administration it would ruin me, which I dare say you are too much my friend to advise."

Kintore explained that the parliamentary seat for which James Keith aimed "depends on E. Findlater who always goes alongst with the Court, and gives his interest to the person recommended by the ministry." As noted earlier, the 5th Earl of Findlater, was a loyal Whig and a Walpolean representative peer of Scotland. He had welcomed Cumberland on 11 April 1746 and contributed money to his troops.[53] Kintore regretted his inability to provide more support to his cousin, and he hoped that their letters would not be intercepted. Despite his caution, the former Scottish and English Grand Master was distrusted by Albemarle, who on 2 January 1747 reported from Edinburgh to Newcastle that "Ld Kintore" and his political colleagues are "in their hearts Jacobites," for "craft and cunning they all abound with."[54] Over the next years, Kintore's Jacobite kinsmen and Masonic brothers would expect James Keith to lead renewed assaults on the Hanoverian regime.[55] General Oglethorpe, who was accused of treason by Cumberland, acquired multiple accounts of the trials and "martyrdoms" of his fellow Masons Kilmarnock, Balmerino, and Derwentwater.[56] He stayed in touch with James Keith and later joined him in Prussian military service, where the severely wounded Scot died in his arms.

In England government concerns about the dissident Masons intensified, while Richmond believed that the royal "brother," Prince Frederick, continued to harbor Jacobite sympathies. He advised Newcastle to "fear neither the Prince of Wales, nor the Pretender; tho' the first I thinke is doing all he can for the last."[57] For Richmond, the prince's

---

[52] *HMC. Ninth Report of the Royal Commision on Historical Manuscripts. Part I. Report and Appendix* (London, 1883), Appendix, 228b-29b. Elphinstone Papers.

[53] W. Cramond, *Plundering of Cullen House.*

[54] Albemarle, *Albemarle Papers*, 357-58.

[55] D. Zimmerman, *Jacobite Movement*, 43, 57, 83, 91-92, 101.

[56] Oglethorpe Library Catalogue, #1704

[57] Richmond, *Correspondence*, 212.

re-organization of the opposition was tantamount to treason, and his attitude extended to all the Masons who supported Frederick. Charles Calvert, 5th Baron Baltimore, became leader of the prince's party, which especially annoyed Richmond, who had initiated him at an unusual outdoor lodge meeting on top of a hill in 1730.[58] Baltimore then had the gall to assist in the initiation of Prince Frederick in 1737. Horace Walpole acknowledged that Baltimore was "the best and honestest man in in the world, with a good deal of jumbled knowledge; but not capable of conducting a party."[59]

Richmond also remained suspicious of Lord Morton, who stayed on in France for five months after his release from the Bastille. Morton later told John Byrom, his Jacobite Masonic friend, that the papers with an alphabet and cipher found by the Parisian police were the shorthand lesson that Byrom had given him.[60] Lady Morton added that rumors about the death of Charles Edward were false, for she has "seen both him and his brother at Paris since that affair; the elder brother has a much better character abroad than the younger." While Morton continued to play a publicly loyal role, his dealings with French and Swedish scientists over the next decades would keep the shadow of Jacobitism hovering over him.[61]

Throughout the Jacobite uprising, Orrery spent much time with Dr. King, but none of their correspondence survives from those months, so it is unknown what they were actually doing. Orrery's name was given to the government for suspected complicity in the rebellion, but they did not move against him, almost certainly because of Chesterfield's protection of his old friend. On 7 July 1746 Lady Orrery wrote from Ireland that she feared the Jacobite trials would detain her husband in London, and she wanted assurance in his hand that "Lord Chesterfield has obtained leave for your absence."[62] Chesterfield did not want the government to interrogate Orrery, who had been privy to the lord-lieutenant's earlier negotiations with Ormonde and the Jacobites. After safely returning to Ireland, Orrery later wrote Thomas Birch that "Lord Chesterfield's influence, like the departing sun, has left a warm and serene sky behind it."[63]

Orrery had also collaborated with Watkin Williams Wynn, who was prepared to militarily support Charles Edward but was thwarted by the unexpected retreat from Derby. In her 7 July letter Lady Orrery indiscretely wrote that she assumed that Orrery

> will see our worthy friend Sir Watkin Williams' three fine Seats, and also many an Honest uncorrupted Welsh heart, the honest blood which streams thro'both our veins, I imagine, derived from our noble Welsh Ancestors, and still imagine that I trace the noble spirit of these Antient Britons…in my Laelius. They contemned wealth on dishonourable terms, servitude to the Saxons, and retired with their Liberty and their Poverty to…the wilds of Wales; my Laelius rejects Court bribes and Court offers, and retires to poor tho' peacefull shades.

---

[58] *Leeds Mercury* (7-14 April 1730).
[59] H. Walpole, *Correspondence, XIX, 360.*
[60] J. Byrom, *Remains,* II, part 2, 434.
[61] M. Schuchard, *Emanuel Swedenborg,* 585-86, 615-18.
[62] Orrery, *Orrery Papers,* I, 235.
[63] *Ibid.,* I, 320.

While the Jacobites, French, and Swedes continued to plan for another campaign, loyalist writers in England boasted of what they hoped was the final victory over the rebels. Conflicting interpretations of the events soon issued from rival Masonic writers. In October 1746 the *Gentleman's Magazine* featured "A Song to the Tune of the Freemasons," which praised George II and Cumberland for defeating the "popish pretender" and breaking "the vile shackle of Gallic Invention."[64] In November Colley Cibber, the Whig Mason and poet laureate, published his "Ode for his Majesty's Birthday," in which he boasted "Tis done! The turmoil's past,/ The Northern storm is over!"/ Rebellion now has breath'd her last,/ And hostile sounds are heard no more."[65] He then launched into praise of Cumberland:

> `Tis he! `tis he! the pride of fame,
> William return'd the shouts proclaim!
> William, with Northern laurels crown'd!
> William the hills and vales resound!
> What numbers fled, what numbers fell,
> Culloden's glorious field shall tell!
> Culloden's field the muse shall fire
> And sing the Son, and charm the sire.

Moses Mendes responded with a satirical epigram against "Old Colley," as he and his Jacobite Masonic friends expressed their disgust at Cumberland's brutality towards the defeated rebels at Culloden.[66]

One non-Jacobite Mason, the young Scottish writer Tobias Smollett, was in London when news arrived of the victory at Culloden.[67] His fellow Scot, Alexander Carlyle, recorded that so riotous was the mob celebrating the Hanoverian victory that they walked home with drawn swords. Smollett counseled silence, "lest the mob should discover my country and become insolent. For John Bull…is as haughty and violent tonight, as a few months ago he was abject and cowardly, on the Black Wednesday when the Highlanders were at Derby."[68] Carlyle wrote that Smollett was not a Jacobite, "but he had the feelings of a Scotch gentleman on the reported cruelties that were said to be exercized after the Battle of Culloden." Smollett was moved to write "The Tears of Scotland," and when advised to suppress it, he defiantly added a seventh stanza "exuding spirited independence and concern for his native land." Published anonymously in Edinburgh, the poem was "well-received" in England as well as Scotland, especially when set to music:

> Mourn, hapless Caledonia mourn
> Thy banished Peace, thy Laurel torn!
> Thy Sons, for Valour long renown'd,
> Lay slaughter'd on their native Ground!
> Thy hospitable Roofs no more

---

[64] *Gentleman's Magazine*, 16 (October 1746), 552.
[65] *Scots Magazine*, 8 (November 1746), 521.
[66] UGLE: MS. 1860. Men.
[67] For Smollett's Masonic affiliation and friendship with French *frères*,, see Richard Jones, *Tobias Smollett in the Enlightenment* (Lanham, 2011), 9-10, 98.
[68] "Tobias Smollett," *ODNB*.

> Invite the Stranger to the Door;
> In smoky Ruins sunk they ly,
> The Monuments of Cruelty!
> ....
> What foreign Arms could never quell,
> By civil Rage and Rancour fell!
> ....
> The Sons against their Fathers stood!
> The Parent shed his Children's blood!
> Yet, when the Rage of Battle ceas'd,
> The Victor's Soul was not appeas'd;
> The Naked and Forlorn must feel
> Devouring Flames and murd'ring Steel![69]

In his defiant seventh stanza, he vowed to never forget his country's fate: "In spite of her insulting Foe,/ My sympathizing Verse shall flow." A hand-written copy of "The Tears of Scotland," dated 1746, was preserved by the Masonic circle of Mendes, Dr. King, and Byrom.[70]

Smollett then anonymously published a satire on Cope, "a General famous for an expeditious retreat, tho' quite not so deliberate as that of the ten thousand Greeks from Persia; having unfortunately forgot to bring his army along with him."[71] He sarcastically lamented that the muse must sleep while "such bright names in constellation blaze," as Newcastle, Grafton, Granville, Bath, and other corrupt politicians. For years he nurtured resentment against the ministers and military perpetrators of the slaughter at Culloden, and his searing indictment of their inhumanity and indiscriminate killing would later be published in his *Complete History of England* (1757-58), a work that produced exaggerated charges that he was a secret Jacobite.[72]

As the policy of "fire and sword" continued in Scotland, the captured English rebels also suffered severely. John Byrom became the target of Hanoverian writers because of his expressions of outrage over the brutal treatment of the prisoners from the Manchester regiment. Nine of them were hung, drawn, and quartered on Kennington Common in London in July 1746. The *Gentleman's Magazine* reported that Colonel Francis Towneley, who had served in the French army under Berwick, was still alive after hanging for five minutes. The hangman then took a butcher's cleaver and severed the head, cut out the bowels and heart, and flung them into the fire.[73] The heads of Towneley and George Fletcher were then impaled on spikes at Temple Bar. Those of Thomas Siddall and Thomas Deacon were preserved in brine and sent to Manchester, where they were impaled and displayed at the city's exchange. Unlike Kilmarnock and Cromarty, the Manchester rebels did not plead guilty and boldly proclaimed the justice of their cause, in letters that were widely circulated.

As noted earlier, there was an overlapping membership of Non-jurors and Freemasons in Manchester, and Byrom was friendly with many of them. At considerable risk to

---

[69] Tobias Smollett, *The Tears of Scotland* [Edinburgh, 1746], 1-4.
[70] London, Grand Lodge: MS. 1860. Men.
[71] Tobias Smollett, *Advice, and Reproof. Two Satires, first published in 1746 and 1747* (London, 1748), 3-4.
[72] Tobias Smollett, *A Complete History of England* (London, 1757-58), IV, 673-77.
[73] *Gentleman's Magazine* (16 July 1746), 383.

himself and his family, he anonymously published a series of attacks upon the more merciless supporters of the policies of Cumberland and his Hanoverian partisans. In November 1746 he sent to the *Gentleman's Magazine* an extract from an article issued by Josiah Owen, a radical Presbyterian minister. In "A Letter from Manchester," Owen had charged that "Jacobite, non-juring, and even popish principles are now making a greater progress here than ever."[74] Even worse,

> The two rebel heads are revered and almost adored, as trophies of martyrdom. The father of one of them (who is a non-juring bishop) as he passes by`em, frequently pulls off his hat, and looks at them with a solemn complacential smile. Some suppose he offers up a prayer for them, others to them. His church daily increases, and he is in the highest credit.

Byrom, who was close to the father, the minister and physician Thomas Deacon, added his anonymous reply to the "Letter from Manchester," in which he defended the pious Deacon, criticized the oppressive military presence in Manchester, and scorned Owen as a credulous Don Quixote, who fantasizes about terrible giants who are only a "few innocent fulling-mills, chimeras of his disordered brain." Fulling mills were used to pleat or gather garments in order to make them fuller (a business in high demand as plaids and kilts became fashionable among the "infatuated" Jacobite sympathizers). Byrom was especially offended by Owen's mockery of "the tender relation subsisting betwixt father and son," for "what but the very dregs of party-spleen could prompt this man to find fault with doctor's behavior, on the first sight of the remains of his dead child?"

Owen, as "Philopatriae," responded in December 1746 with a furious attack upon Byrom and Deacon, charging that the latter had "absolv'd Justice Hall and Parson Paul at the gallows, after the rebellion of 1715" and "declared publicly to them at Tyburn, that the fact for which they dy'd was meritorious."[75] He mocked Byrom's attempt "to gloss over the worship of the *rebel skull divinities* fix'd up at the Exchange: What, asham'd of your *Tyburn* gods?... To offer up a prayer to rebel martyrs, to invoke their intercession and assistance, is *too absurd*. But are you aware, Sir, that this is an absurdity daily practis'd in the *Church of Rome*?" In January 1747 Byrom anonymously replied that Owen and his radical partisans "have always used the *cry of popishly affected*, to run down the steadiest friends of our ecclesiastical establishment."[76] Most shamefully, Owen heightened his attack with "a personal invective against Dr D[eacon], every article of which, except his having three sons in the rebellion, which I doubt not was the misfortune of many an honest *brother dissenter*, is false as the Dr himself will, at a proper time, make appear."[77] He then appended his poem, "Receipt for one that hath the spleen too big, Or sourish blood that turneth all to whig":

> Take a Nonjuror, put him in the news,
> Whate'er he does, or says, or thinks, abuse.
> Look, gesture, motion construe all to crime;
> Small reason serves, if you but nick the time.

---

[74] Josiah Owen, "Letter from Manchester," *Gentleman's Magazine* (16 November 1746), 579-80.
[75] *Ibid.*, 688-91.
[76] *Ibid.*, vol. 17 (January 1747), 76-77.
[77] *Ibid.*, vol. 18 (February 1748), 206-07.

> His very virtues, adding what suffices
> Of rancid spite, shall all appear as vices.
> Hint he's a priest, a Jesuit in disguise,
> Or any nonsense else, or any lies.

Byrom was further offended by a sermon, *The False Claims to Martyrdom Consider'd*, preached in Manchester by Benjamin Nichols, chaplain of the Whig Earl of Uxbridge, in which those who criticize the "most legal and merciful manner" of executions seek to "prejudice the Minds of the Credulous and undiscerning," by branding the government officials "with the opprobrious Names of Cruelty and Persecution." [78] Byrom fought back with his anonymous pamphlet, *An Epistle to a Friend* (1747), occasioned by Nichols' sermon. On the title-page was his poem, which seemed to express his own Masonic ecumenicism:

> Out of the Church, to fix our English Doom,
> There's no Salvation, say some Priests of Rome:
> Affirm, there's no Salvation to be had.
> The same poor Bigotry, on either Side,
> Would make Salvation float upon the Tide:
> Alike the Smithfield and the Tyburn Flame;
> For neither Pope nor Parliament can Damn.[79]

In his long versified response to Nichols, Byrom stressed that "Ev'n rigid Laws, when they condemn, condole,/ And pray to God for Mercy on the Soul." However, the lines that would get him in more trouble were, "Divine Sermon! little understood,/ If they who preach thee, not content with Blood,/ Justly perhaps, perhaps ********[unjustly] shed," followed by the preacher's "fear,/Lest Heav'n should err – and *Jacobites* be there."[80] Is a "preaching Protestant" obliged to "imitate the worst/ That Rome can practice, and pronounce Men curst?/ Can diff'rent Politics, or diff'rent Faith,/ Afford a Plea for such enormous Wrath?" Expressing sympathy for Nichols, a young, inexperienced preacher, Byrom urged him to "Leave to the low-bred O – ns of the Age/ Sense to bely, and Loyalty to rage;/ Wit to make Treason of each Cry and Chat,/ And Eyes to see false worship in a Hat." In a note, Byrom explained that that O – n was "a Furious and Fanatic Preacher in the Neighbourhood of Manchester."[81] Finally, both priest and penitent may differ "in their Prince's Name," but they "hop'd their Saviour was the same," while the penitent hoped that "the Sacrament of Christian Love/ Might be his Passport to the Realms above."

Meanwhile, as the trials of the rebels continued in London, their supporters in Edinburgh defied the government's suppressive measures. On 24 December 1746 Colonel Borland wrote Albemarle that "a surprising, audacious and impudent attempt" was made on 20 December to celebrate Charles Edward's birthday.[82] Several "societies" were to

---

[78] Benjamin Nichols, *False Claims to Martyrdom Consider'd* (London, 1746), 21.

[79] [John Byrom], *An Epistle to a Friend* (London, 1747), title-page.

[80] *Ibid.*, 7-9.

[81] *Ibid.*, 26-30.

[82] Albemarle, *Albemarle Papers*, I, 248. His birthday was 20/31 December, depending on which calendar was used.

meet (including the Freemasons), and the women wore tartan gowns with white ribbons. The guards were ordered to arrest them, but the forewarned ladies managed to change their dress in time. Despite their continuing resistance, the Jacobite Masons were disgusted when one of their own, John Murray of Broughton, betrayed them and turned king's evidence against Lord Lovat and others of their former colleagues in rebellion.

On 4 December 1746 Thomas Birch wrote Orrery that "Secretary Murray has, I believe, earned his pardon by his discoveries, and even confronted our State Prisoners before the Privy Council."[83] And, indeed, Murray did name Orrery as a plotter, but Chesterfield evidently prevented his arrest.[84] In March 1747, during the trial of Lovat, Murray made such wide-ranging accusations, including "hearsay" charges against Barrymore, Wynn, and Cotton, that Lord Talbot, the Lord Chancellor, stopped his testimony, saying, "I object to the witness's proceeding to give evidence which does not relate to the point in question; he has mentioned the names of several honourable gentlemen, who are my friends."[85] Horace Walpole commented that "It is imagined the Duchess of Norfolk would have come next upon the stage," suggesting that her husband would then be implicated by Murray (if not by the "accomodationist" duchess herself). It was no coincidence that William Talbot, 1st Earl of Talbot, was a confidant and supporter of the Prince of Wales.[86]

After Lovat's execution in April, Newcastle refused to honor his dying wish that he be buried in Scotland, because the government feared that his clan would rise in rebellion "at his burial where it is their custom to meet in great numbers."[87] Despite his unsavory reputation, Lovat still had admirers in Scotland, and they despised Murray as an informer. Murray's Masonic brothers, by unanimous vote, inked over all references to the traitor in the lodge book of Canongate-Kilwinning.[88] One foreign Masonic observer of Lovat's beheading was the Abbé Niccolini, who, according to Horace Walpole, was "a great deal shocked, but he comforts himself with the knowledge he thinks he has gained of the English constitution."[89] As noted earlier, Niccolini was an admirer of Chevalier Ramsay, when the latter served as tutor to Charles Edward Stuart. While visiting England in 1747, he was welcomed by the Prince of Wales, who greatly valued his company, much to the disgust of Walpole. On 10 October 1747 Mann wrote to him that the Tuscan minister Richecourt, an anti-Jacobite Mason, is "angry that Niccolini is such a favourite with the Prince and is desirous he should know that in his heart he [Niccolini] wishes much better to the Santi Apostoli [the Pretender's Palace at Rome] than to St. Giacomo [St. James's Palace in London]."[90]

In England Murray's betrayals were welcomed by the Hanoverians, and the former Whig Grand Master Raymond prosecuted Thomas Astley and Edward Cave for printing an objective account of Lovat's grueling trial in the *London Magazine* and the *Gentleman's*

---

[83] Harvard. Houghton: Eng.MS. 218.2, vol.5, f.11.

[84] J. Murray, *Memorials*, 466.

[85] H. Walpole, *Correspondence*, XIX, 381.

[86] G. Young, *Poor Fred*, 205.

[87] H. Walpole, *Correspondence*, XIX, 387.

[88] J. Murray, *Memorials*, xii

[89] H. Walpole, *Correspondence.*, XIX, 382.

[90] *Ibid.*, XIX, 441.

Magazine (March 1747), calling the account a "breach of privilege."[91] Raymond pressed the frightened journalists for more information on their sources, but they remained frustratingly vague and had to be released. Though Lovat was not widely admired in England, some observers sensed that the old man had been bullied in an unfair trial. In a poem "spoken extempore on Lovat's execution," a lover of "all those who will and dare be honest in the worst of times" portrayed the decapitated Jacobite Grand Masters and excoriated the Masonic betrayer, Murray:

> None but the hangman, Murray, or some tool,
> Could from his heart say Lovat was a fool.
> Yet ev'ry coxcomb will explain and teach
> The chain of causes that surpass his reach.
> When soft Kilmarnock, trembling, came to bleed,
> He fell a traitor and a wretch indeed.
> His coward soul the canting preacher awes,
> He weeps and dies a rebel to the cause.
> `Twas hope of pardon; `twas fanatic fear;
> And none but Hanoverians dropt a tear.
> Brave Balmerino, who no words can paint,
> Embrac'd his martyrdom and died a saint.
> He sprang triumphant to a better state,
> By all confest, superior to his fate.
> If Ratcliffe's youthful crimes receiv'd their due,
> Ratcliffe was steady, bold and loyal too.
> This much be said, to palliate his offence,
> Howe'er he liv'd, he died of a man of sense.[92]

Finally, addressing the hypocrisy and opportunism of those politicians who worked with Lovat over the years, the author concluded that "If he had won (for there the difference lies),/ That very crowd his triumph would attend/ Who lately came to view his noble end."

James Boswell, scion of an ancient Scottish Masonic family, later remembered that Samuel Johnson was so moved by the Jacobite executions that he would recite passionately from memory the following poem, which had appeared in the *Gentleman's Magazine* (17 April 1747), at the same time as Cave printed Lovat's trial.[93] Johnson's sympathy for the rebel Masons did not extend to Lovat:

> Pity'd by gentle minds Kilmarnock dy'd;
> The brave, Balmerino, were on thy side;
> Radcliffe, unhappy in his crimes of youth,
> Steady in what he still mistook for truth,
> Beheld his death so decently unmov'd,
> The soft lamented, and the brave approv'd.
> But Lovat's end indiff'rently we view,

---

[91] Cobbett, *Parliamentary History*, XIV, 57-61.

[92] R. Forbes, *Lyon in Mourning*, 239-40.

[93] Boswell's ancestor, John Boswell of Auchinleck, was a Scottish Mason in 1600, and James was an active member; see M.Schuchard, *Rstoring the Temple*, 233-34.

True to no King, to no religion true:
No fair forgets the ruin he has done;
No child laments the tyrant of his son;
No tory pities, thinking what he was;
No whig compassions, for he left the cause;
The brave regret not, for he was not brave;
The honest mourn not, knowing him a knave.[94]

Johnson's friend Ralph Griffiths, bookseller and journalist, published anonymously *Authentic Copies of the Letters and Other Papers Delivered, at their Execution, by the Nine Rebels who Suffer'd Death on Wednesday, July 30, 1746, on Kennington Common* (London, 1746), which sympathetically portrayed the last words of Colonel Francis Towneley and his fellow Manchester rebels. He followed this in December with another anonymous work, *Ascanius; or The Young Chevalier, a True History. Translated from a Private Manuscript Privately Handed About at the Court of Versailles. Containing a Particular Account of all that Happened to a certain Person during his Wanderings in the North, from his Memorable Defeat in April 1748, to his final Escape, on the 19th of September in the Same Year* (London, 1746). Despite the hyperbole and sensationalism of his narrative, Griffiths was actually well-informed about Charles Edward's movements and companions, and he gave an emotional account of the prince's horror when he heard that his troops begged for "Quarter" but were refused it: "The Duke's People, exasperated against us to an uncommon Degree, sacrificed every Man that could not fly beyond the Reach of their Fury."[95]

Griffiths claimed, disingenuously, that Charles Edward could not believe that Cumberland could be capable of "such unsoldiery, such inhuman Arts and Means of Revenge" against his own people. He also held out the hope that the Jacobite campaign was not over, for when the prince first met with Louis XV, the French king affirmed, "You have suffer'd much my P----- [Prince], you have acquired immortal Honour, and we trust you will one day reap the Fruits of your extraordinary Merit." Griffiths was summoned to Westminster and charged with publishing "dangerous propaganda" after each of these works appeared, but he managed to talk his way out of imprisonment.[96]

In *Ascanius* Griffith reported that "the old Duke of Athol (Tullibardine) had been forced to surrender, after having in vain skulked about the Sea Coasts, in hopes of getting off; and after having not only killed his Horse, but flung himself into a bad State of Health, through the excessive Fatigue he had undergone."[97] As noted earlier, Atholl/ Tullibardine had allegedly served as regent of the Order of the Temple after Mar and until Charles Edward's elevation in Holyrood Palace. After his surrender and imprisonment in Dumbarton Castle, the English commander described him as "a most polite well-tempered person, heartily tired of the French schemes and politics and if need be a strong advocate against them, consequently an object of his Majesty's wonted clemency."[98] However, Tullibardine had participated in three Jacobite rebellions, and there

---

[94] J. Boswell, *Life of Johnson*, 130; *Gentleman's Magazine*, 17 (April 1747).
[95] [Griffiths, Ralph], *Ascanius* (London, 1746), 19, 53, 64.
[96] "Ralph Griffiths," *ODNB*.
[97] Ralph Griffifths, *Ascanius*, 40.
[98] H. Tayler, *Jacobite Epilogue*, 45-46.

was to be no mercy. If he had not died in the Tower on 9 July 1746, he would have joined his Masonic brothers Kilmarnock, Balmerino, and Derwentwater in decapitation.

What is suggestive about Griffiths's interest in Tullibardine is that he was familiar with Jacobite Freemasonry and in 1798, in the wake of the French Revolution, he (or his son) rejected the anti-revolutionists' charge that "liberty and equality form the essential and perpetual secret creed of the Free-Masons:

> Certain it is that this body, during the [17ᵗʰ-century] civil wars, and during the protectoral [Cromwellian] republic, fostered an excessive zeal for regal power, and a disloyal leaning towards Popery; that in its congregations and interior assemblies, was plotted the Restoration; and that its attachment to the dynasty of the Stuarts not only survived their exile, but outlived the rebellion in 1745.[99]

Griffiths thus echoed Ramsay's account of the role of Stuart Freemasonry in the Restoration of Charles II in 1660, and he recognized the persistence of Jacobite influence in the fraternity after 1746.

One surprising Masonic defender of the Jacobite peers, including the much-criticized Lord Lovat, was Orator Henley. In 1745, when he issued his *faux*-Jacobite orations, he was acting as an *agent provocateur*, an explanation he secretly sent to Pelham and Newcastle. In February 1746 he had lectured on Anglo-Scots relations with the provocative title, "The King of the North Shall Return."[100] But after Culloden, he was genuinely outraged at Cumberland's treatment of the Scots, which he denounced as "inhumane and stupid." Graham Midgley reports that in June he delivered "A very curious Dissertation on the treatment of Rebels":

> [He] returned in discourse after discourse to the fates of the Scots lords executed for treason, being especially moved by the bravery and dignity of Lord Balmerino, and later defending the aged Lord Lovat as he hopelessly and without assistance stood trial for his life. It was his preaching on Lord Lovat which brought matters to a head and enabled his enemies to succeed where they had failed in '45.[101]

It was perhaps these pro-Jacobite discourses, as well as his Hanoverian Masonic pieces, that John Byrom collected, but they were listed only as "Henley" publications (1727-55) in his library catalogue.[102] On 30 November, while Henley preached on Lord Lovat and prayed for the deliverance of Scotland, a government agent broke into his house and took away manuscripts, while other conspirators "raised a hullabaloo in the Oratory to divert attention." In a prearranged plan, he was then arrested, and the machinery of justice "moved surprisingly – even suspiciously – swiftly." He was charged with seditious expressions "tending to alienate his Majesty's Subjects from their Duty and Allegiance."

Among his examiners were Pelham and Chesterfield, who knew about his earlier service to the government and who recommended his dismissal "as an impudent fellow,

---

[99] *Monthly Review*, 25 (1798), 503. Ralph Griffiths and his son George Edward edited *The Monthly Review* from June 1749 onwards. The early issues often reviewed works by Tory and Jacobite writers such as Dr. King.
[100] G. Midgley, *Orator Henley*, 239-43.
[101] *Ibid.* 239.
[102] John Byrom, *Catalogue of the Library of the Late John Byrom* (London, 1848), 105.

without sufficient reason for him to be dangerous." Henley later asked for a blessing on Chesterfield, who "when false Witnesses rose up against us," had "Justice and Humanity not to push ye Power of ye Courts…and dismiss'd ye Cause."[103] Over the next months, Henley was careful not to offend again, and he issued loyalist statements and confessions that "were just a little too contrite to be true."[104] Though he no longer used Masonry to support Hanoverian policies, he resumed his criticism of the government's cruel policies toward Scotland. His appeal to the government and public to "Tolerate one English Cervantes in the Pulpit" was apparently effective, and he continued his exuberant and bizarre orations until his death in 1759.

Romantic stories emerged about the role that Flora Macdonald played in Charles Edward's escape, when she helped him dress in female garb. Dr. King composed two odes in Latin to the new Jacobite heroine, "Who in the royal youth preserv'd the Isle":

> She led thro' treach'rous firths and ev'ry storm
> The hero lurking in the handmaid's form.
> ………………………………………………………..
> What thanks, O wondrous maid, to thee we owe!
> As long as verse shall soar or canvass glow
> So long thy name, thy praises shall remain,
> The pencil's labour and the poet's strain.[105]

King was even more lavish in praise of the Stuart prince, whose portrait provoked the following lines: "But, lo! The Heroe meets our wishing eyes./ See C-----s himself in living colours rise!":

> What god-like man! What sweetness mix'd with grace!
> What vigour flushes in the princely face!
> What spirit sparkles in the radiant eyes!
> What bold sedateness foes and fiends defies!
> ………………………………………………………..
> Yet thee, in council sage, in battle strong,
> Thee, highly worthy our Apollo's song,
> Thee, unrelated with the first success,
> Thee, undejected in the last distress…[106]

Meanwhile in Italy, despite the papal bull against Freemasonry, a party of Scottish and English travelers defiantly mocked the ban. On 14 February 1747 Mann wrote to Walpole about their behavior during the masked entertainments of Carnival:

> Last night there was a great ball in the Via della Pergola at which many of the English represented freemasonry. Their habits were pretty, and Denis the French dancer, who is a master mason, composed a dance on purpose, which succeeded very well. The Italians liked it as a masquerade, which was all they knew of it. They danced it twice with great applause, but the third

---

[103] *Ibid.*, 242.
[104] *Ibid.*, 243-45.
[105] R. Forbes, *Lyon in Mourning*, III, 67. English translation from the Latin of Dr. King.
[106] *Ibid.*, III, 68.

time the people were offended that their *tresconi* [country dance] was interrupted, and had not General Salin threatened to put all the fiddlers into
prison, the *tresconi* would have got the better. The impresarios are all offended, and Lord March was so angry with them that he proposed that each
of the nine freemasons should fight an impresario. They intended to appear
in the same habits at the ball on Thursday night, but this fracas has made
them alter their minds.[107]

The twenty-two year old William Douglas, 3rd Earl of March, was accompanied by
three fellow Scots, who were introduced to Cardinal Albani by Mann and Fane, diplomats
and former members of the Florentine lodge.[108] Albani regularly reported to the British
ministry about the efforts of Jacobites to seduce British visitors to Rome, and he assiduously tried to keep them away from Stuart sympathizers.[109] He was only partially successful with March, who on his return to England joined the Leicester House group centered
on the Prince of Wales, thus adding a Scottish Freemason to the prince's opposition
party.

In London, during the months of the rebellion, the opposition Mason James Thomson and his Scottish Whig friends kept a low profile, while they opposed the Jacobites
but worried about the carnage and damage to their homeland. After the rebels retreated
from Derby, he began work on a play, *Coriolanus*, in which he drew parallels between the
Stuart prince and the Roman hero ("a noble, rebellious leader camping outside his own
capital, then withdrawing"), which expressed Thomson's relief at this turn of events.[110]
Though Thomson showed some sympathy for the Roman/Jacobite rebels, in the end
they were traitors and were killed; when he concluded, "Then this be the star by which
we steer/ Above ourselves our COUNTRY should be dear," he meant the united kingdom of Great Britain. He also continued work on *The Castle of Indolence. An Allegorical
Poem. Written in Imitation of Spencer*, which was not published until 1748. Mary Jane Scott
observes that,

> in *The Castle*, the Stuarts can be associated with the anti-Christ Wizard
> Archmago. The Jacobites would be among those deceived followers of the
> Catholic, Stuart "Christian inflam'd by black desire"… Thomson sees them
> as enemies of the virtuous and progressive society which is the goal of the
> consummately Whig, Hanoverian, and Protestant British Knight… it is his
> duty to profess his own – and his fellow Scots – loyal allegiance to the Han-
> overian government and to work toward the greater good of united Brit-
> ain.[111]

In 1745 Thomson had been recruited by Fielding to anonymously contribute to *The
True Patriot*, and he may have also assisted on his friend's next political publications. By
the time of the last issue of *The True Patriot* on 17 June 1746, Fielding had become "a
strenuous advocate for the ministry," and by 1747 he served as "the ministry's leading

---

[107] H. Walpole, *Correspondence*, XIX, 364-65.
[108] "William Douglas, 3rd Earl of March," Ingamells, *Dictonary*; ODNB.
[109] Lesley Lewis, *Connoisseurs and Secret Agents in Eighteenth-Century Rome* (London, 1961),, 123-30.
[110] M. Scott, *James Thomson*, 238-39.
[111] *Ibid.*, 279.

propagandist."[112] During the months of the rebellion, he evidently learned about the role of Jacobite Freemasonry in supporting the Stuart cause, and he began to make odd references to the fraternity. In *Ovid's Art of Love Paraphrased, Being a New Art of Love Adapted to the Present Times* (1747), he described a Cretan procession, in which "a vast Multitude was heard, while many Kinds of strange Instruments, like those of the miserable Masons, accompanied the Voices."[113] He remembered the Scald Miserable Masons who had mocked the Grand Lodge processions, with riders on jackasses banging away on bizarre instruments.[114] In his preface to his sister Sarah's book, *Familiar Letters Between the Principal Characters in David Simple* (1747), he commented "that these nice Touches will, like the Signs of Masonry, escape the Observation and Detection of all those, who are not already in the Secret."[115] But it was in *the Jacobite's Journal*, which he published from 5 December 1747 to 5 November 1748, that he made his most serious charges against Scottish Freemasons as not only Jacobites but Jews.

The executions and transportations of Jacobites and the continuing harsh repression in Scotland created a backlash of popular sympathy for "Bonnie Prince Charlie" and his supporters. The year 1747 began with a formal declaration by Frederick, Prince of Wales, of a new opposition party. When Frederick's party acquired some Scottish members of Parliament, charges emerged that he was a Jacobite sympathizer. The prince not only gained the release of Flora Macdonald from prison but took into his household Catherine Walkinshaw, sister of Clementina, Charles Edward's mistress in Scotland. In May Dudley Ryder, a loyalist Whig, warned that "the Jacobites have appeared publicly again," with encouragement from the heir to the throne.[116] While Frederick determined to make himself the true heir to Stuart legitimacy, a Tory faction, calling itself "the Independent Electors of the City and Liberty of Westminster," attracted many disaffected Masons. At its anniversary feast, Jacobite toasts were given, and a government spy was severely beaten. The more militant Electors sought revenge for the execution in 1746 of the Welsh poet David Morgan, an earlier member, who had fought with Charles Edward.

Though the Whig ministry had expected John Coustos's narrative about his sufferings as a Hanoverian Freemason to undermine Jacobite Masonry, he was distressed that the book did not sell well. In late 1746 Coustos petitioned Newcastle for financial help, reminding him that he had sent the duke a copy of his book *before* the 1745 rebellion, but he did not bother him "during the disturbance."[117] Newcastle must have pressured the Grand Lodge to help him, for on 16 May 1747 the usually absentee Grand Master, William, Lord Byron, sponsored a benefit performance at Drury Lane for Coustos, attended by loyalist Freemasons. Coustos sang a ballad "at the particular desire of The Grand Master," and over the next three years he would sing and act at Masonic benefit performances.[118]

---

[112] J. Downie, *Political Biography*, 159-60.

[113] Henry Fielding, *The Lover's Assistant, or, New Year's Gift; Being a New Art of Love* (London, 1759), 59. No copy of the original edition survives.

[114] As reported in *The Daily Advertiser* (25 April 1745); see R. Berman, *Schism*, 127-28.

[115] Sarah Fielding, *Familiar Letters Between the Principal Characters in David Simple* (London, 1747), xix.

[116] G. Glickman, "Parliament," 132.

[117] British Library: Newcastle Add. MS. 33,054, f. 313.

[118] Philip Highfill, Kalman Burnham, Edward Langham, *Biographical Dictionary of Actors, Actresses* (Carbondale, 1975), IV, 12. I am grateful to Ric Berman for this information.

In autumn 1747 opponents of Grand Lodge Masonry and its affiliated architects saw an opening when the controversial, nearly-finished Westminster Bridge began sinking into the Thames. Ten years earlier Pope had entered the fray with attacks on one of the proposed architects Thomas Ripley, a rival of the Burlington faction. Ripley, trained as a carpenter and operative Mason, gained prominence through his work on Houghton Hall for his patron Robert Walpole. An indignant Vanbrugh wrote in 1721 that when he met with Ripley's name in the newspaper, "And Esquire to it," such a "Laugh came upon me, I had like to Beshit myself."[119] In 1731 Pope defended Burlington and scorned not only Ripley but his avaricious patron: "Heav'n visits with a taste the wealthy fool,/ And needs no rod but Ripley with a rule."[120] In 1737,when Ripley campaigned for the Westminster Bridge commission and planned to use wooden rather than stone supports, Pope renewed his mockery: "Who builds a bridge that never drove a pile?/ Should Ripley venture, all the world would smile."[121]

Ripley's design was also opposed by that obstreperous Mason, Batty Langley, who despite their shared politics, countered the operative Mason with his own eccentric design. Opposing all the plans were the Thames watermen, former supporters of the Duke of Wharton and still considered anti-government. In a heated context of lottery schemes, stock-jobbing, and bribery, Desaguliers helped his Huguenot-Masonic protégé Labelye win the contract, and Henry Herbert, 9th Earl of Pembroke, became head of the commission overseeing the project. As a Grand Lodge Mason and friend of the late Walpole and George II, Pembroke helped create the image of the bridge as a Whig-Hanoverian project. Thus, when it began collapsing in 1747, the opposition and Jacobites issued poems and ballads which linked it to the corruption and imminent collapse of the Hanoverian state.

In November an anonymous poet published *The Downfall of Westminster-Bridge; or, My Lord in the Suds. A New Ballad* (1747), in which he mocked the military arrogance, corruption, and greed of the government as the cause of the collapse. With the Whig press still issuing panegyrics to the Duke of Cumberland, the author began, "I sing not of Battles, nor do I much chuse/ With *too many* Vict'ries, to burden my Muse:/ I sing not of Actions that rise to Renown;/ But I sing of a monstrous huge *Bridge* tumbling down."[122] He made clear that he supported Lord Burlington and the City of London, then governed by the Jacobite Mason George Heathcote, who were not consulted in the planning:

> The first they referr'd unto a Committee,
> Who brought it about, in spight of the City;
> The latter they heeded not – so it were done,
> – Whether by a *Hod-Carrier*, or a B--------*n* [Burlington],
> O, B--------*n!* pardon the Use of your Name,
> On a Subject inferior by much to your *Fame*;
> Whilst others decay, like their Mortar and Stones.

---

[119] H. Colvin, *Biographical Dictionary*, 870-71.

[120] *Ibid.*, 870.

[121] Alexander Pope, *Imitations of Horace* (1737), Book II, Epistle 1 ll.185-86.

[122] Anon., *The Downfall of Westminster-Bridge; or, My Lord in the Suds. A New Ballad* (London, 1747), 1-6.

After massive and sometimes fraudulent fund-raising schemes, which ended up being charged to the whole nation, the enormous committee finally selected the architect, with the encouragement of his aristocratic patron:

> The Money thus rais'd, they straight sought for a Man,
> That of this great Work should sketch out a Plan;
> And he must be a Man – that could Bridges erect,
> *A Free Mason* – at least – and a good *Architect.*
> *Such* _____ was: _____ and a Peer of nice Taste,
> And he was the Person – they pitch'd on at last...

Though the author did not give their names, he referred to Labelye and Pembroke as Freemasons and architects, but after the bridge's collapse, Pembroke was embarrassed and angry: "My L – d, when he heard it, he rav'd, storm'd and swore,/ That he'd ne'er undertake to build a Bridge more."

Hinting at the parallel with the sinking state of Great Britain (and Grand Lodge Masonry), the poet concluded:

> But however that be, e'en let it decay;
> And continue to sink – till it sinks quite away:
> Of G---t B----n's Follies we've enough yet in sight,
> Altho you and your Bridge were in Thames plung'd down right.

While the anonymous poet drew on opposition and Jacobite themes, the Hanoverian Mason Batty Langley countered him with a loyalist treatise, *A Survey of Westminster Bridge, As `tis now Sinking into Ruin* (1748), in which he drew on Whiggish xenophobia and anti-Gallican prejudice to portray Labelye as a Frenchified "Swiss Pretender": "It is such Encouragement being so given to *Foreign Pretenders,* that is the *Bane* of English Artists," while "in Honour to my Country," we have "as good Artists and other Workmen (Natives) as any other Country in the World."[123] Two years later, when Pembroke died (allegedly from a stroke brought on by his "outrageous passion" at a meeting of the bridge committee), Chesterfield remembered that he had told the architect earl, "that ever since the pier sunk, he has constantly been *damming and sinking.*" The rowdy Thames watermen cheered and chanted that "now the great {pier/peer} is quite gone."[124]

Meanwhile, in 1747-48, as the war with France dragged on, reports circulated that the French, with Swedish and Prussian support, were collaborating with Charles Edward for a new invasion, this time including Ireland. On the Continent and in Sweden, *Écossais* lodges expanded and flourished, often with covert government support. Fielding evidently became aware of the developing higher degrees, which infused esoteric, mystical, and chivalric themes into traditional Masonic symbolism. Thus, in the first issue of *The Jacobite's Journal* (6 December 1747), he posed as John Trott-Plaid, Esq., who was not afraid to "appear as a Jacobite. A Title which Men assume in the most public manner in Taverns, in Coffee-Houses, and in the Street."[125] The *faux* Scottish narrator planned to explain "the Esoteric Doctrines of our Sect, which are perhaps as mysterious as those of

---

123 Batty Langley, *A Survey of Westminster Bridge, As `tis now Sinking into Ruin* (Londonr, 1748), Iv, vii.

124 H. Walpole, *Correspondence*, XX, 108.

125 H. Fielding, *Jacobite's Journal*, 91, 95.

Free Masonry itself. As to the Exoteric, they will, I apprehend, be easy enough to explain, as indeed they principally consist in one Article, viz. *in Drinking*."

In issue two (12 December), Trott-Plaid explained the illustration on the title-page in which a sword-bearing woman and her drunken husband, both dressed in plaid, ride an ass, led by a Catholic monk carrying a copy of the Tory paper, *The London Evening Post*:

> The *Mystery of Jacobitism* doth not, like that of *Free-Masonry*, exclude the Female World; for tho' all *Jacobites* are not, as some wicked Whigs have represented us, *old Women*, yet Women we have in great Numbers among us, who are as learned in the Knowledge of our Mysteries, and as active in the Celebration of our Rites, as any of the Male Species...
>
> In our *Esoteric* Doctrines there is indeed no Difference... But in our *Exoteric* it is otherwise; for *Drinking* belongs particularly to the Men, and Fighting to the Women. Not that I would insinuate that none of our women drink; for, indeed, some do very plentifully: But this with them is maintained rather to be *Esoteric* than *Exoteric*; for whenever they exceed three or four of our principal *Jaco-Treaso*-Healths, it is always performed in the *Sanctum Santorum*, where, when the Women are assembled alone, Rites are performed no wise inferior to those celebrated by our Men at their Mystical *Revels*; or, indeed, to those which were formerly instituted to the *Bona Dea*; nay, perhaps, equal to the famous *Orgia* performed by the *Bacchanalian Women* of old Time.[126]

Fielding was obviously trying to counter the popular accounts of Jacobite heroines, such as Flora Macdonald and Jenny Cameron, and the widespread sympathy (even romantic infatuation) for Bonnie Prince Charlie among women throughout the British Isles. However, he seemed unaware that in *Écossais* Freemasonry, women were often affiliated in "androgynous lodges" and played an honored role as protectresses of the fraternity.[127] In Ireland a tradition developed that Jenny Cameron was a Freemason; Philip Crossle notes that this was not surprising since "Female Lodges are very common in France."[128]

In issue three (19 December), Trott-Plaid continued his Jacobite-Masonic analogies, and he hinted at the mystical themes ("inward and spiritual Doctrines") developed in *Écossais* systems:

> Tho' I have divided the mysterious Doctrines of Jacobitism into Esoteric and Exoteric, in Imitation of the Doctrines of antient Philosophy, yet we do not imitate those Philosophers in revealing the Exoteric only to the Vulgar: In this Instance we rather resemble the Free-Masons, who communicate their whole inestimable Secrets to the whole Body; for, indeed, as they are equally adapted to the Understandings of all, there can be no Reason why they should be imparted only to the Few.

---

[126] *Ibid.*, 98.

[127] Robert Collis, "Chivalric Muses: The Role and Influence of Protectresses in Eighteenth-century Jacobite Fraternities," in Maire Cross, ed., *Gender and Fraternal Orders in Europe from 1200 Until the Present* (Basingstoke, 2010), 102-32.

[128] P. Crossle, "Freemasonry in Ireland," 104.

> I know some impudent Whigs pretend, that we are ashamed of our Es-
> oteric, or inward and spiritual Doctrines, … I shall here publish the principal
> ones to the World; such as every Jacobite must, and doth, and will maintain
> in Defiance of all the Argument, or Reason which hath been, or may be,
> urged against them.[129]

Fielding then listed the "Mysterys" of Jacobitism, defining them as the beliefs that the Hanoverians claimed to be absolute and universal among Stuart sympathizers – i.e. that kings are divinely appointed and infallible; that passive obedience must be paid to tyrants and destroyers of the "established Religion of the Country"; that "a Popish Prince may be a Defender of the Protestant Church," etc. Since three of the four convicted Jacobite Masonic leaders were Protestants, with only Derwentwater a Catholic, Fielding argued that "the profoundest Mystery" was the notion of a "Protestant-Jacobite." It was crucial to his propaganda campaign that the Jacobites, who in England and Scotland were majority Protestant, be painted as papist autocrats. In issue four he made his last explicit reference to Freemasonry, quoting a report in *The St. James Evening Post* about a quarterly meeting of "the Free and Accepted Masons," in which several lodges "paid in a large Sum of Money for their poor and indigent Brethren," to which Fielding added a note: "To wit, we suppose, the Scald Miserable Masons."[130] He thus got in a final, open jab at the opposition Masons.

However, Fielding would continue to criticize Jacobite Masons without mentioning their fraternal affiliation. In January 1748 he renewed his attack on the former Walpolean Mason and recent (feigned?) Jacobite supporter, Orator Henley. He claimed that Trott-Plaid served as Censor of Great Britain and heard a petition from "Orator Handlie" on 14 January 1747. The petitioner prayed to be "Crier of the Court, offering to write, preach, or swear anything, and to profess any Party or Religion, at a cheap rate," but Trott-Plaid rejected his plea.[131] Fielding also launched a series of attacks on the Jacobite Mason, Thomas Carte, whose enormous, four-volume *General History of England*, began appearing in December 1747. In February Fielding published "A Letter to John Trott-Plaid, Esq; from Duncan Mac-Carte, a Highlander, concerning the History of Thomas Carte, an Englishman," which when read by Trott-Plaid's Court of Criticism was found "to contain Wit and Humour, and was ordered to be recommended. And the said Book of Thomas Carte, the Englishman, was ordered to be taken into Custody."[132]

What provoked the real government censors was Carte's footnote in which he told the story of Christopher Lovell, a laborer of Bristol who in 1716 was allegedly cured of scrofula after being touched by James III in France.[133] The story was immediately attacked as fallacious and treasonable in a pamphlet by a supposed Jacobite Highlander, "Duncan MacCarte," which inspired Fielding to add it to Trott-Plaid's on-going saga. The actual author was Samuel Squire, a politically-ambitious Whig churchman, who in October 1745 argued that even thinking positively about disaffection to the government

---

[129] H. Fielding, *Jacobite's Journal,* 105.

[130] *Ibid.,* 449.

[131] *Ibid.,* 133.

[132] *Ibid.,* 145-46.

[133] Paul Monod, "Thomas Carte, the Druids and British National Identity" in Monod, Pittock, and Szechi, *Loyalty and Identity*, 133-34.

should be considered treasonous, even if the perpetrator never contributed to or acted in the Jacobite cause.[134] In January 1748 Squire, as "Duncan MacCarte a Highlander," published *A Letter to John Trot-Plaid, Esq; Author of the Jacobite Journal, Concerning Mr. Carte's General History of England*, which he dedicated (mockingly) to the Duke of Beaufort, Earl of Arran, Oxford scholars, and other Jacobite supporters of Carte's historical work.

From his ironic stance, Squire worried that Trott-Plaid had revealed too many of the "Mysteries"of the Jacobites, but he was relieved that he kept secret their plans to rescind all royal and government "Grants, Honours, Peerages, Patents, etc. given since the Williamite Conquest," when they achieve the Restoration.[135] He charged that Carte's voluminous history, the "famous Code of the Jacobites," was actually written by "the whole Jacobite Junto," and he disparaged the story of Christopher Lovell's healing by James III's royal touch. Spurred by MacCarte's pamphlet, Fielding's "Court of Criticism" indicted Carte on 17 February for "not having the Love of Truth before his Eyes, nor weighing the Duty of an Historian, but being moved and seduced by the instigation of the wicked Spirit of Jacobitism." He published the Lovell story "with a manifest Intention of imposing on weak and credulous People," to which "the Prisoner pleaded Not Guilty."[136] The Hanoverian attacks on Carte were so effective that on 7 April the City of London withdrew its annual subsidy to the author for his historical project, and on 21 July the Whigs won the City election, for "the first time in many years."[137]

Fielding used Carte as a convenient target to criticize the "new" opposition formed under the Prince of Wales, especially the Protestant Jacobites, "those inflammeable Gentlemen," who can be incensed to produce sedition and violence. Trott-Plaid urged Carte, the "great Author," in his next book to produce a dissertation

> on Jacob's Stone brought from Scotland by Edward I and now placed under the Coronation-Chair at Westminster. Demolish our Adversaries with this Stone: be very particular about the Prophecy *Ni fallat Fatum Scot, &c* – which has always been looked on to have had a primary Completion, when the Stuarts first ascended the Throne.[138]

This reference to the ancient Irish-Scottish tradition that this was the stone which served as Jacob's pillow opened the door to Fielding's most incendiary attacks upon the Scottish Jacobites, whom he accused of being not only Masons but Jews. On 27 February he included an extract from the *Daily Advertiser* about the conversion to Christianity of "a Jew, eminent for his great Knowledge of the Hebrew and Chaldee Languages, "at the Meeting-House in Paul's Alley," to which he added his note, "We wish some Jews in Change-Alley would turn Christian."[139] He possibly targeted the Mendes brothers, Jacobite Masons, who were successful stockbrokers. Some weeks later, he would make more explicit analogies between Jews and Jacobites.

---

[134] Samuel Squire, *A Letter to a Tory Friend. Upon the Present Critical Situation of our Affairs* (London, 1746), 9-10.
[135] Samuel Squire, *A Letter to John Trot-Plaid, Esq....by Duncan MacCarte a Highlander* (London, 1748), 29, 14-17.
[136] H. Fielding, *Jacobite's Journal*, 168-71.
[137] H. Walpole, *Correspondence*, XIX, 425.
[138] H. Fielding, *Jacobite's Journal*, 196-97.
[139] *Ibid.*, 460.

On 26 March Fielding announced his recognition that his ironic role as Trott-Plaid was misunderstood by many readers, so he had his Scottish persona renounce Jacobitism and begin straightforward Hanoverian propaganda, especially targeting Scotland's long tradition of being an essentially Jewish, Covenanted nation.[140] He was evidently informed that Scottish poets were proudly affirming that Jewish heritage and were issuing satires on the English/Hanoverian pork-eaters. Alexander MacDonald proclaimed that the embattled Gaelic language had been spoken in Eden and was the precursor of Hebrew; he then lampooned George II as a boar, who was followed by "pig-snouted Hanoverians."[141] Other bards targeted "that swine King George,/ Son of the sow from Germany," and warned, "When the sow's been singed and her brood of piglings salted/ The broadsword and the plaid ne'er again will be forbidden."[142] Thus, on 21 May Fielding began his new anti-Semitic, anti-Scottish campaign:

> I have often amused myself with comparing the People called Jacobites with the People called Jews; between whom I find a stricter Analogy than perhaps can be discovered between any other two Sects.
>
> Both of these are well known to found their whole Faith on certain Traditions, the Truth of which they take for granted, tho' never so contradictory to Reason, or the Nature of Things. The Jewish Rabbins have, indeed, shewn a more fertile Genius than the Jacobite, in the Number of their Inventions, and a happier Cast of Thought in the Pleasantry of them; but in one Instance, I think, they rather fall short; for the Jacobite Traditions seem to me rather more surprising and miraculous than the Jewish.
>
> To mention one only; the Jacobite Rabbins tell us, that on Friday, Feb. 6. 1684, one of the Angels, I forget which, came to Whitehall at Noon-day, without being perceived by any one, and brought with him a Commission from Heaven, which he delivered to the then Duke of York, by which the said Duke was indefeasibly created King of England, Scotland, and Ireland....
>
> Again, it is the unhappy Fate of both these People, who have been alike deprived of their own divinely constituted Kings, to live under Governments which they hold to be amnable and diabolical, and no Allegiance nor Submission to be due to them: But, on the contrary, are daily hoping and looking for their Destruction.[143]

Fielding then outdid himself by claiming that the Jacobites have copied the Jews by putting a distinguishing mark upon themselves:

> I mean in the Humour of Circumcision, which at present prevails so universally among the Jacobites equally with the Jews. The Original of this Practice was set on Foot, as I am told, soon after the Battle of Culloden, and was performed in Memory of that Victory, or as they call it Massacre, which

---

[140] Arthur Williamson, "The Jewish Dimension of the Scottish Apocalypse: Climate, Covenant, and World Renewal," in Yosef Kaplan, ed., *Menasseh ben Israel and his World* (Leiden, 1989), 7-30, and "A Pil for Pork-Eaters," 237-58.

[141] D. Thomson, *Alasdair*, 123-24, 130.

[142] J. Cambell, *Highland Songs*, 101, 253.

[143] H. Fielding, *Jacobite's Journal*, 281-83.

derives its Name from that Place. From that Day the Custom hath been universal; and I am credibly informed there is not a Jacobite now in England who is uncircumcised.[144]

On 9 July he featured a letter from "Abraham Adams," the Parson Adams in Fielding's novel, *Joseph Andrews*, to John Trott-Plaid, in which the parson criticizes the earlier etymology of Jacobite and argues that it comes from the Hebrew for "Supplanter." He informs the no-longer Jacobitical Trott-Plaid that "these people are ever looking and hoping for the Destruction of Government. You would have found them in their Synagogues, not supinely looking, but zealously and fervently praying for our Destruction."[145] Their party-colored coats (plaids) are meant to imitate the coat of Jacob's favorite son, but the most inveterate and poisonous sort may be clothed in "every Kind of Habit" and are often found dressed in black on the banks of the Isis. Fielding thus began his attacks on Dr. King and his Jacobite colleagues at Oxford. These garments disguise "that Mark in the Flesh" (circumcision) which they have chosen to distinguish themselves "since they were smote at Culloden." Indeed it is well they wear the mark of any religion, "for a Rebel to such a Government as ours is at present, bears no Mark of a Christian about him."

In August Fielding quoted a report that George Mackenzie, "late Earl of Cromarty" (i.e. attainted), and his family have left London for Devonshire, adding his note that "If Ovid had been obliged to have exchanged Scotland for Devonshire, he had never written his Tristia."[146] Given his investigations of Freemasonry, he must have known that Cromarty had served as a Grand Master in Scotland. In October he continued his linkage of Jews and Jacobites by arguing that both love slavery, as exemplified in the writing of Thomas Carte.[147] As the last weeks of *The Jacobite's Journal* sputtered to an end, he managed thus to link Jews, Jacobites, and Freemasons in his concluding, unholy trio.

---

[144] *Ibid*, 284.

[145] *Ibid.*, 331-33.

[146] *Ibid.*, 480.

[147] *Ibid.*, 411-12.

CHAPTER TWENTY-THREE

DISAPPEARANCE OF ONE YOUNG PRETENDER, EMERGENCE OF THE OTHER (1748-1750)

Hail Stuart! Much suff'ring Youth! Yes, I foresee...
Scotia, for Genius fam'd and gallant deed,
Has yet her Bards to sing, her Chiefs to bleed; –
Yet Freedom shall be Hers, her Kings shall reign,
For know, Culloden was not lost in vain.

William Hamilton, *Written at Rouen, in France, in the Year of our Exile*, 1749.

To time alone...and certain Contingencies, must be left the unravelling of this Mystery.

A Letter from Henry Goring...Occurrences which happened to the Prince during the course of his mysterious Progress (London, 1750).

When Fielding published the last number of *The Jacobite's Journal* (5 November 1748), he explained that he had launched his pro-Hanoverian propaganda because "A strange Spirit of Jacobitism, indeed of Infatuation, discovered itself at the latter End of the Year 1747, in many Parts of this Kingdom, which was at the same Time engaged in a dangerous and successless War" against France.[1] In order to stop the increasing support for this "epidemical madness," he unleashed a campaign of satire and ridicule in the persona of Trott-Plaid to dissuade the misguided Tories, Non-jurors, Jacobites, and disaffected Scottish Whigs from backing new invasion plans. Finally exhausted by the years of war, England and France spent the months of April to October 1748 negotiating terms for the peace treaty of Aix-la-Chapelle, with the English pressing for the expulsion of the Stuart prince from French territory.

When the treaty was finally ratified, which included the expulsion of Charles Edward, Fielding used his farewell article in *The Jacobite's Journal* to praise "that happy Peace which the present glorious Administration have, much to their own Honour and the public

---

[1] H. Fielding, *Jacobite's Journal*, 424-26.

Good, secured to this Nation." With the apparent French rejection of the Stuart cause, he boasted that the hopes of the Jacobite party "are in a manner, plucked up by the very Root: And their Projects are as much the Contempt of every honest and sensible Briton, as their Principles were before." He was especially pleased when Louis XV ordered the arrest of the defiant prince at the door of the Paris opera house on 10 November – an act that provoked widespread French disapproval of the "shameful" treatment of the young hero. Ironically, the Hanoverian propaganda campaign (and Cumberland's brutality) created a backlash that led to revived Jacobite sympathy in Britain, to activation of Jacobite lodges in England, and to an international expansion of *Écossais* Freemasonry.

As the impaled heads of executed rebels gradually decomposed, the Jacobite Mason John Byrom continued to protest the government's barbarity, which led to frequent Hanoverian attacks upon him. In March 1748 the radical Presbyterian minister Josiah Owen raised the stakes in his polemical duel with Byrom by publishing a lengthy pamphlet, *Jacobite and Nonjuring Principles, Freely Examined, in a Letter to the Master-Tool of the Faction at Manchester*, published in March 1748. Targeting Byrom as the master-tool and Dr. Deacon as his collaborator, he accused them of "preaching up Politeness with Dunghill Breeding, and under Pretence of advocating for the true Catholic church," and "laboring to introduce the Worship of Dunghill-Gods." [2] He charged Byrom with hypocrisy for posing as a Whig when among his Royal Society and Masonic friends in London.

Byrom admitted to his wife that he expected to be asked questions about Owen's charges by his London acquaintances, "Most whereof are desperate Whigs, and loth to allow a man his liberty."[3] He then tried to take advantage of these Whig Masonic friends to gain clemency for young Charles Deacon and other Manchester prisoners. In June he recorded a dinner with Folkes, Montagu, Charles Stanhope, and Lord Harrington, when they asked him many questions about the Young Pretender and his circumstances when he was at Manchester:

> I told them what I knew and thought without any reserve, and took the opportunity of setting some matters in a truer light than I suppose they had heard them placed in, especially Ch. D-----[Deacon]. They were all very free and good natured, and did not seem offended with anything that I took the liberty to enlarge upon. When Mr. Folkes came away…he said that what had passed might possibly occasion young D's. liberty, that they were not violent in their tempers, and that he took notice that they listened very much to what I had been telling them of Manchester affairs.[4]

Byrom was so encouraged by "the joyous talk of yesterday" that he composed a Latin poem and gave it to the "candid nobles," Stanhope and Harrington, hoping they would influence a decision of mercy:

> Three brothers – I shall only speak the truth –
> Three brothers, hurried by mere dint of youth,
> Incautious youth, were found in arms of late,

---

[2] Josiah Owen, *Jacobite and Nonjuring Principles, Freely Examined, in a Letter to the Master-Tool of the Faction at Manchester*, 2nd ed. (Manchester, 1748), iv-viii.

[3] J. Byrom, *Remains*, II, part 2, 431.

[4] *Ibid.*, 444.

And rushing on to their approaching fate.
One, in a fever, sent up to be tried,
From jail to jail delivered, died.
……………………………………..
The third was then a little boy at school,
That played the truant from the rod and rule;
The child, to join his brothers, left his book,
And arms, alas! Instead of apples took.
Now lies confined the poor unhappy lad –
For death mere pity and mere shame forbad –
Long time confined, and waiting Mercy's bail.
Two years confined amidst the horrors of a jail.
…………………………………………..
He is my countryman, my noble lords,
And room for hope your genius affords;
Be truly noble; hear a well meant prayer,
And deign my fellow-citizen to spare.[5]

In June Byrom was disappointed that Richmond had not read the Latin verses that Stanhope passed on to him, but he continued his campaign.[6] In July Folkes took him to Richmond's house, where he met with several of the duke's Grand Lodge colleagues (Montagu, Henry Fox, and Stukeley). Byrom noted with surprise the presence of "Charles Ratcliffe's son (that was executed)," who had been released to France after his father's death. James Radcliffe had returned to London, where he struggled for months to legally obtain his family's inheritance to support his widowed mother and her children. One wonders what he felt in 1748, as Byrom pleaded with Richmond for mercy on Charles Deacon, for he must have known that the duke had urged the rapid execution of James's own father, who was Richmond's cousin. The unrelenting duke now echoed Nichols's and Owen's argument against the Deacons and responded that "the father and son not repenting…God himself did not pardon without repentance."[7] Byrom recorded, "I did not care to give the reply for fear of exasperating." Charles Deacon was transported to Antigua, where he soon died; thus, the grieving doctor lost all three of his sons.

Josiah Owen also scorned the mystical and esoteric interests of Byrom and Deacon, calling the latter "Dr. Paracelsus" and both men disciples of the "seditious" Jacob Boehme. Certainly, Byrom's library catalogue reveals his extensive reading in Hermetic, Rosicrucian, and Cabalistic works.[8] At this time, many initiates of the *Écossais* high degrees (in Scotland as well as Europe) combined esoteric studies with elevation in the fraternity. Byrom met frequently with Scottish Masonic friends, such as Lord Morton and Thomas, Lord Erskine. He was especially anxious to help John Forbes, Master of Pitsligo, whose father Lord Pitsligo was hiding out in caves and bogs in Scotland, as loyalist troops continued to search for him: "Various romantic anecdotes suggest a benign Lear-like figure, haunting the moors dressed as a mendicant."[9] John Forbes travelled

---

[5] *Ibid.*, 456.
[6] *Ibid.*, 448-51.
[7] *Ibid.*, 450-51.
[8] J. Byrom, *Catalogue*, *66*, 106, 157-63, 187, 191, 222, etc.
[9] D. Shuttleton, "Jacobitism," 35.

to London to try to get his father's attainder reversed on technical grounds, and Byrom recorded: "I did see the Master of Pit.[sligo] when he was here; we passed an evening together, only two of us, to our mutual satisfaction; he made me a present of a book written by his father."[10] He wrote his daughter Beppie that "I shall be a Scotchman by and by; but half of `em are gone over to Flanders."

Beppie joined many other female Jacobites in the defiant wearing of plaid, which infuriated Owen.[11] He accused Dr. Deacon of dressing his young students "in the Livery of Rebellion":

> Is it not to convince the World, that there is no Heresy in Scotch Plaid, when wore only as a Badge of Romish superstion? …That Plaid Politics and Popery are this Gentleman's Aversion? Whence it is that your Ladies disarm themselves of their other Attractions, and distinguish themselves by Party Dress and Rage?[12]

Adding to the corruption of the young was the placement of Thomas Carte's *History of England* – his "political Romances "– in the library, thus poisoning "that fountain of Science, the public Library of Manchester" with "the very Dreggs of Party Spirit."

When Byrom, "the Master Tool of Faction," moved to London in 1748, Owen lost his local target, but his cause was further propagated by Henry Fielding, who increasingly targeted Dr. King, with whom Byrom collaborated in London, as the fomenter of "Plaid Politics."[13] King joined Byrom in trying to get help for Lord Pitsligo, whom he had met either in Scotland or when the Scot and his son visited Bath and possibly Oxford in 1737.[14] King later wrote a fulsome tribute to Pitsligo, "the *rara avis in terris,*" who never spoke evil of any man: "It is no wonder that such an excellent man…should be universally admired and beloved, insomuch, that I persuade myself he has not one enemy in the world."[15] While government troops still searched for him, he was "protected by men of different principles" (Scottish Whigs), and King wrote:

> It was not ambition, but a love for his country, and conscientious regard for his duty, which drew this honest man into the rebellion of 1745. A great prince, who had been well informed of my Lord Pitsligo's character, would immediately have pardoned him, and have restored the little estate which he had forfeited.[16]

King and Byrom were aware that Pitsligo was the anonymous author of the preface to the Marquis de Marsay's *Discourses on Subjects Relating to the Spiritual Life, Translated from the French* (1749), published in Edinburgh by the Jacobite Ruddiman brothers. In 1748-49, while his son labored to get his attainder reversed, Pitsligo took comfort in supporting the mystical writing of Marsay, a French Protestant, who was condemned by rationalist critics:

---

[10] J. Byrom, *Remains*, II, part ii, 471-72.
[11] *Ibid.*, 434.
[12] J. Owen, *Jacobite and Nonjuring*, 157.
[13] J. Byrom, *Remains*, II, part 2, 453.
[14] H. Tayler, *Jacobite Court*, **107**.
[15] Williqm King, *Political and Literary Anecdotes of His Own Time* (London, 1819). 145.
[16] *Ibid.*, 146.

> It is a great Pity that some well-meaning Persons, great Friends of the Letter of Christianity, are such Enemies to the Spirit of it, as to fly out against all internal Operations on the Soul; calling them *Enthusiasm, Fanaticism,* whatever their Spleen and Aversion can suggest! All the Derision and ill Names given to revealed Religion by *Deists* and *Atheists,* are employed by some of the Clergy, and their Lay-disciples, against what they call *Mysticism,* as the worst Name they can invent.[17]

As a friend of the Scottish mystics and Masons who believed in second sight, Pitsligo asked, "Cannot God make known to whom he pleases an Infinity of future Events, by Signs or Voices, or whatever Way he thinks fit to choose?"[18] He further described the three states of initiation utilized by the mystics, "the purgative, the illuminative, and the unitive," and "Analogy, a Resemblance between natural and spiritual things." Though he did not mention Ramsay, whose themes were strikingly similar, he did refer to his late friend's spiritual heroes Bourignon, Fenelon, Guyon, Poiret, the Philadelphians, as well as "Jacob Behmen's Writings (dark as they are)." Finally, he hinted at the Christian Cabalistic notion of the androgynous Adam (or Adam Kadmon), while strongly defending the Cabalists' and Ramsay's belief in universal restoration (or *Tikkun*).

Pitsligo addressed the Preface to "J.F. Esq.," his neighbor and son-in-law, James Fergusson, Lord Pitfour, who served as his defence council in the effort to get his attainder reversed. Pitfour had boldly defended the Jacobites captured at Carlisle, and he was evidently a Freemason, who shared Pitsligo's spiritual and ecumenical beliefs.[19] In an unpublished "Second Letter" to Pitfour for a second volume of Marsay's works, Pitsligo responded to the attacks upon his Preface by free-thinkers, deists, and Christians of all "Denominations." He also revealed that he haunted the coffee-houses in disguise, where he heard arguments about the Preface:

> As my name is a little known in that small unfinish'd piece of Work, I get sometimes a little Diversion in hearing the Objections of different Partys; but unless the Charge be very heavy, as for instance That the Writer is a Despiser and Hater of all Churches and Church-men, a Deist in a Mask and the like; in that case I only say "I believe the man has meant no such thing."[20]

The elderly philosopher certainly needed some amusement, when he slipped out of his wilderness hideouts, for the English House of Lords overturned the positive verdict made in 1749 by the Scottish court of session, and his attainder was thus maintained until his death in 1762.

While King and Byrom tried to help their Scottish friends and "brothers," Fielding went after Dr. King as a dangerously seditious Jacobite. He had especially criticized the student rioters at Oxford, who in February 1748 were reportedly inspired by Dr. King to proclaim "King James forever" and to curse George II. A pamphlet war about the

---

[17] Marquis de Marsay, *Discourses on Subjects Relating to the Spiritual Life* (Edinburgh, 1749), 2.

[18] *Ibid.*, 3, 15, 19, 30.

[19] Pitfour was a member of the Edinburgh Musical Society, which initially met in a Masonic chamber and which had an overlapping membership with the lodges; see Jennifer Macleod, "The Edinburgh Musical Society: Its Membership and Repertoire, 1728-1797" (Ph.D. Dissertation: Edinburgh University, 2001), 235, 244.

[20] D. Shuttleton, "Jacobitism," 51.

Oxford disturbances was waged between Hanoverians and Jacobites, which led Orrery (now resident in Ireland) to worry about King's safety.[21] The uproar led the government to attempt to strip the chancellorship from the Earl of Arran, Ormonde's brother, and replace him with a Whig.

Fielding had especially mocked the wearing of plaid at the Lichfield races in summer 1748, when Jacobite sympathizers, including many disaffected Masons, boldly taunted the Hanoverians.[22] He wanted George II's ban against wearing any item of Highland dress, especially plaids, to be implemented in England as well as Scotland. Scots who violated the law would be subjected to transportation to the king's plantations. These suppressive efforts only emboldened Dr. King's Masonic supporters, such as Moses Mendes, John Byrom, John Ellis, and their circle. Ellis composed "Tartana or the Pladdie. An Allegorical Rhythm" (1748), which was headed by the epigraph, "Let us not weaken still the weaker side by our Divisions – Addison's *Cato*".

In the version published in 1782, the poem seemed aimed at reconciliation between political factions, as it featured debates between ladies wearing different colors – blue from the Hanoverian Garter wearers, yellow from rural folks, green from poetic bards, and, Jove's favorite, red as the source of all the colors and worn by Jove's "chief favourite Rosaline," the "fairest maid/That ever danc'd in chequer'd shade."[23] The poet comments that "In all the fire of furious rage/ Men for mere colours thus engage." Jove finally decides on the "chequer'd" plaid of Rosaline:

> `Ye all are lovely when ye join
> To grace the Plaid of Rosaline.
> And this be Albion's future lore;
> Leave party's treacherous bait, no more
> No more be dupes to France as heretofore.
> View Britain's Monarch, good and great,
> Upon whose royal breast are seen
> Honour'd, by turns, both blue and green;
> Where virtue ever finds its worth,
> Of southern, or of northern birth.[24]

However, in the MS. version written in 1748, there was a decidedly more Jacobite tone. A reader, probably Mendes, added the comment, "Under the character of Rosaline is a compliment to the celebrated Miss F----- M-----," after "her protection of the P---- in S---t---d." The references to Flora Macdonald and Charles Edward were then made clear in the additional lines:

> Hence then in Hieroglyphic Tartan,
> Array the Youth – the modern Spartan!
> Born to deliver my plunder'd Nation/
> From Knaves, and Fools, and Usurp----n [Usurpation].[25]

---

[21] D. Greenwood, *William King*, 182-85.
[22] Owen, *Jacobite and Nonjuring*, 369.
[23] John Ellis, "Tartana, or the Plaidie. An Allegorical Poem," *European Magazine* (August, 1782), 151-52, 234.
[24] *Ibid.*, 235
[25] London, Grand Lodge Library: MS. 1860. Men.

Mendes shared Ellis's admiration for Flora, as suggested by his poem, "My bonny North-ern Lassie" (MS. in the Grand Lodge notebook). Dr. King, an admirer of Flora and a good friend of Ellis and Mendes, would certainly approve of this version of "Tartana or the Pladdie."

From May to August 1748 Mendes seemed to think of Masonic traditions when he anonymously wrote the librettos for two oratorios composed by Handel, *Solomon* and *Susanna.* Though the identity of the librettist has long puzzled scholars, Andrew Pink draws on material in the Grand Lodge notebook to argue convincingly for Mendes's authorship.[26] He points to an unpublished poem by Ellis:

> A very great friend is,
> To the making oratorio's [sic]:
> ....
> When he was alone
> He wrote Solomon,
> And robb'd the poor man of his glory;
> If it had not been Handel'd
> It might have been candl'd,
> And the Jew beat for spoiling the story.[27]

Handel avoided partisan politics and was supported by George II and, after initial hostility, by the Prince of Wales, but his known librettists maintained opposition atti-tudes. William Gibbons argues that his librettist Nicola Haym, an Italian-born musician of German-Jewish descent, drew on Chevalier Ramsay's *Travels of Cyrus* for the oratorio *Orlando* (1733) and included Masonic elements in the narrative.[28] From 1735 onwards, Handel's most important librettist, the wealthy landowner Charles Jennens, was a Non-juring Jacobite, who was friendly with Dr. King and Edward Holdsworth, whom Horace Mann charged with carrying Jacobite letters and Stuart portraits to England.[29] Jennens not only wrote the script for Handel's famous *Messiah* (1741-42), but the work was "en-tirely his brainchild."[30] As a practicing architect who worked closely with operative master masons, Jennens was almost certainly a "brother." Thus, he would have been receptive to Mendes's Masonic and opposition/Jacobite symbolism in the libretto of *Solomon.*

Pink suggests that Mendes pointed to Frederick, Prince of Wales, and his wife Augusta as patrons of the opposition:

> *Solomon* is a glorification of Frederick's character (he had been a Freemason since 1737), expressing hope for a revived nation at peace with itself (repre-sented by the building of the Temple) and at peace with its neighbours

---

[26] Andrew Pink, "Solomon, Susanna and Moses: Locating Handel's Lost Librettist." I am grateful to Dr. Pink for sending me a copy of his full paper, which is published in a condensed version in *Eighteenth-Century Music*, 12 (2015), 211-22. My quotes are from the longer version, which hopefully will be published in the future.
[27] UGLE: MS. 1860.Men
[28] William Gibbons, "Divining Zoraster: Masonic Elements in Handel's Oratorio," *Eighteenth-Century Life*, 34 (2010), 70-71. Haym had allegedly written the libretto before his death in 1729.
[29] H. Walpole, *Correspondence*, XIX, 172n.12.
[30] Ruth Smith, "The Achievements of Charles Jennens," *Music & Letters*, 70 (1989), 161-90; and her article, "Charles Jennens," *ODNB*.

(represented by Solomon's meeting with the Queen of Sheba), all Patriot ideals for their vision of Britain under Frederick.

According to Thomas Carte, at this time the Tories and Jacobites agreed to collaborate with Prince Frederick in defending Dr. King and the University of Oxford from governmental persecution.[31] Byrom recorded that the prince met Lord Lichfield, a Jacobite friend of King, in the park, and asked him if he had read Bolingbroke's book about a patriot king, "and "his Lordship answering that he had, the Prince told him, Well, my Lord, I shall be that patriot King."[32] Orrery, who was worried about the Whig attacks on Dr. King, continued to privately toast James III, while also turning towards the opposition party of Frederick.[33]

As a former student and current friend of Dr. King, Mendes apparently agreed with this strategy. Moreover, he suggested Frederick's affiliation with opposition Masons in his lines about Solomon's Temple. His description of God as "Almighty pow'r, who rul'st the earth and skies,/ And bade gay order from confusion rise," echoed Masonic terminology for the Grand Architect, while his description of the columns of Jachin and Boaz as "Golden columns, fair and bright," and of the sculptured cherubim "display'd/ O'er the ark," drew on Masonic temple symbolism.[34]

Prince Frederick as Solomon was presented in contrast to satirical portrayals of his father, George II, which poked fun at the king's poor political judgment and his sexual indiscretions. A scurrilous print, "Solomon in his Glory" (1738), continued to circulate, in which George was portrayed as a libidinous King Solomon, in a disheveled state, sprawled across the throne with his kingly robes awry, being stroked on the thigh by his [German] mistress, Madame Wallmoden.[35] In 1749, one year after Frederick as Solomon the faithful husband was portrayed by Mendes and Handel, the reprinted 1738 satire was the subject of government prosecution of obscene prints. In an unpublished poem, probably written in the same period as the Handel librettos, Mendes criticized the worship of money and power by the Hanoverian government:

> O Thou who makest Mankind thy sport,
> Ador'd by all, but most at Court,
> And viewing with two partial eyes
> Made Oxford fall and Walpole rise.
> While the proud Monarch from his Throne,
> Is said to pray to thee alone.[36]

Then in lines that were relevant to his portrayal of Prince Frederick, but also implicitly targeting King George, he wrote:

> Adultry in the higher place,
> Seems to give vice superior grace,

---

[31] E. Cruickshanks, *Political Untouchables*, 111.

[32] J. Byrom, *Remains*, II, part 2, 492.

[33] "John Boyle, 5th Earl of Orrery," *ODNB*.

[34] Georg Friedrich Handel, *Solomon. An Oratorio* (1749). The attribution of the libretto to Newburgh Hamilton is no longer accepted. <http://opera.stanford.edu/iu/libretti/solomon.htm>.

[35] A. Pink, "Solomon."

[36] UGLE: MS. 1860. Men. "Imitation of the 35th Ode of the 1st Book of Horace."

And as for simple fornication,
If that be sin, Lord help the nation.

In *Susanna*, Frederick and his wife were portrayed as a chaste and loyal couple, who hope to elevate Britain out of its state of corruption and war; thus, the Chorus of Israelites sings:

How long, O Lord, shall Israel groan,
In slavery and pain?
Jehovah, hear thy people's moan,
And break th' oppressor's chain![37]

Joachim replies that "Our crimes repeated have provok'd His rage,/ And now He scourges a degen'rate age." These words echoed the current criticism of the Whig ministry expressed by opposition Patriots, disaffected Masons, Jacobites, and members of the Mendes-Ellis-King circle. Ruth Smith points out that audiences in Handel's time were highly skilled in the art of interpreting allegory, which could "be double, even contradictory, allowing the author an air of injured innocence if challenged on the more provocative reading."[38]

Ambiguous, allegorical writing became especially important to Jacobites in the late 1740s, as Hanoverian writers launched an intense campaign against the continuing Jacobite activities and popular sympathy for the executed rebels. Mendes's friend Byrom was accused by Owen of avoiding prosecution by writing in verse:

Instead of Argument he'll give you a Catch: Instead of Reason a Rhime: Doggrel instead of Demonstration… [He'll] endeavour to fire away the Devil of Loyalty and Whiggism out of the Nation, by writing------Verses. Thus, as the py'd Piper of Hamel…charm'd away all the Brunswick Rats with his Music, so our Poetical Scaramouch would chase out of our Land, to adopt his own Expression, all Hanover Rats with a Ballad.[39]

On 10 February 1749 Fielding "formally published" his rollicking novel, *The History of Tom Jones, A Foundling*, of which six chapters had been drafted before the 1745 rebellion. He dedicated it to George, 1st Baron Lyttelton, and John Russell, 4th Duke of Bedford, formerly members of the Patriot opposition but now government place-holders. Bedford's political apostasy led to his being horse-whipped by a plaid-wearing Jacobite mob at the Lichfield races.[40] Through their influence Fielding had also been commissioned as magistrate for the County of Middlesex, and he pledged to Bedford that he would "completely serve the Government" in his new office.[41] Bedford was affiliated with the Grand Lodge, which perhaps influenced Fielding's benign references to Freemasonry in *Tom Jones*. He compared the negotiations and concessions within marriage, "well-known to most husbands," to "the secrets of free-masonry," which "should be divulged to none

---

[37] Georg Friedrich Handel, *Susanna. An Oratorio* (1749). http://opera.stanford.edu/iu/libretti/susanna.htm.

[38] Ruth Smith, *Handel's Oratorios and Eighteenth-Century Thought* (Cambridge, 1995), 211.

[39] J. Owen, *Jacobite and Nonjuring*, viii.

[40] E. Cruickshanks, *Political Untouchables*, 107.

[41] "Henry Fielding," *ODNB*.

who are not members of that honourable fraternity."[42] He referred to the secret signs of the initiates: "There surely is no general sympathy among knaves; nor have they, like freemasons, any common sign of communication." Fielding had no problem with the loyalist Masonry of Bedford's Grand Lodge.

However, in the novel, he did not extend any sympathy to the Jacobite Masons who had been decapitated or hung, drawn, and quartered. He based the moderate Whig character, Squire Allworthy, on Ralph Allen, friend of the late Alexander Pope, and made Allworthy counter the critics of the rebels' executions with a mild but firm opinion:

> though Mr Allworthy did not think, with some late writers that mercy consists only in punishing offenders, yet he was as far from thinking that it is proper to this excellent quality to pardon great criminals wantonly, without any reason whatsoever. Any doubtfulness of the fact, or any circumstance of mitigation, was never disregarded; but the petitions of an offender, or the intercessions of others, did not in the least affect him. In a word, he never pardoned because the offender himself, or his friends, were unwilling that he should be punished.[43]

In other words, Allworthy would have agreed with Cumberland's and Richmond's rejection of petitions for mercy submitted for the rebel prisoners.

Despite Fielding's strong defense of the government, he had been stung by the virulent criticism flung at him by opposition writers, who scorned his government-subsidized, anti-Stuart and anti-Catholic propaganda in *The Jacobite's Journal*. Thus, in his novel, he adopted a more humorous tone in his portrayal of the west-country Jacobite, Squire Western, a hard-drinking, fox-hunting, profanity-spouting but hospitable and loveable buffoon. His acquaintance with such characters when he rode the western circuit apparently influenced his less strident characterization. In the conclusion of Part I, Western lashes out at his citified, sophisticated sister, who considers him almost sub-human:

> Do you think no one hath any understanding, unless he hath been at court? Pox! The world is coming to a fine pass, indeed, if we are all fools, except a parcel of roundheads and Hanover rats! Pox! I hope the times are a-coming that we shall make fools of them, and every man shall enjoy his own... I hope to *zee* it, sister, before the Hanover rats have eat up all our corn, and left us nothing but turneps to feed upon.[44]

In Part II, much of it written after the quelling of the rebellion, Fielding took on a more serious tone, making the young Jones expound pro-Hanoverian, pro-Protestant speeches, while trying to join the government troops:

> The sergeant had informed Mr Jones that they were marching against the rebels, and expected to be commanded by the glorious Duke of Cumberland. By which the reader may perceive... that this was the very time when the late rebellion was at its highest; and indeed the banditti were now marched

---

[42] Henry Fielding, *Tom Jones*, ed. John Bender and Simon Stern (Oxford, 1996), 75, 204.

[43] *Ibid.*, 88-89.

[44] Fielding, *Tom Jones*, 280.

> into England, intending, as it was thought, to fight the king's forces, and to attempt pushing forward to the metropolis.
> Jones had some heroic ingredients in his composition, and was a hearty well-wisher to the glorious cause of liberty, and of the Protestant religion. [45]

Jones cannot believe that "there should be a party among us mad enough" to desire the placing of the Stuart family "again on the throne."[46]

To emphasize the madness and irrationality of Jacobitism, Fielding portrayed Mr. Partridge, Jones's Jacobite companion, as a superstitious and gullible Catholic in order to mock the many prophecies and stories of second sight that circulated in Scotland. Partridge is so obtuse that he thinks Jones is on his way to join the rebels, and he reports to him his conversation with a "popish priest," who said that "the Catholics did not expect to be any gainers by the change; for that Prince Charles was as good a Protestant as any in England."[47] When Jones rejects both the prince's Protestantism and right to the crown, Partridge replies that "all the prophecies I have ever read speak of a great deal of blood to be spilt in the quarrel, and the miller with three thumbs, who is now alive, is to hold the horses of the three kings, up to his knees in blood." Jones calls this "stuff and nonsense," for "Monsters and prodigies are the proper arguments to support monstrous and absurd doctrines. The cause of King George is the cause of liberty and true religion. In other words, it is the cause of common sense."

Fielding also featured a scene in which the lovely Sophia Western, the object of Jones's affection, is absurdly misidentified as Jenny Cameron, the Jacobite heroine, while her drunken, blustering father proclaims that he will never let her marry "a lord on any account; I hate all lords; they are a parcel of courtiers and Hanoverians, and I will have nothing to do with them."[48] Western appalls his citified sister by "swearing that all the Londoners were like the court, and thought of nothing but plundering country gentlemen... They have beggared the nation, but they shall never beggar me. My land shall never be sent over to Hanover." In the final reconciliation of all parties and marriage of Tom and Sophia, Fielding affirmed that "a conquered rebellion strengthens a government." Though the exiled Charles Edward Stuart would not have agreed with that conclusion, he was entertained by Fielding's comic narratives and ordered English and French editions of *Tom Jones* and *Joseph Andrews*, which he read with his French mistress.[49]

On 1 April 1749 Richard Rawlinson was pleased that the long-awaited opening of the Radcliffe Library at Oxford would soon occur, and he noted its importance to Jacobite (and Masonic) developments: "On the 13th instant is to be the great day for opening Dr. Radcliffe's Library, and Mr. Carte's history [of England] will be the first book placed in it."[50] Dr. King was to preside over the ceremony, and his Jacobite friends at Oxford invited Charles Edward to the opening, "where they assure him of a better reception than the University had at Court lately."[51] Though the prince could not accept the invitation,

---

[45] *Ibid.*, 321.

[46] *Ibid.*, 414.

[47] *Ibid.*, 381, 898.

[48] *Ibid.*, 503-04, 736, 777, 825.

[49] A. Lang, *Pickle*, 96.

[50] Stickland Gibson, "Francis Wise, B.D., Oxford Antiquary, Librarian, and Archivist," *Oxoniensia*, 1 (1936), 183.

[51] Andrew Lang, *Pickle the Spy* (London, 1897), 52.

exiled *Écossais* supporters were soon delighted by King's defiant performance. Despite ~~~od of Whig pamphlets attacking him, the "Old Trumpeter of Liberty Hall" was not ~~imidated, and on 13 April he gave an inflammatory oration in Latin, which included ~~~epeated calls for "*redeat*" (return, restore). The Jacobite Masons considered King a brother, and his support for the design and construction of the library was seen as emblematic of his traditionalist views of the fraternity.

For over a decade, King had worked closely with the Masonic architect James Gibbs on the design and construction of the Radcliffe, while he also collaborated with operative stonemasons on the renovations of St. Mary's Hall. Murray Pittock argues that Gibbs included Stuart and Catholic elements in his interior and exterior designs, expressing "the silent symbolic language of Jacobitism."[52] King characterized Gibbs as "the most famous Architect," whom he loves, for he "was formerly my Host, and one, whom I knew to be the most humane and friendly Person living."[53] Like King, Gibbs was close to Thomas, Lord Erskine, to whom he would later leave his estate in gratitude for the favors granted him by Erskine's father, the late Earl of Mar, who had launched Gibbs on his architectural career. After Erskine's initiation in the Kilwinning Lodge in Edinburgh in 1736, he devoted himself "to the study of Freemasonry," and he was elected Grand Master of Scotland in 1749.[54]

In mid-May Horace Walpole wrote Mann about King's defiant speech and its encouraging effect on the Jacobites, who believed that the Prince of Wales had become sympathetic to their cause:

> The Parliament continues sitting…We were to have some chastisement for Oxford, where, besides the late riots, the famous Dr. King, the Pretender's great agent, made a most violent speech at the opening of the Radcliffe Library. The ministry denounced judgement but, in their old style, have grown frightened, and dropped it. However, this menace gave occasion to a meeting and union between the Prince's party and the Jacobites, which Lord Egmont had been laboring all the winter. They met at the St. Alban's Tavern, near Pall-mall, last Monday morning, an hundred and twelve Lords and Commoners. [55]

The outreach to Prince Frederick by Jacobite Masons such as Beaufort, Wynn, and Dashwood aimed to produce collaboration with disaffected Tory and Whig Masons. But the charges of Jacobite sympathy would lead to even harsher treatment of the prince by his father and the Whig government.

As controversy swirled about King's oration, his enemy John Burton published *Remarks on Dr. K – g's Speech before the University of Oxford* in January 1750. He targeted King's lavish praise of Dr. John Radcliffe, the late physician, whose bequest made the construction of the great library possible. He determined to smear Radcliffe as a Jacobite by linking him with the recently executed Jacobite Grand Master, Charles Radcliffe, Earl of

---

[52] M. Pittock, *Material Culture*, 49-53.
[53] William King, *A Translation of a late Celebrated Oration, Occasioned by a Lible* (sic), entitled, Remarks on Doctor K—g's Speech (London, 1750), 32-33.
[54] James Saunders and Robert Wright, *A History of the Lodge of Alloa No. 69, 1757-1957* (Alloa, 1957), 9-11.
[55] H. Walpole, *Correspondence*, XX, 50-51.

Derwentwater. He rejected King's praise of the physician's piety and claimed that his supposed generosity was motivated by "mere Vanity":

> What gives no small Confirmation to this Charge against our Speech-maker's Hero, is a Story I have read… that he offered to make a younger son of the *Derwentwater* Family his Heir instead of the University of O----d, if that Family would but consent to let the youth change his *Religious* Principles. The *Political* Principles of that Family, tho' they were the more absurd for being separated from their *Religious* ones, the Doctor, it seems, had no quarrel with.[56]

By "indulging his Vanity," the doctor hoped to "usurp" the Derwentwater arms by insinuating "that He was of the same family, to which he did not bear even the most distant Relation."

King's most controversial lines were his repeated calls for restoration – "*Redeat*," restore the Stuart age of Astraea and save Britain from corruption and degeneration. In a rather bizarre interpretation, Burton asserted "I cannot doubt but by Astraea he meant JENNY CAMERON. For as our Speech-maker measures every Body's Christianity by their J------sm [Jacobitism] , he might well call her Christianissima," for "she was a kind of Guardian to the young P-------r [Pretender], without whom our Speech-maker thinks there can be no Virtue in this Land."[57] Carried away, Burton then charged the abstemious, teetotalling King with "Feasting and Whoring" and bragging that he can furnish "an extraordinary Degree of Venereal Heat."

For King, who was angered by the government's prosecution of Dr. John Purnell, Oxford vice-chancellor, for being too merciful to the student rioters, the signs were ominous for the university's future. In 1748, when the chancellorship of Cambridge became vacant, there was strong support to name the Prince of Wales to the position, but George II vetoed it. Instead, the Duke of Newcastle was appointed, "after much political maneuvering," and he wrote the Whig Bishop of London that "Cambridge is as meritorious as the other [Oxford] is justly to be censured." Over the next decades, Newcastle would manage the university according to his Hanoverian political agenda.

Dr. King was appalled by Newcastle's lavish celebrations at the university, and he warned that if Oxford, like Cambridge, declined "into the Vale of Vice…we should not even deserve a *Patriot Prince*."[58] Among King's "*Redeats*," was the plea to withstand such political interference in the university:

> That whenever our noble and excellent Chancellor [the Jacobite Earl of Arran] shall depart (long hence, I hope) we may not see in his Place a Master, haughty, unmerciful, avaricious, illiterate, impious; but an easy and benign Ruler… That the Office of Vice-Chancellor may be always conferred upon a Man, holy, social, learned… That, the Designs of pernicious Men being

---

[56] Phileleutherus Londinensis [John Burton], *Remarks on Dr. K—g's Speech at the University of Oxford* (London, 1750), 20.

[57] *Ibid.*, 40.

[58] W. King, *Translation*, 13.

frustrated, no one may be invested with such Power…to violate our Laws himself, or exhort others to violate them![59]

Burton responded furiously to the criticism of the unnamed Newcastle:

> What could our Speech-maker say more than to warn the University not to follow the late Example of her Sister in chusing a C---------r [Chancellor] who is well affected to our present Happy E----------t [Establishment] …The noble Person, lately chosen into That High Office by the University of Cambridge, is the Reverse of that abominable Character in every particular.[60]

The government was so angered by King's oration and Oxford's continuing Jacobitism that they tried to name the Duke of Cumberland as successor to Chancellor Arran, in the event of his death, but Arran's longevity frustrated this plan (he died in 1758).[61]

The many responses, pro and con, to the "*Redeat*" oration, often reflected the political divisions within Freemasonry. William Mason, a loyalist Mason and ambitious Cambridge churchman, published *Isis, an Elegy* (1749), in which he criticized the Jacobite sedition of teachers and students at Oxford, sitting on the banks of the river Isis: "See! Gothic Licence rage o'er all my coast./ See! Hydra Faction spread it's impious reign,/ Poison each breast, and madden ev'ry brain."[62] Under the influence of instructors like King, the sons of Isis "deal their insults thro' a peaceful land,/ And boast while Freedom bleeds, and Virtue groans,/ That Isis taught Rebellion to her Sons." On 1 July 1749 Mason composed an "Ode to Music," which was performed at Cambridge for the installation of his hero Newcastle as Chancellor.

Mason was answered by the young Thomas Warton in *The Triumph of Isis, a Poem. Occasioned by Isis, an Elegy* (1749). Warton's late father was a friend of Pope and a popular Jacobite professor of poetry at Oxford, whose early satire on George I, "The Turnip-Hoer," was still recited in university taverns. Warton was a traditionalist Freemason, and he undertook a lifelong study of Gothic architecture and the operative stonemasons who developed its style and stone-carving techniques. In his tribute to Dr. King, he connected Oxford's grand Gothic buildings with King's call for freedom from political interference. He linked Mason's elegy with "the venal sons of slavish Cam," who hope to shake Oxford's lofty towers and send "persecution…o'er yon spiry temples."[63] While Cambridge's senates revere "titled slaves," Oxford's "Gothic spires in ancient grandeur rise,/ And dare with wonted pride to rush into the skies." The "proud dome" of Radcliffe joins the ancient architecture as "fair Learning's amplest shrine." He praised King's oration as the inspiration for noble thoughts: "He blends the Speaker's with the Patriot's fire;/ Bold to conceive, nor timorous to conceal,/ What Britons dare to think, he dares to tell."

The Scottish writer John Cleland, an opposition Mason, anonymously translated portions of King's oration for publication in *The Monthly Review* (November 1749), in which he praised the library left by Dr. Radcliffe as "A magnificent; one might have added, a

---

[59] *Ibid.*, 53-54.

[60] J. Burton, *Remarks*, 44.

[61] He was succeeded by the Jacobite John Fane, 7th Earl of Westmorland.

[62] For Mason's Masonic affiliation, see Marie Mulvey Roberts, *British Poets and Secret Societies* (London, 1986), 27; William Mason, *Isis, An Elegy* (London, 1749), 13, 15.

[63] Thomas Warton, *The Triumph of Isis* (London, 1749), 4-7, 9.

princely foundation, had any thing in these times been less the practice of *princes* than munificence, or encouragement of arts and sciences."[64] Noting that "this piece of eloquence" had made "so much noise," he featured the "*Redeat*" sections and stressed King's criticism of government corruption and persecution. As an opponent of Newcastle's policies, Cleland enjoyed King's characterization of the new chancellor of Cambridge as "insolent, hard, rapacious, unlearned, and profligate."

Among the more moderate Whig Masons, Martin Folkes did not agree with the attacks on Dr. King, and in April 1749 he wrote Orrery that "I was with our friend Dr. King."[65] Orrery had barely escaped prosecution for his own Jacobitism, and he now more publicly identified himself with the Prince of Wales's party. But he still supported King, and he wrote from Dublin that "a virulent paper or pamphlet against Dr. King has been shewn to me," and though the author "is very dull," yet "his kind of scurrility" should be answered: "In the meantime the Doctor appears to me like a noble Eagle flying high in the air and basking himself in the Sun, while his enemies are like so many frogs croaking in a dirty pool, and constantly pelted, whenever they thrust up their heads thro' the scum of the water."[66]

It was the Jewish Jacobite Mason, Moses Mendes, who most fervently came to the orator's defense, albeit anonymously, for he shared the disgust King expressed for "those detestable Informers, who have so embroiled our Affairs of late."[67] The Oxford scholar Richard Blacow had charged King with responsibility for "the treasonable riot," and he subsequently published a detailed account of his alleged complicity. Mendes responded with an unpublished poem, "On the Dignified Informer":

> From selling Ale see BLACO rise,
> A Cannon roaring horrid Lies;
> Prompt to inform and to foreswear,
> Plotting from Rags he us'd to wear,
> To seat himself in Sacerdotal Chair.[68]

In an ambitious Spenserian poem, *The Blatant Beast* (1749), not published until 1792, Mendes paid tribute to King and his Oxford colleagues who continued to stand for principle in a world of political mendacity.[69] Though Mendes's editor notes with some puzzlement that chivalry was "at something of a low ebb in the 1740s" in England, the poet seemed to draw on the revival of chivalric and Templar themes in Jacobite and *Écossais* Freemasonry.[70] He portrayed "good PETER EREMITE" as a son of true religion, "of whose great deeds in Tasso you may read;/ He `gainst Infidels, in per'lous fight/ By counsel wise did Christian GODFREY lead."[71] In Tasso's *Gerusalemme Liberata* (1591), Godfrey of Bouillon was portrayed as the great crusader who led the Knights Templar.

---

[64] "Oratio in Theatro Sheldonio…A Guielmo King," *Monthly Review*, 2 (November 1749), 69-72.

[65] Orrery, *Orrery Papers*, II, 52.

[66] *Ibid.*, II, 66-67.

[67] W. King, *Translation*, 41.

[68] UGLE: MS. 1860. Men.

[69] *European Magazine*, 22 (November, December 1792), 331-46, 417-22.

[70] Editorial comment on "The Blatant Beast," I quote from the online version. http://spenserians.cath.edu/TextRecord.php?=GET&textsi. I quote from the online version.

[71] *Ibid.*, 7

Tasso's book was the favorite reading of the Stuart king, James VI and I, and it was replete with praise of the architects and stonemasons who built the great Crusader castles.[72] Mendes was not only familiar with Tasso's crusader themes, but through his friendship with Dr. King he may well have been aware of Ramsay's chivalric Masonic discourse and eulogies to the Bouillon family, of the late Derwentwater's desire to re-establish Freemasonry on its ancient chivalric basis, and of the Stuart prince's alleged role in the Order of the Temple.

Mendes's knight, Sir Pelleas, sets out to reform the decadent political and religious world, portrayed as the Blatant Beast, and he is soon accompanied by the second-sighted Peter Eremite, who expresses an ecumenical vision which echoes Ramsay's Masonic universalism: "our Religion teaches, gentle youth,/ To serve all men, for all, I hope, shall rise/ On the last day, and dwell in yonder skies." Against this pious hope for universal regeneration, is "madding Zeal, that with an iron hand/ Would hold the free-born mind in slavish tyes," that uses military force to thin "the frighted land." When the two pilgrims come to "the island's chiefest town," they see a magnificent edifice with many pillars, on which "the polish'd marble cast a glittering sheen,/ And well the craftsman work'd, who hew'd the stone, I ween."[73] However, all the marvelous constructions have been defiled by false patriots, who succumb to bribes and places and leave their reforming agendas behind. It has been suggested that Mendes's chief target was David Mallet, the Scottish opposition poet, who had joined the government: "For he who late appear'd in patriot guise,/ And for a while in borrow'd colours shin'd,/ Was just now quitting the godlike enterprize,/ To join the losels vild whom erst he did despise."[74]

But some true patriots held out, such as Gilbert West, a former "Cobham Cub," who was not tainted and who shared Mendes's interest in Spenser and chivalric literature. Even more admirable were the defenders of Dr. King and Oxford, such as Thomas Warton, whose *Triumph of Isis* (1748) had celebrated the independence of the university and the glories of its Gothic architecture. Mendes greatly admired this work, and he later employed Warton as tutor to his son. Sir Pelleas is told "to pursue the BEAST,/ That doth the world with his infection stain," an infection which has now reached Oxford, where some disloyal sons of the university act as informers and place-seeking parasites.[75] Fortunately, many more sons, led by Dr. King (unnamed), are courageous enough to defend her against the Blatant Beast: "Hail, RHEDECYNA! by oppression great,/ Arise, and still assert the glorious cause." Mendes's unwavering support of Dr. King would soon be rewarded on 19 June 1750, when King personally handed him the certificate making him a Master of Arts in Oxford, an honor made possible by Mendes's recent conversion to Christianity.[76]

Mendes was also pleased that his friend Paul Whitehead, still linked with the opposition Masons, rallied to Dr. King's cause and wrote a poem, "To Dr. King," which praised his battle against informers:

[72] For Stuart and Masonic interest in Tasso's work, see M. Schuchard, *Restoring the Temple*, 274-77.
[73] M. Mendez, "Blatant Beast," 12.
[74] *Ibid.*, 15
[75] *Ibid.*, 8-9
[76] With his conversion, Moses followed family tradition, for his grandfather was a Portuguese Marrano, a professing Jew who played a public role as a Catholic; V. Lipmann, "Moses Mendes," XIV, 41-42.

> Oft have I heard, with clam'rous note,
> A yelping Cur exalt his throat
> At *Cynthia's* silver rays;
> So, with blaze of Learning's light,
> When you, O King, offend his sight,
> The Spaniel *Blaco* bays.[77]

The years 1749 and 1750 saw a resurgence of Jacobite enthusiasm, as many Britons sympathized with the rebels and resented the continuing corruption of the Whig government. The Duke of Richmond recognized the seriousness of the Jacobite demonstrations at the Lichfield races, and he had recently tried to block a repeat visit to England by James Butler, kinsman of Ormonde and Arran, who in 1743 had attended the races, met with many Jacobites, and prepared for Louis XV a long list of Stuart supporters.[78] Murray of Broughton had informed on the Jacobites who collaborated with Butler when he testified before the government committee.[79] On 25 April 1748 Richmond wrote Newcastle that Prince Charles of Lorraine wanted to purchase forty horses for Louis XV and some more for himself, but Richmond asked if he should "let him know that the Monsr Butler he formerly sent here was not Welcome & that wee knew him to be a a rascally Jacobite agent for the pretender."[80] Butler had hoped to again take advantage of the Jacobite attendance at the Lichfield races to glean more intelligence for a new Stuart initiative. In September 1749 Dr. King attended the races and compiled a list of 275 Jacobite sympathizers who attended.[81]

Though Butler's visit was blocked, Louis XV sent to London his personal intelligencer, the Comte de St. Germain. The mysterious Rosicrucian Mason took advantage of his musical talents to ingratiate himself with various Whigs and especially with Lord Morton, former Grand Master and still suspected of private Jacobite sympathies. In April and May 1749 Morton hosted St. Germain in a series of performances at his London residence, which were colorfully described by Jemima, Marchioness Grey, daughter-in-law of the Whig Chancellor Hardwicke. She granted him great talent as a violinist but mocked his extravagant and passionate gestures:

> Woe! Be to the Person within the reach of his Eye! For he makes Love so violently they must have a most Inflexible Countenance to stand it… we were very much entertain'd by him or at him… I mean the Oddness of his Manner which is impossible not to laugh at, otherwise you know he is very sensible & well-bred in Conversation.[82]

She continued that "he is an Odd Creature, & the more I see him the more curious I am to know something about him. He is everything with everybody," and talks philosophy with Morton's guests (many of whom could be unwitting sources of information for the count's employer, Louis XV). One wonders if he contacted his old friends, the Prince of

---

[77] P. Whitehead, *Poems*, 224.

[78] E. Cruickshanks, *Political Untouchables*, 39-41.

[79] J. Murray, *Memorials*, 457.

[80] Richmond, *Correspondence*, letter #408.

[81] D. Greenwood, *William King*, 186.

[82] David Hunter, "The Great Pretender, Monseiur le Comte de Saint-Germain," *The Musical Times*, 144 (2003), 4-44.

Wales and Lord Chesterfield. His intelligence efforts in 1749 evidently impressed the French king, who would subsequently send him on even more important secret missions.[83]

In December 1748 the Jacobites in France were alarmed by reports that the Duke of Richmond would be sent to Paris as ambassador. John Towneley, who had fought with Charles Edward in Scotland, wrote from Paris that Richmond "is our hottest enemy, which makes me tremble for the prince, because he [the duke] carries to extreme his loyalty to the House of Hanover."[84] Towneley urged all the exiled Jacobites to appeal to Louis XV to reject the appointment. He did not know that his letter was intercepted by the English, but he was relieved when Richmond declined the appointment. However, the duke and Newcastle became especially worried in February 1749, when Charles Edward suddenly disappeared from Avignon and began nine years of incognito wandering in search of support from foreign courts. The prince hoped to take advantage of the Earl Marischal's friendship (and Masonic bonds?) with the Prussian king in order to gain Frederick II's support for a new enterprise.[85] Dr. King was privy to the overtures to Prussia, and he added a tribute to Frederick II in a footnote to the printed version of his Radcliffe oration.[86] Marischal would later report to the Prussian monarch that Dr. King was one of only two people in England "dans le secret" of the international plotting and that he was "homme d'esprit, vif, agissant."[87]

The most imaginative and audacious plan was put forth by the former *Écossais* Grand Master Hector Maclean, protégé of the late Earl of Mar, who counted upon his international Masonic network to support the enterprise. As noted earlier, the current Grand Master in Scotland was Thomas Erskine, son of Mar, who cautiously moved from opposition to supporting the government, but whom the Jacobites believed was a secret sympathizer. After Maclean's 1747 release from prison in London, he returned to France, where he resumed his close friendship with Charles Edward, and he discussed his project with the prince before the latter's departure from Avignon. In February-March 1749 Maclean proposed to Richelieu a new Jacobite rising that would involve 5,000 French landing on the east coast of Scotland with 4,000 Swedes landing on the west coast.[88] The Jacobite clans would join the liberators, and reports circulated that the Macleans were eagerly awaiting the arrival of the Swedes. The leading Swedish Masons, Tessin and Scheffer, were the main proponents of the project, and they utilized their "interior organization" of *Écossais* initiates to outwit the omnipresent Hanoverian spies and their Swedish informers. They would soon be assisted by Lord Macleod, son of the attainted Grand Master Cromarty, who had become a high-ranking Swedish Mason.[89]

The ministry's concern about a new Swedish-Jacobite initiative was further provoked when an anonymous pamphlet appeared in London bookshops in December 1749, with

---

[83] For his future espionage work, see M. Schuchard, *Emanuel Swedenborg*, 531, 537, 547-50.

[84] NA: SP 98/56, f. 276 (9 December 1748).

[85] F. McLynn, *Charles Edward Stuart*, 391, 400-01.

[86] W. King, *Translation of Oration*, 51.

[87] D. Greenwood, *William King*, 238.

[88] R. McLynn, *Charles Edward Stuart*, 395; University of Nottingham: Pelham MS. NeC2086. Report of Aleister MacDonnell ("Pickle the Spy").

[89] M. Schuchard, *Emanuel Swedenborg*, 464-65. Macleod's elaborate Swedish Masonic certificate is currently preserved in the Scottish Record Office: #6035/1/168. A photo of it is in Schuchard, *Masonic Esotericism*, 72.

the long title, *A Letter from H--- G-----, Esq. One of the Gentlemen of the Bed-Chamber of the Young Chevalier, and the only Person of his own Retinue that attended him from Avignon, in his late Journey through Germany, and elsewhere. Containing many remarkable and affecting Occurrences which happened to the P----- during the course of his mysterious Progress. To a Particular Friend.* The letter was signed, "Sir Henry Goring, Lithuania, 13 September 1749." In February 1749 Charles Edward and Goring suddenly left Avignon and began the decade of secret travels to various courts in search of support for another invasion. They were assisted by an *Éccosais* network of sympathetic *frères*, and rumors swirled that the prince was the secret Grand Master, the "unknown Superior," of the Masonic Knights Templar.[90] Frank McLynn observes that

> Charles Edward was always at least one step ahead of those who sought him. His abilities at playing a Scarlet Pimpernel role were pronounced. The prince would have been a perfect secret agent… Techniques of disinformation, the art of disguise, the ability to cover his tracks, all these came as second nature to Charles Edward. This helps to explain…the achievement involved in his "invisibility" during the obscure years from 1749 to 1758…[when] the combined espionage efforts of Europe could not get a proper fix on a man who arguably was the greatest celebrity of the time.[91]

Andrew Lang reports that when Charles Edward was arrested, "a pair of compasses was found on him," which he speculates could be used in a suicide, but it is more likely that the compasses could be used in Masonic initiations.[92] Goring himself had been initiated in 1730 in the Bear and Harrow, the Duke of Norfolk's lodge, and in the letter supposedly written by him, there are suggestions of a Masonic significance to the prince's itinerary. In Lyons the mysterious Chevalier La Luze called on the prince and engaged him in top secret negotiations.[93] The chevalier knew no English and spoke French and Italian in a foreign accent. In Strasbourg, at a second meeting, Goring learned that "the Title of Chevalier La Luze was only assumed to conceal a character of a much greater Note; and that he who was distinguished by it, was a Person whose extraordinary Talents had gained him the Confidence of one of the wisest Princes in Europe." Goring now understood "the Motives which induced the P----- to take this journey." The only person whom Charles Edward trusted with La Luze's packet was George Kelly, translator of Ramsay's discourse and companion of the prince in Holyrood Palace.

The ultimate destination of the prince was Sweden, and in the unpublished Stuart Papers there survives the draft passport, handwritten by Charles, to travel to Sweden, for which he received a "Commission au Soleil d'Or Milite de Bretagne."[94] The Latin word "Milite," or soldier/knight, was often used in the Templar high degrees, and the Grand Master's name was usually given in Latin, "Eques a Sole Aureo." I have argued elsewhere that the Swedish Masons Nils Bielke and Emanuel Swedenborg were possibly mentioned

[90] J. Tuckett, "The Origin of Additional Degrees," *AQC*, 32 (1919), 24; L. Trebuchet," Références," 95-126; M. Schuchard, *Emanuel Swedenborg*, 752-54.

[91] F. McLynn, *Charles Edward Stuart*, 382.

[92] A. Lang, *Pickle the Spy*, 39.

[93] Henry Goring [?], *A Letter from H---- G-----* London, 1750), 6-8, 16-17.

[94] Stuart Papers: Box 2/114. For details about the Swedish passport and the possible involvement of Nils Bielke and Swedenborg in its transmission, see M. Schuchard, *Emanuel Swedenborg*, 465-71.

in the passport as companions for the prince, and the Templar title suggests that La Luze was possibly the Masonic adventurer Johann Samuel Leucht (Leucht is German and Luz Spanish for "light"). Leucht was a crypto-Jewish alchemist who claimed to be a special emissary from the Order of the Temple in Scotland.[95] His later critics claimed that his Templar rites were nothing more than "le vieux système Suèdois."

In the narrative, the prince undergoes many heroic and chivalrous adventures (including his rescue of a near-naked virgin from a burning fire), before he embarked in "a small trading Vessel, bound for a Port where he knew himself impatiently expected, having some Time before dispatched a Messenger to notify his coming." Upon landing in the unnamed port (Stockholm), he unexpectedly met with "Mr M------- of L------y, whom he thought had been one of the number of those that fell at Culloden." [96] Andrew Lang thought the author referred to Donald MacDonnell of Lochgarry and rejected the story as a fabrication.

However, the details seem to better fit Lord Macleod, who was indeed in Sweden. "Mr M----" informed the prince that "on hearing of some Regiments which were forming in that Kingdom, he had come thither with an Intention of entering into some one or other of them."[97] In January 1750 Macleod wrote his father that Tessin had introduced him to the royal family and the leading senators, and he was delighted that so many were of Scottish descent.[98] The "Goring" author claims that during the three week stay in that kingdom, the prince was "royally, though very secretly, entertained by the *** and other Persons of the highest rank, who were interested in the great Affair depending."[99] The prince was pleased that "the Fidelity of Mr. M------" was rewarded with a Captain's Commission in the Army." Macleod wrote his father that he will join the regiment of Baron Hamilton, a Scottish-descended Swede and strong Jacobite, and he subsequently corresponded with and provided a liaison between Jacobite agents in Sweden, Prussia, and Scotland.

After leaving Stockholm, the Prince and Goring sailed to Lithuania, from where Goring wrote his unnamed London friend, "To time alone, my dear Friend, and certain Contingencies, must be left the unravelling of this Mystery." One attempt to unravel it was later published by the so-called Sobieski Stuarts, who claimed to be the illegitimate grandsons of Charles Edward. In *Tales of the Century* (Edinburgh, 1847), they embellished Goring's story with details of the prince's participation in Masonic ceremonies in the Grand Lodge at Stockholm.[100] They reported that "his jewel, as Grand Master of the Grand Masonic Lodge of Stockholm, is still preserved there," and that they received this information from Sir Ralph Hamilton, member of the Grand Lodge of Stockholm, and Baron de Rondeau.[101]

Despite their reputation for mendacity, these 19th-century Stuart "Pretenders" reported accurately on certain information in the unpublished Stuart Papers, and their

---

[95] See R. Gould, *History*, III, 356-57; R. Le Forestier, *Illuminés*, 153-58.
[96] H. Goring, *Letter*, 39-42. Hugh Douglas identified the kingdom as Sweden and the northern port as Stockholm; see his *Jacobite Spy Wars: Moles, Rogues, and Treachery* (Stroud, 1996), 206.
[97] H. Goring, *Letter*, 40.
[98] Sir William Fraser, *The Lords of Cromartie* (Edinburgh, 1876), I, ccxliii; II, 232-33.
[99] H. Goring, *Letter*, 42.
[100] John Sobieski and Charles Edward Stuart, *Tales of the Century* (Edinburgh, 1847), 48-49.
[101] For further information on their informants, see M. Schuchard, *Emanuel Swedenborg*, 472-73.

account should not be summarily ignored. Andrew Lang, who was unaware of the Swedish-Masonic context, initially scoffed at Goring's Swedish account and concluded that the letter was a Jacobite tract, meant to keep up the spirits of the faithful. However, "it is probable that the author really had some information, though he is often mistaken, or fables by way of a `blind'."[102] Lang later conceded that there was some truth in the Sobieskis' stories: "they were not, as I supposed, the inventors of their own romance."[103] He also concluded that Charles Edward did indeed visit Sweden.

Meanwhile, back in London in December 1749, the actress-author Eliza Haywood was arrested for selling and distributing the Goring pamphlet. Haywood had earlier acted in (and possibly co-wrote) *The Female Freemason* (1732), and in recent years she had moved from opposition Whig to full-fledged Jacobite sympathies.[104] In *The Parrot* (1746), she reported rumours of the Young Pretender's movements, denounced the suppression of the Jacobite rebellion of 1745, and offered a sympathetic portrait of a young Jacobite who was hung, drawn and quartered.[105] In *Epistles for the Ladies* (1749-50), she lamented the exile of Charles Edward after the peace of Aix-la-Chapelle: "From Astrea to a very worthy Gentleman under great Misfortunes, and obliged to take Shelter in a Foreign Realm where he was also ill-treated."[106] Praising him for showing virtue and courage despite adversity, Astrea notes that "Your very Enemies indeed confess you have Talents to give a double Lustre to Prosperity, and it is the Hope of your Friends, who are all the honest and disinterested, that you will yet have an Opportunity of exerting them, which is a Day sincerely wished, and ardently prayed for."

One of those "honest" friends was Watkins William Wynn, with whom she maintained a secretive and confidential relationship, which was relevant to her role in publishing the letter from Henry Goring. Haywood wrote an ode "On the Birth of the first-born Son of Sir Watkin Williams Wynne, Bart.," who was born on 8 April 1749. She revealed her indebtedness to him and promised to discharge some kind of duty requested by him: "Let me the Debt, which Truth and Love,/ And mighty Gratitude demand,/ Well as I may, discharge."[107] This apparently involved her taking on writing projects for her patron: "The reigning Prince let *Colley* sing,/ And tune to royal Praise the venal String." She then urged, "Do Thou, O *Wynne*! But smile upon my Lays;/ Let me thy licens'd Laureat be." The birth of his first son and heir means Wynn's reformist, opposition, and Jacobite efforts will continue: the "beauteous Babe" becomes "The Father all in Miniature Charms confest," for each social virtue and noble aim "The little Patriot-Infant's Charms proclaim." In conclusion, "A second Patriot born,/ And *Albion's* Hopes restor'd. Auspicious Day!" Kathryn King suggests that the repeated use of "Patriot" refers to both the Prince of Wales and to Charles Edward Stuart, though the provocative use of "restor'd" seems to point more to the latter.[108]

---

[102] A. Lang, *Pickle the Spy*, 472.

[103] Lesley Graham, "Robert Louis Stevenson's `The Young Chevalier,'" in A. Macinnes, K. German, and L. Graham, *Living with Jacobitism*," 200-01.

[104] For the controversies about her political beliefs and loyalties in 1749-50, see Kathryn King, *A Political Biography of Eliza Haywood* (London, 2012), 177-91.

[105] P. Spedding, *Bibliography*, 525.

[106] Eliza Haywood, *Epistles for the Ladies* (London, 1749-50), I, 167-68.

[107] *Ibid.*, II, 345-49.

[108] K. King, *Political Biography*, 179-81.

In the months between the birth of his son and his accidental death on 26 September 1749 (he fell from his horse during a hunt), Wynn and his close friend Dr. King were aware of the international plotting for a new Prussian-Swedish-Jacobite enterprise, and he may well have informed Haywood about the plan. One of her Epistles, "From Camilla at Berlin to Astrea in London," hints at Charles Edward's negotiations with Prussia and Sweden, while he proposes a marriage alliance with Frederick II's youngest sister, Princess Amelia. Camilla describes the Prussian king as a patriot prince, who encourages the arts and who maintains a closet of portraits of contemporary heroes. Among them is one that Camilla suggests is a match for the miniature that Astrea wears on her wrist, which as Kathryn King points out, features the Stuart prince.

Haywood's praise of Frederick the Great was echoed by Dr. King, when he added a footnote with praise of the Prussian monarch to the published, translated version of his Oxford oration.[109] In another footnote, he added a long, fulsome tribute to the recently deceased Wynn, who had attended the Radcliffe dedication and who collaborated with King in Jacobite plotting:

> *Heavens! What a Man! How glorious! Alas! How mortal!*... how vigilant an Assertor of public Liberty! How able and ready a Defender and Patron of our University! Who was one of the few (the very few, such is the Degeneracy of the Age) who follow Virtue, even for the Sake of Virtue; and rejected the Trappings of courtly Splendour, and all Titles, while equal to the highest.[110]

As noted earlier, Marischal would characterize King as one of only two people in England who were privy to the secretive Prussian-Swedish-Jacobite plotting. Was Wynn the other one? The answer may have resided in Wynn's "compromising papers," which his widow burned on the night of his death.[111]

Given the intense secrecy maintained by all the parties involved in the international planning, Haywood's tribute to the Prussian king's ability to maintain such secrecy becomes relevant to similar themes in the letter from Goring. In Camilla's letter from Berlin, she describes how Frederick shut himself up because he was working on an affair of great importance, "the Dispatch of which he did not think proper to entrust to his Secretaries, or any other of his Ministers."[112] His confidential collaborators were George and James Keith, who hoped to implement Maclean's ambitious plan, and they used their Masonic networks to maintain the intense secrecy (in Sweden all the collaborators were Masons). As noted earlier, Wynn was reportedly a Mason, and his newborn son – the object of Haywood's eulogy – seemed to carry on a family tradition when decades later he established a Masonic lodge on the family estate of Wynnstay.[113] Hinting at her inside knowledge of the plot, Haywood had Camilla write from Berlin to Astrea: "Hence it is, Madam, that Councils of this Monarch remain so impenetrable a Mystery, and that his Designs are so seldom disappointed; nor is the Secrecy he observes, of less Advantage to

---

[109] W. King, *Translation of a Late Celebrated Oration*, 50-51.
[110] *Ibid.*, 47-50.
[111] P. Thomas, "Jacobitism," 300.
[112] E. Haywood, *Epistles*, II, 369.
[113] "Watkin Williams Wynn, 4th Baronet," *ODNB*.

the Success of his Affairs abroad, than it is to preserve a due Order and Tranquility at home."[114]

Eliza Haywood has often been claimed, controversially, as the author of the *Letter from H---- G-----*, but I suggest that she was the compiler and editor of papers given to her by agents of Wynn and Dr. King, who had received the information from their exiled Jacobite co-conspirators. Given the reality of the Swedish-Prussian-Jacobite plotting, the letter from Goring takes on greater political significance.[115] The English government definitely believed so, and on 9 December 1749 Haywood and her booksellers were arrested and charged with publishing a "Scandalous Seditious and Treasonable Pamphlet."[116] In their depositions before Lovell Stanhope, brother of Chesterfield and a Justice of the Peace for Westminster, the booksellers were evasive as they tried to protect themselves and Haywood. They agreed that her servant delivered the pamphlets to their shops, but they were not sure if she was the author. Her servant in turn testified that in mid-November 1749 loose papers were anonymously dropped at Haywood's shop, and her mistress ordered her to stitch them into books. Because she was ill, Haywood herself was not examined until 14 January 1750, when she testified that anonymous works were often dropped at her shop, and though she "has been an author many years," she "never wrote any thing in a political way."

Some days before Haywood's examination, she had been identified as the author by Ralph Griffiths, writing anonymously, in *The Monthly Review* (January 1750):

> The noted Mrs. H---d, author of four volumes of novels well known, and other romantic performances, is the reputed author of this pretended letter; which was privately conveyed to the shops, no publisher caring to appear in it; but the government, less scrupulous, took care to make the piece taken notice of, by arresting the female veteran we have named; who has about 800 copies of the book.[117]

In 1746 Griffiths had been prosecuted for publishing pro-Jacobite works, but he pleaded with Newcastle to excuse his "foolish Whim" and promised to write anti-Jacobite works in the future.[118] He was released in January 1747, "but he had not finished playing with fire," and he provoked a new prosecution in November 1749 by publishing John Cleland's notorious *Memoirs of a Woman of Pleasure*. As noted earlier, the Scottish Cleland was an opposition Mason and an admirer of Dr. King's Oxford oration. Thus, he may have provided information on Haywood's friendship with Wynn, a co-conspirator with King, for Griffiths "appears to have had inside information on Haywood."[119]

After the confiscation of Haywood's Goring pamphlet, an anonymous Jacobite determined to keep the story circulating, and he published *A Conference Lately held Betwixt H---G-----, Esq.; and a certain E-----h L--d at A-----* [English Lord at Avignon] *in Pursuit of his*

---

[114] E. Haywood, *Epistles*, II, 369.

[115] For details of this plotting, see D. Zimmerman, *Jacobite Movement*, 67-69,81-97; F. McLynn, *Charles Edward Stuart*, 378-92. M. Schuchard, *Emanuel Swedenborg*, 454-56, 463-73.

[116] The following details draw on the narrative and documents in J. Spedding, *Bibliography*, -520-29, 749-58.

[117] "A Letter from H--- G----," *The Monthly Review* (January 1750), 167.

[118] Lewis Knapp, "Ralph Griffiths, Author and Publisher, 1746-1750," *The Library: The Transactions of the Bibliographical Society*, 4th s. vol. 20 (1939), 197-213.

[119] K. King, *Political Biography*, 181.

Travels through Europe, relating to a great but unfortunate P----e [Prince] (1750). In a dialogue with the English Whig, Goring portrayed the Stuart prince as a paragon of virtue, chivalric values, and liberal (almost republican) principles. After the "English Lord" recites all the stereotypical horrors of Roman Catholicism, Goring manages to convince him that Charles Edward would not only support the Church of England but grant liberty of conscience to all his subjects. In an appended poem, "A Birth-Day Ode," written in honor of the prince's birthday on 31 December, the author calls for heaven to "bless the God-like Youth," for Britons to rouse their "native martial Spirit," and "to Arms repair/ Your Wrongs in warlike Sounds declare."[120] This was much more dangerous stuff than Haywood's publication, and it shows why the government was concerned about the original Goring pamphlet.

One bookseller who did not protect Haywood was John Joliffe, who on 18 January 1750 wrote to Thomas Ramsden, an official in the secretary of state's office, asking for "a line" from him that would get Lovell Stanhope, the examiner, to "erase" his name from the charge. Joliffe reported that "at the time this affair happened I was employd in assisting Ld. Trentham at his Election in printing bills" and was not at home when the pamphlets were delivered to his home.[121] For over twenty years he has behaved himself "in a dutiful manner to ye present Government," and hoped that he would not "suffer the Imputations of disaffection to a Government" which he had "always endeavoured to serve." This context of Whig political maneuvering and surveillance over booksellers (using informers) provides a provocative context for Haywood's arrest and for the Jacobite-Masonic significance of the Goring pamphlet.

Joliffe's reference to his work for Lord Trentham in the Westminster elections of November 1749 points to a defiant and dangerous effort by the Jacobites and their Tory collaborators to defeat the government's candidates. Since 1747 the Independent Electors of Westminster, whose stewards included Orrery, Wynn, Lichfield, Oglethorpe, and the London alderman George Heathcote, toasted the Pretender and his cause at their annual meetings ("To all those that dare be honest"), leading to charges that they were a "Jaco-Independo-Rebello-Plaido" society.[122] There was a large contingent of Jacobite and opposition Freemasons in the society, including Heathcote ("the Friend of Liberty"); William Howard, Viscount Andover, and Sir James Dashwood, both of whom had been initiated in the Jacobite lodge in Rome; and Lord Ward who had earlier served as the crypto-Jacobite Grand Master of the Grand Lodge of England.[123] The most daring of the campaigners was Alexander Murray, brother of David Hume's friend, Lord Elibank, who "undoubtedly was fully aware" of the project (which became known as "the Elibank Plot").[124]

In autumn 1749 the Independent Electors saw an opening when Granville Leveson Gower, Viscount Trentham, was forced to run again for his parliamentary seat, and the Independent Electors nominated George Vandeput to oppose him. Trentham was the

---

[120] Anon., *A Conference Lately held Betwixt H--- G----, Esq; and a certain E----h L---d* (1750), 46-47.

[121] J. Spedding, *Bibliography*, 756-57.

[122] E. Cruickshanks, *Political Untouchables*, 108-09; and *Oglethorpes*, 6.

[123] R. Sedgwick, *History*, II, 520.

[124] Ernest Mossner, "New Hume Letters to Lord Elibank, 1748-1776," *Texas Studies in Language and Literature*, 4 (1962), 435.

son of Lord Gower, a former Jacobite and Patriot, who had gone over to the government, much to the disgust of his former colleagues. Trentham was also the brother-in-law of Bedford, who called upon Richmond, his fellow Whig Mason, and George Payne, former Grand Master, to exert all their powers to gain the election for Trentham. Bedford employed John Broughton, the famous pugilist and loyalist Mason, to lead "Broughton's Bruisers" in a campaign of physical and financial intimidation on the small businessmen and craftsmen who defied the wealthy, aristocratic, and royal inhabitants of Westminster.[125] In response the Prince of Wales, an opposition Mason, summoned his chairmen to defy "Bedford Bruisers" at the hustings, and his Leicester House coterie provided financial support to Vandeput. [126]

Paul Whitehead, who had earlier lampooned Broughton and his bullying patron, the Duke of Cumberland, led a vigorous and virulent propaganda campaign against Trentham and his Grand Lodge supporters, Bedford, Richmond, and Broughton. He personally headed great mobs and wrote songs and paragraphs in support of Vandeput, and he soon became the *bête noire* of the Hanoverian Masons. Chetwode Crawley describes their counter-attack:

> In the heat of the contest, Mr. Trentham's supporters bethought themselves of the unpopularity Paul Whitehead had earned at the hands of the Freemasons in 1741. They got hold of the original plate of *Mock Masonry*, or had it retouched or re-engraved, and issued it at the head of a manifesto purporting to come from the rascaldom of St. Giles's – the Scald Miserables – to their fittest representatives, the Directors of the Mock Procession.[127]

Titled "The Cavalcade of the Mock Free Masons, in their Procession from St. Giles's to Whitechapel Dunghill," the engraving included the inscription: "The Representation of the Independent Society of SCALD-MISERABLE Masons to P--l W-----d [Paul Whitehead] and E-----e C----y [Esquire Carey]."

At the height of the rival demonstrations, Bedford called on his protégé Henry Fielding to anonymously attack Whitehead and his Vandeput supporters in a move that almost backfired because of Fielding's widespread unpopularity. As a Westminster justice of peace, Fielding had warned Bedford in July of a planned seditious attack by a large body of disaffected sailors:

> I have recd Informations of upwards of 3000 Sailors now in Arms abt. Wapping and that they threaten to march to this End of Town this Night, under Pretence of demolishing all Bawdy Houses. I have an Officer and 50 Men and submit to yr. Grace what more Assistance may be necessary. I sent a Messenger five Hours ago to the Secretary of War but have yet no Answer.[128]

---

[125] Joseph Grego, *A History of Parliamentary Elections and Electioneering. From the Stuarts to Queen Victoria*, new ed. (London, 1892), 107-22; Nicholas Rogers, "Aristocratic Clientage, Trade and Independency: Popular Politics in Pre-radical Westminster," *Past and Present, 61 (1973), 70-106.*

[126] *Ibid.*, 94.

[127] W. Crawley, "Mock Masonry," 137-38.

[128] M.C. and R.R. Battestin, "Fielding, Bedford, and the Westminster Election of 1749," *Eighteenth-Century Studies*, 11 (1977-78), 153.

Though there was much popular support for the sailors' claim that they had been cheated and mistreated by the owners of the brothels, Bedford and Fielding ordered the military to suppress the mob, and then insisted on the execution of a hapless young wigmaker, Bosavern Penlez, in October. The opposition accused Trentham of refusing to use his influence to secure a pardon for Penlez.

While Paul Whitehead exploited the volatile situation in a multi-pronged propaganda effort, Fielding reverted to his earlier political strategy of charging the opposition with sedition, Jacobitism, and Papism. Under Whitehead's direction, pamphlets were published claiming that "Mr. Justice Trotplaid" (Fielding) prevented the arrest and confinement of the "Bruisers" and rioters on Trentham's side, while Fielding not only directed but himself wrote counter pamphlets attacking "Paul Blackhead" and "Paul Wronghead."[129] Bedford ordered and paid for the publication of 13,000 copies of *The Covent Garden Journal* (5 December 1749), which claimed to be authored by Paul Wronghead, though Fielding was the main contributor.[130] Under "Foreign Affairs," he wrote mock news items from Rome and Paris which associated the anti-court party with papists and Jacobites, while portraying the Dutch-descended Vandeput as alien and un-English. When Trentham was declared the victor by a narrow margin, mass protests led to a months-long "scrutiny" of the election, which fueled even more discontent and eventually contributed to a new Masonic development, in which disaffected Irish residents – many with Jacobite backgrounds – began to organize the "Antients" as rivals to the "Moderns" in the Grand Lodge.

As the rival political and Masonic factions agitated, a branch of *Écossais* Masonry operated under the radar in London and other port cities. As discussed earlier, the Royal Order of Heredom of Kilwinning was brought from France to London ca. 1741, and it was subsequently propagated by the engraver Lambert de Lintot, who had been an officer of volunteers under Colonel MacMahon in Rouen.[131] Some Masonic historians argue that the Royal Order of Heredom drew on the Templar and Jewish mystical themes expressed by Chevalier Ramsay, and it definitely considered the kings of Scotland as hereditary Grand Masters. A Scottish native, William Mitchell, who had been initiated into the Royal Order in France in 1749, travelled to London in July 1750, where the presiding Grand Master named him provincial Grand Master of the Order for a chapter at The Hague.[132] Provocatively, given the seriousness of international Jacobite plotting at this time, the rituals of the order become significant.

During chapter meetings, a seat was kept vacant for the use of the royal Grand Master "should he care to attend."[133] Drawing on Scottish nationalist traditions of the role of Robert the Bruce at the battle of Bannockburn, the order claimed that after his victory over the English, Bruce rewarded the Masons and Templars who served him.[134] The rituals were also influenced by Cabalistic traditions, and the Grand Master was given the title of *Nasi*, Hebrew for "Prince." Norman Hackney, the main examiner of the

---

[129] *T—t—m and V—d-t. A Collection of the Advertisements and Hand-Bills, Serious, Satyrical, and Humorous, Published on Both sides during the Election for the City and Liberty of Westminster, begun November 22d, 1749*, 23, 30, 42.

[130] M. Battestin, "Fielding," 167-68.

[131] W. Wonnacott, "Rite of Seven Degrees," 63-98.

[132] R. Péter, *British Freemasonry*, III, xiv.

[133] R. Lindsay, *Royal Order*, 19.

[134] N. Hackney, "Some Notes," part 1, p. 32.

manuscripts, suggests that "somewhere in the background was a Noble Grand Master who took little or no active part in the conduct of the order," while "Sir Robert R.L.F." was the representative of "Nasi," with wide powers in south Britain.[135] That the honorary Grand Master "in the background" was Charles Edward Stuart was revealed by Lambert de Lintot in 1774, when he succumbed to political pressure and removed the prince from his role as "Grand Master, Grand Commander, Conservator, Guardian of the Pact and Sacred Vow of the Christian Princes."[136]

The connection of the Royal Order with the Jacobite exiles in Rouen was relevant to the hopes in 1749-50 of Robert Strange and William Hamilton of Bangour that the defeat at Culloden did not deal a death-blow to the Stuart cause. Strange engraved a portrait of Hamilton, which included the latter's poem, "Written at Rouen, in France, in the year of our exile, 1749":

> Hail, Wallace! Gen'rous Chief! Who singly brave,
> When all were trembling round, aspir'd to save:
> Hail, Bruce! Intrepid King! Beset with foes,
> Who, from defeat, to fame and empire rose:
> Hail, Stuart! Much suff'ring Youth! – yes! I foresee
> Imperial crowns and certain palms for thee.
> The Land thy Fathers rul'd has oft been view'd
> Enthrall'd unbroken, and vanquished unsubdu'd!
> Scotia, for Genius fam'd and gallant deed,
> Has yet her Bards to sing, her Chiefs to bleed; –
> Yet Freedom shall be Her's, her Kings shall reign,
> For know, Culloden was not lost in vain.[137]

Hamilton presented the portrait with the inscribed poem to Sir Stuart Threipland, a Jacobite Mason and fellow exile.

In London Mendes and his friends shared the optimism of Strange and Hamilton. Mendes was arguably the author of "A Birthday Ode for 1750," which featured the refrain, "Royal Exile soon return."[138] Like the Scottish exiles, he believed that Culloden would be revenged: "When on Culloden's plain, in William's form,/ Inhuman slaughter led the rising storm," but somehow "scap'd my Prince the fury of the day," though "wrong'd triumphant and in bondage great." Soon "justice indignant shall snatch up her sword/ The times shall be chang'd, the K----[King] be restor'd." Mendes or Ellis also copied a long, unpublished poem by John Byrom, calling for the return of the prince to the British shore. In "An Invitation from Horace, Ode 5 Lib. 4," Byrom captured the positive hopes and expectations of the Jacobites and their Masonic brothers:

> Favorite of Heaven! No longer let thy Subjects mourn
> Thy tedious absence, or despair thy safe return.
> Return, return, and bring with thee
> Thy truest Emblems, Love and Liberty.

---

[135] *Ibid.*, part 2, p. 6.
[136] Lintot's letter of 19 June 1774 is reproduced in W. Wonnacott, "Rite of Seven Degrees," 75.
[137] W. Hamilton, *Poems*, xvii.
[138] UGLE: MS. 1860 Men.

With thy long wish'd for presence glad this Isle;
'Tis want of that alone she grieves,
And Hopes of that alone she lives,
Let her not then expire, bemoaning thy Exile…
………………………………………………
With no less ardent Wishes, Sovereign Prince,
Thy Country does implore,
Thy safe Arrival (her Deliverance)
Once more to bless the British Shore.

………………………………………………
This, this our morning Pray'r, our Toast at night,
Till Thou'rst Restor'd, and all again is Light.[139]

In September 1750 these dreams of "return" were secretly but briefly fulfilled when Charles Edward made a clandestine journey to London. McLynn reveals that the visit was "designed to prepare a pre-emptive strike," in case George II died and Cumberland attempted to seize power, "either by a military coup or, more likely, through summoning Parliament and having his brother Frederick declared *non compos mentis*."[140] The distrust of Cumberland was even shared by the Pelhams and other Whig ministers. In the event of the demise of "the Elector," Charles Edward wanted to "be able either to beat Cumberland to the punch or to manipulate Frederick into declaring a Stuart restoration." Before leaving France, he sent the former Grand Master Maclean to Boulogne to await orders, and he planned to report on Maclean's plan for a Jacobite-Prussian-Swedish invasion. For several months, the prince had arranged the purchase of 26,000 guns and bayonets, plus 4,000 broadswords for use in Scotland.[141] He further planned to utilize members of Ogilvy's regiment, which had a large *Écossais* contingent who were initiated in Royal Arch rituals and who maintained connections with sympathetic Swedish Masons.

On 16 September Charles Edward and Lieutenant John Holker, an *Écossais* Mason and veteran of the Manchester and Ogilvy regiments, appeared suddenly at Lady Primrose's house on Essex Street.[142] Startled, she pretended not to recognize the prince since she had Whig as well as Jacobite card-playing guests. They then convened a meeting of the Jacobite leadership in a house in Pall Mall, who included Dr. King, Oglethorpe, Beaufort, Westmorland, and some fifty other sympathizers. Years later, after Dr. King had lost faith in the cause, he described with jaundiced hindsight the meeting:

I received a note from my Lady Primrose, who desired to see me immediately. As soon as I waited on her, she led me into her dressing-room, and presented me to ———— [Charles Edward]. If I was surprised to find him there, I was still more astonished when he acquainted me with the motives which had induced him to hazard a journey to England at this juncture. The impatience of his friends who were in exile had formed a scheme which was

---

[139] *Ibid.*

[140] F. McLynn, *Charles Edward Stuart*, 397-99.

[141] D. Zimmerman, *Jacobite Movement*, 86-90.

[142] For Holker as Mason, see André Kervella, "Le Secret du Grand Orient de Bouillon," *La Règle d'Abraham*, 39 (2017), 150.

impracticable; but although it had been as feasible as they had presented it to him, yet no preparation had been made, nor was anything ready to carry it into execution. He was soon convinced that he had been deceived, and therefore, after a stay in London of five days only, he returned to the place from whence he came.[143]

King added that he had long conversations with the prince, and "for some years afterward held a constant correspondence with him, not indeed by letters but by messengers.*" The asterisk pointed to a footnote which explained that "These were not common couriers, but gentlemen of fortune, honour, and veracity, on whose relations I could entirely depend." One of these couriers was Thomas Carte, close friend of the late Ramsay, who maintained contacts with *Écossais* Masons on the Continent.[144] To King's description of the prince, he added another footnote that "the Chevalier Ramsay, the author of Cyrus, was Prince Charles's preceptor for about a year; but a court faction removed him."[145] In 1783 the elderly Charles Edward described his London meeting to the Swedish king, Gustaf III, as well as his visit with Colonel Arthur Brett to examine the exterior parts of the Tower, "one part of which they thought might be beaten down with a petard."[146] In order to counter the anti-Catholic propaganda of the Hanoverians, the prince also converted to the Anglican church in a ceremony that reportedly took place in James Gibbs's church of St. Mary le Strand, which was fraught with Jacobite symbolism.

On 22 September the prince returned to France, and travelled to different capitols in search of foreign supporters, while English agents desperately tried to determine his location (there were orders to assassinate him if found). Unfortunately, the untimely death of Hector Maclean in November removed a key player from the international enterprise. Despite the prince's disappointment at the timidity and caution of the English Jacobites, his visit helped plant the seeds for what became the Elibank Plot, in which King, Beaufort, Westmorland, Carte, Oglethorpe, and Alexander Murray would play leading roles. It was perhaps no coincidence that in the secretive meetings of the Royal Order in London, the initiates enacted the taking of the Tower and passing over the bridge, actions central to the emerging plot.[147]

One non-Jacobite Scot who seemed to be privy (but not sympathetic) to the increasingly vengeful and esoteric themes in *Écossais* Masonry was David Hume, who was still friendly with the Jacobite Masons Michael Ramsay and Allan Ramsay, the artist. He also knew the former Grand Master of Scotland and England, Lord Morton, and the current Grand Master of Scotland, the Jacobite Lord Eglinton (1750-51).[148] In September 1746 Hume had been invited to join a military expedition to Canada by his kinsman General James St. Clair, descendant of the ancient Scottish Masonic family, who in 1735 purchased and restored Roslin Chapel, considered the spiritual home of Scottish-Stuart Masonry. As noted earlier, the general purchased the castle and chapel from William St. Clair, who served as Scottish Grand Master in 1736. Though General St. Clair was a loyal

---

[143] W. King, *Anecdotes*, 196-97.

[144] D. Zimmerman, *Jacobite Movement*, 95, 233n.139.

[145] *Ibid.*, 200.

[146] Lord Mahon, *The Decline of the Last Stuarts* (London: W. Nicol, 1843), 76.

[147] R. Lindsay, *Royal Order*, 12, 109.

[148] Roger Emerson, "Hume and the Bellman, Zerobabel MacGilchrist," *Hume Studies*, 23 (1997), 9-28.

Hanoverian, who had served under Cumberland, he was privy to the Stuart traditions of Scottish Freemasonry. Ordered to divert the 1746 expedition to an attack on L'Orient in France, the reluctant general was defeated and faced much criticism on his return, when he was vigorously defended by Hume.

As the brother of an attainted Jacobite and family friend of many others, General St. Clair opposed their political principles but maintained a relatively tolerant attitude towards them. Like Hume, he hoped to persuade them to change their politics while still remaining cordial. This context explains Hume's linking of their Scottish colleague, Dr. James Fraser, who served with them in the L'Orient expedition, to his attack on the Independent Electors of Westminster in late 1750. In a "complicated joke," Hume mocked Fraser, described by Ernest Mossner as "a hot-headed Highlander, a rabid Jacobite," for his support of the Independent Electors and especially for his collaboration with Esquire Carey, the Freemason who helped Paul Whitehead organize the procession of Mock Masons.[149] Hume hoped that his satire would cure Fraser of his mistaken politics, for "no man who loves his country, can be a friend to that gentleman, considering his late as well as former behavior."

While drafting his attack on the Jacobite Fraser and the opposition Mason Carey, Hume also produced an anonymous broadside, *The Petition of the Grave and Venerable Bellmen (or Sextons) of the Church of Scotland to the Hon. House of Commons*, which was so controversial that he could not get it printed in Edinburgh (it appeared without the printer's name later in 1751). In this satire, Hume revealed his awareness of the esoteric developments within Jacobite Masonry. Responding to the effort of Presbyterian ministers and sextons (bellringers, grave-diggers) to have their salaries raised by the English parliament, Hume sided with the Whig establishment and landowners to oppose the petition and to satirize a variety of targets.[150] Roger Emerson argues that behind the wit, there was a clear intention "to mock scripture, to cast doubt upon the lineage and functions of Christ the Saviour, and incidentally to point out the foolishness of Freemasonry and the danger of joining too closely both politics and religion – a sin of which both Covenanters and Jacobites had been guilty."[151]

The petition was presented by "Zerobabel MacGilchrist," a Highlander and religious fanatic, resident in Buckhaven in the parish of Wemyss, whose chief heritor and landowner was James, 5th Earl of Wemyss, who served as Scottish Grand Master in 1743-44. As noted earlier the Wemyss family were Jacobites, and the earl's son Lord Elcho was commander of Prince Charles's lifeguard in 1745-46, and then escaped to France. Emerson speculates that Hume had earlier met Elcho in France, when the philosopher was spending time with the Chevalier Ramsay and Michael Ramsay. He further argues that the name "Zerobabel" (Hume's pun on meaningless "zero" and incoherent "babel") points to the role of the Biblical Zerubbabel's role in leading the Hebrews out of Babylon and then presiding over the re-building of the second Temple of Jerusalem. These themes were featured in James Anderson's *Constitutions*, where in 1723 Zerubbabel was named "General Master Mason of the Jews," and in 1738 as "Provincial Grand Master in Judah,"

---

[149] Ernest Mossner, *The Life of David Hume*, rev. ed. (1954; Oxford, 1980), 236-37; .David Hume, *The Life and Correspondence of David Hume*, ed. John Hill Burton (Edinburgh, 1846), I, 305-14.

[150] M.A. Stuart, "Hume's 'Bellman's Petition': The Original Text," *Hume Studies*, 23 (1997), 3-7.

[151] R. Emerson, "Hume," 10.

under the Grand Master Cyrus.[152] Hume probably remembered the conclusion of Ramsay's *Travels of Cyrus*, when Cyrus calls upon the Jews to "go up to Jerusalem, and build the House of the Lord God of Israel," and he may have heard of Ramsay's praise of Zerubbabel in his Masonic oration. The role of Zerubbabel as Grand Master was elaborated in the Jacobite rituals of the Royal Arch and the Royal Order of Heredom and Kilwinning, which emerged with new energy in England and Scotland in 1750.[153]

Hume shared the broadside and his satire on Fraser with another Scottish friend, Dr. John Clephane, who would have understood the Jacobite and Masonic allusions, for he had met many *Écossais* Masons on the Continent. His father was "out" in 1715 and went into exile in Antwerp, where John joined him in 1725.[154] The son studied medicine under Boerhaave in Holland and, after his father's death, returned to Scotland, earning his M.D. from Aberdeen in 1729. In the early 1740s he served as a travelling tutor in France and Italy to young men, several of whom were Stuart sympathizers. In 1743 in Italy he was suspected by "a Great Man" of being a Jacobite. [155] A sophisticated connoisseur of the arts, he arranged the purchase of an important painting for Lord Elcho, whom he apparently met in Italy, when the Jacobite Mason was meeting with James III.[156] In February 1751, Hume sent his satire on Fraser to Clephane, noting that his old colleague's Jacobitism is probably "incurable," but he does not want "a quarrel betwixt Fraser and me; he is an honest, good-humoured, friendly, pleasant fellow," though "a little turbulent and impatient."[157]

While abroad, Clephane became aware of the increasing esoteric interests of many *Écossais* Masons. He wrote to a Welsh friend about the Continental vogue for magic, noting that the French court was deeply imbued with occultism: "The present [King] with the help of old Merlin or Nostradamus seems to have gone further in the black art than his great grand-father; is it not odd that where there are kings, there this art flourishes; I am sorry to say it, I do not know a country in Europe where it is not practiced."[158] In 1739-40, at the time of Louis XV's alleged Masonic affiliation, the Comte de Argenson worried about the king's increasing preoccupation with mysticism and "spiritual books"; even worse was his egalitarian relationship with his "little puppets," the Masonic members of his inner circle.[159] In 1743, when Clephane described Louis XV's occult interests, the king was involved with the Comte de Saint-Germain, a Rosicrucian Mason, whose chemical work he encouraged while also using him as an intelligence agent. Hume assumed that Clephane would sympathize with his mockery of the Jewish identification of the radical Covenanters, when he made the Bellman "more Jew than Christian in his outlook." He would also understand the allusion to Zerubabbel with its hint at the Jewish

[152] J. Anderson, *Constitutions* (1723), 19, and (1738), 223-24.

[153] UGLE: BS.624 Roy. "Royal Order of Scotland: Letter Book" (typescript), 44-45, 128-137.

[154] "Dr. John Clephane," in J. Ingamells, *Dictionary*.

[155] Philip Jenkins, "John Clephane: A Scottish Traveller in Eighteenth-century Europe," *National Library of Wales Journal*, 22 (1982), 421.

[156] Francis Russell, "Dr Clephane, John Blackwood and Batoni's `Sacrifice of Iphigenia,'" *Burlington Magazine*, 127 (1985), 892.

[157] David Hume, *The Letters of David Hume, 1727-1765*, ed. J.Y.T. Greig (1932; Oxford, 2011), I, 148-49.

[158] P. Jenkins, "John Clephane," 423.

[159] Marquis d' Argenson, *Journal and Memoirs of the Marquis d'Argenson*, ed. K.P. Wormeley (Boston, 1902), I, 255, 260, 295.

mystical themes of the exiled Jacobites who joined the Royal Arch and Royal Order of Heredom systems of Masonry.

As the turbulent years of 1749-50 concluded, the Masonic fraternity and its members – Whig and Tory, Hanoverian and Jacobite – would face many new challenges, which continued to be expressed in the writings of the rival brothers. Two prominent Whig Grand Masters died, the Duke of Montagu in July 1749 and the Duke of Richmond in August 1750. The field seemed clear for Frederick, Prince of Wales, to become the iconic figurehead of British Masonry. However, with the sudden death of the Hanoverian "Young Pretender" in 1751 and the virtual disappearance of the Stuart "Young Pretender" from 1749 to 1758, Freemasonry would split into increasingly antagonistic factions, which mirrored the changing political context of a Britain and Europe in a continuing state of war.

EPILOGUE

SCHISMS :

ANTIENTS VERSUS MODERNS, ROYALISTS VERSUS REPUBLICANS, NATIONALISTS VERSUS IMPERIALISTS (1751-1788)

> Our domestic enemies undermine some parts of the Wall... We do not like such patch-work; they build with untempered mortar; nor can they ever cement with us, till they get better materials, and better workmen.
>
> Dean Swift, quoted in Earl of Orrery, *Remarks on the Life and Writings of Dr. Jonathan Swift* (Dublin, 1751).

> The number of antient masons, compared with the moderns, being as ninety-nine to one, proves the universality of the old order...a circumstance peculiar to antient masons.
>
> Laurence Dermott, *Ahiman Rezon* (London, 1764).

> At the beginning of the American war, the Americans at Boston wrote the Pretender to engage him to put himself at their head...the republicans were as determined as the Bostonians in their desire for a Prince of the House of Stuart to be their chief.
>
> Louis Dutens, *Mémoires d'un Voyageur qui se Repose* (Paris, 1806).

Throughout 1750 Frederick, Prince of Wales, had worked with his eclectic party – composed of disaffected Whigs, Tories, and Jacobites – to plan a take-over of the ministry and the removal of his brother, the Duke of Cumberland, from the military. Unfortunately, the prince unexpectedly died on 20 March 1751, and his "Leicester House" political project fell apart.[1] His widow immediately ordered two confidants (the

---

[1] He was hit hard by a cricket ball and died of a resultant abscess.

2nd Earl of Egmont and Dr. Matthew Lee) to burn all his writings and documents, warning them that "the King might seize the Prince's papers – that they were at Carlton House – and that we might be ruined by these papers."[2] Thus, any additional evidence for Frederick's usage of Freemasonry to promote his political aims disappeared in the flames. The frightened princess then threw herself at George II's feet and vowed her loyalty, leading a disappointed Egmont to record, "I now plainly see she has been flattered into a total reliance on the King and has thought it necessary for her own purpose to abandon all the Prince's friends."

One of those friends was Orrery, who had been considered for a place in a future coalition ministry. However, he did not fully trust Frederick and along with Dr. King, he maintained his private Stuart sympathies. Orrery wrote or transcribed a satire that "mocked the prince's posturing" – what he considered his two-faced political opportunism.[3] A dissembling Frederick declares,

> I love with all my Hart,
> The Hanoverian Part,
> And for its Settlement
> My Conscience gives consent:
> ....
> The Tory Party here
> Most hateful doth appear;
> I ever have denied
> To be on Charlie's side.[4]

An anonymous Jacobite wrote a more cruel evaluation of the prince, which soon won popular notoriety and permanently damaged his reputation:

> Here lies poor Fred
> Who was alive and is dead:
> Had it been his father,
> I had much rather;
> Had it been his brother,
> Still better than another;
> Had it been his sister,
> No one would have missed her;
> Had it been the whole generation,
> Still better for the nation;
> But since `tis only Fred
> Who was alive and is dead
> There's no more to be said.[5]

On 28 August 1751 Orrery signed the preface to his biography, *Remarks on the Life and Writings of Dr. Jonathan Swift...in a Series of Letters from John Earl of Orrery, to his Son, the Honourable Hamilton Boyle*, first published in November 1751, which soon became a best

---

[2] A. Newman, "Leicester House Politics, 1750-60." 198, 205.

[3] G. Glickman, "Parliament," 137.

[4] Orrery, *Orrery Papers*, II, 316.

[5] J. Walters, *Royal Griffin*, 223.

seller. Orrery's frankness about Swift's secret marriage, character defects, senile deterioration, and recent sycophantic companions provoked strong rebuttals from his Irish friends. But Orrery always avowed his respect for the dean's courage, intelligence, and wit, and he tried to deflect the recent portrayal of Swift as a Jacobite, published by the radical Irish nationalist Charles Lucas, who claimed to have long known the dean.[6] Lucas later blamed the delay in publishing Swift's *History of the Last Four Years of the Queen* on the fear of Swift's friends that his and their Jacobite sympathies would be revealed.[7]

With the Whig ministry concerned about continuing Jacobite intrigues, Orrery admitted that Swift in 1713 had been considered a Jacobite by the common people in Ireland, who threw stones and dirt at him.[8] He argued that Swift's "clearing himself from Jacobitism" resided in his acceptance of the Williamite Revolution, even though he decried its "unavoidable bad consequences."[9] Finally, his admired but flawed hero was "neither Whig nor Tory, neither Jacobite nor Republican. He was DOCTOR SWIFT." Orrery also reminded readers of Swift's usage of imagery drawn from operative Masonry, when he quoted Swift's criticism of Gilbert Burnet's Whiggish *History of the Reformation* (1713):

> [Bishop Burnet] thanks God, there are many among us who stand in the breach…[but] it is a breach of their own making… The Wall of our church and country is built of those who love the constitution in both. Our domestic enemies undermine some parts of the Wall, and place themselves in the Breach; and then they cry, We are the Wall. We do not like such patch-work; they build with untempered mortar; nor can they ever cement with us, till they get better materials, and better workmen.[10]

Orrery knew that his "brother" Swift had been identified as the author of the *Letter from the Grand Mistress of the Female Free-Masons*, when his own publisher, Faulkner, allowed his London agents to publish the work under Swift's name in 1746.

Orrery's caution about Swift's alleged Jacobitism (caution which Lucas deemed dishonest) was understandable at this time. The earl's confidant Dr. King was deeply involved in the Elibank Plot, which included plans for a diversionary attack from Ireland.[11] Orrery's exiled kinsman, the one-eyed Lord Clancarty, undertook to go "with what men he could pick out of the Irish Brigades & land them upon his own Estate," land which overlapped with that of Orrery.[12] Besides Dr. King, Charles Edward counted upon a network of Jacobite Masons – Goring, Kelly, Carte, Blantyre, and the Keith brothers – to maintain the secret communications and planning. Collaborating with the British Masons were their Swedish "brothers" Scheffer and Tessin, whose Scottish protégé and fellow Mason Lord Macleod corresponded with Lord Elibank.[13] The Swedes worked with

---

[6] Robert Mahoney, *Jonathan Swift: The Irish Identity* (New Haven, 1995), 14.

[7] Jonathan Swift, *The History of the Four Last Years of the Queen*, ed. Charles Lucas (London, 1758), v-vii.

[8] Orrery, John Boyle, Earl of, *Remarks on the Life and Writings of Dr. Jonathan Swift*, 3rd rev. ed. (Dublin: George Faulkner, 1752), 49-50.

[9] *Ibid.*, 248.

[10] *Ibid.*, 215-16.

[11] F. McLynn, *Charles Edward Stuart*, 405, 410

[12] D. Zimmerman, *Jacobite Movement*, 83, 268 n.96.

[13] For Sweden's involvement in the Elibank plot, see M. Schuchard, *Emanuel Swedenborg*, 489-94.

Marischal, now Prussian ambassador to France, and their Prussian *frère* Frederick II, who despised George II and currently admired the Stuart prince.

But the driving force was Lord Elibank's brother Alexander Murray, leader of the Independent Electors, who was charged with violence and intimidation in the Westminster by-election in early 1751 and was imprisoned for refusing to go down on his knees and beg pardon from the House of Commons.[14] When he was later released, a huge mob carried him aloft while shouting "Murray and Liberty!" Murray then fled to France, where he met with Charles Edward to plan the kidnapping of George II and his family, the seizing of the Tower, and the removal of the Hanoverian ministry. Though the Scottish, Irish, French, Swedish, and Prussian participants were determined to succeed, the reports of "Pickle the Spy," a treacherous mole in Charles Edward's entourage, led to exposure of the plot and the execution in June 1753 of Dr. Archibald Cameron. The philanthropic physician had fought in the `45, protected the hunted Charles Edward, and then acted as a liaison between Scotland and Europe.[15] The government believed that Cameron was an emissary of the Prussian king, who planned to send 15,000 men to aid a Jacobite invasion, but they convicted him on his attainder from 1745 in order to protect the identify of "Pickle."

Dr. Cameron was a Freemason, and he had utilized the international fraternal networks of the participants in the Elibank Plot. Thus, it was fitting that his bravery on the scaffold was compared to that of his hero and fellow Mason, for it was reported that "He met the last great enemy with as much intrepidity and as much decency as even the great Balmerino."[16] In the last Jacobite execution in Britain, he was hung, drawn, and quartered. The anti-Jacobite Horace Walpole wrote Mann that Cameron "died with the greatest firmness. His parting with his wife…was heroic and tender"; he was appalled at the brutality of the execution, commenting that the Scot was attended by a Non-juring clergyman who was "not content with seeing the Doctor hanged, [but] he let down the top of the landau for the better convenience of seeing him disembowelled!"[17] Samuel Johnson responded to the execution by vilifying George II "as one who, upon all occasions, is unrelenting and barbarous."[18]

From the Jacobite perspective, the Elibank Plot subsequently "fizzled out in confusion, bitterness and much dejection."[19] It is unclear if Orrery was privy to the plot, but he would surely have approved of it, even if passively. Writing from Marston on 5 August 1752 to Carte, the main courier between Dr. King and the Stuart prince, he hoped Carte would soon visit him. He then seemed to explain his reason for not joining in a project (the plot?) that Carte proposed, partially on grounds of ill health:

---

[14] F. McLynn, *Charles Edward Stuart*, 403.

[15] "Pickle" was Aleistair MacDonald of Glengarry, who placed himself "at the very heart of Jacobite deliberations," with the result that "the recipe for disaster was complete"; see F. McLynn, *Charles Edward Stuart*, 403.

[16] For his Masonic affiliation, see Inna Bell, "Building the New Rome: Charles Cameron as the Architect of Catherine the Great's New Eternal City" (M.A. Thesis: Brigham Young University, 2012), 27; for comparison with Balmerino, see R. Forbes, *Lyon in Mourning*, 41-42, 130.

[17] H. Walpole, *Correspondence*, XX, 384.

[18] "Archibald Cameron," *ODNB*.

[19] D. Zimmerman, *Jacobite Movement*, 113.

Another reason for my retirement is an absolute conviction that it is to no purpose to endeavor to save a Country which is resolved not to be saved. I have seen so many instances to confirm this melancholy opinion that the idle hopes of vain and visionary minds appear to me as airy bubbles not in the least to be regarded. My wishes for my Country will be the same to the last hour of my breath. My opinion of my Countrymen grows indeed less and less favourable every day. But, to say truth, we are a declining People: destined, I fear, to absolute destruction. We have had our Day. It ended with Queen Ann. Since her time all has been Confusion and Discontent at Home; Folly and False Politics abroad: not to mention that Spirit of Slavery and Irreligion that is spreading itself throughout the several parts of the three Kingdoms. These are undeniable Truths. What then have we to hope? Or from whence?[20]

Nevertheless, Orrery urged Carte to send him information on his contacts in France, where his friend was busily coordinating communication between the multi-national plotters.

In the wake of Prince Frederick's death in March 1751, the British opposition had lost its Masonic figurehead. Despite doubts about his sincerity and abilities, the disaffected Masons had counted on Frederick to overcome the prejudices and incompetence that had so weakened the Whiggish Grand Lodge of England.[21] It was perhaps no coincidence that in July 1751 dissident Irish Masons in London formed the Antients' Grand Lodge, which officially divided the British system into competing factions. Within three years, the Antients' claimed nearly forty lodges, while the now-scorned "Moderns" steadily lost ground. Led by an immigrant Irish painter, Laurence Dermott, member of a mixed Protestant-Catholic family, the Irish dissidents determined to reclaim the "authentic," seventeenth-century traditions of Scots-Irish Freemasonry, the same ones that Jonathan Swift revealed in his *Letter from the Grand Mistress* (1724). [22]

To further publicize his claim to be the recipient of the true historical and ritual tradition, Dermott published *Ahiman Rezon: or, a Help to a Brother* (London, 1756), which included the text of "Solomon's Temple, an Oratorio," by James Eyre Weeks, with music composed by the organist of St. Patrick's Cathedral, as it was performed in a Dublin lodge. As noted earlier, in 1745 Weeks had urged Chesterfield to assume the role of the late lamented Swift. In a later edition of *Ahiman Rezon*, Dermott boasted about the successful expansion of the Antients' system and the wide sales of his book by featuring a quote from Swift on the title-page:

As for his Works, in Verse or Prose,
I own myself no Judge of those;
Nor can I tell what Criticks thought 'em,
But this I know, all People bought 'em.
Swift.[23]

---

[20] Orrery, *Orrery Papers*, II, 116-17.
[21] On the Whigs' "Masonic misrule," see R. Berman, *Schism*, 118-50.
[22] M.K. Schuchard, "Some Ancient Scots-Irish-Swedish Sources for `Antient' Freemasonry," published online at www.icom.fm, and in the forthcoming printed *Proceedings of the International Conference of Masonic Research Lodges* (Toulon, 2018).
[23] Laurence. Dermott, *Ahiman Rezon*, 3rd ed. (London, 1778).

Dermott also echoed Swift's statement that "The Branch of the Lodge of Solomon's Temple" is "the Antientist and Purest now on Earth."[24] Swift further claimed that the Grand Master Fergus "was carefully instructed in all the Arts and Sciences, especially in the natural Magick, and the Cabalistical Philosophy...Speaking of the *Cabala*, as *Masonry* was call'd in those Days." Dermott drew on this Scots-Irish tradition and on his knowledge of Hebrew and Jewish texts to argue that Free-Masonry received its name at the building of Solomon's Temple, when "the whole Mystery was communicated to very few," when "the Masons at Jerusalem and Tyre were the Greatest Cabalists* then in the World."[25] The asterisk pointed to a note that Cabalists are "People skilled in the Cabala, i.e. Tradition, their secret Science of expounding divine Mysteries, etc." In "A Prayer said at the Opening of the Lodge, etc., used by Jewish Free-Masons," the Hebrew brothers plead, "number us not among those that know not thy Statutes, nor the divine Mysteries of the secret Cabbala."

Among the predominantly Irish working-class and small-business subscribers to *Ahiman Rezon* there were a significant number of Jews, who were perhaps attracted to the Jewish themes developed in the Royal Arch and other higher degrees, despite the ultimate Christianization of the rituals.[26] These "non-craft" degrees were not accepted by the Modern Grand Lodge. Claiming that the Royal Arch is "the Root, Heart, and Marrow of Free-Masonry," Dermott praised York Masonry, long dominated by Jacobites, for possessing its secrets.[27] In a second edition of *Ahiman Rezon* (London, 1764), he tied the Antients more firmly to the Cabalistic traditions of seventeenth-century Stuart Masonry by linking his system to Rabbi Jacob Jehudah Leon, whose Masonic activities and visit to the Stuart court in London in 1675 were discussed in Chapter One of this book. As noted earlier, Leon's heraldic coat of arms, featured on his booklet describing the Tabernacle and Temple, was reportedly adopted by Irish Masons in the 1680s.[28]

Thus, when Dermott featured Leon's design on the new edition of *Ahiman Rezon*, he was harking back to an "antient" Stuart and Irish tradition. In 1759-60 in London, he viewed an exhibit of Leon's models and studied his explanatory booklets, which were displayed by a grandson of the rabbi. He further claimed that Leon was a brother Free-mason, a point relevant to the Jews who flocked to the Antients' lodges:

> N.B. The free masons arms in the upper part of the frontispiece of this book, was found in the collection of the famous and learned hebrewist, architect and brother, Rabbi Jacob Jehudah Leon...[who] built a model of Solomon's temple...[which] was exhibited to public view...in London... At the same time, Jacob Judah Leon published a description of the tabernacle and the temple, and dedicated it to his Majesty, and in the years 1759 and 1760 I had the pleasure of perusing and examining both these curiosities...

---

[24] J. Swift, *Prose Works*, V, 329.

[25] Laurence Dermott, *Ahiman Rezon* (London, 1756), xiv, 43.

[26] The development of the "Antient" degrees led Dr. Isaac Wise, a leader of 19th-century Reform Judaism and a Scottish Rite Mason, to affirm that "Masonry is a Jewish institution whose history, degrees, charges, passwords, and explanations are Jewish from the beginning to end, with the exception of only one by-degree and a few words in the obligation"; see *The Israelite* (1855).

[27] L. Dermott, *Ahiman Rezon* (1756), 47.

[28] M. Schuchard, *Restoring the Temple*, 698-707.

As these were the arms of the masons that built the tabernacle and the temple, there is not the least doubt of their being the proper arms of the most antient and honourable fraternity of free and accepted masons, and the continual practice, formalities and tradition, all regular lodges, from the lowest degree to the most high, i.e. THE HOLY ROYAL ARCH, confirms the truth hereof.[29]

Dermott repeated the rule in Anderson's *Constitutions* (1723) that a Mason should never "be concerned in plots against the state," though a brother who is a rebel against the state could maintain his "indefeasible" relation to the lodge.[30] However, he added a contradictory new caveat that "if a brother should be so far unhappy as to rebel against the state, he would meet with no countenance from his fellows; nor would they keep any private converse with him, whereby the government might have cause to be jealous, or to take the least umbrage." Suggesting some ambiguity in his political position, he added a footnote to "The Secretary's Song," in which he expanded Anderson's comment on the alleged organization by Freemasons of the Porteous Riots. Dermott claimed that the Scottish people broke the murderer out of prison, ordered him to kneel down, "which was also done by the whole Company, who joined him in Prayers," and then "hawled him up as they do on board a Man of War. It is remarkable that they all wore white leather aprons, which (by the by) is a certain Proof that they were not Free-masons."[31] In this odd comment, Dermott reinforced the Masonic identification of the rioters by garbing them in traditional aprons but then disclaimed that identification, presumably because they no longer paraded in their aprons. Ric Berman suggests that Dermott, who was often scathing in his comments on the Moderns, meant the aprons comment to be ironic.[32]

From its inception in 1751, Dermott tried to recruit an aristocratic Grand Master, beginning with Lord George Sackville, whose father the 4th Duke of Dorset, served as the loyalist Lord Lieutenant of Ireland. Sackville refused Dermott's invitation, explaining that he was headed to Ireland to serve as Grand Master of the Irish Grand Lodge. A waspish Horace Walpole claimed that Sackville was a notorious lecher who collaborated in Ireland with Archbishop George Stone in maintaining libidinous seraglios.[33] Dermott then unsuccessfully solicited the 4th Earl of Inchiquin, Orrery's admired friend, and next the 4th Earl of Chesterfield, Orrery's and Swift's former colleague. He finally succeeded with Lord Mountjoy, now the 1st Earl of Blessington, who accepted the position in 1756.[34] Mountjoy had been a supporter of Swift and was included on the list of Jacobite sympathizers provided to the French government in 1743. One wonders what Orrery and Dr. King thought about these developments, for both had become disillusioned with English opposition Masonry in the wake of the failed Elibank plot.

---

[29] Laurence Dermott, *Ahiman Rezon*, 2nd ed. (London, 1764), xxxiv-xxxv.

[30] *Ibid.*, 25, 15.

[31] *Ibid.*, 109.

[32] Richard Berman, private communication (5 November 2015).

[33] R. Sedgwick, *History*, II, 400. Archbishop Stone was accused of "sexual degeneracy" in a series of pamphlets in the 1750s; see J. Kelly and M. Powell, *Clubs and Societies*, 227.

[34] R. Berman, *Schism*, 36-41.

In 1754 Dr. King anonymously published *The Dreamer*, a strange allegorical satire on English governance and culture, in which he mocked the timidity and hypocrisy of the English Jacobites and high Tories, as revealed in their ineffective support of the rebellion of 1745 and Elibank plot of 1750-53. Caricaturing George II in the persona of "Hercules" and his sycophants as "Herculeans," King lamented the decline of the opposition "Antiherculeans," who had failed to rise to the military challenges. Thus, the loyalist Herculeans argue that "the Antiherculeans are, indeed, a numerous sect":

> sometimes over their cups, they grow tumultuous, and proceed to threatenings. But there is no danger to apprehend from them: They are not formed for great enterprises: They have little judgment, and less courage; …they have no manner of confidence in one another. So that 'tis in our power to create suspicions and jealousies amongst them, as often as we find expedient, and suitable to our interest, and the purposes of our administration.[35]

When the Whig "informer" Blacow charged that King was not only the seditious author of *The Dreamer* but was actually born in Ireland, King indignantly replied that he would be proud to be Irish, especially because of the brilliance and wisdom of his late friend Jonathan Swift. He hoped that the spirit of Swift would descend upon him as he wrote his Gulliverian satire. King also drew on Pope's Rosicrucian-Jacobite allegories in *The Rape of the Lock* (1714), when he traced the noble beginnings and subsequent degradation of "The Rosicrucians; or, Knights of the Rosy Cross." Given the current popular identification of Rosicrucians with Freemasons, King's allegory can be read as a lamentation on the failure of Swiftian Freemasonry and Jacobite Rosicrucianism to maintain and implement their original ideals.

Perhaps remembering the Masonic beliefs of his late friend Ramsay, King described the Rosicrucians as an ancient, "order of Knighthood," which was "greatly respected, while they strictly observed the statutes of their founder":

> the primitive Rosicrucians employed their whole revenues in entertaining the pilgrim and the stranger, and in feeding the poor and hungry…. While they were temperate, vigilant, and laborious, they preserved their independency, and enjoyed with honour as great immunities, as the present Knights of *Malta*.[36]

As noted earlier, Swift in his *Letter from the Grand Mistress* linked the Knights of Malta with the Knights of St. John of Jerusalem as Masonic lodges and praised them for adorning the "Antient Jewish and Pagan Masonry with many Religious and Christian Rules."[37] King then lamented that the Rosicrucians have "now entirely departed from all the rules of their institution, and are become proud and luxurious, covetous and ambitious."[38]

This narrative of decline paralleled that of the Hanoverian Grand Lodge of England which, as Ric Berman documents, was suffering under the absentee and inept leadership of William Byron, 5th Lord Byron, who served as Grand Master in 1747-51: "Indeed,

[35] William King, *The Dreamer* (London, 1754), 193-94.
[36] *Ibid.*, 65-66.
[37] J. Swift, *Prose Works*, V, 329.
[38] W. King, *Dreamer*, 65-67.

there was only one instance when he offered his imprimatur to freemasonry or was otherwise supportive," when in 1747 he attended as Grand Master at a theatrical performance, which was advertised as featuring the singer "Mr Custos," who was "long confined in the Inquisition in Portugal on account of his freemasonry."[39]

Perhaps harking back to Stuart military Masonry before the formation of the Hanoverian Grand Lodge, King further criticized contemporary Rosicrucians:

> It will be proper to inform you...that the Rosicrucians are not Knights of chivalry. They are neither trained to arms, nor acquainted with those maxims of honour and gallantry, which form a modern hero. In case of a foreign, or domestick war, they rather chuse by their harangues to inspire their neighbours with courage, than give any proofs of it themselves.... However, there are some, among them, who have been so bold as to gird their loins with the sword: and their present great master is as full of martial ardour, as he is of piety and devotion; and is ever prepared, in time of danger, both to pray and fight for his friends and country... I have known as excellent men of this order, as are to be found in the whole human species...[40]

King knew that Derwentwater and Ramsay had determined to revive the ancient chivalric traditions of Stuart Freemasonry, and he was evidently informed by Ezekiel Hamilton that the quasi-Masonic Order of Toboso was a military order of knighthood. Moreover, King was possibly privy to Charles Edward's (alleged) installation as Grand Master of the Order of the Temple in Edinburgh in 1745. He had spent an evening with the prince in London in 1750, and three years later, when he participated in the Elibank plot and drafted the allegories in *The Dreamer*, he had not *yet* lost faith in the young Stuart claimant, whom he believed to embody not only "martial ardour" but "piety and devotion" by converting to the Anglican church while in King's company. The "Old Trumpeter of Liberty Hall" still revered the Earl Marischal, an old-style Jacobite Mason and Tobosan, whom he expected to lead an invasion force in the early 1750s.

The question arises of whether King was aware of Laurence Dermott and the dissident Irish Masons who organized the "Antients" Grand Lodge and determined to implement more practical and generous assistance to their needy or impoverished brothers. By making their system of Freemasonry a benevolent, social welfare society, they countered the selfish and callous attitude of the corrupted modern Rosicrucians (Freemasons?), described by Dr. King as affluent politicians and aristocrats who considered "all persons of a lower degree, such as hunters, traders, husbandmen and mechanics" as mere "beasts of burden," who "are created for the sole use and pleasure of their superiors."[41] Instead, Dermott enumerated the great men in history who "were not only poor Men, but many of them of a very mean extraction. The wise philosopher Socrates was the son of a poor stone-carver" (i.e, an operative Mason).[42] He compared his "lower degree" Antient brothers to those upper class, Modern Masons, who were "preferr'd to Places or Offices of great Trust, and dignified with Titles of Honour, without having the least claim to Courage, Wit, Learning, or Honesty."

---

[39] R. Berman, *Schism*, 129.

[40] W. King, *Dreamer*, 71-72.

[41] *Ibid.*, 206.

[42] L. Dermott, *Ahiman Rezon* (1764), xxix-xxx.

Over the next decades, both the Antients' lodges and the Royal Order of Heredom and Kilwinning attracted Masons who challenged the once-dominant Modern Grand Lodge. And despite the stubbornly prevailing "conventional wisdom" among historians that Jacobitism was crushed at Culloden, the Stuart prince continued his travels and negotiations to launch new multi-national restoration projects. Hampered by his growing alcoholism and tumultuous relationship with Clementina Walkinshaw (suspected unjustly of being a Hanoverian spy), the prince still dreamed of a military invasion. In 1759 the Duc de Choiseul, ambitious French foreign minister and Freemason, was pressured by Stuart sympathizers and "influential Masons" at Louis XVs court to launch serious negotiations with Sweden for a new assault on Britain.[43] He met with Charles Edward and assured him that "nothing would be done without him, only through him, and always for him."[44]

Choiseul then implemented "financial operations on what was at the time a gigantic scale" in order to fund the projected Jacobite-French-Swedish invasion. Utilizing the old *Écossais* networks, Choiseul ordered the Baron de Blantyre, former comrade of Derwentwater and Ramsay, to return to Sweden to work with his Masonic brothers Scheffer and Tessin. Lord Macleod in Sweden contributed to the plan, and his father, the attainted former Grand Master Cromarty, was named by French ministers as a potential supporter in England.[45] Eventually frightened by the enormous financial demands, Louis XV and Madame de Pompadour backed off. They employed the Comte de Saint-Germain, still a Rosicrucian Mason, to subvert Choiseul's plan, and the last serious Jacobite attempt fizzled out in a tragi-comical duel of rival alchemical Masons and Cabalistic Rosicrucians (Saint-Germain versus Casanova).[46]

In the 1760s, many French, Swedish, and Prussian lodges still considered Charles Edward to be their hereditary Grand Master, and it is possible that the aged Lord Chesterfield joined their ranks.[47] Among the manuscripts of the Royal Order of Heredom of Kilwinning, there is a startling account of the seventy year-old Chesterfield in 1764 performing rituals of initiation into the order.[48] If the account is accurate, it is possible that the Antients' approach to Chesterfield revived his old interest in Rosicrucianism, which was earlier stimulated by the Comte de Saint-Germain. By the 1770s Lambert de Lintot had developed the rituals of the Royal Order into an elaborate, theatrical, and artistically compelling rite. His masterful engravings of the detailed symbolism of Heredom and

---

[43] Claude Nordmann, "Choiseul and the Last Jacobite Attempt of 1759," in Eveline Cruickshanks, ed., *Ideology and Conspiracy: Aspects of Jacobitism, 1689-1982* (Edinburgh, 1982), 201-21; for Choiseul as Mason, see Frank McLynn, *Charles Edward Stuart*, 533: for the Jacobite-French collaboration with Swedish Masons, see M. Schuchard, *Emanuel Swedenborg*, 528-52.

[44] D. Zimmerman, *Jacobite Movement*, 143-44. He disputes the Whig claim that Charles Edward was drunk during their meeting or that Choiseul worried about his alcoholism.

[45] "Mackenzie, George, 3rd Earl of Cromarty," *ODNB*.

[46] M. Schuchard, *Emanuel Swedenborg*, 529-34, 546-50, for the Masonic duel of Cabalistic-Rosicrucian wits between Saint- Germain and Giacomo Casanova, which was recounted in Casanova's *History of My Life*, trans. Willard Trask (New York, 1962), V, 107-19, 126-44, 178-79, 264-66.

[47] For the French belief in Charles Edward's Grand Mastership, see Alain Le Bihan, *Francs-Maçons et Ateliers Parisiens de la Grande Loge de France au XVIIIe Siècle* (Paris, 1973), 104-118, 146-50.

[48] Grand Lodge, London: BS.624. "Royal Order of Scotland Letter Book," Letter 128.

Kilwinning would later influence the Swedenborgian Masons in William Blake's circle and even, arguably, Blake himself.[49]

However, in 1774, when the government became alarmed at reports of Charles Edward's contact with the American rebels, Lambert and seventy of his lodge members shifted from Jacobite to opposition Whig support. On 19 June they voted to remove Charles "III" from his role as Grand Master of the Royal Order:

> The Wise and Sovereign Chapter of the Knights of the Eagle Rose Croix assembled have decided to recognize His Royal Highness Henry Frederick Duke of Cumberland...for Grand Master, Grand Commander, Conservator, Guardian of the Pact and Sacred Vow of the Christian Princes, in the place of the said Charles Edward [erasure here] at present [erasure] for the reasons alleged in the present Chapter, and particularly that they will give no recognition to any constitution in the name of the said Charles Edward, in the three kingdoms of Great Britain, as contrary to our present deliberation and to the vows we make...for the prosperity of the House of Brunswick.[50]

Complicating the pledge of loyalty made by Lambert's lodge was the fact that Henry Frederick, was not the "Butcher" Duke of Cumberland, but the fourth son of the late Frederick, Prince of Wales, earlier leader of opposition Masonry. Henry Frederick was alienated from his older brother, now King George III; he set up a court in opposition to the king and cooperated with the disaffected Whigs.[51] In 1774 he also served as Grand Patron of the Royal Arch, which Dermott and the Antients considered the "root, heart and marrow of masonry."[52]

From the time of its founding in 1751, the Antients' system spread rapidly in the British Isles, with Ireland and Scotland eventually accepting its Grand Lodge. By 1764 Dermott could boast that the Antients, at home and abroad, outnumbered the Moderns by "ninety-nine to one."[53] In the North American colonies it became the dominant form of Freemasonry and played an increasing role in resistance to English imperial policies.[54] Charles Edward took an intense interest in the American rebellion and, according to Frank McLynn, "Almost certainly, some kind of invitation was made by the Bostonians in 1775 that he should be the figurehead of a provisional American government."[55] Louis Dutens reported that at the beginning of the American war the republicans and rebels at Boston wrote to Charles Edward, because they wanted "a Prince of the House of Stuart for their chief."[56] Sir Walter Scott informed Washington Irving that he had seen in the unpublished Stuart Papers a memorial addressed to Charles Edward "from some adherents in America, dated in 1778, proposing to set up his standard in the back

---

[49] M. Schuchard, "Secret Masonic History," 40-51.

[50] W. Wonnacott, "Rite of Seven Degrees," 75. For the background of Lambert's change of allegiance, see M.K. Schuchard, "Some Ancient Scots-Irish-Swedish Sources for `Antient' Freemasonry."

[51] "Henry Frederick, Duke of Cumberland and Strathearne," *ODNB*.

[52] L. Dermott, *Ahiman Rezon* (1756), 47.

[53] L. Dermott, *Ahiman Rezon* (1764), xxvii.

[54] Ric Berman, *Loyalists and Malcontents: Freemasonry and Revolution in the American Deep South* (Goring Heath, 2015).

[55] F. McLynn, *Charles Edward Stuart*, 519.

[56] Louis Dutens, *Mémoires d'un Voyageur qui se Repose* (Paris, 1806), III, 31-32.

settlements."[57] One wonders how many of these American supporters were Antient Masons or believers in the prince's Grand Mastership.

When France entered the war on the colonists' side, "fleeting visions" were conjured among the prince's followers "of another Jacobite descent on England."[58] An equally fascinated observer of the American revolution was Gustaf III of Sweden who, though a staunch royalist, admired the rebels, praised their victories over the English, and foresaw the revolution as ushering in a new world of American democracy and dominance. In October 1776 he wrote:

> It is a most interesting spectacle this, of a state that creates itself. If I were not what I am, I should go to America to follow at close view all the vicissitudes of this new Republic... Perhaps this is the century of America, and the new republic...may some day put Europe under tribute as she for two centuries had made America pay tribute. However this may be, I cannot help but admire their courage and applaud their audacity.[59]

In the revolutionary 1780s, as various Jacobites became Jacobins, Gustaf determined to preserve the Stuart traditions of royalist Freemasonry, and he travelled to Florence to consult with Charles Edward. As discussed earlier, in emotional secret ceremonies the two re-enacted the building of the Temple and Charles "III" named Gustaf his successor as Grand Master of the Masonic Order of the Temple. He gave the Swedish king an official document to read to his Masonic brothers in Stockholm:

> We Charles Edward, by the Grace of God, Sovereign Chief and Hereditary Grand Master of the Holy Order of the Knights of St. John of the Temple,...last Prince and legitimate Heir of the Royal House of the Stuarts, to all those dear and respectable brothers who read the present letters patent, *Salut*.[60]

He signed the document with his Masonic sigil and a Templar cross.

Despite the determination of Gustaf and Charles Edward to keep the ceremony and transaction secret, news about it soon leaked out. The elderly Horace Mann, former member of the Whig lodge in Florence, wrote that the Swedish king has taken steps, "which though they may appear ludicrous, are not less certain."[61] Ignorant about the past forty years of *Écossais* Masonic developments, Mann was puzzled by the desperate efforts of the Duke of Brunswick to secure the Templar Grand Mastership for himself and the German lodges: "I must own that I never thought the Society of Free Masons was looked upon in Germany to be of such importance, as to excite the ambition of two such princes to be at the head of them." Twenty years earlier, his Whig correspondent Horace Walpole had dismissed English Grand Lodge Freemasonry as a "transient national folly."[62]

---

[57] Washington Irvng, *Abbotsford and Newstead Abbey* (London, 1835), 48. Irving visited Scott in 1816. Like other important documents in the Stuart Papers possessed by the British government, the memorial has since disappeared.

[58] Stuart Papers: 497/119.

[59] Amandus Johnson, *Swedish Contributions to American Freedom, 1776-1783* (Philadelphia, 1953), 151.

[60] P. Mollier, "Les Stuarts," 69-70. My translation.

[61] Kew: NA/ FO 79/3. Mann to Udny (30 December 1783).

[62] H. Walpole, *Anecdotes*, III, 725.

*

* *

For historians of eighteenth-century literature, to follow Mann and Walpole in dismissing Freemasonry as an insignificant political and cultural influence is to ignore the complex international context in which so many poems, novels, plays, letters, diaries, pamphlets, and oratorios reflected the tensions and rivalries within the British and global fraternity. By re-examining Masonic developments in the light of the decades-long struggle between Jacobites and Hanoverians, Tories and Whigs, and between English, Scottish, Irish, and Welsh "brothers," we can gain new insights into the imaginative and behavioral world of many major and minor writers in the British Isles. And we can enlarge that British literary territory to trace its expansion in Europe and the New World.

ABBREVIATIONS OF FREQUENTLY CITED WORKS

AQC	*Ars Quatuor Coronatorum.*
Bodleian	Bodleian Library, Oxford.
BL	British Library, London.
DNB	*Dictionary of National Biography.*
EMC	*Early Masonic Catechisms*, eds. Douglas Knoop, G.P. Jones, Douglas Hamer (1943; Manchester, 1963).
EMP	*Early Masonic Pamphlets*, eds. Douglas Knoop, G.P. Jones, Douglas Hamer (1945; London, 1978).
Heredom	*Heredom: Transactions of the Scottish Rite Research Society.*
HMC	*Historical Manuscripts Commission.*
NA:SP	National Archives, State Papers, Kew.
ODNB	*Oxford Dictionary of National Biography.*
Stuart Papers	Royal Archives, Windsor (microfilm).
TJHSE	*Transactions of the Jewish Historical Society of England.*
UGLE	United Grand Lodge of England, Library, London.

BIBLIOGRAPHY

MANUSCRIPTS: For large MSS. collections, the folio numbers are given in the footnotes.

London, British Library:
  Evelyn MS. 173.f.9
  Sloane MS. 3323.f. 209; MS. 3342, "Minutes of the Royal Society, 1699-1712."
  Add. MSS. 49360.ff. 1-95: "Minute Book of the Board of Brothers."
  Add. MSS. 22539-25541. Carteret Papers.
  Add. MSS. 32793. Waldegrave and Newcastle Papers.
  Add. MSS. 33054. Newcastle Papers.
  Add. MSS. 32703; 32801-82; 73999.
  Althorp MSS, box B8 (2-6 November 1731).

Kew, National Archives,
  State Papers. SP 78/203, 204; 85/16, 19; 95/23, 96, 100; 98/32, 35, 36, 37, 41 56, 84; 105/124.
  FO 79/3. Mann to Udny (30 December 1783).

London, Royal Society MS.
  Register Book, IX, ff. 240-52.
  Journal Book, XI (1714-20), ff. 108-10, 116, 122.

London, United Grand Lodge of England:
  MS 1860. Men.
  BS.624. Roy. "Royal Order of Scotland Letter Book."

London, Wellcome Collection:
  MS. 5744, Ramsay, Letters #6-7.

Oxford, Bodleian Library:
  MS. Eng. Misc. C.444. "Martin Folkes's Italian Journal" (1733).
  MS. Eng. Hist.d.103
  MS. Eng. Hist.218.2, vol. 4.
  MS. 2591.d. 6 [7]. "Library and Collection…of Earl of Cork and Orrery" (1732).
  MS. Locke, C. 31.
  Carte MSS. 100; 225-27; 230-31.
  Calendar of Carte MSS, vols. 72-73.
  Rawlinson MS. Poet. 11, ff. 74-75; 133. ff. 162-96; MS. C.136, f.147, "Masonic Miscellanies"; MS. D1198/247.

Oxford, Christ Church College Library:
  MS. "A Catalogue of the Library of Charles late Earl of Orrery (1732)."

Nottingham, University of Nottingham:
  Pelham MS. NeC2086. "Report of Aleister Macdonnell (Pickle the Spy)."

Windsor, Royal Archives.
  Stuart Papers (microfilm): 59/100; 84/104; 90/illeg.; 92/136; 93/111; 95/110; 101/137; 116/104; 117/28; 142/141; 169/80; 192/98; 194/159; 222/13; 234/138; 303/6; 343/22; 493/19.
  Box2/114. Charles Edward Stuart's Passport to Sweden.

Edinburgh, Scottish National Library:
> Advocates MS. 32.4.2.

Edinburgh, Scottish Record Office:
> MS. 6035/1/168. Lord McLeod's Masonic Certificate.

Edinburgh, Royal Order of Scotland Archive:
> MS. Norman Hackney, "Some Notes on the Royal Order of Scotland."

Galway, Ireland. Dioscesan Archives:
> "Papers of Sir Charles Wogan."

Cambridge, Massachusetts. Harvard University. Houghton Library:
> Eng.MS. 218.2; 218.4F. Orrery Papers.

Linköping, Sweden. Stiftsbibliotek:
> MSS. Bref till A.B. Benzelius en Yngre," V, f.40.

Stockholm, Sweden. Riksarkiv:
> Anglica, #211-12. Gyllenborg Correspondence (1711); Gallica, #330. Scheffer's Journal (10 September 1745).

BOOKS, ARTICLES, DISSERTATIONS:

Abbey, C.J. and J.H. Overton, *The English Church in the Eighteenth Century* (London, 1878).

Acton, Alfred, *Letters and Memorials of Emanuel Swedenborg* (Bryn Athyn, 1955).

Adamson, Henry, *The Muses Threnodie* (Edinburgh, 1638).

Aitken, George, *The Life and Works of John Arbuthnot* (1892; New York, 1969).
> *The Life of Richard Steele* (1889; rpt. New York, 1968).

Akerby, George, *The Life of James Spiller, the Late Famous Comedian* (London, 1729).

Albemarle, Willem Anne van Keppel, 2nd Earl of, *The Albemarle Papers*, ed. Charles S. Terry (Aberdeen, 1902).

Aldridge, A.O., "Shaftesbury's Rosicrucian Ladies," *Anglia*, 103 (1985), 297-319.

Allardyce, James, *Historical Papers Relating to the Jacobite Period, 1699-1759* (Aberdeen, 1895).

Anderson, James, *No King-Killers* (London, 1715).
> *The Constitutions of the Freemasons (1723) and (1738)* (facs. rpt. Abingdon, 1976).
> *The Lord Looseth the Prisoners* (London, 1737).

Anderson, John, *The Book of the Chronicles of His Royal Highness William Duke of Cumberland* (Edinburgh, 1746).

Anonymous, in chronological order:
> *Caledonia's Farewell* (Edinburgh, 1685).
> *To All Godly People in the Citie of London* (London, 1698).
> *A New View of London* (London, 1708).
> *Historical Account of the Union Betwixt the Egypians and Israelites* (Edinburgh, 1709-10).
> *No King-Sellers* (London, 1715).
> *A Letter from the Lord Vi---- B----ke, to the Rev. Dr. S---t* (London, 1715).
> *Dr. S----'s Real Diary* (London, 1715).
> *Tryal of Francis Francia for High Treason* (London, 1717).
> *The Character of Sultan GALGA* (London, 1718).
> *Anti-Priapeia* (London and Edinburgh, 1720.
> *Love's Last Shift: or, the Mason Disappointed* (London, 1720).

Some Memoirs of the Life and Writings of John Toland (London, 1722).

Remarks Upon a Jacobite Pamphlet…entituled Female Fortitude (London, 1722).

By a Member of the Antient Society of Fremasons, A Vindication of the Reverend Dr. Snape and Dr. Sherlock (London, 1722).

The Free Masons: An Hudibrastick Poem (London, 1723).

A Seasonable Apology for Mr. Heidegger (London, 1724).

The Biter Biten (Dublin, 1725).

The Printer's Petition to the Poetical Senate Assembled in Grub-Street (Dublin, 1726).

The Dublin Scuffle (Dublin, 1730).

An Epistle from the Lord B-----ke to the Duke of W-----n (London, 1730).

A Candid Answer to a Letter from a Member of Parliament to his Friends in the Country, Concerning the Duties on wine and Tobacco (London, 1733).

The Devil's Almanac (London: M. Cooper, 1745).

A Sketch of the Life and Character of Mr. Radcliffe (London, 1746).

A Conference Lately Held Betwixt H[enry] G[oring], Esq., and a Certain E[nglish] L[ord] (1750).

The Complete Free Mason, or Multa Paucis, for Lovers of Secrets (1763), ed. J.T. Thorp (London, 1924).

Arbuckle, James, *A Panegyric on the Reverend Dean Swift* (London, 1730).

Arnold, Ralph, *Northern Lights: The Story of Lord Derwentwater* (London, 1950.

Arbuthnot, John, *A Sermon Preach'd at the Mercat Cross of Edinburgh* (Edinburgh, 1706).

A Catalogue of the Capital and Well Known Library of Books, of the late Celebrated Dr. Arbuthnot (London, 1779).

The Correspondence of John Arbuthnot, ed. Angus Ross (München, 2006).

Argenson, René Louis de Voyer, Marquis d', *Journal and Memoirs of the Marquis d'Argenson*, trans. K.P. Wormely (Boston, 1902).

Argyll, Duke of, *The D--- of A-----'s Letter to the Right Honourable Sir ----- ----* (London, 1740).

Arlington, Henry Bennett, Earl of, *the Right Honourable Earl of Arlington's Letters to Sir William Temple*, ed. Thomas Babington (London, 1701).

Armitage, Edward, "Robert Samber," *AQC*, 11 (1898), 103-32.

Ashmole, Elias, *The Institutions, Laws, and Ceremonies of the Most Noble Order of the Garter* (1672; facs. rpt. London, 1971).

The Antiquities of Berkshire (London, 1819).

Assigny, Fifield d', *Poems on Several Occasions* (London, 1730).

An Impartial Answer to the Enemies of Free-Masonry (Dublin, 1741.

A Serious and Impartial Enquiry into the Cause of the Present Decay of Freemasonry in the Kingdom of Ireland (Dublin, 1744).

Assigny, Marius d', *The Art of Memory* (London, 1697).

Atterbury, Frances, *The Memoirs and Correspondence of the Reverend Francis Atterbury, D.D., Bishop of Rochester*, ed. Folkestone Williams (London, 1869).

The Miscellaneous Works of Bishop Atterbury, ed. John Nichols (London, 1798).

Aubrey, John, *Remains of Gentilisme and Judaisme* (London, 1688).

Miscellanies, 2nd rev. ed. (London, 1721).

Backsheider, Paula, *Daniel Defoe: Ambition and Innovation* (Baltimore, 1989).

Baigent, Michael and Richard Leigh, *The Temple and the Lodge* (1988; London, 2013).

Baigent, Michael and Bernard Williamson,"Sir Christopher Wren and Freemasonry: New Evidence," *AQC*, 109 (1996), 88-89.

Baillet, Adrien, *La Vie de Monsieur Descartes* (Paris, 1691).

Bain, R. Nisbet, *Gustavus III and his Contemporaries* (London, 1894).

Baine, Rodney, *Defoe and the Supernatural* (Athens, 1868).

Baker, C. H. Collins and Muriel Baker, *The Life and Circumstances of James Brydges, First Duke of Chandos, Patron of the Liberal Arts* (Oxford, 1949).

Bakounine, Tatiana, *Le Répertoire Biographique des Francs-Maçons Russes* (Bruxelles, 1940).

Baldi, Marieluisa, *Verisimile non Vero: Filosofia e Politica in Andrew Michael Ramsay* (Milan, 2002).

Bancks, John, *Proposals for Printing by Subscription, Miscellaneous Works in Prose and Verse* (London, 1737).

Barbier, E.J.F., *Chronique de la Regence et Regne de Louis XV, 1718-1763 (Paris, 1885).*

Barker, Richard, *Mr. Cibber of Drury Lane* (New York, 1939).

Barnett, R.D., "Mr. Pepys' Contacts with the Spanish and Portuguese Jews in London," *TJHSE*, 29 (1986), 27-33.

Barrell, Rex, *Francis Atterbury (1662-1732), Bishop of Rochester, and His French Correspondents* (Lewiston, 1990).

Barrett, John, *An Essay on the Earlier Part of the Life of Swift* (London, 1808).

Batham, C.N., "Chevalier Ramsay: A New Appreciation," *AQC*, 81 (1968), 280-310. "The Grand Lodge of England (1717) and its Founding Lodges," *AQC*, 103 (1990), 22-23.

Battestin, Martin, *A Henry Fielding Companion* (Westport, 2000). "Fielding, Bedford, and the Westminster Election of 1749," *Eighteenth-Century Studies*, 11 (1977-78), 143-85.

Behre, Göran, "Gothenburg in Stuart War Strategy, 1649-1760," in Grant Simpson, ed., *Scotland and Scandinavia, 800-1800* (Edinburgh, 1990), 90-99.

Bell, Inna, "Building the New Rome: Charles Cameron as the Architect of Catherine the Great's Eternal City" (M.A. Thesis: Brigham Young University, 2012).

Bell, John, *Rhymes of the Northern Bards* (Newcastle upon Tyne, 1812).

Benimeli, José Ferrer, *La Masonería, Iglesia, e Illustracíon* (Madrid, 1976-77).

Bennett, G.V., *The Tory Crisis in Church and State, 1688-1730* (Oxford, 1975).

Benson, William, *A Letter to Sir J---- B-----, by Birth a Swede, but Naturaliz'd and now a M--- of the Present Parliament* (London, 1711). *A Second letter to Sir Jacob Banks* (London, 1711).

Berland, Kevin, "Chesterfield Demands the Muse: Dublin Print Culture, Poetry and the `Irish' Voice," *Eighteenth-Century Ireland*, 17 (2002), 121-45.

Bergquist, B.J., *St. Johanneslogen den Nordiska Första* (Stockholm, 1999).

Berman, Ric, "The Architecture of Eighteenth-Century English Freemasonry" (Ph.D. Dissertation: University of Exeter, 2010). *The Foundations of Modern Freemasonry: The Grand Architects, Political Change and the Scientific Enlightenment, 1714-1740*, rev. 2nd ed. (2012; Brighton, 2015). *Schism: The Battle that Forged Freemasonry* (Brighton, 2013.

Loyalists and Malcontents: Freemasonry and Revolution in the American Deep South (Goring Heath, 2015).

Espionage, Diplomacy and the Lodge: Charles Delafaye and the Secret Department of the Post Office (Goring Heath, 2017).

"Freemasonry, the London Irish, and the Antients Grand Lodge," in Christopher Murphy and Shawn Eyer, *Exploring Grand Lodge Freemasonry* (Washington, D.C., 2017), 241-79.

Bernheim, Alain, "Ramsay's *Discours* Revisited," www.ordo-abchaos.org/ordo/Docs

Beswick, Samuel, *The Swedenborg Rite* (New York, 1870).

Billington, James, *The Icon and the Axe* (New York, 1966).

Black, Jeremy, *The English Press in the Eighteenth Century* (1987; London, 2010).

"A Failed Attempt at Censorship: the British Diplomatic Service and Pöllnitz's *Histoire secrete de la Duchesse d'Hanover*," *Quaerendo*, 18 (1988), 211-17.

Blackett-Ord, Mark, *Hell-Fire Duke: Life of the Duke of Wharton* (London, 1982).

Blom, J.M., "The Life and Works of Robert Samber (1682-1745?)," *English Studies*, 70 (1989), 507-50.

Bogdan, Henrik and Jan Snoek, eds., *Handbook of Freemasonry* (Leiden, 2014).

Bongie, Laurence, "Voltaire's English, High Treason and a Manifesto for Bonnie Prince Charlie," *Studies on Voltaire and the Eighteenth Century*, 171 (1977), 7-29.

Bonneville, Nicholas de, *La Maçonnerie Écossoise comparé avec des Trois Professions et le Secret de Templières de 14e Siècle* (Hamburg, 1788).

Bord, Gustave, *La Franc-Maçonnerie en France de Origines à 1815* (1908; facs. rpt. Paris, 1985).

Bourne, H.R. Fox, *The Life of John Locke* (New York, 1876).

Boyer, Abel, *The Political State of Great Britain* (London, 1717).

Bramston, James, *The Man of Taste. Occasion'd by an Epistle of Mr. Pope's on that Subject* (London, 1733).

Bregoli, Francesca, "Jewish Scholarship, Science, and the Republic of Letters: Joseph Attias in Eighteenth-century Livorno," *Alef*, 7 (2007), 96-181.

Brooks, E. St. John, *Sir Hans Sloane* (London, 1954).

Brooks-Davies, Douglas, *The Mercurian Monarch: Magical Politics from Spenser to Pope* (Manchester, 1983).

"Pope's Alchemical Epic: the Mystery of the King in the *Dunciad*," *Studies in Mystical Literature*, 3 (1983), 41-73.

Browne, James, *History of the Highlands and of the Highland Clans* (Glasgow, 1840).

Browne, Peter, *A Letter in Answer to Christianity Not Mysterious* (Dublin, 1697).

Browne, Simon, *Jewish and Popish Zeal Described and Compared* (London, 1715).

Bruce, Henry, *Life of General Oglethorpe* (New York, 1890).

Bruce, Maurice, "The Duke of Mar in Exile, 1716-1732," *Transactions of Royal Historical Society*, 4th s., 20 (1937). 61-82.

Bruno, Giordano, *The Expulsion of the Triumphant Beast*, trans. Arthur Imerti (New Brunswick, 1964)

Bullock, Christopher, *The Cobler of Preston* (London, 1716).

Burman, Charles, *Memoirs of that Learned Antiquary, Elias Ashmole* (London, 1717).

Burns, Robert, *The Best Laid Schemes: Selected Poetry and Prose of Robert Burns*, ed. Robert Crawford and Christopher MacLachlan (Princeton, 2009).

Burton, John, Phileleutherus Londinensis, *Remarks on Dr. K—g's Speech at the University of Oxford* (London 1750).

Büsching, A.F. von, *Beiträge zu der Lebens Geschichte Denkwürdiger Personen* (Halle, 1783-89).

Bushnell, Nelson, *William Hamilton of Bangour: Poet and Jacobite* (Aberdeen, 1957).

Byrom, John, *An Epistle to a Friend* (London, 1747).

    Catalogue of the Library of the Late John Byrom (London, 1848).

    The Private Journal and Literary Remains of John Byrom, ed. Richard Parkinson (Chetham Society, 1855).

Caesar, Mary, *The Journal of Mary Freman Caesar, 1724-1741*, ed. Dorothy Potter (Lewiston, 2002).

Calendar of State Papers, Domestic Series, of the Reign of Anne, 1702-1703, ed. R.P. Mahaffy (London, 1916).

Cameron, Charles, "On the Origin and Progress of Chivalric Freemasonry in the British Isles," *AQC*, 13 (1905), 156-80.

Campbell, Colen, *Vitruvius Brittanicus* (London, 1715).

Campbell, John Lorne, *Highland Songs of the `45* (1933; Edinburgh, 1984).

Carpenter, Audrey, *John Theophilus Desaguliers: A Natural Philosopher, Engineer, and Freemason* (London, 2011).

Carr, J.C., "Gorgons, Gomorgons, Medusists, and Masons," *Modern Language Review*, 58 (1963), 73-78.

Carte, Thomas, *The Life of James, Duke of Ormonde* (Oxford, 1735-36).

    A Full Answer to a Letter from a By-Stander (London, 1742).

    General History of England (London, 1747-55).

Carter, Jennifer and Joan Pittock, eds., *Aberdeen and the Enlightenment* (Aberdeen, 1987).

Casanova, Giacomo, *History of My Life*, trans. Willard Trask (New York, 1966).

Cawthorn, James, *Poems by the Rev. Mr. Cawthorne* (London, 1771).

Caywood, Desmond, "Freemasonry and the Knights of Malta," *AQC*, 83 (1979), 71-95.

Centlivre, Susanna, *The Gotham Election, a Farce* (London, 1715).

Chambers, Robert, *Traditions of Edinburgh* (Edinburgh, 1869).

Champion, J.A. I., "Enlightened Erudition and the Politics of Reading in John Toland's Circle," *The Historical Journal*, 49 (2006), 11-41.

Chance, James Frederick, *British Diplomatic Instructions, 1689-1789. Volume I. Sweden, I, 1689-1727* (London, 1922).

Chapman, Paul, "Jacobite Political Argument in England, 1714-1766" (Ph.D. Dissertation, Cambridge University, 1983).

Cherel, Albert, *Un Aventurier Religieux au XVIIIe Siècle, Andrew Michael Ramsay* (Paris, 1925).

Chesterfield, Philip Stanhope, Lord, *A Vindication of a Late Pamphlet, intituled, The Case of the Hanover Troops Considered* (London, 1743).

    The Drapier's Letter to the Good People of Ireland (Dublin, 1745).

    The Drapier's Second Letter to the Good People of Ireland (Dublin, 1745).

    The Works of Lord Chesterfield, ed. Lord Mahon (New York, 1855).

Private Correspondence of Chesterfield and Newcastle, 1744-1746 (London, 1930).

The Letters of Philip Dormer Stanhope, 4th *Earl of Chesterfield*, ed. Bonamy Dobrée (London, 1932).

Chetwood,William Rufus, *The Generous Free-Mason* (London, 1731).

A General History of the Stage (Dublin: E. Rider, 1749).

Chevallier, Pierre, *Les Ducs sous l'Acacia, ou les Premiers Pas de la Franc-Maçonnerie Française, 1725-1743* (Paris, 1964).

La Première Profanation du Temple Maçonnique (Paris, 1968).

Histoire de la Franc-Maçonnerie (Paris, 1974).

Cibber, Colley, *The Non-juror. A Comedy* (London, 1718).

Love's Last Shift; or, the Fool in Fashion (London, 1720).

A Letter from Mr. Cibber to Mr. Pope (London, 1742).

An Occasional Letter from Mr. Cibber to Mr. Pope (London, 1744).

Clark, Jane, "Lord Burlington is Here," in Toby Barnard and Jane Clark, eds., *Lord Burlington: Architecture, Art And Life* (London, 1995), 252-60.

Clark, Jonathan.C.D., *The Memoirs and Speeches of James*, 2nd *Earl Waldegrave* (Cambridge, 2002).

Clark, T.E. and H.C. Foxcroft, *A Life of Gilbert Burnet* (Cambridge, 1907).

Clark, W.M., *Tales of the Wars; or, Naval and Military Chronicle* (1836).

Clarke, J.R., "The Establishment of the Premier Grand Lodge: Why in London and Why in 1717?" *AQC*, 76 (1963), 1-8.

Clergyman in the Isle of Sky, *The Young Pretender's Destiny Unfolded* (London, 1745).

Cobbett, William, *Parliamentary History of England…1733-1737* (London, 1811).

Coleborne, Bryan, "James Arbuckle and Jonathan Swift: New Light on Swift's Biography," *Eighteenth-Century Life*, 11 (1987), 170-80.

Colin, Armand, "Correspondance inédit de Montesquieu," *Revue d'Histoire de Litterature de France* (March-April 1982), 179-262.

Colley, Linda, "The Loyal Brotherhood and the Cocoa Tree: the London Organization of the Tory Party, 1727-1760)," *The Historical Journal*, 20 (1977), 77-95.

Collier, John [Tim Bobbin], *The Blackbird. A Poem. By T.B.* (Amsterdam [Manchester], 1741).

The Miscellaneous Works of Tim Bobbin (Manchester, 1778).

Collins, Anthony, *A Discourse Concerning Ridicule and Irony in Writing* (London, 1729).

Collins, John Churton, *Jonathan Swift: A Critical Biography* (London, 1893).

Collis, Robert, "Patrick Gordon and his Links to Stuart and Jacobite Freemasonry," *Faravid*, 28 (2004), 73-90.

The Petrine Instauration: Magic, Esotericism, and Science at the Court of Peter the Great (Leiden, 2011).

"Hewing the Rough Stone: Masonic Influence in Peter the Great's Russia, 1689-1725," in A. Onnerfors and R. Collis, *Freemasonry and Fraternalism*, 33-61.

"Jolly Jades, Lewd Ladies and Moral Muses: Women and Clubs in Early Eighteenth-century Britain," *Journal for Research into Freemasonry and Fraternalism*," Equinoxonline (2012), 215-24.

"The Order of Toboso: A Pan-European Jacobite Fraternal Network, c. 1726-1739," in Pierre-Yves Beaurepaire, et al., eds., *Diffusions et Circulation des Pratiques Maçonnique XVIIIe-XXe Siècles* (Paris, 2013), 141-56.

"'To a Fair Meeting on the Green': The Order of Toboso and Jacobite Fraternalism," in A. Macinnes, *Living with Jacobitism*, 125-38.

Colvin, Howard, *The History of the King's Works* (London, 1963).

"A Scottish Origin for English Palladianism," *Architectural History*, 17 (1974), 168-82.

A Biographical Dictionary of British Architects, 3rd ed. (New Haven, 1995).

Coman, Anthony, "Walpole's Annotations in a Copy of `Love of Fame, the Universal Passion,'" *Notes & Queries* (December, 1979), 552.

Conder, Edward, *Records of the Hole Craft and Fellowship of Masons*, eds. Louis Williams and Robin Carr (1894; facs.rpt. Bloomington, 1988).

"The Hon. Miss St. Leger and Freemasonry," *AQC, 8 (*1895*)*, 16-19.

Conlon, L., "Freemsonry in Meath and Westmeath," www.meath.org./lodges/lodge_131.html

Connell, David, "The Collection of William Dugood, FRS – Jeweller, Scientist, Freemason, and Spy," *Journal of the History of Collections*, 21 (2009), 33-70.

Conner, T.P., "The Making of *Vitruvius Britannicus*," *Architectural History* (1977), 14-30.

Cooper, Antony Ashley, Third Earl of Shaftesbury, *Second Characters or the Language of Forms*, ed. Benjamin Rand (1914; rpt. New York, 1969).

Complete Works of Third Earl of Shaftesbury. Standard Edition, ed. Gerd Hemmerich and Wolfram Benda (Stuttgart, 1981).

Corp, Edward, ed., *L'Autre Exil: Les Jacobites en France au Début de XVIIIᵉ Siècle* (Montpellier, 1993).

"Melfort: a Jacobite Connoisseur, *History Today* (October 1995), 41-46.

ed., *Lord Burlington—The Man and His Politics* (Lewiston, 1998).

"The Jacobite Presence in Toulouse in the Eighteenth Century," in Sophie Dulucq, ed., *Genealogies Rêvées* (Toulouse, 2004).

The Stuart Court in Italy, 1719-1766 (Cambridge, 2011).

"The Scottish Community at Saint-Germain after the Departure of the Stuart Court," in A.Macinnes, *Living with Jacobitism*, 27-37.

and Eveline Cruickshanks, eds., *The Stuart Court in Exile and the Jacobites* (London, 1995).

Coudert, Allison, *Leibniz and the Kabbalah* (Dordrecht, 1995).

The Impact of Kabbalah in the Seventeenth Century: The Life and Thought of Francis Mercurius Van Helmont (Leiden, 1999).

Coustos, John, *The Sufferings of John Coustos, for Free-Masonry, and for His Refusing to Turn Roman Catholic in the Inquisition at Lisbon* (London, 1746).

Coxe, William, *Memoirs of the Life and Administration of Sir Robert Walpole* (London, 1798).

Craig, W.H., *Life of Lord Chesterfield* (London, 1987).

Cramond, William, *The Plundering of Cullen House by the Rebels* (Buckie, 1887).

Cranston, Maurice, *John Locke: A Biography* (1957; London, 1966).

Crawford, Robert, *Scotland's Books* (New York, 2008).

Crawley, W.J. Chetwode, "Early Irish Freemasonry and Jonathan Swift," in Henry Sadler, *Masonic Reprints and Historical Revelations* (London, 1898), vii-xxxvi.
> *Caementaria Hibernica* (1900; facs. rpt. Bloomington, 2002).).
> "Notes on Early Irish Freemasonry, No. VII," *AQC*, 16, part 1 (1903), 69.
> "Mock Masonry in the Eighteenth Century," *AQC*, 18 (1905), 129-52.
> "Contemporary Comments on the Freemasonry of the Eighteenth Century," *AQC*, 18 (1905), 205-06.

Cross, A.G., "British Freemasons in Russia during the Reign of Catherine the Great," *Oxford Slavonic Papers* (1971), 43-72.

Crossle, Philip, "Freemasonry in Ireland, circa 1725-31," *Lodge of Research, No. CC. Ireland. Transactions for the Year 1924* (Dublin, 1931).

Cruickshanks, Eveline, ed., *Political Untouchables: The Tories and the `45* (London, 1979).
> ed., *Ideology and Conspiracy: Aspects of Jacobitism in 1688-1759* (London, 1982), 179-200.
> *Charles XII of Sweden: A Character and Two Poems* (Brisbane, 1983).
> "Lord North, Christopher Layer and the Atterbury Plot," in E. Cruickshanks and J. Black, *Jacobite Challenge*, 92-106.
> *Lord Cornbury, Bolingbroke and a Plan to Restore the Stuarts, 173-1735* (Royal Stuart Papers, 27 (1986).
> *By Force or Default? The Revolution of 1688-89* (Edinburgh, 1989).
> "Lord Cowper, Lord Orrery, the Duke of Wharton, and Jacobitism," *Albion*, (1994), 27-40.
> *The Oglethorpes: A Jacobite Family, 1689-1760.* Royal Stuart Society, Paper XLV (1995).
> "The Political Career of the Third Earl of Burlington," in T. Barnard and J. Clark, *Lord Burlington*, 201-16.
> *The Glorious Revolution* (London, 2000).
> and Jeremy Black, *The Jacobite Challenge* (Edinburgh, 1988).

Curll, Edmund, ed., *Whartoniana* (London, 1727).
> and Howard Erskine-Hill, *The Atterbury Plot* (New York, 2004

Daly, Augustin, *Woffington: A Tribute to the Actress and Woman*, 2nd ed. (1888; Troy, 1891).

Daniel, Stephen, *John Toland: His Methods, Manners, and Mind* (Montreal, 1984).

Daynes, Gilbert, "The Duke of Norfolk, 1730-1731," *AQC, 29 (1926), 109-10.*

Dee, John [?], *The Rosie Crucian Secrets*, ed. E.J. L. Garstin, (Wellingborough, 1985).

Defoe, Daniel, *The Second-Sighted Highlander* (London, 1715).
> *What if the Swedes Should Come?* (London, 1717).
> *An Account of the Swedish and Jacobite Plot* (London, 1717).
> *The Plot Discovered: or, Some Observations upon a late Vile Jesuitical Pamphlet, Written and Published by desperate Agents and Understrappers of Count Gyllenborg* (London, 1717).
> *Some Account of the Life and Most Remarkable Actions of Georg Henry, Baron de Goertz* (London, 1719).
> *The King of Pirates* (London, 1720).
> *The History of the Blacks of Waltham in Hampshire* (London, 1723).
> *Librorum ex Bibliothecis Philippi Farewell, D.D., et Danielis De Foe. 15 November 1731* (London, 1727).
> *An Essay on the History and Reality of Apparitions* (London, 1727).

The Political State of Great Britain (London, 1730).

The Letters of Daniel Defoe, ed. George Healey (Oxford, 1955).

A Tour through the Whole Island of Great Britain, eds. G.D.H. Cole and D.C. Browning (1724-26; New York, 1962).

De Hoyos, Art and Brent Morris, *Freemasonry in Context: History, Ritual, Controversy* (Lanham, 2004).

Denistoun, James, *Memoirs of Sir Robert Strange, Kt., the Eminent Engraver, and His Brother-in-law, Andrew Lumiston, Private Secretary to the Stuart Princes at Rome* (London, 1855).

Dermott, Laurence, *Ahiman Rezon, or a Help to a Brother* (1756; rev. ed. London, 1764).

Desaguliers, Jean Theophilus, *The Newtonian System of the World* (London, 1728).

A Course of Experimental Philosophy (London, 1744).

Désaguliers, René and Roger Dachez, "Chinese Thought and Freemasonry in the Eighteenth Century," in A. de Hoyos and B. Morris, *Freemsonry in Context*, 145-61.

Dickins, Lilian, and Mary Stanton, eds., *An Eighteenth-Century Correspondence, Being the Letters... to Sanderson Miller, Esq. of Radway* (London, 1910).

Dickson, David, *Old World Colony: Cork and South Munster, 1630-1830* (Cork, 2005).

Dickson, M.K., *The Jacobite Attempt of 1719*. Scottish History Society, 19 (Edinburgh, 1895).

Dielemans, G., "Een maconnicke (liefde) Brief uit Maastricht A.D. 1658," *Acta Macionica*, 10 (2000), 181-82.

Donaldson, William, *The Jacobite Song* (Aberdeen, 1988).

Doran, John, *The Book of the Prince of Wales* (London, 1860).

London in the Jacobite Times (Boston, 1877).

Douglas, Hugh, *Jacobite Spy Wars: Moles, Rogues, and Treachery* (Stroud, 1996).

Downes, Kerry, *Vanbrugh* (London, 1977).

Downie, J.A., *A Political Biography of Henry Fielding* (London, 2009).

Draffen, George, "Early Charters of the Royal Order of Scotland," *AQC*, 62 (1951), 325-26.

"Freemasonry in Scotland," *AQC*, 83 (1979), 366.

Drury, Stephen, "Lodge St. John Kilwinning Kilmarnock, no.22: an Historical Sketch 1734-1992," *Year Book of the Grand Lodge of Antient Free and Accepted Masons of Scotland* (Edinburgh, 1993).

Dryden, John, *The Works of John Dryden*, ed. E.N. Hooker and H.T. Swedenberg (Berkeley, 1956).

Duffy, Christopher, "Hidden Sympathies: the Hessians in Scotland in 1746," in Monod, Pittock, and Szechi, *Loyalty and Identity*, 120-31.

Dutens, Louis, *Mémoires d'un Voyageur qui se Repose* (Paris, 1806).

Edenborg, Carl-Michael, *Gull och Mull* (Magister-uppsats I idéhistoria vid Stockholms Universitet, September 1995).

Ehrenpreis, Irwin, *Swift: the Man, His Works, and the Age* (London, 1962).

Einberg, Elizabeth, *William Hogarth: A Complete Catalogue of the Paintings* (New Haven, 2016).

Eisler, William, "The Construction of the Image of Martin Folkes (1690-1754): Art, Science and Masonic Sociability in the Age of the Grand Tour," *The Medal*, 58, part 1 (Spring 2011), 4-29; part 2 (Autumn 2011), 4-16.

Ekman, Eero, *Highlights of Masonic Life in Nordic Countries* (Helsinki, 1994).

Elcho, David, Lord, *A Short Account of the Affairs of Scotland in the Years 1744, 1745, and 1746*, ed. Evan Charteris (Edinburgh, 1907).

Ellis, John, "Tartana, or the Plaidie. An Allegorical Poem," *European Magazine* (August 1782), 151-52, 234-35.

Emerson, Roger, "Hume and the Bellman, Zerobabel MacGilchrist," *Hume Studies*, 23 (1997), 9-28.

Enright, Brian, "Richard Rawlinson: Collector, Antiquary, and Topographer" (Ph.D.Dissertation: Oxford University, 1956).

Entick, John, *The Freemason's Pocket Companion* (Edinburgh, 1765).

Erskine, Stuart, "The Earl of Mar's Legacy to Scotland, and to his Son, Lord Erskine," *Publications of Scottish Historical Society*, 26 (1896), 141-247.

Erskine-Hill, Howard, "'Avowed Friend and Patron': the Third Earl of Burlington and Alexander Pope," in T. Barnard and J. Clark, *Lord Burlington*, 217-29.

Ettinger, Amos, *James Edward Oglethorpe: Imperial Idealist* (Oxford, 1936).

Evelyn, John, *Acetaria* (London, 1699).
> *Miscellaneous Writings*, ed. William Upcott (London, 1825).
> *The Diary of John Evelyn*, ed. E.S. de Beer (Oxford, 1996).

Ewald, Alexander, *The Life and Times of Prince Charles Stuart*, new ed. (London, 1883); plus 3rd ed. (1904).

F.J.U., "Quotations from Evelyn, *AQC*, 46 (1993), 225.

Fagan, Patrick, *Catholics in a Protestant Country: The Papist Constituency in Eighteenth-Century Dublin* (Dublin, 1998).
> *A Georgian Miscellany: Irish Poets of the Eighteenth Century* (Dublin, 1989).
> *An Irish Bishop in Penal Times: The Chequered Career of Sylvester Lloyd, OFM* (Dublin, 1993).
> *Ireland in the Stuart Papers* (Dublin, 1995).

Faucher, Jean-André, *Dictionnaire Historique des Francs-Maçons* (Paris, 1988).

Fay, Bernard, "Les Origines et L'Esprit de la Franc-Maçonnerie ," *Le Revue Universelle*, 66 (1936), 175.

Fenwick, Hubert, *Architect Royal: The Life and Works of Sir William Bruce* (Kineton, 1970).

Ferguson, Robert, *A Brief Account of Some of the Late Encroachments and Depredations of the Dutch upon the English* (London, 1695).

Ferguson, William *Scotland's Relations with England: A Survey to 1707* (Edinburgh, 1977).

Ferrone, Vincenzo, *The Intellectual Roots of the Italian Enlightenment* (New Jersey, 1995).

Fielding, Henry, *The Coffee-House Politician* (London, 1730).
> *The Miser* (London and Dublin, 1733).
> *Miscellanies* (London and Dublin, 1743).
> *The Life Story of Mr. Jonathan Wild, the Great* (1743; Dublin, 1754).
> *A Serious Address to the People of Great Britain*, 3rd rev. ed. (London, 1745).
> *The Lover's Assistant…A New Art of Love* (London, 1759).
> *The Jacobite's Journal and Related Writings*, ed. W.B. Coley (Middletown, 1975).

The True Patriot and Related Writings, ed. W.B. Coley (Middlown, 1987).

Tom Jones, ed. John Bender and Stern (Oxford, 1996).

Fielding's Library: An Annotated Catalogue, eds. Frederick Ribble and Anne Ribble (Charlottesville, 1996).

Fielding, Sarah, *Familiar Letters Between the Principal Characters in David Simple* (London, 1747).

Fifoot, Cecil Herbert, *Lord Mansfield* (Oxford, 1936).

Firth, C.H., "Killing No Murder," *English Historical Review*, 7 (1902), 308-11.

Fischer, John Irwin, *Swift's Poetry* (Gainesville, 1978).

Fisher, Wilfrid, "A Cavalcade of Freemasons as Recorded in *The Gentleman's Magazine* for 1732," *AQC*, 76 (1963), 44-60.

Flynn, M.W., *Men of Iron: The Crowleys in the Early Iron Industry* (Edinburgh, 1962).

Forbes, Robert, *The Lyon in Mourning*, ed. Henry Paton (Edinburgh, 1896).

Forbes, William, *A Pil for Pork-Eaters* ([Edinburgh], 1705).

Foster, Harold, *Edward Young: The Poet of Night Thoughts, 1683-1765* (Alburg, 1986).

Foxon, D.F., *English Verse, 1710-1750* (Cambridge, 1975).

Francovich, Carlo, *Storia del la Massoneria in Italia* (Firenze, 1974).

Fraser, William, *The Earls of Cromartie* (Edinburgh, 1876).

The Scotts of Buccleuch (Edinburgh, 1878).

Memorials of the Family of Wemyss of Wemyss (Edinburgh, 1888).

Friedman, Terry, *James Gibbs* (New Haven, 1984).

"A `Palace worthy of the Grandeur of the King': Lord Mar's Designs for the Old Pretender, 1718-1730," *Architectural History*, 29 (1986), 102-13.

Fritz, Paul, *The English Ministers and Jacobitism between the Rebellions of 1715 and 1745* (Toronto, 1975).

Fuller, Jean Overton, *Comte de Saint-Germain* (London, 1989).

Garden, George, *The Case of the Episcopal Clergy*, 2nd rev.ed. (Edinburgh, 1703).

Gaspar, Julia, *Theodore von Neuhoff, King of Corsica* (Newark, 2013).

Gauci, Perry, "Sir Robert Clayton," in Eveline Cruickshanks, Stuart Handley, and D.W. Hayton, *The House of Commons, 1690-1715* (Cambridge, 2002).

Gay, John, et al, *Three Hours After Marriage* (London, 1717).

Gerrard, Christine, *The Patriot Opposition to Walpole: Politics, Poetry, and National Myth* (Oxford, 1994).

Aaron Hill: The Muses' Projector, 1685-1756 (Oxford, 2003).

"Geschichte der Freimaurer Brüderschaft in Schweden und Norwegen," *Latomia*, 7 (1846), 175-92.

Gibbons, William, "Divining Zoroaster: Masonic Elements in Handel's Oratorio," *Eighteenth-Century Life*, 34 (2010), 65-82.

Gibson, Strickland, "Francis Wise, B.D., Oxford Antiquary, Librarian, and Archivist," *Oxoniensia*, 1 (1936), 173-95.

Gilbert, John T., *History of Dublin* (Dublin, 1903).

Gildon, Charles, *Canons: or the Vision. A Poem addressed to the right Honourable James Brydges, Earl of Caernarvon* (London, 1717).

Gilmour, Ian, *Risings, Riots, and Revolution: Governance and Violence in Eighteenth-Century England* (London, 1993).

Glendinning, Miles, Ranald Macinnes, and Aonghus Mackechnie, eds., *A History of Scottish Architecture: From the Renaissance to the Present Day* (Edinburgh, 1996).

Glickman, Gabriel, "Andrew Michael Ramsay (1683-1743), the Jacobite Court, and the English Catholic Enlightenment," *Eighteenth-Century Thought*, 3 (2009), 293-329.

"Parliament, the Tories and Frederick, Prince of Wales," *Parliamentary History*, 30 (2011), 120-21.

Glozier, Matthew, "The Earl of Melfort, the Court Catholic Party, and the Foundation of the Order of the Thistle," *Scottish Historical Review*, 79 (2000), 233-38.

Goldie, Mark, "The Roots of True Whiggism," *History of Political Thought*, 1 (1980), 195-236.

Gooch, Leo, *The Desperate Faction? The Jacobites of North-East England, 1688-1745* (Hull, 1995).

"The Derwentwater Library," *Recusant History*, 30 (1922), 120-29.

Goodricke, Charles A., *Ribston...Seat of the Goodricke Family* (London, 1902).

Goring, Henry, *A Letter from H---- G----- (London, 1750).*

Gottrand, Gustave, "On the Antiquity of Lodge 'La Parfaite Union,' at Mons, Belgium," *AQC*, 10 (1897), 50-58.

Gould, Robert Freke, *History and Antiquities of Freemasonry*, 3rd rev. ed. (1882-87; New York, 1951).

"Masonic Celebrities: William Stukeley, M.D.," *AQC*, 6 (1893), 127-38.

"Masonic Celebrities: The Duke of Wharton, G.M., 1722-23, *AQC*, 8 (1895), 115-55.
Military Lodges: The Apron and the Sword (London, 1899).

Goulden, R.J., "VOX POPULI, VOX DEI: Charles Delafaye's Paper Chase," *The Book Collector*, 28 (1979), 368-90.

Graham, Lesley, "Robert Louis Stevenson's 'The Young Chevalier,'" in Macinnes, German, and Graham, *Living with Jacobitism*, 197-208.

Graham, Michael, *The Blasphemies of Thomas Aikenhead: Boundaries of Belief on the Eve of the Enlightenment* (Edinburgh, 2008).

Grantham, Ivor, "A Pre-1717 Reference to 'Free masons,'" *AQC*, 59 (1948), 196-97.

Gratton, Silvio, *Trieste Segreta* (Trieste, 1987).

Greenwood, David, *William King, Tory and Jacobite* (Oxford, 1969).

Gregg, Edward, "The Jacobite Career of the Earl of Mar," in E. Cruickshanks, *Ideology*, 179-200.

Grego, Joseph, *A History of Parliamentary Elections and Electioneering, from the Stuarts to Queen Victoria*, new ed. (London, 1892).

Grell, Ole, Jonathan Israel, and Nicholas Tyacke, eds., *From Persecution to Toleration: The Glorious Revolution and Religion in England* (Oxford, 1991).

Grey, Ian, "Peter the Great in England," *History Today*, 6 (1965), 225-34.

Guerinot, J.V., *Pamphlet Attacks on Pope, 1711-1744* (London, 1969).

Guite, Janetta, "The Jacobite Cause, 1730-1740: The International Dimension" (Ph.D. Dissertation: MacMaster University, 1987).

Gyllenborg, Carl, *Reason and Gospel Against Matter of Fact: or, Reflections upon two Letters to Sir Jacob Banks* (London, 1711).
Letters which Passed between Count Carl Gyllenborg, the Barons Goertz, Sparre, and Others Relating to the Design of Raising a Rebellion in His Majesty's Dominions to be Supported by a Force from Sweden (London, 1717).

Halliday, James, "The Club and the Revolution in Scotland," *Scottish Historical Review*, 45 (1966), 143-59.

Hamill, John," The Jacobite Conspiracy," *AQC, 113 (*2000*)*, 97-113.

Hamilton of Bangour, William, *The Faithful Few* (Edinburgh, 1734).
> *The Poems and Songs of William Hamilton of Bangour*, ed. James Paterson (Edinburgh, 1850).

Hammond, Eugene, *Jonathan Swift: Our Dean* (Newark, 2016).

Hancox, Joy, *The Byrom Collection* (London, 1992).
> *The Queen's Chameleon: The Story of John Byrom* (London, 1994).

Hans, Nicholas, "The Masonic Lodge in Florence in the Eighteenth Century," *AQC*, 71 (1958), 109-12.

Harland-Jacobs, Jessica, *Builders of Empire: Freemasons and British Imperialism, 1717-1927* (Chapel Hill, 2007).

Harley, Sir Edward, *A Scriptural and Rational Account of the Christian Religion* (London, 1695).

Harrington, James, *The Oceana and Other Works*, ed. John Toland (1771; Aalen, 1963).

Harris, Eileen, "Batty Langley: a Tutor to Freemasons (1696-1751), *Burlington Magazine*, 119 (1977).

Harris, John, *William Talman: Maverick Architect* (London, 1982).
> *The Palladian Revival: Lord Burlington, His Villa and Garden at Chiswick* (New Haven, 1994).
> "The Architecture of the Williamite Court," in R.P. Maccubin and M. Hamilton-Philips, eds., *The Age of William III and Mary II: Power, Politics and Patronage (1688-1702)* (Williamsburg, 1989), 227-33.

Harris, Michael, *Newspapers in the Age of Walpole* (London, 1987).

Hart, Vaughan, *Art and Magic in the Court of the Stuarts* (London, 1994).
> *St. Paul's Cathedral, Christopher Wren* (London, 1995).

Hashinima, Katsumi, "Jonathan Swift and Freemasonry," *Hitotsubashi Journal of Arts and Sciences*, 38 (1977), 13-22.

Hatton, A.F., "The Early Minute Book of the Lodge of Dunblane," *AQC*, 67 (1955), 84-119.

Hatton, Raghnild, *Charles XII of Sweden* (Cambridge, 1968).

Hay, Richard, *A Genealogie of the Saintclaires of Rosslyn* (Edinburgh, 1835).

Haywood, Eliza, *Epistles for the Ladies* (London, 1749-50).

Hearne, Thomas, *Reliquiae Hearniana*, ed. Philip Bliss, 2nd ed. (London. 1869).
> *Remarks and Recollections of Thomas Hearne*, ed. C.E. Doble (Oxford, 1894-1921).

Heidenreich, Helmut, *The Libraries of Daniel Defoe and Philip Farewell* (Berlin, 1970).

Heidner, Jan, *Carl Reinhold Berch* (Stockholm, 1997).

Heilbrun, J. L., *Physics at the Royal Society during Newton's Presidency* (Los Angeles, 1983).

Heinemann, F.H., "John Toland and the Age of Enlightenment," *Review of English Studies*, 20 (1944), 125-46.
> "John Toland, France, Holland, and Dr.Williams," *Review of English Studies*, 25 (1949), 346-49.

Henderson, George D., *Mystics of the North-East* (Aberdeen, 1934).
> *Chevalier Ramsay* (London, 1952).

Henley, John, *Oratory Transactions*, II, 3rd ed. (London, 1728).
  The Hyp-Doctor; *The Hyp-Doctor/Freemason* (1730-42).
Hervey, John, Lord, *Lord Hervey's Memoirs*, ed. Romney Sedgwick (London, 1952)
  Some Materials towards Memoirs of the Reign of King George II, ed. Romney Sedgwick
  (London, 1931).
  and William Pulteney, *Sedition and Defamation Display'd*, ed. Alexander Pettit (New
  York, 1997).
Hextall, William, "Orator Henley, M.A., 1692-1756," *AQC*, 29 (1916), 68-75.
Hickes, George, *The Spirit of Enthusiasm Exorcized*, 4th rev. ed. (London, 1709).
Higgins, Ian, *Swift's Politics: A Study in Disaffection* (Cambridge: Cambridge UP, 1994).
  "Swift and the Jacobite Diaspora," in Hermann J. Real and Helgard Stover-Lei-
  dig, eds., *Reading Swift: Papers from the Fourth Münster Symposium on Jonathan Swift*
  (Munich, 2003), 87-103.
  "Jonathan Swift's Memoirs of a Jacobite," in A. Macinnes, K. German, L. Gra-
  ham, *Living with Jacobitism,"* 71-84.
Highfill, Philip., Kalman Burnim, Edward Langhans, *Biographica Dictionary of Actors, Ac-
  tresses, Musicians, Dancers* (Carbondale, 1984).
Higham, F.M.G., *King James the Second* (London, 1934).
HMC. Second Report of the Historical Manuscripts Commission (London, 1871).
HMC. Report on the Manuscripts of the Earl of Eglinton, ed. Sir John Stirling Maxwell, (Lon-
  don, 1885).
HMC. 29: 13th Report. Portland MSS, Appendix ii (London, 1893-94).
HMC. Ninth Report of the Historical Manuscripts Commission, Part II: Appendix (London,
  1884).
HMC. Report on the Manuscripts of His Grace the Duke of Portland (London, 1901).
HMC. Calendar of the Stuart Papers (London, 1902-03).
HMC. Report on the Manuscripts of the Earl of Mar and Kellie, Preserved at Alloa House (Lon-
  don, 1904).
HMC. Report on the Manuscripts of the Right Honourable Lord Polwarth (London, 1911).
Hobhouse, Stephen, *William Law and Eighteenth-Century Quakerism, including some Un-
  published Letters and Fragments of William Law and John Byrom* (London, 1927).
Hogarth, William, *The Works of William Hogarth*, eds. John Nichols and George Steevens
  (London, 1810).
Hogg, James, *The Jacobite Relics of Scotland*, 2nd series (Paisley, 1874).
Holmes, Richard, "James Arbuckle and Dean Swift: Cultural Politics in the Irish Con-
  fessional State," *Irish Studies Review*, 16 (2008), 431-44.
Hooke, Robert, *The Diary of Robert Hooke*, eds. H.W. Robinson and W. Adams (London,
  1935).
Hopkins, P.A., "Sir James Montgomerie of Skermorlie," in E. Corp and E. Cruick-
  shanks, eds. *Stuart Court in Exile*, 51-56.
Horgan, D.M., "Popular Protest in the Eighteenth Century: John Collier (Tim Bob-
  bin)," *Review of English Studies*, n.s., 48 (1997), 310-31.
Howard, Carol, "A Female Freemason on Stage? Eliza Haywood's Patriotism at Henry
  Fielding's Haymarket Theatre," in Laura Engel, ed., *The Publics Open to Us All:*

Essays on Women in Performance in Eighteenth-Century England (Newcastle, 2009), 128-55.

Howell, James, *The Wonderfull and Most Deplorable History of the Latter Time of the Jews* (1652; London, 1653).

Howell, T.B., ed., *A Complete Collection of State Trials* (London, 1809-28).

Hoyos, Arturo de, "The Mystery of the Royal Arch Word," in A. de Hoyos and B. Morris, *Freemasonry in Context*, 209-30.

Hoyos, Arturo de, and Brent Morris, eds., *Freemasonry in Context: History, Ritual, and Controversy* (Lanham, 2004).

Huehner, Leon, "The Jews of Ireland: an Historical Sketch," *TJHSE*, 5 (1902-05), 226-38.

Hughan, William J., "The Ancient Stirling Lodge," *AQC*, 6 (1893), 108-11.

    Memorials of the Masonic Union of A.D. 1813 (London, 1874; also, rev. ed. John Thorpe (Leicester, 1913).

    Origin of the English Rite of Freemasonry, especially in Relation to the Royal Arch Degree (London, 1884).

    "Origins of Masonic Knight Templary in the United Kingdom," *AQC*, 18 (1906), 91-93.

    "The Three Degrees of Freemasonry," *AQC*, 10 (1897), 143.

Hume, David, *The Life and Correspondence of David Hume*, ed. John Hill Burton (Edinburgh, 1846).

    The Letters of David Hume, 1727-1765, ed. J.Y.T. Greig (1932; Oxford, 2011).

Hunter, David, "The Great Pretender, Monsieur le Comte de Saint-Germain," *The Musical Times*, 144 (2003), 4-44.

Hunter, Michael, *John Aubrey and the Realm of Learning* (London, 1975).

    "'Aikenhead the Atheist': the Context and Consequences of Articulate Irreligion in the Late Seventeenth Century," in Michael Hunter and David Wooton, eds., *Atheism from the Reformation to the Enlightenment* (Oxford, 1992).

    The Royal Society and its Fellows, 2nd ed. (London, 1994).

    Science and the Shape of Orthodoxy (Woodbridge: Boydell, 1995).

    The Occult Laboratory: Magic, Science and Second Sight in Late Seventeenth-Century Scotland (Woodbridge, 2001).

Hurlo Thrumbo, *The Merry-Thought: or, the Glass-Window and Bog-House Miscellany* (London, 1731).

Ingamells, John, *A Dictionary of British and Irish Travellers in Italy, 1701-1800* (New Haven, 1997). Plus on-line edition.

Ireland, John, *A Supplement to Hogarth Illustrated* (London, 1798).

Irving, Washington, *Abbotsford and Newstead* (London, 1835).

Israel, Jonathan, *The Anglo-Dutch Moment: Essays on the Glorious Revolution and Its World Impact* (Cambridge, 1991).

Jackson, A.C.F., "Rosicrucianism and its Influence on Craft Masonry," *AQC*, 97 (1894), 115-50.

Jacob, Margaret, *The Radical Enlightenment: Pantheists, Freemasons, and Republicans* (London, 1981).

    Living the Enlightenment: Freemasonry and Politics in Eighteenth-Century Europe (New York, 1991).

Jeffrey, Paul, *The City Churches of Christopher Wren* (London, 1996).

Jenkins, Philip, "Jacobites and Freemasonry in Eighteenth-century Wales," *Welsh History Review*, 9 (1978), 391-406.

"John Clephane: a Scottish Traveller in Eighteenth-Century Europe," *National Library of Wales Journal*, 22 (1982), 416-26.

Jerdan, William, ed., *Letters from James, Earl of Perth, Lord Chancellor of Scotland, to his Sister, the Countess of Erroll.* Camden Society, 33 (London, 1845).

Jesse, John H., *Memoirs of the Pretenders and Their Adherents* (London, 1845).

Johnsen, Arne Odd, "Jacobite Officers at Bergen, Norway, after the Battle of Culloden," *Scottish Historical Review*, 57 (1978), 186-96.

Johnson, Amandus, *Swedish Contributions to American Freedom, 1776-1783* (Philadelphia, 1953).

Johnson, Charles, *The Cobler of Preston* (London, 1716).

Johnson, Melvin J., *Freemasonry in America Prior to 1750* (Cambridge, MA, 1817).

Johnson, Samuel, *London* (London, 1738).

Marmor Norfolciense (London, 1739).

A Compleat Vindication of the Licensors of the Stage (London, 1739).

The Vanity of Human Wishes (London, 1749).

Jones, Bernard, *The Freemasons' Guide and Companion*, rev. ed. (London, 1956).

Jones, Claude, "Locke and Masonry," *Neuphiloglogische Mitteilungen*, 67 (1966), 72-78.

Jones, Henry, *The Bricklayer's Poem* (Dublin, 1745).

Jones, Richard F., *Lewis Theobald: His Contribution to English Scholarship* (London, 1966).

Josephson, Ragnar, *L'Architecte de Charles XII: Nicodéme Tessin á la Cour de Lous XIV* (Paris, 1930).

Kanter, Sanford B., "Archbishop Fenelon's Political Activity: the Focal Point of Power in Dynasticism," *French Historical Studies*, 4 (1965-66), 320-34.

Katz, David, *The Jews in the History of England* (Oxford, 1994).

"The Jews of England and 1688," in O. Grell, J. Israel, and N. Tyacke, eds., *From Persecution*, 217-49.

God's Last Words: Reading the English Bible from the Reformation to Fundamentalism (New Haven, 2004).

Kelly, George, *A Letter from George Kelly to a Friend in London* (London, 1736).

Memoirs of the Life, Travels and Transactions of the Revd. G.K. [George Kelly] (London, 1736).

A Catalogue of the Books… being the Library of Mr. George Kelly (London, 1737).

Kelly, James, and Martyn Powell, eds., *Clubs and Societies in Eighteenth-Century Ireland* (Dublin 2010).

Kennedy, Maeve, "Bonnie Prince Charlie portrait found by art historian Bendor Grosvenor," *The Guardian* (23 February 2014).

Kervella, André, *Aux Origines de la Franc-Maçonnerie Française (1689-1750)* (Rouvray, 1996).

La Maçonnerie Écossaise dans le France de la Ancien Régime, les Années Obscures (1720-1755) (Paris, 1999).

La Passion Écossaise (Paris, 2002).

Francs-Maçons au Duché de Bouillon (Neufchâteau, 2006).

Le Mystère de la Rose Blanche: Franc-Maçons et Templiers au XVIIIe Siècle (Paris, 2009).

Le Chevalier Ramsay, Une Fierté Ecossaise (Paris, 2009).

"Le Secret du Grand Orient de Bouillon," *La Règle d'Abraham*, 39 (2017), 111-53.

Kilmarnock, William Boyd, 4th Earl of, *The Chronicle of Charles, the Young Man* (Edinburgh?, 1745).

King, E.J. and the Earl of Scarborough, *The Grand Priory of the Hospital of St. John of Jerusalem in England* (London, 1924).

King, Kathryn, *A Political Biography of Eliza Haywood* (London, 2012).

King, William, *The Toast* (Dublin, 1732; London, 1736).

Miltoni Epistola ad Pollionem (London, 1738).

The Bench. An Eclogue. Occasion'd by the War between England and Spain (London, 1741).

A Chiding Letter to S.P.Y.B. in Defence of Epistola Objurgatoria (London, 1744).

A Translation of a Late Celebrated Oration, Occasioned by a Lible (sic), entitled , Remarks on Doctor K—g's Speech (London, 1750).

The Dreamer (London, 1754).

Political and Literary Anecdotes of His Own Time (London, 1819).

Kirk, Robert, *The Secret Commonwealth and a Short Treatise on Charms and Spirits (1691)*, ed.S. Sanderson (London, 1976).

Knapp, Lewis, "Ralph Griffiths, Author and Publisher, 1746-1750," *The Library: The Transactions of the Bibliographical Society*, 4th s., vol. 20 (1930), 197-213.

Knoop, Douglas, "The Mason Word," *AQC*, 51 (1938), Prestonian Lecture.

Knoop, Douglas, G.P. Jones, and Douglas Hamer, *Early Masonic Catechisms*, rev. ed. (1943; Manchester, 1963). Cited as *EMC*.

Early Masonic Pamphlets (1945; London, 1978). Cited as *EMP*.

Koon, Helene, *Colley Cibber: A Biography* (Lexington, 1986).

La Créquinière, *The Agreement of the Customs of the East Indians with Those of the Jews*, [trans. John Toland] (London, 1705).

Lamberty, Guillaume, *Mémoires pur server a l'historie du XVIIIe Siècle* (La Haye, 1727-31).

Lamm, Martin, *Olof von Dalin* (Uppsala, 1908).

Landa, Louis, *Swift and the Church of Ireland* (Oxford, 1954).

Lang, Andrew, *Pickle the Spy, or the Incognito of Charles Edward*, rev. ed. (London, 1897).

The Companions of Pickle (London, 1898).

A History of Scotland from the Roman Occupation (Edinburgh, 1907).

and A.E.W. Mason, *Parson Kelly* (London, 1900).

Langley, Batty, *Ancient Masonry* (London, 1736).

A Survey of Westminster Bridge (London, 1748).

Lansdowne, George Granville, Lord, *The Genuine Works in Verse and Prose of Lord Lansdowne* (London, 1742).

Lantoine, Albert, *Histoire de la Franc-Maçonnerie Française* (Genève, 1982).

Lawrie, Alexander, *The History of Masonry* (Edinburgh, 1804).

Le Bihan, Alain, *Francs-Maçons et Ateliers Parisiens de la Grande Loge de France au XVIIIe Siècle* (Paris, 1973).

Lee, Francis, *Apoleipomena* (London, 1752).

Lee, William, *Daniel Defoe: His Life and Recently Discovered Letters* (London, 1969).

Le Forestier, René, *Les Illuminés de Bavière et la Franc-Maçonnerie Allemande* (Paris, 1914).
  La Franc-Maçonnerie Templière et Occultiste au XVIIIe et XIXe Siècles , ed. Antoine Faivre (Paris, 1970).

Leibniz, Gottfried Wilhelm, *Sämtliche Schriften und Briefe* (Berlin, 1923-93).

Leijonhufud, Sigrid, ed., *Carl Gustaf Tessins Dagbok, 1748-1752* (Stockholm, 1915).

Lenman, Bruce, *The Jacobite Risings in Britain, 1689-1746* (London, 1980).
  "Physicians and Politics in the Jacobite Era," in E. Cruickshanks and J. Black, *Jacobite Challenge.*

Lennox, Charles, Earl of March, *A Duke and His Friends: The Life and Letters of the Second Duke of Richmond* (London, 1911).

Lepper, John Heron, *The Difference Between English and Irish Masonic Rituals Treated Historically* (Dublin, 1920).
  "The Earl of Orrery, Chevalier Ramsay, John Kempe," *AQC*, 35 (1922), 76-78.
  and Philip Crossle, *History of the Grand Lodge of Free and Accepted Masons of Ireland* (Dublin, 1925).

Leslie, Charles, *The Fall of Virtue, or the Iron-Age* (Edinburgh, 1738).
  On the Scarcity of the Copper Coin. A Satyr (Edinburgh, 1739).
  Masonry. A Poem (Edinburgh, 1739).
  Mum. A Political Ballad for the Present Times (Edinburgh, 1740).
  The Masque of Patriotism and Truth: or, the Court Fool (London, 1743).

Levine, Joseph, *Dr. Woodward's Shield* (Berkeley, 1977).

Levy, Arthur, "The Origins of Scottish Jewry," *TJHSE*, 20 (1959-61), 129-62.

Lewis, Lesley, *Connoisseurs and Secret Agents in Eighteenth-Century Rome* (London, 1961).

Lindsay, Lord Alexander W.C., *Lives of the Lindsays* (Wigan, 1840).

Lindsay, Colin, 3rd Earl of Balcarres, *Memoirs of the Revolution in Scotland, 1688-1690.* Bannatyne Club, 71 (Edinburgh, 1841).

Lindsay, Robert Strathern, *History of the Mason Lodge of Holyrood House* (Edinburgh, 1935).
  The Royal Order of Scotland (Edinburgh, 1970).

Lipton, Marcus, "Francis Francia—the Jacobite Jew," *TJHSE*, 11 (1928), 190-205.

Little, Bryan, *The Life and Works of James Gibbs, 1682-1754* (London, 1955).
  Sir Christopher Wren: A Historical Biography (London, 1979).

Lock, F.P., *The Politics of Gulliver's Travels* (Oxford, 1980).
  Swift's Tory Politics (Newark, 1983).

Locke, John, *The Correspondence of John Locke*, ed. E.S. de Beer (Oxford, 1976).

Loeber, Rolf, "Early Classicism in Ireland before the Georgian Era," *Architectural History*, 22 (1979), 49-63.

Luynes, Duc de, *Mémoires du Duc de Luynes sur la Cour de Louis XV* (Paris, 1860).

Lyon, D. Murray, "The Royal Order of Scotland," *The Freemason* (4 September 1880), 393.
  History of the Lodge of Edinburgh, Mary's Chapel, No. 1 (London, 1900).

Lysons, Daniel, *Collectanea. Advertisements and Paragraphs, relating to the Celebrated Orator Henley* (Strawberry Hill, n.d.).

Macaulay, James, "The Seventeenth-Century Genesis of Hamilton Palace," in John Frew and David Jones, eds., *Aspects of Scottish Classicism* (St. Andrews, 1988), 17-24.

Macbean, Edward, "The Master Masons to the Crown of Scotland," *AQC*, 7 (1894), 101-15.

Macgregor, ed., *Sir Hans Sloane* (London, 1994).

Macinnes, Alan, Kieran German, Lesley Graham, eds., *Living with Jacobitism, 1688-1788: The Three Kingdoms and Beyond* (London, 2014).

Mack, Maynard, *Collected in Himself: Essays Critical, Biographical, and Bibliographical on Pope and Some of His Contemporaries* (Newark, 1982).
    Alexander Pope: A Life (New Haven, 1985).

Macray, William, *Annals of the Bodleian Library at Oxford*, 2nd rev. ed. (Oxford, 1890).

MacDonald, Alexander, *A Gaelick and English Vocabulary* (Edinburgh, 1741).

Mackenzie, Allen, *A History of the Lodge Canongate Kilwinning* (Edinburgh, 1888).

Mackenzie, Niall, "'A great affinity in many things': Further Evidence for the Jacobite Gloss on 'Swedish Charles,'" *The Age of Johnson*, 12 (2001), 255-72.
    "A Jacobite Undertone in 'While Ladies interpose'?" in Jonathan Clark and Howard Erskine-Hill, eds., *Samuel Johnson in Historical Context* (Houndsmill, 2002), 265-94.
    Charles XII of Sweden and the Jacobites. Royal Stuart Papers, LXII (London, 2002).

Maclean, J.P., *A History of the Clan Maclean* (Cincinnati, 1889).

Macleod, Jennifer, "The Edinburgh Musical Society: Its Membership and Repertoire, 1728-1797" (PhD. Dissertation: Edinburgh University, 2001).

Macleod, Wallace, "More Light on John Coustos," *AQC*, 95 (1982), 117-19.
    "The Hudibrastic Poem of 1723," *AQC*, 107 (1994), 9-50.

Mahon, Philip Henry Stanhope, Lord, *The Decline of the Last Stuarts* (London, 1843).
    History of England from the Peace of Utrecht to the Peace of Versailles, 1713-1783 (London, 1853).

Mahoney, Robert, *Jonathan Swift: The Irish Identity* (New Haven, 1995).

March, Henri-Félix, *L'Origine de la Franc-Maçonnerie et l'Histoire du Grand Orient de France*, 2nd rev. ed. (Paris, 1986).

Marchmont, Earls of, *A Selection from the Papers of the Earls of Marchmont*, ed. G.H. Rose (London, 1831).

Martin, Martin, *A Description of the Western Islands of Scotland* (London, 1703; rev. ed. 1716).

Marsay, Marquis de, *Discourses on Subjects Relating to the Spiritual Life* (Edinburgh, 1749).

Maruzzi, Pericle, *La Stretta Observanza Templare e il Regime Scozzese Rettificato in Italia nel Secolo XVIII* (1928; Roma, 2000).

Mason, William, *Isis. An Elegy* (London, 1749).

Matthews, William, "The Egyptians in Scotland: the Political History of a Myth," *Viator* (1970), 289-306.

Mayhew, George, "Swift and the Tripos Tradition," *Philological Quarterly*, 45 (1966), 85-101.

McGilvary, George, *East India Patronage and the British State: The Scottish Elite and Politics in the Eighteenth Century* (London, 2008).

McLeod, Wallace, "Additions to the List of Old Charges," *AQC, 96 (1983), 98-108*.

McLoughlin, *Grand Masters of the Grand Lodge of Ireland, 1725 to 2010* (Dublin, 2013?).

McLynn, Frank, *Charles Edward Stuart: A Tragedy in Many Acts* (1988; Oxford, 1991).
    1759: The Year that Britain Became Master of the World (2004; New York, 2007).

McLynn, Pauline, *Factionalism among the Exiles in France: The Case of Chevalier Ramsay and Bishop Atterbury*. Royal Stuart Papers, Royal Stuart Society 33 (Huntington, 1989).

McParland, "Edward Lovett Pearce and the New Junta for Architecture," in T. Barnard and J. Clark, *Lord Burlington*, 151-65.

Meaney, Lisa, "Freemasonry in Munster, 1726-1789" (MA Thesis: Mary Immaculate College, Limerick, 2005).

Mellor, Alec, "The Mystery of the Jacobites and the Craft," *Transactions of the Phoenix Lodge*, No. 30, 3 (1971-72).

Melville, Lewis, *The Life and Writings of Philip, Duke of Wharton* (London, 1913).

Mendes/Mendez, Moses, *A Collection of the Most Esteemed Pieces of Poetry…by the late Moses Mendez* (London, 1767).

    The Blatant Beast http://spenserians,cath.edu/TextRecord.php?=GET&texts.

Meston, William, *The Knight* (Edinburgh, 1723).

    Old Mother Grim's Tales (Edinburgh, 1737).

    The Poetical Works of William Meston , 6th ed. (Edinburgh, 1767).

Midgely, Graham, *The Life of Orator Henley* (Oxford, 1973).

Miller, James, *An Epistle from Dick Poney, Esq., Grand-Master of the…Scald Miserable Masons* (London, 1742).

Miller, Sanderson, *The Diaries of Sanderson Miller of Radway*, ed. William Hawkes (Bristol, 2005).

Mirala, Petri, *Freemasonry in Ulster, 1733-1831* (Dublin, 2007).

    "Masonic Sociability and its Limitations: the Case of Ireland," in J. Kelly and Martyn Powell, *Clubs and Societies*, 315-31.

Mitchell, David, *The Jesuits: A History* (London, 1980).

Mnemon, Stanislaus, *La Conspiration du Cardinal Alberoni* , *La Franc-Maçonnerie et Stanislaus Poniatowski* (Cracovie, 1909).

Mollier, Pierre, "Les Stuarts et la Franc-Maçonnerie: Le Dernier Épisode," *Renaissance Traditionelle*, 177-78 (2015), 59-73.

Monod, Paul, *Jacobitism and the English People, 1688-1788* (Cambridge, 1988).

    "Painters and Party Politics in England, 1714-1760," *Eighteenth-Century Studies*, 26 (1993), 378-89.

    "Pierre's White Hat: Theatre, Jacobitism, and Popular Protest in London, 1689-1760), in E. Cruickshanks, *By Force or Default*, 161-79.

    "Thomas Carte, the Druids and British National Identity," in Monod, Pittock, and Szechi, *Loyalty and Identity*, 132-48.

    Solomon's Secret Arts: The Occult in the Age of Enlightenment (New Haven, 2013).

Monod, Paul, Murray Pittock, and Daniel Szechi, *Loyalty and Identity: Jacobites at Home and Abroad* (Houndsmill, 2010).

Montagu, Lady Mary Wortley, *The Complete Letters of Lady Mary Wortley Montagu*, ed. Robert Halsband (Oxford, 1996).

Moore, John Robert, *A Checklist of the Writings of Daniel Defoe* (Hamden, 1971).

Morabin, Jacques, *The History of Cicero's Banishment*, [trans. George Kelly] (London, 1725).

Morbach, Phillipe, "Les Régiments Écossais et Irlandais à S.Germain-en-laye: Myth ou Réalité Maçonnique?,"in E. Corp, *L'Autre Exil,"* 143-55.

Morgan, David, *The Country Bard: or, the Modern Courtiers* (London, 1741).

Morley, Henry, *The Earlier Life and the Chief Earlier Works of Daniel Defoe* (London, 1889).

Morris, Corbyn, *A Letter from a By-Stander to a Member of Parliament* (London, 1742).

Moss, W.E., "Freemasonry in France in 1725-1735," *AQC*, 47 (1934).

Mossner, Ernest, *The Life of David Hume*, rev. ed. (1954; Oxford, 1980).

    "New Hume Letters to Lord Elibank, 1748-1776," *Texas Studies in Language and Literature*, 4 (1962), 431-60.

Mothu, Alain and Charles Porset, "A Propos du Secret des Francs-Maçons: une Référence Jacobite (1705)?," in Charles Porset, ed., *Studia Latamorum and Historica: Mélange offerts à Daniel Ligou* (Paris, 1998), 326-33.

Murdoch, Steve, "Soldiers, Sailors, Jacobite Spy: Russo-Jacobite Relations, 1688-1750," *Slavonica*, 3 (1996-97), 7-8.7-27.

Murphy, Sean, "Irish Jacobitism and Freemasonry," *Eighteenth-Century Ireland*, 9 (1994), 75-82.

Murray, David, *Robert and Andrew Foulis and the Glasgow Press* (Glasgow, 1913).

    Some Letters of Robert Foulis (Glasgow, 1917).

Murray, John, *George I, the Baltic, and the Whig Split of 1717* (London, 1969).

Murray of Broughton, John, *Memorials of John Murray of Broughton*, ed. Robert F. Bell (Edinburgh, 1898).

Mylne, Robert S., *The Master Masons to the Crown of Scotland and their Works* (Edinburgh, 1893).

Nelson, Henry, *The Speech of the First Stone Laid in the Parliament House to the Government, February 3rd, 1728* (Dublin, 1728).

Neveu, Bruno, "Un Roman de Spiritualité: *Les Voyages de Cyrus* du Chevalier Ramsay," in *Écriture de la Religion, Écriture du Roman. Mélanges de la Littérature et de Critique offerts à Joseph Tans* (Lille, 1979), 11-27.

    "La `Science Divine' du Chevalier Ramsay," in Denise Leduc-Fayette, ed., *Fenelon: Philosophie et Spiritualité*, (Genéve, 1996), 177-96.

Newman, Aubrey, "Leicester House Politics, 1748-51," *English Historical Review*, 76 (1961), 577-89.

    "Leicester House Politics, 1750-60," *Camden Miscellany*, 4th s. (1969), VII. 85-228.

    "Politics and Freemasonry in the Eighteenth Century," *AQC*, 104 (1991), 36-49.

Nicholas, N.H., *The Statutes of the Order of the Thistle* (London, 1828).

Nichols, John, *Literary Anecdotes of the Eighteenth Century* (London, 1812).

Nichols, J.B., *Anecdotes of William Hogarth* (London, 1833).

Nihtinen, Atina L.K., "Field-Marshal James Keith: Governor of Ukraine and Finland, 1740-1743," in A. Mackillop and Steve Murdoch, eds., *Military Governors and Imperial Frontiers c. 1600-1800: A Study of Scotland and Empires* (Leiden, 2003), 99-118.

Nisbet, Alexander, *A System of Heraldry, Speculative and Practical* (Edinburgh, 1722).

Nordmann, Claude, *La Crise du Nord au Début de XVIIIe Siècle* (Paris, 1962).

    Grandeur et Liberté de la Suède, 1660-1792 (Paris, 1971).

    "Choiseul and the Last Jacobite Attempt of 1759," in E. Cruickshanks, *Ideology and Conspiracy*, 201-21.

    Gustave III: Un Démocrate Couronné (Lille, 1996).

Nugent, Claude, *Memoir of Robert Nugent, Earl Nugent* (New York, 1898).

Nugent, Robert, *Political Justice* (London, 1736).

    An Essay on Happiness (London, 1739).

An Epistle to the Right Honourable, Sir Robert Walpole (London, 1739).

O'Ciardha, Eamonn, *Ireland and the Jacobite Cause, 1685-1766: A Fatal Attraction* (Dublin, 2002).

"'A lot done, more to do': The Restoration and Road Ahead for Irish Jacobite Studies," in P. Monod, M. Pittock, and D. Szechi, *Loyalty and Identity*, 71-105.

"Jacobite Jail-Breakers. Jail-Birds: the Irish Fugitive and Prisoner in the Early Modern Period," *Immigrants and Minorities* (2013), 1-27.

"The Bones and Marrow of History: Irish and Latin Sources for the History of Early Modern Ireland," in A. Jackson, ed., *A Handbook of Irish History* (Oxford, 2013), 439-61.

Odell, Thomas, *Characters: An Epistle to Alexander Pope, Esq., and Mr. Whitehead* (London, 1739).

Oglethorpe, General James Edward, Catalogue of Library. Sotheby's Sales Catalogue (5 May 1788).

O'Higgins, James, *Anthony Collins: The Man and His Works* (The Hague, 1970).

Olin, Martin, *Nicodemus Tessin the Younger* (Stockholm, 2004).

Önnerfors, Andreas, "From Jacobite Support to a Part of the State Apparatus—Swedish Freemasonry between Reform and Revolution," in Cécile Révauger, ed., *Franc-maçonnerie et Politique au Siècle des Lumières* (Pessac, 2006), 203-25.

and Robert Collis, eds., *Freemasonry and Fraternalisim in Eighteenth-Century Russia*, Vol. II (Sheffield, 2009).

Ormsby-Lennon, Hugh, *Hey Presto! Swift and the Quacks* (Newark, 2011).

Orrery, E.C.Boyle, Countess of Orrery, *The Orrery Papers* (London, 1903).

Orrery, John Boyle, Earl of, *Remarks on the Life and Writings of Dr. Jonathan Swift*, 3rd rev. ed., (Dublin, 1752).

Letters from Italy, in the Years 1754 and 1755, ed. William Duncombe (London, 1773).

The Library and Collection of Autograph Letters of the Right Honourable the Earl of Cork and Orrery (London: Christie, 21 November 1905), #11.

Ouston, Hugh, "York in Edinburgh: James VII and the Patronage of Learning in Scotland, 1679-1688," in John Dwyer, Roger Mason, and Alexander Murdoch, eds., *New Perspectives on the Politics and Culture of Early Modern Scotland* (Edinburgh, 1983), 133-55.

Owen, Joshua, "Letter from Manchester," *Gentleman's Magazine*, (16 November 1746), 579-80.

Jacobite and Nonjuring Principles, Freely Examined, in a Letter to the Master-Tool of Faction at Manchester, 2nd ed. (Manchester, 1748).

Parker, E., Philomath, *A Complete Key to the New Farce, call'd Three Hours After Marriage* (London, 1717).

Parkinson, R.E., "The Lodge in Trinity College Dublin, 1688," *AQC*, 54 (1941), 96-107.

"*An Answer to the Pope's Bull* and *An Impartial Answer to the Enemies of Freemasonry*, 1741," *AQC*, 77 (1964), 151-55.

Parry, Graham, "John Talman Letter Book: a Life in Art," *The Walpole Society*, 59 (1997), 3-179.

Patai, Raphael, *The Hebrew Goddess* (Jerusalem, 1967).

    The Jewish Alchemists (Princeton, 1994).

Paton, Henry, "Papers about the Rebellions of 1715 and 1745," *Publications of the Scottish History Society*, XV, *Miscellany*, 1st vol. (1893), 519-21.

Paton, Norrie, *The Jacobites: Their Roots, Rebellions and Links with Freemasonry* (Fareham, 1994).

Patten, Robert, *The History of the Rebellion*, 2nd rev. ed. (London, 1717).

Paul, Robert, ed., *Letters and Documents Relating to Robert Erskine, Physician to Peter the Great, Czar of Russia, 1677-1720*. Miscellany of Scottish Historical Society, II (1904).

Pelagius, Porcupinus, *The Processionaid* (London, 1743).

Pellizzi, C. Matteo, "The English Lodge in Florence in the Eighteenth Century," *AQC*, 105 (1992), 129-36.

Penrice, Gerard, *A Genuine and Impartial Account of the Remarkable Life and Vicissitudes of Fortune of Charles Radcliffe, Esquire* (London, 1747).

Perau, Abbé, *L'Ordre des Francs-Maçons Trahi* (Amsterdam, 1745).

Péter, Róbert, Cécile Révauger, and Jan Snoek, eds., *British Freemasonry, 1717-1813* (New York, 2016).

Petrie, Charles, *The Jacobite Movement: The First Phase, 1688-1736* (London, 1948-50).

Pettit, Alexander, "Packaging Heterodoxy: Oratory Henley's Free-mason-oratorial Puffs," paper presented at Annual Meeting of American Society for Eighteenth-Century Studies, Pittsburgh, PA., April 1991).

Philomath [Neve, Richard], *The City and Countrey Purchaser and Builder's Dictionary* (London, 1703).

Pick, Frederick, "Preston – the Gild and the Craft," *AQC*, 58 (1948), 105.

Pierce, Mildred Weeks, "The Literary Life and Position in the Eighteenth Century of John, Earl of Orrery" (Ph.D. Dissertation: Smith College, 1948).

Pink, Andrew, "Solomon, Susanna and Moses: Locating Handel's Lost Libretto," *Eighteenth-Century Music*, 12 (2015), 211-22.

Pininski, Peter, *The Stuarts' Last Secret: The Missing Heirs of Bonnie Prince Charlie* (East Linton, 2002).

Pinkus, Philip, "A Tale of a Tub and the Rosy Cross," *Journal of English and Germanic Philology*, 59 (196), 669-79.

Pirie, Valerie, *His Majesty of Corsica: The True Story of the Adventurous Life of Theodore I* (London, 1939).

Pittock, Murray, "Jacobitism in the North East: the Pitsligo Papers in Aberdeen University Library," in J. Carter and J. Pittock, *Aberdeen*, 69-76.

    Poetry and Jacobite Politics in Eighteenth-Century Britain and Ireland (Cambridge, 1994).

    Material Culture and Sedition: Treacherous Objects, Secret Places (Houndsmill, 2013).

    Plot, Robert, *The Natural History of Oxfordshire* (Oxford, 1677).

    The Natural History of Staffordshire (Oxford, 1686).

Plot, Robert, *The Natural History of Oxfordshire* (Oxford, 1677).

    The Natural History of Staffordshire (Oxford, 1686).

Poole, H., "Masonic Song and Verse in the Eighteenth Century," *AQC*, 40 (1928), 7-28.

Pope, Alexander, *Windsor Forest* (London, 1713).

The Plot Discover'd; or a Clue to the Non-juror, 2nd ed. (London, 1718).

The Dunciad. An Heroic Poem (Dublin/London: A.Dodd, 1728).

The Dunciad Variorum, with the Prolegomena of Scriblerus (London, 1729).

An Essay on Man (London, 1734).

The New Dunciad: As it was Found in the Year 1741 (London, 1742).

The Dunciad in Four Books. Printed According to the Copy Found in the Year 1742 (London, 1743).

The Works of Alexander Pope, eds. John Wilson Croker and Whitwell Elwin (London, 1871-89).

The Correspondence of Alexander Pope, ed. George Sherburn (Oxford, 1934).

The Poetical Works of Alexander Pope, ed. Herbert Davis (Oxford, 1966).

Popkin, Richard, "So, Hume Did Read Berkeley," *Journal of Philosophy*, 61 (1964), 773-78. "Some Aspects of Jewish-Christian Theological Interchange in Holland and England, 1640-1700," in J. Van den Berg and E.G.E. Van der Wall, eds., *Jewish-Christian Relations in the Seventeenth Century* (Dordrecht, 1988), 3-32.

Pound, Ricky, "The Master Mason Slain: the Hiramic Legend in the Red Velvet Room at Chiswick House," *English Heritage Historical Review*, 4 (2009), 154-63.

Prichard, Samuel, *Masonry Dissected*, 3rd ed. (London, 1730).

Racine, Louis, *Oeuvres de Louis Racine* (Paris, 1808).

Ramsay, Allan, *Poems* (Edinburgh, 1721). *A Collection of Scots Proverbs* (Edinburgh and London, 1737).

Ramsay, Chevalier Andrew Michael, *Histoire de la Vie de Fenelon* (Paris, 1723). *The Travels of Cyrus* (London, 1727). *The Travels of Cyrus*, 4th ed. (London, 1730). *A Plan of Education for a Young Prince* (London, 1732). *Histoire du Vicomte de Turenne* (Paris, 1735). *The Philosophical Principles of Natural and Revealed Religion, Unfolded in a Geometrical Order* (Edinburgh, 1748-49).

Rawlinson, Richard, *Bibliotheca Rawlinsoniana* (London, 1756).

Ray, John, *A Compleat History of the Rebellion from its Rise, in 1745, to its Total Suppression, at the Glorious Battle of Culloden* (London, 1746).

Richmond, Charles Lennox, Duke of, *The Correspondence of the Dukes of Richmond and Newcastle, 1724-1750*, ed. Timothy J. McCann (Lewes, 1984).

Robb, Nesca, *William of Orange* (1962; London, 1966).

Robbins, Alfred, "The Earliest Years of English Organized Freemasonry," *AQC*, 22 (1909), 67-89. "Dr. Anderson of the Constitutions," *AQC*, 23 (1910), 6-34. "Frederick, Prince of Wales, as a Freemasons," *AQC*, 29 (1916), 326-35.

Roberts, J.M., *The Mythology of the Secret Societies* (1972; London, 1974).

Roberts, Marie Mulvey, *British Poets and Secret Societies* (London, 1986). "Science, Magic, and Masonry in Swift's Secret Texts," in Marie Mulvey Roberts and Hugh Ormsby-Lennon, eds., *Secret Texts: The Ltierature of Secret Societies* (New York, 1993), 97-113. "Hogarth on the Square: Framing the Freemasons," *British Journal for Eighteenth-Century Studies*, 26 (2003), 251-70.

Roberts, Michael, "The Dubious Hand: the History of a Controversy," in his *From Oxenstierna to Charles XII* (Cambridge, 1991), 144-203.

Robertson of Struan, Alexander, *Poems on Various Subjects and Occasions* (Edinburgh, 1749*)*.

Robinson, John M., *The Dukes of Norfolk* (Oxford, 1982).

Robinson, John R., *The Last Earls of Barrymore, 1769-1829* (London, 1894).

Robison, John, *Proofs of a Conspiracy Against All the Religions and Governments of Europe*, 3rd rev. ed. (1797; Philadelphia, 1798)

Rogers, Charles, *The Modern Scottish Minstrel* (Edinburgh, 1846).

Rogers, Nicholas, "Aristocratic Clientage, Trade and Independency: Popular Politics in Pre-radical Westminster," *Past and Present*, 61 (1973), 70-106.

"Popular Protest in Early Hanoverian England," *Past and Present*, 70 (1978), 70-100.

Rogers, Pat, "The Waltham Blacks and the Black Act," *The Historical Journal*, 17 (1974), 465-86.

"The Symbols in Pope's One Thousand Seven Hundred and Forty," *Modern Philology*, 102 (2004), 90-94.

The Alexander Pope Encyclopedia (Westport, 2004).

Documenting Eighteenth Century Satire: Pope, Swift, Gay, and Arbuthnot in Historical Context (Newcastle upon Tyne, 2012).

Romanell, Patrick, "Some Excerpts from the Mellon Collection of John Locke's Medico-Philosophical Papers," *Journal of the History of Ideas*, 25 (1964), 107-16.

Roth, Cecil, *Anglo-Jewish Letters* (London, 1938).

"The King and the Kabbalist," in his *Essays and Portraits in Anglo-Jewish History* (Philadelphia, 1962), 139-64.

Roth, Norman, "Social and Intellectual Currents in England in the Century Preceding the Jew Bill of 1753" (Ph.D. Dissertation: Cornell University, 1978).

Russell, Francis, "Dr. Clephane, John Blackwood and Batoni's `Sacrifice of Iphigenia,'" *Burlington Magazine*, 127 (1985), 890-93.

Ryan, David, "The Dublin Hellfire Club," in J. Kelly and M. Powell, *Clubs and Societies*, 332-52.

Blasphemers & Blackguards: the Irish Hellfire Clubs (Dublin, 2012).

Sadler, Henry, *Masonic Reprints and Historical Revelations*, introd. Chetwode Crawley (London, 1898).

"Inaugural Address," *AQC*, 23 (1910), 327.

Sallengre, Henri Albert de [Boniface Oenophilius], *Ebrietatis Encomimum; or the Praise of Drunkenness*, [trans. Robert Samber] (1723; facs. rpt. New York, 1910).

Samber, Robert, *Roma Illustra* (London, 1722).

Sambrook, James, *James Thomson, 1700-1748* (Oxford, 1991).

Saunders, James, and Robert Wright, *A History of the Lodge of Alloa, No. 69, 1757-1957* (Alloa, 1957).

Savage, Richard, *Of Public Spirit in Regard of Public Works* (London, 1737).

The Poetical Works of Richard Savage, ed. Clarence Tracy (Cambridge, 1962).

Schiel, Katherine West, "Early Georgian Politics and Shakespeare: the Black Act and Charles Johnson's *Love in a Forest* (1723), Shakespeare Survey Online@ Cambridge UP, 2007.

Schröderheim, Elis, *Anteckningar till Konung Gustaf IIIs Historia* (Örebro, 1851).

Scott, Abbot Geoffrey, "Thomas Southcott," *English Benedictine Congregation History Commission Symposium* (2002), 1-5.

Scott, Mary Jane, *James Thomson: Anglo-Scot* (Athens, 1988).

Schröderheim, Elis, *Anteckningar till konung Gustav IIIs historia* (Örebro, 1851).

Schuchard, Marsha Keith, "Freemasonry, Secret Societies, and the Continuity of the Occult Traditions in British Literature" (Ph.D. Dissertation: University of Texas at Austin, 1975).

"Swedenborg, Jacobitism, and Freemasonry," in Erland Brock, ed., *Swedenborg and His Influence* (Bryn Athyn, 1988), 359-79.

"Yeats and the Unknown Superiors: Swedenborg, Falk, and Cagliostro," in M. Roberts and H. Ormsby-Lennon, *Secret Texts*, 114-68.

"The Secret Masonic History of Blake's Swedenborg Society," *Blake: An Illustrated Quarterly*, 26 (1996), 40-51

"Leibniz, Benzelius, and Swedenborg: the Cabalistic Roots of Swedish Illuminism," in R Richard Popkin and Gordon Weiner, eds., *Leibniz, Mysticism, and Religion* (Dordrecht, 1998), 84-106.

"Swift, Ramsay, and the Jacobite-Masonic Version of the Stuart Restoration," in Richard Caron, ed., *Ésoterisme, Gnoses & Imaginaire Symbolique: Mélanges offerts à Antoine Faivre* (Leuven, 2001), 491-505.

"Dr. Samuel Jacob Falk: a Sabbatian Adventurer in the Masonic Underground," in Matt Goldish and Richard Popkin, eds., *Millenarianism and Messianism in Early Modern European Culture* (Dordrecht, 2001), 203-26.

Restoring the Temple of Vision: Cabalistic Freemasonry and Stuart Culture (Leiden, 2002).

Why Mrs. Blake Cried: William Blake and the Sexual Basis of Spiritual Vision (London, 2006).

"Les Rivalités Maçonniques et la *Bulle in Eminenti,*" *La Règle d'Abraham*, 25 (2008), 3-48.

"La Revue *The Post Man* et les *Constitutions de Roberts (1722)*, *La Règle d'Abraham*, 30 (2010), 3-62.

"Jacobite versus Hanoverian Claims for Masonic `Antiquity' and `Authenticity,'" *Heredom*, 18 (2010), 225-58.

Emanuel Swedenborg, Secret Agent on Earth and in Heaven: Jacobites, Jews, and Freemasons in Early Modern Sweden (Leiden, 2012).

"The Political-Masonic Background to the 1738 Papal Bull *In Eminenti,*" *Heredom*, 23 (2015), 55-106.

"Politique et Ésotérisme Maçonnique. Les Racines Stuartistes du Titre de Grand Maître Caché de Bonnie Prince Charlie, Part 1," *La Règle d'Abraham*, 38 (December 2016), 45-66; Part 2 (September 2017), 59-109.

Masonic Esotericism and Politics: The "Ancient" Stuart Roots of Bonnie Prince Charlie's Role as Hidden Grand Master. La Règle d'Abraham, Hors-série no. III (Juin 2017).

"Some Ancient Scots-Irish-Swedish Sources for `Antient' Freemasonry," published on-line at www.icom.fm; and in printed *Proceedings of the First International Conference of Masonic Research Lodges* (Toulon, 2018).

"Swift, Ramsay, and `the Cabala, as *Masonry* was Call'd in Those Days,'" *English Language Notes*, 56 (2018), 97-118.

Schwartz, Hillel, *The French Prophets* (Berkeley, 1980).

Scott, Mary Jane, *James Thomson: Anglo-Scot* (Athens, 1988).

Scott, P. H., *Andrew Fletcher and the Treaty of Union* (Edinburgh, 1994).

Scott, Sir Walter, *The Prose Works of Sir Walter Scott* (Paris, 1830).

Sedgwick, Romney, ed., *The History of Parliament: The House of Commons, 1715-1754* (London., 1970).

Seton, Bruce Gordon, *The House of Seton: A Study of Lost Causes* (Edinburgh, 1941).

Sgard, J., *Dictionnaire des Journalistes, 1600-1789* (Grenoble, 1976).

Shackleton, Robert, *Montesquieu* (Grenoble, 1977).

Shaftesley, John, "Jews in Regular English Freemasonry," *TJHSE*, 25 (1977), 150-209.

Shane, Arthur, "Jacob Jehudah Leon of Amsterdam (1602-1675) and His Models of the Temple of Solomon and the Tabernacle," *AQC, 96 (1983)*, 146-69.

Shellabarger, Samuel, *Lord Chesterfield* (New York, 1935).

Sherburn, George, "The Fortunes and Misfortunes of `Three Hours After Marriage,'" *Modern Philology*, 24 (1926). 91-109.

Sheridan, Thomas [father], *Catalogue of the Books in the Library of the Rev. Thomas Sheridan* (Dublin, 1739).

Sheridan, Thomas [son], *The Life of the Reverend Dr. Jonathan Swift*, 2nd ed. (1784; London, 1787).

Shield, Alice, *Henry Stuart, Cardinal of York, and His Times* (London, 1908).
  and Andrew Lang, *The King Over the Water* (London, 1907).

Shore, Donald, *Highland Legends and Fugitive Pieces of Original Poetry* (Edinburgh, 1859).

Shuttleton, David "Jacobitism and the Millennial Enlightenment: Alexander, Lord Forbes of Pitsligo's `Remarks on the Mystics,'" *Enlightenment and Dissent*, 15 (1996), 33-56.

Simms, J.G., "John Toland (1670-1722), a Donegal Heretic," *Irish Historical Studies*, 16 (1969), 304-20.
  "Dean Swift in County Armagh," *Seanchas Ard Mhacha: Armagh Diocesan Historical Society*, 6 (1971), 131-40.

Simpson, J. Percy, "Brother Moses Mendez, Grand Steward, 1738," *AQC*, 18 (1905), 104-09.

Simpson, John, "Arresting a Diplomat, 1717," *History Today*, 35 (1985), 32-37.

Sire, H.J.A., *The Knights of Malta* (New Haven, 1994).

Sirr, Harry, "J. Morgan his *Phoenix Britannicus*, with Notes on his Other Works," *AQC*, 19 (1906, 127-36.

Skeet, Francis, *The Life of the Right Honourable James Radcliffe, Third Earl of Derwentwater* (London, 1929).

Sleigh, John, "The `45," *Notes & Queries*, 3rd s. 4 (14 November 1863), 392.
  "Prince Charles Stuart at Leek in the `45," *Notes & Queries*, 4th s., vol. 3 (5 June 1860), 532.
  "The Stuarts and Freemasonry, *Notes & Queries*, 4th s., vol. 4 (17 July 1869), 66.

Smith, James Fairburn, *The Rise of the Ecossais Degrees*. Proceedings of the Lodge of Research of the Grand Chapter of Royal Arch Masons of the State of Ohio, vol. X (Dayton, 1965).

Smith, Laurence, "Charles Boyle, 4th Earl of Orrery" (Ph.D. Dissertation: Edinburgh University, 1994).

Smith, Ruth, "The Achievements of Charles Jennens," *Music and Letters*, 70 (1989), 161-90.
Handel's Oratorios and Eighteenth-Century Thought (Cambridge, 1995).

Smythe, James Moore, and Leonard Welsted, *One Epistle to Mr. Pope* (London, 1730).

Smollett, *The Tears of Scotland* (Edinburgh, 1746).
Advice, and Reproof. Two Satires, first published in 1746 and 1747 (London, 1748).
A Complete History of England (London, 1757-58).

Sobieski, John, and Charles Edward Stuart, *Tales of the Century* (Edinburgh, 1847).

Sorrow, Obadiah, *A Letter from a Quaker...to Philip, Duke of Wh----n, at Madrid in Spain* (London, 1726).
The Spectator, ed. Donald Bond (Oxford, 1965).

Spedding, Patrick, *A Bibliography of Eliza Haywood* (London, 2004).

Spence, Joseph, *Letters from the Grand Tour*, ed. Slava Klima (Montreal, 1975).
Observations, Anecdotes, and Characters of Men and Books, ed. Joseph Osborne (Oxford, 1996).

Sperry, David, "A Study of Daniel Defoe's Tour of Great Britain" (Ph.D. Dissertation: University of Illinois, 1950).

Speth, G.W., "Two New Versions of the `Old Charges,'" *AQC, I* (1888), 127-29.
Masonic Reprints of the Lodge Quatuor Coronati, #2076 (Margate, 1891).

Spurr, Michael, "William Stukeley: Antiquarian and Freemason," *AQC*, 100 (1987), 113-30.

Squire, Samuel, *A Letter to a Tory Friend. Upon the Present Critical Situation of our Affairs* (London, 1746).
A Letter to John Trot-Plaid... by Duncan MacCarte a Highlander (London, 1748).

Stephens, F.G., *Catalogue of the Prints and Drawings in the British Museum* (London, 1870).

Sterling, James, *Poetical Works* (Dublin, 1734).
Statutes of the Religious and Military Order of the Temple (Edinburgh, 1843).

Stevens, F.G. and E. Hawkins, *Catalogue of Prints and Drawings in the British Museum* (London, 1877).

Stevens, John, *The Journal of John Stevens*, ed. Robert H. Murray (Oxford, 1912).

Stevenson, David, "Masonry, Symbolism and Ethics in the Life of Sir Robert Moray, FRS," *Proceedings of the Society of Antiquaries of Scotland*, 114 (1984), 405-31.
"The Scottish Origins of Freemasonry," in Jennifer Carter and Joan Pittock, eds., *Aberdeen in the Enlightenment* (Aberdeen, 1987), 36-39.
The Origins of Freemasonry: Scotland's Century, 1590-1710 (1988; Cambridge, 1993).
The First Freemasons: Scotland's Early Lodges and Their Members, 2nd ed. (1988; Edinburgh, 2001).
"James Anderson: Man and Mason," *Heredom*, 10 (2002), 93-138.

Stewart, A.T.Q., *A Deeper Silence: The Hidden Roots of the United Irishmen* (London, 1993).

Stewart, Larry, *The Rise of Public Science: Rhetoric, Technology, and Natural Philosophy in Newtonian Britain* (Cambridge, 1992).

Stewart, Margaret, "Lord Mar's Gardens at Alloa, c. 1700-1732," in J. Frew and D. Jones, *Aspects*, 33-40.

The Architectural, Landscape and Constitutional Plans of the Earl of Mar, 1700-32 (Dublin, 2016).

Stewart, Trevor, "'It is of a Service to the Public to shew where the Error is": A Re-examination of the Visit to Edinburgh by the Reverend Dr. John Theophilus Desaguliers," *AQC*, 119 (2006), 198-233.

Stranks, C.J., *The Life and Writings of Jeremy Taylor* (London, 1952).

Stuart, M.A., "Hume's `Bellman's Petition': the Original Text," *Hume Studies*, 23 (1997), 3-7.

Stukeley, William, *The Commentaries, Diary, & Common-place Book of William Stukeley* (London, 1980).

Sullivan, John, *John Toland and the Deist Controversy: A Study in Adaptations* (Cambridge,1982).

Sullivan, Maureen, ed., *Colley Cibber: Three Sentimental Comedies* (New Haven, 1973).

Summerson, John, *Architecture in Britain, 1530-1830* (London, 1935).

Sutherland, Lucy, "Samson Gideon: Eighteenth-Century Jewish Financier," *TJHSE*, 17 (1951-52), 79-90.

Swedenborg, Emanuel, *An Introduction to the Word Explained*, ed. Alfred Acton (Bryn Athyn, 1927).

   Concerning the Messiah About to Come, trans. Alfred Acton (Bryn Athyn, 1949).

   Swedenborg's Dream Diary, trans. Anders Hallengren, ed. Lars Bergquist (West Chester, 2001).

Swift, Jonathan, *The Public Spirit of the Whigs* (London, 1714).

   Letter from the Grand Mistress of the Female Free-Masons to Mr. Harding the Printer (Dublin, 1724).

   The Grand Mystery, or the Art of Meditating, 2nd rev. ed. (London, 1726). [attributed to Swift].

   A Modest Proposal for Preventing the Children of Poor People from being a Burthen to their Parents or Country (Dublin, 1729).

   Memoirs of Capt. John Creichton, Written by Himself (Dublin, 1731).

   Verses on the Death of Dr. Swift, D.S.P.D.,...Written by Himself, November 1731 (London, 1739).

   Catalogue of Books, the Library of the late Rev. Dr. Swift (Dublin, 1745).

   The Works of Jonathan Swift (Dublin, 1746).

   Miscellanies. By Dr. Swift (London, 1746), XI, 170-86.

   The History of the Last Four Years of the Queen, ed. Charles Lucas (London, 1758).

   The Works of Jonathan Swift, D.D....Arrang'd by Thomas Sheridan, A.M., rev. ed., ed. John Nichols (London, 1803).

   The Works of Jonathan Swift, ed. Sir Walter Scott (Edinburgh, 1824).

   The Drapier's Letters, ed. Herbert Davis (Oxford, 1935).

   Journal to Stella, ed. Harold Williams (Oxford, 1948).

   Irish Tracts, 1728-1733, ed. Herbert Davis (Oxford, 1955).

   A Tale of a Tub, eds. A.C.Guthkelch and D.Nichol Smith (Oxford, 1962).

   The Prose Works of Jonathan Swift, ed. Herbert Davis (Oxford, 1962).

   The Poetical Works of Jonathan Swift, ed. Herbert Davis (London, 1967).

   The Complete Poems of Jonathan Swift, ed. Pat Rogers (New Haven, 1983).

Gulliver's Travels, ed. Paul Turner (Oxford, 1998).

The Correspondence of Jonathan Swift, ed. David Wooley (Frankfurt am Main, 2001).

Journal to Stella, ed. Abigail Williams (Cambridge, 2013).

Swinfen, John, *The Objections of the Non-subscribing London Clergy, against the Address of the Bishop of London* (London, 1710).

Szechi, Daniel, *1715: The Great Jacobite Rebellion* (New Haven, 2006).

Tafel, Rudolph L., "Swedenborg and Freemasonry," *New Jerusalem Magazine* (1869), 266-67.

Tait, A.A., "The Protectorate Citadels of Scotland," *Architectural History*, 8 (1965), 12-17.

The Tatler, ed. George Aitken (New York, 1899).

Tayler, Henrietta, *The Jacobite Court at Rome in 1719* (Edinburgh, 1938).

Jacobite Epilogue (London, 1941).

A Jacobite Miscellany: Eight Original Papers on the Rising of 1745-1746 (Oxford, 1948).

and Alaister Tayler, *Jacobite Letters to Lord Pitsligo, 1745-1746* (Aberdeen, 1930).

and Alaister Tayler, *The Stuart Papers at Windsor* (New York, 1939).

Temple, William, *Miscellaneous Essays*, ed. Samuel Holt (Ann Arbor, 1963).

Tessin, Georg, *Die Deutsche Regimenter der Krone Schweden* (Köln, 1965).

Theosophical Transactions of the Philadelphian Society (1697).

Thomas, Peter, "Jacobitism in Wales," *Welsh History Review*, 1 (1960-63), 279-300.

Thompson, Derick, ed., *Alasdair Mac Mhaighstir Alasdair: Selected Poems* (Edinburgh, 1996).

Thompson, E.P., *Whigs and Hunters: The Origin of the Black Act* (New York, 1975).

Thomson, James, *The Prospect. Being the Third Part of Liberty* (London, 1736).

Agamemnon. A Tragedy (London, 1738).

Tancred and Sigismunda. A Tragedy (London, 1745).

James Thomson, 1700-1748. Letters and Documents, ed. Alan McKillop (Lawrence, 1958).

Thorpe, J.T. "Rite Ancien de Bouillon," *Masonic Reprints*, IX (Leiceister, 1926), 22-31.

Thory, Claude Antoine, *Acta Latamorum* (Paris, 1815).

Thulstrup, C.H.I., *Anteckningar till Svenska Frimuriets Historia* (Stockholm, 1892).

Thune, Nils, *The Behmenists and Philadelphians* (Uppsala, 1948).

Timpanaro, Maria, *Tommaso Crudeli* (Firenze, 2003).

Toland, John, *Christianity Not Mysterious*, 2nd ed. (London, 1702).

Letters to Serena (London, 1704).

Adeisidaemon (London, 1709).

The Art of Restoring, 6th ed. (London, 1714).

Reasons for Naturalizing the Jews in Great Britain and Ireland (London, 1714).

Tetradymus (London, 1720).

Pantheisticon; or the Form of Celebrating the Socratic Society (1720; London, 1751).

Tomlinson, Howard, "The Ordinance Office and the King's Forts, 1660-1714," *Architectural History*, 16 (1973), 5-25, 72-76.

Tracy, Clarence, *The Artificial Bastard: A Biography of Richard Savage* (Cambridge, 1953).

Trebuchet, Louis, *De l'Écosse à l'Écossisme: Les Deux Siècles Fondateurs, 1598-1804* (Marseille, 2015).

Trench, Charles Trevenix, *Grace's Card: Irish Catholic Landlords, 1690-1800* (Cork, 1997).

T[rentha]m and V[andepu]t, *A Collection of the Advertisements and Hand-Bills, Serious, Satyrical, and Humorous, Published on Both Sides during the Election for the City and Liberty of Westminster, begun November 22d, 1749.*

Troyer, Howard, *Ned Ward of Grub Street* (Cambridge, 1946).

Tryon, Thomas, *Tryon's Letters Domestic and Foreign* (London, 1700).

Tuckett, J.E.S., "Some Further Light on J. Morgan of the *Phoenix Britannicus*," AQC, 26 (1913), 71-82.

"The Royal Society and Freemasonry," *AQC*, 28 (1915), 57-58.

"The Early History of Freemasonry in France," *AQC*, 31 (1918), 7-21.

"The Origin of Additional Degrees," *AQC*, 32 (1919), 5-53.

"Dr. Begemann and the Alleged Templar Chapter in Edinburgh in 1745," *AQC*, 33 (1920), 40-62.

"The French-Irish Family of Walsh," *AQC*, 38 (1925), 189-96.

"Prince Charles Edward Stuart, G.M.," *The Builder Magazine*, 11 (1925), 53-66.

Tudor-Craig, Algernon, *Catalogue of the Contents of the Museum at Freemasons' Hall* (London, 1938).

Tunstall, William, Charles Wogan, etc., *Poems of Love and Gallantry. Written in the Marshalsea and Newgate, by several of the Prisoners taken at Preston* (London, 1716).

Uglow, Jenny, *Hogarth: A Life and a World* (London, 1977).

Valentin, Hugo, *Judarnas Historia I Sverige* (Stockholm, 1924).

Varey, Simon, "Hanover, Stuart, and the *Patriot King*," *British Journal for Eighteenth-Century Studies*, 6 (1983), 13-19.

Vieler, Douglas, "As it Was Seen—and As it Was," *AQC*, 96 (1983), 77-97.

Voitle, Robert, *The Third Earl of Shaftesbury, 1671-1713* (Baton Rouge, 1984).

Waite, Arthur Edward, *The Brotherhood of the Rosy Cross* (1924; New York, 1993).

Walker, D.P., *The Ancient Theology: Studies in Christian Platonism from the Fifteenth to the Eighteenth Century* (Ithaca, 1972).

Walpole, Horace, *The Correspondence of Horace Walpole*, ed. W.S. Lewis (New Haven, 1937-84).

Ward, Edward, *The Lord Whiglove's Elegy* (London, 1715).

The Dancing Devils: or, the Roaring Dragon (London, 1724).

Durgen. Or, a Plain Satyr upon a Pompous Satyrist (London, 1728).

Apollo's Maggot in his Cups (London, 1729).

Ward, Robert E., *Prince of Dublin Printers: The Letters of George Faulkner* (Lexington, 1972).

Warton, Thomas, *The Triumph of Isis* (London, 1749).

Watson, Robert, *The Political Works of Fletcher of Salton* (London, 1798).

Weatherup, D.R.M., "Swift in County Armagh," *Review: Journal of Craigavon Historical Society*, vol. 7, no. 3 (1987).

Weeks, James Eyre, *The Cobler's Poem*, 2nd ed. (Dublin, 1745).

Rebellion. A Poem (Dublin, 1745).

François Weil, "Chevalier Ramsay et la Franc-Maçonnerie," *La Revue d'Histoire Litteraire de la France*, 63 (1963), 27-78.

Wemyss, Alice, *Elcho of the '45*, ed. John Gibson (Edinburgh, 2003).

Wesley, Samuel, *The Pig and the Mastiff. Two Tales* (London, 1725).

Poems on Several Occasions (London, 1736).

and Thomas Fitzgerald, *Georgia. A Poem. Tomochichi* (London, 1736).

Wharton, Philip, Duke of, *The True Briton* (1722-1723).

Philip Duke of Wh---n's Answer to Obadiah Sorrow (Dublin, 1727).

The Humble Petition of his Grace Ph—p D. of Wh----n to a Great Man (London, 1730).

The Life and Writings of Philip Late Duke of Wharton (London, 1732).

Bibliothecarum…de ducis Wharton (London, 1733.)

The Fear of Death. An Ode by the Late Duke of Wharton (London, 1739).

Whitehead, Paul, *Manners: A Satire* (London, 1739).

The Gymnasiad, or Boxing Match (London, 1744).

The Poems and Miscellaneous Compositions of Paul Whitehead (Dublin, 1777).

"Wildair, Harry," *The Sermon Taster, or Church Rambler* (London, 1723).

Willes, Richard, *The Bishop of Salisbury's Speech in the House of Lords upon the Third Reading of the Bill to Inflict Pains and Penalties on Francis (late) Bishop of Rochester. 15 May 1723* (London, 1723).

Williams, Harold, *Dean Swift's Library* (Cambridge, 1972).

Williams, W.J., "Alexander Pope and Freemasonry," *AQC*, 38 (1925), 11-48.

"Nathaniel Blackerby," *AQC*, 38 (1925), 106.

"The Use of the Word `Freemason' before 1717," *AQC*, 48 (1937), 140-98.

Williamson, Adam, *The Official Diary of Lieutenant-General Adam Williamson, Deputy Lieutenant of the Tower of London, 1722-1747*, ed. J.C. Fox (London, 1912).

Williamson, Arthur, "The Jewish Dimension in the Scottish Apocalypse: Climate, Covenant, and World Renewal," in Yosef Kaplan, ed., *Menasseh ben Israel and his World* (Leiden, 1989), 7-30.

"`A Pil for Pork-Eaters': Ethnic Identity, Apocalyptic Premises, and the Strange Creation of the Judaeo-Scots," in R.B. Waddington and Arthur Williamson, eds., *The Expulsion of the Jews: 1492 and After* (New York, 1994), 237 58.

Wills, Rebecca, *The Jacobites and Russia, 1715-1750* (West Linton, 2002).

Witek, John, *Controversial Ideas in China and Europe: A Biography of Jean-François Fouquet, S.J.* (Rome, 1982).

Wodrow, Robert, *Early Letters of Robert Wodrow*, ed. L.W. Sharp (Edinburgh, 1973).

Wogan, Sir Charles, *Female Fortitude…Narrative of the Seizure, Escape, and Marriage of Princess Clementina Sobieski* (London, 1722)

The Rescue of Princess Clementina (Stuart): A 1719 Adventure of the Irish Brigade. French ed. of 1745, trans. Cathy Winch (Belfast, 2008).

and William Tunstall, *Poems of Love and Gallantry* (London, 1716).

Wolf, Lucien, "Anglo-Jewish Coats of Arms," *TJHSE* (1894-95), 153-57.

Wonnacott, William, "Charles, Duke of Richmond, Grand Master, 1724-15," *AQC*, 30 (1919), 176-201.

"The Rite of Seven Degrees in London," *AQC*, 39 (1926), 63-98.

Wood, Anthony à, *Athenae Oxonienses*, ed. Philip Bliss, 3rd rev. ed. (London, 1813).

Woodward, John, "Of the Wisdom of the Ancient Egyptians," *Archaeolgia*, 4 (1776), 212-310.

Wooley, James, "Arbuckle's `Panegyric' and Swift's Scrub Libel: the Documentary Evidence," Irwin John Fischer and Donald Mell, eds., *Contemporary Studies of Swift's Poetry* (Newark, 1981), 191-209.

Wren, Christopher [son], *Parentalia* (London, 1750).

Wren, Christopher, "Sir Christopher Wren's Report on the Abbey in 1713, to Dean Atterbury," *Wren Society*, 11 (1934), 15-20.

"A Note on the Place of Sir Chr. Wren's Death and His Funeral in 1723," *Wren Society*, 18 (1941), 181.

"Discourse on Naval Architecture," *Wren Society*, 19 (1942), 140.

Wright, Austin, *Joseph Spence: A Critical Biography* (Chicago, 1950).

Wright, F. Alison, "The Layburnes and their World circa 1620-1720: The English Catholic Community and the House of Stuart (Ph.D. Thesis: St. Andrews University, 2002).

Wright, Herbert G., "Some English Writers and Charles XII," *Studia Neophilogia*, 15 (1943), 105-31.

Wright, Thomas, *England Under the House of Hanover*, 3rd ed. (London, 1849).

Wright, William, *The Comical History of the Marriage-Union Betwixt Fergusia and Heptarchus* (Edinburgh and London, 1706).

Yarker, John, "Drummond-Earls of Perth," *AQC*, 14 (1901), 138.

Yates, Frances, "The Art of Ramon Lull," *Journal of Warburg and Courtauld Institute*, 17 (1954), 115-68.

The Art of Memory (London, 1966).

Young, Edward, *Love of Fame, the Universal Passion* (1727; Dublin, 1728).

Two Epistles to Mr. Pope (London, 1730).

Night the Second. On Time, Death, and Friendship (London, 1742).

Night the Sixth. The Infidel Reclaim'd (London, 1744).

The Complaint. Or, Night Thoughts (London, 1744).

The Consolation (London, 1745).

Zimmerman, Doron, *The Jacobite Movement in Scotland and in Exile, 1746-1766* (London, 2003).

Zitser, Ernest, "The Petrine Round Table: Chivalry, Travesty, and Fraternalism at the Court of Peter the Great," in A. Onnerfors and R. Collis, *Freemasonry and Fraternalism*, 7-32.

INDEX

ABOUT THE AUTHOR

After studying at Tulane University, the University of Vienna, and Makerere University in Uganda, Marsha Keith Schuchard earned a Ph.D. from the University of Texas at Austin for her dissertation, "Freemasonry, Secret Societies, and the Continuity of the Occult Traditions in English Literature" (1975). She then worked as a medical writer and international lecturer in drug abuse prevention before returning to literary, cultural, and political history, which led to the publication of over fifty scholarly articles and four books: *Restoring the Temple of Vision: Cabalistic Freemasonry and Stuart Culture* (Leiden: Brill, 2002); *Why Mrs. Blake Cried: William Blake and the Sexual Basis of Spiritual Vision* (London: Random House, 2006); *Emanuel Swedenborg, Secret Agent on Earth and in Heaven: Jacobites, Jews, and Freemasons in Early Modern Sweden* (Leiden: Brill, 2012); and *Masonic Esotericism and Politics: The "Ancient" Stuart Roots of Bonnie Prince Charlie's Role as Hidden Grand Master* (Columbia, SC: Gauthier Pierozak Éditeur, 2017). She lives in Atlanta, Georgia.

Made in the USA
Middletown, DE
21 July 2019